MARKETING

MARKETING

David W. Cravens
Texas Christian University

Robert B. Woodruff
The University of Tennessee

 ADDISON-WESLEY PUBLISHING COMPANY

READING, MASSACHUSETTS • MENLO PARK, CALIFORNIA • DON MILLS, ONTARIO • WOKINGHAM, ENGLAND
AMSTERDAM • SYDNEY • SINGAPORE • TOKYO • MEXICO CITY • BOGOTÁ • SANTIAGO • SAN JUAN

Sponsoring Editors: Frank J. Burns, Cindy M. Johnson
Development Editor: Robert Hartwell Fiske
Production Supervisor: Mary Clare McEwing
Text Designer: Roy Howard Brown
Production Editor: Barbara G. Flanagan
Art Editor: Dick Morton
Copy Editor: Chere Bemelmans
Permissions Editor: Mary Dyer
Production Artist: Lorraine Hodsdon
Photo Researcher: Linda Finigan
Illustrator: Intergraphics
Cover Designer: Marshall Henrichs
Manufacturing Supervisor: Hugh J. Crawford

Part and Chapter Opening Photo Credits: pp. 2–3, Courtesy of Sears, Roebuck & Company; p. 4, Courtesy of McDonnell-Douglas; p. 28, Photo courtesy of Wang Laboratories, Inc.; pp. 56–57, Courtesy of Sheraton; p. 58, Courtesy of Odetics, Inc.; p. 90, Courtesy of Transamerica Corp.; p. 116, Courtesy of Burke Marketing Services, Inc.; p. 146, Courtesy of International Business Machines, Corporation; p. 174, Courtesy of Burke Marketing Services, Inc.; p. 202, Photo courtesy of Gerber Products Company; pp. 236–237, Courtesy of First Interstate Bancorp; p. 238, Courtesy of Snugli, Inc.; p. 274, Courtesy of Genetic Systems Corporation; p. 302, Courtesy of General Mills, Inc.; pp. 332–333, Courtesy of Xerox Corporation; p. 334, Photo courtesy of Nixdorf Computer Corporation; p. 362, Courtesy of the Coca-Cola Company; p. 388, Courtesy of A. C. Nielsen Company; p. 410, Photograph by Michael Puig, used with permission from Transco Energy Company, Houston, Texas; pp. 436–437, Photo courtesy of SCM Corporation, Gary Gladstone, photographer; p. 438, Photo courtesy of InterNorth, Inc., p. 468, Photo courtesy of The Chicago Mercantile Exchange; pp. 504–505, Photo courtesy of The Goodyear Tire & Rubber Company; p. 506, Photo courtesy of Miles Corporate Archives, Miles Laboratories; p. 536, Designed and produced by Pie in the Sky Company, San Mateo, California; p. 574, Courtesy of Cromemco; pp. 606–607, Courtesy of Chesebrough Pond's, Inc.; p. 608, Photograph courtesy of General Foods Corporation (MINUTE is a registered trademark of General Foods Corporation); p. 638, Courtesy of Binney & Smith; p. 670, Photo courtesy of General Mills, Inc.; pp. 698–699, Photo courtesy of Wyle Laboratories—Photographer: Marvin Silver, Mariposa, California; p. 700, Courtesy of International Business Machines Corporation; p. 730, Photograph by Michael Puig, used with permission from Transco Energy Company, Houston, Texas.

Library of Congress Cataloging in Publication Data

Cravens, David W.
  Marketing.

  Includes index.
  1. Marketing.   I. Woodruff, Robert B.   II. Title.
HF5415.C6943   1986   658.8   84-24357
ISBN 0-201-10840-2

ABCDEFGHIJ-MU-89876

To the Marketing Profession

Preface

As the world moves toward 1990 the analysis, planning, and implementation of effective marketing strategies will be essential to the successful performance of business and other organizations. The purpose of *Marketing* is to offer a challenging, complete, interesting, and current examination of introductory marketing, attuned to the needs and preferences of instructors and students. The planning and development of *Marketing* were guided by three objectives: (1) to provide greater managerial emphasis than other basic marketing books, (2) to expand consideration of important analyses used in the planning and control of marketing strategy, and (3) to examine marketing management from a strategic rather than tactical perspective. Central to the design of the book and its supporting package is recognition of the exciting and rapidly expanding role of marketing in business practice. Several key features distinguish *Marketing* from other introductory books.

Professional approach to marketing. It is important to challenge rather than entertain students, including those not planning to pursue marketing careers. Marketing management should be recognized by all students as a professional area of expertise, critical to the success of business and nonbusiness organizations.

Hands-on analysis approach. The text shows the relationship between analysis of macroenvironmental forces, market identification, analysis of buyers, analysis of competition, and forecasting in providing a sound information base for strategy development. The text also goes the next step and links analysis to the development of overall marketing strategy as a roadmap for company operations. Tactical decisions and implementation are of little consequence without a strategy to guide them.

Service orientation to the instructor. A complete package has been developed to help the instructor deliver an effective learning situation. The package has a tested multiple-choice test bank with a mix of difficulty levels and applications, extensive visual aids for classroom use, and other aids. Furthermore, the publisher offers a strong after-the-sale service program.

Highly current and readable text. The text and readings book are based on the literature of the 1980s, using only the most time-tested readings from earlier periods. The text extensively illustrates and demonstrates the application of marketing management to organizations in the United States and around the world. Special features called Marke-TALK, MarkeTOOL, and MarkeTECH help students not only to see marketing in practice, but also to understand how marketing strategy is formulated and carried out. The writing style of the authors is intended to be professional, yet interesting and readable. Easy-to-understand visuals have been created by award-winning designers to enhance the professional nature of the presentation.

Value for the student. The objective of the innovative text design is to create excitement and involvement for today's career-oriented student. We have deliberately chosen a professional rather than a multicolor candy-stripe presentation. The image conveyed by a marketing principles book is important in establishing marketing management as a professional and challenging area of study for all students. The intent of the design is to focus student attention on the content and substance of marketing in an interesting and challenging manner. The design of the book, the presentation of its content, the supporting package, and the practical nature of the approach to marketing management combine to create maximum value for the student.

DESIGNED FOR THE FUTURE

Marketing was designed to support the learning environment of the late 1980s and 1990s. We have made a serious effort to identify the needs and wants of instructors and students by conducting various marketing research studies. Focus group interviews were held at each major stage in the development of the text. Discussions with faculty and students provided important insights into teaching needs, priorities, and text content. Many helpful reviewers offered important critical evaluations of the manuscript and suggestions at various points in its development. Acknowledged experts in several specific marketing areas reviewed applicable portions of the manuscript. All these inputs played a very important role in shaping the content and delivery of the text. *Marketing* and the supporting package clearly are based on users' needs and preferences.

Research and study of market trends indicate that an important transition is underway in introductory marketing courses. This change is marked by greater concern for the analysis and strategy aspects of marketing in an organization, recognition of the critical importance of customer satisfaction to business success, and the expanding interest in marketing by students not majoring in marketing. Career-oriented students are aware of the critical role of marketing in a competitive and changing environment. We have a responsibility to provide these students with a cohesive and complete introductory coverage of marketing management. This is the only course that will be taken by most students. We have attempted to anticipate these trends with our approach and emphasis. Although *Marketing* is designed for the future, it covers all the various concepts and topical areas that academic people and practicing professionals consider essential. You should find no gaps in the topical coverage.

Marketing emphasizes the various decisions faced by managers in all kinds of organizations. Traditionally, the domain of marketing included manufacturing, wholesaling, and retailing companies. Today marketing management is practiced by organizations as different as hospitals, universities, zoos, charities, religious groups, and government units and by professionals as diverse as accountants, architects, and lawyers. The examples and illustrations used in the book represent this broad range of organizations and demonstrate modern marketing management in action.

In moving from markets to marketing actions, our objective is to encourage a sense of involvement and participation by the student. Throughout the text a strong emphasis is given to how marketing should be carried out in an organization, and each principle is supported by an illustration of marketing practice. Recognizable firms, their messages and experiences, both favorable and unfavorable, are featured, in order to bring the business world into the classroom and help students see marketing in the world around them. Although the company's situation may change in the future, it serves as a concrete illustration of the application being discussed. We have avoided developing a reference book that merely describes marketing terms, activities, and functions. The reader is presented with the basics but is also offered an interesting and complete action-oriented coverage of marketing from a managerial perspective.

ORGANIZED FOR ACTION

A brief review of the table of contents will show that chapters are not included on services marketing, not-for-profit marketing, and business or industrial marketing. Specialized coverage of these topics tends to fragment the basics of marketing management. Instead, we have carefully and extensively placed applications of marketing to not-for-profit, industrial, international, and service organizations into the content of each chapter. Services marketing is such a central part of the practice of marketing management today that it deserves complete coverage throughout the book, and we have integrated it where appropriate. The result is a coherent framework following the marketing manager's sequence of analysis, planning, implementation, and control activities. The reader will see marketing principles as they are realized in practice.

At the same time, the organization and coverage of the book offer considerable flexibility in the assignment of topics by the instructor to facilitate course design according to teaching priorities and desired emphasis of particular topics. Parts 3 through 6 can be offered in any order, and all or selected chapters in each part can be used. The first chapter in each part includes an integrating overview for all of the chapters in the part.

A MANY-FACETED VIEW OF MARKETING

We have made a major effort to illustrate the dynamic, exciting, and challenging nature of marketing without disrupting the flow of the text. An understanding of marketing management and the development of marketing strategies can help students cope with today's rapidly changing business environment, regardless of their particular career choices. By reading the special features throughout the book, students will discover more about marketing in action, how it is changing, and how it is practiced.

Each chapter begins with an opening vignette selected to introduce and illustrate marketing as a part of the students' everyday world. MarkeTALK features present actual applications of marketing in greater depth than an in-text example will allow. MarkeTECH items show how computer-related technology is changing the practice of marketing in communications, decision analysis, and other activities. MarkeTOOL features show students how to perform selected marketing tasks such as analyzing competition, estimating market share, and predicting customer preferences that are used to support marketing decision making.

Between selected chapters, essays provide "a special look" at topics important to future marketers. Written by individuals professionally involved in these areas, these essays provide a perspective on and emphasis to these segments of our economy and society.

At the end of each chapter, exercises assist each student in building a portfolio of marketing management capabilities that he or she will take into the workplace. End-of-chapter discussion questions provide an opportunity to comprehensively review and apply chapter materials. The end-of-chapter cases present a wide variety of marketing management situations involving large and small companies, various products and services, consumer and business markets, and companies facing both problems and opportunities. The cases enable students to apply the concepts, analysis techniques, and decision making approaches discussed in each chapter.

TEACHING AND LEARNING SUPPORT

Marketing is a complete teaching and learning package developed to enhance the educational process. The physical design of the book is intended to promote student interest and learning, while avoiding distortion and fragmentation by the careful integration of exhibits and illustrations into the flow of the discussion. Text material is presented in a large, easy-to-read format. The uncluttered layout focuses the reader on the content in an interesting and stimulating manner. The advertisements in black and white encourage students to concentrate on the strategy and message of the organization being represented and to view the ad as a professional rather than merely as a consumer. Carefully developed captions explain the strategic implications of the ad and how these relate to the principle being studied.

Development of the package of student and teacher aids was driven by the reality of teaching the principles of marketing course in many schools today. Large lecture sections are becoming commonplace, discussion sections are increasingly rare, and tight budgets limit assistance and support to faculty. Development of the package received attention on a par with the text. Key priorities were assigned to lecture support aids, exercises that do not require a small section setting, and high-quality test support.

The *lecture support* package includes a comprehensive set of transparencies featuring key exhibits from the text, additional exhibits and illustrations from other sources, and diagrams that synthesize text discussion. Ten to fifteen acetates are available for each chapter. The instructor is also provided lecture outlines, and a complete set of transparency masters in the course planner, to facilitate lecture preparation. Case discussion notes, additional sources of information, answers to text questions, and a film and video bibliography are provided in the Instructor's Manual.

The *exercise enhancement* package provides four types of student assistance. The Learning Guide, by Diana Miller of the University of Northern Colorado, enables students to practice with multiple-choice questions, work on exercises to reinforce and apply text content, and focus on essentials for classroom and test preparation. The *Marketing TOOLKIT,* software and workbook for the microcomputer written by Robert Schaffer of California State Polytechnic University at Pomona, offers further student activities that can be used as homework, lab work, or project assignment materials. Its analysis and decision support modules are keyed to the text, and the complete student guide eliminates the need for instruction from faculty. Importantly, the hands-on decision-making experience based on analysis does not require the time demands of a realistic simulation game. *Marketing in Action,* an integrated readings and case book developed by Andrew Forman of the University of Tennessee, offers additional insight into the practice of marketing management. The cases provide a variety of situations for analysis and marketing strategy development, and the readings further illustrate the breadth and dynamics of marketing. The length of the readings and cases facilitates their use in class discussion and assignments. A comprehensive instructors manual for *Marketing in Action* is available in the parent Instructor's Manual. Finally, *Jazz: A Case Study* (a six part case of approximately sixty pages) is available free to adoptors for use as a project, outside reading, or simply as an ongoing illustrative case. Written by Victoria Crittenden for the principles student, it follows the planning, development, and implementation of the marketing plan for the Jazz software introduced in early 1985 by the Lotus Development Corporation. It, too, is accompanied by complete case notes and usage guidelines.

The *testing support* package includes approximately 2,500 fair and unambiguous test questions produced by a team of teacher/developers with the heavy involvement of the authors. The questions were edited and class-tested by Dianne Barlar, University of West Florida, an experienced teacher at the principles level with graduate training in educational technology. Review, editing, and class testing were also provided by the authors. The questions are classified for ease of use according to difficulty and type of question. The microcomputer (TESTGEN II) test generator system provides all test items on diskette for easy test creation, enabling printing of test and answer keys. Instructors can also add their own items and revise those provided.

The entire teaching-learning package for *Marketing* represents a dedicated effort to present marketing management as a challenging, interesting, and essential business function. We ask both teachers and students to critically evaluate our efforts, and we encourage your feedback and suggestions for improving the book and the supporting materials.

Fort Worth, Texas   D. W. C.
Knoxville, Tennessee   R. B. W.

Acknowledgments

Many people and organizations contributed to the development of *Marketing*. It represents the ideas and efforts of various individuals in addition to the authors. Faculty colleagues, students, business executives, corporations, and executives in nonbusiness organizations have provided important concepts, insights, and materials for the book. We have benefited substantially from students' suggestions and comments. While we assume responsibility for the end result, the contributions of many others were essential in the development of this book.

Various individuals provided helpful comments and recommendations on the manuscript and other aspects of planning and developing the book and package. Included in our thanks are many focus group participants from each region of the country, who offered valued consultation and ideas at important stages during the writing process. Several conscientious reviewers who devoted time and talent to helping us improve the manuscript deserve special recognition.

Gerald Albaum, University of Oregon
W. Thomas Anderson, Jr., University of Texas at Austin
Venkatakrishna V. Bellur, Niagara University
Peter D. Bennett, The Pennsylvania State University
William C. Black, Louisiana State University
Michael J. Cavanaugh, Mercy College
Melvin Crask, The University of Georgia
Ellen Day, The University of Georgia
Phillip E. Downs, Florida State University
Calvin P. Duncan, University of Colorado, Boulder
Andrew M. Forman, University of Tennessee
Linda L. Golden, University of Texas at Austin
Donald H. Granbois, Indiana University
Jon M. Hawes, The University of Akron
Del I. Hawkins, University of Oregon
John C. Keyt, East Tennessee State University
A. H. Kizilbash, Northern Illinois University
Leonard Konopa, Kent State University
Kathleen A. Krentler, San Diego State University
Ruth H. Krieger, Oklahoma State University
Nancy Lambert, Northeastern University
Irene Lange, California State University, Fullerton
Marilyn Leibrenz, George Washington University
Kent B. Monroe, Virginia Polytechnic Institute and State University

Michael Peters, Boston College
Kenn L. Rowe, Arizona State University
Robert E. Spekman, University of Maryland
John Walton, Miami University of Ohio
Richard F. Wendel, University of Connecticut
Terrell G. Williams, Utah State University
Robert F. Young, Northeastern University

We appreciate the important commitment made by the people responsible for particular components of the supporting package for the book. Our special thanks go to Andrew Forman, University of Tennessee, for developing the readings and casebook, *Marketing in Action*. We thank Diana Miller, University of Northern Colorado, for preparing a user-friendly *Learning Guide*. The efforts of Robert Schaffer in designing the microcomputer package, *Marketing TOOLKIT*, represent an important contribution in the use of computer technology to facilitate student learning. The team comprised of A. Dianne Barlar, Beth C. Barnes, Shanna Greenwalt, Gary J. Gaeth, John Keyt, Diana Miller, and Robert C. Harris provided essential assistance in the preparation and evaluation of the test bank. We really appreciate their help. We thank Charles W. Lamb, Texas Christian University, for developing the special feature on marketing by nonprofit organizations; Leonard Berry, Texas A&M University, for preparing the special feature on services marketing, and Mary Jane Sheffet, Indiana University, for writing the special feature on public policy.

The artists, editors, designers, and production personnel of Addison-Wesley Publishing Company provided a wide range of supporting assistance for the project. The enthusiasm and commitment of these dedicated professionals to the book is sincerely appreciated.

A special thank you is extended to Sue Cravens and Nancy Robbins for their excellent work in typing the manuscript and assisting on many other important aspects of the project. We also appreciate the assistance of our graduate assistants in helping on various aspects of the supporting package. Finally, we are greatly appreciative of the support and encouragement of Dean Edward Johnson and Dean Warren Neel.

As authors we acknowledge the essential need for a team effort in moving a book from conception to completion. We sincerely thank the many contributors to the project.

About the Authors

DAVID W. CRAVENS

David W. Cravens is Professor of Marketing at the M. J. Neeley School of Business at Texas Christian University, where he holds the Eunice and James L. West Chair of American Enterprise Studies. He concentrates his teaching and research efforts in the areas of marketing strategy and sales management. Dr. Cravens is author of *Strategic Marketing, Strategic Marketing Cases and Applications,* and *Marketing Decision Making: Concepts and Strategy,* as well as numerous essays and articles. He is currently serving on the editorial board of the *Journal of Marketing* and the *Journal of Personal Selling and Sales Management.*

ROBERT B. WOODRUFF

Dr. Robert Woodruff is Professor of Marketing in the College of Business Administration at the University of Tennessee, Knoxville. As a teacher, researcher, and writer, Dr. Woodruff's work has been primarily aimed at understanding consumer information processing and satisfaction, as well as advancing the role of market analysis in marketing. He is co-author of *Marketing Decision Making: Concepts and Strategy* and author of journal articles and papers on consumer behavior and market analysis. Dr. Woodruff serves as a consultant to businesses on market opportunity analysis, image analysis, and marketing planning.

Contents in Brief

Contents

MARKETING

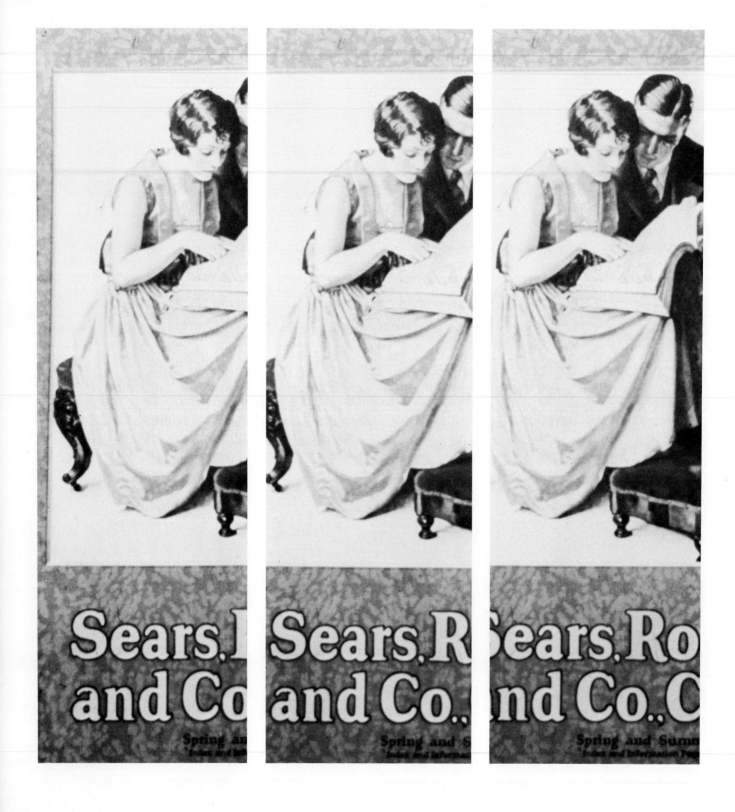

Part One

Marketing
Management

1 Marketing: An Overview

When you finish this chapter, you will understand

☐ How marketing affects everyone

☐ The nature and scope of modern marketing

☐ Why marketing activities are necessary to carry out exchange between buyers and sellers

☐ How marketing management has developed into its present form

☐ The key role of the marketing concept in meeting customer needs

Marketing reaches into outer space as big business competes for rights to televise programs worldwide via satellite.

Outside Shanghai Far East Gold & Silver Ornament Company forty shoppers are tussling for position and the chance to buy gold jewelry when the shop opens in an hour. Inside Shanghai Fabric Company an old man wearing an arm band and a no-nonsense expression is keeping the customers at the counter to four deep, holding back the rest with a long pole. In an alleyway Huangpu District Industrial Company is stacking its sale merchandise on wooden crates while customers surge around, snapping up cut-price T-shirts and socks.[1]

Meanwhile, hovering overhead well beyond the borders of any country, U.S. communications satellites are attracting big-business television marketers. So far, twelve companies have filed more than sixty applications with the Federal Communications Commission to market televised programs by satellite to Canada, Mexico, the Caribbean, and other distant locations.[2]

FROM THE STREETS OF SHANGHAI to the stretches of space, marketing is everywhere. The domain of marketing knows no bounds: It is local and regional, national and multinational, global and, of late, extraterrestrial. Because marketing affects society in so many ways, it is important to understand what marketing is and why it is an essential activity in both developing and advanced social systems.

Besides shopping in Shanghai and satellites in space, marketing encompasses a host of activities that touch our lives in many ways. Marketing accounts for a substantial portion of every dollar spent to purchase goods and services. Marketing creates millions of jobs and is the driving force behind many successful corporations. People are in daily contact with marketing when purchasing everything from hamburgers to hospital services. The television programs we watch and the magazines and newspapers we read are available at little or no cost because of the advertising expenditures of companies. Business firms, government agencies, universities, hospitals, and even public zoos rely on marketing to inform customers about and persuade them to use their goods and services.

In this chapter we first explore what marketing is all about and why it is relevant to everyone. Next we examine how the practice of marketing has developed into its present role and scope. Finally, the critical role of the marketing concept in business practice is discussed.

WHAT IS MARKETING?

Although people are frequently in contact with marketing activities, many are not aware of marketing's true nature and scope. In fact, some people consider advertising and marketing to be one and the same, although advertising is only one aspect of marketing. In this section we discuss why marketing is essential in our society. Then we examine marketing functions and institutions and how they bridge the discrepancies between producers and consumers. Finally, we look at the nature of marketing from the societal, managerial, and consumer perspectives.

Why marketing is needed

Let us start with the fundamental, well-accepted idea of a **need or want,** which is an uncomfortable feeling of deprivation or a desire that can cause people to act, usually by purchasing and consuming goods and services. Consider food. What are your alternatives for meeting this need? You have essentially two options: provide for your own needs by living off the land, or trade with or purchase from others who have the food you need. Early in the history of civilization, people learned that if each person specialized in doing one or a few things and then exchanged goods or services with others, needs and wants could be better satisfied.

The advantages of specialization create a need for exchange. **Specialization** means that each person concentrates on a particular work activity instead of trying to provide for all of his or her needs. By focusing on one activity such as baking bread, a person can become very efficient at the task. This efficiency—specialization—can improve our standard of living over what it would be if we tried to produce all the goods and services we need or want. To meet needs it is often necessary to give an item or perform a service in return for something considered of equal value. This trading activity is called **exchange,** which is a supplier's providing a good or service to a consumer in return for a payment. Money is commonly used to accomplish exchange in many societies. Barter or trading one good or service for another is an alternative to the use of money as a means of exchange.

The clear logic of specialization can be shown through a simple example. Suppose you are an experienced computer systems analyst earning $20 an hour. You want a Nikon FG 35mm programmable camera, which in 1985 sold for less than $180 in discount camera stores in New York. Your earnings from nine hours of work (disregarding income taxes) are enough to purchase the camera. Consider how long it would take you to build the

If it were not for the specialists who built the Nikon FG camera, beginners would not be able to take such "great pictures." (Courtesy of Nikon, Inc.)

Exhibit 1.1 Where your money goes

Food, beverages	**$20.60**
Food at home	$13.30
Food away from home	$ 4.80
Alcoholic beverages	$ 2.50
Housing	**$16.50**
Transportation	**$14.10**
New, used vehicles	$ 4.20
Vehicle operation, upkeep	$ 8.70
Public transportation	$ 1.20
Household operations	**$13.70**
Furniture, appliances	$ 2.10
Utilities, telephone	$ 6.80
Other supplies, furnishings	$ 4.80
Medical care	**$10.40**
Clothing, jewelry	**$ 7.40**
Recreation	**$ 6.30**
Personal business	**$ 5.30**
Private education, research	**$ 1.50**
Religious, welfare activities	**$ 1.40**
Personal care	**$ 1.40**
Tobacco	**$ 1.20**
Foreign travel, net	**$ .20**

SOURCE: "It's Consumers Who Really Rule the Roost," *U.S. News and World Report,* April 26, 1982, p. 37. Reprinted by permission.
Note: Since the breakdowns total $100, you can read the figures as percentages (for example, 16½ percent on housing).

Exhibit 1.2 Specialization creates a need for exchange

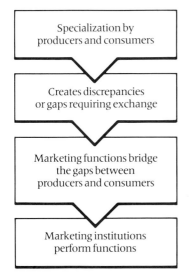

camera. Most of us could not build the camera in nine hours. By becoming efficient at certain tasks, we can improve our standard of living over what it would be if we tried to produce all the goods and services we want or need.

Exchange is the purpose of marketing. Marketing consists of the performance of those activities that result in exchanges. These activities were limited early in history. Over time, however, advanced **marketing systems** evolved: Vast networks of organizations such as manufacturers, distributors, wholesalers, retailers, and other firms together perform many essential functions needed to move goods and services from the point of production to the point of consumption.

Marketing functions and institutions

Defining marketing functions. An interesting profile of how people spend their money is shown in Exhibit 1.1. Each category shown contains products and services marketed by some company, organization, or individual. We are able to obtain a product or service because a firm makes it available through some form of distribution, such as a retail store or a catalogue; establishes a price; and communicates its availability and features by activities such as promotion through advertising and salespersons.

Buyers and sellers are brought together by **marketing functions.** To get a product or service to customers in the desired form, businesses must perform marketing functions such as buying, storing, transporting, assembling, sorting, grading, packaging, advertising, securing information, financing, billing, and services after the sale. These activities account for a substantial portion of each dollar spent on the items shown in Exhibit 1.1.

It is difficult to obtain accurate estimates of the amount of the sales dollar accounted for by marketing because of incomplete data on expenditures for marketing and differences in opinion about what constitutes marketing costs. Some estimate that 50 percent or more of the sales dollar is spent on marketing costs. One source cites 70 to 80 percent of the selling price of a typical consumer product such as a bottle of Maalox antacid as the cost of bringing the product to market.[3] Included are packaging, transportation, storage, marketing research, advertising, selling, and other costs. Advertising alone accounted for more than $85 billion in the United States in 1984.[4]

In view of the amount of the sales dollar spent on marketing activities, it is not surprising that many people are employed to perform marketing tasks for retailers, wholesalers, manufacturers, transportation firms, and other organizations; these jobs are estimated to exceed one quarter of the U.S. workforce. Millions of people are employed in sales positions alone, and selling is only part of total marketing activities. (If you are considering a career in marketing, opportunities in the field are discussed in Appendix C at the back of the book.)

The creation of gaps. Marketing functions are needed to match consumers' needs and wants through exchange as described in Exhibit 1.2. **Producers** are the organizations and individuals that create goods and services. **Consumers** are the individuals, households, and organizations that use the goods and services to meet their needs and wants. A **discrepancy or gap** is a difference in preference between producers and consumers concerning *what* is produced, *where* it is produced, or *when* it is produced. **Marketing**

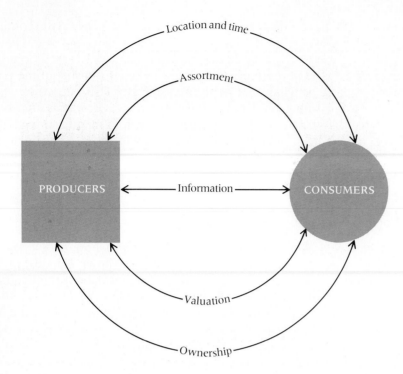

Exhibit 1.3 Specialization creates a gap between producers and consumers

institutions perform the functions necessary to satisfy what, where, and when the consumer wants to purchase. Although some marketing functions are performed by manufacturers and consumers, marketing institutions such as department stores and catalogue showrooms have developed to assist further in bridging the gap between producers and end-users of products and services.

Consider the time and costs that would be involved in shopping for food by going directly to firms such as Oscar Mayer, General Mills, and Stokely-Van Camp. You would find it difficult to purchase one package of hot dogs, a single box of Wheaties, or a can of pork and beans because these firms are not staffed to handle small transactions. The producers are set up to handle case and car load shipments, but homemakers normally do not wish to purchase a case of pork and beans. Cereal produced in Minneapolis must be made available to consumers in Atlanta, and tomatoes picked in July may not be wanted until September. These gaps between producers and consumers, such as differences in quantity, location, and desired time of purchase, are bridged by marketing functions. Let us take a closer look at why gaps between producers and consumers are created and how they are bridged by marketing functions.

Bridging the gaps. The nature of the gap between producers and consumers of goods and services is illustrated in Exhibit 1.3. Characteristics of this gap are as follows:

- *Location and time.* Differences exist as to where and when producers and consumers want to sell and buy. Transportation and storage of products help eliminate this gap by making the product available to the consumer at a convenient location and time.
- *Assortment.* The quantity and scope of products offered by a single producer (e.g., food products) may not meet consumers' needs. Marketing organizations such as food wholesalers stock a wide range of

food brands, transporting orders to retail supermarkets one or more times a week.

■ *Information.* Producers and consumers need information about each other to make decisions concerning what to produce and consume. Buyers' needs and wants help producers decide what to manufacture. Consumers evaluate information about the availability and features of products and services to guide their purchase decisions.

■ *Valuation.* A mechanism is needed for establishing a value on goods and services that is suitable to buyers and sellers. Price and terms of the sale (e.g., cash, credit, discounts) must be established.

■ *Ownership.* The transfer of ownership between buyers and sellers must be accomplished. Also involved are warranty provisions and after-purchase services.[5]

Several examples of the marketing functions that bridge gaps between producers and consumers are shown in Exhibit 1.4. These examples illustrate the range of possible activities. Not all functions are performed for every product and service. Consumers may be willing to perform some functions to obtain low prices or other trade-offs, such as taking an appliance to a service center to be repaired rather than having a repairman call. Contrast, for example, the services provided by a full service department store with a catalogue showroom discount store such as Best's or Service Merchandise. Both offer many of the same products. The showroom typically has lower prices, but it does not provide many of the services offered by the department store, such as sales clerks to explain product features, charge accounts, repair services, and gift wrapping.

Several examples of marketing institutions are also listed in Exhibit 1.4. Like producers and consumers, marketing institutions have specialized to perform certain marketing functions. For example, wholesalers are firms that buy products such as groceries and electrical supplies in large quantities and resell them to retailers. The role and scope of these and other marketing institutions are discussed in Chapters 13 and 14.

The nature of marketing

Marketing can be defined from three perspectives: societal, managerial, and consumer. Each point of view of marketing highlights different aspects, although all generally correspond to the American Marketing As-

Exhibit 1.4 Marketing bridges gaps between producers and consumers

Kind of Gap	Marketing Functions to Bridge Gaps	Marketing Institutions That Perform Functions
Location	Transportation, distribution, and facilities location	Airlines, truckers, railroads, wholesalers, retailers, and direct marketers
Time	Inventory accumulation and storage	Wholesalers, warehouses, retailers, and other marketing intermediaries
Assortment	Assembling, sorting, grading, and packaging	Wholesalers, processors, government graders, and packaging firms
Information	Marketing research, advertising, personal selling, sales promotion, and information services	Marketing research firms, manufacturers' salesforces, sales agents, advertising agencies, and government services
Valuation	Pricing, terms, and transfer of risk	Manufacturers, intermediaries, and facilitators such as insurance firms
Ownership	Purchasing, financing, billing, and servicing	Manufacturers, intermediaries, and facilitators

sociation definition of **marketing** as the process of planning and executing conception, pricing, promotion, and distribution of ideas, goods, and services to create exchanges that satisfy individual and organizational objectives. A brief look at each point of view will help you understand the nature of marketing.

Macromarketing or societal perspective.   **Macromarketing** is the total process of marketing in society that links the supply and demand for the goods and services produced in the economy. It is concerned with the total network of institutions and individuals participating in the marketing process, information regarding the operation and performance of this marketing system, and the ways in which marketing should be carried out to satisfy the objectives of society and optimize social benefits, including the delivery of a material standard of living to society.[6] Thus this **societal perspective** of marketing focuses on the entire system or network rather than on a specific marketing organization. Macromarketing encompasses such societal issues as the quality of life, the productivity of marketing, deregulation of industries, product safety, environmental contamination, and consumer information.

Individuals and groups that hold this broad view of marketing include government regulators, social scientists, consumer crusaders, and elected officials. For example, the deaths caused by contaminated Tylenol in 1982 led to the development of actions and policies to safeguard society from product tampering. The issue and its implications extended far beyond individual firms. Industry and government representatives became involved because of the potential threats of tampering.

Recalling our previous discussion of shopping in Shanghai, it is interesting to see the changes that are occurring at the macromarketing level as China shifts from a centrally planned economy toward experimentation with an open market system.

> China's new economic policy is called the responsibility system, and it aims to stimulate production by offering rewards and incentives, encouraging free-market trading and even tolerating a bit of private ownership. The responsibility system has been phased into use on two-thirds of China's state farms and factories since it was adopted at a 1978 party congress, and the Chinese say it eventually will be countrywide.[7]

Although the success of the open market system in China is far from certain, it illustrates a macromarketing issue.

Managerial perspective.   The **managerial perspective** prevails at the micro or organizational level. Executives and managers are interested in managing their organization so that customers will be satisfied and the organization's performance targets will be reached. Thus the managerial perspective considers marketing in a specific organization and the management of its marketing activities. Marketing in an organization encompasses all the decisions that are made and implemented to obtain a favorable response from target customers. **Marketing management** is identifying and selecting one or more market targets (customer groups) and planning and implementing a program of activities (products, distribution, pricing, and promotion) to serve the needs and wants of the people or organizations in the market target and to achieve the organization's marketing objectives.[8] Note that this definition is applicable to business firms as well as to other organizations concerned with customer satisfaction. (The example of Campbell Soup described in Marketalk indicates the kinds of concerns that are important to marketing managers.)

Consumer perspective. Marketing, from the **consumer perspective,** is the activities of consumers directed toward satisfying needs and wants through

*Marke*TALK //

Campbell Soup: Cooking up a separate dish for each consumer group

EVER SINCE R. Gordon McGovern took the helm at Campbell Soup Co. in 1980, the old-line food processor, known best for its soups and its Pepperidge Farm, Swanson, Franco-American, and Godiva products, has been undergoing a rapid and remarkable transformation. The 56-year-old McGovern has been working feverishly to shift the company's emphasis from production to marketing.

McGovern started by reorganizing Campbell's four divisions into about 50 business groups and making group managers responsible for the marketing, manufacturing, and profit and loss of their units. He believes this structure fosters entrepreneurship and brings "the managers much closer to the market."

"There's a tremendous feeling of urgency because an overseas company could come in here with innovative packaging and technology and just take us to the cleaners on basic lines we've taken for granted for years," McGovern says, pointing to the success of Japanese companies selling *ramen* noodles in the dry-soup category. "They've made a penetration at the low end of the American food market just as they did with cheap cars, and they are going to smash into a lot of other things," he worries.

To keep that from happening to Campbell, the push is on to target the consumer and improve quality. "I think we've had some serious problems in losing touch with our markets," says McGovern. Last year he raised industry—and company— eyebrows when he publicly labeled the Swanson TV-dinner line "junk food." McGovern insists: "It was great in 1950, but in today's world it didn't go into the microwave; it didn't represent variety or a good eating experience to my palate." Campbell has set up Project Fix to improve the quality of its old standbys, and

the Swanson line has been bolstered by the new, high-priced Le Menu entrées.

McGovern's goal for Campbell is "to be positioned with consumers as somebody who is looking after their well-being." Last fall the company set up a health and fitness business unit, and in May it bought a small maker of fitness and sports medicine products. Campbell is also emphasizing segments such as frozen foods, fish (it acquired Mrs. Paul's Kitchens Inc. in 1982), juices (a new Pepperidge Farm apple juice hit the market recently), and produce (Campbell now sells fresh mushrooms).

The program is working. For the last two fiscal years, average tonnage rose 6.5%—exceeding the 5% goal and an improvement over the previous two years, which showed an average decline of 2%. "Our share of market is holding and in some cases building," McGovern says. Mrs. Paul's, for example, reversed a market share decline, going from 24% to 27% in a year.

Much of the new strategy hinges on targeting the consumer. "My 83-year-old mother doesn't eat like my son," McGovern observes. "And my daughters eat differently than their parents, and we eat differently from the people around the corner." So Campbell will gear particular products and ads to specific groups and even do regional marketing. For instance, it will sell its new, spicy Ranchero Beans only in the South and Southwest.

But Campbell also wants new products that will have national appeal. Its Prego spaghetti sauce has been a big winner and a breakthrough product for Campbell. For the fiscal year ended Aug. 1, Prego ran up sales of around $100 million, even though it was not in national distribution for the full year. It is now the No. 2 sauce behind Ragu, grabbing a 22% share.

Prego almost did not get made. The former Campbell policy was that a new product had to show a profit within a year, and the payout on Prego was expected to be three years. Herbert M. Baum, vice-

president for marketing, notes that in the 10 years before Prego, Campbell had only two major new-product successes— Chunky Soups and Hungry Man dinners—"and both were nothing more than glorified line extensions." But because the policy held back product development, then-Chief Executive Officer Harold A. Shaub changed it, and Prego, which was started in 1978, went national in September, 1982. Campbell has recouped its investment in Prego. In all, there are now 20 to 30 new U.S. products in various test-market stages. One of these is Juice Works, a line of fruit-juice blends without added sugar, aimed at children. Research on the line included 6,000 evaluations by kids.

Advertising strategy is also being rethought. Campbell used to cut ad spending at the end of a quarter to boost earnings. Besides hurting the brands, "it gave us a terrible reputation among the media," says Baum. Spending is now up—and continuous. Ad expenditures for fiscal 1983 rose 39% over the previous year, to $144 million. This year's budget will be $175 million. And the message focuses on the nutritional benefits of its products. "Soup is good food" is an example. Previously, Campbell had relied on the sing-and-sell approach: "M-m-m good" was its slogan for years.

McGovern, who rose through the ranks at Pepperidge Farm, sees his role as one of leader and goader. He voices strong opinions on Campbell products. He calls the new Pepperidge Farm Star Wars cookies "a travesty," saying they do not fit the brand's high-quality, upscale adult image and are faddish. Plus, at $1.39 a bag, "it's a lousy value," says McGovern. But he didn't veto them because, he concedes, "I could be wrong."

Clearly, McGovern is challenging managers to do better, to respond to the market faster, and to develop products "that consumers perceive to be in their best interest." He seems to be getting his message across.

Reprinted from the November 21, 1983 issue of *Business Week* by special permission; © 1983 by McGraw-Hill, Inc.

//

the exchange process.[9] Buyers are interested in using their resources to gain as much satisfaction as possible from the goods and services that they purchase. As we discuss in Chapters 5 and 6, all buyers do not measure satisfaction in the same way, and economic rules of behavior do not always apply. For most people, the physical product or service is only part of the "bundle of value" purchased. For example, a product may be perceived as a socially important item, just as the automobile is viewed by many people as more than a means of transportation. The consumer view of marketing focuses on those activities performed to achieve this goal of satisfaction. When people consider buying a microwave oven, for example, they may visit stores for demonstrations, talk with friends, and consult published information such as *Consumer Reports* magazine and advertisements for the product. Selecting the brand that best satisfies their particular needs is how these consumers view marketing.

Because of the different objectives and concerns of the participants in the exchange process, each views marketing somewhat differently. A person may occupy more than one role, however. Marketing managers are also consumers, and elected officials may also be business managers.

The managerial perspective, or marketing management, is the primary focus of this book. A managerial orientation includes the marketing of products as well as services, organizations, people, places, ideas, and other intangibles. Hospitals, schools, public transportation, art galleries, and many other organizations are concerned with marketing their goods and services. Even political parties market their candidates to the public, as was clearly illustrated by the 1984 presidential election. Still, it is important to keep the societal and consumer perspectives in mind as you consider the various issues, problems, and decisions associated with marketing management.

THE DEVELOPMENT OF MARKETING

The nature and scope of marketing have changed over time. To help understand marketing's changing composition, let us look at its development to the present time. You should recognize that any attempt to slice history into sections of time must be arbitrary. We have divided our look at the development of marketing into three parts: the beginning of marketing, the key stages in the development of modern marketing, and finally, future trends in the marketing field.

The beginning of marketing[10]

The shift from self-sufficiency to specialization triggered the beginning of marketing. In some cultures, marketing began even before specialization. It has existed for thousands of years, going back to the time when individuals began bartering and trading instead of supplying all of their own needs and wants. From this simple exchange process, a need developed for people and organizations to specialize in completing exchanges between suppliers.

Era of self-sufficiency. Hans B. Thorelli argues convincingly that marketing began with Adam and Eve.[11] They each probably concentrated on certain tasks that resulted in intrahousehold marketing transactions, which was

Today's Chevrolet

Welcome aboard

Camaro Berlinetta. Above, the night sky is black, punctuated by the flickering of stars and planets. Below, the white lines of the roadway snake deep into the unknown. Ahead, the blue-green glow of your instrument cluster advises you all systems are go on board Starship Camaro. This is not science fiction. This is Berlinetta.

Starship control central. Climb in. Buckle up. Adjust the retractable push-button instrument pods so your hands never have to leave the wheel in controlling vital functions. Turn the key and watch the system monitor perform seven preflight tests as the engine sparks to life. Blip the throttle and watch the vacuum-fluorescent tach dance to

The Camaro—a drive to work or a journey to outer space. It's sometimes as much the excitement and promise of power as it is the practicality that appeal to car buyers. (Courtesy of Campbell-Ewald Company, Warren, Mich., and Chevrolet Motor Division, GMC, Warren, Mich.)

Starship Camaro.

the rhythm of your right foot.
To orchestrate your voyage, dial up a symphony on the pivoting Delco stereo and optional graphic equalizer. (Radio may be deleted for credit.) Now, put it in gear, give it some gas and watch the digital speedometer numbers multiply. Set the available electronic speed control at your desired

cruising speed. Your journey has begun. **Enter a new realm.** Camaro Berlinetta is a higher form of terrestrial transportation. So climb on board and grab hold of the future.
Today's Chevrolet. Bringing you the cars and trucks you want and need. That's what Taking Charge is all about.

analogous to sales and purchases between different business units within a modern corporation. This first family was both a producing organization as well as a consuming household.

Regardless of exactly when marketing began, its rudiments gradually have developed in every society throughout the history of civilization.

Open markets. Moving beyond self-sufficiency, households grouped together into clans and tribes for mutual benefit. Specialization developed even further to meet an entire group's needs for food and protection. Eventually trading between tribes occurred, cities evolved, and rules for producers and consumers developed. The formation of trading markets within these early cities was a major force in the promotion of competition and economic development.

The guild system. This system, ending in Europe with the seventeenth century, was the last stage before what we know today as modern marketing began to emerge. A guild was a strictly controlled association of skilled craftsmen and merchants. The system provided some degree of quality assurance by regulating entry into trades and controlling the performance of guild members. Guilds performed marketing functions but only to a limited degree.

> Beyond user experience the reputation of sellers was based on word of mouth rather than advertising. There was little need for marketing research, and there were relatively few middlemen. Physical distribution for any but locally produced goods was a major marketing cost element. Prices were typically fixed by guild decision, but the church as well as secular tradition or authority tended to have firm ideas of what constituted the "just price," which a guild could not markedly exceed without risking opprobrium or even more tangible reprisals. The most confining aspects of the guild system, of course, were its hamstringing effect on innovation and its narrow confinement of individual economic freedom and initiative.[12]

Modern marketing

Specialization in the performance of marketing functions as well as in the production of goods was an important element in the development of modern marketing.

Development of marketing intermediaries. The marketing specialist offered one key benefit to both the producer and the consumer: **Marketing intermediaries** greatly increased the efficiency of exchange, linking producers with end-user consumers of goods and services. These specialists, functioning as middlemen, performed functions such as distribution, pricing, and promotion. Exactly when these functions developed and in what form are difficult to establish. Consider, for example, the role of marketing intermediaries more than 300 years ago in Japan. A member of the Mitsui family around 1650 opened what may have been the first department store. The merchant performed many of the intermediary functions that would be incorporated into Sears, Roebuck policies 250 years later. He purchased goods for his customers, developed sources of production, and offered a large assortment of products. Mr. Mitsui also recognized the emergence of a new group of potential customers, an urbanized new gentry and a new bourgeoisie. This new venture into retailing was the beginning of Japan's largest retail chain, the Mitsukoshi stores.[13]

The development of marketing has not occurred at the same rate throughout the world. Marketing developed in Europe later than it did in the United States. Exchanges between producers and consumers consisted primarily of the functions of personal selling and distribution until the beginning of the twentieth century in the United States. Illustrative of the nineteenth century was the traveling huckster, often with a wagon full of wares, calling on rural households. These intermediaries between buyers and sellers greatly increased the efficiency of exchange, although the marketing functions were not performed or managed as a coordinated set of activities. By eliminating the need for consumers to make direct contact with producers of goods and services, intermediaries reduced the number of transactions for both producers and consumers. The rural consumer could obtain several different items from one supplier.

Production orientation. The industrial revolution encouraged a **production orientation,** which meant the selling of a product the producer decided to make with little regard for the buyers' actual desires. Even though the orientation was clearly self-centered it survived for several decades, beginning during the nineteenth century in the United States for the following reasons:

> First, to achieve mechanization managers almost by definition had to give most of their attention to the problems of production technology. "Producibility" was the key concern, "what we are good at making" is what we made— and then sold. Producibility and the realization of scale economies both called for high degrees of standardization that in the eyes of many consumers must have meant quality reduction. Second, the enormous cost savings in mass production were reflected in heavy price reductions relative to handicrafted products. Hence, most consumers were happy to buy factory-made products even in cases when it meant accepting a quality reduction. Third, the new division of labor implied a great centralization of production but also great decentralization of consumption epitomized by the mass market.[14]

A production orientation is widespread today in many less-developed countries (LDCs) and controlled economies such as the USSR.

Sales orientation. Cyrus H. McCormick (1809–1884) was one of the early users of marketing as a central function of the business enterprise.[15] He is remembered for inventing the mechanical grain harvester for use on farms. He also used several of the concepts and tools of modern marketing including market research and analysis, the concept of market standing, pricing policies, personal selling and service, stocking of parts, and installment credit. McCormick had used all these marketing methods by 1850—fifty years before businesses began to use them widely in the United States. Clearly, McCormick's firm was far ahead of most in the practice of marketing.

Early in the twentieth century, college-level courses were offered covering some aspects of marketing, although the term *marketing* was not used in the titles. Dr. J. E. Hagerty, a professor at Ohio State University, later commented on the state of development of marketing during his doctoral work at The Wharton School in 1899.

I called the subject on which I was working the Distribution of Industrial Products. Strange as it may seem to us now relatively few seemed to be interested in the subject. For a long time it had been assumed that if goods were produced they would be sold, and there was no need in studying the methods of selling them.[16]

His observations were published in the first issue of the *Journal of Marketing* in 1936. Thus modern marketing's foundations began to emerge in the early 1900s. Nevertheless, development of the practice of marketing as it exists today occurred over several decades.

Although a few innovative firms such as Sears, Roebuck and Company, Procter & Gamble, and General Electric recognized the potential of marketing in the 1920s and 1930s, a **sales orientation,** in which there is a heavy emphasis on only the functions of selling and distribution, continued with most firms until after World War II. Until the early 1950s, shortages of consumer goods meant firms could sell everything that they could produce. During this period selling and marketing were often viewed as two separate activities, and many considered marketing and advertising to be the same.

Consumer orientation. Although there are still companies that maintain a production or sales orientation, a consumer orientation developed rapidly in the United States in the 1950s. The purpose of a **consumer orientation** is to find out what consumers want and then to produce it at a profit. Consider, for example, the experience of the McDonald's restaurant chain, whose management has done an impressive job of applying consumer-oriented marketing methods.

The McDonald's hamburger empire was launched in 1961 by Ray A. Kroc when he purchased a regional fast-food chain owned by the McDonald brothers.[17] Kroc expanded the firm's concept of offering a limited menu at low cost while maintaining consistent quality standards.

McDonald's marketing research is conducted on a continuing basis to monitor customers' wants. This information is used to plan food offerings suitable for the people McDonald's is targeting in the marketplace. Food quality, store appearance, and other aspects of retail operations are monitored on a regular basis. McDonald's stores are carefully located in areas where market opportunities exist. In 1985 the chain was the leading fast-food retailer with nearly 8000 outlets throughout the world. Sales were approaching $4 billion. By focusing on the consumer, the firm chalked up an impressive growth record in only 25 years.

During the 1960s and 1970s the practice of marketing advanced at a rapid pace, fueled by professionals trained in business schools and experienced in developing innovative marketing programs to meet the needs of target customers. Companies such as McDonald's, Procter & Gamble, International Business Machines, and General Electric became acknowledged leaders in the marketing profession. By the early 1980s, industries that had never seen the need for marketing rapidly began to add marketing professionals to their executive staffs. The new marketing challenge was particularly apparent in deregulated industries such as banking, transportation, and telecommunications.

A good example of these changes is AT&T, which operated as a huge utility and had little need for marketing until the mid-1980s. By agreeing, however, to spin off its twenty-two regulated local telephone companies in

COUNT US IN

On March 27, we announced our entry into the computer business.

In fact, we've been involved in computer technology for over 40 years. Many of the industry's basic inventions came from AT&T Bell Laboratories, from the transistor to the UNIX™ operating system, the "brain" behind many of today's most sophisticated computers. We've been making computers for our own use for years. But it wasn't until the formation of the new AT&T that we could market computers broadly.

Our approach.

We bring more than just another computer to market. We bring precisely the communications and networking know-how that the industry's next great growth stage depends on.

Business people today want computers that can talk to each other. They want computers that serve more than one workstation at a time to lower the cost per user. And they want a lot more reliability than they're getting.

AT&T Computers are built from the molecules up to *share* processing power and to communicate swiftly and naturally.

And AT&T Computers set a new standard in reliability. Because they were designed for the most demanding business application—telecommunications. Each of the thousands of AT&T Computers in the nationwide telephone network handles millions of real-time transactions every day with an average of less than 10 minutes downtime a year.

Our products.

Our entry into the field is not a single computer. It is a *family* of computers. The broadest first-day offering in the industry's history. It is a fully integrated line of multi-user, multi-tasking computers. Each is designed to take full advantage of UNIX System V. That means computer users can mix and match AT&T Computers with hardware or software from a variety of sources. So they can take advantage of this year's innovation without having to abandon last year's.

Our computers range from desk-top systems serving up to 18 users to very large systems serving over 150. There's also a high-speed local network to tie them all together. Plus a *PC Interface* that allows personal computers (which used to operate in isolation) to communicate with each other and with AT&T Computers.

Initially, we're making AT&T Computers available to resellers and sophisticated data users who can develop applications that meet a broad range of needs. Soon, we'll offer our own applications for all kinds of businesses.

This is just the beginning. You'll be hearing more from us soon.

Count on it.

AT&T

Industry observers say that AT&T—with its financial strength, technological expertise, and burgeoning marketing ability—will be the only company large enough to mount a serious challenge to IBM's dominance of the data processing market. (© 1984 AT&T)

1984, AT&T became free to enter the highly competitive world of data processing. "We intend to play in the [computer] market and play in it well," proclaimed James E. Olson, vice-chairman of AT&T and head of AT&T Technologies, which makes and markets the new machines. Signs of AT&T's increasing emphasis on marketing already are apparent. Mayford Roark, executive director of systems at Ford Motor Company, says that "AT&T comes across as having a much more aggressive marketing organization than before."[18] How fast and how well this giant can shift from a technology orientation to a consumer orientation is uncertain. Nevertheless, it is clear that marketing will be an important factor, not only in the area of data processing but also in their core business of providing telephone services since they must now compete against firms like MCI and Sprint.

Moving toward 2000

In *The Third Wave*, Alvin Toffler indicates that the modern marketing system that started developing 300 years ago is now in place and that society's future challenge is to use the exchange network to improve life and the future of civilization itself.

> One might plausibly argue that the construction of this elaborate structure of human relationships, and its explosive diffusion around the planet, was the single most impressive achievement of Second Wave civilization, dwarfing even its spectacular technological achievements. The step-by-step creation of this essentially sociocultural and psychological structure for exchange (quite apart from the torrent of goods and services that flowed through it) can be likened to the building of the Egyptian pyramids, the Roman aqueducts, the Chinese Wall and the medieval cathedrals, combined and multiplied a thousandfold.[19]

He suggests that, with this structure in place, the marketing task will be to maintain, renovate, and update it. Toffler offers a convincing evaluation of the present advanced state of development of the marketing system in the United States and throughout the industrialized world. Marketing promises to play a central role in business firms and other organizations as we move toward the twenty-first century. Learning to function in this complex marketplace will be an increasing challenge to managers, and business success may depend not only on efficient use of this exchange network but on an ability to operate strategically within it.

Marketing and business success. Major economic and social changes during the 1980s have made marketing a new priority for many firms, as described by *Business Week.*

> As companies define marketing more clearly, they no longer confuse it with advertising, which uses media to let consumers know that a certain product or service is available. In essence, marketing means moving goods from the producer to the consumer. It starts with finding out what consumers want or need, and then assessing whether the product can be made or sold at a profit. Such decisions require conducting preliminary research, market identification, and product development; testing consumer reaction to both product and price; working out production capabilities and costs; determining distribution; and then deciding on advertising and promotion strategies.[20]

Looking ahead to the next twenty years, the fiercely competitive business environment that is expected to prevail simply will not allow firms in many industries to succeed unless they develop and maintain strong marketing capabilities. Of course, good marketing cannot overcome faulty products, slow delivery, and other operating problems. Rather, marketing must be part of a total company effort aimed at customer satisfaction. The prevailing business environment highlights the critical role of marketing in providing the competitive edge that the production and sales orientation provided in their day. The importance of marketing as the cutting edge of business strategy was recognized by many different businesses in the 1980s.[21] This new awareness of the marketplace was particularly significant in industries that no longer were protected from the vagaries of consumer selling by regulatory statutes—industries such as airlines, railroads, banks, telecommunications, and financial services. These firms as well as many others were faced with the challenge of achieving profitable growth in an environment of product proliferation, intense competition, and escalating marketing costs.

Although the marketing profession has matured, it is by most standards a young profession. Marketing executives are being called on to play a much greater role in guiding the future strategies of corporations than in the past. For example, Apple Computer's new president, John Sculley, is an experienced and highly regarded consumer-goods marketer recruited from PepsiCo Inc. In the past, Apple concentrated more on developing new technologies than on understanding the dynamics of the marketplace. Apple's recruitment of Sculley is one of the more visible signs that marketing has become the new corporate priority.[22]

To close our discussion of how critical marketing has become to business success, let us consider an interesting marketing application in the arts. The director of the Houston Grand Opera—a former opera singer and a graduate of Columbia University's Graduate School of Business—has successfully applied marketing, management, and financial concepts and methods to his organization. David Gockely, the director, comments on his growth and diversification strategy: "With increasing competition, ever-escalating production costs, and reduced government subsidies, the future of an organization like ours will depend on our ability to aggressively market a broad range of products to more and more people."[23] The Houston Grand Opera's business performance record for the decade ending in 1981 was impressive. Season subscriptions more than tripled to 13,500, performances went from 27 to 400, and the budget reached $7 million. The organization has been very skillful in applying planning, budgeting, marketing, and other business techniques. Nancy Sasser, the assistant director, comments: "We spend a lot of time marketing our product; monitoring our cash flow and investments; and forecasting ticket sales, contribution levels, and day-to-day production costs."[24]

Future trends. To a large extent future trends in the practice of marketing will present challenges similar to those experienced during the decade ending in 1985. These trends include a rapidly changing business environment, a critical need by business to understand markets and competition, and a challenge to managers to adjust marketing strategies to changing conditions. The future promises to differ from the past in one important aspect: The nature and scope of social and economic changes in the future are likely to occur at a much faster rate than in the last ten years. These changes include

- Intense and complex global competition because of slow growth in many markets throughout the world and excess production capacity in many industries
- An increasing complexity of people's needs and wants for goods and services
- Emergence of new firms because of deregulation of industries such as financial services, transportation, and communications
- Movement of less developed countries into the application of modern marketing practices.

These changes will result in both opportunities and threats to all persons with careers in business. An understanding of the nature and scope of professional marketing concepts and practices will be important in coping with future challenges. The strong market-centered focus of business planning in the future will require all business professionals, including those in accounting, finance, marketing, management, sales, advertising, human resources, and distribution, to have a basic knowledge of marketing management.

A new era of marketing practice may be emerging. Although its nature and scope are not clear, this stage of development includes an expanded view of managerial marketing. This evolution of business purpose apparently represents a response to the rapidly changing environment. Philip Kotler describes this trend as **megamarketing,** organizations seeking to anticipate, influence, and help direct environmental change rather than merely responding to changes after they occur. This suggests that marketing people may pursue a more active societal role in the future. This perspective recognizes government officials, public-interest groups, and the news media as targets of an organization's marketing efforts.[25] Thus factors such as political power and public opinion formation become marketing concerns of businesses (see "Rethinking the Marketing Concept," a Marketalk in Chapter 3).

THE MARKETING CONCEPT

The **marketing concept** is a belief about the proper way to manage a business or an economic system. Our final task in this chapter is to examine the marketing concept, which spells out the guidelines necessary for a business to provide customer satisfaction. In our brief look at McDonald's and AT&T, we examined the marketing concept's contribution to an organization's performance. For you to see more clearly how the marketing concept helps a consumer-products marketer and a communications giant, we need to examine the requirements for using the concept.

The marketing concept consists of three logical requirements.

1. Examine people's needs and wants as the basis of deciding what the business (or economy) will do.
2. Select the best way to meet the consumer's needs that are targeted by the firm.
3. Achieve the organization's performance objectives by meeting the needs satisfactorily.

Although these guidelines are not complicated, deciding *how* to implement them is not obvious as evidenced by the many organizations that do not follow the marketing concept. A closer look at each requirement will give you an idea of its key features and what must be done to adopt the marketing concept. Our perspective will be that of the business firm.

Customer needs and wants

The customer's needs are often far from obvious, yet they represent the focal point for the decision of what a business will be. Two key issues exist: first, how to identify consumers' needs and second, how to determine which of these an organization should serve.

Identifying needs and wants. Understanding the needs and wants of the people and organizations in the markets of interest to the enterprise is critical to business success. Gaining this understanding requires skillful analysis of market size, growth trends, customer characteristics, industry profiles, and key competitor strengths and weaknesses. Analyzing and tracking market trends demand a close working relationship between corporate and marketing managers and marketing researchers.

The Kroger Company, second largest supermarket chain in the United States, has done an impressive job of finding out what its customers want.

> Up to a quarter of a million shoppers in communities throughout the Midwest and South will be grilled during in-depth interviews this year by researchers working for the Kroger Co. supermarkets. The results of those interviews will be gone over with a fine-tooth comb back in corporate headquarters in Cincinnati. "The fundamental strength of this company is in listening to what the customers are telling us," says Kroger Chairman Lyle Everingham.[26]

Management must stay in touch with the marketplace by direct contact or by the use of customer research. In large firms direct contact with customers is not always feasible. Many companies are finding marketing research essential to discover people's needs. Research eliminates the necessity for management's trying to guess customers' needs, which is a dangerous way to make decisions.

Determining which needs to serve. A **market target** is the group of people or organizations to which a company decides to market its product or service. All operations of the firm revolve around the market target decision. The alternatives range from serving all (or most) buyers using a mass strategy, or serving one or more segments using a different strategy for each segment. **Market segmentation** is targeting one or more specific groups within a market.

There are clear indications that market segmentation is becoming the dominant strategy of many successful firms. Serving a specific portion of the market is a particularly promising option for companies that are not market leaders for two reasons: (1) high market share is often linked to strong business performance, and (2) serving a segment of a product-market is often the only feasible way for many firms to gain and hold a market share. (See Marketool to learn how companies calculate market share.) While the market target decision alone will not guarantee high performance, it can be the first step in building a high-performance marketing program.

Avoiding a product focus. One real advantage of the marketing concept is that it avoids concentrating too much attention on the product while failing to consider the potential buyers' needs and wants. Consider, for example, Polaroid's entry into the home movie market in the late 1970s. Management apparently assumed that people had a need for instant movies, as they did for instant photographs. The camera and projector were expensive, the film quality was lower than conventional movies, and people apparently did not want the instant movies.[27] The spontaneous enjoyment of sharing

MarkeTOOL

How to Calculate Market Share

MARKET SHARE frequently is used to compare a firm against its competitors. It is a useful basis to compare firms for a particular period and over several time periods. Marketing objectives (see Chapter 2) are sometimes stated as increasing or maintaining the market share position of a company for a particular product. Thus market share measures are important information for marketing planning and control. Market share is calculated as follows for a specified time period such as one year:

$$\frac{\text{Sales by company N}}{\text{Total industry sales}} \times 100 = \text{market share (\%)}.$$

Suppose company N sold $1.23 million of widgets in 1985, compared to total industry sales of $21.4 million in the same year:

$$\text{Company N's market share} = \frac{1.23}{21.4} \times 100 = 5.7\%.$$

Market share also can be computed based on the number of units sold. When selling prices vary because of quality and features offered by different firms in an industry, unit market share should be analyzed carefully to avoid misinterpreting the information. For example, a company whose prices are relatively high compared with other firms in the industry will have a market share that is higher on a *dollar* basis than it is on a *unit* basis.

Product planning

Placement channels

CUSTOMER SATISFACTION

Pricing decisions

Promotion strategy

Exhibit 1.5 Elements of the marketing mix

Notes that get noticed. 3M Company wittily addresses itself to the business community, a principal user of its note pads. (Courtesy of 3M)

an on-the-spot snapshot was lost in the more complicated process of projecting an instant movie. The product failed to generate enough sales to make it a profitable venture for Polaroid, and it was withdrawn from the market. It seems logical that marketing research should have been used to test the probable response of people to the concept of instant movies before a decision was made to invest in the development and marketing of the product.

Meeting customers' needs and wants

The second requirement of the marketing concept is to select the best way to meet the organization's target customers' needs and wants, which will be the basis for the design and implementation of the marketing program. The **marketing program** comprises the *product* or service (quality, features, packaging, durability, etc.), its *placement* or distribution (when and where it is made available), its *price*, and its *promotion* (advertising and sales efforts). Thus the critical issue is how to combine these elements (called the four Ps of marketing) into a total company effort. This coordinated program, which is used to obtain favorable response from target customers, is also called the **marketing mix** (or marketing offer). As Exhibit 1.5 suggests, the blending of the marketing mix components into an integrated program designed to deliver customer satisfaction is essential if the benefits of the marketing concept are to be realized. The increasing importance of service after the sale, considering the complex range of products available today, may in the future require breaking out service from the product component into a separate marketing program component.

Meeting customer needs is the responsibility of everyone in the company. Everyone from the production worker to the chief executive officer should be responsible for delivering customer satisfaction. One important aspect of developing the marketing program is organizing people so that efforts in the various activities will be coordinated. Someone in the firm must be responsible for planning and coordinating the marketing mix. Often, the marketing manager assumes this responsibility, although in some companies it is assumed by the president.

Results through customer satisfaction

Customer satisfaction, the process of meeting customer needs, is what business is all about. Managers that are perceptive about *what* needs to serve and *how* to serve them will be successful more often than those who do not give proper attention to these critical tasks. Unfortunately, the marketing concept does not indicate how to do these things, only that they should be done. (An interesting example of applying the guidelines of the marketing concept to an industrial product is described in Marketalk.) Moreover, it is essential that the firm's efforts in providing customer satisfaction be planned and managed in a manner such that revenues (sales) less the costs of the marketing program provide an acceptable profit margin for the company. Not-for-profit organizations (those not in the business of making money) should balance costs against either revenues or some measure of social benefit so that losses do not occur.

The ability of Kroger's management to achieve high profitability on a continuing basis has been impressive. During the 1970s the company's return on equity (assets minus liabilities) more than doubled to approximately 17 percent, yet long-term debt was less than half that carried by most major chains.[28] As one analyzes Kroger's operations, it is clear that management has implemented the requirements of the marketing concept. They know their customers, and they monitor people's changing requirements in supermarket buying. Kroger's services are carefully designed to meet these needs, and they are altered when necessary to adjust to changing conditions. One interesting example of finding a need that offered a new opportunity was Kroger's venture into plants and flowers in 1979.

> Kroger is the largest florist in the country. From a standing start just two years ago, Kroger now has 400 flower shops in its almost 1,300 stores doing up to 4% of sales volume, and the company expects to have about 700 in two years time.[29]

The company's movement into twenty-four-hour shopping, delicatessens, bakeries, seafood markets, and other areas is indicative of management's continuing consumer research and design of programs and services to meet needs and deliver customer satisfaction at a profit. Kroger's success illustrates the full potential of the marketing concept.

*Marke*TALK ///

The marketing concept behind Quick Metal

TO ROUND OUT OUR LOOK at the marketing concept, let us examine how one company satisfied the basic requirements of the concept and achieved some spectacular results by applying marketing management to an industrial (business) market. The company is the Loctite Corporation and its product is Quick Metal, a puttylike adhesive for repairing broken and worn machine parts.

Quick Metal's predecessor was a runny green liquid packaged in a plain red bottle with the uninformative name of RC,601. Dissatisfied with the performance of RC,601, management tried a new approach when planning for Quick Metal. In early 1979, marketing management initiated a marketing research project to determine what customers wanted from an adhesive. Interviews were conducted over a six-week period with approximately thirty equipment designers and production engineers and forty maintenance workers. Interestingly, the research led to targeting the new product toward maintenance people, instead of the previously targeted equipment designers. It was discovered that a designer is likely to be hes-

itant to try an unfamiliar product, whereas a maintenance worker has the authority to buy anything that will put a stalled production line back into operation.

Management developed a coordinated marketing program to launch Quick Metal into the marketplace. The name was selected to convey what the product could do for the customer rather than its chemical composition. Advertising copy was designed to explain the product's features and ease of use. For example, one slogan stated, "Keeps machinery running until the new parts arrive." Pricing was aggressive at $17.75 for a 50-cc tube, yielding an 85-percent gross margin for the manufacturer. Because one tube could eliminate 800 hours of machine downtime, however, the cost was small by comparison to the benefit provided. A program was initiated to call the 695 Loctite independent distributors daily to encourage sales. Incentives were offered to employees and distributors. Management carefully blended the different components of the marketing mix.

Introduced in October 1980, sales reached $2.2 million by April 1981. Management estimated that sales of only $320,000 would have occurred under the firm's prior marketing management methods. The research and planning paid off. Management also gained useful informa-

tion about its salesforce, and the benefits carried over to sales of other Loctite products.

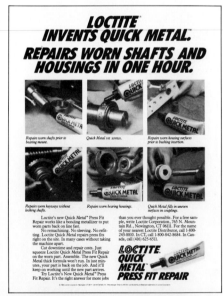

It wasn't simply changing the name from RC,601 to Quick Metal that increased the sale of the product. Loctite's management researched and planned each part of the marketing mix before this ad introduced Quick Metal to the industrial marketplace in 1980. (Courtesy of Loctite Corporation)

SOURCE: Bill Abrams, "Consumer-product techniques help Loctite sell to industry," *Wall Street Journal*, Apr. 2, 1981, p. 29. Reprinted by permission of the *Wall Street Journal*, © Dow Jones & Company, Inc. 1981. All rights reserved.

///

SUMMARY

Marketing affects the daily lives of virtually everyone. The marketing function consumes a large part of every dollar spent on products and services. Marketing functions are essential to complete the exchange process and to reduce the number of transactions between producers and consumers. Marketing management is a critical factor to business success and promises to grow in importance in the decade ahead.

Marketing is an essential function in any society in which specialization of labor occurs instead of each person or living unit providing for its own needs. Specialization creates a need for exchange because there is a gap between producers and consumers of products and services. This gap consists of location and time, assortment, information, valuation, and ownership discrepancies. The purpose of marketing functions is to bridge the gap. Marketing institutions such as wholesalers and retailers have developed to perform the marketing functions that producers and consumers do not handle themselves.

Marketing can be defined from a societal, managerial, or consumer perspective. Exchange is central to all the points of view of marketing. Marketing management is the primary focus of this book, although the societal and consumer points of view should be kept in mind as we examine the various issues, problems, and decisions associated with marketing management.

Marketing has developed over thousands of years, although most of what we call modern marketing has occurred in the twentieth century in the United States. Selling and distribution dominated the marketing function during its early development. As the exchange process expanded from simple barter and trade, the need for marketing specialists came about. The creation of a customer as a specific job of management began in Japan in the mid-1600s. Cyrus H. McCormick shaped the basic tools of marketing in the United States in the mid-1800s.

The marketing concept spells out the requirements for an organization if it is to deliver customer satisfaction, starting with determination of the customer's needs and wants as the basis of deciding business purpose. This is followed by deciding how best to meet the needs and wants to be served by the organization, and then achieving the organization's performance targets through customer satisfaction. Identifying needs and wants and deciding which people or organizations to select as market targets is one of management's most demanding responsibilities. Meeting needs and wants requires a coordinated company effort to design and implement a marketing program (mix) consisting of the product or service, placement, price, and promotion. The marketing concept states the requirements for customer satisfaction but does not indicate what needs to serve or how to serve them. Determining what needs to serve and how to serve them is the purpose of this book.

KEY TERMS

needs and wants	marketing functions	marketing institutions
specialization	producers	macromarketing
exchange	consumers	societal perspective
marketing systems	discrepancies or gaps	managerial perspective

marketing management   sales orientation   market segmentation
consumer perspective   consumer orientation   marketing program
marketing   megamarketing   marketing mix
marketing intermediaries   marketing concept   customer satisfaction
production orientation   market target

QUESTIONS FOR REVIEW AND DISCUSSION

1. Refer to Exhibit 1.1 and list companies you can think of that market food or beverages, housing, transportation, and household operations.

2. During the next decade how will economic conditions affect the marketing efforts of companies?

3. How did systems for exchange evolve?

4. One of the characteristics of the gap between producers and consumers is the difference in location and desired time of purchase. What are the four other characteristics of the gap between producers and consumers?

5. Marketing bridges the gaps between producers and consumers. Give examples of the marketing functions that bridge these gaps.

6. Consumers may be willing to perform some of the functions to bridge the gap between producers and consumers to obtain lower prices and other trade-offs. For example, they shop at catalogue showrooms. What are some other ways consumers bridge the gap?

7. In this book marketing is viewed from a managerial perspective. From what other perspectives can marketing be viewed?

8. A societal perspective concern is consumer protection. The deaths from contaminated Tylenol in 1982 caused a number of changes in the drug industry. Discuss some of these changes.

9. Describe your understanding of marketing from the managerial perspective.

10. How have marketing intermediaries increased the efficiency of exchange?

11. Cyrus H. McCormick was an early user of marketing in business. Discuss his contribution to modern marketing.

12. McDonald's is the leading fast-food retailer in the world. What modern marketing management methods does this firm utilize?

13. The marketing concept is a statement or philosophy about the proper way to manage a business or an economic system. What are the three requirements of the marketing concept?

14. Customer needs and wants are not always obvious. List some ways in which people's needs and wants for goods and services can be identified.

15. Polaroid experienced marketing myopia when it introduced instant movie cameras. What is marketing myopia and how does following the marketing concept help avoid it?

BUILDING YOUR PORTFOLIO

Based on your experience with retailers in your hometown or the town in which you are going to school, select two retailers. The first retailer should be a firm that you know is practicing the marketing concept. The second firm should be an organization that has not been successful in implementing the marketing concept. Prepare a detailed analysis of each retailer, discussing customer needs served by the firm, how the firm is attempting to meet customer needs, and the results that are being achieved. You may find it helpful to talk with people in each firm in developing your analysis of how well the firm is following the guidelines provided by the marketing concept. In addition, customers of each firm can provide you with useful information about how well they are satisfied with the services and products marketed by each retailer.

NOTES

1. June Kronholz, "Buying spree: Chinese learn the joy of shopping as leaders stress consumer goods." *Wall Street Journal,* Oct. 26, 1983, p. 1.
2. "The complicated task of providing satellite service to foreign countries." *Broadcasting,* Mar. 12, 1984, pp. 75–76.
3. Tom Steinert-Threlkeld, "Information: An invisible new industry." *Fort Worth Star-Telegram,* June 6, 1982, p. 20.
4. *Advertising Age,* Feb. 2, 1984, p. 31.
5. An expanded discussion of these gaps can be found in William McInnes, "A Conceptual Approach to Marketing," Reavis Cox, Wroe Alderson, and Stanley J. Shapiro (Eds.) *Theory in Marketing,* second series, Homewood, Ill.: Irwin, 1964, pp. 51–67.
6. William Lazer and James D. Culley, *Marketing Management.* Boston: Houghton Mifflin, 1983, 11–12.
7. Kronholz, op. cit.
8. David W. Cravens, Gerald E. Hills, and Robert B. Woodruff, *Marketing Decision Making* (Rev. Ed.). Homewood, Ill.: Irwin, 1980, p. 16.
9. Philip Kotler, *Marketing Management: Analysis, Planning and Control* (4th ed.). Englewood Cliffs, N.J.: Prentice-Hall, 1980, p. 19.
10. The following discussion is based on Hans B. Thorelli, "Concepts of Marketing: A Review, Preview, and Paradigm," in P. Varadarajan (Ed.), *The Marketing Concept: Perspectives and Viewpoints.* College Station, Tex.: Texas A&M University, 1983, pp. 2–37.
11. Ibid., p. 5.
12. Ibid., p. 8. Reprinted by permission.
13. Peter F. Drucker, *Management: Tasks, Responsibilities, Practices.* New York: Harper & Row, 1974, p. 62.
14. Thorelli, op. cit., p. 10. Reprinted by permission.
15. Drucker, op. cit.
16. J. E. Hagerty, "Experiences of an early marketing teacher." *Journal of Marketing,* July 1936, p. 22.
17. "The burger that conquered the country." *Time,* Sept. 17, 1973, p. 84.
18. "AT&T takes its first giant step into commercial computers." *Business Week,* Apr. 9, 1984, p. 100.
19. Alvin Toffler, *The Third Wave.* New York: Morrow, 1980, p. 286.
20. "Marketing: The new priority." *Business Week,* Nov. 21, 1983, p. 93.
21. Ibid.
22. George Getschow, "Houston's P.T. Barnum of opera thrives by emphasizing marketing, bottom line." *Wall Street Journal,* Mar. 9, 1982, p. 45.
23. Ibid.
24. "Marketing: The new priority." op. cit., p. 96.
25. "Kotler: Rethink the Marketing Concept," *Marketing News,* September 14, 1984, pp. 1, 22.
26. Eammonn Fingleton, "250,000 unpaid consultants." *Forbes,* Sept. 14, 1981, p. 147.
27. Mitchell C. Lynch, "Instant movies falter: Is Polaroid's chairman wrong for a change?" *Wall Street Journal,* Aug. 9, 1979, pp. 1, 29.
28. Fingleton, op. cit.
29. Ibid., p. 148.

Case 1.1

Rent-a-Frog

RENT-A-FROG is a student business organization at Texas Christian University, Fort Worth, Texas. (The TCU mascot is a frog.) The business was started in 1983, patterned after a similar program at Southern Methodist University. The parent company, Scholastic Marketing Corporation of Dallas, plans to expand to other college campuses.

The organization supplies students to perform a variety of services for campus clients and people in the community. A "frog" can be rented at hourly rates from $4 to $50, depending on the service. Jobs vary from babysitting to modeling. Rent-a-Frog's prices may be high for such jobs as petsitting and babysitting, but most of

their services are priced under the going market rate. For example, professional movers will charge from $30 to $45 per hour with minimum of a half-day use. Rent-a-Frog will give you a student mover for $15 an hour with no constraints and little if any quality difference. People needing services are encouraged to contact Rent-a-Frog by telephone. The availability of Frog services is communicated through newspaper articles and other means.

Using a mail survey, Rent-a-Frog determined that 65 percent of its customers are Ph.D.s or medical doctors. The company's service areas are located around country clubs in the community.

Workers are recruited through word-of-

mouth, bulletin board announcements, and school publications. Students who work for Rent-a-Frog are interviewed and must provide references. Each person signs a contract. Jobs are assigned on the basis of talents and availability. Clients are asked to evaluate all services provided so that service quality will be maintained.

By mid-1984, Rent-a-Frog had job requests exceeding the number of students available. Plans were underway to expand into travel services and franchising. All in all, Rent-a-Frog was operating on a successful basis, providing jobs to students, supplying services to people in the community, and generating revenues in excess of costs.

QUESTIONS

1. Is Rent-a-Frog following the guidelines of the marketing concept?

2. Describe the marketing mix used by Rent-a-Frog.

Case 1.2

Pilgrim Industries

LONNIE "BO" PILGRIM, 55, wants to know if the Texas consumer will buy a boneless, uncut, whole chicken that can be cooked and served like a thick-cut ribeye steak or any boneless slab of meat.

Pilgrim, chief executive for Pilgrim Industries and East Texas poultry entrepreneur from Pittsburg, Texas, says he has developed the "world's first fresh, boneless chicken" for the supermarket meat counter.

He heads a company which produces about 375 million pounds of dressed poultry and 36 million dozen table eggs annually and which entered the namebrand, retail consumer market to compete with Holly Farms in 1983.

And this longtime marketer of Pilgrim's Pride poultry already is testing the consumer's reaction to the new deboned

SOURCE: Worth Wren, Jr., "Pilgrim cuts through chicken industry," *Fort Worth Star-Telegram,* March 25, 1984, p. 4G. Reprinted by permission.

product, at $2.36 a pound retail through three Fresh Approach specialty food stores in Dallas. The test is expected to continue six weeks, while Pilgrim's marketing advisers formulate the company's final advertising strategy for the supermarket and restaurant trades.

But Pilgrim is not one of those press-shy executives. He has taken his product to the news media and sought reporters' and editors' critiques of the product, which is about 2 inches thick and averages about 2 pounds per package.

It'll be "the biggest thing to happen in the meat counter in 40 years," Pilgrim said modestly while in Fort Worth. "We take out all the bones without putting a cut in the skin" of the chicken carcass as it moves through the usual processing plant disassembly line, he said.

How his company's workers do it—at the rate of about five minutes a bird, he says—will remain a secret, Pilgrim said. He is still seeking patents on the process,

the apparatus used in the process and the product.

"Just like Coca-Cola does it, that's how I do it," Pilgrim said, tongue in both sides of his cheek.

Whatever this technique and special equipment might be, Pilgrim boasts that his industry-speed deboning process sure beats the heck out of the home chef spending one to three hours cooking a chicken and then deboning it.

Pilgrim isn't talking about the boneless chicken parts, such as breast fillets that already are found commonly in the supermarket display cases. He isn't talking about a whole chicken cut into parts and away from the bones. He is talking about a whole chicken carcass, "with all the meat intact in the original position and minus only the neck, liver, gizzard, heart, tail, wing tips and bones."

Pilgrim said he started on his project to develop the deboning process almost four years ago.

"If there was boneless beef, why not boneless chicken, the whole chicken?" he verbalized his reasoning. "The Japanese sell 60 percent of their retail chicken deboned. But they were cutting it up and deboning it."

Pilgrim said the trail led him to a seminar to demonstrate how to debone a fresh chicken for women attending Texas A&M Research and Extension Center in Dallas. By then, last fall, Pilgrim had figured out how to do it in 20 minutes.

Later, having his company's workers trying the process in the chicken processing plants, Pilgrim found that the unperfected technique he developed at home after work was "exhausting to the wrists of the workers."

At that point, Pilgrim returned home, bought two chickens and set to work on the apparatus, knife and shackle which would alleviate the exhaustion problem, he said. Having done that, Pilgrim vows

that he has developed the process for commercial production.

Pilgrim's wholesale price on the deboned chicken is $1.86 a pound, but he says the company will drop that figure to $1.79 a pound.

"What the stores will do with it is for them to decide," he said. But he estimates that the retail price will range from $2.24 to $2.49 a pound.

"Why would consumers pay almost three times the price of a whole chicken with bones to get one without bones?" Pilgrim was asked.

"You have the whole bird selling for 89 cents a pound, but you lose 50 percent of the weight in bones" and other inedible components, he said. "You have to look at the other boneless meat items in the counter, beef, pork, fish and turkey, and they're priced from $2.50 to $5.50 a pound."

"Then you get to the point you've got to

figure convenience, and you're only paying for the meat," Pilgrim said.

For example, boneless chicken breasts are now selling at $3.89 a pound; so a whole boneless chicken might do well at $2.36 a pound, he said.

"Consumers like a fork-and-knife dish," Pilgrim said, referring to the fast-food chains' recent moves with fried chicken fillets, strips and nuggets.

He's already convinced that consumers will accept his product in droves, and to prove it, he has developed a collection of "Recipes for Pilgrim's Pride Fresh Boneless Whole Chicken." Broiled is one of Pilgrim's favorite ways to fix it.

But what about all those bones? Pilgrim said the company sends all bones, inedible parts, blood and feathers to the company's own rendering plant in Mount Pleasant, where the components are transformed into protein ingredients for livestock feed or pet food.

QUESTIONS

1. Do people have a need for a boneless chicken?

2. What do you think of Lonnie Pilgrim's planned marketing program?

2 Marketing Strategy and Management

When you finish this chapter, you will understand

☐ How the marketing concept guides decision making by company managers who determine marketing strategy

☐ How analyses of the situation are used in a professional approach to marketing management

☐ The major kinds of decisions and activities for which marketing managers are responsible

☐ That marketing managers must work with managers of other business functions for marketing strategy to work

Professional marketing managers are increasingly using computers to perform analyses of the marketplace and to assist in planning and controlling marketing strategy.

The 1980s have ushered in a rapidly changing situation for banks in the United States. Even the largest banks are looking over their shoulders at the threat of new and powerful competition from outside the banking community. Companies such as Merrill Lynch, American Express, and Sears, Roebuck and Company are moving into banking markets, and doing so quite successfully. Customers are changing, too. People are becoming more comfortable with electronic banking as evidenced by the increasing use of automated teller services.

What's more, consumers have shown increased willingness to use nonbank companies as sources of financial services: Note the success of cash management accounts offered by brokerage houses, which have seriously eaten into deposits previously going into banks.

Many banks are developing strategies to deal with the growing challenge of this changing situation. For instance, ways have been developed to share their automated teller machines with each other. This move allows a bank to expand services to customers living in an

area broader than a community or even a state—perhaps eventually creating the means for banks to become national companies. Electronic banking networks will be able to match the services of new competition from nonbank companies, which operate on a national scale. Also, linking computers opens the door to electronic funds transfers between a variety of locations such as home and retail stores. Responding to customer needs, banks have been able through services such as these to remain competitive in a rapidly changing environment.[1]

OF LATE, BANKS HAVE BECOME INCREASINGLY RESPONSIVE to the needs of the marketplace. With an onslaught of new nonbank competition banks have begun to pay more attention to marketing strategies. Business success depends on finding ways to meet customer needs and wants profitably in the face of changing situational forces. Increased competition from nonbanking financial companies and changing customer needs and wants for financial services illustrate some of these forces. Companies must continually stay on top of changes to remain competitive. Only then can managers design and carry out actions that best take advantage of opportunities as well as counter threats. Because the success of these actions is dependent on how customers in markets respond, marketing managers play a very important role in meeting this challenge.

In this chapter, we present an overview of marketing management's responsibilities with special emphasis on how they are interrelated. The discussion serves as a roadmap for the entire text because subsequent chapters explore more fully these responsibilities. Importantly, the principles and approaches advocated as part of marketing management can be applied by marketing professionals at all levels, including a salesperson appointed to a sales territory, a sales manager responsible for the performance of several salespersons, a brand manager assigned to one of the company's brands, or a division marketing manager accountable for the coordination of an entire product line.

MARKETING MANAGEMENT IN ACTION

Marketing management's responsibilities

Marketing managers spend their time designing and carrying out marketing strategy. **Marketing strategy** selects the particular customers whose needs and wants the company can meet profitably, sets objectives for desired performance, and explains how the company is to use the marketing mix to achieve these objectives. Strategy takes into consideration the strengths and capabilities of the company and applies them to the way customers' needs are to be met. Also considered are the many and varied factors that help to shape customers' purchase decisions and the marketing strategies of competitors. K mart's recent decisions concerning its clothing lines provide an interesting illustration. Previously, many people had a low opinion of K mart's clothing quality, so sales were limited to low- and lower-middle-income customers. Furthermore, competition had been intensifying, offering quality brands at attractive prices. The new marketing strategy is to upgrade K mart's reputation as a place to shop for clothing having respectable quality and following fashion trends. Management believes that the change in strategy is necessary to achieve higher sales by attracting more middle-income customers away from competitors. The company is counting on its strong clout with suppliers to get better-quality clothing and on its reputation for bargain prices to make the strategy work.[2]

Marketing strategy provides important guidelines for managers who must make many tactical decisions. *Tactics* put strategy into operation. Managers make specific choices concerning components of the marketing mix that determine how strategy will be carried out. K mart's managers had to choose specific clothing brands that have respectable quality and are fashionable, had to set prices for each brand, had to select sizes, colors, and styles to carry, and had to communicate the new reputation to customers. These are the tactical decisions that transform the strategy into a real offer to customers.

As shown in Exhibit 2.1, marketing management looks easy enough—design and carry out a marketing strategy that satisfies selected customers' needs, and sales will flow back to the organization. A closer look, however, raises questions that marketing managers must answer first:

- Who are the customers in markets that the company can profitably sell to?
- What are their needs and wants?
- What marketing mix will best satisfy these needs, and does this mix capitalize on the company's strengths?
- Does the marketing mix offer significant advantages to customers over the competition?
- What level of sales will result from the mix?
- What financial and other resources will have to be committed to the marketing mix?
- Will the sales justify the costs of carrying out the marketing strategy?

Exhibit 2.1 Companies use marketing strategy to attract sales from markets

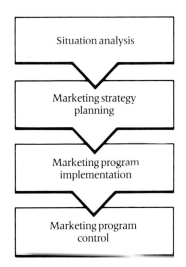

Exhibit 2.2 Marketing management's responsibilities

These questions often are difficult to answer. Even with good answers to these questions, there are no guarantees that management's strategy will work as intended. Unexpected factors such as a change in strategy on the part of a competitor may suddenly appear, or problems in carrying out strategy may crop up. For these reasons, managers must use a systematic approach to fulfilling their responsibilities. This approach, referred to as marketing management in Chapter 1, involves analyzing the situation for opportunity, planning a marketing strategy to meet the needs and wants of selected customers, implementing this strategy to obtain sales, and controlling the strategy's performance.

Exhibit 2.2 presents marketing management as activities—analysis, planning, implementation, and control—that are linked in a logical flow. Analysis of the situation helps marketing managers understand the many factors that influence opportunity to attract sales from customers in the face of competition. A well-designed marketing strategy provides the direction for implementing the strategy. Finally, control follows up on implementation to see that the strategy is working as intended.

Like a chain, marketing management is only as strong as its weakest link. For example, a highly creative marketing strategy cannot work if it is poorly implemented. Nor can a well-implemented but poorly conceived marketing strategy achieve its objectives. RCA's experience with its videodisk player, an electronic device for playing video programming from recordlike disks, shows the consequences of marketing strategy going awry. When videodisk players were introduced in 1981, RCA's management predicted that they would be the hottest selling electronic product of the decade. Marketing strategy intended to gain customer acceptance of the product as part of a home entertainment and information center that would include a television, personal computer, and videotape recorder. The strategy failed, and in 1984 RCA decided to withdraw the product from the market. Apparently, customers were not interested in videodisk players because they could not record television programs. Perhaps a more penetrating analysis of the situation would have helped RCA's management choose a strategy that did not place the videodisk player in such direct competition with the much more popular videotape recorder.[3]

Applying the marketing concept

Marketing management begins with the marketing concept. As explained in Chapter 1, this concept is a philosophy of how a business should be run. Marketing decisions determine how a company meets its customers' needs and wants, and sales and ultimately profits depend on how successful those needs and wants are satisfied. The marketing concept's emphasis on profits means that managers must be highly selective in choosing which customers have needs and wants that the company is capable of satisfying. The threat of competition forces a company to look for ways to use its strengths, whatever they may be, to advantage in doing so.

The marketing concept appears deceptively simple, but experience has shown that applying the concept in practice can be difficult. Even the best of companies can have difficulty finding a successful marketing strategy. Consider Sears, Roebuck and Company's retailing business. The company has built a respected reputation for responding to customer needs through its merchandise and service mix. Yet, Sears has lost customers in the past

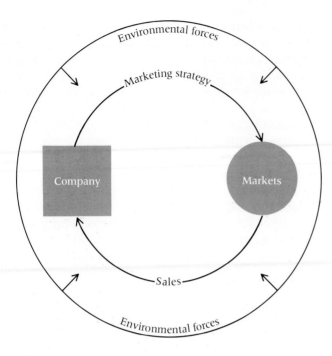

Exhibit 2.3 Marketing strategy's environment

decade by trying several marketing strategies that have not worked well:

- Upgrading their reputation by selling expensive, high-fashion merchandise (clothing, furs, jewelry) to attract high-income customers. Not only were these customers not interested in the Sears label, but the store's traditional customers were not pleased with the higher prices.
- Becoming known for having many styles, models, and colors of merchandise to attract customers who typically shopped in specialty stores. This strategy did not work.
- Establishing a reputation for matching prices of the discount stores. Sales went up, but profits went down.[4]

Sears' problems with marketing strategy illustrate a common fact of business life. Meeting customers' needs and wants profitably is complicated because many influences on sales are hard to understand and difficult if not impossible to control. Coping with these influences is an essential part of a marketing manager's responsibility, as highlighted by Exhibit 2.3. We begin our discussion of marketing management by examining the process of analyzing the situation.

ANALYZING THE SITUATION

A professional approach to marketing management is based on this key principle: Analyses must precede action. Marketing management hinges on designing a successful marketing strategy that uses company strengths to meet customer needs and wants in the face of many outside influences or forces. Thus marketing managers are expected to understand the nature of these forces and what can be expected of them in the future. Analyses of the situation are the information activities that provide this understanding. (See Marketalk on the importance of analysis for Marriott Corporation.)

Two major kinds of analyses that provide information for marketing planning are (1) *internal* analysis of company strengths and weaknesses and (2) *external* analysis of environmental forces influencing opportunity in markets.

*Marke*TALK ///

Analysis and marketing strategy are a winning combination for Marriott Corporation

MARRIOTT CORPORATION is one company that does analysis before taking action. Some years ago, management became convinced that growth in existing businesses—Marriott's hotels, restaurants, food service, and theme parks—would slow down by the 1980s. Management began immediately to search for new strategies. First, the decision was made to stay with businesses related to what the company does best—provide accommodation services for people. This decision substantially narrowed the search for new opportunities.

Subsequent analysis showed that customers staying in moderately priced motels were unhappy with the competition, long dominated by chains operating units built mostly in the 1960s. Out of this analysis, strategy for Courtyard Hotels was born. Large rooms, small size (150 units), standardized designs, and minimal services were conceived to provide good-quality accommodations at low rates. Marriott tested the Courtyard strategy by opening three units near Atlanta. The results have demonstrated a winning idea, and plans now call for opening 300 new Courtyards by 1990. Although competition is heavy—Holiday Inn, Howard Johnson's, and Ramada Inns, to name a few—management believes that the new strategy can capture enough sales to make the opportunity attractive.

With Courtyard Hotels under way, management searched for other opportunities. Again, analysis was used, and it revealed a market among upwardly mobile people for suites rather than for single rooms. From this information came the idea for all-suite hotels having about 250 units per hotel. Locations are planned for suburban areas and medium-sized cities without ex-

isting Marriott hotels. Because people are willing to pay more for suites, these hotels will generate a higher percentage of revenues from the rooms than do traditional hotels. Studies have shown that after staying in a suite hotel, customers are no longer satisfied with regular hotels.

Other opportunities also have been found. In keeping with the company's strengths, Marriott's management is developing time-sharing condominiums at resort locations and total life care facilities for the elderly. Marriott's impressive growth rate of 20 percent per year attests to the wisdom of using analysis to guide the design of marketing strategy.

Bill Marriott has honed his company's planning and research operations. Michael Dickens, president of Guest Quarters, which owns nine all-suite hotels, says, "Marriott is like Procter & Gamble Co. It analyzes and investigates so thoroughly that everyone knows it's coming. But it does its job so well that it doesn't matter." (Courtesy of Marriott Corporation)

"Our handy airport Marriotts offer the same crisp professionalism as our downtown hotels."

Bill Marriott
President, Marriott Corporation

"Once airport hotels were just places to sleep if a flight got cancelled.

Now thousands of busy business travelers use them every day as centers to meet, hold conferences, and finalize deals–without the hassle or delay of ever going 'into town'.

Marriott pioneered the enhancement of airport hotels, and we've worked hard to see that all our facilities really are full-service hotels. They offer the same polish, the same first-class restaurants and meeting rooms, the same express check-out system you'll find in our downtown and suburban hotels.

In fact, the only thing different you'll notice about the airport Marriotts in the cities below is that they're all within a quick five to ten minutes of the terminal–by way of a Marriott courtesy shuttle.

I have to make sure we do things right. After all, it's my name over the door."

Marriott
HOTELS•RESORTS
800-228-9290

Atlanta	Charlotte, NC	Dallas/Ft. Worth	Houston (2 Hotels)	Miami/commercial	New York	Rochester	Tampa
Austin	Chicago	El Paso	Irvine, CA	trans. only	Orlando	San Antonio	(2 Hotels)
Buffalo	Cleveland	Grand Rapids	Kansas City	Minneapolis/St. Paul	Philadelphia	Seattle	Washington, DC
Charleston, SC	Columbus	Greensboro, NC	Los Angeles	Nashville		St. Louis	(4 Hotels)

SOURCE: "Bill Marriott's grand design for growth: Upscale and down in the lodging market," *Business Week*, Oct. 1, 1984, pp. 60–62.

///

Analyses of company strengths and weaknesses

Successful marketing strategy selects market opportunities that take advantage of company strengths, or equally important, that do not expose company weaknesses. For instance, Xerox's copier sales and service capabilities are an acknowledged strength. Management's challenge is to figure out how to use this strength as the firm moves toward the 1990s. Office equipment needs for copiers alone will decrease, and the need for equipment systems performing many tasks in an integrated fashion will increase. Thus, the sales and service organization must adapt in order to cope with this new market opportunity.

An analysis of company strengths and weaknesses looks inside the organization for those capabilities that have been or can be particularly successful in attracting sales in markets (the strengths) as well as for problems or difficulties in matching what other companies can do (the weaknesses). Strengths or weaknesses may lie in many areas of a company's operations, such as reputation in certain markets, management skills, product research and development, product quality and variety, after-the-sale service, selling, cost efficiency, and distribution.

Internal self-appraisal analyses help to shape marketing strategy. For one thing, a company must carefully select which customers and which needs and wants it can most successfully meet. For another, marketing

Xerox Corporation promotes its office automation capabilities in its Team Xerox advertising campaign. Rather than strain its resources by building all the pieces of the office of the future, as its original strategy called for, Xerox has used management analyses to decide to link up with and even sell other vendors' equipment. Still, the company expects office automation gear to constitute half its revenue by 1990. (Courtesy of Xerox Corporation)

Exhibit 2.4 The environment unleashes forces influencing marketing strategy

strategy should be built around those activities that the company can do best. Interestingly, even companies that sell similar products may not see a particular market and its opportunity in the same way because they may not see themselves as having the same capabilities. The competitive battle between McDonald's Corporation, Burger King Corporation, and Wendy's International for fast-food restaurant markets illustrates the point. McDonald's, by far the largest company of the three, goes after both children and adult markets. It promotes a quality-food image and has exceptionally fast and efficient service. McDonald's also spends much more on promotion than any of its competitors. Its management believes that these capabilities are the company's strengths. In contrast, Burger King and Wendy's compete by concentrating on adult markets and by emphasizing differences in their menu items. Burger King in particular was bold enough to take on the industry leader, McDonald's, by making direct comparisons between its broiled hamburger and McDonald's fried product. Obviously, the two competitors see their strengths as different from those of McDonald's and have developed different marketing strategies as a result.[6]

Analyses of external environment

A professional marketing manager uses **environmental analyses** to look outside the company to find and assess external forces that affect marketing strategy. There are many forces that must be analyzed as shown in Exhibit 2.4. Some forces are largely beyond the control of managers, such as national and international economies, forces of nature, and social and cultural characteristics of people. Some forces can be influenced in a limited way, particularly technological innovation and legal and political forces. AT&T's management, for example, was able to bargain with the U.S. government to be allowed to sell to markets that were previously legally barred from the company.

Finally, a few forces can be greatly influenced by a company, particularly through marketing strategy. Both competitors and customers clearly react to marketing mix decisions, as do organizations that distribute the company's product (the resellers such as retail stores). Suppliers also can affect marketing strategies by affecting the availability and cost of those items and services a company must have to implement a strategy.

Environmental forces can present either threats or opportunities for a company. A fascinating aspect of human decision making is that different managers may see the same situation differently: One manager may see a threat from a force and another may see an opportunity. In part the difference may lie in each manager's view of company strengths and weaknesses. But being able to creatively mold a company's strategy to emerging forces is a crucial managerial skill. Information describing the U.S. population provides an interesting illustration because it reveals an important trend taking place: The population is getting older. Part of the evidence is a 20 percent decline in the number of teenagers during the 1980s. Many companies see this social trend as a threat and have cut back on marketing programs aimed at teenagers. A few firms, like U.S. Shoe Corporation, are doing just the opposite. A few years ago, U.S. Shoe decided to purchase Ups 'n

Marke**TECH** □ □ □ □ □ □ □ □ □ □ □ □ □ □ □ □ □

Companies use computers to market their services

THEY ARE NOT HOUSEHOLD NAMES now, but they could be soon. Viewtron, Keycom, Pronto, and HomeBase are brand names of companies forming a new industry that Booz Allen & Hamilton, the well-respected consulting firm, predicts will grow to $30 billion in sales by the mid-1990s. The industry provides computerized services to homes in the United States. Some companies, such as Keycom, send information directly to a home computer, and others, such as Viewtron, require that customers buy a special computerlike terminal that displays words and pictures on television sets. All are taking advantage of the growing ease with which many Americans are using small computers.

SOURCE: Martin Mayer, "Coming fast: Services through the TV set," *Fortune*, Nov. 14, 1983, pp. 50–56.

The opportunity appears exciting, but two stumbling blocks have yet to be overcome. First, price for the services, when everything is considered, is high. Either a terminal or a personal computer must be purchased, a $600 or more front-end cost. Some systems require purchasing software and special add-on equipment such as a telephone hookup (modem). In addition, there are monthly service charges and per-use telephone charges. The industry has been anxiously looking to the market to see how willing people are to pay these prices.

Equally difficult is the question of what specific services to computerize and make available to households. Banks and retailers are betting that people want services aimed at easing the task of making transactions. Chemical Bank's Pronto service allows customers to check their balances, transfer funds between different accounts,

and pay bills from selected businesses—all at any time of the day or night. In contrast, publishers are computerizing information by forming data banks that can be tapped on request by users. For instance, the Knight-Ridder newspaper chain offers Viewtron, which supplies a wide variety of information including national news from Associated Press, area Little League baseball scores, the entire Grolier encyclopedia, official airline schedules, and road maps. Information comes in color layouts, and the system can be used twenty-four hours a day for $12 per month and a $1 per hour telephone charge.

The rush is on to find ways to add the computerized services that people want. As illustrated by Chemical Bank's $20 million investment for Pronto, the stakes are high just to get into this business. But more and more companies are betting that the payoff will be worth it.

□ □

Downs, a shoe store chain catering to teenagers. Even with the decline in their numbers, management saw that teenagers are influential with their parents when family shopping and brand decisions are made.[7]

Analyses and decision making

All analyses are intended to help managers make important decisions. Although environmental analyses may influence decisions throughout a company, our concern is with decisions leading to marketing strategy. For marketing managers, the analyses are especially important for finding markets, deciding how to compete, and assessing whether the return from a marketing program is worth its costs. For instance, communications technology now enables a variety of information services to be provided to people in their homes (see Marketech). Banks, retailers, and publishers all see this force as opening huge new markets for services such as shopping at home, buying and selling stocks, making bank transactions, and keeping informed about world events.[8]

Finding markets. Analysis helps managers determine which kinds of people (or organizations in the case of business markets) are most likely to buy from the company. These people are customers in markets whose needs and wants must be met. Thus, all marketing strategy revolves around finding markets having attractive opportunity. For instance, companies that are moving into home information services cannot assume that everyone is a customer. Instead, they must be selective by identifying markets for each particular service.

Deciding how to compete. How successfully one company meets customers' needs and wants affects the sales opportunity for other companies. The battle between companies for customers' purchases is the essence of competition. Volkswagen of America, the U.S. subsidiary of the German automobile manufacturer, felt the effect of competition when it lost sales to other car manufacturers in the first half of the 1980s. Its percentage of all U.S. automobile sales went down to 2.6 by 1983 after a 7.2-percent high in 1970. With the sales loss, Volkswagen's reputation for reliable, efficient, high-value cars was tarnished. The company had problems with product quality, but that was only part of the reason for the market share decline. Another cause has been the influx of popular Japanese brands—Toyota, Honda, and Nissan—into U.S. markets.[9]

Assessing the return. All marketing managers want to know if they are going to get a desired return for their efforts. Companies measure return in different ways: sales, percent of sales of the product by all competitors (market share), profits, and return on investment. All these measures are based on sales and therefore assessing the return requires predicting the amount of sales that can be achieved from markets. Analyses are needed to make these predictions or forecasts. Essentially, good forecasts are dependent on knowing who customers in markets are, how they will respond to competitors' marketing mixes as well as that of the company, and how other environmental forces are affecting their purchase decisions.

As you can see, the foundation on which marketing strategy decisions is based is sound environmental analyses. These analyses do not eliminate the need for managers to exercise judgment and creativity when deciding on strategy. An interplay between environmental analyses and sound judgment will always be part of successful marketing decision making.

MARKETING STRATEGY PLANNING

Marketing strategy is formulated from key decisions that guide a company's entire effort to achieve sales or other responses from markets. A marketing plan describes these decisions. More formally, a **marketing plan** is a blueprint for action establishing the company's market targets, setting objectives to accomplish in these markets, and specifying how the marketing mix will be used to achieve the objectives (see Exhibit 2.5).

Exhibit 2.5 Planning a marketing strategy

Selecting target markets

Many companies have learned that they cannot sell their products to anyone and everyone. Some people cannot afford to buy. Others do not need or want to buy their products and so are not likely to become customers. A more practical approach is to select **target markets** comprising customers (people or organizations) to whom the company's management wants to present its marketing mix or offer. Typically, managers choose target markets that want specific benefits that the company can readily provide. Commodore International, for instance, decided to concentrate its computer sales in home-use markets where it has achieved approximately 60 percent of the market share. Even in the United States where incomes are high, Commodore recognizes that only about 25 percent of all households will buy home computers in the foreseeable future. The rest have no need or lack the funds to buy. The company concentrates on targets within this 25 percent, particularly those who want a respectable quality product at a very attractive price.[10]

Companies that sell products to other organizations also select target markets. The challenge is the same—to choose customers who are seeking benefits that the company is good at offering. Timken Company uses this principle by selling to manufacturers of durable goods (e.g., automobiles, heavy machinery, oilfield equipment) who want high-quality steel alloys at a competitive price.[11]

Analyses of the company's strengths and weaknesses and of the environment are needed to sort out which markets have the best opportunity. Managers look for those markets that have needs or wants the company can meet, are not overly saturated with competition, and are large enough to be profitably served. Hasbro Industries is a case in point. After a disappointing performance in its toy operations in the late 1970s, management decided to reevaluate its target market strategy. Rather than sell toys for children of all ages, many of whom are fickle in their choice of toys, Hasbro's management decided to concentrate the company's marketing mix on the fastest growing segment of the market for toys—preschoolers between the ages of two and five. Analysis showed that this group is less influenced by faddish trends in toys. By selling long-lived toys, costs of developing new products can be substantially reduced. Furthermore, management learned that an effective edge over the competition can be maintained by keeping prices low relative to already entrenched competitors such as Mattel, Fisher-Price, and Milton Bradley.[12]

Faced with a more complicated market and competitive situation, Gillette has been battling a French competitor, Société Bic, for dominance in razor-and-blade markets. The market contains consumers who differ on how important price is in their purchase decisions. Bic, with its disposable razor, has been a particular threat to the low-priced segment of the market. Gillette was vulnerable because it had concentrated more on the higher-priced Trac II and Atra razors. To counter Bic, Gillette had to set a higher priority on the low-priced market group by bringing out its own brand of disposable razor, Good News. Gillette also decided to step up competitive pressure on Bic in all markets where they compete, including razors, lighters, and pens. Management believes that Bic will have a tougher time competing for the U.S. disposable razor market if they have to meet competitive threats in other markets as well.[13]

Hasbro's and Gillette's handling of their situations demonstrates the critical role that careful selection of market targets plays in a company's marketing and overall business strategy. This decision is dictated as much by what competitors are doing and other environmental forces as it is by the needs and wants of customers in markets. Selecting market targets in which a company can be very competitive is the first step in marketing planning, and it provides essential guidelines for the next steps of setting marketing objectives and designing the marketing mix.

Setting marketing objectives

For each market target, marketing managers must establish what must happen with customers for the company to take advantage of opportunity. A **marketing objective** is a statement about the kind and level of performance that is realistically attainable by the company's marketing mix aimed at target markets.

Marketing objectives can be set in several different performance areas. *Revenue-related objectives* state the contribution that each target market is expected to make to the company's financial well-being. Sales, market share, and profit objectives are commonly set for this purpose. *Market position objectives* state how a company's product is expected to compare to that of the competition, particularly in the minds of customers. Typical position objectives concern desired company and product reputation or image such as for product quality, prestige, value for dollars spent, or superior after-the-sale service. Finally, companies set *marketing mix objectives* for each mix component including introducing new products, creating awareness through advertising, and setting sales quotas for salespersons.

Marketing objectives state where a company wants to be after a period of time. Exhibit 2.6 describes marketing objectives for a clothing store. Time periods set by the store's management are mostly for one year, but range from as short as six months to as long as two years. In practice, managers set periods that are shorter (e.g., a month or a quarter) or longer (e.g., five or more years) depending on the difficulty of achieving objectives.

The marketing mix is the means by which managers achieve their objectives. Thus, objectives help managers develop ideas about what the company must offer to customers. What marketing mix actions by the clothing store in Exhibit 2.6 do you think are suggested by the objectives?

Exhibit 2.6   Marketing objectives for a clothing store's marketing plan

Marketing Performance	Statement of Objective	Time Period to Complete
Sales	To increase sales by 15% among families; 20% among singles	One year
Market Share	To maintain a market share of 13% among families and singles	One year
Market Position	To be perceived by shoppers as a casual clothing store with outfits for the whole family	Two years
Competitive Advantage	To reinforce the store's reputation for brand-name merchandise at below competitive prices	One year
Product	To expand merchandise offerings for females and for children under 10	One year
Advertising	To increase awareness by 50% of the frequent sales offered by the store	Six months

Although you know little about the store, you probably can think of several good ideas. For example, the store must sell men's, women's, and children's clothing. The clothing should fit customers' impression of casual clothing. In addition, advertising themes should stress price-off sales.

A marketing objective is only as useful as it is realistic. What determines whether an objective is, in fact, realistic? In part, the company's strengths and weaknesses are a factor. Look once more at Exhibit 2.6. Suppose it would take an advertising budget of $35,000 to accomplish the advertising objective. The store, however, cannot afford more than $20,000. The objective to increase awareness is unrealistic in this instance simply because the store does not have the resources to achieve it. Environmental forces are also factors: The strategies of competitors, the size of markets, customers' preferences, and technological feasibilities are some of these.

Designing a marketing mix

Having set marketing objectives, managers are ready to design the marketing mix. To attract sales from target markets, a company must have something of value to exchange. Management's challenge is to use the marketing mix to create this value in the form of benefits that customers seek. Furthermore, every company must establish a market position against the competition. **Market position** refers to the way in which a company uses its marketing mix to create in customers' minds an important advantage or combination of advantages for buying from the company rather than its competitors. Advantages might be superior product quality, lower price, a more prestigious image, more convenient location, extra services, or any of a number of others (see Chapter 8 for more on positioning).

Market position is readily evident when comparing the marketing strategies of companies selling similar products used for similar purposes. Consider the cosmetics business, which is dominated by large companies such as Revlon, L'Oreal, Maybelline, and Noxell Corporation (maker of Cover Girl). Three smaller companies, Del Laboratories, Paco Rabanne, and

Georgette Klinger, have found ways to compete against the giants through successful but very different market positions:

■ Del established strong distribution of its brand, Sally Hansen Hard as Nails, through mass retailers like K mart, and concentrated its product line on meeting special wants, including strengthening soft or damaged nails.

■ Paco Rabanne found an attractive market satisfying men's wants for cologne and skin care products. The company's advertising cleverly appeals to both men and women because both sexes buy these products—men for themselves and women as gifts for men. Product advantages are built around medical benefits, and the company promotes its medical expertise in skin care problems. The strategy has worked. Sales for Paco Rabanne Parfums doubled in the four years after this market position was selected.

■ Georgette Klinger discovered that service to customers as they use skin care products provides an effective market position. The company sells a wide range of products through its own salons in New York, Chicago, Beverly Hills, Dallas, Palm Springs, and Bal Harbour, Florida. At each salon, experienced cosmetologists and sales consultants help customers get the maximum benefit from these products. When customers cannot get to a salon, they can call a toll-free number to get advice on skin care treatment.[14]

Exhibit 2.7 summarizes the major components of a firm's marketing mix. We briefly review each one here. Later chapters provide an in-depth look at the decisions required to develop the marketing mix.

Product. At the heart of a marketing mix is the product. A **product** is a combination of tangible or intangible performance capabilities or benefits that are designed to meet particular customer needs and wants. Marketing managers play an important role in making product decisions because they understand customers' needs and wants, competitive strengths and weaknesses, and other environmental forces. This knowledge is essential to pinpoint the combination of benefits that will best attract sales.

Exhibit 2.7 Components of the marketing mix

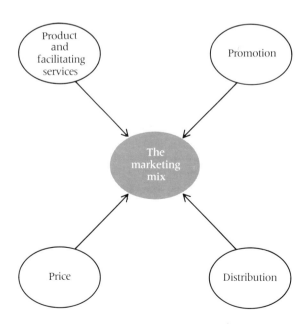

Consider Canon's current strategy in the U.S. camera market.[15] Management of the Japanese camera manufacturer is aggressively going after sales from the large amateur photographer market. The product component of the mix was instrumental in making inroads into this market. A line of high-quality cameras was designed that included a selection on price and degree of automation (from completely manual to fully automatic). Benefits of Canon's cameras are that clear, sharp pictures can be taken with little effort and amateurs who do not know much about cameras can quickly become comfortable using them.

As Canon's decisions on products illustrate, most companies make or sell more than one product. Whole lines of products that differ in benefits like features, quality, and prices are offered to market targets in order to give customers a choice. Not everyone wants exactly the same thing. Thus a product line enables a company to reach more people in markets than the company could with a single product. Decisions are made on what products to add to the line, when to drop products from the line, and how the products in a line relate to each other.

Customers may need help with a product after the sale to get full benefit from using it. Companies build **facilitating services** into their marketing mixes to satisfy these needs (see Marketalk). These services include product repair, credit, guarantees, centers for receiving and dealing with complaints, gift wrapping, delivery, and instruction on how to use the product. Canon's network of repair centers across the United States is one of several facilitating services that management has made an integral part of its marketing mix. Services help to sell the company's products, and they can have residual advantages for company managers, too. Procter & Gamble recognizes this fact by using information from its complaint service to spot problems with products that need correcting.[16]

Services are costly. Thus management must decide how important services are going to be in the total selling effort for the company's products. Some companies like K mart offer very few services, preferring instead to rely on other components of the marketing mix to attract customers. Other companies such as Sears include many services in their mix to provide a competitive edge in markets. If services are offered, managers must select which ones to include in the marketing mix. Furthermore, decisions are needed on how to price the services and how to make them available to customers.

Promotion. Contrary to what you may have heard, good products do not sell themselves. A company must tell customers what the company and its products have to offer them. **Promotion** is a company's most important way of delivering this information. For target markets, promotion informs customers of benefits, reminds them of these benefits from time to time, and persuades them to buy the company's products. Canon's managers know that amateur photographers want information to help them decide what camera to buy. The company has substantially increased its advertising in recent years to tell the market about its camera product line. Salespersons work with stores to show their personnel how to explain to customers the benefits of its cameras as well as how to use them. In addition, special sales promotions such as camera displays in the stores and price-off deals are used to attract customers.

*Marke*TALK ///

Facilitating services become important marketing tool

IMAGINE that you are an American who is caught in war-torn Beirut. You want to get out of the country quickly, but the banks are closed down, and you cannot get any money to pay for your way out. What would you do?

This frightening circumstance actually happened to the Lebanese-born sister of a man from the Midwest. The problem was to get enough money—$3,000—to the woman so that she could pay her hotel bill and book passage on a ship leaving for Cyprus. The woman could write a check, but no one would cash it because her bank could not honor it. Not knowing what else to do, the brother called American Express' Southern Region Operations Center in Fort Lauderdale. As an American Express cardholder, he thought that funds could be obtained through his card. Fortunately, American Express was able to help.

By means of telexes (twenty-eight in all), communication was established between the woman's hotel in Beirut, the Florida operations center, and a Lebanon

SOURCE: "Making service a potent marketing tool," *Business Week*, June 11, 1984, p. 164.

branch of American Express International Banking Corporation (AEIBC). Recognizing the seriousness of the situation for the woman trapped in Beirut, American Express' service personnel worked around the clock to provide the money in one day. Because of the complexity of the situation, personnel from different shifts became involved in the activities. The cardholder's credit was checked, and special authorizations were obtained from the card division and AEIBC's headquarters to cash a check that would, in all likelihood, bounce. The story has a happy ending because the AEIBC branch cashed the $3,000 check for the woman, thereby enabling her to leave Beirut safely. Furthermore, two American Express employees received "Great Performer" cash awards for their instrumental role in the incident.

Providing such a personal service is not done easily or inexpensively. American Express alone spends $150 million per year on the communication and computer equipment, data banks, personnel, and training needed to provide facilitating services to its cardholders. Many other companies are making similar financial commitments. However, the payback can be enormous. Personal service ties the com-

pany's customers more closely to them. Furthermore, a wealth of market information is obtained in the process of providing the services and getting feedback from customers. Among the information routinely collected are (1) demographics; (2) measures of advertising's impact; (3) problem merchandise by model, nature of defect, and where distributed; (4) customers' concerns; (5) product life; and (6) new product ideas. That information can mean more profits down the road. Not surprisingly, a number of companies—including American Express, General Electric, Sony, IBM, Procter & Gamble, and Whirlpool—have elevated facilitating services to a high-priority component in their marketing offers.

Enthusiasm for facilitating services in marketing programs is rapidly growing among businesses. These services may be just the edge a company needs in a highly competitive marketplace. Listen to what one American Express executive, Louis B. Gerstner, Jr., chairman and CEO of American Express' Travel-Related Services Company, has to say: "Service is our most strategic marketing weapon. It's the only way we can differentiate our product in the marketplace."

///

Putting together effective promotion involves many decisions. There are different forms of promotion that a company can use, including advertising, personal selling, sales promotions, and publicity. Many of these are evident in Canon's promotion described above. A company's total promotion is a combination of these forms that management believes is best. Furthermore, decisions are made for each form of promotion to determine who is to receive the information, what is said and how it is said, how the information is to be delivered, and how much should be spent.

Distribution. When buying a product, consumers frequently seek convenience. Managers use **distribution,** the network of company departments and other businesses that make products available to buyers, to provide this benefit. To reach the amateur photographer market Canon has developed an extensive distribution system made up of specialty camera stores, large discounters such as K mart and Target stores, mail-order houses, and catalogue ordering services of mass merchandisers such as Penney's. These retailers link Canon's distribution department (storage, shipping functions) with customers in markets.

In practice, a company can sell directly to end-users, or can arrange to have other firms deliver and sell to these end-users. When other firms are

In promoting its AE-1 product through this advertisement, Canon focuses on its ability to provide customer satisfaction, a benefit that amateur photographer John Newcombe endorses. (Courtesy of Canon U.S.A., Inc.)

used, decisions are made on what types and how many of these firms to include in the channel. And management must ensure that these firms are providing the desired assistance. Members of the channel can help promote the company's products, make sure enough supply is on hand for end-users at all times, and see that price is competitive. The company must motivate the channel firms to provide this assistance, however. Thus a company works closely with channel firms to ensure that they are supporting the company's selling effort.

Price. All products have a cost to produce, distribute, and promote. Managers set **price,** the amount that customers must pay to purchase the product, to cover these costs and to contribute to the financial performance of the company. Of course, customers judge whether the benefits of the purchase are worth the price. Managers face the challenge of finding a price that provides a desired return to the company, and at the same time, causes customers to feel that the purchase is worthwhile. Canon astutely recognized that amateur photographers are sensitive to the price of a camera. Through means such as innovative manufacturing and substitution of less expensive materials, Canon has been able to lower its prices and provide more value to customers. Canon's sales have climbed as a result.

Pricing decisions are complicated by the fact that a company sells its products through a channel of distribution. A manufacturer like Canon, for instance, sets a price that retailers in its channel pay to get Canon's cameras. In turn, these retailers set prices that consumers pay. Canon's managers must consider what price will motivate the retailers to sell its cameras aggressively, and at the same time, what price should be charged to consumers to make the cameras competitive. Decisions on price should simultaneously accomplish both purposes.

Managers usually price not one product, but a whole line of products. Each product's price may affect the sales that other products in the line enjoy. If Canon were to price its top-of-the-line camera too low, for example, sales of its economy camera might suffer. Thus managers look for the opportunity to use the price of one product to protect or enhance the sales of other products in the line.

Marketing mix decisions combine into a program. One of the greatest challenges in marketing is to coordinate decisions among the marketing mix components. Each component can contribute to the effectiveness of the other components. Benefits built into a product must be promoted. Price must cover the costs of producing, distributing, and selling a product, and at the same time, should contribute to the image that people have of product quality, prestige, or service. Distribution can support the offering of services and make the product convenient to get. As you can see, there are many possible ways in which the mix components are interrelated. Only when the many individual mix decisions are blended together does a company have a coordinated marketing program.

Consider the part of Canon's marketing mix devoted to a new product. To penetrate the amateur photographer market, Canon redesigned its 35mm camera. Management wanted a camera that is simple to use and inexpensive to produce. Product research and development staff accomplished these objectives and the Canon AE-1 was born. New design features enabled management to bring down the price. Promotion told customers how easy the camera is to use, how good the picture quality is, and how inexpensive getting this picture quality can be. Distribution was shifted toward more mass retailing to get the camera to the large market. All the components of the marketing mix were neatly coordinated to develop a successful competitive position for Canon's AE-1.[17] The success of AE-1's marketing mix is also a tribute to management's keen understanding of the marketing situation.

Marketing is one of several functions in a company requiring resources. Thus marketing must compete for a company's resources with other functions like production, research and development, and financial control. Decisions are made, usually high up in a company's management, on how much to spend on the marketing program. Marketing, like any other function, must justify its use of funds when these allocation decisions are made.

MANAGING A MARKETING PROGRAM

Marketing management involves much more than planning a marketing strategy. Someone has to see that plans are put into action and that they are working successfully. Far more of a marketing manager's day-to-day work goes into implementing and controlling marketing plans than is devoted to the actual planning itself. Managing a marketing program includes both implementation of the marketing mix and control of the strategy's performance.

Implementing marketing programs

Implementing a marketing program consists of the many activities needed to put the marketing program into operation.[18] The following illustrations will help you see how involved the implementation task is: redesigning a product to improve its benefits, making sales presentations to customers, hiring salespersons, assigning salespersons to sales territories, motivating salespersons to sell enthusiastically, negotiating a price, working with manufacturing and distribution departments to get a preferred delivery schedule for customers, working with an advertising agency on a campaign, hiring media to carry advertisements, negotiating terms with dealers, and helping a customer learn how to use the product. Managers spend the majority of their time and effort on implementation simply because so much must be done to carry out a marketing mix as it was planned.

The implementation task can be organized into five types of activities: (1) budgeting, (2) staffing, (3) communication, (4) coordination, and (5) motivation. **Budgeting** is a transition step between planning and implementation occurring when managers convert a plan into a budget. A budget lists the different tasks that have to be done to carry out a plan, the projected cost of each, and the period of time over which each task is to be completed. It acts as a checklist to guide implementation.

Staffing involves assigning persons with appropriate expertise to each task. These persons may be company employees. Or outside agents like an employment agency or an advertising agency may be contracted to get the needed skills.

Communication is needed to convey information about the plan to those who are responsible for its implementation. For example, a sales manager conducts a sales meeting to explain to the field salesforce their role in a plan. As another illustration, a product manager meets frequently with managers of the company's advertising agency to explain the strategy and resulting advertising objectives of the plan.

Coordination is needed whenever more than one person is taking part in the plan's implementation. Each person must do his or her activity on a schedule that ensures that all activities are done in the proper sequence. An IBM salesperson, for instance, may request that a specially designed brochure be sent to prospects in the sales territory in advance of sales calls. The salesperson coordinates with advertising personnel to see that the brochures are mailed before he or she calls on the customers.

Motivation means giving incentives to those people who are responsible for carrying out plans. An incentive might be a bonus for salespersons who exceed their sales quotas. It can be an inspirational talk delivered by a product manager to a field salesforce explaining how vital the salespersons are to the plan's success. In fact, anything that inspires people to do their best when carrying out the marketing plan is motivation.

Let us take a minute to look at an actual plan's implementation. The president and the merchandise manager of The Young Look, a regional chain of jeans stores, developed a marketing strategy to change its market position among customers.* Strategy centered on becoming more of a casual wear store. Implementing the plan required approximately a two-year lead time to accomplish all the objectives. Among the many implementation tasks were

- Contracting with suppliers of casual clothing brands
- Finding a new name for the stores conveying to customers a casual wear clothing image
- Rearranging store interiors to display prominently the expanded merchandise lines
- Retraining sales clerks to sell casual wear in addition to jeans
- Working with the advertising agency to develop new communications to announce the change in merchandise lines
- Estimating costs of all activities in the plan
- Pricing all new merchandise
- Developing new merchandise displays with accompanying signs for placement in the stores
- Developing a new merchandise return service for customers
- Hiring additional merchandise buyers to handle the increased buying required to expand the merchandise line

Controlling marketing programs

Marketing plans do not always work as well as managers intended them to do. Even the best of companies experience this difficulty. In 1984, for instance, McDonald's Corporation came under fire from critics saying that the company's marketing strategy was not as effective as in the past. They pointed out that McDonald's reputation for high-quality hamburgers was slipping. Furthermore, price-cutting moves were questioned as not helping to restore the quality image.[19]

Why do marketing plans sometimes perform poorly? There are three possible reasons: (1) the marketing strategy may not be very good for the situation, (2) implementation of strategy may be weak, or (3) the situation may have changed unexpectedly causing the strategy to become inappropriate. McDonald's problems seemed to be due to their slow reaction to changes in competition and markets. Wendy's and Burger King have used advertising aggressively to demonstrate that their hamburgers are bigger than Big Macs. What's more, greater concern for health among Americans caused customers to look at McDonald's menu more critically.[20] Many big chains already offer salad bars, but D'Lites of America, the nation's first fast-food chain specializing in healthful meals, is a new competitor going head to head with industry giants like McDonald's:

> By offering healthier versions of mainstream fast-food items to the growing legions of fitness-conscious Americans, the upstart company intends to carve out a niche in the $32 billion fast-food market.[21]

Experienced marketing managers expect performance of marketing plans to go awry from time to time. They guard against letting problems get out of hand through control activities. Controlling a marketing program

---

* The name of the store chain has been changed for proprietary reasons.

Once it realized that beef and buns alone did not appeal to the appetites of many potential customers, Burger King revised its marketing program to offer salad bars. (Courtesy of Burger King Corporation)

means using information to become aware of problems and to find out why they are occurring, and then taking corrective actions. Management's challenge is to spot problems in time to take action before problems reach a crisis point. Control is best conducted as a sequence of steps as shown by Exhibit 2.8.

Setting performance standards. Control begins with performance standards. These standards define what successful performance should be and are derived from marketing objectives. Consider the following sales objective: "to increase this year's sales of the company's product by 12 percent over last year's total sales." The performance standard becomes the 12-percent increase. Similarly, standards are derived from market share, market position, and marketing mix objectives.

Measuring performance. When standards are used, managers must obtain accurate information that measures actual performance. Each kind of performance standard—sales, market share, awareness, image, and others—requires a different type of measure. Importantly, the measure must provide information on exactly the same type of performance as stated in the standard. In the case of a sales standard, a marketing manager must have

Exhibit 2.8   Steps in marketing management's control responsibility

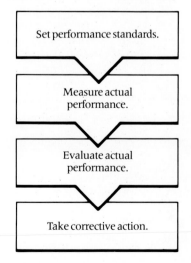

information showing actual product sales to see if the standard has been met.

Evaluating performance. Actual performance is evaluated by comparing it to the standard. Performance that is below the standard signals a problem. For example, a district sales manager regularly compares sales of each salesperson in the district with sales quotas (i.e., sales standards) to spot problems. Salespersons meeting or exceeding quota are performing well and will not need extra attention. The sales manager can concentrate on those salespersons and territories with sales below their quotas.

Evaluation continues as a manager searches for reasons that explain why the problem occurred. Additional information is needed from various sources to explore possibilities. A major department store in a southern city, for instance, spent millions of dollars on a new store near a large market. Management expected that at least 80 percent of shoppers from the market area would feel that the store was a convenient place in which to shop. Management was stunned when a market survey showed considerably less than 80 percent felt that way. A trip to the new store showed that construction on the parking area and access roads was far behind schedule. The construction equipment and condition of the area around the store made it difficult for shoppers to get to the store. Given these unforeseen uncontrollable conditions, the 80-percent standard was too ambitious for the allotted time period.

As these examples illustrate, managers must have information about internal and environmental forces to fully evaluate performance. Periodically updating analyses of the situation provides this information. Seeing performance problems and understanding their causes greatly eases the task of deciding on the corrective action to take.

Taking corrective action. Corrective action decisions usually change one or more parts of the marketing plan. Market targets might be broadened, objectives altered, or some aspect of the mix adjusted to bring performance back in line. Suppose a manager finds out that changes in environmental forces have caused a sales performance standard to become unachievable with the current marketing mix. Corrective action in this case might involve setting a lower sales objective. Or target markets might be changed to expand the customer base from which to draw sales.

Correcting decisions also can result in changes to the marketing plan's implementation. The basic strategy is retained, but new activities are used to carry it out. For instance, a district sales manager may help a below-quota salesperson develop a more efficient scheduling of prospects to increase the number of sales calls. Or a brand manager may deliver a motivational talk at a meeting of salespersons to encourage them to put more effort into their selling. In general, the key to control is management's ability to creatively determine what it will take to bring performance in line with the standard.

MARKETING AND THE BUSINESS FUNCTIONS

Marketing's involvement in analyzing the situation and developing, implementing, and controlling marketing strategy places a special responsibility on marketing managers. They must work closely with managers from nonmarketing departments that play a part in marketing strategy. Aside from top management, the managers that have the most impact on marketing management are managers of finance, distribution, production, and product and research development.

Marketing strategy, of course, takes its lead from top management. Board chairpersons, presidents, and other executives at the highest levels set goals and objectives that determine the company's directions. For example, Dart & Kraft had tried for several years to diversify from its main food lines (e.g., Kraft cheeses and salad dressings, Sealtest ice cream, Parkay margarine) into nonfood products such as Kitchenaid appliances, Tupperware, and Duracell batteries. Marketing strategies were needed for each product line. Recently, top management decided to get back to the food business that the company knows best. Resources are being shifted toward the food product lines, and directives call for expansion through new products. Marketing managers have had to shift attention to finding new food product opportunities and developing marketing strategies for them.[22]

Marketing strategy typically demands that all aspects of a company's capabilities be used. Products must be designed to offer selected benefits, they must be produced and distributed conveniently to customers, financial resources must be allocated for the marketing mix, and services must be organized and implemented to support the sales and use of products. Only by marshaling the expertise of people in the other business departments can marketing strategy be planned, implemented, and controlled. Because the marketing mix is centered on performing successfully in target markets, marketing managers are in a unique position to coordinate decisions and actions of these managers.

Effective cooperation between departments in a company is a give-and-take proposition. Managers in departments outside marketing must understand what goes into a marketing strategy and its implementation. At the same time, marketing managers must understand the objectives, problems, and decision-making procedures of managers in these other departments. Dart & Kraft, for example, has improved cooperation between managers in marketing and product research and development by establishing a group of special-product managers who have responsibility for developing new product ideas. Research and development staff work with these product managers to push the new product effort forward.[23] Cooperation works best when supported by top management, as Dart & Kraft has found out.

SUMMARY

Professional marketing management involves many different activities. Analysis of the situation begins the process. Managers must first understand their own company's strengths and weaknesses. Analysis also is necessary to learn about the environment in which the company is vying for sales. Customer needs and wants, strengths and weaknesses of competition, and other environmental forces combine to affect market opportunity and therefore are carefully considered when developing marketing strategy.

Analysis provides the information base for planning a marketing strategy. Strategy begins to emerge when management selects target markets. Managers cannot hope to develop a successful marketing mix without knowing the customers to whom the company is selling. Because a company cannot satisfy everyone's needs and wants, targets are singled out comprising customers for whom a company has an advantage in meeting their needs and wants.

For each market target, marketing managers specify the kinds of performance expected from markets. These expectations are marketing objectives. Objectives are only meaningful if they are realistic in light of the market situation. Thus, analyses must guide the setting of these objectives.

Marketing objectives serve as guidelines for planning a marketing mix. A mix is the combination of product, facilitating services, promotion, distribution, and price offering benefits to target markets. Coordination among these components is essential to develop a strong market position.

Marketing strategy sets the stage for action. Plans must be implemented by delivering the marketing program to customers in target markets. Developing a list of activities and associated costs and timing of implementation (budgeting), assigning responsibility to people with the proper skills (staffing), providing information about the marketing plan to those involved in its implementation (communication), arranging the activities of different parties (coordination), and providing incentives to get the activities accomplished (motivation) all play a vital role in implementation.

Following implementation marketing managers must control the performance of marketing strategy laid out in the plan. The control steps allow marketing managers the chance to improve a marketing plan's performance. Spotting problems, finding out why they occurred, and taking appropriate corrective action should be a part of every marketing manager's responsibility.

Finally, planning, implementing, and controlling marketing strategy requires cooperation from managers in departments throughout a company. Top management, product research and development, production, finance, and distribution are particularly important. Although marketing managers do not have authority over these functions, they are in a unique position to provide the necessary coordination.

KEY TERMS

marketing strategy	product	budgeting
environmental analyses	facilitating services	staffing
marketing plan	promotion	communication
target markets	distribution	coordination
marketing objective	price	motivation
market position		

QUESTIONS FOR REVIEW AND DISCUSSION

1. What are the four major responsibilities of marketing management?

2. What is a marketing strategy?

3. What is the relationship between marketing management and marketing strategy?

4. What is the relationship between the marketing concept and marketing management?

5. Explain the two major types of analyses that marketing managers must perform to develop a marketing strategy.

6. What are the questions that analyses of the situation answer?

7. What does market position mean? Give an example of a company that you think has a successful market position.

8. What are the three important types of decisions that together make up a marketing strategy?

9. Should a large food company such as Kroger select everyone as its target market? Why or why not?

10. What is a marketing objective? Explain three different types of marketing objectives.

11. What are the factors that make an objective realistic?

12. How do marketing objectives help design a marketing mix?

13. What are the components of a marketing mix?

14. Can decisions be made concerning one component of the marketing mix that are independent of the decisions concerning the other components? Why or why not?

15. What are the activities that marketing managers perform to manage a marketing program? How do they differ?

16. Is analysis of the situation needed for control?

17. Do managers from departments outside of marketing play a role in marketing management? Why or why not?

18. How can top management help with marketing management?

19. What are the steps in controlling the marketing program?

BUILDING YOUR PORTFOLIO

Choose any well-known, national company that sells consumer products of interest to you. Gather information to help you describe marketing strategy for one of the company's brands. Sources of information include (1) company product brochures; (2) newspaper, magazine, and radio and television advertisements; (3) store visits to see how the brand is sold; (4) the brand's package; (5) company annual reports; (6) government reports such as SEC 10-K reports and *U.S. Industrial Outlook;* (7) periodicals such as *Business Week, Fortune, Forbes, Newsweek,* and *Time;* (8) newspapers such as *The Wall Street Journal,* and *The New York Times;* and (9) research company reports such as Standard & Poor's, Simmons Study of Media and Markets, and Dun & Bradstreet.

Based on this information describe the company's marketing strategy. Try to say as much as you can about the brand's market targets, marketing objectives, and each component of the marketing mix. What do you believe is the market position of the brand? What are the strategy's strengths and weaknesses?

NOTES

1. For an excellent discussion of electronic banking, see "Information processing: Electronic banking." *Business Week,* Jan. 18, 1982, pp. 70–80.
2. Steve Weiner, "K Mart upgrades clothing lines to draw more customers and change firm's image." *Wall Street Journal,* Apr. 3, 1984, p. 1.
3. Laura Landro, "RCA reaches crossroads on future of its troubled videodisk player." *Wall Street Journal,* Sept. 13, 1983, p. 35; and "Videodisc dream is over: RCA." *Advertising Age,* Apr. 9, 1984, pp. 4, 68.
4. "How Sears became a high-cost operator." *Business Week,* February 14, 1981, pp. 52–53.
5. "Information processing: The new lean, mean Xerox." *Business Week,* Oct. 12, 1982, p. 132.
6. "The fast-food war: Big Mac under attack," *Business Week,* January 30, 1984, pp. 44–46.
7. Mark N. Dodosh, "Widely ignored teen market has a lot of spending power." *Wall Street Journal,* June 16, 1982, p. 1.
8. Martin Mayer, "Coming fast: Services through the TV set." *Fortune,* Nov. 14, 1983, pp. 50–58.
9. Robert Ball, "Volkswagen's struggle to restore its name." *Fortune,* June 27, 1983, p. 100.
10. "Cool heads are trying to keep Commodore hot." *Fortune,* July 23, 1984, p. 36.
11. "A bolder Timken streamlines its steel plants to finesse tough markets." *Business Week,* Oct. 8, 1984, pp. 94, 99.
12. "Hasbro Industries: Playing catch-up in toys by aiming at preschoolers." *Business Week,* Sept. 5, 1980, pp. 85–86.
13. Linda Snyder Hayes, "Gillette takes the wraps off." *Fortune,* Feb. 25, 1980, pp. 148–150.
14. "How three companies are making it in makeup." *Business Week,* Sept. 17, 1984, pp. 97, 100, 104.
15. "Japanese camera makers: A 35 mm shot at America's mass market." *Business Week,* July 2, 1979, pp. 88–89; and Louis Kraar, "Japan's Canon focuses on America." *Fortune,* Jan. 12, 1981, pp. 82–88.
16. "Making service a potent marketing tool." *Business Week,* June 11, 1984, pp. 164–170.
17. Kraar, op. cit.
18. For an excellent discussion of implementation, see Thomas V. Bonoma, "Making your strategy work." *Harvard Business Review,* March–April, 1984, pp. 69–76.
19. "The fast-food war: Big Mac under attack." op. cit., pp. 44–46.
20. Ibid., p. 44.
21. "D'Lites: The pioneer of 'healthy' fast food goes on a growth binge." *Business Week,* Sept. 10, 1984, pp. 136–140.
22. "Dart & Kraft turns back to its basic business—food." *Business Week,* June 11, 1984, pp. 100, 105.
23. Ibid.

Case 2.1

Chrysler Corporation

FOR YEARS, U.S. AUTO MAKERS have used world fairs and auto shows to display their latest blue-sky designs. But few of the gee-whiz marvels that went into these "cars of the future" ever made it into production. Radar brakes, driverless vehicles, and automatic raindrop detectors were all hits during the 1950s. This year, Chrysler Corp. is using the New Orleans fair as a showcase for an electronic gadget that seems as farfetched as any of them. But it may be the exception to the rule: The system employs radio signals from orbiting satellites to pinpoint the vehicle's location on a computerized map.

Satellite navigation systems have been around for a long time, but Detroit seemed to be the last place in the world that they would be used. Most experts foresaw little application beyond the military, except in such specialized tasks as oil exploration and the positioning of ships and commercial aircraft. The reason was cost: Ground-based systems that compute locations from satellites sell for upwards of $100,000. However, Chrysler, as well as General Motors Corp. and Ford Motor Co., is hotly pursuing the development of such locator systems for use in cars. And they are now convinced that such systems can be produced economically enough that they may be on the family car by the end of the decade. "I don't see a $500 system as being out of reach," says George J. Dellas, plant manager for the Chrysler Huntsville Automotive Electronics Division.

The system in Chrysler's sporty white "concept" car that is on display in New Orleans replaces the traditional glove compartment—cluttered with wrinkled paper maps—with a video display screen located under the dashboard. At the beginning of a trip, a map of the United States stored on a laser videodisc appears on the screen. By touching the screen, the driver can zoom in on a particular part of the map, say a state or a detailed street map of a city. At the same time, the computerized system continuously calculates the location of the car from satellite signals. The vehicle shows up as a symbol on the screen and moves across the map as the car travels down a highway. The com-

puter can even display the best route to a location.

Ford and GM have similar systems, except they currently use videotape cartridges to store the map data. All three auto makers are taking advantage of recent moves by major mapmakers such as the American Automobile Assn. to encode their maps in digital computer data so that they can be quickly updated to include such information as road construction. "Anything you would find on an AAA Triptik could be programmed into a computer," observes Ronald A. Dork, staff development engineer at General Motors Technical Center.

What makes these automobile locators work is a military satellite navigation system called Navstar. By 1988 the federal government plans to have launched 18 satellites that will blanket the globe with radio signals and allow computers to calculate the location of an object to within a few feet. Although the system is intended mainly for military navigation, the government plans to make it commercially available to anyone who wants to buy or build the ground equipment to tap the satellites' signals. Navstar satellites will continuously broadcast the precise time and their current positions, which will allow a ground-based computer to locate its own position by measuring the time that the signals take to reach it from at least four satellites. A coded signal for military use will allow a position to be calculated to within 50 ft. or less. Another signal for commercial users will permit a position to be figured to within 300 ft. or so.

The government is still undecided over whether to encode the commercial signal as well and charge a user fee. Congress has considered a user fee, but it is being opposed by the Pentagon. "It's not a desirable thing to do," says Captain Robert J. Munn, branch head for navigation and environmental satellites on the staff of the chief of naval operations. "It would be a monumental effort and could price [the service] out of the market." Auto makers are confident that Congress will back off from its position on charging a fee. "The government wants to encourage civilian usage," explains Jacques Mosier, who heads Ford's satellite navigation project.

But the Pentagon satellite navigation system might get some competition from high-technology entrepreneurs. Geostar Corp., in Princeton, N.J., hopes to launch

three satellites in geostationary orbit over the United States by the end of 1987 and to build a low-cost navigation system that will be even more sophisticated than Navstar. Geostar believes that its system could be less costly to use than the government's because it would rely on a network of central computers, rather than installing computers in autos to make the location calculations for the users. Such ground stations would simply be radio receiver-transmitters that would display data on small screens—something that could be priced at only about $500, the company figures. The company expects to charge customers for the time they use the system, and it estimates that fees will average about $20 a month.

Geostar, which has so far raised $4.2 million in private financing for initial development costs, still has some fancy fund-raising ahead before it can launch its own satellites. "You have to be talking on an order of magnitude of $100 million even to play," admits President Gerard K. O'Neill. Currently, Geostar is trying to drum up interest for its system among major trucking companies. The company argues that its system would allow a shipper to know the precise whereabouts of its trucks at any time.

For now, though, auto makers are designing their systems to work with the government's Navstar system. All three are in a position to be in production on their locators by the time the satellite system is operational. They are now conducting marketing studies to assess the potential demand for them. Designers already believe that, priced at $2,000, the locator systems would make sense as an option in luxury autos. "There will always be people who would buy it in a high-end luxury car," says Ford's Mosier. "If cost comes down enough, there will be a lot of people who will want it." To tap the mass market, auto makers believe the retail price must be down in the $500-to-$1,000 range. And they are convinced that such a price can be reached, primarily because the cost of computer power is still dropping rapidly.

The auto companies have major efforts under way to build computer technology into their cars. Computers are now doing such jobs as controlling engine functions, monitoring brakes, and even keeping track of gas mileage. And automotive computer applications are becoming increasingly sophisticated. One model of the

1985 Buick Riviera, for example, will contain a cathode-ray-tube (CRT) video screen that will display a wide range of information for the driver.

With such screens being planned for installation in cars, the cost of adding the computer necessary to calculate a car's location from satellite data will drop significantly. "Once you've got the CRT, locator systems are a fantastic use for it," says an automotive engineer.

QUESTIONS

1. Chrysler wants to determine if there is opportunity to sell the computerized dashboard map. How would analyses of the situation be helpful to Chrysler's marketing managers for this purpose?

2. What marketing strategy decisions must be made?

3. What functions (or departments) of Chrysler's organization would have to cooperate with marketing to plan the marketing strategy?

4. What do you think might be some of the marketing objectives for the product?

5. Which components of a marketing mix should be included in the marketing program?

Case 2.2

Stride Rite Corporation

STRIDE RITE CORPORATION has long been respected for making and selling high-quality children's shoes and for its fitting services that help parents find the proper shoe for their child. By being customer-oriented and maintaining a strong brand-name recognition in markets, the company has been a high performer in the

SOURCE: Johnnie L. Roberts, "By concentrating on marketing, Stride Rite does well despite slump for shoe makers," *The Wall Street Journal*, Feb. 23, 1983, p. 31. Reprinted by permission of *The Wall Street Journal*, © Dow Jones & Company, Inc., 1983. All rights reserved.

U.S. shoe industry. Several trends, however, have led the company in new directions. First, competition from imported brands had taken more than 60 percent of all shoe sales by 1984. Second, management noted declining birth rates in the 1970s and saw their children's market become less attractive as the company moved into the 1980s.

In the past decade, marketing strategy has been broadened to include shoes for other markets while retaining the emphasis on brand-name recognition. For instance, Stride Rite is going after adults in suburbs and cities who want boots for weekend life-styles with its Herman boots

line. It also expanded into women's casual shoe markets with Grasshoppers and Sperry Top-Sider brands.

Most recently, the company is trying to develop a strong market position in athletic shoes with its Pro-Ked line. Marketing strategy centers on improving the Pro-Ked image for quality athletic shoes, expanding distribution to reach more customers, competing on price, and adding new products (e.g., running shoes) to the product line. Competitors have voiced concern because of Stride Rite's well-respected reputation for developing good marketing strategies and implementing them well.

QUESTIONS

1. What functions or departments in Stride Rite's organization should be involved in implementing the company's athletic shoe marketing strategy?

2. Describe activities and decisions required to implement the strategy.

3. Should management expect problems with the marketing strategy? Why or why not?

4. How can Stride Rite's management guard against possible poor performance from the athletic shoe marketing strategy?

Part Two

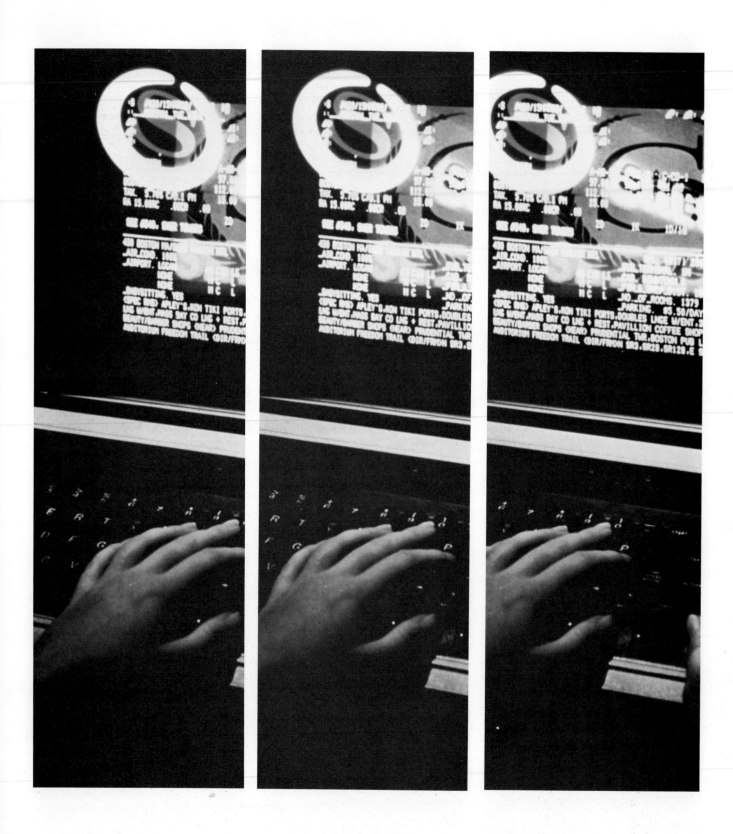

Market
Targeting

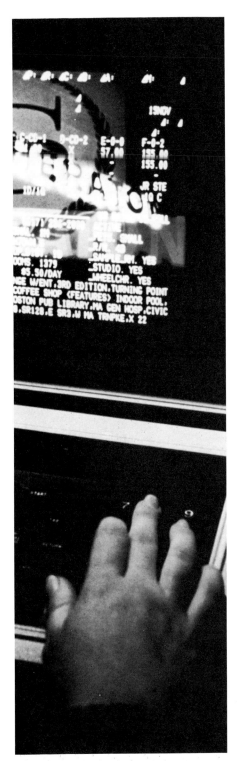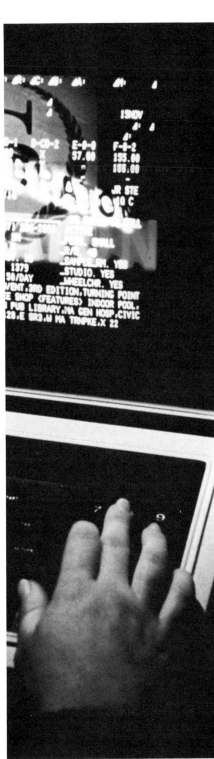

3 Marketing's Environment

When you finish this chapter, you will understand

☐ The nature of important environmental influences on marketing

☐ The major types of influences that affect the success of marketing decisions

☐ How key trends and changes in environmental forces affect marketing decisions

☐ How an organization scans the macroenvironment for influences on marketing decisions

Odetics hopes that the invention of its versatile robots will open new markets. Firefighters and firms dealing with dangerous contamination are likely customers.

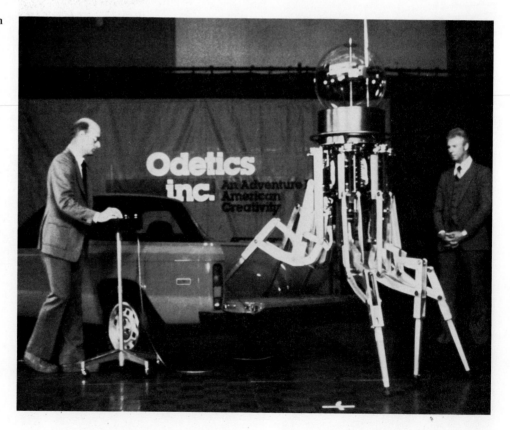

Few managers have ever felt such tremendous uncertainty about the future as those at American Telephone and Telegraph as January 1, 1984, approached. The breakup of this giant corporation was the result of years of legal battles between the company and the Federal Trade Commission (FTC). Management did not want to be split apart, but a court ruled that it would be in the best interests of telecommunications markets if AT&T did not have such a dominant, monopolistic position. As a result of the breakup, AT&T's assets decreased from $148 to $40 billion.

The new streamlined AT&T offers long-distance, communications, and information services and develops, manufactures, and distributes communications and information equipment. Divisions responsible for local telephone service and telephone directories were spun off into independent businesses. The effect is to create opportunity for more and different competition for all the new companies involved.

Think about the impact of the FTC's action on the marketing responsibility of managers in these companies. Western Electric, the manufacturing arm of AT&T, is free from the regulation that previously limited its operations. Management can pursue any product and service opportunities that it wants. AT&T quickly used this freedom to enter computer markets and is considering other product-line expansions. Furthermore, management can now charge whatever prices it deems appropriate.[1]

AT&T's REACTION to governmental intervention illustrates one of the greatest challenges for professional marketing managers: understanding and dealing with important influences on company decision making and performance. More than this, however, managers must also attempt to anticipate these influences and their direction to plan effectively rather than to react badly. Exhibit 3.1 shows the result of organizational changes at AT&T caused by the breakup. These changes provide only a glimpse into new opportunities (as well as lost opportunities) open to management. As one illustration, the name change from "Long Lines Department" to "Interexchange Organization" signals a more extensive move into long-distance services. At the same time, AT&T has given up the twenty-two operating companies handling local telephone services. Influences such as those affecting AT&T make up the environment for marketing. More specifically, **marketing's environment** is the set of forces, external to the marketing manager's job position, that are either partially or completely uncontrollable but have a substantial impact on the success of decisions made by that manager.

This definition leaves the door wide open for many different kinds of influences that make up marketing's environment. In some ways, the sheer number of environmental influences makes the marketing manager's job full of uncertainty. How managers deal with uncontrollable forces can make the difference between success and failure.

Because the environment is such an important fact of life for marketing managers, fully appreciating their challenge requires understanding the impact of environmental forces on decision making. The discussion in this chapter will help you gain an understanding of these forces and how marketing managers can deal with them. We begin by building a perspective of the makeup of the marketing environment. Then, each of the major types of environmental forces is examined in greater detail. Finally, we introduce and illustrate the process by which marketing managers study environmental forces.

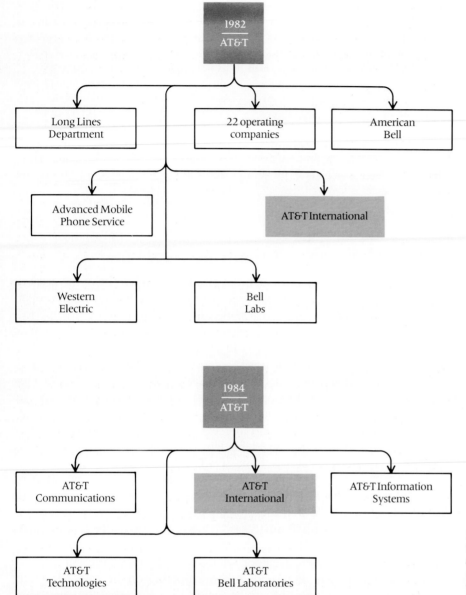

Exhibit 3.1 Governmental action leads to major changes in AT&T's organization and operation

SOURCE: *AT&T: 1982 Annual Report* and correspondence with AT&T Communications. Used by permission.

MARKETING'S ENVIRONMENT

To understand marketing's environment, we begin by describing the different types of forces. Each type comes from a different source and can have different kinds of effects on marketing decisions. First, we illustrate the types of forces by taking a step inside a company. Then, we put the forces together into a total picture of what managers face.

Environmental forces illustrated

Consider the situation faced by a marketing manager for American Hospital Supply Corporation, a manufacturer and distributor of drugs, supplies, and equipment for health care organizations. The manager is developing a marketing strategy for the next five years. Many of the uncontrollable forces that this manager faces are events happening outside American Hospital Supply. Surprisingly, though, not all of them are external. The manager need only look around the company for forces affecting marketing strategy. People in departments outside of marketing make decisions that partly determine what the manager can do. No strategy can be effectively implemented without adequate funding. Yet, gaining this support is not automatic. Financial managers at American Hospital Supply develop financial strategy by setting goals and allocating funds accordingly. Marketing is only one user of these resources, and so it must compete with other departments (e.g., production, research and development, shipping, and accounting services) for funds.

Working with financial managers illustrates the challenge of coping with the environment inside the organization. More generally, all forces that arise from the formal organizational structure and from interactions with employees make up marketing's **intraorganizational environment.**

Looking outside American Hospital Supply, the marketing manager knows that there is competition coming from other companies selling similar products. Drug companies such as G. D. Searle & Company, Pfizer, and McNeil Pharmaceutical are carrying out marketing strategies designed to attract sales, sales that might otherwise have gone to American Hospital Supply. Furthermore, customers—hospitals, clinics, doctors' offices, and surgery centers—make important buying decisions that determine how successful American Hospital Supply's marketing strategies are. When hospitals cut back on purchases of many products to cope with decreased patients and increased costs, a difficult situation is created for companies trying to expand sales to hospital markets. Finally, American Hospital Supply must deal with suppliers of chemicals, production equipment, transportation services, and many other products and services required in the daily operation of its business. These suppliers have their own goals and business strategies. Their decisions have an important effect on the costs, terms, and availability of resources that American Hospital Supply purchases from them, and so these suppliers' actions can be a factor in developing marketing strategy.

Suppliers, competitors, and customers constitute marketing's **task environment.** The term *task* refers to what the company is doing to meet the needs and wants of customers in target markets. Thus the task environment brings together the groups that most directly affect the company's success in serving these target markets. The task environment includes only these immediate external groups because they most directly influence this task. Understanding and responding to this environment is primarily a marketing responsibility.

Finally, a marketing manager should look beyond the task environment for more general forces that may eventually affect suppliers, customers, and competitors and their actions. External, partially or fully uncontrollable forces that influence and change the task environment make up marketing's **macroenvironment.** Currently, managers at American Hospital Supply are facing a momentous population change: People in the United States are becoming more highly educated. In turn, with greater education, people will become more knowledgeable about alternative health care treatments. An outgrowth of this trend is that in the future people will probably take a more active role in decisions made jointly by patient and doctor concerning their health care. How will this trend affect American Hospital Supply? One way might be shrinking hospital markets as more patients are treated in other health care facilities or use more outpatient services in their homes.

Forces combine to form marketing's environment

Marketing's environment is a combination of forces arising from all three major components: (1) the intraorganizational environment, (2) the task environment, and (3) the macroenvironment.[2] As Exhibit 3.2 illustrates, an astute marketing manager looks outward from a particular job to forces inside and outside the company that affect decisions being made. The manager determines what is happening in the environment and then uses marketing to respond to, and sometimes influence, these forces.

The arrows in the diagram emphasize that forces from all levels act on a marketing manager simultaneously. One-way arrows pointing toward the marketing manager show largely uncontrollable forces, and two-directional arrows show those forces that are able to be at least partially influenced. For instance, rising education of a population is uncontrollable by managers of a single firm. However, suppliers', competitors', and customers' decisions are partially influenced by a marketing manager through marketing mix decisions. In the following sections we examine each of the three types of environments more closely.

Exhibit 3.2 Marketing's environment combines forces from the intraorganizational environment, task environment, and macroenvironment.

INTRAORGANIZATIONAL AND TASK ENVIRONMENTS

The intraorganizational environment

Dealing with people in an organization is an essential part of a manager's job. These people include those in marketing who work for the manager such as salespersons assigned to a sales manager. Also, there are important people outside the manager's area of responsibility who are not under his or her direct supervision. These other people have their own views, objectives, and ways of doing things, which sometimes can be detrimental to what the manager wants to do. For example, a large, well-known pharmaceutical company introduced a new nonprescription drug that had the backing of a powerful member of the board of directors. The drug did not perform as expected in spite of a well-developed and executed marketing mix. The marketing vice-president eventually recommended dropping the product altogether, but the board member would not accept that recommendation. As a result, the product was kept in the product line and a series of marketing managers tried hard to improve performance without much success.

In contrast, other people in the company can be a tremendous help to a marketing manager if they are carefully cultivated. For example, a salesman for Continental Group, a large manufacturer of metal cans and many other products, recognized the importance to his customers of getting cans shipped on time. He worked closely with personnel in the shipping department to ensure that his customers' orders were scheduled properly. He took the time to personally get to know shipping people, he called frequently to check on progress of orders, and when possible he made concessions on delivery schedules. The shipping personnel responded very well to the salesman's prodding. Equally important, customers appreciated the expedited delivery service and were more inclined to award sales contracts to the salesman. As you can see, ability to sway other people in an organization may have to rely on interpersonal skills such as persuasion rather than direct authority.

Organizations also have a formal structure that assigns decision-making responsibility, sets procedures for making and implementing decisions, and determines guidelines for operations. These organizational features impose constraints and safeguards on marketing decision making. You can see these features at work in the management of a sales force. Salespersons typically are expected to meet specific objectives for areas of performance such as sales, number of calls on customers, and number of new customers contacted. These objectives not only guide the actions of salespersons, but also influence many decisions by managers who are overseeing the salespersons (e.g., hiring new salespersons and reassigning salespersons to new territories).

In a large organization, authority for making marketing decisions is divided among managers. (In Chapter 22 we discuss marketing organization more fully.) Advertising and personal selling in a company such as Procter & Gamble are handled by two departments. Coordination between decisions on these two parts of a marketing program is not easy to accomplish. Ever-present is the danger that advertising strategy will not support personal selling strategy. Procter & Gamble has dealt with this situation by using an important kind of marketing manager called a **brand manager** (some companies use the title **product manager**) who has marketing planning responsibility for one or a group of related brands. An important advantage of this position is the manager's ability to oversee and coordinate decisions in different departments that affect a brand's total marketing strategy.

A marketing manager, or for that matter any manager, must have a sound understanding of the organization and how it works. Although the organization is largely uncontrollable from the viewpoint of a marketing manager, ample opportunity exists to become familiar with its limitations and flexibility for decision making. For instance, practically every organization collects information of various kinds, yet that information may not be automatically given to all in the company who might benefit from it. One aspect of getting to know an organization is to learn about information that is available. A sales manager might take advantage of these organizational resources by requesting a marketing research report containing information collected for product development to help salespersons improve the content of their sales presentations to customers.

The task environment

Marketing managers occupy an interesting position in a company. Besides dealing with managers inside the organization, they are responsible for dealing with outside groups having power or influence over a company's performance in markets. The most central of these groups is customers. Because customers are the primary source of revenue, a majority of marketing management's energies are devoted to generating this revenue through sales. Other groups in the task environment are important because they also influence customers or because they partly determine what a company can do to sell to customers.

Suppliers and intermediate sellers. One way to understand the makeup of the task environment is to think of a firm as part of a channel of distribution stretching from suppliers to markets. Exhibit 3.3 shows the major participants in this channel. A firm's managers must interact with both suppliers and intermediate sellers because their actions are crucial to the success of a marketing strategy. Each level in the channel is made up of separate companies with managers who are trying to achieve their own purposes. The number of these companies and their approaches to achieving these purposes become factors for managers to consider when planning marketing strategy.

An interesting illustration concerns marketing strategy decisions made by large computer companies such as IBM, Digital Equipment Corporation, and the Japanese company NEC. As popularity of personal computers and related products grew, most manufacturers were not equipped to effectively reach and sell to the many buyers in business and consumer markets. Their salesforces were geared toward selling fewer but much larger computers. They did not have experience selling many small machines and standard software packages to a large number of individuals. New strategies had to be implemented that included setting up several alternative distribution channels to reach buyers.

IBM was one of the first to change marketing strategy in response to the realities of the new markets. Its management developed a distribution

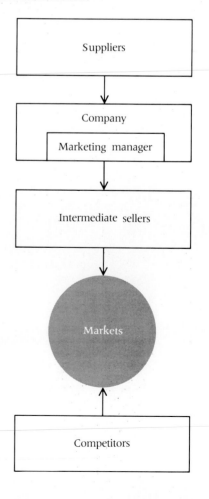

Exhibit 3.3 Central participants in the task environment

The Model 100™ was the first computer to employ liquid crystal display (LCD) technology. New technology alone, however, does not sell a product. Pitching its product to students is part of a marketing strategy that may help this portable computer succeed where IBM's PCjr did not. (Courtesy of Radio Shack, a division of Tandy Corporation)

network through Computerland, a successful franchise retail chain of computer stores accounting for more than 25 percent of U.S. retail computer sales.[3] In addition, IBM has continued to expand retail distribution by adding its own IBM retail stores as well as signing other chains to carry its products. At the heart of IBM's strategy is its ability to get independent retailers such as Computerland to provide enthusiastic selling support for its brands.

IBM could not dictate to Computerland what the arrangement would be. Rather, extensive negotiation was required to work out arrangements agreeable to both companies. For example, one aspect of their arrangement concerned the division of responsibility for sales to organizations buying in large volume versus sales to individuals (small business owners, managers, and consumers) who buy one or a few personal computers at a time. IBM wanted to handle large volume sales with its own sales staff and let the retail stores sell to individuals. Computerland wanted the freedom to sell to both kinds of customers. Negotiation is the only way to arrive at a solution, and it is an important way in which marketing managers gain cooperation from task environment players.

Markets. Markets are made up of people. These people bring their own experiences, opinions, and attitudes to buying decisions for products and services. A business firm influences, but cannot dictate exactly, what customers will buy and use. For this reason, the nature and makeup of markets is part of the task environment. Marketing managers face the ongoing responsibility for learning about people in markets so that effective marketing mixes can be created.

Let us continue the personal computer illustration. Markets for this product have presented obstacles for firms such as IBM and Apple Computer to overcome. When the market grew beyond knowledgeable hobbyists, sales were increasingly made to people who came into the buying situation knowing little about computers or how to use them. Most of these buyers were interested in computers because of a particular need (e.g., word processing, bookkeeping in a small business, home finances), and yet many were afraid of the machines.[4] Markets had to be approached in a special way. Marketing strategy of manufacturers (and retailers) was aimed at educating adult buyers to overcome their fear of computers. For the longer run, special programs were designed for use in primary, secondary, and vocational schools to create computer literacy among young people.

As the selling of personal computers illustrates, marketing mixes must be adapted to best take advantage of opportunities created by markets. Furthermore, as markets change, marketing strategies also must change. In the early 1980s, IBM introduced and aggressively marketed its PCjr in part to meet an emerging market for a portable home computer to complement a machine purchased previously. In 1985, however, the market changed, and so did IBM's marketing strategy: A depressed home computer market caused the company to stop production of its highly touted PCjr.

Competition. Every marketing manager is acutely aware that other organizations are competing for sales in its target markets. Very broadly, **competition** refers to the marketing actions of all organizations that are aimed at taking sales from a company's target markets. In free enterprise economies, such as the United States, Canada, Europe, and other parts of the free world, competition is a powerful yet largely uncontrollable influence on a company's success. Even in societies with closed economies, there is more competition than one may believe. In China approximately 45,000 farmers'

A holding company created by the AT&T divestiture, US WEST capitalizes on the powerful image of the American West: The independence, determination, and pioneering spirit of an unfolding country are also in this newfound company. US WEST believes that regulators ought not to protect their business from competitors and advocates that they be allowed to compete fairly and equally to preserve financial viability. (Courtesy of US WEST)

Bring on the competition.

We are not AT&T anymore. The rules have changed. And so have we.
    As the holding company for Mountain Bell, Northwestern Bell and Pacific Northwest Bell, we welcome our new competitive environment with a new and competitive organization.

We have learned from our past that regulation cannot shelter us from competition. So, today, wherever we find competition, we advocate deregulation. It is our belief that our customers and our shareowners are best served by the laws of the marketplace. Start thinking of us as a growth company. If you

haven't already, you will soon. We are not a utility. And we are not acting like one.
    Find out how we're different than the other companies created by divestiture. For a 32 page report, call 1-800-828-2400 or write US WEST Report, 7800 East Orchard Road, Englewood, Colorado 80111.

U S WEST

Mountain Bell. Northwestern Bell. Pacific Northwest Bell.
And a growing number of unregulated companies.

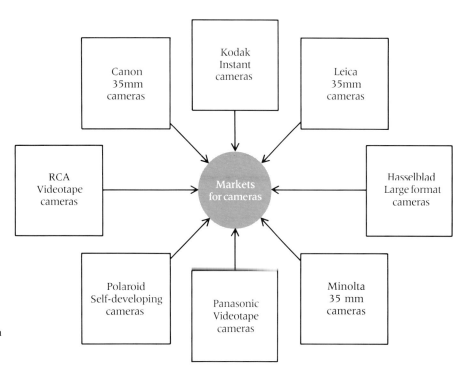

Exhibit 3.4 Companies competing with Kodak for sales show different types of competition at work

markets have emerged since the cultural revolution to compete with the state-run food stores.[5]

Understanding competition as part of the task environment begins when managers sort out different kinds of competition. Competition is much more than similar brands of the same product vying for the same customers as represented by Heinz ketchup taking on Del Monte ketchup. There are other less obvious forms of competition. Consider the task environment facing marketing managers at Kodak, the U.S. manufacturer of Instant cameras. Exhibit 3.4 may help you recognize some of the types of competition with which Kodak must deal.

- *Brand competition.* The most readily identifiable form of competition is between different brands of essentially the same type of product: **brand competition.** Kodak's Instant cameras must compete with Polaroid's Sun cameras, both of which are completely automatic and sell for approximately the same price. It is the most direct competition because of the similarity between brands. Brands that are alike offer similar benefits and are most likely to attract the same customers.

- *Product type competition.* Products that do not look similar may still compete with each other if they are bought and used for essentially the same purpose. We use the term **product type competition** to recognize this fact. One reason that people buy cameras is to record events (birthdays, anniversaries, basketball games). Different kinds of cameras can be used to provide a visual record of memorable events. For this reason, Kodak's still-picture Instant cameras face real competition from other different types of cameras such as 35mm cameras, large-format cameras, and videotape cameras. Companies such as RCA and Panasonic are also in competition with Kodak because they make videotape cameras. Because each type of camera may appeal to somewhat different market groups, the competition may be less direct than brand competition, but real nevertheless.

■ *Need competition.* Customers cannot buy everything they want. They make choices concerning which needs and wants to satisfy immediately, and which ones are less important and can be postponed. In this sense, buying a camera may compete with other luxury products such as tennis rackets, furniture, and food processors. Whenever customers place priority on some needs or wants over others, the corresponding products designed to satisfy those needs face **need competition.** Kodak's ability to get a sale in part depends on a customer's wanting a camera more than products satisfying competing needs.

■ *International competition.* Overlapping all other competition is **international competition** from brands and product types sold by companies from other countries. (The competition shown in Exhibit 3.4 includes both U.S. and foreign-based companies competing with Kodak for camera sales.) Some of Kodak's most powerful competitors are located in Japan (Canon, Panasonic, and Minolta) and Germany (Leica).

Task environment analysis. The task environment is arguably the most important of all the environments for determining the success of marketing strategies. Because of the central role of markets in this environment, marketing managers must understand what to expect from it. Fulfilling this responsibility can only come from finding and using appropriate information for decision making, which is the purpose for market opportunity analyses. We discuss analyzing the task environment in greater depth in Chapters 4 through 8.

THE MACROENVIRONMENT

Moving further from the company, beyond the task environment, a skilled marketing manager looks for important trends and changes in the macroenvironment. Task environment participants—markets, suppliers, intermediate sellers, competition, and the company itself—are influenced by the larger environment in which they all reside. Although an infinite number of macroenvironmental forces are possible, they usually can be divided into the five major categories shown in Exhibit 3.5: legal and political, social, technological, natural, and economic environments.

Legal and political environment

Look back to Exhibit 3.1, which describes how legal action by the U.S. government affected AT&T. In the United States, rarely does the government have such a severe and disrupting impact on a private organization. Yet, AT&T's experience demonstrates the necessity of analyzing the **legal and political environment**—the actions (e.g., laws, regulations, decrees, and political influence) of decision makers in governmental positions that affect the strategies of an organization.

This environment increasingly is becoming international in scope as governments are taking a close look at foreign companies selling products

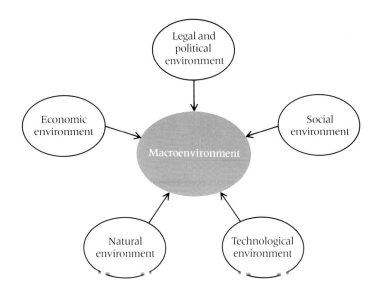

Exhibit 3.5 Categories of macro-environmental forces

in their countries.[6] In the early 1980s, the U.S. government required Japanese automobile companies to limit the number of cars imported into the country. Rationales for this import quota were politically motivated. For one, the Japanese government placed strict controls on the business that American companies could do in Japan. A natural reaction to these controls was to place similar controls on Japanese products imported to the United States. For another reason, sales of Japanese cars were seriously hurting the sales of American automobiles in the American market. Import quotas in the United States were a way of helping domestic automobile manufacturers remain competitive with the Japanese in U.S. markets.

The larger international companies are recognizing that their success is dependent on the political stability of countries in which they are selling.[7] Managers must negotiate with increasingly demanding government officials who have their own national interests at stake. Futhermore, as more companies expand internationally, there will be greater competition for each country's markets. The result is greater bargaining power for government officials.

Managers have learned from experience that the international legal and political environment includes an often confusing difference between the laws of various countries. What is illegal in one country may be acceptable, or at least tolerated, in another country. An illustration concerning the copying of popular brands should help you see how these differences affect marketing strategy. In recent years, the number of counterfeit brands coming from Taiwan has increased dramatically. Eveready batteries, Apple computers, Vaseline Hair Tonic, and Cartier watches are just a few of the famous brands that have been illegally copied. The government of Taiwan does not condone such practices, but its view of counterfeiting is more lenient than the view of the government of the United States and other Western countries. Trying to curb the practice in Taiwan is not as easy as it might be in a country with a different political attitude toward counterfeiting.[8]

On a national level, a country's political and legal environment also affects companies. Typically there is a maze of different laws and regulations to understand. Different aspects of this environment may limit business or can create opportunities. The antitrust laws of the United States that were used as the legal rationale for breaking up AT&T both limited the company's operations and created opportunities, as we have seen. For another component of business, the U.S. government's assistance to entrepreneurs and small businesses through loans and technical advice has been a boon. This favorable political climate, as well as other factors, has caused the number of new companies to jump from 93,000 in 1950 to 600,000 a year in the early 1980s.[9]

In the United States, the practice of using regulations to maintain competition or to regulate monopolies in which competition does not exist is changing. Maintaining competition is still of uppermost importance to the legal system. But more governmental effort is being directed toward protecting consumers, monitoring business for unethical practices, and mandating corrective actions when unethical practices are found. (See A Special Look at Public Policy and Marketing, following this chapter.) For instance, Hawaiian Punch was required to put on packages the percentage of fruit juice in its drinks to correct a consumer misconception about the content.[10] As a country's government changes the kinds of issues with which it is concerned, managers need to keep informed of the changes and analyze their impact on company and marketing strategy.

Even at the state or community level, the legal and political environment can impose constraints on firms or create market opportunities. For instance, South Carolina strives hard to attract new business. Because the population is not wealthy, bringing in new business is a way to help the economy grow. Once in the state, government works with businesses to help them prosper.

Social environment

As you might expect, the number of, and differences among, people in a population exert powerful influences on marketing. No matter where a consumer-products company conducts its business (in a country, region, state, or city), markets come from that area's population. Even firms that sell to other organizations, the industrial goods companies, are affected by population characteristics because all firms depend on consumer demand to keep an economy growing. The cultural, demographic, and life-style characteristics of people in a geographic area, or the **social environment,** influence consumer demand.

The importance of the social environment can be grasped by considering what happens when a company tries to sell a product in a foreign country where managers do not understand the local population. People in a country share opinions and attitudes about various things, a characteristic we call **culture.** Pepsodent found out about culture the hard way when it used promotion in Southeast Asia to show that Pepsodent toothpaste whitens teeth. This theme works well in the United States because white teeth are socially desirable. But, it was not effective in an Asian country where people deliberately chew betel nuts to stain their teeth to achieve social prestige.[11]

Managers gain insights into the social environment by studying the **demographic characteristics** of an area's population. Demographic

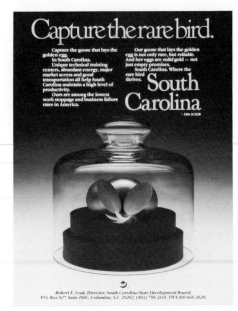

State and city alike try to attract new businesses. The difference between these two approaches is that the South Carolina campaign is publicly sponsored—the state government itself endorses and finances the advertising— whereas the Boston campaign is privately sponsored—the local business community is responsible for promoting the city. (Top: Courtesy of South Carolina State Development Board; bottom: Courtesy of Robinson Associates, Inc.)

Exhibit 3.6 U.S. population census study shows a trend toward higher percentages of adult women working

| Year | Total* | Single† | Selected Women's Groups | |
			Married with Spouse Present†	Widowed or Divorced†
1965	36.7%	40.5%	34.7%	35.7%
1970	42.6	53.0	40.8	36.2
1975	46.0	57.0	44.8	37.7
1980	51.1	61.5	50.1	41.0
1982	52.1	62.2	51.2	42.1

*Numbers are percentages of all women over the age of 14 (for 1965) or over 16 (for all years after 1965).
†Numbers are percentages of all women in the defined groups.
SOURCE: *Statistical Abstract of the United States: 1984*, Washington, D.C.: U.S. Department of Commerce, Bureau of the Census, 1983, p. 412.

characteristics are data about people describing their (1) innate physical characteristics (age, gender, race), (2) key possessions (education, income, occupation, type of housing), and (3) social arrangements (marital status, family size). Demographic information can tell the astute manager a lot about the purchases that people are likely to make. We can best understand this point by considering three of the more significant demographic changes occurring in the U.S. population.

■ *Increasing number of women in the labor force.* As Exhibit 3.6 shows, from 1965 to 1982, the percentage of adult women in the labor force rose from 36.7 percent to 52.1 percent. Furthermore, the women who are in the labor force are not confined to any particular group. Look at Exhibit 3.7. Notice that in 1982 percentages were high for women of all marital status and all ages up to 64 years old. These numbers mean that women of all ages are working.

The increase in working women has affected dramatically the demand for all kinds of products and services. Some of the more obvious

Exhibit 3.7 Women working in the U.S. labor force are coming from all marital status groups and most age groups

| Women's Marital Status | Women's Age Groups | | | | |
	16–19	20–24	25–44	45–64	65 and over
Married, spouse present in household*	50.8%	62.2%	62.6%	47.8%	7.1%
Single	51.5	75.7	83.0	64.8	13.0
Other status (divorced, widowed, separated)	53.4	67.7	77.8	60.5	7.9

*Percentages are the 1982 proportion of all women in the respective age group and marital status group who are working outside their home.
SOURCE: *Statistical Abstract of the United States: 1984*, Washington D.C.: Department of Commerce, Bureau of the Census, 1983, p. 412.

ones are child-care services, microwave ovens, home-cleaning services, quick-preparation food products, and restaurant meals.

■ *Aging of the population.* Persons in the famous post–World War II "baby
boom" are now reaching middle age. Coupled with increases in the
average life span of Americans, we can expect tremendous growth in
the older age groups for years to come. By the year 2050 there will be
more people older than 65 years of age than people younger than 18,
and more people 85 and older than there were people 65 and older in
1950.[12]

Implications of the changing age structure are enormous. Already
hospitals and other medical services are aggressively going after opportunities to cater to the elderly. Retirement communities are thriving.
Entertainment services such as motels, restaurants, and movies give
discounts to the elderly to attract their business. Many other opportunities to satisfy the unique needs and wants of the elderly will be
spotted in the future by creative marketing managers.

■ *A steady shift from farm and blue-collar positions toward white-collar and
service jobs* (see Exhibit 3.8). The growth of white-collar jobs—professionals, teachers, managers, administrators, salespersons, and clerks—
is particularly important. John Naisbitt in *Megatrends* says that more
white-collar workers signifies a shift from an industrial economy to an
information economy:

Now more than 65 percent of us work with information as programmers,
teachers, clerks, secretaries, accountants, stockbrokers, managers, insurance
people, bureaucrats, lawyers, bankers, and technicians. And many more
workers hold information jobs within manufacturing companies. Most Americans spend their time creating, processing, or distributing information.[13]

In other words, the U.S. business base is becoming decreasingly
oriented toward making things (products) and increasingly skilled at
supplying, handling, and using information. Marketing should benefit
greatly from the information economy because gathering and using
special kinds of information is a key marketing manager skill, as we
demonstrate throughout this text.

Studying the social environment can progress to learning about peoples' life-styles. **Life-styles** refer to the particular ways that people lead
their lives including time, money, and energy spent on work and leisure
activities. Many marketing managers now accept that life-styles affect
which products and services are desired. Consider the life-style decisions

Exhibit 3.8   Occupations chosen by Americans
point to a changing economy

Occupation	1970	1975	1982
White collar	48.3	49.8	53.7
Blue collar	35.3	33.0	29.7
Service	12.4	13.7	13.8
Farm	4.0	3.4	2.7
Totals	100.0%	100.0%	100.0%

SOURCE: *Statistical Abstract of the United States: 1984,* Washington D.C.: U.S. Department of Commerce, Bureau of the
Census, 1983, p. 417.

Scene: Bachelor apartment, Chicago.
Time: 7:02 p.m.
Cast: One hungry guy. One T-bone done to a T.

And Stouffer's® Fettucini Alfredo,
in another outstanding performance.

**Turn the side of your plate into a star attraction.
With Side Dishes. From Stouffers.®**

Recognizing the proliferation of
single-person households, Stouffer's now
offers one-portion products. Ten years
ago this ad might have read:

  Scene: Family kitchen, Toledo.
  Time: 5.30 P.M.
  Cast: One busy wife. And one hungry
          family to feed.

(Courtesy Stouffer Foods Corporation)

being made by many Americans: (1) young people are deciding to delay marriage, but live away from their parents' home, (2) adults of all ages are deciding to divorce, and (3) older people are choosing to maintain their home after all the other members are gone.[14] An outgrowth of these life-style trends is that an increasing number of households comprise single persons or unrelated persons living together. These nonfamily households are smaller than families and therefore do not need as large a size of many household products (e.g., cereal, milk, ovens, refrigerators, and dish-washers), to mention just one implication.

Of all the macroenvironmental forces, the social environment seems to get the most scrutiny. And rightly so. Cultural, demographic, and life-style characteristics of a population play a crucial role in determining what people need and want. Marketing managers must be able to study populations to spot market opportunities ready to be tapped now as well as those that are emerging

Technological environment

The **technological environment** refers to the capabilities of a country and its industries to produce and distribute products and services. These capabilities are the driving force behind a business system's ability to meet market needs and wants. The most visible result of technology comes from the truly new and exciting products. Videocassette recorders, lasers for surgery, communications satellites, and robots are just a few of the more recent innovations of which you may have heard. New products open new market opportunities and help customers meet needs in more interesting and more efficient ways. G. D. Searle & Company is one company on the technological edge. It uses genetically altered bacteria enzymes to help make its aspartame sweetener, NutraSweet.[15]

Technology has a less visible, more behind-the-scenes impact on business success, too. Innovation in package designs, materials, production methods, and distribution techniques can change demand for products and services: Brik Pak, a U.S. subsidiary of a Swedish company, successfully introduced "paper bottles" for packaging fruit drinks and other beverages. The new package keeps the product fresh on the shelf for months. Perhaps you have seen Hi-C, Ocean Spray, Del Monte, and Gatorade use paper bottles for their drinks. Spaceage materials such as graphite and boron are helping companies offer new designs of skis, tennis rackets, golf clubs, and other sporting equipment. Additionally, new designs in industrial robots are changing the nature of manufacturing and improving the quality of products by taking over the more dangerous and tedious jobs from workers.

Technology also affects the other categories of macroenvironmental forces. New ways of doing things can alter the behavior of people. Consider the combined effect of cable television and home computers on consumers' shopping habits. With a computer hooked up to a television set, a consumer can get access to shopping information services that display products on the screen. Products can then be ordered with the push of a button. The impact on all retailing will be interesting to watch.

Counterbalancing these many benefits of technology are potential costs. Costs can show up in high product price as well as in undesirable impacts on other aspects of our lives. We have seen how oil spills can cause tremendous damage. Costs of trying to prevent these spills as well as the costs of cleaning them up should be charged against the technological development of drilling and transportation capabilities. Technological costs are prevalent in many products and services. Computer crimes, increased risk of cancer from food additives, and loss of privacy as organizations accumulate information are just a few that are widely publicized. Yet, most would agree that on balance, benefits of most new technology outweigh its costs.

The potential for technology to influence business success is enormous. Companies must participate in the advancement of technology related to their products or services or watch competitors move ahead. At the same time, managers also must monitor the advance of technology to keep from being surprised by a new development. Continual monitoring is the only way to see innovation coming far enough in advance to develop a strategy to deal with it.

Countries also use technology to compete. An indication of a country's technological effort is its industries' research and development (R&D) activity. The United States is a world leader, spending twice as much on R&D as Japan and all other Western countries combined.[16] Undoubtedly, the technological edge of the United States is a major factor in the strength of its economy and of its products and services in world markets.

Natural environment

The **natural environment** includes the forces of nature as well as availability of natural resources that influence the success of company strategies. Some natural forces such as fire, lightning, and floods are unpredictable, and so managers can do little to plan for them. Other forces of nature are becoming more predictable. For these, forecasting is a key to providing the information that managers need to incorporate these factors into business decisions. For instance, weather patterns can influence demand for many products and services, as the ski resort industry found out in the early 1980s when snow falls were less than normal. Scientists are beginning to shed light on the causes of weather, and weather forecasting has improved dramatically. Many industries including fishing, farming, vacation resorts, and airline services can expect to benefit from these new techniques (see Marketalk).

The natural environment also provides raw materials for producing goods and services. Availability of these materials has a far-reaching impact on all products that use them. Shifting oil prices since the early 1970s illustrate the impact of shortages and surpluses on product supply and demand. The Organization of Petroleum Exporting Countries (OPEC) demonstrated to the world what a shortage of a key resource such as oil can do to the health of economies. OPEC raised prices by some 1200 percent from 1973 to 1982, setting off a worldwide recession.

At the same time, consumers, companies, and even governments continually adapt to changes in the natural environment. Behavior adjusts so that problems in the natural environment are dealt with. OPEC found out that people gradually responded to higher oil prices by engaging in conservation efforts, and when possible, using other fuels. Oil companies ran advertisements encouraging people not to use as much oil-derived products

*Marke*TALK ///

Weather watch

NEXT TIME THE WEATHERMAN forecasts gusty winds, soft-drink companies might want to beef up their advertising. Soda pop consumption curiously increases with wind velocity. And when storm clouds form, the climate may be just right for a barrage of hot cereal ads. Research indicates that's when cereal eaters are most likely to treat themselves to an extra bowl.

Struggling to get the most for their advertising dollar, some marketers have started paying close attention to such meteorological trivia. "Weather can change people's habits and taste preferences enough to boost consumption of a product by 50% to 100%," declares Fred Ward, a former TV weatherman and one of the founders of Advertiming, a new service in New York that uses computer models to match product usage with weather conditions.

SOURCE: Ronald Alsop, "Companies look to weather to find best climate for ads," *Wall Street Journal,* Jan. 10, 1985, p. 29. Reprinted by permission of *The Wall Street Journal,* © Dow Jones & Company, Inc., 1985. All rights reserved.

It's just common sense to advertise beer and suntan oil more heavily in the summer and cold medicine and ear muffs more in the winter. But now some companies are monitoring the daily weather outlook to help them select the best times to run their commercials. Vitt Media International Inc., New York, one of the partners in Advertiming, claims it can buy local TV and radio time with just 24 hours notice.

Connecticut Radio Network Inc. in Hamden, Conn., also provides weather guidance, placing ads for Campbell soup before snow-storms strike and devising a chapped lips index for Blistex based on temperature, wind and humidity. Soon, the company's Mediarology service plans to alert Quaker Oats Co. to impending cold snaps in some of its cereal markets.

With media costs rising rapidly, "we're looking for every bit of leverage we can get," says George Mahrlig, director of media services at Campbell Soup Co. "Based on reaction from the supermarket trade and consumers, we believe the winter storm ads have given us an edge." This winter, Campbell will boost its storm ad budget 50% to about $750,000.

Whenever a storm is forecast, radio ads are aired urging listeners to stock up on soup before the weather worsens. After the storm hits, the ad copy is changed to tell people to relax indoors and warm themselves with soup. Connecticut Radio Network monitors the weather in more than 30 cities, 24 hours a day, for Campbell. Barry Berman, the network's president, says he sometimes has to roust radio salesmen from bed to schedule the ads.

Consumers' perception of the weather often is more important than meteorological readings alone. Mr. Ward of Advertiming notes that people eat soup and hot cereal when it's cloudy because they "feel colder." Likewise, Mr. Berman might not urge Quaker Oats to run more ads when the thermometer reads 16 degrees in Chicago, but he probably would if the temperature dipped to 25 in Atlanta. Says Mr. Berman: "We have to measure the misery index."

Connecticut Radio Network has turned down some companies. An aspirin manufacturer wanted to time its ads to run when a cold spell was about to begin. But research revealed that people buy more aspirin whenever they run out, regardless of the weather.

///

such as gasoline and kerosene. Furthermore, countries were spurred by the higher prices to find new sources of oil outside OPEC's control. All these actions created a surplus of oil in the middle 1980s and a welcome fall in prices.[17]

Natural resources are limited. The delicate balance between supply and demand for these resources can influence the ability of business to meet market needs and wants. Furthermore, most people agree that business, partly through responsible marketing practices, has an obligation to conserve and protect the natural environment. Conserving resources for future generations is one practical reason. For instance, companies that produce aluminum have encouraged return of aluminum cans for profitable recycling to conserve the metal. Availability of natural resources and their prices will always be factors in business decisions.

Economic environment

Of all the macroenvironmental forces, you are probably most familiar with the economic environment. The **economic environment** comprises the actions of business that directly affect the purchasing power of organizational and consumer buyers. Although there are many economic forces, two of the most influential in this decade have been unemployment and inflation.

Jobs are the primary source of purchasing power for most consumers. For this reason, the level of unemployment often is used as a barometer of economic health. In the United States, unemployment during the 1980s has been disturbingly high, reaching double digits in the early part of the decade. Many fear that the current situation is symptomatic of a long-run economic change. Cheap labor in countries such as Korea, Taiwan, and Brazil has already led to loss of employment opportunities for U.S. workers.

*Marke*TALK //

Rethinking the marketing concept

MARKETING EXECUTIVES and managers should rethink the marketing concept and two of its tenets—the "4Ps" and the "uncontrollable environment," advises Philip Kotler, professor of marketing, Northwestern University, Evanston, Ill.

"The marketing concept is a management orientation that holds the key to achieving organizational goals (and) consists of the organization determining the needs and wants of target markets and adapting itself to delivering satisfactions more effectively and efficiently than its competitors," Kotler wrote in his 1980 book *Marketing Management: Analysis, Planning, and Control.*

This view of marketing, like many others, reflects the theories described by E. Jerome McCarthy, professor of marketing, Michigan State University, East Lansing, in his 1960 textbook *Basic Marketing.*

McCarthy likened the marketing concept to three concentric circles: the inner circle is the customer; the middle circle consists of the "controllable" marketing mix factors of product, price, place, and promotion (the 4Ps); and the outer circle consists of the "uncontrollable" economic, social, cultural, political, resource, and technology factors of the external environment.

Kotler and other marketing thinkers have always contended that the marketing manager's job is to select and control the marketing mix factors that can help the company best adapt to the uncontrollable external environment.

But Kotler has changed his mind! At a recent meeting of the alumni of NU's Kel-

logg Graduate School of Management, he announced: "Like Galileo, I am ready to recant, but in this case, out of my own volition.

"I now believe that marketers *can* influence the environment in which the firm operates and do not simply have to accept it and adapt to it. More firms are awakening to the possibility of environmental management through strategic investments and influence. Firms need not accept a reactive mode of thinking and planning, but a proactive mode.

"I am currently working on a concept I call 'Megamarketing: The Fourth Wave.' I think that the orientation of our discipline has evolved from distribution to sales to marketing to megamarketing."

Kotler defined megamarketing as "the application of economic, psychological, political, and PR skills to gain the cooperation of a number of parties in order to enter and/or operate successfully in a given market."

Megamarketing, he said, "expands the idea of who the marketing targets are— they may include government officials, public-interest groups, the news media, etc.—and the marketing-mix tools. There are really six Ps, with *political power* and *public-opinion formation* added.

"The environment must be managed as well as the marketing mix. This may be the essence of creative strategic thinking," he said.

The traditional marketing concept, Kotler said in an interview, is too restrictive and does not seem to apply to all firms in all industries.

"We've always had great faith in the marketing concept. We believed that if you offered a good product at the right price in the right place and promoted it properly, you would succeed. But sometimes that just isn't true. You can do everything right and still fail. Simply creating

incentives to buy isn't enough. The 4Ps are insufficient.

"If you are an American marketer of electric appliances, and you want to sell your products in Japan, you have to do more than the 4Ps. The 4Ps don't tell you how to overcome the gatekeepers, invisible tariffs, and import restrictions that virtually prohibit your products from being sold in Japan. This is a megamarketing problem that requires marketers to make big changes in the external environment.

"You need to use the other two Ps—political power and public-opinion formation through public relations—to solve such a problem. If your products are being blocked by gatekeepers, you may have to pressure your embassy officials to work on opening up the gates.

"You may have to lobby government officials to change the trade agreements. Or you may have to run a series of advocacy ads to inform the public about the foreign country's policies and generate public support of your efforts.

"A similar problem is faced by U.S. pharmaceutical manufacturers wanting to market in Indonesia. On the domestic side, if you want to open up a store in a certain city, but zoning laws prohibit it, you'll have to exert political power to change the laws. In other words, if power is being used against you, you have to fight back with power.

"Marketers are always looking at economic factors and rational factors, but they fail to study political science. They should examine the conflicts, the special-interest and pressure groups, the vested interests, the political realities, and create appeals in those arenas.

"Marketers can no longer sit back and adopt a defensive posture when power is being used against them. They have to go out there and influence the external environment."

SOURCE: "Kotler: Rethink the marketing concept," *Marketing News,* Sept. 14, 1984, pp. 1, 22. Used by permission of the American Marketing Association.

//

Technology in the form of robots also will take jobs. Furthermore, the combination of both factors may cause a widening gap between workers' present skills and the skills needed by business in the future.[18]

Inflation, higher prices for essentially the same products and services, has been a worldwide problem for more than a decade. In recent years, inflation has been highly resistant to change even in the face of economic slowdowns. Called *stagflation,* this economic phenomenon causes loss of buying power because prices go up without offsetting increases in job opportunities. World leaders worry particularly about what happens in the United States because of the impact that such a huge economy has on the economies of other countries.

No company's managers can understand customers' buying patterns without examining the impact of economic forces on purchase decisions. Consider the effect of inflation on spending. Surprisingly, it seems to cause people to save less and spend more. Perhaps consumers buy more because they feel that waiting will mean paying more for the same product. Determining inflation's impact on specific products and services, however, is more difficult. Some products and services sell better in times of inflation, and others sell worse. Unraveling the mystery of inflation's impact on consumer buying is only one illustration of a company's need for careful analyses of the economic environment. (See Marketalk about rethinking the marketing concept, which suggests that marketers can sometimes influence the environment in which a firm operates.)

MACROENVIRONMENTAL SCANNING

Each of the three categories of environments for marketing must be analyzed using different methods. Only very infrequently would formal studies be used to assess the interorganizational environment. (See Chapter 22 for discussion of one such study called a marketing audit.) Instead, marketing managers usually rely on astute observation and experience from interactions with other personnel to learn how to work successfully in the organization. Especially important is attaining a realistic understanding of the company's strengths and weaknesses. Moving outside the firm, analyzing the task environment is the special province of the marketing manager. Consequently, we devote considerable discussion of this activity in Part Two of the text. For now, gaining insight into analyzing marketing's environment is accomplished by concentrating on the macroenvironment.

Discovering and evaluating macroenvironmental forces are ongoing activities in a well-managed organization. The technique for this activity is **macroenvironmental scanning,** which refers to gathering and using information on macroenvironmental forces to identify new trends, project trends into the future, and analyze implications for corporate and marketing decisions.

Scanning environments

Marketing managers typically want three questions answered concerning a macroenvironmental force: (1) What is the force like now? (2) Will the force change in the future? (3) What is the direction and magnitude of change expected? The thrust of these questions is toward the future because managers must make decisions now to adapt to, or in some cases influence, each macroenvironmental force as it will be in the months or years ahead. Exhibit 3.9 shows the steps for macroenvironmental scanning ordered into a logical sequence. Let us examine each step.

Identify forces. Macroenvironmental forces lie within one or more of the five categories previously discussed (you may want to review quickly Exhibit 3.5). To spot the most relevant forces, a marketing manager begins by considering decisions that must be made. In some instances, there may be only one force of consequence to a decision. A bank's marketing manager, for instance, is most concerned with the trend in interest rates, an economic force affecting mortgage purchases by consumers, when deciding whether to offer a new variable interest rate service. For more complicated decisions, more than one force may have to be scanned, such as when IBM made its historical decision to enter the market for personal computers. Management had to consider social (educational attainment of consumers, work requirements, life-styles), technological (advances in microprocessor chips, display screens), and economic (discretionary income, inflation, interest rates) forces.

Gather information on trends. Information for environmental scanning comes from many sources including (1) government statistics, (2) customer attitude and opinion studies, (3) patent applications, (4) economic forecasting models, (5) studies and reports done by the media such as *The Wall Street Journal* and *Business Week,* (6) polling of managements' opinions, and (7) studies done by independent research organizations and universities. With so much available, rarely would a manager want to rely on only a few sources. The challenge at this step is to seek a mix of various information sources so that all aspects of a macroenvironmental force are covered.

In many cases, information can be accumulated and organized in a way that highlights historical trends. Trends are regular patterns of change over time, and they are important to discover because they help the manager see how a force will change in the future. Exhibit 3.10 shows information arranged to help you see a trend. Can you see why many forecasters, after looking at this information, predict an increase in nonfamily households? Notice that from 1970 to the present there has been a steadily increasing percentage of nonfamily households and a corresponding decrease in percentage of family households. The regularity of the change over so many years suggests that a trend is taking place.

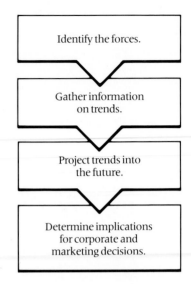

Exhibit 3.9   Steps in a macroenvironmental scanning sequence

Exhibit 3.10   Changing household composition

	1970	1980	1981	1982
Total households	100.0	100.0	100.0	100.0
Family households	81.2	73.7	73.2	73.1
Married-couple family	70.5	60.8	59.8	59.4
Other family, male householder	1.9	2.1	2.3	2.4
Other family, female householder	8.7	10.8	11.0	11.3
Nonfamily households	18.8	26.3	26.8	26.9
Male householder	6.4	10.9	11.3	11.3
Female householder	12.4	15.4	15.5	15.6

SOURCE: Arthur J. Norton, "Keeping up with households," *American Demographics,* Feb. 1983, p. 20. Reprinted by permission.

Project trends into the future. The value of macroenvironmental scanning information lies in helping a manager predict change. Prediction begins by simply projecting past trends into the future. Consider Exhibit 3.10 again. What prediction would you make concerning the number of nonfamily households in 1990? You could make a rough forecast by calculating the average annual change from 1970 to 1982, and then assume that this average change will continue to hold from 1982 to 1990.

More refined predictions also can be made by considering related factors when projecting a trend. Suppose you want to forecast future increases in nonfamily households. You could consider what is happening to social trends causing nonfamily household formations (divorces, later marriages, and elderly maintaining households after all other family members are gone). Of course, this additional analysis takes more time and effort, but often the improved results are worth these costs. (See Marketool for a discussion of whether there is a trend toward a vanishing middle-income class.)

MarkeTOOL

Analyzing reasons for environmental trends yields surprising insight

AFTER EXAMINING the most recent population income figures for the United States, many persons in the media and in academia have made a disturbing prediction—the middle-income class is vanishing. On the surface, the figures seem to show a decline in the size of the middle-class households (as a percent of all households), and greater polarization of people into the high-income (more than $35,000) and low-income (less than $15,000) groups. If the conclusion is true, the marketing implications are enormous. For instance, companies that sell luxury products and services such as exclusive vacation resorts, videocassette recorders, and large-screen televisions can be optimistic about future market opportunity. But companies that cater to the middle class—such as those that sell basic appliances, casual-wear clothes, and fast-food—would be seriously hurt.

Is this trend really happening? One researcher for the Conference Board, a well-respected business research organization, says that there is no such long-term trend. Instead, the data show a short-term adjustment to other factors. How this conclusion was reached provides an interest-

ing look into proper analysis of environmental trends.

Having isolated a trend, the first step is to look for corollary trends that might explain the primary trend (in this case the decline of the middle class). Important corollary trends happening during the 1970s included (1) an influx of the post–World War II "baby boomers" (the 70 million children born between 1946 and 1965) into the job market; (2) a growing number of persons who are more than 65 years of age; (3) more households headed by a woman (caused by more divorces and separations); and (4) more households in which both husband and wife work. All these trends were spotted from analysis of demographic information collected by the U.S. government.

The next step is to analyze how the corollary trends are affecting the primary trend. Take a minute to assess how the four trends just listed have influenced the trend of the disappearance of the middle class. Persons born during the baby boom years are entering the job market at relatively low income causing expansion of the group earning less than $15,000. An increased number of elderly persons and households headed by women can be added to this group. These factors explain why the percentage of households earning less than $15,000 rose during the 1970s.

The larger percentage for the group earning more than $35,000 generally is attributed to an increasing number of households with two spouses working.

The last step is to see if the factors causing the primary trend will continue to change in the same way. If so, then the primary trend should continue. But if the corollary trends do not continue, then neither will the primary trend. The Conference Board has concluded that the four corollary trends will not continue to change as they have in the 1970s. Their research indicates that the baby boomers are moving increasingly into more middle-income and higher job positions. This factor alone should stop the shift toward lower-income households. Furthermore, there is an upper limit beyond which the other demographic and social trends will not go. For instance, not all women want or need to work outside the home, meaning that the percentage of working women will stop well short of 100 percent.

The conclusion from this analysis is that the middle-income group has been hit by adjustments in the 1970s, but it certainly is not disappearing as many have said. There is a moral here: Information must be analyzed cautiously and with an eye toward underlying causes before it can be used to predict the future.

SOURCE: Bernie Whalen, "The 'vanishing' middle class: A passing demographic aberration," *Marketing News*, May 25, 1984, p. 1, 6, 7.

Determine implications for marketing. The payoff from environmental scanning occurs when managers are faced with important decisions. Because success of these decisions is influenced by macroenvironmental forces, predictions of change help managers assess the risks and opportunities from alternative courses of action. Sometimes action might be taken to try to alter the predicted trend itself as happens when a company uses advertising and lobbyists to sway politicians' votes on an issue. More commonly the marketing challenge is to make decisions that creatively take advantage of opportunities presented by a trend in the macroenvironment. Howard Head and Prince Manufacturing Company had the foresight to see that new materials such as aluminum, graphite, fiberglass, and boron, when used in the manufacture of tennis rackets, allow much greater flexibility in designing more functional shapes and size of the racket head. As a result, Prince aggressively marketed an innovative oversized racket line and has since become the pace setter in tennis racket sales for the rest of the industry.

Developing strategy for a firm based on macroenvironmental trends is a creative process. Information never replaces the imagination and sound judgment of managers. Information only helps managers make better use of these talents.

Applications for marketing

Understanding the macroenvironment is crucial for marketing. An amazing amount of help can be provided for marketing decision making by periodically scanning these forces. Some of the marketing decisions that can

Prince became the top-seeded tennis racket maker because it convinced many players that it's easier to hit a tennis ball with a big racket than with a little one. The larger racket, quite believably, has a bigger "sweet spot"—a nebulous concept that generally refers to the area of the racket where a player should get the solidest hit. (Courtesy of Prince Manufacturing, Inc., owner of registered trademark Prince)

benefit include the following:

- Developing new product ideas
- Selecting new target markets
- Deciding when to drop a product
- Deciding what extra services to offer with a product
- Deciding what role promotion should have in an overall strategy
- Deciding whether and how best to change distribution to better reach markets
- Deciding on prices that communicate value to markets

As you read through the chapters of this book, try to spot when macroenvironmental scanning played a part in the marketing decisions being discussed. As you will see, findings from scanning are frequently applied in marketing and business practice.

SUMMARY

One reason that marketing managers get so excited by their profession is the ever-present challenge of dealing with the many environmental forces. There is no doubt that marketing's environment creates uncertainty and adds risk to marketing decision making. Yet, a corresponding reward comes from anticipating the environment correctly and putting into practice a marketing strategy that works well under the circumstances. Of course, every marketing manager must develop key skills to cope with these environmental forces.

One of these skills is having a sound grasp of what marketing's environment includes. As we discussed early in the chapter, there is not one environment. Instead, there are three levels of the environment that surround a marketing manager. These are the intraorganizational environment, the task environment, and the macroenvironment. The intraorganizational environment is limited to the confines of an organization. Rules and proper procedures must be followed. Furthermore, no marketing manager can survive without working with others in the firm. Developing a sound understanding of the organization combined with well-polished interpersonal skills are essential for dealing with the intraorganizational environment.

The task environment gets special consideration in this book because it is so important to planning a marketing strategy. Participants in the task environment—markets, suppliers, intermediate sellers, competition, and the company itself—all have a vested interest in a company's strategy, and their actions are instrumental in determining the strategy's success. Marketing managers have primary responsibility for analyzing the task environment and building strategies to deal with it. Furthermore, marketing is becoming increasingly intertwined with strategies being developed for the entire firm.

Finally, the outermost level is the macroenvironment, which comprises five major categories of forces: legal and political, social, technological, natural, and economic. Each is a source of uncontrollable trends that not only influence the success of marketing decisions, but can have an impact on the entire operations of a company. For this reason, managers throughout a firm must be alert to the trends and changes taking place.

Marketing often plays an important role in analyzing macroenvironmental forces because its managers have important information and analysis skills developed from evaluating the task environment. Macroenvironmental scanning gave us our first look at an analysis procedure. This procedure is based on gathering information describing current forces, projecting these forces into the future, and analyzing implications for company decisions. Learning about the task environment, to which we turn in Chapter 4, expands on this straightforward procedure.

KEY TERMS

marketing's environment	brand competition	demographic characteristics
intraorganizational environment	product type competition	life-styles
task environment	need competition	technological environment
macroenvironment	international competition	natural environment
brand manager	legal and political environment	economic environment
product manager	social environment	macroenvironmental scanning
competition	culture	

QUESTIONS FOR REVIEW AND DISCUSSION

1. What does *uncontrollable* mean when applied to environmental forces?

2. What are the three types of environments faced by marketing managers?

3. Does marketing's environment include only forces that come from outside a marketing manager's organization?

4. In what ways does the macroenvironment differ from the task environment?

5. What skills should a marketing manager have to deal effectively with marketing's intraorganizational environment?

6. Which functions of a business (finance, accounting, etc.) are most important for marketing managers to know how to work with?

7. List three trends (other than the ones discussed in the chapter) in the social environment of the country of your choice that are having an important impact on marketing decisions. Why did you pick these trends?

8. List three trends (other than the ones discussed in the chapter) in the economic environment of the country of your choice that are having an important impact on marketing decisions of companies. Why did you pick these trends?

9. Who are the major participants in the task environment?

10. What are the major forces making up marketing's macroenvironment?

11. How can macroenvironmental scanning be used by marketing managers to help make important marketing decisions?

12. Describe three different kinds of competition faced by a company.

BUILDING YOUR PORTFOLIO

Many environmental trends are going on right now that are having momentous impact on business. You can acquire excellent experience in using environmental information for marketing by going through the macroenvironmental scanning steps. First, choose a key economic or social trend that you have heard about and would like to analyze further. Then, apply the macroenvironmental scanning procedure discussed in this chapter so that you can make marketing recommendations for a company of your choice. For example, you might analyze the impact of rising interest rates on the marketing strategy of a condominium construction company. Or how will declining birth rates in the United States affect marketing strategy of Gerber Products, the baby food manufacturer? Follow the step-by-step procedure presented in the chapter: (1) select a trend, (2) gather information from available library sources, (3) project the current trend to 1990, and (4) create recommendations for the company's market targets and/or marketing mix that you believe will respond to the trend you have evaluated.

NOTES

1. The information for this illustration came from Brian O'Reilly, "Ma Bell's kids fight for position." *Fortune*, June 27, 1983, pp. 62–68; Carol J. Loomis, "Valuing the pieces of eight." *Fortune*, June 27, 1983, pp. 70–73, 76–78; and *AT&T: 1982 Annual Report*.
2. The classification of environmental forces into intraorganization, task, and macroenvironment is based on the discussion in David W. Cravens, Gerald E. Hills, and Robert B. Woodruff, *Marketing Decision Making Concepts and Strategy*. Homewood, Ill.: Irwin, 1980, pp. 52–54.
3. Dennis Briskin, "Exec Computerland: A retailer's perspective." *Softalk*, June 1983, pp. 22–23, 25–28.
4. Virginia Inman, "Learning how to use computers is frightening experience for many." *Wall Street Journal*, Apr. 12, 1983, pp. 37, 42.
5. Hans B. Thorelli, "First survey of China's 'middle-class consumers' finds 8% own refrigerators, but 75% own TVs." *Marketing News*, Feb. 18, 1983, p. 16.
6. Stephen Blank, John Basek, Stephen J. Kobrin, and Joseph LaPalombara, *Assessing the Political Environment: An Emerging Function in International Companies*. New York: The Conference Board, 1980, p. 2.
7. Ibid.
8. Louis Kraar, "Fighting the fakes from Taiwan." *Fortune*, May 30, 1983, pp. 114–116.
9. "'Restructuring of America'—when, where, how and why." *U.S. News & World Report*, Dec. 27, 1982, and Jan. 3, 1983, p. 49.
10. "FTC now conducts attitude research before entering costly legal battles." *Marketing News*, May 16, 1980, p. 1.
11. David A. Ricks, *Big Business Blunders: Mistakes in Multinational Marketing*. Homewood, Ill.: Irwin, 1983, p. 65.
12. Gregory Spencer and John F. Long, "The new Census Bureau projections." *American Demographics*, Apr. 1983, p. 26.
13. John Naisbitt, *Megatrends*. New York: Warner Books, 1984, pp. 4–5.
14. Arthur J. Norton, "Keeping up with households." *American Demographics*, Feb. 1983, p. 18.
15. "Biotech comes of age." *Business Week*, Jan. 23, 1984, p. 85.
16. "The U.S. still leads the world in R&D spending." *Business Week*, June 20, 1983, p. 122.
17. "Special report: The collapse of world oil prices." *Business Week*, Mar. 7, 1983, pp. 92–94.
18. A. F. Ehrbar, "Grasping the new unemployment." *Fortune*, May 16, 1983, pp. 106–112.

Case 3.1

First Methodist Hospital*

THE ADMINISTRATOR for First Methodist Hospital, James Henry, was reviewing alternative solutions to a marketing problem. Data from a marketing research study confirmed that the hospital was losing patients from its market area to other hospitals (see the table). In 1970, First Methodist received 85.6 percent of all patients in its market area who stayed one or more nights in a hospital during the year. By 1982, that percentage had dropped to 70.2 percent. Clearly, a very worrisome long-run slide in share of patients was in progress. Actions taken in the past had not slowed the trend, so different approaches were needed.

Since 1980, First Methodist has made several improvements that Mr. Henry hoped would stem the loss of patients to competitors. These improvements included

* This illustration is based on an unpublished report describing a market opportunity analysis and marketing strategy recommendations presented to administrators of First Methodist Hospital (name is disguised for proprietary reasons).

- Adding a new wing to the hospital
- Purchasing more sophisticated diagnostic equipment including a new computed tomographic scanner
- Upgrading the physician staff with better-trained people

Promotion of the hospital was previously confined to news items reported by local media and a brochure describing the hospital and its staff. The brochure is handed out to patients as well as periodically mailed to people in the market area. All promotional activities have been planned and implemented by one person, Ms. Clara Morgan.

Mr. Henry met with Ms. Morgan to discuss how promotion could be used to help the hospital stop the share-of-patients performance slide. Both agreed that people in the area needed to be much more informed of the hospital's excellent facilities and its highly qualified staff of doctors. They decided to meet with the doctors to discuss their promotion ideas.

As the meeting with the doctors progressed, Mr. Henry noticed that the doc-

tors seemed to be upset with the promotion ideas. Finally, one of the doctors spoke up, "We do not think it is right to promote doctors. Doctors are professionals, not products. You can't sell us like you sell toothpaste!" Neither Mr. Henry nor Ms. Morgan knew how to react to this comment, and they were not sure what to do next.

Percent of patients from market area using First Methodist Hospital versus all other hospitals

Year	First Methodist's patient share (%)	All other hospitals' patient share (%)
1970	85.6	14.4
1973	82.3	17.7
1976	78.5	22.5
1979	75.1	24.9
1982	70.2	29.8

QUESTIONS

1. In which of the three categories of marketing's environment do the doctors fall?

2. Do Mr. Henry and Ms. Morgan need the cooperation of the doctors to go ahead with their promotion ideas? Why or why not?

3. Should the doctors be concerned at all by the slide in share of patients received by First Methodist Hospital? Why or why not?

4. How would you try to sway the doctors to accept the promotion ideas? Explain your arguments in favor of promoting the doctors that you would present.

Case 3.2

Mountain Central National Bank

THE PRESIDENT of Mountain Central National Bank, Ms. Arlene Cannon, sat in her office one day and thought about changes going on around her. She wanted to assess how these changes were affecting the bank's performance. Some of her thoughts follow.

After a long history of protection of and support for banks, the U.S. government is changing its approach by backing off on both regulation of banking practices and its willingness to use federal resources to

bolster a weak bank. This change has opened the door for nonbank organizations to offer traditional banking services. For instance, securities firms are offering essentially savings account services, called cash accounts, which have interest rates that generally are higher than those of banks. At the same time, new opportunities are opening up for banks. The more aggressive banks are offering a wider variety of services including insurance, stock brokerage, and security underwriting for a

broader range of securities.

Capabilities for handling and moving information are expanding. Financial transactions (deposits, withdrawals, transfer of funds, payment of bills) are becoming highly computerized. Furthermore, automated teller machines are becoming more widely accepted, allowing a bank to offer services to customers twenty-four hours a day.

Finally, Ms. Cannon remembered a magazine article that she had read that discussed trends evident from the latest U.S. population census study. One trend that stuck in her mind is that more and more households have two or more adults working outside the home. Another is that the percentages of households earning less than $15,000 and more than $35,000 are increasing, whereas the percentage of households earning $15,000 to $35,000 is shrinking.

Ms. Cannon was afraid that she had not yet discovered all important trends of which she should be aware. She was also perplexed about all the implications for her bank's marketing strategy.

QUESTIONS

1. Which of the categories of marketing's environment are foremost in the president's mind?

2. From your reading and experience, do you know of any other environmental trends that will affect the bank's performance in markets? If so, what are they?

3. What aspects of the bank's marketing strategy will be most affected by these environmental forces? (Hint: You may want to look back to Chapter 2 to review the kinds of marketing decisions that determine marketing strategy.)

A Special Look
Public Policy and Marketing

DR. MARY JANE SHEFFET

The marketing of a product or service is subject to many different types of restrictions and regulations. Many of these are imposed by government regulatory agencies such as the Federal Trade Commission (FTC) and the Consumer Product Safety Commission, whereas others are laws passed by Congress and enforced by the Antitrust Division of the Justice Department, the FTC, the Food and Drug Administration, and the Federal Reserve. Still other restrictions and regulations are the result of judicial decisions that interpret and apply existing laws. The legal environment affects all aspects of marketing a product including new product development and design, place (distribution), pricing, and promotion. It is imperative that marketers stay informed about these issues and incorporate this information in all phases of product development and marketing. Although the public policy environment of the 1980s has been marked by a shift toward less government intervention and deregulation, such a shift does *not* imply an unregulated marketplace. Examination of each of the four functional areas of marketing will show which regulations apply to it and how potentially costly lawsuits can be avoided.

PUBLIC POLICY AND MARKETING'S FOUR Ps

Product

Title I of The 1975 Federal Trade Improvements Act, better known as the Magnuson-Moss Warranty Act, requires that manufacturers *clearly* state the terms of their warranties and that these warranties be displayed and readily available to consumers in stores for all products that cost more than $25. Although the law does not require a manufacturer to provide either a full or limited warranty, Congress hoped that by requiring the display of warranty information in the stores manufacturers would feel pressured to offer warranties and provide consumers with additional information to help them make better purchase decisions. Warranty protection is also guaranteed by the state-enacted Uniform Commercial Code, which defines two types of warranties, express and implied. Manufacturers create express warranties when they claim a product will perform certain functions. Claims are made not only in advertisements and by the materials in the box (e.g., instructions), but also by what is printed or shown on the box or container in which the product comes. An express warranty can also be created by a retailer when the product is displayed in the store or when a salesperson makes promises about a product when selling it. Express and implied warranties are not created when a product is sold "as is." When

About the Author: Dr. Mary Jane Sheffet is an assistant professor of marketing at Indiana University at Bloomington. She received her B.A. degree from Occidental College in 1968 and her M.B.A. and Ph.D. degrees from UCLA. Dr. Sheffet has written a number of articles for journals including *Journal of Marketing, Journal of Public Policy and Marketing,* and *Journal of Advertising.*

that phrase is used the buyer must inspect the product carefully because no guarantee of quality is being given by the seller.

Recent courts have been interpreting product liability law in ways that extend more protection to consumers. The concept of strict liability means that consumers no longer have to prove that a manufacturer was careless or negligent when designing or manufacturing a product but only that an accident-causing defect was present in the product when it left the control of the manufacturer. Delayed manifestation cases in which injuries such as cancer may not develop until years after exposure to a product have become numerous. Many of these products (e.g., asbestos) may not have been known to be dangerous when first used. Manufacturers and retailers thus must be very careful not only to design and manufacture safe products but also to communicate the benefits and warn of the possible dangers of their products so they can avoid misunderstandings, misuse, and costly accidents.

Distribution

As is discussed elsewhere in this text a product can be distributed in many ways. A manufacturer may choose to sell directly to the final user or may use a variety of middlemen. When a manufacturer sells to independent dealers whether they be wholesalers, jobbers, or retailers the potential exists for antitrust problems because the manufacturer and its dealers do not always agree about how a product should be handled. When such disagreements result in the termination of a dealer the potential for antitrust problems is high: Terminated dealers are highly motivated to sue. The Supreme Court's decision in the GTE Sylvania case in 1977 specified that *nonprice* vertical restraints, or distribution systems imposed on dealers by a manufacturer such as exclusive territories, were to be examined under the rule of reason. Further, this opinion stated that an economic analysis was to be done that looked at both interbrand competition (dealers selling different brands) and intrabrand competition (dealers selling the same brand). If interbrand competition was vigorous and there were several strong brands in the market then a manufacturer could legally restrict the territory in which a dealer could sell or the location from which that dealer could sell. Thus, Sylvania could legally prevent its San Francisco dealer, Continental T.V., from opening another store in Sacramento.

Price

There are two areas of pricing in which antitrust law applies: price fixing and price discrimination. Horizontal price fixing, or when sellers of different brands of the same product get together to agree on what price to charge, has always been a per se violation of the antitrust laws. Vertical price fixing, also known as resale price maintenance, which involves one manufacturer setting the retail price of its product, has not had such consistent treatment. An early Supreme Court decision, Dr. Miles Medical (1911), declared such vertical price fixing to be illegal. During the early 1930s state "fair trade" laws were passed and federal legislation, the Miller-Tydings Act of 1937 and McGuire Act of 1952, was enacted exempting these vertical price-fixing agreements from the federal antitrust laws. Thus a manufacturer who wanted to ensure a high level of pre- and postsale service from its dealers could use resale price maintenance to protect these dealers from free-riding discounters who sold the product but did not provide any service. The Consumer Goods Pricing Act passed in 1975 ended fair trade and was followed by vigorous pursuit by both the Antitrust Division of the Justice Department and the Federal Trade Commission of manufacturers suspected of using resale price maintenance. This pursuit of vertical price fixers was abruptly ended, however, when the Reagan administration took office. Representatives of the Reagan administration argued that the GTE Sylvania rule applied to nonprice restrictions should also be applied to resale price maintenance and as long as there was vigorous interbrand competition such intrabrand pricing restrictions should be legal. This position was presented to the Supreme Court in the recent Monsanto (1984) case but the Court rejected this reasoning and ruled that any price-fixing agreement, whether horizontal or vertical, is per se illegal. Thus, a manufacturer can "suggest" a retail price for its product but cannot terminate a dealer solely for failing to charge it. If a terminated dealer is a discounter the manufacturer must be able to prove that the dealer was terminated not solely because of its price-cutting activities but because that dealer failed to live up to some other provisions of its dealer's agreement (e.g., did not maintain a well-trained salesforce or perform adequate warranty service).

The Robinson-Patman Act (1936) prohibits price discrimination when the effect is to lessen competition or to tend to create a monopoly unless the price differences can be cost justified, the products are not of the same grade or quality, or the lesser price is charged to meet but not beat a legal price charged by a competitor. This law is still in effect, and over the years there have been numerous cases involving illegal price discrimination within the channels of distribution. The provisions of this law, however, are extremely complex, and it is often very difficult for a manufacturer to be certain that all of the prices charged the various channel members are completely legal. Whereas the number of government-instituted cases under this law has been lessening, private lawsuits, that is, one company suing another, continue to be filed.

Advertising and promotion

The 1970s saw numerous deceptive advertising cases brought by the FTC. It was during this decade that "corrective advertising" orders were first written that required a firm to spend part of its advertising budget to correct a misperception, deceptive statement, or misleading impression made by an advertisement. Some of the products involved in corrective advertising orders were Profile Bread, Hi-C fruit drink, Hawaiian Punch, Ocean Spray cranberry juice, and Listerine mouthwash.

In 1971 the Advertising Substantiation program, which required advertisers to provide data backing up performance claims made in their advertisements, was established. Thus, when Firestone claimed that its Super Sport Wide Oval Tire stopped 25 percent quicker the Commission demanded that Firestone prove it. Advertising substantiation was requested from all companies in several industries, including the air conditioner, tire, and shampoo industries, when the program was first established. Current FTC Chairman James C. Miller III, reflecting the current movement toward less government interference in business, has stated that advertisers must now have such data available if an advertised claim is challenged but the

After Kellogg began using its *All-Bran*® cereal advertising campaign to communicate the National Cancer Institute's message that a high-fiber, low-fat diet may reduce the risks of some kinds of cancer, two federal agencies had different views about the campaign. The Food & Drug Administration questioned whether the Kellogg campaign was permissible or whether its use of health claims transformed *All-Bran*® cereal into a drug that must face federal approval. The Federal Trade Commission, on the other hand, publicly praised the campaign as an example of how food advertising can help convey useful dietary information to consumers. (© 1983 Kellog Company. All rights reserved. Kellog's® and All-Bran® are registered trademarks of Kellog Company.)

EVEN A 250 POUND LINEBACKER WOULDN'T RIDE THIS WITHOUT A HELMET.

He's tough. He's trained. He's a professional athlete. And he knows the value of safety gear. He wouldn't step on a football field or jump on a skateboard without a helmet. For starters.

A lot of kids just aren't that smart. Especially when it comes to skateboards. So if you're going to buy your child a skateboard this year, don't stop shopping after you've bought the board.

Buy a helmet. Elbow pads. Knee pads. And gloves. Because at speeds of up to 50 miles per hour, safety gear is the only thing between your child and the pavement.

Send for free safety information on skateboards. Write: Wheels, Washington, D.C. 20207. Or call: 800-638-2666 (Hotline for the Hearing-Impaired: 800-638-2690).

CPSC

The U.S. Consumer Product Safety Commission, Washington, D.C. 20207.

Created by the Consumer Product Safety Act of 1972, the Consumer Product Safety Commission, advertising in magazines like *Family Circle*, here reminds parents of the pitfalls of play. The CPSC estimates that as many as 20 million Americans are injured each year by consumer products. (Courtesy of U.S. Consumer Product Safety Commission)

data need not be submitted to the FTC before the advertisement can be shown. Chairman Miller believes that the marketplace will police and prevent deceptive advertising through private lawsuits and self-regulation.

Self-regulation is most evident in the advertising industry's efforts, which include the National Advertising Review Board (NARB) and the National Advertising Division (NAD) of the Council of Better Business Bureaus. Complaints about advertisements are solicited from consumers and competitors, and if an advertiser fails to satisfy NAD with its substantiation of a challenged claim, the complaint goes to a NARB panel. If the advertiser refuses to make the NARB's suggested changes the matter is referred to the FTC. Most cases are resolved by the NAD, however, and do not reach the NARB or the FTC. Advertising Review Board, which screens any advertisement challenged by a competitor as being deceptive, and the Better Business Bureau, which also has a reviewing board to rule on challenged advertisements, help eliminate deceptive advertising.

FUTURE TRENDS

Whereas the focus of the 1980s and the Reagan administration is on deregulation, it is obvious that this does not mean "no regulation." Although the FTC and other regulatory agencies may be less intrusive and promote a more "free market" climate, American businesses must still operate within the legal boundaries set by the antitrust laws and the regulatory and judicial bodies responsible for enforcing those laws.

4 Analyzing Market Opportunities

When you finish this chapter, you will understand

☐ The role that market opportunity analysis plays in marketing decision making

☐ The major factors that determine market opportunity

☐ How marketing managers go about finding and evaluating markets for products and services

☐ How to evaluate a company's competition for market opportunity

☐ How managers can estimate the amount of sales that can be obtained from markets

When they define a market, managers specify the geographic area as well as the kinds of people or organizations that are likely to use their product.

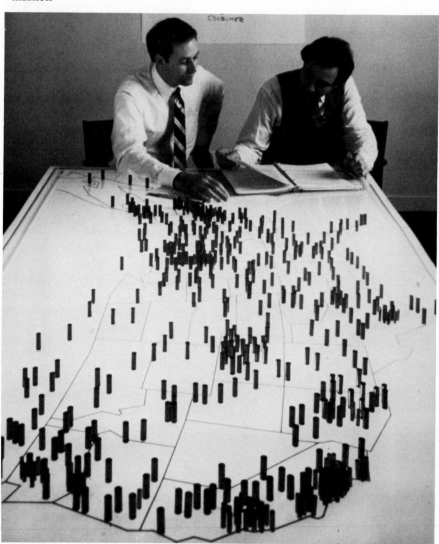

Eastman Kodak Company, the sleeping giant of the photography business, awakened to a changing marketing environment in the 1980s. For most of the company's history, Kodak had maintained a dominant position in its markets. But that dominance now is being threatened.

Competition finally is making serious inroads into Kodak's position. Most worrisome are the strong marketing strategies of Japanese companies including Fuji Photo Film Company, Konishiroku Photo Industry Company, Sony, and Sharpe. The American company, 3M, also is making waves. Competitors seem to be attacking Kodak on two fronts. They are undercutting Ko-

dak's prices on traditional products while providing quality. At the same time, competitors are bringing out innovative new products to chip away at some of Kodak's market share.

Kodak has also seen the growth in amateur photography, the lifeblood of its business, drop from 13 percent to approximately 6 percent during the past two decades. While this market remains important, Kodak must look to new markets to maintain profitability.

Kodak is responding with new strategies that include (1) expansion into new markets with nonphotographic products, (2) new emphasis on technological development, and (3) more aggressive marketing of film and photographic pa-

per products to worldwide markets with special emphasis on Japan, West Germany, Southeast Asia, the Middle East, and Brazil.

At the heart of Kodak's planning for new marketing strategies is a keen understanding of market opportunities. Management is expanding its effort to learn more about what is going on in markets. It created the new position, director of market intelligence. Worldwide market research is being coordinated through this position. What's more, a team of strategic planners has been formed to seek new growth opportunities in areas other than consumer photography.[1]

SUCCESSFUL MARKETING STRATEGIES rarely are developed through guesswork. Increasingly, professional marketing managers are assessing carefully the environmental situation before planning a marketing strategy. Kodak's response to slowed growth and increased competition in photography markets aptly shows that planning begins by building a sound understanding of **market opportunity,** the opportunity to convert potential sales in a defined market for a product or service into actual sales. The primary way of learning about this opportunity is through a **market opportunity analysis** (MOA), which is the gathering and analyzing of information about products, buyers, and competition to determine what marketing strategy is needed to convert potential sales into actual sales and the amount of these sales to expect.

In this chapter, we expand on the nature and purpose of an MOA. Because its objective is to learn about the opportunity to achieve sales from markets, we begin by explaining what a market is. Then we introduce a step-by-step procedure for conducting an MOA. Finally, we examine these steps in depth so you can see how marketing managers use information for making marketing decisions.

WHAT IS A MARKET?

Unfortunately, the term *market* is used loosely by many people. You probably have heard the terms *European Common Market, world market, youth market, high-income market, supermarket, stock market,* and *the marketplace.* Obviously, all these uses of *market* do not have the same meaning. In our discussion of MOA, **market** means a group of people (or organizations) with the ability and willingness to buy a product or service for consumption. This definition highlights five key ideas that characterize a market: (1) a group of people (or organizations), (2) ability to buy, (3) willingness to buy, (4) product or service, and (5) consumption. Let us examine each of these ideas.

People

Markets are made up of people who make purchase decisions. After all, a marketing mix must convey that the product meets the needs and wants of persons who decide whether and what to buy. We use the term *customer* to refer to these purchase decision makers.

Sometimes customers and users of a product are not the same persons. When this happens, marketing managers define markets as comprising customers rather than users because customers are the primary target for marketing programs. As you know, Gerber Products makes baby food. Clearly, babies are the primary users of Gerber's baby food. But babies play little if any role in purchase decisions for baby food, particularly concerning which brand to buy. Gerber must convince parents of the benefits of buying its products. Thus, parents of babies make up Gerber's market.

Ability to buy

For people to be customers, they must have ability to buy. Ability to buy usually means having financial resources to make a purchase. Those people who cannot afford to buy a company's product are not customers. Income determines what people can afford, as do savings, borrowing power, and assets convertible into money (e.g., a trade-in). Information on these characteristics can be used to screen people in populations from markets.

Occasionally, other factors can limit which people are able to buy a product. Underage people legally cannot buy alcoholic beverages, for instance, and physical handicaps can prevent people from buying and using some products and services. In general, anything that prevents a person from buying keeps that person from being a customer in a market.

Willingness to buy

Not all people who can buy a product want to. To be a customer a person also must be willing to buy, which means that he or she has the desire to buy the product. The most important factor that creates the desire to buy is having a need or want that the product can satisfy. However, many related factors such as life-style, likes and dislikes, values, and social pressure also give rise to needs and wants. As a result, finding customers can be quite a challenge.

Interestingly, willingness to buy does not depend on ability to buy. Most everyone wants some products or services that they cannot afford. Furthermore, all of us can afford some products that we do not want to buy. Therefore, a person must have both ability and willingness to buy to qualify as a customer.

Products or services

A product (or service) has certain benefits. In fact, customers look at a product as a combination of benefits. Think of a condominium. It offers apartment-style living, no responsibility for upkeep of grounds, and ownership of the unit. This combination of benefits makes condominiums different from other types of housing such as apartments and houses. Benefits of condominium living are desired by some but not by others. The corresponding market is partly determined by what these benefits are.

Babies are their business, but no longer their only business. Still, Gerber is a well-known and trusted name in baby food and nonfood products. Ninety-seven percent of supermarkets carry Gerber foods; in fact, in most stores Gerber is either the exclusive baby food brand or shares shelf space with only one competitor. Even low-cost generic competition disappeared in the late 1970s because parents did not trust the unknown products. (Courtesy of Gerber Products Company)

We prepare peas for Leslie.

At Gerber, we think Leslie is a very special person. So we prepare peas in a very special way. Although the common garden pea is uncommonly rich in vitamin A, important B vitamins and C, some of these riches last for only a few hours after the pea is picked. In that short time, we begin to capture the nutrients so essential to Leslie's good health. Peas are just one example of the Gerber commitment to produce wholesome baby food. And there are probably easier, less costly ways to prepare them. But we didn't skimp on the other 30 million babies we've helped feed since we began. And we aren't about to start with Leslie.

Gerber
Babies are our business...and have been for over 50 years.

We know a lot about food because we care a lot about babies.

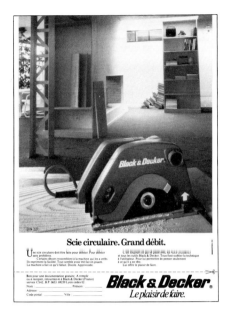

Scie circulaire. Grand débit.

Black & Decker
Le plaisir de faire.

Until recently, Black & Decker's Italian subsidiary made tools for Italians, and its British subsidiary made tools for Britons. When Lawrence Farley became president in 1982—he won the job by selling the globalization concept to the Black & Decker board—the company was experiencing fierce competition from Japanese power-tool makers like Makita, which had already embraced a global strategy. (Courtesy of the Black & Decker Manufacturing Company)

A product's price also helps determine which people are customers. Only people with sufficient financial resources can afford a particular price. A condominium's price is affordable for some persons but too high for others. If price is lowered, more people can afford to buy. Raise price and some people will be driven from the market.

The influence of product price and benefits on ability and willingness to buy means that a market exists only with respect to a particular product or service. One way to see the significance of this idea is to consider a group of people with a need or a want that no existing product satisfies. Many people probably wanted to view television programs at their own convenience long before the home videocassette recorder was invented. Was this group a market at that time? You may be surprised to learn that it was not. Because no product existed (i.e., no videocassette recorder), there was no way to determine if people with the desire also had the ability to buy. Furthermore, if there is no product there are no benefits for people to desire. As you can see, markets exist only for specified products, and different products have different markets.

Consumption

Markets comprise people who are buying for consumption. *Consumption* means that the product is used to satisfy the need or want the product was designed to meet. Consider a camera. It is bought for consumption if the customer's intent is to use it to take pictures, the primary purpose for which a camera is designed. But retailers that buy cameras for resale are not buying for consumption and therefore are not in the camera market.

Consumers are not the only ones who buy products for consumption. Organizations, as Chapter 6 will make clear, also buy for consumption. A newspaper publisher buys cameras for its reporters and photographers to use in performing their jobs. The publisher has a need or want (i.e., taking pictures for publication with news stories) that cameras can satisfy. Organizations that buy a product with the intent to use it as part of their ongoing operations make up an industrial market for that product.

Other characteristics of markets

Two additional characteristics are important for understanding markets. First, a market is confined to a specific geographic area. Change the area and the market also changes. (See Marketalk, which discusses global, or world, markets.) The market for cameras in Peoria, Illinois, is different from the market in San Diego simply because San Diego is located in a different and much larger area. Differences in buying ability and life-styles that create needs abound. On a larger scale, U.S. markets for cameras are not the same as Mexican markets for the same product. At the outset, a marketing manager must define the geographic area within which an MOA searches for markets. These areas can be a country, a region in a country, a state, a city, or any other area of importance to the manager.

Another important characteristic of markets concerns the dimension of time. An MOA must search for opportunity within a defined time period. Management may decide that the period should be long (e.g., several years in the future or more) or short (e.g., several months ahead to a year or two) or somewhere in between, depending on the decisions being made. A

*Marke*TALK ///

More companies offer world brands to world markets

ON THE INTERNATIONAL scene, a fascinating debate is taking place among managers in advertising agencies and business firms with sales around the world. Until recently, most experts agreed that markets for products are notably different from country to country. The conventional wisdom was that marketing mixes—brand names, package designs, product size, distribution channels, advertising, even prices and services—must be tailored to meet the unique needs in each country's markets. Procter & Gamble cannot, so the argument goes, sell Ivory soap in France as they do in the United States because the average French citizen has personal care habits very different from the average American.

SOURCE: Dennis Chase, "World brand trend grows," *Advertising Age,* Mar. 19, 1984, pp. 3, 74; and Bill Saporito, "Black & Decker's gamble on 'globalization,'" *Fortune,* May 14, 1984, pp. 40–42, 44, 48.

Some international companies are taking a new, innovative approach. They are creating world brands for world markets. A *global,* or *world, brand* is a company's product that uses essentially the same marketing strategy in all markets entered around the world. Makita Electric Works, the Japanese power tool manufacturer, uses this strategy by selling the same power drill to Germans as it sells in Japan and other countries. Furthermore, in all countries where it is sold, the power drill uses similar advertising and is priced low relative to its competition.

Success of a world brand depends on finding world markets. Ignoring country boundaries, marketing's challenge is to show that people everywhere have similar demographic characteristics, life-styles, and most important, desire for product benefits to be attracted to world brands. Makita is counting on people around the world wanting a good, dependable power

drill for a low price. More generally, many argue that technology and mass communications are reducing the distinctions between countries and creating similar consumption behavior.

The advantages of a world brand and world market strategy are that companies can achieve cost economies from having standardized products and marketing programs. Cost is lowest when a company sells the same product to everyone, uses the same advertising, and offers the same services. In turn, lower costs allow a company to charge a lower price, which adds to sales volume. Many well-known companies including Coca Cola, Black & Decker, British Airways, and Toyota are already using the world brand and world market strategy. Their successes should attract others.

///

decision on whether to introduce a major new product may require looking ahead five or more years, whereas a decision to change pricing strategy—a decision more easily reversed if it is not working—may need to evaluate market opportunity for only the next year or two.

Markets can and do change over time. Change in a market can show up as growth, decline, a shifting makeup of customers, or all three. A market situation that has experienced all these changes recently is industrial markets for robots in Japan. Between 1979 and 1981, Yaskowa Electric Manufacturing Company experienced a rapid increase in demand for robots. Its sales jumped more than 450 percent in this short time. Then demand leveled off for the next few years as customers, primarily automobile and related manufacturing firms, cut back on purchases. In response, robot manufacturers such as Yaskowa broadened their markets by seeking robot sales from companies in industries other than those tied to automobiles and by looking for markets in other countries.[2] An MOA helps managers identify and evaluate the implications of these time-oriented changes for marketing strategy.

MARKET OPPORTUNITY ANALYSIS

How should a market be analyzed for opportunity? Exhibit 4.1 shows the major steps in an MOA. We briefly review these steps to help you grasp the procedure as a whole. Then in the remainder of the chapter, the steps are discussed in greater detail to help you see what marketing managers can

Between 1974 and 1983, American Express defined prestige as success and attainment, targeting primarily males in their "Do You Know Me?" advertisement campaign. Today many people seem to be defining prestige as "leading an interesting, varied, and unexpectedly rich life." The "Interesting Lives" campaign has been so successful that the number of women who have applied for the card has more than doubled. (Courtesy of American Express Travel Related Services Company, Inc.)

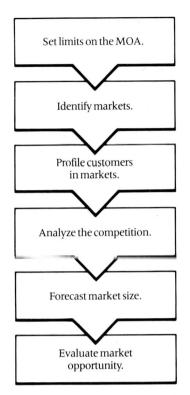

Exhibit 4.1 Steps in a market opportunity analysis

learn about market opportunity and how the information can be used to develop a marketing strategy.

- *Setting limits.* Market opportunity analyses must be tailored to meet the information needs of managers. Illustrations of typical decisions requiring an MOA and the corresponding limits on scope are shown in Exhibit 4.2. Notice that the decision faced by a manager places restrictions on the MOA. In every case the decision specifies a company brand for which there are markets of interest to the manager. Furthermore, the nature of the decision helps set a reasonable time period and geographic area within which the MOA must search for opportunity.

- *Identifying markets.* As we have seen, not everyone living in a geographic area is a customer, no matter what the product or service is. One purpose of an MOA is to identify the types of people (or organizations) who are customers in markets. American Express is one company that has used analyses to identify customers in its credit card markets. The company is most interested in persons who have the financial ability to use the card, are in occupations in which business use of the card is quite likely (e.g., traveling, entertaining customers), and who lead travel-related life-styles. Furthermore, American Express is making a special effort to attract women to its card as a way of increasing sales.[3]

- *Profiling customers.* Marketing managers use an MOA to build a description of what customers are like as people in order to know how to cater to them with a marketing mix. Using customer descriptions to visualize customers as people helps managers anticipate what benefits they seek when making a purchase.

Exhibit 4.2 Marketing decisions define the scope of MOAs

Marketing Decisions Requiring an MOA	Product Focus	Time Period	Geographic Area
A Schwinn salesperson is asked to present a selling plan for bicycles in his sales territory.	Bicycles	6 months	Sales territory
A district sales manager for IBM is reassigning salespersons to territories within her district.	Computers	1 year	A 4-state district
Speech Systems developed a voice-operated typewriter that can transcribe dictation into typewritten copy with 95% accuracy; management must decide when and how to introduce the product into markets.	Typewriters	5 years	The nation

■ *Analyzing competition.* Rarely does a company have an entire market to itself. Other companies are vying for customers by also trying to meet their needs. Thus market opportunity for a company depends on how well it performs against the competition. To attract cardholders, American Express is competing with Carte Blanche, Visa, MasterCard, and other more specialized credit services. An MOA can help marketing managers keep track of what competitors are doing in markets, and assess competitors' strengths and weaknesses.

■ *Forecasting market size.* Every marketing manager wants to know, "How much sales can I get from this market?" Therefore, an MOA must predict expected sales. When evaluating female markets, American Express needed to know the volume of sales that could be achieved by attracting women who met the income, occupation, and life-style criteria as a separate market for its credit card. Management estimated that its 2½ million women who had cards were only about 20 percent of U.S. women who met these criteria, indicating substantial room for growth.[4]

■ *Evaluating market opportunity.* Payoff from an MOA comes when all the information has been collected and marketing managers use it to evaluate market opportunity. The bits and pieces of information must be fitted together into an overall picture of the nature of the opportunity. Consider once more American Express's decision to attract the female market. This decision was based on what these women wanted, how well and with what benefits the competition was attracting them, and whether the market was large enough to generate enough sales to justify costs of targeting them.

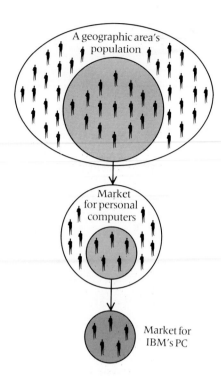

Exhibit 4.3 **IBM's PC brand market comes from the market for all personal computers that is located in the geographic area's population**

This brief overview is intended to help you see the coverage and application of an MOA as a total activity. As we discuss each step in more detail, keep in mind that an MOA is not finished until all the steps are put together. Before reading further, you may want to look once more at Exhibit 4.1.

SETTING LIMITS AND IDENTIFYING MARKETS

Until management chooses a product with specific attributes and benefits as the focus for an MOA, no one can identify who the customers are.[5] As you now know, these attributes and benefits help determine who has ability and willingness to buy. Furthermore, if markets cannot be identified, competition cannot be pinpointed and forecasts of sales cannot be made. The product selected already may be selling in markets or it may be nothing more than a concept for a proposed new product. In fact, providing market opportunity information for new product decisions is one of the most important applications of an MOA, though certainly not the only one.

Markets for products, markets for brands

Understanding the term *product* is so important to the task of identifying markets that we start by expanding on earlier ideas of what it means. Every organization offers a product (or service) for sale. Consider the microcomputer, or personal computer. Apple Computer has its line of personal computer products including the Macintosh, Lisa, Apple IIe, and Apple IIc. IBM also has a product line with easily recognized names including the PC (short for personal computer), PC AT, PC/XT, and PCjr. For convenience, this notion of product is called a brand. More formally, a **brand** is a combination of attributes and benefits that is offered for sale by a particular organization. A brand can be a product or a service as long as it is being sold by an organization.

Another way to think of the concept of a product is as a particular form characteristic of brands of competing companies. Several companies, competing for sales in the same markets, usually have brands that have similar attributes and benefits. A personal computer is a product form because it has certain defining characteristics—it costs less than $10,000, has limited memory and storage capabilities, is small enough to place on a desk, and can be programmed for various applications. These characteristics are common to all brands of personal computers: They differentiate personal computers from other, different products (e.g., minicomputers, mainframe computers, and calculators). We use the term *product type* to refer to this meaning of product. More specifically, a **product type** is a combination of attributes and benefits that similar competing brands have in common.

Finding markets

The distinction between product type and brand is quite important for marketing managers who are looking for markets. Take a minute to think about the source of markets. We already know that markets ultimately come from an area's population. Yet, which people in the population are customers? To answer this question, we can apply a very important principle: The market for a company's brand comes from the larger market for the corresponding product type. Look at Exhibit 4.3. Customers for IBM's PC are individuals and organizations who are attracted to IBM's marketing mix as opposed to those of other brands. But only someone who wants to buy a personal computer (the product type) will be making a purchase choice of one brand instead of another. This fact means that the market for IBM's PC comes from people who are customers for a personal computer (i.e., the product type market).

Marketing managers can apply this principle to the task of locating markets for their company's brand. This task should be done in steps, as shown in Exhibit 4.4. Because populations contain markets, the first step is to learn about the population in the geographic area. The next step is to find markets for the product type, remembering that no product type has everyone in the population as customers. Finally, market targets for a company's brand are chosen from these product type markets.

Analyzing populations. In many countries, a wealth of information is available about citizen and business populations. Most of this information is collected by governments such as the Bureau of the Census in the United States and Statistics Canada in Canada. A **population analysis** is a procedure for using this information to look for indications of market opportunity.

Exhibit 4.4 Steps for identifying markets with opportunity

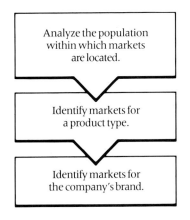

Analyze the population within which markets are located.

Identify markets for a product type.

Identify markets for the company's brand.

This analysis begins by describing the size and growth of the population. Growth in populations is one source of growth in markets. Next, the types of people who make up the population are examined. Population demographic characteristics such as income of households, occupations, and employment provide insight into people's ability to buy a product. Other demographic characteristics including marital status, household size, and education give clues to life-styles that indicate desire for the product. Finally, a population analysis may uncover macroenvironment forces in an area that can affect markets. Most important, the economic climate, as indicated by the level of interest rates, inflation, and types of businesses providing jobs, can say a lot about ability to buy a product.

Identifying product type markets. Taking the next step, identifying product type markets, usually requires market research information. **Marketing research** refers to gathering information through studies that ask people questions or observe what they do. (Market research is discussed in detail in Chapter 7.) These studies are needed to find out who customers of the product type are and what they like. Through experience, companies have worked out several different kinds of studies for identifying product type markets.[6]

- *Describe current customers of a product type.* Often a product type has been sold by companies for a while. A study can be conducted to find out which people have bought the product in the past. This approach works if the same kinds of people as those who have bought in the past will buy in the future.

- *Describe customers of competing product types.* Sometimes a company can take advantage of there being other competing product types that satisfy the same or similar needs and wants. A study can be used to find out who these people are. Public transportation services satisfy people's need to get from one place to another in a city. A competing product that people use for this need is the automobile. Therefore, if a company is looking for new markets for a bus service, a study of automobile users may help locate them.

- *Describe customers of a complementary product type.* A complementary product type is used jointly by customers with the product type of interest. Automobiles and gasoline, toothpaste and toothbrushes, and tennis rackets and tennis balls are illustrations of pairs of complementary products. If a complementary product has been sold for a while, a study can be conducted to find out who has bought it. These same customers also may be customers for the product type of interest.

- *Describe kinds of people who are in selected use situations in which a product type can be used.* This approach uses a study to find out which people are most likely to be in situations creating needs or wants that a product type is designed to satisfy. A bus service is designed to move people between specific locations in a city at particular times as designated by its route and schedule. A study that finds out when and where in the city people travel on a regular basis might reveal markets. Discovering who goes to work between 7:00 and 9:00 A.M. and returns between 4:00 and 7:00 P.M. and the locations to which they travel helps locate people in the commuter situation, one for which bus service benefits are best designed to match.

■ *Describe kinds of people who prefer a product type.* Markets can be identified by studying people's preferences (i.e., what they like and do not like) for a product type. Every product type has certain attributes and benefits that some people prefer and others do not. Markets are found by searching for people with preferences for what the product type has to offer. To locate markets for bus services a study can search for people who prefer key benefits such as low cost, regular schedules, on-time stops, and specified pickup points.

Identifying markets for a brand. The last step in the market identification task is to identify possible markets for a company's brand. This step comes early in the MOA, and so managers are not yet ready to select target markets. All that can be done is to see what the target market options are.

Managers begin with the principle that target markets for a brand are most likely to come from a market for a product type. The entire market may become the target market. Or a company may want to consider drawing target markets from only a portion of the product type market. American Express took this latter approach by aiming its credit card at the specific group in the credit card market that includes persons with high-income occupations and life-styles. Similarly, Budget Rent-a-Car goes after rental car customers (i.e., a service type market) who seek an economy-price benefit. For this approach to work, additional studies are needed to find out how a product type market can best be broken down into market groups, called segments, in which each group has customers who are looking for similar benefits.

Finally, a brand may be sold to customers who are in a market for another product type. Different product types can compete for satisfying the same need, and so customers may be persuaded to switch from one product type to another. A case in point is Compugraphic Corporation, a maker of typesetting machines for printing documents. Its management decided to target toward markets for office typewriters. Typewriters and typesetting machines, very different product types, have traditionally attracted different markets. Compugraphic's management believes, however, that benefits of typesetting can appeal to business customers of typewriters.[7]

PROFILING CUSTOMERS IN MARKETS

Identifying markets is the most important step in the entire MOA. All other analyses that follow are intended to further describe and evaluate opportunity in these markets. Finding out more about customers is one of these analyses.

Customers have requirements

Customers rarely purchase for no reason: They seek benefits from a product or service. Not all benefits are inherent in the product or service itself. Consider credit card customers again. Some might want the prestige associated with the card (advertising-related benefit), a low annual charge for using the card (price benefit), and easy procedures to follow to qualify for the card (credit application benefit). The product and related benefits that customers expect to receive when they purchase and use a product or service are called **market requirements.**

Sometimes an MOA can discover market requirements simply by asking customers what benefits they want. There are, however, situations in which people may not want to or cannot answer questions about market requirements. An experienced marketing manager is alert to these more hidden requirements. A very interesting illustration came up in an MOA for condominiums. Some condominium customers do not understand the advantages of condominium living, but will not admit this fact to people conducting a market research study. Yet people will not buy an expensive product like a condominium if they do not understand its benefits and costs. Other means are needed to draw out requirements in a more indirect way. Bringing customers together in groups and getting them to discuss a product and its use is a frequently used approach. Individuals often are more open about discussing benefits that they want when they see others feel the same way.

Customers respond to influences

When deciding to buy a product, customers are typically influenced by a number of different factors. Some factors, such as needs and wants, past experience with products, and likes and dislikes, come from the personal characteristics of customers. Others come from the environment around them including the situation in which the product is to be used, a government regulation specifying how a product must be used, or an advancement in technology. Regardless of the factors, if they influence customers' buying decisions, managers should know about them. An MOA must examine both task environments and macroenvironments to look for these influences. (See Chapter 3 for a discussion of these environments.)

Customers need to be profiled

All information collected by an MOA that describes customers in markets consitutes a **customer profile.** A profile helps marketing managers understand who customers are and what they are like as people. In fact, a good profile should enable a manager to mentally visualize a picture of the real, "flesh and blood" people in markets. With practice, marketing managers become extremely adept at using profiles to look for market requirements, to find influences on customers, and to anticipate how customers will respond to a marketing mix.

An interesting illustration of customer profile information is shown in Exhibit 4.5, which describes selected characteristics of customers of records and albums. Note that there are two profiles, one for hard rock buyers and one for soft rock buyers. Separate profiles are needed to show how these market segments are different. Another notable aspect of profiles is the variety of information in them. No one or even a few facets of customers are adequate. Managers must know quite a lot to get a good understanding of market requirements and purchase influences. The many facets that might be covered are further discussed in Chapters 5 and 6, which examine consumer and industrial buying behavior. After you have studied those chapters, you will have an even more complete understanding of what a customer profile may contain.

For practice, use the profile in Exhibit 4.5 to try to figure out some of the market requirements of hard and soft rock buyers. Hard rock customers do not want to hear music that blends rock and country music, as some popular artists have tried to do. They are more easily introduced to the music of new singers and bands than are soft rock customers. On the other hand, soft rock customers do not want a heavy, harsh sound to their music. They also want to know more about songs and artists, and they want songs from their favorite artists.

The payoff from customer profile information comes when marketing managers plan a marketing mix. Understanding buyers guides managers when selecting between alternative target markets. Furthermore, customer profiles suggest important objectives to achieve and help create marketing mix programs to attract these buyers. To illustrate, information in Exhibit 4.5 was very helpful for managers who design record and album advertising. The two segments require different approaches. Advertisements aimed at the hard rock market should not contain much information but instead show models and scenes expressing aggression, adventurousness, risk, and

Exhibit 4.5 Customer profile information describing buyers of records and albums

Hard Rock Market	Soft Rock Market
Moderate to heavy listeners, with one third listening to music more than four hours a day.	Moderate to heavy listeners, with one quarter listening to music more than four hours a day.
Very knowledgeable about music.	Moderately knowledgeable about music.
Consider themselves to be aggressive, rugged, and adventurous; enjoy activities that involve risk; seek sensation.	Consider themselves to be cautious and conservative, practical, and introverted.
Describe themselves as friendly, funloving, energetic, and active.	Believe they are old fashioned, traditional, and like to belong.
Have very little brand loyalty to stations or products.	Have strong brand loyalty.
Prefer to plan activities.	Tend to buy the music of certain artists repeatedly.
Are not information seekers; do not read ads for information; do not evaluate technical specifications before buying.	Seek information and study technical specifications before buying.
Have very strong dislikes, such as for country music.	Dislike intensely the heavy, hard rock music.
Do not like to be part of a team or formal groups.	When at a store to buy one album, will often buy five or six other records or albums.
Do not see themselves as upscale, sophisticated, or prosperous.	Are between the ages of 18 and 34, low to middle income, and somewhat more likely to be female than male.
Do not see themselves as traditional, cultured, peaceful, or serene.	
Think of themselves as being "with it."	
Are between the ages of 13 and 24, low to middle income, about evenly divided between males and females.	

SOURCE: "Before using music, recording artists in ads, study music preferences of target audiences," *Marketing News*, May 15, 1981, Section 2, p. 8. Reprinted by permission of the American Marketing Association.

activity. In contrast, soft rock customers respond favorably to technical information in advertisements.

ANALYZING THE COMPETITION

Having profiled markets, an MOA then describes and evaluates competition. Before we discuss what an analysis of competition should include, let us see how competition influences market opportunity.

Competition's impact on market opportunity

Competition can expand market opportunity for all companies serving a market. Usually, customers must learn something about a product and its benefits before they will purchase it. The marketing mixes of competing companies, when considered together, help customers gain an understanding of the product and encourage more people to enter a market. A fascinating illustration comes from the market for personal computers. Exhibit 4.6 shows how growth can take place as competitive marketing mixes reach more and more customers. Between the mid-1970s and the mid-1980s, sales of personal computers grew from practically nothing to $12 billion.[8] People have had needs that a personal computer could satisfy for much longer than the last decade. But only when competitors developed easy-to-use machines and software, lowered prices, expanded distribution, and taught people how to use the power of the computer did customers flock to make purchases. The market grew in size largely because firms branched out into different kinds of customer segments. Sales from customers who buy for home use have grown to more than $2 billion.[9] The most explosive growth, however, has come from business applications.

Competition also has a negative impact on a company's market opportunity. This impact comes from the vying of competitors for a percent share of markets. Each competitor tries to persuade customers to buy its brand rather than the brands of other firms. In this way, the success of one competitor holds down the percent share of markets that another company can enjoy. Witness IBM's strong marketing program for its brand of personal computer, PCs, which has eaten into the percentage of total business and home use sales previously garnered by competitors. Just one and a half years after entering these markets in the early 1980s, IBM had captured 19 percent of these sales.[10]

Exhibit 4.6   Competition helps expand market opportunity

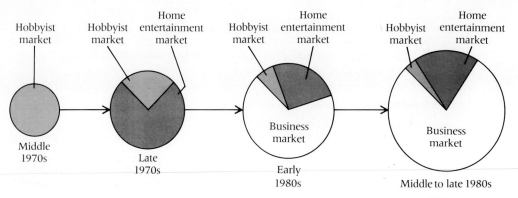

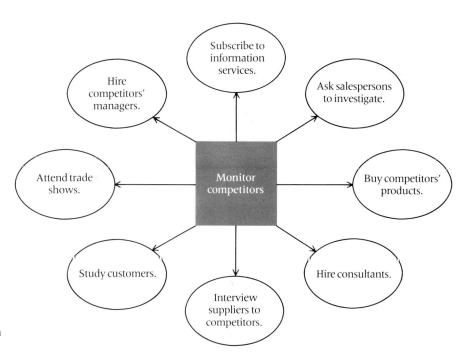

Exhibit 4.7 Monitoring competitors' marketing programs requires information from many sources

Evaluating the competition

A wealth of information can be gathered about competitors.[11] Exhibit 4.7 shows many of the ways that well-managed companies keep up with the activities of competitors. With experience, a marketing manager can sift through this information to look for indications of competition's effect on market opportunity. Although some clues come from the financial strength of competitors, the most significant help comes from learning about their marketing strategies.

Financial information. A competitor's ability to attract sales in markets is determined partly by its financial strength. It takes money as well as managerial talent to successfully plan and implement a marketing strategy. Marketing managers learn a lot about the ability of a competitor to compete in a market by analyzing financial information. An executive at Honeywell effectively used this kind of information when he noted, "One competitor was making a little more noise in the marketplace, but after we looked at the balance sheet, we found out he probably couldn't mortgage any more; his profitability had turned down; his asset utilization had become less efficient; and there wasn't much he could do."[12]

Marketing strategy information. Every competitor has a marketing program that it uses to attract customers. The best competitors use marketing to build an advantage over others by meeting selected customer market requirements better than do other companies. There are many possibilities. A company might try to win customers by offering benefits such as product superiority, product innovation, price economy, distribution convenience, a chic image, or after-sale service. Marketing managers must learn what these advantages are as well as uncover any weaknesses in a competitor's marketing program (see Marketool).

MarkeTOOL

A handy tool for evaluating competitors

THE DIRECTOR OF Business Planning and Research for Borg-Warner Corporation argues strongly for evaluating competition as part of the preparation for marketing planning. He comments on the importance of knowing your competition and offers a worksheet to guide the analysis.

Companies engaged in industrial marketing, especially those with high technology products, often focus their planning on internal programs for product development and technology. Other more progressive firms tend to look at external forces such as market trends, but still do not focus on competition when planning.

While it is valuable to consider both internal and external forces, the competition factor should not be overlooked. So for each product-market segment, you need to ask questions such as

- Who are the major direct and indirect competitors today? Will they be the same five years from now?

- What share of market does each competitor have in this segment and what are they likely to have in the future?

- What are the key ingredients for success in this segment and how do competitors rate on each ingredient?

- What are my competitor's strategies today and what are they likely to be in the future? If I "leapfrog" the competition, what will be their reaction?

- How do I describe the management "style" of my competition? Are they conservative engineering-oriented businesses or entrepreneurial marketing-oriented risk takers?

The answers to these questions will serve as the foundation of a successful business strategy. They can also help you properly channel resources toward profitable growth opportunities which match your strengths while attacking the weaknesses of competitors.

A competitor evaluation technique involves the analysis of key success factors vs. competitor strengths in specific

SOURCE: Milton Shapiro, "Effective industrial market planning requires techniques for evaluating competitors," *Marketing News*, Apr. 4, 1980, p. 6. Used by permission of the American Marketing Association.

business segments. The first step is to call on two or more managers knowledgeable about competition in the particular segment.

The experts should gather in a distraction-free room for about three hours. A blackboard or flip chart is required, and a facilitator from outside the business being analyzed should be present to record the information and keep the process flowing. Here is the format to follow for this analysis (see worksheet below):

Step 1: Determine the key competitive success factors in the segment and look at them from the viewpoint of the buyer. In one example these were: full line, qualitative and metallurgy technology, price, availability, geography/freight, customer service response, and reputation image.

Step 2: Rank the factors in order of importance. On the basis that all factors listed account for 100% of success, give each one a percentage weight.

Step 3: List the major competitors that account for at least 80% of the segment being analyzed across the top of the form.

Step 4: Starting with the first success factor, rank each competitor in order. The most successful competitor would be ranked No. 1 and so forth. On the basis of 10 being the best possible—a perfect for the factors being rated—assign a number from one to 10 to each competitor. List these one-to-10 factors in the left hand side of each box. Continue this process in turn for each of the success factors listed.

Step 5: Calculate the competition strengths for each factor by multiplying the percentage weights by the one-to-10 factors assigned. Add the strengths for each competitor and yourself. Add the "Total Strategic Muscle" and determine the "Share of Strategic Muscle" for each competitor and yourself. Finally, compare this share with your best estimate of current market share.

Competitor evaluation worksheet

Key Competitive Success Factors	Percentage Importance Weights	Your Strengths		Competitor 1		Competitor 2	
		Rating	Weighted Rating*	Rating	Weighted Rating*	Rating	Weighted Rating*
Full line of products	15	(6)	90	(10)	150	(8)	120
Technology expertise	20	(8)	160	(7)	140	(9)	180
Price	20	(8)	160	(5)	100	(7)	140
Availability	10	(7)	70	(9)	90	(8)	80
Geography/ freight	10	(9)	90	(6)	60	(8)	80
Customer service	20	(9)	180	(7)	140	(8)	160
Reputation image	5	(4)	20	(7)	35	(9)	45
Totals	100		750		715		805
Share			0.33		0.31		0.35

* Determined by multiplying the weights (second column) by the corresponding rating.

Evaluating the competition is essential to plan a marketing strategy. The challenge is to figure out how to win customers from the competition. Consider Cordis Corporation, which developed a new line of heart pacemakers that were technically more advanced than the competition. Management expected cardiologists (heart doctors) to buy and use the product because it was better. Unfortunately, sales did not grow as predicted. Managers were eager to know why, so salespersons were asked to see what competitors were doing. They found out that competitors were offsetting Cordis's technical advantage by offering bonus gifts for purchases of their brands. Sales improved quickly after Cordis increased its efforts to educate doctors about its superior pacemaker and began giving free equipment bonuses for buying its brand.[13]

Predicting competitors' actions

Knowing what competitors currently are doing is only a start. Marketing managers must anticipate how competitors will act in the future. Probably the most frequently used basis for predicting competitors' actions is a cataloging of how they have responded in the past to the changing task environment and macroenvironment (though, as Marketalk reveals, other tactics sometimes are used). Many companies have predictable management styles that dictate how they will react to a particular situation. The challenge is to use past actions to learn about their styles. This approach is evident in a comment made by a manager at Honeywell about one of his company's competitors.

> *Company A.* Here's a company that uses high technology to be a product leader. For it, technology is a way to get new products, and every time I look at this company it has a whole brochure of brand new products. The company is going to get there right away. It comes out with fairly low cost; it sticks to growth markets; and its philosophy is highly profitable through initial monopoly in the marketplace. In other words, it's the only game in town.
>
> Profit on any product starts big, and when the competition finally decides it has to come in, the profitability drops. Whenever competition gets tough, Company A gets out.[14]

Managers do not have to rely solely on what competitors have done in the past. Sometimes a competitor will give advance signals of a change in marketing strategy. Maybe the company is testing a new product in some market areas, or perhaps it has alerted wholesalers and retailers to expect a change in price on brands in its product line. By looking for these signals, management can be forewarned of a marketing strategy change.

Finally, a marketing manager who sees a change coming in the task environment or macroenvironment can try to deduce how competitors will respond if they act in a logical way. Suppose a homebuilder sees interest rates rising and a slump in the economy coming. Both of these macroenvironmental factors might put homes financially out of reach of many customers. How do you think homebuilders will respond? One logical prediction is that competitors will redesign homes to be smaller and more affordable. During the early 1980s when the times were poor for the housing industry, many builders adopted this strategy.[15]

*Marke*TALK ///

Snooping on the competition

HOW WOULD YOU like to know your competitors' sales plans, key elements of their corporate strategies, the capacity of their plants and the technology used in them, who their principal suppliers and customers are, and a good bit about new products your rivals have under development? No, you don't have to break any laws to get this information. While illegal corporate espionage makes headlines occasionally, it probably accounts for only a small fraction of corporate intelligence-gathering. There are many other ways you can find out what your competitors are up to that are completely legal, if sometimes ethically questionable.

The legal use of intelligence-gathering techniques has increased dramatically as more and more companies learn how cheap and effective it is. United States corporations known to collect intelligence on competitors include Ford Motor Company, Westinghouse Electric, General Electric, Emerson Electric, Rockwell International, Celanese, Union Carbide, and Gillette. Digital Equipment Corporation and Wang Laboratories both have batteries of competitor analysts. Nor is snooping limited to companies that make highly engineered hardware. Enterprises such as

Chemical Bank, the USV Laboratories subsidiary of Revlon, the specialty grocery products group of Del Monte, General Foods, Kraft, and J. C. Penney are all busy monitoring what the other guy is doing.

Companies have always needed to know what competitors were doing—so why more so now? The answer, in a word, is competition. Businessmen believe competition has intensified and become global. In industries where growth has slowed, executives realize that most of the increased business they need will have to come out of the hides of their competitors. In addition, the corporate strategy vogue of the 1970's has left as a legacy the thought that competitive intelligence is a necessary ingredient in executing strategic plans. Henry P. Allessio, a founding partner of Easton Consultants of Stamford, Connecticut, says flatly, "You can't get there from here without it." Companies realize that, without taking the behavior of competitors into account, their strategic plans don't work. Says Harvard Business School Professor Michael Porter, a guru of strategy, "If your competitors respond the wrong way to your 'right' move, they can make the right move wrong."

Obtaining competitive information is getting easier these days. Electronic data bases, which store information to be retrieved by computer, are proliferating. Some 2,000 are now available. One, called Economic Information Systems, published by a subsidiary of Control Data Cor-

poration, lists the names and locations of industrial facilities along with estimates of each plant's dollar volume of output, number of employees, and the share of market that its production represents. Another data base, called Investext, published by Business Research Corporation of Brighton, Massachusetts, gives subscribers the full text of research reports on companies by security analysts and investment bankers.

There are now even services that monitor such data bases for you. Selective Dissemination of Information (or SDI), offered by data base distributors such as Dialog Information Services, provides subscribers with surveillance and periodic reports on competitors' appearances in data bases. Unfortunately, some of the information in these data bases is inaccurate, irrelevant, or stale. But nuggets can be found—and competitive intelligence is a bits-and-pieces business. Says Michael Porter, "Once you have 80 percent of the puzzle, you begin to see things in what people say that you didn't see when you had 20 percent."

Competition in the competitive intelligence business is getting as rugged as in the industries the snoopers monitor. Leonard Fuld, managing director of Information Data Search, discovered, for example, that a competitor had enrolled in one of his seminars under an assumed name. During another seminar his lecture notes and source book were stolen.

///

FORECASTING SALES IN MARKETS

Marketing managers always want to know how much market opportunity is in markets. **Forecasting** market size, the process by which predictions are made of the amount of sales that markets will yield, is included in an MOA for this purpose. This activity should be attempted only after the markets have been defined, customer profiles constructed, and the competition evaluated. Information and analyses from these prior components of the MOA are valuable aids to forecasting.

Deciding what to forecast

Several questions must be answered to decide exactly what a forecast should predict.

1. For what product (product type or brand) will the forecast be made?
2. Over what time period will the forecast be made?
3. Within what geographic area will the forecast be confined?

4. For what market (or markets) is the forecast being made?

5. Under what market condition assumptions does the forecast hold?

Product type and brand forecasts. Marketing managers are most interested in estimating sales for the company's brand. A **brand sales forecast** estimates how many units (or dollars) of a particular brand will be sold. Brand sales forecasts can be summed over all brands to yield a **company sales forecast.**

Sometimes a manager wants to know the sales that can be expected for a product type. This estimate is a **market forecast,** which predicts total sales for all companies selling brands of that product type. Suppose a marketing manager for Miles Laboratories, the maker of Alka Seltzer, wanted a forecast of the sales of all antacids (Alka Seltzer is one of several brands of antacids). This sales estimate is a market forecast because it is the sum of sales of all antacid brands including Alka Seltzer, Tums, and Rolaids.

Length of time forecasted. A forecast covers a designated future period of time. How a forecast is used dictates the proper time period. A sales manager for Miles Laboratories who wants sales forecasts to set short-term goals for the district needs correspondingly short-run forecasts, maybe only looking ahead a few months. Other purposes, such as determining how much to expand the sales force, require longer-terms forecasts.

Geographic area coverage. Forecasts of sales must be made for a designated geographic area. Each Miles Laboratory salesperson forecasts sales only for his or her territory. In contrast, the Miles Laboratories' marketing manager is more likely to use a national forecast. In each case, the geographic area for which the marketing person is responsible dictates the proper coverage for a forecast.

Defined markets. Managers should specify the market for which a forecast is to be made. An estimate may be for an entire market for a brand or product type, or it could be for a segment. Again, management's use of the forecast determines the appropriate market.

Market situation assumptions. Accuracy of forecasts often depend on how well factors that influence sales, the **market conditions,** are anticipated. The task environment yields many of these conditions. The extent of marketing by competition and the makeup of customers and their needs help determine the situation in which sales will take place. Macroenvironmental forces such as economic conditions, government regulations, population changes, and social and life-style changes also are market conditions.

Within a given period, market conditions cause sales opportunity in a market to have a finite upper limit, which is called **market potential.** As competing companies increase their marketing efforts, actual sales should increase. At some point, however, further increase in marketing efforts becomes less and less effective in getting more sales. Exhibit 4.8 illustrates this decrease in effectiveness. As companies selling the product type expand their marketing from M1 to M2, sales increase from S1 to S2. The increased marketing may reach more customers as well as convince some customers to buy more. But no amount of marketing can expand product type sales beyond market potential. At that point, most customers have been reached and they are buying all that they want. Realistic forecasts of sales must recognize this limit. Clearly, as market conditions change over time, so will market potential and the sales opportunity being forecasted.

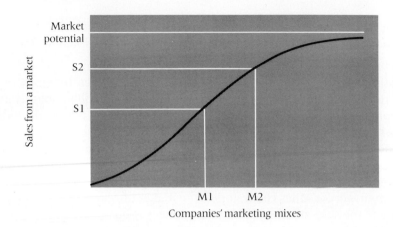

Exhibit 4.8 No amount of marketing can move sales past market potential

The fact that customers' needs, wants, and buying power; companies' marketing mixes; and macroenvironmental forces affect product type and brand sales has an important implication for forecasting. A forecast must be founded on specific assumptions about each of these market conditions. The accuracy of forecasts depends on how accurate the assumptions prove to be. Thus, only prior analysis of markets and competition by the MOA can provide the information for making realistic assumptions.

How forecasts are made

No one has found a single best way to forecast sales in all situations. In practice, one of several available techniques must be chosen that best fits a forecasting situation. Exhibit 4.9 shows one way of categorizing alternative forecasting techniques. Within each of these categories, mathematical techniques and informed judgment techniques, there are three different approaches. Each alternative uses markedly different kinds of information and different procedures for arriving at a forecast.

Mathematical techniques. Often facts are available about how a market has been growing in the past. Past sales for a product type or brand might be readily extracted from records kept by a company or other organization. Or

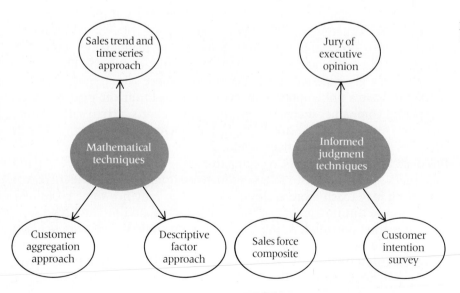

Exhibit 4.9 Alternative techniques for forecasting sales from markets

facts from past studies of populations and customers in markets can be obtained. Whatever the source, the information or data tell us something about sales or purchase trends that have, in fact, been happening historically.

Mathematical forecasting techniques use mathematically stated relationships or models to derive a forecast from these historical data. Thus, they are based on finding a strong link between the past and the future. Using data describing the past market situation, the forecaster looks for a regular pattern of change. Then, by assuming that this change will continue into the future, mathematical procedures determine how to project the pattern to estimate future sales. In essence, most mathematical techniques are simply ways to predict the future from past trends. Some examples of mathematical techniques should help you see how they work.

- *Sales trend and time series approaches.* A company may have a record of sales (for a product type or brand) for several time periods. Analyzing how sales have changed from one period to the next may uncover a regular pattern of change indicating growth or decline. Sales for future periods might be forecast by projecting the pattern to future periods. A salesperson might use past sales in her territory to see if regular growth is evident. Suppose she finds that over the past three years, the average growth in sales for each quarter has been 4 percent of the previous quarter's sales. She can forecast next quarter's sales by multiplying last quarter's sales by 104 percent.

- *Descriptive factor approaches.* Information may be available that describes past sales and environmental factors that are known to influence sales. Mathematical approaches are available to estimate the increase in sales for a product type or brand based on predictions of changes in these forces. A sales manager may have, in addition to sales records, information on population growth in her district and on interest rates for the past three years. If these two factors are important influences on purchase decisions of customers, she can apply predicted change in population growth and interest rates to estimate how much sales growth is indicated.

- *Customer aggregation approaches.* If information is available on N, the number of customers in a market, and R, their extent of use of a product, then simple calculation of $N \times R$ yields an estimate of sales. Applying this technique, a salesperson can count the number of customers in her territory, estimate the usage of each product by each customer, and then multiply these numbers together to get next quarter's sales.

Informed judgment techniques. Markedly different approaches to forecasting are available when mathematical techniques cannot be used. Managers can solicit help from people who have some special knowledge of the market and factors influencing sales. These people are "informed" so their opinions or judgment about future sales are reasoned estimates. **Informed judgment techniques** use the opinions of these knowledgeable people, and differ largely according to who provides the forecast and how the opinions are obtained.

- *Jury of executive opinion.* Informed judgment may come from managers of the company, managers from other organizations such as research and advertising firms, and outside consultants. Usually, several persons are recruited to ensure that a variety of experiences and points of view are brought to bear on the forecast. The forecasting procedure is used to obtain a consensus of the participants. This technique was used by a merchandise manager for a large department store who wanted a sales estimate for a line of cameras. To get an annual sales estimate, the manager called together the advertising manager, store manager, store buyers, and the camera department manager to discuss the opportunity for sales. Together, they reached a consensus sales forecast for the camera line.

■ *Sales force composite.* Company salespersons can be a source of informed judgment. Each salesperson is asked for a forecast of sales in his or her assigned territory. A manager for a precision tool manufacturing company turned to this technique when he polled salespersons to get opinions of annual sales in each territory of a new tool about to be introduced for sale. All opinions were summed to get a company sales forecast.

■ *Customer intention surveys.* Customers themselves may be able to give opinions about future sales. Customers who plan for purchases decide when and how much to buy. With a market research study, customers can be interviewed concerning their intentions to purchase a product type or brand within a given time period. Sales estimates are derived from these intentions. The precision tool manufacturer's marketing manager might obtain additional estimates of sales by calling customer companies to ask for their estimates of need for the new precision tool.

Selecting the best forecasting approach

When selecting a forecasting approach the marketing situation for which a forecast is needed should be considered. Criteria can be established to serve as standards for evaluating alternative approaches. Criteria commonly used for this purpose include

1. Is information available to implement the approach?
2. Is the information relevant for the forecast period?
3. Is the cost of obtaining required information reasonable?
4. Will managers using the forecast understand and accept the estimate from this approach?
5. Is there sufficient time to go through the forecasting procedure required by the approach?
6. Will the resulting forecast be sufficiently accurate?
7. Do we have forecasters with sufficient technical skills to develop a forecast using the approach?

EVALUATING MARKET OPPORTUNITY

Forecasts reveal opportunity

An experienced marketing manager looks for indication of growth and competitive impact on market opportunity by examining the differences between the market potentials, market forecasts, and sales forecasts. As an

Exhibit 4.10 Forecast of sales for artificial turf surfaces

Type of Forecast	Demand Forecasts*	
	Existing Markets	New Markets
Market potential for artificial grass	$9,000,000	$18,000,000
Market forecast for artificial grass	7,000,000	500,000
Sales forecast for artificial grass	3,400,000	0

* Although these demand forecasts are illustrative, they are representative of estimates actually made in an analysis of market opportunity for a division of a large, well-known company.

Illustration, Exhibit 4.10 provides one-year forecasts of sales of artificial grass sports surfaces (e.g., for football, baseball, and soccer fields). Management of Safe Turf, a manufacturer of artificial grass, scanned the numbers to seek clues to market opportunity.

First, notice how much greater market potential is in new markets than in existing markets: $18,000,000 versus $9,000,000. Artificial grass primarily has been used for large playing fields for football, baseball, and soccer (the existing markets). Forecasts show that market potential is twice as great for applications to other sports such as golf and tennis (the new markets).

Second, manufacturers of artificial grass surfaces apparently are expected to get almost all sales from existing markets: $7,000,000 versus $500,000. This conclusion is surprising because the new markets look more attractive. However, many artificial grass manufacturers are held back by the high cost of building a distribution system to serve the vastly more spread out new markets. Finally, Safe Turf is apparently planning to concentrate solely on existing markets in which the company anticipates having a large percentage of all product type sales: $3,400,000/$7,000,000 = 49 percent. Management should have an excellent reason for not entering the lucrative new markets to justify this decision.

Evaluation uses entire market opportunity analysis

Evaluating market opportunity should use all information from an MOA, not just the forecasts. Customer profiles and competition's strengths and weaknesses are major factors in selecting a target market. One key consideration is the degree to which the company can meet customer's market requirements. The MOA provides the description of these requirements. Managers also must consider the company's and the brand's capabilities to meet these requirements. Perhaps you wondered why Safe Turf did not plan to go after the new markets. The reason was that management believed that the company could not afford to develop the distribution system needed to reach these markets. Only by understanding the market's requirements for convenience when buying artificial turf could managers reach this conclusion.

Market opportunity is difficult to tap without having some advantage over competitors. The analysis of competition is essential for revealing competitors' strengths and weaknesses. Again, managers must consider their company's capabilities to match strengths and to exploit weaknesses to see if an advantage can be found. Returning to the artificial grass illustration, Safe Turf did have competitive advantages—a longer-lasting turf, a longer guarantee, and more reliable repair services than the competition—that related directly to important market requirements of customers in existing markets. For this reason, management felt comfortable staying with existing markets. The sales forecast reflected the conclusions that management had reached from the entire MOA.

SUMMARY

Market opportunity analysis plays a vital role in a marketing manager's job responsibility. Without MOAs, developing a marketing strategy would be like shooting at a moving target in the dark. MOAs allow marketing managers to select target markets with attractive opportunity, set realistic marketing objectives, and design marketing mixes that meet market requirements of customers in an advantageous way.

The approach to market opportunity analysis presented in this chapter can be adapted to fit the needs of marketing managers at all levels in a company. A salesperson preparing for a district sales meeting can use an MOA to plan a selling approach for the territory, a product manager can use it to plot strategy for a brand, and a top marketing executive can follow the procedure to plan marketing strategy for a line of related brands.

After setting limits on the scope of the MOA, the next step is to identify markets for a product. Customers who have ability and willingness to buy the product are grouped into markets. Then the MOA profiles what customers are like as "flesh and blood people." The profiles help marketing managers understand what benefits buyers expect (the market requirements) and what influences are affecting buying decisions.

Meeting market requirements adequately is not enough. Competition for market opportunity comes from other brands of the same product type, and from other product types that satisfy the same needs and wants. A successful company must find some advantage over competitors in meeting market requirements to gain market opportunity. Understanding the strengths and weaknesses of their competition is essential for managers to plan a marketing strategy that achieves that advantage.

Finally, to commit resources to a market, managers must show a planned return to the company. Market opportunity analysis can help here, too, because sales in one important kind of return for marketing managers to demonstrate. Forecasting market size is the way in which managers gauge how much sales return a market will yield. By evaluating the differences between market potential, market forecast, and sales forecast, valuable insights are gained into the magnitude of opportunity.

KEY TERMS

market opportunity	brand	marketing research
market opportunity analysis (MOA)	product type	market requirements
market	population analysis	customer profile

forecasting
brand sales forecast
company sales forecast

market forecast
market conditions
market potential

mathematical forecasting
  techniques
informed judgment techniques

QUESTIONS FOR REVIEW AND DISCUSSION

1. A marketing manager for RCA made the following comment: "The number of people 65 and older in this country is increasing dramatically. We ought to look into this elderly market." Do the elderly constitute a market for televisions, radios, and other entertainment products sold by RCA? Why or why not?

2. Suppose you worked for Prince Manufacturing Company, the leading maker of tennis rackets. Your job is to sell Prince's line of rackets to sporting goods stores, specialty tennis stores, tennis pro shops, and department stores. Does your market comprise these retailers? Why or why not?

3. Do people who have the desire or willingness to buy a product make up that product's market?

4. In what ways does a population analysis help identify markets for a product?

5. How does a product type differ from a brand?

6. Explain three kinds of studies that a company can use to identify markets for a product type.

7. What does the term *market requirements* mean? Choose a product that you recently bought and describe your market requirements for this purchase.

8. Explain two ways in which a marketing manager can use a customer profile.

9. Does competition always limit the market opportunity available to a company?

10. Describe two types of information that management should use to evaluate competitors.

11. How can a marketing manager predict what a competitor will do in the future?

12. What are the differences between an estimate of market potential, a market forecast, and a sales forecast?

13. Can sales of a product ever exceed market potential? Why or why not?

14. Describe three techniques for forecasting sales in markets.

15. Should the forecasting technique that provides the most accurate forecast always be used by a marketing manager?

16. Is a forecast of sales in markets the best indicator of market opportunity for a company? Why or why not?

BUILDING YOUR PORTFOLIO

Choose any product of interest to you that is regularly advertised on television and in magazines. You may choose either a product type or a brand. Create a file of these advertisements by clipping them from magazines and taking notes on television ads. From this information develop a customer profile of the kinds of people in target markets for the product. That is, describe the kinds of people who you think these advertisements are trying to reach. You should get clues from the types of models used in the advertisements, the scenes and situations shown, and from what is said in the ads.

After you have a customer profile, test your results by seeing what you can find out from published sources about customers for the product that you selected. There are many sources in your library that you can consult including (1) periodicals (*Business Week, Fortune, Forbes, Time, Newsweek*); (2) newspapers (*The Wall Street Journal, The New York Times*); (3) government reports (*U.S. Industrial Outlook*); and (4) standardized information services (*Simmons Study of Media and Markets, Standard and Poor's Industry Surveys*). You may also want to interview people in local businesses (salespersons, store managers) to get their opinions. From this information, construct another customer profile for the same product. Then compare the two profiles to see how well they match.

NOTES

1. This illustration is based on information in "Corporate strategies: Kodak fights back." *Business Week,* Feb. 1, 1982, pp. 48–54, and correspondence with Kodak.
2. "Robots bump into a glutted market." *Business Week,* Apr. 4, 1983, p. 45.
3. Bill Abrams, "American Express is gearing new ad campaign to women." *Wall Street Journal,* Aug. 4, 1983, p. 1.
4. Ibid.
5. For a more complete discussion of this idea see Robert B. Woodruff, "A systematic approach to market opportunity analyses." *Business Horizons,* Aug. 1976, pp. 57–58.
6. For more discussion of approaches for identifying markets, see George S. Day, Allan D. Shocker, and Rajendra K. Srivastava, "Customer-oriented approaches to identifying product markets." *Journal of Marketing,* Vol. 43 (Fall 1979), pp. 8–19.
7. "Compugraphic: Trying to move typesetting from the shop to the office." *Business Week,* July 2, 1984, p. 89.
8. Joel Dreyfuss, "More power to the PC chains." *Fortune,* May 14, 1984, p. 83.
9. Peter Nulty, "Cool heads are trying to keep Commodore hot." *Fortune,* July 23, 1984, p. 38.
10. Janet Guyon and Erick Lareson, "New Apple chief expected to bring marketing expertise gained at Pepsi." *Wall Street Journal,* Apr. 11, 1983, p. 29.
11. "You have to know where to look, who to ask to find data about new markets, prospects." *Marketing News,* Feb. 5, 1982, p. 8; and Milton Shapiro, "Effective industrial marketing requires specific techniques for evaluating competitors." *Marketing News,* Apr. 4, 1980, p. 6.
12. " 'Key issue': Its key issue in strategic planning: Johnson." *Marketing News,* June 1, 1979, p. 6. Used by permission of the American Marketing Association.
13. Steven Flax, "How to snoop on your competitors." *Fortune,* May 14, 1984, p. 29.
14. " 'Key Issue,' " op. cit. Used by permission of the American Marketing Association.
15. "Urge building small homes to end market slump." *Marketing News,* Oct. 29, 1982, pp. 1, 8.

Case 4.1

The North American Soccer League

AS PLAYERS in the North American Soccer League (NASL) were booting in professional soccer's seventeenth season last month, a new regime at the league's New York City offices was kicking around marketing plans, something the league has been sorely lacking.

"I'm not saying all the teams are bad marketers, but some are atrocious," says new NASL president Howard Samuels, 64, who made his fortune as cofounder of Kordite (it introduced Baggies). One team, for instance, sold $500,000 in corporate sponsorships last year, while another sold none. True, the NASL gets only cable TV coverage, but Samuels blames amateurish marketing for the league's $25 mil-

SOURCE: "Pro soccer's new kick," *Sales & Marketing Management*, May 16, 1983, p. 27. Copyright © 1983; reprinted by permission.

lion loss last year.

A recent A. C. Nielsen survey shows that 8 million U.S. youngsters up to college age play soccer. Counting their families and friends, the study estimates that there are 25 million U.S. soccer fans, mostly upper middle-class whites. "So that's a market," says Samuels, "but how do you translate that market into a successful pro venture?"

Samuels's answer is to banish some ex-jocks from the executive suite and bring in professional marketers. As marketing chief, he hired Alan Levine, a veteran of Phillip Morris and Standard Brands, who, so far, has taken the following steps to maximize non-TV revenues:

- Hired a merchandiser away from Lord & Taylor to establish department-store team shops for licensed goods.

- Brought in Procter & Gamble marketer Ed Tazzia to write the NASL's first marketing plan.

- Ran seminars on group ticket sales and developed a marketing newsletter for franchisees.

The NASL's biggest hope is Team America, an all-star squad culled from league teams that will play a full season schedule and preen for World Cup competition. A season sponsorship of Team America costs $300,000 vs. as little as $10,000 for other teams.

QUESTIONS

1. Do the president and marketing chief of the NASL need a market opportunity analysis? Why or why not?

2. Are the "8 million U.S. youngsters up to college age" who play soccer the market for the soccer league? Are the "25 million soccer fans" the market?

3. What is the competition faced by the soccer league? Are the soccer teams in the league the competition for each other?

4. Is "maximizing non-TV revenue" a good statement of the market opportunity sought by the NASL?

5. What are the most important characteristics of market opportunity that should be studied before developing a marketing plan for the NASL?

Case 4.2

Chesebrough-Pond's

CHESEBROUGH-POND's is a diversified company with many well-known brands including RAGU', VASELINE, PRINCE MATCHABELLI, and PRINCE Manufacturing Company. Forecasting brand sales for so many products is difficult because each one is sold in different markets. Consider sales for two of Chesebrough-Pond's product categories for the ten-year period from 1973 to 1982 (in thousands of dollars).

Tennis equipment	1982 56,888	1981 35,376	1980 18,039	1979 9,520	1978 7,143
	1977 5,052	1976 2,946	1975 1,165	1974 1,151	1973 500
Health and beauty aids	1982 271,311	1981 269,533	1980 238,811	1979 223,415	1978 198,540
	1977 179,484	1976 163,183	1975 146,071	1974 134,755	1973 125,129

SOURCE: Chesebrough-Pond's *Annual Report*, 1982. Used by permission.

QUESTIONS

1. Which product category, tennis equipment or health and beauty aids, has the larger market opportunity?

2. In what ways is market opportunity different for these two product categories?

3. Speculate on the market situation factors that might be causing the differences in market opportunity that you see.

4. Can these sales data be used in forecasting sales for the next five years? Why or why not?

5 Consumer Buying Behavior

When you finish this chapter, you will understand

☐ How analyses of consumer behavior can help marketing managers carry out their responsibilities

☐ Questions that marketing managers must answer with buyer behavior analysis

☐ How the personal makeup of consumers affects their purchasing decisions

☐ The major environmental influences on consumer purchasing

☐ How consumers make purchase decisions when the product is highly relevant to their needs, wants, and life-styles

☐ How consumers make purchase decisions for products or services that have little relevance to their lives

Personal interview studies conducted in shopping centers are a popular technique for learning about consumers' reactions to new product ideas.

In a family with both husband and wife present, who does the everyday household activities—cooking meals, cleaning bathrooms, washing dishes, vacuuming, and other similar tasks? Marketing managers in hundreds of companies selling household care and food products—soaps, detergents, vacuums, kitchen appliances, cleansers, frozen foods—are quite interested in the answer. They know that those people who actually use products often have an influence on what is purchased.

Some managers would rely on personal experience for an answer. A male marketing manager could conclude that housewives do these household activities simply because his wife does them in their home. Another manager might rely on a stereotype about who does what in households. For instance, the stereotype of the so-called traditional housewife held by many in the United States may cause a manager to guess that the housewife does the household chores.

Basing decisions on personal experience and stereotypes is always dangerous. Consider the results of the study, "Men's Changing Role in the Family of the 1980s."[1] Some of the statistics may surprise you. Of the sample of *men* in the study,

- Thirty-two percent shop for food
- Seventy-four percent take out the garbage
- Forty-seven percent cook for the family
- Fifty-three percent wash the dishes
- Twenty-nine percent do the laundry
- Twenty-eight percent clean the bathroom
- Thirty-nine percent vacuum the house
- Eighty percent take care of children (in households with children younger than twelve)

THE STUDY OF HUSBANDS' ROLE in families illustrates an important fact of business life—buyers do not always behave as marketing managers expect them to. Carefully analyzing buyers' behavior often reveals surprising insights that become instrumental when designing a marketing strategy. As husbands become increasingly involved in household chores, many companies will rethink their approaches to selling their products and services. Some companies have already begun: Advertisements for laundry soap occasionally show men washing clothes.

Conducting and using analyses of buyer behavior are specialties of the marketing manager. As we explain in Chapter 4, finding markets with opportunity, uncovering market requirements that buyers expect to have met, and forecasting sales depend on having a sound understanding of buyer behavior.

Marketing managers are particularly interested in buyer purchase decision making. Proper design of a marketing mix can influence buyer's product and service choices. For this reason, our view of buyer behavior emphasizes purchase decision making—**buyer behavior** refers to the actions of persons directly involved in purchasing and using a product or service including the decision processes that lead to a purchase choice and the satisfaction or dissatisfaction experienced as a result of the purchase.[2]

Buyer behavior is not quite the same for every product or service purchased. Choosing a restaurant in which to celebrate a birthday is not like choosing a brand of cereal or a copying machine for an office. There are similarities in the way that customers make purchase decisions, however, and from these similarities we can derive questions that buyer behavior analyses try to answer. This chapter and chapter 6 help you understand these questions and how marketing managers can answer them.

BUYER BEHAVIOR AND MARKETING MANAGEMENT

In Chapter 2, the major responsibilities of marketing management are presented as a sequence of interrelated activities: analyzing the situation, planning marketing strategy, implementing marketing strategy, and controlling marketing strategy. Analyzing buyer behavior is part of analyzing the situation, and it provides information on market opportunity for each of the other marketing management activities.

Buyer behavior and marketing planning

Understanding buyer behavior plays an important role in planning marketing strategy. Each of the marketing planning decisions—selecting market targets, setting marketing objectives, and designing a marketing program—is guided primarily by what managers' know and believe about the behavior of buyers in markets.

Selecting market targets. The entire marketing plan is based on the market target decision. Who will most likely buy the product or service? How are they different from people who are not buyers? These questions are answered by analyzing buyer behavior. The battle for market share among the major beer breweries—Anheuser-Busch, Miller, Pabst, and others—is a case in point. Each company has similar market targets, of which the most important is frequent beer drinkers. This market segment comprises people who typically are between the ages of twenty-one and forty, are in both white-collar and blue-collar occupations, and are sports enthusiasts. Whereas frequent beer drinkers are only 20 percent of all beer drinkers, they buy approximately 80 percent of the beer sold. You can see why the breweries have used buyer behavior analysis to find out who they are.[3]

Setting marketing objectives. Many marketing objectives are really statements about the desired or predicted behavior of buyers in one or more target markets. Consider a sales objective. When managers state a sales objective they are, in fact, predicting how many buyers will purchase the company's product as well as the quantity each will buy. Similarly, a market position objective is actually stating the impression of a company or its brand that management wants buyers to have.

Analyzing buyers helps managers set objectives that are realistically achievable. Knowing who buyers are, how many there are, what they want from a product, and the like focuses management's attention on what behaviors are possible and important to seek from buyers. Beer brewery managers are very concerned with buyers' impressions of beer brands because they know that little product difference exists among the brands. Thus establishing a certain brand image with beer drinkers is an important marketing objective. Analyzing buyer behavior helps uncover an image to portray that will best influence sales of the brand. Miller's Lite beer used this approach and initially captured 60 percent of low-calorie beer sales before Budweiser started making a comeback.[4] Their advertising relies on professional athletes including Bubba Smith, Dick Butkus, and Marv Throneberry who create an image of rugged men enjoying Lite's low-calorie, less-filling benefits while getting a true beer taste.

Designing a marketing mix. The marketing mix provides the means by which a company meets requirements of customers. Understanding these requirements and other factors that influence buyers can be instrumental in shaping the mix. Seagram and Sons recognized this fact when it developed a successful marketing mix for a wine that subsequently showed two years of sales growth in the early 1980s—more than five times as much as sales increases for the wine category of which it is a part. The vice-president of marketing services attributed much of the success to sound buyer behavior analysis. As one illustration, studies showed that wine drinkers are likely to try other types of wine of the same brand once they have found a brand they like. This finding encouraged Seagram to develop a line of wines under the one brand-name label.[5]

Buyer behavior and implementation and control

Implementing marketing mix decisions often involves choosing between alternative ways to achieve the same purpose in market targets. Which alternative is best usually depends on how buyers will react to each one. Buyer behavior information can help managers evaluate the alternatives by examining their impact on buyers. Implementation became an important issue for one company that makes equipment used by hospital outpatients to monitor heartbeat and blood pressure because it needed a brand name for its products. Management wanted the name to help buyers understand the purpose of the equipment. Results of studies indicated that LifeScan was the best brand name for this purpose.[6]

The contribution of buyer behavior analysis extends all the way to marketing control activities. Information on buyer behavior is frequently used to measure how well a marketing plan is working in practice. Furthermore, buyer behavior analyses also may help explain why problems are occurring. Only when managers are aware of problems and their causes can decisions be made to correct them. Administrators of Johnson County Hospital faced this situation. They approved and implemented a marketing plan centered on building a reputation for treating respiratory ailments.* Follow-up buyer behavior analysis was necessary to find out if the strategy was working. Studies showed whether consumers' opinions concerning the hospital's reputation as a treatment center for respiratory ailments were improving and whether the number of patients admitted for respiratory-related treatments was increasing. The number of referrals of patients with respiratory ailments from other hospitals was checked periodically. When problems were spotted, further studies of buyers uncovered the cause and guided decisions to get performance back on line.

Donald E. Peterson, president of Ford Motor Company, aptly summarizes the critical importance of companies' maintaining a strong understanding of customers.

> Survival in a rapidly changing market requires not only that we adapt to change but that we anticipate change. To do this, we have to understand the people we serve: their needs and desires, their hopes and dreams, their fears and misgivings, their habits and hobbies, and the way the live. It means caring enough to ask questions and listen and respond in ways that make sense.[7]

A VIEW OF CONSUMER BUYING BEHAVIOR

Knowing what questions to ask about customers is at the heart of properly applying buyer behavior analysis. These questions are derived from a general view of the nature of buying that is based on thousands of studies

---

* Although the name of the hospital is fictitious, the situation described is real.

Exhibit 5.1   A model of consumer buying behavior

conducted over many years. We begin our discussion of this view by considering **consumer buyers,** persons in families and households who are purchasing goods and services for personal use to satisfy needs and wants.

Consumer buying model

Exhibit 5.1 shows a general model of consumer behavior. This model shows the three importance factors involved in consumer behavior: (1) the outside environmental influences on buyers, (2) the personal makeup of buyers, and (3) the process by which consumers decide what to buy and use.

External environmental influences to which consumers respond include the marketing mix components of a company. Consumers use information concerning product benefits, promotion, value for price, purchasing convenience provided by distribution, and help from facilitating services when they make purchasing decisions. Other influences such as opinions of families and friends affect consumers but are not part of the marketing mix. The personal makeup of consumers also influences buying behavior. A consumer's past experience and other personal characteristics influence the buying decision. A few of the many personal characteristics are needs and wants, experiences with products from past purchases, and likes and dislikes. A consumer's personal makeup combines with outside influences to influence how he or she decides what to buy and use. Purchase choices are the result of actions taken by consumers that determine the process of reaching a decision as well as their reaction to the outcome of the decision. Some of these actions are behaviors that can be seen, such as going to a store, reading newspaper advertisements, or pulling a product off a shelf. Others are not observable, such as thinking about the advantages and drawbacks of a product. Yet both kinds of actions are involved in the purchase decision-making process.

The model guides analyses

Having a general view of buying as portrayed by a consumer behavior model enables marketing managers to ask the right questions about consumer buying. These questions are

1. Who are the consumer buyers who make up markets?
2. What factors influence their buying decisions?
3. How do consumers make buying decisions?

The remainder of the chapter discusses how marketing professionals answer these questions. We introduce basic notions about consumer behavior gleaned from the great volume of studies that have been done.

Practical applications of these notions for marketing management are illustrated to help you see the crucial importance of analyzing buyers before making marketing decisions.

PERSONAL MAKEUP OF CONSUMER BUYERS

The starting point for analyses of consumer behavior is to find out which people are in a market. A **consumer market** is a group of people in households having both the ability and willingness to buy a product or service to satisfy a need or want. Not everyone in a population is part of a product's market. Thus marketing managers must identify not only who has the resources but also who has a sufficiently strong need or want to be willing to buy the product or service. Once these consumers are found, analyses find out what they are like as people.

Who are consumers in markets?

Obviously, most consumer markets are so big that managers cannot get to know everyone in person. For this reason, marketing managers look for ways to describe what is typical of buyers in markets. Demographic and life-style characteristics of buyers commonly are used for this purpose.

Demographic characteristics. People can be described using physical (age, gender, race), social (marital status, social class, household size), and economic (income, education, employment) characteristics. We call these demographic characteristics. Many such characteristics exist, and studies must be conducted to find out which ones best describe buyers in markets.

Exhibit 5.2 presents an interesting example of using demographic characteristics to identify customers in the market for solar water heaters.[8]

Exhibit 5.2 Demographic characteristics of solar water heater consumers in four segments of the market

	Comfortables	Aspirants	Established	Affluents
Average age	About 35	Under 30	About 46	35 to 44
Average income	$43,300	$23,800	$27,800	$77,900
Education	College	High school	College	College
Number of wage earners	2	1 or 2	1	2
Family size	3 to 4	3 to 4	4 to 5	3 to 5
Race	White	White	White	White
Sex	Male	Male	Male	Male
Time lived at current address	3.9 years	3.3 years	More than 7 years	Less than 3 or more than 5 years
Percent of total market	42%	30%	22%	6%

SOURCE: Heather S. York and M. Lynne Keener, "Cluster analysis reveals four consumer segments in solar heater market," *Marketing News,* Apr. 30, 1982, p. 8. Reprinted by permission of the American Marketing Association.

Exhibit 5.3 Study reveals eight male life-style groups

Group I. "The Quiet Family Man" (8% of total males)
 He is a self-sufficient man who wants to be left alone and is basically shy. Tries to be as little involved with community life as possible. His life revolves around the family, simple work, and television viewing. Has a marked fantasy life. As a shopper he is practical, less drawn to consumer goods and pleasures than other men.
 Low education and low economic status, he tends to be older than average.

Group II. "The Traditionalist" (16% of total males)
 A man who feels secure, has self-esteem, follows conventional rules. He is proper and respectable, regards himself as altruistic and interested in the welfare of others. As a shopper he is conservative, he likes popular brands and well-known manufacturers.
 Low education and low or middle socio-economic status; the oldest age group.

Group III. "The Discontented Man" (13% of total males)
 He is a man who is likely to be dissatisfied with his work. He feels bypassed by life, dreams of better jobs, more money and more security. He tends to be distrustful and socially aloof. As a buyer, he is quite price conscious.
 Lowest education and lowest socio-economic group, mostly older than average.

Group IV. "The Ethical Highbrow" (14% of total males)
 This is a very concerned man, sensitive to people's needs. Basically a puritan, content with family life, friends, and work. Interested in culture, religion, and social reform. As a consumer he is interested in quality, which may at times justify greater expenditure.
 Well educated, middle or upper socio-economic status, mainly middle aged or older.

Group V. "The Pleasure Oriented Man" (9% of total males)
 He tends to emphasize his masculinity and rejects whatever appears to be soft or feminine. He views himself a leader among men. Self-centered, dislikes his work or job. Seeks immediate gratification for his needs. He is an impulsive buyer, likely to buy products with a masculine image.
 Low education, lower socioeconomic class; middle-aged or younger.

Group VI. "The Achiever" (11% of total males)
 This is likely to be a hardworking man, dedicated to success and all that it implies, social prestige, power and money. Is in favor of diversity, is adventurous about leisure time pursuits. Is stylish, likes good food, music, etc. As a consumer he is status conscious; a thoughtful and discriminating buyer.
 Good education, high socio-economic status, young.

Group VII. "The He-Man" (19% of total males)
 He is gregarious, likes action, seeks an exciting and dramatic life. Thinks of himself as capable and dominant. Tends to be more of a bachelor than a family man, even after marriage. Products he buys and brands preferred are likely to have "self-expressive value," especially a "Man of Action" dimension.
 Well-educated, mainly middle socio-economic status, the youngest of the male groups.

Group VIII. "The Sophisticated Man" (10% of total males)
 He is likely to be an intellectual, concerned about social issues, admires men with artistic and intellectual achievements. Socially cosmopolitan, broad interests. Wants to be dominant, and a leader. As a consumer he is attracted to the unique and fashionable.
 Best educated; highest economic status of all groups; younger than average.

SOURCE: From a study by the Newspaper Advertising Bureau as reported in William D. Wells, "Psychographics: A critical review," *Journal of Marketing Research*, Vol. XII (May 1975), p. 201. Used by permission.

The study uncovered not one group of buyers, but four different groups or segments, each of which has its own typical buyer. By comparing the groups, managers quickly can see how people in one segment are different from people in the other segments. Labels are given to each group (comfortables, aspirants, established, and affluents) to identify them easily.

Demographic descriptions are only a start for consumer behavior analysis. Yet, even this little information helps managers see that only some consumers in a population are good prospects for sales. Furthermore, the descriptions help managers begin to form a picture of the kinds of people toward whom they are aiming the marketing mix. For instance, Exhibit 5.2 should help you see that only some people in the United States will buy solar water heaters, and you now can visualize who they are. Of course, further analysis is needed to see which persons to select as market targets.

Life-style. Another popular way to determine who is in a product's market is to study life-style characteristics. Life-style refers to people's overall pattern of living, including how they spend their time, energy, and money.[9] Life-style is reflected in their opinions concerning things and events in their lives as well as their interests and activities. The products and services that consumers choose to buy often reflect the life-style they have chosen to live.

Exhibit 5.3 should help you see how life-style studies can be used to identify markets. Eight male life-style groups were identified from answers that men in the United States gave to 300 questions about their activities, interests, and opinions. The exhibit briefly summarizes the characteristics of each group. From the descriptions you can see how each group's life-style is markedly different from the others.

By appealing to two different life-styles, Bombay Gin hopes to capture a larger market share. (Courtesy TBWA Advertising, Inc., photography Frank Farrelli)

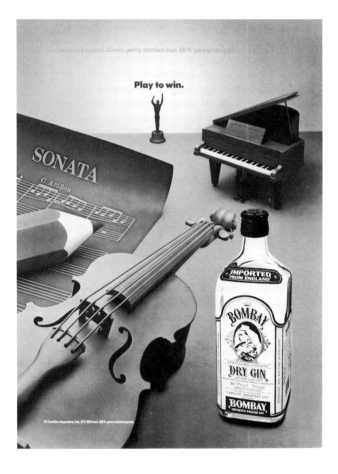

Life-style studies are valuable when they uncover in which life-style groups a company's product is used most. These groups become high-priority target markets. For instance, some men in all eight groups in Exhibit 5.3 drink beer, but the groups in which men drink the most beer are the He-Man, the Pleasure Oriented Man, and the Sophisticated Man. For domestic air travel one gets a different picture. Men who use domestic airlines are most likely to be in the Sophisticated Man, the Achiever, and

*Marke*TALK //

The nine American life-styles

THE TERM *VALUES* covers the attitudes, beliefs, opinions, hopes, fears, prejudices, needs, desires, and aspirations that, taken together, govern how one behaves. One's interior set of values—numerous, complex, overlapping, and contradictory though they are—finds holistic expression in a lifestyle.

The values and lifestyles (VALS) typology developed by SRI International is an attempt to analyze and systematize the values and lives of Americans to discover why people believe and act as they do. It comprises four groups that are subdivided into nine lifestyles, each intended to describe a unique way of life defined by its distinctive array of values, drives, beliefs, needs, dreams, and special points of view. The four groups are: need-driven (Survivor and Sustainer lifestyles), outer-directed (Belonger, Emulator, and Achiever lifestyles), inner-directed (I-Am-Me, Experiential, and Societally Conscious lifestyles), and combined outer- and inner-directed (Integrated lifestyle).

Here are brief descriptions of each of the nine American adult lifestyle groups:

- **Survivors.** Characterized by extreme poverty, America's 6 million Survivors tend to be despairing, depressed, withdrawn, mistrustful, rebellious about their situation, and conservative. Most are poorly educated, ill, and old. Of all segments of the U.S. population, they are the most likely to think things are changing too fast.

- **Sustainers.** Also driven by poverty, the 11 million Sustainers of the United States tend to be angry, distrustful, rebellious, combative people who often

feel left out of things. Unlike Survivors, they have not given up hope. They are the least satisfied of any lifestyle group with their financial status and the most anxious to get ahead economically. Many Sustainers tend to be "streetwise" and are often involved in the underground economy.

- **Belongers.** By far the largest segment, with about 60 million people. Belongers typify what is generally regarded as middle-class America; they are traditional, conforming, conservative, moral, nonexperimental, family-oriented, and patriotic—the most "old fashioned" of the VALS groups. Their key drive is to fit in, not to stand out.

- **Emulators.** These people are intensely striving, ambitious, competitive, and ostentatious, but they are also very hard working, fairly successful, and ask more of themselves than do Belongers. Approximately 13 million Americans fall into this category, a turbulent transition stage between the established, self-confident lifestyles of Belongers and Achievers.

- **Achievers.** These are the 35 million Americans who are at the top of the outer-directed groups. They have built "the system" and are now at the helm. They are a diverse, gifted, hard-working, self-reliant, successful, and happy group. As embodiments of the "establishment," they tend to be staunchly conservative and politically and socially opposed to radical changes.

- **I-Am-Mes.** The youngest of the VALS groups (the average age is 21), these 6 million Americans are in a tumultuous transition from the outer-directed way of life in which they were raised to inner direction, involving discovery of

new interests and setting of new life goals. The confusion of this stage is evident in the tendency of the I-Am-Me individual to be both contrite and aggressive, demure and exhibitionistic, self-effacing and narcissistic, conforming and wildly innovative.

- **Experientials.** Because they are generally older than the I-Am-Mes, Experientials have removed themselves further from the outer-directed lifestyles in which they were brought up. They seek direct, vivid experience, either through deep personal involvement in ideas and issues or through hedonism and experimentation. Numbering approximately 11 million, they are very well educated and hold well-paying technical and professional jobs; unlike Achievers, however, they are politically liberal and have little faith in institutional leaders.

- **Societally Conscious.** These 15 million Americans are primarily concerned with societal issues, trends, and events. They are successful, influential, and mature—the inner-directed equivalent of the outer-directed Achievers. Though a diverse group, they share the belief that humans should live in harmony with nature and with each other and that the nonmaterial aspects of life are more important than the material.

- **Integrateds.** Not many people have attained a truly integrated outlook on life—perhaps only 3 million Americans. These are the people who have put together the decisiveness of outer direction with the penetration of inner direction. Integrateds reflect both Achiever and Societally Conscious qualities: They are both makers and movers, observers and creators; they are open, self-assured, self-expressive, and often possessed of a global perspective.

SOURCE: Arnold Mitchell, "Nine American lifestyles," *The Futurist*, Aug. 1984, pp. 4–6. Reprinted by permission.

//

the Ethical Highbrow groups.[10] (See Marketalk for another perspective of American life-styles.)

What are consumers like as people?

Demographic and life-style studies demonstrate the value of understanding what people in markets are like. Life-style, however, is only part of the personal makeup of buyers. Several other important characteristics influence purchase decisions, and companies increasingly are expanding studies to search for a whole constellation of such characteristics. The rationale for such large and expensive studies is that the more a manager knows about customers, the more likely a successful marketing program can be designed specifically for target markets. Let us briefly examine the more important factors that describe what people are like.

Motives. A foundation on which marketing is built is that customers have a purpose in mind when they buy a product or service. Researchers have gone to great lengths to discover these purposes by looking for **motives**— "enduring predispositions that direct behavior toward certain goals"[11]— that lead to purchases. Probably the best known list of motives is Abraham H. Maslow's motive hierarchy. He believed that people had different kinds of motives that are arranged in order of importance:

- Physiologic motives direct people toward behavior that satisfies the basic needs of hunger and thirst.
- Safety motives lead to behavior that keeps a person safe from physical harm including satisfying needs for shelter and avoiding pain.
- Belonging motives direct behavior toward satisfying needs for acceptance by important other people.
- Esteem motives lead people to behave in a way that causes other people to think highly of them.
- Self-actualization motives direct behavior toward realizing one's full potential as a person.[12]

Although Maslow's classification is intuitive rather than based on facts from studies, it highlights an important idea—some motives must be satisfied before other motives can become forces for action. Few people can be influenced by self-actualization motives if they are continually hungry or fear for their safety. Marketing managers should look for those motives that currently are guiding consumer behavior.

Personality. People often react to a variety of different situations in a similar way. These enduring reaction tendencies form a person's **personality.** We typically describe a person's personality by using traits such as aggressive, sociable, relaxed, and willing to take risks. For example, a sociable person likes to be with other people, is outgoing and friendly, and seeks out people in many different kinds of situations.

Identifying personality traits of customers in target markets can help managers understand what product benefits are important or why a particular product benefit is desired. This knowledge can be invaluable when promotion is created. Many companies use advertising to appeal to typical personality traits of their target audiences. For example, Ford Motor Company portrays strong, rugged outdoorsmen in their small-truck advertising to appeal to the masculine and aggressive personality traits of buyers.

Values. Because we grow and live with others, we develop values. A **value** is a very important feeling about how good or bad performing an activity or achieving a goal is. To illustrate a value, many people in the United States feel that having an education is important for success. Interestingly, one study showed that people with different values have different preferences for product characteristics and product types. This finding explains why many young people who place more value on having an exciting life and experiencing pleasure than do their parents are more likely than their parents to prefer styling and high speed in cars.[13]

Beliefs and attitudes. Through experience with products and services consumers develop a variety of beliefs and attitudes. **Beliefs** are opinions or facts that a person holds to be true. Your beliefs about Coca-Cola might be that it is inexpensive, sweet, carbonated, and has many calories. Beliefs may be based on either direct use of the brand or what a consumer has heard about it. We all have beliefs about things with which we are familiar. Marketing managers, however, are interested primarily in consumers' beliefs about their company and its brands.

Attitudes are feelings of like and dislike toward something such as a product, a company, an idea, or a person. Attitudes can be very specific feelings toward individual characteristics of that object. Think of your attitudes toward Coca-Cola. You may like its low price, sweet taste, and carbonation, but dislike its calories. Attitudinal feeling also may be toward the object as a whole, as is the case if you like (or dislike) Coca-Cola.

Beliefs help form attitudes. You must believe that Coca-Cola is sweet before you can like its sweet taste. Furthermore, the combination of beliefs and attitudes toward a product's characteristics determines the extent to which a consumer likes the product as a whole. If you like Coca-Cola, it is probably because you have more likes toward the brand's important characteristics than dislikes.

Marketing managers study consumers' beliefs and attitudes because of their important role in purchase decisions. Given a choice, consumers usually buy what they like best and are less likely to buy what they do not like. Attitudes are more enduring and resistant to change than beliefs; therefore, many companies try to influence their customers' attitudes by changing their existing beliefs or creating new beliefs. Consider Buick's marketing program to reach the "yuppie" (young urban professionals with high incomes) market. Studies have shown that yuppies want "taut suspension, quick steering, smart acceleration, and high quality."[14] Through redesign of Buick models, a price lower than European competitors, and promotion, the marketing program is aimed at getting the target market to believe that the cars have performance, comfort, and value. If the yuppies' attitudes toward Buicks improve, more sales should result.

Does personal makeup change?

Some characteristics of consumers are permanent parts of their makeup. Personality, values, demographic characteristics, and to a lesser extent life-styles typically cannot be changed by the marketing program of a single company. Other characteristics, however, including motives, beliefs,

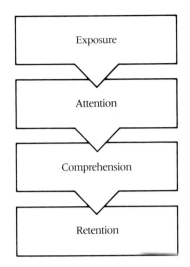

Exhibit 5.4 Steps in consumers' perception process

and attitudes can be influenced. How this influence takes place requires understanding the way in which a marketing mix can affect consumers. Two processes that consumers use to receive and act on information are instrumental: perception and learning.

Perception. Marketing managers know that two people can view exactly the same marketing mix of a company and react in different ways. One person may see the Chevrolet Corvette as a sports car because it is sleek and fast. Another person may see the Corvette as a "muscle car" built for speed but with little of the superior handling expected from sports cars. Part of the reason for this well-known phenomenon is **perception,** the process by which people receive, interpret, and remember information coming from the world around them. Exhibit 5.4 shows the steps in the process.

For a moment try to visualize a man walking down an aisle in a supermarket. All the products shelved on either side of the aisle have gained *exposure* because they are in physical proximity to him. The opportunity exists for the man to notice them. Suppose the man looks to his right and his eyes stop when he sees the cartons of ice cream in a freezer about halfway down the aisle. He is paying *attention* to these cartons because he notices their features such as size, shape, and brand name.

The man picks out one carton from the freezer, looks at the list of ingredients, and thinks, "This ice cream is all natural and very rich." *Comprehension* has taken place because he interpreted something about the ice cream based on his understanding of the information on the carton. Finally, the man remembers an advertisement that he saw earlier in the week explaining how the ice cream was made from all natural ingredients, confirming his impression of the brand. The advertisement's information had gained *retention* because the man remembered it during the time that passed between his seeing it and his decision to purchase the brand.

How does the perception process cause different reactions to the same information (such as that provided by a marketing mix)? The answer lies in the extremely selective way in which people receive and use information. Because the shopper was interested in buying ice cream, he did not walk down all the aisles in the store. Thus products in some aisles were not seen or touched. In effect, they were screened out through *selective exposure.* By looking only for ice cream and ignoring all other products on shelves in the aisle, the man used *selective attention* to further screen out other products. He simply did not let his eyes or hands or any of his other senses notice products that were not of interest.

After reading the carton, the shopper reached his own interpretation of the ice cream's benefits. He did not think that the ice cream was too fattening or possibly spoiled because it had no preservatives. Through *selective comprehension* he chose to believe that the ice cream was "all natural and very rich." Remembering the one advertisement out of all the advertising the man had been exposed to in the past week shows *selective retention* taking place. People only remember a fraction of what they see and hear.

Marketing managers have become creative and resourceful in dealing with these selective perception mechanisms. The task is not easy because so much information from marketing and nonmarketing sources competes for consumers' attention. Marketing managers must find a way to (1) be interesting to target market consumers, (2) be relevant by showing that what the company has to offer is aimed at meeting consumers' needs and wants, and

(3) be different from the competing sources of information, particularly competitive firms, so that the company stands out.

Learning. Although a few characteristics of consumers such as the need to satisfy hunger and thirst (physiologic motives) are innate, most of consumer behavior is learned. **Learning** refers to changes in what consumers believe, in their attitudes, and in how they behave that occur through experience.

Consumers can learn in any of three different ways. First, consumers learn when they are either positively or negatively *rewarded by experience.* Positive rewards make people feel good, usually by satisfying a need or want. Because consumers like to feel good, a positive reward is reinforcing by increasing the chances that the consumer will behave in a similar way the next time the need or want comes up. Negative rewards have just the opposite effect. Learning by rewards establishes a powerful rationale for the marketing concept (discussed in Chapter 1). Getting what you want from a product is rewarding. Thus designing marketing programs that meet customer needs and wants reinforces their purchase choice and can influence them to make the same choice again the next time the product or service must be purchased.

Consumers also learn through *repeated association.* Rewards do not have to be present. Learning occurs through rehearsal or seeing the same thing repeatedly. For instance, frequent advertising showing rugged men using Ford pickup trucks in rough situations causes some consumers to associate ruggedness and durability with the Ford name. Notice that there is no particular reward for making the association. This kind of learning suggests that marketing managers communicate with consumers repeatedly over time to encourage these associations.

Finally, consumers learn through *insight.* Using the power of reasoning, consumers rely on related past experience and incomplete new information to draw conclusions. In this way, they can deal with new situations for which they have limited direct experience. Learning about new products can happen in this way. Prince Manufacturing Company recently brought out a new type of tennis racket, one that is much larger than even the oversized rackets in the company's product lines. Even before a consumer has the opportunity to buy and use the new racket, learning takes place. Experiencing other oversized rackets, inspecting the new racket to see its shape and materials, and examining already-formed beliefs about Prince's reputation as a racket manufacturer help a consumer learn various beliefs about the new racket. None of these experiences is the same as having used the racket repeatedly, and yet the consumer may learn to like the new racket enough to buy it. You can see from this illustration the value of having a strong brand reputation among consumers when a company brings out a new product.

ENVIRONMENTAL INFLUENCES ON CONSUMERS

Consumers' behavior constantly is influenced by what is going on around them. A marketing program must take environmental factors into consideration or risk failure. As an illustration, consider an important marketing challenge for American automobile dealers—how to sell to an increasing percentage (approximately 40 percent in 1982) of car buyers who also happen to be women. Many women want to show their independence and not be patronized or feel threatened by a car's technical features. They want special features such as security systems in cars. Dealer salespersons must adjust their sales presentations to women to help them cope with having to buy and later use a car on their own without help from others.[15] Exhibit 5.5 presents some of the more important environmental influences on consumers.

Marketing program influences

One of the most important influences on consumer decision making is the marketing programs of companies. Each company's program helps create awareness of products offered for sale, educate consumers about what those products can do for them, and helps them form preferences for one product over others. Consumers use the information created by all facets of a marketing program to help them find out what is available, to form likes and dislikes, and to later make up their minds about what to buy. Magic Chef planned a marketing program to improve its reputation for having innovative new products for higher-income households. The company is designing, distributing, and promoting new products with extended capabilities. It has added to its product mix a refrigerator that makes ice cream, a refrigerator with a wine rack, and microwave ovens with fancy features. Products such as these and the accompanying promotion are aimed at influencing consumers to believe that the company is a "leader in innovative products."[16]

Marketing's impact on consumers is even more powerful when all the marketing programs of competing companies are considered together. The variety of information provided through promotion, the continuous stream of new and improved products, and the widespread distribution of these new products help consumers learn over time what to buy to satisfy particular needs and wants. Surprisingly, marketing may even help consumers

Exhibit 5.5 Environmental influences on consumer decision making

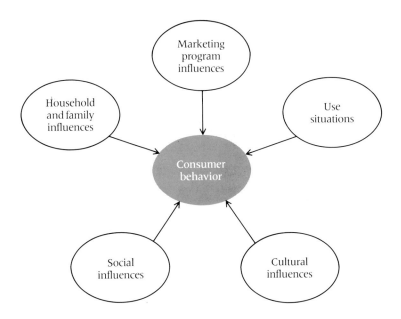

better understand what their own needs and wants are. In this way, marketing develops markets for types of products. Consider all the marketing programs of drug companies. They play an important role in educating consumers about the recognition and treatment of diseases, from common colds to hypertension and heart disease. At the same time, sales of drugs used for these diseases grow as consumers learn the benefits of their use (see Marketalk).

Use situations

Another outside influence is **use situation,** which refers to those characteristics of the immediate time and place in which a person will use a product or service. Situational influences include people present, time of day or season, aromas, weather, pressure to finish a task, or anything else that is part of the immediate surroundings but not part of the person using the product or its marketing mix.[17] For example, consider a husband and wife who want to take special relatives out to dinner. The use situation includes the relatives' presence and their impressions of the occasion, the conversation that will take place, interruptions that may impede conversation, and how much time they can spend at the restaurant.

*Marke*TALK ///

Drug companies use marketing aimed at consumers to build sales of prescription drugs

SOME COMPANIES have to educate consumers to recognize a need or want for products. Drug companies that sell prescription drugs for serious diseases are a case in point. Because doctors prescribe these drugs, the drug companies typically have aimed their marketing programs toward doctors rather than consumers. Yet, consumers buy and use the drugs once they are prescribed. Recognizing that consumers decide when to seek a doctor's help and can influence choice of brand of drug, several drug companies are redirecting some of their promotion toward consumers.

Pfizer has run advertisements that help consumers recognize the symptoms of diabetes. The messages alert people to the se-

riousness of the disease and the need to be checked by a doctor if any symptoms are present. Pfizer expected to increase sales of its drug, Diabinese, as more consumers with diabetes are diagnosed. Management was right. Although the Pfizer advertisements did not mention the drug's brand name, in one year sales of Diabinese increased more than 15 percent. At the same time, many consumers who might have gone untreated now are being helped because the advertising educated them to previously unrecognized symptoms.

Promoting directly to consumers has worked so well that many prescription drug companies are using or considering this approach. For instance, Ciba-Geigy Corporation wants to educate consumers about hypertension; Boots Pharmaceuticals promoted an antiarthritic drug; and Merck & Company has run consumer advertisements for a pneumonia vaccine. Some companies are even running adver-

tisements comparing prices to show consumers which are the lower-priced drug brands.

Using promotion to educate consumers about diseases and drugs also has its critics. Although most doctors are in favor of advertising that discusses disease prevention, they, some pharmaceutical companies, and consumer groups including the Women's Health Network are critical of the promotion of brand-name drugs. All are concerned that patients will request that an advertised drug be prescribed even though they do not know all the factors involved in its use. Doctors would have to spend more time explaining the alternatives. Furthermore, the drug companies are worried that promotion of drugs could lead to increased price competition, which would reduce their profit margins. In spite of these objections, promotion directly to consumers probably is here to stay.

SOURCE: "Going to the public with ads for prescription drugs," *Business Week,* May 21, 1984, pp. 77, 81.

///

Use situation is important because people can anticipate the situation they will be in when using the product or service. The situation, in turn, affects the benefits that consumers seek when buying the product or service. A marketing manager who understands what the use situation is can build a corresponding marketing program with benefits tailored to meet consumers' expectations in that situation. Restaurants that specialize in creating a unique dining atmosphere are successfully applying the use situation by catering to consumers who wish to have a special evening out.

Cultural influences

People in a country share values, ideas, beliefs, and attitudes about a wide variety of issues, appropriate behavior, and objects (including products such as automobiles and houses) that together form a culture. Culture has an impact on buying behavior because it determines what people will accept. A refrigerator manufacturer learned the hard way about culture's influence on buying when an advertisement of its refrigerator showed it stocked with ham. Unfortunately, the advertisement was run in Middle Eastern countries where for religious reasons Moslems do not eat ham. These consumers were offended, and they rejected the product being advertised.[18]

Within most countries are **subcultures,** pockets of people who share values, ideas, beliefs, and attitudes different from the dominant culture of the country. Subculture may be based on the ethnic origin of consumers. For example, French Canadians, living primarily in Quebec, share the language and cultural heritage of France rather than of Canada. Other subcultures may be based on religion (a Catholic subculture), race (a black subculture), or geographic concentration (the southern subculture in the United States). Marketing programs can be aimed at subcultures as target markets. Grocery stores in a French Canadian area do this by altering advertising messages and food selections to cater to the preferences of that subculture.

Most countries also have a social class structure along with culture. A **social class** is a large group of people who are held in approximately equal esteem; share similar cultural values, ideas, beliefs, and attitudes; and tend to socialize among themselves rather than with people from other social classes. People arrange social classes into a hierarchy of esteem and importance. Exhibit 5.6 shows a social class structure in the United States; it should help you see how belonging to a social class can influence consumer behavior. As you read the descriptions of the classes, try not to be offended by the words used. Their purpose is to show how people themselves describe social classes. You may not like the fact that people are judged by others to be in higher or lower social classes, but the phenomenon is real and must be considered by marketing managers.

A company may select target markets according to social class. For example, some department stores target middle and upper classes, whereas others target working-class people. J. C. Penney, for years perceived as a discount store, has lately been offering higher-priced clothing such as Santa Cruz separates and Halston fashions to appeal to a more middle- and upper-class clientele. Zayre department stores, on the other hand, appeal to

Exhibit 5.6   Social class structure in America

Upper Americans
   Upper-Upper (0.3%)—The "capital S society" world of inherited wealth, aristocratic
      names
   Lower-Upper (1.2%)—The newer social elite, drawn from current professional, cor-
      porate leadership
   Upper-Middle (12.5%)—The rest of college-graduate managers and professionals;
      life-style centers on private clubs, causes, and the arts
Middle Americans
   Middle Class (32%)—Average-pay white-collar workers and their blue-collar friends;
      live on the "better side of town," try to "do the proper thing"
   Working Class (38%)—Average-pay blue-collar workers; lead "working class life
      style" whatever the income, school background, and job
Lower Americans
   "A lower group of people but not the lowest" (9%)—Working, not on welfare;
      living standard is just above poverty; behavior judged "crude," "trashy"
   "Real lower-lower" (7%)—On welfare; visibly poverty-stricken; usually out of work
      (or have "the dirtiest jobs"); "bums," "common criminals"

SOURCE: From a study reported in Richard P. Coleman, "The continuing significance of social class to
marketing," *Journal of Consumer Research,* Vol. 10 (Dec. 1983), p. 267. Reprinted with permission from
the *Journal of Consumer Research,* 10 (December) 1983.

working-class consumers by carrying low-priced, modest quality name
brand merchandise and by having a no-frills interior to their stores.

Social influences

Consumers can be influenced by a wide variety of people. Consumers
looking for support, information, or advice concerning a purchase may be
influenced by friends, co-workers, neighbors, teachers, and people in social
organizations such as a garden club. Some of these influences come from
reference groups, groups composed of two or more people who share
values and beliefs concerning acceptable behavior. Other influences come
from **opinion leaders,** persons whose opinions a consumer seeks.

Marketing managers must be aware of these influences on purchase
decisions. Interaction among consumers certainly is not controllable by a
manager, but actions may be taken to make sure the influence is positive.
Consider again Johnson County Hospital, which completed a study of its
markets. One important finding was that people relied almost entirely on
others in the county for information about both doctors and hospitals, as
indicated by Exhibit 5.7.

Exhibit 5.7   How consumers find out about doctors and hospitals

Information Source	Doctor (%)	Hospital (%)
Recommendation by a friend	30	21
Recommendation by a doctor	26	35
Recommendation by a relative	20	17
Opinion of someone who works in local hospital	11	18
Recommendation by an employer	4	4
Listing in the telephone book	3	3
Advertisement	1	1
Another source	5	2

SOURCE: Unpublished report of a study of health care needs in a county served by a
Tennessee hospital.

HALSTON III. *From head to toe.*
Because there's nothing more beautiful than a confident woman.

You're looking smarter than ever. JCPenney.

"You're looking smarter than ever" is JC Penney's theme for the new fashion campaign to inform shoppers the store is changing. The company is well into a five-year, $1 billion store modernization program that is designed to counter shrinking profits and smaller sales gain. (Courtesy JC Penney Company)

Based on these results, what marketing actions would you take if you were the administrator of Johnson County Hospital? Notice that two notably important sources of influence are doctors and hospital employees. One action you might take is to build and maintain strong relations with the doctors who use the hospital and with staff employees. Perhaps discussions with these opinion leaders can enlist their help in the promotional effort. Another action might be to ensure that patients using the hospital are satisfied with their care so they will talk positively about the hospital to their families and friends. In these ways, the hospital can reach people in the county through favorable opinions communicated from one person to another.

Household and family influences

A sometimes overlooked fact of consumer buying is that often families, not individuals, make purchase decisions. Many products, such as furniture, cars, food, linen, and televisions, are used by all persons in a family. Other products may be purchased by one person but used by someone else in the family. Consider the following facts:

Although the size of the teenage market has declined and is not expected to grow for the next 10 years, marketers should not ignore 13- to 19-year-olds: A soon-to-be-released Young & Rubicam Inc. study shows that their disposable income is growing (56% work full-time or part-time, and 48% receive a weekly allowance) and that brand loyalties developed during these teen years are lasting. Y & R also reports that 60% of teens have a hand in making out the family grocery list, and 40% select the brands to be bought. Further, as the number of working mothers increases, teens will be relied on more heavily for family shopping. Right now, 34% of teen females and 18% of males do some major food shopping each month.[19]

To see how marketing managers use information on family purchase decision making, we continue the Johnson County Hospital illustration. The market study discovered that decisions on what doctor to use are made jointly by husbands and wives in approximately one-half of the families studied. In many other families surveyed, each spouse had some influence on the other's decision. How can the hospital's managers apply this information? For one thing, target markets must be considered as comprising husbands and wives. For another, promotion of the quality of treatment in the hospital must be directed at both spouses, even though only one is likely to use the hospital at one time.

HOW CONSUMERS DECIDE TO BUY

Our discussion to this point has concentrated on personal and environmental factors that influence consumer behavior. Now we consider how consumers make purchase decisions, the aspect of consumer behavior of central interest to marketing managers. Purchase decision making refers to the steps that consumers go through beginning with problem recognition and ending with choice and postchoice satisfaction.[20]

High-involvement decision making

Not all consumer decision making is alike. **High-involvement decision making** is used for purchases that are related to important motives or values or are significantly relevant to a life-style. For these items, the purchase decision process is likely to be extensive and to take a measurable amount of effort. **Low-involvement decision making** is used for purchases that are not relevant to the consumer. This process is typically much shorter than high-involvement decision making. Let us start with the high-involvement purchasing process, the steps of which are shown in Exhibit 5.8. As you read about the steps, visualize a young couple, the Hansens, who are purchasing a camera.

Problem recognition. The Hansens, while looking through the family's photograph album, were displeased to discover that many of their pictures seemed fuzzy. Later in the week, Mr. Hansen talked with a friend experienced in photography, who pointed out that the Hansen's camera was totally automatic and could not be focused for each picture. That night, the Hansens decided that their camera was not adequate for their picture-taking needs and resolved to purchase a new camera.

The Hansens experienced *problem recognition*, a realization that the present solution to a need or want does not match the preferred solution.[21] This realization can happen quickly, in a matter of seconds, or take a while, days, weeks, or even months, to occur. For the Hansens problem recognition took days because they had to learn about cameras and photography before they concluded that their camera was not what they ideally wanted.

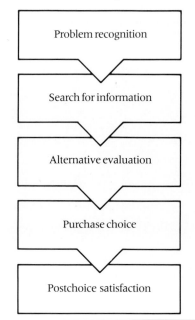

Exhibit 5.8 Consumer decision making for a high-involvement product

Search for information. Problem recognition leads to an intention to buy a product or service. A consumer, however, may not immediately know what to buy. The Hansens were not sure what type or brand of camera they wanted. They needed information to help them decide. *Search for information* includes all those activities that a consumer does to get information about purchase alternatives. Recalling from past experience and seeking information from outside sources such as family members, friends, advertising, salespersons, and packages are part of a search.

Many high-involvement purchases require information from outside sources. The Hansens were in the process of high-involvement decision making because a new camera was expensive, the choice was important to them, and neither knew much about cameras. They needed to learn what types of cameras were available other than the kind they already had, and what benefits these types of cameras had to offer. New information has value when it helps consumers learn about product and brand alternatives, allowing them to make a more informed choice.

Alternative evaluation. When consumers find several purchase alternatives, they proceed to *alternative evaluation,* which involves determining how well an alternative meets needs and wants. Both beliefs and attitudes play important roles in helping a consumer see which alternative is best. Returning to the Hansens, through information search they learned that cameras have attributes such as interchangeable lenses, adjustable focus, and easy to use controls. These attributes enable the camera to deliver benefits. Some attributes are more important than others because they are more instrumental in determining whether a product alternative will satisfy needs and wants. These attributes become criteria for evaluating products.

Beliefs link criteria and attitudes together in helping consumers evaluate alternatives. Although many different beliefs may develop from information search, the most important beliefs concern the criteria. The Hansens picked out several criteria important to them including price, adjustable focus, interchangeable lenses, and light weight. As they learned about cameras, the Hansens were able to evaluate each one based on what they believed it had in the way of attributes they wanted. As they acquired beliefs, they formed attitudes toward different brands. Generally, the better a product performs on attributes used as criteria, the more a consumer will like it.

Sometimes people directly compare different alternatives. Each alternative will have definite strengths and probably some weaknesses, too. When deciding which alternative they most prefer, consumers may weigh the strengths against the weaknesses of each one, making trade-offs between attributes. In this way, strong features compensate for weak features. Market researchers sometimes call this kind of evaluation process *compensatory product evaluation* because trade-offs on attributes are being made. The Hansens used this kind of evaluation only for the two brands they seriously considered for purchase. They weighed the strengths of Canon and of Minolta (e.g., a wide variety of lenses, light weight, well-placed controls) against the weaknesses of each (e.g., high price, larger size). The more the strengths of a brand outweighed its weaknesses, the more the Hansens liked it.

What happens when there are many products and many criteria on which to evaluate products? The compensatory approach would take too much time and effort. Imagine the Hansens trying to evaluate ten different cameras on ten different criteria! They would be overwhelmed with all the possible considerations. When there are many alternatives, consumers screen them by using *noncompensatory product evaluations*. This term means that alternatives are eliminated from further consideration if they do not meet a particular requirement on one or a few criteria considered one at a time. The Hansens followed this approach by setting a price limit of $200 for the camera. They did not consider any brand costing more than $200, no matter what other criteria it met.

You can easily see important implications of noncompensatory evaluations for marketing strategy. A company's product must first meet the requirement on the screening criteria or the brand will not be considered as a purchase alternative. Nikon, the Japanese manufacturer of high-priced cameras, seems to understand this point because it has been widening its product line by offering models over a broader price range. An important advantage of this strategy is the greater likelihood of getting the Nikon brand considered by consumers who use price as a screening criterion.

Purchase choice. Alternative evaluation leads to *purchase choice*—that is, either the consumer buys or does not buy. In reality not one but several choices are being made. Some possibilities include

- *What product to buy.* Sometimes two or more product types compete for the same need. A consumer first chooses which product to buy.
- *What brand to buy.* Even for the same type of product, a consumer must choose which of several brands to buy.
- *When to buy.* The timing of the purchase is a decision. A consumer must decide whether to buy immediately after evaluating products and brands or to wait for a while to buy.
- *Where to buy.* Consumers are faced with an increasingly large number of options as to where to buy a brand. There are often competing stores as well as nonstore options. Mail-order, catalogue, and electronic shopping are a few nonstore ways to buy that are becoming popular.
- *How to pay.* A consumer may pay cash or defer payment with credit cards, bank loans, store credit, or other means.

These choices are interrelated because a decision on one aspect can affect decisions on another. Suppose the Hansens decided to buy a 35mm, single lens reflex camera (a type of camera) and preferred a Canon to a Nikon (brand preference). Will they buy a Canon? Not necessarily. The store that carries Canon may not accept the Hansens' credit card, or the Hansens may feel more comfortable buying at a store that handles Nikon, but not Canon. As a result they could end up purchasing their second favorite brand, Nikon.

Postchoice satisfaction. Consumer behavior continues after a purchase decision has been made as consumers evaluate the product purchased during and after using it. This evaluation causes *satisfaction* or *dissatisfaction*, an emotional response to the performance of a product or service. Do you remember coming out of a restaurant with a warm, pleasant feeling as you thought of the fine meal you just had? That feeling is satisfaction. Of course, satisfaction also has a negative side. You may have read a book that did not entertain you as much as you wanted it to, and you felt disappointed or frustrated. Those feelings are dissatisfaction.

How do these feelings arise? Consumers set standards for the performance of the purchased brand. A standard may be as simple as expecting the brand to perform as well as it has in the past, or the standard might be that the brand purchased should perform as well as that of the brand previously owned.[22] The Hansens' standard seemed to be the performance of their previous camera. They bought a Canon 35mm camera and were very satisfied with the improved pictures compared to those taken with their old camera.

Having satisfied customers is especially important to marketing managers because these feelings can influence what consumers do in the future. Most businesses depend on customers coming back to buy again as well as getting favorable "word-of-mouth" advertising as one customer talks to another. The following finding from a consumer behavior study demonstrates the payoff to automobile businesses of customer satisfaction:

> The payoff can be handsome. Technical Assistance Research Programs Inc. (TARP), a Washington consulting firm that specializes in consumer behavior, found that a disgruntled car owner will vent his frustrations to 16 people. But a satisfied customer will burble the good news to eight people and is likely to buy four more cars of the same make over the next 12 years.[23]

Applying decision-making information. Companies go to great lengths to learn about customers' decision making. This information is valuable because it yields insights into customer market requirements. Results from studying problem recognition explain what people want when using a product. Studying search and evaluation helps managers understand how consumers find and evaluate alternative products and brands (see Marketool). Determining how consumers make choices lets managers know what must happen to complete a sale (e.g., if credit is needed, what consumers do when their favorite brand is not available). Evaluating customers' satisfaction enables managers to see what is necessary to ensure satisfied customers in the future. These insights are well worth the cost of studying consumer purchase decision making.

Low-involvement decision making

High-involvement purchasing can be a rather extensive, step-by-step decision-making process. Not all products and services are purchased in this way. Products such as salt, paper towels, laundry soap, pencils, lightbulbs, and toothbrushes usually are not particularly important in a consumer's life. Thus there is not much incentive to expend a lot of effort or time on search for information or evaluation of alternatives. Furthermore, consumers may not even have noticeable likes or dislikes at the time of purchase of a low-involvement product.

Look at Exhibit 5.9 and compare it to Exhibit 5.8. You can see that low-involvement decision making has a slightly different sequence of steps than does high-involvement decision making. The major difference is in the evaluation of alternatives. When high-involvement products are purchased, each alternative is evaluated before a choice is made. But when a low-involvement product is bought, little of this aspect of purchase decision

Exhibit 5.9 Low-involvement consumer decision making

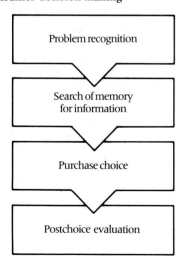

making occurs prior to choice. A consumer may buy a brand for the first time without comparing it to any other and without really liking or disliking it. Because little if any evaluation takes place, there is also little need for information search from outside sources.

MarkeTOOL

Image studies probe how consumers evaluate alternatives

THROUGH EXPERIENCE, consumers develop images of brands, and these images can influence their purchase choices. An image is the impression that comes to mind when a person thinks of a brand, including his or her overall attitude toward it.

The payoff from studying these feelings comes when marketing managers gain insights into why consumers have the images that they do. An *image study* identifies beliefs that are contributing to a positive image as well as those that are contributing to a negative image. Managers can decide how best to reinforce the favorable beliefs, and if necessary, to try to change beliefs that are not positive.

A department store chain in a medium-sized southern city used an image study to evaluate marketing strategy for a new store that had just opened. Management knew from previous studies that customers had certain attributes they sought in a store in which they shopped for fashion clothing, for example, quality merchandise, variety of merchandise styles and sizes, and friendly salespersons. A complete list of attributes is shown in the diagram. Consumers participating in the image study were asked to express beliefs concerning the extent to which the new store and two of the competing stores offered these attributes. The results as shown to management are image profiles portrayed in the diagram. For each attribute, the average belief ratings are shown for the three stores. Ratings on the left side identify those that are contributing to a positive image, while the further to the right the rating is the more it detracts from a positive image. All ratings together, as connected by the lines or dashes, reveal a profile that describes image over all the attributes.

The images explain how consumers are evaluating the three stores on important criteria for choosing a place to shop. The new store has been successful in many ar-

eas in building a strong image. The store interior (pleasantness and shopping efficiency), services, merchandise (quality and variety), and salespersons (friendliness and helpfulness) are strengths and should be reinforced through the store's marketing program. Management, however, saw that price was one of several weaknesses to correct. After doing some comparative shopping, managers found out that the new store's prices were com-

parable to other stores for similar quality merchandise. Thus, promotion was needed to change consumers' erroneous beliefs about price. Convenience to the store was improved as other stores opened in the mall area and as access roads and parking were improved. Promotion helped inform customers of these improvements to change consumers' beliefs about convenience.

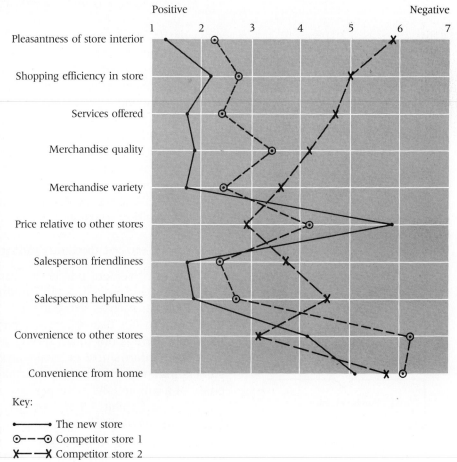

Key:
•——• The new store
⊙– –⊙ Competitor store 1
✕– –✕ Competitor store 2

Low-involvement purchasing has important implications for a marketing program. For example, consider the challenge for Proctor & Gamble as they introduce a new brand of dishwashing soap. Knowing that soap is a low-involvement product, what general guidelines for promotion do you think Procter & Gamble should follow?

Procter & Gamble would waste money if it used advertising to educate consumers about all the soap's features and benefits. Consumers probably would not listen to the advertising because they are not involved with the soap purchase. Procter & Gamble must concentrate on getting people to try the brand. Simple messages about its most important benefit might be coupled with incentives to use it the first time. For instance, one approach often employed for low-involvement products is to distribute samples or coupons, which encourage consumers to try the product without obligation. Advertising might help by informing consumers that the new product is available in stores. Setting a low price and distributing widely to get the product in front of consumers wherever they are shopping can effectively support this strategy, too.

SUMMARY

Successful marketing plans do not just happen by chance but are derived from the insight gained from learning about markets. Most importantly, a marketing plan must lay out exactly how the company is going to meet buyers' market requirements for a purchase. These requirements can only be fully understood by analyzing buyers in advance of designing the plan. Implementing and controlling marketing plans also benefit from buyer analyses showing how well the marketing program has been received by buyers and where any problems with the program may lie.

Analyzing buyers is really a process of using information to answer several key questions. Managers must know who buyers are to select the best target markets for the company. They must understand what influences customers' buying decisions so that the marketing program can be tailored to fit in with these influences. Finally, marketing managers must know how buying decisions are made to know what requirements have to be met, and how to reach people who are making the decisions.

Although answering such straightforward questions seems simple, analyzing buyers takes experience and skill. Personal makeup, such as demographic and life-style characteristics, motives, personality, values, beliefs, and attitudes, are important influences on consumers' decision making. They help determine needs and wants and affect how consumers make decisions. Some aspects of personal makeup are permanent such as demographic makeup, personality, and values. However, through perception and learning consumers use information to change other aspects such as motives, beliefs, and attitudes. Thus marketing managers can influence consumers by using marketing programs to help people learn about products and services.

Consumers respond to influences from their environment such as the marketing program, use situation characteristics, culture, social class status, and family or household members as well as on past experience. Marketing managers must be aware that the influence of the company's marketing program is operating along with the many other influences from these other uncontrollable sources. Only by understanding these sources can the program be designed to have the greatest impact on consumers.

Perhaps the most important skill needed to analyze buyers is having a sound perspective on buyer behavior. A commonly used perspective views buyer behavior as a decision-making process in which consumers follow steps to make purchases that satisfy needs and wants. The steps for high-involvement purchases include problem recognition, search, evaluation, purchase choice, and satisfaction or dissatisfaction. Because the purchase is important, consumers are likely to spend significant effort during the steps. In contrast, low-involvement purchases are made much more quickly, often with much less search or evaluation prior to purchase.

KEY TERMS

buyer behavior	beliefs	social class
consumer buyers	attitudes	reference groups
consumer market	perception	opinion leaders
motives	learning	high-involvement decision making
personality	use situation	low-involvement decision making
value	subcultures	

QUESTIONS FOR REVIEW AND DISCUSSION

1. Why is purchase decision making the central focus for the definition of buyer behavior?

2. How can analysis of buyer behavior help a manager develop a marketing strategy?

3. How can analysis of buyer behavior help a manager implement a marketing strategy?

4. How can analysis of buyer behavior help a manager control a marketing strategy?

5. What three questions must a marketing manager be able to answer about buyer behavior?

6. How can demographic characteristics of consumers be used to help managers define target markets?

7. Can life-styles of consumers be used to define target markets? Why or why not?

8. What are the most useful aspects of a consumer's personal makeup for helping managers understand what people in target markets are like? Why did you choose these aspects?

9. What is a use situation? Why should a marketing manager be concerned about target market consumers' use situations?

10. Is it possible to always identify one individual as the one who made the final purchase decision for a product or service? Why or why not?

11. How does social class influence consumer behavior?

12. What is an opinion leader?

13. Is a company's marketing mix an influence on consumer behavior? Why or why not?

14. If a company is successful in getting consumers' attention with a marketing program, is the program guaranteed to be successful? Why or why not?

15. How are beliefs and attitudes related to each other?

16. What are the three ways in which consumers learn about products and services?

17. Explain the difference between high-involvement and low-involvement decision making.

18. How are attributes, criteria, beliefs, and attitudes involved in consumers' evaluation of alternative products or services?

19. What is problem recognition? Does consumer purchasing always begin with problem recognition?

20. What is consumer satisfaction? Why should marketing managers be concerned about consumers' satisfaction with their company's products?

21. Under what circumstances would a consumer search for information?

BUILDING YOUR PORTFOLIO

Do you think you can use consumer behavior information to predict the purchase choice of a real consumer? Select a student who has recently bought a brand within a product or service category. (Cameras, sports equipment, restaurants, watches, clothing, transportation products, or grooming aids are product or service categories you might try.) The brand should have cost more than $10. Do not ask the student what type of product or brand he or she purchased within the product category. Instead, develop a list of questions for your consumer that are derived from the chapter's discussions of consumer behavior. You may ask anything you want *except* what product or brand they actually bought.

Record your consumer's answers to these questions. Evaluate the answers and use your results to predict what product type and brand your consumer actually purchased. Finally, go back to the consumer and find out what he or she actually purchased.

How close was your prediction? If you predicted correctly, answers to which questions helped you the most (e.g., life-style, attitudes, beliefs, motives, values)? If your prediction was wrong, where did you miss—on product type, brand, or both? What additional questions might you have asked to do better?

NOTES

1. "Large numbers of husbands buy household products, do housework." *Marketing News,* Oct. 3, 1980, pp. 1, 3.
2. A similar definition is found in James F. Engel and Roger D. Blackwell, *Consumer Behavior.* Chicago: The Dryden Press, 1982, p. 9.
3. "Big beer's Titanic brawl." *Time,* Aug. 16, 1982, p. 48.
4. Ibid.
5. "Action-oriented research spells success for new Seagram wine." *Marketing News,* Jan. 9, 1981, p. 4.
6. Bernie Whalen, "Hightech research approach yields memorable, meaningful brand names." *Marketing News,* May 13, 1983, p. 1.
7. "Consumer preference must be reflected in every level of corporation." *Marketing News,* Dec. 11, 1981, p. 13.
8. Heather S. York and M. Lynne Keener, "Cluster analysis reveals four consumer segments in solar water heater market." *Marketing News,* Apr. 30, 1982, p. 8.
9. For more discussion of the meaning of life-style, see Emanuel Demby, "Psychographics and From Whence It Came," in William D. Wells (Ed.), *Life Style and Psychographics.* Chicago: American Marketing Association, 1974, pp. 9–30.
10. William Wells, "Psychographics: A critical review." *Journal of Marketing Research,* Vol. XII (May 1975), p. 202.
11. Engel and Blackwell, op. cit., p. 303.
12. Abraham H. Maslow, *Motivation and Personality.* New York: Harper & Row, 1954.
13. Donald E. Vinson, "Personal Values: An Approach to Market Segmentation," in Kenneth L. Bernhardt (Ed.), *Marketing: 1776–1976 and Beyond.* Chicago: American Marketing Association, 1976, p. 316.
14. "Detroit's new goal: Putting yuppies in the driver's seat." *Business Week,* Sep. 3, 1984, p. 46.
15. "Wine, baubles, and glamour are used to help lure female consumers to Ford's showrooms." *Marketing News,* Aug. 6, 1982, p. 1.
16. "Magic Chef's new recipe calls for upscale appliances." *Business Week,* June 20, 1983, p. 73.
17. Russell W. Belk, "Situational variables in consumer behavior." *Journal of Consumer Research,* Vol. 2 (Dec. 1975), pp. 157–164.
18. David A. Ricks, *Big Business Blunders.* Homewood, Ill.: Dow Jones–Irwin, 1983, p. 66.

19. "Teenagers: Rising in income and firm in brand loyalty." *Business Week,* Apr. 23, 1984, p. 51. Reprinted from the Apr. 23, 1984 issue of *Business Week* by special permission, © 1984 by McGraw-Hill, Inc.
20. Engel and Blackwell, op. cit., pp. 21–38.
21. Ibid., p. 301.
22. Robert B. Woodruff, Ernest R. Cadotte, and Roger L. Jenkins, "Modeling consumer satisfaction processes using experience-based norms." *Journal of Marketing Research,* Aug. 1983, p. 296–297.
23. "Detroit's tonic for lemon buyers." *Business Week,* Apr. 4, 1983, p. 54.

Case 5.1

Prince Manufacturing

PRINCE MANUFACTURING, the company that made the king-size tennis racket famous, is taking a swat at new markets. For the first time in its nine-year history, the company is coming out with two new racket sizes: one smaller than its standard model and a superlarge racket that a sporting goods salesman describes as a "garbage can cover." The Princeton, New Jersey, company wants to keep its leading 30% share in a racket market that's lost its bounce. According to the National Sporting Goods Association, only three million rackets, valued at $170 million, were sold in the U.S. last year vs. over eight million at the 1976 peak.

Prince became the top-seeded weapon maker because it convinced many players of the none-too-surprising proposition that it's easier to hit a tennis ball with a

SOURCE: Brian Dumaine, "Prince gets into some new rackets," *Fortune,* Oct. 29, 1984, p. 78. Reprinted by permission.

big racket than with a little one. Prince's popular 110-square-inch full-size racket is based on a 1975 U.S. patent awarded to Howard Head, the inventor who founded Head Ski Co., a maker of skis and tennis rackets. His patent covers rackets varying in size from 85 to 130 square inches. (A standard racket face is about 70 square inches.) Head, who joined Prince Manufacturing a few years after his company was bought by AMF, decided to market only the 110-square-incher, which became the most popular high-priced racket on the courts. Prince kept this full-size racket selling by adding models made of exotic materials—magnesium ($115 suggested retail price), graphite ($250), and boron ($450).

Prince will now try to exploit both the large and small ends of Head's patent. The new $125 supersize magnesium racket has a 125-square-inch head, which pushes the size limit under International Tennis Federation rules. Prince is pitching the supersize specifically to the doubles player, and it should appeal mainly to

players who like to plant themselves at the net and block the ball back. Even the company admits that the supersize isn't designed for ground strokes from the baseline.

Prince's other new racket, a 90-square-incher, *is* meant for those long hard shots more typical of singles play. This entry competes in the market for mid-size rackets, the slammers recently taken up by such pros as John McEnroe and Jimmy Connors. This is where the action is—sales are expected to increase 15% this year. AMF's Head and Kennex, a Taiwanese brand, dominate this part of the market with rackets slightly smaller than Prince's patented size. Prince claims that its new mid-size racket has a 38% bigger sweet spot than Head's best seller. Sweet spot is a nebulous concept that generally refers to the area of the racket where a player should get the most solid hit. George Vaughn of Head, based in Plainsboro, New Jersey, says, "If I put all the rackets claiming larger sweet spots together, they'd go to the West Coast."

QUESTIONS

1. What environmental influences on consumer tennis racket buyers might be causing the drop in tennis racket sales to the current level of 3 million?

2. Might changes in the personal makeup of tennis racket buyers also be causing the drop in tennis racket sales?

3. What information concerning consumer behavior of tennis racket buyers does Prince Manufacturing's marketing managers already have as evidenced by the case discussion?

4. Do you feel that the consumer behavior information you identi-

fied (for question 3) is adequate for planning a marketing strategy to accompany the introduction into markets of the new supersized and midsized tennis racket models? Why or why not?

5. Assuming that the consumer behavior information you identified (for question 3) is the extent of what management knows, suggest additional buyer behavior information that would help Prince's managers develop a marketing plan for each of the two new tennis racket models.

Case 5.2

Howard Johnson Co.

SHORTLY AFTER G. Michael Hostage took over as chairman of Howard Johnson Co., he announced plans to overhaul the company. At that time, the dowdy chain

SOURCE: "Howard Johnson: Is it too late to fix up its faded 1950s image?" *Business Week,* Oct. 22, 1984, p. 90. Reprinted by special permission; © 1984 by McGraw-Hill, Inc.

hadn't refurbished any of its orange-roofed hotels or restaurants for nearly 20 years and was losing market share rapidly. Hostage set out boldly to update the chain's image as well as its properties.

Although Hostage now claims that HoJo has made "a quantum leap" toward catching up with rivals, most outsiders describe

the move as more of a crawl. About $350 million has been spent so far on a program to build a new chain of flagship hotels, renovate existing lodging, and upgrade the restaurant chain, but a negative image persists. "I don't think anybody could pull [a turnaround] off," says J. Willard Marriott Jr., chief executive of Marriott Corp. Howard Johnson "has too much outdated

product that they can't do anything with."
Adds one company watcher: "The orange
roofs are still real dogs."

To make matters worse, Howard Johnson's British parent, Imperial Group PLC, is equally pessimistic about the company's progress. Imperial Chairman Geoffrey C. Kent, who lured Hostage from Continental Baking Co., is facing pressure from the board to dump him—and HoJo. Since 1980, when Imperial purchased the Quincy (Mass.) company, sales have grown only 22%, to $750 million. Earnings have been consistently flat, reaching $38 million before interest or taxes last year.

Industry sources say the British conglomerate's search for a buyer has sparked much interest—primarily for the real estate—but no offers. Hostage himself is trying to put together a leveraged buyout but has been unable to raise the financing. Analysts estimate that because of the strong dollar, Imperial could sell HoJo for about half the $630 million it paid for the company without losing money.

Nonetheless, Hostage, 51, is plunging ahead with the company's face-lift. The keystone of his turnaround strategy is Howard Johnson's new Plaza-Hotels. So far, Hostage has opened eight of the mid-priced, full-service hotels and hopes to open 100 more within five years, at an average cost of $20 million each. But competition is tough in HoJo's traditional market segment, and many of its rivals—chains such as Holiday Inns, Best Western, and Ramada Inn—began upgrading their facilities several years ago, while Howard Johnson clung to its faded, 1950s, turnpike image.

As a result, HoJo's average occupancy rate is a few percentage points below the industry average of 68%. HoJo has refurbished nearly all of the company-owned lodges and hotels—about 25% of the 500 total—but it has rehabilitated less than one-third of its franchised properties. Hostage says the remainder will have to renovate by mid-1987 or lose their franchises. But operators have been reluctant, and more than 40 franchisees have left the system since 1982.

As franchisees flee, Hostage is trying to restructure the managements of the hotels HoJo owns. He has merged the staffs of restaurants and hotels that are at the same location and given them greater control. Bettering the chain's infamously undependable service has suddenly become a priority. Hostage created the company's first national sales staff, updated the antiquated reservation system, and boosted the company's advertising budget to $5.8 million from virtually nothing. He also is performing major surgery on HoJo's restaurants—changing menus and replacing vinyl booths with wooden tables and chairs.

A no-nonsense manager who worked his way through business school washing dishes and digging sewers, Hostage admits the restaurants' bad reputation is a difficult burden. "The only way we're going to make a substantial difference," says the former Marriott executive, "is to do something dramatic." Hostage plans to close as many as 100 marginally profitable restaurants and is converting the company's one-hundred turnpike restaurants into Burger King Corp. franchises—a belated admission that fast food has replaced

HoJo cola and hot dogs as travelers' staples.

The company is testing four concepts and will implement two of them at existing HoJos. Two of the test restaurants, Pickle Lily's and Bumbershoots, resemble HoJo's 200-unit, highly profitable Ground Round chain, which aims its inexpensive fare at the young-adult drinking crowd. One-year-old Bumbershoots, which already is ringing up $2.5 million a year, replaced a traditional HoJo that produced annual sales of $750,000, Hostage says. Volume has nearly tripled at Pickle Lily's as well. Paddywacks, the third concept, is a moderately priced coffee shop catering to families. Hostage has high hopes for HoJo's first Deli Baker Ice Cream Maker, a restaurant with take-out counters.

Despite the superficial changes, Hostage has done little to correct the company's shortage of able managers. He did begin college recruiting last year, nabbing four of the top 10 graduates from Cornell University's restaurant management program. But again, critics say Hostage is moving too slowly in hiring and in ridding the company of unproductive employees.

Hostage firmly believes that Howard Johnson can catch up with its rivals but figures it will take three years—far too long for Imperial. And sources say prospective buyers, unwilling to defer investment returns, would sell off chunks of the company. Either way, it appears the orange roofs that dotted American highways for 60 years are going the way of roadside Burma Shave signs.

QUESTIONS

1. Can advertising alone change Howard Johnson's image among consumers? Why or why not?

2. Explain the ways in which consumers' images can be changed.

3. What specific information about consumers' purchase decision-making process should Howard Johnson's managers have to determine what adjustments in the company's marketing program are needed to change the company's hotel and restaurant image?

4. Should Howard Johnson's managers be concerned about environmental influences on their target consumers? Why or why not?

5. Could changes in the personal makeup of consumers be causing part of Howard Johnson's performance problems? Why or why not?

6 Industrial Buying Behavior

When you finish this chapter, you will understand

☐ That many different kinds of organizations buy goods and services

☐ The ways in which industrial buying behavior differs from consumer buying behavior

☐ How buyers in industrial markets are identified

☐ The environmental factors that influence industrial buying decisions

☐ How industrial buying decisions are made

IBM educates as it promotes because industrial buyers are often less informed about the optimum use of computers in their organizations than they are about other purchases.

An emerging technology has captured manufacturing companies' attention. Coming out of product development laboratories and onto production lines are machines that can see. Using computers to analyze and interpret images coming from one or more cameras, the vision systems can duplicate some of the skills of a human observer. Robotic Vision Systems has sold a system that can see in three dimensions and is used to guide a robot that welds and checks ship propellers. Many manufacturing companies welcome the prospect of having vision systems replace human eyes for quality control, for guiding robots, or for other repetitive jobs requiring vision.

Sales of vision systems are still small—$80 million in 1984. One problem is convincing buyers—usually plant engineers—that the machines can do the job expected of them. Apparently, these engineers have strong opinions about what the machines should be able to do to satisfactorily replace workers. They also worry that vision systems will not stand up to the rough environment of the factory. Another problem is that buyers want machine vision systems tailored to their unique needs. Thus sellers cannot mass produce the systems to gain economies of scale cost advantages. Instead, vision systems have to be custom built for each customer.

In spite of the problems, the vision systems are here to stay. As a manager for a consumer product manufacturer said, "We know we have to apply this technology in the next five years."[1]

IN THE WORLD OF BUSINESS, considerable buying and selling goes on between organizations. Sellers such as Robotic Vision Systems must develop, implement, and control marketing strategy for markets in which customers are employees of buyer organizations. Success of a strategy depends on identifying viable markets and meeting the needs and wants of buyers in those markets. For instance, to build the emerging market for machine vision systems, Robotic and other sellers will have to overcome buyers' objections to current visions systems. Thus analyzing buyer behavior is as important a responsibility for marketing managers in companies selling to organizations as it is for companies selling to consumers.

Although many of the concepts of consumer buying behavior apply to purchasing by organizations, organizational buying differs in important ways from consumer behavior. For this reason, we devote this chapter to examining the buying behavior of organizations. The first section defines organizational or industrial buying behavior. Next, we look more closely at how industrial buying behavior differs from consumer buying. Subsequent sections examine important ideas about how organizations make purchase decisions.

DEFINING INDUSTRIAL BUYER BEHAVIOR

Organizations as buyers

Many different kinds of organizations buy products and services. Some of these differences are evident in the way the U.S. government classifies organizations. Exhibit 6.1 shows the number of establishments of each type in the classification. Although these numbers do not approach the size of consumer markets, literally thousands of organizations buy products and services. We use the term **industrial buying** to refer to purchasing by these organizations.

Most organizations are quite small. One way to measure size is by number of employees. Exhibit 6.2 shows the percentage of all manufacturers in each of five different size categories. Notice that 67.5 percent of manufacturers have fewer than twenty employees, and less than 1 percent

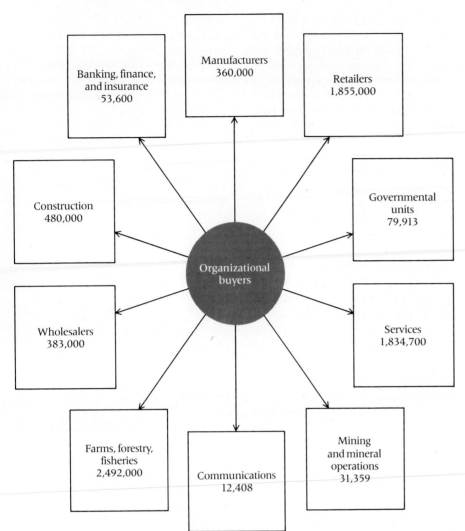

Exhibit 6.1 Organizations in the United States making up industrial markets for products and services (1977–1978)
SOURCE: *Statistical Abstract of the United States: 1984*, Washington D.C.: Bureau of the Census, U.S. Department of Commerce, 1983.

have one thousand or more employees. The largest manufacturing firms account for the majority of value added (the value added by a manufacturer to a raw material or commodity) and shipments of products. As buyers, the relatively few large manufacturers account for the bulk of all purchases by manufacturers. The same pattern also holds for the other types of organizations.

Organizations buy a wide variety of products and services. Products for resale, buildings, plant and office equipment, furniture, supplies of all kinds, raw materials, packaging, and services such as insurance, finance, advertising assistance, and transportation are purchased in the normal course of running a business. Much of this industrial demand exists because of the economy's purpose of satisfying consumer needs and wants. For instance, your demand for soft drinks creates more than just a consumer market. As Exhibit 6.3 suggests, many industrial markets are created including those for aluminum cans, cacao beans, business insurance, and bottling services. All this buying and selling is necessary just to get that soft drink into your hands.

Exhibit 6.2 Size of manufacturing organizations in the United States (1977)

| | Number of Employees in Organization | | | | |
	Less than 20	20–29	100–249	250–999	More than 999
Percentage of establishments	67.5	22.3	6.1	3.4	.6
Percentage of employees	6.5	18.8	18.0	29.1	27.5
Percentage of shipments	2.2	15.6	16.2	29.8	34.2
Percentage of value added	5.1	15.4	15.8	29.5	34.2

SOURCE: *Statistical Abstract of the United States: 1984,* Washington, D.C.: Bureau of the Census, Department of Commerce, 1983, p. 775.

Do organizations or consumers purchase a larger volume of products and services? As shown in Exhibit 6.3, a great many transactions between organizations are necessary to get a single consumer product such as soft drinks to the location where consumers conveniently can buy it. For this reason, sales to organizations are far greater than sales to consumers.

Exhibit 6.3 Your demand for soft drinks creates many industrial markets

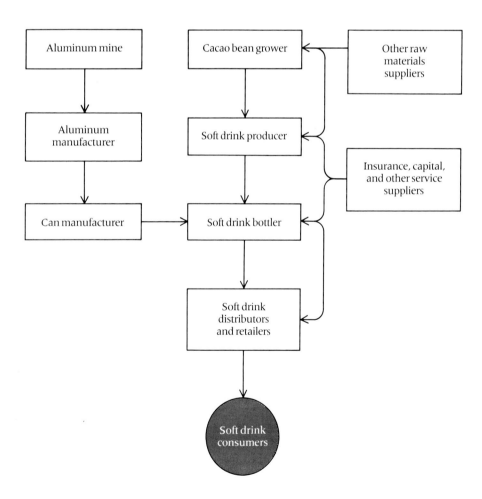

Industrial buying behavior defined

With only slight modification, the definition of buyer behavior from Chapter 5 also can be used to get a clear picture of what we mean by industrial buying behavior. After all, our central concern for purchase decision making does not change. **Industrial buying behavior** is the actions of organizations and their employees directly involved in purchasing and using a product or service, including the communication and decision processes that lead to the purchase choice and the satisfaction or dissatisfaction resulting from the purchase.

DIFFERENCES BETWEEN CONSUMER AND INDUSTRIAL BUYING BEHAVIOR

Many aspects of consumer buying behavior discussed in Chapter 5 also are true for industrial buying. Both consumer and industrial buyers use a decision process, are looking for certain benefits from a product, and react to environmental influences. Nevertheless, there are important differences. As industrial buying behavior is analyzed in this chapter, look particularly for differences in the following areas: (1) setting for buying, (2) technical knowledge of buyers, (3) goals for buying, (4) contact with buyers, and (5) number of people involved in the purchase. Let us briefly consider these differences now.

Setting for buying

Both consumer and industrial purchasing decisions are made within the setting of **buying units.** For the consumer, the unit is a family or household; for the industrial buyer, the unit is an organization. Usually an organization has a more formal chain of command and assigned responsibilities for its employees than does a family. These factors influence who is involved in the buying decision as well as the way in which buying activities are carried out.

The influence of the organization is evident when a quality control instrument is purchased by a large drug manufacturer such as Pfizer. A plant manager decides whether the instrument has priority over other needs. If the purchase is authorized, then quality control engineers, with help from the purchasing department, evaluate types of instruments for the intended application. Finally both the engineers and purchasing personnel decide on the seller.

Not all industrial buying is as involved as that for the quality control instrument. Some purchases such as stationery, paper clips, typewriter ribbons, and pencils do not require much time and effort. Furthermore, the majority of organizations are small with simple organizational structures, which limits the number of people involved in a purchase. For instance, when a small trucking firm purchases an office typewriter, the owner decides when and what to buy although the secretary probably influences the purchase. This situation is not much more complicated than many family buying decisions.

We're proud of our tiny part in the space shuttle program.

Thousands of products have contributed to the successful launch and return of the space shuttle, Columbia. And our products were among the tiniest.

By design.

Entran manufactures a broad line of ultra-miniature accelerometers and pressure transducers. These tiny, high accuracy instruments have very little mass to interfere with the system being tested, and won't distort your test scale.

Because they are so small they can be mounted almost anywhere for the ultimate in applications flexibility. And they leave plenty of room for other electronics.

Our devices have been used to obtain critical test data for the Columbia throughout its development. From the early scale-model wind tunnel tests, to main engine testing, through full-scale vibration testing of the entire shuttle and into actual flight.

Now our devices will be used to gather data for a series of intricate on-board experiments.

Our products are rugged enough to function in the toughest applications.

To find out how our tiny accelerometers and pressure transducers can help you, please write to: Entran Devices, Inc., 10 Washington Avenue, Fairfield, NJ 07006. Or call (201) 227-1002.

Pressure transducer.
EPI-080, only 0.080" diameter.

Accelerometer.
EGA-125D, less than 0.5 gram.

Entran Devices, Inc.
(Our tiny products help make big projects possible.)

Business buyers represent their firms as well as themselves. Generally well trained and experienced, they state exacting specifications for the goods they buy. As a result, factual or rational appeals are used often in industrial advertising. (Courtesy Entran Devices, Inc.)

Technical knowledge of buyers

Organizational buyers often are more knowledgeable about the products or services being purchased than is the typical consumer. Consider further Pfizer's purchase of a quality control instrument. Quality control engineers, because of their educational training and job experience, know a great deal about the design and operation of the different instruments being evaluated. Even persons in purchasing, who probably have little formal technical training, develop their technical capability from past experience, working with other employees, reading literature, talking with salespersons, and observing products used in the plant.

Selling to industrial buyers must take buyers' technical knowledge into consideration (see Marketalk). Industrial salespersons also must have extensive product knowledge, and advertising for an industrial product generally must convey more technical information than does a typical consumer advertisement.

There are important exceptions to this general rule. Sometimes marketing managers must deal with industrial buyers who know very little about what they are buying. For instance, when computer companies sell to businesses, they may encounter persons—owners, managers, secretaries, clerks—who do not understand how computers work or how to use fully their benefits.[2] Part of computer companies' promotion has been to educate industrial buyers to build higher sales volumes. In contrast, many consumer markets have a small segment of persons who have considerable knowledge of the product. Wine connoisseurs, stereo buffs, and do-it-yourselfers are just a few illustrations. These exceptions demonstrate differences between industrial and consumer buyers that are more a matter of degree than of kind.

*Marke*TALK ///

Industrial selling based on knowing the buyer

SALESMANSHIP at AmCast Industrial Corp. used to involve little more than what company officials referred to as "chasing smokestacks"—a description for the process of driving from one customer to the next to make sales calls.

But that phrase isn't used much anymore at the Dayton, Ohio parts maker, which, until last December, was known as Dayton Malleable Inc. AmCast, like a lot of other Rust Belt companies, has had to change its ways.

No longer are its sales representatives mere glad-handers, skilled at wining and dining purchasing agents in hopes of getting a share of available orders. Today, they are college graduates with metalworking backgrounds, who not only deal

with buyers but with customers' engineers, marketing specialists and manufacturing personnel as well. The purpose: to get involved early on in the business plans of potential customers.

The changing strategy at AmCast is part of what some sales experts see as a revolution in industrial marketing. "Smokestack industries are realizing the need to be involved in the customers' decision making process," says Richard G. Hodapp, president of Managing Process Inc., a Cincinnati marketing firm. Once a supplier gets order specifications, it's too late to do anything but react, Mr. Hodapp says.

Aggressive industrial marketing isn't totally new. For years Timken Co., in Canton, Ohio, has designed bearings to meet customers' needs rather than waiting for them to place orders. But new technology and increased competition are pushing more industrial concerns into sophisticated marketing.

Trucking deregulation, for instance, is spurring Cleveland's Leaseway Transpor-

tation Corp. to use computers to show customers how to haul goods more effectively and cheaply. Leaseway beefed up its marketing department to 20 people, from just two in 1981. In the past, Leaseway simply hoped that customers such as General Motors and Sears Roebuck would prosper, because "the more they sold, the more we hauled," says Chuck Lounsbury, vice president of sales and marketing.

The Big Three auto makers have also given impetus to the new marketing methods, partly because they are asking suppliers to share more of the research and development costs associated with engineering new autos. To be able to provide for those needs, car industry suppliers have had to become a lot more knowledgeable about technological trends—both in terms of what the auto companies are likely to want and in terms of what areas the supplier might be best able to address.

///

Goals for buying

Consumers buy for personal use to satisfy needs and wants or for use by others close to them. Industrial buyers also buy to satisfy needs and wants but typically those of their organization, not strictly for themselves. Organizational needs and wants often are economically based causing industrial buyers to weigh costs against benefits, many of which can be translated into dollars and cents.

Even in industrial buying decisions, the buyer's personal goals must be considered.[3] After all, people make industrial buying decisions. Marketing managers sometimes have difficulty knowing which kind of goal is more important to the buyer. For instance, an industrial purchaser of metal cans, a product that does not differ much from supplier to supplier, considers such organizational goals as cost, quality control, package safety, and delivery time when choosing a supplier. The buyer, however, may like to be entertained and let this personal goal influence the size of orders given to different suppliers. An industrial seller has little choice but to respond to both types of goals (see Exhibit 6.4).

Contact with buyers

A national consumer-products manufacturer sells to hundreds of thousands or millions of buyers. Rarely can the company afford to deal directly with each one (direct-to-consumer sellers such as Tupperware and Avon are exceptions). Usually channels of distribution must be set up to reach such vast markets. In contrast, a national manufacturer of industrial products works with far fewer buyers. At one extreme, McDonnel Douglas, the aircraft manufacturer and defense contractor, bids for contracts from a limited number of buyers—armed forces branches of governments in the United States and a relatively few other countries. At the other extreme, even a seller of widely used, standardized products such as cleaning supplies may reach only a few hundred or thousand industrial buyers.

Industrial markets usually are more geographically concentrated than consumer markets. Factors such as proximity to labor markets, raw materials, and transportation facilities often dictate an industry's location. For instance, the automotive industry in the United States is a huge market for many products such as plastic, steel, and tires. Much of the buying by the automotive companies is centered primarily in the Midwest where headquarters and major plants are located. The combination of a small number of buyers and geographic concentration means that there is more direct selling to industrial markets than to consumer markets.

An important advantage of short channels of distribution is that buyer and seller personally interact. Not only are salespersons an important influence on purchase decision, but increased opportunity exists for the seller to learn firsthand about buyer behavior. Consumer-products manufacturers, working through lengthy channels, are more dependent on market studies for buyer behavior information.

Number of people involved in the purchase

The number of people involved in a single consumer buying decision is small because of the limited size of households. Many people may be involved in an industrial buying decision depending on the size of the organization. In a small business such as a flower shop, purchasing may be done by the owner. In large organizations, the number of people affecting a buying decision may include personnel from departments such as production, advertising, purchasing, research and development, engineering, and distribution.

Exhibit 6.4 Organizational and personal goals can influence industrial buying decisions

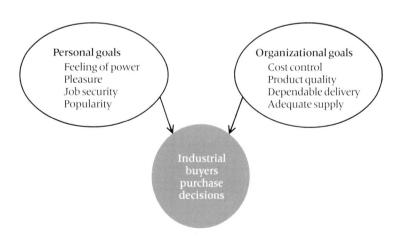

Derived demand

Purchases by industrial buyers are influenced by demand in their own markets. This is called **derived demand** and simply means that industrial buyers adjust their purchases according to the outlook for their sales, buying more when sales are growing than when they are not. In the late 1970s and early 1980s, automobile manufacturers in the United States suffered a period of low sales. Because fewer automobiles were being sold to consumers, Ford, GM, Chrysler, and the other automakers cut back on purchases of everything used to manufacture automobiles from labor to materials such as steel and tires (see Exhibit 6.5). Thousands of industrial sellers suffered because of the reduced buying.

The up-and-down swings in sales for industrial products can be greater than for consumer goods. Industrial buyers make forecasts of their own sales, which become a factor in purchase decisions, and use inventories to adjust purchases to their needs. General Motors, for example, will cut back purchases of many supplies in anticipation of a forecasted dip in sales, using up inventories for current production.

Reciprocal demand also is possible, which means that two companies can be both buyer and seller at the same time but for different products. Suppose an insurance company wants to sell a major medical insurance program to a computer manufacturer. At the same time, the computer manufacturer is trying to win a contract from the insurance company for the purchase of computer hardware and software. Both companies want to sell to each other, and although the sales are supposed to be independent, buying decisions on one may influence the other.

Studying industrial markets

Marketing managers for industrial sellers must consider the nature of industrial buying when learning about market demand. Yet, differences between consumer and industrial buying behavior mean that the two kinds

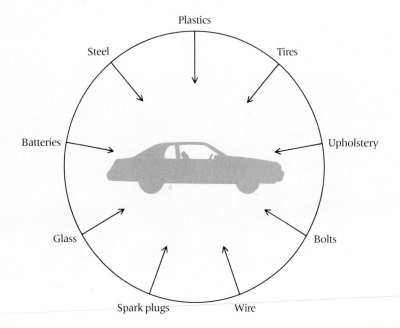

Exhibit 6.5   Sales of many industrial manufacturers are derived from automobile demand

Exhibit 6.6 A model of industrial buying behavior

of buying cannot be studied in exactly the same way. For this reason, some new ideas, not described in Chapter 5 on consumer buying, are needed to understand industrial buying.

As with consumer behavior, a general view of industrial buying should guide analysis. This view is shown by the industrial buying model in Exhibit 6.6. The most important aspect of industrial buying to sellers is the purchase decision making of buyers. Outside environmental influences, characteristics of the organization, and the makeup of individual buyers also are important because they influence the way purchase decisions are made as well as their outcome. Notice that this model directly parallels the consumer model discussed in Chapter 5.

Because the general views of industrial and consumer buying are similar, questions that an industrial seller's marketing managers want answered about industrial buying behavior are the same. These questions are

1. Who are industrial buyers in markets?
2. What factors influence their purchase decisions?
3. How do these buyers make purchase decisions?

ORGANIZATIONAL BUYERS IN MARKETS

Planning marketing strategy demands that sellers find out who target markets comprise. Because buying is by organizations, an industrial seller usually looks for types of organizations in markets. Many sellers also attempt the more complicated step of trying to discover which people in buying organizations are involved in a buying decision.

Classifying organizations

Industrial market opportunity analysis begins by classifying buying organizations using factors such as sales volume, number of employees, repeat sales, geographic location, size of purchase order, and products or services sold.[4] In a way, these factors are similar to the demographic characteristics used to group consumers into markets. Of these, classifying by products or services sold is the most important. What a customer company sells determines the products and services it must buy to keep the operation going. Consider Alcoa, which produces rigid container sheet aluminum for use in manufacturing aluminum cans. Approximately 95 percent of these cans are used for packaging soft drinks and beer.[5] Alcoa sells its product to can manufacturers and directly to beverage firms that manufacture their own cans. As suggested by Exhibit 6.7, identifying these industrial markets helps managers see target market opportunities.

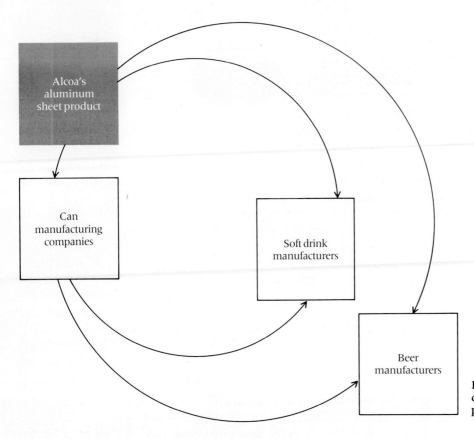

Exhibit 6.7 Alcoa breaks out markets comprising companies making and packaging with cans

Standard Industrial Classification (SIC) codes is a classification scheme used by the U.S. government (and private information companies such as Dun and Bradstreet) to group U.S. organizations into categories for purposes of organizing and presenting statistical information on them. These codes are numbers assigned to types of organizations designated by the products or services they sell and by the nature of their operations. They start with two-digit codes that divide all organizations into ten industry groups:

01–09: Agriculture, forestry, fishing
10–14: Mining
15–17: Contract construction
20–39: Manufacturing
40–49: Transportation and other public utilities
50–59: Wholesale and retail trade
60–67: Finance, insurance, and real estate
70–89: Services
91–97: Government: federal, state, local, international
    99: Others

Each of these groups is divided into subgroups. The subgroups provide more detail on products sold or the nature of operations. For instance, Exhibit 6.8 shows SIC code classifications for different manufacturing subgroups. Using published information organized by these codes, marketing managers can find out how many organizations fall into a category, number of persons employed by organizations in the category, sales volume for the category, and other information useful for market opportunity analyses.

One application of this information is to evaluate volume of potential sales from various industrial market segments.

Once industrial customers have been classified by type of business, other characteristics may help identify the most important organizations. Size is especially revealing. Usually, a few firms account for most of the purchases of a product or service. It is widely believed that the 80–20 rule applies to industrial markets: about 80 percent of a company's sales are made to 20 percent of its customers. Knowing which buyers are the most important 20 percent allows industrial sellers to target these buyers with special programs.

Identifying buyers in organizations

The next task is to find out which persons in customer organizations are involved in the purchase decision since marketing programs must be aimed at these persons. J. David Lyons, vice-president of Data General Corporation, described the challenge for his company, which sells computers and information systems for business applications:

> As changing customer needs arose and new applications were developed, our customers weren't solely the technical specialists and marketing information

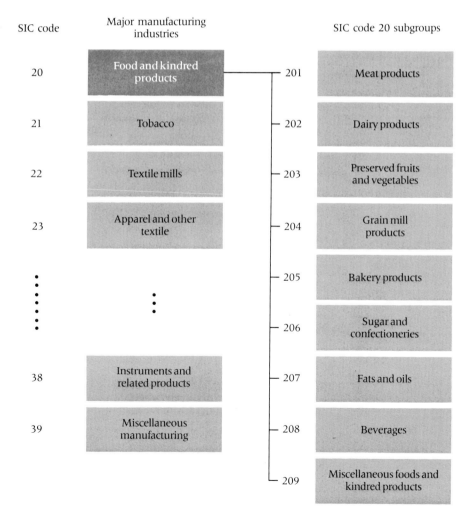

Exhibit 6.8 Standard Industrial Classification (SIC) code subdivisions for manufacturing

SIC code	Major manufacturing industries		SIC code 20 subgroups
20	Food and kindred products	201	Meat products
21	Tobacco	202	Dairy products
22	Textile mills	203	Preserved fruits and vegetables
23	Apparel and other textile	204	Grain mill products
		205	Bakery products
		206	Sugar and confectioneries
38	Instruments and related products	207	Fats and oils
39	Miscellaneous manufacturing	208	Beverages
		209	Miscellaneous foods and kindred products

systems managers who understood how the technical specifications of systems would translate into solutions for their needs.

Our new customers—executives, managers, and professionals without technical degrees—had to be approached through distribution channels matched to their needs.[6]

The most obvious persons participating in a company's purchase decisions are **purchasing agents or managers.** A purchasing agent typically is responsible for identifying suppliers of a product, collecting information on suppliers and their products, negotiating price for a purchase order, and working with suppliers' salespersons. In some companies, a purchasing agent is a low-level manager who is more involved in the implementation of a purchase order than in the actual decisions on what to purchase. A current trend, however, is to upgrade purchasing. Several companies including Du Pont, Sperry-Rand, and Kaiser Aluminum have created the position vice-president of purchasing to head that function and to give it high-level authority in the company. This trend recognizes that purchasing is a source of cost savings and improved profitability. After all, purchasing expenditures often are as high as 50 to 60 percent of a company's sales dollars.[7]

Some companies also use **buying committees,** or a collection of persons assigned responsibility for purchase decisions. In a small organization, the buying committee may be the board of directors. For instance, the board of directors of a small tennis and swimming club with annual purchases of more than $250,000 approves all purchases. In a large organization, a buying committee comprises managers from various departments including purchasing, finance, distribution, production, and engineering.

Formal lines of purchasing authority in an organization do not always indicate all personnel who are involved. An important concept describing buying by organizations is the **buying center**. The buying center includes all members of an organization who participate in a purchase decision.

Exhibit 6.9 Buying center roles for a telecommunications purchase

Buying-decision Role	Illustration
Initiator	Division general manager proposes to replace the company's telecommunications system.
Decider	Vice-president of administration selects, with influence from others, the vendor the company will deal with and the system it will buy.
Influencer	Corporate telecommunications department and the vice-president of data processing have important say about which system and vendor the company will deal with.
Purchaser	Corporate purchasing department completes the purchase according to predetermined specifications by negotiating with or receiving bids from suppliers.
Gatekeeper	Corporate purchasing and corporate telecommunications departments analyze the company's needs and recommend likely matches with potential vendors.
User	All division employees who use the telecommunications equipment.

SOURCE: Thomas V. Bonoma, "Major sales: Who *really* does the buying?" *Harvard Business Review*, May–June 1982, p. 113. Reprinted by permission of the *Harvard Business Review*. An exhibit from "Major sales: Who really does the buying?" by Thomas V. Bonoma (May/June 1982). Copyright © 1982 by the President and Fellows of Harvard College; all rights reserved.

How many of the world's 15 largest airlines are served by our data communications systems?

All of them.
Motorola is a world leader in advanced electronics for memory, logic and voice and data communications.

MOTOROLA / codex

Corporate advertisements help create an awareness of a firm and its business and also help build a firm's reputation. General in nature, these ads are often useful to influence top-management members of the buying center. (Courtesy Motorola Inc.)

Experience shows that buying center participants may play different buying-decision roles, usually known as *initiator, decider, influencer, purchaser, gatekeeper,* and *user.* Exhibit 6.9 defines these roles in the context of a telecommunications purchase decision.

Buying centers demonstrate that considerable joint decision making goes on in many industrial buyer organizations. Joint decision making involves interaction among personnel as they discuss aspects of the purchase, which may lead to disagreements (over what to purchase, when to purchase, product attributes desired, etc.). Thus marketing managers should find out who has the power in the buying center.

Sometimes power is vested in a formal job position such as a purchasing agent. However, there does not seem to be a consistent relationship between a person's department and the power to make buying decisions. Thus marketing managers must use other clues to discover who should be the target of the seller's marketing program. One source of this information is industrial salespersons who observe communications between people in the buying organization and often can see where the power lies.[8]

INFLUENCES ON INDUSTRIAL BUYING

Growth in the economy, shortages of raw materials, and the like influence industrial buying decisions as well as economic factors such as cost of funds. Actually, many factors are influential. Exhibit 6.10 lumps these factors into five major categories.[9]

Environmental influences

A buying organization's environment is packed with two kinds of influences on purchasing. Nonmarketing influences including government regulations, changes in demand for the buying organization's products,

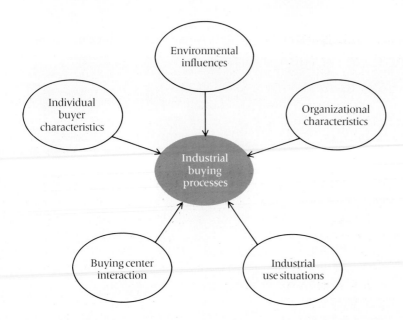

Exhibit 6.10   Influences on industrial purchasing

technological innovations, cost of funds, and shortages of supplies cause buyers to adjust purchases of products and services. Marketing influences from the marketing programs of industrial sellers also are important factors.

Markets for hospital supply companies illustrate both kinds of influences.[10] During the 1980s hospitals have become increasingly conservative with their purchasing dollars. They have been hit by a rapidly changing environment. The U.S. government changed rules covering reimbursements for Medicare patients, cutting into cash flows for hospitals. New surgical techniques have been developed that minimize damage to surrounding tissues and thus decrease hospital stays. Furthermore, competition for patients is coming from new sources, reducing demand for traditional hospital services. In response to these environmental influences hospitals have cut back purchases of construction, equipment, drugs, and supplies.

Hospital supply companies are changing marketing strategy to maintain sales growth. Baxter Travenol Laboratories has developed product lines for other segments of health care markets such as home health care products. At the same time, its hospital products are being packaged with services to help hospitals with cost control and increased productivity. Their strategy is not aimed at getting hospitals to buy more in total, but to buy more from Baxter.

Organizational characteristics

One of the more important differences between consumer and industrial buying is the impact of the organization on industrial purchasers. Characteristics of the organization that affect industrial buying decisions are that goals are set, responsibilities are assigned, and personnel must adhere to formal procedures.

Goals set at the highest level in a buying organization can filter down to buying decisions. Consider a goal set by many companies: to sell quality products. This goal affects purchasing because purchasing managers also stress quality when they buy machinery, materials, and supplies for production. Even goals or objectives set at low levels in an organization can be important. As an illustration, the purchasing department is judged by the amount of money saved on purchases over what other departments in the organization could do if they did their own purchasing. The objective of saving money can cause purchasing personnel to place great emphasis on price and on soliciting bids from selling companies to get the lowest price.

Buying organizations have a formal structure and decision-making authority is assigned to departments and personnel. In some companies authority is given to personnel on a high level, such as a centralized purchasing department headed by a vice-president. In others authority is given to a purchasing committee. These are also informal roles among personnel, such as the amount of influence exercised by the user of a product. Uncovering these roles can be quite a challenge for the seller because they may not be very visible to outsiders.

Purchasing procedures also are important to understand. A purchase procedure refers to steps that the purchaser must go through to make a purchase, and it can influence the purchase decision made. For instance, many purchases by the federal government must use a bidding procedure. Product specifications are detailed, and suppliers submit bids for the purchase order. Because each bid is for essentially the same specifications, lowest price is the dominant factor in the selection of supplier.[11]

In general, marketing managers must "play by their customer's rules" by conforming to buying organizations' goals, buying responsibilities, and buying procedures. Managers, however, need not view these organizational characteristics as constraints. A creative evaluation of buyer organizations may uncover opportunities. For example, managers at Baxter Laboratories noticed the growing importance of cost control objectives of hospitals and saw an opportunity for consulting services to help hospital administrators achieve these objectives.

Industrial use situations

Industrial buyers as well as consumers anticipate a use situation when they buy. Aspects of the use situation may affect significantly the benefits expected from the selling company when a purchase is made. For instance, some drug companies use special instruments to precisely measure temperature when sterilizing containers for intravenous drugs. This measurement is part of their quality control, so if an instrument breaks an entire production operation may be shut down. Buyers for drug companies, anticipating this situation, expect extremely fast repair services from instrument manufacturers as part of the purchase agreement.

Buying center interaction

Studying buying center interaction can help marketing managers understand how buying decisions are reached and who is involved in the process. The buying decision may be influenced from unexpected sources. In addition, disagreements can lead to conflict between members, which later may influence the buying decision.[12] For example, a purchasing manager and a quality control engineer, both sitting on a buying committee, can disagree sharply over the importance of price relative to quality and timing of delivery. In arguing for their points of view, each person is attempting to sway the purchase decision.

Marketing managers get ideas for selling strategy by learning about why conflict is taking place and how it may be resolved. Suppose that the purchasing manager has final authority in disputes with the quality control engineer. The seller should target primarily the purchasing manager and highlight the instrument's competitive price. If the purchasing manager and engineer decide to resolve the conflict through compromise by weighing price, product quality, and delivery equally, then a different selling strategy is needed. Both purchasing manager and engineers may become targets, and communication about the instruments should go beyond price into these other benefits.

Individual buyer characteristics

Each person in a buying center has personal goals, personality traits, opinions and attitudes, experience, and other characteristics that influence purchases. A seller's challenge is to learn about these characteristics so marketing programs can be tailored to the individual makeup of buyers. Most of the characteristics that describe consumers—values, personality, beliefs, attitudes, motives—also apply to industrial buyers.

Industrial salespersons are in an ideal position to learn about buyers' makeup. The astute salesperson keeps a record of characteristics noted during sales calls that later may be used to plan a sales presentation. A buyer with an assertive personality might want to be in charge during a sales call and not want to waste time with idle conversation. For this buyer, the salesperson should plan an efficient presentation concentrating on quickly explaining the product's benefits. Another buyer, who has a more amiable personality, may prefer a low-key presentation.[13]

ORGANIZATIONAL BUYING DECISIONS

The many industrial buying influences that we have discussed are important because they affect what buyers do when making purchase decisions. They should be examined in the context of the steps taken during purchasing. Thus, planning industrial marketing programs depends on understanding how industrial buyers make buying decisions. Fokker, a Dutch airplane manufacturer, was fortunate to have managers who followed this principle when the company developed an airplane seating one hundred passengers for short-haul trips. The company was up against powerful competition from Boeing, McDonnel Douglas, and British Aerospace for sales to Swiss Air Transport Company. To improve Fokker's chance of getting the Swiss Air order, management studied how the choice between competitors would be made. They found out that Swiss Air buyers considered fuel economy, efficiency of the cockpit instrumentation (particularly for operating in the heavy fog common in Switzerland), and price as key criteria for evaluating aircraft. Obtaining this information enabled Fokker to make both product design and marketing changes.

To learn about industrial buying behavior marketing managers must study the process from beginning to end. Collectively, persons in a buyer center go through a series of steps when ordering products or services from a seller.[14] These steps make up the process of purchase decision making. The exact steps and sequence, however, depend on the type of buying decision being made.

Types of decision processes

Industrial buyers' decision processes depend on whether the product has been purchased previously and how much information is needed to make a choice. These factors suggest that purchasers face three types of decisions.[15]

New task decisions. A purchase decision that must be made for a product or service for which managers have little or no previous purchasing experience is called a **new task decision.** With this type of purchase decision, considerable information is sought to evaluate many alternatives. Buying center involvement by personnel from different departments is greatest during a new task decision. A company buying its first corporate jet airplane makes a new task decision.

Modified rebuy decisions. When a company must purchase a product or service to replace one that has been used in the past, a **modified rebuy decision** is made. This type of decision involves considering alternatives other than the product bought previously, so managers must gather new information. A university that wants to purchase computer equipment to replace its current system would make a modified rebuy decision.

Straight rebuy decisions. A manager makes a **straight rebuy decision** when the product or service being purchased is one that has been bought frequently in the past. Managers have extensive purchasing experience on which to rely and usually reorder from the supplier used previously. Because straight rebuys are more routine than new task or modified rebuy decisions, they are likely to be handled primarily by the purchasing department. Some straight rebuys become so systematic that a computer reorders with scarcely a helping human hand (see Marketech). A straight rebuy decision is made when a construction firm reorders nails from a supplier.

Decisions made by purchasers

During an industrial buying process three specific decisions that combine to determine a purchase are important: (1) authorizing a purchase, (2) specifying the product's attributes and performance benefits, and (3) selecting the supplier. In large organizations, each decision may be made by different people. Thus the makeup of the buying center can shift during a decision process. Although organizations differ in how authority for purchasing is allocated, Exhibit 6.11 lists key personnel likely to be involved in the buying center for important purchases.[16]

Steps in the buying decision process

The steps of an industrial buying process are not the same for all organizations or even for all products or services purchased by an organization.[17] Each organization develops its own purchasing procedures. Further-

Marke**TECH** □ □ □ □ □ □ □ □ □ □ □ □ □ □ □ □ □ □

Computer-to-computer ordering has dramatic impact on both purchasing and selling

THE ADVENT OF THE COMPUTER has brought a new way to purchase and sell industrial products: A purchasing agent can go to a computer terminal instead of a salesperson to make a purchase order. The order of a product is entered into a computer terminal at the purchasing company, and then it is electronically sent to a computer terminal at the seller company (or it is sent to a third computer acting as a "mailbox" where it waits to be called by the seller's computer). At the seller's warehouse, the order is filled by selecting products from inventory, a carrier is hired to deliver the order to the buyer, and proper bills are sent to the buyer. All this happens without any face-to-face interaction between buyer and seller.

SOURCE: James H. Huguet, Jr., "Computer-to-computer ordering: The sales/marketing implications," *Marketing News*, Sept. 14, 1984, pp. 1, 31.

Computer-to-computer ordering is a recent innovation, but it is catching on. The drug and food industries are leading the way in adopting this new approach. The cost savings is the primary reason given for its use. One study estimates that the grocery industry will save $196 to $324 million in one year. Savings come from fewer contacts between salespersons and purchasing managers.

As electronic ordering catches on, the relationship between industrial buyers and sellers will change markedly. Traditionally, sellers have relied on personal contacts between salespersons and their purchasing counterparts in buying firms. Computer-to-computer selling will reduce the importance of these relationships. Furthermore, the personnel needs of both buyer and seller companies will decline as personal contacts occur less frequently. Purchasing decisions will be based in-

creasingly on objective criteria that a computer can evaluate and become more centralized in home offices.

Computer-to-computer ordering should change the challenge facing people in sales. Centralized buying will mean dealing with larger accounts. For instance, rather than selling to individual stores in a supermarket chain, a seller will work with centralized buyers for the chain. Each account will involve complicated negotiations to set up the computerized ordering system. Thus many sellers will shift to selling teams comprising managers with financial, marketing, distribution, and planning skills. These teams also will have to know their customers well to sell long-term purchasing arrangements. Although these changes will take years, many companies are looking ahead and planning for the inevitable shift.

□ □

more, some steps included in a new task or modified rebuy decision (information search and evaluation of different suppliers) usually are not necessary for a straight rebuy decision. There are steps, however, which are common to many decisions, particularly for new task or modified rebuy purchases. These steps are (1) recognizing a need, (2) determining product specifications, (3) searching for information and evaluating suppliers, (4) negotiating a purchase order, and (5) evaluating product and supplier performance.

Need recognition. Industrial purchasing processes begin when a need for a product or service is recognized. This step can occur in many different ways. At one extreme, need recognition is routine, such as for straight rebuy decisions. Anticipating this kind of need, a company may negotiate a contract with a supplier to replenish inventories on request. When an inventory drops to a prespecified level, purchase orders are filled out by a clerk and sent to the supplier.

At the other extreme, a need for a product can arise because of events that happen in specific situations. Consider a drug company's purchase of an instrument for measuring temperature. Need for purchasing the instrument may arise because

- A quality control engineer notices that an instrument measuring temperature in a group of conclaves (large ovens used in sterilization) has broken and cannot be repaired.

- A plant expansion is being planned making room for more conclaves in which temperature must be monitored for quality control.

Exhibit 6.11 Purchasing decisions made by managers from different departments in a firm

Buying decision	Buying center involvement
Purchase authorization	Top management
Product specifications	Engineers Product users Purchasing agents Outside consultants
Choice of supplier	Purchasing agents Engineers Lawyers

- A government regulating agency increases the accuracy level that must be maintained when measuring temperature in the conclaves, and existing instruments are not able to meet the new standard.

- A quality control engineer sees a new type of instrument at a trade show and requests that the instrument be tried.

- A research and development department has received approval for testing a new drug under varying temperature conditions, and an extremely accurate instrument is needed for the testing.

- An instrument salesperson demonstrates to a quality control engineer an improved instrument recently developed by the vendor's company.

These need recognition situations demonstrate a central principle of industrial purchasing: Products and services are purchased to solve problems or to respond to new opportunities. For example, look at the third situation. If accuracy of existing instruments does not meet the new regulation, buying companies must purchase new instruments. Because the stipulated accuracy must be met, accuracy of instruments will be a crucial factor in a purchase decision as will getting delivery in time to comply with the regulation.

Typically, problem recognition leads to a request for authorization to purchase a product. Top management can handle authorizations in one of two ways. First, conditions may be established in advance, and when they are met a purchase authorization is automatic. This approach is most likely to be used for straight rebuy decisions. For instance, a condition might be depletion of inventory of a supply item to a prespecified level. Second, purchases may also be authorized at the time of each request. Final authorization may come at that time or later in the decision process after costs have been determined.

Product specifications. Having recognized a product need, members of the buying center must determine **product performance specifications.** Specifications include benefits important to the user of the product as well as nonproduct criteria important to the buying organization. Furthermore, each member of the buying center often has his or her own specification that must be met, and some of these may conflict. For instance, consider the following comment made by a marketing manager for DunsPlus, seller of personal computing systems that integrate hardware, software, and service.

American Technical Services tries to stimulate need recognition by describing its capabilities to potential customers. (Courtesy American Technical Services, Inc., Tucker, Ga.)

May we give you a hand?

If your plant equipment is starting to show its age, you're probably asking yourself these questions: Should I be upgrading? Automating? Should I be looking into distributed control systems as so many other companies are doing?

What you may need is an experienced instrument engineering services company like ATS that offers turnkey capabilities.

ATS operates eight offices nationwide, and offers complete engineering design plus the services of highly skilled technicians to put that design to work for you.

We do existing systems analysis, feasibility studies, system design, vendor selection and procurement. We also provide installation, start-up, checkout and calibration and responsive on-going support.

Our objective is to put into your hands the instrument capabilities necessary to keep your operations working at maximum efficiency.

And though we think of ourselves as part of your in-house engineering team, we don't join the payroll. You use us only when you need us. And you pay us only when you use us.

We at ATS are organized to do jobs big and small. So whether you need a turnkey boiler revamp or one-day-a-month maintenance, we can support you.

Let us lend you a hand and we'll provide a service capability that shows results. Call or write us today for complete details.

American Technical Services

ATS

P.O. Box 1047
Tucker, Georgia 30084
(404) 934-3113

Industrial ads like this one are a way of reaching prospects who may be unavailable to salespeople; they are also an effective means of paving the way for salespeople when they do call. (Courtesy Endevco Corporation)

Within the last year, about 80% of these corporations [*Fortune* 1350 company customers] have created special departments or committees to purchase and support personal computing. These departments, often called "information centers," form an additional layer of decision making between the marketer and actual end user.

And the buying needs of these information centers are quite different from the needs of the business people, who simply want to use PCs to solve problems. They are concerned with the ability to standardize their hardware and software purchases so that large numbers of employees can be supported efficiently.

They also consider the conflicting objective of customization. And, like any quantity purchaser, they are concerned with price, delivery, service, etc.[18]

The result of this step is a list of specifications that sellers must meet. Specifications range from general statements of performance requirements to detailed listings of product attributes, price, and support services. For example, specifications for a drug manufacturer's temperature measurement instrument include

- Accuracy of measurement within specified tolerance
- Ability to handle multiple sterilizer conclaves
- Stability of measurement under different conditions in the plant
- Ability to print out temperature readings on paper
- Compact and lightweight for moving up and down aisles in a plant
- Easy to read temperature readouts
- Price limit per unit
- Twenty-four-hour repair service for instrument breakdowns

Specifications usually are derived from studying product users and their needs and are written by technical experts such as engineers and knowledgeable users. A buying committee may determine specifications, as when a college of business at a large state university purchased a large order of personal computers for faculty and students. The committee, comprising computer center personnel and faculty with extensive microcomputer experience, discovered that faculty and students wanted easy access to the university's mainframe computer. Thus, part of the specifications included a communications link between all microcomputers and the university's central computer.

Information search and supplier evaluation. New task and modified rebuy decisions require that information to evaluate alternative products and suppliers be obtained. Purchasing agents and managers act as gatckeepers by gathering relevant information for buying center members to use. A wide variety of information sources are available to the skilled purchasing manager including trade advertising, trade shows (see Marketalk), direct mail literature, visits from vendors' salespersons, professional conferences, and talking with purchasing managers from other firms.

Companies that sell products being considered for purchase, called **suppliers,** also are evaluated. If the number of suppliers is large, industrial purchasers screen them to identify a few that are further evaluated. For instance, Chrysler Corporation uses a group of ten to fourteen technical persons and interested users to evaluate the price and performance of computer hardware and software and their suppliers. They pare the acceptable list to three or four for a purchase decision.[19]

Procedures for evaluating suppliers are similar to those for evaluating products. Criteria are developed that describe the kinds of performance desired from a supplier. Performance of a supplier might include speed of delivery, offering of support services such as repair, and price. Then alternative suppliers are evaluated against these criteria. If a screening process is used to reduce a large number of suppliers to a workable number, one or a

MarkeTALK //

Trade shows bring industrial buyers and sellers together

AN IMPORTANT PART of many industrial companies' marketing programs is the trade show. Usually held in a large convention center in a major city, these shows offer a place where sellers can display their products and talk directly with representatives of buyer companies. At some shows, a seller's objective is to sign orders for products. At others, contacts are made that set up sales calls. Consider Acco's participation in a National Office Products Association show in New York City.

SOURCE: Susan Buchsbaum and Mark K. Metzger, "Show and sell," *Inc.*, May 1984, pp. 64–76.

By show's end, Acco had a few hundred sales prospects, most of them lined up the way Greg Hewitt, an Acco field sales manager, lined up Lionel Eltis. With a few studiously nonchalant questions, Hewitt determined that Eltis, the owner of a small chain of stores in Louisiana, could be a serious customer. Then Hewitt set to work, quickly but deftly eliciting everything he needed to know about Eltis's company—for example, its size, number of stores, and distributor operation—to set him up for a sales call. Before the conversation had ended, Hewitt had put Eltis's name, and the name of his buyer, on a standardized card that would soon go into Acco's sales system.

Some companies go to trade shows simply to keep their name in front of customers. Others see an economic benefit from making contact and sales presentations to buyers. In 1981, the Trade Show Bureau estimated the cost of a contact at a trade show to be $68, compared with an average cost of $178 for a industrial salesperson's sales call as measured by the McGraw-Hill Laboratory of Advertising Performance in the same year. Furthermore, studies by these same organizations show that an industrial salesperson took an average of five calls to make a sale, whereas only one call was needed when the sales lead came from a trade show. These comparisons provide powerful support for the value of trade shows in getting buyers and sellers together.

//

few criteria probably will be used. For instance, many companies quickly weed out small suppliers who do not have broad product lines.

An important tool for choosing criteria for evaluating products and suppliers is a **value analysis.** At the heart of value analysis is a study of the function that a product must perform. For example, a drug manufacturer might state the function of a temperature measurement instrument: "To measure whether temperature in a sterilizer unit exceeds the level needed to ensure sterilization." The analysis then determines which of several alternative products can perform the function at the lowest cost while maintaining desired quality. The drug manufacturer would evaluate alternative instruments to see which ones can measure the temperature level with the needed accuracy at the least cost.[20]

Negotiating a purchase order. Determining which supplier gets a purchase order may involve a **bidding** procedure, in which offers are obtained from suppliers to sell at a specified price. For example, the U.S. government is frequently required by law to purchase from the lowest-price bidder. When a large state university, a state government institution, purchased personal computers, several suppliers were invited to bid for the order. Each supplier submitted a bid showing the price for which it would fill the order as specified. This procedure helps get the lowest price for a list of specifications.

Another way to select a supplier is to use a **request for proposal.** The purchasing company sends a letter to selected suppliers or makes a general announcement inviting proposals for a purchase order. Each supplier sends back a written offer that explains how all specifications are to be met, terms of delivery, and the price charged. This procedure is common when purchasing services such as marketing research or financial resources.

Finally, the final supplier selection may be made by negotiating a **contractual agreement.** Contracts frequently are used for straight rebuy decisions when a company decides to renew a purchase agreement with a supplier. Contracts usually cover purchases over a specified period of time.

A buyer may not limit the purchase to one supplier. When practical, many organizations prefer to have more than one supplier of a product. This tactic keeps the buyer from being overdependent on a single supplier. General Motors routinely uses this tactic by purchasing a fixed percentage of its orders for various types of steel from each of several producers. Should something unforeseen happen to one supplier (e.g., a strike at a key steel plant), the buyer can shift purchases easily to others.[21]

Performance evaluation. Industrial buyers typically evaluate how well suppliers have met their commitments. For a smooth relationship to continue each must work with the other. The buyer should make the specifications of the purchase clear to the supplier, and the supplier must follow through on promises made when the purchase order was accepted.

The purchasing department usually is responsible for periodically evaluating a seller's performance. Evaluation begins with a review of the criteria that were used to select a supplier. These criteria now become performance standards that the seller must meet.

One set of standards concerns the performance of the product or service in its use application. A questionnaire may be sent to users of the product to get their observations. If possible, technical measurements of performance will be used. For example, a drug manufacturer periodically will test its temperature measurement instruments to determine whether specified levels of accuracy are being achieved.

Delivery times also are checked. A supplier is given a specified amount of time within which to make a delivery. For a purchasing company to meet its own schedules these delivery times must be met. When the purchase order calls for periodic deliveries of the product over a prespecified time span, delivery times must be monitored periodically.

Evaluating a supplier enables the industrial purchaser to determine if performance is satisfactory. Furthermore, satisfaction with current orders can be an important factor in future supplier selection decisions. This simple fact drives suppliers to meet the performance requirements of purchasers.

SUMMARY

Satisfying the needs and wants of consumers requires a complex network of businesses and other organizations. Raw materials, labor, energy, and other resources must be converted into products and services that then are delivered conveniently to consumers' markets. Manufacturers, wholesalers, retailers, government, and service suppliers purchase many products and services for this purpose. In this way, industrial markets are created in which purchases are made by organizations.

Industrial buying behavior has some similarities to consumer buying because people do the buying in organizations as well as in families and households. There are important differences, however, between the two types of buying. Thus special attention should be given to understanding industrial buying behavior.

To plan marketing strategy, marketing managers must know (1) who industrial buyers are, (2) what factors influence buying decisions, and (3) how buyers make purchase decisions. Identifying industrial buyers begins by classifying organizations. Characteristics such as products produced by the buying organizations, size, geographic location, and order volume are useful for this purpose. Then the seller must determine which persons in a buying organization are involved in the purchase. Purchasing agents and managers, buying committees, engineers, product users, and top management may at one time or another be in a buying center.

Many kinds of influences act on members of a buying center during a purchase. These influences fall into five categories: environmental influences, organizational characteristics, use situation, buying center interaction, and individual buyer characteristics. Each influence can be studied to determine its effect on the outcomes of industrial buyers' purchase decisions.

All purchases are based on a decision process, but not all processes are the same. New task, modified rebuy, and straight rebuy decisions do not all require the same process. Furthermore, different decisions must be made during the process including authorizing a purchase, developing purchase order specifications, and selecting suppliers. Each of these decisions may be made by a different mix of people in a buying center, and each decision uses different steps. Certain steps, however, are common to many industrial purchase decisions: recognizing a need, determining product specifications, searching for information and evaluating suppliers, negotiating a purchase order, and evaluating product and supplier performance.

KEY TERMS

industrial buying

industrial buying behavior

buying units

derived demand

reciprocal demand

Standard Industrial Classification
  (SIC) codes

purchasing agents or managers

buying committees

buying center

new task decision

modified rebuy decision

straight rebuy decision

product performance specifications

suppliers

value analysis

bidding

request for proposal

contractual agreement

QUESTIONS FOR REVIEW AND DISCUSSION

1. What is industrial buying behavior?

2. How is industrial buying behavior different from consumer buying behavior?

3. Are there any ways in which industrial buying behavior is similar to consumer buying behavior?

4. What are ways to classify industrial buyers into markets?

5. Do purchasing agents make buying decisions in organizations? Why or why not?

6. How does a buying center differ from a buying committee?

7. Explain five influences on industrial buying decisions.

8. Explain the difference between new task, modified rebuy, and straight rebuy industrial buying decisions.

9. What are the steps in an industrial buying decision process?

10. Does a straight rebuy decision process have the same steps as a new task or modified rebuy decision process?

11. Explain how use situation is related to the problem recognition step in the industrial buying decision process.

12. Explain how industrial buyers select suppliers.

13. What is value analysis?

14. How is industrial buyer satisfaction determined?

15. Should a seller be concerned with industrial buyer satisfaction? Why or why not?

16. What is the difference between the product evaluation and supplier evaluation steps in an industrial buyer decision process?

BUILDING YOUR PORTFOLIO

Pick any business firm of interest to you and located nearby. It can be a manufacturer, distributor, a retailer, or a service firm. Also pick a product that you know the company buys. The product can be one that involves a new task, modified rebuy, or straight rebuy decisions. Develop a list of questions that you think are necessary to find out how purchase decisions for the product are made by people in that firm.

Set up an interview with someone involved in the firm's purchasing, for example, the owner, a purchasing agent, or an engineer. Ask your questions and record the person's answers. After reviewing the information you received, outline a sales presentation that you would make to the purchaser to convince the firm to buy the product from you. For this task you may assume that you work for a seller of the product you chose, and you can refer to that seller's brand.

NOTES

1. The basis for this illustration is John W. Dizard, "Machines that see look for a market." *Fortune,* Sept. 17, 1984, pp. 87, 88, 92, 96, 100, 104.
2. Peter Nulty, "The computer comes to main street." *Fortune,* Sept. 6, 1982, p. 79.
3. Thomas V. Bonoma, "Major sales: Who *really* does the buying?" *Harvard Business Review,* May–June 1982, p. 116.
4. "Measures exist for segmenting industrial markets." *Marketing News,* Apr. 1, 1983, p. 11.
5. Bill Saporito, "Alcoa rolls the dice once more." *Fortune,* Aug. 6, 1984, pp. 53–56.
6. "Computer firm lands big accounts by marketing information management systems, not hardware." *Marketing News,* Oct. 12, 1984, p. 41.
7. Gregory D. Upah and Monroe M. Bird, "Changes in industrial buying: Implications for industrial marketers." *Industrial Marketing Management,* Apr. 1980, pp. 117–118.
8. Bonoma, op. cit.
9. These categories are discussed in Fredrick E. Webster and Yoram Wind, "A general model for understanding organizational buying behavior." *Journal of Marketing,* Vol. 36 (Apr. 1972), p. 15; and in Jagdish N. Sheth, "Research in industrial buying behavior— Today's needs, tomorrow's seeds." *Marketing News,* Apr. 4, 1980, p. 14.
10. This illustration is based on information in "How two hospital suppliers are faring in a penny-pinching era." *Business Week,* June 18, 1984, pp. 54, 56, 60.
11. Robert M. Springer, "If approved, new rules will make government a better buyer." *Marketing News,* June 25, 1982, p. 12.
12. Michael J. Ryan and Morris B. Holbrook, "Decision-specific conflict in organizational buyer behavior." *Journal of Marketing,* Vol. 46 (Summer 1982), pp. 62–68.
13. Jack R. Snader, "Amiable, analytical, driving, or expressive? Base marketing style on prospect's behavior." *Marketing News,* Mar. 16, 1984, Section 2, p. 3.
14. The decision process idea is evident in widely cited models of industrial buying behavior including those discussed in Webster and Wind, op. cit., pp. 12–19; Jagdish N. Sheth, "A model of industrial buyer behavior." *Journal of Marketing,* Vol. 37 (Oct. 1973), pp. 50–56; and Jean-Marie Choffray and Gary L. Lilien, "Assessing response to industrial marketing strategy." *Journal of Marketing,* Vol. 42 (Apr. 1978), pp. 20–31.
15. C. W. Faris, "Market Segmentation and Industrial Buying Behavior," in R. Moyer and J. Vosburgh (Eds.), *Educators' Proceedings.* Chicago: American Marketing Association, 1967, pp. 108–110.
16. Buying center participation by different personnel is discussed in Choffray and Lilien, op. cit., pp. 27–28; and Wesley J. Johnston and Thomas V. Bonoma, "The buying center: Structure and interaction patterns." *Journal of Marketing,* Vol. 45 (Summer 1981), pp. 143–156.
17. Wesley J. Johnston, "Industrial Buying Behavior: A State of the Art Review," in Ben M. Enis and Kenneth J. Roering (Eds.), *Review of Marketing.* Chicago: American Marketing Association, 1981, pp. 77–78.
18. Kathleen M. Groll, "Battle big boy's big ad bucks with target marketing." *Marketing News,* Sept. 14, 1984, p. 3. Reprinted by permission of the American Marketing Association.
19. "The bewildering array of options facing users." *Business Week,* July 16, 1984, p. 86.
20. For more discussion of value analysis, see B. Charles Ames and James D. Hlavacek, *Managerial Marketing for Industrial Firms.* New York: Random House, Business Division, 1984, pp. 42–47.
21. Steven Flax, "How Detroit is reforming the steelmakers." *Fortune,* May 16, p. 34.

Case 6.1

Scovill's Yale Security Group

SCOVILL INC.'S Yale Security Group has a hit on its hands. Hotelkeepers are lining up to buy Yale's electronic locking system, which uses credit-card-size pieces of paperboard to replace brass keys. Yale wasn't first on the market with electronic locks, but a two-year push has made it the leader of the young business.

Keeping that top position pickproof may be tough. Electronic lock technology is advancing quickly, and other companies have an eye on the hotel market, which is a fat niche. Some 800,000 hotel doors are prospects for electronic locks, which sell for between $165 and $250 apiece. Overall, lockmakers estimate a market of $15 million to $20 million for

SOURCE: Robert Norton, "Scovill's smart locks click," *Fortune*, Sept. 17, 1984, pp. 51, 54. Reprinted by permission.

electronic products, vs. $600 million in sales for all locks.

Yale's locking system, installed in 50 hotels, uses a computer at the front desk and a microprocessor in every door lock to make a unique key for each guest. A code on the guest's card key is scanned by the room lock. If it is correct, the card will open the door. Once it accepts a new card, the lock invalidates keys issued to previous guests. Since the lock is "changed" for each guest, lost or stolen keys are not a security problem, and the cards are much cheaper than the 75 cents it costs to make metal keys. A big plus for the hotel is that if a master card—which acts like a master key—is lost or stolen, locks can be quickly recoded.

Unique, a privately held firm based in Hong Kong, pioneered the first electronic system in 1978, but hotelkeepers say it has since sat on old technology. Yale's

closest rival is Security Systems Inc., a privately held firm in Troy, Michigan, that has contracts to install 25 systems this year under the brand name of Saflok. Some hotel purchasing agents give Saflok the edge in technology, but both lockmakers are racing to add new features to their products.

Several small companies are readying similar products, and the major producers of conventional locks are set to enter the electronic market as well, among them Ingersoll-Rand (Schlage locks), Kidde (Sargent), and Emhart (Russwin). The industry shakeout may come with the advent of "smart hotels." Within ten years, experts think, hotel rooms will be wired so that everything from climate control to security is run from the front desk. Lockmakers who can best integrate their products with the new technology will be winners.

QUESTIONS

1. Is an electronic door lock likely to be a new task, modified rebuy, or straight rebuy purchase decision for hotels?

2. Who in a hotel's management would be involved in the buying center?

3. From the information given, what specifications do you think a hotel would list for an electronic lock purchase?

4. What do you think would cause a hotel to recognize a problem

that electronic locks can solve?

5. Do you see any influences on purchase decisions of which marketing managers at Yale should be aware?

6. How would the decision by hotels to purchase electronic locks be different from consumers' decisions to buy electronic locks for their homes?

Case 6.2

TeleVideo Systems

ONCE UPON A TIME the plot of the Tele-Video fairy tale seemed to all but guarantee a happy ending: North Korean immigrant Philip K. Hwang starts a computer terminal company in his California garage in 1975. Eight years later sales hit $169 million a year, while annual earnings in-

SOURCE: Brian Dumaine, "Fast-climbing Tele-Video falls off the beanstalk," *Fortune*, Sept. 17, 1984, p. 51. Reprinted by permission.

crease 128% a year, compounded, from 1980 through 1983. But lately the plot has taken an unpleasant twist. In the quarter that ended in July estimated profits plunged 85% to less than $2 million, on sales that fell 8% to $41 million. What pulled Hwang off the magic beanstalk was an ill-timed move in the personal computer business and fierce competition in computer terminals from a new company founded by another Asian immigrant.

TeleVideo Systems boomed as a maker of terminals, which lack the brain power of personal computers and are hooked up to large computers. Hwang's strategy was to manufacture low-priced terminals in South Korea with more features than the other guy's. According to Dataquest, a California market research firm, TeleVideo became the leader among independent terminal makers with 16% of a $650-million-a-year market.

TeleVideo ventured from the business it knows best, computer terminals, into the personal computer market two years ago. It did well with a high-powered multiuser system, one that could perform a number of tasks for a number of users all at the same time. Then last November the company announced its first IBM-compatible PC. Computer experts hailed it as a competitively priced machine, and TeleVideo spent $16 million on a national advertising campaign. But by the time the company got into full production, the market was so overcrowded that retailers were loath to order, leaving TeleVideo with PCs it can't move.

To salvage his personal computer business, Hwang has adopted a daring strategy. He is shifting his marketing emphasis from the retail market to distributors who sell directly to large users and to computer companies that will repackage TeleVideo's computer and then sell it under a different name.

QUESTIONS

1. How would a personal computer purchase by an organization be different from a personal computer purchase by a consumer?

2. What are possible influences on organizations' purchase decisions that TeleVideo's marketing managers should understand?

3. What effect will the new personal computer marketing strategy have on organizations' buying decision processes?

4. Describe and explain the four most important kinds of information that TeleVideo's marketing managers should gather concerning organizational buyer behavior when purchasing personal computers. Would your answer be different for computer terminal purchases?

5. What type of decision would be made by an organization buying personal computers—new task, modified rebuy, or straight rebuy? Would your answer be different for computer terminals?

7 Marketing Information Systems and Marketing Research

When you finish this chapter, you will understand

□ The kinds of data that go into a marketing information system

□ How data are converted into information by a marketing information system

□ Why marketing managers must plan and use a marketing information system

□ The steps in planning marketing research for use in marketing decision making

□ Why marketing managers must be involved in the marketing research process

□ How marketing research fits into an overall marketing information system

Split-cable television systems enable researchers to compare advertising among control and test groups side by side within a single market location.

The Breast Examination Center of Harlem (BECH) faced a marketing problem. Opened in 1979, the New York City clinic's purpose is to fight the high mortality from breast cancer among black women more than 35 years of age. Unfortunately, many of these women saw a doctor only after their cancer was advanced. Although the clinic offered free breast examinations, it was not attracting women from the target group. Young women outside Harlem were the primary users. BECH's staff was puzzled as to how to increase the percentage of its patients from its target market.

BECH's management set out to discover why the target women were not using the clinic. Women in the target group were asked about the clinic's location, the free breast examination program, and their fears of cancer. The results clearly showed that women from Harlem knew little about the clinic or its purpose.

Promotion was an answer to the clinic's marketing problem. A first attempt was to use 30-second television and radio advertisements. Records of women using the clinic showed that this approach was not successful. BECH tried another approach. Approximately 14,000 personalized letters were sent to women in the target group, which invited them to call the clinic for an appointment for a free breast examination. The mailing successfully made women aware of the location and services of BECH. Furthermore, it reduced some of their fears of breast cancer.[1]

MANAGERS OF THE Breast Examination Center of Harlem found out what every marketing manager must understand: Having information is a key to successful decision making. The clinic's managers, faced with the problem of not attracting the targeted women, relied on research to discover that the target women knew little about the clinic. The managers decided to use promotion to inform the women of the clinic's location and program. Management also used information to find the proper promotion approach. Without the foresight to get information before taking action, the managers of BECH may have been unsuccessful in solving their problem. As two marketing experts have emphatically stated: "A strategic plan can be no better than the information on which it is based."[2]

In this chapter, we examine how marketing managers obtain and use information for decision making. First we discuss principles of marketing information planning. Then characteristics of a marketing information system are explained to show how information from several sources can be coordinated and delivered to marketing managers. Finally, we examine marketing research, one of the important sources of marketing information.

MARKETING INFORMATION PLANNING

Information for marketing decision making must be planned, not left to chance. Marketing managers need timely, accurate, and relevant information, yet want to avoid being inundated with too much information. Achieving these objectives means that the flow of information from the various sources to the managers who use it must be controlled. Meeting this challenge is the purpose of **marketing information planning.** Let us see how this planning works.

Pertinent information is power

To paraphrase a well-known saying, pertinent information is power (see Marketalk). The right information enables managers to make decisions that they may otherwise not have been able to make. For instance, managers of Ryder Truck Rental had a difficult problem targeting customers, primarily manufacturers and wholesalers, for its service. Management solved the problem by developing a list of likely customers in the United States and Canada. As its trucks became available in an area, key information on targeted customers (name, address, person to contact, probable type of truck needed, etc.) was sent immediately to the area's salespersons so that they could make sales calls. The information for targeting is an important factor in Ryder's success, as the vice-president of market planning and research acknowledges:

> Developing an accurate, comprehensive data base and organizing specific marketing techniques for putting that data to work have played a pivotal role in the success of our company.
>
> It is difficult to isolate revenue results and tie them directly to a component of a marketing program. However, we are certain that since we began the targeted marketing program, our growth (from $200 million in 1972 to $1 billion today) has exceeded the rest of the industry's by a wide margin.[3]

*Marke*TALK //

Political parties learn that information is power

IN THE OLD DAYS, political parties relied heavily on personal persuasion—the so-called arm-twisting—to get people to vote for their candidates. Arm-twisting is still a big part of politics, of course, but lately politicians are becoming much more sophisticated. They have learned to use the tools and techniques of market opportunity analyses, just like those employed by businesses. The computer and creative application of information have revolutionized the way political parties plan for a campaign.

The Republican National Hispanic Assembly, a group within the Republican National Committee, used available data in a very creative way to locate and sign up those unregistered voters who would be most likely to vote for its candidates. A computer was primed with data from a list of people with driver's licenses in a state. A second list of all registered voters in the state was also fed in. The computer examined both lists, searching for all people on the driver's license list who were not registered voters. The result was a third list of all unregistered adults in the state. Census data provided income, median home cost, and other socioeconomic characteristics. James L. Bruite, the Assembly's executive director, describes the last step in the analysis: "This group is then run through a

SOURCE: "The powerful new machine on the political scene," *Business Week*, Nov. 5, 1984, pp. 58, 62.

program that recognizes Hispanic surnames, and out pops your target list of upwardly mobile Hispanics." All of these data are widely available to anyone, but it is the way in which analysts put the data together to find the target potential voters that indicates how far political strategists have come in knowing how to study their constituents.

Much like companies use data on customers, the political parties are studying their voter segments. "Information is power," is the way Richard B. Wirthlin, the President's pollster, puts it. Through surveys, or polls, and other information, the parties learn about the makeup of voters across the nation. They know who votes as well as how they vote. Politicians also are able to listen to voters almost daily and find out what is important to them. For instance, in the last presidential election, a poll showed that after the first Reagan–Mondale debate support for the President was eroded among eighteen-to thirty-year-old voters. Immediately after receiving that information, Reagan stepped up campaigning to young people and talked about issues that they were interested in.

Studying the competition is also part of a market opportunity analysis, and the political parties have astutely benefited here, too. With the help of computers, strategists can study the positions of opponents as reflected in speeches and statements. The Republicans took advantage of these

kinds of data in the last presidential election by cross-indexing over 50,000 speeches, statements, and stories in the news media to glean where their opponents stood on the issues. The party's strategists could then devise responses most likely to influence the voters. Furthermore, split-second tactical decisions were made to counter the opposition as the campaign moved along.

An indication of the degree to which the computer is gaining favor with political parties is the success of the first commercially available software program for political analyses. Called Campaign Manager, it costs $750 and does a variety of tasks from fund-raising mailings to analysis of data from polls. Sales in one election year exceeded $500,000. The market for the program comes from the hundreds of thousands of political offices that are contested each two-year election period—from school board members to mayors to legislators. Clearly, analyses are being used by political strategists at all levels of public office campaigning. Thomas B. Hofeller, the director of computer services for the Republican National Committee, comments on the widespread use of computerized analysis in political campaigns: "What has happened over the past two years is the arrival of the microprocessor in a big way on the American political scene. It's in vogue and it's affordable, even in small campaigns."

///

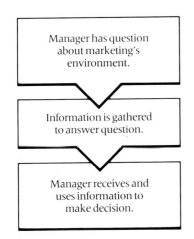

Exhibit 7.1 Pertinent information describes marketing's environment

Information is only pertinent if it answers questions that managers raise when they must make important marketing decisions. Information planning at Ryder Truck Rental started with a marketing question: Who are target customers for sales calls? Information needed to answer this question was identified and made available to managers. Importantly, marketing managers, who are users of the information, were involved throughout the process of planning and providing it.

The questions likely to be raised by marketing managers concern marketing's environment (macroenvironment, task and intraorganizational environments; see Chapters 2 through 6). Marketing decisions generally are aimed at influencing some aspect of these environments (customers, competitors) and in turn will be affected by environmental forces. Thus information helps managers understand the environment sufficiently well for proper decisions to be made (see Exhibit 7.1).[4]

Some questions are asked repeatedly, and information is regularly gathered and reported. For instance, a department store manager wants to know the volume of sales of each product line daily and weekly so that prices, promotion, and ordering decisions can be made. Product-line sales data are reported routinely each day with totals at the end of the week. Other questions are asked on an irregular basis, and information must be tailored at the time of the question to provide answers. For instance, new information must be gathered if the department store manager wants to know whether customers will buy a new product being considered. A study of customers' opinions of the product may answer the manager's questions.

How data are obtained

Information begins as facts and opinions about marketing's environment that we call **data.** Facts are numbers, words, or symbols that describe something about activities, transactions, or events that have happened or are happening now. For instance, historical sales volumes for a product; number, names, and characteristics of competitors; number and characteristics of a company's customers; and last quarter's percent growth in the economy are a few of the many facts that are used by marketing managers. Opinions are ideas that people believe to be facts or are their predictions of events. A study that asks customers whether they will buy the company's brand in the future yields opinion data. Because these customers have not actually bought the brand at the time of the study, they only can render an opinion about future behavior.

Information planning requires knowing where data are located and how they are obtained. Essentially, marketing data have three main sources: (1) internal data in company files and records, (2) external data gathered by marketing intelligence, and (3) external data gathered by marketing research.

Internal data. Every organization daily accumulates and records an amazing amount of data. **Internal data** describe the volume of transactions and activities of a company including orders, shipments, purchases, inventory, accounts receivable, expenditures, and previous studies. Companies store internal data in many places—accounting records, department files, internal correspondence (letters, memorandums, and reports), and even in employees' minds. Some of these data go into external reports such as stockholders' reports and tax statements. However, these data also are available to managers for decision making. For example, a brand manager may decide to increase advertising in one area of the country after seeing data indicating that sales of the company's product have decreased.

Marketing intelligence. Organizations set up procedures for scanning events in their macroenvironment and task environment. This scanning is called **marketing intelligence** and makes use of employees, other people, and published sources to gather data. For instance, salespersons for Flexatard Company, a manufacturer of dance and fitness bodywear, fill out weekly reports for managers listing the following information for each store visited: whether it is a new or established sales account, its location, what lines it carries, store buyer's requests, complaints and compliments on products, local economic conditions, and special marketing actions taken by the store (promotion, price specials, new products).[5] These data help managers plan marketing programs for store accounts.

There are so many sources of marketing intelligence that data tend to come into the firm in bits and pieces (see Exhibit 7.2). These sources must be coordinated so data forming a complete picture of environmental events are regularly sent to managers. Campbell Soup Company is one that performs this activity well. It combs sources such as government reports to keep up with demographic trends (e.g., slowing of population growth, increased growth among nonwhite groups, increasing family units but decreasing family size, increase in single-person households and elderly people). At the same time, the company studies technology related to food (e.g., biotech improvements in food production). Interestingly, this intelli-

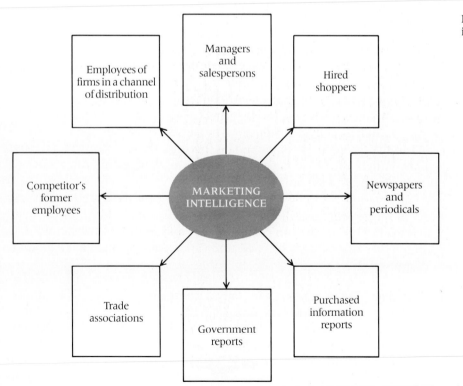

Exhibit 7.2 Sources of marketing intelligence information

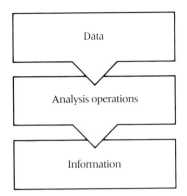

Exhibit 7.3 Analysis creates information from data

gence demonstrated the nutritional value of soup as well as people's concern for health. Campbell then developed the positioning strategy reflected in its slogan "Soup is good food," which is aimed at establishing soup as a healthy snack food.[6]

Marketing research. When marketing managers' questions cannot be answered with internal or intelligence data, managers use **marketing research,** the systematic gathering, analysis, and reporting of data to answer managers' questions concerning a specific marketing problem, opportunity, or decision. Projects or studies are designed to generate only the data needed for a specific decision. For instance, when Procter & Gamble's managers wanted to know how much sales to expect from its new brand of aspirin, Encaprin, a three-month study of consumers' purchases was conducted in a test-market city. Results helped managers decide to introduce the product across the United States (see Marketalk) [7]

Analyzing data for information

Data are not typically in a form that is useful for managers and must be analyzed to yield information on which managers can act. **Data analysis** is operations made on data to provide summaries, descriptions of relationships, and conclusions drawn from the data. In other words, analysis converts data into information (see Exhibit 7.3). For example, Procter & Gamble's marketing research test yielded sales data for Encaprin. The original form of the data was a list of numbers, each one measuring the unit sales of the new pain reliever for one week of the three-month test. Managers,

Marketing intelligence information helped Campbell Soup create the theme of its new advertising strategy, which focuses on the nutritional benefits of its products. "Soup is good food" has replaced its "M-m-m good" slogan of many years. (Courtesy of Campbell Soup Company)

*Marke*TALK ///
Phantom products

MARKET RESEARCHERS call it an "aided awareness" test. It goes something like this: "The following is a list of denture adhesive brand names. Please answer yes if you've heard the name before and no if you haven't. Okay? Orafix? Fasteeth? Dentu-Tight? Fixodent?"

Simple enough. But the results aren't always simple. When such a test was given to a group of denture wearers, 16% said they recognized the Dentu-Tight brand name. Funny. Dentu-Tight doesn't exist.

It's not funny at all, though, to the mythical Dentu-Tight's real competitors, who have spent millions of dollars to promote their own brand identity. Nor was the same phenomenon funny to the number one fastfood chain, McDonald's, a sponsor of the Olympics. In one audience awareness study, 32% of those surveyed believed that Burger King was a sponsor. It isn't.

That's called "spurious awareness," and it is a major problem for advertisers. Yet many companies ignore it—to their peril, thinks Joseph Smith, a consumer psychologist and president of Oxtoby-Smith Inc., the 28-year-old, Manhattan-based market research firm that is behind the Dentu-Tight findings and other studies on the problem.

Marketers have always pretty much taken product awareness for granted, says Smith. "You have reason to believe that if you spend X dollars on a felicitous advertising campaign, you will get a certain proportion of people in the intended market to know about you." But that assumption isn't always true.

Spurious awareness may begin at an early stage in an advertising campaign or

SOURCE: Raymond Goydon, "Phantom Products," *Forbes*, May 21, 1984, pp. 202, 204. Used by permission.

even before. If product awareness starts at zero, says Thomas Dupont, Oxtoby-Smith's director of research and also a psychologist, then that twilight zone between zero and something greater than zero may be much more important than previously thought. Until recently it was assumed to be negligible, a factor unworthy of measurement. But when Oxtoby-Smith decided to do some benchmark studies on the awareness of some new health and beauty products, Dupont noticed that spurious awareness "hovered around 8%." So consistent were the readings that Dupont created an 8% spurious awareness discount factor: When a survey showed 25% awareness for a product for which no benchmark had been established, the real level of awareness was about 17%.

But Dupont soon realized that wasn't precise enough. For products outside the health and beauty field, spurious awareness fluctuated greatly. Dentu-Tight's 16% mark was soon bested by results obtained in surveys for other new products, ranging from pasta to soft drinks. In one case, a proposed addition to an existing product line was already thought to exist by about 50% of those surveyed. When half the population believes a product you haven't yet introduced already exists you could be in big trouble. Your marketing efforts can verge on chaos. Advertising budgets can be easily misspent, and give results that send the wrong signals to product managers.

What happens if you ignore the spurious awareness factor? Dupont provides an illustration: "Before we hit on all this, we had a case in which the awareness [of a new product] was 70%, but first purchase was almost nil. The company therefore concluded that it didn't need more 'intrusive' advertising—telling people about the product—but, instead more persuasive

advertising. In fact, the spurious awareness for that product was so high that the reverse was true. The direction given to the advertising agency by the company was completely wrong."

Such problems are particularly important now in a boom time for marketers, when hundreds of new products are being introduced. "In 1983 some 1,803 products, representing some 3,791 flavors, colors and varieties, were introduced in the supermarket and drugstore area alone," says Martin Friedman, editor of Dancer Fitzgerald Sample Holdings, Inc.'s *New Product News*. That's the highest level in 20 years. So you may not want to spend a lot of money on advertising if you are not able to accurately test its effectiveness.

What's at the root of spurious awareness? Probably that the sounds and images of advertising messages often have no direct behavioral impact: People listen with only half an ear, so that the messages just seem to float around unconnected in the head. But when the proper stimulus comes along—say, a call from a market research company—connections are made, genuine or mistaken. "People often don't want to say they don't know," says Dupont, "so they create a plausible answer." The more plausible the name, the more likely people will think they have heard of it. In the arena of spurious awareness, Dentu-Tight will beat Lockjaw any day.

What can marketers do? At the very least, spurious awareness should prompt marketers to question the validity of advertising effectiveness measures on which they now rely. As Smith puts it, "Unless we can parse out that which is invented from that which is substantive, we are going to continue to make errors in assessing our advertising and introducing new products."

///

however, wanted to know whether growth in sales justified introducing the product into all markets. Analyzing the numbers, such as calculating the average change in week-to-week sales, yielded the desired information. As this illustration demonstrates, managers seldom want data; they want information.

Sometimes data are transformed immediately into information by persons collecting the data. For example, a salesperson may see a competitor's new brand in the stores (data), and conclude that the competitor is testing the brand for later introduction (information). More typically, data must be formally analyzed before being sent to marketing managers. Tools for analysis are needed; these include models and statistics.

Models. **Analysis models** describe a relationship between selected environmental factors. Relationships typically are stated in mathematical terms so data can be applied to the model. For instance, to calculate average growth rate for Encaprin's sales from the test data, a simple model such as the following is needed:

$$\text{Sales growth rate} = \sum_{t=1}^{n} (S_t - S_{t-1})/n,$$

where Σ is the sum of the calculations in parentheses, S_t is sales in week t, S_{t-1} is sales in the week immediately before week t, and n is the number of weeks in the three-month test.

Interestingly, managers have their own models—ideas of how their business world works—that guide their decisions. Every store manager for K mart has an idea, based on experience, of how store prices of products influence consumers' purchase decisions. Personal models help marketing managers determine what information is important. Because analysis models must coincide with personal models, managers should be involved in decisions on how to analyze data.

People who are specialists in planning information can help managers select the best model for a particular decision. Consider AT&T's application of computer simulation, a computer model that approximates real conditions and thereby describes how the environment works. The marketing decision was whether to introduce a new product, data terminals, into industrial markets. AT&T's specialists convinced managers to use simulation to describe how industrial buyers make purchase decisions for data terminals and how marketing programs influence these buyers. With simulation, managers analyzed how the market would likely react to different marketing programs.

To use models data are needed. The computer simulation required that AT&T conduct marketing research to get data on (1) benefits that buyers believed important in data terminals, (2) how buyers would trade off one benefit against another if they could not have everything they wanted in a single terminal, (3) the benefits that competitive products offered, and (4) an estimate of the total demand in markets for data terminals. The data were applied by the simulation model to determine the market share that each product design could expect under various monthly rental rates. Managers selected a design and price combination that was predicted by the model to achieve an 8 percent market share. After four years of sales, the marketing program actually achieved a market share at just less than 8 percent, proving how well the simulation model worked.[8]

Statistics. Usually data have to be manipulated in some way before they can be used by a model. **Statistics** refers to manipulations that organize data and help discover important differences among the data. Calculating averages, comparing two averages to see which is larger, calculating ratios, grouping numbers into categories, adding columns of numbers, and picking out the exceptional numbers in data are illustrations.

As you can see, statistics and models go hand in hand to provide the key information on which to base marketing decisions. Usually marketing managers use this information to determine the best of several alternatives. A model formalizes the criterion or criteria on which the judgment of "best" is to be made. Then data are inserted into the model to apply the criterion or criteria. Returning to AT&T's simulation model, it helped managers see which product design and price combination would yield the highest market share. In this case, "highest market share" is a decision criterion analyzed by the model and marketing research data.

We have discussed the ingredients for marketing information planning. Let us see how these ingredients fit together into a marketing information system.

MARKETING INFORMATION SYSTEMS

Information is needed on an ongoing basis to plan, implement, and control marketing strategy. Well-run companies meet this need by developing and using a marketing information system. A **marketing information system (MIS)** is a combination of people and equipment organized to systematically gather data about marketing's environment, to analyze the data for information, and to deliver the information to managers who use it for marketing decisions.[9] Building an information system, as one expert notes, is not easy, but it can change the way decisions are made.

> [An MIS] means hiring people with marketing science skills. It means organizing data bases and putting them in usable form. It means building a portfolio of models and analytical techniques directed at important company issues. It means integrating problem-solving and problem finding within the marketing function using the marketing science intermediary to facilitate the process. A strong system does not spring up overnight. It takes two or three years of evolution and development, but it can lead to new styles of marketing management.[10]

Building an information system

An MIS comprises both data on the marketing environment, which managers must have to make successful decisions, and the managers who seek information for decision making. Essentially a company designs an MIS to manage the flow of data, including their conversion into information, from the marketing environment to the marketing managers who must take action in that environment. Exhibit 7.4 shows the important components of the system that link environment and manager.

Building an information system must start with the decisions being made by managers for which information is needed. Most decisions concern how to use the marketing mix components most effectively to achieve objectives. For example, a sales manager makes decisions such as the following:

- How many salespersons are needed to cover an area
- What kinds of training a salesperson should have to be effective with customers
- How salespersons should be motivated to sell to customers to achieve sales objectives

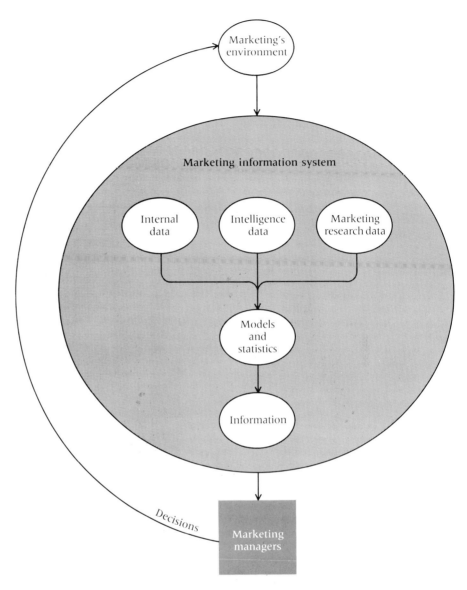

Exhibit 7.4 A marketing information system

- The amount of salespersons' time that should be spent looking for new customers as opposed to selling to current customers
- If salespersons should be devoting more time to some customers, less time to others
- If salespersons should be changing sales presentations to counter what competitors are doing

As you can see from these illustrations, making marketing decisions requires understanding the effect of marketing mix components on the environment, particularly on customers and competitors. Pressure to make decisions leads managers to ask two questions of an MIS: What is happening in the environment? and How is marketing going to affect the environment? Exhibit 7.5 provides illustrations of both questions.

As you look at the illustrations in Exhibit 7.5, notice that some questions ask for information that describes events, and others ask for information concerning relationships between one event and another. Each question calls for different models and statistics. For instance, consider information describing events. When a manager at AT&T wanted to know the kinds of industrial customers that buy data terminal products, marketing research was used to discover characteristics of companies buying the product (e.g., their size, geographic location, need for the product, type of business). The event described is customer purchasing. A simple model that matches data on companies that have purchased with data on their characteristics is all that is needed.

Questions that describe relationships between events are more difficult to answer and often require more sophisticated models and statistics than questions that just describe events. Returning to AT&T's situation, managers also wanted to know the relationship between product data, terminal product designs, price alternatives, and probable share of all sales of the product. Analysis required that data on customers and competitors be used with a sophisticated computer simulation model to provide the answers. In general, a company's MIS becomes more sophisticated as the difficulty of the questions that managers expect the system to answer increases.

Exhibit 7.5 Questions marketing managers ask and answers they expect from a marketing information system

Questions	Illustrations
What is happening in the environment?	What kinds of people are buying the product? Why are these people buying while others are not? When competitors raised their price, what happened to our sales? How will higher interest rates in the economy affect customers' purchases? What new technologies are coming along to improve product benefits for customers?
What is the relationship between marketing and the environment?	How much will sales increase if two more salespersons are hired and assigned to territories? Will competitors lower their prices in retaliation if we lower our price? Which of two advertising campaigns will yield higher sales? How much market share can we expect if the company introduces this new product? Can we increase repeat sales if we offer credit?

Using a marketing information system

An MIS quickly becomes ineffective if the information is not delivered to managers who are in a position to act on it. At the same time, a company does not want key information to get into the wrong hands. For these reasons, effective procedures for delivering information are essential. Two major concerns are security and getting information to the most likely user.

An MIS can be misused easily if information is inappropriately altered or delivered to the wrong people. Although computers have greatly enhanced MIS capabilities, heavy reliance on them also increases security problems. For example, a disgruntled computer programmer can wreak havoc on an MIS by altering data, statistical operations, or models. Furthermore, theft of information by outsiders is an ever-present problem.

Getting the right information to the right managers is crucial. Yet managers at various levels in a company and with a range of responsibilities can place a wide variety of information demands on the system. Consider information for planning marketing strategy. Marketing managers must evaluate a broad range of factors from the macroenvironment and task environment to understand the conditions under which the strategy must work. At the same time, a number of managers—in advertising, product divisions, and sales—are planning for their functions. An MIS must be accessible to all these managers with timely and relevant information.

Even after marketing plans are complete, managers need information for making implementation decisions. For example, Zales, the jewelry retailer, decided to target new segments. The strategy included relocating Zales' stores to be close to these segments. The MIS had to supply information to answer managers' questions that came up during the location decisions:[11]

- Where do target customers live and shop?
- Which and how many retailers serve the target customers' needs?
- Is the area's target segment growing?
- Are there enough customers in the area to support another store?
- Can the market be entered without taking sales from existing stores?
- Can the store be profitable in the area?

Finally, an MIS must provide information to help managers monitor a strategy's performance during and after implementation. Initially, information helps set standards for evaluating performance. With standards in place, information is collected at regular intervals (daily, weekly, monthly, quarterly) to show how well actual performance compares with these standards. For example, a marketing executive for a mail-order company routinely studies trends in sales from orders. The information helps him evaluate performance of the company's marketing program against sales objectives or standards and take action when improvements are warranted.[12]

Our discussion of a marketing information system demonstrates the contribution that information makes to marketing management. To take a closer look at the task of information planning within the system, we examine marketing research to see how information can be tailored to help with a specific marketing decision.

MARKETING RESEARCH PLANNING

Marketing research is a valuable tool for getting data on marketing's environment. It is justified when the value of new information in making a decision is greater than its costs. To get the most value for the cost, marketing research should be planned carefully so only the most pertinent information is provided. Planning requires that both managers and research specialists go through a sequence of steps: (1) defining the problem or opportunity, (2) setting information objectives, (3) deciding on sources of data, (4) deciding on a research design, (5) analyzing data, and (6) reporting research results (see Exhibit 7.6). To help you understand how these steps are applied in practice, we follow an actual marketing research process implemented by Goode Memorial Hospital, a county hospital in a southern state.*

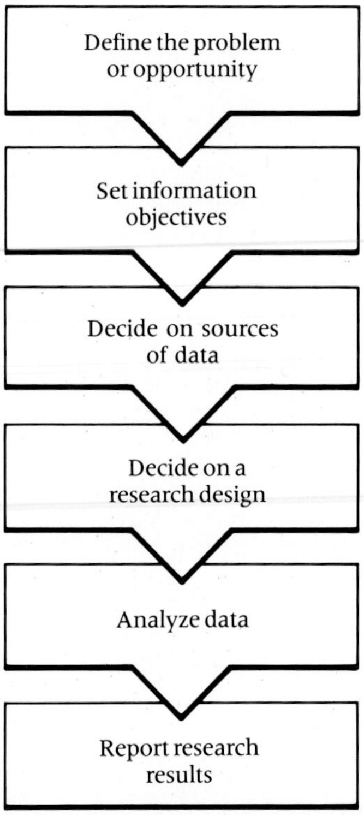

Defining the problem or opportunity

Marketing decisions solve a problem, take advantage of an opportunity, or both. A **problem** arises when the performance resulting from implementing a previous decision is not meeting the standards set for it. Goode Memorial Hospital considered itself the primary health care facility for residents of the entire county. This purpose was translated into a key marketing objective: at least 90 percent of the county's residents requiring hospital care be admitted to Goode Memorial. A study of hospital usage, however, indicated that the actual percentage was only 70 percent and dropping. A market share problem was clearly evident.

At times a marketing manager discovers an opportunity for the company and must decide how best to take advantage of it. An **opportunity** is a set of environmental circumstances that enables the company to improve its performance. At the same time that the market share problem was discovered, Goode Memorial saw an opportunity to reach out into the community with new services (e.g., a prescription drug filling and delivery service for the elderly).

Marketing research can help managers primarily in two ways. First, information enables managers to define more clearly the problem or opportunity as well as its cause. Goode Memorial Hospital's administrators were not sure why they were losing patients to hospitals outside the county, nor did they know what particular new services were needed by county residents. Market research helped discover reasons for both. Second, information enables managers to identify and weigh the advantages and disadvantages of alternative courses of action. Usually a problem can be solved or an opportunity exploited in more than one way, and managers may not know which is best. This dilemma faced Goode Memorial's administrators. They were at a loss as to how to get market share up to former levels. Furthermore, as mentioned previously, they were not sure which additional services to offer. Research helped them deal with these decisions.

Exhibit 7.6 The marketing research planning process

---

* This illustration is based on an actual project performed for a hospital. The name of the hospital has been changed for reasons of confidentiality.

Setting information objectives

Generally, marketing managers use marketing research to answer questions about specific aspects of marketing's environment. Formulating good questions becomes the basis for setting **research objectives,** statements specifying what is to be learned about selected marketing environmental forces likely to affect decisions. Marketing managers must be directly involved with setting the objectives because only they know which answers will make a difference when an alternative marketing action is chosen.

If managers know almost nothing about the environmental forces relevant to a decision, *exploratory research objectives* are set to find out what might be causing a problem or creating an opportunity. If managers know some of the environmental forces that are occurring, they can set *descriptive research objectives,* which guide research toward testing managers' understanding of these forces and what can be expected from them. Finally, if managers believe that a relationship exists between factors and want to know what the relationship is, *cause-and-effect research objectives* are set to test how one or more factors cause changes in another factor. Goode Memorial Hospital's administrators set research objectives by first discussing the performance problem and potential opportunities. They formulated a tentative list of research objectives to guide research toward questions the administrators wanted answered. Then they reviewed the list to eliminate objectives that were not essential for the decisions. The following list shows the marketing research objectives finally determined:

1. To learn about the role that patients and their families play when health care facilities are chosen
2. To learn about county residents' opinions of Goode Memorial Hospital
3. To learn about county residents' opinions of competitive hospitals
4. To determine residents' awareness of competitive health care facilities including nonhospital services
5. To find out which hospital residents would choose for selected kinds of treatments
6. To find out the needs that county residents have for health care facilities and services
7. To determine the likelihood of county residents using new health care services such as wellness centers, drug and alcohol abuse programs, and physician referral services
8. To determine what information sources residents use to learn about doctors and hospitals

Some objectives were aimed at discovering reasons for the market share problem (items 2, 3, 4, and 5), and the others guided marketing research toward discovering opportunities for new services. Rarely would one research project cover all three kinds of objectives (exploratory, descriptive, cause-and-effect). Goode Memorial concentrated on exploratory (items 1, 6, and 8) and descriptive (items 2, 3, 4, 5, and 7) objectives to learn about the hospital's task environment. Administrators did not believe that they were able to formulate cause-and-effect objectives.

Deciding on sources of data

In the United States, there is an $11 billion industry devoted to supplying data and information to organizations.[13] Some of these suppliers sell standardized reports to all customers, that is, every report contains the same data. Examples of these reports (which are probably in your library) are *Predicasts, Standard & Poor's Industry Surveys,* and *Sales & Marketing Management's Buying Power Data Service.* The government is also an important supplier of information. U.S. Bureau of the Census reports and the *U.S. Industrial Outlook* are probably the best-known examples. Data provided in published form from commercial and government suppliers are called **secondary data** because the data have been collected previously, but not specifically to assist in making a particular marketing decision.

Other suppliers of information customize research for their clients, providing exactly the information requested. A company also may decide to collect its own marketing research data. In either case, new data that are collected expressly to assist in making a specific marketing decision are called **primary data.** Information availability, quality, timeliness, and cost considerations generally dictate whether primary data are needed. Goode Memorial decided to gather primary data because neither internal data nor intelligence data answered their questions and no relevant secondary research data were available. The hospital was willing to postpone marketing decisions and spend funds to get information it needed for decisions.

Deciding on a research design

If primary data are needed, research decisions are made to determine what and how data should be collected. A **research design** is a plan for conducting the study. Marketing managers seldom are involved heavily in making these choices: They usually are made by someone with specialized marketing research skills. Nevertheless, a marketing manager must understand how the research design determines the nature and quality of the resulting information. Exhibit 7.7 shows the key characteristics and corresponding options for the research design.

Types of research. There are three basic types of marketing research that correspond to the three types of marketing research objectives. **Exploratory research** provides data that help managers discover environmental forces affecting a marketing decision. It is best used when managers are not well informed about what is happening in the environment. For instance, the manager for a racket club saw that sales of indoor court time was low for two of the eight courts, and he had no idea why. An exploratory study revealed that people believed that the lighting was poor on those two courts.

Descriptive research is used when managers suspect that a particular environmental factor is important but want to know more about it. Sometimes a manager may have a hypothesis that states the expectation of how two or more forces are related. For example, a manager of a jeans store believed that people less than thirty years of age (first factor) were the most frequent buyers of jeans (second factor). A descriptive study confirmed this hypothesis by analyzing data on the number of people in each age group who bought jeans.

Exhibit 7.7 Determining a marketing research design

Design Characteristics	Options
Type of research	Exploratory Descriptive Experimental

Method of sampling	Nonprobability
	  Convenience sample
	  Quota sample
	  Judgment sample
	Probability
	  Simple random
	  sample
	  Stratified sample
	  Cluster sample

Method of collecting data from sample	Observation
	Interviewing
	  Mail questionnaire
	  Telephone
	  Personal

Timing data collection	Cross-sectional study Time series study

Experimental research is used when cause-and-effect objectives have been set. Usually a manager wants to know how one factor will cause a change in another factor. An experiment isolates the cause-and-effect relationship between the two factors by eliminating the possibility that other factors not of interest will affect the data. For example, if the product manager for Alka-Seltzer, an antacid sold by Miles Laboratories, wanted to know how sales would change if prices were raised, experimental research could provide the answer if conducted in the following way: First, several similar cities (same size, mix of demographic characteristics, distribution, competition, and so on) are selected. In some of the cities, price is raised for a specified number of weeks. In the other cities, price is not changed. Sales of Alka-Seltzer are compared in all the cities to see how price caused sales to change.

Sampling. Marketing research can collect data from and about people, events, and objects such as products or stores. For simplicity, let us concentrate on data from people. People usually studied are current or prospective buyers, although suppliers, competitors, or intermediate sellers also may be the focus of the study. If all people in a group of interest, called a population, are included in the study, the result is a *census*. Censuses rarely are done because they are extremely time consuming and expensive. The U.S. Bureau of the Census conducts a census study of the U.S. population every ten years, which costs billions of dollars and takes years to complete.

Fortunately, most studies need not get information from all people in a population. Conclusions can be drawn about the population by obtaining data from a sample. A **sample** is a subset of people selected from the population. The opinion polls that gauge how people in a whole country will vote in an election are based on data from samples of at most a few thousand people.

Two sampling methods are used: nonprobability sampling and probability sampling. In **nonprobability sampling,** the selection of people is based on the researcher's judgment. One type is a *convenience sample* in which only people who are easiest to recruit are included. For example, the owner of a restaurant puts comment cards on the table for diners to fill out because he is interested in how satisfied diners are. Only those diners who decide to fill out the card are included in the sample; it usually is not known if they represent all diners. In a *quota sample* the researcher specifies the desired characteristics of the sample. For example, in a study of travel behavior the rescarcher specified that at least 40 percent of the sample be men. A quota that the sample must meet is forty percent men. In a *judgment sample,* the third approach, people are chosen based on the researchers' judgment that they are important for the data wanted. Suppose a study needed a sample of people in industrial customers' buying centers. The researcher may first contact purchasing agents in each company, who are asked to name people in the company who also are involved in a purchase decision. The researcher uses judgment to decide which of these additional people to include in the sample. Notice that quota sampling is a special case of judgment sampling.

Nonprobability sampling techniques usually are relatively easy and inexpensive to implement. Furthermore, the researcher can control the extent to which certain kinds of people are included in the sample, which helps it be representative of the population. The major drawback of all nonprobability samples is that judgment substitutes for systematic procedure in the selection process. As a result there is no way to evaluate how much error in the data is caused by using a sample rather than by obtaining data from a census. Nonrandom sampling can be justified for exploratory research, but it generally is not recommended for descriptive or experimental research.[14]

In **probability sampling** systematic procedures, not judgment, are used to select members of a sample. These procedures ensure that every person from the population has a known probability of being selected for the sample. Consequently, the researcher can evaluate the amount of error in data caused by using a sample rather than a census. This advantage comes at a cost because probability samples are more expensive and difficult to obtain than nonprobability samples.

There are three major types of probability samples. For a *simple random sample* people are selected from a population in such a way that each person has an equal probability of being selected. For instance, a camera store drew a sample from its credit customers by randomly selecting names from a listing of these customers. Of 800 customers 200 were selected: each member on the list had a 200/800 or 25 percent chance of being included in the sample.

For a *stratified sample* another step is added to the random sampling procedure. First the population is divided into groups called strata. The basis for division is chosen judgmentally, but it must be an important factor for determining who to include in a representative sample. For example, if management believes that income is an important factor influencing people's attitudes, then researchers planning an attitude study can form income strata. Then a simple random sample is selected from each strata.

For a *cluster sample* a population is divided into clusters before the sample is taken. As with strata, clusters are formed based on judgment. A cluster sample differs from a stratified sample because only a sample of the clusters are selected for obtaining data, though each cluster has a known probability of being selected. Either a census or a sample is drawn from these clusters. The error from using a sample rather than a census can be evaluated more easily when a probability procedure such as cluster sampling is used. It was partly for this reason that Goode Memorial Hospital decided to use this technique. Cluster sampling frequently is used because it can be done at low cost for a given size sample. For instance, clusters may be city blocks. By interviewing everyone on randomly selected blocks rather than randomly selected people throughout the city, interviewing costs can be held down.

Methods of data collection. Data from a sample can be obtained from an observation study or an interview study. In an **observation study** people's behavior (what they are doing at the moment) is observed and recorded. Researchers themselves or electronic observation equipment may watch what people do. Suppose managers of a supermarket want to find out which aisles in the store have the heaviest traffic. An easy way to get pertinent data is to watch how shoppers move through the store, going from aisle to aisle. Cameras and checkout scanners could also be used (see Marketech).

Marke**TECH** □ □ □ □ □ □ □ □ □ □ □ □ □ □ □ □ □ □

Technology helps marketing researchers

TECHNOLOGY IS REDUCING costs and improving the ease with which marketing research data are gathered. Two illustrations are checkout scanners and electronic questionnaires. Scanners are devices for reading bar code information from product packages. Used in a checkout lane of a supermarket, scanners, when hooked up to electronic cash registers, help keep track of inventory and reduce costs of hand-marking products. As the number of supermarkets using scanners has increased, marketing researchers have applied the technology to gathering data for analyzing consumer behavior. For example, a coffee manufacturer can get quick feedback on how many items of its brand, and those of competitors, have been sold each week.

Another application has been to run experiments. Suppose the coffee manufacturer wants to see which of two advertisements works best at getting sales. The company can run each advertisement in similar cities. With the cooperation of se-

SOURCE: Edward Tauber, "Purchase transaction analysis of UPC data identifies buying habits," *Marketing News,* Jan. 11, 1980, p. 10.

lected supermarkets, scanner data on purchases of the manufacturer's brand from the cities can be compared and which advertisement generated more sales will be indicated.

Opportunities for learning from scanner data are great. Some marketing researchers are getting randomly selected shoppers to present an identification card to a supermarket checkout clerk. By inserting an identification number, purchases of each shopper can be recorded for all products in the shopping cart. Only three types of data are on the scanner record: brands purchased, number of units of each brand purchased, and price paid. The data can be used, however, to discover aspects of buying behavior such as (1) combinations of products that usually are purchased, (2) products purchased most frequently when the total bill is high versus low, (3) amount spent in a product category, (4) whether one or multiple brands were purchased in a product category, and (5) how many items were bought in a product category.

Marketing managers can answer many questions from the data. For example, consider data on combinations of products

purchased. Managers may look for opportunities to promote several products in the same campaign. Furthermore, new product opportunities may be uncovered for products that can complement those sold by the company. As another illustration, data on price and purchases of competing brands can be used to see if price is a key factor in determining market share.

A second technology is the electronic questionnaire. These devices can ask questions of people virtually anywhere (in a store, in a restaurant, at an airport, at the checkout counter of a hotel). People answer each question by pushing a button, choosing one of several alternatives. Data are recorded immediately in the machine and can be easily and quickly transmitted to a computer. An important advantage is the speed with which data can be gathered, analyzed for information, and sent to managers for action. A hotel may use electronic questionnaires to obtain feedback on customer satisfaction with its services. The hotel manager can get daily information to help spot problems as they arise (poor food service, dirty bathrooms, slow checkout) and in time to correct them before business is hurt severely.

□ □

Exhibit 7.8   Questionnaire questions

1. If you get sick and need a doctor, who chooses your doctor? (Please check the one answer that *most often* describes what happens.)
   ____ me
   ____ my spouse
   ____ me and my spouse together
   ____ someone else in my home
   ____ someone else not living in my home

2. If your spouse gets sick and needs a doctor, who chooses the doctor?
   ____ me
   ____ my spouse
   ____ me and my spouse together
   ____ someone else in my home
   ____ someone else not living in my home
   ____ does not apply

3. Think back to all those times that you or someone in your home had to be admitted to a hospital. How *often* did *the doctor* pick the hospital that was used?
   ____ always
   ____ almost everytime, but not always
   ____ about half the time
   ____ sometimes, but not often
   ____ never
   ____ do not know

4. If your doctor wanted to admit you to one hospital and you wanted to go to another hospital, which of the following actions would you take?
   ____ go to the hospital my doctor chose
   ____ try to convince the doctor to use the hospital I chose
   ____ go to another doctor who practices in the hospital I chose
   ____ take some other action

Another way to gather data about people is to conduct an **interview study.** Questions are placed into a carefully arranged list forming a *questionnaire,* which is then delivered to the people in the sample, called *respondents.* Their answers to the questions are recorded as data. The questions are selected according to the marketing research objectives. The questions shown in Exhibit 7.8 were asked to provide data to meet Goode Memorial's marketing research objective item 1 (see page 187). Clearly, which questions to include on a questionnaire are of great concern to managers who will later use the data.

When planning an interview study, researchers must decide how to deliver the questionnaire to respondents. Most questionnaires are delivered in one of three ways. A **mail questionnaire** is designed so respondents can complete it without assistance. One is sent to each respondent. Because Goode Memorial had limited funds for their research, needed the data quickly, and were asking questions not easily obtained in a personal interview or by telephone, managers decided to use a mail questionnaire. Although this technique is the least expensive of the interview studies, it has several drawbacks. Many people in the sample may not return the questionnaire because they lack time or motivation. Thus the percentage of questionnaires mailed that are returned (the *response rate*) can be low, causing concern about how accurate data are. Response rates in practice vary widely from less than 10 percent to more than 90 percent.

An increasingly popular alternative to a mail questionnaire is a **telephone interview.** Interviewers call people in a sample and ask them questions over the telephone. Answers are recorded immediately by the interviewer, who often uses an electronic data entry terminal that looks something like a personal computer. Using the telephone is a faster process of getting data than the other methods, and response rates usually are high. It is less versatile, however, because only simple, easy-to-answer questions can be asked.

A third method of delivery is a **personal interview.** Interviewers ask questions of respondents face-to-face and record their answers. Personal interviews may be one-on-one with each respondent questioned individually, or group interviews may be used. A popular form of group interviewing is the **focus group interview.** Each interview is conducted by a moderator who asks questions of eight to ten respondents in a group. The moderator's job is to "focus" the group's attention on a topic of interest. Questions are general, however, and respondents are encouraged to talk with each other about the topic. The give-and-take discussion that ensues is an excellent way to draw out and probe respondents' thoughts and feelings on the topic. The group's support encourages respondents to express comments they might not make in a one-on-one interviewing situation.

Focus group interviews are particularly valuable for exploratory research. The results are not representative of a population because the samples are quite small and recruited using nonprobability techniques. Nevertheless they do provide an in-depth look at how consumers think and react. For example, Its For Levi, a regional chain of jeans stores, used focus group interviews with groups of eight to ten adults from families to learn how jeans and jeans stores are chosen by family members. The results from the discussions suggested that wives play a key role in these decisions. They buy jeans for themselves without influence from other family members, buy

In 1981 an AT&T service number helped Quaker Oats not only collect market data but also promote its Cap'n Crunch cereal. Kids could call a toll-free 800 number to find out if they had won a bicycle. The promotion generated a staggering 24 million calls and increased Cap'n Crunch's share of the cereal market by one-third. (Copyright © 1984 AT&T Communications.)

jeans for their husbands, and are opinion leaders for their children. A subsequent mail questionnaire study that included more persons than the discussion groups confirmed these findings. Focus groups are inexpensive, can be done quickly, and are good for helping managers get ideas for marketing decisions.[15]

When should observation instead of an interview be used? Neither is always best and so the answer depends on several considerations.[16] First, the researcher must think about the types of data required. Generally, an interview is more versatile than observation because a greater variety of data can be gathered. For instance, if a marketing manager wants to understand customers' unobservable characteristics such as beliefs, attitudes, values, and motives, then an interview clearly is preferred. Both observation and interviews can yield data on behavior, but interviews record respondents' perceptions of their own or others' behavior.

Second, observation is a more objective way of getting data on behavior than is an interview, as it does not depend on a respondent's memory. For example, Miles Laboratories wanted to find out how well a new brand of children's vitamins was selling in a city. Observation was used to audit sales: The number of units sold in a sample of stores was counted. Interviewing people, on the other hand, would have yielded less accurate data because some people might have forgotten how many units they purchased, or might not want to say whether or how much they purchased.

Finally, observation can be more time consuming and expensive than an interview. Observation studies only measure current behavior and so must wait for that behavior to take place. An interview can proceed immediately. In general, versatility, objectivity, and cost of data must be evaluated to select the best approach for a study.

Timing data collection. Many marketing research studies collect data at one point in time. A **cross-sectional study** observes or questions respondents once, and data from that single time are analyzed for information. For instance, when Zales, the jewelry store chain, decided to go after new target markets, a cross-sectional study of "active jewelry purchasers" was conducted. The study yielded data on purchases, likes and dislikes of jewelry types, uses of jewelry, and demographic characteristics. Results of the study demonstrated that segments exist.[17]

Cross-sectional studies are not good for analyzing changes taking place in a company's marketing environment. Another approach is needed that collects data at more than one point in time. This technique is called a **time series study,** which can be thought of as a series of cross-sectional studies done at regular intervals. For example, Procter & Gamble's three-month test of its new aspirin product, Encaprin, illustrates a time series study of consumer purchases.[18] Sales were measured at regular intervals during the three months. Each time sales data were collected, a picture of consumer purchasing was revealed. The data of most interest, however, were the change in sales from period to period, which allowed management to see sales growth. A time series study is more expensive and takes longer to complete than a cross-sectional study. It was for these reasons that Goode Memorial decided on a cross-sectional rather than a time series study: The hospital administrators were under pressure from their board of directors to develop a marketing strategy as quickly as possible. There was not time to conduct a time series study. Furthermore, administrators believed the cross-sectional technique would be sufficient for uncovering reasons for Goode Memorial Hospital's market share problem and for learning what direction to explore with respect to new market opportunities.

Analyzing data

Analyzing data from a marketing research study uses statistics and models to answer managers' questions. Most managers first want to know what kinds of people were respondents in the study. Data describing respondents, such as their age, gender, occupation, frequency of use of the product of interest, and income, help answer this question. The entire analysis proceeds in this fashion—questions are posed by management and the appropriate data are analyzed for information to answer each one. For every question, researchers must choose the proper statistics and models. Their application summarizes the data and searches for comparisons that managers want to know about.

Administrators of Goode Memorial Hospital asked the following question: "How do people rate our hospital compared with our major competitor?" This question is good because people do rate competitors and often use the one they rate highest. The administrators did not read the 400 or more questionnaires returned by respondents to get the answer. The answer was provided more simply as follows: average (a statistic) ratings across the entire sample for each hospital on each of several performance dimensions were computed. Then a statistical model was used to test whether the average ratings for Goode Memorial were different from the corresponding ratings for the major competitor.

The results of this analysis are shown in Exhibit 7.9. Each respondent rated Goode Memorial Hospital and its competitor on specific criteria that

Exhibit 7.9 Comparing Goode Memorial Hospital with its major competitor

	Average Rating	
Criteria	Goode Memorial*	Major Competitor
Cleanliness of hospital	2.2	2.0
Reasonableness of cost	3.0	2.7
Quality of nursing care	2.2	2.0
Many specialists	2.4	1.4
Moderness of building and equipment	2.2	1.7
Friendliness of nurses and technicians	2.2	2.1†
Credit availability	2.7	2.4
Quality of food service	2.4	2.3†
Orientation programs	2.6	2.2
Family members' opinions	2.5	2.0
Convenient location to home	1.5	2.4
Visiting hours strictly controlled	2.7	2.2

* 1 = essential to have and 5 = not at all important
† Not statistically significantly different

typically are used to judge hospitals. The criteria are listed in order of importance, the most important at the top and the least important at the bottom. Each average rating in the two columns was computed by summing all respondents' ratings and then dividing by the number of respondents. These ratings were compared to discover which differences were significant (i.e., that cannot be explained only by a sample being used instead of a census). All but two of the differences were significant.

The most exciting part of marketing research comes during **data interpretation,** when conclusions are drawn from the analysis. Notice in Exhibit 7.9 that for all criteria except Convenient location (which is next to last in importance) the competitor had higher ratings. From the data analysis, administrators concluded that Goode Memorial Hospital had a reputation problem. This information explained why the competitor was able to draw away patients, particularly for more serious kinds of treatments.

Reporting marketing research information

How well marketing research can be applied by managers depends in part on how the data and analyses are communicated. Managers always have the option of not using the results and basing decisions on other factors, such as their experience. If the marketing research is to be accepted, the results must have **validity** (the data measure what they were intended to measure) as well as suggest actions to take. A good report of a study should not dwell only on information. It must also comment briefly on the study's safeguards that ensure valid data, present interpretations of results in a way that marketing managers can understand easily, and suggest appropriate marketing actions. A marketing research report with these features was presented to the administrators of Goode Memorial Hospital. It explained the objectives of the research, the research design, and the analyses performed so the administrators would have confidence in the report. The report also presented information and recommended marketing decisions suggested by that information. For example, one recommendation, derived from analysis of data in Exhibit 7.9, concerned improving the hospital's reputation among people in the county. Goode Memorial needed to be perceived as more friendly and concerned about the patient than the competitor. Retraining the staff to better interact with patients was suggested to improve Goode Memorial's reputation.

Another recommendation was to build a strong reputation for providing specialty treatment in at least one, or preferably a few, health care areas (e.g., heart, eye, lung, or emergency care). The reputation in the specialty area should carry over to improve the hospital's overall image. These recommendations, in addition to others on providing new services, helped the administrators properly apply the marketing research study to the marketing problems and opportunities at hand.

SUMMARY

Ability to find and use information for decision making is the hallmark of a professional marketing manager. This ability must be learned by acquiring information skills. Marketing managers need information because they must make decisions that affect and are affected by marketing's environment. Information helps a manager understand and predict these environmental forces.

Information does not appear by chance; it must be planned. In the large context of an organization, information is best controlled by marketing information planning. Data are obtained from internal sources, marketing intelligence, and marketing research. Once obtained, data must be analyzed. Tools for analysis include models and statistics.

To obtain and coordinate information on an ongoing basis to plan, implement, and control marketing strategy, well-run companies use a marketing information system (MIS). The MIS gathers data, analyzes them for information, and delivers information to marketing managers according to their needs. A sound MIS is a significant aid to a professional approach to marketing management. But managers must have the information skills to enable them to interact with the system.

Finally, marketing research planning is a sequence of steps that enables primary data to be gathered, analyzed, and communicated to management as information for decision making. This process includes defining the problem or opportunity, setting information objectives, deciding on sources of data, deciding on a research design, analyzing data, and reporting information. Marketing research cannot be left to information specialists: Managers must be involved in the process to ensure that exactly the information needed is provided. At each step of the process, managers and information specialists must work together.

KEY TERMS

marketing information planning	research objectives	interview study
data	secondary data	mail questionnaire
internal data	primary data	telephone interview
marketing intelligence	research design	personal interview
marketing research	exploratory research	focus group interview
data analysis	descriptive research	cross-sectional study
analysis models	experimental research	time series study
statistics	sample	data interpretation
marketing information system (MIS)	nonprobability sampling	validity
problem	probability sampling	
opportunity	observation study	

QUESTIONS FOR REVIEW AND DISCUSSION

1. What is marketing information planning?
2. How are data and information related? How are they different?
3. What are the three main sources of marketing information?
4. What is an analysis model? How is statistics related to analysis models?

5. Explain the components of a marketing information system.

6. If you wanted to find out what prices your competitors are charging, what source of information would you use?

7. If you wanted to know sales of your brand for the last three years, which source of information would you use?

8. What are the steps in the marketing research planning process?

9. How is a problem different from an opportunity?

10. Do marketing managers ever set exploratory marketing research objectives? Why or why not?

11. How is an exploratory research objective different from a descriptive research objective?

12. How is a descriptive research objective different from a cause-and-effect research objective?

13. Give examples of secondary and primary data.

14. Suppose you wanted to recommend a research design. What decisions would you have to make?

15. Should marketing managers always expect that probability sampling will be used for marketing research? Why or why not?

16. Suppose you wanted to learn more about how members of a family go about purchasing a car. Would you use an observation or an interview study? Explain the reasons for your answer.

17. If you wanted to know how many people shop in your store each week, would you use an observation or an interview study?

18. Explain the difference between a cross-sectional and a time series study. Give an example of each one.

19. Is marketing research planning best left up to information specialists? Why or why not?

BUILDING YOUR PORTFOLIO

Knowing where to get information for marketing decisions is an important marketing skill. This project will help you become more familiar with intelligence and marketing research sources. Your task is to compare the attractiveness of two states in the United States (or any two geographic areas in your country on which you can get data) as markets for appliances. Pick any two states that are close to each other and of similar land size (e.g., Indiana and Illinois, Alabama and Georgia, Missouri and Colorado). Write down your guess as to which state has more opportunity.

Using library sources, gather all relevant data on these two states such as population size, age breakdowns, average income, effective buying income, number of businesses, employment, and retail sales. Find as much data as you can that are pertinent. Then analyze the data by making comparisons between the two states to draw conclusions about which one has the larger market for appliances. (Hint: use the data to indicate residents' ability and willingness to buy appliances.) How accurate was your original guess?

NOTES

1. The basis for this illustration is Iders Marsh, "Social marketing: How advocacy groups use research, advertising, PR to alter behavior." *Marketing News*, May 13, 1983, Section I, pp. 26–27.
2. David B. Montgomery and Charles B. Weinberg, "Toward strategic intelligence systems." *Journal of Marketing*, Vol. 43 (Fall 1979), p. 41.
3. Gordon J. Bingham, "Marketing data base ups revenue for Ryder Truck Rental." *Marketing News*, June 25, 1982, Section 2, p. 3.
4. Montgomery and Weinberg, op. cit., pp. 41–52.
5. "Send in the sales force." *Sales and Marketing Management*, Mar. 14, 1983, pp. 57–58.
6. "Soup maker bets future on monitoring technological, consumption changes." *Marketing News*, Oct. 12, 1984, p. 44.
7. Eleanor Johnson Tracy, "Testing time for test marketing." *Fortune*, Oct. 29, 1984, p. 75.
8. This illustration was drawn from "Attitude research, conjoint analysis guided Ma Bell's entry into data-terminal market." *Marketing News*, May 13, 1983, Section 1, p. 12.
9. For a similar definition, see John D. C. Little, "Decision support systems for marketing managers." *Journal of Marketing*, Vol. 43 (Spring 1979), p. 11.
10. Ibid., p. 25.
11. Craig E. Cina, "Selecting store locations: A market-driven approach." *Marketing News*, Sept. 14, 1984, p. 41.
12. "How computers remake the manager's job." *Business Week*, Apr. 25, 1983, p. 69.
13. "Report on $11 billion information industry finds it fragmented, dynamic, overlooked." *Marketing News*, Oct. 12, 1984, p. 27.
14. Gilbert A. Churchill, Jr., *Marketing Research*. Chicago: The Dryden Press, 1983, pp. 344–348.
15. Bobby J. Calder, "Focus groups and the nature of qualitative marketing research." *Journal of Marketing Research*, Vol. 14 (Aug. 1977), pp. 353–364.
16. Churchill, op. cit., pp. 174–176.
17. Cina, op. cit.
18. Tracy, op. cit.

Case 7.1

Steelcase

STEELCASE hit on a new product idea for office furniture markets. The Grand Rapids, Michigan, company developed office furniture systems designed for a variety of office environments. The systems include coordinated furniture (desks, chairs, tables, bookshelves) that business pur-

SOURCE: "Company markets office furniture as total package instead of components," *Marketing News*, Oct. 26, 1984, p. 23.

chasers can buy as a package. Studies of types of office environments such as for secretaries, computer programmers, and executives guided Steelcase in designing a product line of these packaged systems. This concept offers increased cost effectiveness and more efficient use of space than competitors' products. The brand name was basix.

Steelcase has also developed a program to help purchasers determine their user's furniture needs and requirements. This

program enables purchasers to select the most appropriate furniture system from the company's product line. As the vice-president of marketing said, "We see basix as a major step forward in the evolution of system's furniture. Because of its logic and simplicity, basix will significantly enhance both facility management and asset control."

Marketing managers must plan a marketing strategy for the basix systems product line.

QUESTIONS

1. What are the key marketing decisions that Steelcase's marketing managers must make?

2. List five important questions that must be answered by Steelcase's marketing information system (MIS) for marketing managers to plan the marketing strategy.

3. Which of the kinds of data in the company's MIS—internal,

intelligence, and/or marketing research—would most likely be needed to answer each question?

4. Assuming at least one of management's questions must be answered by marketing research, what steps would you take to answer that question?

Case 7.2

Big Brothers of Fairfax County

BIG BROTHERS OF AMERICA is a social service program designed to meet the needs of boys ages six to eighteen from single-parent homes. Most of the boys served by the program live with their mothers and rarely see or hear from their fathers. The purpose of the program is to give those boys the chance to establish a friendship with an interested adult male. Big Brothers of America was founded on the belief that an association with a responsible adult can help program participants become more responsible citizens and better adjusted young men.

SOURCE: Gilbert A. Churchill, Jr., *Marketing Research*, Third Edition. Copyright © 1983 by CBS College Publishing. Reprinted by permission of The Dryden Press, CBS College Publishing.

The Fairfax County chapter of Big Brothers of America was founded in Fairfax in 1966. In 1971, United Way of Fairfax County accepted the program as part of its umbrella organization and now provides about 85 percent of its funding. The remaining 15 percent is raised by the local Big Brothers agency.

Information about the Big Brothers program reaches the public primarily through newspapers (feature stories and classified advertisements), radio, public service announcements, posters (on buses and in windows of local establishments), and word-of-mouth advertising. The need for volunteers is a key message emanating from these sources. The agency phone number is always included so people wanting to know more about the program can call for information. Those calling in

are given basic information over the telephone and are invited to attend one of the monthly orientation sessions organized by the Big Brothers program staff. At these meetings, men get the chance to talk to other volunteers and to find out what will be expected of them should they decide to join the program. At the end of the session, prospective volunteers are asked to complete two forms. One is an application form and the other is a questionnaire in which the person is asked to describe the type of boy he would prefer to be matched with as well as his own interests.

The files on potential Little Brothers are then reviewed in an attempt to match boys with the volunteers. A match is made only if both partners agree. The agency stays in close contact with the pair, and monitors their progress. The three counselors for the Big Brothers program serve as resources for the volunteer.

The majority of the inquiry calls received by the agency are from women who are interested in becoming Big Sisters or from people desiring information on the Couples Program. Both programs are similar to the Big Brothers program and are administered by it. In fact, of fifty-five calls concerning a recent orientation meeting, only five were from males. Only three of the five callers actually attended the meeting, a typical response.

While the informational campaigns and personal appeals thus seemed to have some impact, the results were also generally disappointing and did little to alleviate the problem of a shortage of volunteer Big Brothers and the shortage grows weekly.

Big Brothers of Fairfax County felt a lack of awareness and accurate knowledge could be the cause of the shortage of volunteers. Are there men who would volunteer if only they were made aware of the program and its needs? Or is the difficulty a negative program image? Do people think of Little Brothers as problem children, boys who have been in trouble with the law or who have severe behavioral problems? Or could there be a misconception of the type of man who would make a good Big Brother? Do people have stereotypes with respect to the volunteers—for example, that the typical volunteer is a young, single, professional male?

QUESTIONS

1. What are the marketing problems facing Big Brothers of Fairfax County?

2. What are the questions that managers of Big Brothers should have answered to help resolve these problems?

3. Which of the kinds of data—internal, intelligence, and/or marketing research—are needed to answer these questions?

4. What steps would you take to answer these questions?

8 Market Targeting and Positioning

When you finish this chapter, you will understand

□ Why the market target decision is important

□ What market segmenting is all about

□ How markets can be divided into market segments

□ The steps that are necessary in segmenting a market

□ The types of information used to segment markets

□ How market targets are selected by marketing managers

□ The concept of positioning products and services

To many parents, Gerber is synonymous with baby foods. After an unsuccessful sojourn into adult-food markets, Gerber again concentrated on the target markets where it has incredible strength: parents who buy baby food and nonfood products.

Pan American World Airways flight 110, which leaves JFK International for Rome every day at 6:45 P.M. and returns as flight 111 the next day, is virtually a private New York-to-Rome shuttle for Mario Perillo, 56, president and owner of Pearl River, N.Y.–based Perillo Tours. Since 1974, when his firm started buying air tickets exclusively from Pan Am, Perillo estimates that his firm has flown some 90,000 people to Italy and back. It's the only destination Perillo serves. . . . Of Pan Am's estimated 146,000 round-trip passengers to Italy annually, Perillo Tours accounts for 15%. His firm is now Pan Am's single biggest customer.

The Perillo family has been selling all-inclusive package tours to Italy since 1945, when Perillo's father, Joseph, started the operation, and even before Pan Am began to fly 377 Strato-cruisers to Rome in one-way trips of 17 hours. Perillo used to sell charter flights until he negotiated a deal with Pan Am to buy regular flights at a discount—a draw for a budget-minded traveler. A normal economy-class round trip to Italy now runs $1,200 on Pan Am. Perillo's $1,500 package includes air fare and ground transfers, meals, hotels, and sightseeing for two weeks. His sales reached $30 million this year.[1]

PERILLO TOURS has targeted a specific group of people for its customers: budget-conscious persons, families, and groups who want to visit Rome for two weeks on a sightseeing tour. Attractive prices can be offered by concentrating on a single service. Understanding customer needs and wants and deciding which people (or organizations) a firm should try to satisfy can have a critical effect on the future performance of any organization, large or small. Management rapidly is recognizing that mass or shotgun approaches to serving markets are both costly and ineffective in generating sales for many kinds of products and services.

In this chapter, we examine mass and selective approaches to serving customers, and then consider how market segments or niches can be formed. Next, the characteristics used to describe market segments in consumer and industrial markets are considered, and the criteria important in deciding which people or organizations to target are examined. Finally, we discuss positioning the marketing effort to serve the firm's target customers.

MASS VERSUS SELECTIVE APPROACHES

A company has great flexibility regarding its choice of which customers to serve. The options range from targeting all people (or companies) that have a need or want for a particular product type (or service) to concentrating on only a specific group of people within the total market. A market target may be the total market or one or more specific groups within the total market. Let us examine these market target options.

Mass marketing and segmenting defined

Mass marketing is a firm's deciding to serve all or most of the people (or organizations) that have needs or wants for a specific product type with the same marketing program. Thus the mass market is the total market. All people in the market represent potential customers. A firm is using a mass market approach when it offers the same marketing mix (product, placement, price, and promotion) to everyone in the market. Although a mass (or undifferentiated) approach will not satisfy completely all buyers, it can be effective if the needs and wants of most buyers are similar. There are other reasons why a company may target the mass market. If the market is new, enough information may not be available to break up the mass market into parts. The absence of competition also may suggest using a mass

Do you ever feel guilty about loving clothes? I do sometimes...and then I get over it. Next to friends, sex, work, books, tennis, my Lhasa Apso and my husband—not in that order—I get more pleasure from buying and wearing beautiful clothes than nearly anything! My favorite magazine says following and then creating your own fashion isn't immoral, illegal, or full of calories, so go! And they show me beautiful pages of inspiration every month. I love that magazine. I guess you could say I'm That COSMOPOLITAN Girl.

One of my most satisfying relationships is with a magazine.

COSMOPOLITAN®
A PUBLICATION OF THE HEARST CORPORATION

In the ads, That Cosmopolitan Girl is usually single, 21, and white. Don Schultz, professor of advertising at Northwestern University, says, ''This campaign is target marketing at its finest. People will say it's tacky, . . . but [Cosmo] knows who they want to talk to and they speak directly to them.'' (Courtesy of *Cosmopolitan* magazine)

approach. Finally, serving the mass market may be necessary to obtain the sales volume needed to make the venture profitable.

Market segmenting is dividing the total market into two or more parts, such that the people in each part have relatively similar needs and wants for a particular product type or service, and designing different marketing programs for different segments. Each part of the market is designated a **market segment** (or **market niche**). The basis for a segment (or differentiated) approach is that the marketing mix appropriate for the people in one segment is not appropriate for the people in another segment. A company may decide to market to a single segment, a few segments, or all or most of the segments in the total market. The distinction between mass and segment approaches is illustrated in Exhibit 8.1. In the mass approach a single marketing program is designed to meet the needs of the entire market. In contrast, when using the segment approach, a marketing program is tailored to the needs of the people in each segment selected. For example, each segment targeted by a firm has a unique marketing program. Note that the marketing program differences between segments may apply only to certain parts of the program such as the use of different channels of distribu-

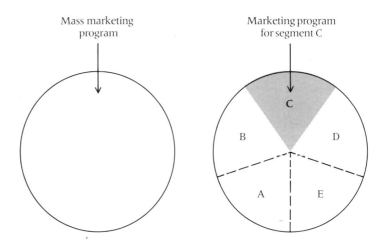

Exhibit 8.1 Mass versus segment approaches

tion or advertising media. Thus, uniqueness can be accomplished without altering all of the marketing program components.

The key feature of a segment approach is that the people in a particular segment will be more responsive to a marketing program that meets their needs than will be people in another segment to the same program. Thus the objective of segmenting is to place people (or organizations) into the same segment if they are expected to respond similarly to a particular marketing program that has been designed to meet their needs. In contrast, people in other segments will not respond favorably to the same program. The assumption is that there are differences in response between segments; otherwise, there is no reason to use a segmenting approach. Response is measured by the volume of the product purchased, frequency of purchase, or other measures of patronage. (See Chapter 21 for more about market response.)

An example will be helpful in illustrating differences in response. Suppose a market has been divided into two segments, A and B. Each segment

(Below) The debut of *Wild Concerto* was a great success. Originally published in trade size—that is, as a hardcover book—this bestseller has had such popular appeal that Worldwide Library later brought it out in a 4″ × 7″ paperback, mass market size. (Courtesy of Harlequin Sales Corp.)

(Below, right) Minnetonka Inc., recognizing that gum disease has become the number 1 dental problem in the United States, found a niche for itself by becoming the first to offer a toothpaste with plaque-fighting ingredients. By also putting Check-Up into a new dispenser it managed to pump up its sales to more than 2 percent of all toothpaste sold in 1984. (Courtesy of Minnetonka, Inc.)

*Marke*TALK ///

Payless Cashways segments the home improvement market

SEVERAL COMPANIES have selected as market targets consumers who do their own home improvement work rather than hire contractors. Firms that are marketing to the do-it-yourselfer include Color Tile (floor covering), Stanley Works (hand tools), Sherwin-Williams (paint), Black and Decker (power tools), and Payless Cashways (home building supplies). This market is experiencing explosive growth and is expected to hit $115 billion by 1990, approximately three times the size of the market in 1981.

---

* "Payless: Zeroing in on suburbia," *Business Week*, Sept. 7, 1981, pp. 104, 108.

Payless Cashways has been particularly successful in the do-it-yourself building market. Sales in 1985 were approaching $1400 million, up from $383 million in 1979. Net profits rose rapidly during the same period, reaching $37 million in 1984. An important feature of the Payless marketing approach was its choice of the customer group that the firm began targeting in the early 1980s.

Currently, Payless' biggest customer category is made up of college-educated, white-collar workers in their mid-30s, with family incomes of more than $30,000 annually. Women make up 24% of the market, and that figure is

growing. In general, the do-it-yourselfer is young, upwardly mobile, usually owns a house, and is willing to devote time and energy to enhance what is commonly his largest investment.*

In 1981 the company began conducting customer research to refine its understanding of target customers for use in guiding advertising and sales promotion efforts. Interestingly, unlike other lumberyard and home improvement center competitors, management has discouraged contractors' and builders' purchases by not offering them discounts. Management wants to concentrate on serving the needs and wants of do-it-yourself customers.

///

has one million people. The people in each segment are exposed to an identical marketing mix. That is, the same product is offered to both segments A and B through the same distribution channels (e.g., department stores), at the same price, with the same advertising media and message, and with equal personal selling effort. After twelve months, total sales of the product are $10 million in segment A and $2 million in segment B. The response to the marketing program by the people in segment A is clearly much higher than in segment B. This example highlights the basic reason for segmenting. In many markets the responsiveness of people to the same marketing mix varies between segments. Thus by grouping people with similar responsiveness into segments, marketing results often can be improved.

Segmenting often is desirable in large mature markets when competition is strong and clear differences exist in buyer responsiveness. By selecting one or more segments in which a firm has advantages over competition, a strong market position can be established, and segments in which intensive competition exists can be avoided. The real test of the value of segmenting is whether it will prove to be more profitable to a company than following a mass marketing approach. Buyers benefit from firms tailoring marketing programs to the specific needs of the people in the segment. Perillo Tours (discussed earlier) demonstrates how a firm can increase sales and profits by specializing on a particular segment of the market. (See Marketalk for an additional application of segmenting.)

Steps in selecting a market target

Market segmentation is deceptively simple. It often is easy to find differences among the people or companies that constitute the total market for a product or service. The important issue is whether differences in factors such as income, age, life-style, and product use will be useful in

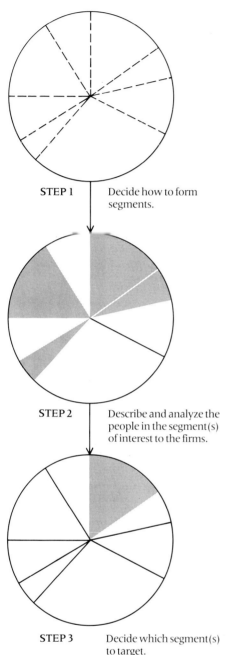

STEP 1   Decide how to form segments.

STEP 2   Describe and analyze the people in the segment(s) of interest to the firms.

STEP 3   Decide which segment(s) to target.

Exhibit 8.2   Steps in selecting a market target

Exhibit 8.3   Factors used to form market segments

guiding the targeting of a firm's marketing efforts. Careful analysis must be conducted by management to determine if real segments exist and, if so, whether the firm should target its marketing efforts toward one or more of the segments.

The major steps in selecting a market target are shown in Exhibit 8.2. Step 1 is deciding how to divide a market into segments. Selecting the basis of segmenting is very important. Many factors can be used to establish segments. When a segment is correctly formed, the people in that segment will respond similarly to a particular marketing mix. Step 2 is learning about the people in each segment of interest to the firm. Sources of information include customer profiles and competitor analysis. Step 3 is deciding which segment or segments to target, or instead deciding to use a mass approach because segment analysis may indicate no real advantages to be gained by using a segment approach. In the following sections we look closely into what is involved in each of the steps in selecting a target market.

An illustration will show what is involved in identifying market segments. Architect James Hamill and engineer Earl McKinney launched their architecture firm in Lexington, Kentucky, in 1978.[2] By 1983, Hamill & McKinney had ninety employees, offices in six cities, many clients, and revenues of nearly $5 million a year. Architecture is not an easy profession to break into considering the 70,000 architects fighting for business in the mature new construction market. How did they do it? Beyond their acknowledged professional capabilities, two features of their business approach stand out. First, they decided to specialize in restaurants, a rapidly growing segment of the construction market. Hamill's experience as head of the architecture department at Jerrico (designers of Long John Silver's seafood restaurants) especially enabled them to attract this segment. Thus the type of building to be designed was the basis of forming segments. Second, they aggressively marketed their services using personal selling, advertising, and high-quality services delivered quickly to meet clients' deadlines. In 1982 the firm spent more than $100,000 for magazine advertisements, trade shows, direct mail, and travel to call on prospective customers. Their use of aggressive marketing is particularly interesting, given the lack of concern (and sometimes distaste) for promotion by many professional people. Yet professionals in several fields such as medicine, law, dentistry, architecture, and accounting are beginning to recognize the need for targeting prospective customers and developing programs to meet clients' needs.

FORMING SEGMENTS

Factors used to form segments

Three factors are popular for dividing total markets into segments as shown in Exhibit 8.3. These are (1) the characteristics of the buyer or user, (2) the characteristics of the product that are desired by the buyer, and (3) the purchase-use situation.[3] Some examples of the target segments of different companies are shown in Exhibit 8.4. Let us examine how these three factors are used to form segments.

Exhibit 8.4 Examples of target segments

Company	Target segment
Lane Bryant stores (women's retail apparel stores)	Women 16 and older needing "special-sized" clothing
Dossier magazine (monthly magazine covering Washington, D.C., society)	Affluent, socially conscious D.C. residents
Weight Watchers International (weight-loss clinics)	Overweight people who want to become serious dieters
Snap-On Tools (socket wrenches and other hand tools)	Professional mechanics needing durable hand tools
Stanley Works	Do-it-yourself home improvement homeowners
Estée Lauder (cosmetics)	Women who patronize higher-price and quality department stores

Buyer or user characteristics. Characteristics of people (or organizations) can be used to divide total markets into segments. Characteristics used by consumer-product markets include age, race, income, occupation, life-style, geographic location, and physical characteristics such as size and weight. Socioeconomic and demographic characteristics are popular with marketers because advertising media (television, newspapers, magazines, and radio) can be selected so that the audience corresponds to the market niche a firm is trying to reach. Useful characteristics for segmenting industrial markets include type of industry, size, geographic location, and management orientation (e.g., conservative). A closer examination of some of the popular buyer characteristics for segmenting consumer markets will demonstrate how segments are identified.

Geographic segmentation is widely used to divide national markets into regional, state, and local segments. Suppose, for example, you have a new product that you plan to market to the Hispanic segment of the U.S. population. Approximately 70 percent of the U.S. Hispanic population can be found in ten metropolitan areas (see Exhibit 8.5). Geography, as a basis of segmentation, allows the marketer to concentrate marketing efforts in selected areas such as the ten cities listed in Exhibit 8.5. Regional preferences often are used to segment specialty products. For example, hominy grits are popular in the South, western wear is marketed aggressively in the West, and sailboat retailers are concentrated near the east, west, and gulf coasts and large inland bodies of water. Other geographic variables include temperature, terrain, and population density.

Demographic segmentation uses variables such as age, income, and gender to divide consumer markets. Age, for example, frequently is related to preferences for various products. Because the relative size and growth rate of different age groups vary, identifying the relevant age groups for a firm's products is important. An interesting analysis of age group composition, size, and growth rate for Canada is shown in Exhibit 8.6.

Suppose a company planned to introduce a new snack product in Canada in 1980 aimed at persons between the ages of thirty-five and forty-four. What were the growth prospects for this group from 1980 to 1990? As you can see, it was the fastest growing age segment in the Canadian population. Of course, growth by age group does not indicate how many persons

Exhibit 8.5 Hispanics: The top markets

Area of Dominant Influence	Population
1. Los Angeles	3,133,000
2. New York	2,355,000
3. Miami	790,000
4. Chicago	734,000
5. San Antonio	718,000
6. San Francisco	686,000
7. Houston	552,000
8. McAllen-Brownsville, Tex.	480,000
9. Albuquerque, N.M.	389,000
10. El Paso, Tex.	388,000

SOURCE: Strategy Research Corporation, Miami. Reprinted with permission from the December 5, 1983 issue of *Advertising Age.* Copyright 1983 by Crain Communications, Inc.

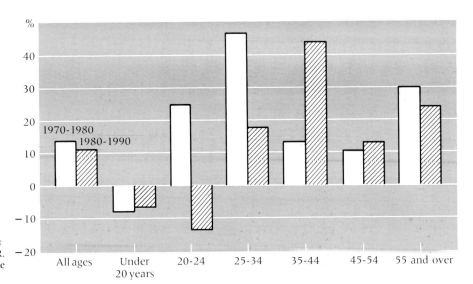

Exhibit 8.6 Age group growth in Canada, 1970–1990

SOURCE. *Handbook of Canadian Consumer Markets* 3rd edition, compiled and edited by Carolyn R. Farquhar and Carole FitzGerald (Ottawa: The Conference Board of Canada, 1984), p. 11.

are in the category. Importantly, in 1985, 3.5 million persons were estimated to be between the ages of thirty-five and forty-four, approximately 14 percent of the total population. Because age group composition can be forecast accurately several years into the future, age represents a useful basis of segmentation. As an illustration, Exhibit 8.7 projects the growth of this age group in Canada from 1980 to 2000. As indicated, products aimed at these people should experience substantial sales growth through the year 2000.

Psychographic segmentation uses variables such as life-style, social class, and personality. Psychographic information about buyers is more difficult to identify and interpret than is geographic or demographic information. Nevertheless, psychographic information can better discover *why* people buy goods and services than can other types of information. Consider the following life-style information obtained from a national survey of 500 men and women between the ages of twenty-five and forty-nine:

- Sixty-seven percent considered leisure and recreation to be necessities rather than luxuries.
- Sixty percent agreed that "vacation is not the time to cut corners to save money."

Exhibit 8.7 Projections of the growth of the number of persons between the ages of thirty-five and forty-four in Canada (millions of persons)

SOURCE: *Handbook of Canadian Consumer Markets,* 3rd edition, compiled and edited by Carolyn R. Farquhar and Carole FitzGerald (Ottawa: The Conference Board of Canada, 1984), p. 10.

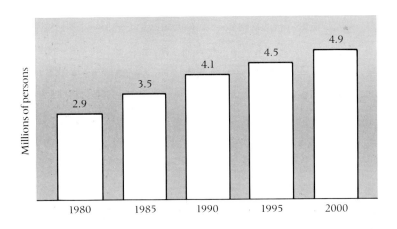

- A widespread underlying concern was identified regarding social isolation, rejection, and happiness.
- Seventy percent said they would not become "tied down to long-term financial responsibilities."
- In general, the group was more interested in enjoying the present than in worrying about the future.[4]

These and other study findings indicate promising future sales prospects for products that meet this age group's life-style needs. Examples include health clubs, vacations, games, and other products that "enhance direct communications between human beings."[5]

Whereas the potential of using psychographic information as a basis of segmentation is exciting, the high costs and complexity of marketing research needed to identify market segments are likely to discourage widespread use of psychographic segmentation. Moreover, psychographic factors probably account for only part of the differences between buyer groups in a market. Incorporating psychographic information into market analysis nevertheless has proved beneficial for some firms.

The profile of Spiegel's new target market shown in Exhibit 8.8 illustrates how life-style provides an important guide to targeting Spiegel customers. Note how various life-style characteristics are highlighted in the Spiegel target customer profile. An important influence on Spiegel's decision was the marketing research findings that indicated the rapid shift of the traditional housewife into the workforce. This expanding economic base and changing life-style of American women were important factors in the decision.

Desired product characteristics. Product characteristics such as product features, price, quality, service, warranty, and performance attributes can be used to form market segments. Hartmarx, a manufacturer of medium- to high-priced men's suits, provides an interesting example of market segmenting based on product price and style. The wide range of brands and prices offered by Hartmarx is shown in Exhibit 8.9. The use of product attributes to form segments involves matching the attributes to specific needs and wants of buyers. Note, for example, that Hartmarx offers different styling choices for men's apparel in the same price range (e.g., Henry Grethel, Austin Reed, and Christian Dior Monsieur). A closer look at some

---

Exhibit 8.8   Spiegel targets upscale career women

Profile of Spiegel's New Target Customer

The career-oriented woman between the ages of 25 and 54,

Who responds to fashion,

Who recognizes quality,

Who is extremely pressed for time,

Who appreciates the convenience of direct (catalogue) marketing,

Who has a median household income of $34,000+, and

Whose demands for service and convenience are not being met by the typical department store.

SOURCE: "Spiegel turns a new page," *Chain Store Age Executive,* May 1983, pp. 125–126.

Exhibit 8.9 How Hartmarx uses price and style to form market segments in the men's apparel market

Retail Price	Contemporary	Designer/ Personality	Traditional	Forward Fashion
$525+	Hickey-Free-man–Walter Morton			
$450–$500	Jaeger	Christian Dior Grand Luxe		Walter Holmes–Soci-ety Brand
$325–$450	Hart Schaffner & Marx		Graham & Gunn	
$255–$375		Christian Dior Monsieur Pierre Cardin	Austin Reed of Regent Street	Henry Grethel
$215–$275		Nino Cerruti	Racquet	
$170–$245	Jaymar Allyn St. George	Johnny Carson		
$120–$180	Kuppenheimer			

SOURCE: Hartmarx's 1984 *Annual Report,* p. 17.

of the variables used in segmenting by desired product characteristics illustrates the usefulness of this basis of segmentation.

Price segmentation is used by various types of retailers. Consider Toys R Us, the successful discount toy retailer, who is targeting people who want low prices. The chain typically does not run sales. Instead, everyday prices are extremely low. In contrast Makers' Mark whiskey is priced high and the firm's advertising message is that "It tastes expensive and is."

Instead of remaining in direct competition with Sears, Penney, and Wards, Spiegel's management decided to go after Saks Fifth Avenue, Bloomingdale's, and other upscale department stores. The company's strategy, reflecting the changing life-styles of its target customers, shifted from a price to a fashion orientation. (Courtesy of Spiegel)

Benefit segmentation is based on the type (or types) of benefits offered to the buyer by the product or service. People buy products as a way of meeting their needs. People's needs vary so they seek products with benefits that satisfy their needs. As an illustration of benefit segmentation, the toothpaste market has been divided into the following categories based on benefits:

Sensory segment comprises people who are interested in flavor and appearance of the product.
Sociable segment comprises people who want bright teeth.
Worrisome segment comprises people who are interested in preventing decay.
Independent segment comprises buyers who are not loyal to any brand. They perceive no differences between brands and typically buy on the basis of low price.[6]

The worrisome segment is the user group that Crest dominated for many years. In the 1980s Crest encountered aggressive competition from other brands for buyers in this segment.

Consider this illustration. Jerome Schulman, a seventy-year-old entrepreneur, identified a profitable segment for toothpaste based on the benefit provided.[7] Troubled with canker sores, fever blisters, and other problems, Schulman, a chemist, developed a toothpaste to respond to these problems. Priced three times higher than most brands, the product is targeted to people who have bleeding gums and sensitive teeth. Shane (Hebrew for *tooth*) was selling well in 1983 without a multimillion-dollar advertising budget or the endorsement of the American Dental Association. It was carried in more than 700 drug and food outlets in the Chicago area.

The purchase-use situation. The purpose of the purchase and how the product is used may be useful information in forming market segments. Examples include size and frequency of purchase, where the purchase was made, importance of purchase, how the product will be used, and various other aspects of the purchase-use situation. Some examples of segmentation by use situation show the value of this segmentation scheme.

Volume segmentation, or the extent of product use, provides a useful basis of segmentation for some products. User categories include heavy, medium, and light users. For example, light coffee drinkers might represent a market segment for instant coffee because users would not want to spend the time to brew their own coffee. Other product features such as size of a coffee pot and ease of preparation could be used to meet the needs of different user groups. For volume segmentation to be effective, product features of each brand must appeal to particular user groups. For example, if the same product or brand meets the needs of heavy, medium, and light users equally well, there is no need segment by product use.

Consider, for example, people's needs for away-from-home food and beverages. This market can be divided into eating occasions involving family, social, and business meals. Different types of eating establishments correspond to each use category. Family meal occasions may include fast-food outlets, family-style restaurants, and cafeterias. Other examples of markets in which *user-occasion segmentation* may be appropriate are air travel (e.g., business, pleasure, and special tours) and hotel accommodations.

Multiple segmentation factors. Often, as illustrated in previous examples, multiple segmentation factors may be used to form segments. Several factors such as age, income, and life-style may together identify a specific segment within a market. Of course, if segmentation is carried to its limits, each person (or company) would be a segment. This degree of segmentation is not practical in many markets. The objective is to recognize and identify distinct segments that represent feasible targets.

An illustration will show how multiple factors can be used to identify a market segment. Let us consider how one company screens prospects for automobile insurance to determine if they fall into the market segment the firm wants to serve. A small California automobile insurer, Twentieth Century Insurance Company, has targeted as its customers mature, stable persons that drive conservative automobiles and represent low risks.[8] The company operates by mail and phone, offering insurance rates that are far below those of its competition. Promotional costs have been kept low because Twentieth Century has not advertised for several years. Management studies loss statistics to identify the characteristics of good and poor insurance risks. Included in their analyses are potential indicators of risk such as age, driving records, automobile types, neighborhoods, and marital status. Here are some of the questions you might be asked if you called the firm regarding insurance rates.

> Are you less than twenty-five years of age?
> Are you married? For how long?
> How many cylinders does your car have?
> What type of transmission?
> Do you have any mental or physical impairments?
> Have you ever been denied insurance?[9]

Answer two or three questions wrong, as half the callers do, and Twentieth Century will not send out an application. Of those that return applications, 15 percent are rejected. Thus an important aspect of Twentieth Century's marketing approach is identifying low-risk segments of the market for automobile insurance.

Popular bases for segmenting business markets

Whereas many of the factors used to segment consumer markets can be used for business and organizational markets as well, there also are some differences in segmentation factors. A look at some of the widely used segmentation bases for business markets will highlight the similarities and differences.

Geographic segmentation. Segmentation by location is often more feasible in business markets than in consumer markets. Similar types of businesses tend to concentrate in certain areas. Also, there are fewer firms in business markets than persons in consumer markets. For example, if you are marketing a product or service that is used in new building construction, only ten cities in the United States represent a major portion of new building construction. The ten cities and the construction volume for each are shown in Exhibit 8.10. Note the heavy concentration of new construction in Texas, accounting for approximately one-third of the total for the ten metropolitan areas.

Industry segmentation. Often companies in the same industry have similar needs for products. Segmentation by industry category is a useful method of targeting marketing efforts. Industrial-products companies sometimes assign salespersons to specific industry groups, which enables the salespersons to become knowledgeable about buyer needs and wants. International Business Machines used industry segmentation when it first began developing computer systems. This specialization helped IBM determine computer application requirements, equipment and software needs, and product marketing guidelines. The illustration of the architecture firm earlier in the chapter is another example of segmentation by industry or type of business.

Usage or volume purchased segmentation. Because business buyers vary in their needs for goods and services, segmentation based on volume purchased is a useful way to group industrial buyers into similar use categories. The Quaker Chemical Company has an interesting approach to volume segmentation. Quaker is a producer of specialty chemicals for use in various processes such as steel manufacturing. The company concentrates its marketing efforts on buyers whose chemical requirements exceed $50,000 a year. Salespersons have only a few accounts so they can study the customers' operations in depth, which enables the salespersons to determine where and how Quaker's chemicals can be used by the customers.

Benefit segmentation. Business, like consumers, seek benefits from products that satisfy their needs.

> In industrial marketing heavy emphasis is given to service before and after the sale, to product performance, and to technological needs. For highly technical equipment the important benefits may be unique to each buyer. In such cases benefit segmentation would result in one customer in each segment. Such uniqueness prevents a generalized strategy. There are, however, some benefits that are common to most industrial purchases. These benefits include price, terms of sale, performance, quality maintenance, integrity, service after the sale, deliveries according to schedule, and efficient handling of complaints.[10]

Interestingly, brands of industrial products often vary in the extent to which they meet buyers' needs. For example, a manufacturer of motors learned by comparative testing of a key competitor's product that its own motor used

Exhibit 8.10 The ten most active metropolitan areas in building construction (in millions)

	1982	1981	Percent change
1. Houston	$5,790	$5,818	−0.5
2. Dallas–Fort Worth	4,616	4,007	15.2
3. Los Angeles	3,320	4,553	−27.1
4. New York	2,876	2,821	2.0
5. New Orleans	2,579	882	192.4
6. Washington	2,569	2,741	−6.3
7. Chicago	2,363	2,634	−10.3
8. Denver	2,300	2,296	0.2
9. San Francisco	2,161	1,909	13.2
10. Atlanta	1,884	1,527	23.5

SOURCE: First City Bancorp., F. W. Dodge division, McGraw-Hill Information Systems; reprinted with permission from the December 5, 1983 issue of *Advertising Age.* Copyright 1983 by Crain Communications, Inc.

substantially less fuel at high speeds, but substantially more fuel at low speeds than the competitor's motor. Thus, for buyers using the motors at high speeds, the firm had an advantage over the competitor's motor.

We now consider the criteria that can be used to evaluate the usefulness of a segmenting scheme.

Have real segments been identified?

Because it is often easy to break into groups the people or organizations that a market comprises (using factors such as age, location, and use situation), it is essential that we have some gauge as to whether actual segments have been identified. As we discussed previously in the chapter, a key issue is whether differences in responsiveness to a marketing mix exist between segments.

Differences in responsiveness. If actual segments have been found, the people in a segment will respond similarly to a particular marketing mix, and those in all other segments will respond differently to that same marketing mix. Segmenting consists of first identifying the segments in a market, then selecting one or more segments to be targeted by the firm, and finally designing a marketing mix (product, distribution, price, advertising, and personal selling) that is suitable for each target segment. When the proper marketing mix is selected for a particular segment, the people in the segment will respond more favorably to that mix (i.e., buy more of the product) than will the people in any other segment.

Other considerations in segment formation. Suppose segments have been formed such that response differences to a marketing mix clearly exist between segments. What other considerations are relevant to the marketer? Four criteria (in addition to response differences) may be important in determining if segmenting is feasible and appropriate for a particular company.

■ Can the people in each segment be *identified*? What are their characteristics?

For example, a major manufacturer of western boots determined that lifestyle was an important factor in boot purchases. Yet management was unable to find demographic and socioeconomic factors that could describe boot purchasers.

■ Is it *feasible* to aim a different marketing mix at each segment of interest?

As an illustration of this criterion, a specialty import retailer found wide variations in the characteristics of buyers from store to store and region to region. Moreover, it was clear that different advertising media would be needed to communicate with buyers in different locations. Yet the costs of such focused media coverage were prohibitive for the retailer.

■ Will the sales revenues obtained through market segmenting, less the costs of marketing to the segment, yield acceptable profits? In other words, is segmenting *worth doing*?

A jewelry retailer located in a downtown area served a broad customer base that included people with a wide range of demographic and socioeconomic characteristics. Targeting specific groups within this broad base was prohibitive because of the costs of promotion. Instead, one-page newspaper advertisements were used to appeal to various buyers by featuring many different jewelry items.

■ Will the segments identified today remain *stable*? If customer needs and wants change rapidly over time, the segments formed may not exist in the future.[11]

This problem is often encountered with new products. Until buyers gain experience with a new product it may be difficult to identify specific needs and wants.

Let us consider segmentation of the U.S. market for diet foods. Look at Exhibit 8.11. Suppose you are concerned with how to appeal to both cosmetic dieters and serious dieters.[12] Cosmetic dieters want to lose weight but are not as committed to the task as are serious dieters. H. J. Heinz's Weight Watchers foods were first aimed at serious dieters.

> The theme: Guilt. An ad appearing in women's magazines shows a double-chinned woman staring dolefully at a plate of lasagna—from behind bars. "Eat without feeling guilty," the text says of Weight Watchers lasagna. "You can enjoy without feeling like a criminal." Television spots in certain cities employ a devilish-looking character called Mr. Temptation.
>
> When Heinz broadens its target to include cosmetic dieters, the company's ad executives acknowledge, the fine line between the effective and the offensive will become even finer. Cosmetic dieters are typically female, college-educated, between 24 and 44 years old. They have previously used some other figure-improvement product, anything from diet salad dressing to control-top pantyhose.
>
> A target market that includes cosmetic dieters can't be reached by ads with the chubby type of model Heinz uses now. Alfred O. Wittemen, marketing manager at Camargo, believes the campaign has to appeal to "basic instincts," such as sex appeal and sensuality, thus requiring the use of models he describes as "something between Bo Derek and Shelly Winters." If the products don't succeed, he says, "it certainly won't be because we haven't committed people, machines, time and a lot of capital to them.[13]

The Weight Watchers illustration clearly indicates the differences in responsiveness between serious and cosmetic dieters to one element of the marketing mix—advertising message. The descriptive profile identifies the cosmetic dieters. Advertising messages will be different for serious and cosmetic dieters. The serious and cosmetic dieters apparently represent sizable markets, given H. J. Heinz's interest in the segments. In addition, people's needs for weight loss are not likely to change rapidly. Thus the segments appear to meet all five criteria for formation of real segments.

Once segments have been formed, the next step in selecting a market target is to describe and analyze the people (or organizations) in each segment being considered as a market target by a company (see Exhibit 8.2).

DESCRIBING SEGMENTS

Recall our earlier discussion of the various price, quality, and style segments for men's suits that Hartmarx serves (see Exhibit 8.9). For example, the Hickey-Freeman brand is positioned in the high-priced (more than $500), high-quality, and contemporary-styling segment of the market. Although this is a logical basis of forming a market segment, additional information is

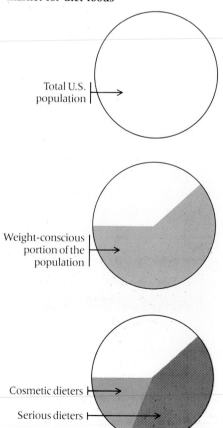

Exhibit 8.11   Segmenting the U.S. market for diet foods

Total U.S. population

Weight-conscious portion of the population

Cosmetic dieters

Serious dieters

"Weight Watchers new Chicken Cacciatore and new Beef Oriental are like having Rome and Hong Kong in the fridge." *Lynn Redgrave*

"See what I mean? Chunks of chicken with spaghetti, ripe tomatoes, green peppers, black olives and mushrooms basking in an Italian style tomato sauce. Yum. Strips of beef on rice with tomatoes, Oriental snow peas and water chestnuts, sitting crisply in a savory brown sauce. Yum, yum. Yet neither glorious dish is a threat to my size 10 wardrobe. That's Weight Watchers for you."

Weight Watchers® Frozen Foods. This is living, not dieting.

Weight Watchers targets this ad at cosmetic dieters who can identify with Lynn Redgrave. These are attractive women who value pleasure and adventure, but they're also weight-conscious. (Courtesy of Foodways National Inc. and Doyle Dane Bernbach Advertising)

needed to (1) identify potential buyers of Hickey-Freeman suits, (2) determine their specific needs and wants, and (3) guide the design of an appropriate marketing mix. The major kinds of information needed for describing market segments are

- Descriptions of the people or organizations in the segment
- Estimates of the size and rate of growth of the segment
- Distribution channels used to reach customers and prospects
- Identification of major competitors
- Marketing mix guidelines[14]

The objective is to learn as much as possible about each segment that is of interest to a company. A closer look at each group of information will show how the information assists a company in *deciding* whether to go after the segment and how to *design* a sound marketing mix for each segment to be targeted by the firm.

Customer profiles

The same information used to form segments also can be used to develop descriptions of the people or organizations each segment comprises (see Exhibit 8.3). Information about buyer characteristics, the use situation, and product characteristics is useful in profiling the people (or companies) that make up the market segment.

The market research conducted by Ford Motor Company for its compact cars—Ford Tempo and Mercury Topaz—indicates the usefulness of customer profiles. In the early stages of the planning for the new compact, Ford researchers found in analyzing its customers that

Ford was getting a stodgy image, and its customers were growing old with the company. The average Fairmont buyer was 50 years old and had an income of less than $24,000—a customer who bought a car only when the old jalopy couldn't make it out of the driveway.[15]

The compacts were designed to appeal to young and affluent persons and to establish a new image in a market crowded with dozens of look-alike models.[16] Styling decisions, advertising strategy, price decisions, and various other aspects of planning were guided by information from the customer profile of Ford's target customers for the company's car.

Consider this profile of the customers targeted by Goya Foods. Goya, whose annual sales exceed $150 million, distributes a line of 700 Hispanic speciality foods to grocery stores.[17] Goya's customer base consists of Caribbean emigrants mainly from Puerto Rico, Cuba, and the Dominican Republic living in New York and the mid-Atlantic states and south Florida. Customers are young Hispanic families with several children who are loyal to the Goya brand. Supermarkets represent approximately 50 percent of Goya's sales. Management is considering expanding into other geographic areas.

Let us look at how Goya's management could analyze new market opportunities. Based on the information shown in Exhibit 8.5, Los Angeles represents the most promising geographic area for Goya's market expansion after New York. Texas is also a promising Hispanic market. Both of these market expansion areas differ from the highly concentrated Caribbean Hispanic areas in New York and Miami because food preferences in these areas differ from those in New York. Research into consumer food preferences should be a first step in evaluating expansion alternatives.

Size and growth estimates

Trends in the total market for a product may not indicate what is happening in particular segments. Consider, for example, the comparison of consumption of coffee, soft drinks, and beer shown in Exhibit 8.12. Coffee consumption had declined substantially by 1982 compared with 1966 yet both soft drinks and beer consumption increased. Interestingly, consumption of instant and decaffeinated coffee increased. For example, General Foods' Sanka brand market share of regular coffee increased from 2 percent in 1978 to 3.7 percent in 1982.[18] Thus the trend in the total market for coffee is totally misleading if you are interested in a particular use category such as decaffeinated coffee.

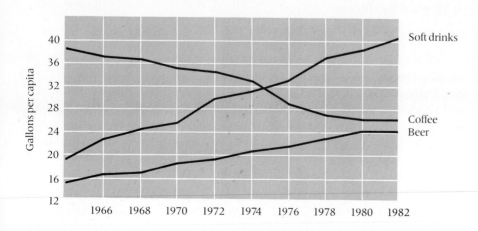

Exhibit 8.12   Growth trends for coffee, soft drinks, and beer
SOURCE: John C. Maxwell, Jr., Lehman Brothers Kuhn Loeb Research; reprinted with permission from the May 9, 1983 issue of *Advertising Age*. Copyright 1983 by Crain Communications, Inc.

Exhibit 8.13   Growth in national defense expenditures by program and service

Program and Service	National Defense Expenditures (billions of 1972 $)		Change 1982/87 (%)
	1982	1987	
Total	80.1	118.5	48
Military Personnel, Total	20.9	21.8	4
Operations and Maintenance, Total	27.9	37.8	35
Army	6.8	9.0	32
Navy	8.4	10.8	29
Marines	.6	.8	14
Air Force	7.3	10.6	45
Other	4.8	6.5	35
Procurement, Total	19.1	40.7	113
Army	4.4	9.0	105
Navy	7.4	12.9	74
Marines	.2	.7	250
Air Force	6.9	17.1	148
Other	.2	.9	350
Research and Development, Total	8.6	10.6	23
Army	1.6	2.1	31
Navy	2.5	3.6	44
Air Force	3.8	3.4	−11
Other	.7	1.5	114
Military Construction, Total	1.0	3.3	230
Army	.2	1.0	400
Navy	.3	.8	166
Air Force	.3	1.2	300
Other	.2	.3	50
Family housing, total	.7	1.3	86
Other than Department of Defense	1.7	3.0	77

SOURCE: U.S. Department of Commerce, Bureau of Industrial Economics, *1981 U.S. Industrial Outlook*, Washington, D.C.: U.S. Government Printing Office, Jan. 1983, p. XLI.

Both the size of the segment market and the expected rate of growth are important in determining if the segment represents an attractive market opportunity. Look at the comparison of U.S. national defense expenditures by program and by branch of military service shown in Exhibit 8.13. Note the changes in both the sales volume and growth trends for the different program components. For example, Air Force research and development expenditures are estimated to decline by 11 percent in 1987 from 1982 levels, whereas Army construction will increase 400 percent over the same period.

Methods of distribution

The channel of distribution used for a particular product determines the customers that will be exposed to the product. It therefore is important to identify alternative distribution channels and the end-user customers served by each channel. Distribution channels that provide access to the customers a firm wants to target must be found. For example, Goya Foods' 120 salespersons deal directly with their 9300 grocery store clients and pay special attention to the family-owned shops located in Hispanic neighborhoods.[19] The firm also prepares its own Spanish-language advertising. Firms such as Campbell Soup and General Foods have found it difficult to market Hispanic foods working through middlemen and food brokers (independent selling agents). Goya's direct contact with retailers has been more successful than the use of traditional food distribution channels.

An example illustrates the importance of understanding how products move through distribution channels to market segments. The market for personal and small business computers can be divided into three large segments.

- Home hobby computers less than $1000 targeted to teenagers and hobbyists
- Home and business computers between $1000 and $4999 targeted to serious home users, students, and professionals
- Small business computers between $5000 and $30,000 targeted to small businesses and professionals

The methods of distribution to the three segments clearly are different. The low-priced computers are distributed through mass merchandise retailers (e.g., Target Stores), mail-order marketers, and various other retailers. The middle-priced computers often are found in computer stores and selected retailers, and there is some overlap in distribution methods used for the low-and middle-priced segments. In contrast, the $5000 to $30,000 segment is served by retail business specialists and by direct customer contact using field sales personnel.

Information is needed on all aspects of product distribution from manufacturer to the end-user of the product. This information includes the types of firms operating in the distribution channel; services provided; and discounts offered to distribution organizations such as distributors, retailers, and agents.

Major competitors

The key competitors operating in a market segment should be identified and evaluated. Typically, all firms in an industry do not serve all segments in the market. An interesting comparison of brands of saber saws for cutting wood using a saber-type blade is shown in Exhibit 8.14. Note the variations in price and performance characteristics. These brands probably serve several segments such as serious do-it-yourselfers, professional carpenters, casual users, and hobbyists. A firm should focus on its key competitors. Note also in Exhibit 8.14 that some firms have several models undoubtedly aimed at different customer segments based on price and quality features.

Marketing mix guidelines

The last part of describing segments is to determine the type of marketing mix that is appropriate for each segment. Guidelines are established regarding product features, distribution approaches, prices, advertising, and personal selling. Let us return to the three personal and small business computer market segments to illustrate how the marketing mix varies among the three segments. Two components of the mix, the price and quality range and distribution approaches, already have been discussed.

The low-priced computer is heavily advertised by the producer. Price competition is intense. A shake-out of weak or unprofitable competitors is

Brand and model	Price	Speed of sawing wood	Scroll cutting	Plunge cutting	Vibration	Estimated quality of construction	Switch/speed control *	Weight, lb.
VARIABLE-SPEED MODELS								
SKIL 515	$90	◒	◉	◒	◒	◉	T	5½
SKIL 500	80	◒	◉	◒	◒	◉	T	5½
SKIL 492	70	◒	◉	◒	◒	◒	T	5½
BLACK & DECKER 7566	100	◉	○	◒	◒	◒	T/D	5¾
SEARS Cat. No. 1729	80 +	◒	◉	◒	○	◉	T	5½
SEARS Cat. No. 1840	100 +	◒	◒	◒	○	◉	T/D	6
WEN 531	62	◒	◒	○	○	○	B	4½
SEARS Cat. No. 1072	60 +	○	◒	◒	◒	◒	T	4½
SKIL 497	40	○	◒	◒	○	○	T	3½
SEARS Cat. No. 1070	50 +	○	◒	◒	○	◒	T	4
BLACK & DECKER 7578	62	○	○	○	○	○	S	3½
BLACK & DECKER 7580	40	○	◒	○	○	◓	S	2¾
SEARS Cat. No. 17215	40 +	◓	◒	◒	○	○	S	3½
TWO-SPEED MODELS								
SKIL 487	46	○	◒	◒	○	○	S	3½
BLACK & DECKER 7530	31	○	◒	○	○	◓	S	2¾
WEN 501	44	○	◒	○	◓	○	S	3
SEARS Cat. No. 1718	20 +	◓	◒	◒	○	○	S	3½
SINGLE-SPEED MODELS								
MILWAUKEE 6245	169	◉	◒	◒	◒	◉	P	4¾
MAKITA JG 1600	128	◒	◉	○	◒	◉	P	3¼
BLACK & DECKER 7504	21	◓	◒	◓	○	◓	S	2¼

Exhibit 8.14 Saber saw ratings

* T = trigger; T/D = trigger for on-off, separate dial for speed; B = button; S = slide switch; P = paddle.

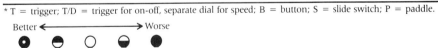

Better ←――――――――→ Worse

◉   ◒   ○   ◓   ●

likely to occur as this segment moves toward maturity. Recall, for example, Texas Instruments' exit from this segment in 1984. Marketing the middle-priced computer also involves substantial advertising although costs fall more heavily on retailers than on producers. Service and software availability are likely to be important factors in the brand choice decisions of buyers. For the high-priced computer, service, professional reputation of the manufacturer, software, and personal selling are important parts of the marketing mix to be aimed at users. It is not surprising that IBM has the largest market share in this segment because IBM is strong on all these marketing mix characteristics.

After segments have been formed and each one of interest is described and analyzed, the final step in market targeting is to decide which segment or segments to target (see Exhibit 8.2).

MARKET TARGETING

Sometimes it is not feasible to form market segments. A company may decide instead to use a mass approach, as did Tokyo's Kikkoman Shoyu Company when it introduced its soy sauce in the United States in the early 1970s.[20] From market studies, management learned that Japanese-Americans had become so westernized in their eating habits that they did not represent an attractive market segment. Kikkoman decided instead that its market target would be the American adult population as a whole. The firm also learned from its studies of American consumers that penetration of the U.S. market for soy sauce would require educating Americans about soy sauce, emphasizing its versatility. With only a few major brands serving the market and no apparent advantages to be gained through use of a segment approach, Kikkoman's management wisely decided on a mass market approach, beginning in San Francisco and using a **roll-out** or region-by-region introduction. This method allowed the firm time to refine its marketing approach, capitalizing on experience gained in one region before moving into another.

The Kikkoman example illustrates the impressive business insights and capabilities of the Japanese. They seem to have an unusual ability to analyze consumer behavior and to choose the right strategies for meeting peoples' needs. Firms in the United States and throughout the world have felt the impact of these successes in cameras, watches, televisions, automobiles, and many other lines. The Japanese were successful in penetrating the

Soy to the world.

For more than a thousand years, soy sauce has been a key ingredient in Japanese cooking, enhancing the taste of meat, fish and vegetables.

Since 1630, Kikkoman has brought this special seasoning to people everywhere.

Today, Kikkoman's naturally-brewed blend of quality and tradition is enjoyed in over 80 countries. It's a taste that has won more than 30 international awards. And has made Kikkoman the world's number-one selling soy sauce.

So add the Kikkoman touch to your taste. And discover what some of the world's best cooks have known for centuries.

KIKKOMAN CORPORATION
339 Noda, Noda City, Chiba 278, Japan
KIKKOMAN FOODS, INC., P.O. Box 69, Walworth, Wisconsin 53184, U.S.A.
KIKKOMAN INTERNATIONAL INC., 50 California Street, Suite 3600, San Francisco, Calif. 94111, U.S.A.
KIKKOMAN TRADING EUROPE GmbH.
Duisburger Strasse 3, 4040, Neuss, F.R. Germany

World Renowned Quality Since 1630.

Enjoyed today in more than eighty countries, Kikkoman has become the world's number 1 selling soy sauce. Had management decided on a segment approach to marketing their product in the United States instead of a mass market approach, such success would have been far more difficult to achieve. (Courtesy of Kikkoman Corporation)

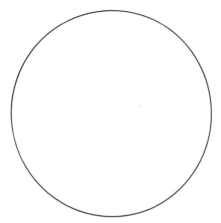 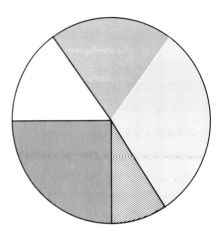

Mass Approach
Response differences do not exist.
Limited (or no) competition.
Company dominates the market.
Product characteristics favor mass approach (e.g., commodity type product).
Economical production costs require high volumes.

Segment Approach
Response differences exist.
Strong competition from many firms.
Company has small market share in the total market.
Product characteristics favor segment approach (e.g., different models of saber saws).

Exhibit 8.15 Conditions favoring mass and segment approaches

mature Scotch whiskey market. By importing malt whiskey in bulk, blending it with local spirits, and selling the product as scotch, Suntory claimed that in 1980 its brand had the largest sales in the world, exceeding even Johnnie Walker Red.[21]

First we examine the conditions favoring mass and segment targeting. Then segment targeting options are discussed.

Mass and segment targeting

Several of the conditions that favor mass and segment market target approaches are highlighted in Exhibit 8.15. A close examination of these factors indicates the major reasons for selecting one approach instead of another.

Mass approach. In today's complex marketplace, companies using mass approaches are clearly in the minority when compared with the number of firms that target specific segments. Nevertheless, in some instances a mass approach may be appropriate if the conditions shown in Exhibit 8.15 are met. If customer differences in responsiveness to a marketing mix do not exist, there is really no reason to break up the market into segments. This condition probably occurs more frequently in new markets in which buyers lack experience and exposure to the product. Similarly, in new markets competition may be limited, thus eliminating one reason for segmenting. For example, Ultrasuede fabric initially did not experience much competition from other brands. Additionally, firms with a dominant share of the market may not benefit from segmentation assuming they are using a mass approach. De Beers, with its global diamond cartel, has no real need to segment its market, other than into commercial and consumer markets. The product's characteristics (e.g., quality) may not be such that they can be modified to fit the needs of different segments. Segmentation does exist for diamonds at the retail level based on price and quality. Finally, mass production may be required to produce the product at cost levels necessary to gain profitable sales volume. Examples include chemicals such as antifreeze that require giant processing plants.

Segment approach. Peters and Waterman, in their 1982 bestseller, *In Search of Excellence,* discuss the results of their studies of excellent companies.

> A very large share of the companies we looked at are superb at dividing their customer base into numerous segments so they can provide tailored products and service. In doing so, of course, they take their products out of the commodity category, and then they charge more for them. Take Bloomingdale's. The heart of its success is the boutique, and each boutique is tailored to a unique service or a modest-sized set of customers.[22]

Clearly, segmenting is the logical choice for serving many markets, and Peters and Waterman found that segmenting often leads to profitable performance for the companies that use it as the basis for targeting customers.

As shown in Exhibit 8.15, the conditions that favor segmenting are the opposite of those that are supportive of a mass approach: differences in responsiveness, many aggressive competitors, small market share, and product characteristics that can be differentiated from competitors' products and products offered to other segments by a firm.

Suppose the market, competitive, and product conditions favor segmenting. Let us look at the possible options using a segment approach.

Segment targeting options

The alternatives for targeting segments range from serving a single segment to targeting all segments in a market. The three target market options shown in Exhibit 8.16 indicate the possibilities that are available to a firm.

Single segmenting. **Single segmenting,** or targeting one segment within the total market, is as popular an option for firms with limited resources as it is for firms with highly specialized capabilities that meet the needs of a single segment of end-users in the market. The firm's marketing program can be designed to meet the needs of the people or companies in the segment. This approach to the market also is called **concentrated marketing.**

> Volkswagen has concentrated on the small-car market; Hewlett-Packard on the high-price calculator market; Richard D. Irwin, on the economics and business texts market. Through concentrated marketing the firm achieves a strong market position in the particular segments it serves, owing to its greater knowledge of the segments' needs and the special reputation it acquires. Furthermore, it enjoys many operating economies because of specialization in production, distribution, and promotion. If the segment is chosen well, the firm can earn a high rate of return on its investment.[23]

The negative side of serving a single segment is that all of your eggs are in one basket, and thus this option involves more risks than the other segment options. Management must continuously monitor for changes in customer needs and wants as well as for threats from competition.

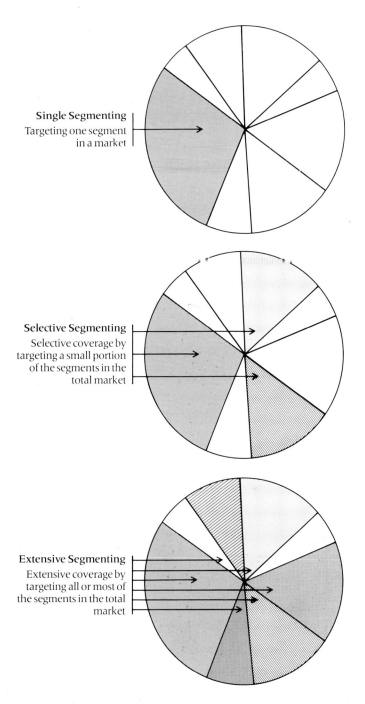

Single Segmenting
Targeting one segment in a market

Selective Segmenting
Selective coverage by targeting a small portion of the segments in the total market

Extensive Segmenting
Extensive coverage by targeting all or most of the segments in the total market

Exhibit 8.16 Company options for targeting market segments

Selective segmenting. Targeting a few segments, or **selective segmenting,** offers many of the advantages of going after a single segment while eliminating the risks. The major requirements for selective segmenting are sufficient resources and knowhow to meet the needs of multiple segments. This option is popular with several industrial-products firms in which segments are formed by type of industry or type of application of the product. For example, a small manufacturer of industrial parts decided to concentrate on four industry segments out of a total of thirty-five industry groups. The four industries were lock manufacturers, electronic equipment, typewriter manufacturers, and transportation equipment. Specific companies were targeted within each industry group. Limiting the markets to four industry groups enabled the firm's sales and manufacturing personnel to become knowledgeable about customers' needs. Trying to serve all thirty-five industries would have been impossible because of its small staff.

Extensive segmenting. With **extensive segmenting,** a firm targets many or even all different segments of the market. The demands on resources and expertise are substantial. Referring to Exhibit 8.16, each arrow aimed at a market segment represents a different marketing mix. Thus it is necessary to develop, implement, and manage a group of marketing programs, one for each segment. Whereas some of the mix components may be the same across all segments, some variation exists between each of the marketing mixes. If a mass strategy is used, only a single marketing program is necessary. Thus, extensive segmenting is expensive compared with a mass approach. This option is popular for the large firms in an industry. Hartmarx, discussed earlier in the chapter, employs extensive segmenting in the men's suit market. There are also major advantages associated with extensive segmenting. For example, marketing research information can be used for several segments. In some instances the same marketing mix component, such as personal selling, can be used for more than one segment.

We turn finally to an examination of how a firm assembles a marketing mix to meet the needs of a market target.

Not just a set of four wheels and an engine, an automobile also fulfills psychological and other customer needs. Manufacturers differentiate their automobiles according to the needs they fulfill. One car can be positioned as a "status" product, another as a "performance" product, even if the cars themselves are similar. If automobiles were marketed solely on the basis of their specifications (the number of cylinders, the size of the engine, and so on), customers would perceive them as being very much alike. (Courtesy of Toyota Motor Sales)

POSITIONING

In this section we define positioning, illustrate its use, and indicate some of the ways products and services are positioned.

What is positioning?

Positioning is the buyer's overall perception of a brand, product line, or company that results from the impact of the firm's marketing mix on the buyer. This image or state of mind results from the marketing actions taken by a company such as product offer, distribution channels, price, advertising, and personal selling. **Product positioning** is the image or perception in the mind of the buyer that distinguishes it from competition.

The product is the focal point of positioning because distribution, price, advertising, and personal selling all are working toward positioning the product in the eyes and mind of the buyer. A marketing executive discusses positioning.

> At the bottom line, positioning is really a state of mind, a perceptual set in the minds of consumers. . . . Ideally, this "perceptual" positioning (over which a marketer has only limited control) is a direct result of actions in support of the positioning strategy (over which a marketer has complete control). But it is not necessarily so. This is because a strategy goes through many filters before it is perceived. These include the product, the package, the pricing structure, the promotional mix, and importantly, the advertising. In effect, the consumer is like a sponge, soaking up information from all such communication sources and generating his or her own perceptions.[24]

Positioning then consists of two stages: (1) the actions taken by the marketer to position the product with the buyer and (2) the buyer's perception of how the product is positioned. Of the positioning of General Foods' Stove Top Stuffing and Bristol-Myers' Small Miracle hair conditioner, Stewart Hegelman, vice-president of Grey Advertising in New York, said,

> Selling Stove Top as an anytime potato or rice substitute instead of as a substitute for mom's Thanksgiving homemade stuffing was brilliant positioning.
>
> Bristol-Myers' Small Miracle hair conditioner was a loser because of the wrong positioning. The product was designed to be used after every third shampoo, but consumers shunned the idea. . . . Consumers aren't interested in function or economy, they just want beautiful hair.[25]

Marketalk discusses how Irish Spring bar soap was positioned by consumers.

How companies position

Although positioning is ultimately in terms of the buyer's perceptions, the actions taken by firms through their marketing efforts provide the information buyers process in reaching their perceptions. There are several ways that a company can position.

- *Attribute.* A product is associated with an attribute, product feature, or customer benefit. For example, promotion for Viva paper towels stresses durability, using demonstrations in advertising.

*Marke*TALK //

Positioning Irish Spring

LINDEN A. DAVIS, JR., senior vice president at McCaffrey and McCall, describes how Irish Spring bar soap was perceived by buyers when it was introduced.

At the time that Colgate was developing and launching Irish Spring, the popular manufacturer's conception of the bar soap market was that it consisted of a complexion bar segment and a deodorant bar segment. Colgate Palmolive had entries only in the complexion bar segment, and had been losing its share. The deodorant segment was dominated by Armour-Dial and Procter and Gamble. Men were considered the principal users of deodorant soaps, and women of

SOURCE: Earl L. Bailey, ed., *Product-Line Strategies;* New York: © 1982 The Conference Board, page 37.

complexion bars. The logical positioning, which aimed at providing Colgate with an entry in the deodorant segment, was a "manly deodorant soap." Tactical considerations involved a unique, green, striated product (which supported a "double-deodorant" story) and a high-impact perfume.

Irish Spring, supported by heavy promotional spending, became a big success. Research indicated, however, that it was something more than a male deodorant soap. For another, it was perceived quite strongly as a refreshing soap, a new attribute in the bar soap market. Almost certainly, this was a new segment in the market. As evidence of this, consider the later launching of Coast with a refreshment and invigoration theme and just a hint of deodorant reassurance.

With Irish Spring, Colgate got something it had not bargained for. Fortunately, it turned out happily. The point is that consumers "positioned" Irish Spring in a way, I am sure, that was much different from what was intended. Colgate's positioning strategy resulted in a different perceptual positioning. In this case and always: It is consumers who position. To lose sight of this consideration—even early on—is a big mistake. The key question is: How will this product be perceived?

Colgate's experience with Irish Spring emphasizes that positioning is the consequence of how the buyer perceives the marketing mix. Marketers can attempt to influence position by their marketing actions but the ultimate position is determined by the buyer.

//

The easy way to position a product in a person's mind is to be first. What's the first name in rent-a-cars? Hertz. What's the first name in computers? IBM. Though you may not consider Perrier to be the first name in soft drinks, the company here brilliantly proclaims itself as such. Perrier knows that the first company to occupy a position in the mind is hard to dislodge. (Courtesy of Great Waters of France, Inc.; Art Director: Joe LaRosa; Illustrator: Milton Glaser)

- *Price and quality.* This position may involve stressing high price as a signal of quality or emphasizing low price as an indication of value. Neiman-Marcus positions according to the high-priced strategy, and K mart has successfully followed the price and value strategy, although in recent years the firm has been attempting to gain a more upscale image using national brands and higher-quality K mart brands.

- *Use or application.* During the last few years, telephone advertising has stressed communication with loved ones using the "reach out and touch someone" campaign. Stressing uses or applications can be an effective means of positioning the product with the buyer.

- *Product user.* This strategy involves positioning by association using a personality or type of user. Revlon's introductory positioning of the Charlie cosmetic line by associating it with the life-style profile of liberated women is illustrative of this strategy.

- *Product class.* The objective here is to position the product as being associated with a particular category of products such as positioning a margarine brand with respect to butter.

- *Competitor.* The Avis rental car positioning as number two is an example of positioning against specific competitors. Positioning against competitors is involved to some extent in any positioning strategy.[26]

Finally, it should be emphasized that firms may use a combination of more than one of these six ways of positioning. An interesting method for positioning brands is discussed in Marketool.

Positioning a service

The difference between positioning a product and positioning a service usually is slight. In fact, Al Ries and Jack Trout, authors of *Positioning: The Battle for Your Mind,* maintain that about the only difference is that in a product advertisement the visual element (the picture) is dominant, whereas in a service advertisement the verbal element (the words) is dominant. This theory makes sense because a product is obviously tangible and a service usually is not. Services are more likely than products to be successfully advertised on the radio.

As an example of positioning a service, consider the strategy used for Western Union's Mailgram, their electronic mail service. The original positioning theme developed for Mailgram was "Mailgram: Impact of a telegram at a fraction of the cost." By referring in the slogan to Western Union's well-known telegram service, advertisers were able to relate quickly to potential customers; Mailgram was understood easily because it was compared with the telegram, a service with which customers already were familiar. As a service as speedy as but less costly than the telegram, the positioning of Mailgram was immediately apparent. Although this advertising campaign compared one Western Union service with another, the positioning concept was sound: In eight years, Mailgram's revenues increased from $3 million to $80 million a year.[27]

MarkeTOOL

How Chrysler analyzes brand position

ALTHOUGH THEY HAVE been in use for some time at consumer-goods companies that sell generic items such as razor blades and cat food, *brand position maps* (or *perceptual maps*) have only recently become a valuable tool for positioning automobiles.

The following marketing map is based on research conducted by the marketing department at Chrysler Corporation. The map shows how car makers are currently trying to calculate differences between their products.

Chrysler draws a series of such maps about three times a year, using responses to customer surveys. The surveys ask owners of different makes to rank their autos on a scale of one to 10 for such qualities as "youthfulness," "luxury," and "practicality." The answers are then worked into a mathematical score for each model and plotted on a graph that shows broad criteria for evaluating customer appeal.

Chrysler recently concluded that its Plymouth, Dodge, and Chrysler models all needed to present a more youthful image. By trying to position a model into an uncluttered space on the map through changes in areas such as styling, price, and advertising, Chrysler believes it can successfully carve out a distinctive segment in the market.

The upper right quadrant of the map looks like a possible positioning opportunity for a firm such as Chrysler. Today the company is moving away from its past conservative image. A classy new design with spirited performance aimed at young people might be a good prospect.

SOURCE: John Koten, "Car makers use 'image' map as tool to position products," *The Wall Street Journal,* Mar. 22, 1984, p. 11. Reprinted by permission of *The Wall Street Journal,* © Dow Jones and Company, Inc. 1984. All rights reserved.

Map axes and points:
- Top: Has a touch of class / A car I'd be proud to own / Distinctive looking
- Bottom: Very practical / Provides good gas mileage / Affordable
- Left: Conservative looking / Appeals to older people
- Right: Has spirited performance / Appeals to young people / Fun to drive / Sporty looking

Points: Lincoln, Cadillac, Porsche, BMW, Mercedes, Chrysler, Buick, Oldsmobile, Pontiac, Conservative, Ford, Chevrolet, Datsun, Toyota, Dodge, Plymouth, VW

SUMMARY

Deciding what people or organizations to serve in the marketplace is an important decision for a company. The choice of people or organizations to whom a company markets its products is a company's market target. This target may be all or most of the people that have needs or wants for a specific product. If so, the firm is using a mass marketing approach. Alternatively, the market target may be one or more market segments within the total market. Market segmenting is dividing the total market into two or more parts, so that the people in each part have relatively similar needs and wants for a particular product or service. Market segmenting is used by many firms.

The major steps in selecting a market target are (1) deciding how to divide a market into segments; (2) studying the characteristics and needs and wants of the people or organizations in each segment of interest to the firm; and (3) deciding which segment or segments to target, or instead to use a mass approach.

A market can be divided into segments using the characteristics of the buyer or user, the characteristics of the product, the purchase-use situation, or all three. An important issue is whether real segments have been formed because it is not difficult to break a market into groups using one or more characteristics from the three factors. The basic requirement for segment formation is that differences in responsiveness to a marketing mix must exist between segments. When the proper marketing mix is selected for a segment, the people in that segment will respond more favorably to that mix than will the people in any other segment. The additional criteria for determining if segmenting is feasible and appropriate are the ability to identify the occupants of each segment, the feasibility of targeting each segment of interest with the appropriate marketing mix, the financial attractiveness of segmenting, and the stability of the segments over time.

The objective of step 2 in selecting a market target is to learn as much as possible about each segment of interest to a firm. The information often used to describe market segments includes descriptions of the people (or organizations) in the segment, size and rate of growth of the segment, distribution channels used to reach customers and prospects, identification of major competitors, and marketing mix guidelines. This information is needed to help the company decide whether to market to the segment and to guide the design of a proper marketing mix for each segment to be targeted by the firm.

Step 3 involves the choice of what people or organizations will be a company's market target or targets. A mass approach may be selected, or instead one or more segments will be targeted by the firm. A mass approach may be favored if response differences do not exist, competition is limited, the firm has a strong market position, product characteristics favor a mass approach, economical production costs require high volumes, or all five. Generally the conditions favoring a segment approach are the opposite of those favoring a mass approach. A firm may choose to target one segment, a few segments, or all or most of the segments in the total market.

Positioning essentially is how the product is perceived by the buyer. Positioning is the consequence of more than the product. Distribution channels, price, advertising, and personal selling help position a product with people in the marketplace. Whereas the firm establishes the basis for positioning, the product's ultimate position is determined by the buyer, not the marketer.

KEY TERMS

mass marketing	demographic segmentation	selective segmenting
market segmenting	psychographic segmentation	extensive segmenting
market segment	roll-out	positioning
market niche	single segmenting	product positioning
geographic segmentation	concentrated marketing	

QUESTIONS FOR REVIEW AND DISCUSSION

1. How would you explain market segmentation to a group of first-year business students?

2. What is the major difference between mass marketing and segmenting?

3. How is a market segmented?

4. What basis could be used by an architectural design firm to segment its market?

5. Discuss the types of factors that are used to segment markets.

6. Why are demographic and socioeconomic variables such as income, age, gender, and social class popular with marketers as bases for segmenting markets?

7. Develop illustrative customer profiles of the segments targeted by Revlon and Esteé Lauder. What are the major differences between the segments served by the two cosmetics firms?

8. Suppose a firm has divided its market into five parts on the basis of age and life-style. How should the marketing manager determine if actual market segments have been identified?

9. Do you think that market segments exist within the Hispanic sector of the U.S. population? Why?

10. What information should be included in a description of a market segment?

11. Under what conditions might a mass approach be better than a segment approach?

12. Explain the difference between selective and extensive segment targeting by a firm.

13. What is the relationship between positioning and the marketing mix?

14. What is the buyer's role in positioning?

15. To what extent are market targeting and positioning interrelated?

BUILDING YOUR PORTFOLIO

Using the method Chrysler used to create a brand position map (see page 230), develop a list of attributes (e.g., juvenile, sophisticated, nutritious) that you can use to create a map for soft drinks. Construct a map of four quadrants that indicates distinct tastes or different life-styles, and determine which attributes are indicators of each quadrant. You might want to ask your friends and neighbors to help you rank the soft drinks for each of the attributes you list. Consider the following soft drinks (add or substitute others that are popular in your area): Hires root beer, Canada Dry ginger ale, Diet Coke, Pepsi Light, Wyler's lemonade, Hawaiian Punch, Kool Aid, Citrus Hill orange juice, Ocean Spray cranberry juice, and Perrier mineral water. Position the results on your map. Do the results surprise you? Do you believe that the brands' marketing mix (promotion, price, distribution, product features) fits their position, as you have identified it, in the market?

NOTES

1. "These seats are taken." *Forbes,* Oct. 11, 1982, p. 227.
2. This illustration is based on Sanford L. Jacobs, "Emphasis on marketing keeps small architecture firm busy." *Wall Street Journal,* Apr. 25, 1983, p. 25.
3. David W. Cravens, *Strategic Marketing.* Homewood, Ill.: Irwin, 1982.
4. Bill Abrams, "Middle generation growing more concerned with selves." *Wall Street Journal,* Jan. 21, 1982, p. 25.
5. Ibid.
6. Russell P. Halcy, "Benefit segmentation: A decision-oriented research tool." *Journal of Marketing,* Vol. 32 (July 1968), p. 3.
7. Bill Abrams, "A new toothpaste takes off, promoted by single employee." *Wall Street Journal,* May 26, 1983, p. 29.
8. The account is drawn from John Merwin, "Skimming the cream." *Forbes,* May 11, 1981, p. 67, 71.
9. Ibid., p. 67.
10. G. David Hughes, *Marketing Management.* Reading, Mass.: Addison-Wesley, 1978, p. 207.
11. Cravens, op. cit., p. 172.
12. Thomas Petzinger, Jr., "Heinz tries to reshape demand for Weight Watchers' products." *Wall Street Journal,* July 17, 1980, p. 23.
13. Ibid.
14. Cravens, op. cit., p. 183.
15. Douglas R. Sease, "Dealers turn: Ford awaits the payoff on its 4-year gamble on new compact car." *Wall Street Journal,* May 4, 1983, p. 1.
16. Ibid., pp. 1, 22.
17. Roger Lowenstein, "Branching out: Goya Foods Inc., No. 1 in Hispanic market, aims to broaden base." *Wall Street Journal,* Mar. 23, 1982, pp. 1, 15.
18. John C. Maxwell, Jr., "Coffee sales dip continues." *Advertising Age,* May 9, 1983, p. 82.
19. Lowenstein, op. cit., p. 1.
20. John E. Conney, "Selling American: Top soy sauce brewer in Japan shows how to crack U.S. market." *Wall Street Journal,* Dec. 16, 1977, pp. 1, 29.
21. Alan L. Otten, "Scotch firms dilute 100-proof gloom." *Wall Street Journal,* Sept. 23, 1980, p. 39.
22. Thomas J. Peters and Robert H. Waterman, Jr., *In Search of Excellence.* New York: Harper & Row, 1982, p. 182.
23. Philip Kotler, *Marketing Management,* 5th ed. Englewood Cliffs, N.J.: Prentice-Hall, 1984, p. 270.
24. Linden A. Davis, Jr., "Market Positioning Considerations," in Earl L. Bailey (Ed.), *Product-Line Strategies.* New York: The Conference Board, 1982, p. 37.
25. "Agency exec explores reasons why new products fail." *Marketing News,* Aug. 3, 1984, p. 16.
26. This discussion is based on David A. Aaker and J. Gary Shansby, "Positioning your product." *Business Horizons,* May–June, 1982, pp. 56–58. Copyright, 1982, by the Foundation for the School of Business of Indiana University. Reprinted by permission.
27. Al Ries and Jack Trout, *Positioning: The Battle for Your Mind.* New York: McGraw-Hill, 1981, pp. 183–190.

Case 8.1

Blair's Restaurant

BLAIR IS PLANNING to open a restaurant in her hometown, which has a population of 30,000. After attaining a business degree at the university in the town, Blair took a few restaurant management courses at a trade school and worked for six months in a restaurant in a nearby city. Blair is sure that she can manage the restaurant, but she is not sure of the type of restaurant she wants to open.

SOURCE: R. Arnold, M. Capella, and D. Smith, *Strategic Retail Management,* © 1983, Addison-Wesley, Reading, Massachusetts, p. 230, Fig. 7.1. Reprinted by permission.

The university is the dominant feature of the town. There are about 16,000 students at the university; about half live in dorms, the others in apartments. Only about 1,000 live more than ten miles from the town. Almost half the city residents are connected with the university; 3,000 are employed by the university. The median family income in the city is $27,000. Only 30 percent of the students qualify for financial aid. A study Blair did in a marketing research course indicated that the adult townspeople ate dinner out in the town an average of twenty times a year, about half the time at fast-food restau-

rants. They typically spent about $12 when they ate in conventional restaurants and $3 when they ate at fast-food restaurants. They ate lunch out an average of six times a month and spent about $3.50 per meal.

Students ate out much more often. Non-dormitory students ate dinner out once a week and spent about $5.50 per meal. Dorm students ate dinner out twice a week and spent $6 each time. Dorm students normally ate lunch in the school cafeteria. Nondorm students ate lunch out three times a week and spent $2.50 each meal.

QUESTIONS

1. What other data would you want about the adult townspeople and the students, the two target markets that Blair has identified, before deciding on what kind of restaurant to open?

2. Which market do you think is best? Why?

3. What marketing mix would you use to reach the selected market?

4. Could you appeal to both markets? How?

Case 8.2

Noxell Corporation

NOXELL CORPORATION—marketer of the popular Noxzema and Cover Girl brands of makeup and skin cream—has found success in a segment of the $11 billion cosmetic industry that its haughtier rivals disdain: the mass market. Its products are aimed primarily at teenagers and evoke the image of fresh-faced, natural beauty. Widely distributed and heavily advertised, Noxell's brands are easily recognizable by either their low price or, in the case of Cover Girl, model Cheryl Tiegs, whose visage has graced the line's ads and packages for an astonishing 10 years.

Content to sell its products in chains such as K mart Corp. and F. W. Woolworth Co., the family-controlled company has let others vie for the more

Reprinted from the February 14, 1983 issue of *Business Week* by special permission; © 1983 by McGraw-Hill, Inc.

prestigious, but cutthroat, department and specialty store business. That approach, derided by some as stodgy, has nonetheless given Noxell's balance sheet an in-the-pink glow. While most of its flashier rivals would rather forget 1982, Noxell plumped up its earnings 9.7% over the previous year, netting $20 million on a 12.3% sales gain to $261.9 million.

The determination to sell exclusively through mass merchandisers is based on Noxell's belief that chic department store displays, which gloss a brand's image and hold out the promise of fat profit margins, do not always help the bottom line. The reality is that when selling through department stores, cosmetic companies are usually obliged to lease counter space for their lines, keep large inventories on hand, and pay commissions to sales people.

Noxell reaches its customers through

outlets that usually display cosmetics on economical self-service racks, with retailers depending on low margins and quick turnover for success. Its product line is deliberately limited: Cover Girl sells only seven shades of liquid face makeup, while chief competitor Maybelline offers 20. "We don't want to burden the storekeeper with too many shades," explains Robert W. Lindsay, Noxell's vice-president and secretary.

Low price has always been a company tenet. And this past year, as the economy worsened, Noxell's products thrived as cost-conscious consumers traded down from more expensive lines. As a result, Noxell's centerpiece Cover Girl line—priced from $1.25 to $3.75—enjoyed a 20% sales gain and a 10% growth in units through last September. Maybelline Co. posted unit sales increases of 6% to 7% during that time, says David C. Brittain, president of Schering-Plough Corp.'s U.S. cosmetic division, the marketer of Maybelline. Competitors Revlon Inc. and Avon Products Inc. saw their profits drop 33% and 19%, respectively, during the first nine months of 1982.

Still, some industry observers detect corporate crow's feet. Noxell, they say, has not been able to capture the increasingly large over-30 market. Sales of the company's 69-year-old Noxzema were flat last year, and to revive the product Noxell has started a new ad campaign called "Dry is a lie." But the campaign—spotlighting both Noxzema and 12-Hour Acne Medication—is aimed at teens, using magazines such as *Seventeen* and TV shows such as *Happy Days* and *Laverne and Shirley.*

While Lindsay insists that "we already have the older customer," doubts run strong. Critics note that the skin care market is growing about 6% annually and that Noxell should have expanded Noxzema into night or eye creams. They cite the success of low-price Oil of Olay, aimed at the woman in her thirties, which has grown fifteen-fold to almost $150 million in sales since Richardson-Vicks Inc. acquired it in 1970.

Noxell has made attempts to woo the "older" woman. Its moisturizing lotion, RainTree, introduced during 1980, "never got off the ground," says industry consultant Alan G. Mottus. The trouble was that Noxell did not anticipate that others—including Soft Sense by S. C. Johnson & Sons Inc. and Vaseline Dermatology Formula, marketed by Chesebrough-Pond's Inc.—would enter the hand- and body-lotion market after it had tested RainTree.

The company mounted another attempt to capture the over-30 crowd in 1976, by introducing Moisture Wear makeup as part of its Cover Girl line. But after six years, the product has eked out only $14 million in sales. George L. Bunting Jr., 42, president and chief executive, says Moisture Wear is "still in its infancy." One problem may have been a blurry image. Once a part of the Cover Girl line, it was aimed at older users. To sharpen the brand's focus, Noxell is using older models.

Noxell has spread Cover Girl brand's popularity across a wider age group by keeping model Tiegs, now 35, as its spokeswoman for more than a decade. "The active, attractive girl-next-door image is how the working woman likes to view herself," says Diana K. Temple, cosmetic industry analyst with Salomon Bros. And to boost Tiegs's image, Noxell consistently spends about 22% of annual sales on advertising, well above the industry average of 7% to 9% of sales.

The growth figures indicate that this strategy is a winner. Cover Girl accounted for more than 50% of Noxell's sales in 1982, up from 47% in 1981. In addition Cover Girl, with about 13.5% of the lower-price cosmetic market, is growing faster in both dollar and unit sales than Maybelline, which holds nearly an 18% share. Both are well ahead of Revlon's low-price Natural Wonder line, with about 5% of the market.

While company executives say they are making every attempt to go after new markets in the makeup and skin care business, Bunting acknowledges that he is looking for an acquisition, perhaps in another field. Some think Noxell may look for household cleanser products, since it already distributes Lestoil and is test-marketing another, called Kind. But Bunting says the unabashedly conservative company, which carries no long-term debt on its books, will not change its ways. He states: "We don't have to change to continue to grow."

QUESTIONS

1. How can Noxell identify and reach women in the over-thirty age group?

2. How is Noxell affected by the current composition of families and households?

3. What market target strategy (segmentation or mass) is Noxell using?

Part Three

Products and Services

9 Product Management

When you finish this chapter, you will understand

☐ That products have tangible and intangible characteristics

☐ How consumer and industrial products are classified

☐ How services differ from goods

☐ Why products have life cycles

☐ The characteristics of the various product life-cycle stages

☐ The relationships among a product item, line, and mix

☐ The nature and importance of product-service portfolio management

Sparked by seeing African women carry babies in shawls tied to their bodies, Snugli developed a product to satisfy parents' needs for a comfortable, safe, nurturing method of carrying their babies.

In 1964, shortly after Ann and Michael Moore returned from working with the Peace Corps in West Africa, their first child, Mande, was born in Evergreen, Colorado. Ann carried her daughter home from the hospital in African fashion using a shawl to strap the child to her back. This experience marked the beginning of a company called Snugli, whose sales in 1981 reached $4.5 million. Ann Moore wanted to carry her baby close to her body but found the shawl difficult to use. She designed a pouchlike device (Snugli) made of cloth that straps to the adult's chest or back. The business began as a hobby to handle the requests of other parents for Snuglis. As more people were exposed to the innovative soft baby carrier, demand for the product grew. By 1972 sales had reached 300 items per month. In 1975 Snugli received the top rating for soft carriers from *Consumer Reports* magazine. In 1982 the firm had more than 200 employees and was marketing the product using a national force of sales representatives.[1]

As illustrated by Snugli, products are developed to meet the needs and wants of customers. If a product does not provide customer satisfaction, it will not be successful. The products or services offered by an organization represent why it is in business. Deciding what products to offer, when to modify them, and when to eliminate those that have outlived their usefulness is important in determining the success of both business and not-for-profit organizations. Likewise, the product or service is the starting point in developing a marketing program because deciding what distribution channels to use, how to price the product, and how to advertise and sell it is not possible until the product or service to be marketed has been chosen.

This chapter begins with the definition of a product. Then we look at how products are classified, and how products and services differ. Next, the important idea of the product life cycle is examined. This is followed by a discussion of how products are grouped to form product lines and product mixes. Finally, we consider managing the product-service portfolio. This chapter sets the stage for discussion of new product-service planning in Chapter 10.

WHAT IS A PRODUCT?

A product is what it is perceived to be. Thus a product is more than something with physical characteristics. The customer's perceptions of a product or service often are the result of an assessment of both tangible and intangible factors or attributes (Exhibit 9.1). Moreover, these perceptions vary according to each brand of a product category, such as watches. For example, a person may perceive a Rolex watch as prestigious, durable, accurate, and expensive and a Timex watch as having attributes opposite to Rolex. Interestingly, Seiko offers a Rolex look-alike at a small fraction of the price of the Rolex, aimed apparently at those buyers who want the prestigious watch but are unable or unwilling to pay the price.

A variety of tangible and intangible factors leads to the perceptions buyers have about brands. The dirty lobby of a hospital may raise questions in a patient's mind concerning the quality of the hospital's medical services. The high price of an electronic device may serve as a proxy for determining quality, which the buyer is unable to evaluate. Our perception of a retailer may extend to products carried by the retailer. The informal welcome aboard and flight briefing of an airline captain may help calm a nervous passenger. After-the-sale service and the warranty or guarantee are also part of the product. Chapter 11 considers the aspects of product. Thus if a

Exhibit 9.1 Illustrations of tangible and intangible product and service perceptions

Tangible Perceptions
The *feel* of an Ultrasuede coat
The *look* of a 20-carat diamond
The *sound* of a stereo music system
The *accuracy* of a temperature measurement device

Intangible Perceptions
The *prestige* of owning a Porsche automobile
The *safety* of an airline service
The *value* of an investment advisory service
The *competence* of a television repair service

product is something more than a commodity such as corn or wheat, the product represents the buyer's perceptions of its various attributes. Some of these perceptions may be favorable and some may be unfavorable. When one cannot make a direct evaluation of a product or service, proxies are evaluated: the reputation of a jeweler is considered when a diamond ring is purchased.

Thus a product offers benefits to satisfy one or more needs or wants of a customer and involves an exchange between the user and the provider. Some benefits ultimately may become liabilities, such as an automobile that does not operate properly. Note that the term *product* is often used to mean service as well, although we should recognize certain distinctions that exist between products and services. These differences are discussed later in the chapter as well as in A Special Look at Services Marketing, the essay following this chapter.

How Products Are Classified

Whereas several schemes have been developed for use in classifying goods and services, two popular approaches are to classify according to

- The *buyer* of the good or service, in which products typically are designated consumer or industrial products
- The *industry* producing the good or service

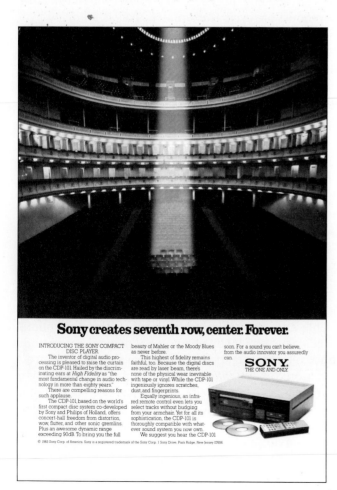

The tangible sound of a Sony CD player and the intangible elegance of dining at the Parker House are attributes that contribute to customers' perceptions of this product and this service. (Courtesy of Sony Corporation of America and Parker House)

Goods and services purchased for consumption by a person, family, or household are called **consumer products,** and products purchased by an individual or organization for use in producing or distributing goods and services are called **industrial products.** Note that the essential distinction between the two categories is based on the *use* of the product or service rather than what it is. An automobile purchased by a family is a consumer good; an automobile owned by a corporation and assigned to a salesperson is an industrial good. Other examples of consumer goods and services include bicycles, fishing equipment, life insurance, clothing, television sets, and contact lenses. Steam turbines, janitor services, and trucks are industrial goods and services.

The industry basis of classification deserves brief mention because a wide range of sales, market share, and other data are available in industry categories from government agencies, trade associations, and marketing research firms. There are several industry-based classification schemes, but the most complete and most widely used is the Standard Industrial Classification (SIC) system developed by the U.S. Department of Commerce.

The SIC system is popular with industrial firms. It is used for sales analyses, forecasting, and market segmentation. Several information services offer listings of companies and plants classified by SIC. Each year the Department of Commerce, Bureau of Industrial Economics, publishes industry trends and projections by SIC code in the *U.S. Industrial Outlook,* which contains extensive data on all industries. Chapter 6 discusses the industry classification of products in more detail.

In the remainder of this section we discuss the buyer classification of goods and services, in which products are designated as consumer or industrial.

Consumer products

Considering the broad array of products and services that people buy, selecting a basis of classification that is useful for items such as video games, apparel, appliances, life insurance, and coffee is a major challenge. Several methods have been proposed for classifying consumer products. One method that has been popular with marketers since it was first proposed in the 1920s is classification according to how the product fits into the consumer's buying patterns.[2] The system designates purchases as convenience, shopping, and specialty products. The following discussion of these categories describes their characteristics and indicates some of the differences in the marketing approach used for each category.

Convenience products. Many of our everyday purchases fall into this category. Included are soft drinks, health and beauty aids, food, magazines, and gasoline. **Convenience products** typically are relatively inexpensive purchases, and limited effort is made to identify and evaluate purchase alternatives. Consider, for example, the small amount of time devoted by most of us to purchasing a candy bar, a can of baked beans, or a writing pad. Because of the consumer's unwillingness to spend much time looking for convenience items, they are often widely available. Many different retail outlets carry soft drinks, cigarettes, and candy. Thus distribution is an important factor in marketing convenience products.

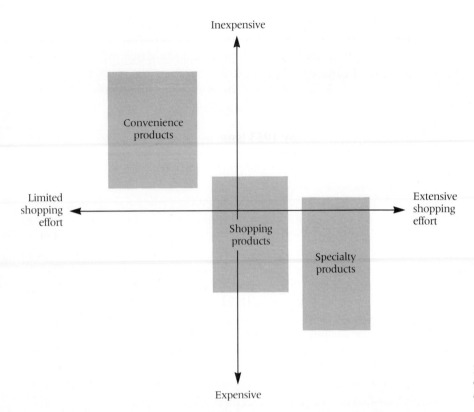

Exhibit 9.2 Illustrative comparison of consumer products according to price and amount of shopping effort

Convenience products normally are marketed by several suppliers, so competition is strong and profit margins are tight. Buyers often have developed brand preferences as a result of experience in the use of products. Some of us prefer Pepsi and others prefer Coke or another brand. Nevertheless, we may be willing to substitute one brand for another when our favorite brand is not available. To develop and keep brand preference, producers of convenience products spend huge amounts of money on advertising and promoting their brands. Because some of these products are purchased on impulse—that is, purchased with little or no forethought—exposure to the buyer is important. Consider, for example, the wide array of items available to you in the racks next to the checkout stand in supermarkets and other retail outlets.

Shopping products. As shown in Exhibit 9.2, these items involve more shopping effort than convenience products and are often more expensive. **Shopping products** involve comparing brands, stores, or both on the basis of features such as price, quality, and style. Shopping products include television sets, automobiles, furniture, skis, and wristwatches. These examples highlight an interesting aspect of product classification. What is a shopping product for one buyer may be a convenience item for another. Some buyers may walk into an appliance store and purchase a television set after shopping for five minutes. Others may shop in several stores, extensively compare brands, and extend the search process for several days. Note that the reason for purchase may also affect the shopping effort expanded. If a buyer's only television set is beyond repair, the effort to obtain a new one may be greatly compressed.

The importance of the purchase typically is higher for shopping goods than for convenience items. The buyer is willing to spend more time and effort choosing a shopping product because of the importance of the decision. Importance may be based on the purpose of the purchase such as a gift for a special person or the size of the purchase. The reason for the purchase may shift a product from one classification to another. For example, a fragrance purchased for personal use may be a convenience product because the buyer has developed a strong brand preference.

Specialty products. The January 1983 issue of *Ultra* magazine carried an advertisement for Extraordinary Perfume offered by Giorgio cited as "The Best-Selling Fragrance in Beverly Hills." The advertisement was scented with the perfume. One ounce was available for $150. This product along with other exclusive items such as Godiva chocolates and Brooks Brothers' clothing is a specialty product. Purchasing **specialty products** involves increased effort by the buyer owing to the particular attraction of the item.[3] They are typically expensive, available on an exclusive or selective basis from retail outlets, and often possess unique characteristics that help establish an image with the buyer. Because of limited availability of the specialty good in the marketplace, the buyer must expend some time and effort to obtain the product.

The marketing of specialty items sometimes involves some type of status appeal, for example, saying that the product is popular with movie stars. Buyers often exhibit strong brand loyalty for these products and thus do not evaluate alternative brands. Moreover, compared to alternative brands, specialty goods and services carry high price tags, which help establish an exclusive image for the items. Buyers are reached through advertising media that concentrate on specialty products such as *New Yorker* magazine. Alternatively, the image of the retailer may establish products it offers as specialty items. Consider this item in the world-famous *Neiman-Marcus Christmas Book 1984.*

Can you identify each of the products in these three ads as convenience, shopping, or specialty items? What characteristics of each product caused you to place it into its category? (Published Courtesy of General Mills, Inc., RCA, and Godiva Chocolatier, Inc.)

James Galanos' design for N-M is a floor-length regality in rare white ermine. Wrapped in clouds of white fox at neck and cuffs, and decorated with hand-attached rows of ermine tails. One of a kind, and subject to prior sale. $50,000.00. Fur origin: White ermine from U.S.S.R. and fox from Norway.

Exhibit 9.3 Illustrative summary of characteristics of consumer goods and services

Convenience Products
Frequently purchased
Little or no shopping effort
Relatively inexpensive
Widely available in stores
Advertised aggressively by manufacturers
Competitively priced

Shopping Products
Occasionally or infrequently purchased
Substantial shopping effort (prices and product features)
Purchase decision important to buyer
Prices often vary between stores
Less available than convenience products

Specialty Products
Infrequently purchased items
Shopping effort varies
Item has unique characteristics
High margin, prestige pricing
Very selective distribution

Note how this item helps establish a specialty image for the other products shown in the catalogue, although the prices of several items are modest compared with the coat. For example, also shown in the catalogue is a pair of knee-high stockings priced at $6.

The characteristics of convenience, shopping, and specialty products are summarized in Exhibit 9.3. Note that the characteristics are illustrative rather than exhaustive, because particular items within a category may display other characteristics. It is also important to recognize that the product classification is from the consumers' point of view. A multimillionaire may purchase an expensive piece of clothing as a convenience good. Of course, it is unlikely that many convenience goods would ever fall into a shopping or specialty category, regardless of the buyer.

Another basis of classification of consumer and industrial products that should be mentioned is product durability. Items that are used many times such as a refrigerator are classified as **durable products.** Examples of durable products include television sets, electric razors, automobiles, and silverware. Alternatively, products that are consumed immediately or after a limited number of uses are designated **nondurable products.** These items include foods, cut flowers, beverages, and adhesive tape. Often the nondurable item is something that is purchased again after it is consumed. Thus the marketing approach used for nondurables seeks to build brand loyalty to enhance repeat purchases.

Industrial products

Business and industrial firms and other organizations such as government agencies purchase industrial products for two primary purposes: (1) to carry out production and distribution activities, and (2) to become an integral part of the items that are produced. The major classification categories that correspond to these uses are shown in Exhibit 9.4. Let us look briefly at each category.

Facilities. *Facilities* include the buildings and other structures used to produce and store products. Examples are a factory, a railroad siding, an oil refinery, and a shopping mall. The marketing of facilities often involves several parties such as architect-engineering design firms, contractors, real estate developers, and leasing firms. The buyer may be the user (e.g., General Motors), or a developer may lease space to users such as Sears, insurance brokers, and dentists. A not-for-profit hospital is also classified as a facility.

Equipment. *Equipment* is used to perform functions for industrial firms and other organizations such as manufacturing, movement and storage, maintenance, and office services. Equipment ranges from heavy agricultural tractors that sell for more than $100,000 to typewriters used in offices. A multimillion dollar computer system used by a bank holding corporation is another example of equipment used to produce goods and services. Purchases of equipment involve purchasing agents and, depending on the type and importance of the equipment being purchased, other technical and management personnel. For example, the decision to purchase a computer system in a large university may be made by a committee consisting of faculty and staff. Identifying and communicating with the key people influencing the purchase decision for equipment are of major importance in marketing industrial equipment (see Chapter 6).

Supplies. *Supplies* are the many and varied items used in production and distribution operations that are not incorporated into finished products. Examples include gasoline, disposable face masks, word processor paper, safety gloves, chemicals for cleaning, and lubricants. Supplies are used for three major purposes: (1) maintenance (paint for buildings), (2) repair (welding rod to fix broken machine parts), and (3) operating and production supplies (electroplating chemicals). For many of these products the purchasing department primarily is responsible for the buying decision. Manufacturers often employ independent salespersons to distribute their

Exhibit 9.4 Classification of industrial products

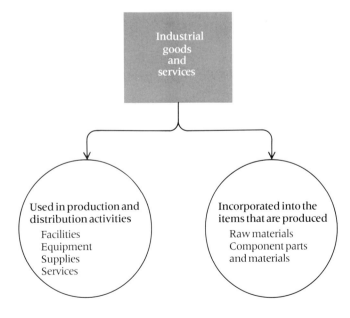

products to industrial end-users. By selling a variety of supplies offered by noncompeting manufacturers, distributors can reduce marketing costs.

Services. *Services* include public accounting, architectural design, cleaning, advertising, management consulting, and other functions that are needed in production and distribution operations. Because of the intangible nature of services, the person (or persons) representing the supplier often serves as a surrogate for tangibility. Thus the potential buyer may be influenced by how the supplier's representative dresses, talks, writes, presents proposals, works with prospects, responds to questions, initiates ideas, and demonstrates understanding of the client's business.[4]

Raw materials. We turn now to the items that become part of the products that are produced. *Raw materials* are the various substances such as metals, woods, agricultural produce, chemicals, and other goods that are transformed in production processes into products. Steel is processed into automobile fenders; crude oil into gasoline; livestock into steaks, roasts, and ground beef; and lumber into furniture and houses. Depending on the importance of raw materials to final cost of the item produced, commodity price fluctuations may have a major impact on the item's selling price. Some companies trade in commodity futures as a hedge against price fluctuations of important raw materials. Purchasing the firms that supply raw materials is another strategy for hedging against both price ups and downs and shortages.

Component parts and materials. Most producers do not manufacture all the *component parts and materials* that go into their products. These items are assembled into products during the production process. Typically, they are ready in the purchased form to become part of the product. Through specialization suppliers often can produce and distribute parts and materials more economically than can a single firm. Also, the expertise needed for the various components that make up a finished product may call for several different technical capabilities. For example, the manufacturer of a refrigerator designs and assembles the appliance; other parts such as motors and electrical controls are purchased from outside suppliers. Both the quality and price of component parts and materials are of critical importance to the purchasing firm because they affect the performance and competitiveness of the final product. The supplier of these items often is involved in meeting specifications, warranty provisions, and other requirements imposed by the buyer.

HOW SERVICES DIFFER FROM GOODS

Because of the growing importance of services in many developed countries and some important differences between goods and services, a discussion of services is appropriate at this point in the chapter.

What is a service?

An important distinction between a good and a service is that a **service** is intangible; it cannot be seen, tasted, or felt. The service is not a physical entity. Like a good, the purpose of a service is to provide customer satisfaction. Typically, the service is produced at the time of consumption. The buyer actually experiences the production process. Inventories of services are not produced in advance of use.

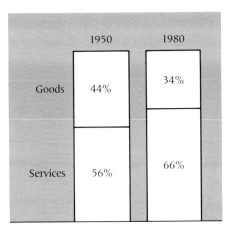

Exhibit 9.5 How each dollar spent for goods and services is split
SOURCE: U.S. Department of Commerce, 1981.

Economic importance of services. Shown in Exhibit 9.5 is a comparison of how each dollar spent for goods and services produced in the United States from 1950 to 1980 is split. Note the substantial growth in services, a trend that is expected to continue throughout the 1980s. The 1980 output of goods and services amounted to $2.6 trillion, with consumer purchases accounting for 64 percent, government purchases for 20 percent, and business investments for 16 percent.[5] Several examples of consumer and business service organizations are shown in Exhibit 9.6.

Types of service businesses. Although we considered services in our discussion of how products are classified, a closer examination of the types of service businesses is warranted, given the importance of the service sector. The types of services fall into two categories: equipment based and people based.[6] Examples of *equipment-based services* are an automated teller machine that processes banking transactions, a heavy equipment operator who digs trenches, and an airline crew that supplies flight service. *People-based services* involve human beings as the major component of the delivery system. Examples include professional services such as lawyers, doctors, day-care personnel, and funeral directors (see Marketalk about Service Corporation International). Note that both equipment-based and people-based services typically involve some of each category.

Characteristics of services

Whereas both goods and services are intended to meet needs, services differ from goods in several ways. Some distinctions are that

- Products are tangible and services are intangible
- Services are conveyed or rendered, and products are produced
- Services often are perceived as the people who render them
- Products lend themselves to image-making, but services do not
- Unlike products, services cannot be designed and tested in laboratories[7]

Exhibit 9.6 Organizations that provide consumer and business services

Consumer
Hospital Corporation of America (hospital services)
ChemLawn Corp. (lawn care)
E. F. Hutton (financial services)
KinderCare (baby sitting)
Budget Rent-A-Car (automobiles)
Blue Cross of California (health insurance)
NYNEX Corporation (telephone services)
New York City Police Dept. (safety)
Southern Company (electric power)
Dental Care Systems (dental franchisers)

Business
Federal Express (package delivery)
A. C. Nielsen (marketing research)
Pinkerton's (security services)
Brown & Root (construction)
Saudia Arabian Airlines (air travel)
Sheraton Hotels (lodging)
Western Temporary Services (employees)
Chicago Board of Trade (futures trading)
Arthur Andersen (public accounting)
Young & Rubicam (advertising agency)

*Marke*TALK //

Service Corporation International: A market-driven service company

ALTHOUGH THE DEATH RATE in the United States declined to a record low in 1982, Service Corporation International (SCI), the largest funeral service and cemetery company in North America, should continue to grow through 1990. Its growth will be accomplished through acquisitions and diversification into related business areas such as the GUARDIAN PLAN and flower shops. In the decade ending in 1984, SCI's sales increased from $75 to $235 million.

Service Corporation International . . . today announced that the acquisition

SOURCE: Service Corporation International, news release, Jan. 23, 1985.

activity in its current fiscal year to end on April 30, 1985 should be the second greatest in the Company's history.

B. B. Hollingsworth, Jr., President, reported that this year's acquisition activity to date includes businesses cumulatively owning 11 funeral service operations and 12 cemeteries with total annual revenue of approximately $16,000,000. In addition, agreements in principal exist for the purchase in February 1985 of an additional three funeral homes and three cemeteries. Annual revenues of the completed and currently scheduled fiscal 1985 acquisitions should be surpassed only by those of IFS Industries, Inc., which was merged with the Company in December 1981.

"The businesses," Hollingsworth

said, "are located in twelve different states and reflect SCI's ongoing program of acquiring prominent, geographically diverse firms within our funeral service and cemetery lines of business. In addition, these firms will provide an expanded base for our GUARDIAN PLAN and prearranged funeral marketing program."

With the addition of the firms acquired so far this year, SCI, through its subsidiaries, will own and operate 292 funeral homes, 63 cemeteries, 42 flower shops and other related businesses. The Company will serve 230 cities in 29 states, the District of Columbia and five provinces of Canada. SCI also markets funeral prearrangement programs in 12 of these states and two of the Canadian provinces.

//

Service marketers try to provide buyers with an image to associate with their services. NYNEX uses advertising that promotes itself as a competent, aggressive company that intends to succeed. (Courtesy of NYNEX Corporation)

Services and goods as a continuum

In 1978, G. Lynn Shostack, a vice-president of Citibank, observed that all goods and services fall along a continuum, ranging from tangible to intangible, in contrast to the commonly held view that services and goods are dichotomized as opposites (funeral services versus instruments).

The output of companies can be positioned at various locations on this scale. A tangible such as an expensive automobile is more than rubber, metal, and upholstry: It carries an image of prestige, comfort, service, and dependability. Likewise, an intangible such as a college education is not entirely intangible—buildings, classroom furniture, and books are all highly tangible. Shostack positioned a number of products and services, placing salt at the tangible extreme and teaching at the intangible extreme.

Based on this observation, Shostack proposes that the approach of "opposites" be used when communicating about your product or service to the markets. An intangible service should be described with tangible ideas and a tangible good with intangible ideas. Thus, TWA does not sell "floating through space" but rather 747 airplanes, tasty meals, and attractive cabin attendants. And Revlon, with its tangible product line, sells hope, not cosmetics.

Shostack's argument is appealing. An intangible suffers from an unclear, nebulous perception, and descriptions of it do not communicate the same ideas to all buyers. Therefore the advertiser must give specific examples of the nature of the service—modern airplanes, desirable meals, helpful attendants. On the other hand, a tangible item may need some broader appeal—some excitement. Differentiation should be in terms of nonphysical images and values.[8]

PRODUCT LIFE CYCLES

How often have you heard someone comment that a particular product has reached maturity? Many products eventually reach a stage of maturity and saturation of the market. Sales of citizens band radios boomed in the late 1970s; today this market is saturated. Annual sales of 8mm home movie cameras in 1983 were a small fraction of sales a decade earlier. The concept of a **product life cycle (PLC)** is used to describe the various stages a product moves through from its initial introduction into the market. Let us look at the PLC to learn more about its characteristics and its usefulness to marketing managers.

Stages of the product life cycle

The PLC shown in Exhibit 9.7 portrays a typical pattern of sales with four identifiable stages: introduction, growth, maturity, and decline. Each stage corresponds to how sales of the product are doing, such as increasing in the growth stage. Also shown in Exhibit 9.7 is an illustrative profit curve associated with the PLC. Note that the PLC describes an industry pattern of sales and profits, not the sales of a particular company. Typically the term

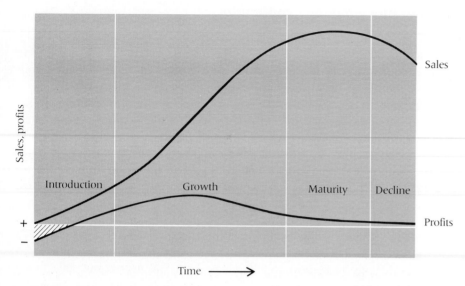

Sales, profits

Introduction | Growth | Maturity | Decline

+

−

Time ⟶

Exhibit 9.7 Illustrative product life cycle and profit curves

product refers to a specific product category such as color television or some specific subcategory (color television consoles). Also, the life cycle in one country is not likely to be the same as in another country. For example, sewing machine sales have reached maturity, and even decline, in most industrialized nations. In many developing nations the sewing machine PLC is in the growth stage.

First, each stage of the PLC is discussed. Next, we examine some of the important characteristics of the PLC followed by a look at marketing guidelines for each stage. Finally, variations of the typical PLC shown in Exhibit 9.7 are discussed.

Introduction stage. The **introduction stage** is the beginning of the life of a product or service. The product must succeed in the introduction stage or it will never reach the next stage. Often, new products are not profitable until they move beyond the introduction stage because marketing costs are high and revenues are not large enough initially to cover expenses. It is not uncommon for new products to lose money during the introduction stage. Mead Corporation spent more than $27 million over six years on its computerized information service, Lexis (which provides legal information), before finally making money in 1977. Three years later, Mead introduced Nexis (which provides general news) and expects it to be profitable by 1985.

Typically, price is at its highest level at this stage (excluding the effects of inflation). The objective of marketing efforts is to make buyers aware of the product and to encourage them to try the product. Free samples of inexpensive products may be distributed. Promotional efforts to encourage purchase such as discount coupons and demonstrations also are popular for new products. Distribution channels often are important for a new product because wholesalers and retailers must be encouraged to carry the product. Personal selling is focused on creating awareness and informing users and distribution firms about the use and features of the new product. For instance, a major feature of ChemLawn Corporation's CarpetClean service, which was introduced in 1981, is the money-back guarantee offered by the firm for all of its services.

Growth stage. A successful product moves from introduction to growth. At the **growth stage** revenues should be increasing faster than expenses and the product should be generating profits (see Exhibit 9.7). Promotion continues to be important in expanding the customer base. Competition is likely to develop during growth because of the apparent success of the new product. Prices typically remain high but may be lowered during the growth stage if necessary to counter competitive threats. Profit margins are normally the highest during the growth stage.

Videocassette recorders (VCRs) moved into the growth stage in the early 1980s. Sales of VCRs in units increased from approximately 30,000 in 1976 to nearly 1.4 million in 1981.[9] Competition began to intensify during this period and prices declined from the early life-cycle highs with VCRs costing in excess of $1,000. The VCR life cycle appears to be following the traditional pattern shown in Exhibit 9.7. By the mid-1980s the product began to mature. Continued increases in sales were expected although the rate of growth from 1986 to 1990 was expected to slow compared to the period from 1980 to 1986.

Maturity stage. Sales reach their highest level at the **maturity stage.** Intensive competition often develops bringing pressure on prices and profit margins. The duration of the maturity stage varies among products, although it is normally longer than the other PLC stages. Market segmentation frequently occurs during the maturity stage. Some companies may decide to exit from the market because profits are low and market growth prospects are limited. Firms with high market shares are able to produce at lower costs than competitors because of experience and high volume production. Prices during this stage are lower than during the earlier stages and relatively stable among competitors. Product improvement is a popular strategy for companies attempting to extend the PLC and to establish an advantage over competition. During this stage the shape of the PLC shown in Exhibit 9.7 may be altered owing to product improvement and other changes.

Nabisco's Ritz Crackers celebrated its fiftieth anniversary in 1984.[10] It has been the most popular and best-selling cracker in the world. This product's life span is remarkable for a snack food. Ritz has maintained a position in the maturing stage for decades. Prices are low compared with other crackers, and Ritz's appeal seems to be well-entrenched in the minds of consumers. The marketing approach used for Ritz is interesting.

> What makes Ritz's strength in the marketplace even more remarkable, though, is that it has not come from aggressively marketing its brand but rather from finding a viable position and sticking with it. "From the beginning, Ritz has been a brand that stressed high consumer satisfaction," says Nicholas Romano, Nabisco's marketing manager for Ritz. "People feel good after they eat a Ritz, and that was the whole point of the advertising, even from the start."[11]

Decline stage. Eventually the sales of many products begins to decrease. The **decline stage** may lead to complete elimination of the product from the marketplace or a sales decline that extends over a long time period. Some products remain in the decline stage indefinitely. Marketing expenditures

GORE·TEX®
fabrics

A recent *Business Week* article described W. L. Gore & Associates, Inc. as "a company where everybody is the boss." It is largely because workers rely on their own initiative that the maker of Gore-tex fabrics remains as entrepreneurial today as it was twenty-eight years ago when the business was born. (Courtesy of W. L. Gore & Associates, Inc.)

often are reduced in this stage. Weak competitors exit from the market. Market leaders may find this period profitable owing to reduced marketing expenditures and reduced competition.

The manual typewriter was clearly in the decline stage in the mid-1980s. The complete demise of the manual typewriter appeared likely by 1985, its existence threatened by electric and electronic models and computer printers. In 1966, some 500,000 manual typewriters were sold compared with only 10,000 in 1984.[12] The product was essentially dead, a victim of new technology. Exhibit 9.8 shows several examples of products at different stages of their life cycles in 1983.

Characteristics of the product life cycle

Illustrative pattern of the product life cycle. The shape of the PLC is not the same for all products. The shape shown in Exhibit 9.7 is generally representative of the trend of sales over time for various products. The exact PLC for a specific product must be determined. Nevertheless, recognition of the general pattern of sales and profits during the life of a product is useful in guiding marketing activities at each stage in the cycle. We should note that events may occur that will alter the shape of the product life cycle. For example, a major improvement in the performance, cost, or attractiveness of a product may cause an upward shift in the sales curve because an increased number of people will want to buy the product.

Length of the product life cycle. The time span between introduction of a new product and maturity varies among products. In general PLCs are getting shorter and shorter, especially in the introductory and growth stages. The fast-food industry reached maturity in less than two decades. A shakeout of competitors in the personal computer market is already occurring, yet the

Exhibit 9.8 Examples of products at each life-cycle stage (1983)

Introduction
Instant 33mm slide film
Videotex information services

Growth
Cordless telephones for home use
Gore-tex waterproof fabric

Maturity
Hand-held calculators
Fast-food hamburger restaurants

Decline
Railway passenger services
Black-and-white television sets

first personal computer was introduced a scant ten years ago. Companies dropping out of a market indicate that it is reaching maturity. Estimates are that 1986 sales of personal computers will reach $21 billion.[13] Factors that may shorten a PLC include appearance of new products, rapid market entry and market development by many competitors, and changes in the needs and wants of potential buyers.

As Exhibit 9.9 shows, PLCs for three innovative technologies defy the typical four-stage pattern. From 1964 to 1976 IBM introduced only two families of mainframe computers. When the technology began to change rapidly, introductions came more often, so that from 1976 to 1980 four

Exhibit 9.9 Product life cycles are not what they used to be

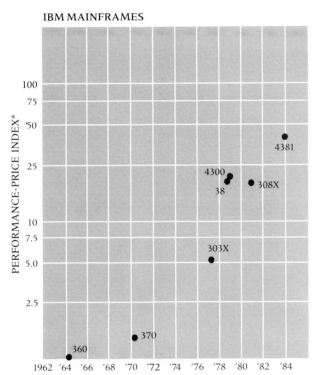

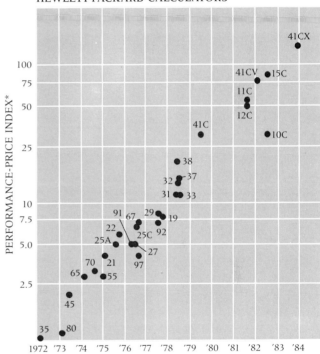

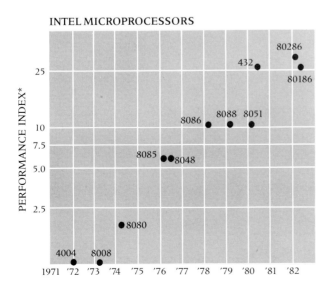

*The performance-price index is a ratio of processing speed to introductory price for IBM mainframes. For the Hewlett-Packard calculators, performance is judged by the amount of memory and number of functions the model can perform. Intel's microprocessors are plotted according to performance (speed) alone because prices have fallen so sharply that if a performance-price index were used, some would have to be plotted off the page.

Note: Products are shown by model number.
SOURCE: Susan Fraker, "High-speed management for the high-tech age," *Fortune*, Mar. 5, 1984, p. 64. Reprinted courtesy of *Fortune* Magazine.

mainframes were announced. Hewlett-Packard did not begin selling calculators until 1972. So quickly did the technology evolve (twenty-three models in eight years) that calculators entered their mature phase by 1980. Finally, Intel's microprocessors have been coming along so steadily that no life cycle has yet emerged.[14]

Management implications of the product life cycle. Assuming that the general life-cycle pattern shown in Exhibit 9.7 applies for a particular product, the implications are clear. As the product moves through the life cycle, profits will decline. Maintaining increasing profit levels will require improving the product to extend its life cycle (and profitability) or introducing new products. In addition, at some point the product may outlive its usefulness and be discontinued.

Product life cycle marketing guidelines

Although a product should be examined in its unique market and competitive setting to determine specific marketing guidelines, several of the kinds of changes in marketing actions that may occur over the PLC are suggested in Exhibit 9.10. These actions should be viewed as illustrative

Exhibit 9.10 Illustrative marketing guidelines over the product life cycle

Effects and Responses	Stages of the PLC			
	Introduction	Growth	Maturity	Decline
Competition	None of importance	Some emulators	Many rivals competing for a small piece of the pie	Few in number with a rapid shakeout of weak members
Overall strategy	Market establishment; persuade early adopters to try the product	Market penetration; persuade mass market to prefer the brand	Defense of brand position; check the inroads of competition	Preparations for removal; milk the brand dry of all possible benefits
Profits	Negligible because of high production and marketing costs	Reach peak levels as a result of high prices and growing demand	Increasing competition cuts into profit margins and ultimately into total profits	Declining volume pushes costs up to levels that eliminate profits entirely
Retail prices	High, to recover some of the excessive costs of launching	High, to take advantage of heavy consumer demand	What the traffic will bear; need to avoid price wars	Low enough to permit quick liquidation of inventory
Distribution	Selective, as distribution is slowly built up	Intensive; employ small trade discounts since dealers are eager to store	Intensive; heavy trade allowances to retain shelf space	Selective; unprofitable outlets slowly phased out
Advertising strategy	Aim at the needs of early adopters	Make the mass market aware of brand benefits	Use advertising as a vehicle for differentiation among otherwise similar brands	Emphasize low price to reduce stock
Advertising emphasis	High, to generate awareness and interest among early adopters and persuade dealers to stock the brand	Moderate, to let sales rise on the sheer momentum of word-of-mouth recommendations	Moderate, since most buyers are aware of brand characteristics	Minimum expenditures required to phase out the product
Consumer sales and promotion expenditures	Heavy, to entice target groups with samples, coupons, and other inducements to try the brand	Moderate, to create brand preference (advertising is better suited to do this job)	Heavy, to encourage brand switching, hoping to convert some buyers into loyal users	Minimal, to let the brand coast by itself

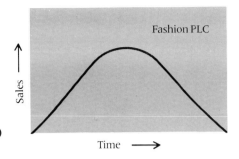 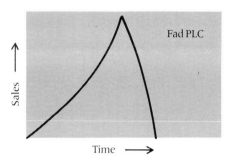

Exhibit 9.11 Product life cycles (PLC) for fashions and fads

and are probably more applicable to consumer products than industrial products. Exhibit 9.10 offers a useful contrast between the PLC stages. Note, for example, the changes in retail prices at the various PLC stages.

It is interesting to compare the personal computer market to the characteristics of the maturity stage of the PLC shown in Exhibit 9.7. The following description of the personal computer market in 1983 shows a close correspondence to several characteristics of the maturity stage:

- More than 150 companies were building personal computers and another 300 had jumped into the aftermarket (supplemental equipment).
- Each firm was trying to build a brand position.
- Profits were holding firm for the market leaders although price cuts were likely to lead to some erosion of profits.
- Competing firms were aggressively expanding distribution.
- The proported advantages of each brand were advertised.[15]

By 1985 personal computers appeared to be moving toward the maturity stage of the PLC, although it was not clear whether the growth stage was complete. Some firms had already stopped producing personal computers.

Fashions, fads, and other variations

Some products do not follow the general pattern of the PLC shown in Exhibit 9.7. The most obvious exceptions are fashions and fads. Illustrative PLCs for fashions and fads are shown in Exhibit 9.11. A **fashion** is a style or trend in clothing and other accessory items that gains acceptance and grows to a peak in sales, then disappears as the fashion loses its appeal. The decline may occur more abruptly than shown in Exhibit 9.11. Interestingly, some styles, such as in clothing, reappear in the future. For example, over the last several decades, the width of men's coat lapels has moved from wide to medium to narrow and of late, back again to wide.

A **fad** is a product that becomes popular quickly and dies suddenly. Examples include hula hoops, pet rocks, and citizens band radios. These products accumulate most of their sales volume in a few months or years, and after sales hit a peak, they fall rapidly to zero or a trivial volume compared with peak levels.

Extending the product life cycle

Finally, we must consider the question of "whether the product life cycle is an inevitable force to which companies must adopt their marketing efforts or whether the firm's marketing strategy can change the course of the product life cycle."[16] Either point of view may apply in some situations. Clearly, marketing efforts can alter and extend the sales curve. For example, after a sales decline in the late 1970s, General Foods had measurable success marketing its Jell-O products in the early 1980s. In 1970 the typical household bought 15.6 packages of Jell-O, compared with only 11.4 in 1979.[17] Rather than let the product decline further, management decided to try to revive Jell-O sales. Companies have found changes in advertising, packaging, pricing, formulation, and sometimes brand names are effective in rejuvenating mature products. The marketing approach used with Jell-O was to promote the brand as an exciting salad and dessert option at a budget price. More recently, Coca-Cola Company has reformulated its soda by changing its taste (see Marketalk). Apparently, management did not correctly estimate the extent of brand loyalty that existed for the original Coke brand. Old Coke was reintroduced three months after the new formulation replaced the original Coke.

Extending the PLC through marketing expansion can be accomplished in various ways. Greater usage by existing customers can be encouraged. Another option is to use marketing efforts to attract new users.

> Marlboro cigarettes was 30 years old when Philip Morris scrapped its advertising directed at women (Marlboro had been offered with either white filters or red "beauty tips" that hid lipstick stains) and switched to cowboy ads. Sales soon outraced production capacity; today Marlboro is the top-selling U.S. cigarette.[18]

Ovaltine, Pet Evaporated Milk, Miss Breck hair spray, Bon Ami cleanser, and Arm & Hammer baking soda are among brands recently saved from the graveyard. Note that these examples are brands within a specific product category. Brand revival is often more feasible than reviving the PLC for an entire product category such as coffee or tea.

The powerful forces of the external environment often play a major role in shaping the PLC of all products. In most instances, this influence is probably more powerful than the marketing efforts of a particular firm, or even an industry. Some industry efforts have been successful in building product sales. For example, industry promotional efforts led to increased consumption of turkeys by encouraging people to eat them on occasions other than holidays. Similar efforts have been successful for other agricultural products.

PRODUCT LINE AND PRODUCT MIX

So far we have been concerned with a single product. Because most firms offer different products and several items within product categories, it is useful to delineate the possible product offerings. Two key decisions must be made regarding the possible product offering—determining the depth of the product line and selecting the product mix to be offered by a particular firm.

Product mix, line, and item defined[19]

Product mix (also designated product assortment) is the total product offering of a particular firm, composed of lines of products and individual items. For example, General Mills offers a diversified mix of consumer

*Marke*TALK ///

Coca-Cola: Marketing coup or monumental blunder?

April 24, 1985:

The folks at Pepsi-Cola couldn't be more tickled.

After all these years—87, to be exact—of competing with front runner Coca-Cola in the $50 billion worldwide soda market, they feel quite thoroughly vindicated.

If imitation is indeed the highest form of flattery, then yesterday, they believe, Coca-Cola paid them the ultimate compliment.

Amid incredible hoopla and hyperbole, Coke announced it is changing the taste of its soda for the first time in the company's 99-year history. Coke will be smoother, the company said, more refreshing, and somewhat sweeter.

Pepsi celebrated by taking out a full-page newspaper ad and declaring Friday a company-wide holiday.

Coke, Pepsi crowed, now will be "more like Pepsi."

"This is terrific," gloated Pepsi spokesman Maurice Cox from the company's Purchase, N.Y., headquarters. "We couldn't be more delighted and pleased. If it were not for the kind of progress and success we've had over the years, they would not be reformulating."

Coke executives say they were experimenting a few years ago with a formula for what eventually became Diet Coke when

SOURCES: Wendy Fox, "Coke changes; Pepsi celebrates," *The Boston Globe*, April 24, 1985, pp. 1, 13, and "Old Coke is it; to return with a 'Classic' label," *The Boston Globe*, July 11, 1985, pp. 1, 10. Reprinted courtesy of *The Boston Globe*.

they happened on what they thought was a much tastier—if slightly more caloric—version of regular Coke. They tried it out on about 190,000 consumers nationwide and in Canada.

"Consumers in blind taste tests all across the continent have told us they prefer the new taste of Coca-Cola to the original by an overwhelming majority," Robert C. Goizueta, chairman and chief executive officer of the Coca-Cola Co. said yesterday at a press conference in New York.

"Some may choose to call this the boldest single marketing move in the history of the packaged goods business," he said. "We simply call it the surest move ever made."

July 11, 1985:

The Coca-Cola Co. yesterday stunned the soda-sipping world by announcing it would reintroduce the original Coca-Cola within several weeks.

Less than three months after it proclaimed, with great hoopla and high hopes, that it was changing the formula of the nation's No. 1 soft drink, the company admitted it is bowing to consumer pressure and bringing back what is apparently, for a great many people, the favorite.

New Coca-Cola will remain on the market alongside the old—which is being renamed "Coca-Cola Classic"—prompting company executives to say in their official statement, "Everyone wins."

"Over 40 million consumers every day in the US enjoy today's Coca-Cola," according to the statement released from Coke headquarters in Atlanta, "but thou-

sands of dedicated Coca-Cola consumers have told us they still want the original taste as an option.

"We have listened and we are taking action to satisfy their request."

Although the company has said that its taste tests show consumers prefer the new Coke to the original, Coke drinkers' complaints have been loud and highly publicized. Coca-Cola has said it has received 1,500 calls a day about the new Coke.

Gay Mullins, a retired businessman in Seattle, sued to require Coke to change back to its old formula. The case was thrown out of court.

Yesterday, a spokesman for Mullins' group, Old Cola Drinkers of America, took full credit for the switch. "We are elated," he said. "We're going to have a victory party tomorrow. I know why they did it—because we raised such a ruckus."

. . .

As might be expected, the people at PepsiCo Inc. pooh-poohed Coke's announcement and maintained their superiority.

"We're not surprised by it," sniffed company spokesman Ken Ross. "We now have the opportunity to compete against one product that was losing very badly to Pepsi . . . and against one product the public hates.

"It doesn't seem to pose too tough a challenge."

Industry analysts viewed yesterday's announcement as a smart and clever marketing decision in the face of consumer outcry rather than a corporate admission of defeat.

///

products, divided into five major business areas: consumer foods, restaurants, toys, fashion, and specialty retailing. Tom's Foods, General Mills largest domestic snack-food business, offers more than 300 varieties and sizes of bagged chips, snacks, and cookies. (Note that we could refer to the product mix of just Tom's Foods which comprises three major product lines: chips, snacks, and cookies.)

Product line is a set of specific product items that logically fall together because of one or more common bonds such as performing the same function, meeting the same user need, using the same distribution channels, or having comparable price ranges. Lines composed of items that perform the same functions are probably the ones we are most familiar with such as Kodak's line of slide projectors. The width and depth of each firm's particular product line varies considerably, as we discuss in the following sections. For example, Procter & Gamble's chip line consists of only one item, Pringles, whereas Tom's Foods offers many items.

Product item refers to a specific unit or model within a product line. It may be identified by its price, size, features, model number, or other characteristics that establish the item's identity from all others. Note that product item does not distinguish between two identical items with different serial numbers (e.g., two Chevrolet Camaro Sport Coupes sitting side-by-side in a General Motors dealer's showroom).

Depth of the product line

Because a product line may range from a single item to many items, we need to look at what is involved in determining the **depth** (or length) **of the product line.** A Coca-Cola Company executive comments on this decision.

> Product lines come in all lengths. Some are very short with two or three sizes, styles, or flavors—such as Hellmann's, Skippy, or Chicken of the Sea. Some are quite long—like Birdseye, Campbell's or Diet Delight—and a few go as far as several hundred items, like the Gerber baby products. . . . What is the optimal length of a product line? Is it 2 or 20 or 200? For each of the brands just cited, the current number of products in the line may be optimal. Obviously, no single length is optimal for all brands or trademarks, or in all circumstances.[20]

Several considerations may be important in deciding the depth of the product line. Certainly the *profitability* of adding items to the line is an essential factor. The *customers* served also may influence the decision. For example, a line with several items may enable the brand to appeal to more than one target group of customers. Likewise, what the *competition* is offering may influence the line decision. Production, distribution, or marketing *efficiencies* may be enhanced with a deep line of products. The *impact on sales* of other items should be evaluated. Will a new item enhance sales of other items or steal sales from them? A firm's taking sales from its own existing brands by introducing a new brand is called **cannibalization.** For example, Coca-Cola's new Diet Coke brand cannibalized sales from Tab. Finally, the *reaction* of the firms in the distribution channel must be considered. For example, will retailers react favorably to stocking a new soup flavor? Displaying the flavor will require reducing shelf space of another flavor or brand.

Width of the product mix

The **width of the product mix** refers to how many different product lines are offered by a company. As in the case of the product line depth, product mix varies substantially from one company to another. Management may decide to add product lines to increase the rate of growth in sales and profits, lower dependence on a single product line as the only source of sales and profits, or use cash that is not needed to support the existing product line. Usually the additions to the product mix are related to the existing line (or lines). Consider, for example, Kraft's mix of product lines.

> Dominant in the dairy section with all kinds of cheeses and bottled fruit juice, Kraft is also big in several different grocery categories—jams and jellies, packaged dinners, salad dressing and mayonnaise, to mention a few. Kraft's optimal number is obviously a lot higher than most.[21]

Exhibit 9.12 Product mix of the Gillette Company

	Width of the Product Mix			
	Blades and Razors	Toiletries	Writing Instruments	Lighters
	Trac II	Adorn	Paper Mate	Cricket
	Atra	Toni	Flair	S.T. DuPont
	Swivel	Right Guard		
	Double Edge Super adjustment	Silkience		
Depth of the Product Line(s)	Lady Gillette	Soft and Dri		
	Super Speed	Foamy		
	Twin injector	Dry Look		
	Techmatic	Dri Idea		
	Three-piece	Brush Plus		
	Knack			
	Blades			

Kraft's product mixes are concentrated on various food items. Some firms have product mixes that are quite diversified into different product and market categories. For example, Tenneco's product mix includes oil and gas production, gas transmission, shipbuilding, automotive parts, farm equipment, real estate, and financial services. In Chapter 23, we take a closer look at product mix options when we discuss business planning.

The product mix of the Gillette Company is shown in Exhibit 9.12. The company, founded in 1903 by King G. Gillette, initially offered only the safety razor and blades. Today Gillette dominates the world market for wet shaving razors and blades. Thus the razor and blade line is quite deep. Gillette started to expand into the other lines shown with the acquisition of the Toni Company in 1948. Interestingly, the razor and blade line has consistently over the years been the firm's most profitable line.

MANAGING THE PRODUCT-SERVICE PORTFOLIO

So far in this chapter we have established several basic guidelines that are useful in managing products including describing product characteristics, indicating methods for classifying products, presenting the product life-cycle concept, and determining product line and product mix. In the remainder of the chapter, we discuss some key issues in managing the various products offered by a firm.

Evaluating products

Because many organizations market several specific product or service items, regular evaluation of the portfolio of products is an important management activity. A **product portfolio** consists of the entire product offering of an organization such as a business firm or some unit within the organization. The portfolio may represent one or more lines of products. The essential idea underlying portfolio evaluation is that each product item may vary according to (1) the attractiveness of the market opportunity of the product and (2) the product's strengths and limitations against competing products. The information gained from evaluation is helpful in deciding how to manage each product item. Let us take a closer look at how market attractiveness and product strength are used to evaluate products.

Market attractiveness. One common way of measuring attractiveness is the estimated future rate of growth of the market, because a rapidly growing market offers a more attractive opportunity than a market that has reached maturity. Of course, the size of the market for a product also is important. A market for a product that has twelve million potential buyers is more attractive than one with one million potential buyers. Other factors that may be used to gauge market attractiveness include intensity of competition and profit margins. The objective is to determine the market attractiveness of the products in the portfolio.

Product strengths. When evaluating a product's strengths, a company's product capabilities are compared with the competition. A popular gauge of business strength is company market share compared with competition. For example, Kellogg dominates the cold cereal market, holding a 39 percent market share in 1983 compared with General Mills' 23 percent, General Foods' 16 percent, Quaker Oats' 9 percent, Ralston Purina's 6 percent, and Nabisco's 4 percent.[22] These firms together account for approximately 97 percent of the total market for cold cereal.

Results of evaluation. An illustrative product portfolio evaluation is shown in Exhibit 9.13. One of four actions may result from product evaluation:

1. The decision to make no changes may be made in the plans for the product. For example, making major modifications to product D is not likely to improve product strength very much, given its already strong position.
2. Product modification may be appropriate for certain products to strengthen their competitive position. For example, improvements in product C might make it more desirable to buyers than competing products.
3. Some products may not be worth continuing because of low market attractiveness and weak product position. Product E, for example, may be a candidate for elimination from the firm's product portfolio. Likewise, product B may require too much financial support to move it into a stronger position.
4. Finally, evaluation of the product portfolio may indicate that new products are needed to complement existing ones or to replace products that will reach maturity in the future.

We turn now to a brief look at product modification, dropping products, and planning for new products. A more extensive discussion of new products is the topic of Chapter 10.

Modifying existing products

The basic reason for **product modification** is to make the product better and thus more attractive to buyers. A product may also be modified to overcome a deficiency that has been identified. Modifications to products include improving materials, changing design, improving performance, re-

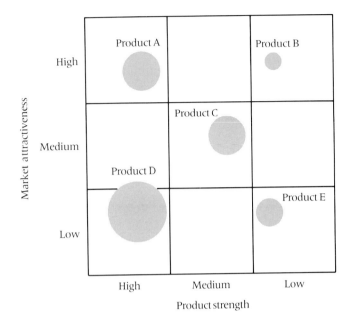

Exhibit 9.13 Illustrative evaluation of a product portfolio*

* Size of circles indicates sales volume for products

ducing cost, changing style, and reducing size and weight. The term **product rejuvenation** is sometimes used to describe a product modification intended to help extend the product's life cycle. Modifications typically fall into two categories. The quality of the product may be improved such as when television manufacturers in the 1970s began replacing tubes with solid-state transistor systems. Alternatively, the styling and features of the product may be changed. Styling changes are common in clothing, appliances, and automobiles. Seiko has masterfully modified watch styles over time, offering a continuing stream of new face designs and features such as time in three zones.

A modified product has been changed in some way from the original product. The modification may offer increased quality, new features, style changes, different ingredients, or some other alteration that retains the primary identity of the original product yet differs from it in some tangible way. The addition of NutraSweet to many food items is an example of product modification. In fact, most of the products in which NutraSweet is used have been **line extensions;** that is, the brand names for these products are retained and the products are not changed except for the addition of the new sweetener, or, in the case of other line extensions, for the use of a new flavor, size, or model.

Often, in the promotional messages about their products, firms will designate as new a product that has actually been modified. And, in some instances, distinguishing between what is clearly new rather than modified is difficult. For example, when the first calculator wristwatch was introduced, it retained the basic features of a watch, yet the calculator capability should probably be considered as something new rather than as an added feature. Thus we would classify the product as new.

Quality modifications. Quality and functional modifications take many forms, such as developing new materials to enhance performance (e.g., Gore-tex rainwear), or adding features (e.g., free traveler's checks to enhance the attractiveness of a savings institution's money market account or adding electronic memory controls to an electric coffee maker). Cost reduction is also a reason for product modification. Consider this illustration. Illinois Tool Works (ITW) is a company unknown to most people. Its products are fasteners that hold together buildings, washing machines, and computers.[23] In trying to help its customers improve the cost and performance of their products, ITW sometimes takes customers' products apart, studies how they are assembled, and then designs new fasteners that will reduce costs or improve performance. Interestingly, from ITW's point of view the fastener is a new product, but from ITW's customers' point of view the fastener is a modification in their building or appliance.

Style modifications. Style modifications are concerned with the aesthetics of the product. Style modifications may apply to products such as clothing or services such as hair styling. Clothing fashions developed by name designers are periodically altered. Style modification may even apply to people as when the image of a political candidate is altered. For example, a candidate that comes across in television interviews and public appearances as too aloof may be coached to help him or her be perceived as more down-to-earth.

Eliminating products

One possible consequence of product evaluation is the identification of candidates for elimination from the firm's line of products. Phasing out products that have outlived their usefulness often can improve financial performance. Every product in the line should be evaluated periodically to determine if poor-performing products can be improved through modification or by alteration of the marketing approach. If not, dropping the products should be considered. Deciding whether to eliminate a product often depends on both direct and indirect factors. An example of product elimination was RCA's decision in 1984 to drop the videodisk player. Introduced in 1981, the product, designed to play disklike records with both sound and pictures, never attained enough sales to become profitable.

Direct reasons for dropping products. Sales and cost analysis is often a first step in targeting candidates for product elimination. Examining a product's sales and costs may indicate that its cost exceeds its revenues. A product that is losing money or barely breaking even is not making a worthwhile financial contribution. An important question is finding out why the financial performance of the product is poor. With a new product, immediate profitability may not be feasible. Products in later life-cycle stages normally face more demanding profit standards than new products. In some instances, the mature product can be modified to make it more acceptable to buyers. If the estimated financial return from this action is favorable, then management may decide to keep the product. Alternatively, a change in the way the product is marketed may improve revenues or reduce costs. For example, aiming at a market segment may improve customer response, and through concentration on a particular target group of customers, marketing costs may be reduced.

Other factors influencing the drop decision. Some situations may cause management to keep a product even though its financial performance is unac-

Using creative designs, Seiko offers exciting styles and features intended to appeal to different people and interests. This particular ad ran in six different magazines, including *Sports Illustrated*, *Esquire*, and *Fortune*. (Courtesy of Seiko Time Corporation)

ceptable or marginal. Factors that may influence the product drop decision include

- The need to keep the product because its elimination will have a negative effect on the sales of other products in the line. For example, supplies or parts used in the product make important profit contributions to the firm.

- The product may contribute to overhead costs that will not disappear if the product is eliminated.

- Other firms in the distribution channel may be irritated if the product is eliminated and perhaps unwilling to aggressively market the supplier's other products.

Thus various customer, channel of distribution, and operating factors may influence the product elimination decision in addition to the financial performance of the product.

Adding new products

Deciding to develop a new product normally represents a large financial commitment by a firm, and substantial risks are involved. Nevertheless, because of the consequences of products reaching the maturity stage in their life cycles, most companies must introduce new products to maintain and improve their competitive positions in the marketplace.

Because the distinction beween a new product and one that has been modified is sometimes fuzzy, we attempt to distinguish between the two. A **new product** is an item not previously offered by a company that substantially differs from existing products in function, design, features, or method of production. We should note that most new products are not revolutionary innovations (see Marketech). Chapter 10 is devoted to a discussion of new product planning.

SUMMARY

The products or services offered by an organization represent why it is in business. Deciding what products to offer, when to modify them, and when to drop them is a major determining factor to the success of any organization. The product represents the starting point in building a marketing program.

The buyer's perceptions of a product or service are often based on an assessment of both the tangible and intangible attributes of the product. To be a product, a good or service must offer benefits that satisfy some of the buyer's needs and wants. Products provide satisfaction and involve some form of exchange between the user and the provider.

The wide variety of products available in the marketplace requires some method of classification of products. Goods and services are broadly classified as consumer and industrial products. Consumer products are purchased by individuals, families, or households and are designated as convenience, shopping, or specialty items. Industrial products may be used to produce or distribute goods or services, or incorporated as materials and component parts of products produced by an organization. Another classification sometimes used for both consumer and industrial products is durables

Marke**TECH** □ □ □ □ □ □ □ □ □ □ □ □ □ □ □ □ □ □

Transferring technology to new applications

OFTEN NEW PRODUCTS are based on existing technology that is innovatively applied to new use situations. The Magic Marker–type marking pen has been in use for many years. Recently the cosmetics industry adopted this idea and put nail polish in a pen.

Chesebrough-Pond's introduced its new "Polishing Pen" in late 1984, eighteen months after a research manager saw its potential for applying nail polish. Like

SOURCE: "How Chesebrough-Pond's put nail polish in a pen," *Business Week,* Oct. 8, 1984, pp. 196, 200.

most new product ideas, moving from one use situation to another was not an easy task.

The pen-type nail polish offers ease of use and fast drying, key advantages for working women. Industry observers are optimistic concerning sales. Some estimate that pen sales will account for half of the market in a few years.

The new product was a consequence of Chesebrough-Pond's new policy to encourage laboratory employees to experiment with their own ideas as long as the ideas are related to the company's business. One-half day each week can be used for this purpose. John D. Cunningham

recognized the potential of the pen applicator and devoted company time plus many weekends to the project.

Getting the bulky nail enamel to flow like ink was a major problem in the project. Obtaining fast drying was another challenge. Working with other research and development personnel and suppliers, Cunningham eventually overcame the problems. The new product was introduced in late 1984.

It will be interesting to track the progress of this product in the marketplace. Some users indicate problems in applying the polish saying that the tip deteriorates, resulting in a streaky finish.

□ □

and nondurables. Durables are subject to continuous use, and nondurables are consumed after one or a few uses. Finally, type of industry is a useful basis of classification.

Services differ from goods in that services are intangible and thus perceived in terms of the provider. Buyers often look for indirect ways to evaluate services, such as their impressions of the salesperson that sells the service.

The concept of the product life cycle (PLC) was introduced to show how industry sales and profits vary over the life of a product. Most products move through four identifiable stages in their lives: introduction, growth, maturity, and decline. The existence of the PLC provides a partial explanation of why a continuing stream of new products is essential for many companies to achieve their growth and profit objectives. Perhaps most important from a marketing perspective is that the role and importance of distribution, pricing, advertising, and personal selling change as a product moves through its PLC.

Product line and product mix designations are helpful in organizing the portfolio of specific product items offered by a firm. A product line contains specific product items that share common characteristics on the basis of function, type of benefit provided, method of distribution, or other common bond. A product mix is the total group of products of a company. The mix of many firms is made up of two or more lines.

Regular evaluation of the product portfolio is essential. The results of evaluation may indicate that product performance is satisfactory, the product should be modified, the product should be eliminated, or new products should be developed. Product modification involves a change in the quality, feature, style, or composition of an existing product. A new product is an item new to the firm that differs from existing products in function, design, features, or method of production.

KEY TERMS

consumer products
industrial products
convenience products
shopping products
specialty products
durable products
nondurable products
service
product life cycle (PLC)

introduction stage
growth stage
maturity stage
decline stage
fashion
fad
product mix
product line
product item

depth of the product line
cannibalization
width of the product mix
product portfolio
product modification
product rejuvenation
line extensions
new product

BUILDING YOUR PORTFOLIO

Ben-Gay, a pain remedy for treating rheumatism, backache, and other pains, was patented in Paris near the end of the nineteenth century. In the early 1980s, Pfizer began promoting Ben-Gay as product for use before exercise. Today, Ben-Gay has the leading market position with an estimated 35 percent of the market for topical analgesics.*

Read the *Advertising Age* article cited in the footnote. Prepare an analysis of the marketing of Ben-Gay over the different stages of the life cycle, indicating the important marketing considerations at each life-cycle stage. Base your discussion on the product life-cycle material contained in the chapter and the article. Include in your discussion the differences in customer needs between the time of initial introduction of Ben-Gay and today. Another source of information is Pfizer's current *Annual Report,* which provides an overview of corporate operations and the Consumer Products business segment, of which Ben-Gay is a member.

QUESTIONS FOR REVIEW AND DISCUSSION

1. Discuss the tangible and intangible attributes of Joy perfume or a BMW automobile.

2. Using the classification schemes discussed in the chapter, classify the following products:

   Lotus 1-2-3 personal computer software
   Wheaties cereal
   Deere farm tractor
   Portland cement

3. What are the essential differences between a convenience product and a shopping product?

---

* Belinda Hulin-Salkin, "Pfizer's Ben-Gay warms up a broader market," *Advertising Age,* Sept. 24, 1984, p. 54.

4. Identify several specialty products.

5. Distinguish between a consumer product and an industrial product. Is it possible for a product to be both?

6. How are services different from physical products?

7. How do people evaluate services they are considering for purchase?

8. What is the purpose of the product life cycle?

9. Why do not all products follow the same product life cycle?

10. Discuss the difference between a product mix and product line.

11. Why does the marketing mix change as a product moves through its life cycle?

12. What is the distinction between depth of the product line and width of the product mix?

13. Discuss what is involved in evaluating a product portfolio.

14. Distinguish between a product modification and a new product.

NOTES

1. This account is based on Eric Morgenthaler, "Baby-carrier maker succeeds playing it close to the vest." *Wall Street Journal*, Apr. 23, 1982, pp. 1, 29.
2. Melvin T. Copeland, "Relation of consumers' buying habits to marketing methods." *Harvard Business Review*, Vol. 1 (Apr. 1923), pp. 282–289.
3. Ibid.
4. Theodore Levitt, "Marketing intangible products and product intangibles." *Harvard Business Review*, May–June 1981, p. 100.
5. *U.S. News & World Report*, Apr. 26, 1982, p. 50.
6. Dan R. E. Thomas, "Strategy is different in service businesses." *Harvard Business Review*, July–Aug. 1978, p. 161.
7. G. Lynn Shostack, "Marketing a service." *Bankers Magazine*, Vol. 160, No. 1, 1977, pp. 42–43.
8. Robert T. Davis and F. Gordon Smith, *Marketing in Emerging Companies*. Reading, Mass.: Addison-Wesley, 1985, pp. 26–27.
9. Ann Hughey, "Sales of home-movie equipment falling as firms abandon market, video grows." *Wall Street Journal*, Mar. 17, 1982, p. 33.
10. "If it's not broken, don't fix it." *Forbes*, May 7, 1984, p. 132.
11. Ibid.
12. *Wall Street Journal*, Mar. 22, 1984, p. 1.
13. "The coming shakeout in personal computers." *Business Week*, Nov. 22, 1982, pp. 72–75, 78, 83.
14. Susan Fraker, "High-speed management for the high-tech age." *Fortune*, Mar. 15, 1984, p. 64.
15. "The coming shakeout in personal computers," op. cit., p. 72.
16. Yoram J. Wind, *Product Policy: Concepts, Methods, and Strategy*. Reading, Mass.: Addison-Wesley, 1982, p. 57.
17. Bill Abrams, "Jell-O's revival shows sales can grow with older products." *Wall Street Journal*, Sept. 11, 1980, p. 29.
18. Ibid.
19. These definitions are based on *Marketing Definitions: A Glossary of Marketing Terms*, compiled by the Committee on Definitions of the American Marketing Association. Chicago: American Marketing Association, 1960.
20. Albert G. Munkelt, "Optimal Breadth and Depth of the Line," in Earl L. Bailey (Ed.), *Product-Line Strategies*. New York: The Conference Board, 1982, p. 34.
21. Ibid.
22. John C. Maxwell, Jr., "Cereal milks '83 gains." *Advertising Age*, May 28, 1984, p. 32.
23. "More than meets the eye." *Forbes*, June 26, 1978, p. 76.

Case 9.1

Ralston Purina Company

RALSTON PURINA CO. likes to brag of its humble origins as an animal feed store on the St. Louis riverfront. But there was nothing humble about the agricultural and grocery products company's diversification drive in the 1970s.

By the end of the decade it was running a Colorado resort, breeding shrimps in Panama, growing mushrooms from Connecticut to California, fishing for tuna in the Pacific and Atlantic oceans, and operating its own canneries (one of which was in Pago Pago). In the U.S., it operated the Jack in the Box fast-food chain and, in Europe, it chased the cat and dog food market. It even arrogated to itself the civic duty of buying the St. Louis Blues, the hometown hockey team, and its stadium, which, in homage to its very own trademark, it renamed the Checkerdome.

Today, however, humility once again pervades Ralston. Having come a cropper from its extravagant expansion, the company is pulling in the reins. William P. Stiritz, the chairman and chief executive who took control last January, has decided to jettison much of the smorgasbord that comprised the company's portfolio. "Our future growth," he says, "will come primarily through aggressive new product development in our core businesses"—animal feed, grocery products, and restaurant operations.

Stiritz, 48, has already dumped the tuna-catching, mushroom-raising, and European-based pet food businesses. And he has publicly promised to unload any others that do not pull their weight.

But this back-to-basics approach, coupled with his admitted interest in acquisitions that would dovetail with core businesses, is anything but fail-safe. "Ralston is staking its future on the [same] terribly mature markets that provoked it to seek growth elsewhere in the 1970s," warns a skeptical competitor. Indeed, all of the businesses that Stiritz plans to grow seem to be trapped by tough markets, hot competition, or both:

Sales of animal feed by the AgriProducts Group, Ralston's oldest and largest operation, have been bludgeoned by the depressed U.S. farming economy and by the fiscal plight of Mexico, where the company does considerable volume.

SOURCE: "Ralston Purina: Dumping Products That Led It Away from Checkerboard Square," *Business Week,* Jan. 31, 1983, pp. 63–64. Reprinted from the Jan. 31, 1983 issue of *Business Week* by special permission; © 1983 by McGraw-Hill, Inc.

In sales of breakfast cereals, Ralston still trails Kellogg, General Mills, and General Foods, although it made some market gains in the last two years. But ominously, Kellogg recently announced a new line of cereals that is being positioned to go head-to-head with Ralston's Chex brands, a move that could eventually take a large bite out of Ralston's sales. "We may all be tested by Kellogg," says one competitor, "and Ralston may be tested first." Ralston, however, is more secure as No. 1 in pet foods, because it has consistently invested in many new products.

The entire fast-food business, including such giants as McDonald's, Burger King, and Wendy's International, is currently faced with not only a glut but also an accelerating decline in sales growth. The same factors threaten growth for the Jack in the Box chain, despite current healthy earnings.

Obviously, there is a dangerous drop in Ralston's two biggest businesses: grocery products and agricultural goods. Despite steady $1.9 billion sales, grocery products profits were down sharply because of the $122 million aftertax write-off of the three divestitures. But there is less reason for the 31% drop in operating profits from AgriProducts: Its sales dropped only 15% to $2.1 billion. All told, total sales dropped to $4.8 billion in 1982, down from $5.1 billion in 1981, while profits nosedived 60% to $69 million from $174.8 million.

Stiritz argues that with the three big money losers out of the way, "We're now going to be able to spend our time doing what we do best." And this downhome confidence coupled with his low-key style has permeated the company. Managers are encouraged by the stark contrast to his predecessor, R. Hal Dean, who retired last year at 65. It was Dean, a flamboyant dealmaker, who entwined the skein of acquisitions that Stiritz is now unraveling. Those acquisitions paid off initially, but in latter years almost all of them backfired. In his later years with the company, the autocratic Dean also aroused the enmity of many analysts. Some felt they were being misled or stonewalled about Ralston's future. Indeed, following one acrimonious analysts' meeting in 1978, Ralston's stock plummeted 8% in two days.

Dean was equally cavalier with his employees. Insiders claim he publicly belittled his managers' ideas and suggestions, eroding their self-confidence. By contrast, Stiritz places employees at their ease, encouraging them to deliver their best. Says

one: "The operations guys know that Stiritz wants to emphasize new products and will give them a quick go-ahead on a good idea."

William M. Jones, president of AgriProducts, cites several examples, such as a feed supplement that a hog farmer can mix with his own corn. Jones will also go after "the new rural market"—small farmers, horse owners, and breeders of chickens, rabbits, and dogs. Since such potential customers are usually too small to order feed in bulk, the company will offer its products in small packages through lawn and garden shops. In the past, says Jones, this market has fallen between the cracks of Ralston's distribution. New for Ralston, too, is the $280 million-a-year birdseed market. Jones will market feeders equipped with a new line of fruit-added feed.

American farmers remain the backbone of the business, and Jones believes that they will get the upturn they need within two or three years. To be ready for it, Ralston has acquired four existing feed plants and built three new ones in the past year to provide better geographic distribution. Altogether, claims Jones, "We are changing the definition of what we are from being one of the leading feed companies to one in which we are a leading company serving the entire agricultural industry."

The pet food strategy is simpler: maintain and solidify the lead that Ralston already has, says William P. Lacey, president of the Grocery Products Group. A variety of new products, backed by extensive advertising, won back some of the market share lost in the late 1970s.

But the toughest battle that faces Ralston may be in the cereal business. Lacey insists that Ralston "will be launching some major new products in the next two years." New cereals, however, carry heavy advertising costs, and in the slow growth, competitive marketplace, may not bring commensurate gains.

Outsiders look for improved earnings, given Stiritz's willingness to shed other money losers. The hockey team, but not the Checkerdome, may be sold to a Canadian group, and the shrimp business and the Colorado resort are candidates for imminent divestiture.

One survivor is likely to be the small protein technologies division. Ralston scientists have developed protein isolates used in many foods, as well as soy-based polymer products used in paper and paperboard coatings. This operation, a Dean startup, is now moving into the black, insiders say.

In the meantime, the chairman has advanced Ralston's cause with at least some company critics. "I wouldn't have believed he could do so much in such a short time," says analyst Alan S. Greditor of Drexel Burnham Lambert Inc. But Greditor, along with those other analysts who have expressed cautious praise for what Stiritz has accomplished in his first year on the job, still has some reservations. "He has proved that he is an excellent operating guy, but I'd like to see how well he handles a major acquisition," Greditor says.

Many others are waiting to see what Stiritz does next. So far he has done little more than what most top executives usually do when brought into problem-fraught businesses: They take big write-offs the first year, setting the scene for better results down the line. Stiritz's own strategy has pushed him into seeking growth from the very businesses that his predecessor saw as peaked. Whether he can do so remains to be seen.

QUESTIONS

1. Describe how Ralston's restaurant operations are experiencing the problems associated with a mature market.

2. What factors should be considered in deciding whether to drop one of Ralston's products?

3. What is a major difficulty in monitoring product life cycles in a firm such as Ralston Purina?

4. What are some of the product management issues associated with Ralston's entry into the birdseed market?

Case 9.2

Briggs & Stratton Corporation

AMID THE LAVISH BEER and auto commercials on Super Bowl XVII was an unlikely newcomer to high-price national television—Briggs & Stratton Corp., the Wauwatosa (Wis.) supplier of engines for lawn mowers, generators, and small industrial equipment. The $400,000 spent on the 30-second commercial kicked off Briggs & Stratton's new offensive strategy, one that will include spending $4 million on TV and consumer magazine advertising this year—quadruple its 1982 spending. The reason for the marketing blitz: After years of dominating the small engine market, the company is facing its first serious foreign competition. "The real battle over the next five years is with the Japanese," says Frederick P. Stratton Jr., president and chief executive. "I hate to admit it, but Japan has set a new standard for quality."

With a reputation for solid if not particularly innovative products and an unparalleled service network, the 73-year-old company is the leader in the $1.5 billion world market for small engines. But customers complain that in recent years it has become complacent and vulnerable. "They are kind of like the General Motors of the small lawn-mower engine industry," notes Kendrick B. Melrose, president of Toro Co., which buys Briggs & Stratton engines for its mowers. "But their weakness is that they have become so dominant that they haven't responded quickly with innovative new products."

Now, the company is being forced to act. The sluggish domestic and world-wide economy has whipsawed its earnings over the past three years. In the first half of its 1983 fiscal year ending June 30, Briggs & Stratton's earnings fell 25% to $14.7 million, while sales slipped 7% to $298 million. Even more ominous, Japanese manufacturers are making inroads into the market as both engine suppliers and manufacturers of end products. "We are determined to build consumer awareness of our product and maintain our leadership position," says 43-year-old Stratton, the soft-spoken, bookish grandson of one of the company's founders.

As part of a broad strategy to beat back Japanese competition, particularly from Honda Motor Co., the company has put together a six-member marketing staff to push its engines not only with its traditional commercial customers but also with the mass merchandisers that sell two-thirds of all lawn and garden equipment. "We are trying to get them [mass merchandisers] to request Briggs & Stratton engines on end products," says L. William Dewey Jr., executive vice-president. The company is also strengthening its relations with the 25,000 dealers who sell and service its engines.

On the product front, the company is working with industrial designers to improve the appearance of its engines by adding such cosmetic features as chrome and spiffy new decals. But even more important, Briggs & Stratton has recently introduced engines for both lawn and industrial applications that have reduced noise levels and electronic ignitions.

The new stance is drawing approval from customers. "Briggs & Stratton know they are under attack, and they are working much closer with us and distributors," says Tony A. Malizia, chairman of the Snapper Power Equipment unit of Fuqua Industries Inc. Still, he is not convinced that the company has completely shaken its complacency. He cites its failure to introduce a two-cycle engine for hillside mowing to compete with one from Japan's Suzuki Motor Co.

For the time being, Honda, which entered the U.S. market six years ago as a supplier to Snapper and two years later introduced its own branded products, is aiming only at the high end of the lawn mower business. But the company has already grabbed a large share of the small

SOURCE: "Briggs & Stratton's new hard sell," *Business Week*, Feb. 14, 1983, pp. 42, 46. Reprinted from the Feb. 14, 1983 issue of *Business Week* by special permission; © 1983 by McGraw-Hill, Inc.

recreational generator business, and it says that lawn mowers and generators will become its "third major line" behind autos and motorcycles.

Clearly, advertising alone will not do the trick for Briggs & Stratton. Some skeptics doubt that a component manufacturer can effectively advertise directly to a consumer. But Chief Executive Stratton argues that the company's advertising, combined with its clean balance sheet, modern plant, and new product commitment, will carry the day. Says he: "We are not going to let the Japanese take this market from us."

QUESTIONS

1. At what stage is the small engine in its product life cycle? What actions appear necessary for Briggs & Stratton regarding the firm's small engine?

2. Why is the rate of technological change for engines important to Briggs & Stratton?

3. What options should Briggs & Stratton consider for extending the mature stage of the product life cycle for small engines?

4. How has Briggs & Stratton begun to deal with product improvement?

A Special Look
Services Marketing

Dr. Leonard L. Berry

The U.S. economy *is* a services economy. In 1982, 50 million persons, or almost 56 percent of the total U.S. nonagricultural workforce, were employed in the services sector. In contrast, the goods-producing sector employed only 24 million persons or approximately 27 percent of the nonagricultural workforce. Whereas goods industries contributed approximately 31 percent to our national income in 1982, services industries contributed 52 percent.

The point of these statistics is not to belittle the importance and contribution of goods industries such as agriculture, mining, construction, and manufacturing. Rather, it is to stress that those of you reading this textbook will work in an economy dominated by services.

UNDERSTANDING SERVICES

In the years ahead, as consumers you may spend at least half of your disposable income for services such as rent, medical care, airline tickets, restaurant meals, electricity, long-distance telephone calls, loan interest, insurance premiums, and basketball games. In fact, if you were to list all the services you have used in the last twenty-four hours, you might be surprised at the length of your list. If you have used fewer than seven services, you have either just spent a very uninteresting twenty-four hours or you do not yet have an understanding of what constitutes a service and how it differs from a good. Let us explore several characteristics of services.

Concept of intangibility

The fundamental distinction between a good and service is that a good is an *object* (automobile, dress, drill press) and a service is a *performance* (housecleaning, exercise class, dry cleaning). In essence, services are intangible. Unlike goods, they cannot be seen, touched, smelled, tasted, tried on for size, or stored on a shelf. We use services but do not possess them. We may spend hundreds of dollars on a trip for airfare, taxis, hotel rooms, restaurant meals, and entertainment, yet we return home with little other than memories and laundry. As college students, you are spending a considerable amount of money for an educational service that is invisible to the naked eye.

The importance of intangibility to marketing can be realized by walking through a department store and an office of a financial institution such as a bank, savings and loan, securities broker, or insurance firm. In the department store goods are everywhere—colorful goods, goods that are

About the Author: Dr. Leonard L. Berry is Federated/Foley's Professor of Marketing and Retailing Studies at Texas A & M University. Dr. Berry is coauthor or coeditor of many articles and eight books, including *Marketing Financial Services* with James H. Donnelly, Jr., and Thomas W. Thompson (Dow Jones–Irwin, Inc., 1985) and *Bankers Who Sell* with Charles M. Futrell and Michael R. Bowers (Dow Jones–Irwin, Inc., 1985). Dr. Berry was instrumental in the American Marketing Association's adding a Services Marketing Division in 1984 and will serve as president of the American Marketing Association in 1986–1987.

interesting to look at, goods that can be touched, goods that in many instances will sell themselves. The department store is full of "things." Not so with the financial institution office, which, except for furnishings, forms, and people, will mostly be empty. No goods sit on shelves to be touched or inspected. The contrast is striking. Back-to-back visits to the two types of companies are recommended for anyone believing that the concept of intangibility is only academic nonsense.

Intangibility poses some special challenges for services marketers. What do services marketers picture in advertising if the product itself is invisible? How do they brand their product if there is no tangible object on which to place the brand? How do they stimulate "impulse buying" in their stores when there are no products to display on the shelves? Should those of you reading this essay work in service organizations—and many of you will—you may have to grapple with these very questions.

Concept of inseparability

A second characteristic of services is that production and consumption are inseparable, that is, the customer must be present for the service to be performed. You must be present, for example, to get your hair cut, your teeth examined, or your pulse taken. You must be on the airplane to receive the airline's service and in the classroom to receive the educational institution's service.

In effect, inseparability means that the customer is *in the service factory* and experiences directly the production of the service. How service personnel conduct themselves in the customer's presence—how they act, their facial expressions, their "tone of service," what they say, what they do not say, their overall appearance—can determine whether the customer buys from the firm again. If a worker in an appliance factory has a bad attitude, is poorly dressed, or has body odor, the buyer of the appliance will never know. The appliance is purchased at a location and time different from where and when it was made. The appliance producer and appliance consumer never meet. However, if a medical doctor has an uppity attitude, a restaurant waiter and unkempt appearance, or a taxi driver body odor, customers' perceptions of the service are affected. Accordingly, a central challenge for many service businesses is orchestrating the behaviors of personnel interacting with customers so that the service actually rendered will be what the marketer and the customer want it to be.

A second aspect to the concept of inseparability and a second way that the behavior of service personnel is orchestrated is through *buyer involvement.* That is, buyers frequently play a major role in the production of a service. For instance, hairdressers are often influenced by their customers' hairstyling suggestions, and insurance coverage is largely determined by the interaction between the representative and his or her client.

Concept of perishability

Nothing is quite so perishable as an airline seat, a hotel room, or an hour of a consultant's time. If these are not used when they are available, they cannot be inventoried or stored. Almost all services suffer because their output cannot be inventoried. The question for services, then, is, in the short run, given a certain capacity, how can a balance between output and sales be maintained when there is no inventory capability?

Concept of heterogeneity

Although Holiday Inn may train all its reservation clerks in exactly the same way, there is no way to ensure that service in San Francisco will be the same as service in Boston. Depending on the mood and motivation of the clerk, the same services will differ among locations and over time.

Furthermore, many services are difficult to evaluate in advance of purchase. As experience has shown, the quality of professional services such as law, medicine, and dentistry varies widely. Yet obtaining an objective evaluation of these services is difficult and is based primarily on the advice and experience of friends and associates. Although extreme cases of inadequate service usually are publicized, information about more modest variations in the quality of services is not available to buyers. As a consequence, buyers of services seek indirect ways to gauge the quality and reliability of services. These ways include the appearance of service facilities, appearance and courtesy of personnel, testimonials by well-known persons, past accomplishments of the service, and experience of known and trusted people.

FUTURE TRENDS AND CHALLENGES

The challenges posed to services marketers by intangibility, inseparability, perishability, and heterogeneity mean that the following marketing strategy issues will become increasingly important:

1. *Managing evidence.* Because services are intangible, customers tend to be especially attentive to tangibles associated with the service (e.g., the appearance of the service facility and service providers) for clues con-

The U.S. Postal Service has chosen to picture an eagle in advertising its Express Mail "next day service." This well-known American symbol does effectively convey the intangibles of "speed, reliability, and economy." (Reproduced with the permission of the United States Postal Service)

Positioning themselves differently to try to capture market share, dating services in the Boston area like Relationships, Inc. compete with countless others, including Boston Sportslovers, Young Professionals, the Single Gourmet, and Cultural Companions.

cerning the service's quality. Marketers will devote increasing attention to "managing this evidence" so that it conveys the desired image of the service.

2. *Making the service tangible.* Clever services marketers will try to find ways to make their services more tangible because advantages are associated with marketing tangibles compared with intangibles. For example, credit card companies are able to market credit services as though they were goods because of the existence of the tangible plastic card, which can be branded, brightly colored, pictured in advertisements, and carried around by customers.

3. *Marketing to attract employees.* Because services are performances, it makes sense to focus marketing attention and resources on the performers. More and more services marketers will recognize the potential of using marketing ideas and tools to better attract, keep, and motivate the kind of employees (internal customers) who can and will perform the service the right way. By satisfying the wants and needs of internal customers, labor-intensive organizations upgrade their ability to satisfy the wants and needs of external customers.

4. *Differentiating from competitors.* Service organizations frequently have difficulty differentiating themselves from competitors because of the product's intangibility as well as—in many instances—uninspired marketing. In banking, for example, competing banks often have similar names, buildings, services, rates, machines, and advertisements. It is no wonder then that to many customers all banks are alike. A key marketing opportunity for many service firms lies in finding ways to be institutionally distinctive. Using marketing to position the organization and to define its reason for being from the customer-prospect's perspective will rightfully occupy the energies of services marketers in the years ahead.

5. *Developing retention and relationship marketing.* Service marketers are recognizing the opportunities involved in developing formal marketing programs for existing customers. It is frequently easier and more cost efficient to sell additional services to existing customers than to sell the first service to a noncustomer. Nevertheless, it is not uncommon for service firms to virtually ignore customers they already have in favor of customers they do not have when it comes to developing next year's marketing plan. The tide is beginning to turn, however, and more companies are emphasizing *retention marketing* (nonpersonalized strategies to keep and improve existing customer business, such as the airlines' frequent flier programs) and *relationship marketing* (personalized, client-based strategies to maintain and increase present business, such as banks' "personal banker" programs).

Services marketing is different in subtle but powerful ways. Understanding these differences is important. After all, the services economy is not something in the faraway future. The services economy is here; it is real; it is now.

10 New Product Planning

When you finish this chapter, you will understand

☐ Why new products are essential to the survival and growth of companies

☐ The major stages in moving new product ideas into commercialization

☐ How new product ideas are generated and screened

☐ The activities included in new product and marketing plan development

☐ How new products are tested before market introduction

☐ What is involved in introducing new products and why some new products fail

☐ The available organizational approaches for coordinating and managing new product activities

Biotechnology—the new science of manipulating microorganisms such as these—is generating new product lines unimagined a few years ago. For example, Monsanto will introduce a growth hormone for cattle in 1987, while Du Pont experiments with products to diagnose and treat cancer.

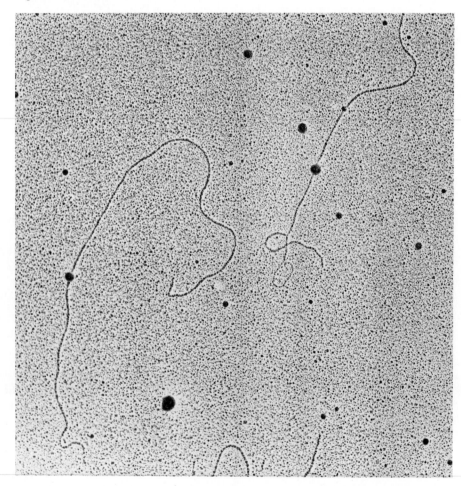

To keep up with the Ewings in Texas, it helps to subscribe to *Ultra*. . . . *Ultra* already has become required reading for upper- or would-be upper-class Texans. *Ultra* is strong in how-to articles: where to buy gold-heeled cowboy boots, for example; how to go helicopter hiking in the Cariboo Mountains; how to serve caviar mousse and dress the servants (in togas) for a real Lone Star–style party, and how to evaluate duck vs. goose for Christmas dinner.

Inasmuch as such questions never have been and never will be relevant to some millions of native-born Texans, *Ultra* has already found a few detractors. "The ultimate obnoxious expression of the gauche parvenu mentality. . . . no redeeming social or cultural value," a letter to the editor goes. Says another: "*Ultra* reflects much of what I don't want Texas to be with affluent snobbery, glossy overpriced artifacts and disjointed suggestive literature."

Harsh words for what "is surely the finest piece of literature available" in Texas today, according to Christopher Harlepp. Mr. Harlepp owns a Ferrari, a Mercedes-Benz and two BMWs. He also subscribes to *Ultra*, a monthly, along with 70,000 other Texans whose names originally were selected from country-club membership lists and other such sources to get free copies. Since then, the magazine's management has decided to sell subscriptions, at a special price of $12 a year, to the public. The newstand price is $2.50 a copy.

Houston real estate developer Harold Farb, who founded *Ultra*, calls it an "upbeat" magazine for an "upscale" audience. Mr. Farb is a Texas partygoer and amateur singer and recordmaker. He gets publicized in his own magazine.

Karl Sternbaum, former proprietor of a Florida printing plant, is *Ultra*'s editor. He considers himself an authority on the Texas rich. In Dallas, he says, they are "conservative and cerebral"; in Houston, "new and flashy," and in El Paso and San Antonio, a "closed society." Beneath it all, however, he says they are really "down-to-earth" folks.

Mr. Sternbaum is proud that *Ultra* is being produced right in Texas by some of the best magazine people in the business. They mostly come from New York.[1]

Published for more than five years, *Ultra* can no longer be considered a new product. The magazine today enjoys success partly because of the planning that went into it. For instance, the promotion of the magazine is targeted to appeal to Texans who are socially conscious or who aspire to be: *Ultra* is "the talk of Texas"; it's "enticing, spirited, and lavish"; and it "encompasses Texas traditions while setting new trends." (Courtesy of *Ultra* magazine)

ULTRA IS A NEW PARTICIPANT in the highly competitive magazine market. Nevertheless, certain specialty magazines have performed quite well. The targeting and positioning of *Ultra* are quite innovative. Aimed at wealthy people in a single state, the magazine provides them with a custom-tailored offering of feature articles and topics. As is the case with most new products, the financial risks of market entry are high but the rewards could be exciting if the magazine is successful.

Planning for new products is an essential activity for organizations. Without new products most businesses cannot survive. New products must be planned carefully because product development is costly and failure rates are high.

In this chapter we discuss how new ideas are developed into commercial products. We first examine the major steps involved in moving new product ideas to the marketplace. Building on this overview of new product planning, we discuss searching for and evaluating new ideas and look at what is involved in new product development. Test marketing, a technique sometimes used to gauge market success, is described, and how new products are introduced into markets is considered. The chapter concludes with a discussion of organizational approaches for product management.

MOVING NEW IDEAS INTO COMMERCIALIZATION

It usually is not difficult to recognize a totally new product. If a firm is first to enter the market with the product, then a new product life cycle is initiated. A product may be new because it is unique, such as a device that records picture and sound from a television set—the VCR when it was first introduced, for instance. Alternatively, the product may function differently from existing products, as, for example, the microwave oven. In all instances a product that is new starts as an idea and involves a company developing and launching it in the marketplace.

Why new products or services?

Why do companies develop and introduce new products? Part of the reason is that sooner or later products become obsolete. They mature and then decline in their product life cycle. Change is the way of life for the innovative organization.

> Above all the innovative company organizes itself to abandon the old, the obsolete, the no longer productive. It never says: "There will always be a market for a well made buggy whip." It knows that whatever human beings have created becomes obsolete sooner or later—usually sooner. And it prefers to abandon its obsolete products itself rather than have them made obsolete by the competition.[2]

New products may also increase sales and profits. Additionally, a diversified mix of products can protect a company from a sudden drop in the sales of a particular product line. The Gillette Company, the leading firm in the razor industry, continually is introducing shaving and other products such as writing instruments, toiletries, and grooming aids. Aggressively developing products is an essential part of Gillette's business strategy designed to extend the lives of existing products and initiate new product life cycles. An example of Gillette's new product development program is Brush Plus, an all-in-one brush and shaving-concentrate system introduced in 1984. Gillette is illustrative of many firms whose managements recognize both the importance of new products and the financial demands associated with developing and introducing new products.

Many new products fail even after careful development and testing. For example, in 1982 Hershey Foods Corporation's management was enthusiastic about the potential of Hershey's Frostin', a line of ready-to-spread cake frostings. By late 1983, the success of the product was doubtful, and in 1984, Hershey's Frostin' was withdrawn from the marketplace. Nevertheless, according to Hershey's president, the firm is commited to new product development.

> As we see the future of our businesses, we believe there is continuing significant opportunity for many new products, in both the grocery and confectionery fields, in our pasta products, and in new service concepts and techniques . . . which will place continuing demands upon our financial resources.[3]

Stages in new product development

The six major stages in moving a new product idea into the marketplace are shown in Exhibit 10.1. In stage 1, promising new ideas for products are generated in company research and development laboratories or from other idea sources such as customers. Ideas are screened by managers and technical people in stage 2 to identify promising new product candidates. Ideas that appear attractive after they have been screened undergo product development (stage 3), the stage in which how to make the product is determined. For instance, decisions as to flavor, composition, packaging, and processing must be made for a food product such as a new cereal. While the product is being developed, planning associated with marketing also is underway in stage 4. Questions such as what to name the product, how to price it, what distribution channels to use, and how to promote it must be answered. Some of these questions are not resolved fully until the testing in stage 5 is complete. Testing may involve asking people to try the product as well as introducing the product into the market in selected test cities, as was done with Gillette's Brush Plus in Peoria and Tucson. Finally, if the test results are favorable, the product moves to commercialization (stage 6) and is introduced nationally or regionally.

The six stages of new product development provide a general description of how new products move from the idea stage into the marketplace. Depending on the product, industry, and company, specific activities in each stage may vary. For example, complex industrial products often require extensive time and effort in product development, whereas a new type of certificate of deposit developed by a bank may necessitate only a minimal amount of time. The Marketalk about Armour's Boneless Turkey illustrates the stages in new product development.

Mix of new product introductions

Because new products vary as to degree of newness they can be placed into categories.

New-to-the-world products. New products that create an entirely new market

Exhibit 10.1 Stages in new product development

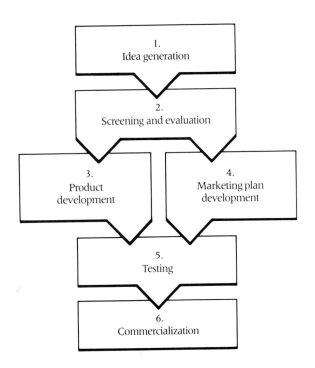

New product lines. New products that, for the first time, allow a company to enter an established market

Additions to existing product lines. New products that supplement a company's established product lines

Improvements in or revisions to existing products. New products that provide improved performance or greater perceived value and replace existing products

Repositionings. Existing products that are targeted to new markets or market segments

Cost reductions. New products that provide similar performance at lower costs[4]

*Marke*TALK ///

Moving the Boneless Turkey from idea to market

ARMOUR'S GOLDEN STAR Boneless Turkey provides an interesting new product case study that illustrates the stages in new product development. The opportunity to encourage people to move turkey out of the holiday-only category was clearly attractive to Armour. Interestingly, the idea of a boneless turkey came from a company salesperson who reasoned that consumers would buy turkey more frequently if a hassle-free, nonprocessed product was available. Their salesperson was right, although moving the idea to market was a major undertaking. As you read through the following description of how the new product was developed, tested, and introduced into the market, note the close correspondence to the stages shown in Exhibit 10.1:

All indicators showed that the timing was right—turkey consumption was up 25% over the previous five years, and a continued steady rise was projected for the foreseeable future.

Armour began by polling a nationwide, random sampling of consumers during which market researchers discussed the boneless turkey concept and carefully explained that the suggested product was not intended to replace the traditional holiday bird, but rather was to be used for family meals on a year 'round basis.

The results of this survey showed that the boneless turkey concept was right on target. First, it would be more economical because without the bones, every morsel of meat paid for is meat

that gets eaten. Second, cooking time would be reduced conserving both homemaker time and household utility bills. Next, the product was a natural product, not processed, and would provide all the natural turkey taste and texture without the bother associated with refrigerating and cooking a whole bird. And finally, it would be a welcome addition to the homemaker's list of nutritional meal possibilities.

With the concept of the new product firmly established, Armour's research and development food specialists set out to produce the first boneless turkey for testing.

A number of whole-bodied turkeys were carefully deboned, and extensive cooking methods developed to arrive at the best possible product for presentation to the first of what would eventually evolve into hundreds of consumer test panels. These test panels confirmed the tremendous consumer interest of the first survey, and enabled Armour to proceed with the development of a prototype boneless turkey for limited test production.

Next, 500 prototype boneless turkeys were distributed to consumers for in-home tests during which every detail from label instructions to sliceability to taste was reported on exhaustively. Each consumer was prodded for every reaction, every opinion—no matter how minor—regarding the product's ease of preparation, its natural turkey flavor and texture and serving convenience.

The result! Over 85% of the in-home testers said they would buy boneless turkey for year 'round family dining.

With such high marks from consumer panelists, Armour then proceeded with the extensive fine tuning and large scale consumer testing that would further en-

sure the product's success in the mass marketplace.

Engineering and manufacturing worked out production logistics; Armour home economists triple-checked cooking times, temperature and other preparation directions trying to anticipate every flaw, every possible problem that could cause consumer disenchantment. And Armour's packaging experts finalized the plastic covering for the product itself, as well as the containers used to ship them to retail outlets nationwide.

And while all this was going on, the most efficient techniques were being developed to debone turkeys on a full scale production basis so that the final product would consist of precisely the natural portion of white and dark meat, carefully covered with its own attached skin and wrapped in a stretch netting to hold it all together.

Once it was demonstrated that boneless turkeys could be produced to precise specifications, Armour's marketing, advertising and sales staff swung into action to introduce the new product.

Los Angeles and Sacramento, California, were selected as tests markets, and a special introductory TV commercial was developed to educate consumers that Armour's new boneless turkey consisted of the natural meat of a whole turkey—that only the bones are gone, and that it should not be confused with the more familiar processed turkey roll.

The test marketing of the boneless turkey on the West Coast was highly successful and put the final stamp of approval on the nearly two years of development, testing, engineering, marketing and advertising effort that went into bringing the new product to market.

SOURCE: "Beating the odds!" *Go Greyhound,* Nov. 3, 1980, pp. 6–7. Courtesy the Greyhound Corporation.

///

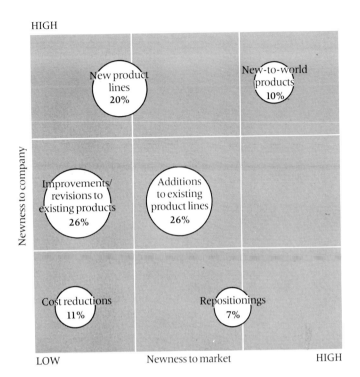

HIGH

New product
lines
20%

New-to-world
products
10%

Improvements/
revisions to
existing products
26%

Additions
to existing
product lines
26%

Cost reductions
11%

Repositionings
7%

Newness to company

LOW   Newness to market   HIGH

(Size of circle denotes number of introductions relative to total)

Exhibit 10.2 Categories of new products in terms of newness to the company and marketplace

SOURCE: *New Products Management for the 1980s,* New York: Booz, Allen & Hamilton, Inc., 1982, p. 9. Used by permission.

Note that our discussion in Chapter 9 designated three of the categories as modifying existing products. These include improvements in or revisions to existing products, repositionings, and cost reductions.

Booz, Allen & Hamilton, management consultants, has estimated the percentages of new product introductions for each category, which are shown in Exhibit 10.2. Each category is positioned according to newness to the company and market. Interestingly, the firm's research indicates that the high-risk new-to-the-world and new product line categories account for only 30 percent of all introductions yet represent 60 percent of the most successful new products.

FINDING, SCREENING, AND EVALUATING IDEAS

Sources of ideas

Idea generation is the process of producing new product ideas. Ideas may be generated within the company or by sources outside the firm such as customers. Ideas come from many sources including company research and development laboratories, employees, inventors, customers, marketing research, and competitors. Maintaining a flow of new product ideas calls for the cultivation of many idea sources. No one source should be relied on to supply ideas. Both persistence and a willingness to take risks may count as much as innovation in finding and developing new products.

Companies that recognize the importance of new ideas have developed organized approaches for finding, encouraging, and evaluating ideas. The management of Cordis Corporation, a producer of heart pacemakers and other biomedical products, recognizes the importance of both new technology and understanding customer needs in guiding new product planning. The president of Cordis made the following changes to keep the firm in touch with the marketplace:

> Weldon [the president] increased his sales force by 305 and broadened its responsibilities. Cordis salesmen no longer merely sell. They collect marketing data for product improvement, participate in conceptual discussions of new products, and coordinate worldwide sales for all products. Weldon created Cordis' first autonomous marketing department, and Cordis' soon will launch its first project born of collaboration between marketing and research: a radiological angiographic product.[5]

It is important that responsibility be assigned to a person (or group) for collecting and evaluating new product ideas.

How are ideas screened and evaluated?

Often new product ideas go through a series of evaluations, including screening, customer testing, and business analysis.

Screening new product ideas consists of placing each idea into one of two categories: (1) ideas that receive further comprehensive evaluation before a decision regarding development is made and (2) ideas that are rejected. Several factors often are considered in determining whether to continue evaluation or to reject an idea. Most of the screening criteria fall into the following categories:

- Product features and limitations
- Market opportunities
- Competitive factors
- Company technical and marketing capabilities
- Financial considerations

After developing a list of relevant criteria, a judgmental evaluation of the idea is made usually by a team of key managers and specialists. In some firms a new product idea committee performs the screening function. In

Crystal clear. Wafer thin. Flawless in its composition. Inscribed with a channel through which two opposing circles of light travel at extraordinary speed. This is the heart of the Micro Optic Gyroscope, developed by Northrop Corporation's Precision Products Division, Norwood, MA. Using micro-electronics, the difference in resonance between these two circles of laser light is measured, exactly. The Micro Optic Gyro combines precision measurement with greatly reduced cost. From the worldwide leader in precision inertial instruments.
Northrop Corporation, 1800 Century Park East, Los Angeles, California 90067 USA

NORTHROP
Making advanced technology work

Creative energy. Unaware of time. Generating new ideas. In the continuing pursuit of quality, performance, reliability. In aircraft, electronics, services.
Northrop Corporation, 1800 Century Park East, Los Angeles, California 90067 USA

NORTHROP
Making advanced technology work

The idea generation and creative working environment that are encouraged by Northrop Corporation are illustrated by these two corporate ads. The Micro Optic Gyroscope displayed here is one product of this environment. (Courtesy of Northrop Corporation; *left*, photographer: Per Volquartz; *right*, photographer: Jeffrey Corwin)

Exhibit 10.3   Guides for concept testing of industrial products

Clarify the function or functions the new product would perform, possible situations in which it could be used, and how it would be used

Portray the product's characteristics in terms that will be understood readily by the respondent

Provide a comparison of the product's likely physical and performance characteristics with those of any existing competitive products that perform a similar function

Cite the product's principal advantages and disadvantages

Indicate an expected price or price range

SOURCE: E. Patrick McGuire, *Evaluating New-Product Proposals*, New York: The Conference Board, 1973, p. 65.

other firms the review may be done by the executive who is responsible for approving new idea development.

Customer testing is obtaining an evaluation of a new product idea from potential customers. **Concept testing** is one useful technique for measuring customer reaction to a proposed new product. The product concept is described to a sample of potential customers. They are told about the features of the product, and if appropriate, shown a sketch or description of the product. The concept test does not provide an opportunity for a person to look at (other than a sketch), hear, feel, or try the product. Thus the test can provide only a rough gauge of customer reactions. It can be used for consumer products, industrial products, and services in instances when the services can be described adequately. Several guidelines for concept testing industrial products are shown in Exhibit 10.3. Concept testing also can be used to help define a product idea after the decision has been made to develop the product or service. The advantages and limitations of concept tests are listed in Exhibit 10.4.

Other research techniques may be used to identify promising new product ideas and to evaluate customer reaction to the ideas. For example, a focus group can be used to brainstorm various aspects of product planning. These interviews are conducted with a small group of people (see Chapter 7). A trained interviewer either asks broad questions or leads the group in identifying questions or issues associated with a topic (e.g., the desired features of a proposed basic marketing textbook).

Exhibit 10.4   Advantages of concept tests

Concept testing can be done quickly and before the product prototypes need be developed.

It can often be done early enough to make any project modifications indicated at little cost.

It is relatively inexpensive as compared with later-stage research possibilities.

It involves less danger of premature disclosure of the concept to competitors than does test marketing.

It can help planners make sound choices from among alternative concepts being considered.

It can help define and prove the existence of a suitable target market.

It can assist planners in developing the right product and appeals for that market.

SOURCE: E. Patrick McGuire, *Evaluating New-Product Proposals*, New York: The Conference Board, 1973, p. 34.

Comprehensive analysis of new product ideas is usually the last step before the decision is made to either drop an idea or to move it into development. This aspect of idea evaluation is called **business analysis,** which is an estimate of the financial attractiveness of the new product to the firm after it is introduced into the market. This analysis often includes financial projections, market analyses, and other projections of feasibility and performance. Included in the analysis are sales projections, profit margins, development costs, and other aspects related to the proposed business venture.

Booz, Allen & Hamilton learned from a major study of more than 700 U.S. industrial and consumer goods companies that managers estimate their new products' contribution to growth will rise one-third for sales and 40 percent for total profits during the 1980s. Not surprisingly, given the importance of new products, many firms are refining new product idea screening and evaluation procedures.

> Greater effort is going into the "homework" phase, during which companies screen new product ideas by "looking at corporate goals, doing the analytical work, business analysis, and market research." Out of this comes a pared-down list of products that will be developed and produced.
> Much of the market research "homework" available to companies will depend on increasingly sophisticated methods, using demographics, psychographics, and other tools to attain a deeper understanding of the potential customer's specific needs.[6]

DEVELOPING THE PRODUCT AND THE MARKETING PLAN

If a product idea is not rejected, it moves into the development stage. At the same time, several important marketing decisions are made.

Product development

Product development is the process of transforming an idea into an actual product: The product development stage is the beginning of the design of the new product. During the development process, customer reaction may be obtained at various times. Gillette's experience in developing the antiperspirant, Dry Idea, highlights the long road from idea to a marketable product.

> The product concept of a dry roll-on was established through consumer research in 1975.
> R & D people began work, and by late 1976 on the third try the lab came up with a product that scored well on tests on women recruited to sweat in a 100-degree "hot room" for hours.
> By the summer of 1977 the product was judged ready for market introduction.
> Management decided not to test market the product, and launched it nationwide in August 1978 after completion of the marketing plan for Dry Idea.[7]

Thus a major development effort that spanned three years was required to develop Dry Idea and its marketing plan.

Developing the marketing plan

Important marketing decisions can be resolved during product development. If the firm waits until product development is complete before developing a marketing plan, market introduction will be delayed substantially. Several marketing activities and decisions can be undertaken including

- Deciding what people or firms to use as the target market
- Investigating names for the product
- Testing the advertising and sales promotion program
- Designing the package
- Selecting distribution channels
- Analyzing price

Although all details of the marketing plan may not be completed during product development, major progress can be made. As an illustration, consider the name research conducted for Dry Idea by Richard Goldberg, the 28-year-old product manager assigned marketing planning responsibility for the new product.

> Mr. Goldberg's first job was to pick a name and develop an advertising strategy with Batten, Barton, Durstine & Osborn, Inc., the New York agency. More than a dozen names were tested on consumers. Among the rejects: Drynamite ("It sounded too much like a drain cleaner"), Feel Free (consumers thought it might be a tampon) and Omni and Horizon, both now names of cars.[8]

TESTING THE PRODUCT AND THE MARKETING APPROACH

Testing is the next stage of the new product development process. Efforts during this stage normally are concentrated on obtaining customers' reactions to the product as it is used regularly and market testing in limited areas such as test cities.

Use tests

The **use test** gauges how the intended user feels about the new product after actually using it. Samples of the product may be distributed to consumers for in-home tests and their reactions may be questioned during in-depth interviews. Typically, the use test measures reaction to the product in a plain wrapper. The company and brand normally are not identified so the user's reaction is concentrated on the attributes of the product rather than perceptions about the firm supplying the product. Because of this, the use test is somewhat artificial. Nevertheless, by comparing the new product to competing items in a use situation, important information about the product can be obtained. The use test does not measure customer reaction to the marketing approach planned for the product. Test marketing is used for this purpose.

Test marketing

Because test marketing is sometimes used to test and refine marketing plans, we need to look closer at this phase of new product planning. **Test marketing** is introducing a new product or service in a limited market area to predict the ultimate success of the product when it is introduced nationally and to test the planned marketing strategy. Market tests usually are conducted in one or a few cities. The basic idea underlying a market test is to sample market response in a limited market area and then project the test results to the national or regional target market. Test marketing is a form of marketing research. (See Marketech in this chapter and in Chapter 21 for more on test marketing.) Let us take a closer look at *why* and *where* market tests are conducted, and then we consider some of the problems involved in market tests.

Why and where market tests are conducted. Market tests are conducted for two primary purposes: to estimate the sales and profits that will result from full-scale introduction of the new product and to try out and refine the marketing approach planned for the product. Achieving both aims depends greatly on the similarity of the test cities to the national market. Management must know if the test results are indicative of what will happen when

Marke**TECH** □ □ □ □ □ □ □ □ □ □ □ □ □ □ □ □ □ □

Test marketing: A way of life for Sensormatic Corporation

AT SENSORMATIC CORP., test marketing is a commitment to "a way of life" for the Deerfield Beach, FL, manufacturer of electronic anti-theft devices. Last year the company conducted extensive tests on two new surveillance systems. This year testing could be stepped up, depending upon the number of new products and systems it develops. Considering that its executives estimate that fully 90% of their market is untapped by *anyone,* more testing seems inevitable. Competitive information about new products is treated as secret by the company—but it's no secret that no new Sensormatic product will appear without testing. This was not always the case.

Fifteen years ago, when it introduced its first anti-theft "alligator tags" (they trigger an alarm when anyone exits a store without paying) the company was $10 million in debt. Propelled by anxiety, and unable to find customers, company president and co-founder Ronald G. Assaf offered the untested system to retailers free. But easily detected drawbacks, including false alarms and breakdowns, outweighed the system's merits. A year later only 25 retailers were using the system, 24 for free, 1 on lease. Indeed, it was another four years before the company turned a profit, $191,000 on sales of $3.8 million. It was an expensive and well-learned lesson.

Says Lou Chiera, product manager for the company's SensorGate, an electronic surveillance system for supermarkets, "What happens in a lab isn't what happens in the field. We've learned from experience if you test something in an engi-

neering laboratory you don't see the actual real-life situation, a unique cash register that may react differently to your system or even the type of floor you have to put the system in."

The SensorGate was developed to cut down on pilferage in such high-theft areas of supermarkets as packaged meats and health and beauty aids, which account for 90% of the merchandise lost to shoplifters. The system consists of magnetically sensitized labels which are attached to the goods and swinging store exit gates with electronic transmitters. Any tagged item not rung up by a checker triggers an alarm. The cost is $4,750 for a single or double gate per aisle and $4,275 each for two or more aisles. Tags are 2½¢ apiece, fully discounted.

First tests of the system were launched close to two years ago in southern Florida units of the Winn Dixie grocery chain, located near Sensormatic's headquarters. Says Chiera, "We usually test close to the plant so that we can easily get back to our designers and engineers for anything that requires changes. After the changes are made they can go out and monitor the systems so that we don't have to make any drastic changes halfway into the marketing of the product."

A major change that resulted from this strategy was the development of the single-gate system. Says Chiera, "Everyone in the building has a feel for the product. But even with that you get the real feel and the needs only in the marketplace. What we found in our earliest efforts was that a large number of stores have narrower checkout aisles that can't handle our double gates, so we came up with the single-gate as well as the double-gate system." Doing that saved his company considerable time and money. "If we hadn't test marketed," Chiera says, "we would have

lost six months of actual time in researching sales to get the bugs out."

Eight supermarkets and 15 liquor stores throughout the country participated in the tests, with the final trials set to wrap up next July at two units of Ralphs Grocery Co., in Pasadena and Redondo Beach, CA. (Chiera estimates there are over 620,000 potential installations for his system in the U.S. and Europe; 2,000-plus systems were sold at the recent Food Marketing Institute Show in Chicago.) Says Chiera, "We started on a selective basis to test market, and we could have made claims based on localized testing. But the selling job is easier when store managers in different parts of the country actually see what the system can do."

Feedback, which comes from focus groups, on-site interviews by company monitors, and electronic data tied into the system, is used as a selling tool. Says Chiera, "If a store has scanning, it can track the movement of a given item, and we recommend that as one way to test the system's efficiency. To prove its cost effectiveness, we suggest plugging in 10 different items before and after it is installed. The store manager can then track how many went through the register."

Chiera says that without the tests "we wouldn't have moved as fast as we have. We would have been limited to selling to those who automatically believe that the system works, this without proof, because they are in a very high crime area and suffer a severe shrinkage problem."

Despite a $24 billion a year shoplifting bill most retailers, however, have to be persuaded with hard facts before they protect themselves. Brad Kane, corporate marketing chief, and Chiera agree. After two years of test marketing, Sensormatic is convinced it has the hard facts prospects demand.

SOURCE: "Test marketing," *Sales and Marketing Management Magazine,* Mar. 12, 1984, pp. 84, 87, 88. Copyright © 1984. Reprinted by permission.

□ □

Exhibit 10.5 The nation's most popular test markets

Albany-Schenectady-Troy	Louisville*
Albuquerque	Lubbock, TX
Amarillo	Madison*
Atlanta	Memphis
Bakersfield*	Miami
Bangor*	Milwaukee
Binghamton, NY	Minneapolis-St. Paul
Boise*	Nashville
Boston	Oklahoma City
Buffalo	Omaha
Burlington*	Orlando-Daytona Beach
Charleston, SC*	Peoria
Charleston, WV	Phoenix
Charlotte	Pittsburgh
Chattanooga*	Portland, ME
Chicago	Portland, OR
Cincinnati	Providence
Cleveland	Quad Cities: Rock Island & Moline, IL,
Columbus, OH	Davenport & Bettendorf, IA
Dallas-Fort Worth	(Davenport-Rock Island-Moline
Dayton	metro market)
Denver	Richmond, VA*
Des Moines	Roanoke-Lynchburg*
Erie, PA	Rochester, NY
Evansville*	Rockford*
Fargo, ND	Sacramento-Stockton
Flint*	Salt Lake City*
Fort Wayne	San Francisco
Fresno	St. Louis
Grand Rapids-Kalamazoo-Battle Creek*	San Antonio
Green Bay, WI	San Diego
Greensboro-Winston-Salem-High Point*	Savannah*
Harrisburg*	Seattle-Tacoma
Houston	South Bend-Elkhart*
Indianapolis	Spokane
Jacksonville, FL	Springfield-Decatur-Champaign, IL*
Kansas City, MO	Syracuse
Knoxville*	Tampa-St. Petersburg
Lexington, KY	Tucson
Little Rock*	Tulsa
	Wichita-Hutchinson*

* New this year.
SOURCE: *Sales and Marketing Management Magazine,* Mar. 12, 1984, p. 104. Copyright © 1984. Reprinted by permission.

the product is introduced nationally. For example, can a 10 percent market share for the product in two test cities, Denver and Chicago, be used as an estimate of how the product will sell nationally? While no city is a perfect proxy for an entire market, several have proved to be reasonably good indicators of national and regional markets. The nation's most popular test markets are listed in Exhibit 10.5.

A good test city should contain people who correspond to those in the target market for the new product. An ideal city should be a scaled-down replica of the national market. Geographically isolated cities ensure that sales results will not be contaminated by persons from nontest cities purchasing the product. Other characteristics of good test cities are listed in Exhibit 10.6.

The advantage of test marketing is that the product can be tried in the marketplace at a small fraction of the costs of a national introduction. Because the risks of new product failures are extremely high, spending a million dollars in a test market to learn that the product probably will fail

Exhibit 10.6   A checklist for selecting
test markets

In choosing a test market, many criteria need to
be considered, especially the following:

Typical of planned distribution outlets

Relative isolation from other cities

Availability of advertising media that will cooperate

Diversified cross-section as to ages, religion,
cultural-societal preferences, etc.

No atypical purchasing habits

Representative as to population size

Typical per-capita income

A good record as a test city, but not overly used

Not easily "jammed" by competitors

Stability of year-round sales

No dominant television station; multiple newspapers, magazines, and radio stations

Availability of retailers that will cooperate

Availability of research and audit services

Free from unusual influences, such as one industry's dominance or heavy tourist traffic

SOURCE: *Sales and Marketing Management Magazine,* Mar. 15,
1982, p. 72. Copyright © 1982. Reprinted by permission.

clearly is better than spending millions of dollars on a national introduction
that fails. Consider this account of Bristol-Myers attempts to enter the
$250-million-a-year market for cold remedies. Interviews were conducted
with 600 consumers to determine their preferences in cold remedies.

> Bristol concocted three products to fill the bill: Dayphen, without sleep-induc-
> ing antihistamines; Clinicin, an easy-to-swallow lozenge; and Comtrex, to
> relieve multiple symptoms. . . . Lacking antihistamine, Dayphen failed to
> dry the nasal passages of cold sufferers sufficiently. Clinicin was accepted well
> enough to be sold in test markets—but there it failed to meet test goals, and
> was dropped. But Comtrex, test-marketed in Spokane, Wash., and Rockford,
> Ill., sold 40 percent above Bristol's projection.[9]

How a product is tested. The test market attempts to create a situation similar
to the national market. Ideally, buyers should not know that the product is
being tested, although this often is difficult to accomplish. The product
should be in the form and package intended for the national market. The
product must be distributed to the types of retail outlets planned for the
national market and sold at prices being considered for the national market.
Advertising, sales promotion (e.g., free samples), and selling efforts also
should be launched as planned for full-scale introduction of the product.

Because testing may be used to evaluate marketing program components (e.g., price, amount of advertising, effectiveness of coupons) some
parts of the marketing effort may be varied from one city to another. For
example, the product may cost $1.69 in Spokane and $1.99 in Denver to
help determine which price generates the most favorable profit contributions after taking into account differences in sales and price.

Marketing research usually accompanies testing to obtain the information needed to evaluate test results. For example, information on the characteristics of buyers can be used to see if test market buyers correspond to

those considered to be the target market for the new product. Information also is often collected on how many first-time buyers repurchase the product and the sales of competing products or brands before and after the test. One problem in interpreting test results is adjusting for the actions of competitors during the test. Some have been known to make unusual changes in their marketing efforts during competitors' tests to sabotage the results. For example, a major cut in advertising by a key competitor during the test could artificially inflate the test product's sales.

INTRODUCING NEW PRODUCTS INTO THE MARKET

Commercialization is the final stage in moving new products into the marketplace. Market introduction begins after completing test marketing, or after completing development when test marketing is not conducted. (Not all new products are market tested.) Introduction follows one of two avenues: The product may be launched immediately into the national market or it may be moved into the market in stages, one geographic area at a time. This roll-out approach may be favored when the supply of the product is limited or when market tests were not conducted. Alternatively, a product may be launched nationally because a lead can be gained on competition, because full production is necessary to obtain cost advantages in production, or because no other reasons favor introducing the product to one area at a time.

Market introduction is the commercialization stage of new product planning. When the product reaches stage 6, it is ready to begin moving through its life cycle. Because some products are dropped soon after market introduction, we need to consider what makes a product successful. The reasons for new product failure also offer important guidelines for avoiding failure.

What is a successful product?

Whether a new product is successful really depends on the performance criteria established by the managers of the firm that introduced the product. A broad gauge of success is whether the product remains on the market after a reasonable trial period. In an extensive study involving 700 firms conducted by Booz, Allen & Hamilton, these facts were uncovered.

> Between 1976 and 1981, the companies surveyed introduced a total of 13,311 items. Of those entries, 35% were unsuccessful; an earlier Booz Allen study found a 33% failure rate between 1963 and 1968. In both surveys, success was determined by each company's own criteria. (When a successful product is defined as one that is still on the market, only 23% of the new items in the past five years are flops.)
>
> Most of the new products since 1976 weren't strikingly new, though. Half were either additions to or modifications of existing products. Only 10% were what Booz Allen calls "new to the world." But of the products that companies rated as their biggest winners, 27% were "new to the world."
>
> Although marketers may not be improving their new-product batting average, they are becoming more efficient at developing products. Today only seven ideas need to be seriously evaluated to find one successful product, compared with a 58:1 ratio in the 1968 study. One reason: earlier weeding of ideas that are weak or don't fit a company's overall strategy.

New-product spending also is more efficient. Today successful entries account for 54% of total new-product expenditures, compared with 30% in 1968. Capital investment as a percent of total new-product spending has fallen to 26% from 46% in 1968.[10]

Note, for example, the success in recent years of improving the number of new product ideas weeded out early in the product planning process.

Perhaps the best gauge of product success is whether the product performs up to the standards management set before it was introduced. For example, new ready-to-eat cereals are often evaluated on the market share they attain. Kellogg's management in 1982 indicated that Nutri-Grain cereal was a success because it had gained a 1 percent share—successful by traditional industry standards.[11] (The market leader, Kellogg's Corn Flakes, has only about a 5 percent market share.)

Why products fail

Several examples of successful and unsuccessful products are shown in Exhibit 10.7. According to some experts, 30 percent of unsuccessful new products fail because they answer no important need, and another 40 percent fail because they perform inadequately.[12] Let us take a closer look at these and other reasons for new product failure.

No real advantage. A product with no real advantage over existing products fights an uphill battle against established products. A product that copies existing ones may be successful in new markets, but even then products with unique features and advantages usually prove to be more successful. Polaroid's instant movie camera failed because it was too costly and of low quality compared with available 8mm systems and users did not want instant developing.[13]

Fifteen months after its entry into the home computer market, IBM stopped production of its PC*jr*. Junior got off to a bad start: Its $1500 price and "Chiclet" keyboard so slowed sales that not even a 20 percent price cut and a free upgrade to a conventional keyboard could move the machines. (Courtesy of IBM Corporation)

Exhibit 10.7 Examples of new product winners and losers

Winners

Radio Shack TRS-80 personal computer
Federal Express overnight mail service
Ragu spaghetti sauce
E.T.—The Extra-Terrestrial
Diet Coke
Loctite Quick Metal industrial adhesive
Lear Jet small commercial aircraft

Losers

Ford's Edsel automobile
DuPont's Corfam synthetic leather
Campbell's Oriental soups
Polaroid instant movie camera
Susan B. Anthony $1 coin
Concorde supersonic aircraft
RCA videodisk player

Technical problems. No matter how much technical effort is put into developing a new product, it may not meet performance expectations. The results of research and development are not certain. The problem arises when a lot of money already has been spent on development and management decides to introduce a product even though its performance characteristics are not as good as originally expected. If the gap is too large between desired and actual product characteristics, the product will fail at the commercial stage.

Lack of or faulty marketing research. Either the lack of marketing research or faulty research may cause a new product to fail. Users thought Campbell's Oriental chicken soup was too bland and the beef teriyaki had a peculiar odor. A panel of the company's advertising and business executives, tasting by sipping from teaspoons, not surprisingly failed to spot the problems.[14] The results of comprehensive use tests might have indicated that the product should not be introduced. Good research information also can help determine product characteristics, market target decisions, and product positioning.

Poor timing. There are risks of being too early or too late in entering a market. Ford introduced Edsel, a fast, high-powered automobile, in 1957 when the industry was banning high horsepower and the economy was moving into a major recession. Other problems in planning plus poor timing cost Ford $350 million.[15]

Faulty execution. Preoccupation with the development of a new product and neglect of the commercial stage sometimes occurs in industrial products firms with highly technical products. An industrial products firm's vice-president comments: "Managers should be selected to stay with the project during commercialization until it matures into a new business or as a product line within the existing organizational structure.[16]

Factors beyond management's control may cause products to fail. For example, competition may occupy a stronger position in the marketplace than was anticipated from test market results and other testing efforts. Apparently, Hershey's Frostin', a product that obtained favorable response from retailers and consumers, was unable to gain sufficient market share to make the venture profitable. Strong competition was encountered from Duncan Hines and Betty Crocker brands. Government regulations and controls also may affect a new product's success. For example, the Food and Drug Administration's approval must be obtained before a firm can introduce various drugs. Finally, company personnel may favor some new products and not others for political reasons. For example, a division manager may not favor a new product idea that will be produced and marketed in another division. The complexity of the modern corporation also makes communication among the people involved in product planning difficult.

Analyzing a failure

A look at why a new industrial chemical first performed well in the market and subsequently failed offers a useful example of the importance of a complete product evaluation and planning program. The experience is described by a company executive.

The product was a specialty chemical, the company's first entry into this field. Testing was successful, and outside manufacturing arranged with some difficulty. For several years we sold all we could make, and by the second and third years of full marketing achieved substantial volumes. We realized that this success was to some extent due to the shortage of similar chemicals [in that period]. What we did not fully realize was, firstly, that our product was being sold and used as if identical with the market leader's product, in spite of instructions to the contrary on our labels and advertising; and, secondly, that the third-year sales largely represented precautionary buying in case the shortage continued. Then the market turned down, the market leader's product became freely available, and our product, with its reputation damaged by the results of wrong application, started a sales decline from which it was never to recover.

We have identified plenty of reasons for these sad events. Not necessarily in order of importance, here are some of them:

1. Our own laboratory tests showed measurable superiority over the market leader. These tests were not usually confirmed by the less precisely controlled trials of customers' technical people. However, we remained convinced for some time that our assessment was "right."
2. The product was intrinsically more expensive to make than its major competitor, and therefore required a premium in the market; however, the premium could not be sustained unless the product was recognized to be superior by the user. (In addition, our costs increased sharply during the introductory period along with those of all other organic chemicals.)
3. We started the program with a small sales force and a select group of supposedly highly motivated distributors. In the context of the product shortage it was easy for these distributors to sell that product without bothering to explain how it should be used, and they also failed to observe the subsequent stockpiling of material. Our own sales force, besides being highly optimistic by disposition, was much too small to second-guess the distributors.
4. We were followed into the market about two years after our own introduction by a number of similar compounds. These were dismissed in our planning as offering no performance advantage over the market leader. They were, however, respectable compounds, aggressively promoted by large companies, and they forced the market leader to accept lower profit margins, which hurt us as a high-cost producer.[17]

Thus the ultimate failure of the product in this instance was caused by not sufficiently testing user reaction, high production costs, no apparent superiority to support higher prices, and marketing inadequacies. Inadequate market knowledge was a central contributor to the failure of the specialty chemical.

Buyers' adoption process for new products

The adoption and diffusion of innovation offers useful insights into how buyers adopt new products. Early work by rural sociologists stimulated the interest of marketing researchers.[18] The essential basis of the research was that if opinion leaders could be encouraged to adopt an agricultural innovation, this could encourage other people to try the innovation. The analogy to new products prompted marketing professionals to investigate adoption findings.

Study of the adopters of various innovations suggests that (1) new product adopters move through specific stages in their adoption process; (2) the characteristics of adopters vary depending on how quickly they adopt an innovation after it becomes available; and (3) adoption research may offer useful guidelines for new product planning.

Adoption stages. Rogers[19] has developed a useful description of the process of adopting a new product.

Awareness. The potential buyer becomes aware of the existence of an innovation.

Interest. The person obtains additional information about the innovation.

Evaluation. Interest stimulates the potential buyer to evaluate whether to try (purchase) the innovation.

Trial. A positive evaluation of the innovation leads to trial.

Adoption. Finally, favorable results from trial use cause the buyer to accept the adoption for continued use.

Characteristics of adopters. Adoption research has led to the classification of people into the adopter categories shown in Exhibit 10.8. Note that the proportion of adopters in each category is arbitrarily determined. For example, the first 2½ percent of the total adopters are designated innovators, the next 13½ percent early adopters, and so on.

The important marketing issue is determining the characteristics of those who adopt an innovation early in the process. Once identified, initial marketing efforts can be directed to these people. Rogers has hypothesized the following profile of early adopters:

> The relatively earlier adopters in a social system tend to be younger in age, have higher social status, a more favorable financial position, more specialized operations, and a different type of mental ability from later adopters. Earlier adopters utilize information sources that are more impersonal and cosmopolite than later adopters and that are in closer contact with the origin of new ideas. Earlier adopters utilize a greater number of different information sources than do later adopters. The social relationships of earlier adopters are more cosmopolite than for later adopters, and earlier adopters have more opinion leadership.[20]

The results of marketing research into the characteristics of early adopters have not been as useful as the adoption stages. Awareness of buyers' information needs at each stage is helpful in marketing program design.

Marketing implications. Several interesting new product planning guidelines are suggested by the adoption stages. Note, for example, the similarity with the stages and the buyer decision process for all products discussed in Chapters 5 and 6. Note also that various advertising and promotional messages are often targeted to the adoption stages of interest and evaluation for

Exhibit 10.8 Classification of adopters of innovations

SOURCE: Reprinted with permission of The Free Press, a division of Macmillan, Inc., from *Diffusion of Innovations* by Everett M. Rogers. Copyright © 1962 by The Free Press.

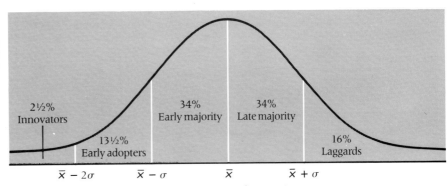

Time of adoption of innovations

new products. The trial stage explains the use of extensive sampling of new consumer products. The favorable experience resulting from a free trial of a product can encourage further use and adoption. (See Marketalk.)

RESPONSIBILITY FOR PRODUCT PLANNING

It is essential that company efforts for product planning be organized. Planning and coordinating product activities involve virtually everyone in an organization, including marketing, manufacturing (or operations in distribution organizations), accounting and finance, and human resources. Responsibilities for product planning often are divided between two or more business functions. To ensure that product management activities are properly coordinated, special organizational arrangements have been developed by some companies. A major study of new product practices in 148 companies uncovered two practices common to many companies' attempts to ensure better direction for new product development: (1) pinpointing responsibility for initiating and coordinating new product ventures and for keeping programs on schedule and (2) formalizing organizational arrange-

*Marke*TALK ///

Planning new products is difficult but exciting

POLAROID has seen Japan's vision of the future of photography—but isn't yet convinced it will work. That vision is a filmless camera that Hitachi Ltd. believes will revolutionize picture-taking even more than Polaroid Corp. instant photography has. The camera records images on a tiny magnetic disk, or "video floppy." These electronic pictures can be viewed immediately on a television screen or turned into color snapshots with a separate printer.

Hitachi offered Polaroid the marketing rights to the new camera a year ago but was turned down flat. "The prints aren't very good," explains Polaroid scientist Conrad H. Biber. "A true photographic company can't come out with a product that mediocre."

Biber's opinion isn't deterring a half-dozen Japanese companies, however. A flurry of filmless cameras is expected to hit the U.S. in the next year or so. Canon Inc. plans to join Hitachi in unveiling an electronic-imaging camera late this year or early next. And Sony, Minolta, Matsushita's Panasonic, and Copal, the biggest pro-

SOURCE: Alex Beam and Otis Port, "The filmless camera is here, but will it sell." *Business Week,* Apr. 15, 1985, pp. 151, 154. Reprinted from the April 15, 1985, issue of *Business Week* by special permission, © 1985 by McGraw-Hill, Inc.

ducer of camera shutters, will likely follow in 1986. That's not all. A dozen more Japanese giants, including most major camera makers, are in the final stages of development with similar products.

While filmless photography hangs like a sword over the $9 billion U.S. photography market, it won't fall right away. Because of its high price tag, almost no one believes electronic imaging will dent consumer markets before 1990. After Polaroid's turndown, Hitachi decided to market the camera itself and will roll it out later this year at about $2,000.

Still, the goal of filmless camera makers is to get production lines humming so they can lower prices to around $500, a level that should start stirring consumer interest. "We never worry about price points for new products and new technologies," says Michael P. Schulhof, president of Sony Corp. of America's Sony Industries Div. "If the idea has merit, there's always some segment of the population that will buy it, regardless of cost. Then we can refine it and bring down the price."

Even though Polaroid and Eastman Kodak Co. say they have a wait-and-see attitude, the two U.S. photography giants seem to be taking the long-term threat seriously. In January, Kodak created a Consumer Electronics Div., and its mission includes electronic imaging. Kodak's electronic camera technology is equal to Japan's, claims Wilbur J. Prezzano, general manager of photo products. The new division, he adds, "won't be distracted by our traditional interest in photography." And in May, Polaroid plans to open a new Microelectronics & Materials Center to house its $25 million-a-year electronics research effort, which accounts for about 20% of the company's total research budget.

Apart from lowering the new camera's price, the most pressing concern for researchers in Japan and the United States is improving picture quality. That has been the main hangup since Sony Corp. unveiled its much-ballyhooed Mavica camera in 1981. Critics charge that the current technology produces prints comparable to those from cheap diskfilm cameras. Consumers flocked to buy the simple-to-use cameras, but many were disappointed with the photo quality. "The resolution is so poor, electronic cameras are a nonissue right now," says Ian D. Robinson, president of Photographic Consultants Ltd. in Cambridge, Massachusetts. Gripes Herbert Keppler, editorial director of *Modern Photography*: "It'll be the year 2000 before people get a decent electronic image from a printer."

The quality of the pictures produced by

///

ments for ensuring close cooperation between marketing, research and development, and other functions concerned with new products.[21]

Some of the organizational approaches that are used to assign responsibility for planning and coordinating both new and existing product activities are new product committees, product managers, new product departments, and venture teams. A more detailed discussion of the marketing organization is provided in Chapter 22.

New product committees

Some firms appoint managers from various departments to committees responsible for planning and coordinating product activities. A **new product committee** generally is concerned with reviewing new product ideas, selecting ideas for development, and reviewing new product planning activities. A product committee also may be used to decide what products to drop. A product **task force** is similar to a committee except it usually is formed for a particular project such as developing a new product. The committee operates on a continuing basis, whereas the task force is formed for a particular task and then disbanded after the project is complete.

//

the new cameras is determined by a special type of semiconductor chip with a light-sensitive grid on its surface. This grid is made up of about 360,000 tiny photocells. An image falling on the grid triggers an electrical signal from each cell that varies with the intensity of the light. The result is a TV-like image with 360,000 "dots" called pixels. By contrast, a Kodachrome slide contains more than 18 million pixels and thus produces a sharper and far more detailed picture.

Yet even the doubters concede that electronic imaging is making exceptionally rapid progress. Gary W. Hamann, who experiments with electronic systems on the "future floor" of Polaroid's headquarters complex, notes that an imaging chip containing 1 million pixels, which can produce snapshot-quality images, has already been demonstrated.

If today's electronic cameras can't compete with Kodachrome, they can take picture suitable for reproduction in newspapers. News photographers, along with commercial and industrial applications, are the first targets for the filmless cameras. During the Los Angeles Olympic Summer Games, prototype cameras from Sony and Canon were used by photographers from the Japanese newspapers *Asahi Shimbun* and *Yomiuri Shimbun*, respectively, who relayed their photos by phone

to Japan in time to make the morning editions.

While image quality still isn't quite good enough for regular newspaper use, Harold G. Buell, assistant general manager for news photos at Associated Press, expects electronic imaging to improve to the point where filmless cameras can replace regular cameras. Once imaging chips with 10 million pixels are developed, Buell adds, "that's when photography leaves the publications field" altogether, even at high-quality magazines such as *Architectural Digest*.

As for consumers, electronic photography may soon begin sneaking into homes through the back door, in the guise of "TV projectors" that eliminate the rigmarole of setting up a slide projector and screen. Fuji Photo Film Co. this month introduced its $200 Fujix machine for displaying color photos on TV—after the photos are transferred onto a standard video floppy by a photofinisher. Such hybrid systems are "cheaper and more viable today than a total electronic approach," says Eugene G. Glazer, a photo industry expert at Dean Witter Reynolds Inc.

Electronic imaging proponents believe that the average camera buff will not hold out for Ansel Adams quality. "The consumer of today is a television person," says James D. de Merlier, marketing di-

rector for Minolta Corp.'s Photographic Div. "He doesn't know from the quality that Bert Keppler wants. He knows from what he sees on television. So if the cameras are priced right and offer certain features, people might accept a lower level of quality than even we think."

The new photography will indeed offer some unique features. With a home computer, a photographic illiterate could set up an "electronic darkroom" and crop, enlarge, and perhaps visually enhance his pictures, then churn out prints on a home printer that would work much like a color copier.

Electronic photography will also offer consumers the ability to "peek, pick, and print" only good photos, notes Richard D. Schwartz, an analyst at E. F. Hutton & Co. He thinks affluent people will gladly pay extra up front for this feature to save on film-processing costs later. "A lot of people are tired of plopping down a $10 bill and picking up a yellow bag of prints," only some of which are good enough to keep.

So the future may arrive sooner than Kodak and Polaroid expect. And maybe it will work after all.

//

Unless a firm has no new product activities, at a minimum a new product review and coordination committee should be appointed. Depending on the amount of new product activity, the committee may operate continuously or be formed as the need arises. Committees are not notably effective in managing projects and programs, so a member of the committee should be assigned responsibility for day-to-day product planning. A group of people cannot direct the various activities of ongoing projects. For example, it is not feasible to convene a committee every time a problem arises, a decision must be made, or a question requires an answer.

Scrivner, a large grocery wholesaler, uses a committee to evaluate new food items offered by food processors. The huge number of new food items that comes out each year precludes the wholesaler from carrying all of them. The committee, comprising top management, finance, operations, purchasing, and marketing executives, meets every two weeks to review new products offered by suppliers, deciding to stock some of the items and rejecting others.

Product managers

A product manager is responsible for planning and coordinating activities of a particular product brand, product line, or related group of products. Typically a product manager is an individual or a manager of a small group of people. In some firms the manager has responsibility for both new and existing products. In other situations only new products are involved. Proctor & Gamble is the leader in the use of brand management, having launched the approach more than fifty years ago. Product and brand management organizations are used in many firms including General Foods, General Electric, and Aladdin Industries.

Although the responsibilities of the product manager vary among firms, they typically include coordination of new product development activities, marketing program development (e.g., product specifications, distribution, price, and promotion), marketing research, and commercial development. Depending on the type of firm and product complexity, the background of the product-brand manager may include either technical or marketing experience. For example, product managers for complex industrial electronic products often have engineering experience and training. Regardless of the complexity of the product, marketing management capabilities also are important in product-brand management positions.

The product manager normally does not have authority over all product activities such as designing, manufacturing, packaging, advertising, and selling. For example, a product manager may be assigned to the marketing department with responsibilities for advertising, researching the market, and providing product assistance for the salesforce. Product managers of manufacturers maintain regular contact with manufacturing and engineering, although normally they cannot direct the activities of these departments. For example, the product manager would not have the authority to initiate a product or package design change, although recommending this and other actions would be part of the person's responsibility. In firms with technical products, a product manager may be assigned to engineering or research and development and would be responsible for coordinating those functions with sales and advertising. A brand manager is responsible for a particular brand and normally is assigned to the marketing department. The brand manager's scope of responsibility is similar to a product manager assigned to a marketing department except his or her effort is concentrated on a particular brand such as Crest toothpaste or Pringles potato chips.

New product departments

New product organization may be formalized by establishing a department. Often the department manager reports to the research and development or marketing chief executive. The **new product department** is responsible for coordinating all aspects of new product planning, although part of the actual work on new products is done outside the department. Otherwise, the department would have to duplicate all the business functions involved in moving new product ideas into commercialization. Departmental status gives the manager more power than a committee or product manager to get things accomplished. This type of organization can be found in firms with both industrial and consumer products. Activities of new product departments include locating and evaluating new product ideas, coordinating product development, developing a marketing plan, testing, and commercialization.

Venture teams

A modification of the new product department is the **venture team.** The team consists of key people representing various business functions such as manufacturing, research and development, marketing, and accounting and finance who work with the product venture from idea to commercialization. Businesses that develop and introduce major new products involving new production facilities, new markets, and substantial additions to personnel find that a venture team is useful in building the new business operation. If the new product represents a new business, then the venture team forms the core of managers who will launch and develop the new business. Providing venture team management with suitable incentives and rewards appears to be important in achieving success.[22]

International Business Machines has developed two interesting versions of the venture team approach, called *independent business units (IBUs)* and *special business units (SBUs),* for use in exploring business opportunities beyond the scope of IBM's main business.

> The rationale for IBM's little units is straightforward. "To manage new ventures with the same controls and procedures used for developing a whole new mainframe would inhibit them," explains James Hewitt, head of the IBM Information Network, an IBU that offers time-sharing and other computing services. IBM styles its new units as "companies within the company" and itself as their "venture capitalist." Each IBU manages its own finances, manufacturing, and marketing, while SBUs depend on the parent to handle one or more of these.[23]

SUMMARY

A new product begins as an idea, moves through development, and is launched into the marketplace. Moving new products into commercialization is both risky and expensive. Yet a continuing stream of new products is essential to growth and profitability of most firms. The major stages in new product planning are (1) generating ideas, (2) screening and evaluating ideas, (3) developing the product, (4) developing the plan for marketing the product, (5) testing the product and the marketing approach, and (6) commercially introducing the product. A new product may be aborted at any of the four product planning stages.

Stages 1 and 2 of new product planning are locating and screening and evaluating ideas. Research and development laboratories are one of several idea sources, rather than the primary source. Other sources are employees, inventors, customers, market research, and competitors. Once ideas are identified they are subjected to a series of evaluations including screening, customer testing, and business analysis. Screening reduces the stock of ideas to a small number that can be subjected to comprehensive analysis. Comprehensive analysis includes customer testing, which seeks to gain a reaction from potential users to the product idea, and business analysis, which is an estimate of the financial attractiveness of the product. Business analysis concentrates on financial projections, market analyses, and other projections of feasibility and performance.

An idea that is considered promising after evaluation is complete moves to product and marketing plan development. In stage 3, the product is developed, and the marketing plan is prepared concurrently in stage 4. Product development primarily is a technical task conducted by engineers and scientists that may consume years of effort and many millions of dollars. Several marketing planning activities can be completed while the product is under development, including selecting the market target, investigating names, designing the package, testing advertising and sales promotion, and selecting distribution channels.

Testing, stage 5, consists of use tests and market tests. Use tests are trials of the product by intended users. These tests are somewhat artificial because they do not take place in a market setting. Instead, samples are given to people who agree to try the product. Use tests are conducted before market tests, which are extremely expensive. The market test is actually introducing the product in selected test cities.

Commercialization, stage 6, is the last step in the new product planning process. If test results from stage 5 are positive, the product is ready to be moved into the market either one geographic area at a time (roll-out) or nationally. Companies may gauge the success (or failure) of a new product by whether it performs up to standards set for it. Some of the reasons products fail include faulty marketing research, faulty execution, and technical problems. Company efforts must be organized for product planning. The need for pinpointing responsibility and developing organizational arrangements for product planning is clear from studies of new product planning practices in many different companies and industries. Some of the popular organizational approaches for new product planning are new product committees, product managers, new product departments, and venture teams.

KEY TERMS

idea generation	product development	task force
screening	use test	new product department
customer testing	test marketing	venture team
concept testing	commercialization	
business analysis	new product committee	

QUESTIONS FOR REVIEW AND DISCUSSION

1. Why is it important for firms to develop and introduce new products on a continuous basis?

2. What marketing management decisions should be considered during product development (stage 3)?

3. Why are several functional areas of an organization involved in the stages of new product development?

4. What types of information sources could be helpful in developing new product ideas for an electronic products firm?

5. What are the advantages and disadvantages of concept tests?

6. Why might the stages of new product development span a long period of time, perhaps several years?

7. What are the advantages (and limitations) of test marketing compared with the use test?

8. What are some characteristics of a good test market city?

9. Why might a firm launch a new product into the market in all geographic areas instead of using a roll-out approach?

10. What are some ways a firm can measure new product success?

11. Why do many new products fail?

12. What type of firm may choose to employ a venture team to plan and coordinate product activities? Why?

13. Why is it important for product-brand managers to be skilled in marketing management?

14. Why are new product committees often not effective in managing new product projects?

BUILDING YOUR PORTFOLIO

One of the most perplexing product management problems faced by many specialty retailers is selecting a merchandise mix that will tend to balance sales over most of the year. For example, sales of boats and motors are highly seasonal. Most of a boat retailer's sales fall within the spring and summer months. Assume you have been asked by a pleasure boat retailer to recommend other products (or services) that could be added to the boat line to help balance sales over the year rather than only during a six-month period. What product additions do you suggest? Keep in mind that the objective is to use the retailer's existing facilities, people, and experience.

NOTES

1. Noreen O'Leary, "*Ultra:* A magazine for Texans who want to dress the servants right." *Wall Street Journal,* Jan. 5, 1982, p. 1. Reprinted by permission of the *Wall Street Journal,* © 1982 Dow Jones & Company Inc. All rights reserved.
2. Peter F. Drucker, "The innovative company." *Wall Street Journal,* Feb. 26, 1982, p. 15.
3. *1982 First Quarter Report and Report of Annual Meeting of Stockholders.* Hershey, Penn.: Hershey Foods Corporation, 1982, p. 14.

4. *New Products Management for the 1980s.* New York: Booz, Allen & Hamilton, 1982, pp. 8–9.

5. "Cordis: Building marketing muscle to pump up strength in biomedicine." *Business Week,* Dec. 20, 1982, p. 63.

6. "Listening to the voice of the marketplace." *Business Week,* Feb. 21, 1983, pp. 90, 94.

7. This account is based on Neil Ulman, "Sweating it out—Time, risk, ingenuity all go into launching new personal product." *Wall Street Journal,* Nov. 17, 1978, pp. 1, 41.

8. Ibid., p. 41.

9. Gail Bronson, "Creation of Comtrex: Marketing hit gives Bristol-Myers relief." *Wall Street Journal,* Mar. 10, 1980, p. 37.

10. Bill Abrams, "Despite mixed record, firms still pushing for new products." *Wall Street Journal,* Nov. 12, 1981, p. 27. Reprinted by permission of the *Wall Street Journal,* © Dow Jones & Company, Inc., 1981. All rights reserved.

11. John Koten, "For Kellogg, the hardest part is getting people out of bed." *Wall Street Journal,* May 27, 1982, p. 29.

12. "Agency exec explores reasons why new products fail." *Marketing News,* August 3, 1984, pp. 9, 16.

13. Michell C. Lynch, "Instant movies falter: Is Polaroid's chairman wrong for a change?" *Wall Street Journal,* Aug. 9, 1979, pp. 1, 29.

14. Betsey Morris, "Getting stirred up." *Wall Street Journal,* July 16, 1982, p. 12.

15. An interesting description of the Edsel failure can be found in William H. Reynolds, "The Edsel ten years later." *Business Horizons,* Fall 1967, pp. 39–46.

16. Edward N. Aqua, "Don't neglect new products during their crucial first six months, nurture them." *Marketing News,* Apr. 16, 1982, p. 14.

17. David S. Hopkins, *New-Product Winners and Losers.* New York: The Conference Board, 1980, pp. 18–19. Copyright 1980 The Conference Board. Used by permission.

18. Everett M. Rogers, *Diffusion of Innovations.* New York: Free Press, 1962.

19. Ibid.

20. Rogers, Ibid., p. 192.

21. Hopkins, op. cit., p. 23.

22. Shelby H. McIntyre and Meir Statman, "Managing the risk of new product development." *Business Horizons,* May/June 1982, pp. 51–55.

23. Peter D. Petre, "Meet the lean, mean new IBM." *Fortune,* June 13, 1983, p. 78.

Case 10.1

Manufacturing Supply Company

IN ONE OPERATING DIVISION of a company manufacturing supply items, an interdepartmental team spent 10 months last year studying answers to the question: "How can we improve our methods of developing and bringing to market our new and improved products?"

Results of this teamwork included a new "standard operating procedure," a detailed checklist for guiding product development methods, a standard form for use in appraising each new product proposed, an activities sheet for reporting progress on projects, and some organizational adjustments.

The twin anchors of the revised organization are a screening committee for new-product ideas, and a project evaluation and review team. The screening committee is new, and the review team replaces the former new-product committee. Each has regular monthly meetings.

The screening committee evaluates each proposed product in terms of its potential to exceed minimum targets for sales volume and profitability, as well as its uniqueness, producibility, and conformity to the capabilities of the division. If an idea seems promising at first blush, it is assigned to a "sponsor." It is the sponsor's duty to coordinate market surveys and other preliminary screening, and to complete a "Product Development Proposal"—a one-page form on which esti-

SOURCE: David S. Hopkins, *New-Product Winners and Losers*, Report No. 773, New York: The Conference Board, 1980 pp. 24–26. Copyright 1980 The Conference Board. Reprinted by permission.

mates are made of the size of the total market, the new item's probable share of that market, projected sales volume, unit price and gross profit for each of the first three years after introduction, plus the particulars of anticipated developmental costs and return on investment.

After a new-product idea has successfully passed the scrutiny of the screening committee, it gains the status of a proposed project. It is then subject to further study by the project evaluation and review team, chaired by the vice president of new product development. The principal tasks of this interdepartmental team are to recommend approval or rejection of each proposed project, to maintain all current projects under review, and to revise project priorities when necessary. Each approved project is assigned to a "project leader," who becomes responsible for selection of a "project team."

Membership of a project team comprises the project leader, the "sponsor" (i.e., the person who first guided the new idea through the screening committee), and representatives from product management, industrial engineering, marketing research, quality assurance, and other functions as required.

A project leader is expected to "ride herd" on the assigned project by maintaining a "critical-path" chart encompassing a detailed checklist of more than 100 steps to be taken during the product development process. The main headings appearing on this checklist are business analysis, design criteria, preliminary design, design review, field trial, final design, documentation, production plan-

ning, sales and marketing, and, lastly, production release. Each of these main headings is divided into a number of subheadings, which often are further subdivided. By way of illustration, under the main heading "design review" there are eight subheadings, just one of which—"quality assurance"—covers the following six points: materials evaluation, testing costs, test fixtures, standard test methods, sterilization qualifications considerations, and regulatory considerations.

Each project leader reports progress once a month to the project evaluation and review team by means of an "activities sheet" which notes significant milestones, individuals responsible for key activities, and the scheduled and actual start and completion dates for each step in the project.

Several major benefits reportedly are expected from this refocusing of organization and procedures for new-product development after the current "shakedown" phase has been completed:

- By ensuring that a greater amount of marketing research and careful planning is done up front, before any significant engineering time has been devoted to a new product, the proportion of successful projects having a superior financial payoff is expected to rise.
- Greater use of project planning and project teams should raise the odds of setting and achieving completion dates.
- Improved monitoring and control of new-product projects should help the division to meet its sales and profit objectives for new products.

QUESTIONS

1. What are the advantages of Manufacturing Supply's new product development process?

2. Why is it necessary for so many functional areas to be involved in new product planning?

3. Do you have any recommendations to management for improving the new product planning process?

Case 10.2

Sara Lee

MANY PRODUCT CATEGORIES have been experiencing economy-driven changes that blur the lines between once-distinct product segments as consumers trade down or substitute products.

The sweet goods category is one example of how economic conditions expand product categories and force into competition marketers that might never have battled for market share.

Kitchens of Sara Lee, still the leader in the frozen baked sweet goods category, has suffered as a result of unit volume declines that reflect such an expansion of the market. Like the products of other sweet goods marketers, consumption of Sara Lee products also has been eroded by the "fitness trend" and new competition from fresh goods marketers—Entenmann's, in particular. While Sara Lee, a unit of Consolidated Foods Corp., never lost much of its share in the frozen baked sweet goods arena (it now hovers around 40%), unit volume was sluggish and its strength in the baked sweet goods category as a whole had diminished.

"The sweet goods category includes mixes, store-delivered items and in-store bakery goods" along with frozen products, noted Richard Sharoff, vp-retail marketing at Sara Lee, in a recent interview at the company's headquarters. Today, he said, the homemade segment is major competition. "What we want to do is offer products in ready-to-eat form that offer options to that, and we see opportunities in that area."

Sara Lee officials were not always so collected about unit volume losses. Attempting to stem them, the company last year tested fresh baked goods in Chattanooga and Nashville in cooperation with Dallas-based Campbell-Taggart (now a subsidiary of Anheuser-Busch), which distributed the products (*Advertising Age,* Sept. 14, 1981). P. Frederick Kahn, senior vp of Consolidated Foods' frozen sweet goods group and chief executive officer of Sara Lee, now calls the experiment "a little test that probably got more notice than it deserved."

The project, he said candidly, "was hastily conceived and it didn't prove much. At the time, we were concerned

SOURCE: Janet Neiman, "Sara Lee reacts, tries basketful of new sweets," *Advertising Age,* Dec. 27, 1982, p. 4. Reprinted with permission from the Dec. 27, 1982, issue of *Advertising Age.* Copyright 1982 by Crain Communications, Inc.

about turning around our retail business, but I have confidence that we can get the [frozen] category to grow" exclusive of a fresh baked goods approach.

The attempt was so faulty that, although neither executive would rule out the possibility of Sara Lee reentering the fresh baked goods arena at some time in the future, they expressed strong doubts about it. "I have a hard time seeing how we ever could compete in the [fresh baked goods] business profitably," Mr. Kahn said.

Now, Sara Lee's emphasis is on unit volume, rather than market share. "Sara Lee has always succeeded in increasing its market share," Mr. Kahn said.

Mr. Kahn and Mr. Sharoff pinpointed new products and more aggressive consumer advertising programs as the means to reverse the unit volume damage. Consumers seem to be responding. After reporting continued unit volume declines for fiscal 1982, ended July 3, the company, with fiscal '82 sales of about $330 million, "stabilized" sales during the first six months of calendar 1982, and had sales increases during the last half. The second-half figure includes an estimated 7% increase in case sales for the last quarter of calendar 1982 over the same period last year.

Sara Lee has never been a slouch in the realm of product development, even though the company didn't even have a new product development department as recently as a year ago. Rather, the company has proven itself prescient of food trends. However, apparently unable to find the niches to satisfy both itself and its consumer base, it has been forced to back down from many new products only to watch later entries in other categories follow up on its instincts with great success.

It pegged the smaller household, diet-conscious and convenience goods movements quite early, for instance, and unsuccessfully entered Sara Lee Cakes for Two, Sara Lee Light 'n Luscious and Sara Lee frozen entrees. (Sales of Cakes for Two turned out to be "tradeoff" sales in which consumers bought the smaller products rather than the original sizes, "at a price disadvantage," Mr. Sharoff said.)

The company is hoping such mistakes won't occur under its current set of new product criteria, and with a new product development unit established this year.

New Sara Lee products now must meet consumer needs by entering "potential growth markets"; broaden Sara Lee's participation in the frozen baked goods category; be "outstanding products," and represent products "the competition couldn't copy easily, if ever."

During 1982, Sara Lee introduced such new products as Puddin' in-the Middle, New York Style Cheese Cake and a reformulated line of coffee cakes. (Puddin' in-the Middle has been a stellar performer, and the company recently announced it would extend the original four-item line to six, with the addition of lemon cake-lemon pudding and banana cake-banana pudding items.)

Mr. Kahn and Mr. Sharoff say the company is deemphasizing line extensions and moving instead toward new categories.

One thing Sara Lee is concerned with is giving more attention to the consumer, in terms of marketing as well as consumer need. "We're investing heavily in marketing programs, with the focus of advertising increasingly [on] consumers." Declining ingredients costs have made that effort easier, he noted.

Early in the year, the company, via agency Foote, Cone & Belding, Chicago, broke two campaigns: A tv and print effort supporting the repackaged line of layer cakes themed, "What's your Sara Lee fantasy," and a testimonial tv drive for coffee cakes directly striking at Entenmann's (*Advertising Age,* Feb. 15, 1982). Although a spokeswoman at the time referred to the advertising as "choreographed", the two campaigns in fact were highly detached; Mr. Sharoff admitted in the interview that the "fantasy" campaign was a "false start" that was run only because the company "had already committed" to it.

Midyear, Sara Lee introduced Puddin' in-the Middle with a tv spot stressing the real pudding in every bite and through the year continued its earlier "bake sale" and "cake break" promotions and backed the reformulated, repackaged coffee cakes with print couponing and rebates.

This year's efforts provide a good contrast with the past few years, when consumer advertising dwindled to almost nothing (Mr. Sharoff now says it "wasn't what it should have been") and trade promotion was intensified. In '82, Sara Lee ran five flights of three to five weeks of tv, which, in his words, is "heavier than it's been" in years and "not too bad for a company that hasn't had any."

QUESTIONS

1. Discuss the possible reasons why Sara Lee's management successfully identified new consumer eating trends (e.g., smaller households) but failed to benefit from the opportunities.

2. Can you describe the market target of one of Sara Lee's product lines?

3. What suggestions can you offer Sara Lee's management to identify potential new product ideas?

4. What are advantages and disadvantages of test-marketing products such as those offered by Sara Lee?

11 Branding, Packaging, Servicing, and Product Safety

When you finish this chapter, you will understand

☐ Why businesses assign brand names to their products

☐ The options companies have in branding their products

☐ What is involved in brand name selection

☐ The actions taken by firms to protect their brand names

☐ The various functions performed by product packaging

☐ The role of product service and warranties in the marketing mix

☐ Several product safety and product liability issues

Customers look for this alligator when they want a classic, well-bred look in sportswear. Until recently, counterfeiters were very successful at exploiting the logo's popularity. However, new federal and state laws imposing jail sentences and substantial fines will deter counterfeiters in the future.

By 1982 Izod-Lacoste alligator apparel sales were more than $450 million, compared with $15 million in 1969. The alligator, which is really a crocodile, originated in 1926 when the French tennis star Rene Lacoste, nicknamed "Le Crocodile," wore a polo shirt with a crocodile emblem on it. The shirt was marketed in France in 1933. The brand reached the United States in 1951, imported by the Izod division of David Crystal Apparel Company. Later the company obtained the license to sell clothing with the Lacoste label. General Mills bought David Crystal in 1969. Today the popular alligator can be found on a wide range of apparel items from belts to bathrobes. And General Mills' lawyers are constantly fighting copycats.[1]

THE IZOD-LACOSTE ILLUSTRATION clearly demonstrates the power that a strong brand identity commands in the marketplace. Companies spend huge amounts of money to attract and hold the buyers of their branded goods and services. Not surprisingly, by 1984 Izod was facing strong competition from foxes, tigers, horses, and other wildlife on shirt fronts that had been the alligator's exclusive habitat.[2] Not only did Izod's management fail to anticipate competition, but, perhaps more of a problem, they failed to capitalize on the shirt's popularity and to update its sportswear lines. A new chief executive was appointed who indicated that Izod's future marketing strategy would be to sell fashion, not alligators. By early 1985 General Mills' management had decided to sell the Izod unit. A brand name, however strong, cannot alone perform the complete marketing task.

In this chapter we look at branding issues and practices and several other aspects of products. First we consider what is involved in making branding decisions and how company brands are protected from others who try to obtain the benefits of established brands. Next, we discuss several aspects of the packaging and servicing of products. Finally, product safety, product liability, and recalling faulty products are examined.

Exhibit 11.1 Illustrations of trademarks (*Top to bottom:* Courtesy of the Coca-Cola Company, Atari, and the Eastman Kodak Company)

BRANDING DECISIONS

How brands are identified

A **brand** is "a name, term, symbol, or design, or a combination of them that is intended to identify the goods or services of one seller or groups of sellers and to differentiate them from those of competitors."[3] A brand usually is communicated to the buyer by a **brand name** or **brand mark.** Examples of brand names are Charlie (Revlon's cosmetic line), Coors (beer), and Caterpillar (earth-moving equipment). A brand mark is a logo design; for example, Aigner leather goods are identified by their distinctive dark red color and by the metal "A" symbol attached to the goods.

A **trademark** is a legally protected name or symbol. It may be the entire brand name or some part of the brand.[4] More than 500,000 active trademarks are registered at the U.S. Patent Office, and 25,000 new ones are added each year. A **service mark** is used in the sale or advertising of services to identify the services of one person and distinguish them from the services of others. Recall the notation of an ® or Reg. TM or Reg. SM on products and packages and in advertising messages. These symbols indicate that the trademark or service mark is registered with the U.S. government. Several trademarks and symbols are shown in Exhibit 11.1. Companies sometimes "bank" trademarks, although to do so, a firm must sell the product commercially to qualify for trademark registration. A **banked**

trademark is one for which a firm has registered a trademark even though management has no immediate plans to launch a major marketing effort for the brand. In 1980 Seven-Up filed applications for 138 brand names![5] Trademarks are not considered banked by the government until they have been registered for several years. Law suits often occur because of the unauthorized use of one firm's trademark by another firm. We examine trademark and patent protection after completing our discussion of branding decisions.

Why products are branded

Product identity. The purpose of branding is to establish the brand's identity. For frequently purchased items such as soft drinks, beer, cigarettes, and dog food the extent of brand loyalty (repurchase of the same brand) often determines the long-term success of the brand. The advantages gained from branding by the marketer are many. Branding establishes a unique identity and brand position for a product. The brand name or mark serves as a proxy for the buyer, incorporating all the buyer's preferences for the various attributes offered by the product. Once a manufacturer or retailer establishes a strong brand position with buyers, competitors have a difficult time stealing buyers away from the brand. When brand identity applies to several product items in a line, market introduction of additions to the line is less costly and more likely to be successful when the same brand name is used. For example, additions to the Charlie cosmetic line were aided by the favorable brand image gained through the initial introduction of Charlie perfume. Many new product items enjoy similar advantages from their ties to established brands.

Distributors, dealers, and retailers recognize the benefits of marketing either established brands of their own (e.g., J. C. Penney) or those of well-known manufacturers. For example, a grocery wholesaler is far more likely

PURE WOOL

(*Above*) The Wool Bureau, Inc., a nonprofit organization subsidized by wool growers of the Southern Hemisphere, has registered this trademark to help identify for the consumer wool yarn and wool products that meet high standards for tensile strength, color fastness, mothproofness, and shrink-resistance.

(*Above*) "Thank you for calling Procter & Gamble concerning the malicious and false stories about our company's trademark," began the toll-free message by which P&G tried to combat persistent rumors alleging that its man-in-the-moon logo is satanic and that the company is involved in devil worship. In 1985, P&G reluctantly decided to remove its 103-year-old symbol from product packages because of a rebirth of the rumors. (Courtesy of the Procter & Gamble Company)

Brands are promises.   **So is this.**

(*Left*) General Foods Corporation recently adopted a new corporate symbol that company chairman James L. Ferguson said "reflects the fundamental change that has been taking place at General Foods since 1980. We have made substantial progress toward our mission to be the world's premier food and beverage company. Our new corporate symbol is a signal of that progress, of our confidence for the future and of our continuing commitment to provide superior consumer satisfaction in all our products." (Reprinted courtesy of General Foods Corporation)

CORNING
That little blue flower. And a whole lot more.

Corning Ware's "little blue flower" has long adorned this cookware. The logo design has come to symbolize the versatility of a product that's usable in the freezer or in the oven, in the microwave or on the table. (Courtesy of Corning Glass Works)

Exhibit 11.2 Percentages of adults who would not switch from their favorite brand to a generic brand

Product	Percent 1978	1981
Beer	48	48
Sinus remedies	50	44
Dog food	28	38
External analgesics	35	38
35mm film	44	37
Cartridge film	33	32
Instant film	38	32
Margarine	29	26
Canned soup	29	25
Potato chips	26	22
Snack crackers	25	22
Aluminum foil	16	13

SOURCE: Bill Abrams, "Brand loyalty rises slightly, but increase could be fluke," *Wall Street Journal,* Jan. 7, 1982, p. 2. Reprinted by permission of the *Wall Street Journal,* © Dow Jones & Company, Inc., 1982. All rights reserved.

to stock a new product offered by an established supplier such as Procter & Gamble or General Mills than an item offered by an unknown producer. Wholesalers and other distribution firms know that suppliers with strong brand positions will promote their brands aggressively and thus encourage potential users to try the brands.

Brand loyalty. Consumers of goods and services also benefit from branding. Buyers often judge product quality based on their knowledge of the products offered under the brand name. For example, established names such as Kodak, IBM, Kraft, and Sony often influence buyers purchasing new or unfamiliar products. A buyer may reason as follows: "My Sony television has performed well so I am going to purchase a Sony videocassette player-recorder." Likewise, once experience has been gained with a particular brand, buyers are assured of consistent quality in future purchases. Of course, unknown brands may offer comparable quality at low prices, but often the consumer has no basis of evaluating the unknown brand other than by trying it. Thus buyers frequently purchase established brands.

Brand loyalty, or a customer's predisposition to purchase a brand repeatedly rather than to sample unknown brands, varies by product category and it appears to shift over time for a given product. The J. Walter Thompson advertising agency surveyed 2500 adults, asking them if they would switch from their favorite brand to a generic (unbranded) product costing one-half the price of their favorite brand. Exhibit 11.2 shows the findings based on the percentage of adults who indicated that they would *not* switch. Because the conditions for a brand switch (50 percent saving) were rather sizable, the percentages probably understate the true proportion of buyers who are brand loyal. Also, the survey indicates what respondents said they would do rather than what they actually purchased. Nevertheless, it is clear that strong brand preferences exist for a substantial portion of buyers of various products.

Branding options

Management first must decide whether to use a **manufacturer's brand** or a **middleman's brand.** A manufacturer's brand is owned by the manufacturer, whereas a middleman's brand is owned by some organization in the distribution channel other than the manufacturer. An example of a middleman's brand is the Kroger brand of foods. **Private brand** refers to brands owned by retailers and other distributors of products such as Kroger, A&P, Skaggs Alpha Beta, Revco, K mart, and Radio Shack. In some instances, large retailers may own some of the producers of the private brands. For example, Sears has part-ownership in some of its major suppliers. The feasibility for a manufacturer or middleman to establish a brand depends on the firm's size, resources, product, and management's preferences. Some manufacturers such as Kellwood Company (apparel for men, women, and children) have their own brands and also produce private brands for retailers such as Sears. A brand may be available nationally (**national brand**) or only marketed in certain geographic areas (**regional brand**).

A firm can follow one of several approaches to branding its products. Let us look at the alternative ways of branding a product or service.

Individual brand. **Individual branding** is using a brand name for a single product item such as toothpaste (Crest), beer (Miller), or spaghetti sauce (Ragu). Note that there may be different sizes of a single brand. Individual brands are quite popular with many consumer-products firms that produce and market frequently purchased nondurable products. Individual brands normally are used by manufacturers rather than retailers because the promotional support of individual brands usually is too costly.

Although marketing an individual brand is costly, this branding approach is well suited to product categories in which sales opportunities are large enough to justify the advertising, sales promotion, and other marketing activities needed to gain sufficient market share to make the brand profitable. The management of single brands by producers is so demanding that firms such as Procter & Gamble may assign a brand manager to each of their brands. One characteristic of the individual brand is that if it encounters problems such as contamination or poor performance, the problems normally will not adversely affect the firm's other brands. An individual brand may also be at a disadvantage because it cannot benefit from the franchise that has been established by other products.

A firm offers only one brand if it is a single brand company; alternatively, it may offer multiple brands. **Multiple branding** is used by large manufacturers of soap, toothpaste, cereal, and clothing. The objective may be to target various market segments by marketing brands with a variety of features and prices. Multiple branding is also a way of getting more extensive distribution through different types of middlemen while restricting certain brands to particular retailers.

Family brand. When management places one or more entire lines of products under one brand name, the practice is called **family branding.** Examples include Sears Craftsman tools and Kenmore appliances. By placing several products under one brand name, marketing costs can be shared and introducing (or deleting) product items is facilitated. Family branding is particularly appropriate when one or more lines of products are interrelated on the basis of function, use, or other characteristics (e.g., tools). There are two major disadvantages of family branding. First, any problems that are encountered by any of the items in the family may affect all the other items. Second, specific product items may not receive enough marketing effort (e.g., attention by salespeople) to enable the products to become successful.

Corporate brand. **Corporate branding** establishes product identity with the corporate name. It is similar to family branding except the brand name applies to all products offered by a company or division of a company. Smuckers has been extremely successful in using the company name to brand its line of jams and jellies. Corporate branding is popular with retailers and producers of various consumer and industrial products. Examples include Stanley Works (tools), Exxon, U.S. Steel, The Limited (women's apparel), and J. C. Penney. Corporate branding also is appropriate for services such as airlines, hotels, and restaurants. (See Marketalk for a detailed look at corporate branding.)

Combination branding. **Combination branding** is stressing both the company name and the individual or family brand name in product marketing efforts. For example, a new cereal brand produced by Kellogg's, the established industry leader, certainly benefits from the company's image in the marketplace. Interestingly, some firms do not seem to care whether the buyer knows who is the manufacturer, and instead, they concentrate on building the position of individual or family brands. This is probably because the corporate name has no particular identity with buyers. Alternatively, Eastman Kodak stresses both the corporate name and family brands (e.g., instantmatic cameras) in its marketing efforts.

Franchise extension

Another branding practice that has become popular in recent years consists of using proven brand names to identify new products, often not closely related in function or use to the original brand. **Franchise extension** enables a company to enter a new business through the leverage of its most valuable asset—the consumer awareness, goodwill, and impressions conveyed by its brand name.[6] Examples of capitalizing on proven brand names include Sunkist orange soda, Minolta copiers, and Bic shavers. ChemLawn is using a franchise extension strategy for its pest-free, tree and shrub, and carpet cleaning services. Some experts argue that the use of franchise extension often does not work, citing several examples of failures including Certs gum, Eveready alkaline batteries, Pall Mall menthol cigarettes, and Diet Pepsi. Nevertheless, franchise extension continues to be used in new product development.

> Black & Decker Mfg. Co., a big brand in power tools, will soon be out with a line of men's grooming aids, specifically hair dryers. . . . The line will be called Black Tie Grooming Tools for Men.
> In another move, the Coca-Cola Co. brand name will begin appearing on men's and women's activewear.[7]

The advantages of franchise extension are that it capitalizes on an existing customer base and reduces promotion costs because of the new product's association with an established brand name. The lack of specific identity of the new product may lead to weak performance. Many considerations may lead to success or failure of franchise extension. Ries and Trout

*Marke*TALK //

Controversy over corporate brands

IF THEY DIDN'T KNOW it a year ago, chances are many TV viewers are well aware by now that Nabisco Brands Inc. is the company behind the brand name on Oreo cookies, Planters nuts, Life Savers candy and Fleischmann's margarine. Nabisco has tried hard to forge the link, tacking a three-note corporate jingle onto the end of all its commercials.

The reasoning: If you like Oreos, you will also feel warmly about Planters once you learn they're both part of the same corporate family. "We believe the rub-off effect will be especially beneficial in getting people to try new Nabisco products," says W. Lee Abbott, vice president, marketing services.

Although some marketing consultants dispute that logic, more companies are

attempting to connect their corporate names with well-known consumer-product brands. ITT Corp., for example, is running print ads with the tag line, "All in the family," to tell investors and consumers it owns such businesses as Sheraton hotels, Burpee seeds, and Scotts lawncare products.

Beatrice Cos., meantime, is spending $23 million to spread the word that it sells everything from Stiffel lamps to Martha White grits. Using the slogan, "You've known us all along," a typical commercial breezes through a litany of 14 products and drops the Beatrice name 18 times. The rationale is similar to Nabisco's, but Beatrice started cold with virtually no name recognition and a much greater hodgepodge of products than Nabisco. Says Nabsico's Mr. Abbott: "There's a significant question as to whether consumers who like Samsonite luggage will find that reason enough to also buy Beatrice Food products."

Big industrial companies, brokerage

houses, and conglomerates have long used corporate advertising to make a flattering impression with customers and investors. But corporate advertising by packaged-goods companies raises a basic question: Do consumers really care to know who makes the multitude of mouthwashes, detergents, and snack foods they buy?

Some advertisers say "yes," claiming that people nowadays are more quality conscious than ever, even when buying food and toiletries. "Corporate advertising gives a product an edge," says Keith Reinhard, chairman of the ad agency Needham Harper & Steers USA. "Consumers often can't see much difference between products when confronted by a lot of labels at the grocery store. Knowing something about a company's philosophy and reputation can help to decide the brand they choose."

Many marketers, however, still believe it's more sensible to put all their money into brand advertising. Procter & Gamble Co. takes the view that its brands must

///

cite Bayer's non-aspirin franchise extension as essentially unsuccessful. Yet the failure may not be due to franchise extension.[8] Other firms with new brand names such as Datril have not been able to gain much market share either against Tylenol, the dominant firm in the market.

Brand name selection

Up to this point little has been said about how the names of brands are selected. This is an important decision. Although some names are chosen with little or no deliberation, most firms devote considerable effort to the task.

Pansy Ellen Essman identified a need that was not being met.[9] She designed a sponge product to cradle a child in the bath, freeing the parent's hands to clean the baby easily. She selected the brand name, Pamperette, which had many of the important characteristics of a good brand name: (1) It provided a clear product *identity,* (2) it suggested both *function* and *benefits*—pampering while bathing, (3) it implied *quality,* and (4) it was *easy to remember* and *simple to pronounce.*[10] The major problem was that it was not different enough from names of other baby care products. Procter & Gamble objected to the name because it was similar to the name of its brand of disposable diapers, Pampers, so Essman experienced a $2000 packaging loss and changed the name to Pansy-ette.

Selecting a good brand name normally is much more involved than was Essman's choosing a name for her line of infant care products. How should a firm go about choosing a brand name? A study of 200 consumer-

///

make it on their own without corporate advertising support. Chesebrough-Pond's Inc. experimented a few years ago with corporate ads but has stopped running laundry lists of such brands as Vaseline, Q-Tips, and Health-Tex. Says Ron Ziemba, corporate communication director, "Corporate advertising could be a negative if one product gets a shaky reputation and has a harmful rub-off effect on the others."

Corporate promotions can be important in building consumer confidence for marketing big ticket items like cars and appliances. But Thomas Garbett, a Waterford, Conn., corporate advertising consultant, contends that the parent company's image is usually inconsequential for low-cost impulse items. "If you invest in a pack of chewing gum and don't like it," he says, "it's no great loss."

Mona Doyle, a market researcher in Philadelphia, agrees, noting that consumers have made it clear "they don't care who owns what." She criticizes the Bea-trice ads as being irrelevant to most people, but says corporate advertising can succeed if there is a specific message that people will find useful or interesting.

Richardson-Vicks Inc., for example, found it helpful to catalog such brands as Oil of Olay and Clearasil when introducing itself as a new company in 1981. The ads followed the spinoff of the consumer businesses from Richardson's prescription drug operations. To rebut its junk-food image, Frito-Lay, a subsidiary of PepsiCo Inc., has placed corporate ads in women's magazines, showing all its snack foods and arguing that potato chips are a good source of vitamins. And currently, Campbell Soup Co. is trying to create an aura of a company concerned about people's physical well being by running eight-page booklets on stress and fitness in *Reader's Digest*.

Tony Adams, research director for marketing at Campbell, maintains that corporate advertising by packaged-goods companies can be merely an ego trip. "Some of our friends in the food business are doing ads that look like a patchwork quilt," he says. "They're talking to themselves."

But Nabisco and Beatrice say they are pleased with results so far from their promotions. Nabisco's consumer research found 85% recall of the three-note melody.

Beatrice is still assessing the effects of its commercials, which appeared frequently during the summer Olympics. It believes the ads "quite satisfactorily" increased awareness of the company name. Whether that translates into increased sales remains an open question. "This year, we're positioning Beatrice as warm and caring because that's what consumers say they are looking for and not getting from companies," says Greg Carrott, a management supervisor at Marsteller Inc., Beatrice's ad agency. "Next year, when a new Beatrice logo is plastered all over packages in the supermarket, it will mean something special to shoppers."

///

product manufacturers' brand name selection procedures identified the following commonly used steps:

1. Decide what role the name is to play in marketing the product, and indicate what criteria should be satisfied by the name (such as describing product benefits).
2. Identify possible names and screen them against the criteria to pinpoint the most promising candidates.
3. Use marketing research to test customer reaction to the names.
4. Determine if another firm already has staked a claim to the name (trademark search).
5. Select the brand name that best satisfies management's objectives and fares best in customer tests.[11]

A name may be chosen by a marketing research firm such as NameLab that specializes in name research (see Marketech) or a marketing executive who has experience in name determination. Name selection also is important for industrial products. Recall, for example, the adhesive illustration discussed in Chapter 1. The name Quick Metal clearly possesses many advantages over RC-601, the brand name it replaced.

It is also important to evaluate the meanings in different languages of the words used in brand names. During test marketing in Brazil, it was discovered that the word Fudgies, the brand name Kraft had chosen for one of its candies, sounded like an obscenity. The name was changed to "Fadgies."[12] General Motors' trademark of a few years ago, "Body by Fisher," translates into "corpse by Fisher" in Flemish. Pepsi's advertisement, "Come

Marke**TECH** □ □ □ □ □ □ □ □ □ □ □ □ □ □ □ □

How NameLab works

NAMELAB IS A PROMINENT commercial-names factory. That is, NameLab is in the business of naming things, usually products or companies. Two of NameLab's more famous creations are Sentra (the car) and Compaq (the company).

Names such as Sentra and Compaq, says founder Ira Bachrach, are "attributive nouns"—symbolically appropriate images or evocative sounds that are NameLab's stock in trade. Consumers accept them as a quality of the product such as its size or color, Bachrach explains, but understand that the name also expresses the product's characteristics. For instance, in Sentra's case, the idea was to denote safety and security.

SOURCE: Robert A. Mamis, "Name-calling," *Inc.*, July 1984, pp. 67–69. Reprinted with permission, *Inc.* magazine, July 1984. Copyright © 1984 by Inc. Publishing Company, Boston, Mass.

To get an angle on the product or corporate attributes that NameLab needs to work with, Bachrach insists that each client take part in a three-hour meeting to agree on a ranked list of messages to be expressed in the name. NameLab then relies on its computer for an appropriate combination of semantic and symbolic fragments that Bachrach has arranged by the thousands. (Symbolic fragments are meaningful roots from dozens of languages including Greek, Latin, Saxon, and Breton that contribute to American English. Semantic fragments are visible and meaningful elements of existing names in the category.)

Because a name can be made up of two or three fragments, mathematically there are millions of possibilities. Most, however, are nonsensical and so are dismissed from consideration. Eventually, Bachrach ends up with 300 or more sensible, or

somewhat sensible, combinations. From these, about twenty of the strongest are selected for detailed analysis.

Each promising name is then reshaped according to NameLab's rules of name function to enhance performance in areas such as impact, aesthetics, memorability, uniqueness, vocabulary fit, internal or external reference, shelf selling, and flicker perception. Then a short list of major candidates is searched for trademark potential.

Later, there is a second meeting at which the client is presented with the recommendations, each of which is analyzed symbolically—from where it was derived, how it positions itself among similar items, and what it is apt to mean to the public. Finally, the client picks one and uses it.

□ □

Alive with Pepsi," created consternation in Germany where the literal translation was "to come alive out of the grave." A detergent company advertises that its product is particularly suited for cleaning the really dirty parts of the wash. The company blushingly withdrew its boasts under fire of plummeting sales in Quebec, where words in its advertisements corresponded to the American idiom "private parts."

Generic products

A **generic product** is a specific product item such as paper towels, canned green beans, or a drug that has no brand name. The key advantage of a generic product, as highlighted in the following example, is low price:

> CHLORDIAZEPOXIDE hydrochloride is scarcely a household name. But it's no stranger to many households under its trade name: Librium, the anti-anxiety prescription drug.
>
> What's the difference between the two? Essentially this: the Librium produced by Hoffmann-La Roche costs $43.65 per 500 10-mg. tablets; the same quantity of chlordiazepoxide hydrochloride turned out by a handful of other drug companies costs $5.20.[13]

The comparison is perhaps unfair because Hoffmann-La Roche spent many millions of dollars developing the drug, obtaining approval for its use from the Food and Drug Administration, and gaining market acceptance for the product. For many generic products the price gap between them and branded products is not as large as it is for Librium. There also may be differences in quality. Nevertheless, generic products in many categories have gained substantial market share during the last several years. Consider, for example, the profit potential for the generic drugs when the patents expire on the drugs shown in Exhibit 11.3.

A major opportunity for generic versions of products exists when the buyer is assured of comparable or at least acceptable quality to branded items plus lower prices. Generic products are essentially commodities, such as wheat, cattle, and coffee beans, so the basis of competition is essentially price. Some generic products benefit from consumers' image of the retail outlet that sells them. If the buyer has a favorable perception of the retailer, then this perception may be carried over to the generic products carried by the retailer. Generics pose major threats to brands with weak market positions.

PROTECTING BRANDS

How do firms protect their proprietary positions with products? Protection is achieved through two main avenues: through legal means and by secrecy. Legal protection can be obtained by registering trademarks and obtaining patents. Additionally, firms attempt to keep secret the design or ingredients of their products. Apparently, only a handful of people know the exact formula for Coca-Cola. First we discuss what is involved in gaining legal protection for brands and then shown how some firms find it profitable to license brand names.

Patents and trademarks

In the United States the Patent and Trademark Office in the Department of Commerce processes applications of companies and persons who want to register names (trademarks) or designs of products and processes (patents). Because the patenting practices of countries throughout the world vary, we concentrate our discussion on the U.S. patent system.

Obtaining a patent. A **patent** is an exclusive property right to an invention and is issued by the Commissioner of Patents and Trademarks, U.S. Department of Commerce. The inventor has the right to exclude others from making, using, or selling an invention for a period of seventeen years in the United States, its territories, and possessions. A patent cannot be renewed except by act of Congress. The patent may apply to the design or composition of a product or to the process used to produce the product. By offering legal protection to innovators, there is a substantial incentive for investing

Exhibit 11.3 Major drugs coming off patent, 1982–1985

Generic name	Brand name	Maker	1981 Sales* (millions of dollars)	Category	Expiring
Norgestrel	Ovral	Wyeth	$ 80	Oral contraceptive	1982
Cephalothin	Keflin	Lilly	48	Antibiotic	1982
Methyldopa	Aldomet	Merck	220	Antihypertensive	1984
Ibuprofen	Motrin	Upjohn	200	Antiarthritic	1984
Propranolol	Inderal	American Home	50	Cardiovascular	1984
Chlorpropamide	Diabenese	Pfizer	75	Antidiabetic	1984
Diazepam	Valium	Hoffmann-La Roche	200	Tranquilizer	1985

* Estimated
SOURCE: Stan Kulp, "No pale imitations: Generic drugs enjoy vigorous growth," *Barron's,* May 10, 1982, p. 18.

time and effort on potentially patentable ideas. Obtaining a final patent often requires a few years. Because of the legal process involved, attorneys who specialize in patent law usually handle the filing with the Patent and Trademark office.

Determining whether an application duplicates an existing patent is quite involved, considering that classified patent search files of the Patent and Trademark office contain more than 22 million documents distributed among 100,000 subdivisions of technology.[14] Each year some 250,000 new U.S. patent documents and 280,000 new foreign patents are added to the files. One criticism of the U.S. patent system is that the risks of revealing new product information to competition are greater than the rewards of protection. By knowing the details of a design as revealed in the patent application, a competitor may be able to develop a design similar in function that is sufficiently different from the original that it does not represent a patent infringement.

Protecting a trademark. Trademarks are registered by the Commissioner of Patents and Trademarks on application by persons or companies who distinguish, by name or symbol, a product used in commerce subject to regulation by Congress. Gaining protection of names and logos is not as complicated as is the patenting of designs. Whereas registration is initially for a period of twenty years, there is no time limit for trademark protection providing the brand is marketed actively. Other guidelines for trademarks are that the protection applies to a name or a mark rather than a function that would be patentable. You should not register your family name because anyone else with the same name is entitled to use it for commercial purposes. Of course, the name or logo that is registered must not be similar to any existing name.

> Goldhirsh Group is *Inc.*-ing up the works for Metro Magazines' *Manhattan, inc.,* a glossy monthly book focusing on business in Manhattan.
>
> Goldhirsh, publisher of *Inc.,* . . . filed suit in federal court against Metro, charging it with trademark infringement. The suit seeks an injunction prohibiting Metro from using the abbreviation *inc.* in its logotype.
>
> Even though *Manhattan, inc.* uses a lower case ''i'' in its logotype, Bernard Goldhirsh . . . said, ''We feel it's an infringement on our mark.''[15]

Some guidelines for maintaining exclusive rights to a trademark are shown in Exhibit 11.4.

One possible consequence of a successful trademark is that people will treat the trademark as the name for a type of product instead of as a designation for one particular brand of the product.[16] When this happens the trademark no longer identifies and distinguishes the goods of the manufacturer, and thus becomes generic. Brand names that have become generic are aspirin, cellophane, celluloid, escalator, kerosene, lanolin, linoleum, milk of magnesia, shredded wheat, and thermos (see Exhibit 11.5). In early 1983, Parker Brothers Monopoly game joined the ranks of trademarks ruled generic by the courts.[17] The more specific the name applies to the product rather than its function, the stronger is the brand protection.

Licensing trademarks and patents

Brand names sometimes become valuable assets for their owners, over and above the use for which the names were originally intended. **Licensing** a trademark is selling to another party the right to use a brand name

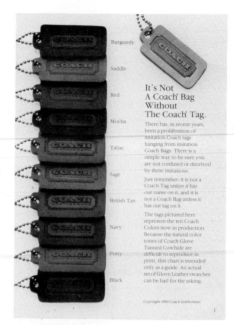

As is true of many other prestigious products, there has been in recent years a proliferation of imitation Coach Bags. In this advertisement, Coach Leatherware reminds readers that ''it is not a Coach Tag unless it has our name on it, and it is not a Coach Bag unless it has our tag on it.''

Exhibit 11.4 Maintaining exclusive rights to a trademark

Vigilance is the key to maintaining exclusive rights to a trademark. Companies must not only educate the public and the media on proper use of their trademarks, employees and advertising agencies must also be taught a few simple rules. Basically, the rules are these:

1. **A trademark must be distinguished from other words in print, even if only by capitalizing it**
   For example, Herculon olefin fiber or HERCULON olefin fiber is correct. But herculon olefin fiber or Herculon Olefin Fiber are incorrect uses of a trademark.

2. **Whenever possible, a trademark notice should follow the mark**
   If that is impossible, it should be used at least once in copy and preferably, the first time the mark appears. If the trademark is registered in the U.S. Patent and Trademark office, the registration notice ® or "*Reg. U.S. Pat. & Tm. Off." should be used. If the trademark isn't registered, TM or Trademark of Widget International can be used.

3. **The trademark should always be used with the generic name**
   Therefore "Vaseline petroleum jelly is good for burns," would be correct but "Vaseline is good for burns" would be wrong. The simple way to remember this is to think of the trademark as a proper adjective.

4. **Trademarks should never be used in the possessive form**
   "Karastan's fine quality" is wrong but "Karastan carpets' fine quality" is correct.

5. **Trademarks should always be used in the singular**
   They aren't nouns so they can't be made plural. So "Band-Aid brand adhesive bandages are good for cuts," is correct but "Band-Aids are good for cuts" would be wrong.

6. **Thinking of the trademark as a proper adjective is perhaps the best way to avoid two common pitfalls**
   Never use a trademark as a verb or common adjective. "Simoniz your car" is wrong but "Polish your car with Simoniz paste wax" is correct. "Buy a Dacron shirt" is an example of using a mark as a common adjective but "Buy a shirt made of Dacron polyester fibers" is correct.

7. **Companies should identify their ownership of a trademark**
   For instance, "Plexiglas is a registered trademark of Rohm & Haas."

SOURCE: Ellen M. Kleinberg, "Trademarks: The care and feeding of brand name identities," *Industrial Marketing*, Oct. 1980, p. 62. Reprinted with permission from *Industrial Marketing*, now known as *Business Marketing*, October 1980. Copyright 1980 by Crain Communications, Inc.

Exhibit 11.5 Brand names—preserved and lost

Many companies have successfully preserved their trademarks, despite the fact that their brand names have become virtually synonymous with an entire product category and are often incorrectly applied to products made by other manufacturers.

Band-Aid (Johnson & Johnson)	Q-tips, Vaseline (Chesebrough-Pond's Inc.)
Coke (The Coca-Cola Co.)	Ritz crackers (Nabisco Brands Inc.)
Formica (American Cyanamid Co.)	Scotch tape (3M)
Jeep (Jeep Corp.)	Styrofoam (Dow Chemical Co.)
Jell-O (General Foods Corp.)	Technicolor (Technicolor Inc.)
Kleenex (Kimberly-Clark Corp.)	Teflon, Orlon (E. DuPont de Nemours & Co.)
Magic Marker (Berol Corp)	Windbreaker (Men's Wear International Inc.)
Ping-Pong (Parker Bros.)	Xerox (Xerox Corp.)

Some of the most common nouns in the English language started out as brand names before going generic.

aspirin	escalator	shredded wheat
cellophane	kerosene	thermos
celluloid	lanolin	yo-yo
cola	milk of magnesia	zipper

SOURCE: Dsana Sammons, "The name of the game," *INC.*, Sept. 1983, p. 89. Reprinted with permission, *Inc.* magazine, Sept. 1983. Copyright © 1983 by INC. Publishing Company, Boston, Mass.

normally for purposes not in competition with the original brand use. In some instances licensing may allow similar use of the brand name in noncompeting geographic areas. In 1983 the licensing of names and characters was estimated to be a $21 billion industry, growing from approximately $7 billion in 1978.[18] (The $21 billion represents retail sales of licensed products.) In 1983 the E.T. name alone was carried on more than 200 items! The very popular 1985 Rambo movie about Vietnam was the basis for launching a variety of licensed products.

Both parties in a licensing agreement can benefit from the arrangement. The originator can increase profits at little additional cost. The firm that obtains the license creates instant identity for its products. Consider the following account of the Smurf, the blue gnome with the white stocking cap:

> The Smurfs have brought . . . financial rewards to Wallace Berrie Co., a toy manufacturer in Van Nuys, Calif., and the exclusive North American licensee for Smurfs. The brainstorm of Belgian artist Pierre Culliford, Smurf-like items will account for at least $650 million in retail sales in 1982. Culliford gets 5% of the wholesale price of Berrie-manufactured items, plus a portion of the estimated 7% royalty other companies pay Berrie to use the Smurf trademark.[19]

Licensing is not restricted to brand names. Licensing of patented products and processes also occurs. The practice particularly is popular between companies in different parts of the world. In these instances the intended use or application is similar to the original so the firm holding the patent must first decide if it wants to offer the product in the market or markets of interest to the firm seeking a license.

By placing reminder ads like this one, Xerox Corporation has so far been able to preserve its well-known and much abused Xerox trademark. Xerox Corporation rightly fears that people who refer to a ''xerox'' instead of a ''photocopy'' will dilute their products', indeed their corporate, identity.

PACKAGING

An estimated 90 million tons of packaging is used in the United States alone, not to mention the rest of the world.[20] The industry that provides this huge quantity of packaging has more than $50 billion in sales, which is more than either steel mill or textile industry sales. Most of us consider a package as something that contains and protects the product. For many products the package performs several other important functions in marketing and distributing the product. Let us take a closer look at the marketing functions performed by the package and some issues associated with packaging.

What does the package do?

Exhibit 11.6 highlights the functions of the package. Although a package may not always perform all the functions, several may be present in a particular package application. A close look at each packaging function provides insight into the various ways the package may contribute to the marketing efforts for a product.

Protection. The Tylenol package tampering incidents resulting in the deaths from poisoning that occurred in 1982 offer sobering evidence of the critical importance of packaging. McNeil Consumer Products Company, the producer of Tylenol, withdrew all Extra-Strength Capsules from the market until the package could be redesigned to reduce the threat of tampering. Protection, of course, involves more than protecting the product from tampering. Foods, drugs, and other perishables must be protected from deterioration and damage during shipment and handling when stored and displayed. Exposure to light and air causes some products to deteriorate.

Containment. Packaging may also be essential to contain. Items such as paints and other liquids require a container. Lawn fertilizer and other materials must be held together while they are transported and stored.

Promotional labeling. The package can be used to promote a brand. The color of the package may be used to attract the buyer and create a favorable impression. Philip Morris, the nation's biggest tobacco company, has launched a new brand of cigarettes called Players, and it has decided to package the product in an elegant black box. By deciding on black, the company is breaking a long-standing taboo against using what, for the tobacco industry especially, is regarded as a morose color. "The American brands are finally waking up to elegance in packaging," says Jerry Nestos of England's Dunhill cigarettes. Or, as one advertising executive remarked, "They're creating extra value through the beautiful black box."

Promotional messages and pictures often are printed on packages. For example, a food package may show an appetizing food item prepared with the product in the package. Sometimes a company's other brands are shown on the package, and coupons for price reductions may be included inside the package or printed on the outside.

Information labeling. In addition to promotional information, labeling information may include composition of the product, warnings about the product, instructions for using the product, and suggestions for product applications. Consider the following labeling information shown on a 6-ounce box of Pepperidge Farm Croutons:

- Serving suggestion: great for soup, salad, and snacks
- A notation that the product contains no artificial preservatives
- Nutrition information per serving and a list of ingredients

Exhibit 11.6 Functions performed by packaging

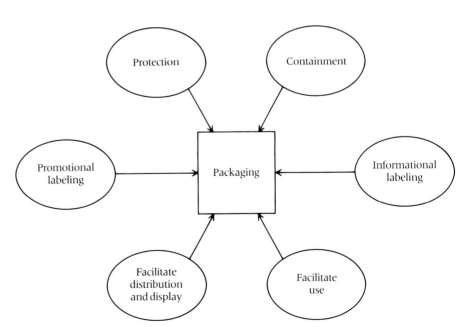

- Brief description of Pepperidge Farm
- Instructions on how to open the package and how to use the croutons in soups and salads
- A recipe for cocktail mix and crouton combinations
- Suggestions to try other listed Pepperidge Farm croutons
- Information on the packaging inside the box
- Universal product code symbol for supermarket optical scanning

Facilitation of distribution and display. For some products the size, shape, and strength of the package are important in assisting in the movement of the product through distribution channels. Package design should include consideration of how the product will be transported and stored as it moves through distribution channels to the consumer. Packaging also can assist retailers in displaying products in stores.

Facilitation of use. The package may provide consumers of the product with useful aids. For example, some beer six-packs are designed so they can be placed in a refrigerator to serve as dispensers. Tape for sealing packages often is attached to easy-to-use dispensers. Powdered soups are packaged in single portions for ease in preparation. Quaker State's new motor oil containers were designed for ease of use (see Marketalk). Some packages are designed for reuse after the product is consumed. For example, instant coffee and tea bags sometimes are packaged in containers that can be used to store other foods.

It wasn't long after Philip Morris began packaging its Players brand of cigarettes in an elegant black box that R. J. Reynolds began to promote Sterling, its own brand of black-box cigarettes. Recognizing that there is a market for a prestige-image product, R. J. Reynolds has gone a step further by using such slogans as "It's only a cigarette like Porsche is only a car." (Advertisement courtesy of Philip Morris Incorporated)

*Marke*TALK ///

Quaker State introduces a new motor oil container, but so does Pennzoil

PHASED INTRODUCTION is under way for a new type of motor oil container which Quaker State Oil Refining Corp., Oil City, Pa., hopes will boost its share of the do-it-yourself market.

"This will significantly affect the 70% of the driving public who replenish and replace their own motor oil," predicts Walter B. Cook, executive vice president of refining and marketing for Quaker State.

"The new container with a built-in pouring funnel is leakproof and spillproof and eliminates the need for messy spouts required with the composite cans that most oil comes in. Further, it is more durable for trunk storage and can be recapped after part of a quart is used."

Motor oil traditionally has been sold in quart cans with metal tops which must be punctured, much like soft drink cans of the pre-pop top era. A funnel is needed to pour the oil into a car's engine, and even that is no guarantee against some spillage. Moreover, the can cannot be resealed.

Marketing studies confirmed strong consumer preference for the new container—a white plastic bottle with indented sides for grasping and a neck for direct pouring.

"Compared to the composite can, it is modern and attractive," Wood said, "and it can be recapped when partial quarts are used."

Quaker already commands 20% of the $2.5 billion motor oil market, and it is banking on the new packaging giving it

an opportunity to carve out a larger share of the do-it-yourself segment. The firm won't disclose its sales projections for the new bottle, but its research shows "overwhelming consumer preference" for the packaging.

Leaking and collapsed containers, spouts puncturing sides of cans, spillage during the pouring operation or when some oil is left in the can, and dirt getting into open cans have been chronic complaints of the 90 million Americans who change their own oil, and the new packaging addresses all those problems, Cook said.

"To succeed in serving this market, you have to understand mass merchandising techniques, and that includes packaging," he said. "The motor oil quart can is one of the last vestiges of the pre-mass merchandising era.

"Our participation in the packaging revolution is long overdue. What held it back was the tremendous volume involved in motor oil—literally tens of millions of quarts per day in the entire market.

"With that volume, a few cents per container quickly adds to millions of dollars per year. And to move that volume, you have to fill the containers at extremely high speed."

Once technical problems were surmounted and the company confirmed the bottles were an economical alternative to composite containers, research was conducted to assure officials that a market existed for the bottles.

Focus groups and mall intercepts conducted throughout the country demonstrated a significant number of consumers would buy Quaker State after trying it in

the bottle. Those studies formed the basis for the ad campaign, which is themed "Say good-bye to America's favorite can of motor oil."

"These studies also told us what kind of container would be most preferable," Cook said. "Our studies were conducted with a round, green plastic bottle we had been using for limited production. Consumers told us they preferred a white bottle and one that was easier to grasp.

"They also preferred one which was easier to open and yet tamper evident."

He expects other major oil manufacturers to convert to plastic bottles as soon as possible, but a lengthy conversion process is involved, and he says Quaker State "will enjoy a substantial lead time."

Eleven months later, however, in January 1985, Pennzoil Co. introduced a new rectangular plastic container for motor oil.

Consumer research and field tests conducted by Pennzoil revealed a preference for the rectangular-shaped bottle over round plastic containers like the Quaker State bottle.

The Pennzoil containers are leak-proof and tamper resistant, feature resealable lids to assure clean storage, and can save retailers 50% in shelf space compared with round bottles.

"The rectangular container stores more conveniently in auto trunks and is more efficient for adding oil under the hood," says Frank Turner, executive vice president, Automotive Products Division. "This package option—combined with our already strong brand loyalty—will give us a decided advantage in the highly competitive motor oil market," Turner said.

SOURCE: "Quaker State expects sales gains with new packaging system for oil," *Marketing News*, Feb. 3, 1984, pp. 6–7; and "Marketing briefs," *Marketing News*, Jan. 18, 1985, p. 2. Reprinted from Marketing News, published by the American Marketing Association.

///

Some packaging issues

Buyer satisfaction. Consumers do not always like the physical packages that contain the products they purchase. Exhibit 11.7 lists the percentage of 145 respondents who indicated dissatisfaction with the packaging of specific products.

A survey by the Package Designers Council, a trade group, found that consumers ranked these package characteristics as important (the most important is listed first): extends storage life of the unused portion, indicates contents by the package graphics, can be resealed, and can be easily

Exhibit 11.7 Percentage of 145 respondents who indicated dissatisfaction with the packaging of these products

Product	Percent	Product	Percent
Lunch meat	77	Noodles	49
Bacon	76	Lipstick	47
Flour	65	Nail polish	46
Sugar	63	Honey	44
Ice cream	57	Crackers	44
Snack chips	53	Frozen seafood	40
Cookies	51	Nuts	39
Detergents	50	Cooking oil	37
Fresh meat	50	Ketchup	34

SOURCE: Bill Abrams, "Packaging often irks buyers, but firms are slow to change," *Wall Street Journal*, Jan. 28, 1982, p. 23.

stored.[21] Still another survey about household products packaging found that people were most often irked by spray cans that do not spray. Close runners-up included cans with tear-off tabs that cut fingers, transparent food cartons that hide the bad parts of the contents, boxes with crushed cookies, drippy meat packages, and hard-to-unroll toilet tissue.[22]

Because package design involves a number of considerations in addition to the buyer's needs and wants, the final package often represents a compromise between costs and functions. For example, a change to a new material may facilitate resealing the container but increase the cost of the product: Will the buyer be willing to pay the added cost? Consumer research may help answer questions as to what the buyer wants in a package and his willingness to pay for the added features. Packaging designers continually must be concerned with the costs of packages and the benefits provided by them.

Environmental contamination. Packages may become potential environmental contaminants. Metal cans, particularly aluminum, will not decompose. Other packaging materials may offer similar problems in keeping highways and parks free from waste. Packaging materials that emit dangerous chemical smoke when burned must be avoided or carefully labeled to warn people attempting to dispose of the packages. Another area of concern is the packaging of radioactive materials.

Government regulation. Certain aspects of packaging are of concern to federal, state, and local governments. For example, package labels for cigarettes and saccharin must include statements of the potential hazards of using these products. The areas of major concern relative to government regulation of packaging are labeling, safety, and contaminating the environment. Government regulations, which involve both the package and the product, are discussed later in the chapter when safety and liability issues are considered.

Packaging and the marketing program. The package often represents an important part of the marketing program. For example, Pillsbury adopted a green packaging design for its Green Giant frozen vegetable line to create a strong brand identity in the freezer case. The color, shape, function, and information contained on the package all contribute to marketing the product. Because nonmarketing people may be responsible for deciding how to package a product, marketing's needs relative to the package must be incorporated early in the design process. The technical aspects of the packaging should be coordinated closely with the marketing aspects of the package.

SERVICING PRODUCTS

Products whose parts and components wear out or fail to function properly for other reasons must be repaired. Providing product service is essential to maintaining customer satisfaction for many durable consumer and industrial products.

Objectives and responsibility for service

Servicing products can be used as an important advantage over competitors. Consider the following account of the importance of service for Caterpillar Tractor Company's customers described by one of their dealers, John Fabick of Fenton, Missouri:

"When something goes wrong with his equipment, you can't provide service fast enough for him."

Fabick also has an airplane based at a nearby airport to speed deliveries of parts.

In this ad, Weyerhaeuser Company mentions several benefits to using corrugated packaging: its compactness, its cost-effectiveness, its color capability. Also implied here is that corrugated packages are not potential environmental contaminants, as are, for instance, metal cans. (Courtesy of the Weyerhaeuser Company)

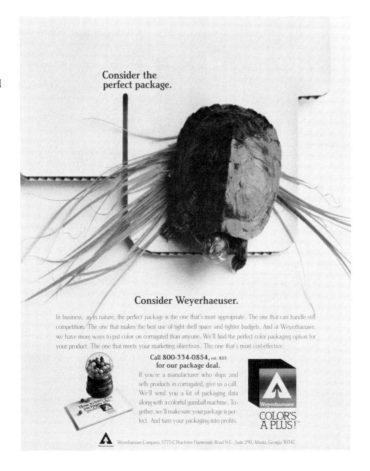

Because most Caterpillar dealers are larger and better capitalized than competitors, they're able to offer customers a better supply of parts and a wider selection of equipment. Caterpillar dealers also are responsible for all equipment operating in their territory whether or not it was purchased from them, an arrangement that few competitors have with their dealers.[23]

Role of product service. Service performs three primary functions:

1. Protecting the customer base by maintaining customer satisfaction during the use of the product
2. Enhancing the product's salability
3. Generating income that may range as high as 15 to 30 percent of a corporation's total revenue.[24]

Of course, the importance of the three functions will vary by firm and by type of product.

Responsibility for service. The servicing of products may be accomplished by authorized distributors or dealers, service organizations operated by the manufacturer, or independent service companies. Service during a warranty period normally is arranged by the manufacturer. After warranty, the need for service often results in the formation of independent service organizations. There are clear indications that many people are not satisfied with available arrangements for servicing the products they own. *"Consumers* are growing unhappier over the products and services they buy. Topping the list of complaints—high prices, high interest, poor quality, inadequate service and repair, and products breaking down too quickly."[25] The service inadequacies are due, in part, to the increasing complexity of products, electronic technology used in a wide variety of new products, and the sheer number of new goods that are produced and sold each year.[26] Obtaining reliable and economical services for products promises to be of increasing concern to both producers and users. Consider, for example, the difficulty today of obtaining proper service at acceptable prices for your automobile. It is common to return two or three times to an automobile repair center to have a problem corrected.

Product warranties

A **product warranty** is a written or oral statement provided by a manufacturer to the buyer that spells out the firm's responsibilities if the product or service proves to be defective.[27] The warranty guarantees the integrity of the product for a specified time period. Thus the warranty or guarantee is an explicit promise that the product is suitable for the use intended and the producer will stand behind the product or service it provides. The Magnuson-Moss Consumer Product Warranty Act of 1975 established provisions regarding statement and enforcement of warranties by manufacturers. In general the legislation improved warranty information available to consumers. According to one source the costs to manufacturers of servicing and repairing products under warranty range from a fraction of 1 percent to more than 10 percent of the firm's net sales.[28]

An example of a product warranty statement for Snap-on Tools is shown in Exhibit 11.8. Snap-on has the reputation for being extremely cooperative on warranty claims. Professional mechanics know that the

Exhibit 11.8 An example of a product warranty statement

LIMITED WARRANTY

Snap-on will replace or service, after inspection, at its cost, all *Snap-on* hand tools or parts thereof which fail to give satisfactory service when returned to a *Snap-on* representative or branch warehouse.

Any *Snap-on* or *Blue Point* equipment item which fails to give satisfactory service or for which parts have become defective within the stated warranty period will be serviced or replaced when returned to a *Snap-on* representative or branch warehouse. The customer is responsible for prepaying any transportation charges connected with service under this Limited Warranty. This Limited Warranty is null and void if the customer or any other person, other than an authorized representative of *Snap-on*, has made any attempt to service or alter the unit prior to its delivery to a *Snap-on* representative or branch warehouse.

Snap-on shall not be liable for loss of product use or other incidental or consequential costs incurred by the purchaser or user of its tools and equipment, and all implied warranties are expressly excluded. Additional warranty language may accompany specific *Snap-on* products.

SOURCE: Snap-on Tools Corporation, Kenosha, Wisconsin.

company and its independent dealers will stand behind the tools they sell. The major reasons for providing warranties are to assure the buyer that the producer will stand behind the product, to define the manufacturer's liabilities and responsibilities, and to be competitive with other firms that offer warranties on similar products.[29] In some instances buyers can purchase extended warranties, for example, for automobiles and appliances. In the 1980s warranties on new homes became quite popular.

Service contracts have become popular for various appliances and equipment used in homes and offices. They are essentially a form of service insurance. The owner can purchase a service contract that provides service for a specified length of time. If service is needed during the period covered by the contract, the owner can obtain the service at no additional charge or lower than would be necessary without the contract. Sears offers service contracts on various appliances and other items. Service contracts are available for office equipment such as copiers, typewriters, and computers.

Offering a warranty requires that many issues be considered. Although specific warranties vary quite a bit, several basic elements normally are present in any warranty statement.

1. The name and address of the firm (or firms) that is the warrantor
2. The specific buyers to whom the warranty is extended
3. The particular elements or parts of the product that may be covered by the warranty
4. The time duration of the warranty

Holiday Inns, Inc. found that offering a money-back guarantee on accommodations not only helped it gain a second chance with unhappy customers but also helped improve its service. Since Holiday Inns began advertising the guarantee program in 1983, the evaluation forms it distributes to its guests have grown increasingly positive. Moreover, the hotel chain has had to pay refunds to only a tiny fraction of its customers. (Reprinted with the permission of Holiday Inns, Inc.).

5. The seller's responsibilities under the forms of the warranty
6. Use and maintenance conditions necessary for the warranty to be applicable
7. How the buyer should obtain service under the warranty
8. The exceptions and exclusions that apply
9. If arbitration is to be used to resolve warranty disputes, what procedures will be followed[30]

SAFETY AND LIABILITY ISSUES

Faulty products may lead to user injury, unhappy customers, and costly legal battles. We consider several issues associated with product safety and discuss responsibility for safety. Finally, we examine the task of recalling unsafe or faulty products.

Safety issues

Safety hazards. Countless people are injured every day because products are faulty or misused. The following statistics were cited in the mid-1970s by the National Commission on Product Safety:

> Accidents outside the workplace involving consumer products produce 20 million injuries each year. An estimated 110,000 of these injuries reportedly result in permanent disability, and 30,000 persons die each year in product-related accidents.[31]

When the consequences of industrial accidents involving products are added to consumer accidents, the problem of safety becomes increasingly critical. Product safety is clearly an important national and international issue.

Soaring costs. While injury and death are in themselves critical concerns of consumers, government, and industry, the costs associated with unsafe products further document the importance of product safety in society today. Johnson & Johnson said that the cost of temporarily withdrawing its prescription drug, Zomax, from the market would reduce the firm's 1983 after-tax earnings by $20 million.[32] Several people died apparently from allergic reactions to the drug, although there was no conclusive evidence that the drug caused the reactions.

The costs of unsafe products go far beyond product recalls. The number of product-liability suits filed increases every year, as does the amount of money paid in settlements. One study conducted in 1975 of the seventy-nine largest incidents of loss indicated that settlements made to injury victims and their survivors were approximately nine times greater than their economic loss sustained up to the time of the settlement.[33] Rising liability insurance premium costs during the 1980s indicate the impact of liability claims on insurance costs. Malpractice suits for medical services illustrate that safety issues also extend into the services areas.

Consumer misuse. There are numerous incidents of the misuse of products. Some may be the responsibility of the user although the incidents are of obvious concern to the producers of the products. For example, Lever Brothers Sunlight brand of dishwashing liquid was introduced in 1982.[34] The product smelled like lemons, contained 10 percent lemon juice, and had pictures of lemons on its front label. Another product, Minute Maid 100% Pure Lemon Juice, had a package with a similar shape and color and pictures of lemons on it. Here is one report of consumer misuse.

> When 33 adults and 45 children recently became ill, reportedly after mistaking five-ounce samples of Sunlight dishwashing liquid for lemon juice, it reopened a debate, which has been going on for at least 10 years, about the use of edibles in non-food products.[35]

The unusual aspect of this incident is that adults were involved. Accidental consumption of such products is more common with consumers less than five years of age. Helping prevent product misuse is one major concern of package designers.

When one considers (1) the hazards of faulty products and the associated injuries and deaths, (2) the costs to both consumers and industry (not to mention the costs of government agencies), and (3) various other problems owing to misuse and accidental consumption, we can well understand that product safety and liability are major concerns in society today.

Who is responsible?

Four groups are involved in product safety: government, business, product users, and consumer groups. Let us look at some of the activities and responsibilities of each group.

Government. Several federal, state, and local government agencies and various safety statutes are concerned with product safety. Beginning in the 1960s, Congress moved aggressively into the regulation of work and product safety. Some of the more well-known statutes are

- National Highway Traffic Safety Act (1966)
- Coal Mine Health and Safety Act (1969)
- Clean Air Amendments (1970)
- Occupational Safety and Health Act (1970)
- Consumer Product Safety Commission Act (1972)[36]

Even with the proliferation of agencies and statutes, consumers seem to want more. A 1983 survey found that nearly three-fourths of respondents said that Congress was not watching out for their interests and two-thirds contended that the president is not doing enough to protect the public.[37]

Business. What functions and activities related to product safety are the responsibility of business? A study of approximately 300 manufacturing firms conducted by The Conference Board, a nonprofit business research group, identified the following product safety functions performed by many of the firms:

Evaluating and testing the safety of new and existing products
Studying product-safety failures
Maintaining liaison with regulatory agencies
Preparing product-use instructions

Educating employees in product safety matters
Setting quality control standards for products
Reporting safety defects to regulatory agencies
Offering safety education programs to users[38]

In the past, manufacturers were liable only if they were proved negligent or careless in what they made or how they made it. Today, however, the sterner concept of **strict liability** states that if a defect in a product legally is established, the manufacturer is liable, regardless of the precautions taken. Business firms therefore must not only assume a major responsibility for product safety, they must anticipate the injuries that may result when consumers use their products inappropriately. Although users must share the responsibility because many safety problems are caused by consumers, they are less liable than product manufacturers.

Product users. Each of us as consumers should assume some responsibility for learning how to use products that may be unsafe when used improperly. Reading and following the instructions provided by the manufacturer will eliminate many misuse problems. We can benefit from proper product use by reducing injuries and preventing product price increases caused by liability claims against manufacturers.

Consumer groups. Several consumer special interest groups are actively involved in various aspects of product safety. For example, Consumers Union (CU), the research organization that tests products and publishes the results in the magazine *Consumer Reports*, typically evaluates safety features of products. In some instances, products are rated as unsafe or as potential hazards. Some industry critics have argued that CU is overconservative and sometimes unreasonable. In 1983 one of the debates between industry and CU centered on the potential hazards of kerosene heaters. Kero-Sun, the largest U.S. marketer of the heaters, sued CU for $82 million because of CU's October 1982 report stating that the heaters create pollution levels indoors that may pose a health hazard.[39]

Product recalls

If the potential safety consequences of a faulty product are serious and widespread, a recall may be necessary. A recall by a manufacturer may involve buyers' returning the product to a dealer for repair, replacement, or refund of the purchase price. The impact on both company reputation and operating costs is often substantial. A look at General Motors Corporation's experience with the Chevrolet Citation and other X-cars, which were supposed to be one of the automotive breakthroughs of the 1980s, highlights the scope of product recall. Exhibit 11.9 provides a summary of X-car recalls since its introduction. Consider the costs associated with repairing the cars, not to mention the adverse publicity associated with the recalls.

Product recalls are perhaps an inevitable consequence of increasingly complex products, aggressive consumers, and cost cutting by manufacturers. The product recall involves four important communications considerations that should be planned carefully.

1. Effective initial announcement
2. Easy product-model identification by the consumer

Exhibit 11.9 A summary of X-car recalls

	Problem	Number of Cars
September 1979	Deficiency in material of automatic transmission cooler hose—possible leak and fire hazard (1980 models)	225,000
	Fatigue cracks in steering gear mounting plate (1980)	160,000
October 1979	Improper installation of turn flasher unit (1980)	236
October 1980	Incorrect routing of power-steering hoses—possible fire hazard (1981)	25,400
March 1981	Possible flaw in electrical ground cable (1981)	105,000
August 1981	Possible rear-wheel lockup and loss of control (1981)	47,000
March 1982	Faulty clamps on fuel-filler and vent-pipe hoses (1982)	150,000
	Possible scraping of clutch cable against left front brake line (1982)	5,000
January 1983	Possible failure of brake hoses to meet standards (1982)	8,500
February 1983	Possible rear-wheel lockup (1980)	240,000

SOURCE: Douglas R. Sease, "X-Cars, once GM's pride, getting a shoddy reputation with owners," *Wall Street Journal*, Mar. 3, 1983, p. 23. Reprinted by permission of the *Wall Street Journal*, © Dow Jones & Company, Inc., 1983. All rights reserved.

3. Adjustment offer to the consumer
4. Adjustment fulfillment by the manufacturer or authorized representative[40]

Some firms establish task forces to handle a recall. Most important, basic guidelines for recall should be established in advance of the need to recall products by firms whose products might be subject to recall.

SUMMARY

In this chapter we considered several of the issues and tasks associated with branding decisions, protecting brands, packaging, servicing, and safety and liability. An incredible amount of money is spent each year branding, packaging, and servicing products. Product accidents and liability claims further increase the costs of product-related activities.

A brand is a name, term, symbol, design, or combination of these. The brand usually is communicated to the buyer through a brand name, brand mark, or both. A trademark is a legally protected name or symbol that may be the entire brand name or some part of it. Branding serves two purposes: First, it is the means by which consumers identify the product, and second, it is a way in which a company can obtain brand loyalty from buyers. Firms have several branding options. A manufacturer must decide whether to market its own brand (manufacturer's brand), to produce private brands for middlemen (middleman's brand), or to do both. Likewise, middlemen must elect to market manufacturer's brands or to contract for the production of products to be marketed under their own label. Some firms assign a brand name to a single product (individual branding) and others use the brand name to identify one or more lines of products such as Sears Craftsman tool line (family branding). Product identity also can be achieved using the company name such as Stanley Tools. Combinations of these options also are used. Another branding practice, franchise extension, consists of using existing brand names for new products not closely related in function or use to the original brand. The selection of a brand name is an important decision. A brand name may be chosen by an executive in the firm or a marketing research firm. Generic products—which have no brand name—are growing in importance. The major advantage to the consumer is low cost.

Brand protection is accomplished through legal means and by secrecy. Legal protection is obtained by registering trademarks and obtaining patents. Secrecy is maintained by internal procedures and practices designed to protect confidential information about products and manufacturing processes. The licensing of trademarks and patents has become a booming industry.

One normally thinks of a package as something to contain and protect the product inside. For many products the package is important as a means of promoting the product and informing the buyer. The package may play an important role in facilitating distribution, display, and use of the product. Important packaging issues include responding to the buyer's needs and wants, balancing costs against packaging benefits, preventing environmental contamination from packages, responding to the concerns of government, and using the package in marketing products.

Providing after-the-sale product service is essential to obtain and keep customers for many firms. A good service program can be used as an important advantage over competition. It also can be a means of generating sales and profits. Service functions are performed by manufacturers, middlemen, and independent service organizations. Complex products, inadequate service facilities, and unhappy customers have established the service function as a high priority area in many firms. Product warranties provide a way for manufacturers to spell out the firm's responsibilities if the product or service is defective during the specified warranty period. The warranty can be an effective marketing tool by assuring the buyer of satisfactory performance of the product for the duration of the warranty.

Manufacturers must be aware of product safety and liability issues. Both faulty products and misuse of products can lead to user injury, unhappy customers, and costly legal battles. The soaring costs of product liability compound the safety problem. Those responsible for product safety include government, business, product users, and special consumer groups such as Consumers Union. Product recall is the means by which an unsafe product is taken off the market. Johnson & Johnson's removal of Tylenol capsules from the market in late 1982 owing to their contamination is an example of the huge efforts and costs associated with product recalls.

KEY TERMS

brand	banked trademark	national brand
brand name	brand loyalty	regional brand
brand mark	manufacturer's brand	individual branding
trademark	middleman's brand	multiple branding
service mark	private brand	family branding

corporate branding   generic product   product warranty
combination branding   patent   service contracts
franchise extension   licensing   strict liability

QUESTIONS FOR REVIEW AND DISCUSSION

1. Explain the term *banked trademark.* What is required to obtain this trademark?

2. One advantage the marketer gains from branding is that it establishes a unique identity and brand position for a firm. List other advantages branding has for the marketer.

3. How do consumers of goods and services benefit from branding?

4. Private branding refers to those brands owned by retailers and other distributors of products. What determines the feasibility for a distributor to establish a brand?

5. The objective of using multiple brands of the same product type is to try to appeal to different customer needs by marketing brands with different features and prices. Give examples of companies that use multiple branding.

6. When entire lines of products are placed under one brand name it is known as family branding. What are the advantage and disadvantages of this branding approach?

7. What are the important characteristics of a good brand name and what steps are used by many firms for brand name selection?

8. How do generic products benefit consumers? What threat do they pose to brand name products?

9. One way firms protect their proprietary positions with products is through the legal protection of obtaining a patent. How does obtaining a patent protect a company?

10. Trademarks are registered by the Commissioner of Patents and Trademarks on application by individuals or companies who distinguish, by name or symbol, a product used in commerce subject to regulation by Congress. How difficult is it to register a trademark and what benefits are gained by a firm that goes through this process?

11. Licensing is the sale of the right to use brands or patented products and processes. What benefits are derived from a licensing agreement? What is involved in licensing patented products and processes?

12. Packaging performs several important functions in marketing and distributing products. Enumerate some of these functions.

13. Package design involves compromises between considerations such as buyers' needs and wants, environmental problems, and governmental regulation. What factors within these areas have an effect on packaging?

14. Product service performs three primary functions for a company. Discuss these functions.

15. Many people are not satisfied with the available arrangements for servicing products. Who services products and what contributes to the service inadequacies?

16. What is a product warranty; what do warranties guarantee consumers?

17. What are the major reasons manufacturers provide warranties to consumers? How much do warranties cost manufacturers?

18. Four groups are involved in product safety. Who are they and what are their responsibilities regarding product safety?

19. What does a product recall entail and what are the costs to the manufacturer?

20. What can the marketing manager do to prepare for potential recalls? Develop an outline of a product recall procedure.

Building Your Portfolio

■ Select a product category and identify several brands of the product within that category. Prepare a description of the quality and features of each brand including price, availability in various types of retail outlets, and advertising. Because all brands do not compete directly, identify which brands appear to be competing with each other and in what types of outlets. Possible product categories are 35mm single lens reflex cameras, 19-inch color television sets, fast foods, tennis rackets, toothpastes, sleeping bags, and instant potatoes. (Hint: *Consumer Reports* may be a good place to look for information.)

■ Look at a package of a brand of cereal. Prepare a complete analysis of the functions performed by the package. Select a second cereal brand and compare its package functions with the first package. Indicate what you consider to be the strengths and limitations of each package. What improvements in the packages can you suggest?

Notes

1. This illustration is based on Lawrence Ingrassia, "Those little alligators on clothes sell big, breed imitators, impostors and detractors." *Wall Street Journal*, Dec. 1, 1981, p. 31.
2. Bill Saporito, "When business got so good it got dangerous." *Fortune*, Apr. 2, 1984, p. 62.
3. Committee on Definitions, *Marketing Definitions: A Glossary of Marketing Terms*. Chicago: American Marketing Association, 1960, p. 8.
4. Ibid., p. 10.
5. Bill Abrams, "Practice of naming new products upset by ruling on trademarks." *Wall Street Journal*, Oct. 16, 1980, p. 31.
6. Bill Abrams, "Exploiting proven brand names can cut the risk of new products." *Wall Street Journal*, Jan. 22, 1981, p. 27.
7. "New items christened with old names." *Advertising Age*, Oct. 1, 1984, p. 80.
8. Al Ries and Jack Trout, *Positioning: The Battle for Your Mind*. New York: McGraw-Hill, 1981, p. 128.
9. John A. Byrne, "It scared the bejejebers out of me!" *Forbes*, Jan. 31, 1983, p. 48.
10. See Dennis J. Moran, "How a name can label your product." *Advertising Age*, Nov. 10, 1980, pp. 53–56; and Daniel J. Doeden, "How to select a brand name." *Marketing Communications*, Nov. 1981, pp. 58, 61.
11. James McNeal and Linda Zeren, "Brand name selection for consumer products." *MSU Business Topics*, Spring 1981, pp. 35–39.

12. "A Krafty solution." *Advertising Age,* Feb. 21, 1983, p. M-18.
13. Stan Kulp, "No pale imitations: Generic drugs enjoy vigorous growth." *Barron's,* May 10, 1982, p. 13.
14. Yoram J. Wind, *Product Policy: Concepts, Methods, and Strategy.* Reading, Mass.: Addison-Wesley, 1982, p. 186.
15. *"Inc.* sues new book." *Advertising Age,* Oct. 1, 1984, p. 74.
16. Sidney A. Diamond, *Trademark Problems and How to Avoid Them,* 2nd ed. Chicago: Crain Communications, 1981, pp. 143–177.
17. Richard L. Gordon, "Monopoly name doesn't pass go." *Advertising Age,* Feb. 28, 1983, pp. 3, 69.
18. "E.T. and friends are flying high." *Business Week,* Jan. 10, 1983, p. 77.
19. Ibid., p. 77.
20. Walter McQuade, "Packagers bear up under a bundle of regulations." *Fortune,* May 7, 1979, p. 180.
21. Bill Abrams, "Packaging often irks buyers, but firms are slow to change." *Wall Street Journal,* Jan. 28, 1982, p. 23.
22. ———, "Consumers want improved packaging." *Wall Street Journal,* June 28, 1984, p. 32.
23. Harlan S. Byrne, "What recession? A leaping Caterpillar is a wonderous thing, even its rivals agree." *Wall Street Journal,* Apr. 19, 1976, p. 12.
24. William H. Bleuel and Henry E. Bender, *Product Service Planning.* New York: AMACOM, 1980, pp. 16–17.
25. *U.S. News & World Report,* Feb. 28, 1983, p. 12.
26. "Repair people struggle to keep up with glut of breaking products." *Wall Street Journal,* Jan 5, 1981, pp. 1, 8.
27. E. Patrick McGuire, *Industrial Product Warranties: Policies and Practices,* Report No. 800. New York: The Conference Board, 1980, p. 1.
28. Ibid., p. 13.
29. Ibid., p. 2.
30. Ibid., p. 24.
31. E. Patrick McGuire, *The Product-Safety Function: Organization and Operations.* New York: The Conference Board, 1979, p. 1.
32. "J&J sees removal of Zomaz costing $20 million in 1983." *Wall Street Journal,* Mar. 8, 1983, p. 10.
33. E. Patrick McGuire, *The Product Safety Function: Organization and Operations.* New York: The Conference Board, 1979, p. 2.
34. This account is based on Lynn G. Reiling, "Consumer misuse marrs sampling for sunlight dishwashing liquid." *Marketing News,* Sept. 3, 1982, pp. 1, 12.
35. Ibid., p. 1.
36. McGuire, op. cit., p. 3.
37. "Tomorrow." *U.S. News & World Report,* Feb. 28, 1983, p. 12.
38. McGuire, op. cit., p. 53.
39. "The kerosene-heater controversy." *Consumer Reports,* Jan. 1983, p. 20.
40. David L. Malickson, "Are you ready for a product recall?" *Business Horizons,* Jan./Feb. 1983, pp. 31–35.

Case 11.1

ChemLawn CarpetClean

CHEMLAWN CORPORATION was 14 years old in 1983. Sales had grown to $228 million and profits to $12.6 million. During this period ChemLawn had evolved from a lawn care company to a multiservice company providing lawn care, tree and shrub care, carpet cleaning, and pest elimination services. 1983 was the first year that all services used the ChemLawn name. Marketing research and test market experience supported the advantages of this approach compared to creating new names for each service. If a unique name were used for each service, the buyer would not know that the service was offered by ChemLawn. Thus, whatever favorable brand awareness gained from

SOURCE: *1983 Annual Report,* ChemLawn Corporation.

lawn care services would not apply to their ChemLawn services. Moreover, promotional efforts would need to be focused on each service.

All services emphasize ChemLawn's strong guarantee of satisfaction by using the slogan, "ChemLawn Guarantees," in advertising and on all trucks. Management's commitment to this marketing approach was based on the assumption that consistency of name and advertising should increase overall marketplace awareness and should facilitate the expansion of ChemLawn's new services.

ChemLawn's CarpetClean service is relatively new. In 1983 test marketing continued in 18 markets. The results encouraged the belief that by providing guaranteed satisfaction and using strong introductory marketing support, ChemLawn can achieve a leadership position in the large, fragmented carpet cleaning

market that has been served by a large number of very small businesses throughout the U.S. Sales increased to $3,018,000 in 1983, an increase of 86 percent over 1982.

The two markets using this strong introductory approach exceeded their sales goals for 1983. In 1984, CarpetClean is expected to have its first million dollar market. All other CarpetClean test markets will be strengthened in operations staff and marketing support in 1984. Television will be added to the testing program.

A number of supplemental services can add importantly to the sales and profit opportunity of carpet cleaning. In particular, these include the application of a carpet fiber protector, already offered by Carpet-Clean, and upholstery cleaning. Upholstery cleaning was tested in several markets in 1983 and will be expanded in 1984.

QUESTIONS

1. What are the major advantages of ChemLawn's franchise extension strategy for marketing carpet cleaning services?

2. What potential disadvantages may exist by management's decision to market all services under the ChemLawn name?

3. How important is ChemLawn's guaranteed satisfaction in the firm's marketing mix?

4. Are there other services that ChemLawn should investigate as possible areas of business expansion?

Case 11.2

McNeil Consumer Products

THE MAKERS OF TYLENOL face long—but not impossible—odds as they begin the herculean effort to save one of history's most commercially successful products.

The task of rebuilding sales will take months at a minimum and millions of dollars in advertising, marketing, testing and packaging—perhaps to no avail.

That was the prospect as McNeil Consumer Products Company, a subsidiary of

SOURCE: Judith B. Gardner, "When a brand name gets hit by bad news," *U. S. News & World Report,* Nov. 8, 1982, p. 71. Copyright © 1982 U. S. News & World Report, Inc. Reprinted by permission.

Johnson & Johnson and manufacturer of the over-the-counter drug, resumed advertising in late October, 25 days after the first of at least seven deaths from cyanide-laced capsules of Extra-Strength Tylenol. Capsules were withdrawn from the market nationwide, at an after-tax cost of 50 million dollars, and sales of regular Tylenol tablets have fallen sharply.

The 60-second spots, which aired on network television for four days, featured McNeil's medical director, Dr. Thomas N. Gates. The company will reintroduce capsules in new tamper-resistant containers "as quickly as possible," he told viewers. "Tylenol has had the trust of the medical profession and a hundred million Ameri-

cans for over 20 years. We value that trust too much to let any individual tamper with it. We want you to continue to trust Tylenol."

Only time will tell if McNeil and Johnson & Johnson will be able to restore consumer confidence in the product and regain market leadership. History shows that negative publicity, particularly with deaths involved, can kill a product—

■ Procter & Gamble stopped manufacturing Rely tampons at a loss of 75 million dollars in 1980 after the item was linked with deaths from toxic-shock syndrome.

■ Bon Vivant Soups, Inc., filed for bankruptcy in 1971 after a botulism death was traced to its vichyssoise and the Food and Drug Administration recalled all Bon Vivant products.

- The demise of Chevrolet's rear-engined Corvair in the 1960s and Ford's compact Pinto in the 1970s was linked, in part, to controversies over safety. The Corvair's handling and stability were faulted by consumer advocate Ralph Nader, and design defects of the Pinto were implicated in fires after rear-end collisions.
- Firestone incurred huge losses in recalling 20 million steel-belted radial tires that were found to separate under some conditions. Production of tires under the name 500 was halted in 1978.

Still, it is possible for companies and industries to recover from devastating publicity through aggressive marketing and advertising, especially when consumers don't hold the maker to blame.

Cranberry sales have rebounded from a cancer scare that erupted just before Thanksgiving in 1959. Only a small portion of berries were found to have been contaminated, and the government was accused of overreaction in telling people not to eat them. The industry eventually branched out into a variety of related products, such as juice, to bolster business year-round.

Tuna fish remains a household staple, years after a government-ordered recall and emergency testing in 1970 for unsafe levels of mercury. Similarly, the public still buys canned mushrooms, despite incidents of botulism in 1974.

DC-10 aircraft are in wide use after negative publicity from a 1979 crash in Chicago that killed 275 people, and the subsequent grounding of all DC-10s for inspection.

Nevertheless, many experts doubt that Tylenol can ever regain its commanding leadership among over-the-counter pain relievers. "The brand has suffered a mortal wound," contends Benjamin Lipstein, marketing professor at the Graduate School of Business Administration of New York University.

Some doubt that even the name can survive. "The chances are less than 50 percent," says David W. Flegal, marketing executive with Oxtoby-Smith, a New York research and consulting firm. Explains Flegal: "When a brand name is so clearly established and then is so tarred and feathered, it is difficult or impossible to ever separate the two in consumer's minds."

Beyond that, consumers have a wide choice of other painkillers to buy, and many are likely to turn to the alternatives.

With an increasingly skeptical public, say marketers, appeals to "trust us" might fall on deaf ears.

Despite the odds facing Johnson & Johnson, however, no one is writing off the product entirely.

For one thing, the rash of copycat taintings of other over-the-counter drug products could actually help Tylenol sales. "The more the public perceives that this is an industry problem, the better off Tylenol will be," says Stephen A. Greyser, marketing professor at Harvard Business School.

Furthermore, the FDA has cleared the firm of wrongdoing. And new government requirements for tamper-resistant packages may help restore public confidence in Tylenol and other products. They also mean that all firms will be saddled with higher costs for new packaging.

Finally, few people underestimate the business savvy of Johnson & Johnson, which pushed Tylenol to the top of its line and built tremendous consumer loyalty. "They are by far one of the smartest and most aggressive marketers in this business," says Lipstein.

Ultimately, it's not the marketing experts who will determine Tylenol's fate, but a jury of millions of consumers who seek relief from pain. The verdict is yet to be known.

QUESTIONS

1. Should McNeil Consumer Products Company have anticipated the possibility of tampering, and introduced tamper-proof packaging before the cyanide incidents?

2. Evaluate the pros and cons of reintroducing the product under the Tylenol brand name.

3. How does the Tylenol incident differ from Procter & Gamble's death-linked problems with Rely tampons?

4. By early 1983 it was clear that Tylenol was well on the way to regaining its market position as a leading pain killer. Why were the experts wrong?

Part Four

Distribution

12 Marketing Channels

When you finish this chapter, you will understand

□ The vital role of the channel of distribution in marketing many goods and services

□ How various flows, including the physical flow of the product, serve as the connecting links for the channel network of organizations

□ How channels of distribution are organized

□ The types of channels that are available

□ How a channel of distribution is selected by a company

□ The important factors in channel selection and choice of channel participants

In 1983 Nixdorf Computers distributed, through a network of channel organizations, 16,000 computer systems and 60,000 display systems to thirty-nine countries.

A marketing channel of distribution consists of the organizations that work together to move goods and services from producers to end-users. A look at the marketing plan of Ricoh of America, the U.S. subsidiary of Japan's largest copier manufacturer, demonstrates how the channel of distribution is a major part of the firm's marketing approach in the United States, which accounts for nearly half of the world copier market. Management of the firm is committed to building a strong dealer network as a means of establishing a market share position in the competitive office copier market. Each dealer has an exclusive sales territory, thus ensuring that no competing firms in the territory will sell Ricoh copiers. Sales revenue estimates for 1984 were $300 million.

The firm began marketing its copiers in the United States in April 1981. Although the dealer network was central to Ricoh's marketing plan, major advertising, sales promotion, and public relations programs were also part of the marketing approach. To strengthen Ricoh's management team, marketing talents were acquired by attracting executives from IBM and Xerox.[1]

RICOH'S MANAGEMENT carefully researched the U.S. office equipment market before entering it, learning in the process several weaknesses of competitor's marketing approaches. Marketing research discovered the following:

- Poor communications between office equipment manufacturers and their dealers

- Inadequate quality control in production

- Erratic and unreliable parts supply

- Too much competition within trading areas, resulting in price erosion, particularly of low-priced equipment

- Manufacturer financing programs forced dealers to carry a larger inventory than they needed or reasonably could sell

- Inconsistencies in technical training programs

- Inconsistencies in sales training programs[2]

The problems uncovered by the research highlight the importance of the participants in the distribution channel. The findings also identify several functions of the channel organizations. Ricoh's marketing plan was designed to eliminate the problems. For example,

> The major sticking point in dealer-manufacturer communications is the availability of replacement parts and supplies, and Ricoh has addressed that with a satellite communications system. U.S. parts inventory updates are sent each morning to Japan, and the stockpile is replenished daily with a shipment from the Orient.[3]

Surprisingly, given Xerox's strong brand image, Ricoh is the number-one manufacturer of copiers in the world on a unit basis, trailing only Xerox on a revenue basis. Ricoh has more than 40 percent of the Japanese market and is Europe's most popular brand. Nevertheless, Ricoh's performance in the U.S. market could depend heavily on management's success in building a strong distribution network.

The illustration provides an appropriate introduction to the topic of marketing channels of distribution. In this chapter we discuss the need for distribution channels, flows in distribution channels, and channel organization, including a discussion of channel participants, channel configuration, channel forms, and channel behavior. Finally, an overview of the design and management of channels is presented.

WHY CHANNELS ARE NEEDED

Ricoh probably would have failed if it had attempted to market its copiers by mail to the United States. Building its own company salesforce to sell the copiers to individual accounts would have taken several years and substantial financial resources. It is easy to see that the distribution channel has been influential in this firm's success.

The marketing channel defined

A **channel of distribution** is a network of cooperating organizations that together perform all the activities required to link producers of goods and services to end-users to accomplish the marketing task.[4] This definition has four important implications: (1) organizations work together to accomplish marketing functions (tasks), as implied by the term *network*; (2) channel organizations perform various functions; (3) physical products, information, and money flow among the members of the channel network, as implied by the involvement of a network of organizations; and (4) performing the marketing task involves carrying out the process of exchange between suppliers and end-users of goods and services.

Illustrative channels of distribution for refrigerators are shown in Exhibit 12.1. Note that a manufacturer can reach consumers and organizational end-users in several ways through the marketing intermediaries shown. Whirlpool Corporation, for example, manufactures special model refrigerators for the Sears retail chain, distributes its own brand through wholesalers to independent retailers such as appliance stores, and markets its brand to retail chains. Whirlpool also sells directly to large apartment developers. A manufacturer may use one or a combination of the intermediaries shown in Exhibit 12.1.

Since 1981, Ricoh's U.S. copier sales have grown steadily, and the company now ranks second behind Canon in the number of copiers sold in the United States. Though Canon advertises heavily, Ricoh has relied more on building a strong dealer network. The company has signed more than 300 dealers and plans to add at least 200 more.

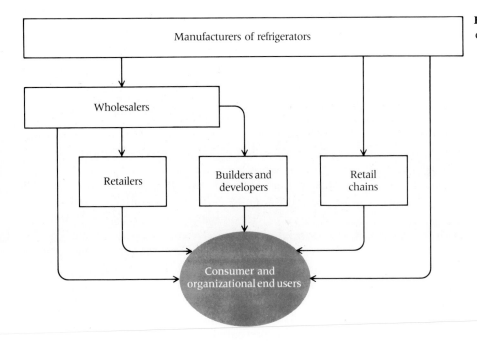

Exhibit 12.1 Illustrative channels of distribution for refrigerators

Justification for intermediaries

Marketing intermediaries link producers to end-users. These middlemen typically are independent businesses that perform various channel functions—specialists in performing various distribution tasks. They often are more efficient in performing these tasks than producers or end-users of goods and services. Intermediaries perform functions in the distribution channel for two reasons: to reduce the number of transactions between buyers and sellers and to balance discrepancies in supply and demand. The Marketalk about Blue Diamond illustrates how important cooperation can be to moving a product through distribution channels.

Reducing transactions. Whenever people stop being self-sufficient, exchange between producers and consumers becomes essential. Recall our look in Chapter 1 at the need for transactions. Division of labor and specialization require that suppliers and consumers perform some type of exchange. Regardless of whether the exchange is accomplished by barter (trade) in a country store or a shopping mall, a transaction is necessary to accomplish the exchange between buyers and sellers. Marketing intermediaries are essential to this function.

Exhibit 12.2 illustrates how intermediaries reduce the number of transactions between buyers and sellers. Without a supermarket intermediary, twenty-five transactions would be necessary between the five producers and the five consumers. Placing the supermarket between producers and consumers reduces the number of transactions from twenty-five to ten. Each consumer and each producer has reduced the number of their transactions from five to one. Considering the hundreds of food items carried in the modern supermarket and the millions of people who shop one or more times each week, the critical function of marketing intermediaries in a

*Marke*TALK ///

Moving nuts through the channel

A LOOK AT HOW PACKAGES of almonds were made available to airlines illustrates the importance of distribution channels in marketing the 2000 Blue Diamond Nut products of the California Almond Growers Exchange, a producers' cooperative owned by 5500 growers. Roger Bacciagaluppi, president of the cooperative, has developed an aggressive marketing effort designed to move almonds from the growers' farms to consumers' stom-

SOURCE: Adapted from Wayne Beissant, "Marketing makes nuts fly," *USA Today*, Feb. 7, 1984, p. 4B.

achs. In 1968 he persuaded American Airlines officials to distribute almonds to passengers. Today, twenty-five airlines hand out 20 million bags a year. Per capita consumption in 1984 was a half a pound a year, double the consumption of 1981.

Bacciagaluppi's strategy was to expose people to the product during airline flights. Although airlines represented only a small portion of total market potential, thousands of people tried the nuts in flights, liked them, and bought more when they got home. Today Blue Diamond controls half of the overall almond market and 50 percent of the retail market. In 1984 California produced 60 percent of the world's almonds—300 million

pounds. Between 1984 and 1990 annual consumption of almonds is expected to double.

The Exchange continually is promoting the use of almonds. New product research and development has generated new products. Almond exports increased from 5 million pounds in 1950 to a record 208 million pounds shipped to eighty-eight countries in 1981. Each member of the Exchange pays a surcharge to cover the expenses of the cooperative. It was 5.4 cents on each 90 cents per pound paid to growers in 1982 and 1983. This money is used as working capital to finance the operations of the organization. The money is paid back four years later to the growers.

///

developed economy is clear. Direct transactions simply are not feasible between producers and consumers with their wide range of needs and wants.

Balancing discrepancies. As discussed in Chapter 1, specialization creates discrepancies or gaps between producers and consumers. A discrepancy is a difference in preference between producers and consumers based on *what* is produced, *where* it is produced, or *when* it is produced. Marketing intermediaries perform the functions necessary to eliminate these discrepancies. Balancing these discrepancies is the central task of marketing intermediaries. *Time and location* discrepancies exist because producers cannot manufacture goods and services when and where each buyer wants them. Production efficiencies require sufficient volume to gain cost advantages, thus the number of production locations is limited. If a cookie processor only made cookies when a buyer requested them, the costs would be pro-

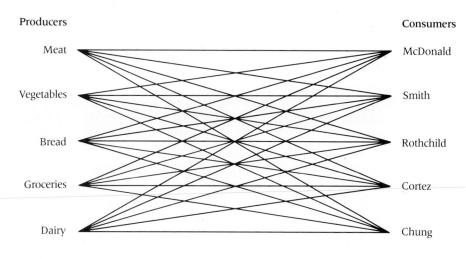

NO INTERMEDIARY: 5 PRODUCERS × 5 CONSUMERS = 25 TRANSACTIONS

Exhibit 12.2 **Reductions in grocery shopping transactions provided by an intermediary**

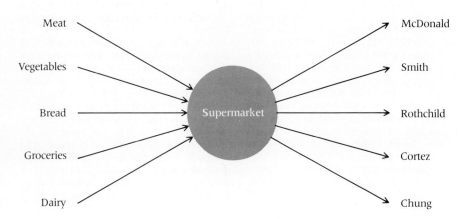

SUPERMARKET INTERMEDIARY: 5 PRODUCERS + 5 CONSUMERS = 10 TRANSACTIONS

hibitive. To provide a package of fifty cookies for ninety-nine cents, thousands must be produced at one time in a limited number of automated production facilities. By shipping the cookies to consumers, transportation helps eliminate location gaps. A storage function normally is required of intermediaries, who hold the item on the shelf or in stock until the buyer is ready for it.

The process of creating *assortments* often is necessary to eliminate gaps between buyers and sellers. **Sorting** pertains primarily to establishing grade categories for minerals and agricultural products such as eggs (grade A jumbo) and beef (choice ground). De Beers, the monopolistic diamond distributor, performs the sorting function for most of the world's supply of new diamonds. **Assorting** is assembling items in stock to satisfy the needs of the buyer. The process of building assortments takes place in a wide variety of marketing intermediary organizations. For example, a building contractor calls a lumberyard, ordering lumber, nails, window frames, and other items needed for a construction project.

Bulk-breaking is another activity intermediaries perform to bridge the gap between producers and end-users. This consists of breaking down large quantities of goods purchased from producers into smaller quantities. For example, a chemical distributor purchases a tank car of acid that is stored in large tanks. Acid is drawn from the tanks into small containers to supply the distributor's customers with desired quantities of acid. Other examples of products that require bulk-breaking are fertilizers, grain, and seeds. Products may be packaged in smaller units when received by the intermediary and stored until needed to fill a customer's order. Alternatively, the entire quantity may be stored in bulk until a customer's order is actually received.

The elimination of discrepancies requires the exchange of *information* within the channel network. Purchase orders are transmitted, invoices are sent, salespeople try to persuade buyers to purchase, customers complain about faulty products, and so on. Information is critical to the functioning of the channel of distribution.

Finally, some means of *valuation* of goods and services is needed, and the transfer of *ownership* between buyers and sellers must be accomplished. Pricing establishes the value of items available for sale. Transfer of ownership is handled by contractual arrangement, receipt of sale, or word of mouth. For example, when a stockbroker executes a "telephone buy order" of common stock for a customer, the purchase and transfer of ownership of the stock is set in motion.

Our look at the need to reduce the number of transactions and to balance the discrepancies between buyers and sellers clearly illustrates why channels of distribution facilitate exchange in developed economies. This, of course, does not mean that the channel of distribution is the only way of linking buyers and sellers. Producers and consumers can and do have direct contact for a portion of the exchanges that occur. The important point is that buyer and seller relying *only* on direct exchange rarely is feasible in a modern marketing system. Channel intermediaries help reduce the number of transactions and, in many other ways, facilitate the exchange process. The sorting, storing, contracting, transporting, and communicating functions performed by intermediaries eliminate the discrepancies between suppliers and consumers.

FLOWS IN DISTRIBUTION CHANNELS

Channel flows

The channel of distribution is a unique business institution because it is a network of organizations. Several flows serve as connecting links for the channel network including physical, ownership, financial, information, and risk. A **channel flow** is the movement of goods or services through the distribution network between two or more channel participants. An example of the physical flow of gasoline through the distribution channel is shown in Exhibit 12.3. The illustration highlights two important characteristics typical to channel flows: (1) several participants are involved and (2) flows occur between various participants. A close look at each type of flow provides a better understanding of their unique characteristics.

Physical flow. Physical flow, the most visible, is the actual movement of the product from one channel participant to another as shown in Exhibit 12.3. The product may not flow through all participants. For example, a manufacturer's agent for a women's apparel manufacturer sells the apparel line to a retail store, and the order is shipped directly to the retailer by the manufacturer. The independent agent is paid a commission on the sale by the manufacturer, who bills, or invoices, the retail store for the amount of the purchase.

The physical flow through the channel illustrates the role of **facilitating organizations** such as transportation firms and warehousing companies. These firms provide specialized services for regular channel participants, and their payment is based on these services instead of the product's sale or exchange value. Among the various facilitating organizations needed to accomplish physical and other flows through the channel are banks, marketing research firms, insurance companies, and advertising agencies.

Ownership flow. The flow of ownership or title through the channel may be different from the physical flow of the product. Some channel participants take title to goods; others do not. For example, the commission agent for the apparel firm previously discussed does not own the apparel. Instead, ownership is transferred from the manufacturer to the retailer. Typically, facilitating organizations do not take title to goods. When purchases such as houses are financed, the firm holding mortgage has a claim against the real estate for the amount of the loan.

Financial flow. Money and credit often move in several directions in the distribution channel. Payment for purchases moves in reverse of the physical flows from the end-user backward to the producer. For example, the producer receives payment from a distributor who is paid by the retailer. The retailer, in turn, receives payment from the consumer. The various facilitating organizations also receive payment for their services. Normally, payment for goods and services covers the cost of the item plus compensation for the channel participant's services and profit. Suppose a grocery wholesaler buys inventory from various food processors and sells the groceries at an average 7 percent margin over product cost. For every dollar of sales the wholesaler has seven cents to cover costs such as interest, storage, depreciation, transportation, insurance, wages and salaries, and various

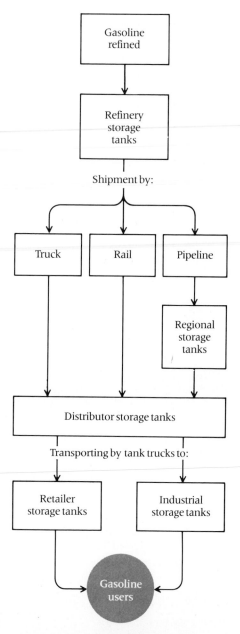

Exhibit 12.3 Illustrative physical distribution flows of gasoline from refinery to gasoline users

other operating expenses. The amount remaining, after all expenses are paid, is the wholesaler's profit before taxes. For grocery wholesalers the average net profit margin is approximately a penny for each dollar of sales.

Information flow. Information is the nerve center of the distribution channel. Information flows in all directions. Orders are transmitted, salespersons communicate with customers, marketing researchers question respondents, distributors estimate future requirements, and so on. Communications within the channel network enable it to function. Faulty information transfer hampers the workings of the channel. Consider the following illustration:

> Iris Lingerie Co. knows how frustrating department-store transactions can be. For several months in 1979, the New York nightgown maker battled Bullock's Wilshire fashion store over $900 that the Los Angeles based Federated unit had deducted without authorization from a $9,700 order. Eventually, after a trade publication wrote about the problem, Bullock's Wilshire paid the $900; it blamed a clerical mistake. The payment for the store's next order, however, also was reduced by $900—another computer error that was hastily solved.[5]

Risk flow. This channel flow is somewhat more difficult to define than the others. Some examples will illustrate how risk flows through the distribution network and how the elimination of risk helps the channel to function.

- Farmers sell their corn in the futures market and eliminate the risk of a price decline. By accepting a specified price in the future, farmers assure themselves of a certain price for their corn.
- Retailers carry insurance on their inventories to avoid the risks of theft and fire.
- College bookstores are allowed by textbook publishers to return all books not sold for a full refund.
- Retailers pay a fee to credit card services such as American Express to avoid risks of offering their own charge services and encountering bad debts.

These are only a few of the many ways that risks flow through the distribution network.

Channel flows for services

Distribution channel flows for services differ to some extent from the flows of tangible products. The most important distinction is that the service itself does not move through the channel as does a physical product. A service may be sold, however, through intermediaries. For example, you may purchase an airline ticket from the airline, a travel agent, or a tour group. The airline pays the travel agent a commission for handling the reservation arrangements and ticketing function.

Typically, channels for services involve only one level of intermediary between the service provider and end-user. In several instances a service provider such as American Airlines also may make direct contact with end-users. Interestingly, during the past few years American Airlines has worked aggressively to strengthen its ties with travel agents. The airline offers agents training, computer services, and other types of assistance. Management apparently has determined that travel agents provide an effective means of marketing airline services.

For everyone who sells on the futures market, which deals in agricultural products, raw materials, and other commodities, someone else must buy. It's risky because options and futures prices can change direction during the course of a day. Traders speak of developing a "feel" for the market or of losing its "rhythm" if they take even a day off. "I don't believe trading is a science," says Brian P. Monieson, chairman of the Chicago Mercantile Exchange. "It's more of an art. You can't plug in a computer that will tell you the way the market is going." (Courtesy of Chicago Mercantile Exchange)

Another characteristic of channel flows for services is that normally ownership does not transfer from one channel participant to another. Instead the service is conveyed to the end-user by the provider. There are no major differences in financial, information, and risk flows between services and tangible products. In general, channels for services are not as long or complex as channels for tangible products because many channel functions are not appropriate for services. For example, if the service is produced at the time of consumption, there is no need for inventory or storage. This obviously is true of services such as haircuts or housecleaning. Intermediaries primarily are involved in performing selling, financial, information, and risk functions.

Distribution profits and costs

Marketing organizations often are criticized because of the high margins believed to exist between production costs and retail selling prices. Surprisingly, net profit margins on sales are quite small for many types of marketing intermediaries. For the six industry groups listed in Exhibit 12.4, net profits (after taxes) range from approximately a penny to less than a nickel. Although the profit margins of some specific retailers and wholesalers are higher or lower than the industry averages shown, on the balance the margins are not excessive. If profits are not out of line for distribution firms, what about costs? Are the costs of distribution responsible for making prices higher than they should be?

Two factors affect distribution costs. First, the functions that are performed in the distribution channel cost money. The more functions that intermediaries must accomplish, the greater the selling price of the product must be to cover the costs. For example, most of us take advantage of the services in a modern supermarket without ever realizing the costs of the many conveniences that are available (which we ultimately pay for). The costs of processing and marketing food account for approximately two-thirds of the retail food dollar.[6] There are wide variations from the average, with cereals and bakery products at the high end and eggs at the low end. Consider this profile of today's food consumer.

> Today's housewife—who is often a wage-earner, as well—wants her sausage precooked, her chicken cut up and ready to fry, her spinach chopped and frozen, her hams cooked and boneless, her rolls ready to pop into the oven and her orange juice squeezed. She also demands a variety of prepared mixes that will, almost instantly and effortlessly, yield everything from cookies and cakes to mashed potatoes and puddings. Thus, today's middlemen serve as converters, processors, butchers and dressers of meat, and even as cooks to the nation. For these additional services they earn a large share of consumer food outlays.[7]

The second factor contributing to distribution costs is efficiency. Many distribution functions are labor intensive. For example, the largest single cost component of food marketing is labor, representing approximately 31 percent of the food dollar. People do not perform repetitive tasks as efficiently as machines. Although major gains in the productivity of intermediaries have been made during the 1980s, distribution efficiencies still do not compare to manufacturing efficiencies. Given the nature of distribution, it is doubtful whether the efficiencies in this area will ever be as high as manufacturing efficiencies. Sorting, storage, transportation, inventory accumulation, theft, spoilage, facilities, and service all contribute to costs.

Exhibit 12.4 Illustrative net profit margins for marketing intermediaries

Industry	1985–1987 Estimated Net Profit Margin On Sales (Average)
Grocery stores	1.0%
Food wholesalers	1.2
Fast-foods	6.8
Drug stores	3.0
Retail chains	2.8
Speciality retailers	4.8

SOURCE: *The Value Line Survey,* New York: Value Line, 1984.

To a large extent distribution costs are due to (1) the demands consumers place on the marketing system and (2) the nature of the distribution function. Thus reducing costs requires improving distribution efficiency or shifting some functions to others—usually the consumer. Firms that advertise low costs because they have "eliminated the middleman" frequently offer limited functions, leaving their buyers responsible for activities such as delivery and credit.

HOW CHANNELS ARE ORGANIZED

Channel participants

A useful channel participant classification scheme is shown in Exhibit 12.5. Participants are either members or nonmembers. The main distinction between member participants and nonmember participants is that the members perform the negotiatory functions of buying, selling, and transferring title. The facilitating organizations (nonmember participants) normally are not considered part of the marketing channel, although this designation is purely definitional. The importance and contribution of the facilitating organizations are not issues because they perform essential functions.

Producers and manufacturers. A wide variety of producing industries exist including steel, electronics, and food. These firms create the product or service that is distributed through the channel. Unless direct contact with final users is made through the manufacturer's salesforce or other direct

By offering services like its "no-stop check-in," American Airlines acknowledges the importance of providing easier ways for businesspeople to travel and recognizes the role that travel agents can play in the carrier's distribution strategy. (Advertisement courtesy of American Airlines and Bozell & Jacobs, Inc.)

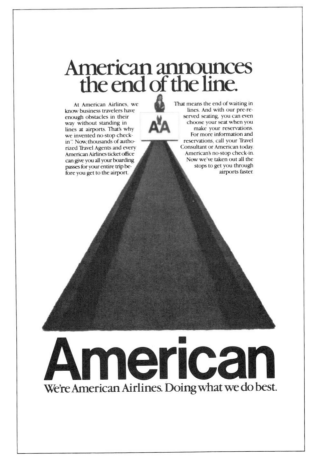

American announces the end of the line.

At American Airlines, we know business travelers have enough obstacles in their way without standing in lines at airports. That's why we invented no-stop check-in? Now, thousands of authorized Travel Agents and every American Airlines ticket office can give you all your boarding passes for your entire trip before you get to the airport.

That means the end of waiting in lines. And with our pre-reserved seating, you can even choose your seat when you make your reservations. For more information and reservations, call your Travel Consultant or American today. American's no-stop check-in. Now we've taken out all the stops to get you through airports faster.

American

We're American Airlines. Doing what we do best.

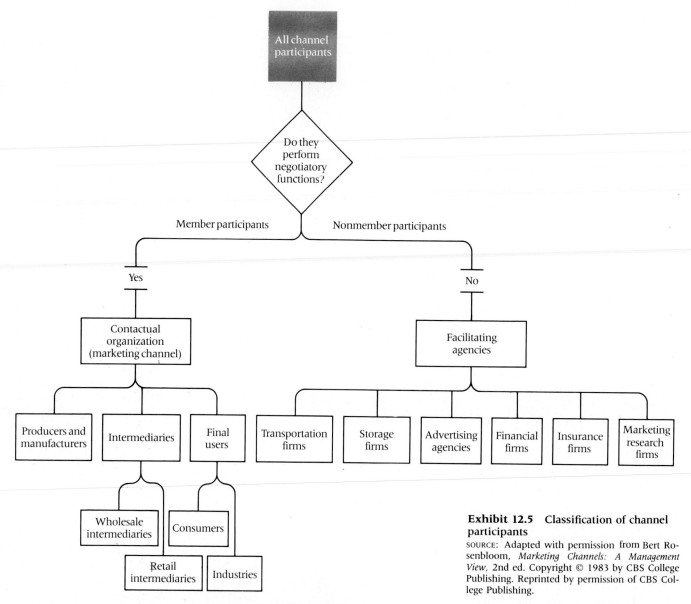

Exhibit 12.5   Classification of channel participants

SOURCE: Adapted with permission from Bert Rosenbloom, *Marketing Channels: A Management View*, 2nd ed. Copyright © 1983 by CBS College Publishing. Reprinted by permission of CBS College Publishing.

means such as mail order, marketing intermediaries are needed to connect producers with end-users.

Marketing intermediaries. Retailers and wholesalers are the channel participants familiar to most people. Many different forms of intermediaries distribute consumer and industrial products and services. Some provide very specialized functions, and few people know that they even exist. For example, agents and brokers are intermediaries that perform the selling function for producers and are paid a commission on the sales they make. Typically, agents and brokers do not take title to the goods they sell. Although most consumers are aware of real estate agents, few realize that food brokers are important in distributing many of the food items available today. Manufacturers' agents sell a vast range of products for industrial uses and represent another type of channel specialist. Because of their importance in performing various marketing tasks, the different types of retailers and wholesalers are discussed in some detail in Chapters 13 and 14.

Facilitating agencies. Facilitating agencies perform special tasks for producers, intermediaries, and final users. (The major types of facilitators are identified in Exhibit 12.5.) Included are marketing research firms, insurance companies, financial services firms, advertising agencies, storage firms, and transportation providers. These organizations perform tasks essential to the functioning of many channels of distribution. For example, most channels could not operate without the credit extended by banks and other financial institutions to various channel participants.

Final users. The consumer and industrial end-users are the final link in the distribution chain. They are different from all the other participants because they consume or use the products and services distributed through the channel. Thus these final users represent target markets for the producers, manufacturers, and marketing intermediaries.

Channel configuration

Intermediaries can be placed into various configurations to form distribution channels. Several alternatives for connecting participants into a channel of distribution are shown in Exhibit 12.6. The position or location in the channel of each type of marketing intermediary is called the *level* in the channel. One may refer to the wholesale level, retail level, or broker level in the channel of distribution. The vertical and horizontal dimensions of channels are sometimes used to describe channel configuration. **Vertical dimension** refers to the alignment of different organizations from producer to end-user. Alternative vertical channel configurations are illustrated in Exhibit 12.6. The **horizontal dimension** refers to the channel participants at a particular channel level. These participants on the horizontal dimension of the channel are similar in type and function. Ethan Allen retail furniture dealers are an example.

An organization often is part of more than one distribution channel. For example, a manufacturer may use wholesalers for distribution to independent retailers while distributing directly to large retail chains. Similarly, a large retail chain may obtain its merchandise from several different channels of distribution. Because of this practice, it is important to distinguish between a single channel and multiple channels. Suppose a manufacturer distributes all its products through department stores to end users. Regardless of the number of department stores involved, the manufacturer has only one channel of distribution.

Multiple channels of distribution exist when more than one type of intermediary is used at a particular level. Multiple channels of distribution are composed of two or more channel linkages between a producer and its end-users. Each of the vertical configurations shown in Exhibit 12.3 is a single channel. American Airlines uses multiple channels because tickets are sold directly to travelers through the airline's sales offices (one linkage) and commissions are paid to travel agents for performing the sales and reservation functions (second linkage). Food producers normally use multiple channels. They distribute directly to large retail supermarket chains, sell to large grocery wholesalers, and may work through food brokers to distribute to small wholesalers and institutions such as hotels and restaurants.

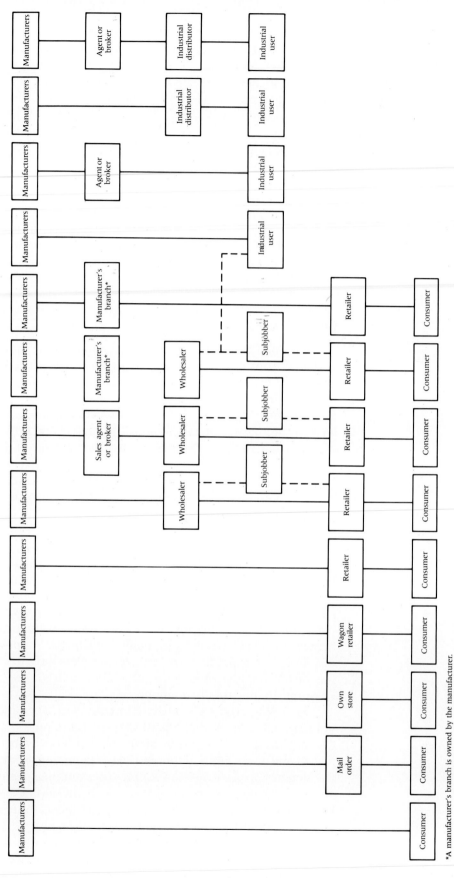

Exhibit 12.6 Illustrative configurations for channels of distribution

*A manufacturer's branch is owned by the manufacturer.

SOURCE: David T. Kollat, Roger D. Blackwell, and James F. Robeson, *Strategic Marketing*, p. 284. Copyright © 1972 by Holt, Rinehart and Winston, Inc. Reprinted by permission of Holt, Rinehart and Winston, CBS College Publishing.

Movie films follow an interesting distribution pattern. Consider the channels of distribution used by movie producers shown in Exhibit 12.7. Distribution through the four channels does not occur at the same time. Distribution begins in the channel on the left-hand side of Exhibit 12.7.

1. The film debuts in U.S. theaters.
2. The foreign opening occurs approximately six months later.
3. Videocassettes are available four to ten months after the U.S. theatrical release.
4. Pay television audiences see the film one year after its debut.
5. Network television airs the film two years after it has been on pay television.[8]

An additional distribution channel not shown in Exhibit 12.7 is the theft of new films and the production of videocassettes, which have become a thriving international racket. Successful films are stolen, reproduced on cassettes, and distributed a few weeks after the debut of the film.

Types of channels

The two types of distribution channels are a conventional channel and a vertical marketing system. All channels of distribution fall into one of the two categories.

Conventional channels. **Conventional channels** are made up of firms that buy and sell from each other and generally cooperate in performing the various channel functions. A major feature of the conventional channel is that each member is independent.[9] The channel is not managed as a coordinated network of organizations. Entry into and exit from the channel normally is not difficult. The independence of the participants in conventional channels sometimes may lead to conflict. The primary concern of the partic-

Exhibit 12.7 Distribution channels for new movies

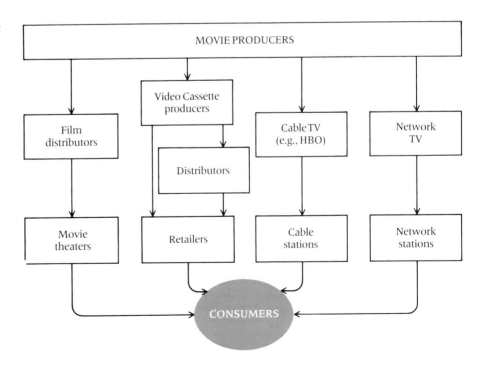

ipants is their own individual performance rather than the performance of the channel.

Consider this description of a conventional channel member. April-Marcus offers a buying service for independent discount retailers. Haunting cutting rooms and manufacturer's lofts, Mike Green tries to buy at cost or below.

> He chats on the phone constantly and follows up good leads with personal visits.
>
> One rainy morning, he travels by cab to a remote section of lower Manhattan at the request of Gene Yoon, a Korean importer. Mr. Yoon's problem is clear from the start: In his cavernous warehouse, some 20,000 out-of-season suits hang unsold and without prospects. "Right now there's no action, Gene," Mr. Green says, softening the news with the hint that a later order will be forthcoming. He will return after calculating which of his stores need the suits and for what selling season.[10]

April-Marcus supplies more than 200 off-price retailers. This market is growing at an annual rate approaching 30 percent. April-Marcus provides a service to both producers and retailers.

> In one such transaction, Mr. Green bought 1,000 Mongolian cashmere sport coats, which House of Darby had made up from overstock fabric in its inventory. Not only does Mr. Green's quick payment save House of Darby from burdensome carrying costs on the excess fabric, but also his order allows its Far Eastern factories to remain operating during slack periods. In exchange, Mr. Green gets the coats for $117 each, or $38 less than the normal wholesale price. April-Marcus stores will sell them for as much as $255, instead of the $350 usually charged by full-price stores.[11]

There are many forms of conventional distribution channels, in which products are sold at regular as well as "off" prices and both industrial and household end-users are served.

Vertical marketing systems. The vertical marketing system has grown rapidly during the last two decades and is the prevailing channel form in many types of retailing today. In contrast to a conventional channel, the **vertical marketing system (VMS)**

- Consists of a network of horizontally coordinated and vertically aligned marketing intermediaries
- Functions as a system with activities coordinated by the managing organization
- Operates at an optimum scale so marketing functions within the channel network are performed at the most advantageous level or position[12]

The three major types of VMSs are corporate, contractual, and administered.

1. A *corporate* system is a distribution channel that is owned by a company. For example, Sherwin-Williams, a paint producer, owns its retail paint and decorating supplies stores and distribution centers. Other examples of corporate VMSs are The Limited in retail women's apparel and Tandy Corporation in electronics stores. Both firms are retailers but also own or control their producers. The corporate system provides the greatest degree of control over channel participants as compared with the contractual or administered VMS. The capital needed to finance ownership of all participants is substantial. Some firms partici-

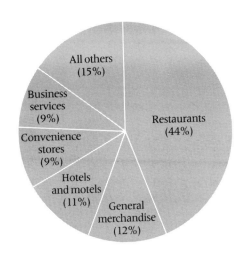

Exhibit 12.8 Retail franchise sales in the United States*

SOURCE: Data from Phillip D. White and Albert D. Bates, "Franchising will remain retailing fixture, but its salad days have long since gone," *Marketing News*, Feb. 17, 1984, p. 14.

* Excluding gas stations and car dealerships.

pate in both corporate and contractual VMSs. For example, McDonald's owns some retail stores and has franchised others through contractual arrangements. Holiday Inn also has both corporate-owned and franchised motels.

2. A *contractual* VMS typically involves a written agreement between the firm that is the channel manager and the other channel participants. At a minimum some basis of formalizing the contractual arrangement must exist. Included in this category are franchise systems such as McDonald's and various kinds of cooperative organizations such as IGA food stores. Three major kinds of contractual arrangements are (a) franchising, (b) wholesaler-sponsored chains, and (c) retail cooperatives. Producer (farmer) cooperatives also exist for various agricultural products. Franchising is clearly the most popular: one-third of all retail sales in the United States and Canada are made at franchised stores. Exhibit 12.8 indicates the percent of sales in each category of franchising. **Franchising** is an arrangement in which a parent company, or *franchisor*, grants a small company or individual, or *franchisee*, the right to do business in a specified manner for a specified period of time in a specified location. Typically, franchisees receive management assistance, training, advertising support, and other aids. For this assistance and support, they pay the franchisor an initial fee plus a continuing charge based on a percentage of sales (see Marketool). The wholesaler- and retailer-sponsored groups are tied together by cooperative arrangements to obtain group advantages in purchasing, distribution, management assistance, and promotion. Ace and True Value hardware stores are examples of retailer cooperatives. Cooperative arrangements provide the small business a means of competing against corporate chains. Although the small business such as a supermarket, drug store, or farmer loses some of its independence, its owner gains operating and marketing advantages through the contractual arrangement.

3. The *administered* channel is less formal than the corporate and contractual channel systems and is coordinated through the power, influence, incentives, and persuasiveness of the channel manager. Manufacturers of consumer goods seek to acquire such influence by combining superior products with heavy advertising to consumers. The administered channel differs only in degree from a conventional channel. "The point at which the conventional channel stops and the administered one begins must be made on the basis of judgments about the degree of effective interorganizational management taking place in the channel."[13] Examples are Lenox in tableware and gifts, Kraftco Corporation in dairy products, and Magnavox in consumer electronic products. As is apparent from these firms, the administered channel arrangement applies to a product or line of products rather than to a complete retail assortment.

Channel behavior

Because channels often are made up of organizations with different corporate affiliations, the relationships between these organizations are a mixture of cooperation and conflict. Organizations differ regarding objectives, preferences, priorities, and control over other firms in the channel.

Channel cooperation. A fundamental premise underlying the formation of a channel of distribution is that the members will cooperate. Unless the channel organizations try to work together in moving goods and services from producer to end-user, the functioning of the distribution channel will be hampered. **Channel cooperation** can be encouraged in several ways. Producers often provide incentives to channel members. For example,

MarkeTOOL

Ever thought of opening a franchise?

BERNARD LEYVA seemed to have an ideal background for striking out on his own with a franchised business. Before buying two Der Wienerschnitzel restaurants in Los Angeles in 1978, he had been a Der Wienerschnitzel district manager for five years.

But Mr. Leyva's restaurants did poorly —location was one factor—and his costs escalated. Last year, Mr. Leyva quit the restaurant business. He vows never to buy a franchise again.

For a would-be entrepreneur, a franchise is often the best route to success. There's the protective umbrella of a larger organization that provides guidance, sets standards and supplies national advertising. And the failure rate is low. By the Commerce Department's count, only 4% of all franchises in the U.S. were discontinued in 1983.

But as Mr. Leyva's experience shows, a franchise isn't a sure way to make a lot of money. While nearly a third of all retail sales last year—$383 billion—was accounted for by franchises, the competition can be intense—especially among restaurants. About 42% of all eating places are franchises, and that includes more than 20,000 hamburger, 12,000 pizza and 10,000 chicken outlets.

The franchisee also pays a price for affiliation with an established chain; he isn't totally independent. It is the franchiser who dictates the terms of the relationship, and those for ending it, too. That's why it is important to investigate thoroughly what one is getting into before signing a franchise contract.

Generally, a franchisee agrees to sell a service or a product under a marketing contract that obliges him to follow the franchiser's formula. The franchiser is paid a lump sum for the right to operate at a particular location and a royalty based on monthly sales. A franchise can cost as little as $1,000 for an Augie's Inc. industrial catering truck to $1.5 million for a Good Taco Co. restaurant.

Since 1978, the Federal Trade Commission has required franchisers to disclose information about their operations to prospective franchisees. Among other details, says Mark J. Klein, a Kansas City, Mo., lawyer, the disclosure will reveal a franchiser's past litigation, which could suggest a lot about how a company operates. "Sometimes the best advice a lawyer can give a client is to stay away from a particular franchiser," he says.

Fifteen states also have registration laws, and some require a franchiser to report audited sales figures. "This shows the franchisee exactly what's in store since, in most cases, his life savings are on the line," says Ronald W. Thomas, former chairman of the North American Securities Administrators Association.

The International Franchise Association, which represents 480 franchisers, says that franchisees aren't gaining much from state registrations, though. Franchisers complain that it is cumbersome and costly to prepare each state's version of disclosure. Some say there's too much information. "I question whether the average investor is able to absorb all of this," says E. Jan Hartmann, president of Ziebart Rustproofing Co., a Troy, Mich., concern that has 365 franchised outlets.

"Our real hope is that the FTC and the states will pursue a uniform disclosure interpretation," says Philip Zeidman, a Washington, D.C., lawyer for the franchisers' association.

No matter what disclosure requirements are, prospective franchisees should be sure they know how the franchiser can terminate a contract or deny renewal. Some state laws ensure that a contract can't be revoked without just cause. But some franchisers have construed breach of contract to include minor "quality control" violations when they wanted to get rid of a particular franchisee.

Before counting up potential profits, franchisees should estimate their overhead costs and take into account factors that might affect them. One way is to ask several established franchisees to talk about their expenses. Mr. Leyva says troubles with his restaurants worsened in 1980 after his building leases, which were tied to the consumer price index, ballooned to $4,100 a month from $2,900.

Many new franchisees are short of cash when they start up. Typically, they will lease their real estate, fixtures and equipment from the franchiser, sometimes at stiff rates. If the business takes a while to get off the ground, it may be impossible to pay the bills. "It's a built-in scenario for disaster," says William H. Manger, a Los Angeles attorney who has represented many disgruntled franchisees.

After buying a franchise, an owner may feel powerless to alter his relationship with the franchiser. But when franchisees join forces, they can win more control over their fortunes. The Midas Dealers' Association, organized in 1971, has "given us the strength to get management to listen to us," says Richard Tobino, owner of a Midas auto muffler shop in Paramus, N.J. The group represents about 80% of the franchisees who run 1,385 Midas outlets. One accomplishment: It negotiated a plan to protect existing shops' territories when Midas started a major expansion program in 1976. Says Mr. Tobino, "Nothing major has affected us without a lot of discussion and compromise with the Midas management."

dealer rebates are popular in the automobile, appliance, and electronics industries. Factory product training is another method of building cooperation in the channel. Some firms offer travel and other incentives to dealers, as when travel retailers such as cruise lines, hotels, and tour services offer free packages to travel agents. Cooperative advertising by supplier and retailer is another means of strengthening relationships between channel members. Establishing service centers by manufacturers to help small retailers with the service function has been used effectively by firms such as General Electric to build channel cooperation.

Channel leadership. Cooperation with channel participants usually is facilitated when one of the members plays a leadership role in the channel. When one firm coordinates, supports, and controls the activities of the other members of the channel, that firm is called the **channel captain.**[14] The captain may be the producer or a marketing intermediary such as a wholesaler or retailer. Power of some form usually is the means by which a channel member obtains a leadership role. Power can be obtained through ownership, contractual ties, or product and company reputations in the VMS. Power in conventional channels is difficult to achieve because often no member has significant resources to gain authority over other channel members. An interesting example of channel power occurred in 1984 when CompuShop, a Dallas-based chain of fifty retail stores, stopped carrying Apple Computer products.[15] The chain announced that it would instead carry AT&T's new personal computer, which is compatible with IBM and Compaq computers. CompuShop was one of six major retailers carrying the AT&T computer. Apple did not have enough power to counteract the influence of AT&T on the retail chain.

Often channel power is based on economic clout. Other means of achieving channel leadership include market coverage, innovative products, brand reputation, and special operating capabilities that are difficult to copy. At this time, manufacturers in most cases are the dominant firm in their channels but this may change as the number of VMSs captained by retailers increases. Examples of manufacturer captains include Deere in farm equipment, IBM in computers, Ethan Allen in furniture, and Exxon in energy. Intermediary captains include De Beers in diamonds, The Limited in women's apparel, and Mervyn's in family softgoods.

Channel conflict. Regardless of the efforts aimed at encouraging cooperation among channel participants, conflicts develop between channel members over issues such as prices, terms, inventories, territorial boundaries, competitors, and functions performed. Conflict occurs in vertical marketing systems as well as in conventional channels. Conflicts between channel members may be at different levels in the channel (vertical conflict) or between firms at a particular level (horizontal conflict).

Vertical conflict occurs when disputes arise between a manufacturer and intermediaries or between intermediaries and channel members at other levels such as retailers and distributors. An example is the irritation of department store and specialty store managers when an apparel manufacturer sells through its own factory outlet discount stores as well as through the retailers' stores. Conflicts sometimes arise because the prices charged at one level of the channel are unacceptable to channel members at other levels. A recurring conflict in fast-food channels concerns the amount retailers pay for supplies purchased from the franchisor.

Horizontal conflict may develop between intermediaries at the same level in a distribution channel regarding various operating policies and activities such as merchandise carried, geographic coverage, and cooperative advertising. For example, industrial distributors sometimes get into disputes regarding the geographic areas covered by each distributor. Violations of exclusive territory arrangements create problems between intermediaries.

What are the options available for resolving conflicts between channel members? The most extreme course of action is to terminate a relationship. Alternatively, legal action may be taken by one or both parties to resolve a dispute or claim. A third option is to try to work out the difference through discussion, negotiation, or arbitration.

DESIGNING AND MANAGING CHANNELS

Should a manufacturer distribute directly to end-users through its salesforce or through a channel of intermediaries? Although direct distribution is used by several firms marketing industrial goods and services and by some consumer-products firms such as Avon and Mary Kay, many manufacturers use longer channels of distribution. A producer may use a distribution channel because the financial resources or the capabilities to market directly to end-users are not available or because using channel intermediaries is more efficient than direct contact by the manufacturer.

Assuming distribution will be through marketing intermediaries, the channel must be designed, channel members selected, and the channel managed in VMSs. Similarly relationships between organizations must be maintained in conventional channels. Channels sometimes are formed by working arrangements between participants. An example would be a soup manufacturer's contract to buy a farmer's carrot crop or a tool wholesaler's effort to find retailers to carry his line of wrenches. Although these activities help establish channels, they are not necessarily the result of a particular channel participant's attempt to design an entire distribution channel. Nevertheless, all channel participants face design decisions of some type.

> For retailers, however, channel design is viewed from the opposite perspective from that of producers and manufacturers. That is, they look "up the channel" in an attempt to secure suppliers rather than "down the channel" towards the market as is the case for producers and manufacturers. Wholesale intermediaries face channel design decisions from both perspectives.[16]

Many of the considerations in channel design apply regardless of the channel level involved. The four major channel design and management activities are

- Identifying channel alternatives
- Selecting channel types
- Choosing channel participants
- Managing channel operations

The following discussion is based on the point of view of a manufacturer or producer concerned with establishing a channel of distribution.

Identifying channel alternatives

Because there may be more than one channel alternative, the first step is identifying the feasible channel options. The producer must decide whether to use a conventional channel or a VMS. If a VMS is to be used, a corporate, contractual, or administered arrangement must be selected. Regardless of whether a conventional or VMS channel is selected, there are three important considerations in identifying channel alternatives: the market target, the distribution intensity, and the functions intermediaries are expected to perform.

Market target. The location and characteristics of the customers and prospects targeted by the firm provide useful information for identifying the best channels for reaching the market target. The channels that provide good access to market target customers are the alternatives that should be considered by management. Thus analysis of the characteristics and location of targeted customers should indicate the distribution channels that will be most effective in reaching the customers. (Occasionally, however, even the most thorough analyses do not result in satisfactory sales, as the Marketalk about remarketing indicates.) In the late 1960s, Ethan Allen's management decided to target middle- to high-income households interested in traditional American furniture and furnishings of medium to high price and quality. This market target suggested using specialty furniture dealers rather than department stores that carry various styles and brands. Dealers would be able to concentrate on Ethan Allen's line because they would not be carrying other lines.

Distribution intensity. A related issue is deciding how intensive distribution will be. For example, should only one retail outlet in a trading area carry the manufacturer's line or should distribution be encouraged in every possi-

*Marke*TALK ///

Inventory remarketing

INVENTORY REMARKETING provides an innovative approach for reducing the risks of introducing new products. Tradewell Industries offers client companies (Polaroid, Fedders, Keds, J. P. Stevens, Quaker Oats, and others) the service of remarketing products they have been unable to sell in satisfactory amounts through normal distribution channels. This is how the service works.

Tradewell establishes with its client a fixed and firm purchase price before the first item is shipped. The maximum transaction commitment is $10 million.

SOURCE: Company information and Mark N. Vamos, "Rescuing flops—or how to buy cat litter and sell sawdust," *Business Week,* Dec. 3, 1984, p. 128.

The client may ask Tradewell to exercise the remarketing option any time within twelve months of the product's introduction.
Tradewell purchases the remaining inventory at the preagreed price.
The product is remarketed according to guidelines determined by the client.

Because clients often insist that Tradewell stay away from their usual channels to avoid disrupting established distributors or retailers, Tradewell finds alternative markets and channels of distribution for manufacturers' unsuccessful products. Consider the following examples:

4.3 million pounds of Crown Zellerbach's unsuccessful Discreet brand cat litter was sold to racetracks and

horse farms as a substitute for sawdust.
Polaroid Corporation's obsolete Zip camera became a premium offer for Johnson & Johnson's Reach toothpaste.
Swift & Company's canned "turkey hams" were sold to institutions such as schools and hospitals to avoid food store distribution as specified by the client.

Tradewell provides an unusual service that meets a need. Sales increased from $7 million in 1977 to an estimated $100 million in 1984. There is no apparent risk to the client because Tradewell does nothing if the product is successful. The up-front price contract with the client is often near the wholesale price of the product.

///

ble retail outlet in the trading area? A range of choices is available. The customer and the type of product involved are both important factors in determining how intensive distribution should be.

Frequently purchased items such as soft drinks, cigarettes, and candy typically involve **intensive distribution,** whereby a product or brand is placed in as many outlets as possible to make it widely available in the marketplace. Consumers are not likely to spend much time shopping for low-cost, frequently purchased items, so the merchandise must be conveniently located in various retail outlets. Low-cost, frequently purchased items that do not obtain wide distribution probably will not achieve satisfactory sales results. Because shelf space is limited in retail outlets, new brands that require intensive distribution may not interest wholesalers and retailers.

Selective distribution is used when a product or brand is placed in a limited number of outlets in a defined geographic area. Ethan Allen uses selective distribution through their nationwide network of Showcase Galleries. Selectivity in distribution may be important to a producer for several reasons. It allows the producer to screen channel intermediaries on the basis of capabilities, location, interest in the product, and competitive products carried. Selectivity often helps convey a favorable image of the brand. By concentrating efforts on a selected group of intermediaries, the manufacturer can provide substantial assistance to its intermediaries and costs can be lowered. Selective distribution helps encourage cooperation in the channel and avoid conflicts between participants.

Selective distribution can be beneficial for all organizations in the channel if effective intermediaries are located. Many industrial and consumer-products firms have moved toward selective distribution during the last few years because of the high costs of marketing. For example, it is often more productive to concentrate on a small percentage of total prospects whose buying power is high. A western boot manufacturer found in analyzing its dealers that less than 25 percent of the total number of dealers accounted for more than 80 percent of sales. One state, Texas, represented more than half of total sales of boots.

Selective distribution has proved to be an important factor in the success of several companies. Examples include Estée Lauder cosmetics, Evan-Picone women's apparel, Polo brand apparel, and IBM personal computers. The use of selective distribution is likely to increase in the future as producers evaluate the costs of serving their channel intermediaries and the results obtained from retailers, dealers, and distributors.

Finally, some products or brands such as Deere & Company farm equipment use **exclusive distribution,** which relies on only one outlet in a defined trading area. Although not widely used, exclusive distribution is appropriate when a product requires tight control, has complex service requirements, or has an extremely prestigious image. The approach is used in distributing expensive imported automobiles, for example. Several manufacturers of industrial products use exclusive distribution. A key issue is whether customers will patronize a retail outlet sufficiently to satisfy sales and profit expectations of the producer. In the case of industrial buyers, the exclusive dealer often calls on the buyer, so there is no problem regarding accessibility. A strong brand identity such as Deere's reputation as a farm equipment producer is an important factor in deciding to use exclusive distribution.

Functions performed by intermediaries. The functions that the manufacturer requires of intermediaries have an influence on the kind of channel to be used. For example, if the product or brand requires service and repair, will distributors or dealers perform this function? Because the range of functions that can be performed by different types of intermediaries generally is established, the task is to match the producers' needs with the capabilities of appropriate kinds of channel organizations.

Selecting channel type

The type of channel selected establishes the channel levels and types of intermediaries to be used. For example, a manufacturer of industrial adhesives may decide to use distributors to reach the industrial users in the manufacturer's market target. Such a channel consists of one level—distributors. It would be necessary to indicate the type of industrial distributors that provide coverage of the target market. Let us examine the criteria that are used in making a decision such as the one just described.

Revenue and cost estimates. A key consideration in channel selection is estimating the revenues to be obtained from a channel alternative and the costs necessary to provide needed support to the channel participants. For example, Ethan Allen's revenues increased from $8 million in 1967 to $174 million in 1978![17] The increase was due to an expanded number of stores and substantial gains in the average sales per gallery. Although the expenses necessary to obtain the revenue increases (e.g., advertising, distributing catalogues, training retailers) were substantial, the profit gains from its Showcase Gallery distribution approach made the firm one of the most profitable in the furniture industry.*

Control of intermediaries. A manufacturer or an intermediary can benefit from having control over several aspects of channel member performance. Examples include pricing, amount of effort allocated to the line, inventory stocking, retail store location and layout, extent of purchases from other suppliers, training salespeople, and advertising.[18] When considering two channel alternatives with equal revenue and cost estimates, the channel that offers the best opportunity for control of participants would be favored. One advantage of a VMS over a conventional channel is the increased opportunity for control by the channel manager.

Legal considerations. Channel arrangements may be affected by legal constraints so it is important that the legal implications of any channel alternative under consideration be investigated by the firm. While many of the federal constraints such as the antitrust laws are concerned with horizontal channel arrangements (e.g., merger of two distributors that would create a monopoly), several constraints also apply to the vertical channel. Territorial allocations, incentives for resellers' employees, commercial bribery, price discrimination by sellers, promotional allowances and services, functional discounts, delivered pricing, vertical integration, and dual distribution may all be limited by law.[19]

---

* In 1979 the firm was acquired by Interco Incorporated.

Channel availability. Finally, the choice of a particular channel ultimately may depend on the channel's availability. Many channel arrangements already exist and their members are not willing to join in forming new channels. Accordingly, the issue may hinge on the feasibility of a manufacturer's joining an existing channel rather than forming a totally new channel.

Choosing channel participants

After selecting the type of channel to be used, management must select the particular firms that the channel network will comprise. Recall the Ricoh illustration at the beginning of the chapter. Once the decision was made to distribute office copiers through exclusive dealers, potential dealers had to be identified, evaluated, and selected. One problem often encountered in selecting channel participants is the lack of good middlemen. For example, Deere & Company's exclusive farm equipment dealer network is the envy of all other firms in the industry. It is highly unlikely that many of Deere's dealers could be persuaded to work with another farm equipment manufacturer.

Assuming that a channel participant is available, selection depends on the extent that the intermediary covers the producer's market target, the estimated performance of the intermediary, the functions required by the manufacturer, and the extent to which the requirements of the producer and the intermediary are satisfied. It is important to recognize that two decisions are being made. First, the producer must decide if a particular intermediary is desired. Second, the intermediary must decide if it wants to become part of the producer's channel of distribution. Thus, the issue is not always what intermediary to select. In some situations the producer must try to persuade the intermediary to carry the producer's product.

Managing channel operations

After channels are formed they normally remain in place for many years. Several of Deere's dealers have been around for decades. Maintaining effective long-term associations requires substantial effort. The ongoing management of channel operations involves two major types of activities: (1) assistance and support and (2) evaluation and replacement.

Assistance and support. Many activities are essential to the overall performance of the channel of distribution. One of the real strengths of a VMS is the programmed approach to training and assisting channel participants by the firm responsible for managing the channel. For example, consider this description of the advantages to the franchisee of working with a franchisor such as McDonald's.

- Their affiliation with an established product name or service gives franchisees an immediate edge over the competition.

- Association with an established name also facilitates obtaining financing. Most franchisors assist franchisees in finding credit sources; some extend credit themselves.

- Tapping the expertise of the franchisor helps minimize risk. In addition, key functions such as national advertising, research, marketing, training, large-scale purchasing and technological innovation are far more effective, extensive, and affordable than they would be if the franchisee were acting independently.

■ As part of a network of similar outlets, a franchised business benefits from referrals by other franchisees or the franchisor.[20]

Evaluation and replacement. An important part of managing channels is regularly evaluating channel participants. For example, dealers may neglect a firm's products or become lax in providing service to customers. Similarly, suppliers may not produce to the quality levels desired by middlemen. Interestingly, evaluation may be conducted by more than one firm in the channel, particularly in conventional channels. Criteria often used to evaluate channel participants include amount of effort expended on the line, volume of sales, customer complaints, communications, payment of bills, and ease of working together.

When the relationship between channel participants is not satisfactory and cannot be improved, one or both firms may decide to end the relationship. Termination is relatively simple in conventional channels, but more involved in the VMS. Termination may have adverse consequences for one or both parties. For example, a dealer with an established group of customers, if terminated by a manufacturer, may persuade many of the customers to purchase a competing line. In some instances unfavorable legal consequences may occur such as a distributor's taking legal action because of the loss of the manufacturer's line.

SUMMARY

A marketing channel of distribution consists of a network of vertically aligned organizations that perform all the activities necessary to link producers of goods and services to end-users and users with producers. Marketing channels are essential to the functioning of any economic system involving division of labor and specialization. The justification for intermediaries is based on the need to reduce the number of transactions between buyers and sellers and balance discrepancies in supply and demand. Discrepancies, which are created by specialization, are eliminated by sorting and creating assortments, exchanging information, valuing goods and services, and transferring ownership.

As a business institution the channel of distribution is unique because it is a network of different organizations. Several flows, including physical, ownership, financial, information, and risk, provide the connecting links between the businesses in the network. A channel participant may not be involved in all the different flows. Physical flow moves products through the channel. Ownership flow transfers title from one participant to another. The financial flow involves the movement of money and credit throughout the channel. Information flow is the nerve center of the distribution channel. The flow of risk also occurs in the channel network.

Because many intermediaries are involved in operating channels of distribution, marketing organizations often are criticized because of the high margins believed to exist between costs and profits. A look at net profits for several kinds of intermediaries does not reveal high profit margins. Whereas distribution costs are substantial, they are largely a function of both the demands consumers place on the marketing system and the labor-intensive nature of the distribution function.

All channel participants can be placed into the categories of producers and manufacturers, wholesale and retail intermediaries, facilitating agencies, and final users. Channels are organized into various configurations of channel participants. The configurations take one of two forms: conventional channel and vertical marketing system (VMS). A VMS is managed as a coordinated network of channel participants by a channel member. Activities of the VMS are programmed so the channel functions as a system rather than as a group of loosely aligned firms characteristic of conventional channels. The relationships between channel participants are often a mixture of cooperation and conflicts.

It is important to recognize that not all manufacturers and producers use channel intermediaries. They may be used if a company does not have the financial resources or marketing capabilities to market directly to end-users. Alternatively, use of channel intermediaries may be more efficient than direct contact by the manufacturer. All channel participants face design decisions of some type. Four major activities are associated with channel design: identifying channel options, selecting channel type, choosing channel participants, and managing channel operations. Management is essential to a vertical marketing system, and management and coordination occur to some extent in conventional channels.

KEY TERMS

channel of distribution	horizontal dimension	channel cooperation
sorting	multiple channels of	channel captain
assorting	distribution	vertical conflict
bulk-breaking	conventional channels	horizontal conflict
channel flow	vertical marketing	intensive distribution
facilitating organizations	system (VMS)	selective distribution
vertical dimension	franchising	exclusive distribution

QUESTIONS FOR REVIEW AND DISCUSSION

1. What is a channel of distribution?

2. Marketing intermediaries facilitate transactions between buyers and sellers. Why is this intermediary function so important?

3. Intermediaries perform certain functions that help eliminate the discrepancies between suppliers and consumers. Explain these functions.

4. Is the channel of distribution the only way of linking buyers and sellers? Support your answer.

5. What are channel flows? What are two important characteristics of channel flows?

6. Physical flow is one of the five types of channel flows discussed. What are the others and what are the characteristics of each?

7. What is the purpose of facilitating agencies in a channel of distribution?

8. Marketing organizations' margins are not unreasonable as is believed by many people. What two factors affect distribution costs?

9. What is the distinction between a single channel and multiple channels?

10. Describe conventional channels of distribution.

11. How does a vertical marketing system differ from a conventional channel?

12. Compare the three major types of vertical marketing systems.

13. Channels are made up of organizations with different corporate affiliations that sometimes causes conflict. In what areas do conflicts occur? What are the options for resolving them?

14. Why do producers decide to go through a distribution channel rather than use direct distribution?

15. Explain the important considerations in identifying channel alternatives

16. Selecting the channel type establishes the channel levels and types of intermediaries to be used. What criteria are used in the selection process?

17. Management must select the particular firms the channel network will comprise. Assuming that a channel participant is available, on what does selection of a channel participant depend?

18. What criteria are used to evaluate channel participants and who does the evaluating for the channel?

BUILDING YOUR PORTFOLIO

Conduct a survey in your city to determine the specific retail stores that carry Rolex watches and Seiko watches. Plot the location of the stores for each brand on a city map. After completing your survey discuss the distribution approach used for each brand. Also indicate the number of stores that carry both brands. Next, go to the library reference section and using U.S. Census tract data study the characteristics of people that reside in the areas adjacent to suburban store locations. Prepare a descriptive population profile for each suburban store.

NOTES

1. This illustration is based on "Copier firm seeks top spot by developing dealer network." *Marketing News,* Oct. 1, 1982, pp. 1, 13.
2. Ibid., p. 1.
3. Ibid., p. 13.
4. Reavis Cox and Thomas F. Schutte, "A Look at Channel Management," in Philip R. McDonald (Ed.), *Marketing Involvement in Society and the Economy.* Chicago: American Marketing Association, 1969, p. 100.
5. Jeffrey H. Birnbaum, "Suppliers accuse big department stores of fudging on bills due and paying late." *Wall Street Journal,* Feb. 11, 1981, p. 56.
6. "What keeps food prices high—and rising." *Citibank,* June 1980, p. 6.
7. Ibid.
8. "How TV is revolutionizing Hollywood." *Business Week,* Feb. 21, 1983, p. 79.
9. William R. Davidson, "Changes in distributive institutions." *Journal of Marketing.* Vol. 34 (Jan. 1970), p. 7.
10. Jeffrey H. Birnbaum, "A menswear buyer for discount stores haunts lofts, cutting rooms to find bargains in volume." *Wall Street Journal,* Mar. 31, 1982, p. 48.

11. Ibid.
12. Davidson, op. cit.
13. Bert Rosenbloom, *Marketing Channels: A Management View.* Chicago: The Dryden Press, 1983, p. 361.
14. Robert W. Little, "The marketing channel: Who should lead this extracorporate organization?" *Journal of Marketing,* Jan. 1970, pp. 31–39.
15. Brian Moran, "AT&T 'Game' to battle IBM." *Advertising Age,* July 9, 1984, p. 64.
16. Rosenbloom, op. cit., p. 136.
17. *1978 Annual Report,* Ethan Allen.
18. Michael Etgar, "Selection of an effective channel control mix." *Journal of Marketing,* July 1978, p. 56.
19. An excellent discussion of channel legal constraints is provided in Louis W. Stern and Adel I. El-Ansary, *Marketing Channels,* 2nd ed. Englewood Cliffs, N.J.: Prentice-Hall, 1982, Chap. 8.
20. "Franchising: A tool for growth in the '80's," *Forbes,* June 7, 1982, Advertisement 4.

Case 12.1

Mervyn's

MERVYN'S STATED MISSION is to achieve superior financial performance by consistently providing its customers with exceptional value in softline general merchandise. This firm commitment to value has enabled Mervyn's to build one of the most successful regional businesses in the retail industry—and will continue to guide Mervyn's in its drive to become a national retail chain.

Mervyn's interprets value as the proper balance of quality, price, fashion, timeliness and customer service.

Quality at Mervyn's begins with an extensive merchandise offering that emphasizes family softgoods, including men's, women's and children's apparel, shoes and accessories, together with linens, bedding, draperies, housewares and toys.

Nearly half of Mervyn's inventory is made up of selected nationally branded items that have long-standing reputations

SOURCE: Dayton Hudson Corporation Annual Report.

for quality. The remainder consists of merchandise bearing Mervyn's own label, or other brand names, many of which are created especially for Mervyn's. Before any private-label goods reach the selling floor, they are thoroughly tested to ensure that their quality is up to Mervyn's high standards.

Mervyn's offers this unique mix of quality merchandise at highly competitive prices that deliver real value to a broad spectrum of customers on a day-in, day-out basis.

Prices are even lower on the merchandise featured in Mervyn's weekly advertising tabloid. A Mervyn's tradition and its primary promotional tool, the tabloid spotlights special prices on a selection of items from every department. Each week nearly 6 million copies of the tabloid appear in over 100 newpapers, reaching an audience of more than 10 million shoppers throughout Mervyn's markets.

Fashion is an important part of Mervyn's value merchandising formula. Mervyn's strategy is to introduce emerging

trends early in their development, offer them throughout their fashion cycle and then move on to the next trend. This approach enables Mervyn's to be fashion-right and price-right at the same time.

Timeliness in Mervyn's value formula means providing customers the right goods at the right time in the appropriate quantities. In fashion merchandise, it's the looks and styles customers want most—when they want them. In basic merchandise, it's the essential softgoods that value-conscious families need most. And in both fashion and basics, it's large assortments and a commitment to being in stock, creating a depth of merchandise selection that is unmatched in softgoods retailing.

Rounding out Mervyn's value offering is a comprehensive package of customer services usually found only in higher-priced retail formats, including credit, alterations, gift wrapping, layaways, departmental service counters, friendly and knowledgeable sales people and an unconditional return and adjustment policy.

QUESTIONS

1. Is Mervyn's part of a conventional channel of distribution or a vertical marketing system? Why?
2. Discuss the marketing intermediary functions performed by Mervyn's.

3. Describe Mervyn's marketing mix.

Case 12.2

Snow*To*Go

SCOTT POULSON founded Snow*To*Go in 1982, offering snowcones in cone-shaped retail outlets in the Fort Worth area. A year later with two retail outlets, president Poulson was planning to build over 100 outlets in 1984. He would be 15 by then. The idea occurred to Poulson at age 9 when he was on vacation eating a snowcone. His idea was to offer snow-cones in small retail outlets that look like snowcones.

SOURCE: This case is adapted from Brian Howard, "Snowcone tycoon at 14 coolly building empire," Fort Worth Star-Telegram, July 30, 1983, p. 17A.

Scott's dad helped him build the first snowcone stand. It took a few years to work out the interior design, shape, and colors. Red and white exteriors were used. The first two stores became very popular. Scott received national publicity and was invited to appear on a national morning news program. During the summer of 1983 several inquiries were made regarding the availability of franchises. A convenience store chain was interested in placing snowcone stands on its premises.

Scott earned about $11,000 in 1982 and estimated clearing $17,000 in 1983 for the snowcone season which runs from May to September. Businesses had provided free

rent and utilities for the stand locations because they helped attract business. A government program pays 85 percent of the wages for the teenagers Poulson hires.

Most of the snowcone-making is done by teenagers, trained by Poulson. He also instructs them in handling the cash register. The cones are shaped like chess pieces. The 12 ounce pawn is priced at 59 cents. Items continue through bishop, queen, king, and castle. A 40-ounce Checkmate Missile is available for $1.99. Twenty-four flavors are available. Bottle bottoms are used to shape the snow—which he says is really snow not the ice used by some vendors.

QUESTIONS

1. What advantages does Scott Poulson's venture have over competition? Can these be duplicated by others?
2. Is expansion by franchising a feasible undertaking?

3. What problems is Scott likely to encounter as he begins to expand his business?

13 Marketing by Retailers

When you finish this chapter, you will understand

□ The important role of retailers in marketing goods and services

□ Why it is necessary for retailers to develop marketing strategies

□ The various types of retailers

□ How differences in merchandise carried, pricing, ownership, and location create different kinds of retailers

□ The reasons why several important trends are occurring in retailing

Buy a Coke and play a computer game, too! New vending options for retail distribution, including electronic games like "Catch-A-Coke," give the company a competitive edge.

If you have had a key duplicated in a small shop inside a retail store in a shopping center, you probably purchased the key in one of the Cole National Corporation's more than 600 key departments. Businesses such as Cole add value to products by performing functions such as cutting metal "blanks" into keys and making dough into bread. Although keys are the company's oldest business, Cole National's sales, which exceed $0.5 billion, are generated by a variety of retail businesses including bakery outlets in malls, prescription eyeware, gifts, arts and crafts, toys, and keys. These different retail activities may seem unusual for a single firm, but there is a clear rationale to Cole's retail businesses as described by management:

We have entered businesses where the fashion elements are secondary in importance. We have entered markets where we would be, or would have the opportunity to become, one of the market leaders. We have brought some uniqueness or value added to every situation from engraving while you wait, to high technology eye examinations, to baking real French bread and cookies in the store, to having computer literate sales personnel in the electronics centers in our toy stores. All of our chains do something distinctive that others find hard to duplicate on a nationwide chain basis. Having operated on a national basis for almost our entire history, Cole National has long since passed over the problems of regional retailers trying to develop national strategies. Also, our systems' foundation was laid down long ago and regular investments are made to keep it up to date. Balanced and controlled growth have been important elements in our long-term financial strategy. While we operate a diversified retail format, we have kept our marketing and merchandising strategic elements consistent and have achieved our growth through disciplined implementation.[1]

COLE NATIONAL'S BUSINESS is specialty retailing. The firm is an example of the new wave of retailers that have moved into various types of retail activity during the past several years. These firms are well managed, profitable, innovative, aggressive, and above all, sharply tuned to consumers' needs and wants. Examples include Payless Cashways in home-improvement supplies; Dayton Hudson in bookstores, Target discount stores, and value-priced department stores; and The Limited in women's apparel. The common feature of this wide range of firms is that they are marketing intermediaries. Each has grown rapidly and profitably, which suggests that they are meeting the needs of buyers and producers.

Because of the wide scope and importance of retailers in performing marketing functions, our objective in this chapter is to examine retailers' roles and functions, the various types of retailers that operate within the marketing system, and the trends that are occurring in these institutions.

ROLE OF RETAILERS

Retailing is the activities involved in selling (or renting) goods and services to end-users, including households, individuals, and others who are purchasing for final consumption. Retailing activities include purchasing goods and services for sale, storing, displaying, pricing, advertising, selling, financing, servicing, and other activities necessary to complete transactions with buyers. The **retailer** occupies the level in the channel of distribution that connects with the final consumer. The term **dealer** also is used to identify certain types of retailers, specifically those handling goods or services purchased by business end-users. To gain a better understanding of the role of retailers it is revealing to look at the size and scope of retailing in the economy today and to examine retailer marketing strategies.

Size and scope of retailing

Importance. The importance of retailing in the United States is conveyed by the following statistics:

■ More than 1.9 million retailers operate in the United States.
■ One of seven working persons (15.6 million in 1983) is employed in retailing.

- Nearly one of five employees in retailing is a manager, so many job opportunities for college graduates are available.
- Most people become entrepreneurs through retailing. Retailing often is easy to enter, although the failure rate of new retailers is quite high.
- Retailing renders a valuable service to customers by reducing the complexities and costs of buying and other marketing functions.[2]

Retailing clearly is an essential activity in business that affects all of us in various ways in our roles as buyers, workers, entrepreneurs, and citizens.

Selected merchandise categories. The sales, employees, and hourly earnings of selected types of retailers are shown in Exhibit 13.1. Some interesting trends are indicated. Department store employment remained nearly constant from 1972 to 1985, reflecting an increase in the number of self-service checkout counters. In contrast, employment in eating and drinking places increased rapidly to 1980 and then remained relatively constant through 1985. The statistics in Exhibit 13.1 indicate how large retailing is in the economy, with total retail sales in 1985 forecast at $1.4 trillion.

Let us take a closer look at food retailing. Major trends in the industry include growth of the number of large combination superstores such as the Skaggs Alpha Beta combination supermarket and drug stores, growth of off-price food warehouse stores, placement of automated teller machines (ATMs) in stores, and growth of the demand for generic products. The following profile highlights some important aspects of the food industry:

- Sales were $250 billion in 1982 compared with $93 billion in 1972.
- Profits in 1982 averaged approximately 1.2 percent of sales.
- By 1985 an estimated 8000 stores had electronic scanners (computer-assisted checkout) compared with 200 in 1977.
- Labor-intensive food retailing employed approximately 2.5 million persons in 1982.
- By 1983 demand was expanding for gourmet-type foods, fresh-baked goods, fresh seafood, and cut flowers.[3]

Exhibit 13.1 Characteristics of selected merchandise categories (in millions of current dollars except as noted)

	1972	1980	1981	1982	Compound annual rate of growth 1972–1982	1983[1]	1984[1]	1985[2]
Retail trade, total								
Sales	440,069	956,655	1,038,790	1,074,561	9.4	1,173,966	1,297,232	1,420,469
Total employment (000)	11,836	15,292	15,395	15,258	2.7	15,281	15,357	15,434
Department stores								
Sales	47,287	94,185	103,609	107,863	8.8	116,658	127,741	139,876
Total employment (000)	1,706	1,805	1,891	1,885	1.3	1,885	1,895	1,900
Apparel and accessory stores								
Sales	24,127	44,487	47,755	51,387	7.5	54,005	58,860	63,569
Total employment (000)	784	964	981	970	2.3	951	970	975
Eating and drinking places								
Sales	36,180	86,612	94,070	104,715	11.0	115,710	127,281	140,000
Total employment (000)	2,860	4,818	4,833	4,781	5.5	4,888	5,018	5,201

SOURCE: U.S. Department of Commerce, *1983 U.S. Industrial Outlook*, Washington, D.C.: U.S. Government Printing Office, Jan. 1983, p. 48-2, and 1985 *U.S. Industrial Outlook*, p. 54-1.
[1] Estimated
[2] Forecast

Improving productivity, often calculated as sales per employee hour, is a continuing problem for food retailers because of the labor-intensive nature of in-store operations. Computerized inventory management and ordering methods have greatly increased efficiency in the industry during recent years.

Risks in retailing. The poor business conditions in the United States and throughout the world in the early 1980s increased the already high risk of failure in retailing.

> Three major retailers were forced into bankruptcy. Wickes Companies is the largest retailer ever to file for bankruptcy, surpassing the W. T. Grant Company failure. In addition, Fed-Mart Corporation, with sales in excess of $1 billion in 1981, ceased operations in 1982, and KDT Industries, a discount retailer with sales of $741 million, also filed for bankruptcy. Moreover, F. W. Woolworth shut down its Woolco discount stores at the end of 1982, and major food retailers closed hundreds of stores. Also in 1982, nearly 900 automobile dealerships failed, along with numerous small- and medium-size retailers.[4]

In addition to the widely publicized failures of major retailers, countless small retailers also failed. Retailing is relatively easy to enter compared with manufacturing because of the limited financial investment required to open a store. Often people with little or no experience start a business. A few learn quickly and succeed, but many fail—usually from causes such as inability to define and reach appropriate target markets or lack of adequate working capital to overcome the low sales of the business's startup period.

Retailer strategies

Marketing management in a retail organization is somewhat different from management in a manufacturing or wholesale organization. The difference becomes apparent when the purchasing functions of retailers are examined. They must decide what products to purchase and what brand or brands of each product to carry. Consider, for example, ComputerLand, a retailer with more than 500 stores throughout the world. With more than 100 brands of desktop computers that retail from $3000 to $10,000, no retailer can effectively handle more than a few brands.

> At ComputerLand, manufacturers must survive a series of evaluations to be represented in the retail chain's centralized inventory, from which more than 300 ComputerLand stores select their merchandise. Only about 20 computer makers are represented today. Typically, a ComputerLand store will carry four to six computer systems. All stores carry the IBM desktop computer; most carry Apple machines. The stores pick and choose among such brands as Commodore, Atari, Fortune, Altos, Cromemco, Xerox, NorthStar and Zenith according to demand in their area, says Ed Faber, president of ComputerLand.
>
> Once selected, a computer system still runs the risk of being dropped if a ComputerLand manager decides it is falling behind the competition. The ComputerLand store in Niles, Ill., recently dropped the Commodore International Ltd. line in part because "it just couldn't compete with the Apple," according to store manager Howard Herbin.[5]

The retailer is faced with two important marketing tasks: deciding what customers to *target* and assembling a *marketing mix*. An important issue that affects both tasks is whether the retailer will manage the distribution channel or instead be a participant in an existing channel. A retail chain such as ComputerLand exercises a considerable amount of power with its suppliers and must make several marketing strategy decisions. In contrast, a McDonald's franchisee primarily is concerned with operational activities because major strategy decisions (e.g., new products, advertising, price) are coordinated by the franchisor.

Targeting. Two major factors help determine the customers a retailer will attract: store location and how the store is perceived by the buyer. Both must be considered when the market target to be served by the retailer is determined. The retailer's market target must first be identified. A location should be chosen that is accessible to the people in the firm's market target. For example, a shoe store targeting upper-middle-class men may be located in the financial district of a major city, such as the LaSalle Street area in Chicago. After selecting a particular location the retailer can further influence the type of people attracted by the store. The merchandise carried, prices, advertising, and personal selling will appeal to some of the people who shop in the store, but not to others. Even the decor of the store can have a marked effect on customers.

> In choosing the Product Centers' decor, IBM revealed retailing naivete. Anxious not to appear cold and remote, it abandoned its traditional icy blue and decorated the centers bright red. "Red doesn't just irritate bulls," remarks Warren Winger, chairman of CompuShop, a Dallas-based chain, "it makes salesmen hostile and alarms customers."[6]

Thus because both location and customer perception of the retailer help determine patronage, the retailer must first identify the market that will be targeted and then locate in a place that is convenient for customers. The marketing program offered by the retailer must also be designed to meet the needs of the market target.

Characteristics of the marketing mix. The retailer's marketing mix consists of the line or lines of merchandise carried, services provided, hours of operation, the type and location of stores, prices, advertising, sales promotion, and personal selling. These actions *position* the retailer by differentiating it from competitors. The chart in Exhibit 13.2 illustrates how retailers differ by merchandise variety (number of different lines carried) and merchandise assortment (amount or depth within each line).[7]

Kids "R" Us is an interesting retailer planning to use the same retail mix strategy for children's wear that has worked so well for toys. Consider this satisfied customer:

> Mrs. Vangrofsky is delighted with the $17 Osh Kosh brand overalls she has found here for $11.97. Kids "R" Us is "going to change my shopping habits for sure," she says. In the past, she has "shopped sales" at fancy department stores like Bloomingdale's, Macy's and Saks Fifth Avenue. But, she says, if Kids "R" Us offers the same merchandise for less money, "why should I go to a department store?"[8]

Kids "R" Us is another example of the explosive growth of off-price retailing. The chain offers large discounts, wide assortments, plenty of parking, fast service, and a liberal return policy. This example highlights an important characteristic of retailing: When the same brands are available to many retailers, price can be used to create an advantage over competition. This is one reason why many retailers market their own private brands.

Manage or be a participant. A key strategic decision is whether the retailer wants to manage the distribution channel or to be a participant. Often this

It's about time you got financial advice that you could understand.

Along with offering insurance, investment, and real estate services, Sears, Roebuck and Co. offers another intangible: trust. Sears believes that Hal Holbrook, whom the public views as very trustworthy, is a suitable spokesperson for its financial services. (Courtesy of Sears, Roebuck and Co., 1984)

decision is made during the process of growth, rather than when the retail business is founded. Typically, the small retailer has no choice but to join an existing channel until the firm grows large enough to be able to influence channel operations. After gaining experience and financial resources, some retailers attempt to manage their channels. One means of doing this is to integrate backward to the wholesaling or manufacturing level. In 1978, The Limited, a women's apparel retailer, acquired Mast Industries, one of the largest apparel contractors in the world. The Limited grew from one store in 1963 to a billion-dollar company in twenty years. The firm has evolved from a channel member to channel captain of a corporate-owned vertical marketing system.

TYPES OF RETAILERS

We come into contact with different types of retailers every day when purchasing goods and services. Retailers can be classified according to (1) merchandise carried, (2) pricing strategy, (3) type of ownership, (4) location, and (5) store or nonstore sales. We discuss each of these ways of classifying retail outlets.

Merchandise carried

One way of distinguishing between retailers is according to whether they carry services or products. Because many of the ways of classifying retailers apply to both goods and service retailers, before we examine merchandise categories we identify several types of services. A wide variety of **service retailers** exists, including public accounting firms, medical and dental services, banks and other financial institutions, airlines, home repair contractors, movie theaters, and pest control firms. A service retailer sells an intangible product rather than tangible goods. Service retailers are growing

Exhibit 13.2 Retailers vary in the variety and assortment of merchandise

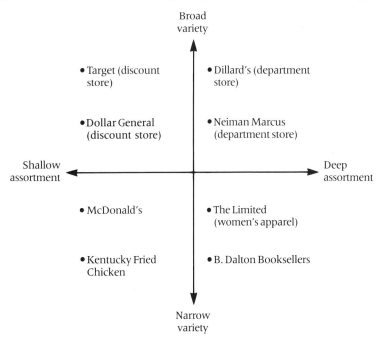

more rapidly in the United States than product retailers. One example is Sears, Roebuck & Company, the world's largest retailer of general merchandise. In addition to Allstate Insurance, which has been a Sears unit for several decades, the department store retailer acquired Coldwell Banker (real estate broker) and Dean Witter (stockbroker) in 1981. Service retailing not only includes business firms but also not-for-profit organizations such as zoos, public transportation, and libraries. Universities as well are retailers of services. Some generate substantial profits from continuing education and executive development programs.

Turning now to merchandise retailers, we saw previously in Exhibit 12.2 how retailers differ according to the variety and assortment of items offered. Retailers can be classified according to the variety of product lines sold. Let us examine the major types of stores.

Department store. Department stores offer more product lines than other retailers and considerable depth of assortment within each line. Many department stores belong to retail chains. These stores provide a wide range of services. A full-line department store carries apparel and soft goods, household linens and dry goods, furniture, appliances, jewelry, and home entertainment products. The three major kinds of department stores are traditional, mass merchandisers, and discount. **Traditional department stores** offer a wide range of merchandise carried in several departments at prices yielding high margins. Merchandise is purchased through sales clerks, and many services are offered including credit, restaurants, hairdressing salons, gift wrapping, and decorating advice. **Mass merchandisers** price goods lower than traditional department stores, provide more limited services, and may process sales through checkout counters. **Discount department stores** offer large discounts, few if any services, austere facilities, and self-service checkout counters. Examples of each are shown in Exhibit 13.3. The existence of high margins between the costs of merchandise offered and retail prices of traditional department stores stimulated the development of various discount retailers. Retailer price strategies are discussed later in the chapter.

Specialty store. **Specialty stores** typically concentrate on one line or a few lines of merchandise. Examples include The Limited (women's apparel),

Exhibit 13.3 Illustrative profile of three department store retailers

Traditional
HUDSON BAY COMPANY
Largest Canadian department store chain, with sales of $5.2 billion and 585 stores.

Diversified into real estate and energy; wholesale and fur business is 13% of sales.

Mass Merchandiser
J. C. PENNEY COMPANY
Third largest general merchandise retailer in the United States, with $14.5 billion in sales.

Private-label products comprise 60% of sales; Penney is increasing emphasis on fashion merchandise and other soft goods.

Discount
DOLLAR GENERAL CORP.
More than 1000 stores in rural Sunbelt locations, with sales of $630 million.

Merchandise mix: soft goods, 54%; housewares, 22%; health and beauty aids, 18%; shoes, 6%; average store size: 5000 sq. ft.

SOURCE: *The Value Line Investment Survey,* 1985.

ComputerLand (small computers), Toys "R" Us (toys), Gordon's (jewelry), and Singer Sewing Centers (sewing machines). Assortment normally is deep, and some of these retailers offer buyers assistance and advice in product use. Specialty stores are a substantial portion of the retailers located in large shopping malls.

Catalogue showroom. **Catalogue showrooms** offer low prices, national brands, and small shopping areas with warehouse space adjacent to retail display areas. By limiting display, theft losses are reduced. Operating costs also are kept low by limiting store personnel. Typically shoppers review the widely distributed catalogues before visiting the store. The buyer must complete an order blank, which is processed, before the item is provided to the buyer at a central location. During the 1970s this form of retailing expanded rapidly. Best Products, Service Merchandise, and Modern Merchandising are the three largest chains today. Best's 1985 sales exceeded $2.4 billion compared with $200 million in 1975.

Food and drug retailers. The profile of the food retailing industry shown previously provides an interesting description of food and drug retailers. Food retailers greatly outnumber drug retailers. The three major types of **food and drug retailers** are supermarket and superdrug stores, convenience stores, and combination stores. **Supermarket and superdrug stores** are large self-service stores that sell high-volume foods or drugs at low margins. Drug stores sell general merchandise lines in addition to prescriptions and health and beauty aids. The typical food supermarket chain makes approximately one penny of net profit on each dollar of sales. High volume and rapid turnover of goods enable these stores to operate profitably on extremely small margins. Usually customers select merchandise from aisles and place it in carts for movement to checkout counters. Most food and drug supermarkets are part of regional or national chains. Few single independently owned grocery or drug stores exist today. Examples of food supermarkets are Kroger, Safeway, A&P, and Winn-Dixie. Drug chains include SuperX, Revco, Walgreen, and Longs.

Convenience stores, of which Seven-Eleven is an example, are much smaller than supermarkets. They offer a limited range of food items to meet the needs of people purchasing frequently used products such as bread, milk, and cigarettes. Prices are higher than supermarkets. Stores are located near residential areas to provide easy access by automobile, and store hours usually are longer than those of other businesses.

Combination stores such as Skaggs Alpha Beta carry many of the items that both supermarket and superdrug stores offer. Combination stores are larger than conventional supermarket or superdrug stores, but they are similar regarding pricing strategies and operating practices. The term **superstore** is also used to describe these large combination food and nonfood retailers. They range in size from 35,000 to 60,000 square feet. Several food chains are building combination-type stores. Giant superstores called **hypermarkets** have become popular in Europe. These combination supermarket and discount department stores are larger than U.S. combination stores and superstores (100,000 to 200,000 square feet), and the merchandise mix is expanded to include appliances, clothing, and several other nonfood and nondrug items. Hypermarkets in West Germany accounted for approximately a 5 percent retail market share in 1970, 13 percent in 1978, and an estimated 16 percent in 1990.[9] By 1990 independents' market share of West German retail sales will shrink to approximately 11 percent compared with 22 percent in 1970.

An interesting U.S. version of the hypermarket is the Price Club, a unique retailing hybrid that is part cash-and-carry grocery and part discount department store.[10] Operating in low-rent warehouse facilities exceeding 100,000 square feet, members are recruited selectively and include local retailers and professionals and employees of certain banks, utilities, and government offices. Retailers find Price's items priced so low that they buy large quantities for resale. For example, Price Club's cigarettes are priced 20 percent less than those in local supermarkets. The retailer does not advertise. Founded in 1976, by 1985 Price Club sales had grown to $1.8 billion generated by 20 warehouse stores in California, Arizona, and Virginia.

New wave of retailers. In addition to the superstores and combination stores that became important in food and drug retailing during the last decade, several other types of retailers experienced rapid expansion. These include hobby and craft centers (Tandycrafts), home decorating specialty stores (Color Tile), paint and decorating supermarkets (Sherwin-Williams home decorating centers), and super hardware stores such as Ace Hardware. Still another firm, Comp-U-Card International, hopes to triple sales to $27 million in its main business—a 60,000-item catalogue available only through personal computers (see Marketech). These new retailers have grown rapidly, and many are more profitable than independent retailers with similar lines. Moveover, they pose real threats to independent retailers because the new retailers obtain sales that previously went to the smaller independents.

Pricing strategies

Retailers offer a wide spectrum of prices from low to high. Substantial variations in the price of the same brand can be found among retailers. Four categories of retailers represent the range of pricing strategies used by retail-

Marke**TECH** □ □ □ □ □ □ □ □ □ □ □ □ □ □ □ □ □ □

Computerizing bargain hunting

COMP-U-CARD INTERNATIONAL offers consumers an in-home shopping service using television sets or personal computers linked to two-way cable systems. Products are viewed and items ordered by telephone. Because electronic shopping is not yet widespread—not enough people have the necessary equipment—bargain hunting using the Comp-U-Card toll-free (800) number has proved successful for the firm.

SOURCE: Peter Petre, "The man who computerized bargain hunting," *Fortune,* July 9, 1984, p. 137. Reprinted by permission from *Fortune* Magazine.

The service can be joined for a $25 annual membership fee. There are more than 700,000 members, and the list is growing every day. Dialing the 800 number enables members to find out what products are available and their prices. Orders are also placed by telephone. Comp-U-Card lists more than 60,000 brand-name products including Whirlpool washers, Panasonic home entertainment equipment, and Wedgewood china selling at 20 to 40 percent below list prices. The firm orders the item for the buyer from the lowest-priced supplier, and the item is delivered by United Parcel Service. Comp-U-Card's

sales in 1984 should exceed $40 million.

Comp-U-Card built its membership base by working through Banc One, an innovative bank holding company in Columbus, Ohio ($7 billion in assets). Free Visa cards were offered with memberships. Mailings were sent to 22 million middle-class households in 1982. The firm has not given up its plans to offer electronic shopping and is running some market tests. Until the need for electronic shopping develops, the telephone ordering system should provide Comp-U-Card with a promising business opportunity.

□ □

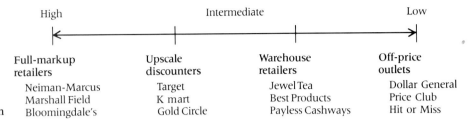

Exhibit 13.4   The retail pricing spectrum

ers. **Full-markup retailers** price to maintain substantial margins between the cost of merchandise and the selling price. Typically, department stores and other full-markup retailers offer a variety of services including attractive and conveniently located stores. Other retailers such as **upscale discounters** pose an increasing threat to high-margin retailers. Upscale discounters often are located near full-price retailers and use low prices to attract business from full-price department and specialty stores. **Warehouse retailers** offer lower prices than upscale discounters in stores that consciously present a "stripped-down" image. Finally, **off-price outlets** operate at the low end of the pricing spectrum, marketing merchandise that may be irregular, manufacturers' closeouts, or otherwise purchased at low cost to the off-price retailer. Examples of retailers using each of the four pricing strategies are shown in Exhibit 13.4.

Type of ownership

Another way of classifying retailers is whether the business is independent, part of a corporate chain, or a member of a cooperative. The **independent retailer** is the predominant type of retailer based on number of stores. Yet based on dollar volume of sales, the independent retailer accounts for approximately one-fourth of total retail sales.[11] Moreover, the importance of the independent retailer for many lines of merchandise continues to decline as **corporate-owned and franchised chains** expand their coverage in the marketplace, particularly in metropolitan areas. Examples of corporate-owned chains are Sherwin-Williams in paint and Radio Shack in electronics. Several fast-food chains have franchised outlets. Joining **retailer cooperatives** such as IGA food stores is one means of gaining some of the advantages of the retail chains while at the same time remaining independent. One of the purported advantages of purchasing a retail store franchise from a corporate franchisor is staying independent but benefiting from the brand name and experience of the chain.

Location

Retailers also can be classified according to where they are located in a metropolitan area. Stores primarily are found in three geographic locations: downtown central business districts, street and highway segments or strips, and shopping centers. Some stores also are located alone throughout a city and in rural areas.

Central business district retailers. During the last twenty-five years many retailers have moved from downtown to suburban locations, following the movement of people from central city locations. Several factors were responsible for the decline of **central business district (CBD) retailers** including traffic congestion, lack of parking, crime, and the convenience of suburban shopping. Nevertheless, a substantial amount of CBD retail activity continues. In several cities, urban renewal programs are revitalizing retailing at downtown locations. The Rouse Company, a leading shopping center developer of downtown areas, has been particularly successful in CBD retail development. For example, Grand Avenue Rouse completed a $70 million downtown mall complex in Milwaukee in 1982.[12] Eight months after the opening the 160 shops continued to attract 60,000 shoppers on a weekend. Near the center of the complex, a Victorian retail arcade, originally built in 1916, was restored and topped by a vaulted skylight and rotunda.

Single store and strip retailers. Some retailers locate away from groups of stores because they can obtain retail store space at reasonable rates and buyers are willing to travel to single store locations. Retailers also often are found along street and highway segments called **strip developments.** For example, such strips frequently are found at the edge of college campuses.

Shopping centers. Shopping centers range from small neighborhood retail store developments with adjacent parking to large, multilevel regional shopping malls. Major features of shopping centers are that they are planned by a developer and space is leased to different retailers. The objective is to obtain a group of retailers that cover a wide range of retail product lines. Expanding this range of retail products may soon be Saturn Corporation—a General Motors subsidiary that by 1990 will produce subcompact

Exhibit 13.5   Illustrative shopping center store layout plan

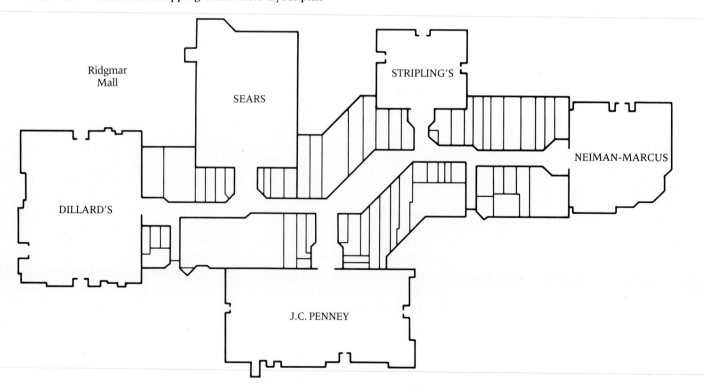

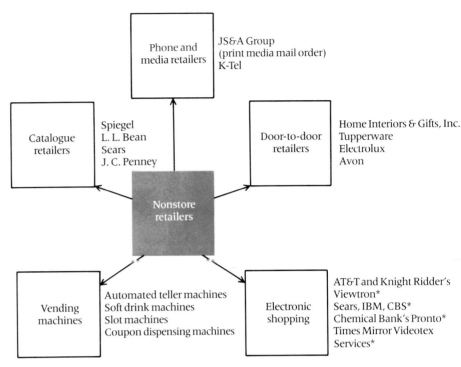

Exhibit 13.6 Types of nonstore retailers

*field testing

cars—which hopes to locate some of its dealerships in nontraditional locations such as shopping malls.[13]

Large malls typically have two or more department stores, called **anchor stores,** that help attract buyers to the mall location. For example, Gimbels and the Boston Store anchor the four-block-long mall in Rouse's Milwaukee downtown complex. Large malls may contain more than 100 retail stores. An illustration of a mall layout is shown in Exhibit 13.5. Food and drug supermarkets are used as anchors for small shopping centers.

Nonstore retailers

This basis of retailer classification is whether consumers travel to a retail store to shop or instead make contact with the retailer by mail, telephone, door-to-door salesperson, vending machine, or electronic methods (see Exhibit 13.6). Moving the product from producer to consumer through the latter channels is called **direct marketing.** More than $150 billion was spent through direct-marketing distribution channels in 1983. Direct marketing, let us emphasize, is not an industry but a distribution channel, and mass merchandisers, merchants who sell their products in stores, are direct marketing's competition.

Mail-order retailers. Mail-order retailing experienced explosive growth during the last decade, although it has been around for approximately 100 years. Sears, Roebuck and Montgomery Ward were well established in catalogue retailing by the early 1900s. Today, many firms are active in this market. For example, in 1982 five billion copies of 4000 different catalogues were placed in mailboxes.[14] In the same year Spiegel, the number-four mail-order retailer, distributed 300,000 copies of a test catalogue entitled *Private Lives,* which featured lingerie, and received 7500 orders averaging $80 each. Sears, Roebuck has two dozen specialty catalogues.

Although statistics on this sector of retailing are difficult to obtain, one estimate placed 1982 sales at $35 billion.[15] Consumers will make 15 percent of their purchases by mail in 1985; and, because catalogue orders are growing faster than in-store purchases, 20 percent of all retail transactions will be made by mail by the end of the decade.[16]

Mail-order food sales, in 1980 alone, reached $700 million, but this was spread over approximately 500 mail-order houses. Despite the huge numbers of catalogue companies, newcomers are still moving into the business, among them

> Des FitzGerald, who last year on some $20,000 launched his Duck Trap River Fish Farm in Lincolnville, Me. to sell smoked trout. FitzGerald expects to turn a profit this Christmas by selling 1,000 boxes of the delicacy at $20 per box.[17]

The fierce competition for customers by mail-order firms quite likely will lead eventually to an industry *shakeout*—some catalogue companies will exit from the market. As this market moves toward maturity, many small firms may not be able to continue to operate profitably. Montgomery Ward dropped catalogue sales in 1985.

Telephone and media retailers. These retailers use telephone contact and advertising media such as television, radio, newspapers, and magazines to inform and persuade consumers to buy their products. Television advertisements often are used in combination with toll-free telephone numbers (numbers preceded by 800) to market records, cookware, and other products. *The Wall Street Journal* and *National Geographic* advertise for subscrip-

Pier 1 imports *by Post*

In 1983 Pier 1 tried marketing its merchandise by mail. Two years later the catalogue venture was halted due to low profit. Though 74 percent of U.S. households purchased a product by mail order in 1985, most catalogue shoppers rated the experience fair to poor, according to a study by Stone & Adler, a direct-marketing agency. Catalogues are useful for comparison shopping and locating unusual products, but many people are reluctant to order through them because of concerns about returning merchandise. (By permission of Pier 1 Imports, Inc.)

tions on radio and television. Many products and services not available in stores are brought to the attention of potential buyers through advertising. Advertisements that ask buyers to telephone or send their orders to the advertiser are a form of direct, nonstore marketing.

Telephone marketing, or telemarketing, has become one of the fastest-growing methods of marketing a wide variety of products including insurance, cameras, stocks, political candidates, and charities. The telephone can be used in two ways to make contact between buyers and sellers: (1) inbound service—taking orders and queries from buyers calling a toll-free (800) number—and (2) outbound contacts—making unsolicited "cold calls" to sell products.[18] One estimate places telemarketing sales of goods and services at $75 billion annually, expanding 15 to 20 percent a year. Outbound calls through telephone service bureaus cost clients $30 to $50 an hour, and inbound calls cost $1 or more each. Although more expensive than direct or media advertising, telemarketing is much less expensive than face-to-face selling. Many industrial product marketers are also using telemarketing.

Door-to-door retailers. Perhaps the oldest form of nonstore retailing is door-to-door, or on-the-premises, selling. These retailers use salespersons to contact potential buyers in their homes and other nonstore locations. The typical compensation arrangement for salespersons is a commission on sales. Some of those retailers such as Fuller Brush, Avon cosmetics, and World Book Encyclopedia call on individual households. Others such as Tupperware persuade a household member to invite friends to a party at which goods will be displayed. Mary Crowley, a successful in-the-home retailer, founded Home Interiors & Gifts in 1957.[19] Today the firm, which sells through in-home parties, has sales of more than $400 million. The firm purchases more than 500 items from twenty suppliers. The items are sold at up to 100 percent markup by an in-home displayer who receives two-thirds of the markup. Displayers, on the average, earn $3500 in commissions a year. Like Avon, Mary Kay Cosmetics, Amway, and Shaklee, successful salespersons are encouraged to become managers and recruit salespersons. A new manager may earn $12,000 a year, and some senior managers earn more than $100,000.

Vending machines. Vending machines are an important part of retailing, dispensing everything from food and beverages to entertainment and coupons. Modern electronic vending machines are capable of performing a variety of tasks. Some of the new soft drink machines can even talk electronically. We come into contact with vending machines in locations such as banks, supermarkets, hotels, offices, and schools. Typically, the products dispensed by machine cost more than if they were purchased in a store. For example, postage stamps from a machine in a hotel lobby cost more than stamps purchased at a U.S. post office. Computerized coupon dispensing machines, however, do not cost consumers a single cent to use. These machines, now largely in the testing stage, are providing mail-in coupons to food store customers while providing greater distribution control to manufacturers. A system developed by Electronic Advertising Network has expanded to approximately 240 supermarkets, including three national chains—Safeway, Kroger, and Skaggs Alpha Beta (see Marketalk).

*Marke*TALK ///

In-store pioneers clip coupon competition

WITHIN THE NEXT FEW months, package-goods marketers will be presented with at least three alternative coupon-distribution schemes, all based on in-store distribution. They are designed to combat the clutter and exclusivity problems found in free-standing newspaper inserts and the rising cost of direct mail.

Although coupon distribution is strong so far—160 billion coupons were distributed last year, up from 142 billion in 1983—advertisers have grown much more vocal in their complaints. And at least three companies feel the time is right to offer alternatives.

Coupon Counter, Westwood, Mass., developer and distributor of an automated in-store coupon vending machine, plans to place its machines in one-third of the country by yearend and nationwide by the end of 1987, based on results in the Boston and Providence, R.I., markets since November.

Actmedia, Westhampton Beach, N.Y., a company that places advertising on shopping carts and in supermarket aisles, plans a national rollout next month of its in-store coupon-distribution scheme. It will use its 3,000-strong field force to distribute coupon books to consumers as they walk into the store during peak shopping periods.

And Retail Insights is gearing up for a test in Chicago this summer of its coupon vending machines.

Unlike Coupon Counter's machines, which print out a fixed number of coupons at a time, consumers will be able to select the coupons of their choice.

At dairy marketer H.P. Hood, Boston, cultured products product manager Michael McManama said he has tested the Coupon Counter system.

"Combining coupon distribution on their system with trade-allowance tie-ins resulted in a 10% redemption rate on cottage cheese and sour cream. That's twice the redemption rate we get from fsis [free-standing inserts] and triple what we get from r.o.p. [run of press]," he said.

Mr. McManama said advertisers will have to be cautious in their use of in-store distribution because of the increased redemption rate, but he added that if all the costs for fsis and in-store distribution are added up, in-store distribution is more efficient.

That's because coupons are distributed

SOURCE: "In-store pioneers clip coupon competition," *Advertising Age,* Jan. 24, 1985, p. 6. Reprinted with permission. Copyright 1985 by Crain Communications, Inc.

only to shoppers, a point emphasized by the promoters of in-store couponing.

Coupon Counter, founded two years ago, began a test program with six machines in April and rolled out 360 dispensers in November. It covers a market that includes 2.4 million households in Rhode Island and the Boston metropolitan area. Mark McLean, vp-marketing, said the coupons dispensed by his machines resulted in a redemption rate three times greater than fsis or direct mail.

While Mr. McLean concedes that high redemption rates have not been a goal of advertisers, he said other features of Coupon Counter result in a favorable promotional package.

To receive coupons from the in-store machine, the consumer must have a Coupon Counter access card. When the card is used, the user's code is read by the machine and, together with a store code, printed on the strip of coupons dispensed by the machine. Thus the identity of each consumer who redeems a particular coupon can be determined later, providing marketers with valuable information.

He also noted that since the coupons are dispensed in the store, their face value can be somewhat less and still result in a sale. Coupons distributed via direct mail or fsis, he said, have an average face value of 25¢. The coupons distributed via the machines, he said, have a face value averaging 20¢.

The machines also seem to solve part of the problem of misredemption by limiting access to consumers who have cards. Further, the machines have a memory that limits consumers to one strip of coupons per store per week.

Participating advertisers pay $8 per thousand coupons distributed, compared with the $5 to $6 per thousand paid to distribute coupons in fsis.

At Actmedia, president Bruce Failing said his approach, the personal distribution of coupons during peak sales periods, offered advantages over the vending machine approach.

"We'll be there force-feeding books of up to 15 coupons to every consumer that walks in the store," he said. "Just imagine what it would be like in a busy supermarket if all you had was a machine. Most shoppers wouldn't bother waiting in a long line just to get their coupons."

Mr. Failing said Actmedia plans additional support for its coupon distribution. Before distributing coupons, he said, his sales force will place promotional display cards in the aisles adjacent to those products for which consumers have coupons. They also will set up a display that fea-

tures all the goods being promoted.

In trial tests around the country, he said, the Actmedia program has resulted in up to 46% more product movement, compared to an average of 15% for fsis and 25% for direct mail.

Mr. Failing also said that fraudulent redemption would decline because of the limited distribution compared with fsis or direct mail.

Actmedia, he said, will begin the rollout of the program next month, with 5,000 stores participating out of the 7,500 stores it serves with advertising. Costs to the advertisers will run $16.50 per thousand coupons distributed, with an additional fee of $2 per thousand coupons printed. Mr. Failing said that although these rates appeared high, the true cost to the advertiser should be calculated on a cost-per-product-moved basis.

That same argument is used by Ned Whitmore, vp-sales of Retail Insight. The company is using an entirely different approach to pricing, but one he said that will result in a low cost-per-product-moved. The Retail Insight machine, known as Video Coupons, is housed in a kiosk and employs laser-disc technology. Standing at the kiosk, the consumer is shown on a video screen pictures of the products being promoted. By pressing a button next to the picture, a coupon is printed in four seconds. If the manufacturer is participating in the bonus coupon offer, a second coupon for another product is printed at the same time.

Each kiosk is programed to display up to 32 different products. The advertiser pays $12,500 per week per product.

Like Coupon Counter, Video Coupons will be able to capture significant information about the consumers selecting and redeeming coupons. The machines are activated by inserting any magnetic-stripe credit card. By reading the stripe, the company can capture the names and addresses of the consumers.

Mr. Whitmore said, however, names would not be released initially. "We are very much concerned about protecting individual rights to privacy. We will still be able to compile demographic information that was previously unavailable."

Mr. Whitmore said his approach offered marketers the most security against misredemption. "Our machines only dispense coupons that the consumer wants, so our redemption rate will be very high."

Video Coupons will begin its test this summer in the Chicago [area], where Mr. Whitmore said he has lined up more than 300 supermarkets.

///

Vending machines are available around the clock, in convenient locations, and normally easy to use. Interestingly, financial institutions have encountered some problems in getting consumers to use automated teller machines because of their perceived complexity. Sometimes, vending machines do not work properly, keeping your money and not dispensing the item you selected. And, once dispensed, a vending machine purchase cannot be returned. For the vendor, theft of coins is often a problem so when selecting machine locations retailers must consider the potential for theft.

Electronic shopping. This new form of retailing, called **videotex,** offers both opportunities and threats to retailers. Videotex is a system for use by households and businesses to retrieve information from remote data bases using a terminal or television set and telephone lines. The major parts of a videotex system are shown in Exhibit 13.7. These systems deliver text and other information services to consumers using television or other video devices for display.

> Videotex can be described as the generic term for a developing, interactive medium that delivers text and visual information directly to consumers. It can be used to reach either mass or tightly targeted audiences in both home and business markets. The user interacts with the system via a handheld keypad, pushbutton console, or keyboard. Desired information is retrieved by user command from one or more public/private data bases through telephone lines, cable or broadcast signals, with text or graphics displayed on a television screen or other video device.[20]

Viewtron, AT&T's first full-service, commercial videotex offering, went into operation in October 1983 in several Florida cities. The system can

Though Telidon NAPLPS, a Canadian videotex company, apparently prospers, Knight-Ridder, Times Mirror, and Honeywell videotex services had not by mid-1985 made any money. Industry experts estimate no real growth until the 1990s: Videotex is still too expensive and hard to use, and no one has figured out just what the consumer wants. (Reproduced by permission of the Minister of Supply and Services, Canada)

A central computer controls the videotex systems. Users communicate with the *host* computer to request information from the *database* which is then sent to the home *terminal*.

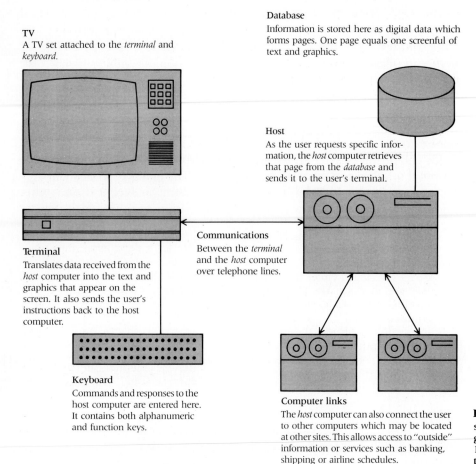

TV
A TV set attached to the *terminal* and *keyboard*.

Database
Information is stored here as digital data which forms pages. One page equals one screenful of text and graphics.

Host
As the user requests specific information, the *host* computer retrieves that page from the *database* and sends it to the user's terminal.

Terminal
Translates data received from the *host* computer into the text and graphics that appear on the screen. It also sends the user's instructions back to the host computer.

Communications
Between the *terminal* and the *host* computer over telephone lines.

Keyboard
Commands and responses to the host computer are entered here. It contains both alphanumeric and function keys.

Computer links
The *host* computer can also connect the user to other computers which may be located at other sites. This allows access to "outside" information or services such as banking, shipping or airline schedules.

Exhibit 13.7   The videotex system
SOURCE: Tom Mach, "High-tech opportunities getting closer to home," *Advertising Age*, Apr. 16, 1984, p. M-60. Copyright Crain Communications.

perform a number of functions including electronic banking and shopping; conveying personal messages; communicating news, sports, and weather information; providing entertainment; and administering problem-solving tests. AT&T, who joined forces with the Knight-Ridder newspaper chain for the Florida venture, believes that some form of videotex service will penetrate as many as 10 million homes by 1990, at which time videotex will be a $15 billion industry.[21] Adding strength to AT&T's conviction is the newly formed joint venture between IBM, Sears, and CBS, who are planning to develop a nationwide commercial videotex service for households with personal computers.

A second, more recent development in electronic shopping comes from CompuSave Corporation. The company offers terminals built into free-standing kiosks (boxlike structures) that do duty as portable catalogue showrooms, selling more than 3000 hardgood items at discounts of 20 to 40 percent. The supermarket chain Stop-n-Shop has already bought the idea and is beginning to install the kiosks in its stores.

> Anthony J. Collura, vice-president of Rini Supermarkets Inc., a member of the Stop-n-Shop group, . . . found that the units "pulled people in" because they broadened the store's offerings. Says Collura: "We could almost become a hypermarket—selling hardgoods as well as food—without the costs."[22]

Growth of nonstore retailing. One expert estimates that nonstore retailing has been growing at least three to four times the rate of store retailing, recognizing, of course, that nonstore retailing is relatively small compared with store retailing.[23] Several factors help explain the popularity of catalogue and other forms of nonstore retailing. One reason is the rapid increase in the number of families in which both spouses work, limiting the amount of shopping time available but providing the income for more expensive nonstore purchases. Ease of communication through 800-number WATS lines has also helped expand nonstore retailing. Other factors also are responsible.

> Direct marketing is among the most identifiable and easily understood incursions of the service economy into the American way of life. Retailing, of course, has always been a service business. But direct marketing does what no store can do. No hassle with parking. No time wasted finding the right size. No lines at the register. Many direct mail orders can be processed as quickly as a conventional retailer can run a credit card check.[24]

TRENDS IN RETAILING

Although many changes in the future will affect the retailing sector, four trends promise to be particularly significant: (1) emergence of new types of retailers, (2) expansion of price competition, (3) increased polarity of retail trade, and (4) acceleration of life cycles.[25]

New retailing forms

Two important developments in retailing during the last decade were the explosive growth of super specialty stores and a new generation of mass merchandisers. Both have siphoned sales and profits from conventional retailers. This new wave of retailers has forced many changes on existing retailers owing to the new retailers' market leadership in the areas of pricing, assortment, store location, and advertising. (Read Marketalk about how many college bookstores are becoming major retail forces by changing their marketing strategy.)

The concept of the **wheel of retailing** helps explain the development of new forms of retailing.[26] The concept suggests that low-status, low-margin, low-price competitors force their way into the marketplace because of the high margins and high prices of existing retailers. Eventually, these new retailers become established and increasingly costly to operate. Then they also become high-margin, high-price merchants susceptible to the low prices of new retailers. The wheel of retailing provides an explanation as to why discounters entered the retailing scene in the 1950s and 1960s. Similarly, catalogue showrooms assaulted department stores, discounters, and other retailers in the 1970s with low prices for name brand merchandise and efficient operations. Now discount chains, superstore mass merchandisers, and outlet stores are being successfully developed. Nevertheless, high-price and high-margin retailers continue to be successful, particularly in specialty lines of clothing, jewelry, furniture, and gifts.

Retailing is changing in other countries as well as in the United States. McDonald's, for example, is Japan's largest restaurant chain with 350 fast-food stores and 1982 sales of $293 million (up 16 percent from 1981).[27] The basic menu is the same as in the United States but several modifications

*Marke*TALK ///

College bookstores learn marketing

ALTHOUGH COLLEGE bookstores typically have been private not-for-profit organizations operated by the university or an independent organization, today they are becoming major retail forces. In 1984, estimated sales of college stores approached $4 billion; by 1987, they are expected to reach $5 billion.

The average student shops at a college store three times a month, spending approximately $300 each year. Several stores reach averages of $400 to $500 per year, and Stanford University averages approximately $900 per student per year. The estimated disposable income of students, faculty, and staff is $40 billion a year. Some stores are attempting to attract the non-

SOURCE: Sharon Donovan, "College bookstores learn marketing," *Advertising Age*, May 7, 1984, p. 80. Copyright © 1984 Crain Communications, Inc.

university community. Alumni also are potential market targets.

Sales ratios run approximately 70 percent for books and 30 percent for nonbook items, with some stores reporting fifty-fifty mixes. Because margins are slim on textbooks and used books, many stores are pushing sales of nonbook merchandise to help improve financial performance. For instance, personal computers and engineering and art supplies help attract off-campus customers.

An aggressive retailer is the Boston University Bookstore—a seven-story building with 70,000 square feet recently renovated at a cost of $9.5 million. Before the university undertook major expansion, the bookstore had been only 9000 square feet.

The B.U. Bookstore advertises to the campus population and to the public with the help of its agency, Allied Advertising. Bookstore general manager Larry Carr estimated that his advertising budget this

year would be $300,000, with next year's projected budget increasing up to 50 percent. A campaign tagged "4.1 miles of books" in radio and print advertisements is aimed not only at 28,000 full-time and part-time students, but at everyone in a twenty- to twenty-five-mile radius. Of the 2.5 million residents in the market area, Mr. Carr has targeted only persons between the ages of twenty and forty-five. But the advertising campaign—on FM stations, the city's two daily newspapers, the campus newspaper, and a group of weekly publications—has been so successful that the bookstore has attracted a full range of customers contributing to the expected sales of $9.5 million for its first ten months of operation.

NOTE: In mid-1985, Cosmopulos, Crowley & Daly took over the Boston University Bookstore account.

///

were made in McDonald's marketing approach as a result of learning about Japanese culture. A Japanese joint-venture partner knew the country and how to set up franchises. Restaurants were built closer to nearby buildings than in the United States, and television commercials were tied closely to Japanese life. And the name "Ronald" was changed to "Donald" because it was easier to pronounce. As mentioned previously West Germany is experiencing rapid growth in hypermarket discount stores.

Expansion of price competition

The logic of why price competition can be successful is at least partially explained by the wheel of retailing. The break-even point of many retailers ranges above 90 percent of sales. Supermarkets, for example, operate on an average net profit margin on sales of 1 percent compared with approximately 7 percent for fast-foods. Some conventional retailers break even in the 80 to 90 percent range of sales but are vulnerable to price competition by other retailers. Cutthroat competition reduces sales volume.

The decline in real income, high inflation, high interest rates, and general economic conditions of the early 1980s have changed the price and value orientation of many shoppers. This trend probably will continue through the 1980s. Some of the retailers that are using price as a competitive weapon are the following:

Pic-A-Dilly: Junior sportswear chain that deep discounts national brands. The chain's labor costs are 6 percent of sales compared with more than 20 percent for a conventional department store.

Bi-Mart: A deep discounter that underprices K mart and Wal-Mart.

Eli-Lilly: Well recognized in the high-margin pharmaceuticals, Lilly is also the leading producer of generic drugs.

Toys "R" Us: The nation's leading retailer of toys uses low prices and efficient operations and has gained the number-one position in the market.

Increased polarity of retail trade

One of the interesting characteristics of the new wave of retailers is that most of these retailers are part of the vertical marketing systems (VMSs) discussed in Chapter 12. You will recall that a VMS consists of distribution channel organizations that are corporate owned, contractually linked (e.g., by franchising), or otherwise tied together through strong administrative power by one organization in the channel of distribution. Retailing is developing at two major extremes: mass merchandising and specialty retailing, and both forms of retailing typically use some form of VMS. Consider this analysis of more than 500 U.S. retail corporations.

■ Those operating primarily conventional outlets have not been able to achieve a sales growth equal to the rate of inflation, and profits as a percent of shareholders' equity or net worth generally have not been equal to the cost of capital.

■ Practically all of the high-growth, high-profit companies have been those that can be described either as large-scale mass merchandisers or intensely specialized stores.[28]

Acceleration of life cycles

The trends in retailing we have examined so far have been concerned with new retail forms, the intensity of competition in the retail sector, and the development of speciality retailing and mass merchandising. The final retailing trend we consider is the length of time required for new types of retailers to reach maturity.

In Chapter 9 we discussed the product life cycle (see Exhibit 9.7): the introduction of a new product and its rapid growth, maturity, and eventual decline unless actions are taken to extend its life cycle. Retailers, like products, tend to move through life cycles, and these life cycles are becoming increasingly short. The traditional department store development spanned more than 100 years from introduction to maturity. Fast-foods reached maturity in less than two decades, whereas speciality retailing such as catalogue showrooms gained maturity in approximately ten years.

As shown in Exhibit 13.8 several retail chains experienced major growth from 1972 to 1984. For example, The Gap, Inc. was founded in 1969 with one small jeans store located near San Francisco State College.[29] This successful retailer had reached sales of $0.5 billion by 1984 and net profits on sales of about 3 percent. The Gap claims to be Levi Strauss' largest customer. Interestingly, management, faced with a fading jeans boom and intense competition, expanded into casual clothes and kept a tight control on expenses. This illustration demonstrates the importance of adjusting to the changing retail environment if a retailer is to survive and prosper.

The Boston University Bookstore doesn't rely only on ads to promote its book and nonbook merchandise. It also uses special programs of "tales and songs and dance from different lands and times," in addition to discount coupons for parents, free balloons for kids, free T-shirts, and surprise package drawings.
(Photography: Jonathan Dempsey Hart)

books, et al.

BOSTON UNIVERSITY BOOKSTORE

Exhibit 13.8 Growth of selected retailers

	Merchandise	Sales (millions of dollars)		Number of Stores, 1984
		1972	1984	
The Gap, Inc.	Jeans and casual clothes	6	525	600
Tandy Corp.	Electronics products	420	2700	9000
The Limited, Inc.	Women's apparel	9	1300	1400
Payless Cashways	Do-it-yourself home improvement supplies	50	1200	160
Color Tile	Do-it-yourself floor and wall covering	30*	280	800

SOURCE: *The Value Line Investment Survey*, 1984.
* 1974 sales

SUMMARY

Retailers are major participants in performing various essential marketing functions such as buying and selling, storing, handling products, transporting, merchandising, financing, servicing, and assuming risks. Retailers provide vital links between producers and end-users of products and services.

The role of the retailer varies significantly from one type to another. There are more than 1.9 million retailers in the United States, employing one of seven people in the total workforce. Retailers, like all business firms, must develop marketing strategies to serve their target markets. Nevertheless, marketing in retail organizations is somewhat different than that of manufacturers and wholesalers. A major determinant of the target market served by many retailers is the location of the retail outlet. Both location and customer perceptions of the retailer help determine who patronizes a store. The retailer's marketing mix consists of the line or lines of merchandise carried, services provided, hours of operation, the type and location of stores, prices, advertising, sales promotion, and personal selling.

Retailers can be classified according to the merchandise carried, pricing strategy, type of ownership, the store's location, and store or nonstore sales. Major types of retailers are department stores, specialty stores, catalogue showrooms, food and drug retailers, and various new retail forms such as home improvement and decorating supermarkets. Four categories of retailers illustrate the range of price strategies for these firms: full-markup retailers, upscale discounters, warehouse retailers, and off-price outlets. Retail stores may be owned by independents, corporate chains, and retailer cooperatives. Retailers primarily are found in three locations: central business districts, street and highway segments or strips, and shopping centers. Nonstore retailers include mail-order catalogue, telephone, vending machine, and door-to-door.

Several important trends are under way in retailing. First, several new retail forms have developed during the last decade. Second, the 1980s have brought on rapid expansion of price competition in retailing. Third, there has been an increased polarity of retail trade to either specialty stores or mass merchandisers, many of whom are part of vertical marketing systems. Finally, new types of stores are moving rapidly to the maturity stage of their life cycles.

KEY TERMS

retailing

retailer

dealer

service retailers

traditional department stores

mass merchandisers

discount department stores

specialty stores

catalogue showrooms

food and drug retailers

supermarket and superdrug stores

convenience stores

combination stores

superstore

hypermarkets

full-markup retailers

upscale discounters

warehouse retailers

off-price outlets

independent retailer

corporate-owned and franchised chains

retailer cooperatives

central business district (CBD) retailers

strip developments

anchor stores

direct marketing

videotex

wheel of retailing

QUESTIONS FOR REVIEW AND DISCUSSION

1. Two important marketing tasks facing retailers are deciding what customers to target and assembling a marketing mix. What important issue affects both tasks?

2. How do store location and the way the store is perceived by the buyer help determine the customers a store will attract?

3. What actions *position* the retailer by differentiating it from competitors?

4. Describe the nature and scope of "off price retailing."

5. What are the three major kinds of department stores and what differentiates department stores from other types of merchandise retailers?

6. Best Products and Service Merchandise are examples of catalogue showroom chains. What characteristics of catalogue showrooms have caused them to become popular with consumers?

7. What are the advantages and disadvantages of franchising?

8. Vending machines are an example of nonstore retailing. What are the characteristics of these machines that attract buyers?

9. Nonstore retailing has been growing at three to four times the rate of store retailing. List several factors that explain this rapid growth.

10. Several trends are expected to have a particularly significant effect on the future of the retailing sector. What are these trends?

11. How does the concept of the "wheel of retailing" help explain the development of new forms of retailing?

12. Retailing is developing at two major extremes: mass merchandising and specialty retailing. Why are these forms of retailing experiencing such high growth and what effect is their growth having on conventional retailers?

13. Explain why retailers, like products, tend to move through life cycles.

BUILDING YOUR PORTFOLIO

David owns and operates three retail men's clothing stores in a large city in the southwest. He has based past decisions about new stores, merchandise carried, and advertising on his twenty years of experience in retailing. As he reviews changes in the retail environment during the last five years, he realizes that the rate of change is faster than it used to be. David has decided that he must study trends in the retail environment more carefully than he did in the past and attempt to estimate the impact of key changes on his business. Identify the external factors that David should evaluate in the future, indicating why they are important. Suggest how he can obtain information on these factors. The information on key environmental factors will be useful in analyzing what kinds of decision alternatives?

NOTES

1. Cole National Corporation, *1982 Annual Report*, p. 5.
2. James R. Lowery, *Retail Management*. Cincinnati: South-Western Publishing, 1983, pp. 4–5.
3. *1983 U.S. Industrial Outlook.* Washington, D.C.: U.S. Department of Commerce, Jan. 1983, pp. 48-2–48-6.
4. Ibid., p. 48-2.
5. Susan Chace, "Marketing grows more vital for desktop computer sales." *Wall Street Journal,* Oct. 22, 1982, p. 25.
6. Peter Petre, "IBM's misadventures in the retail jungle." *Fortune,* July 23, 1984, p. 80.
7. R. Patric Cash, *The Buyer's Manual.* New York: National Retail Merchants' Association, 1979, p. 10.
8. Claudia Ricci, "Children's wear retailers brace for competition from Toys 'R' Us." *Wall Street Journal,* Aug. 25, 1983, p. 21.
9. "West German retailing." *Economist,* June 27, 1981, p. 84.
10. William Harris, "So who doesn't like a bargain?" *Forbes,* Apr. 26, 1982, pp. 148–149.
11. William R. Davidson, "Davidson looks back on his retail outlook for 1970s." *Marketing News,* Mar. 7, 1980, p. 12.
12. Howard Rudnitsky, "Make room, Disney World, Federated and Gimbels." *Forbes,* May 9, 1983, p. 100.
13. "GM's bold bid to reinvent the wheel." *Business Week,* Jan. 21, 1984, p. 35.
14. Gail Bronson, "You name it—you can buy it by mail." *U.S. News & World Report,* May 9, 1983, p. 153.
15. *1982–83 United States Consumer Mail Order Industry Estimates.* Published annually by the Maxwell Sroge Company.
16. Richard Greene, "A boutique in your living room." *Forbes,* May 7, 1984, p. 86.
17. William Harris, "Christmas mail munch." *Forbes,* Dec. 22, 1980, p. 36.
18. Joel Dreyfuss, "Reach out and sell something." *Fortune,* Nov. 26, 1984, p. 128.
19. Anne Bagamery, "Please make me feel special." *Forbes,* Mar. 28, 1983, pp. 88–89.
20. W. Wayne Talarzyk and Robert E. Widing, II, "Introduction to and Issues with Videotex: Implications for Marketing." Working Paper Series WPS 82-16, College of Administrative Science, The Ohio State University, Jan. 1982, p. 1.

21. "AT&T prophesies a $15 billion market for videotex." *Marketing News,* Sep. 28, 1984, p. 20.
22. Marilyn A. Harris, "Electronic retailing goes to the supermarket." *Business Week,* Mar. 25, 1985, pp. 78–79.
23. Davidson, op. cit.
24. Greene, op. cit., p. 88.
25. Many of the concepts and illustrations in this section are based on the studies conducted by Bert C. McCammon, Jr., Director, Distribution Research Program, College of Business Administration, The University of Oklahoma.
26. Stanley C. Hollander, "The wheel of retailing." *Journal of Marketing,* July 1960, pp. 37–42.
27. Michael Doan and Hidehiro Tanakadate, "Ways some U.S. firms crack Japan's market." *U.S. News & World Report,* Aug. 29, 1983.
28. Davidson, op. cit.
29. Howard Rudnitsky, "Widening the gap." *Forbes,* Sept. 13, 1982, p. 205.

Case 13.1

J. C. Penney

J. C. PENNEY, the nation's third largest retailer, announced in early 1983 that the chain's future strategy would be concentrated on clothes and soft goods merchandise, while dropping major appliances, paint, hardware, lawn and garden equipment, and auto service. Clearly, this move represented a major shift in retailing strategy; management planned to spend $1 billion over the next five years to update 450 larger stores.

The basis of the change was an overall assessment of performance combined with the results of several consumer research studies. Some of the major findings were:

SOURCE: Jim Fuquay, "Competitors, analysts, applaud J. C. Penney," *Fort Worth Star-Telegram,* Feb. 6, 1983, p. 1F.

■ Customers shopped Penney's for clothes, linens, and household goods.
■ Sales of women's clothing were being lost to specialty stores.
■ Auto services were becoming increasingly competitive.
■ Aggressive price competition was coming from discount and off-price retailers in hard goods (e.g., refrigerators), hardware, and auto services.

Penney's decision to upgrade its apparel lines was intended to help attract lost customers using designer clothes such as Halston, Adolfo, and Lee Wright. These names would provide prestige to the firm's apparel lines.

The strategy adopted by Penney was influenced by the trends in retailing toward specialization and mass merchandising. Management selected specialization since its customer franchise was strong in the apparel and other soft goods lines. The discontinued lines contributed less than 10 percent of sales. One observer commented on industry trends:

> Basically, it's another chapter in the continuing story of retail specialization. Years ago, department stores blazed the path Penney took, and in recent years specialty merchandising has been an industry buzzword. It means building an image and market presence for certain goods and services and leaving the rest to the other guys.
>
> As Penney explains it, it means putting the store's money where it would do the most good.

QUESTIONS

1. What trend in retailing influenced the decision of Penney's management to drop appliances and auto services?

2. What are the advantages and limitations of the strategy selected by Penney's management?

3. Do you agree or disagree with the decision to offer fashionable clothing to retain customers?

Case 13.2

Fast-food chicken restaurants

FAST-FOOD CHICKEN restaurants are waging a battle for supremacy as hot as grease sizzling in a frying pan.

Fried chicken, once popular primarily in the South, is consumed by so many Americans that restaurants specializing in the dish, mostly for carryout, ring up 4 billion dollars in sales annually. Chicken, in fact, is a major menu item for 192 restaurant chains varying in size from three to 6,000 outlets.

Nearly two thirds of that business goes to Kentucky Fried Chicken. But its domi-

SOURCE: Jeannie Thornton, "The great American chicken war," *U.S. News & World Report,* Aug. 22, 1983, p. 61. Reprinted from *U.S. News & World Report* issue of Aug. 22, 1983. Copyright, 1983, U.S. News & World Report, Inc.

nance is being challenged by aggressive regional chains offering new recipes, expanded menus and eat-in sections. One of them, Mrs. Winner's Chicken & Biscuits, aims at capturing 25 percent of any market within two years of opening its first outlet in the targeted area.

In this heated chicken war, advertising is a major weapon. Kentucky Fried spent nearly 80 million for advertising last year, 27.2 million of it on television. Popeyes Famous Fried Chicken & Biscuits, a 10-year-old chain based in Jefferson, La., will spend 6 million this year for ads, and as much as 9 million in 1984.

Most chains have ambitious plans. In its biggest expansion ever, Kentucky Fried intends to add 1,000 outlets in the next five years to its present 6,500. Fast-grow-

ing Popeyes, with 350 units in 35 states, opens one to three new ones each week and has sold nearly 1,000 franchise options.

Franchises are eagerly sought, since a successful chicken place can run up annual sales of 1 million dollars or more. Some franchise agreements require a commitment to open more than one outlet—from three to 20 for a fee of $10,000 to $25,000 each.

Church's Fried Chicken, the No. 2 chain, concentrated its outlets in black neighborhoods because research found that blacks on average eat seven times as much chicken as whites. Other companies have since followed its lead.

One of them, Chicken George, sharpened its appeal to minority customers in

Baltimore, Philadelphia, Washington, D.C., and Norfolk, Va., by keeping the salt content of its foods low. Salt is a contributor to high blood pressure, prevalent among blacks. The black-owned firm claims its average customer visits one of its outlets three or four times a week, helping individual restaurants ring up sales of as much as 2 million dollars a year—highest in the industry.

Moving away from catering only to the carryout trade, many chains have added tables and chairs. Described as "upscale" by the industry and aimed at middle and upper-middle-class families are places such as Bojangles' Famous Chicken & Biscuits. They feature carpeted floors, salad bars and fancy lights along with higher prices on the menu.

The combination of moderate cost, fast service and pleasant surroundings makes such restaurants appeal to "the family headed by parents who 15 years ago grew up on McDonald's hamburgers," says Steven Rockwell of the Alex Brown investment firm in Baltimore.

As with the burger chains, competition leads the chicken houses to diversify menus. Few offer as wide a variety as the Perdue Chicken Restaurant in Queens, N.Y. It serves chicken salads, sandwiches, soups, quiche, Tetrazzini, Parmesan and cacciatore in addition to chicken fried or roasted.

For their part, the chains have beefed up menus with crispy, spicy and Cajun-style fried chicken, plus corn on the cob, fried okra, rice dishes and biscuits. The introduction of made-from-scratch biscuits sparked an advertising war so intense that Rockwell quips, "You almost wonder what came first, the chicken or the biscuit."

By stuffing their biscuits with eggs, Canadian bacon, sausage or country-fried steak, some restaurants have built a brisk breakfast business that accounts for 30 percent of receipts. "We already have a good start on the day when some of our competitors open," says M. V. Hussung, president of the parent company of Mrs. Winner's Chicken & Biscuits.

The success of chicken has not gone unnoticed by purveyors of other fast foods. A chicken-breast sandwich accounts for 17 percent of sales at the 3,200 Burger King outlets. Wendy's International not only added a chicken sandwich to the fare at its hamburger units, but also now operates 35 Sisters Chicken & Biscuits outlets in six states.

In a new marketing strategy, some Sisters restaurants are being located next to Wendy's outlets. While initially that hurts sales at Wendy's, in the long run "it draws more eating customers to the area," boosting the sales of both restaurants, says company spokesman Denny Lynch.

The rapid growth of the chicken places makes them tempting targets for takeovers by larger corporations. In late July, the two founders of Grandy's Country Cookin', with outlets in suburban areas in 13 states, sold the chain to Saga Corporation for Saga stock valued at 66 million dollars.

Purveyors of chicken see their future as bright. Increasing numbers of two-income families and singles mean more eating out, they say. Other pluses, in their view, are the relatively low price of chicken and a public perception that it is a healthier food than red meat.

Some analysts are not so sure. As with hamburger chains, this fast-food phenomenon may someday approach the saturation point and find its chickens coming home to roost.

	1982 Revenues	1982 Outlets	Outlets Being Added in 1983
Kentucky Fried Chicken	$2,500 mil.	6,396	250
Church's Fried Chicken	$ 424 mil.	1,379	175
Popeyes Famous Fried Chicken	$ 175 mil.	275	85
Chick-fil-A	$ 104 mil.	255	30
Pioneer Take Out	$ 100 mil.	300	30
Bojangles' Famous Chicken & Biscuits	$ 85 mil.	121	104
Mrs. Winner's Chicken & Biscuits	$ 83 mil.	69	54
Lees Famous Recipe Chicken	$ 75 mil.	208	17
Brown's Chicken	$ 74 mil.	139	36
Grandy's Country Cookin'	$ 47 mil.	52	95

Note: Figures are for worldwide sales and outlets.

QUESTIONS

1. How important is store atmosphere for fast-food chicken stores?

2. What competitive problems do the new chains encounter?

3. How can one chain gain a competitive advantage in this chicken war?

14 Marketing by Wholesalers

When you finish this chapter, you will understand

□ The important role of wholesalers in marketing products

□ The various functions performed by wholesalers in distribution channels

□ The nature and scope of wholesaler marketing strategies

□ The characteristics and functions of merchant wholesalers, agents and brokers, and manufacturer-owned establishments

□ The reasons why several important trends are occurring in wholesaling

Newsstands would have to buy and transport a multitude of magazine titles from many different sources without the services of wholesalers.

Steel service centers perform several important distribution channel activities. These firms purchase steel coil (sheets rolled into coils) and bars in large quantities from steel producers such as U.S. Steel, Inland, and Republic. Service centers cut and shape the bulk steel at labor rates substantially lower than those paid by steel producers. Steel centers also deliver faster than producers, which enables their customers to eliminate costly inventory. When steel is ordered from the producers' mills it must be purchased in large quantities, and the time between order placement and delivery is relatively long. Customers of steel service centers include Deere & Company and General Motors. Of course, large firms such as these do not rely on service centers for all of their steel requirements. Nevertheless, steel service wholesalers are increasing their market share of steel sales. One of the firms, A. M. Castle, concentrates on a specific market segment, users of highly engineered metals such as titanium and steel alloys used in aerospace and petrochemical production. Shipments to all steel service centers in 1984 should reach 20 million tons. These wholesalers are attracting customers today because they offer efficient and fast service to steel users.[1]

MANY PEOPLE ARE NOT FAMILIAR with wholesalers because consumers typically are not in contact with these firms to the extent they are with retailers. Because wholesalers usually do not advertise to consumers, awareness is not created by advertising. Nevertheless, wholesaling is an important business activity, providing many manufacturers with a vital link to the consumers of their products. Retailers and business buyers also rely on wholesalers to perform many important distribution functions.

In this chapter we examine the role and functions of wholesalers, identify the types of firms that operate within the marketing system, and discuss several important trends occurring in wholesaling.

ROLE OF WHOLESALERS

Descriptive profiles of an illustrative group of wholesalers are shown in Exhibit 14.1. One of the firms, the Phibro-Salomon Corporation (PSC), is a huge trading firm, yet few people know it exists. The trader's financial performance is ahead of many other wholesalers, with the annual return on equity (assets minus liabilities) ranging from 20 percent in 1979 to 37 percent in 1984.[2] PSC deals in crude oil, oil products and petrochemicals, minerals and metals, ferrous alloys, fertilizers, sugar, and grains. The firm employs approximately 5000 persons. In addition to commodities trading, the company owns various plants for processing materials. It acquired Salomon Brothers (securities broker) in 1981, and owns the Swiss bank, Phibrobank. Net profit margins on revenues are approximately 1.5 percent.

A **wholesaler** is a distributor that performs the functions necessary to supply retailers and other organizational buyers with producers' goods and services. The U.S. Bureau of the Census defines **wholesaling** as "the activities of those persons or establishments which sell to retailers and other merchants and/or to industrial, institutional, and commercial users, but who do not sell in significant amounts to ultimate consumers." A restricted view of wholesaling includes only independently owned and operated wholesalers and excludes manufacturers' branches and offices.

Located in the middle of a channel of distribution, this marketing intermediary simplifies and streamlines the transactions between producers and organizational buyers. The justification for the wholesaler is in the services it performs for suppliers and buyers.

Vie de France has carved a niche for itself by establishing a network of wholesale and retail bakeries and restaurants. "The synergy between our activities

Exhibit 14.1 Descriptive profile of selected wholesalers

Company	Products	Buyers	1984 Sales Volume (Millions of dollars)
Genuine Parts Company	Automotive replacement parts.	Services over 5000 dealers.	2,300
Phibro-Salomon Corporation	International commodities, merchant and securities broker.	Deals in over 150 materials, including crude oil.	30,000
Premier Industrial Corporation	Industrial maintenance products (lubricants, fasteners, etc).	Industrial firms through over 200 U.S. and foreign branches.	380
Durr-Fillauer Medical, Inc.	Distributes pharmaceuticals, drug-store sundries, medical products, and orthotic-prosthetic devices.	Hospitals, pharmacies, and physician's offices.	270
Vallen Corporation	Industrial safety equipment distributor (hard hats, safety glasses, etc.).	Industrial firms in the Sunbelt.	36
Wetterau, Inc.	Nation's fourth largest grocery wholesaler	Distributes to 1700 independent retailers.	2,700
United Stationers, Inc.	Computer-based wholesale distributor of office products.	Serves 8500 dealers throughout the eastern half of the United States and California.	350

SOURCE: *The Value Line Investment Survey* and company reports, 1984.

makes us different,'' says Lloyd Faul, president of the company. The wholesale division, for example, helped support expansion of retail stores . . . by providing both dough and finished products.[3]

Let us now examine what wholesalers do and how they make an important contribution to distribution channels.

What do wholesalers do?

Merchant wholesalers represent the largest industry category, typically performing many wholesalers' functions. Agents and brokers and manufacturers' branches make up the remaining portion of the wholesale industry. As we look at the functions performed by wholesalers, you should recognize that all functions are not performed by all wholesalers. An overview of the functions performed by type of wholesaler is shown in Exhibit 14.2. This comparison is illustrative because there are undoubtedly exceptions as to whether wholesalers always, sometimes, or never perform the functions indicated.

Buying and selling. Central to the services provided by wholesalers is buying from producers and selling to retailers and to farm, governmental, professional, and institutional users. Nonmerchant wholesalers such as purchasing and selling agents, manufacturers' agents, export and import agents, and commission agents facilitate the sale for which they receive a commission typically paid by the producer or other supplier. Such agents do not take title to the goods they sell and normally are not involved in transporting, storing, and other functions involving the physical product.

Merchant wholesalers take title to merchandise and perform many functions in addition to purchasing and reselling goods. These activities include selecting items to be purchased, negotiating terms from suppliers, establishing selling prices, keeping records, and processing orders. The wholesaler serves as an important communications link between producers and organizational buyers. Deciding what to buy is a major activity for firms such as grocery wholesalers. From 1975 to 1982, an average of more than 5000 grocery items were available from producers each year.[4]

Warehousing and product handling. Sorting, assembling, grading, and storing contribute to the value that is added by the wholesaler to the product. For example, an industrial chemical distributor may purchase chlorine in a tank car from a chemical company and then repackage it in small containers for sale to public and commercial swimming pool operators. A tobacco wholesaler may sort tobacco leaves according to type and grade. Maintaining inventories represents a major activity of many wholesalers. Inventory control is an important aspect of product storage. For example, Super Valu Stores, the largest food wholesaler in the United States, uses a $300,000 IBM 4300 computer to assist its retail supermarket customers in analyzing point-of-sale information generated in their stores.[5] Electronic product coding scanners are used at checkout stands to record the item purchased. The firm spends more than $1 million a year to analyze the scanning data, which yields valuable marketing and inventory control information.

Transporting. Many wholesalers transport orders to their customers with a fleet of trucks or vans. For example, rack jobbers (see the section Types of Wholesalers) supplying health and beauty aids use vans to carry a variety of items to retail stores where the jobber stocks display racks with items such as razor blades and toothpaste. Transportation is a substantial expense for some wholesalers. Wetterau's trucks travel more than eighteen million miles yearly transporting products from distribution centers to retailers' stores and warehouses. A food wholesaler's travel, automobile, and truck costs may be the largest expense item, amounting to more than 10 percent of operating expense. Leasing trucks is a popular option for wholesalers to reduce the amount of capital needed to run the business. Leasing activity in 1980 for transportation equipment totaled $3.5 billion.[6]

The grocery wholesaler Wetterau, as part of an ongoing program to improve operating efficiency, has installed electronic trip recorders in each division's truck fleet. These on-board computers provide detailed data that are used by Wetterau to maximize driver efficiency, increase fuel efficiency, and reduce maintenance costs. The trip recorder program produced about $2 million in fuel and labor savings during fiscal year 1984.[7]

Exhibit 14.2 Major wholesaler activities by type of wholesaler

Activity	Merchant Wholesalers	Agents and Brokers	Manufacturers' Branches and Offices
Buying and selling	Yes	*	*
Warehousing and product handling	Yes	No	Mixed
Transporting	Yes	No	Mixed
Management and merchandising assistance	Mixed	No	Mixed
Financing	Mixed	No	Mixed
Returns and repairs	Mixed	No	Yes
Assumption of risks	Yes	No	Yes

* Acts as representative of supplier

Management and merchandising assistance. Wholesalers in several merchandise lines have found that they can help independent retailers compete more effectively with corporate-owned and franchised chains by offering these customers various merchandising and management services. For example, many drug wholesalers offer retail customers inventory management systems including electronic ordering, price labels, inventory and price records, and financial reports and analyses. A wholesaler may provide assistance in store layout, advertising, sales promotion, and financial controls such as retailer accounts receivable analyses. Wetterau provides its retail grocery customers with an impressive array of services including accounting, advertising and merchandising, business counseling, store development, and several computer-based technologic services such as data entry terminal systems, point-of-sale scanning, direct store delivery systems, shelf management and merchandising, price management, and in-store computers.

Financing. Some wholesalers offer financial assistance to retailers in the form of credit, favorable payment terms, and other financial services. By providing financial and other forms of assistance, wholesalers are able to strengthen their positions in the distribution channel. These financial services have helped independent stores compete against chains. Without such financial assistance an independent store may be unable to compete effectively with chain stores.

Returns and repairs. Wholesalers may offer maintenance and repair services. For example, Caterpillar Tractor Company's dealers provide contractors and other heavy equipment users with a full range of services including fast replacement of parts on a worldwide basis. Caterpillar's strong independent dealer network is a major factor in their marketing approach. Equipment customers often are willing to pay a premium price because they know Caterpillar's dealers will provide fast and competent service.

Wholesalers are closer than manufacturers to product users and can respond more quickly to their service needs. An independent retailer may not have the capabilities for service and repair, whereas a wholesaler can handle service needs for many retailers. Wholesalers also play an important part when a manufacturer must recall products.

Assuming risks. Wholesalers take on risks by buying and stocking merchandise that may become obsolete or unpopular, and thus difficult to sell to retail customers. Because they stock in greater quantities than retailers, wholesalers must assume greater risks on their stock. Actions wholesalers take to reduce risks include comprehensively evaluating new brands and lines, bargaining with producers for favorable terms on returning excess inventory, designing inventory control systems, and implementing employee theft controls.

Importance of wholesaling

Our examination of the various wholesaler activities highlights many reasons why both producers and retailers need wholesalers to perform various functions: transactions between producers and retailers are reduced; goods are stored and transported; management, merchandising, and finance services are provided to retailers; returns and repairs are facilitated; and risks are assumed. Consider this example of RCA's purchase of its metropolitan New York distributor, Bruno Appliance Corporation.

"We didn't buy it by choice," says Francis V. McCann, RCA's vice-president for public affairs for the consumer electronics division. "The discount stores—Crazy Eddie's, 47th St. Photo, and the bigger volume stores—were exerting leadership in the market, and we had to do it. But we always wanted to be out of the distribution business. We sold off Chicago, Atlanta, Kansas City, and San Antonio in 1975 and 1976, and we would have sold the others (including Detroit and Southern California) if we could have."[8]

RCA needs wholesalers like Bruno Appliance Corporation. The purchase was necessary to keep the wholesaler operating. Management clearly is indicating that it wants the wholesaling function performed because an intermediary can perform the job better than a producer. Wholesaling is an essential part of an advanced economic system (see Marketool). This is doubly so when producers are located in limited areas and retailers are

MarkeTOOL

When the wholesaler is important in Japan's distribution channels

PLANNING A DISTRIBUTION strategy in Japan involves a careful examination of (1) the types of outlets where the product is or could be sold; (2) the role of wholesalers in distribution and the power balance between manufacturers, wholesalers, and retailers; and (3) incentives that are provided by manufacturers to wholesalers and by wholesalers to other wholesalers and retailers. Competing effectively in the Japanese environment and bringing about change in the distribution system (or creating one's own distribution channels) require careful consideration of trade practices.

Suppose you are the marketing manager of a mayonnaise manufacturer in an industry that is highly concentrated (dominated by a few large firms). In this situation the wholesaler takes the initiative in assembling a range of products and brands for use by retailers. The wholesaler is often the primary organizer of the distribution channel because the firm must assemble a range of other goods. Access to the channel requires the cooperation of the wholesaler. The producer must demonstrate the advantages of its brand to the wholesaler, maintaining good relations to help move the product through the channel.

SOURCE: *Planning for Distribution in Japan,* Tokyo: Japan External Trade Organization, 1982, pp. 23–24. Courtesy of JETRO (Japan External Trade Organization).

Determinants of the distribution entities taking organizing initiative

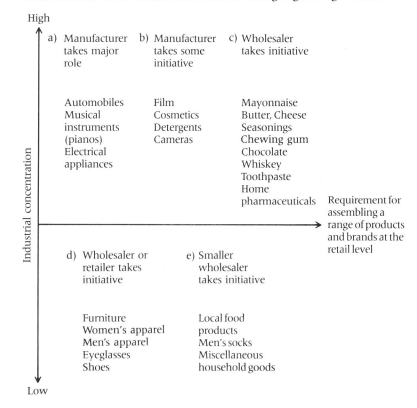

widely dispersed geographically. Wholesalers are marketing specialists, and the various activities they perform to facilitate transactions between producers and retailers and other organizational buyers are vital to efficient operation.

Wholesaler marketing strategies

Like manufacturers and retailers, the wholesaler must make market target decisions and develop a marketing mix appropriate for the targeted customers. Nevertheless, because of the wholesaler's location in the channel of distribution, its marketing decisions differ in several ways from the decisions of producers and retailers.

Selecting market targets. Wholesalers are geographically concentrated; few operate across the nation. Most serve customers in local, state, or regional areas. Within their geographic boundaries, a wholesaler's management can select the characteristics of customers to target. For example, a manufacturer's agent may decide to target certain industries or types of industrial customers. An agent selling safety equipment would concentrate on heavy industry such as steel making, refineries, and power plants. Selectivity in serving customers can be an important factor in the profitability of wholesalers. Cost-effective methods such as catalogue orders and telephone contact can be used to serve customers whose buying needs do not justify face-to-face contact.

Marketing mix composition. The type of wholesaler determines to some extent its *lines and mix of merchandise.* The wholesaler must decide what assortment and line to carry. This choice depends on the willingness of the producer to provide its products to the wholesaler as well as the wholesaler's preferences. Thus the bargaining power of both parties may be important in determining the composition of the wholesaler's product mix. Moreover, the wholesaler must consider the needs and wants of suppliers and buyers and the costs of meeting their requirements.

Wholesalers must perform their various *operations and distribution* functions in an efficient manner. This task is compounded because wholesaler operations are often labor intensive. Efficient cost control, inventory management, and financial management are extremely important in achieving profit levels. Computerized ordering and control systems offer wholesalers important avenues for managing and controlling operations.

Investing in modern, cost-effective *facilities* and equipment is a major step for full-service wholesalers. Automation in materials handling can reduce dependence on labor-intensive functions in warehousing, locating, stocking, and assembling merchandise. Efficient, well-managed facilities can have a positive impact on customers' perceptions of a wholesaler's capabilities.

The extent of flexibility that exists in *pricing* by wholesalers varies from merchant wholesalers to agents and brokers. Merchant wholesalers typically have more choice in the pricing decision than do agents and brokers. Cost plus markup is probably the most widely used method of pricing by wholesalers. A percentage of cost is added to cost to arrive at the price the wholesaler sells to customers (e.g., cost + 10 percent of cost = selling price).

In general, wholesalers do not spend much money on *advertising*, relying instead on producers and retailers to accomplish the advertising and sales promotion function. Because wholesalers work with a relatively small number of suppliers and customers as compared with a household consumer market, it is not surprising that direct mail, telephone contact, and personal selling are used more extensively by wholesalers than is advertising.

Expenditures for *personal selling* are substantial for many wholesalers. Some wholesalers, particularly food and drug, have been criticized for using salespersons primarily as order takers. In contrast, broker and agent wholesalers are often highly paid professionals that rank among the best in selling capabilities.

Often wholesalers' marketing strategies lack cohesiveness. Their marketing programs are not as integrated and targeted as are those of producers and retailers. (An exception is Durr-Fillauer Medical, discussed in MarkeTalk.) Wholesaler organizations, particularly those whose customers purchase regularly and frequently, are clearly oriented toward order taking. In some instances producers' salespersons and management assist wholesalers in developing their marketing programs. Later in the chapter we discuss

*Marke*TALK //

A drug wholesaler's marketing strategy

DURR-FILLAUER MEDICAL, Inc., founded in 1896, distributes pharmaceuticals, drugstore sundries, medical products and orthotic-prosthetic devices. Through its Wholesale Drug, Medical-Surgical and Orthopedic Divisions, the Company supplies hospitals, pharmacies, nursing homes, physician offices and laboratories in addition to manufacturing, fabricating and distributing components for artificial limbs and braces.

The Wholesale Drug Division is one of the largest distributors of pharmaceuticals and drugstore sundries in the Southeast. The Division distributes products to approximately 2,000 independent and chain drugstores and hospital pharmacies through distribution centers located in Montgomery and Mobile, Alabama; Meridian, Mississippi; Shreveport, Louisiana; and Tampa, Florida. Virtually all orders are delivered within 24 hours of receipt in Company-owned vehicles. . . .

The Wholesale Drug Division operates under the same basic strategy as the Medical-Surgical Division—satisfy customer needs, control costs and manage assets to generate the highest possible return. The

SOURCE: Durr-Fillauer Medical, *1983 Annual Report*, pp. 7–8. Courtesy of Durr-Fillauer Medical, Inc.

Division utilizes electronic order entry to maintain a high level of productivity and customer service. During 1983, 96% of all orders in this Division were received electronically.

Wholesale Drug Division revenues experienced substantial growth in all major customer categories in 1983. Sales to all three major customer segments, independent retail drugstores, chain drugstores and hospital pharmacies, increased at least 25%. Sales of pharmaceuticals to hospital pharmacies made this the fastest growing customer segment. During the past five years the Division's percentage of sales to hospitals almost doubled.

Service through innovative ideas and efficient operations continued to be the hallmark of the Division's success. During the last quarter of 1983, the Division introduced "Priceguard," a total marketing program for independent and smaller drugstore chains. Priceguard provides customers with merchandising support, advertising materials and market research assistance. A Priceguard merchandiser will visit each member store monthly to assist in merchandising the entire store layout. Priceguard also includes a coupon redemption service which relieves the pharmacy of troublesome coupon handling. In the few months since Priceguard

was introduced, 265 accounts had joined the program by year-end.

The Division's merchandise shows also received excellent response in 1983 with over 600 Durr-Fillauer customers attending four shows. Each show featured continuing education seminars and exhibits by more than 100 manufacturers.

The Wholesale Drug Division also developed a total program to supply products to providers serving the home health care market. Changing health care delivery systems are expected to create increased long-term demand for home health care. Durr-Fillauer's approach is to supply pharmacies, home health care centers, and providers administering food supplements and antibiotics with the necessary products that will make them highly competitive in the marketplace.

The wholesale drug industry is still in a period of consolidation. The best and most efficiently managed companies will continue to take market share from those less efficient. The changing health care payment system will add further pressures to be innovative and responsive. Durr-Fillauer intends to maintain its leadership position in the Sunbelt states through the best combination of knowledge, marketing systems, service, price and product availability.

//

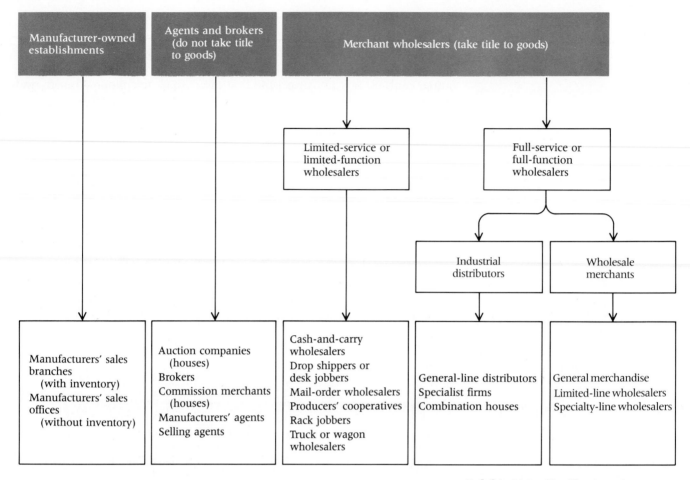

Exhibit 14.3   Classification of wholesaling middlemen

SOURCE: Ralph M. Gaedeke and Dennis H. Tootelian, *Marketing Principles and Applications*, St. Paul, Minn.: West Publishing Company, 1983, p. 256. Reprinted by permission. Copyright © 1983 by West Publishing Company. All rights reserved.

several trends in wholesaling that are changing the nature and scope of the marketing strategies of these marketing intermediaries.

TYPES OF WHOLESALERS

Sales of wholesalers were in excess of $2 trillion in 1982.[9] The U.S. wholesaling industry's share of the gross national product is approximately 7 percent. In 1980 there were about 600,000 wholesaling establishments in the United States.[10]

A classification of wholesaling middlemen is shown in Exhibit 14.3. The three types of wholesalers are merchant wholesalers, agents and brokers, and manufacturers' branches and offices (manufacturer-owned establishments).

Merchant wholesalers

Merchant wholesalers make up the largest portion of the wholesaling industry, accounting for approximately $1 of every $2 of sales, three of every four employees, and four of every five establishments. **Merchant wholesalers** buy, sort, assemble, grade, and store goods in large quantities and sell these goods to retailers and to institutional, farm, governmental, professional, and business users.[11] Merchant wholesalers also offer credit and other services to customers and suppliers. Customers may receive delivery services and management assistance, and suppliers may receive marketing information such as changes in buyers' preferences.

Sales of merchant wholesalers by product category are shown in Exhibit 14.4. Let us take a closer look at the two major types of merchant wholesalers.

Full-service or full-function wholesalers. These wholesalers provide many of the services or functions described in the previous section. Super Valu Stores (sales of $5 billion in 1982), Fleming Companies ($4 billion), and Wetterau ($2 billion) are examples of full-service grocery wholesale mer-

Exhibit 14.4 Sales of merchant wholesalers by product category for 1969 and 1979

SOURCE: U.S. Bureau of the Census, *Monthly Wholesale Trade, December 1979,* BW-79-12, Feb. 1980, p. 3.

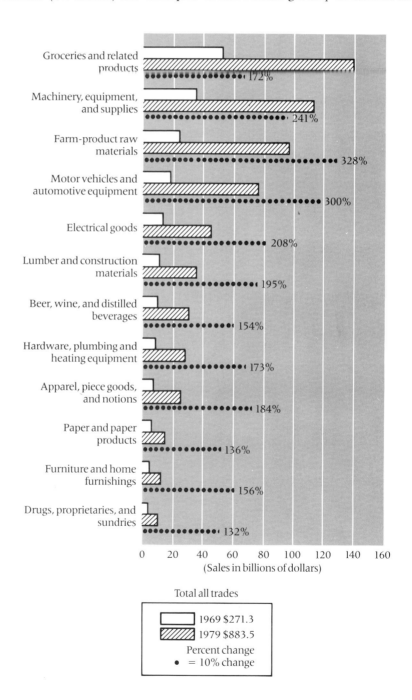

chants. Approximately 400 general line food wholesalers supply food, non-food products, and operating services to small supermarket chains and the 108,000 independent grocery stores in the United States.[12] The food whole-saling industry is steadily consolidating as the large food wholesalers expand their market position by acquiring small wholesalers.

Other examples of general merchandise wholesalers include hardware, drugs, and electrical supplies. Limited-line wholesalers offer a more limited mix of product lines than the general merchandise wholesaler. Specialty-line wholesalers concentrate on a particular line. Industrial distributors (general line, specialist firms, and combination houses) constitute the remaining portion of full-service or full-function wholesalers.

Limited-service or limited-function wholesalers. These wholesalers provide fewer services than the full-service or full-function wholesalers, although each takes title to goods. The major categories of limited-service or limited-function wholesalers are defined as follows:

cash and carry wholesaler: A wholesaler that does not use salespersons but instead allows customers to pick up merchandise from the wholesale location in return for immediate cash payment. Grocery wholesalers often provide this service to small food stores, institutions, and consumers who wish to purchase in case quantities.

drop shipper (desk jobber): A merchant wholesaler operating from an office or showroom that rarely takes physical possession of the goods sold. The customer receives the goods directly from the producer who bills the desk jobber. The desk jobber, in turn, bills the customer.

mail-order house: A retailer or a wholesaler specializing in the sale of goods through orders received by mail. Office supplies such as stationery, business forms, and computer paper are sold by mail.

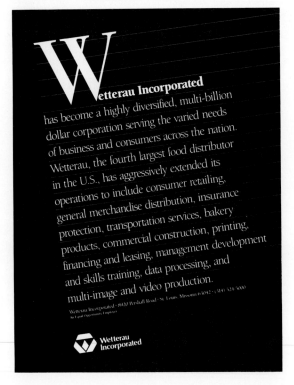

This Wetterau ad is directed toward the general public and the investment community. It also informs other food wholesalers that Wetterau Incorporated is interested in expanding its market position through the acquisition of smaller wholesalers. (Courtesy of Wetterau Incorporated)

In 1984 Land O' Lakes brand butter celebrated its sixtieth anniversary and became the dairy cooperative's first nationally sold product as distribution reached the West Coast. (Reprinted by permission of Land O' Lakes, Inc.)

producers' cooperative (agricultural cooperative): An organization formed by a number of small farmers enabling them to achieve some of the competitive advantages of large-scale marketing. Land O' Lakes is a dairy products cooperative.

rack jobber: A wholesaler that supplies merchandise, sets up displays, and receives payment only for items sold. Magazines sold in supermarkets often are supplied by rack jobbers.

truck wholesaler (truck jobber): A merchant wholesaler that combines the activities of salesperson and delivery person, usually sells for cash, and usually limits stock to nationally advertised specialties and fast-moving items of a perishable or semiperishable nature. Independent truckers purchase agricultural products such as watermelons from growers, transporting and selling them to wholesalers and retailers.[13]

Agents and brokers

Agents and brokers differ from merchant wholesalers in that agents and brokers do not take title to goods and typically provide only limited services to suppliers and customers. These intermediaries normally receive a commission on the sales of the manufacturers' products they represent. Consider, for example, a modern food broker. The primary role of the food broker is to act as a sales representative for the producer. Andorn, Beriga & Danks (ABD), one of the largest food brokers in metropolitan New York, employs 200 people and receives $9 million in commissions (normally 3 percent to 5 percent of sales) from approximately twenty product lines.[14] At least 2700 food brokers operate in the United States, and most of them are smaller than ABD. ABD has half a dozen salespeople whose yearly earnings exceed $100,000. In recent years, many such brokers have added merchandising and management aids for their customers.

Agents. Several kinds of agents perform selling and other limited functions and are paid by a commission on sales. Agents may perform these services for either sellers or buyers.

Manufacturers' agents are salespersons outside the manufacturing organization; they are an alternative to a factory salesforce. Manufacturers' agents often play an important role in the early stages of product life cycles when new manufacturers are entering markets. These firms' limited resources are not sufficient to develop a salesforce. Normally, manufacturers' agents (sometimes called **manufacturers' representatives**) do not handle competing lines of products, although they are likely to handle complementary lines. They offer the manufacturer several advantages including established relationships with buyers, selling experience, selling expenses tied to sales volume, sales costs spread over several manufacturers' lines, and in some instances, technical expertise. Agreements between agents and producers usually are established by contract that specifies operating guidelines such as commission rates, geographic area assigned, exceptions, and basis of termination.

The agent's main function is selling, and he or she typically does not establish prices, advertise, or perform physical distribution functions. The size of the agent organization may range from a single person, often operating out of his or her residence, to a sales organization involving several salespersons. Agents operate in geographic areas as large as a few states or as small as a portion of a state or a city. Successful agents' annual earnings can exceed $100,000. Commissions on sales range from less than 5 percent to 20 percent, depending on the size of purchase, type of product, frequency of purchase, and assistance on how to use the product provided by the agent. Typically, agents' commissions are less than 10 percent. As a small manufacturer grows, its agents may be dropped in favor of a factory sales-force. Because of this, agents must search for new lines on a regular basis.

Selling agents, in contrast to manufacturers' agents, perform all or most of the necessary marketing functions for the producer including pricing, advertising, selling, and distributing. Thus, **marketing agent** is probably a more appropriate name for these organizations. They ordinarily do not take possession of (own) the products they sell, nor do they handle competing lines. These agents market the entire output of one to several manufacturers. Selling agents are popular with small manufacturers that lack the resources and knowhow to perform the marketing function and with producers of seasonal lines. Products include textiles, lumber, furniture, and chemicals.

Commission merchants differ from other agents in that they handle the lines of competing producers and may take possession of the merchandise. Commission merchants commonly sell agricultural commodities produced by small- and medium-sized farms. The agent sells the commodity and charges the producer a commission and expenses. Selling price is based on the prevailing market price at the time of sale. Note that commission agents are not the same as the producers' cooperative previously discussed, which consists of farmer members grouped together to form a marketing cooperative. (Land O' Lakes with 350,000 farmer members is an example of a producers' cooperative.)[15] In contrast to the cooperative, the commission agent normally does not work with the producer on a long-term basis. For example, an independent trucker might contract to serve as a commission agent for a farmer who wants to sell a truckload of watermelons or a load of tobacco.

Brokers. The primary role of **brokers** is to act as go-betweens for buyer and seller. As discussed previously, food brokers represent manufacturers by performing the selling function to wholesalers, retail chains, and institutional buyers. Brokers receive a commission on the sales they make. In addition to foods, brokers are common in real estate, insurance, and securities (stocks and bonds). Normally, brokers do not stock merchandise or provide financing. Brokers fill information gaps between buyers and sellers. They provide a contact point for both parties. Their major contribution is conveying information about the availability of products and the needs of buyers. An auction company is also a broker.

Exhibit 14.5 Examples of merchandise lines of agents and brokers

Manufacturers' Agents	Selling Agents	Commission Merchants	Brokers
Electronic instruments	Textiles	Fruits	Stocks and bonds
Valves	Furniture	Vegetables	Real estate
Apparel	Canned Foods	Tobacco	Grocery products
Machinery	Lumber	Livestock	Insurance
Tools	Chemicals	Grain	

Several examples of the merchandise lines of agents and brokers are shown in Exhibit 14.5. Although a particular line of merchandise is not necessarily restricted to one wholesaler, some lines fall logically into a particular agent or broker category.

A distinction between an agent and a broker historically has been that agents have long-term relationships with sellers whereas brokers have one-deal contract relationships. Today, this distinction is blurring and the terms may become synonymous.

Manufacturers' branches and offices (manufacturer-owned establishments)

The branches and offices operated by manufacturers are the third type of wholesaler (see Exhibit 14.3). These organizations are located throughout the producers' market areas, including foreign countries. They differ from other wholesalers because they are owned and operated by the manufacturer. A **sales office** is normally a smaller organizational unit than the **sales branch** and typically performs only a selling function.

Branches sell and service the manufacturer's products and are likely to carry at least a limited inventory. Some provide financial services including invoicing and credit. A company branch is established when a manufacturer shifts from manufacturers' representatives to its own sales locations. These field units range in function from primarily selling to offering a full range of marketing and physical distribution functions. Examples of companies that operate company offices and branches are Procter & Gamble, IBM, General Electric, and Magic Chef.

Retailers may operate **purchasing offices** in major trade centers such as Chicago, Dallas, and New York. Purchasing offices are buying units located in market centers to take advantage of direct and regular contact with suppliers. Where merchandise or trade marts exist, retailers may occupy offices in these facilities. A **merchandise mart** is a facility where producers display their goods and organizational buyers such as retailers can examine the lines of several manufacturers. Merchandise marts are popular in the apparel and furniture industries. Dallas's World Trade Center illustrates the dynamic development of the use of marts for various other lines of goods. The mart contains a display of products from all over the world including electronics, housewares, and jewelry.

Four types of wholesalers handle exporting goods.[16] The **combination export manager (CEM)** may be a person or an organization that serves as the export representative for several noncompeting firms often with related products. The CEM is compensated by a commission arrangement. CEMs are experienced in selling to foreign markets, have an established network of overseas distributors, and are familiar with export procedures and requirements. **Importers** located in the United States are a second form of export representative. Because they specialize in buying from a particular part of the world, their contacts often are useful for export purposes. The third type of export wholesaler is the **trading company.** These firms are similar to the CEMs, except they represent product lines on a continuous basis and may carry competing brands. Trading companies are large middleman companies, often integrated backward into manufacturing. These firms are part of the channels for products and services sold worldwide and perform a host of services such as buying and selling products, offering trade financing, managing construction projects, conducting research, and consulting with other companies. The major trading companies are located in Europe and Japan (see Marketalk). Most of Japan's imports and exports are handled by trading companies such as Mitsui and Mitsubishi. Finally, producers may have their own company-owned distribution network outside the United States through branches and sales offices.

TRENDS IN WHOLESALING

Wholesaling has not changed as rapidly as manufacturing and retailing, perhaps because of the relative power in many channels of distribution held by producers and retailers. Nevertheless, several major trends are underway in the wholesaling industry. In the 1960s and 1970s, some industry observers suggested that independent wholesalers as a marketing institution would die out because of vertical integration of producers and retailers and the growth of large retail chains for many lines of merchandise. Although these forces certainly have altered the composition of the industry, wholesaling remains a major dynamic segment of business today.

Wholesaler consolidation

Acquisition and consolidation of wholesalers are occurring in several merchandise lines. As discussed previously in the chapter, large food wholesalers are acquiring small firms, causing consolidation throughout the industry. Consolidation in food wholesaling began in the 1970s and will continue through the 1980s. The chief executive officer of Super Valu Stores, Mike Wright, comments on one reason for consolidation—computerizing the warehouse industry.

> Selling out to someone with the necessary capital can become the only way out for the little guy. "By merging with larger companies, the warehouses have capital available to expand their distribution centers and to help their retailers expand by financing their growth," he says. Wright's company has nearly $100 million outstanding in financing for its customers' operating needs.[17]

Wholesaling continues to be a fragmented industry with an extremely large number of small firms. Consolidation is difficult in wholesaling because of the large number of limited-line wholesalers and the lack of firms sufficiently large and motivated to acquire other small firms. The desire for independence by many wholesalers is also a factor.

Targeted marketing strategies

Some wholesalers clearly are moving away from an order-taking orientation toward developing merchandising and management systems for use by their retail customers. The motivation, of course, is to improve the productivity and performance of both the wholesaler and its customers. Consider these illustrations.

> Wholesaling firms are looking to new avenues of potential growth and profits. Fundamental to their survival is the need to boost productivity and enhance profitability through new techniques, innovation, and diversification.
> Drug wholesaling firms are leading in the use of sophisticated methods to

improve profitability. For example one large company is computerizing and diversifying its markets by using automated entry services that link stores to the warehouse; modernizing and consolidating its distribution facilities; and adding new and diversified lines such as school supplies and stationery, nutritional foods, appliances, and small electronic items.

This wholesaler also hopes to implement a full-service merchandising program in all its distribution centers by 1983 and expects to double its interstate chain of voluntary, independent drugstores by 1985.

Some large distributors, as a customer service, are holding educational seminars for their customers to inform them about the products they purchase and resell. One distributor holds quarterly seminars led by a representative of one

*Marke*TALK ///

How Japanese trading companies contribute to trade development

THIS CHART ILLUSTRATES the contribution of general trading companies to the steel industry and to the development of sources of supply and demand. General trading companies are involved first in the development of sources of iron ore (Country A). This involvement typically begins with equity investments in development companies, which seek and draw up initial plans for mining iron ore resources. Next, trading companies make equity investments and provide know-how for setting up transportation companies that will move the ore from the mine to port of loading, and eventually to its foreign destination (Japan). At the same time, the trading company may also invest in storage companies that will construct portside storage facilities. When the iron ore mine actually goes into production and loads of iron ore begin to arrive for shipment, the trading company arranges for ship charters. The large volume of business that trading companies do with major shipping companies allows them to obtain more favorable rates than import-export companies, which deal in much smaller volumes. After the ore has arrived in Japan, the trading company sells it to steel manufacturers, along with other raw materials that come into Japan from a wide variety of other sources. In many cases the development of these other sources of raw materials has also involved trading company participation.

After the processing of raw materials into raw steel or finished steel products, trading companies typically purchase a portion of the output and sell it to export

markets overseas. In many cases the trading company may also play an intermediary role in the domestic market, purchasing steel products from one of the five largest manufacturers of raw steel and selling them to domestic processors.

SOURCE: *The Role of Trading Companies in International Commerce,* Tokyo: Japan External Trade Organization, 1983, pp. 15–16. Courtesy of JETRO (Japan External Trade Organization).

///

of its suppliers. These seminars provide opportunities for suppliers to understand end-users' problems and identify where changes and improvements are needed.[18]

The strategy launched by Wetterau, the food wholesaler, illustrates the aggressive, market-driven orientation of top management. Wetterau is interacting directly with the Kroger Company to develop an innovative approach to cooperation between a wholesaler and retail chain. The strategy is as follows:

> Following the Kroger Company's decision to close its Pittsburgh retail division in 1984, Wetterau entered into negotiations and acquired the rights to 27 stores in that region for lease to independents. This strategy enables Wetterau to expand its customer base in this important market, while providing independents with an opportunity to grow and capture a greater market share. The transfer of these stores to independents is underway. Wetterau and Kroger have formed a separate wholesaling company to supply retail food store accounts in the Michigan area. This innovative joint venture, Foodland Distributors, will provide supermarket operators with a full line of grocery products, general merchandise and support services.[19]

This arrangement between retailer and wholesaler could be the beginning of a new era in the food industry—an era of cooperation and unique business relationships.

Important productivity gains

During the last decade major gains in productivity have been made by wholesalers in product areas ranging from food to industrial products. Trends toward automated operations in distribution including robotics; computerized, direct buyer-seller order linkages; and other applications of technology are strengthening wholesalers' relationships with customers and reducing distribution costs. Innovative warehouse designs are improving accessibility and efficiency for wholesalers. Computerized planning and control are central to the modern wholesaler's operations.

Comprehensive computer capability integrates forecasting, buying, inventory control, order entry, shipping, and invoicing for United Stationers. Consider this description of the electronic order entry system.

> Electronic order entry from dealers' premises makes it easier for dealers to do business with the company. It makes order entry easier, faster and more accurate while efficiently generating documentation that helps dealers operate more profitably.
>
> To its larger commercial dealers, United Stationers offers SCORE (Self-Contained Order Entry), which places desk-top computers on the dealers' premises directly linked to the company's computers through leased telephone lines. Dealers can instantly check available stock and confirm prices even while talking to customers, and then enter orders on the spot. SCORE effectively places the United Stationers' warehouses at the dealers' fingertips, on line in real time.
>
> Two other electronic order entry systems are designed especially for over-the-counter retailers: REDI (Rapid Entry Data Input) and AIM (Automated Inventory Management). They both use a hand-held data encoder with an optical scanning wand to read shelf and item price labels provided and constantly updated by United Stationers.
>
> REDI, the simpler of the two systems, is an order entry system through which dealers scan shelf labels with the wand and then punch in desired reorder quantities of the items scanned which then are transmitted to United Stationers over telephone lines. An ordering decision must be made for each item, requiring a decision-maker on the spot.

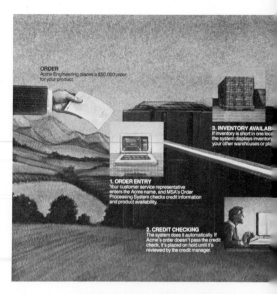

Management Science America, Inc., the largest independent software company, with a customer base of more than 5000 companies, specializes in mainframe applications software. Its order processing systems are one reason that gains in productivity have been achieved by wholesalers. (Courtesy of Management Science America, Inc.)

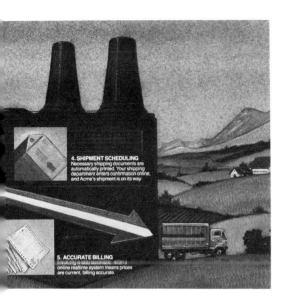

em. It lets you review the status of orders,
es, credit or inventory availability at a
ent's notice. You can change orders easily.
d the system is flexible enough to handle
al requests for shipping vendors, packaging,
ery dates or special handling procedures.
t as important, MSA's online realtime
m helps you control internal costs. It moves
s along without costly error or duplication
ort. It provides current information on
ng, discounts and special sales agreements
individual customers.
d it's a powerful tool for controlling inven-
since you can conveniently check on
tory status daily.
'll find MSA's new Order Processing System

flexible and easy to use. It works with the MSA
Manufacturing System to let you schedule pro-
duction more efficiently. And promise ship
dates to customers more confidently. Of course,
it's also perfectly integrated with MSA's
Financial System.
   If your company is ready for a dramatic
improvement in your order processing, contact
Robert Carpenter at (404) 239-2000. Or write
Management Science America, Inc., 3445
Peachtree Road, N.E., Atlanta, Georgia 30326.

MSA
The Software Company

AIM is a similar but more sophisticated inventory management system because it includes storage in United Stationers' computer of maximum-minimum quantities for each item in each dealer's stock. Ordering the right quantities to meet the intended inventory levels is automatic after the shelf labels are scanned and on-hand quantities are entered. Furthermore, AIM generates stock movement histories and other computer-derived reports to help dealers manage their inventory more effectively.

To serve its dealers even more directly with computer-based management services, United Stationers is offering "COPAS" (Computerized Office Products Accounting System). This is a comprehensive, integrated mini-computer system for use by dealers on their own premises to run their business on a day-to-day basis. It provides dealers with their own order entry, warehouse order picking, accounts receivable, purchasing, accounts payable and general ledger management information systems.

In addition, COPAS provides computer-to-computer telecommunications with United Stationers over regular telephone lines. Item files are preloaded with United Stationers' own 20,000-item inventory file as well as the dealers' own additional items files. This allows the dealers' computer systems to tie in directly with their imprinted catalogs from United Stationers. As with SCORE, dealers know item availability at the time they place their order. Their margins are protected because the system provides for automatic updating of their own computer price files.[20]

The use of new technologies to improve the productivity of distribution is discussed further in Chapter 15.

Product liability

Another trend in wholesaling concerns product liability litigation. Because of the hazardous nature of various products sold such as machine tools, woodworking machinery, heavy-duty automotive and farm equipment, materials handling equipment, electronic goods and components, construction equipment, and power transportation equipment, product liability is a serious concern to wholesale distributors. Many court decisions have held sellers (distributors) as well as manufacturers liable for injuries that occur when such products are used. Many distributors provide installation and service, and even products that are shipped directly to customers involve wholesalers because they perform the selling function. The **Risk Retention Act of 1981** was enacted by the Congress to help wholesalers overcome the rapidly escalating costs of product liability. The act allows wholesaler-distributors to purchase product liability insurance coverage from a commercial carrier on a group basis or to self-insure by forming insurance cooperatives.[21] Before passage of the act insurance rates were becoming extremely costly for wholesalers. For example, the annual premium of one firm increased 400 percent, from $5000 to $20,000, within one year. Using group insurance and cooperative packages should help reduce the problem. It should be noted that product liability concerns are not unique to wholesalers. All of the organizations in the channel have been affected by the high cost of product liability.

SUMMARY

Although there are only about one-third as many wholesalers as retailers, their sales account for a 7 percent share of the gross national product. Wholesalers perform many necessary functions in marketing channels including buying and selling, warehousing and product handling, transporting, providing management assistance to retailers, financing, handling returns and repairs, and assuming risks. Not all of these functions are performed by all wholesalers.

Wholesalers' marketing strategies differ to some degree from other firms owing to the wholesalers' location in the channel of distribution. Most wholesalers are geographically concentrated, so geographic coverage sets boundaries on the target market. Wholesalers' marketing mixes include choices of lines and mix of merchandise carried, operations and distribution, pricing, advertising, and personal selling. Typically, advertising represents a relatively small portion of the wholesalers' marketing budget.

The three major types of wholesalers are merchant wholesalers, agents and brokers, and manufacturers' branches and offices. Merchant wholesalers are the largest category of wholesaler, accounting for approximately four of every five establishments, $1 of every $2 of industry sales, and three of every four employees in wholesaling. Grocery wholesalers account for the largest portion of merchant wholesalers' sales. A major distinction between merchant wholesalers and agents and brokers is that merchant wholesalers take title to goods whereas agents and brokers do not.

Four major trends are underway in the wholesaling industry. First, wholesaler consolidation has occurred in recent years in certain merchandise categories such as food and drugs. Second, wholesalers are adopting aggressive marketing strategies, designed to move them away from an order-taking orientation toward developing merchandising and management systems for use by their retail customers. Third, major gains in productivity have been made by wholesalers. Fourth, product liability has become a serious concern to wholesale distributors.

KEY TERMS

wholesaler	rack jobber	sales office
wholesaling	truck wholesaler	sales branch
merchant wholesalers	truck jobber	purchasing offices
cash and carry wholesaler	manufacturers' agents	merchandise mart
drop shipper	manufacturers' representatives	combination export manager
desk jobber	selling agents	(CEM)
mail-order house	marketing agent	importers
producers' cooperative	commission merchants	trading company
agricultural cooperative	brokers	Risk Retention Act of 1981

QUESTIONS FOR REVIEW AND DISCUSSION

1. What is a wholesaler?

2. Compare and contrast the activities performed by merchant wholesalers and nonmerchant wholesalers (agents and brokers).

3. What are the functions of manufacturers' agents and what advantages do they offer manufacturers?

4. Why is the term *marketing agent* an appropriate name for a selling agent?

5. One of the major types of wholesalers is manufacturers' branches and offices. Explain the role of these wholesalers and indicate how they differ from other wholesalers.

6. What effect on efficiency and cost can investments in modern, cost-effective facilities and equipment have on a full-service wholesaler?

7. Why do wholesalers *not* spend much money on advertising?

8. Several major trends are underway in the wholesaling industry. Describe these trends.

BUILDING YOUR PORTFOLIO

Frontier Plastics has developed a strong yet lightweight stepladder for use in the home. Frontier can produce the ladder at a cost approximately 10 percent higher than aluminum ladders. The material used in the plastic ladder will not conduct electricity, and it weighs about two-thirds as much as a comparable metal ladder. The firm sells its existing line of products to four toy manufacturers. If management decides to produce and market the ladder, a new distribution channel will be needed. Bill Smith, the president of Frontier, is interested in finding out how products such as the stepladder are distributed to consumers. He is particularly interested in learning about the types of distributors and other wholesalers that market this type of product. Prepare a complete analysis of distribution channels for a product such as the stepladder. Describe the types of wholesalers and retailers that carry stepladders. Which distribution channel or channels appear most appropriate for Frontier Plastics, assuming they decide to market the new stepladder?

NOTES

1. Elizabeth Sanger, "Proving their mettle." *Barron's*, July 19, 1984, pp. 13, 20.
2. "Ratings & Reports," 8th ed. *The Value Line Investment Survey*, Aug. 17, 1984, p. 1185.
3. "Vie de France: Putting a French twist on America's daily bread." *Business Week*, Nov. 5, 1984, p. 98.
4. K. O. Carlson, "The supermarket new product scene—1982." *The Nielsen Researcher*, No. 2, 1983, p. 25.
5. Jonathan Greenberg, "Wholesalers." *Forbes*, Jan. 3, 1983, p. 203.
6. "Leasing gets a new lift." *The Morgan Guaranty Survey*, Dec. 1981.
7. Wetterau, Incorporated, *1984 Annual Report*, p. 9.
8. "Why manufacturers are doubling as distributors." *Business Week*, Jan. 17, 1983, p. 41.
9. *1983 U.S. Industrial Outlook*, p. 47-1.
10. *Statistical Abstract of the United States*, 1980, p. 550.
11. *1983 U.S. Industrial Outlook*, p. 47-1.
12. Greenberg, op. cit., p. 202.
13. Irving J. Shapiro, *Dictionary of Marketing Terms*, 4th ed. Totowa, N.J.: Littlefield, Adams, 1981.
14. Harold Seneker, "Food brokering: It's where the action is." *Forbes*, Sept. 17, 1979, pp. 208, 212.
15. James Cook, "Dreams of glory." *Forbes*, Sept. 12, 1983, p. 92.
16. This discussion is drawn from *Export Marketing for Smaller Firms*, 3rd ed. Washington: Small Business Administration, 1971, Chap. IV.
17. Greenberg, op, cit., pp. 202–203.
18. *1983 U.S. Industrial Outlook*, p. 47-3.
19. Wetterau, Incorporated, *1984 Annual Report*, p. 3.
20. United Stationers *Annual Report* for the year ending Aug. 28, 1983, p. 9.
21. *1983 U.S. Industrial Outlook*, p. 47-3.

Case 14.1

Durr-Fillauer Medical-Surgical Division

THE MEDICAL-SURGICAL Division of Durr-Fillauer supplies over 20,000 items and related services to independent and group-related hospitals, physician offices, nursing homes, clinics, laboratories and other health care providers. The Division operates fifteen sales, service and distribution centers in seven states.

In 1983, revenues of the Medical-Surgical Division increased 23% to $102.8 million. Income before taxes increased 18% to $7.7 million compared with pre-tax income of $6.5 million in 1982. At year-end, the Division accounted for 39% of total corporate revenue and 44% of corporate pre-tax income.

The Division's efforts in 1983 were oriented toward satisfying customer needs, while maximizing the utilization of assets, controlling expenses and continuing to pursue profitable growth opportunities.

SOURCE: Durr-Fillauer Medical, *1983 Annual Report*. Courtesy of Durr-Fillauer Medical, Inc.

The key elements in this strategy include asset management, expense control, customer satisfaction and targeted markets.

Average inventory turns for the Division were 9.3 during 1983. The faster inventory turns, the higher the return the Company receives on each dollar invested. The Division's 1983 turnover rate is among the highest for comparable organizations within the industry.

The average collection period also improved in 1983 as did selling, general and administrative expenses as a percentage of revenues. One further aspect which helped overall efficiency was the increased use of electronic order entry in this Division. Over 30% of all orders were received electronically—up from 10% in 1982. Large hospitals and clinics using electronic order entry help reduce our total distribution cost thus allowing a portion of the savings to be passed along to our customers.

Using information obtained as a result of customer-based planning, the Company's sales and marketing programs were further enhanced to meet the specific needs of each customer segment. All of the distribution centers achieved greater market penetration by customer segment utilizing the resulting market strategies.

Future growth for the Division will essentially depend on continuing and expanding with existing strategies: geographic expansion, efficient operations and programs targeted by customer segment. The change in the health care payments program will cause some variations in delivery systems. Outpatient surgery centers, home health care and increased use of nursing homes are a few of the likely areas to benefit from the change. Durr-Fillauer's strategy has tailored the Company's distribution services to meet the changing needs of the health care marketplace.

QUESTIONS

1. What intermediary functions does this wholesaler perform?

2. Describe the Medical-Surgical Division's marketing strategy.

3. What role does inventory turnover play in the financial performance of a wholesaler?

4. How is technology involved in this wholesaler's operations?

Case 14.2

Vallen Corporation

THE NATIONAL SAFETY Council has estimated that in 1980, the most recent year studied, deaths and injuries on the job cost business approximately $30 billion. The Safety Council estimates the average cost of a disabling accident to be $9,400.

Corporations are becoming increasingly aware of the mounting cost of on-the-job claims. The call for industrial safety is resurging. It is no secret that lower accident rates foster higher profits.

SOURCE: Vallen Corporation, *Fiscal 1983 Annual Report*, pp. 9, 11. Designed by Herring Design, Houston.

Although some industries are inherently more dangerous, such as construction, accident rates tend to vary greatly from company to company within the same industry—an indication that industrial safety can be improved through sound programs and a commitment to them. Corporations which establish serious safety programs average a reduction of 38 percent in accidents the first year.

Accident and illness costs are advancing faster than the rate of inflation. For the last several years, the cost of employee lost time due to injuries and occupational illnesses has been rising at an average an-

nual rate of 15 percent. If a company's safety performance is just average, that organization will have more than 2.5 lost workdays per 100 employees per year due to injury or illness. Each lost workday now costs the employer from $10,000 to $14,000. This cost does not include indirect expenses such as associated property damage and administrative time which could account for up to five times the direct accident cost.

Incentives to take safety seriously have increased sharply because costs are threatening to get out of hand. Not only are claims bigger, but more ailments and injuries are coming under the coverage of worker's compensation. Although states determine employee compensation rates, employers pay for their own safety records. They buy insurance to pay the claims, or are self-insured up to a minimum which ranges from $250,000 to $1 million per accident. Most states set payment at two-thirds of the injured worker's wage up to a maximum amount. The bulk of worker's compensation claims, until recently, have arisen from accidents. Companies now face additional large and growing liabilities because of the health effects of substances, such as asbestos, used years before their damaging effects became known. Furthermore, the range of ailments which may be attributed to occupational conditions has expanded. Alcoholism or ulcers can now be interpreted as a response to a stressful working environment.

The cost of establishing a corporate safety and health program, depending upon the magnitude of the program required, could include: supervision and management time; accident investigation; job safety analysis; inspections; safety committees; communications and incentives; training standards; new employee orientation; safety apparel and equipment; fire protection; housekeeping; industrial hygiene; security; off-the-job safety; audiovisual aids; and damage control. These expenditures are often less than the average cost for a lost workday due to injury or illness. Most organizations which invest in a safety program on any scale have found the investment to be more than worthwhile.

Progressive companies are implementing loss-prevention measures into their safety programs. Instituting programs, often through professional consultants, ensures higher safety standards and a boost in productivity and profits.

With the formation of the Occupational Safety and Health Administration (OSHA) in 1971, government regulation of industry increased dramatically. Once regarded solely as a regulatory agency, OSHA has developed a new emphasis: to help industry improve its safety record by stressing human factors, such as training and safety awareness. Evidence exists that most accidents are not caused by unsafe conditions, but by unsafe acts—more than 70 percent of injuries are the result of slips and falls, improper lifting or careless driving. This shift in policy from policeman to consultant by OSHA places the burden of providing a safe workplace and a healthy workforce on the private sector.

Vallen's role in the safety industry is as a major distributor and manufacturer of safety equipment to industry. It distributes a wide range of personal protection equipment and protective clothing, such as goggles, safety glasses, safety hats and protective garments. Other products include fire extinguishers, hoses, nozzles, safety hooks, safety signs, lights and alarms. The Company's manufacturing subsidiary, Encon Manufacturing Co., is a leading producer of such items as eyewash, emergency showers, eye protection products and protective clothing. Vallen manufactures products when it sees a need in the marketplace but cannot find outside suppliers whose products are of acceptable quality. Important customers include chemical producers, petroleum refiners, oil and gas extractors, and the construction industry, all of whom have ac-

knowledged their responsibility to get the job done safely, efficiently, and economically.

Vallen's largest product category is respiratory equipment, including both portable and self-contained units, designed to be worn by workers requiring an independent source of breathable air. This equipment, together with gas detection instruments, is used in industries where work must be done in unbreathable atmospheres, or where workers are exposed to toxic or combustible gases, carcinogens or other dangerous atmospheric particles. The company also maintains service centers which inspect, repair and calibrate respiratory equipment and gas detection instruments.

Vallen also provides industrial safety training for companies concerned with a wide range of occupational hazards such as respiratory impairment, hearing loss, and the physiological dangers of working within confined spaces. Vallen's trained personnel often conduct seminars for individual companies and for safety conferences.

It is management's contention that safety equipment is often made and never used because the equipment is difficult or uncomfortable to use. Vallen believes that workers must be trained in the proper use of safety equipment and offers this service to its customers. There exists a need for more innovative equipment which takes into consideration the comfort of the worker and utilizes the latest technological advances. Vallen will market these products as they are developed.

QUESTIONS

1. Who are Vallen's customers? What customer needs is Vallen meeting?

2. What services could Vallen provide to its customers to assist them with their safety programs?

3. Is Vallen involved in a channel of distribution role other than as a wholesaler?

15 Physical Distribution

When you finish this chapter, you will understand

□ The vital role of physical distribution in marketing products

□ The characteristics of the various physical distribution management activities and their interrelationships

□ The key features and limitations of each transportation mode

□ The problems that occur when the physical distribution system is not functioning properly

□ The objectives of physical distribution management

□ The considerations involved in building a physical distribution system

□ Several important trends affecting physical distribution management

Pipelines ensure the efficient distribution of oil and other liquids and gases. They transport oil from its source to storage locations easily accessed by refineries.

In the transportation industry, United Parcel Service (UPS) is unique. Although it is the biggest single private shipper on most railroads and owns a large fleet of airplanes (it also ships packages on commercial airlines), it is basically a highway carrier with a fleet of more than 62,000 vehicles. It is also by far the largest employer of members of the International Brotherhood of Teamsters (IBT), with approximately 85,000 members on the payroll. Its drivers call on 600,000 factories, offices, and stores each day.[1]

UNITED PARCEL SERVICE REPRESENTS only a small part of the physical distribution of goods through marketing channels, yet the firm's 1982 revenues were more than $5 billion. As companies continue to use speed of transport as an alternative to carrying inventory, UPS's business is likely to grow. Physical distribution costs are a major portion of the selling price for many products, and transportation is only one component of the total cost of physical distribution. UPS offers powerful evidence that private enterprise can improve customer service at competitive costs and still chalk up a strong record of financial performance. UPS performs a transportation service for many organizations and persons. Organizations involved in the physical movement of goods include transportation firms, manufacturers, wholesalers, retailers, and warehouse firms.

First, we examine the role of physical distribution in a developed economy by defining its function and highlighting its importance. Next, we consider the physical distribution decisions that must be made regarding transportation, inventory, facilities, materials handling and packaging, and communications. We discuss how to identify physical distribution problems and what must be done to eliminate the problems. Finally, we describe the essential aspects of managing physical distribution and consider some important trends in physical distribution management.

ROLE AND IMPORTANCE OF PHYSICAL DISTRIBUTION

What is physical distribution?

Physical distribution defined. **Physical distribution** essentially is moving goods from origin to destination. **Physical distribution management (PDM)** is planning, implementing, and controlling the physical flows and storage of materials and finished goods inventory from suppliers, manufacturers, and middlemen to end-users.[2] The term **logistics** is sometimes used instead of physical distribution, particularly when the flow of raw materials, supplies, and parts to producers is considered part of the physical distribution network.

Physical distribution activities. Moving and storing goods throughout the distribution network require that managers make decisions about facilities, inventory, transportation, communications, and materials handling and packaging. The concept of PDM recognizes that these activities must be integrated and coordinated to perform properly the distribution function. Instead of each activity operating independently, the group of activities should be managed as a system because their costs are interrelated: attempting to hold individual costs down (such as shipping by boat rather than by air) may cause the total costs (for example, high costs of inventory and warehousing) to skyrocket (see Exhibit 15.1). Coordinating these activities is considered in detail in the section Managing Physical Distribution.

Production and marketing channel interrelationships. Exhibit 15.2 illustrates the links between the marketing activities and manufacturing activities included in physical distribution. The solid lines indicate marketing activities and the dashed lines show production activities. A coordinated approach to physical distribution integrates both production and physical distribution responsibilities, with one manager overseeing the various activities. Because a coordinated approach to PDM involves several functional areas such as manufacturing and marketing, giving one manager responsibility for all activities may not be accepted readily by the functional managers involved. We return to this issue later in the chapter.

Importance of physical distribution

If importance is measured by the amount of money spent, then physical distribution clearly is important. But more is at stake than costs. Physical distribution activities can drastically alter customer satisfaction. Let us examine both the cost and customer aspects of physical distribution.

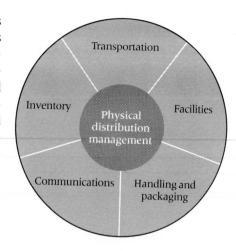

Exhibit 15.1   Physical distribution management activities

Physical distribution costs. Because a wide variety of activities are associated with physical distribution and the activities usually are performed by several functional areas (e.g., sales, purchasing, transportation, and manufacturing), estimating exact costs often is difficult. The National Council of Physical Distribution Management and others indicate that the physical distribution costs of moving goods from producer to final consumer for U.S. and Canadian firms are as much as 20 percent of the gross national product.[3] Physical distribution costs in the U.S. were approximately $800 billion for 1985, assuming that they comprise 20 percent of gross national product. Based on this figure, annual physical distribution costs are

- More than 20 percent of personal income
- Approximately double the size of state and local government purchases
- Approximately 2.5 times federal purchases
- Double nonresidential fixed investment

Thus it is not surprising that PDM is a major concern of many companies, including merchandising and manufacturing firms.

Norfork Southern strives to be an efficient provider of low-cost transportation. In 1984, the railroad had the lowest transportation ratio—transportation expenses to operating revenues—of any major railroad. Norfolk Southern also foresees cost-effective innovations such as a communications network of fiber-optic cables, an expanded use of robotics, and perhaps even satellites to control train operations. (Courtesy of Norfolk Southern Corporation)

A major study of distribution costs yielded cost comparisons of distribution activities as a percentage of sales for U.S. firms, as shown in Exhibit 15.3. Total distribution costs for manufacturing firms are approximately 14 percent of sales compared with 26 percent for merchandising companies. Transportation is one-quarter to one-half of physical distribution costs—the largest cost item for manufacturing firms. Interestingly, inventory carrying is the largest cost component for both consumer and industrial merchandising companies.

Physical distribution and customers. Having a product in the right place and at the right time can affect greatly customer satisfaction. When the physical distribution system satisfies customers' needs and wants, customers will be

Exhibit 15.2   Illustrative physical distribution network*

* Solid lines represent marketing logistics; dashed lines represent production logistics.

SOURCE: J. R. Dowdle, "Physical Distribution," in Earl L. Bailey, (Ed.), *Tomorrow's Marketing*, New York: The Conference Board, 1974, pp. 26–39.

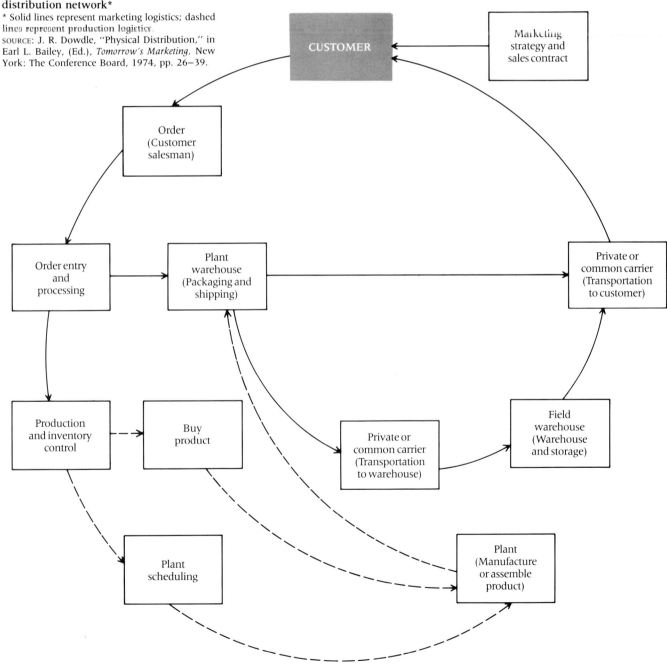

Exhibit 15.3 Physical distribution costs by type of activity (percentage of sales)

	Transpor-tation	Inventory Carrying	Ware-housing	Adminis-tration	Receiving and Shipping	Packaging	Order Processing	Total
All Manufacturing Companies	6%	1%	4%	1%	1%	1%	1%	14%
Chemicals and plastics	6	2	3	*	1	1	1	14
Food manufacturing	8	*	4	*	1	—	*	13
Pharmaceutical	1	—	1	1	1	*	1	4
Electronics	3	3	3	1	1	1	1	13
Paper	6	*	5	*	*	—	*	11
Machinery and tools	5	1	2	1	1	1	1	10
All other	7	1	3	1	1	*	*	14
All Merchandising Companies	7	10	4	1	1	1	1	26
Consumer goods	8	9	4	1	1	1	1	24
Industrial goods	6	14	3	1	*	2	1	26

SOURCE: B. J. LaLonde and P. H. Zinszer, *Customer Service: Meaning and Measurement,* Chicago: National Council of Physical Distribution Management, 1976.
* = less than 1%

favorably inclined toward the company and the brand. Consider this illustration: Steve Stevens, the head of maintenance for a school district near Houston, paid $12.64 for a box of wood screws delivered by a Lawson Products' salesperson, when comparable screws could have been picked up for $4.53 from a wholesaler twenty miles away.

> For Stevens, the arrival of the Lawson salesman has meant more time for his carpenters to fix broken school windows. "Before, they were buying a few screws here and a few there and leaving them around in bags," he says. "It would take them an hour to get to the hardware store and back."[4]

Lawson is a profitable business based on the idea that customers value their time and are willing to pay premium prices for quality and convenience. The firm has five regional warehouses, each stocked to provide customers with 99 percent order fulfillment (which means that 99 percent of all items ordered are available immediately). More than 1000 salespersons sell 17,000 different replacement parts. (See Marketech for a discussion of how Lowe's Companies' Accusale Information Management System keeps track of its extensive inventory.)

Aspects of physical distribution affect customer satisfaction in several ways. Some examples include speed and availability of spare parts, reduction of order-processing time, availability of wide assortments, and shipment of the correct order. Transportation, inventory, and the other activities listed in Exhibit 15.3 work together to help deliver customer satisfaction. Malfunction of any one of the activities can antagonize a customer. The following section, Physical Distribution Activities, examines what is involved in making decisions about these activities.

PHYSICAL DISTRIBUTION DECISIONS

Selecting a transportation mode

General Electric's major appliance group, based in Louisville, Kentucky, bargains with transportation suppliers such as truckers and railroads to reduce the total costs of distribution.

The GE appliance group is overhauling its distribution system. The new strategy involves closing small warehouses that can't profitably stock its full line of appliances. Customer orders will be shipped from regional distribution centers to public terminals or warehouses in secondary markets.[5]

Central to GE's physical distribution strategy is developing an extremely efficient trucking and rail system. Computers are used to keep track of fluctuating freight rates and to target the best mode of transportation for each distribution situation.

Criteria for mode selection. The major transportation modes according to billions of ton-miles transported in 1980 are shown in Exhibit 15.4. (A ton-

Marke**TECH**

Lowe's Accusale Information management system

KEEPING LOWE'S home-improvement stores stocked is a major physical distribution challenge. The firm carries 15,000 different products, 10,000 of which are in each of the retailer's 235 stores. Lowe's maintains an impressive in-stock level of 95 percent.

Lowe's neatly dovetails its distribution systems and its inventory management systems to effect better service to individual stores and therefore to customers. This coordination has reduced the amount of money tied up in inventory, which previously had to be in place to ensure high in-stock status.

Lowe's Accusale system is the information management muscle that allows all this to happen. Today the vast majority of Lowe's merchandise is purchased in North America, with a small but important part of it coming from five Far Eastern nations. This inventory, which supplies more than 60 percent of the retail business, moves into and out of two product distribution warehouses. Lowe's fleet of distribution equipment (56 over-the-road tractors and 188 road trailers) made more than 10,000 deliveries last year, or an average of 42.5 trips to each store. Lowe's distribution fleet accounted for only half of the trips; the rest were handled by trucks operating under contract to the company, known as contract carriers. The 5.5 million miles Lowe's trucks travel from warehouse to stores is cost efficient because each returns by way of a supplier, hauling merchandise back to the Lowe warehouse

for distribution to the store network.

The data processing system determines the selection of merchandise from the location within the warehouse, what the distribution trucks will be loaded with, the schedule for the loaded truck to follow, how long it will take to unload it at the store, where to travel to the vendor to pick up a load of merchandise for back-haul to the warehouse, the schedule for sequential unloading of the truck back at the warehouse, and the optimum position in the warehouse for storage of the new merchandise until it is ready to go out.

The task of determining what each order to each store will consist of has been greatly enhanced with the adoption of a perpetual stock status and inventory system. From the store's computer systems, information on what each store sold during the previous sales hours is gathered nightly. Accusale captures the information on an item-by-item, store-by-store basis and expedites it. In past years, Lowe's ran weekly inventory updates in hard-copy form. Today inventory information is on-line, ready for buyers to use on their terminal screens by 7:30 A.M. This immediacy has reduced the lead time by six days for products to be ordered, which alone saves $24 million annually in inventory funds.

Inventory management through Accusale sets up a system of price discipline, which makes pricing a strategic management decision, not a field salesforce determination. Every item within the company has a company firm price, including commodities. These prices can be and frequently are changed weekly, and a salesperson cannot change them without store office intervention. The second tier of Ac-

cusale-controlled prices is the manager firm price: The manager is able to review and establish a local market price by overriding the company firm price on approximately 400 to 500 items that are competitive in a store's market. The third tier is a builder price that applies to builder customers only on up to 300 items.

The automatic inventory system also enables sales to be forecast and products to be automatically replenished. *Inforem,* the IBM-originated software, generates a sales forecast by item by store, and today more than 5600 items in the warehouses are on the automatic replenishment model. The sales profile is based on a seasonal profile of a family of similar items rather than on precisely specific items. It has a variable response smoothing mode that takes present sales and replenishes stock according to a three-year historical sales model. The entire system tends to eliminate routine clerical decision making from buyers' jobs, which typically covers 200 different items for more than 200 stores. More than 40,000 clerical decisions a week are eliminated.

One of the newest areas data processing is being challenged to improve is selecting the proper channel for an item to travel to a store—whether through the warehouse to stores or from the vendor directly to the stores. The first project the model was asked to solve concerned paint, which previously had been shipped directly to stores. An internally developed model determined that the better channel was through the central warehouse, effecting a savings of forty cents per gallon—a savings, based on last year's sales, of $400,000.

SOURCE: Lowe's Companies, Inc., *Investors' Review,* 1982, pp. 20–21.

mile is the movement of 2000 pounds of freight for one mile.) Typically, several criteria may be considered by a firm when selecting an appropriate mode for a given situation. These include

Cost per ton-mile

Speed: length of time required to move item from origin to destination, or door-to-door delivery time

Frequency: the number of times per time period (e.g., per day) that services are provided from one destination to another

Availability: the number of different geographic origin and destination points served by a particular mode or carrier

Dependability: the extent to which time schedules are met; the reliability of the transporter

Capability: the ability of the transporter to perform necessary transportation functions, including providing needed equipment and personnel[6]

Using these criteria as a basis for comparison, the features and limitations of each transportation mode are shown in Exhibit 15.5. Building on this comparison several examples of the types of goods movement appropriate for each mode are shown in Exhibit 15.6. These examples are illustrative because the mode decision often is influenced by the priorities assigned to the criteria when management selects a specific mode. (Marketalk about Overseas Shipholding Group takes an in-depth look at bulk shipping.)

Impact of deregulation on transportation. Major changes are taking place in the transportation industry, largely as a consequence of deregulation. In 1978 the federal government deregulated the airlines, and in 1980 the trucking and railroad industries. One major consequence is increased flexibility available to shippers who use the combination modes or **multimodal services** offered by transportation firms. A transportation firm such as Burlington Northern, as a result of deregulation, can offer combination mode arrangements instead of only railroad services. Consider this assessment:

> A handful of giant companies are expected to evolve, each offering global door-to-door service. They will use various combinations of truck, rail, aircraft, ship, barge and pipeline for what promises to be a more efficient and finely tuned system of moving and distributing goods.[1]

For example, a canned goods factory may load crates into a Safeway trailer. A crane lifts the trailer onto a railroad flatcar. After the train carries the Safeway trailer to a regional destination, the trailer will be unloaded, and a truck will haul it to Safeway stores. This combination is called **piggyback** (also known as trailer-on-flatcar or TOFC). **Fishyback** is a similar combination of truck and water service, and **birdyback** combines air and land service. Still another multimodal service is **containerized freight,** in

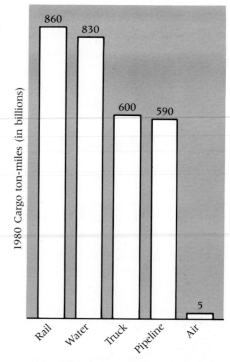

Exhibit 15.4 1980 Cargo ton-miles (in billions), by major mode
SOURCE: U.S. Department of Transportation, *National Transportation Statistics*, DOT-TSC-RSPA-81-8, Sept. 1981.

Exhibit 15.5 Comparison of modes according to various selection criteria

Mode	Cost	Speed	Frequency	Availability	Dependability	Capability
Rail	Medium	Medium	Low	Extensive	Medium	High
Water	Low	Very slow	Very low	Limited	Medium	High
Truck	High	Fast	High	Very extensive	High	Medium
Pipeline	Very low	Slow	Very high	Very limited	High	Very low
Air	Very high	Very fast	Medium	Medium	High	Low

Exhibit 15.6   Examples of goods shipped by transportation mode

Rail
Automobiles, farm equipment, grain, coal, petroleum products

Water
Steel, cement, bauxite, iron ore, automobiles, beef

Truck
Appliances, televisions, apparel, automobiles, milk, meats, foods

Pipeline
Chemicals, petroleum products, natural gas, water

Air
Mail, newspapers, fresh seafoods, flowers, instruments, small parts

which goods are placed in a large standardized container that is loaded on-to a trailer's chassis. Using this system, it is possible to place only the container, and not the truck, onto a ship or flatcar (this latter combination is known as container-on-flatcar or COFC).

This new flexibility in transportation options available to shippers may eliminate several important distinctions between modes that were present before deregulation. Shippers can gain the important advantages of multi-modal transportation systems while eliminating key disadvantages.

Inventory planning and control

Inventories consist of raw materials and parts, work-in-process, and finished goods located at the production location and at various points in the distribution channel. Let us look closer at the purposes of inventory, the costs associated with inventory, and how decisions regarding inventory are made.[8]

Why carry inventory.   Several points in an illustrative distribution system at which inventory stocks may exist are shown in Exhibit 15.7. Some major reasons for carrying inventories are to

1. Reduce delays in producing and distributing products
2. Provide flexibility in production scheduling and ordering materials, parts, and finished goods
3. Have available products when and where buyers want to purchase them
4. Take advantage of purchasing quantities in economical lots

Other reasons for stocking inventories of materials, parts, and finished goods are to provide hedges against inflation, to protect against strikes, and to provide steady employment for employees.

Demand for products may be continuous, staying at relatively constant levels. Alternatively, demand may fluctuate during the year. Finally, demand for products may follow seasonal patterns. Toys, for example, are purchased heavily during the Christmas season.

Inventory costs.   Maintaining an inventory involves these costs.

carrying costs: Costs associated with maintaining inventory stocks such as financing, storage, insurance, and obsolescence
ordering costs: The expenses of placing and processing orders
production costs: The cost per unit produced at a given time (produc-

In 1984, American railroads earned $2.7 billion in profits on $29.5 billion in freight revenue—almost double the numbers of a decade ago. One big reason, in addition to deregulation, is improved technology, making freight railroads competitive with trucks and cargo planes. (Courtesy, Association of American Railroads)

*Marke*TALK ///

The business of Overseas Shipholding Group—bulk shipping

OVERSEAS SHIPHOLDING Group, one of the largest bulk shipping companies in the world, is engaged exclusively in the ocean transportation of liquid and dry bulk cargoes both worldwide and in the self-contained United States. OSG's operating fleet totals seventy-one vessels with a total carrying capacity of 6.5 million deadweight tons. (A deadweight ton [dwt] is a measure of a vessel's cargo capacity.)

Bulk shipping is distinguished from other forms of ocean transport by the types of vessels used, the trades in which they engage, and the manner in which freight rates are determined. Bulk vessels are designed specifically to transport large-volume individual bulk commodities. The vessel's tanks or holds are loaded and unloaded directly by on-board or shipside equipment. Owing to the fast and efficient cargo-handling operations and the long voyages, these vessels normally spend rel-

SOURCE: Overseas Shipholding Group, Inc., Annual Report 1983.

atively little time at loading and discharging facilities.

Tankers and dry bulk carriers usually transport one full cargo per voyage directly from the point of origin of the shipment to the point of destination (although the incidence of multiport loading and discharging of oil cargoes has been increasing). They are not bound to specific ports or schedules and therefore are free to take advantage of chartering opportunities. Bulk vessels are contract rather than common carriers, and charter rates are determined by market forces.

In 1983, the world merchant fleet totaled 633 million dwt, down 2 percent from a year earlier. This decline compares with an annual average growth rate of 5 percent during the previous decade. Oil tankers, the largest segment of the fleet, accounted for 44 percent, or 280 million dwt, after a 21 million dwt net reduction in 1983. This was the sixth successive year of declining world tanker capacity. Dry bulk carriers, transporting a wide variety of commodities including grain, coal, iron ore, and other minerals, accounted for 28 percent, or 178 million dwt. Combination

vessels, able to carry either liquid or dry bulk cargoes, accounted for 7 percent, or 43 million dwt. These bulk ships totaled 501 million dwt, or 79 percent of the total world's merchant shipping tonnage.

Bulk shipping freight rates are highly responsive to changes in supply and demand, and short-term fluctuations are common. OSG tries to minimize the effects of periods of market weakness by a chartering policy that favors medium- and long-term contracts. This policy avoids the sharp rate fluctuations characteristic of the spot, or voyage, markets. Although medium- and long-term charter rates also adjust to changes in supply and demand, the fluctuations are not as extreme.

The various markets in the bulk shipping industry often differ in character and prospects. Demand for particular types or sizes of vessels can remain strong at the same time that weakness prevails in other sectors. Moreover, the development of new types of vessels to meet the requirements of specialized trades is largely independent of market conditions in the main commodity trades.

///

ing small quantities is typically more expensive than producing less frequently in large quantities)

out-of-stock costs: Costs incurred when a customer becomes dissatisfied or purchases from another source if he or she is forced to wait for goods to be ordered

The relationships between inventory size and costs are illustrated in Exhibit 15.8. Note that carrying costs increase whereas ordering, production, and out-of-stock costs decrease as the quantity in inventory increases.

Inventory decisions. Three decisions must be made about inventories: the amount to be carried in stock, the quantity to be ordered when stock is depleted, and when to reorder. These decisions are interrelated. Several decision guides or models are available based on the kind of inventory situation present in a particular firm and the assumptions about costs and demand that correspond to the situation.

An illustrative decision guide is the **fixed-order quantity model,** which can be used when inventory stock is depleted to a reorder level established by management. It is often called the **economic order quantity (EOQ) model,** because it represents an economic balance between ordering costs and inventory carrying costs. That is, the total of the two costs is at a minimum. The model is illustrated in Exhibit 15.9, where the

Exhibit 15.7 Illustrative points of inventory stocks in a distribution system

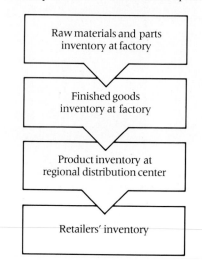

Raw materials and parts inventory at factory

Finished goods inventory at factory

Product inventory at regional distribution center

Retailers' inventory

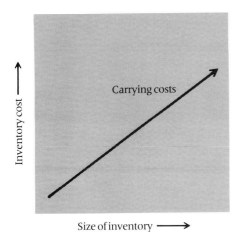

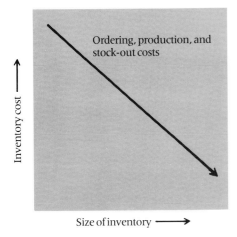

Exhibit 15.8 Illustrative relationships between inventory size and costs

order quantity, Q_1, is fixed and the order frequency varies according to how fast the inventory stock is depleted to the reorder point. The order quantity (Q_1) is determined by minimizing the total cost of ordering plus carrying. Thus Q_1 is the quantity that corresponds to the minimum point on the total cost curve in Exhibit 15.9.

Warehousing

Purpose of warehousing. Warehouses provide the physical space for storing inventories. Warehousing is an essential activity for most firms because it does the following:

1. Achieves production and transportation economies
2. Enables quantity purchase discounts
3. Maintains a source of supply
4. Supports customer service policies
5. Hedges against changing market conditions
6. Overcomes time and space differentials that exist between producers and consumers
7. Helps accomplish the development of an effective physical distribution system[9]

Warehousing and inventories are closely interrelated because one requires the other.

Types of warehouses. Two major kinds of warehouses are public and private. **Public warehouses** (also called **storage warehouses**) are independently owned and provide space on a rental basis to various firms. They are available to store general merchandise and items needing specialized storage such as cold storage and bulk storage.[10] In addition to storage these warehouses may provide other services such as consolidating different shipments, breaking bulk quantities into smaller amounts, packaging, labeling, transporting, and billing. **Private warehouses** (also called **distribution**

Exhibit 15.9 Fixed-order quantity inventory model

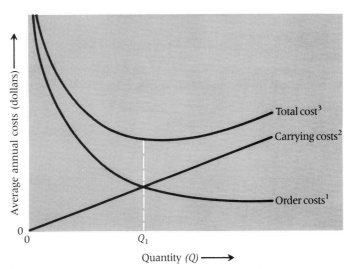

[1]The cost of ordering; this cost decreases as the size of the order increases.
[2]The cost of carrying inventory; this cost increases as larger quantities are ordered.
[3]The combination of ordering cost and inventory cost.

Exhibit 15.10 Factors affecting the choice among types of warehouses

	Types of Warehousing Arrangements		
	Private		Public
Factors	Owned	Leased	
1. Fixed investment	Very high	Moderate; depends on the lease's terms	No fixed investment is involved
2. Unit cost	High, if volume is low	High, if volume is low	Low, since facilities are on "for hire as needed," and fixed costs are widely distributed among users
3. Control	High	High	Low managerial control
4. Adequacy to product line	Highly adequate	Moderately adequate	May not be convenient
5. Flexibility	Low	Low	High; termination of usage can be easily arranged

SOURCE: Adapted from Louis W. Stern and Adel I. El-Ansary, *Marketing Channels*, 2nd ed. Englewood Cliffs, N.J.: Prentice-Hall, 1982, p. 167. © 1982. Reprinted by permission of Prentice-Hall, Inc.

warehouses) are owned (or leased) and operated by the firms whose products are stored in them. Manufacturers, wholesalers, and retailers own and operate warehouses. Several factors that may be important in deciding between public and private warehousing are shown in Exhibit 15.10. Note that the comparisons are from the point of view of a company seeking warehousing for its products. Many firms maintain private warehouses for typical inventory levels, but rent public warehouse space for seasonal demand surges or unusual stockpiling situations.

Regional distribution centers. A **regional distribution center (RDC)** is a large private distribution warehouse located within a geographic area served by a manufacturer, wholesaler, or retailer. The purpose of the RDC is to shorten delivery time and provide improved service to the customers of the firm operating the RDC. These centers became popular during the last decade as a means of providing high levels of customer service at efficient operating levels. As an illustration, Dayton-Hudson has an RDC in Dallas designed to support forty retail stores in the firm's South Central region. These RDCs perform various distribution functions including purchasing, storing, transporting, processing orders, and packaging. Often, the RDCs are linked by computer to each other, to customers, and to the firm's headquarters.

Warehousing functions. In addition to actually storing products, warehousing involves several activities including receiving, movement within the warehouse, selecting orders, and loading onto the transportation carrier.[11] Consider, for example, the activities of a grocery wholesaler. Food products are unloaded from railcars and trucks by forklift truck and moved to storage bins or shelves in the warehouse. When a retail supermarket orders a week's supply of groceries, the items in the order are "picked" from storage spaces, grouped together on wooden bases called pallets or in containers, moved to loading docks, and placed on a truck for transporting to the customer's store. Various forms of paperwork and electronic information processing such as additions and deletions to inventory records and invoicing accompany the movement and storage of warehouse goods.

Warehouse decisions. Management must decide the *number* and *location* of warehouses needed to facilitate the physical distribution function. Trade-offs between warehousing and other physical distribution functions exist. For example, a few large warehouses with sufficient inventory levels can do the job of a large number of small warehouses, provided an adequate transportation network is available to support the large warehouses. Some companies, such as The Limited (women's apparel retailer), use a single strategically located distribution center to serve their stores. The Limited has a 525,000-square-foot center in Columbus, Ohio, with the capacity to serve 700 retail stores throughout the United States. Other firms, such as United Stationers (office products wholesalers), use RDCs. (See Marketalk.)

Materials handling and packaging

These functions are concerned with various aspects of handling products and materials throughout the distribution system. We discuss the importance of packaging for protecting and enhancing the product in Chapter 11, and in this chapter we concentrate on materials handling. It is important, nevertheless, to recognize that packaging may represent an essential aspect of physical distribution systems design.

The physical handling of goods involves inventory, warehousing, and transportation activities throughout the distribution network. Consider, for example, the number of times a box of dishwasher soap is handled as it is moved from point of production to a shelf in a supermarket. From the

*Marke*TALK //

Physical distribution in action

UNITED STATIONERS is a computer-based wholesale distributor. The company distributes some 20,000 office product items made by 380 manufacturers to 8500 dealers.

The Regional Distribution Centers are warehouses averaging 260,000 sq ft, each stocking all 20,000 items listed in the United Stationers catalogs. They are inventory hubs networked by the company's controlled fleet of owned, leased and contracted trucks and its 27 Local Distribution Centers, which are nonstocking re-distribution points averaging 7,800 sq ft.

The Local Distribution Centers are delivery points served from the Regional Distribution Centers. The Regional Distribution Centers send semi-trailers with dealer orders each night to the Local Dis-

SOURCE: United Stationers *Annual Report* for the year ending Aug. 28, 1983, p. 11.

tribution Centers for dealer pickup the next day or for local delivery. In addition, more and more controlled truck routes are being developed for direct delivery from the Regional Distribution Centers or the Local Distribution Centers to the dealers on a pre-arranged, scheduled-time basis. United Stationers also drop ships to the end users in its dealers' names (the company never sells direct to an end-user).

This distribution system provides consistent, dependable (much of it overnight) delivery of 98% of the dealer orders placed. So United Stationers dealers can promise their customers the consistent availability of 20,000 of the most popular brand-name items in the office products industry. This minimizes dealers' inventories, increasing their inventory turns and profits.

United Stationers, in summary, views its role as a wholesaler as more than that of an order-taking warehouse and delivery

operation. It makes itself increasingly more important to dealers by helping them sell more and more profitably. It does this by providing a comprehensive catalog selection, state-of-the-art electronic order entry, innovative merchandising help, the broadest and deepest inventory in the industry, and timely delivery.

Along with its array of direct selling support programs, the company provides dealers with management services they could not afford on their own. The services help dealers run their businesses better with respect to inventory and financial controls, facilities, promotional programs, up-to-date price reporting and computer analysis of operations.

As these services make United Stationers more important to more dealers, United Stationers will achieve its goals of increasing dealer penetration and extending its dealer base.

///

assembly line it is placed in a container of several boxes of soap. The container is fastened with other containers on a pallet, loaded by forklift onto a truck or railcar, shipped to a wholesaler's warehouse, unloaded, and placed in a bin. After remaining in the wholesaler's inventory for a few days, it is picked for loading and transport to the supermarket, where the container is unloaded and opened, and several boxes are placed on the retailer's shelf.

This simple example highlights the many handling tasks involved in the physical distribution of goods. The efficiency of distribution may be notably improved if materials handling activities can be simplified and made increasingly efficient. An important part of the handling function is preventing damage to the products being moved. Although it often is impossible to eliminate damage entirely, minimizing it is essential.

Two important developments are making substantial contributions to materials handling in some firms: (1) **unitizing,** in which as many packages as possible are stacked onto one load (or pallet) and held in place by straps or plastic sheeting, and (2) **containerization,** in which several unitized loads are combined in a container specially designed for efficient handling. As an example, a manufacturer may package a complete retail display (unitizing), shipping several displays to a wholesaler in a container. These packaging techniques reduce handling, decrease damage, and facilitate movement of products through the channel.

Communications and order processing

Communications play a critical role in the physical distribution system, considering the many organizations, individuals, and functions involved in moving goods from producer to end-user. Information-processing equipment such as telecommunications and computers is being used to speed up information flow through the distribution network and to monitor various aspects of physical distribution flows such as inventory levels, shipping status, scheduling, and other essential information.

Order processing. A critical function of the communications flows in the channel of distribution is **order processing**—transmitting by paper or electronics the customer's purchase order. This information indicates the description and quantity of the item requested, delivery dates, destination, and various other instructions. Technology has made electronic order entry possible in many types of business. **Electronic order entry** uses an electronic device to record and transmit a customer's order to the distribution location where the order will be filled, usually faster and more accurately than telephone or mail orders. An example includes optical reading devices used by food retailers to record orders of brands and quantities of products. The information is recorded on magnetic tape for transmission by telephone lines to company warehouses or wholesalers. Some industrial buyers have computer terminals linked to suppliers' computer systems, so that orders are transmitted from the terminal directly to suppliers. Standardized product and brand identification codes have proved useful in electronic order entry. Examples include the universal vendor marking (UVM) and the universal product code (UPC). These bar code markings are displayed on many packages and on the edge of supermarket shelves.

Communications network. The communications network is a critical component in integrating the various physical distribution functions into a total distribution system. Progress in improving the productivity of physical distribution essentially depends on the effectiveness and efficiency of the information system. Effectiveness is designing the information system to perform the proper information processing functions, and efficiency is how cost effectively the functions are performed. Because the array of available equipment is substantial, the major challenge is designing information systems that perform needed functions efficiently.

Now that we have examined the various physical distribution functions it should be clear that the variety of activities and functions that interact in physical distribution creates an opportunity for improving customer services and reducing distribution costs. We turn now to a brief discussion of the benefits to be gained from improving physical distribution activities.

SPOTTING PHYSICAL DISTRIBUTION PROBLEMS

Often problems encountered in the physical distribution of products stimulate efforts to improve physical distribution management. Consider this illustration of how Polaroid Corporation eliminated serious operational problems in distribution.

> New competition from Kodak and a potentially hot new product were about to bring heavy pressure to bear upon the corporate distribution function. It proved to be too much.
>
> Within 12 months, the fast-breaking developments had brought several of Polaroid's eight regional distribution centers to the verge of chaos and had cast the department as the company villain.
>
> "In 1977 it was hectic and 1978 was even worse. We were about to lose [contact with] Paramus at one point," recalls James Grinnell, general manager-distribution in Polaroid's Needham, Mass., headquarters. "Surviving from day to day was a major achievement."
>
> For better or worse, the crisis turned top management's attention to the serious weaknesses that existed in the company's distribution operations and won Mr. Grinnell the "opportunity" to overhaul the system from top to bottom. He was able to buy one year's time to do it.
>
> Despite working under the gun, Mr. Grinnell and his team succeeded in implementing a completely new distribution structure and information system that will take future changes easily in stride. Today, Polaroid's products are flowing smoothly to market, and corporate distribution provides the company's information interface between forecasting, marketing, manufacturing, and purchasing.
>
> Even better, the department is operating with 20 percent fewer people than it had in 1978, while keeping its total budget increase between 1978 and 1981 to only 11 percent—including transportation costs.[12]

Today, Polaroid's distribution system is set up to respond to calls for orders from dealers and sales representatives at five distribution centers. An order is entered into a computer terminal, and inventory is allocated to the order. If the item is out of stock, the customer has a credit problem, or a special purchase order is needed, the computer alerts the account executive while the customer is on the phone.

Problem signals in distribution

Several signals indicate that the physical distribution system is not functioning properly. The major problems fall into the categories of customer service levels, order processing, inventory management, warehousing operations, and transportation and delivery operations.[13]

Customer service levels. To a physical distribution manager, a **customer service level** refers specifically to his or her firm's standards for performance in speed and reliability in making products available to customers. One firm might set a performance standard of three days to deliver merchandise, whereas another might attempt to fill 95 percent of its orders from stock on hand in its warehouse.

If products are not available when and where customers want them, their complaints often indicate distribution malfunctions. Commodore International encountered serious problems in delivering inventory to dealers in late 1983. The following account dramatically illustrates the bottlenecks that may occur when trying to lower costs of one distribution activity while failing to consider its impact on other activities:

> Commodore "vastly underestimated" the number of disk drives that Commodore 64 users would buy, a Commodore spokesman says. Deliveries slowed with a switch from air to sea shipment—the disk drives are made in the Far East—chosen to save about $15 million annually.[14]

The disk drive in a computer is analogous to the transmission in an automobile. Increased demand, slow transportation, and inadequate inventory stocks created the disk drive distribution bottleneck. Distributors and dealers were frustrated and angry. The projected $15 million annual cost reduction in transportation helped cause a malfunction in the distribution system.

Order processing. Errors such as filling a buyer's order incorrectly are both costly to retailers and irritating to customers. The information transmitted on orders is essential. Errors, delays, and incomplete information can cause distribution problems.

Inventory management. Several problems can occur with inventories including stock-outs, incorrect inventory mix, and excess inventory. Commodore discovered the importance of having an adequate inventory of components (disk drives) to be able to sell computer consoles. In fact, one of Commodore's customers threatened to return 150 just-delivered consoles unless the manufacturer provided the add-on hardware.[15] Inventory problems typically involve too much or not enough items in stock. Too much stock leads to excess expenses in carrying inventory and too little creates customer dissatisfaction.

Occasionally a firm's information system is inadequate, and goods that are actually in stock are "lost." This type of mismanagement causes lost sales just as surely as if the merchandise had never been ordered.

Warehousing operations. Efficiency is the key factor in warehousing operations. Examples of problems are damaging products when stocking and loading, incorrectly filling customer orders, theft, and incurring excessive costs in performing warehouse functions. Consider this illustration: A grocery wholesaler with $50 million in sales found warehouse labor costs to be excessive. Analysis of the problem by management revealed high employee turnover (percentage of the workforce terminated). The percentage of new employees with limited experience was high, and they were slow in picking orders from warehouse stock. They were also more error prone than experienced workers.

Transportation and delivery operations. A final source of distribution malfunction may occur when goods are transported from producer to ultimate consumer. Problems may occur because of delay, damage, theft, and costs associated with transporting products. For example, to overcome the disk drive delay caused by sea shipment, Commodore's management airfreighted a rush order of more than 100,000 disk drives from its Far East supplier.[16]

Improving physical distribution

Recognizing several of the problems (and costs) that occur when physical distribution does not function properly, what is necessary to improve distribution? First, management must recognize that effective and efficient physical distribution involves trade-offs between distribution functions. Second, the key to improving physical distribution is approaching the task using a systems approach.

Trade-offs. Our discussion of problems in physical distribution suggests some of the trade-offs that may be made. For example, pressures owing to low inventory stocks can be reduced by increasing the speed of movement of products through the distribution network. Commodore attempted to eliminate inventory pressures by switching to air-freight from sea shipment. Many of the components of the distribution system can be used in place of others. Inventory stocks are substitutes for rapid transportation. Fast communications can reduce the need for warehousing and inventory. Thus the crux of PDM is deciding how to use the different trade-offs to accomplish physical distribution objectives in the most cost-effective manner.

Systems approach. Because of the various activities involved in physical distribution, an effective approach requires managing physical distribution as an integrated system of activities. We saw previously how attempting to minimize transportation costs without taking into account other distribution activities backfired for Commodore International. We also saw the benefits gained by Polaroid from a systems approach to PDM. Let us consider what is involved in putting it all together.

PHYSICAL DISTRIBUTION MANAGEMENT

We focus on three important aspects of PDM, recognizing that our brief look at PDM does not represent a complete examination. First, the objectives of PDM are considered. Next, an overview of what is involved in building a physical distribution system is discussed. Finally, several issues and alternatives in assigning organizational responsibility for PDM are examined.

Objectives of physical distribution management

Two major objectives of PDM are (1) achieving a high level of customer service and (2) keeping the *total* cost of physical distribution as low as possible, given customer service objectives. We discuss each of these objectives.

Customer service objective. Before discussing how to meet this objective, it is essential to understand what it is. To a large extent the specific requirements of good customer service are related: the buyer, the purchase situation, and the product. Nevertheless, most definitions of customer service include the terms *availability, convenience,* and *information.* Thus providing customer service means ensuring that the buyer will

- Get the right product, at the right place, at the right time, and in good condition
- Have to expend a minimum amount of administrative effort to get the goods and pay for them
- Be advised promptly if the supplier is unable or expects to be unable to deliver the complete order on time[17]

Customer service objectives can take many forms such as

- To deliver an item within a specified time after an order is placed
- To have available in stock the requested item a certain percentage of the time
- To hold damage of products transported to a small percentage of total shipment
- To control errors in shipment to a specified percentage

For example, UPS promises three-day delivery of items they transport. Additionally, the amount of damage that occurs with UPS shipments is low.

Delivering customer service is the ultimate PDM objective. The problem is that keeping 100 percent of customers satisfied 100 percent of the time would be prohibitive in terms of costs and probably impossible even if cost constraints did not exist. Nevertheless, high levels of customer service are both feasible and cost effective. Management must determine which aspects of customer service have the greatest effect on patronage and then decide what levels of customer service are appropriate. For example, apparently UPS has determined that three-day service is both acceptable to customers and can be provided at competitive rates.

Total cost objective. Customer service is one aspect of PDM; the total cost of distribution is another. The two objectives are closely related. The higher the level of customer service, the higher the total cost of distribution. Management's challenge is to set objectives for both such that optimal profits will result. The total cost objective emphasizes that the sum of the distribution costs is the issue, not the minimization of the costs of particular physical distribution activities such as transportation, warehousing, or inventory levels. Recall, for example, Commodore's distribution problems created in part by trying to keep transportation costs to a minimum.

Minimizing total cost highlights the importance of managing physical distribution as an integrated set of activities. We next consider what is involved in developing an integrated physical distribution system.

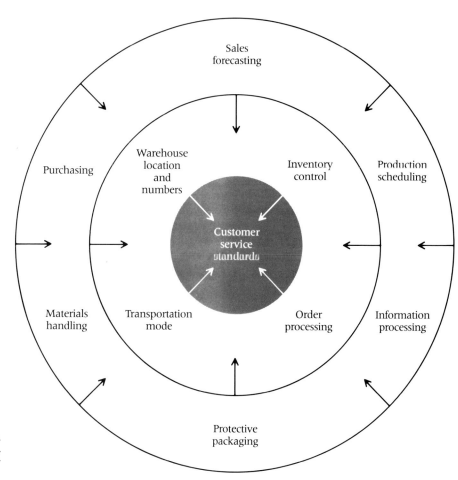

Exhibit 15.11 Components of an integrated physical distribution system

SOURCE: Louis W. Stern and Adel I. El-Ansary, *Marketing Channels*, 2nd ed. Englewood Cliffs, N.J.: Prentice-Hall, 1982, p. 159. © 1982. Reprinted by permission of Prentice-Hall, Inc.

Building the physical distribution system

To implement PDM, managers must coordinate and integrate its various components, as shown in Exhibit 15.11. Customer service standards (objectives) are shown at the center of the system because the physical distribution system's design begins with the objectives and levels management determines appropriate for customer service.

Selecting service levels. Returning to the Commodore International illustration, consider the following statement:

> Wholesale distributors and computer retailers say they have had to return 20% to 30% of Commodore's merchandise because it is defective. Production foul-ups have slowed shipments of high-profit accessories that are crucial to Commodore 64 sales and profit margins. And Commodore has fired almost all of its salesmen and has stopped helping retailers with the advertising costs.[18]

Clearly, Commodore's levels of customer service are inadequate. How does a firm determine which aspects of customer service are important to patronage and the levels of service to establish? Often these decisions are based on consideration of several factors including past experience, customer feedback, competition, and costs. Management must balance both the costs and benefits of customer service.

Estimating the benefit side of the issue is the most difficult. For example, suppose a mail-order firm such as L. L. Bean is considering increasing the percentage of orders that can be filled immediately from 97 percent to 98 percent. How much is 1 percent improvement in the distribution system likely to increase future sales? The effect on sales response is likely to be small and extremely difficult to measure. Thus a typical approach to setting standards is to rely heavily on judgment, experience, and competition. For example, management of a firm such as L. L. Bean may decide that 98 or 99 percent of orders filled immediately is essential. Management at a luxury furniture firm, however, might find accurate order taking and undamaged delivery to be far more important than filling orders from stock. Once established, over time, a firm may adjust service levels based on experience, customer feedback, and costs.

Approaches to designing the system. The complexity of the physical distribution network is clear when you look at the various components shown in Exhibit 15.11 that must be integrated. Some of the trade-offs and interrelationships become quite complex. For example, what impact will more rapid order transmission and processing have on inventory needs? Or, what is the trade-off between faster transportation services and warehouse requirements? Because of these complexities, a typical approach to PDM is to identify two or three of the major contributors to distribution costs and then attempt to design a system that minimizes the total of these costs for specified customer service objectives. Although not a perfect solution, this approach should lower distribution costs. Then, using this system as a base, further refinements can be made over time.

Computer models and other tools for the design of the physical distribution system sometimes are used to analyze single distribution activities such as inventory and combinations of activities such as inventory and transportation decisions. For example, Polaroid's approach to PDM involved computer simulations.

> Through trial and error, the team discovered which elements are the "drivers" of Polaroid's business, and they are now using that information to run simulations of how various changes might affect distribution costs.[19]

The powerful capability of computers is an important tool in PDM regardless of how sophisticated the approach to design is.

Designing an integrated physical distribution system normally requires two years or more for the initial development. Even then, the system is being continually refined and improved, as was described in the example of Polaroid.

Organizational responsibility for physical distribution management

Several business functions participate in physical distribution. Most heavily involved are manufacturing, transportation, purchasing, and marketing. Who is (or should be) responsible for PDM? The responsibility of PDM at Polaroid belongs to a corporate distribution organization. In some firms responsibility is assigned to a single department such as transportation, marketing, or manufacturing, and in others coordinating committees are formed to manage physical distribution. Let us examine some of the considerations in assigning responsibility for PDM.

L. L. Bean's sales in 1984 were below the company's projections, partly because of competitors that offer similar clothing and outdoor gear. Bean hopes to recapture some of this lost revenue by increased customer service. For instance, an L. L. Bean telephone representative can instantly locate any order—particularly helpful the week before Christmas—and all Bean salespeople "know the outdoors" and have the expertise to show customers what to buy and how to use it. (Courtesy of L. L. Bean, Inc.)

Management priorities. Because PDM involves several functions it is critical that those assigned management responsibility not have conflicting interests in a particular function. For example, if the traffic manager is being evaluated according to her transportation expenses and also is asked to coordinate physical distribution, transportation management may cut costs without considering the effects, which was the situation at Commodore when the decision was made to ship by water.

Function most heavily involved. There is some logic to assigning responsibility to the business function that accounts for the largest portion of distribution costs. For example, if 80 percent of costs are in transporting products, then the PDM job could be assigned to this manager. The problem with this approach is that it tends to focus on "what is" rather than "what should be." Perhaps shifting expenses to other physical distribution activities could reduce total costs. Vested interests in function might prevent this from happening, however, as when a long-term, influential employee holds the position of transportation director.

Integration and coordination. The organizational approach that promises the greatest opportunity for integration and coordination should be selected. Many companies such as Polaroid have established separate departments or divisions for PDM. When costs represent a substantial portion of the sales dollar, this approach should be considered.

Step-by-step approach. Most firms that have developed successful approaches to PDM have done so in stages over several years. One expert recommends starting by integrating traffic and warehousing followed in the next stage by integrating order-processing and finished goods inventory.[20] The goal of the third stage should be to totally integrate all physical distribution activities. Of course, the choice of what to include in each stage should consider the physical distribution situation in a particular firm.

TRENDS IN PHYSICAL DISTRIBUTION MANAGEMENT

The uncertain energy situation, high interest rates, consumer demands, and other factors have increased the importance of PDM. Several important trends promise to affect PDM in the last half of the 1980s and beyond.

Transportation deregulation

Transportation deregulation is discussed elsewhere in the chapter so a brief mention here will suffice. The major impact is, of course, to provide far greater flexibility in choice of transportation mode. An interesting speculation is that this flexibility may lead to the formation of companies that will provide PDM services for manufacturers and other firms in the distribution network. A new form of distribution specialist may develop.

Deregulation of transportation services also has certain negative features for transportation users. Services to low-market-demand locations have been eliminated or reduced by many transportation firms, and costs of transporting goods between low traffic areas have increased. Many firms in trucking and air transportation have gone bankrupt, and more are likely to encounter severe financial problems. Productivity will be essential to survival in the transportation services industry. Thus the greater flexibility gained through deregulation may be countered by loss of services and higher transportation costs to some locations. Nevertheless, the advantages for transportation users appear greater than the disadvantages, as the truly effective carriers survive by competing vigorously for business.

Fast transportation offers a means of overcoming high inventory and storage costs. Combining the flexibility of deregulation with innovative use of transportation services offers an exciting potential for improving PDM. Consider these illustrations.

> Leaseway Transportation maintains "tire banks" between two Whirlpool Corp. plants in Ohio so that the 25 trucks serving locations will not be delayed.
>
> Trucks with loading doors on the side are being tested to determine if rail sidings can be turned into truck docks.[21]

New technology

Computers and information processing. The impact of data processing, information management, and other information technologies will be substantial in the decade ahead. Already, terminals in business customer facilities are connected to extensive distribution networks. Computer technology and software will be important in both designing and managing physical distribution systems.

Materials handling technology. Although robots primarily have been used on the production line, their future impact on various aspects of routine and repetitive materials handling could be substantial. Other technologies such as electronic controls and automated warehouse functions already have had significant impact on physical distribution. Advances in materials handling techniques and equipment should contribute to lowering physical distribution costs.

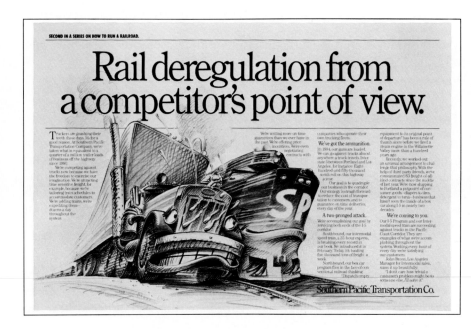

One consequence of a deregulated transportation industry is increased competition. Several months after Southern Pacific Transportation Company ran this ad, Volvo White Trucking Corporation placed its own ad disputing the railroad's findings. It said in part: "Southern Pacific . . . has been claiming in its advertising that the railroads are outperforming trucks. . . . Volvo White . . . did not think that was possible so we conducted a door-to-door delivery test. . . . The door-to-door time for the truck was 45 hours, 6 minutes, and for the railroad it was 67 hours, 26 minutes. . . . remember trucks continue to outscore the railroads." (Courtesy of Southern Pacific Transportation Company)

Customer trade-offs

PDM takes into consideration the trade-offs in distribution functions when designing systems. Limited progress has been made, however, in evaluating alternative trade-offs regarding customers. For example, what aspects of customer service are important to buyers? Marketing research offers useful methods for gaining better insights into customers' needs and wants. For example, will improved communications with customers allow longer delivery times, greater flexibility in products purchased, or other concessions? Clearly, a major factor in improving both the results and costs of physical distribution is understanding customers' needs and wants.

An interesting development regarding the give-and-take aspects between suppliers and buyers on inventory stocking is the adoption by U.S. industries of the Japanese method, called *kanban*, of keeping inventories to a minimum.[22] The **just-in-time (JIT) inventory system** consists of ordering supplies and parts frequently and in relatively small quantities from suppliers located as close as possible to production centers. The gain from this system is that inventory and storage costs are substantially reduced. Although transportation costs may increase using this system, total distribution costs have been reduced in a number of firms. For example, Harley-Davidson Motor Company has reduced inventory costs by $20 million using the JIT system. One consequence of JIT is that it places greater responsibility on suppliers.

International physical distribution

Our earlier look at Commodore highlighted the global management aspects of physical distribution. As trade continues to grow between nations and sectors of the world, global PDM will become increasingly critical. The complexities of fluctuating currency valuation, international trade documents, governmental requirements, theft, and political uncertainties compound the international PDM task.

Physical distribution on an international scale imposes several considerations not present on a domestic basis. For example,

- The rate of damage, loss, or both in international traffic movements is higher than in domestic movements.
- Use of transportation modes varies by country. Water carriage is more popular in Japan and Europe than in the United States and Canada.
- Customer service levels, in general, are lower for foreign customers than for domestic customers owing to length of haul and delays in customs.
- Political and legal factors, competition, economic conditions, and other environmental factors vary widely among countries.[23]

Interestingly, many foreign companies are more experienced in global distribution than are U.S. firms. For example, the Japanese trading companies have a long history of moving goods throughout the world.

SUMMARY

The physical movement of parts and materials to manufacturers, their transformation into products, and the movement of these finished goods through channels of distribution to end-users are essential parts of the physical distribution network. Representing as much as 20 percent of the gross national product, physical distribution offers an important avenue for improving customer service and reducing the total costs of distribution. The activities involved in physical distribution management (PDM) include transportation, warehousing, handling, packaging, inventory, and communications.

Several important and interrelated decisions affect physical distribution. One is selecting a transportation mode or combination of modes. The options include truck, rail, aircraft, ship, barge, and pipeline. This choice may involve considering several criteria including cost, speed, frequency, availability, dependability, and capability.

Decisions regarding inventory planning and control affect physical distribution. Inventory serves as a buffer against demand uncertainties and distribution delays, helping to reduce delays, provide flexibility, enable purchasing economies, and meet buyers' needs and wants. Inventory costs include carrying, ordering, production, and out-of-stock costs. Inventory management involves decisions concerning the amount to be carried in inventory stock, the quantity to be ordered when stock is depleted, and when to reorder. Several models for assisting inventory decision making are available to management including the fixed-order quantity model.

Decisions regarding warehousing are similar to those regarding inventory. Warehousing may be public or private. Each type of warehousing offers advantages and limitations. Warehousing decisions consist of selecting the number and location of warehouses to perform the physical distribution function.

Materials handling is a distribution activity that involves the entire distribution network—inventory, warehousing, and transportation. Preventing damage is an important aspect of materials handling. Finally, communications is a distribution activity that concerns the exchange of information. Information is a critical component of the physical distribution system. New information technology offers PDM a major opportunity for improving the effectiveness and efficiency of the information system.

Several signals may indicate malfunctions in the physical distribution system. Examples of problems include stock-outs, damaged goods, shipping delays, errors in shipment, incorrect quantities, and incomplete orders. Theft also is a major problem in distribution. Improving physical distribution requires assessing the trade-offs among distribution activities and applying a systems approach in developing an integrated physical distribution system.

Managing physical distribution begins by recognizing the two major objectives of PDM: (1) achieving a high level of customer service and (2) keeping the total cost of physical distribution as low as possible, yet consistent with customer service objectives. Customer service means making the product available at a convenient location and informing the buyer if it is unavailable or unlikely to be delivered on time. The total cost objective seeks to keep the total costs of distribution at a given customer service level at a minimum. To implement PDM, appropriate customer service levels are selected and the physical distribution elements are combined into an efficient system. Typically the development of a physical distribution system evolves over several years.

PDM organizational responsibility may be assigned to a coordinating committee or to an existing business function such as transportation or marketing. Some firms have assigned PDM responsibility to the business function most heavily involved in distribution. Firms that have been successful with integrated PDM approaches often have used a step-by-step approach to building the system. The major consideration is that distribution activities be properly integrated and coordinated.

KEY TERMS

physical distribution

physical distribution
  management (PDM)

logistics

multimodal services

piggyback

fishyback

birdyback

containerized freight

carrying costs

ordering costs

production costs

out-of-stock costs

fixed-order quantity model

economic order quantity (EOQ)
  model

public warehouses

storage warehouses

private warehouses

distribution warehouses

regional distribution center
  (RDC)

unitizing

containerization

order processing

electronic order entry

customer service level

just-in-time (JIT) inventory
  system

QUESTIONS FOR REVIEW AND DISCUSSION

1. What exactly is physical distribution management (PDM) and why is it important in marketing products?

2. Discuss the features and limitations of transporting products by air, rail, truck, and ship.

3. Products with what characteristics tend to be shipped by air?

4. Discuss the criteria that are important in selecting a transportation mode for shipping goods.

5. What role does inventory play in the physical distribution of products?

6. Discuss the function of a regional distribution center in moving products from producer to consumers.

7. Identify some of the signals that may indicate that physical distribution problems exist in a distribution system.

8. What is the objective of PDM?

9. How can the conflict between customer service and the cost of operating a physical distribution system be resolved?

10. What is customer service, and what are its objectives?

11. Discuss the advantages and disadvantages of assigning PDM responsibilities to a single department compared with assigning PDM responsibility to a separate department for only PDM.

12. What impact is transportation deregulation likely to have on PDM?

BUILDING YOUR PORTFOLIO

Suppose you must ship a package from your city to Hong Kong. The package is 12 inches high, 12 inches wide, and 8 inches deep. It weighs 14 pounds and is not breakable but the contents will be unusable if they are exposed to temperatures more than 110°F or less than 30°F for longer than six hours. Determine the fastest way to send the package to Hong Kong and the estimated cost. Next, determine the lowest-cost way to send the package. Finally, what factors should be considered when you decide which way to send the package?

To obtain the needed information you should consult actual shipping schedules and freight-cost schedules for the various transportation modes. Because the package is traveling internationally it will be necessary to determine special regulations regarding shipment of goods. Here are some possible sources.

1. Schedules and freight charges are available from individual firms.
2. U.S. Department of Commerce, International Trade Administration.
3. Import-export agencies.

You will need to determine which transportation modes can provide the specialized handling that this parcel demands.

NOTES

1. "Behind the UPS mystique: Puritanism and productivity." *Business Week,* June 6, 1983, p. 66.
2. Donald J. Bowersox, *Logistical Management,* 2nd ed. New York: Macmillan, 1978, p. 3.
3. David P. Herron, "Managing physical distribution for profit." *Harvard Business Review,* May–June 1979, p. 123; and *Distribution Management Handbook.* Toronto: McGraw-Hill Ryerson Limited, 1980, p. 8.
4. William Baldwin, "Dollars from doodads." *Forbes,* Oct. 11, 1982, p. 51.
5. Michael L. King, "Bigger load: Transportation official at GE finds his role rises with fuel prices." *Wall Street Journal,* Dec. 31, 1981, p. 6.
6. Bowersox, op. cit., p. 120.
7. Bill Paul, "Freight transportation is being transformed in era of deregulation." *Wall Street Journal,* Oct. 20, 1983, p. 1.
8. The following discussion is based in part on Don Hellriegel and John W. Slocum, Jr., *Management,* 3rd ed. Reading, Mass.: Addison-Wesley, 1982, pp. 417–421.
9. Douglas M. Lambert and James R. Stock, *Strategic Physical Distribution Management.* Homewood, Ill.: Irwin, 1982, p. 182.
10. Ibid., p. 185.
11. Ibid., p. 187.
12. Patrick Gallager, "To the rescue at Polaroid." *Handling and Shipping Management,* Apr. 1981, p. 68. © 1982 by Penton/IPC, Inc., Cleveland, Ohio.
13. Lambert and Stock, op. cit., p. 47.
14. Dennis Kneale, "Commodore hits production snags in its hot-selling home computer." *Wall Street Journal,* Oct. 28, 1983, p. 31.
15. Ibid.
16. Ibid.
17. *Distribution Management Handbook,* op. cit., p. 60.
18. Kneale, op. cit.
19. Gallager, op. cit., p. 75.
20. Bernard LaLonde, "Strategies for organizing physical distribution." *Transportation and Distribution Management,* Jan.–Feb. 1974, pp. 21–25.
21. "The 'radical change' gives trucking an edge." *Business Week,* May 14, 1984, p. 176H.
22. "How just-in-time inventories combat foreign competition." *Business Week,* May 14, 1984, pp. 176D–G.
23. James R. Stock and Douglas M. Lambert, "Physical distribution management in international marketing." *International Marketing Review,* Autumn 1983, pp. 28–41.

Case 15.1

Alynn Neckwear

ALAN CADAN IS THE entrepreneurial equivalent of the one-man band. He is the owner, founder and chief executive of Alynn Neckwear Inc., as well as its head designer, bookkeeper, salesman, order-taker, typist, shipping clerk and telephone operator.

His four-year-old necktie business booked sales of $1 million last year. Mr. Cadan, 42 years old, runs the business from his house in Stamford, Conn. He is the only full-time employee. He manages that because he is well organized. He's probably that way, he says, because he admired an uncle who was a compulsive organizer. The uncle wrote his own obituary and died on a weekend, his family says, so as not to inconvenience his loved ones.

His wife, Lynn, and their four children, ages 11 to 15, help out. Mrs. Cadan does some bookkeeping and mailing chores and tones down some of her husband's ideas for tie designs, which tend to be clever.

Mr. Cadan's fabrics are made in the U.S. and European mills; a New York City factory turns them into ties. But all of Alynn Neckwear's shipments are from the Cadans' home.

SOURCE: Sanford L. Jacobs, "By being organized, one man builds a thriving tie business," *Wall Street Journal*, Feb. 14, 1983, p. 19. Reprinted by permission of the *Wall Street Journal*, © Dow Jones & Company, Inc. 1983. All rights reserved.

Packing and shipping are the most time-consuming tasks. Everyone in the family packs ties, a chore that extends into the late hours during the Christmas season, when the company ships 50% of its annual volume. Mr. Cadan's 79-year-old mother drove 40 miles a day to help out last year. "It's a one-man business," Mr. Cadan's wife says, "with a lot of elves."

It's also a no-frill enterprise. It is equipped with an old, hand-operated tape machine and a worn bathroom scale.

Mr. Cadan's desk is a door covered with blotting paper that rests on two saw-horses. His office used to be the garage. A $10,000 computer system was acquired last year, but he prefers to use clipboards to keep track of things. The clipboards hang in neat rows on the wall behind the desk. One holds orders to be shipped; another has documents that show when fabric went from the mills to the New York tie-makers. The computer could track the inventory, but it is simpler and quicker to subtract each day's shipments from what's on hand to keep a continuous inventory count, Mr. Cadan says.

The inventory data is on one of the clipboards on the wall. Mr. Cadan can reach it without putting down the phone. "You have to be able to save time if you're doing everything yourself," he says.

The computer is used mostly to make out invoices. Previously, with nearly 1,000 retail stores, 36 mail-order houses and 196 corporations buying his ties, Mr. Cadan sometimes had to spend entire days typ-

ing invoices. The computer also tabulates accounts-receivable and prints monthly statements.

But Mr. Cadan uses a manual system to track accounts receivable. A file at his desk contains unpaid invoices grouped by customer. He says he can update the file faster than he could if the information were in the computer. He also can get current information about an account quicker by pulling the unpaid invoices than he could if he had to depend on the computer.

Mr. Cadan went into the tie business after working 17 years at Chipp Inc., a New York City men's store owned by his father-in-law, Sidney Winston. The years there taught him about retailing and the tie business (Chipp contracts to have its own tie designs made). He also learned that women buy a lot of ties.

Mr. Cadan's current best seller is imprinted with a backward "Hello Handsome" that reads properly when reflected in a mirror. Few men would buy it for themselves, but lots of them wear it when a woman buys it for them, Mr. Cadan says.

His ties wholesale for $7.50 or $10 each. Most retailers mark them up 100%. Tie makers normally set wholesale prices by doubling their manufacturing cost. They don't gross 50%, however, because of unsold inventory and damaged goods. A 30% gross profit is considered average, but Mr. Cadan does better due to his tight operation. The business provides his family with a good income.

QUESTIONS

1. What are Alynn's physical distribution objectives?

2. What role does physical distribution play in this firm's operations?

3. What inventory costs are involved in Alynn's physical distribution system?

4. What suggestions do you have for improving Alynn's physical distribution management?

Part Five

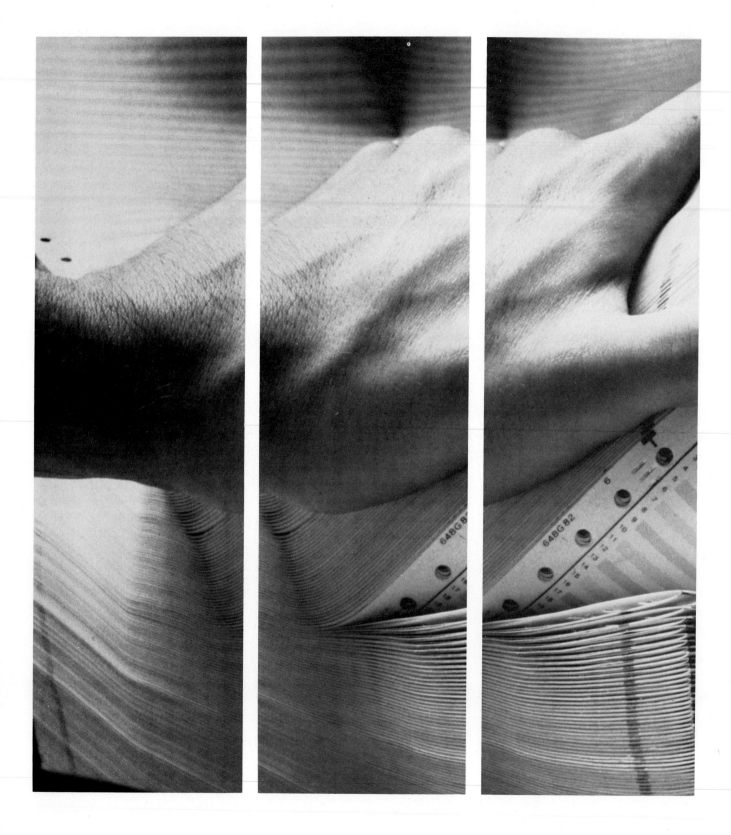

Pricing

16 Pricing Fundamentals

When you finish this chapter, you will understand

☐ How to recognize price in its many forms

☐ The factors from the macroenvironment and task environment that managers consider when making pricing decisions

☐ The factors from inside the company that managers consider when making pricing decisions

☐ How other components of the marketing mix may influence pricing decisions

☐ How price may be used to support other components of the marketing mix

To determine how much a customer owes, a serviceman reads a natural gas meter to see how much gas has been used since the last reading.

Changing demand for silver flatware (knives, forks, and spoons) created a pricing controversy in the industry. Between 1979 and 1980, the price of silver rose nearly 1000 percent, from $5 an ounce to more than $48. Retailers immediately moved to take advantage of consumers' new interest in silver investing. Using inventories purchased earlier at lower costs, many retailers began offering high discounts on silver flatware (up to 50 percent off manufacturers' list prices). The tactic worked, and a boom in the demand for silver flatware ensued. But growth was short-lived as demand slowed with the recession of the early 1980s.

The industry was in trouble. Consumers began to expect the large discounts. To support retailers' discounting practice, manufacturers had to provide lists of suggested prices. Many manufacturers, under intense competitive pressure to maintain market share, went along. As retailers tried to outdo each other, the discounts kept getting higher.

One silver flatware manufacturer, Reed & Barton, argued that list-price discounting was misleading consumers. Management refused to provide a suggested manufacturers' price list, which upset the company's retailers. They demanded that the list be reinstated. Without the list prices as a basis of comparison, these retailers could not easily claim the high discount on their prices that they needed to remain competitive. Reed & Barton did reinstate the list prices, but set them much lower than those of other manufacturers, so that only a 25 percent discount could be claimed. The company then sponsored comparative advertising showing that even with the smaller discount their flatware was less expensive than that of Towle, a major competitor. Towle felt that the advertising was false and sued Reed & Barton. Reed & Barton then filed a suit of its own against Towle, claiming unfair competitive practices.

The whole industry faces a dilemma. The high discounts are expected by consumers. Retailers are forced into offering the discounts to keep their sales up. Yet the discounts have caught the attention of the Federal Trade Commission and some state consumer protection agencies because of their potential to mislead consumers.[1]

AT FIRST GLANCE, setting a price for a product or service may seem relatively straightforward. As the pricing of silver flatware illustrates, however, a complicated mix of conflicting influences must be considered before price can be determined. Flatware manufacturers faced this situation as they looked at costs when setting list prices, and raised them as silver costs went up. At the same time, the manufacturers wanted to set prices that would support their retailers' selling tactics. Consumers of flatware also played a role, as they began to expect high discounts. Then the government forced manufacturers to reconsider their pricing policies. All these factors created uncertainty about the best pricing approach.

Before you can appreciate fully how managers set prices, you must understand the factors that influence prices. In this chapter we examine the nature of price. Then task environmental and macroenvironmental influences on price are discussed. Finally, we examine pricing considerations that stem from within the company.

THE NATURE OF PRICE

As consumers, we are confronted constantly with words indicating price of products and services. Products usually have a price or cost. Services often use other terms: A doctor lists charges for an office visit; a lawyer receives a fee for legal advice; and a bank establishes an interest rate for a loan. In each case, a seller states in advance the amount of money a buyer must exchange to get the benefits of the product or service.

Definition of price

In a free enterprise economy, price plays an important role in guiding the allocation of resources. Products and services of great value to consumers command a high price, and those of less value are priced low to sell.

When an economic system responds to this price mechanism, resources are allocated to products and services for which prices can be set high enough relative to costs to earn profits. (See Marketalk for an illustration of how China is allowing the marketplace to determine prices.) From this viewpoint, price is the value that a buyer exchanges for the benefits of a seller's product or service.[2]

Defining price as a relationship between values—the value given up by the buyer and the value of the product's benefits received—has an important implication for pricing decisions. In practice a seller sets price by establishing the ratio of these values. Suppose Procter & Gamble wanted to increase the price of a cannister of Pringles potato chips. Each one of the following actions accomplishes this purpose:

■ Increase the price charged per cannister.
■ Charge the same price for a smaller cannister.
■ Charge the same price for lower-quality potato chips in the same size cannister.

*Marke*TALK ///

China lets supply and demand forces set prices

AFTER A SUCCESSFUL TEST down on the farm, the Chinese are extending free pricing to the big city. Starting next year, Chinese factories will come under the same system that now lets farmers sell their homegrown produce in "free markets." As a result of that innovation, farm output has jumped by 89% and farm family income has more than doubled since 1978.

The application of free-market methods to industry represents the riskiest move yet by Deng Xiaoping since he began shaking up China's socialist economy in 1978. The Chinese are about to discard their Soviet-style planned economy. For the first time since the Communists came to power in 1949, supply and demand will determine economic planning "This is very revolutionary," says a Hong Kong banker. "It's been in progress for some time, but nothing moves until the party says 'go.'"

Under the new system, state enterprises will function as independent companies responsible for making profits and determining production. They will pay taxes instead of fixed quotas to the central gov-

ernment. Unprofitable factories will be closed as the government slashes subsidies, which have chewed up some 30% of the $65 billion national budget.

In theory, the reforms should straighten out an economy plagued by an excess of unpopular items and by shortages of goods in greatest demand. Warehouses are jammed with unsold stocks of watches, bicycles, and sewing machines, while refrigerators are all but unavailable. Under the new system, prices of products in oversupply will probably be allowed to fall to more realistic levels. To spur production, prices of refrigerators and other popular items may be increased.

But with a decline in subsidies and the removal of many price controls, the Chinese fear a resurgence of hyperinflation. Many Chinese still remember the rampant inflation of the 1940s, when China's currency had so little value that people had to cart it around in wheelbarrows. They worry that if prices rise, they will lose the extra cash they have earned as a result of Deng's reforms. Savings deposits, for example, have almost tripled, to $42 billion, since 1980. "The leaders will have to be very careful," says Luis A. Viada, a vice-president of Citibank's China office in Hong Kong. "In the past few years, they've created a sense of improved quality of life. If they suddenly start floating the price of basic commodities, it will cause real resistance."

Deng is keenly aware of the political risks involved. His opponents, hard-line party veterans who feel their power slipping, would be quick to react if the new policies turn out to be inflationary. The government is calling for prudence, and it plans to go on subsidizing basic commodities such as coal, oil, rice, and steel.

Foreign companies doing business in China are taking a close look at Deng's industrial reforms, too. Although direct foreign investment remains low—totaling $2.6 billion through 1983—China is the biggest untapped market in the world. "I see an upside potential for foreign investors in these reforms," says James Kong, China business development manager at R.J. Reynolds Industries Inc., one of the first foreign companies to sell in China. The price of its China-bound Camel cigarettes is now set by Chinese authorities at whatever level they choose. Says Kong: "This relaxation might mean we can set our own prices according to market forces, too."

China's current pricing system discourages the formation of joint ventures. "Our biggest problem with joint-venture negotiations has been price controls and preset wage levels," says a U.S. executive working on a proposed venture in southern China. Such factors "will now be based more on demand and supply and market value. It will make negotiating a lot easier."

///

Market Access through Countertrade

Metallgesellschaft Services Inc. –
Leaders in countertrade and barter services
for corporations and governments
around the world

Metallgesellschaft has built a thriving business helping businesses and governments consummate huge trade deals. Exchanging one country's or company's product for those of another shows that price is not always an amount of money. (Courtesy of Metallgesellschaft)

Price stated by a seller may not be the price actually paid—the true price. Discounts, free gifts, cost of credit, and other conditions of sale cause the true price to be different from the one stated by the seller. The true price of a shirt bought at a "two-for-one" sale, for instance, is not the stated or "regular" price, but one-half of that stated price.

Bartering and countertrade

Value exchanged for a product or service is not always money (cash or credit). The age-old practice of bartering eliminates the need for money to consummate an exchange. **Bartering** is an exchange in which one product or service is traded for another. Persons near each other geographically often barter. A doctor's patient with little money may offer to build cabinets for the doctor in exchange for medical treatment. Corporations also barter: American Airlines recently traded eight 747s for 15 DC-10s from Pan American World Airways. Even nations barter, though it is called **counter-trade**: The Japanese and Soviet governments agreed to trade with each other for the different kinds of fish caught by each nation.

Countertrade is quite common among nations, accounting for from 25 to 30 percent of all world trade by one estimate.[3] Both bartering and countertrade complicate the price-setting process because there is no medium of exchange and greater bargaining skill is required. Yet, countertrade is growing in popularity, partly because of the increasing risk of extending credit on an international basis.

EXTERNAL ENVIRONMENTAL INFLUENCES ON PRICE

Price is one of the more visible components of a company's marketing mix. Other departments, such as financial control, have a stake in price because of its impact on cash flows. Outside the company, customers consider price when deciding to buy, competitors note prices of competing brands to see where they stand in a market, and governments monitor prices to check for compliance with regulations. Because price has so much significance to these parties in marketing's environment, the number of factors influencing price can be overwhelming (see Exhibit 16.1).

In this section, we discuss the task and macroenvironmental factors influencing price. Managers use macroenvironmental scanning and market opportunity analysis (MOA) to discover and evaluate these influences (see Chapters 3 and 4 for a discussion of these analyses).

Customers' influence on price

Managers strive to set price so that target customers believe that the benefits received from the purchase are worth the value that is given up in exchange. Customers react to the product's price and the rest of the marketing offer by deciding how much of the product to buy. How well the price succeeds depends directly on what customers do because the quantity purchased at a given price determines a company's revenue:

Revenue = price per unit × quantity of units sold.

Suppose Scripto offered its disposable, erasable pen to consumers for $.98. Millions of consumers decide whether and how many pens to buy at that price. If consumers decide, in total, to buy 15,000,000 units, total

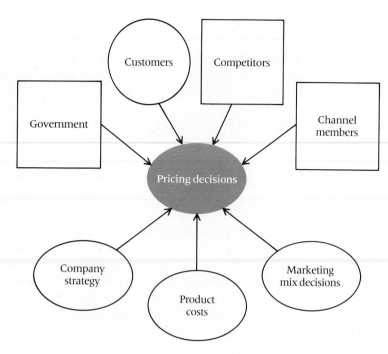

Exhibit 16.1   Influences creating a pricing situation

revenue (at retail) would be $14,700,000: $.98 × 15,000,000. Now suppose that Scripto's management contemplates raising the price to $1.03, and estimates that consumers would buy only 14,000,000 units. Revenue would go down to $14,420,000 because the price increase is more than offset by the fewer units sold. These reactions of customers to different prices are described by a demand curve.

Demand curves and price elasticity. A **demand curve** is a picture of the schedule of quantities of a product or service that customers in a market are expected to buy at different prices. Exhibit 16.2 illustrates a common shape of a demand curve. Notice that the curve is sloped downward from left to right describing an inverse relationship between price and quantity. As the product's price decreases from P1 to P2, the curve indicates that the quantity purchased will increase from Q1 to Q2.

Many products have downward-sloping demand curves. As price goes down the product's benefits become increasingly attractive relative to the value expended. This encourages purchases. Raising prices can have the opposite effect.

Exhibit 16.3 illustrates different shapes of demand curves for a range of products. No two products have demand curves of exactly the same shape because customers' sensitivity to price is different across products. This sensitivity is called **price elasticity** and is measured by the percentage of change in quantity purchased relative to the percentage change in price:

$$\text{Price elasticity} = \frac{(\text{old quantity} - \text{new quantity})}{\text{old quantity}} \div \frac{(\text{old price} - \text{new price})}{\text{old price}}$$

$$= \frac{Q1 - Q2}{Q_1} \div \frac{P1 - P2}{P_1}$$

$$= \frac{\text{Percentage change in quantity purchased}}{\text{Percentage change in price}}$$

Price elasticity information helps managers see how revenue changes in response to a price change. Suppose a company decreased price of its

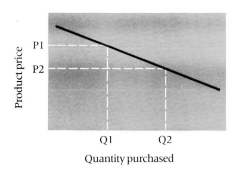

Exhibit 16.2   A typical demand curve

camera brand by 5 percent, and found that sales increased by 10 percent. Price elasticity is −2: 10 percent increase in sales divided by −5 percent decrease in price. The minus sign confirms that there is an inverse relationship between price and quantity purchased. Total revenue from the cameras increases because the greater quantity sold more than offsets the drop in price per unit. A price elasticity of −1 means that total revenue will not change if price is changed. However, if sales increases by only 1 percent when price is decreased by 5 percent, then price elasticity is −1/5, warning managers that total revenue has fallen.

A market is *price inelastic* when customers will purchase about the same quantity despite a large price change (see demand curve D in Exhibit 16.3 for a perfectly inelastic market). In an inelastic market, prices can be raised to increase total revenue because the loss of units sold is offset by the greater amount received per unit. In contrast, a market is *price elastic* when a price change causes a correspondingly greater change in units sold (see demand curve A in Exhibit 16.3). In this situation, management is encouraged to lower price in order to get greater total revenue. In reality, the markets for most products are neither completely elastic nor completely inelastic but fall somewhere between these extremes (see demand curves B and C in Exhibit 16.3). Furthermore, elasticity is not the same over the whole range of prices shown in a demand curve. Suppose BMW, a luxury automobile, is priced at $24,000. At that price, customers may be price inelastic for prices ranging from $24,000 up to $27,000. But eventually the higher prices cause customers to become more sensitive to price. Thus, price elasticity goes up after $27,000.

Managers should be careful to distinguish between a demand curve for a product type and a demand curve for a brand. The markets for product types and brands do not necessarily have the same price elasticity. Think about the market for a new and highly effective cancer drug, a product type, which is likely to be inelastic. A doctor whose patients' lives are threatened by cancer probably will not consider price in his or her decision to use the drug (particularly when insurance pays most of the cost). But suppose four pharmaceutical companies have brands of that type of drug. The market for each brand is more price elastic than that for the cancer drug because doctors can choose among the four brands. Typically, a company's pricing decisions are based on forecasts of price elasticity for the brand.

The concept of a demand curve is important because it demonstrates that price affects customers' buying decisions. However, companies often do not know exactly what demand curves they are faced with, particularly the demand curve for a brand. Three problems arise in practice that inhibit learning about demand curves.

1. Demand curves are affected by nonprice components of the marketing mix.
2. Demand curves are affected by environmental forces.

Exhibit 16.3   Demand curves with differing price elasticity

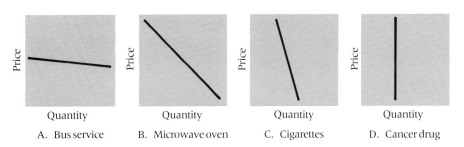

3. Obtaining measures of demand curves requires enormous amounts of information.

Let us briefly consider each problem.

A demand curve essentially holds the nonprice components of a company's marketing mix constant. The curve only portrays what happens to quantity purchased when price is varied, but not product, promotion, distribution, or after-sale services. In reality, marketing managers make pricing decisions along with decisions on the other marketing mix components. Thus decisions on price, in combination with the nonprice components, can change demand curves. Exhibit 16.4 shows that nonmarketing component decisions can cause whole demand curves to shift from one level to another. Notice that at the same price P_1, two different marketing mixes yield different quantities sold, Q_1 and Q_2. For this reason, managers cannot consider price in the absence of the other components of the marketing mix.

A demand curve also assumes the macroenvironmental and task environmental forces are remaining the same over the range of prices. Rarely does this happen in reality. Suppose an insurance company lowers prices on a life insurance policy from $124 a month to $117 a month. An elastic demand curve shows quantity of policies purchased from the company going up. But that increase in sales happens only if competitors do not change price on similar policies. A price decrease by competitors nullifies the price advantage and the insurance company's sales may not change at all. Other environmental factors such as changes in product technology, social trends, changes in the state of the economy affecting employment, and legal changes also can affect the demand curves faced by a company, as Exhibit 16.5 suggests.

Finally, the uncertainties created by marketing mix and environmental forces, in addition to the sheer number of prices and quantities to measure, make the task of measuring entire demand curves nearly impossible. Yet, marketing managers can get information about customers' price elasticities in several ways (see Marketech). First, managers learn informally about elasticity through trial and error. As price changes are made for a product over time, managers watch what happens in the market. This experience helps them form opinions about the sensitivity of customers to price. Sec-

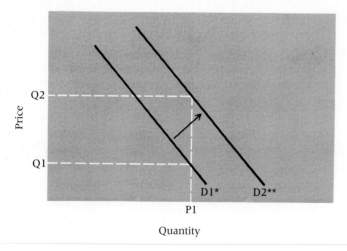

Exhibit 16.4 Decisions on the market mix can shift demand curves

*D1 = demand curve for marketing mix alternative 1
**D2 = demand curve for marketing mix alternative 2

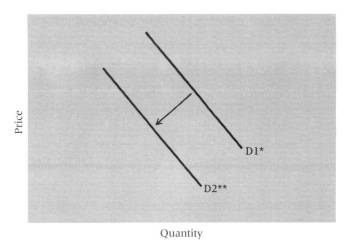

Exhibit 16.5 Environmental forces can shift demand curves

*D1 = demand curve for a brand with current environmental forces
**D2 = demand curve for a brand with changed environmental forces

ond, managers learn by charging different prices in different geographic areas at the same time to see how volume sold varies. If the areas are reasonably alike in every way except for the product's price, the volume differences can be attributed to price.

A third way managers obtain information is by conducting marketing research, in which competing influences on purchases other than price can be carefully controlled. Test marketing is sometimes used to learn about price-demand relationships. Price's effect on buyers also can be studied by having consumers participate in a controlled but realistic shopping situation. Buyers shop in a storelike setting (a room set up to look like or simulate a retail store with shelves, competing products, marked prices, and special displays). Prices are changed systematically for different groups of customers, and their purchases are measured. The simulated store ensures that only the price charged for the test product is different for each group of

Marke**TECH** □ □ □ □ □ □ □ □ □ □ □ □ □ □ □ □ □

Computers help American and United Airlines spot discount price opportunities

UNITED AIRLINES uses its computerized "capacity control" system to plan seating allotments in advance and capture the maximum revenue for each flight. The airline issues few Easy Saver and Super Coach tickets for midweek flights it can fill with business travelers paying full price. Less than 10% of the passengers on such flights might be paying the lowest available fare. But on weekends or late at night, United loads up seats that would other-

SOURCE: Kenneth Labich, "Fare wars: Have the big airlines learned to win?" *Fortune*, Oct. 29, 1984, pp. 26–27. Used by permission.

wise be empty with Easy Saver and Super Coach customers.

American Airlines is also using computers to fight low-cost carriers. The airline employs 130 people who spend their days at computer terminals monitoring ticket sales. The computer breaks down historical selling patterns on flights up to 11 months in advance. It's the job of the operators to make adjustments in the proportion of discount seats offered. If, say, a tour group books a large block of low-cost seats six months in advance, the operator might halt all further discount sales on

that flight. If a flight is not proving as popular with full-fare passengers as the computer predicted, the operator will open up more seats for discounts.

Since the status of each flight is monitored as its date approaches, the balance of discount and full-fare tickets continually changes. A passenger unable to buy a Super Saver ticket on a future American flight when he calls on Monday might get a cheap seat on that same flight if he calls back Wednesday. Like United, American is doing a far better job of containing its losses to discount airlines.

□ □

respondents. Thus managers can attribute differences in quantity purchased to the prices charged.

Psychological meaning of price. The relationship between price and quantity purchased often reflects more than value exchanged for benefits received. Customers can attach psychological meanings to price. Customers sometimes depend on price to indicate quality, especially for products such as appliances, televisions, stockings, and sweaters where quality is difficult to judge. This is known as the **price-quality relationship.** Customers for whom quality is more important than price may choose a higher-priced brand to ensure getting quality. Similarly, customers may use price to judge the prestige value of products such as wine, automobiles, jewelry, and clothing. As one analyst, when explaining why some people want a more expensive and prestigious credit card, put it: "Those who want a prestige card will get a Diners Club or American Express. If you want to buy an expensive car, you tend to buy a Mercedes or a Cadillac, not a souped-up Honda."[4]

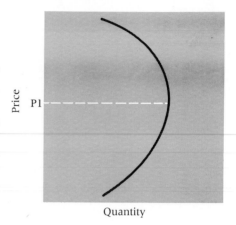

Exhibit 16.6 Demand curve for a prestige product

Exhibit 16.6 illustrates the shape of a demand curve for a product where price was used to indicate quality or prestige. Notice that over a range of prices, up to P_1, the curve slopes upward from left to right. Within this range, higher prices lead to increased quantity sold. At too low a price (below P_1), people may not think the quality or prestige value of the product is very high. Thus increasing price can cause higher sales. However, a company cannot raise price indefinitely. At prices above P_1, the demand curve slopes back to the left as some customers judge the value given up to be too much when compared with the value received. Many luxury products—furs, jewelry, wine, expensive cars, microwave ovens, and stereos— have this kind of demand curve.

The possibility that price is used as an indicator of quality or prestige complicates pricing decisions. The price setter must consider the impact of price on customers' psychological interpretation of the product. Consider the dilemma of managers at Canon, the Japanese camera manufacturer, when tough plastic was substituted for steel in their camera bodies. The plastic was cheaper so some of the savings could be passed on to the customer in the form of lower prices. But if many buyers were using price as an indicator of quality, then Canon would have been taking a risk by lowering price noticeably. Customers may have interpreted the lower price as meaning lower quality and bought other brands. At the same time, if consumers did not notice the price change, then lower price would not have been an incentive to purchase.

A creative company may find an opportunity in the price-prestige relationship. Proper pricing decisions in a coordinated marketing mix can be used to stimulate and maintain customers' interest in the product. One very interesting example of pricing to create value is the pricing of diamonds. De Beers Consolidated Mines of South Africa controls approximately 80 percent of the world's gem diamond supply. Management maintains customers' perception of value by keeping prices high through strict control of the supply of gem diamonds to world markets. The strategy has worked well—in 1980 the price of a flawless one-carat diamond reached an all-time high of $62,000, though it has decreased considerably since then.[5]

Another aspect of customer's influence on price setting is the psychological meaning that may be attached to certain numbers. Some price setters believe that **odd pricing,** setting prices that end in an odd number (e.g., $1.57, $119, $33) or that end just below a whole number (e.g., 99¢, $4.98, $199.99) leads to more quantity purchased than pricing with even or whole numbers. Although the value of odd pricing has not been demonstrated by market research studies, its popularity can be seen by checking prices in grocery stores.[6]

Sometimes customers become accustomed to seeing a particular price for a product. Lack of price changes over a long period of time causes customers to expect the same price in the future. Pricing of candy bars and chewing gum created this expectation after years of being sold for a nickel. Price setters use **customary pricing** when they are convinced that raising the price would cause a large drop in quantity sold and a loss of revenue. The fear is that too many customers would no longer believe that the product is worth the price. Changing the size or quality of the product, such as making a candy bar smaller, is an alternative way to make price adjustments.

Price lining, the setting of specific prices for a line of products with no prices in between, is also based on customers' psychological interpretation of prices. The price setter believes that customers see any prices in between the set prices as psychologically the same. You can see price lining decisions by a tennis manufacturer that has a $50 racket, a $90 racket, a $125 racket, and a $250 racket in its product line. Suppose the manufacturer is considering dropping the price of the $250 racket to $225. If a $225 racket is seen by customers as approximately the same value as the $250 racket, quantity purchased would not increase enough to offset the lower price. Thus the seller has no incentive to lower the price of the $250 racket. Although no strong research supports price lining, its wide use suggests that managers' trial-and-error experiences with pricing indicate that customers see certain prices as similar.

All the psychological effects on price influence the price elasticity of demand curves. Thus managers cannot be sure that the demand curve for a product is a smooth, downward-sloping demand curve like the one shown in Exhibit 16.2. Studies of price and quantity of purchases may be needed to find out how quantity purchased varies with price alternatives.

Price effects over time. Price charged at one point in time may cause customers to adjust their perception of product benefits or to alter the way they use the product in the future. This phenomenon happened as consumers in the United States responded to a decade of rapidly rising costs of oil-based products. Many changed their purchase behavior by reducing dramatically their consumption of gasoline and other oil products. Although the price of oil has decreased in the 1980s, results of a consumer opinion poll suggest that purchases will not go back to former levels.[7]

Understanding how price is used by customers is an essential part of making pricing decisions. Customers' reactions to price through quantity purchased sends an important message to price setters. They rarely have complete freedom to charge whatever price they want. Because customers weigh value given up against benefits received and attach psychological meanings to price, price setters have a limited number of price alternatives that can be considered.

Influence of competition on price

Customers often shop among competitors to find a price they are willing to pay. Price setters therefore must consider what other companies are charging. In some situations, price is set at or less than that of competitors. Car dealers vie with each other in this way by offering discounts off the manufacturer's suggested price to attract customers and discourage them from buying another dealer's cars.

Offering unique benefits that are especially important to customers enables a company to set price higher than that of the competition. Price inelastic markets can be targeted and product quality, prestige, or after-sale services can be used to justify the increased price. Holiday Inn has recently developed a marketing strategy based on this approach. The company is targeting middle- and upper-class business travelers for its Crowne Plaza and Embassy Suite hotels. Both chains offer many services such as complimentary newspapers, interpreters, plush upholstery, and 18-hour-a-day maid service and charge a premium room-rate price.[8] However, management must be careful to maintain the quality, prestige, or service differential to keep customers who are willing to pay the higher price. Volkswagen found out the hard way that it must maintain its reputation for reliability if it is to charge a higher-than-average price. Problems with the Rabbit, a relatively expensive car, caused sales to fall.[9]

Competition's influence on company price decisions depends on the nature of the industry. Industries differ according to the number of competitors, the size and strength of each competitor, and similarity of products among competitors. Four types of industries can be indentified that account for the competitive situations that companies encounter: monopoly, oligopoly, monopolistic competition, and pure competition.

Monopoly. A **monopoly** exists when only one company provides a product or service and customers have no choice of companies to buy from. In this situation, product type and brand demand curves are one and the same. Although strict monopolies are rare in free enterprise economies, near monopolies are more common. A near monopoly exists when one seller controls almost all supply of a product or service. Until the break-up in 1984, AT&T held a near monopoly on local telephone service. And as we discussed previously, De Beers holds a near monopoly over the supply of gem diamonds.

Unlike AT&T and De Beers, many monopolies or near monopolies operate on a local level. A community's power utility, a town's only neurosurgeon, a rural hospital, a city bus system, a commuter train line, and an airport are examples of monopolies. Monopolies may be either permanent (e.g., the bus line, commuter train) or short-term (e.g., because the local racket and fitness club is successful, competitive clubs are drawn into the community).

A company that holds a monopoly has considerable freedom over the prices charged. Price still must be set to attract the desired level of demand. Although competition among brands does not exist, substitute product types may be available to customers. The competitiveness of these product types and customers' needs and ability to buy determine the market elasticity faced by the monopoly company.

In a free enterprise economy, a monopoly is worrisome. The chance exists that the seller will take advantage of the lack of competition by charging unusually high prices relative to the product's cost, a practice known as **price gouging.** When the product is essential for consumers, the monopoly company's prices may be regulated by government as are the rates of power utilities. Or the government actually may operate the service rather than let private business have the monopoly. The U.S. Post Office's first-class service is an example of a government-run monopoly.

Oligopoly. An industry in which a few large sellers control a high percentage of the supply of a product or service is called an **oligopoly.** Although the marketing mixes are different in ways besides price, price is a major influence on buyers' choice of suppliers. In the United States, many of the established manufacturing industries are oligopolies, including automobiles, packaging, appliances, silver flatware, and mainframe computers. Each company's brand demand curve is different from the product type demand curve because of differentiated marketing mixes.

Companies in an oligopolistic industry are sensitive to each other's pricing decisions, and each competitor knows that customers will switch suppliers if prices are too unequal. Because products tend to be similar in oligopolies, when one seller changes price other competitors typically follow suit. **Price leadership** occurs when one or a few, usually larger companies, are consistently the first in the industry to change price.

Oligopolistic pricing is evident in the price battles that have been occurring in the U.S. domestic wine industry. Although many wine producers, both domestic and foreign, sell to U.S. markets, the industry is dominated by less than a dozen large companies including E. & J. Gallo Winery, R. J. Reynolds (Heublein Wines), Seagram (Taylor California Cellars and Paul Masson brands) and National Distillers & Chemical (Almaden). In a fight for market share at the low-price end of the market, Gallo has been the price leader. Using its economy of scale advantage over competitors, Gallo has shaved prices to keep them below those of the other producers. Some competitors such as Heublein have decided to put more of their marketing emphasis on higher-priced, premium wines so that they do not have to compete so directly with Gallo. Other competitors are following Gallo's lead by trying to bring down their prices.[10]

Monopolistic competition. A company faces **monopolistic competition** when its industry is made up of many small firms, no one of which is large enough to stand out as a price leader. Each firm develops a nonprice competitive difference in its marketing mix such as product design, packaging, location, after-sale services, or reputation. These differences allow firms to charge prices either more or less than those of the competition. Thus each company's brand demand curve is slightly different from the product type demand curve.

The hickory chips industry is an interesting example of monopolistic competition. Hickory chips are a food flavoring product sold by hundreds of small producers. The chips typically are sold by mill operations that retain and package the chip residue from their milling processes. Consumers use hickory chips in outdoor cooking to impart a hickory flavor to foods. Because the mills treat hickory chips as a by-product, price generally is kept low.

What would a company have to do to command a premium price for its hickory chips? This question was asked by the president of Genuine Tennessee Hickory Chips, a small producer in Tennessee. The answer lay in finding some way to differentiate the company's brand in the minds of consumers on nonprice components of the marketing mix. First, a unique package was designed that incorporated a plastic window, because management knew that consumers wanted to see the size of the chips before buying (small chips burn up too quickly). Second, advertising emphasized that the hickory trees from which the chips were made grew in a particular geographic area. Supposedly, the chips from hickory trees from that area imparted a unique flavor. These marketing mix differences from competition enabled the company to charge a slightly higher price.

Pure competition. **Pure competition** exists when there are many small sellers with no differences between their marketing offers. Each seller has only a small share of the total market. With nothing to differentiate them, sellers have no freedom to vary price from those of competitors. Brand and product type demand curves are the same. Sellers have no incentive to lower price because each can sell all it wants at the prevailing price. If a seller raises price, its sales will decline rapidly as customers shift to other sellers with lower prices. Pure competition is rare on a national level. Even farming, which at one time was characterized by pure competition, is now dominated by large businesses. Because businesses have so little control over their marketing strategies in pure competition, there is incentive to move to one of the other industry forms.

Price as a competitive weapon. In the United States, most industries are oligopolies or monopolistic competition. Interestingly, companies in these two types of industries have choices as to what prices to set (unlike in pure competition) but at the same time must consider competition's pricing as a key influence on the choices (unlike in a monopoly).

How effective price is as a competitive weapon in these two industry types depends on the size and on the financial and marketing strengths of the competitors. When competing firms in a stable market are nearly equal, one company lowering price often leads to a price war in which everyone lowers price to protect their market share. The result is that everyone loses money. Managers quickly learn that lowering price is often the easiest way for one competitor to counter another. Unless the company's market share increases, the net effect for the initiator of a price reduction may be only less profits (see Marketalk).

If one company has an advantage over competitors, such as being able to produce the product at lower costs, then price can be a powerful competitive weapon. Lowering price creates a difficult situation for the higher-cost competition. If they do not also lower price their sales may drop. If they do lower price their profits will suffer. The lowest-cost seller can maintain higher profits at the lower price. For instance, People Express Airlines lowered fares because management believed that the company could fly at lower costs per seat than the larger and more established airlines (United, American, Eastern, Delta). People Express used this advantage to attract sales from competitors and increase its market share.

Successful pricing depends on anticipating competitors' response to a price being considered. Furthermore, managers need to be forewarned of competitors' price changes to counter the threat. Analyzing the competition, which is part of a market opportunity analysis, is particularly important to maintain constant vigilance on competitors' pricing practices (see Chapter 4 for a discussion of analyzing the competition).

Government's influence on price

Even in a free enterprise economy, government restricts prices that can be charged. These influences vary widely across countries and even by level

EIGHT TIMES THE PHONE IT USED TO BE.

New England Telephone introduces their Choose-A-Carrier Charge-A-Call telephone at Boston's Logan Airport.
It's the first phone to allow subscribers to reach their long-distance companies with just the push of a button.
This courtesy phone provides direct connections to eight additional long-distance companies. There's no local number to remember or look up.
Or, if you prefer you can still make calls the way you always have.
So next time you're in Logan, discover the phone that's eight times the phone it used to be. ⓐ New England Telephone

Alternative carriers like Sprint, MCI, and U.S. Telecom are asking the FCC for a moratorium on price-cut plans by AT&T. Most threatening to them is a 15 percent discount called Pro America, which would bring AT&T's prices for small to midsize businesses extremely close to its competitors'. (Courtesy of New England Telephone)

of government in a country (e.g., federal or state). To illustrate the role of a government in pricing decisions, we consider the influence of the United States government on pricing decisions of U.S. firms.

Federal government actions influence pricing decisions by regulating prices that can be charged and by enacting laws that prohibit certain pricing practices. A regulated industry must submit requests for price changes to a government agency for approval. Industries regulated in the past include railroads, trucking, airlines, and utilities. More recently, many industries, particularly those in transportation, have been deregulated. The government is allowing the market forces of competition to keep prices at a fair level.

The second way in which government influences pricing decisions is by enacting laws that prohibit certain pricing practices. In a free enterprise economy, customers' choosing among competitors acts as a safeguard against a company's charging too high a price relative to costs. If one competitor's prices are too high, customers can buy from another with a lower price. Unfortunately, competition does not always provide the intended safeguard, so government enacts laws to referee situations in which the competition safeguard would otherwise break down. Exhibit 16.7 on page 454 describes important federal laws affecting certain pricing situations.

Price fixing. Suppose the managers of several companies in an industry get tired of the day-to-day pressure of setting prices to meet or beat the competition. These managers get together and jointly agree on the prices each company will charge. This practice is called **price fixing,** and although it may make managers' jobs easier, it takes away customers' freedom to choose the lowest-priced product. As a result, sellers feel less pressure to set prices based on cost and efficiency. The **Sherman Act** and the **Federal Trade Commission Act** outlaw price fixing between companies at the same level in a channel as an illegal restraint of trade in an attempt to monopolize.

Another form of price fixing, **resale price maintenance,** occurs when a firm fixes the price of a product that a firm at another level in a channel of distribution can charge. For instance, a manufacturer of wine, believing that a high price is necessary to maintain a quality image, may try to establish the prices a retailer can charge for the brand. The **Consumer Goods Pricing Act** has made resale price maintenance illegal.[11]

Managers from different firms in an industry are wary of discussing issues related to pricing with each other for fear that it may be construed as price fixing. Even when the intent is not to fix prices, discussions about price could later lead to trouble with the Federal Trade Commission.

Price discrimination. **Price discrimination** is charging different prices to different customers for the same product. An appliance manufacturer who charges one price to K mart and a higher price to Ed's Appliance Store is engaging in price discrimination. If K mart uses the lower price to discount the appliance's price to consumers, sales at Ed's Appliance Store may suffer.

The government is concerned that price discrimination may harm competition. Suppose that many stores like Ed's Appliance Store go out of business because they cannot meet the prices of the large discounters. The net effect might be to lessen the safeguard of competition. The **Clayton Act** and the **Robinson-Patman Act** were passed to prohibit price discrimination when it lessens or injures competition.

Price discrimination is not always illegal. In fact, a considerable amount of price discrimination goes on. One reason is that the laws generally do not apply to pricing directly to consumers. An automobile dealer, for instance, can let salespersons bargain for the best price they can get from each consumer. Other conditions in which different prices may be charged to different customers legally are as follows:

1. When a company can show that it costs less to sell to one customer than to another. For example, a company may offer volume discounts, in which lower-per-unit price is given for high-volume purchases. The

*Marke*TALK ///

AT&T uses price in the fight for long-distance service market share

THE DAYS of low-key, homey, "reach out and touch someone" phone ads are gone. In their place is cutthroat competition to sign up long-distance customers: When MCI Communications Corp. began to offer prospective subscribers in Charleston, W. Va., an hour of free calling for signing up for its service, American Telephone & Telegraph Co. and GTE Sprint Communications Corp. were quick to match the giveaway program. After AT&T cut its long-distance phone rates by 6.1%, MCI responded by dropping its already lower rates by up to an additional 6%.

The contenders knew the long-distance battle would be tough when it started earlier this year (BW—Feb. 13). But now they are finding they have to slash rates, dream up novel promotional gimmicks, and fund expensive advertising campaigns at a pace the telephone business has never known. These marketing tactics are getting so expensive that some observers fear the companies could end up losing more money than they make from new customers. "They are like lemmings marching to the sea," comments Amy L. Newmark, a telecommunications analyst for Cyrus J. Lawrence Inc. "These guys are going to kill each other."

The prize looks worth fighting for. The next two years will be the best chance yet for discounters to grab market share from AT&T, which owns 92% of the $40 billion annual long-distance market. As a result of last January's breakup of AT&T, cus-

tomers in most areas will for the first time be asked to choose their preferred long-distance carrier, which they will be able to reach with the same "1-plus" dialing they now use to call via AT&T—a process called equal access. "It's not a natural market development," says Lee L. Franklin, marketing vice-president at Sprint, "It's a once-in-a-lifetime opportunity."

So carriers are throwing caution—and profit margins—to the winds in those markets, such as Charleston, that already are beginning the equal-access process. They are setting up sales booths on city streets and shopping malls, sending thousands of pieces of direct mail, badgering potential subscribers over the phone, and blanketing TV and radio waves with ads. MCI alone is spending $60 million this year on advertising—up 50% from last year. AT&T's long-distance ad budget this year is estimated at $200 million.

Yet signing up new customers turns out to be more difficult and expensive than alternative carriers had anticipated. For one thing, the local Bell companies running the carrier-selection process have quietly changed the ground rules over the past few months to favor AT&T. Most Bell companies originally had planned to send out ballots asking customers to select one of a limited number of carriers. But that started to look too expensive for the phone companies. So now, all but Northwestern Bell Telephone Co. plan simply to advise customers that "1-plus" dialing is available from carriers other than AT&T—then leave the actual signing of customers to the competitive carriers.

"Instead of causing each customer to make a decision—even if it's just checking

a box for AT&T—they have turned the most remarkable marketing event in history into a nonevent," grumbles Sprint's Franklin. "Now it's a very different marketing proposition—the difficult challenge of creating the need to make a decision."

At the same time, local phone companies are backing away from earlier plans to allocate to all competing carriers those customers who failed to make any choice. That split would have been made by assigning those customers to carriers in the same proportion as customers who had made selections. The vast majority of local phone companies worry, however, that consumers would object to being assigned arbitrarily to an unfamiliar company. So they plan to continue to route via AT&T all calls from customers who have not expressed a choice.

AT&T is also proving to be a tougher and more nimble competitor than expected. It is matching most of its competitors' marketing giveaways—and, in the past few weeks, it has even introduced some innovative promotional and pricing programs of its own. One that has rivals crying foul is an AT&T plan to offer an hour of calls anywhere in the continental U.S., at night and on weekends, for just $9.40. Additional hours will cost $8.20 each, a price equal to or below that of most of AT&T's competitors—and seemingly below its cost of providing the service. "It's predatory pricing," claims William G. McGowan, MCI chairman. But a staff unit of the Federal Communications Commission has approved the plan, and AT&T hopes to put it into effect as soon as the full commission concurs.

SOURCE: "A marketing blitz to sell long-distance service," *Business Week*, July 2, 1984, pp. 86–88. Reprinted from the July 2, 1984 issue of *Business Week* by special permission; © 1984 by McGraw-Hill, Inc.

///

discounts, however, must be available to all buyers who order the designated quantities.

2. When the seller can prove that it offered a different price to a buyer to meet a competitor's price (allowed by the Clayton Act). Recently the Supreme Court expanded the provisions of the Clayton Act to include this condition.[12] A large retail buyer may say to a manufacturer, "Your price is too high. I have a price from your competitor that is considerably lower." The manufacturer can offer the same price as the competitor to that retail buyer without offering the same price to all buyers.

3. When the seller can show that the products are not of like grade or quality. Continental, for instance, can sell aluminum cans to buyers at

///

Perhaps more upsetting to the industry, the fierce marketing battles now seem likely to continue indefinitely. In a little-noticed move, the FCC recently ordered local Bell companies to limit to $5 the fee that they will charge customers to switch carriers after their first choice. Some companies were planning to charge $40 or more, a move that would have restrained some customers from switching carriers again. Says Gregory L. Mann, director of strategic planning for Allnet Communication Services Inc.: "If the only thing holding a customer to you is $5, that's not much." Allnet, in fact, has already offered to pay the $5 fee for those who decide to switch to its service. Says Mann, who expects others to copy that move: "It will become marketing warfare."

Industry leaders desperately hope to confine the warfare to features and promotions—not price, although price is now the main selling point for every carrier but AT&T. They want to transform long-distance service into a normal consumer product, stressing brand identity, quality, and service. "It's going to come down to attributes other than price," predicts John R. Smart, marketing vice-president at AT&T Communications Inc. Adds Sprint's Franklin: "There have been industries that have cut their own throats; I just hope this isn't one of them."

But carriers' attempts to prevent price wars may be in vain. Lured by the glitter of big profits, new, well-heeled competitors are entering the game by building their own networks. United Telecommunications Inc., the nation's second-largest non-Bell local phone company, is planning to spend $2 billion in the next three

years building a 23,000-mi. nationwide fiber optics communications network. Numerous joint ventures between telephone companies and railroads to build regional fiber nets have cropped up recently. At the same time, existing carriers such as MCI, Sprint, and Satellite Business Systems are spending billions to expand their present systems. All this construction could produce more capacity than there is demand for—and result in price-cutting. After all, these new networks are in addition to AT&T's, which is already capable of carrying almost all the traffic in the U.S.

Some carriers, however, are confident that demand will catch up with supply, as such new uses as videoconferencing and data communications require more phone channels. But others, including some of the newcomers, think price cuts are inevitable if the market is to grow fast enough to use all that capacity. Says William T. Esrey, president of United Telecom's Communications Div.: "We believe the economies of the business are such that companies will have to offer service at lower cost than has been publicly expressed." V. Orville Wright, president of MCI, agrees: "Overall pricing of long-distance services will gradually drift downward over the next six years, perhaps by about 30%."

Whether the price cuts will impair margins is the big question. In the short term, admits Wright, "our margins will be squeezed substantially." The reason: At the same time that discount carriers are cutting rates to attract customers, the amount they pay local phone companies for local connections will rise dramatically. They now enjoy a 55% discount over

AT&T because they have lower-quality connections. But that saving will disappear in markets where they gain equal connections.

Discount carriers are counting on cost-cutting to prevent a bloodbath. One big saving will come when the cut-rate companies stop buying lines from AT&T, as they now must to complete calls to locations that their networks do not link. But by 1986 or 1987, MCI and Sprint figure they will have connections to all of the nation's calling areas. "That will eliminate 15% to 20% of our costs," says Wright, adding optimistically, "I see our margins improving rapidly by 1990."

In the end, the fate of the industry may rest with the people who touched off the competition in the first place—the federal regulators. For years long-distance phone rates have subsidized local telephone service, and the FCC has promised to redistribute the burden of this support to telephone users by imposing "access charges." That would lower the connection fees that all the long-distance companies, especially AT&T, pay to local phone companies and would make price cuts more palatable. For now, though, congressional and consumer group opposition to these access charges has stalled the effort.

But the FCC, which is moving toward eventual deregulation of the entire long-distance market, appears determined to impose these user access charges. And as soon as AT&T's market share dips substantially, the FCC would remove many of the regulations it now imposes on AT&T. If that happens, the resulting market battle could make the current fracas look like a minor skirmish.

///

Exhibit 16.7 Important U.S. laws affecting pricing decisions

The Sherman Act (1890):	Outlawed any action specifically intended to restrain national or international trade or intended to create a monopoly.
The Clayton Act (1914):	Outlawed price discrimination and other acts that have the effect of substantially lessening competition or creating a monopoly. Section 2 of the Act is particularly important because it defines illegal price discrimination and establishes conditions under which price discrimination is legal.
The Federal Trade Commission Act (1936):	Established the Federal Trade Commission to enforce the Clayton Act. The Commission has the power to prosecute firms that are thought to be violating the Clayton Act as well as engaging in unfair methods of competition such as deceptive pricing or deceptive advertising.
The Robinson-Patman Act (1936):	Expanded the activities that are considered to be price discrimination. Charging different prices to different buyers for a product of "like grade and quality" is considered illegal if competition is injured, and that injury could be at any level in a channel of distribution. Cost-based justifications for different prices to different customers are allowed as a defense for price discrimination. Price discrimination is also allowed when a company is meeting the price reductions of a competitor. The Act makes illegal the actions of a buyer who knowingly extracts a discriminatory price from a seller.
Consumer Credit Protection Act (1968):	Requires lenders to disclose fully annual interest rates and other financial charges.
Consumer Goods Pricing Act (1975):	Superseded and ended state laws that had legalized price-fixing between different levels in a channel of distribution (e.g., between manufacturer and wholesaler or retailer). This act terminated the Miller Tydings Act (1936) and the McGuire Act (1952), which had legalized resale price maintenance under certain conditions involving interstate trade.

SOURCE: David W. Cravens, Gerald E. Hills, and Robert B. Woodruff, *Marketing Decision Making*, Homewood, Ill.: Irwin, 1980, pp. 517–522; and Kent B. Monroe, *Pricing: Making Profitable Decisions*, New York: McGraw-Hill, 1979, pp. 250–252.

different prices if there is a clear difference in the quality or amount of aluminum used in making the cans sold to the buyers.

4. When the seller can show that competition has not been injured. Charging one price for a national brand and another for a private brand of exactly the same product does not injure competition if customers can choose between them.

The last two conditions in which price discrimination is legal are difficult to defend because "like grade or quality" and "injury to competition" are not well defined. In practice, cost differences in selling to customers is probably the easiest defense to use, so carefully kept cost records are essential.

Predatory pricing. **Predatory pricing** occurs when one company "unfairly" uses price to injure a competitor. The Federal Trade Commission Act is concerned with this practice, which is most likely to happen when a powerful competitor lowers prices to drive a smaller, weaker competitor from a market. For instance, price that is set below cost may be unfair. When AT&T set a low rate on night and weekend long distance telephone calls, the chairman of one competitor, MCI Communications, charged that the practice was predatory pricing because the price was below cost. Carefully kept cost records are essential to defend against such charges. Apparently, AT&T had such records because the Federal Trade Commission approved the low rate.

Deceptive pricing. The government steps in when the potential exists for prices to be deceptive. **Deceptive pricing** occurs when a price is quoted in such a way that the customer is misled about what is actually being paid for the product. A lender that states the interest rate for a loan as 2 percent per month might be deceptive because the rate sounds low until it is converted to an annual rate of 24 percent. The so-called truth-in-lending statute or **Consumer Credit Protection Act** guards against this kind of deceptive practice. Lenders must provide borrowers with information on the true annual interest rates and other charges being made in a credit arrangement.

Many other forms of potentially deceptive pricing practices exist. For instance, retailers' pricing of flatware described in the chapter's opening may be misleading if the manufacturer's list prices are set artificially high. Injury comes when the consumer makes a purchase decision based on the belief that the price offers more value than it does in fact. The FTC has the power to stop such practices.

In reality, pricing decisions are complicated greatly by the many laws with which the price setter must comply. The language used in the laws—"unfair," "injury to competition," products of "like grade and quality," "lessening competition"—often is so vague that a price setter may not know whether a price complies. Legal counsel may be needed periodically to determine whether a particular pricing decision can be implemented.

Channel members' influence on price

Pricing might be easier if managers had to set prices for only end-users. Pricing decisions, however, extend to every level in a channel of distribution. Consequently managers must examine the impact of price on members of the company's channel. Of particular concern is how to use price as an incentive for the channel and avoid potential for conflict.

Price as an incentive. When selling through a channel, a company's total revenue is based on the volume of its product purchased by the channel members and the price they pay. Thus price set by a manufacturer is not the price that the end-user customer sees, but the price that the channel member, a wholesaler or a retailer, pays. In turn, the channel member sets price for its customers. Pricing decisions are concerned with both price to end users needed to generate a desired volume for the entire channel, and price to the channel members that will encourage them to aggressively sell the product to their customers. Scripto was faced with this pricing situation when it brought out its disposable, erasable pen. Market opportunity analysis showed that a price to consumers of $.98 was best. To work back to the price that Scripto should charge, management had to determine what price retailers would pay to Scripto and also sell the product at the desired $.98 to consumers. Suppose retailers needed to make $.30 per pen to achieve their revenue objective. Scripto's price to retailers would be $.68: $.98 retail less the $.30 required by the retailers to sell the product to consumers.

Companies in the channel are concerned with their opportunity for profit from selling various competitors' brands. Their decisions to stock a brand are based largely on two factors: the margin a brand offers and estimated quantity that can be sold. **Margin** is defined as the per unit price received from customers less the per unit price paid for the seller's brand. **Quantity** is the estimated number of units of a seller's brand that can be sold. Putting quantity together with margin yields an estimate of a brand's **profit contribution** to the channel member:

$$\text{Profit contribution} = \text{Quantity} \times \text{Margin.}$$

Manufacturers can influence the channel's profit opportunity in either of two ways. Building a strong appeal for the product ensures that consumers will go to the stores looking for the brand. Thus quantity is increased. Proctor & Gamble has been successful using this strategy. Crest toothpaste is a popular brand, and Procter & Gamble can command cooperation from the channel simply because consumers look for Crest in stores. Management can charge a relatively high price to the channel because although margin is smaller for Crest than for less-popular brands of toothpaste, the quantity sold is high.

A second way that manufacturers can influence the channel's profit opportunity is to offer a larger-than-average margin. A less-popular, lower-sales-volume brand may do this to gain cooperation from the trade. Colgate-Palmolive markets Peak toothpaste, a brand that does not sell as much as Crest, having only a 0.1% market share in 1983.[13] To offset the lower-sales-volume potential, Colgate can offer a lower-than-average price to the channel to increase Peak's margin.

Let us compare the profit contributions of Crest and Peak if they offered the same margin of $.50. Crest, being the considerably more popular brand, will generate more sales to consumers. Suppose that a store's sales of each product are expected to be 10,000 units of Crest and 1000 units of Peak. The profit contribution to the store for each brand is as follows:

Crest: $.50 × 10,000 = $5,000
Peak: $.50 ×   1,000 = $ 500

You can see that the store would be much more interested in selling Crest than Peak solely because Crest's quantity is higher. Peak can offset Crest's popularity somewhat by offering the store a greater margin, say $.75, so that the store makes more revenue on each unit of Peak sold. The higher margin may encourage the store to sell Peak more aggressively and generate higher quantity sold. Suppose that the store now shifts sales of 1000 units from Crest to Peak through a special promotion of Peak. The profit contribution from the two brands changes:

Crest: $.50 × 9,000 = $4,500
Peak: $.75 × 2,000 = $1,500

The store makes more profit contribution in total for both brands by more heavily promoting Peak. At the same time, Colgate enjoys a higher sales volume for Peak.

A seller need not offer permanent price reductions to get cooperation from the channel. Short-term discounts of price are more flexible. The seller can offer discounts at certain times of the year or in return for particular activities requested of the channel. (Types of discounts are discussed in Chapter 17.) Colgate for instance, may offer a discount to retailers if in exchange they give assistance promoting Peak in the stores' local areas, give Peak favorable shelf locations, or offer reduced prices to consumers. The practice of discounting prices to channel members is expanding dramatically in the United States. One estimate puts the growth of these discounts during the past decade at eightfold, from $1 billion to $8 billion.[14]

Exhibit 16.8 The chain of prices in a channel of distribution

Manufacturer's list price (per unit) to end-user customers	$150
Less: 40% discount off list price for retailer's service ($150 × .40 = $60)	60
Price to retailers (per unit)	$ 90
Less: 20% discount off retailer's price for wholesaler's services ($90 × .20 = $18)	18
Price to wholesalers	$ 72

Conflict from pricing in the channel. The concern of the channel for their own profitability can create conflict for the price setter. To gain an advantage over their competitors, channel members may attempt to exercise power over suppliers by trying to get a favorable price, preventing trade competitors from getting a favorable price, or pressuring suppliers not to sell to competitors. Department stores selling name brand children's clothing exercise this power by putting pressure on clothing manufacturers not to supply discount companies such as Toys R Us. The department stores are fearful of losing business to these discounters who offer the same merchandise for a price that is as much as 30 percent lower.[15]

Price can be used as a weapon to thwart the plans of competitors as they try to gain cooperation from the channel. Although the price decision must be legal, short-run profits may be sacrificed to gain market share from competitors. Colgate-Palmolive was hurt by a competitor when Peak toothpaste was introduced. Proctor & Gamble immediately initiated a price discount program for Crest. Retailers stocked up on Crest and so did consumers because part of the discount was passed on to them. As a result, Peak did not sell well.[16]

Properly set, price can be a powerful incentive for the channel to assist in selling a product to consumers, or price can be used to disrupt channel cooperation. A manufacturer must simultaneously consider prices at each level in the channel all the way down to the consumer. Exhibit 16.8 shows the effect of offering discounts to channel members. In this illustration, a manufacturer is selling through wholesalers and retailers to reach end-user markets. Because the channel members charge for their services, there are really three prices being set: (1) price to the wholesaler ($72); (2) price to the retailer ($90); and (3) price to end-users ($150). Many firms approach this complicated multiple pricing task by beginning with the price needed for target markets and working backward to set prices for the channel. The types of selling effort needed from channel members are considered in determining what discounts will be used throughout the year.

PRICING IN THE COMPANY

Price setters must look inside the company for factors that influence price (please review Exhibit 16.1). The strategy of the company, the costs of the product, and components of the marketing mix must all be considered when price is being set.

Company strategy's influence on price

Because price has such a direct impact on revenue, it is particularly visible to top managers charting company strategy. Guidelines are set that determine the role of price in company strategy, or the weight management attaches to price relative to other aspects of strategy. In American business, the weight given to price varies a great deal.

At one extreme, top management may establish price as a central part of the company's approach to attracting customers and differentiating itself from competitors. Customers are encouraged to perceive that they are getting more value than if they bought from a competitor. Safeway Stores, the world's largest food retailer, recently has renewed its determination to become a low-price leader in the industry. The company is coordinating actions to set prices extremely competitive relative to other food retailers.[17]

More generally, the discounting and low-price strategies of many companies such as K mart, Krystal fast-food restaurants, and Commodore International rely heavily on price. Of course, price need not be set low for it to play a large role in strategy. Premium brands of many products are priced relatively high to maintain a strong exclusive reputation. Pampers, Mercedes Benz, and Michelob are but a few of the many brands that use price in this way.

At the other end, some companies do not place much weight on price as part of company strategy. Increased emphasis is given to strategic components such as product quality, innovation, or services. Small and medium-sized firms in particular have great difficulty setting prices competitive with large firms. Thus they must find successful strategies that do not include competing directly on price. Robert H. Waterman, Jr., a director of McKinsey & Company, reported on a study of successful smaller companies:

> All of the successful smaller firms in the study, he said, "thought of themselves as creators and leaders of small market niches, rather than going after positions in huge, established markets. They innovate so rapidly that they don't have to worry about cost position.
>
> "They told me, 'Look, by the time we have to worry about cost, we hope we've moved on to something else. We'll leave it to somebody else to be the low-cost competitor.' They forge their own destinies by creating and innovating their way to success, creating new markets.
>
> "As a corollary, they view themselves as competing on value rather than cost. They create value and tend to get the higher prices for that value."[18]

Cost's influence on price

Within the guidelines set by top management, managers must find price alternatives that exceed the cost of a product. No firm can exist for long if the price for each unit sold does not exceed its cost. Thus cost sets a minimum (or floor) below which price cannot go if a profit is to be made.

Keeping track of all costs is a responsibility for the accounting function of a company. To make the cost information useful for a price setter, separate costs must be kept for each product in a company's product mix. Only then can the price setter examine the cost of a product to establish the floor for price. Even with a sound accounting system, determining product cost usually is difficult. Let us examine a few of the cost complexities that managers must face.

Direct and indirect costs. Every company incurs a variety of costs. **Direct costs** can be traced directly to the product being priced. They are only incurred because the company is producing, distributing, and selling the product in question. Price must be set so that revenue is greater than direct costs if losses are to be avoided. Examples of direct costs are the costs of labor, materials, and machines used to produce the product; advertising; shipping; and product development. Direct costs can be further divided into the following important categories:

- **Fixed costs** do not vary with the volume of a product produced. A machine purchased for $40,000 retains the same cost no matter how many units of the product are produced.

- **Variable costs** vary with the volume of a product produced. Costs of labor and materials used are variable because they increase or decrease in proportion to the volume produced or sold.

- **Total direct costs** are the sum of fixed and variable costs for a product.

- **Per unit cost** is the total direct cost divided by volume of the product produced.

- **Per unit fixed cost** is the total fixed cost divided by volume of the product produced.

- **Per unit variable cost** is the total variable cost divided by volume of the product produced.

Indirect costs are costs that cannot be traced directly to individual products in the company's product mix. Usually called overhead, these costs include salaries for administration, office equipment and supplies, utilities, and buildings.

Whether a price setter should be concerned with indirect costs depends on how these costs are treated. One way is to keep indirect costs separate and not consider them for pricing purposes. This approach is called **contribution pricing** because prices set for a product must yield enough revenue to cover direct costs and make a contribution to total indirect costs and profits. Per unit direct costs establish the floor for price, and other factors such as price elasticity, competition, and legal constraints determine how much above the floor price is set.

Before setting prices, a company may allocate all indirect costs to all products in the product mix, an approach called **total cost pricing.** Accountants determine the method for allocation, though all methods essentially are arbitrary because these costs are by definition not traceable to individual products. Salaries of middle and top managers are indirect costs and might be allocated to each product in proportion to their sales volumes, with higher-sales-volume products being assigned proportionately more overhead costs. After all allocations are made, total per unit cost becomes the floor for pricing a product.

Decisions on what costs to assign a product can influence dramatically its price. Let us return to the pricing of hickory chips, a food flavoring product that is purchased for outdoor cooking. A common practice in the industry is to base price only on the direct costs of producing, distributing, and selling the chips. Because hickory chips are a by-product of saw mills, managers do not allocate any indirect costs to the product, nor do they expect the product to contribute much to overhead. As a result, hickory chips are priced low. If indirect costs were allocated to hickory chips then the price would be set higher because the cost floor is higher.

Costs change with volume. The per unit cost of a product decreases as the volume produced increases partly because of **economies of scale.** These economies occur because per unit fixed cost decreases as volume increases. Per unit variable costs also are lowered due to volume discounts on purchases of materials and supplies.

Another reason costs change with volume is that experience is gained the longer a product is produced. Through trial and error, a company's operations become more efficient. Workers learn how to do their jobs better, and more efficient ways of performing different tasks are found. And technological improvements are likely to be made over time. Many manufacturers, for instance, look for increases in productivity that are made through greater automation, which lead to lower per unit costs.

The effect of experience on per unit cost (in constant dollars) is shown by an **experience curve.**[19] As illustrated by Exhibit 16.9 this curve graphically shows the degree to which per unit cost goes down as cumulative volume goes up over time. When the concept of the experience curve was first introduced, some managers tried to use it in developing company strategy. The central idea was that the company must build volume to take advantage of experience benefits. Building volume required taking market share from competitors, which could be done by lowering price. Profits would be maintained by lowering per unit costs from the benefits of experience as cumulative volume grew over time.

In many industries, this strategy was not successful because management overlooked the reaction of competitors to lowering price.

> When the client company was already a significant player in the market, probably the easiest first step was to cut price in the hope of picking up share. The not infrequent result, unhappily, was a kick-'em, punch-'em, wrestle-'em-to-the-ground price war. "When you start a war, all generally lose," observes Jack Field, vice president of strategic planning at Union Carbide, which says it uses the experience curve, but only as one element in pricing decisions.[20]

The lesson has been well learned. Companies that use the experience curve apply it to forecast per unit costs in the future under assumed increases in volume. These forecasts, however, are only one factor considered in the price decision. Although cost is usually the first consideration, managers cannot forget other influences on pricing.

Marketing strategy's influence on price

To achieve maximum effectiveness, pricing decisions should be coordinated with other marketing decisions. Price may be needed to support decisions on other components of marketing strategy, and decisions on the rest of marketing strategy may help price achieve its purposes.

Pricing supports marketing strategy. Price, in the minds of customers, is frequently interrelated with the total set of benefits being purchased, as previous discussion has made clear. Marketing managers take advantage of this fact by using price to enhance the effectiveness of other decisions.

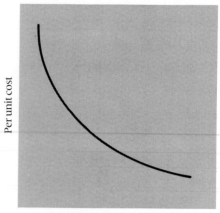

Exhibit 16.9 The experience curve

Market target, product, channel, promotion, and services are important components of marketing strategy that depend on price.

Profitable market targets may be discovered by breaking out segments with customers having different price elasticity. Targeting price inelastic segments of the market for a product increases a company's ability to obtain a higher margin and not sacrifice volume. The more price elastic segments, then, receive a lower price to attract sales.

The airlines apply this kind of segmentation by charging different prices for the same seats at different times. It works well because business travelers flying at peak times are less sensitive to price than are tourist travelers. Companies in a wide variety of industries—appliances, coffee, wine, hotels, rent-a-car services, and home building, to name a few—have taken advantage of price elasticity–defined segments.

Another way in which price can be used to support market target decisions is to help gain faster penetration for a product or a new feature of a product. Penetration means that more and more customers decide to buy and use the product. A relatively low price compared with cost or with competitor's prices can act as a strong incentive to buy from the seller. General Electric took advantage of price as an incentive for buyers by pricing a new digital dishwasher to cover only half the cost of the digital components. Management expected future cost to decrease as sales increased. As a GE senior vice president put it: "I forward-priced it. I took less margin on that product to try to establish the market."[21]

Product-related pricing decisions extend to an entire line of products being sold. Different prices for each product help establish product quality differences in the minds of customers. Consider Whirlpool's full line of refrigerator models ranging in price from a few hundred dollars to $1600 or more. The wide price range cannot be explained only by differences in cost. Rather, Whirlpool uses electronic digital readout controls on its top-of-the-line refrigerator and charges a premium price to create an image of a trend-setting appliance and to separate this model from the middle- and low-priced refrigerators in its mix.[22]

We have already seen how price may be used to increase cooperation from companies in a channel of distribution. Similarly, price can be used to enhance the effectiveness of promotion. Announcing changes in price can be a very important promotional theme, helping promotion contribute to a company's sale performance. Stores such as Its For Levi, a chain of jeans stores, regularly space price-off sales on selected merchandise over the calendar year. The price-off sales give advertising a message and help draw people to the stores, increasing store traffic. Many manufacturers also combine price and promotion, as illustrated by the price rebate advertising of durable product sellers of automobiles, computers, and appliances.

Companies that rely heavily on facilitating, after-sale services as an integral part of their strategy incur substantial added costs to provide them. Frequently, companies do not want to charge a separate price for each service, and so use product price to cover these costs. The pricing dilemma faced by Exxon and other major oil companies demonstrates that this approach only works when price can be kept high enough to offset service costs. For a long time, these companies offered "free" credit with the purchase of gasoline. A recent customer survey showed that availability of credit is very important to consumers when they choose which brand of gasoline to use. Yet the credit expense is becoming prohibitively costly. Gasoline pricing is so competitive that prices cannot be easily raised without losing volume. A price and credit strategy is being implemented as a solution. Credit is offered with gasoline sold at regular prices, and customers who pay cash get a reduced price. Management hopes that the lower price will reduce use of credit over time.[23]

Marketing decisions to support pricing. Marketing decisions on nonprice components of marketing strategy may be made to support a price decision. To justify a price increase, the company may have to demonstrate to people, through product redesign, extra services, and/or promotion, that the increase is justified. On the other hand, to lower price a company may have to change other components of the marketing mix to bring costs down, too. Caterpillar Tractor Company has been successful for decades using a product quality, fast-service, high-price strategy. Recently the company has found that its market share is declining owing to lower-price competitors. Caterpillar reassessed its strategy and decided to become increasingly price competitive. To bring prices down, management has streamlined its distribution system and is more efficiently producing its products. Furthermore, Caterpiller is looking to new and more price elastic target markets to keep sales up.[24]

SUMMARY

Price is determined by the relationship between the value exchanged by the buyer for the value or benefits offered by the seller. Thus anything that affects either of these values can be part of the pricing decision. Furthermore, pricing decisions may not even involve the exchange of money, as buyer and seller can choose to barter for goods or services. In international sales, bartering between countries, called countertrade, is quite common and growing in importance.

Price is very visible to parties in the external environment, and so managers must evaluate the effect of influences coming from this environment. Marketing managers look for prices that will attract the volume of demand desired. Demand curves provide a way to examine how customers react to alternative prices. Many demand curves are downward sloping, indicating an inverse relationship between price and quantity purchased in markets. However, demand curves can be very different among products and services. Price elasticity explains some of the differences because some markets are more sensitive to price as a factor in buying decisions than are others. When markets are price inelastic, managers can raise price and increase total revenue. Price elastic markets cause managers to consider lowering price to increase total revenue.

Price can also have psychological meanings to buyers. When there is little else that the buyer can use to judge prestige or quality, price may help make this judgment. In these situations, higher price may actually lead to more quantity purchased, suggesting that over a certain range of prices the demand curve can be positively sloped. Luxury products such as perfume, expensive cars, fur coats, and jewelry are ones where companies have experienced a direct relationship between price and volume purchased.

Competition also influences pricing decisions. Marketing managers typically are careful to set prices that have a desired relationship to those of competitors. If a company has a superior combination of benefits to offer, a premium price can be charged, keeping price above that of the competition.

On the other hand, management of a company may want to include value as an important part of its offer by pricing below that of the competition. In part, the nature of the industry in which a firm is competing determines how much freedom a seller has to vary price in markets. A monopoly offers the most freedom, while a pure competition industry has the least. Most industries fall in between these two extremes. They are classified as oligopolistic or monopolistic competition industries where some but not complete freedom to set price desired by management exists.

How competition prices vary in relation to other competitors depends on the nature of the relative advantages each has over the others. Low cost sellers try to take advantage of their cost strength by charging lower prices. Other sellers may try to build a benefit advantage, such as quality or service, in order to justify charging a higher price. A market opportunity analysis is needed to evaluate what relative advantages a company has over its competition.

Government, through laws and regulations, limit the price alternatives that managers can consider. Government's aim is to act as a safeguard against pricing decisions that may unfairly take advantage of a monopoly situation or harm competition that is needed to keep price in line with benefits offered. Many pricing practices such as price fixing, resale price maintenance, price discrimination, predatory pricing, and deceptive pricing are outlawed in the United States primarily to protect competition and buyers.

At the same time that price is attracting buyers, it also must act as an incentive to companies in the channel of distribution. Channel companies want to achieve profit contribution objectives from the products they sell. Thus a company must set price to the channel that is enough lower than the price that channel members charge their customers so that these objectives can be met. Otherwise the channel will not have incentive to carry the product or aggressively sell it.

Finally, marketing managers look inside the company for factors that influence pricing decisions. Company strategy, costs, and overall marketing strategy influence prices that can be charged. Price may be needed to support decisions on target markets, product, distribution, and other parts of marketing strategy. At the same time, decisions on other components of the marketing mix may be needed to support a price decision. Lowering costs to enable a price reduction or using promotion to announce a price change are illustrations. Together, the external and internal marketing environments create a complicated pricing situation for marketing managers.

KEY TERMS

bartering	price gouging	Consumer Goods Pricing Act
countertrade	oligopoly	price discrimination
demand curve	price leadership	Clayton Act
price elasticity	monopolistic competition	Robinson-Patman Act
price-quality relationship	pure competition	predatory pricing
odd pricing	price fixing	deceptive pricing
customary pricing	Sherman Act	Consumer Credit Protection Act
price lining	Federal Trade Commission Act	margin
monopoly	resale price maintenance	quantity

profit contribution	per unit cost	total cost pricing
direct costs	per unit fixed costs	economies of scale
fixed costs	per unit variable costs	experience curve
variable costs	indirect costs	
total direct costs	contribution pricing	

QUESTIONS FOR REVIEW AND DISCUSSION

1. Suppose that Hershey Chocolate Company decided to reduce the size of its chocolate candy bar and maintain its forty cent cost to consumers. Does this decision involve pricing? Why or why not?

2. What is bartering? Does bartering eliminate the need for making pricing decisions? Why or why not?

3. How does price affect the revenue that a company receives from a product?

4. What is a demand curve? Why is the downward-sloping demand curve so common?

5. What is price elasticity? In what way does a demand curve show price elasticity?

6. Is a demand curve for a product type (e.g., economy car) the same as a demand curve for a brand of that product type (e.g., Ford Escort)? Why or why not?

7. What are two ways that a company can find out about price elasticity for a brand?

8. What is the price-quality relationship? In what way can this relationship affect pricing decisions?

9. How do pricing decisions in a monopoly industry differ from those in pure competition?

10. How do pricing decisions in an oligopoly industry differ from those in a monopolistic competition industry?

11. Is price an important competitive weapon? Why or why not?

12. Is price fixing always illegal in the United States?

13. Is price discrimination always illegal in the United States? If so, explain why. If not, explain the conditions under which price discrimination is legal.

14. What are "unfair" pricing practices?

15. What is a margin? Explain how margin affects the profits of a member of a company's channel of distribution.

16. Can pricing in the channel create conflict for a manufacturer? Why or why not?

17. Is being the lowest-price seller in an industry always best? Why or why not?

18. How does contribution pricing differ from total cost pricing? Which one leads to a higher price?

19. What is an experience curve? How can an experience curve help with pricing decisions?

20. Explain four ways in which price can be used to support nonprice components of a company's marketing strategy.

BUILDING YOUR PORTFOLIO

Select two products or services, each one from a different type of industry: monopoly, oligopoly, monopolistic competition, or pure competition. You might pick hickory chips (monopolistic competition) and refrigerators (oligopoly). If you pick a service you might consider nonfranchise restaurants (monopolistic competition) and rent-a-car services (oligopoly).

Use the telephone book yellow pages or business section to identify a list of businesses selling the products or services selected. Then, by either telephone or personal visits, obtain a list of competitive prices. Be sure that you specify exactly the same product or service when getting the prices. Obtain as many prices as you can in the time you allocate to this exercise.

The product or service from which industry had the greatest difference between the highest and lowest prices (i.e., the widest range)? Can you explain why the price range is wider for one product (or service) than the other? Is the structure of the corresponding industries a factor?

NOTES

1. The silver flatware industry situation is based on information in "The silverware price war." *Business Week,* Mar. 29, 1982, pp. 160, 162.
2. Kent B. Monroe, *Pricing: Making Profitable Decisions.* New York: McGraw-Hill, 1979, pp. 4, 6.
3. Estimate by *Business Week* as reported in Darryl G. Waldron, "Countertrade: A Framework for Analysis," in Paul F. Anderson and Michael J. Ryan (Eds.), *Scientific Method in Marketing.* Chicago: American Marketing Association, 1984, p. 243.
4. "A new marketing blitz in the war of the plastic cards." *Business Week,* July 23, 1984, p. 126.
5. Peter W. Bernstein, "Cartels: De Beers and the diamond debacle." *Fortune,* Sept. 6, 1982, p. 44.
6. Monroe, op. cit., p. 39.
7. "Energy-guzzling: Most consumers are cured." *Business Week,* Apr. 4, 1983, p. 16.
8. "Holiday Inns opens doors for the upscale traveler." *Business Week,* Apr. 25, 1983, p. 101.
9. Robert Ball, "Volkswagen's struggle to restore its name." *Fortune,* June 27, 1983, pp. 101, 102.
10. "The wine wars get hotter." *Business Week,* Apr. 11, 1983, pp. 61, 65.
11. Ray O. Werner, "Marketing and the United States Supreme Court, 1975–1981." *Journal of Marketing,* Vol. 46 (Spring 1982), p. 76.
12. Ibid., pp. 74, 75.
13. Monci Jo Williams, "The no-win game of price promotion." *Fortune,* July 11, 1983, p. 93.
14. Ibid., p. 92.
15. Kenneth Labich, "Toys R Us moves in on kiddie couture." *Fortune,* Nov. 26, 1984, p. 135.
16. Williams, op. cit.
17. "Safeway Stores: Back to price wars for a company that played it safe." *Business Week,* Apr. 5, 1982, p. 108.
18. "Successful small & medium-sized firms stress creativity, employ niche strategy." *Marketing News,* Mar. 16, 1984, Section 2, p. 22.
19. For a more complete discussion of the experience curve see George S. Day and David B. Montgomery, "Diagnosing the experience curve." *Journal of Marketing,* Vol. 47 (Spring 1983), pp. 46, 47.
20. Walter Kiechel, III, "The decline of the experience curve." *Fortune,* Oct. 5, 1981, p. 140.
21. "Look, Ma, no dials: More major appliances go digital." *Business Week,* Nov. 12, 1984, p. 97.
22. Lisa Miller Mesdag, "The appliance boom begins." *Fortune,* July 25, 1983, p. 56.
23. "Gas credit starts to evaporate." *Business Week,* May 10, 1982, p. 53.
24. "A shaken Caterpillar retools to take on a more competitive world." *Business Week,* Nov. 5, 1984, pp. 91, 92.

Case 16.1

Bausch & Lomb Inc.

FOR THREE YEARS in the early 1970s, Bausch & Lomb Inc. owned 100% of the soft-contact-lens market. It even got away with charging optometrists $25 to attend a class to learn how to fit them. Angered, many were quick to turn to the competitors that entered the market in 1974. By 1978, B&L's market share fell below 50%. But in 1979, the haughty leader started to fight back. It cut prices 28%, to $25 for some lenses, and announced it would meet all prices offered by competitors to high-volume chains (BW—Nov. 17, 1980). B&L's market share quickly exceeded 60%. President Daniel E. Gill declared: "Losing market share now is just not an alternative."

Bausch & Lomb nevertheless continued to cede market share until the middle of last year. It lost ground after two competitors—Cooper-Vision Inc. and Revlon Inc.'s Barnes Hind Hydrocurve brand—introduced extended-wear lenses in 1981, which customers could wear up to a month without having to remove and clean each night, as they must with daily-wear lenses. For two years the B&L competitors owned this new market while Bausch belatedly developed its own extended-wear entry, a thinner version of its daily-wear lens that was suitable for extended wear.

But when the Food & Drug Administration finally approved the lens in April, 1983, B&L's marketing power took over. Within a month, B&L's sales staff had supplies of the new lenses in more than 90% of the 12,000 professional eye-care outlets in the U.S. that sell contact lenses. Within four months, Bausch captured 37% of the EW market and was the No. 1 seller. "We're like IBM," smiles Gill. "We don't have to be first to become first."

How well that clout has paid off began to be noticeable in the first quarter of this year. The company's income rose 26% over the year-earlier period to $10.1 million on a 16% sales gain to $154.3 million. Still, many optometrists continue to grouse about the company's pricing policies, particularly its strong support of chain stores through volume discounts. The *Review of Optometry* says the company's own research reveals that nearly one-third of all optometrists say Bausch is the com-

pany they least prefer to do business with. But another third say they like Bausch best.

Bausch backed its introductory show of marketing muscle with the strongest weapon of all: aggressive pricing. Its entry price of $20 was 50% or more below the industry norm for extended-wear lenses. Analysts assume that competitors' total costs are at least two to as much as five times higher than the $1.10 they estimate it costs B&L to make a lens, yet Cooper-Vision hit back in March with a new, top-quality, high-water lens it offered for about $15 wholesale. Bausch retaliated in April by lowering all its prices even further. Now its high-water model wholesales for $10 to $15, while its basic low-water lens lists at $8 to $13 depending on volume, and a new daily-wear lens has been introduced at a low price of $7 to $12.

April's high sales tripled in May. "I don't think prices will go much lower," says Gill, who admits the current levels suit Bausch's strategy admirably. "We do not set up an umbrella under which others can make big profits," he says. Consequently, he expects a further shakeout of the dozen companies in the business.

Competitor John D. Fruth, president of Ocular Sciences Inc., agrees there will be a shakeout and says Bausch will remain a leader. But he believes B&L's management should take advantage of its market position to raise its pricing umbrella. "I can't think of one other market leader that is also the price leader," says Fruth. "Big Blue didn't take the lead in computers by cutting prices," he says. "If I had the largest sales volume, and the largest sales force, and the oldest franchise, and the broadest product line, I would insist that I get a price-preference delta of at least $3 per lens. They are leaving money on the table that a good marketing operation would not leave."

Many on Wall Street agree. "They had 10 down quarters out of 11, so Wall Street was down on them," says Larry Haimovitch, an analyst with Woodman Kirkpatrick & Gilbreath. At about $19, Bausch's stock is selling near its low for this decade because the Street distrusts deep price discounting. It may have good reason. Gill recently split the company's eye-care business into two parts: A consumer group markets sunglasses and cleansing solutions chiefly through drug stores; the Professional Eye Care Products Group sells lenses. The company's report

shows operating earnings from lenses fell 31% between 1981 and 1983, to $46 million, while sales in the same period rose only 5% to $148 million.

But Gill shows no signs of changing B&L's pricing strategy. One reason: High volume is a critical component of the company's low-cost formula. And the profitable replacement market, which grows each time a new pair of lenses is fitted, now accounts for two-thirds of the total market, up from one-third in 1980. Sales of replacement lenses and sterilizing solutions accounted for 76% of B&L's total U.S. dollar volume from eye-care products last year, says analyst Otto F. Grote, president of Derby Securities Inc. Next year, he estimates B&L will sell 9 million replacement lenses, half the total U.S. replacement market, and an average of one lens per wearer.

New products could make today's market appear antique almost overnight. Barely one-fourth of the 47 million Americans who need vision correction wear soft contacts. That market is expected to grow by 3.4 million new "fits" this year and to expand an additional 20% next year as improvements appeal to more customers. A further 48 million potential bifocal-lens wearers could come into the market as the industry begins to develop lenses that satisfy them. B&L's first-generation lens can fit only a small percentage of the total market, but improvements will rapidly expand the product base—also adding to replacement-lens and solution sales.

Furthermore, tinted lenses are just beginning to woo innumerable vanity customers. Early offerings make light eyes blue, while stronger tints to turn brown eyes blue are being tested. None offer meaningful glare resistance, and in Canada, 20% of the prescriptions sold offer no optical correction whatsoever—simply a cosmetic tint to the eye.

Not surprisingly, Gill says, "This industry is still in its infancy." His goal is to capture "at least 50% of every segment of the lens market" and become a "more broadly based, health-oriented company." He plans to offer three differently priced lenses in each market segment and "to test to see how far we can extend the Bausch & Lomb name in the front end of the drugstore," where sales of its Ray-Ban line of upscale sunglasses have shot up this year. It is test-marketing an anti-irritant eye drop not tied to contact lenses, and prescription eye-care drugs are also a possibility.

The company's strategic emphasis on

SOURCE: "Bausch & Lomb: Hardball pricing helps it to regain its grip in contact lenses," *Business Week,* July 16, 1984, pp. 78–80. Reprinted from the July 16, 1984 issue of *Business Week* by special permission; © 1984 by McGraw-Hill, Inc.

health and eye care will increase this year if Gill can shed, as he hopes to, the bulk of B&L's $217 million instrument business, which lost $16 million during the past two years. Microscopes and telescopes will be retained, but B&L is negotiating a leveraged buyout of two lackluster heavy-industry-oriented instrument units by their managements, while a public offering and spinoff of B&L's strong line of graphic design and drafting equipment will probably be arranged this year. With lens sales booming and the instrument albatross about to be removed, Gill admits: "It feels good to have gotten to where we are."

QUESTIONS

1. What are the key environmental factors affecting Bausch & Lomb's pricing decisions?

2. In what way is price related to Bausch & Lomb's marketing objectives?

3. How is cost affecting Bausch & Lomb's pricing decisions?

4. Should Bausch & Lomb be concerned about the impact of its prices on the channel of distribution? Why or why not?

5. Should Bausch & Lomb continue to price lower than the prices of the competitors? Why or why not?

Case 16.2

Republic Health Corporation

"STEP LIVELY" is the latest marketing slogan of Republic Health Corp., a Dallas-based health care chain that peddles its wares the way Procter & Gamble pushes soap. To lure those with ailing feet to seek surgery at General Hospital of Lakewood in Texas, the company is conducting a newspaper campaign promising reduced rates for a foot examination, a free take-home meal after hospitalization, and a $20 gift certificate toward a new pair of shoes. Notes Chief Executive James E. Buncher,

SOURCE: Eleanor Johnson Tracy, "Cut-rate surgery is luring customers," *Fortune,* Nov. 12, 1984, p. 88. Used by permission.

"We carry on a very aggressive marketing program, and we tend to feature one thing at a time."

The September feature was cataract operations, and as usual Republic stressed its freebies. In a two-week "Gift of Sight" campaign promoted in Southern California newspapers, the bait included a promise to absorb deductibles—$356 for patients with only Medicare insurance—and a $50 gift certificate toward a new pair of glasses. The campaign evoked 2,000 responses, 100 of which resulted in operations.

Republic's reliance on heavy doses of promotion comes at a time when the business of for-profit hospitals is changing rapidly. Medicare and Medicaid spawned the industry in 1965 by flooding it with money—the government reimbursed hospital costs plus something extra. But new Medicare rules are making the business tougher. Last fall the government began phasing in a new policy of paying hospitals a flat fee for a specific treatment. If the hospital does the job for less, it makes money. If the treatment costs more, it loses money. Buncher's advertising blitzes are aimed at getting costs down by keeping Republic's beds filled.

QUESTIONS

1. What are the environmental factors influencing Republic's pricing decisions?

2. Suppose a cataract operation at one of Republic's hospitals costs the patient $543 in hospital charges. What is the true price to the patient for the hospital care (not including the doctor's fees)?

3. How is cost influencing Republic's pricing decisions?

4. In what ways do Republic's pricing decisions assist in its advertising strategy?

17 Price Determination

When you finish this chapter, you will understand

□ The steps that managers follow to determine a price for a product

□ How managers integrate price into the overall marketing program for a product

□ How external environmental and internal company factors affect the determination of price

□ Different kinds of situations in which pricing decisions must be made

Customer demand and supply provided by competition are key factors in determining the prices of futures and options for commodities.

When the market for personal computers exploded in the late 1970's, literally hundreds of firms jumped into the fray and achieved impressive growth and profitability. Vector Graphic, North Star Computers, Intertec Data Systems, Computer Devices, and others like them carved out a share with the better-known companies such as Apple, Tandy Corporation, and Commodore. Demand outstripped supply enabling firms to set prices yielding attractive returns. For a while, management could afford the luxury of only worrying about production schedules and counting the profits. But this prosperity could not last forever.

A shakeout of computer companies has begun. Price setting has become an increasingly important competitive weapon. The better-known companies, now including IBM, have become more aggressive with their pricing. Both dealers and customers have shown more interest in value received from a personal computer. And price reductions of 10 to 20 percent have been common.

Large-volume companies spread costs over large production runs and remain profitable even as prices are squeezed by competition. Small-volume companies, however, are caught in a difficult situation. They must employ strategies offering more product performance and at a lower price. Yet small-volume manufacturers cannot easily lower price and still retain a big enough margin to remain profitable. Some firms—Timex Sinclair, Mattel, and Texas Instruments—have already dropped out, and others such as Atari are in trouble.[1]

As PRICING OF PERSONAL computers demonstrates, factors such as customer demand, costs, and competition force pricing managers to be creative and resourceful in their response to changing market conditions during a product's life cycle. A survey of industrial firms discovered that during the 1980s pricing decisions are becoming an increasingly important aspect of strategy in many companies.[2] Our discussion of price determination in this chapter is particularly timely in light of this development.

Price is not treated with the same importance in all firms. In some, great strategic weight is given to a product's price, which is determined after much research and consideration. In others, the product's price is a smaller part of the marketing mix and is determined by mechanical procedures. Applying only mechanical rules, however, oversimplifies the real pricing situation faced by management. No firm is exempt from macroenvironmental and task environmental forces or from internal cost considerations, and price must reflect these factors.

Our discussion of price determination examines the opportunity to use price in a strategic way, which requires that managers consider how pricing can contribute to achieving company and marketing objectives. Furthermore, managers must have a sound understanding of the many influences on a pricing decision. Using price in a strategic way is best accomplished by having a logical, step-by-step approach to making pricing decisions.

A strategic approach to pricing must also work in a variety of situations created by company strategy, marketing planning for the product being priced, and environmental influences on the pricing decision being made. Setting a price for a new product is a different situation than changing the price of an existing product. Another situation is created when new competitors enter a market with a price discount strategy (see Marketalk). As you read this chapter, look for these situations and how they affect pricing considerations.

Exhibit 17.1 presents a multistep approach to price determination.[3] As we saw in Chapter 16, price must reflect the role that top management has assigned to it in company strategy. The price setter also must look for opportunities to use price to enhance the effectiveness of components of the marketing mix such as product quality, promotion, and services. Decisions on components of the mix may be needed to support price. These considerations establish the role of price in the marketing mix.

Next management establishes pricing objectives and strategy. These guidelines provide a basis for evaluating alternative prices being considered and ensure that prices are being coordinated with other decisions affecting overall marketing strategy. Pricing policies also are set to deal with specific recurring situations.

The preceding steps create the boundaries or range within which price must be set. Typically there is flexibility when choosing among specific prices. Several pricing methods are used in practice to determine the best price within this range. Each requires that managers consider important task environmental or internal factors before choosing the price.

Finally, managers can never expect a price to remain the same over a product's life. Periodically, prices must be changed as influences on price change. Preparing for these changes requires that managers evaluate current prices to anticipate when these price-change decisions should be made.

In the remainder of the chapter we discuss each of the steps in the multistep approach to price determination.

PRICING'S ROLE IN COMPANY STRATEGY

Price has a direct impact on customers, competitors, channel members, the marketing mix, and costs. Price is also influenced by government. These relationships mean that managers from many different departments of a company have a stake in prices set for products. An approach to price determination must recognize this fact by considering the **role of price** in company strategy. In part, this role is the weight that is placed on price

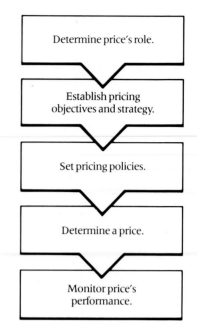

Determine price's role.

Establish pricing objectives and strategy.

Set pricing policies.

Determine a price.

Monitor price's performance.

Exhibit 17.1 A multistep approach to price determination

The Commodore 64 is a very popular computer in the United States, but in Mexico it's the Commodore 16 that sells. The 16 (which was withdrawn from U.S. production) sells for about twice as much as the $100 price that it had in the States but is less expensive than other computers now on the Mexican market. Commodore's main competition in Mexico comes from models made by Apple Computer and Acorn Computers that cost as much as $1000. (Courtesy of Commodore International, Ltd.)

*Marke*TALK ///

Deregulation creates a new pricing situation for the airlines

BEFORE 1978 PRICING for airline routes in the United States was regulated. On individual routes across the United States, very little competition was allowed. Routes were awarded to the airlines by the government. Thus buyers had little choice about which airlines to use. Airline fares also were approved by the government, making prices uniform.

The Airlines Deregulation Act of 1978 changed the entire situation. Airlines' managements are free to charge whatever prices they think best. At the same time, the door was opened to new competition. During the next seven years, twenty-eight new airlines, both regional and national, came into operation. Another twenty re-

SOURCE: "Airlines in turmoil," *Business Week,* Oct. 10, 1983, pp. 98–99; and James V. Cammisa, Jr., "Deregulated airlines are trying to carve out profitable market niches," *Marketing News,* Apr. 13, 1984, p. 3.

ceived approval from the Civil Aeronautics Board to begin operation. As a result, fares for seats on the same routes began to vary considerably.

The older established airlines such as United, American, Eastern, and Delta were caught in a difficult situation. Over the years of regulation, airlines' costs had grown dramatically owing to high labor rates and the high fixed costs of jet aircraft and the equipment to keep them flying. Deregulation took away the airlines' ability to pass these costs on to customers periodically in the form of government-approved fare increases. Additionally new competitors took advantage of the situation by making significant inroads on market share held by the established airlines.

Pricing is being used in different ways as airline competitors go after different marketing niches. Some airlines set price high and appeal to business travelers who

want extra services. Regent Air has adopted this approach by offering a one-way fare of $1610 for a flight between New York and Los Angeles. In return, passengers get gourmet meals, spacious seating, a cocktail lounge, private compartments, and conference rooms. At the other extreme, price wars have developed as discount airlines moved in on the established airlines. People Express, which flies routes in the northeast, Southwest Airlines, and Continental Airlines have all cut frill services and held labor rates down to offer discount fares. The established airlines fought back with deep fare cuts to protect their market share. On routes where established airlines compete against discounters, pricing low helps fill seats on planes so fixed costs can be spread over increased volume. The new pricing situation clearly calls for a more strategic use of price by all airlines.

///

relative to other components of the strategy. For example, a company must decide how much to rely on low price relative to product innovation as part of its strategy for achieving sales and profit goals. The role of price also considers the kinds of contributions that price can make by working with other aspects of strategy.

Top management's decisions on pricing

Top management, when charting strategy for a company, makes decisions that affect pricing flexibility. These decisions tie price to other aspects of strategy. To see how price is influenced by company strategy decisions, consider a **competitive dominance strategy.** This is a strategy of building and maintaining the largest market share in target markets. In turn, high market share may enable a firm to keep price below those of competitors. Gallo Winery owes much of its success to a competitive dominance strategy in the low-priced wine market. Gallo consistently undercuts the prices of competitors to remain the dominant seller in this market. Low price helps generate high-volume sales, which yield cost economies. These cost economies enable Gallo to be profitable while keeping price low.[4]

Other company strategy decisions affect price alternatives, as we shall see. Each decision is the result of top management's confronting issues that arise from a company's relationship with its external environment. How these issues are resolved provides directives to price setters that serve as bases for evaluating pricing alternatives. Alfred R. Oxenfeldt summarizes many of these issues.

Many vital price-related decisions made by top management deal with the following issues: Are we willing to drive competitors from business if we can? Should we inflict serious injury upon them when they have been struck by misfortune? Are we willing to violate the spirit or letter of the law to increase sales? At a different level of concern, pricing decisions are related to price strategy and general competitive policy by questions such as: Should we seek price leadership for ourselves or foster a pattern of price leadership with some other firm as leader? Should we try to shake out the weak firms in the industry to achieve price stability and higher profitability? Should we foster a spirit of cooperativeness among rivals by an avoidance of price competition?[5]

Pricing in the marketing mix

In companies whose product mix is extremely large, setting prices for so many products may seem overwhelming. Try to imagine the difficulty of setting prices for the thousands of products sold in a Target discount store. To cope with the situation, managers may seek a simple rule for calculating price such as: Take cost of a product and add a 50% increase to determine the price to change. The danger in using such rules is that opportunities to use price to achieve overall marketing objectives may be overlooked. Establishing a role for price in the marketing mix helps overcome this pitfall.

Product-line role. In multiproduct companies, price may help achieve objectives for a product line. Price of one product is set in such a way that performance of the entire line of products is enhanced. **Loss-leader pricing** is commonly used for this purpose by setting a low price for one product to increase sales of other related products in a line. You may have noticed that retail stores with sporting goods departments such as Penney, K mart, and Target stores regularly sell tennis balls at or even less than cost, and little if any profit is made. Store managers believe that the low price on tennis balls draws more people into the store's sporting goods department. While there they are likely also to buy related products such as tennis rackets, warm-up suits, and bags, all of which are profitable items in the line.

Timing of sales. Price can help the marketing mix by offering an incentive for customers to buy at certain times of the day, week, month, or year. Management's purpose is to even out production and sales over a period of time so the firm can plan on regular revenue. Detroit Edison has effectively used price in this way by offering steel companies discounted electricity rates during late evening and early morning hours when residential use of electricity is low and demand is reduced. The low rates have successfully encouraged McLouth Steel Corporation and other steel companies to shift some operations to this time period, evenly distributing demand over twenty-four hours.[6]

Coordination. As we saw in Chapter 16, price can have many roles in the marketing mix. Enhancing product quality, building a prestige image, gaining cooperation from the trade, and providing an attention-getting advertising message are some of the more important ones. For price to effectively support the marketing mix, managers in different departments must coordinate their decisions. Suppose a company's management wants to develop a prestigious image for a product. Managers in financial control and product departments, with advise from advertising managers, will jointly set price to

ITALIAN DESIGN ON WHEELS: ABOUT $72,300
ITALIAN DESIGN ON HEELS: ABOUT $60

Nickels

Nickels tries to convey a prestige image for its "Cinema" shoe by suggesting that it has the dash and design of an expensive car. (Courtesy of Intershoe Inc. and Sacks & Rosen)

enhance image impressions among customers, and at the same time, contribute to achieving revenue and profit-related objectives. Then the advertising department must create an advertising theme to communicate the prestigious image that price is helping to establish.

A company must determine how best to achieve this coordination. A high-level executive may mandate that informal coordination take place, a committee may be formed with key managers from the different departments, or a manager from one of the departments, such as a product manager, may be assigned responsibility for coordinating pricing with the other departments. However it is done, pricing's role is the result of interplay among managers from several functional areas including but not limited to marketing.

PRICING OBJECTIVES AND STRATEGY

Depending on pricing's role there is usually considerable lattitude for the way in which price can be used in a marketing mix. Guidelines are needed that provide direction to price setters concerning the specific prices to charge. Thus the next step in the pricing approach is to establish pricing objectives and strategy.

Pricing objectives are statements describing price's expected performance. They formalize the purposes that managers have in mind for price that are consistent with an assigned role. Some objectives such as maximizing long-run profits or maintaining market share link price to more general objectives of the entire business. Other objectives such as encouraging the sale of weak products in the line tie price to nonprice components of the marketing mix. Finally, price objectives may be set to obtain certain kinds of behavior on the part of outside parties important to the company such as customers or competitors. Setting price to discourage competitors from entering a market is this kind of objective.

Exhibit 17.2 provides a list of practical price objectives. Consider Apple Computers, which uses price to enhance the image of the firm and its products. Although it has reduced production costs on its Apple IIe personal computer to as little as $200 to $300 according to one estimate, the company keeps the product's price high relative to the lower-priced home computers sold by Commodore and Atari. Apple does not want to be associated with low-priced computers.[7]

Pricing strategy refers to guidelines that specify how price is to achieve its objectives. Strategy is needed because objectives usually can be achieved in more than one way. For instance, objectives that link price to company performance such as maximizing long-run profits offer no direction as to the specific prices that will best accomplish the objective. A strategy of pricing low relative to the competition considerably narrows the range of alternative prices that are acceptable to the company.

Developing a pricing strategy has the added advantage of encouraging managers to evaluate important influences on price. How customers consider price in their buying decisions, the prices of competitors, and the costs of producing, distributing, selling, and servicing products are particularly important. Premier Industrial Corporation's pricing strategy is to keep prices high relative to the competition and reflects a sound evaluation by management of these factors. The company sells common undifferentiated products such as nuts, bolts, batteries, circuit breakers, lubricating oil, and electronic components in an extremely price-competitive market. Premier has found a way to avoid cutthroat price competition by linking price

---

Exhibit 17.2   Setting pricing objectives to guide managers

Maximize long-run profits.

Maximize short-run profits.

Expand market share.

Maintain market share.

Desensitize customers to price.

Maintain a price-leadership position.

Discourage potential competitors from entering a market.

Encourage competitors to leave a market.

Avoid government investigation and control.

Maintain loyalty of middlemen and get their sales support.

Avoid demand for "more" from suppliers (e.g., labor).

Enhance image of firm and its offerings.

Be regarded as "fair" by end users.

Create interest and excitement about the item.

Be considered trustworthy and reliable by competitors.

Help the sale of weak items in the line.

Discourage others from cutting prices.

Make a product "visible."

Make market attractive to obtain high price for sale of business.

Build customer traffic.

SOURCE: Adapted with permission from Alfred R. Oxenfeldt, "A decision-making structure for price decisions," *Journal of Marketing*, Vol. 37 (Jan. 1973), p. 50.

strategy to product quality and extensive service. For its electronic products, the company's forte is filling orders quickly, and they charge a higher-than-average price for the service. Premier also supplies superior quality and custom-made nonelectronic products and charges a premium price. Customers are willing to pay higher prices in order to get the quality and service benefits. Furthermore, the premium prices more than offset the higher costs of the company's marketing mix. Clearly, its pricing strategy is based on a sound understanding of its own costs, the price inelastic market segments, and competition's use of price.[8]

Companies must be flexible enough to adjust pricing objectives and strategy over time. External environmental influences change over a product's life cycle, as do internal costs, and managers must be alert to new objectives and strategy needed to accommodate them. Two important time-related marketing situations in which managers set specific price objectives and strategy are (1) pricing a new product and (2) pricing an existing product in a company's line from growth to maturity.

Pricing objectives and strategy for new products

Setting price for a new product, particularly one that is truly different from other products, is difficult because of its newness. Managers cannot rely as well on past experience to analyze the factors affecting a product's success. Yet the new product's initial price can have long-lasting impact on the company's ability to tap market opportunity. Consider a price that yields unusually high profits early in the product's life cycle. High initial profits acts as a beacon to attract competitors quickly and the innovating company may not have enough time to establish a strong position with customers. In fact, some firms like Coca-Cola, IBM, and Bausch & Lomb sometimes wait for other firms to innovate, monitor their performance, and then use their huge marketing strength to rapidly jump into the market with a competitive brand.

Time horizon. How far in the future management wants to establish a product's overall performance objectives is reflected in the pricing objective, and this time horizon affects the range of price alternatives that can be considered. Setting a short-run profit maximization objective results in relatively high prices because introductory costs are high for a new product. In contrast, setting a long-run profit maximization objective enables managers to consider a broad range of prices to determine which will best help develop the market.

Customers' price elasticity. Pricing objectives and strategy depend on the extent to which managers believe customers are price elastic. Analysis is needed to find out how customers weigh price against specific product benefit when they make buying decisions. If economical price is an important factor in customers' decision to try the new product, then low prices will attract more sales than high prices. But, when the benefits of an innovative product outweigh price and initial buyers are price inelastic, higher prices may be charged. Furthermore, price objectives and strategy may dictate a high price relative to competition to make the product visible.

Competition's reaction. A truly new product will have little or no immediate competition from similar brands. Nevertheless, competition from product types satisfying the same need is usually a threat. These products can serve as a frame of reference for customers when they evaluate the benefits of the new product.[9] Pricing objective and strategy are needed to establish the relationship of the new product's price to those of these product type competitors. For instance, prices for videodisk players, an innovative product, were set below prices for videocassette recorders because consumers were expected to compare these two products. Interestingly, consumers preferred recorders, even at the higher price, because they offered more benefits. Thus sales of videodisk players suffered.

Pricing managers also must consider how quickly potential competitors can enter the market. If there are barriers to entry, such as a patent on the new product or technical know-how not easily acquired, a long time may pass before competition is a factor. Management does not have to be concerned with the threat of competition moving into markets with similar brands and rapidly forcing price down. The barrier allows the innovating company time to establish a strong position in the market. Polaroid's patents and unique technical know-how established effective barriers to competitor's entry into markets for instant film development cameras, and the company was able to develop this market while remaining virtually unchallenged.

When entry barriers do not exist, pricing may be used to discourage potential competitors from entering a market. Strategy usually involves setting prices relatively low to prevent competitors from getting a high enough price to justify the costs of developing and introducing their own brands. Management may even hold down short-run profitability for a new product to achieve this pricing objective.

Influence of costs. The more innovative a product is, the less experience management has with which to estimate costs. Yet, costs must be forecasted. If per unit costs decrease quickly as volume increases, management will be inclined to set a relatively low price to build sales volume in a short time. But if costs do not vary much with volume, then pricing objectives may dictate that higher prices be considered.

The cost-forecasting problem is facing banks today as they try to sign up customers for home banking services through computers. Costs of the service are partly dependent on the banks' being able to reduce paper in processing customers' accounts such as for paying retail charges. For consumer markets to be developed, retailers have to agree to allow electronic transfers of funds from customers' accounts to these stores' accounts. However, acceptance by the retailers has been difficult to predict because they have to change their accounts receivable systems to accommodate the home banking services.[10]

The following two pricing strategies and related pricing objectives have evolved from these considerations:

1. **Skimming pricing** is setting a high initial price for a new product, relative to the price of a competitive product used as a reference by customers. High price "skims" the market by attracting price inelastic buyers. This strategy works best when (a) buyers who are the first to try a new product place more importance on benefits other than price, (b) the new product offers clear advantages over other products competing for the same customers, (c) per unit costs are not likely to come down quickly with volume sales increases, and (d) competition cannot

quickly enter the market with a similar product at a lower price. Skimming pricing has long-run implications. Management expects to lower price over time to build sales volume and to target more price-elastic markets. Thus later price reductions are planned. IBM is using a skimming strategy with its personal computer products. The PC originally was introduced at a relatively high price. During the next five years IBM brought out five versions of the PC and cut the initial price in half.[11] This strategy has been effective in meeting ambitious sales, market share, and profit objectives.

2. **Penetration pricing** is setting a price low relative to those of competitive products. It is the opposite extreme from skimming. Low price helps the new product "penetrate" the market by gaining quick market acceptance from customers. The result is high sales volumes and market share early in the product's life cycle. Penetration pricing is best used when (a) many potential buyers are price elastic, (b) per unit costs drop substantially with increases in volume, and (c) competition is seriously threatening to enter the market quickly with a similar product. Japanese watch makers such as Seiko effectively used penetration pricing to establish a strong market share in U.S. consumer watch markets. They introduced electronic watches that were extremely accurate and priced lower than Swiss and American brands. The strategy has made competitive retaliation difficult, though Swiss watchmakers such as Longine are fighting back with Swatches, inexpensive, brightly colored plastic watches, some of which have the scent of banana, raspberry, or mint.[12]

Exhibit 17.3 shows pricing objectives that typically lead to skimming and penetration pricing strategies. In practice, these two strategies are merely opposite ends of a whole range of new product pricing strategies. Cost, degree of customer price elasticity, likely competitive reaction, and other factors may cause managers to select a strategy falling somewhere in between the two extremes.

Pricing objectives and strategy for existing products

Factors that affect price change during a product's life.[13] As we saw in Chapter 16, over time per unit costs decrease as volume and production experience increase, competition from similar brands increases, and market size expands, bringing more price elastic buyers. Thus a company must be

Exhibit 17.3 Pricing objectives for skimming and penetration pricing strategies

Skimming pricing objectives
Maximize short-run profits.
Desensitize customers to price.
Enhance image of the firm and its product offer.
Make a product visible.

Penetration pricing objectives
Maximize long-run profits
Discourage potential competitors from entering a market.
Be regarded as fair by end-users.
Create interest and excitement.
Build customer traffic.
Build market share quickly.

flexible enough to change pricing objectives and strategy to better fit evolving pricing situations.

Initiating a price change. A company's management may decide to be the first in an industry to initiate a price change. The decision most often concerns how much to reduce a product's price.[14] As a product becomes established, lowering price can encourage sales, and the company can benefit from cost economies and experience. Furthermore, the threat of competition taking the price initiative is an incentive to lower rather than to raise price. Firestone Tire & Rubber Company, for instance, is keeping prices low to discourage competition from companies in countries such as Japan, Taiwan, and Korea.[15]

There are, of course, situations that cause management to raise a product's price. Price increases may be considered if inflation is increasing product costs, if competitors' costs are rising, or if demand is greater than the industry's ability to meet all customers' purchase requests. The threat of competition undercutting a company's price increase is minimal when these factors are present. More than likely competitors will also raise their prices. We can see this phenomenon in pricing of meals by restaurants. Rising costs of beef have led restaurateurs to increase the price of hamburgers and other beef menu items. Because these cost increases affect all restaurants alike, competition has not forced prices to stay down.

Countering competitors' price changes. When a competitor is the first to announce a price change, management's options are to leave price alone, to meet the competitor's price reduction, or to raise or lower price even more than did the competitor.

The response depends on several considerations: whether other components of the company's marketing mix—product quality, brand prestige, or extensive service—offset the competitor's lower price and whether the competitor's cost structure will sustain the price decrease. The company's pricing objectives (e.g., to maintain market share) and costs at different prices and quantity sold are also factors. When Coca-Cola discounted the price of its soft drink, Pepsi countered with price decreases. The similarity of the brands and the desire to protect its market share gave Pepsi's managers little choice but to follow Coca-Cola's lead. In contrast, Dr Pepper is trying to avoid price competition by targeting segments (largely in the South and Southwest) where it has a strong following based on the drink's distinctive flavor.[16]

Managers must be alert and creative to take advantage of pricing situations during a product's life cycle. Equally important is their ability to use information describing marketing's environment to make appropriate choices of pricing objectives and strategy. Consider Thermos, a manufacturer of "outdoor living products" such as insulated jugs and coolers. These products have reached a maturity in their life cycles and there is intense price competition despite low prices reducing everyone's profits. Management wanted to break out of total reliance on price to compete, and company research discovered that Thermos is well known for quality. A price objective was established to maintain middleman loyalty and sales support. Thermos offered rebates to consumers, which allowed Thermos' channel of distribution to remain competitive on price without eating into their profit margins on each unit sold. Price to consumers was intended to make the product visible. The corresponding pricing strategy was to keep price competitive without deep price reductions. The rest of the marketing mix also was redesigned to build on the strong quality image.[17]

PRICING POLICIES

Most managers encounter recurring pricing issues for which specific rules called **pricing policies** can be established. These policies are helpful because the situations can be anticipated, and managers can simply apply the policy each time the situation occurs to avoid having to spend the time and effort making a new decision. Four areas in which policies often are set concern price negotiation, frequency of price changes, price discounts, and geographic pricing.

Price negotiation

Salespersons are sometimes asked by customers for a discount on price. Managers do not want salespersons to make all decisions on these requests because they are apt to set too low a price. Yet, the managers do not have the time to intervene on price each time a sales negotiation is under way. Perhaps you know that car dealers in the United States face decisions on price-discount requests every day because many customers expect to pay a price lower than the one shown on a car's sticker. Although salespersons want the freedom to negotiate a price that will guarantee a sale, managers know that offering too low a price will erase the profit from selling the car. Thus a **price negotiation policy** is needed to set boundaries around the authority of a salesperson to reduce price. Many sales will take place at prices falling in the boundaries set by the policy, thus saving managers' time.

Determining a price negotiation policy involves striking a balance between maintaining a desired profit margin and setting a price that will influence the buyer to buy. Competition must be considered because they also have price negotiation policies. One option used by many consumer-product retailers is to set a policy of no price negotiation. Managers of restaurants do not allow their waiters or waitresses to bargain over the price of a meal with customers. Department stores, movie theaters, grocery stores, and gas stations also have this policy.

When price negotiation is allowed, managers must establish the lower limit on price that a salesperson can offer. The product's **list price,** the preestablished price normally communicated to customers, provides the base from which reductions are allowed. The lower limit is determined by considering (1) costs of the product, (2) price elasticity of customers, (3) level of understanding that salespersons have of cost, (4) amount of price reduction competitors are willing to let their salespersons negotiate and (5) typical expectations of customers about receiving a price reduction as a condition of sale.

Frequency of price changes

As a product moves through its life cycle, management will face numerous instances in which a new pricing decision must be made. Managers may treat each situation independently, or a **price change policy** may be established that considers the cumulative effect of periodic price decisions on markets and on competitors. A company may establish a policy of having frequent price changes, particularly when the changes are reductions. This policy is most likely to be used to help achieve the pricing objective of creating interest and excitement among customers. For instance, The Brown Squirrel, a retail store selling name brand furniture, has a policy of frequent price changes through periodic sales. Management wants to instill in customers an impression that "something is always happening at The Brown Squirrel store." Frequent price changes are best when (1) customers place a great deal of importance on price, (2) competition has a similar policy of frequent changes, and (3) building traffic and sales volume are important pricing objectives. Frequent price changes can be implemented by periodically reducing price permanently or temporarily reducing price through sales. On the other hand, a policy of infrequent price changes is advised when (1) price is perceived by customers as indicating value, prestige, or quality of a product; (2) competitors will retaliate by undercutting the company's price; and (3) the company wants to avoid government investigation and control.

Price discounts

From time to time, managers may want to encourage members of the company's channel (called the trade) or end-users to act in a desired way. Price is a valuable tool for this purpose because it provides the needed incentive. Offering a discount off list price gains cooperation from the trade. In a similar way, discounts encourage end-users to increase their purchases. When discounts are used periodically, a **price discount policy** may be established to control the amount, timing, and terms of the discounts offered. Four types of discounts are common in practice: trade discounts, promotion discounts, cash discounts, and quantity discounts.

Trade discount. A **trade or functional discount** is a price reduction given in exchange for the trade performing specified functions such as storing the product, providing warranty repairs, training dealers, and marking prices. It usually is stated as a percentage reduction from the list price to end-users. Suppose the list price for a product is $20, and the manufacturer offers a trade discount of 40 percent. The discount determines the price paid by the trade to the manufacturer, which in this case is $12: $20 − .40($20). The 40 percent trade discount is the cost to the seller of the functions performed by the trade, and it is also the margin or revenue that the trade uses to cover its cost and contribute to its profits.

The seller weighs the cost of a discount (lost revenue by not getting the full list price for each unit of the product sold) against the value of the functions performed by the trade. This evaluation is difficult because the seller may not be able to determine easily exactly what function each member of the trade is performing.[18] There may be many wholesalers and retailers, each performing somewhat different functions.

Promotion discount. A **promotion discount** encourages wholesalers and retailers to advertise, set up in-store displays, or otherwise promote the product in their area. It may be given as a discount off price or in the form of a cash payment to the trade. The policy decision concerns how often to offer a promotion discount and how much the discount should be. Considerations include the probable sales volume increase from the local promotions, the cost of the discount, and the advantage of having the trade rather than the manufacturer sponsor the advertising in the local area.

Cash discount. A seller offers a **cash discount** to encourage the trade or end-user to pay for purchases within a specified period of time. Managers must decide on the amount of the discount and the terms of the discount. Suppose a manufacturer states a list price to the retailer of $45 for a product and also stipulates the terms, 3/10, net 30. These terms mean that if the buyer pays the amount owed for the purchase within ten days, 3 percent can be deducted off the price of each unit, but if the buyer does not use the discount, the full amount must be paid within thirty days.

Because the cost of a cash discount must be compared with the value of getting quick payment as well as possibly achieving higher sales, the decision is both a credit policy and a marketing policy. How much early payment is worth depends on whether the discount sufficiently reduces the amount of outstanding debts and the amount of funds tied up in accounts receivable. These are concerns of financial control managers. Marketing managers also have a stake in cash discounts because they are a means for lowering price to increase sales.

Quantity discounts. A **quantity discount** offers a price reduction to encourage customers to buy in volume from the seller. A **noncumulative discount** is given for volume buying on each purchase order. A manufacturer of videotape recorders may offer no discount to customers who purchase less than twenty recorders, a 20 percent discount on orders of twenty to fifty recorders, and a 30 percent discount on purchases of more than fifty recorders. The amount of the discount is based on lower costs of selling more recorders for each purchase and having to process fewer purchases from a customer during the year. The discount also encourages a buyer to purchase a greater amount from the seller at one time.

A **cumulative discount** is given when large purchases are not practical. The nature of the business or the product may require smaller, more frequent purchases. A restaurant cannot purchase large amounts of perishable foods at one time, but must buy small amounts frequently to ensure freshness. The food supplier's management may want to encourage the restaurateur to buy most of its food products from their company rather than from competitors. Quantity discounts based on how much is purchased throughout the year, not on any one purchase, accomplish this purpose.

For quantity discounts management must decide: the number of different volume breaks for which discounts are given, the volume of purchases that qualify for each discount, and the amount of the discounts. Lost revenue from the discounts is balanced against likely increased sales and reduced costs of processing orders. The quantity discount policy of competitors also is a key factor in determining how much sales will increase as a result of a company's own policy.

Discounts determine revenue. Discount policies significantly affect revenue that a company receives. List prices are reduced by discounts so that real prices paid to the seller are considerably less. Suppose a manufacturer of videocassette recorders suggests a list price (to consumers) of $369 on its low-end of the line model. The company sells to large retail chains, elec-

By showing the price of its twelve-year-old Scotch in the equivalent Japanese currency, Chivas Regal appears to be deflecting attention from the U.S. cost of their product compared with other domestic brands and, in fact, implies that consumers are getting a bargain for their buck. (If you've not seen many photographs of American dollars in ads, it has been for good reason: Until 1984, when the U.S. Supreme Court overturned a 1958 law, it was a federal crime to publish photos of U.S. currency in advertising.) (Courtesy of the Seagram Company and Doyle Dane Bernbach Inc.)

tronics stores, and specialty video stores. Management has decided upon a quantity discount of 7 percent for orders over 100 units. Functional and promotional discounts are 35% and 5% respectively for warranty repair handling, inventory, promotion, display, and other services of the retailers. Finally, the cash discount terms are 3/10, net 30. Let us see how these discounts affect the manufacturer's revenue from the sale of 150 units of the recorder to a retail store chain:[19]

Total revenue at list price (150 × $369)	$55,350.00
Less: Quantity discount (55,350 × .07)	3,874.50
	51,475.50
Less: Functional discount (51,475.50 × .35)	18,016.43
	33,459.07
Less: Promotional discount (33,459.07 × .05)	1,672.95
	31,786.12
Less: Cash discount (31,786.12 × .03)	953.58
Net revenue to manufacturer	$30,832.54

The average price per unit received by the videocassette recorder manufacturer is determined by net revenue:

$$\text{Average price} = \frac{\text{Net revenue to manufacturer}}{\text{Number of units sold}}$$

In this illustration, the manufacturer was actually paid a price per unit of $205.55: $30,832.54 ÷ 150 units. The difference between the list price and the average price is $163.45 per unit sold ($369 − $205.55) and represents the cost to the manufacturer of the functions and services provided by the retail chain.

Geographic pricing

One of the most significant costs of a sale is incurred when transporting products from the seller to the buyer. Transportation costs become an issue for pricing when management sets a **geographic pricing policy** establishing how price is to reflect this cost. Policy is necessary because the way that transportation cost is handled affects a company's ability to compete in distant markets.

To help you understand the geographic pricing issue, consider a manufacturer in Pittsburgh that sells aluminum cans to soft drink bottling plant customers in Milwaukee, Denver, St. Louis, and Atlanta (see Exhibit 17.4). Each customer is located a different distance from the seller, so the cost of transporting the cans to each one will be different. The can manufacturer may choose F.O.B. origin pricing or one of several delivered pricing policies to deal with this situation.[20]

F.O.B. origin pricing. F.O.B. means free on board and is a way of telling the buyer that the price is good only at a particular location. **F.O.B. origin** means that the seller's price is quoted from the point of shipment and does not include transportation cost. The buyer must assume responsibility for arranging for transportation and pay its cost. The can manufacturer states its price as F.O.B. Pittsburgh which means that the price is good only in Pittsburgh. The advantage of this policy is that the same price can be quoted

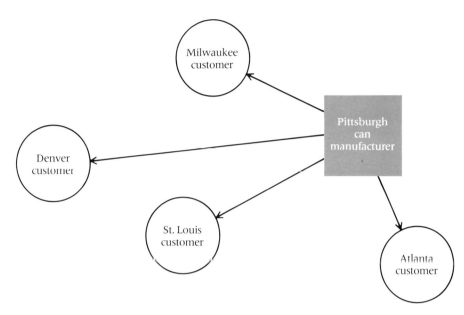

Exhibit 17.4 Geographic pricing considers location of customers

to all customers regardless of their location. Furthermore, the seller does not have to arrange transportation.

F.O.B. origin pricing works best when all competitors in an industry are located in the same geographic area. When competitors are in different areas, however, this policy creates competitive difficulty because buyers consider transportation as part of the cost of a purchase. Thus buying from a competitor nearby reduces their total cost. Unless the seller has a nonprice advantage such as product quality, F.O.B. origin pricing can cause more distant customers to purchase less. Because cans of different manufacturers are so similar, you can see that the Pittsburgh can manufacturer cannot compete on price for the purchases of the Denver customer if another can manufacturer is located closer to Denver.

Delivered pricing policies. The disadvantages of F.O.B. origin have caused many firms to apply F.O.B. destination pricing. Called a **delivered pricing policy,** it determines the amount of transportation costs to be paid by the seller. Companies are most likely to use it when customers are price elastic, competitors are not located in the same area, and nonprice components of a marketing mix do not outweigh price. Single-zone pricing, multiple-zone pricing, F.O.B. with freight allowed, and basing-point pricing are delivered pricing policies.

Single-zone pricing is used when the seller quotes one list price and the same transportation cost for all customers, regardless of their location. The cost is an average cost for all customers in the single zone. The Pittsburgh can manufacturer may quote the same price and average transportation costs to customers in Milwaukee, Denver, St. Louis, and Atlanta. This policy benefits the buyer because it transfers the responsibility for arranging for and paying transportation costs to the seller. Furthermore, because all buyers pay the same delivered price (product price plus transportation costs) more distant buyers pay a lower net amount than under an F.O.B. origin policy. Of course, buyers nearby pay a higher delivered price.

Multiple-zone pricing establishes more than one zone for purposes of quoting delivered prices. Customers in the same zone are charged the

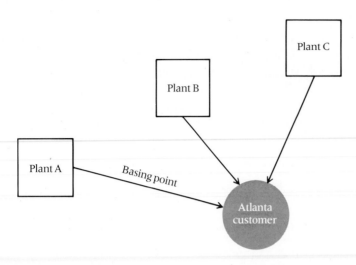

Exhibit 17.5   Basing-point pricing

same average transportation cost and pay the same delivered price. A different cost is quoted for each zone depending on how far the zone is from the seller, on competitive prices in the zones, and on customers' price elasticity. Look again at Exhibit 17.4. The can manufacturer may set up one zone for Denver and St. Louis customers, a second zone for the Milwaukee customer, and a third zone for the Atlanta customer. This policy enables the seller to adjust prices according to price elasticity and competitive price differences in various geographic areas. The pricing flexibility comes at a cost. The seller has the added responsibility of arranging for and paying transportation costs. Customers on either side of a zone's border also may complain about paying different delivered prices even though they are located close together. What is more, customers in the same zone may feel they are being treated unfairly by paying the same price even though their distances from the seller's plant are not the same. Keeping these customers satisfied becomes more difficult.

F.O.B. with freight allowed is a way for the seller to include transportation costs in price and, at the same time, let the buyer arrange for and pay the shipper. The buyer deducts the costs of transportation from the total bill and pays the net amount to the seller. Furthermore, the buyer is free to arrange the lowest-cost transportation available.

Basing-point pricing is yet another variation of delivered pricing policies. The seller establishes one (*single basing-point pricing*) or more (*multiple basing-point pricing*) locations from which to calculate transportation costs. Each location, usually a plant where a product is produced, is a basing-point. Used by companies with more than one production facility, the basing point is not necessarily the plant from which the product is shipped. Exhibit 17.5 shows the can manufacturer's three plants from which shipments are made to the Atlanta customer. Although the manufacturer may ship cans to Atlanta from all three plants, the price quoted to customers is calculated as if the cans were shipped from one plant. If plant A is the basing point, then the transportation cost included in price is the cost from this plant to the Atlanta customer's location. Shipping costs from plants B and C are not considered in the delivered price, although some of the cans may be shipped from these plants. When serving customers in several geographic areas, different basing points may be used depending on the location of plants closest to these customers. The transportation cost is determined by the basing point that yields the lowest delivered cost.

Basing-point policy enables a seller to charge the same transportation cost regardless of which plant actually ships the product, which simplifies price quotes and keeps managers of different plants from feeling they are in competition with each other for the orders from customers. Furthermore, the production schedules for the plants can be controlled without regard for differing numbers of customers located nearest each one. The negative aspect of the basing-point policy is that customers may get upset if the basing point is farther away than the plant that shipped the product but not designated as a basing point. In that situation the buyer pays more than the true transportation cost.

DETERMINING A PRICE

Although pricing's role, objectives, strategy, and various policies help managers determine which prices are acceptable, there usually remains flexibility in the choice of a particular price. In practice, managers have developed several ways to determine what this price should be. Before examining these methods, let us consider marginal analysis, an ideal method of determining price. This ideal serves as a useful framework, as is explained later.

Marginal analysis

Selecting a price requires managers to consider the important influences on price (see Chapter 16). **Marginal analysis** meets this criterion by evaluating changes in revenue and costs as price increases or decreases. It assumes that management wants to find the price that maximizes profits. Let us see how the technique works.

Price and quantity determine total revenue. To apply the analysis a demand schedule showing the quantity of the product that can be sold at alternative prices is needed. Exhibit 17.6 illustrates a demand schedule for prices ranging from $65 to $16. Notice that quantity sold increases as price decreases, indicating a negatively sloped demand curve. The first step in the analysis is to calculate **total revenue** (TR) by multiplying price (P) times quantity (Q): TR = P × Q. Then change in total revenue can be analyzed as price is varied. By moving down the schedule you can see that total revenue increases as price decreases until a price of $26 is reached. Lowering price further decreases total revenue.

Marginal revenue measures the amount of change in total revenue caused by a change in price and quantity sold. From Exhibit 17.6, you can see that marginal revenue is positive but decreases as price drops from $65 to $26. It becomes negative at prices less than $26. The reason for this pattern is that change in total revenue is affected by two offsetting factors: (1) at a lower price each unit sold brings in less revenue and (2) at a lower price more units are sold. Consider what happens when the price is dropped from $51 to $44. Each unit sold brings in $7 less in revenue ($51 minus $44), but at $44, one more unit can be sold (four instead of three). Thus the net effect on revenue is an increase of $23 ($44 from the one more

Exhibit 17.6 Deriving marginal revenue from a demand schedule

Price	Quantity Sold	Total Revenue	Marginal Revenue
$65	1	$ 65	—
58	2	116	$ 51
51	3	153	37
44	4	176	23
38	5	190	14
33	6	198	8
29	7	203	5
26	8	208	5
21	9	189	−11
16	10	160	−29

unit sold minus $21 lost on the 3 units that could have been sold at the higher $51 price). At all prices from $65 to $26, the greater quantity sold more than offsets the lower price, and so marginal revenue is positive. But at prices less than $26, the lower price causes more revenue to be lost than can be gained from the higher quantity sold, and marginal revenue is negative.

The demand schedule is determined by influences on price, such as customers' price elasticity, competitors' prices, assistance from the channel, and the company's marketing mix. Thus marginal revenue encourages managers to consider these factors.

Effect of price and quantity. Because the objective is to maximize profits rather than revenue, marginal analysis also examines costs of producing, distributing, and selling the product. Exhibit 17.7 is a schedule of the costs incurred at each price and corresponding quantity. Fixed costs are added to variable costs to get **total cost.** Notice that total cost rises as quantity sold increases but the amount of increase, measured by **marginal cost,** declines until a price of $33 is reached. As quantity sold increases the company gains the benefits of economies of scale and experience. Per unit costs (total costs divided by quantity) decrease fast enough to offset some of the added cost of producing more units. These benefits, however, become so small as quantity grows beyond that sold at $33, that marginal cost begins to rise again.

Profit-maximizing price. We are now ready to find the profit-maximizing price. Exhibit 17.8 summarizes the important revenue and cost data needed for this purpose. Suppose we started with a price of $65 and lowered it to $58. What happens to profits? Marginal revenue shows that total revenue increases by $51 ($116 minus $65). At the same time, marginal cost indicates that total cost increases by only $30 ($90 minus $60). Thus the price decrease adds $21 to profits ($51 minus $30), and so management is encouraged to make this pricing change. This result illustrates a general rule followed by marginal analysis: *As long as marginal revenue is greater than marginal cost, lowering price yields higher profits; the* **profit-maximizing price** *is found when marginal revenue equals marginal cost because any further price reduction adds more to cost than it does to revenue, and profits will go down.*

Using the data in Exhibit 17.8, you will see that the profit-maximizing price is $29. Actually, a price of either $33 or $29 yields the same amount of

Exhibit 17.7   Deriving marginal cost from a cost schedule

Price	Quantity Sold	Fixed Cost	Variable Cost	Total Cost	Marginal Cost
$65	1	$20	$ 40	$ 60	—
58	2	20	70	90	$30
51	3	20	93	113	23
44	4	20	112	132	19
38	5	20	120	140	8
33	6	20	123	143	3
29	7	20	138	148	5
26	8	20	140	160	12
21	9	20	156	176	16
16	10	20	178	198	22

Exhibit 17.8 Marginal analysis determines the optimal price

Price	Quantity	Total Revenue	Marginal Revenue	Total Cost	Marginal Cost	Profit
$65	1	$ 65	—	$ 60	—	$ 5
58	2	116	$ 51	90	$30	26
51	3	150	34	113	23	37
44	4	176	26	132	19	44
38	5	190	14	140	8	50
33	6	198	8	143	3	55
(29)	7	203	(5)	148	(5)	55
26	8	208	5	160	9	48
21	9	189	−11	176	16	13
16	10	160	−29	198	22	−38

profits—$55. However, at $33 managers would not know that profits are maximized because the marginal revenue of $8 is greater than the marginal cost of $3 (more is added to revenue than is added to cost). Only when you priced at $29 and found that marginal revenue is equal to marginal cost do you know that profits are at their highest.

Exhibit 17.9 should help you visualize why profits are maximized at a price where MR is equal to MC. The graph in (a) shows the quantity Q* where TR exceeds TC by the greatest amount. At low quantities sold (at high prices assuming a negatively sloped demand curve), TC is higher than TR, and a loss would be incurred. As price is lowered to increase quantity, TR rises faster than TC, and profits begin to appear. At some point the loss in revenue from lower price per unit will more than offset revenue gained from more units sold and the TR curve turns down. TC keeps rising, so profits get smaller and eventually become losses. Management wants to find the quantity Q* and corresponding price where the TR curve is at its greatest distance above the TC curve.

The graph in (b) illustrates what is happening to changes in TR and TC as quantity is increased by lowering price. The negatively sloped demand curve for the product is also portrayed. Notice that MR and MC curves intersect at Q*, the quantity at which profits are maximized. By projecting Q* onto the demand curve, P*, the profit maximizing price is found. As you can see, TR is maximally greater than TC at the price and quantity where MR = MC.

Applying marginal analysis in practice. Marginal analysis is difficult to apply directly in practice because the technique requires completely accurate information on demand, competition, and costs. Companies rarely know their complete demand schedules with certainty. There are so many influences on the price-quantity relationship that managers cannot simply rely on experience to estimate quantities likely to be sold at a wide range of prices. As we saw in Chapter 16, price-quantity relationships can be measured in several ways but it is prohibitively expensive and time consuming to try to obtain these measures over the full range of prices required to implement marginal analysis.

Obtaining information on costs also is problematic. A company must have an extremely detailed accounting system to allocate costs to products. Even with such a system, trying to trace all costs to individual products

a) Profits are maximized when TR exceeds TC by the greatest amount

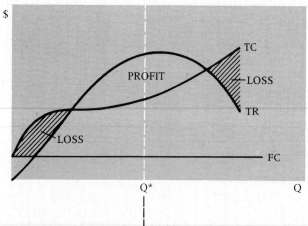

b) TR is maximally greater than TC when MR = MC

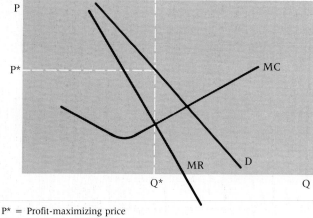

P* = Profit-maximizing price
Q* = Profit-maximizing quantity

Exhibit 17.9   The relationship between marginals and totals

usually is impossible because some costs are shared by more than one product. Furthermore, marginal analysis requires predicting what will happen to costs as quantity is increased or decreased at alternative prices. Experience curve analysis has helped many companies predict the extent to which costs will come down as quantity is increased, so progress is being made here.

Finally, marginal analysis assumes that profit maximization is the price-setting objective. Yet there are many other objectives a company could choose. Even if we could use the technique to find the profit-maximizing price, another price may be selected to meet one of these other objectives.

Marginal analysis is worthwhile to understand because it illustrates the kind of analyses important for price determination. Additionally, it can help evaluate the soundness of methods that companies actually use to set price because actual analyses may fall short of the ideal. Let us now turn to methods of price determination used in practice.

Determining a price in practice

In reality, price is often determined by using information on one of the major influences—cost, demand, or competition—to a greater extent than the other two. Thus methods for determining price can be grouped into three categories: (1) cost-oriented pricing, (2) demand-oriented pricing, and (3) competition-oriented pricing.

Cost-oriented pricing. The most common methods for determining a product price are cost oriented.[21] Two types of cost-oriented methods are target markup pricing and target rate of return pricing.

Target markup pricing (sometimes called **cost-plus pricing**) adds a prespecified or target amount to the per unit cost of a product to determine price. The target amount is a **markup** over cost. As an illustration, the manager of a tennis shop, Professionally Tennis, received a shipment of Wilson Ultra 2 tennis rackets. She looked at the invoice to see the per-racket cost charged by Wilson. Suppose the cost of each racket is $162. The manager wants to achieve a target $88 markup on each racket sold. Price for each racket therefore would be $250: $162 plus $88.

In practice, markups typically are set in percentage terms rather than in dollar amounts. A *markup on cost* is the percentage of the cost of an item that will be added to determine price. A 55 percent markup on the cost of each Wilson racket, for instance, yields a price of $251.10: $162 plus .55($162). A *markup on price* expresses the markup as a percentage of the selling price. A markup of 35 percent on the $250 price of each Wilson racket allows the store to receive $87.50 over the cost of each racket sold.

How do managers determine a markup for a product? For products that consumers buy repeatedly, markups are often those that have been applied historically. Over time managers gain experience with the prices at which a product will sell at desired volumes. This trial-and-error experience leads to "accepted" markups for product categories. The manager of Professionally Tennis knows from experience that markups for tennis rackets must be smaller than those for clothing. Consumers can more easily compare prices of the same racket in different stores than they can clothing, and stores are more likely to compete on price for rackets than they are for clothing. Thus even with markup pricing, customers' price elasticity and competition are judgmentally considered.

A markup also can be established for each product based on a company's costs and desired profit. Costs that are traceable to the product are calculated, and a target contribution to unallocated costs and profit is established as an objective to achieve. The manager of Professionally Tennis figured the direct costs for fifteen Wilson Ultra 2 rackets of display space, interest on money tied up in the inventory, and advertising, which came to $7.50. Then she set a desired amount of contribution to unallocated costs and profits of $80.50. The markup over cost of buying the rackets from Wilson becomes $88 ($7.50 + $80.50).

A markup applied to an item is only a target. There is no guarantee that the item will sell at the desired quantity at the list price. In reality, factors such as customer demand and competition combine to determine how much is sold at a given price. If all items of a product are sold at the list price, then the target margin is achieved. If some items are not sold within a reasonable time, however, price may have to be reduced. The manager of Professionally Tennis has periodic clearance sales on items that remain in inventory too long. A sale price reduces the markup received on a product causing the target markup to be missed, but is necessary to clear the rackets from inventory.

Target rate-of-return pricing, another cost-oriented method, was pioneered by General Motors. This method uses price to achieve a target rate of return on total investment (TROI) that has been established by top management of the company. Price is set for each product so that the quantity sold will yield a revenue and cost relationship achieving the TROI:

$$Pr = AVC + \frac{FC}{Q} + \frac{(TROI \times I)}{Q},$$

where

$$Pr = \text{price per unit of the product sold,}$$
$$AVC = \text{direct variable cost per unit,}$$
$$FC = \text{fixed cost allocated to the product,}$$
$$TROI = \text{target percent return on investment,}$$
$$I = \text{investment or total cost of the product, and}$$
$$Q = \text{quantity of the product sold.}$$

In essence, price is determined by adding a target return to the total cost per unit of the product sold. To illustrate, suppose management wanted to achieve a 20 percent return on the investment made for a product in the company's product mix. Direct variable cost per unit is $5.45, fixed costs are $50,000, and the expected quantity to be sold is 500,000 units. The total investment in the product is equal to fixed costs plus total variable costs and is $2,775,000: $50,000 + ($5.45 × 500,000). Price is determined by applying the above formula:

$$Pr = \$5.45 + \frac{\$50,000}{500,000} + \frac{(.20 \times \$2,775,000)}{500,000}$$
$$= \$5.45 + \$.10 + \$1.11$$
$$= \$6.66.$$

As you can see, achieving a target ROI depends on being able to sell the estimated quantity (Q) at the price set. If the actual quantity sold is less than Q, then the target ROI will not be met. Interestingly, when management sees that sales are going to be less than Q, the pricing method leads to raising price in order to meet the ROI target. Sales that exceed Q yield a ROI that is greater than the target, unless the cost relationships change as might happen if the larger-than-expected sales volume causes inefficiencies in production or distribution.

Estimating Q is not easy. We already know that sales volume at a given price is determined by customers' price elasticity and that estimating elasticity is difficult. A way that managers can deal with this situation is to use break-even analysis. This analysis examines the total number of units of a product, called **break-even volume,** that must be sold if revenue is to equal only costs (notice that no profits are made at this volume):

$$BEV = \frac{FC}{(Pr - AVC)},$$

where

$$BEV = \text{break-even volume,}$$
$$FC = \text{total fixed costs allocated to the product,}$$
$$Pr = \text{price per unit of the product, and}$$
$$AVC = \text{direct variable cost per unit.}$$

Suppose managers for a desk manufacturer are trying to set price for a particular style of desk in the company's product mix. Exhibit 17.10 illustrates break-even volume at a price of $500, a fixed cost of $150,000, and a

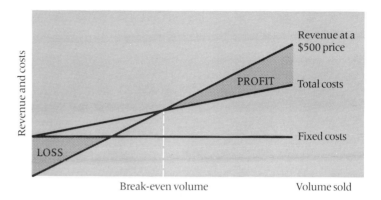

Exhibit 17.10 Break-even volume for desks sold at $500

variable per unit cost of $250. The diagram shows that the company would have to sell 600 desks at $500 each to break even: $150,000/($500 - $250)$. The next step is to estimate whether at least 600 desks can be sold at $500 per desk. If that volume is not likely, then managers repeat the analysis for other alternative prices such as $400, $450, $550, and $600. Examining break-even volumes at different prices helps managers narrow the range of prices that are most likely to yield sales volumes that will lead to the target ROI.

To achieve a target rate of return, sales will have to be above the break-even volume. For each alternative price, the manager must estimate whether enough additional desks can be sold to reach the target rate of return. To achieve a 20 percent rate of return the desk manufacturer would have to sell 900 desks at $500. If management believed that their company could sell this number of desks, then the desks would be listed at $500. If not, other prices would have to be examined in the same way.

In regulated industries such as utilities, a cost-oriented approach to pricing is quite common because cost is the primary justification for making a price change. Cost-oriented pricing is popular in nonregulated industries because of its many advantages.[22] First, with careful record keeping, cost information is available. Second, a product's price can be calculated from a simple formula. This feature is particularly attractive for companies such as a supermarket that must price many products frequently. Third, price based on cost is a legal defense for price discrimination and provides a way to justify price to customers. But most important, managers know that a business will not be around in the long run if prices do not cover costs and contribute to profits.

Cost-oriented pricing also has drawbacks particularly when applied without sufficient consideration of demand and competitive factors. All cost-oriented methods set targets that are achieved only if anticipated sales volumes are reached. If sales estimates are based on factors other than demand—such as on number of units in inventory to be sold or on production capacity—these approaches are unlikely to set the best price. If customers are price inelastic, then a cost-oriented price can lead to lost revenue because the product could have been sold at a higher price. On the other hand, in a market where price competition is intense, price based on costs can cause sales to fall short of the volume needed to achieve the target markup, or target rate of return. The following comment on cost-oriented pricing aptly summarizes the problem.

But no mechanical formula can guarantee a profit. Both cost and profit estimates depend on volume estimates; and volume, among many other things, depends on the right price, whether that price maximizes unit profit right away or not.[23]

Demand-oriented pricing. Companies that use **demand-oriented or value pricing** set price according to the value customers place on the product. From an analysis of market opportunities (MOA), management evaluates how customers perceive the benefits of a product and how valuable these benefits are to them when the product is used. When applied to an industrial product such as a tractor, a computer, or a robot the customer's cost savings from using the product is commonly used as a measure of value to the customer. Du Pont applied a demand-oriented approach to price a new polyethylene resin used to make pipes for transporting water or other liq-

MarkeTOOL

Gauging customer reactions to future price changes

CUSTOMER REACTION to price changes often determines whether a pricing decision meets its objective. Because customers compare values when making product purchases (value given up to get product vs. value received from the product), price is intertwined with other considerations. For this reason, obtaining data on customer reactions to possible prices is difficult.

A marketing research tool that is gaining acceptance for pricing studies is *conjoint analysis*. The tool is particularly attractive because of two features: (1) it gets reactions to prices for a product when compared with other product benefits such as brand name, package size, and quality; and (2) it forces customers to make trade-offs between price and these benefits. Will a customer prefer a more convenient package at a higher price, or a lower price and a less convenient package? These comparisons and trade-offs are similar to what customers do in real-life buying. Furthermore, customers participating in the study do not pay undue attention to price because they are considering nonprice aspects of products, too.

A conjoint analysis study has respondents evaluate alternative product concepts (descriptions of combinations of product benefits available at various prices). A Chicago-based research firm, John Morton Company, uses the format shown in the accompanying illustration. Interestingly, a microcomputer does the interviewing. After familiarizing people with the use of the microcomputer (first two frames), the respondent rates a sequence of alternative concepts, presented two at a time (see the third frame). A respondent chooses the one concept most preferred from a pair (the one on the left vs. the one on the right of the screen) and then picks a number from the 1 to 9 scale indicating how much the chosen concept is preferred over the other. This procedure continues for a number of pairs of concepts, each pair having a somewhat different combination of prices and product benefits.

The data are transferred directly to another, large computer for analysis. The result of this analysis is a set of utilities for each price level, for each brand, and for each performance benefit. A

SOURCE: Linda D. Straube and Bridgid J. Michaud, "Combine microcomputer interviewing with conjoint analysis to study pricing strategies," *Marketing News*, May 13, 1983, Section 2, pp. 1, 11. Used by permission of the American Marketing Association.

COMPUTER ASKS THE QUESTIONS

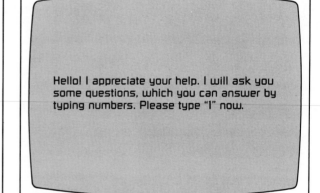

Frame 1

utility is a number between 0 and 1 which measures how much a particular benefit is desired by the customer. The higher the number, the more that benefit is desired. For example, a single respondent's utilities might be as follows:

Price	Utility	Brand Name	Utility	Package Size	Utility
$1.59	.42	Coke	.56	6-can pack	.34
$2.29	.28	Pepsi	.31	2-liter bottle	.66
$2.49	.18	7-Up	.13		
$2.69	.12				

uids. Pipes made with this material had longer life and could withstand greater pressure than pipes made with competitor's materials. Cost savings created by less-frequent replacement were calculated. This value was high and it allowed Du Pont to charge a much higher price for the material than competitors charged for substitute products.[24]

Value pricing can also be used for setting price of consumer products. Using an MOA, managers can learn about the situation in which the product is used and the benefits perceived by customers. The challenge is then to examine how consumers trade off price against benefits (see Marketool). Airlines have successfully applied this value-oriented pricing approach to set fare differentials for seats according to benefits. Price for a seat on a plane is discounted if the buyer will reserve the seat well in advance of the

---

These utilities allow a marketing manager to compare the shares of preference for each brand under different competitive situations and price decisions. For example, suppose Coke priced its 2-liter bottle at $2.49 and Pepsi and 7-Up countered with a price of $2.29. The total utility for each brand would be determined by adding the utilities for brand name, price, and package:

Coke: .18 + .56 + .66 = 1.40
Pepsi: .28 + .31 + .66 = 1.25
7-Up: .28 + .13 + .66 = 1.07

When each brand's total utility is divided by the sum of utilities for all three brands (1.40 + 1.25 + 1.07 = 3.72), share of

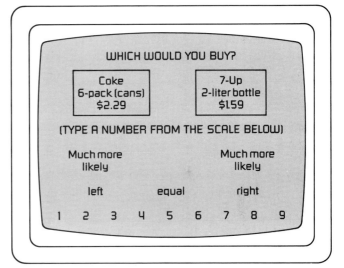

Frame 3

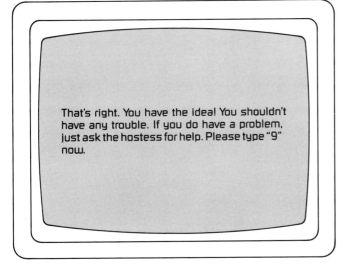

Frame 2

preference is calculated. Coke can examine the impact of charging the higher price by looking at these shares:

Coke: 1.40/3.72 = .38
Pepsi: 1.25/3.72 = .34
7-Up: 1.07/3.72 = .29

In this illustration, Coke would lose about 1 percent of preference share to Pepsi and 7-Up because of the higher price. Notice that at the same price and same package, Coke has a .39 share (.28 + .56 + .66 divided by 3.82, the new total of all utilities). The same approach could be used to evaluate other prices and other competitive situations before deciding on a price.

trip, but is set higher if the traveler does not want to make an advance reservation.[25]

Demand-oriented pricing can extend to an entire product line. Price is set on one product to enhance sales of another product in the line. Our previous discussion of loss-leader pricing is one illustration; another is price lining, which is discussed in Chapter 16.

Although managers who base price on demand do not entirely ignore costs and competition, price does not bear a fixed relationship either to cost or to competitors' prices. (See Marketalk for an interesting illustration of strict demand-oriented pricing.) With proper information, this approach is the best way to ensure that a company does not underprice or overprice its product, as might happen with cost-oriented methods. At the same time, the difficulty of getting information on customers' responsiveness to alternative prices keeps demand-oriented pricing from reaching the full potential of the marginal analysis ideal.

Competition-oriented pricing. As long as customers have a choice among sellers and price is a factor in their purchase decisions, a company's manager should consider how the product's price compares with competitors' prices. But when managers set price primarily to establish or maintain a certain relationship—either below, at, or above—competitors' prices, competition-oriented pricing is being applied.

A number of different situations cause companies to use competition-oriented pricing:

- When a company's top management sets a pricing objective and corresponding strategy with competition foremost in mind. Maintaining market share, building market share, and maintaining price leadership are objectives that require managers to set price in relation to competition. We have already seen how Safeway Stores, People Express Airlines, and Gallo Winery try to maintain price leadership by pricing

MarkeTALK //

An auction is the ultimate in demand-oriented pricing

A CHICAGO CONSTRUCTION firm found a novel way to set prices for new homes. Illinois Communities Division of U.S. Home (ICD), Inc. put some of its new homes up for auction. During the auction customers bid against each other for the purchase of each home for sale. While new home auctions are common in Japan and Australia, in the United States they have only been used to liquidate the inventory of a bankrupt builder or developer. ICD is

SOURCE: "Developer puts new homes up for auction to cut marketing costs and other overhead," *Marketing News*, Apr. 15, 1983, p. 1.

not in financial trouble, but decided to try the auction anyway.

The company's first auction was tried in a suburb of Chicago. Rather than set a price in advance for each home in the development, the auction quickly established the price which customers were willing to pay. People eligible for bidding had to bring a certified cashier's check for $3,500, and a professional auctioneer handled the sales. ICD completely depended on demand since no minimum price was set, and so the homes had to be sold no matter what the high bids were.

After the sale, 15 new homes had been auctioned off at $50,000 to $71,000, with

an average sale price of $61,000. These prices were well below the $80,000 to $100,000 that the builder estimated could have been received if the homes had been sold in the usual way. Clearly, buyers came away with substantial bargains. However, the firm's management was pleased with the results. Substantial cost savings from not having to carry the homes in inventory for very long, not furnishing model homes, reduced advertising, small insurance premiums, and no security costs more than offset the lower prices. More auctions of this type are predicted for the future.

//

low relative to the competition. A company using a penetration pricing strategy for new products when the aim is to develop a market quickly is another illustration.

■ When companies are unable to offer nonprice benefits (product quality, prestige, service) that strongly outweigh price in customers' purchase decisions. Companies may have little choice but to price so as to meet competitors' prices or suffer serious loss of sales and market share. Closely matching prices of competitors is often called **going rate pricing.** As we saw earlier, soft drinks and the deregulated airlines are industries in which the severity of price competition dictates that competition-oriented pricing be used. Another example is the price wars that erupt from time to time among companies selling gasoline.

■ When there is a price leader in an oligopolistic industry. Automobile and steel are examples of industries in which the price leader makes a decision to raise price, usually justified by pointing to cost increases, and other firms follow with price increases of their own. Although cost reasons may cause the price change, the primary rationale for the followers' decisions to raise price is to match the price leader.

In competition-oriented pricing, price may deviate from price based on costs or target markups. In this sense, it can fall short of the guidelines provided by marginal analysis. In all fairness to price setters, competitive pressure on price may leave them little or no freedom to vary price from those of competitors.

Competitive intensity and value of the product as perceived by customers create a **price band** that dictates the amount of flexibility or freedom that a company has to vary price relative to competition.[26] Exhibit 17.11 illustrates the effect of these factors on the width of price bands for different segments of consumer markets for ice cream. When price competition is intense and perceived value of product is low (e.g., in the fair quality segment of generic and store brands), the price band is likely to be narrow, and competition dominates pricing decisions. In contrast, when competition is less intense (i.e., the customer considers nonprice benefits as more important) and perceived value higher (e.g., very good and excellent ice cream segments), the price band is much wider. Each brand has more freedom to set price relative to costs and demand.

Selecting a list price

Having selected a price-setting method, a price for the product can now be determined. This price may become the list price communicated to customers, or management may modify it further in some way. An adjustment might be needed if managers decide that the price is not entirely consistent with pricing objectives, strategy, or policy. Suppose a target markup pricing approach does not yield a sufficiently low price to maintain dealer support, a pricing objective. In this case, price will have to be lowered slightly to bring it in line with the objective.

Price may also be adjusted to reflect considerations not included directly in the price-setting method. Suppose a tentative price has been calculated based on costs and a target markup. Management may adjust this price after considering the probable psychological impact of price on customers (see Chapter 16 for a discussion of psychological pricing). Prices

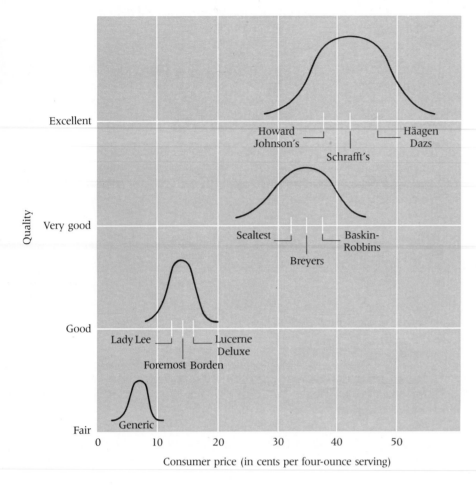

Quality

Excellent

Howard
Johnson's — Häagen
Dazs

Schrafft's

Very good

Sealtest — Baskin-
Robbins

Breyers

Good

Lady Lee — Lucerne
Deluxe

Foremost Borden

Fair   Generic

0   10   20   30   40   50

Consumer price (in cents per four-ounce serving)

Exhibit 17.11   Competition and perceived value of product dictate freedom to price

ending in odd numbers seem to be particularly popular for low-priced consumer products. You probably have noticed that most products in food stores have prices ending in nine or five (e.g., $1.99, $2.35, $.99). Store managers appear to believe that these prices create more attention among customers than prices that end in other numbers.[27] Although target markup pricing is commonly used for food products sold at retail, these adjustments are an attempt to build aspects of demand into price.

Including this step in the overall pricing procedure highlights an important idea about pricing in practice. Rarely should a single method be used to the complete exclusion of the others. Rather, each method offers one of several checkpoints on the feasibility of alternative prices. Determining a target markup on cost, for instance, allows a manager to see the impact on profits of a price. Yet the competitive intensity for that product may limit the ability of the company to charge a high enough price to get the target return. In this situation, the final price is likely to be a compromise between the target markup desired and the necessity of pricing at the "going rate."

MONITORING PRICE'S PERFORMANCE

Opportunities for making pricing decisions do not end when a list price is determined. Managers must be prepared to monitor how well price is achieving its objectives. In spite of the best efforts of managers, an inappropriate price may be set. Furthermore, changes in marketing's environment may dictate new pricing decisions. As one pricing expert noted,

> There are at least three situations in which a price review can and should be initiated. One is when there is a change in the environment, such as the loss of a major account, or an important competitive move. Another is when there is a change in some relevant internal activity or variable. The introduction of new, similar items into the product line or a change in cost structure are typical examples. Finally, prices should be reviewed periodically whether or not these other reasons are present. Given the unstable nature of the business world at this time, it seems prudent to review prices at least every six months.[28]

Monitoring price performance in markets requires gathering information. Pricing objectives provide standards against which actual price performance can be compared. Additionally, managers must monitor the possible reasons for price performance going off target. These reasons generally involve changes in areas such as costs, customers' price elasticity, channel cooperation, or competitive pricing. Knowing when to make changes in prices of products is dependent on the quality and timeliness of information on these changes. Responding quickly with appropriate price decisions can improve performance dramatically.

> The value of a superior pricing information system can often be measured in hard cash. One company, determined to improve its pricing information, started by revising its accounting data to reflect fixed and variable costs accurately by product and by market. By surveying the sales force, it created a pricing history by customer and product type of each key competitor as well as a profile of the buying process of each major customer. Finally, it provided each pricing decision maker with a personal microcomputer, access to three data bases (cost, competitor, and customer), guidelines on pricing strategy, and feedback on individual performance. In less than a year (and at a time of declining market demand), its margins improved by several percentage points, representing almost $25 million in added profits.[29]

SUMMARY

Price setting is a process of skillfully weaving price into the entire marketing mix. It also requires an analysis of the many factors that influence the success of a price in the market. Using price in a strategic way is best accomplished by having a logical multistep approach to pricing decisions. Such an approach includes the following steps: Determine price's role, establish pricing objectives and strategy, set pricing policies, determine a price, and monitor price's performance.

Pricing begins when managers establish the role price is to play in the overall marketing mix. This role is likely to be constrained by top management's strategy for the company. Furthermore, the role must recognize opportunities for using price to help achieve broader marketing objectives.

Pricing's role in a company provides direction for deciding on pricing objectives and a strategy for achieving these objectives. Different situations call for different pricing objectives. For instance, pricing objectives for introducing a new product typically differ from those for existing products in a company's product mix. The forces of competition and customers' price elasticity are particularly important in accounting for these differences. Over time costs also change, as do the needs of channel members in the trade.

Managers quickly learn that certain pricing situations are likely to recur. Policies are established to provide guidelines for making pricing decisions in these situations. Typical situations that call for policy decisions concern price negotiation, frequency and timing of price changes, discounts off price, and pricing to reflect transportation costs.

Pricing's role, objectives, strategy, and policy establish a framework within which to determine a product's price. However, there is usually flexibility to choose among several price alternatives, so a method must be selected for setting price. To evaluate the methods used in practice, a marginal analysis approach to setting price serves as an ideal. It considers the key influences on price by using demand and cost schedules to find the profit-maximizing price. Methods commonly used in practice differ in the weight managers give to these influences. For instance, cost-oriented methods base price primarily on covering costs associated with a product and contributing to profits. The influences of demand and competition receive less attention in this method. In demand-oriented pricing, price is set according to the value customers place on the product, and in competition-oriented pricing, price is set to establish or maintain a certain relationship to the competition.

Cost-, demand-, and competition-oriented methods of price determination are best viewed as checkpoints on the feasibility of alternative prices. Clearly, all influences must ultimately be considered for price to be used in a strategic way. Yet, each of the methods represents a practical way to narrow the range of prices being considered.

Price determined by starting with one of these methods is quite likely to receive further evaluation. A price setter must check to see that the price is consistent with pricing strategy, objectives, and policy. Furthermore, price may be adjusted to better match manager's assessment of other factors not fully covered by the chosen method.

After setting price, managers must monitor price performance. Pricing problems will arise eventually, and so managers must use information to be informed of their occurrence. Corrective action, including price change decisions, can only be made if managers know that current price is not working and why.

KEY TERMS

role of price	price change policy	delivered pricing policy
competitive dominance strategy	price discount policy	single-zone pricing
loss-leader pricing	trade or functional discount	multiple-zone pricing
pricing objectives	promotion discount	F.O.B. with freight allowed
pricing strategy	cash discount	basing-point pricing
skimming pricing	quantity discount	marginal analysis
penetration pricing	noncumulative discount	total revenue
pricing policies	cumulative discount	marginal revenue
price negotiation policy	geographic pricing policy	total cost
list price	F.O.B. origin	marginal cost

profit-maximizing price
target markup pricing
cost-plus pricing

markup
target rate-of-return pricing
break-even volume

demand-oriented or value pricing
going rate pricing
price band

QUESTIONS FOR REVIEW AND DISCUSSION

1. What are the steps in a multistep approach to price determination?

2. How can top management of a company assist in determining price for a company's product?

3. Do financial managers get involved in the price determination procedure? Why or why not?

4. What is loss-leader pricing?

5. Explain four roles that price can play in the marketing mix.

6. What is a pricing objective? Give five examples of pricing objectives.

7. What is a pricing strategy? How is a pricing strategy different from a pricing objective?

8. Compare the advantages and disadvantages of a skimming pricing strategy and a penetration pricing strategy for introducing a new product.

9. Suppose General Motors is planning to introduce a new type of car. The car is an electric-powered economy car for in-town driving. Should a penetration or skimming pricing strategy be used? Explain the reasons for your answer.

10. Under what conditions would a company initiate a price increase?

11. What options does a company have to respond to a competitor's price decrease?

12. What is a price negotiation policy? What are the factors to consider in determining this policy?

13. Why is a policy needed for the frequency of price change decisions?

14. Explain four kinds of price discount policies.

15. What are the advantages and disadvantages of an F.O.B. origin pricing policy?

16. Explain why a company would use a delivered pricing policy rather than F.O.B. origin pricing.

17. Is basing-point pricing preferred to multiple-zone pricing? Why or why not?

18. How well does target markup pricing compare with marginal analysis? Is target rate-of-return pricing any better?

19. How well does value pricing compare with marginal analysis?

20. How well does going rate pricing compare with marginal analysis?

21. Why should a company monitor the performance of a pricing decision?

BUILDING YOUR PORTFOLIO

Set up an interview with a manager of a local business who is responsible for pricing a product or service. The business can be a retail store or dealer, a service company, a distributor or wholesaler, or a manufacturer. Prior to the interview, develop a list of questions about the procedure the manager uses to determine a list price. Be sure that your questions uncover all factors the manager considers important, as well as a pricing formula or method used. Analyze the answers from your interview to reconstruct the price determination procedure. Evaluate the procedure by answering the following questions:

1. Is the procedure a multistep approach to price determination?
2. Can you classify the method used to determine price as cost oriented, demand oriented, or competition oriented? Why or why not?
3. What suggestions do you have for improving the manager's pricing procedure?

NOTES

1. This illustration is based on "The squeeze begins in personal computers." *Business Week,* May 30, 1983, pp. 91, 95; and Peter Nulty, "Cool heads are trying to keep Commodore hot." *Fortune,* July 23, 1984, pp. 36–38, 40, 44–45.
2. Barbara Coe, "Perceptions of the Role of Pricing in the 1980s Among Industrial Marketers," in Patrick E. Murphy et al. (Eds.), *1983 AMA Educators' Proceedings.* Chicago: American Marketing Association, 1983, pp. 235–240.
3. For a more detailed discussion of a multistep approach to pricing see Alfred R. Oxenfeldt, "A decision-making structure for price decisions." *Journal of Marketing,* Vol. 37 (Jan. 1973), pp. 49–50. The author updated this article in 1982 for distribution as a reprint in The Markus Wiener Reprint Series in Business Administration.
4. "The wine wars get hotter." *Business Week,* Apr. 11, 1983, pp. 61.
5. Oxenfeldt, op. cit., p. 50.
6. "Utilities are tempting big customers to turn up the juice." *Business Week,* Oct. 31, 1983, p. 121.
7. Nulty, op. cit., p. 44.
8. Susan Fraker, "Making a mint in nuts and bolts." *Fortune,* Aug. 22, 1983, pp. 131–132, 134.
9. Kent B. Monroe and Albert J. Della Bitta, "Models for pricing decisions." *Journal of Marketing Research,* Vol. 15 (Aug. 1978), p. 415.
10. Maggie McComas, "Banking goes home." *Fortune,* Dec. 10, 1984, p. 150.
11. Bro Uttal, "Is IBM playing too tough?" *Fortune,* Dec. 10, 1984, p. 36.
12. "A last-minute comeback for Swiss watchmakers." *Business Week,* Nov. 26, 1984, pp. 139, 142.
13. Monroe and Della Bitta, op. cit., p. 420.
14. Ibid.
15. "Firestone after the turnaround: Where next?" *Business Week,* Apr. 23, 1984, p. 58.
16. "Coke's big marketing blitz." *Business Week,* May 30, 1983, pp. 58–63.
17. "Thermos hopes to cool competition with a revamped marketing strategy." *Marketing News,* Dec. 23, 1983, pp. 1, 11.
18. Kent B. Monroe, *Pricing: Making Profitable Decisions.* New York: McGraw-Hill, 1979, p. 169.
19. This illustration is similar to ibid., p. 171.
20. For further discussion of these pricing policies see ibid., pp. 183–187.
21. S. E. Heymann, "Cost Considerations," in Earl L. Bailey (Ed.), *Pricing Practices and Strategies.* New York: The Conference Board, 1978, p. 40.
22. J. Fred Weston, "Pricing Policy and the Meaning of Target Return Pricing," in Neil Beckwith, Michael Houston, Robert Mittelstaedt, Kent B. Monroe, and Scott Ward (Eds.), *1979 Educators' Conference Proceedings.* Chicago: American Marketing Association, 1979, pp. 312–313; and S. E. Heymann, op. cit.

23. Gilbert Burck, "The myths and realities of corporate pricing." *Fortune,* Apr. 1972.
24. Benson P. Shapiro and Barbara B. Jackson, "Industrial pricing to meet customer needs." *Harvard Business Review,* Nov.–Dec. 1978, p. 121.
25. Thomas Nagle, "Pricing as creative marketing." *Business Horizons,* July–Aug. 1983, p. 15.
26. This idea is based on a discussion in Elliot B. Ross, "Making money with proactive pricing." *Harvard Business Review,* Nov.–Dec. 1984, pp. 145–155.
27. Kent B. Monroe, "Buyers' subjective perceptions of price." *Journal of Marketing Research* Vol. 8 (Feb. 1973) pp. 70–71.
28. Benson P. Shapiro, "Common Fallacies," in Earl L. Bailey (Ed.), *Pricing Practices and Strategies.* New York: The Conference Board, 1978, pp. 32–33.
29. Ross, op. cit., pp. 154–155.

Case 17.1

Network Television Pricing

THE TELEVISION NETWORKS in the United States face complicated pricing decisions at the beginning of each annual show season. Most of their on-the-air time is allocated to programs that draw viewers organizations want to reach with advertising. The remainder of the time is sold to advertisers as the networks' primary source of revenue. But the networks—CBS, NBC, and ABC—have a limited number of seconds during a season to sell to advertisers, and each available second is a precious product. During the 1983–1984 season, a 30-second commercial on ABC's popular program, "Dynasty," sold for $179,000. A 30-second commercial on an average prime-time show can sell for as much as $75,000.

At the beginning of a season, each network has an inventory of time to sell. Executives first decide how much of the in-

SOURCE: Steven Flax, "Squeeze on the networks," *Fortune*, Sept. 5, 1983, pp. 83, 85, 86, 90, 92, 94.

ventory to sell at the beginning of the season, called up-front sales, and how much to hold back to sell at different points during the season (scatter sales). Although time sold immediately is a sure thing, some time is held back on the gamble that popularity of the programs will increase and the network will be able to command a higher price. Of course, if popularity does not hold up, then advertisers will not pay as much. How much time to hold back hinges on executives' predictions of audiences' reactions to each year's lineup of programs, a very difficult and risky prediction to make.

Advertisers usually try to delay making initial purchases of airtime as long as possible. They know that as the beginning of the season gets closer, a network feels more pressure to accept a lower price for unsold airtime. On the other hand, there is a limited amount of time available, so advertisers cannot wait too long to buy or time they want might be snapped up by their competitors. Usually the first adver-

tiser to negotiate for a time slot breaks the log jam, and up-front sales proceed at a feverish pace. On one day alone, ABC sold more than $170 million of commercial time.

Program ratings and demographic reach information are playing an ever-increasing role in the pricing negotiations. Advertisers want airtime that captures certain kinds of viewers. In many cases, these people are eighteen to forty-nine year olds, live in urban and suburban areas, and are high spenders. The more of these target people in a program's audience, the greater the value of the time and the higher the price that can be charged. Network salespersons must be able to show that programs can deliver these audiences. Furthermore, market research must demonstrate what audiences were actually reached. Sometimes a network will give a guarantee of delivery by agreeing to run additional free advertisements if the research shows a certain audience is not reached during the purchased time slots.

QUESTIONS

1. Is the pricing method used by the networks a multistep approach? Why or why not?

2. What method is used to determine price—cost oriented, demand oriented, or competition oriented?

3. Is a price negotiation policy needed? Why or why not?

4. How can price performance be monitored and evaluated?

Case 17.2

Safeway Stores

SAFEWAY STORES, the largest food retailer in the United States, is facing competition from a new concept in food retailing. A chain of food stores called Cub Foods is moving into Safeway's markets with an off-price or discounting pricing

SOURCE: "'Super warehouses' chomp into the food business," *Business Week*, Apr. 16, 1984, p. 72.

strategy. Cub stores are huge—about twice the size of a typical supermarket. They generate large sales volumes by offering discount prices. By one estimate, Cub stores have more than six times the sales volume of a regular supermarket. The stores bring in more customers and they are also spending, on the average, about twice as much per trip (approximately $45).

Cub stores also are designed to cut down on operating costs. Merchandise is

displayed in manufacturers' cartons, cartons are stacked to the ceiling, and customers pack and carry their own food items. As a result, labor costs are reduced significantly. Cub stores also save by buying directly from some manufacturers. These moves mean that Cub stores can make profits on a lower markup than supermarket competitors. At the same time, the interiors are attractive, well-lighted, pleasant places to shop. Clearly, food shoppers like the concept, and they have been supporting it with their food purchase dollars.

The strategy is dubbed *super warehouses,* and it is so successful that other food retailers, including Safeway, are considering how to respond. Cub Foods is one of the more successful competitive entries, and other super warehouses are appearing across the country.

QUESTIONS

1. Is the pricing method at Cub Foods cost oriented, demand oriented, or competition oriented?

2. Should Safeway use a competition-oriented pricing method? Why or why not?

3. What are alternative ways in which Safeway can use pricing to respond to the new competition from super warehouses?

Part Six

18 The Promotion Mix

When you finish this chapter, you will understand

☐ The process by which organizations communicate with their audiences

☐ The alternative audiences for an organization's promotion

☐ The kinds of decisions that must be made to plan a promotion program

☐ The advantages and disadvantages of the four tools of promotion—advertising, sales promotion, publicity, and personal selling

☐ Management's need to coordinate decisions among the promotion tools

☐ The major factors that management must consider when planning a promotion mix over stages in the product's life cycle

Miles Laboratories has demonstrated a flair for advertising and public relations since 1882, when it introduced "Dr. Miles' Restorative Nervive," a tranquilizer remedy.

PepsiCo's marketing managers knew that consumers preferred Coca-Cola to other soft drink brands. Not surprisingly, Coke's food store market share was higher than other brands, too. Pepsi needed a strategy to improve its market position.

Market research studies revealed that in blind taste tests, more than half of all respondents preferred the taste of Pepsi to Coke. Apparently, Coke's sales performance was based on a strong brand image among consumers rather than on a strong preference for its taste. Armed with this information, Pepsi planned and launched a promotion campaign called "The Pepsi Challenge."

The campaign asked consumers to compare the taste of Pepsi with that of Coke. Its objective was simple: Convert Coke drinkers to Pepsi drinkers by having consumers prove to themselves that they liked Pepsi better than Coke. Advertising showed people sipping unlabeled soft drinks and choosing the one they liked best. Persons usually expressed surprise when they discovered that they had chosen Pepsi. Taste tests were run in stores and malls across the country to continue building the evidence for Pepsi's "more-preferred taste." Signs and displays in food stores also carried the Pepsi challenge theme. Salespersons soon were able to show store managers the increasing popularity of Pepsi, and they encouraged stores to carry the brand in greater volume.

The Pepsi challenge was successful, much more so than previous Pepsi promotion. Sales of Pepsi tripled pre-campaign levels. Moreover, Pepsi was able to take over market share leadership in food stores. Surely this performance was a factor in Coca-Cola's risky decision to counter with "the new taste of Coke."[1]

THE SUCCESSFUL PROMOTION campaign, the Pepsi challenge, illustrates how valuable communication is to marketing strategy. Pepsi creatively informed consumers of its product's good taste. Consumers also were persuaded to try Pepsi, and they were repeatedly reminded that when tested, consumers preferred the taste of Pepsi to Coke. *Informing, reminding,* and *persuading* are the essential tasks of a company's **promotion mix:** the tools that deliver information to an organization's audiences.

This chapter introduces the tools that make up the promotion mix and provides a brief look at the important decisions facing promotion managers. This overview will prepare you for the comprehensive discussion of promotion tools in Chapter 19 and 20. The first section identifies the promotion tools and their purpose. The next section examines a model of communication between an organization and its audiences. Understanding this process will help you see the different decisions that must be made when planning a promotion mix. Then the advantages and drawbacks of each of the promotion tools are assessed, as is the importance of a company's having a mix of tools. Finally, we examine how communications tasks change as marketing's environment changes during a product's life cycle.

PROMOTION COMMUNICATES WITH AUDIENCES

Promotion is the communications function of an organization's marketing mix. Information is delivered to those people in marketing's environment who determine how well the objectives are achieved. Let us begin by seeing who these people are and the means by which a company can communicate with them.

Organizations have many audiences

Well-managed promotion is designed to communicate with particular persons known as the **target audience.** The most common target audience is the company's target markets. In fact, a large part of promotion is aimed at target markets because customers need information to assist them in making buying decisions. There are, however, other important target audiences. One is a company's trade—the wholesalers and retailers in the company's channel of distribution. The trade comprises independent businesses that must be motivated to cooperate in selling a company's product, and promotion can be effectively used for this purpose. Consider what happened to Porsche, the German maker of high-quality, high-priced sports cars, when it tried to eliminate its dealer system in the United States and replace it with agents. Management underestimated the power of the dealers to prevent the changeover, however, and Porsche had to repair deteriorated relations with its dealers. Promotion was essential in Porsche's efforts to rekindle dealers' support. It informed dealers that Porsche would continue to include them in its marketing effort in the United States and assured them of their importance in the future.[2]

Another target audience is the general public in a country. Many organizations want to build a favorable, well-known reputation among citizens. Promotion provides information on the organization and its products or services so that people understand what the organization is and does. In part, future sales are a result of the public's familiarity with the organization. Community mental health centers have used promotion in this way. They find it difficult to draw in potential patients and their families because the causes and cures of poor mental health are not well understood. Promotion is used to inform and remind the public that the stress of modern life can lead to mental health problems and that mental health is an important part of total health. An increased general awareness of mental health should lead to more persons' using community mental health centers.[3]

Other possible target audiences are investors, suppliers, employees, government decision makers, and groups that advocate a point of view on an issue. Any of these audiences can have an impact on how well a company achieves its goals. Promotion may help affect the nature or extent of this impact through communication of information. Cigarette manufacturers use promotion, for instance, to explain to antismoking advocates that whether to smoke is a choice only adults should make, not children. Promotion's purpose is to diffuse antismokers' complaints about the selling of cigarettes.

Tools in a promotion mix

A company has several communication tools that it uses to send information in the form of a message to people in target audiences. The originator or sponsor of a message is the **source,** and people in the target audience are the **receivers** of the information in the message. Each tool is briefly defined.

- **Advertising:** A paid form of nonpersonal communication, carried by the mass media (e.g., television, radio, newspapers, billboards, and magazines) or by direct mail. Receivers clearly understand that the message is coming directly from the source.

- **Sales promotion:** A wide variety of short-term inducements to buy including coupons, point-of-purchase product displays, free gifts, signs, contests, and trade shows. Receivers know that the inducement is coming from the source.

- **Publicity:** Nonpersonal communications primarily in the form of "news" items carried by the mass media. The media are not paid by the source, and the message's origin is often perceived by receivers to be the media and not the source.

- **Personal selling:** Individuals paid by the source (salespersons, other employees, or independent agents) who deliver the source's messages through oral communications with receivers who clearly understand that the message is coming from the source.

A promotion mix is quite often made up of a combination of all four tools. Rarely will each tool be given an equal weight, however. Factors such as the amount of money a company has to spend, the nature of the audiences to be reached, and the purposes for promotion influence how much an organization relies on each tool. Some companies may even forego one or more of them. Currently Häagen-Dazs, the premium ice cream company, does not advertise. The company's management believes that informal recommendations from one ice cream eater to another (so-called word-of-mouth advertising) is sufficient. Eliminating any one of the tools from the mix simply increases a company's reliance on the others.

Promotion strategies

Two types of promotion strategies are regularly used by companies, and each one influences which audiences are targeted for promotion (see Exhibit 18.1). The **push promotion strategy** is dominated by personal selling, trade advertising, and sales promotion, and the promotion mix is aimed primarily at the trade in a company's channel of distribution. Its purpose is to persuade the trade to purchase the manufacturer's product. In turn, the trade "pushes" the product through the channel by aggressively selling it to customers.

The opposite approach is a **pull promotion strategy.** The target audience is primarily end-users, and the promotion mix is dominated by end-user advertising, sales promotion, and publicity. Promotion's purpose is to build a strong image and loyal following among customers so they will go to the retailers in the channel and ask for the manufacturer's product.

Exhibit 18.1 Push versus pull promotion strategies.

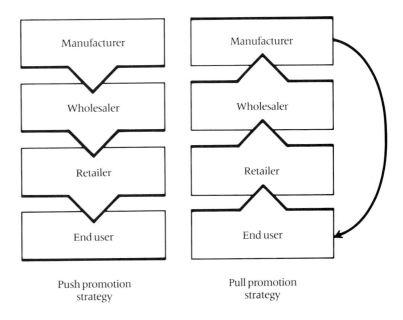

Push promotion strategy

Pull promotion strategy

Retailers, realizing the popularity of the product, order more of it from wholesalers or the manufacturer. Thus the product is "pulled" through the channel of distribution because of the demand created in end-user markets.

Push and pull promotion strategies are opposite ends of a continuum of strategies and differ only in the relative importance of end-users and the trade as target audiences. Most companies use a strategy falling somewhere in between by deciding how much to emphasize each technique to promote their products. A large company such as Procter & Gamble can afford to have a balance between the two. Consumer advertising and sales promotion are aimed at building strong demand for Proctor & Gamble's brands such as Tide detergent, Crest toothpaste, and Pampers disposable diapers. At the same time, Procter & Gamble has a large and well-trained salesforce that calls on retailers. These salespersons are effective at getting the company's product on the retailers' shelves. Of course, the consumer-aimed promotion makes the salespersons' jobs easier than if the brands were not popular.

Equally combining push and pull promotion is expensive. Companies that do not have enough resources to use both effectively are more likely to put their funds into one strategy than to combine them. Splitting limited promotion resources between push and pull strategies may leave to little funds for either to be very effective. But concentrating most resources on one or the other can enable the small company to more closely match the spending of large companies on one target audience (either the trade or end-users). The medium-sized appliance manufacturer Magic Chef put most of its promotion dollars into a push strategy for many years, by concentrating on building a strong relationship with retailers in its channels. Only in the past few years has the company shifted some of its promotion resources to consumer advertising, although it still emphasizes the push strategy.

THE COMMUNICATIONS PROCESS

Most marketing managers know that there is a process by which promotion from a company reaches and influences people in audiences. Importantly, this process can be managed by a company through decisions on the promotion mix. To understand these decisions, you must first understand the communications process.

A communications process model

Exhibit 18.2 presents a model describing the flow of communications between a company and an audience.[4] This model links the five elements of the communications process: the source, the message, the delivery channel, the receiver, and the action taken by the receiver as a result of the communication.

Source of a communication. Communication begins when a source originates a message. The source in our context is an organization—a company, trade association, or nonbusiness organization. Yet in reality, communication can be an *exchange* between an organization and its audience, so people in an audience may also be a source of communication. Consumers sometimes

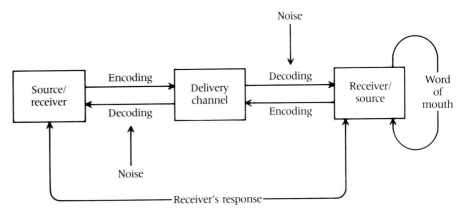

Exhibit 18.2 A model of the communications process

let an organization know how satisfied or dissatisfied they are with its product or service. The model shows a two-way flow to emphasize that communication can move back and forth between an organization and its audiences.

Message. The source creates a message that is intended to inform, remind, and persuade people in the audience. This task is sometimes called **encoding** because it involves putting ideas into words, pictures and sounds that have meaning. Combining words and pictures in an advertisement and writing a letter to an organization complaining about product performance are illustrations of encoding.

Message delivery. A **communications channel** is a means of delivering the message to the audience. Most channels used by organizations are the mass media, which are in the business of carrying messages to large numbers of people. Direct mail and oral communication between a person representing the source and the audience are also used.

Proper channels can help communication be more effective by enhancing the message. The rich color available in television and magazines can make products such as a Stouffer's Lean Cuisine frozen meal or a Pacific Mountain Bartlett pear appear tantilizingly delicious.

Receiver. Receivers are people in a target audience who receive the message by **decoding** or interpreting its meaning. Language, symbols, and pictures are used to convey an intended meaning consistent with the purpose of the communication. But the actual meaning decoded depends on how receivers perceive the message, and may not necessarily be the meaning intended by the source.

Three problems can inhibit decoding. First, receivers in an audience may not see or listen to the messages. Apparently this phenomenon happens often to the United States. One study found that 45 percent of television viewers miss one or more advertisements aired during a half-hour program. The president of the company that conducted the study commented on the findings.

> In many homes, says Elizabeth J. Roberts, president of the nonprofit research concern, viewers were distracted easily and television served "as little more than a 'talking lamp.' " Three-fourths of the people who weren't watching alone were talking to someone else in the room. One-fifth of the viewers were doing household chores, 18% were eating, 17% were reading, 12% were engaged in other leisure persuits and 6% were talking on the phone.[5]

Second, receivers may misunderstand the message. Language, symbols, or pictures selected by the source for a message may not have the same meaning for the receivers. This problem is difficult when promoting in a home country, and even more dangerous when targeting audiences in a foreign market. Consider the plight of an American company that decided to use a phrase from its U.S. advertising campaign to help promote its table napkins to British markets. The phrase was, "You can use no finer napkin at your dinner table." Unfortunately, the British word *napkin* means diaper, so the phrase was interpreted by British audiences as, "You can use no finer diaper at your dinner table." Needless to say, the advertisement was not effective.[6]

Third, distractions during the communications process called **noise** can inhibit effectiveness. Noise is anything that causes a message to go unnoticed or to be misinterpreted. Imagine the following situation: A family is eating dinner. The television is on and a commercial for a dishwasher has just come on the screen. The woman is interested, but as she is listening to the commercial one of her children spills a glass of milk. She turns away from the commercial to help clean up the mess, and only partly hears the announcer say that the dishwasher is "just $499 this week." The woman thought the announcer said $949, which was too high a price for her to consider. She immediately forgets about the commercial.

When the milk was spilled noise was added to the communications process and caused the dishwasher commercial to be ineffective, at least for that potential consumer. Some noise is almost always present in a communications process, and managers often do not have any control over it. Thus a message must be designed to work in the imperfect environments that surround the receiver.

Action as a result of communication. An organization communicates to obtain action from its audience. Typical actions a company desires from its promotion are customers' purchasing the brand, going to a retailer to shop, telling others of the benefits or satisfaction with the brand (shown in Exhibit 18.2 as word of mouth), and being loyal to the company's brand. Desired actions also may be subtle, such as persons developing a good feeling toward the company and its products or forming an intention to try the product. Of course, the action may not be the one that was intended by the source. The receiver may take no action at all, may develop a dislike of the product, may tell others about the disadvantages of the company's brand, or may complain about the brand directly to the company's managers. Promotion's effectiveness is determined by the actions that occur.

Managing the communications process

Promotion decisions guide the communications flow from source to receivers, and in some cases from receiver to receiver through word of mouth. These decisions address five important questions that arise when the promotion mix is planned:

1. Who should receive the message?
2. What actions by the audience are desired?
3. What should the message say to the audience?
4. How should the message be delivered to the audience?

Come to Canada

Waterton Lakes Peace Park, Alberta

Along with its magazine advertising, Canada's Ministry of Tourism, as part of its 1985 summer tourism campaign, placed two-page, full-color ads in several U.S. newspapers. "Come up for a fling!" suggests an East Coast newspaper ad as it describes the summer-long activities available to tourists in New Brunswick, Newfoundland, Prince Edward Island, and Nova Scotia. (Courtesy of Ronalds-Reynolds & Company Limited)

The Endless Surprise.

The spectacular beauty of the world's first international peace park. Soft, mellow nights in our modern cities, where strolling is a pleasure–anytime. Gourmet dining and nightlife to match. And for a change of pace, the heart-pounding thrill of a mountie charge. So much to see, so much to do. Come share the excitement with us this autumn. Canada. The endless surprise.
For information to help plan your trip write: Canadian Tourism, Box 1192, Glenview, Illinois 60025.

AMERICA BORDERS ON THE MAGNIFICENT

Canada

5. How much should be spent on managing the process? (See Marketalk for a discussion of how these questions were addressed by the Canadian government.)

Receivers of the message. The target audience (or audiences) must be selected before the message can be delivered. Only by knowing who is to receive the message can managers know what to say and how to relay the message.

When target markets are the target audiences, a market opportunity analysis (MOA) provides essential information on the makeup of audiences (see Chapter 4). Market definition shows which market segments are candidate target audiences. Additionally, an MOA helps managers understand what these people are like so messages and promotion channels can be tailored to them. Managers at New Jersey Bell effectively used an MOA when they wanted to promote the company's new call waiting service (a tone that alerts a person talking on the telephone that another caller is trying to get through) to the most likely customers. The MOA showed that a target market is families with teenagers. Parents are concerned about reaching their children in an emergency because they know how much teenagers use the telephone. The promotion message was aimed at this audience and explained the convenience of using call waiting to call home when a teenager is tying up the telephone.[7]

MarkeTALK //

Canada uses promotional blitz to attract U.S. tourists

THE CANADIAN GOVERNMENT watched its share of U.S. tourism dollars fall to 15.6 percent, down from 17 percent in 1980. There were 36.2 million American visitors to Canada in 1972 compared with 32.4 million just a decade later. Because each visitor spends an average of $200 a day, this decline meant substantial loss of revenue for the economy. A number of factors accounted for the downward trend—inflation, movement of people in the north to the southeast and southwest portions of the United States, the recession—but the slide was alarming. As Guy Simser, the U.S. Marketing Development Directorate for Tourism Canada, noted, "Once they break the habit of coming here, its hard to get them back."

To find a way to reverse the tourism trend, the Canadian government used marketing research. Studies uncovered that people had two key interests in visiting Canada: the beautiful outdoor scenery and unspoiled wildlife and the fascinating culture, different from that in America. Surprisingly, people are aware of the outdoor beauty, but many did not know of the many cultural and artistic activities in Canada. Furthermore, culture enthusiasts are different from those that want the scenery. Working women and single women in particular are more attracted by culture. They do not want to go out and scale a cliff or go camping. But they do enjoy shopping, theater, outdoor cafés, and the fine arts widely available in Canada.

Armed with this information, Canada beefed up its promotion effort to blitz proportions. The promotion budget was just about doubled to $20 million. A promotion strategy emphasizing the dual benefits of visiting Canada—outdoor beauty and culture—was created. Target audiences included both the trade (tour operators, travel agencies, and conference plan-

ners) and American tourists. And a promotion mix was developed that relied heavily on advertising, publicity, and sales promotion activities. For instance, two message themes were created for advertising: "Come to Canada, the endless surprise," and "America borders on the magnificent—Canada." Advertising media were switched from a concentration in the northern United States to nationwide. Trade shows, dinners, and meetings were held for the trade to win their support. In addition, the arts were promoted by taking Canadian actors, ballet dancers, jazz musicians, and opera singers on tour of U.S. cities, getting wide press coverage at every stop.

The promotion blitz worked. Tourism increased significantly as did inquiries made at Canadian consulates in the United States. And tourists spent more than half a billion dollars more in Canada that year. These results speak well for the well-planned and coordinated promotion campaign put together by the Canadian government.

SOURCE: "Canadian marketing blitz lures U.S. tourists back after decline," *Marketing News,* Aug. 31, 1984, pp. 1, 6. Reprinted with permission of the American Marketing Association.

//

Desired actions by target audiences. **Promotion objectives** are statements specifying exactly what actions are desired by management. There are two types of promotion objectives, sales oriented and communication, and either one or both objectives determine the purpose of the promotion. Managers often want to elicit overt kinds of behavior such as customers' redeeming a coupon, making an inquiry about a purchase, going to a dealer, or buying the product. These are **sales-oriented promotion objectives** because they involve a purchase or behavior leading to a purchase. The other type of promotion objective concerns less-observable actions involving the thinking or feelings of people in target audiences and are called **communications promotion objectives.** They are based on an important idea: Promotion must communicate with an audience before it can eventually influence its members to buy. Several models have been developed to help managers understand promotion's communications task. They are generally called **hierarchy-of-effects models** because they describe a sequence of mental steps that people go through leading to a purchase. Two such models, the **AIDA model** and an expanded hierarchy-of-effects model[8] are described in Exhibit 18.3.

Hierarchy-of-effects models tie communications to customer purchase decision processes (see Chapters 5 and 6). Exhibit 18.4 shows how the steps in these models are related to purchase decision making. A central notion derived from these models is that promotion must accomplish communications objectives (achieving awareness, stimulating interest, building knowledge, gaining liking, and so forth) so people in the target audience will move from problem recognition through search and alternative evaluation

Exhibit 18.3 Models help define communications tasks for promotion

AIDA Model		Hierarchy-of-Effects Model	
Steps	Definition	Steps	Definition
Awareness	Audience becomes aware of a company and its product.	Awareness	Audience becomes aware of a company and its product.
Interest	Audience becomes interested in the company's product as a solution to a problem.	Knowledge	Audience understands what the company and its product can do for them.
Desire	Audience desires to buy the company's product.	Liking	Audience has a good feeling or attitude toward the company and its product.
Action	Audience buys the company's product.	Preference	Audience prefers the company's product more than those of other companies.
		Conviction	Audience becomes convinced that they should buy the company's product.
		Purchase	Audience actually buys the company's product.

Exhibit 18.4 Communication models show how promotion can influence customer purchase decision making

Customer Purchase Decision-making Process	AIDA Model	Hierarchy-of-Effects Model
Problem recognition ↓		
Search ↓	Awareness	Awareness Knowledge
Alternative evaluation ↓	Interest Desire	Liking Preference Conviction
Purchase	Action	Purchase

to purchase. New Jersey Bell telephone service knew that people in families with teenagers (the target audience) must know about the call waiting service and then must think they will like its benefits before they will inquire about it or buy it.

As marketing professionals have learned more about customer decision making, communications models have been more closely scrutinized. We now know that the steps from awareness to purchase shown in Exhibits 18.3 and 18.4 apply primarily to high-involvement decision making (see Chapter 5 for a discussion of involvement as applied to consumer decision making). When customers purchase low-involvement products, the communications steps may change their sequence (see Exhibit 18.5). The major difference is that knowledge, liking, preference, and conviction may occur *after* a low-involvement product is purchased and tried.

Promotional objectives should depend on whether high- or low-involvement purchasing characterizes markets. For high-involvement products such as videotape recorders, expensive cameras, and big-screen televisions, promotion should help lead the target audience through the hierarchy-of-effects steps. In contrast, when a product is low involvement, such as soap, potato chips, cookies, and magazines, promotion's ability to influence overt behavior—the sales-oriented objective—is emphasized. Accomplishing communications objectives (other than gaining awareness) has less payoff simply because customers are not spending much time or effort searching and evaluating alternatives.

Exhibit 18.5 Communication models for different types of customer purchase decision making

High-Involvement Decisions		Low-Involvement Decisions	
AIDA	Hierarchy Model	AIDA	Hierarchy Model
Awareness ↓	Awareness ↓	Awareness ↓	Awareness ↓
Interest ↓	Knowledge ↓	Action ↓	Purchase ↓
Desire ↓	Liking ↓	Interest ↓	Knowledge ↓
Action	Preference ↓	Desire	Liking ↓
	Conviction ↓		Preference ↓
	Purchase		Conviction

What to say to audiences and how to say it. At the heart of the communications process is constructing the right message to influence people to act in the desired way. An effective message grabs the audience's attention, is not misunderstood, and is memorable. Two message-related decisions determine whether these characteristics are achieved. First, **message content** is created describing *what* is to be communicated to target audiences. For instance, when introducing Diet Coke, management decided to tell target audiences that the new product is a "great tasting soft drink that happens to have one calorie, rather than a diet drink that tastes great."[9] This decision led to the promotion message, "Just for the taste of it."

A second decision concerns *how* the message content is to be communicated to the target audience, or **message context.** Some of these context features include the use of color, the scene that is portrayed, the use of large headlines, and the size of the advertisement. Other parts of the company's promotion campaign, such as sales promotion signs and point-of-purchase displays, may communicate the same message content, but in different contexts (see Marketech).

Message content and context decisions rely heavily but not entirely on creativity. Creative designers are guided by information on target audiences as well as by communications objectives. An MOA that describes lifestyles, product benefit preferences, and other characteristics of people tar-

Marke**TECH** □ □ □ □ □ □ □ □ □ □ □ □ □ □ □ □ □

Retailer using computer graphics to print point-of-purchase signs

RETAILERS ARE USING computer-graphics technology to produce signage which increases the effectiveness of promotions while cutting printing costs.

"The system we have has not only improved sign quality but given us the ability, by store, to generate any sign we want with any message needed, almost instantly, and at less cost per sign," reports Edward Porter, executive vice president and chief operating officer of the Milgram's Food Store chain, Kansas City, Mo.

Milgram's is one of a growing number of supermarket and discount-store chains whose signage is produced by the computer-printing method. Its system, an IBM 4341 driving a Flexographic dot-matrix printer, can produce thousands of colorful, custom-made shelf-talkers, signs, labels and other point-of-sale materials for all 41 Milgram and Save Mart stores in the Midwest.

"We were looking for uniformity. Prior to making the switch, we had left a lot of discretion to each individual store. And that system wasn't working too well," said Milgram president Frank Hopfinger. "The signage was either poor or nonexistent. A rare exception was the store which just happened to have somebody artistic enough to make up good signs.

"By printing our signs electronically, we're now getting uniformity. Our stores are more attractive, the signs are moving merchandise, and we've reduced the workload of each store."

Sales of items promoted with the new computer-printed signage "tend to go up dramatically," said Porter, estimating the typical increase at 20% to 40%, depending on the product category.

In addition, the technology saves labor costs. Porter said the computer signage costs $.01 to $.05 compared to "the situation of a clerk making $12 an hour sitting there making conventional signs. Using a computer to do the same work, and getting higher sign quality, makes a great deal of sense."

Alan Chapman, Milgram advertising director, said of the electronic signage sys-

tem: "Store managers think the program is great. We've got computers doing what is essentially a tedious job. It was hard to get people to care about making a sign that goes up one week and comes down the next."

Frank Peak, assistant vice president, adds, "What the system means is that if a manager plans to stack charcoal briquettes nine feet high in an end-of-aisle display, and he wants a super low price to get people excited about it, we'll be able to provide that sign. And I think once we get requests from our stores, we'll start to get more promotional ideas."

Emblem Graphics Systems Inc. Kansas City, Mo., which helped Milgram's set up the electronic-printing program, is currently working with the retailer on a new pricing concept called category signage.

Large, bright, computer-printed end-of-aisle posters will display the prices of items by the ounce—a convenience for the shopper. The items will be listed in descending order by "best-buy" price so shoppers can easily scan the list and find the best bargain by unit price.

SOURCE: "Perk up promotions with computer-printed signage," *Marketing News*, Nov. 9, 1984, p. 46. Reprinted with permission of the American Marketing Association.

□ □

RICOH COPIERS

"RAINY HOTEL"

:30 TV Commercial

SFX: LIGHTNING, THUNDER, RAIN.

SPOKESMAN: A minute of your time. Can anyone name a copier manufacturer that's bigger than Ricoh?

MONK: Xerox.

SPOKESMAN: Ricoh's bigger.

LOOKALIKES: (IN UNISON) IBM?

SPOKESMAN: Ricoh's bigger.

And we got to be bigger than Xerox,

by making precision engineered copiers

like this Ricoh 4060.

MONK: I'm beginning to see the light.

SPOKESMAN: Now are you still overlooking Ricoh and the Ricoh 4060?

Call Ricoh. We respond.

800-526-0890
In NJ 800-452-5757

RICOH
We respond.
Cameras, Facsimile and Office Automation Equipment

Ricoh was once considered Japan's biggest copier company, and some Japanese still speak of making a "ricopy." Ricoh still has 40 percent of the Japanese market, but its name is little known overseas. To combat this, Ricoh now has a huge billboard in Times Square and, as this storyboard shows, is using TV advertising to promote its copiers and their ease of use.

geted for promotion is invaluable for this purpose. As one advertising executive notes,

> Creatives want to understand the consumer, get into his or her mind, and find out what makes the consumer tick. The role of a researcher should be to represent the consumer to the creative by speaking the consumer's language and describing the consumer as a flesh-and-blood human being, not a statistical average extrapolated from a computer printout.[10]

Delivering the message. Having the right message is important only if it can be effectively delivered to the target audience. There are many different types of media from which to choose, and each reaches a different mix of people. The most important media are newspapers, magazines, television, radio, billboards, direct mail, salespersons, store signs, packages, and catalogues. Some of these categories summarize more specific alternatives; in the magazine media category alone, there are hundreds of different magazines.

Decisions on media must take into consideration all the previous promotion decisions. First, managers seek media that reach the same kinds of people as those in target audiences. A heavy machinery manufacturing company such as General Electric primarily uses salespersons to sell to engineers in buying organizations because the target audience is relatively small and includes persons that want a lot of information about products they are going to use on the job. Direct mail is also used because the mailings can be targeted to the individual engineers who are most involved in the buying decision. In contrast, a consumer-products company such as

General Mills that must reach millions of people across a country is likely to rely heavily on the mass media—television, radio, newspapers, and magazines. Managers must also determine the extent to which each medium can effectively enhance the message's ability to achieve promotion objectives. Newspapers are a good choice for making people aware of which stores sell your company's brand, but television may be the better choice to demonstrate how easy the brand is to use. Finally, cost of each medium must also be considered. A company must be able to afford the media selected.

Most companies select a combination of media to deliver messages. A combination of media increases the likelihood that most people in a target audience will be reached because no one medium will typically reach everyone. Furthermore, using different media allows a company to convey more than one message in a promotion campaign.

Budgeting for communications. Media hired by a company to deliver a company's messages set rates for their services. Salespersons' salaries and expenses must be paid. Additionally, many expenses are associated with creating and testing messages.[11] Without careful control by management, costs can easily get out of proportion to the benefits received from a promotion mix. Well-run companies use budgets to control these expenses.

In practice, determining a promotion budget is usually done in one of two general ways: the top-down approach or the bottom-up approach. The **top-down approach to promotion budgeting** is applied when an upper limit or "cap" on how much can be spent for promotion is set by top management—a board of directors, an owner, a president, or a vice-president of finance or marketing. Little or no directives are given to middle- and lower-level management on how the money is to be spent, so a promotion mix is planned that costs no more than the cap. For instance, a company's chief marketing executive may establish a budget limit by taking a certain percentage of forecasted sales and allocating this amount to promotion.

The **bottom-up approach to promotion budgeting** develops a promotion plan by deciding which combination of message content, context, and media is required to achieve specified promotion objectives. The total cost of the plan becomes a recommended promotion budget. This budget is then reviewed by top management for approval. At this point, the use of funds by promotion is weighed against other ways the company has to use that money.

Which budgeting approach is used depends on top management's style as well as on the general approach to planning in a company. The top-down approach is popular when planning is heavily dominated by high-level financial managers who compare promotion's use of funds to return on investment opportunities from other corporate activities, or when managers rely on historical guidelines for planning. These guidelines, such as allocating a certain percentage of forecast sales to promotion, enable top managers to decide on promotion budgets without a detailed analysis of how the budget will be spent.

On the other hand, a company may have a companywide planning system that requires lower- and middle-level managers to begin the budgeting process by planning for their departments. Then the departmental plans are reviewed and combined into a total company plan. In a company such as this, promotion budgeting will use the bottom-up approach.

Evaluating promotion's performance

After developing a promotion plan, a manager's chief concerns are to implement the plan and evaluate its performance. Testing the combined effects of all the promotional tools usually is expensive. If a test market is needed to compare the sales return from different combinations of promotion tools tried in different market areas, it can cost hundreds of thousands of dollars. Other kinds of tests are not so expensive, but can cost thousands of dollars. In practice, managers typically evaluate each component separately in the promotion mix because the information needed is different for each. Think about evaluating the effectiveness of a direct mail advertising campaign. It only may require counting the number of inquiries received. But to measure the effectiveness of personal salespersons requires evaluating several indicators of performance such as comparing sales to quotas, counting number of sales calls made, and subjectively evaluating the quality of personal contacts made with customers. Evaluating the promotion plan is discussed in much more detail in Chapters 19 and 20.

THE PROMOTION MIX

Each of the four promotion tools (advertising, sales promotion, publicity, and personal selling) provides a source of information for buyers, though consumers do not use them all equally nor equally well. A study of housewares shoppers discovered that point-of-purchase displays (a sales promotion device) are frequently used for information on new products, apparently even more often than television, magazine, and newspaper advertising combined.[12] Another study found that consumers believe that too much product information is available, which makes product choice more, not less, difficult.[13]

Because no one of the tools is always best, promotion managers work hard to find the proper combination for a promotion mix. Each tool has qualities that the others do not offer, so understanding these qualities is essential to determining the mix. To help you better appreciate a promotion manager's challenge when choosing a promotion mix, we consider five qualities of the promotion tools: (1) costs (including total costs and costs per contact), (2) ability to target specific audiences, (3) ability to interact with audiences, (4) flexibility in designing content and context of the communication, and (5) ability to reach large audiences with a common message. Exhibit 18.6 summarizes the differences among the promotion tools on these qualities.

Advertising

With the proper choice of media, advertisements can be targeted toward a local city or town, a regional area of several states, or nationally across the country. The geographic coverage by a company's sales effort determines the proper area for promotion. A department store uses newspapers, television, and radio to reach fashion clothing shoppers in a city. At the same time, a fashion clothing manufacturer such as Ralph Lauren uses magazines, television, and newspapers to communicate with selected groups of shoppers in communities across the country.

Exhibit 18.6 A comparison of the qualities of the promotion mix tools

Qualities	Advertising	Sales Promotion	Publicity	Personal Selling
Total cost	Moderate to high	Moderate	Low	High
Cost per contact	Low	Moderate	Low	High
Ability to target specific markets	Moderate to good	Good	Moderate to good	Very good
Interact with audiences	No	No	No	Yes
Communication flexibility	Good	Poor	Good	Very good
Ability to reach large audiences	Very good	Moderate	Very good	Poor

Flexibility to target specific market groups within a geographic area also depends on the media used. Local newspapers are read by broad cross-sections of people in a community. Businesses with correspondingly broad target markets such as grocery stores and department stores can benefit using this medium. But a specialty store such as one that sells women's fashion clothing will not be able to reach the clientele in its narrow market with newspapers because most persons in a newspaper's audience are not interested in high-fashion, expensive clothing. On the other hand, the women's clothing shop may be able to efficiently reach its target markets by sending an advertisement through the mail directly to select clientele on a mailing list.

AMERICA'S FAVORITE SIX PACK.

PROUD SPONSORS OF THE U.S. OLYMPIC TEAM.
ANHEUSER-BUSCH, INC - ST. LOUIS • THE WORLD'S LEADING BREWER USA

In 1985, the Federal Trade Commission decided that it would not ban advertising in broadcasting for alcoholic beverages; it will, however, monitor individual ads to prevent any deceptive claims. Currently, all forms of alcohol are advertised in the print media, but only beer and wine use television and radio advertising—media voluntarily not used by the makers of distilled spirits. (Courtesy of Anheuser-Busch, Inc.)

"Here's #5 of my 17 reasons why H&R Block should prepare your taxes."

Henry W. Block

REASON #5: If the IRS audits your return, H&R Block goes with you at no extra cost.

An IRS audit can be an anxious time for any taxpayer. But, if you're audited, Block will go with you at no extra cost. Not as a legal representative, but to explain how your return was prepared. We're always ready to stand behind you, year-round.

H&R BLOCK®

THE INCOME TAX PEOPLE

17 reasons. One smart decision.

The future for tax preparation services looked dim indeed when President Reagan announced a new tax plan supposedly so simple that two out of three Americans wouldn't even have to file returns. But H&R Block, which prepared 10 percent of all U.S. returns in 1984, wasn't bothered: "Going from fourteen rates to three rates only affects the tax tables. It doesn't make the tax preparation process any simpler," says president Thomas Block. So long as Block's business continues to boom, its advertising will continue to answer customers' questions. (Courtesy of H&R Block, Inc.)

Total costs of advertising are moderate to high, primarily because of the expense of using media. But cost must be evaluated in relation to the number of persons in a target audience that are reached, and on this basis cost of advertising per contact reached is low. Anheuser-Busch, brewer of Budweiser, Michelob, and other beers, spent $20 million on television advertising during the three weeks of the 1984 Summer Olympics.[14] The huge audience watching television coverage of the Olympics, many of whom were sports fans in beer target markets, made Anheuser-Busch's cost reasonable. Of course, only a big company can afford to spend large amounts of money for a short period of time. Many smaller companies are prevented from even considering expensive national exposure such as that provided by the Olympics.

Generally, there is a direct correspondence between total cost of a medium and the number of people in that medium's audience. A local newspaper's advertising rate is low compared with national advertising on network television because the audiences differ so much in size. Of course, other factors such as the expense of reproducing the advertisement also affect cost.

Advertising is an impersonal form of communication, which means that there is no face-to-face interaction between the advertiser and members of the audience. Although advertising is effective at reaching large audiences, it is unable to respond to an audience's questions and objectives. To partially overcome this deficiency, a company may try to anticipate some of the audience's questions so advertising message content can address them.

Some messages are easily communicated to audiences, and others are not. Thus managers consider the versatility of each promotion tool for delivering particular messages. Procter & Gamble had to consider versatility of promotion tools when management discovered through consumer research that its household cleaner, Spic 'n Span, was typically used only for heavy spring cleaning. For much of the year the product was not used. Management wanted to encourage consumers to use the brand more frequently. Promotion was created to suggest other uses of Spic 'n Span such as cleaning bathroom tubs and sinks without scratching them. Television advertising was chosen because it could visually demonstrate the brand's ability to handle these situations.[15]

Sales promotion

Drawing conclusions about sales promotion is difficult because so many different activities fall into this category. Point-of-purchase signs and displays, free samples, coupons, cents-off promotions, trade shows, premiums, and contests are not at all alike, but they are lumped into this category. Nevertheless, some observations can be made.

Total costs of sales promotion are moderate, particularly when compared with advertising and personal selling. Sales promotion does not require mass media or salespersons, although sometimes one or the other carries the sales promotion. For instance, a coupon offering a price reduction for a purchase of a pizza dinner may be placed in a newspaper. Furthermore, sales promotion usually has a short-run impact on sales because its objective is to increase sales immediately; it is not used continuously as is advertising or personal selling. A cents-off special may be used to get consumers to try a new pizza topping, but it would not likely be made a permanent price reduction.

Most sales promotion activities are moderately effective in reaching large audiences. Audience size varies considerably with the way in which the message is distributed, and so cost per contact is at best moderate. When sales promotion messages are delivered through stores, these stores must agree to carry a manufactuer's point-of-purchase displays and signs, and so audience reached depends upon how many stores cooperate with a sales promotion. Free samples of a product mailed to potential customers reach only those on a mailing list, which can vary from a few hundred persons or less to many thousands. When sales promotion is tied in with advertising, such as when a coupon is included in an advertisement, the audience reached is comparable to the reach of that tool.

Sales promotions can be aimed either directly to customers or to the trade. Through in-store activities that reach buyers when they are ready to buy or by using mailing lists, sales promotion is efficient in reaching buyers without wasting effort on nonbuyers. Similarly, activities directed at wholesalers and retailers can pinpoint target audiences.

Sales promotion activities are most often impersonal means of communication because no interaction with customers takes place. One exception is a **trade show,** where sellers set up exhibits to show their wares to dealers or end-user customers. People who operate the exhibit can talk with customers who stop by to see the company's products. Yet even at the trade show the prevailing thought is to use exhibit time to identify potential customers and get essential information about them. Thus limited interaction takes place. When the trade show is over, salespersons can take over the selling task.

> On the trade show floor, familiar selling caveats are out. Limited time, not patience, is the main factor. The goal is to identify potential customers as quickly and conclusively as possible, to eliminate abruptly anyone who is not

a prospective buyer, and to capture swiftly, on a lead card, all the information necessary for contacting a likely client once the show ends.[16]

Except for the trade show, sales promotion activities typically lack flexibility, as only simple messages can be communicated. Additionally, many of these activities are strictly short-run inducements to buy the product immediately such as free gifts with purchase, cents-off specials, coupons, and free samples. More complex arguments for trying the product would have to be communicated by other promotion tools.

Publicity and public relations

Many companies try to ensure favorable promotional value from newsworthy activities by managing the release of information to the press. News stories carried by the media have high believability, which can help achieve promotion objectives. New and exciting products or services, in particular, benefit from publicity. When the personal computer began to emerge as a product for both managers and consumers, the public was deluged with news stories about it. *Time* magazine even gave the personal computer its "Man of the Year" award in 1983 in recognition of its impact on society. Computer companies such as IBM, Apple, and Commodore supplied information for these stories, which played an important part in increasing people's familiarity, understanding, and eventually acceptance of this product.

Some companies establish a **public relations** function to gain public understanding and acceptance of its goals and image as well as of management's point of view on issues of concern to the welfare of the organization. A variety of means are used for this purpose including arranging for managers to speak on behalf of the company at public functions, developing company history materials, and producing films on subjects important to the company. Publicity, which is usually limited to marketing-related activities for a product or product line, often becomes a part of the larger public relations activity.

Publicity and public relations typically use the same mass media as does advertising. Yet there are major differences between the two. The company does not pay media to carry its publicity and public relations messages, so there is no media cost to a company. On the other hand, the company loses control over the content of the news stories. Suppose a newspaper sends a gourmet critic to dine at a new restaurant to write a review column on the menu, service, and decor. The restaurant may go all out to serve a satisfying meal, but the critic has a free rein on what to say in the paper's column.

Although publicity and public relations costs are low compared with the other promotion tools, only the media costs are free. Other costs involved in planning, execution, and control are incurred by the company. Thus managers must plan for the proper use of these resources by setting objectives, deciding what information to release and how to deliver it to the press, and deciding how publicity and public relations should be coordinated with the rest of the promotion mix.

Publicity and public relations information is more likely to be believed by its audience than information from the other tools.[17] People typically do not associate it with the self-interest motivation of a company, a motivation that is apparent in advertising, personal selling, and sales promotion. Think about the newspaper's gourmet critic again. Potential diners are more likely to believe the gourmet critic's saying the food served by the new restaurant is "extraordinary" than an advertisement carrying the same message.

Publicity and public relations items may also get prime locations in the media.[18] These same or similar locations are often impossible to get for advertising, or at the very least would be quite expensive. Knoxville, Tennessee, benefited from nationwide publicity, including being on the front pages of some newspapers, because it was selected as the most liveable city in the United States based on a study of cities' quality of life. Local administrators received excellent coverage by many media and used the story to attract businesses and people to the area. The city could not have duplicated the publicity it received by using advertising.

Because publicity and public relations so frequently use the same media as does advertising, they similarly reach large audiences, can target audiences through selecting appropriate media, and provide communication flexibility. They also have the same limitation of not being able to interact with audiences, though some public relations activities involve speakers who are in face-to-face contact with their audience. On the other hand, news items are not repeated as is an advertising message. For these reasons, publicity and public relations are rarely ever considered as a substitute for advertising.

One expert summarizes the payoffs from using publicity and public relations (PR) in a promotion mix.

1. Leverage. PR will sharply boost reach, add frequency, and increase believability for only incrementally more than the amount companies already spend on other marketing techniques. The cost is usually in the mid-five to low-six figure range.
2. Efficiency. PR can gain free exposure in media a company couldn't or wouldn't consider advertising in. It can also acquire space in media that don't accept advertising such as newsletters, house organs, and certain trade journals.
3. Techniques. PR does the work a company's lawyers, finance department, and ad agency don't want to do: booklets, fact sheets, seminars, trade shows, films, and, of course, publicity.
4. Sales. Publicity can generate inquiries and traffic. It can sell products and services as well as ideas and opinions. Dryden & Palmer, Norwalk, Conn., manufacturer of the original rock candy, is amazed at the number of inquiries it still receives from a *Wall Street Journal* story that was published on its business nearly a year ago.[19]

Personal selling

Personal selling is the most expensive of the promotion tools, especially when the cost of making a contact with a customer is considered. In addition to salary, there are the expenses of getting the salesperson to and from customers. One study estimated that in 1982 expenses for meals, lodging, and automobile rental for a single salesperson averaged $641 per week in the United States and $732 in Canada.[20] Dividing these expenses by an average number of calls made, the same study found that each call averaged $81.25.[21] When salary and other expenses are added to these figures, the total cost of keeping a salesperson on the road can average $75,000 each year.[22] In spite of these costs, advantages of personal selling compared with the other tools encourage many companies to rely heavily on personal selling in their promotion mix.

Familiarity with a sales territory allows salespersons to target customers with high potential for buying. Furthermore, sales calls involve face-to-face interaction with buyers, and so personal selling is more flexible in tailoring a message to individual customers than are the other promotion tools. A salesperson can make presentations of the company's offer, answer questions raised by customers, and respond to any of their objections or concerns. Additionally, the customer can often try the product.

A salesperson can also turn to a variety of communications equipment and visual aids to enhance a sales presentation. Videotapes, slide projectors, overhead projectors, tape recorders, and movies are increasingly being used by the well-equipped salesperson. Gould's medical products division, for instance, developed very effective videotape presentations demonstrating a new portable transducer (a product that allows blood pressure to be digitally read). Salespersons carry videotape recorders on sales calls to show the tape to customers.[23]

Many firms are turning more and more to **telemarketing,** which involves salespersons making contacts with customers by telephone rather than in person. A recent report issued by the Distribution Research and Education Foundation estimated that by 1990 telephone salespersons will make up 50 percent of the average wholesale distributor's salesforce. In 1980, the figure was 30 percent. At Louisiana Oil & Tire Company, all ten of the traveling salespersons were brought inside and put at a bank of telephones. Since then the company's telephone bill has increased by $6000 a month, but other sales expenses have declined by $15,000 a month. More important, says Gregory Martin, sales manager, is that sales have doubled.[24]

When telemarketing was introduced, many firms rejected it and public sentiment was against it. In fact, some groups, claiming that it was an invasion of privacy, proposed laws to ban or limit it. However, firms are finding they can establish the same rapport over the telephone as they can person-to-person (see Marketalk). "Telemarketing isn't just how to talk on the phone," says a telephone consultant. It may take three to six months before a program starts to pay off. Success depends on (1) an analysis of which accounts can best be sold by telephone and which accounts require face-to-face contacts, (2) knowledge of company policies and product lines, (3) extensive training in telephone techniques, and (4) a good personality. The telephone salesperson must be enthusiastic to create interest and thick-skinned to handle dozens of rejections per day.[25]

Another development is **teleconferencing.** This technique also puts salespersons in direct contact with customers without their having to travel. But it goes one step further than telemarketing by using television and telephone hookups so that salespersons in one location can see and talk with several customers in different locations.[26] Television adds face-to-face contact, while avoiding the high costs of travel for salespersons. (See Marketech in Chapter 20 on videoconferencing.)

Coordinating the promotion mix

To get the most return from a promotion mix, the tools must be coordinated. At the heart of this task is setting sound promotion objectives derived from a marketing strategy plan. Then important promotion activities required to achieve these objectives can be allocated to each promotional tool. Chemical Bank of New York successfully followed this procedure when it combined advertising and sales promotion to attract savings deposits. Advertising portrayed Chemical Bank as a neighborhood bank with branches conveniently located. As a short-run incentive to attract depositers, medallions were offered as a sales promotion premium. These medallions were minted with popular scenes from the neighborhoods in which the branches were located and supported the neighborhood bank marketing strategy.[27]

Coordinating the promotion mix usually is easier for a small company than for a large one. A small company's total promotion effort is sufficiently limited so that one manager or one department can handle the task. Thus coordination automatically occurs simply because so few persons are involved in the effort.

As a company grows the problem of synchronizing promotion activities mounts. Large companies assign each promotion tool to a different department that handles the extensive planning and implementing required. Exhibit 18.7 illustrates an organizational allocation of promotion responsibilities for a large organization. Publicity is handled by advertising when no public relations function exists. But in companies that use public relations, publicity is likely to be assigned to that department. Sales promotion may be assigned to a separate department or it may be divided between advertising and personal selling. Consumer contests, price promotions, couponing, premiums, and free samples may be supervised by the advertising department. Point-of-purchase activities such as special displays, signs, and contests directed toward the trade are likely to be coordinated by the personal selling department.

When promotion management is divided among departments, the need for coordination among the different tools mushrooms. One way to

*Marke*TALK //

Telemarketing requires special professionals

IT'S NO SURPRISE THAT an industry built on the spoken word has its own language. Telemarketers call the people on the lines "communicators." A telephone campaign is known as "the program." "Outbound" telemarketing—in which a communicator calls a name on a list to make a sales pitch—is valued more highly than "inbound," which has the communicator merely taking the calls and recording the order of someone ready to buy.

In suburban and rural areas, communicators are often housewives, students, and retirees. In large cities, dancers and musicians fill many positions. Telemarketing companies like to hire actors: they don't sound as if they're reading a script and they know how to deal with rejec-

SOURCE: Joel Dreyfuss, "Reach out and sell something," *Fortune*, Nov. 26, 1984, p. 128. Reprinted by permission from *Fortune* Magazine; © 1984 Time Inc. All rights reserved.

tion—a necessary asset for the job. Potential employees are auditioned over the phone to determine if their voices are pleasant and their manner assertive. Most work part-time, at salaries from $3.45 an hour to $8 or more.

Communicators read from a sheet of paper, a set of plastic-coated flip-cards, or a computer screen—and are not allowed to improvise. The script begins with "Hello" and ends with "Thank you" and has pat responses to foreseeable customer objections in between. Supervisors often listen in to make sure the job is getting done. Telemarketing clients may also eavesdrop to get a feel for customer reaction. Communicators work four- to six-hour shifts and may have to meet a quota of ten or more calls per hour.

Despite the pressure, Deborah Abney, 29, says she loves her job at New York's Campaign Communications Insti-

tute. When she started, three years ago, the first person she called hung up on her and she broke into tears. Now, 120,000 calls later, Abney says she can tell within the first or second response if she's going to make a sale. Andrea Purcell, 27, a seven-year CCI veteran, welcomes more business use of telemarketing. It's easier to do business-to-business selling than to win consumers at home, she says: "Business people make decisions. You don't have to beat around the bush." Ed Jupp, 29, who went to New York from Ohio two years ago to become an actor, divides his time between a theatrical agency during the day and the 6 P.M.-to-midnight shift at CCI. He was attracted to telemarketing because of flexible hours—and steady pay—but now finds that it helps his daytime job. He hires actors for crowd scenes and bit parts—and often finds them among fellow communicators.

///

Exhibit 18.7 Large organizations assign promotion mix tools to different departments

ensure coordination is to assign responsibility for it to a high-level executive such as a marketing vice-president. Another is to have the heads of the different departments informally coordinate with each other, or to staff a promotions committee. A third option used by some companies such as Procter & Gamble is to assign product or brand managers to each brand in its product mix. Brand managers typically have direct responsibility for advertising, most of sales promotion, and sometimes publicity (if there is no public relations department). They must work with sales managers to obtain the desired personal selling effort.

PROMOTION MIX CHANGES DURING A PRODUCT'S LIFE CYCLE

As a product goes through different stages in its life cycle, marketing strategy usually changes as the marketing environment shifts. New promotion objectives are formulated and corresponding strategies are created. Examining how promotion changes with the product's life cycle will enable you to better understand the important factors that influence management's decisions on the proper promotion mix. These factors are (1) technical complexity of the product, (2) intensity of competition, (3) ease of understanding product benefits by customers, and (4) amount of money available for promotion.

Introductory stage

Introducing a new product into markets is a special challenge for managers because potential customers are not yet familiar with the product or the supporting aspects of the marketing mix (price, service, where the product can be bought). Promotion helps people become aware of the product as well as understand what benefits it has to offer. Developing awareness and knowledge are the typical communications objectives at this stage, and introductory promotion campaigns are usually large relative to later campaigns. For instance, Nestlé has introduced new coffee products with as much as $50 million in promotion in an attempt to communicate a premium image and target consumers with particular taste preferences. Because coffee drinkers are numerous and widely dispersed, advertising and sales promotion dominate the effort.[28]

When a product is truly new and different from other products, there is little or no competition from similar brands in the introductory stage. But there is usually competition from other product types. The promotional mix must demonstrate the advantages and benefits of the new product type over those of existing competitive product types. This promotion purpose was very apparent when microwave ovens were introduced. Promotion concentrated on convincing customers of the safety and convenience of microwave cooking compared with conventional gas and electric ovens.

The weight given to each promotional tool also depends on the ease or difficulty of explaining product benefits to customers. For uncomplicated products or knowledgeable customers the nonpersonal tools—advertising, sales promotion, and even publicity—can be heavily relied on to take advantage of their ability to reach large audiences economically. Many consumer products such as shampoo, toothpaste, frozen food, and cereal are introduced with heavy advertising and sales promotion campaigns. Publicity may also be important to gain public awareness and interest, but only if the new product has news value. In contrast, if the product is difficult to understand or is very expensive, such as industrial products, personal selling must be relied on. Introducing a new type of airplane to commercial airline or corporate jet markets, for instance, will have a promotion mix dominated by personal selling.

Finally, the amount of money that a company can devote to promotion will also influence the makeup of the mix during introduction. Limited resources mean that small companies will have a different communications mix during introduction than would a large company. Low-cost tools such as sales promotion and publicity will have to play an increased role. And personal selling will probably be used more than advertising, because advertising media costs are so high. A company with no more than $150,000 available for promotion could support two or more salespersons for one year but could not support a national advertising campaign.

Growth stage

As a product moves into the growth stage, competition from similar brands increases, and customers become familiar with the company's brand and what it has to offer. The market is still expanding, so increased revenue from product sales is likely to be available for marketing activities. At the same time, marketing objectives change as profits increase and maintaining market share is emphasized.

Promotion objectives need to be changed to respond to the shifting situation. Gaining awareness and understanding remains important as long as markets can be expanded. Additional competition from similar brands, however, increases management's concern with how to position its brand against these competitors. The effect of increased competition on the promotion of microwave ovens is that the advantages of individual brands such as Thermodore and Amana's Radarange are now emphasized.

Publicity typically declines in importance after a product's introduction because the news value of the product is lost as the public increasingly becomes familiar with it. Exceptions are products such as personal computers, satellite communications, and organ transplants that are unusually important to society. For products such as these, publicity may continue. A company's emphasis on advertising versus personal selling will continue to be determined by the size and dispersion of target audiences, amount of resources available, technical complexity of the product, and ability of customers to easily understand its use. Sales promotion may decrease in importance during the growth stage as customer interest builds and the company cuts back on expenses to increase profits.

Maturity stage

The promotion mix continues to change as the product moves into the maturity stage. Competition from similar brands becomes very intense, probably surpassing the threat from existing competitive product types. Of course, there is the constant threat of a new product type being developed that will outdate the company's brand and push it into decline.

Promotion objectives continue to shift from awareness and knowledge toward proper image positioning of the brand against similar competitive brands. Furthermore, brand similarity among competition means that non-product benefits (low price, convenience, after-sale services) rather than product benefits may be emphasized. Consider the credit card companies such as American Express, MasterCard, and Carte Blanche. They are increasingly emphasizing peripheral services such as insurance benefits and a prestige image as selling points to win customers, maintain market share, and increase profits.

Personal selling may become important at this stage. Services provided by salespersons can give one company an advantage over another. For instance, competition among the major companies selling metal cans to soft drink, beer, and other manufacturers of consumer products is no longer based much on product benefits. American Can, Continental Group, and others produce essentially equivalent products. The ability of their salespersons to build a strong relationship with customers is crucial to gaining an advantage over competitors. Salespersons work hard at providing service to customers including expediting orders, troubleshooting problems that arise in customers' plants involving use of cans, and arranging price discounts.

Sales promotion often regains importance during the maturity stage because management is fighting to achieve short-term sales objectives in the face of intense competition. Techniques such as contests, price promotions, and coupons are used to keep customers interested. Advertising reminds customers of benefits and persuades them to buy the company's brand. Publicity is difficult to use in the maturity stage because the product has lost its news value. Only important changes in the product will be interesting to the press.

Decline stage

Promotion in the decline stage depends on the company's corporate and marketing strategies to deal with the severity of competition, the waning interest of customers, and the great difficulty of achieving profits. Decline is actually a key decision stage in which a company determines whether it wants to stay with its product or pull out of the market it is in and move into others. If the decision is to pull out, then promotion is likely to be severely cut back to reduce costs and maintain as much cash coming into the firm as possible. In the meantime, a way to get out is sought.

If the company decides to stay in the market with the product, then promotion is coordinated with the marketing strategy for coping with the situation. One option is to try to innovate by changing the product significantly. If this strategy works, then the life cycle returns to the introductory stage and promotion's role changes accordingly. Another option is to try to build market share as other companies decide to leave the market. Emphasizing low price, services, or a premium image aimed at special market segments are all possible strategies for weathering the decline stage. Promotion will take its direction from the strategy selected, and any of a number of mixes are possible.

SUMMARY

The promotion mix is a company's way of informing, reminding, and persuading people in target audiences. While communication between a company and an audience is a two-way process, our concern is with managing the flow of communications from a company through delivery channels to target audiences. Steps in the process highlight important decisions that managers make to plan and control a promotion mix.

Planning begins when promotion managers select target audiences. For the majority of promotion effort, target markets are the target audiences. Management must also determine what actions promotion should accomplish. Setting either sales-oriented or communications promotion objectives serves this purpose. Hierarchy-of-effects models provide a very useful guide for setting different kinds of objectives, particularly the communications objectives.

Objectives guide the creative development of a message's content and context, as does a market opportunity analysis of target audiences. Many different media alternatives can carry these messages to target audiences, and no one of them is best for all audiences, objectives, and messages. Thus managers select a combination of media that the company can afford, that reach the desired audience, and that enhance the communication capabilities of the message.

Communicating with audiences is expensive. While the primary cost is for the media, there are also costs such as conducting market research, creatively designing messages, and testing messages. Managers develop budgets that help ensure that costs of promotion are in line with benefits. A budget is a plan showing the categories for expenses, and the amount of expenditures approved for each one.

During and after promotion is implemented, it should be evaluated to see if objectives are being accomplished. Measuring the effectiveness of promotion should recognize that the tools can support each other in achieving overall promotion objectives. In fact, the total effectiveness of an entire promotion mix can be more than the sum of the individual effectiveness of each tool.

Planning a promotion mix requires understanding the advantages and disadvantages of the tools of advertising, sales promotion, publicity and public relations, and personal selling. Properly blending these into a promotion mix depends on managers' assessment of each one's (1) costs, (2) ability to target specific audiences, (3) ability to interact with audiences, (4) flexibility in designing content and context, and (5) ability to reach large audiences.

To get the most benefit out of the entire promotion mix, the different tools must be coordinated. The size of a company can influence how this coordination is achieved. Small companies group the promotion activities under the responsibility of one or a very few managers who work closely together. In a large company, the extent of promotion usually requires that the different tools be managed in several departments, which makes coordination difficult. A chief marketing executive, informal interaction by heads of communication departments, and brand managers are some of the ways in which companies achieve coordination.

Finally, promotion managers must be alert to opportunities to adjust the promotion mix over a product's life cycle. The size of the market, the familiarity of customers with the product, the nature and extent of competition, the marketing objectives set for the product, and the familiarity of audiences with a product are all factors that change over time. Promotion must also change to provide the kind of communication needed for the marketing situation.

KEY TERMS

promotion mix	communications channel	message context
target audience	decoding	top-down approach to promotion budgeting
source	noise	
receivers	promotion objectives	bottom-up approach to promotion budgeting
advertising	sales-oriented promotion objectives	
sales promotion		trade show
publicity	communications promotion objectives	public relations
personal selling		telemarketing
push promotion strategy	hierarchy-of-effects models	teleconferencing
pull promotion strategy	AIDA model	
encoding	message content	

QUESTIONS FOR REVIEW AND DISCUSSION

1. What are the different kinds of audiences for a company's promotion?

2. What are the four tools of promotion, and how do they differ from each other?

3. Do all four tools have to be in a promotion mix? Why or why not?

4. How can a communications process be managed?

5. What are the factors in a communications process that can cause a source's message to be ineffective?

6. What are five important questions that arise when the promotion mix is planned?

7. How does the top-down approach to promotion budgeting differ from the bottom-up approach?

8. How does a push promotion strategy differ from a pull promotion strategy?

9. Under what circumstances would a company rely more heavily on advertising than on personal selling in the promotion mix?

10. What advantages do publicity and public relations have compared with advertising?

11. What are the major advantages of sales promotion?

12. Which promotion tool is most costly?

13. What are two developing trends in personal selling?

14. How can a company coordinate its promotion mix?

15. In what ways is a promotion mix likely to differ in the introductory and maturity stages of a product's life cycle?

16. Does the promotion mix need to be changed when moving from an introductory to a growth stage in a product's life cycle?

17. Is promotion unnecessary in the decline stage of a product's life cycle?

BUILDING YOUR PORTFOLIO

Companies that sell the same product use different promotion mixes. You can see this by evaluating promotion of companies in an industry. Choose two companies that sell a consumer product: two manufacturers, two retailers, or a manufacturer and a retailer. For example, you might pick two camera manufacturers such as Kodak and Polaroid, or select Polaroid and a local camera store.

Gather information on the promotion mixes of the two companies. First, see if the companies are in standardized information services such as Dun & Bradstreet, Leading National Advertisers (LNA), Value Line, and Standard & Poor's. If so, you can find out how much each spends on promotion. Then clip or record advertisements for the companies from the mass media (newspapers, magazines, radio, television, billboards, direct mail). Also note whether sales promotion activities are tied in with advertising (coupons, free gifts, contests, stamps, etc.). Go to stores that sell the product and gather information on sales promotion such as special product displays, point-of-purchase signs, cents-off sales, contests or games, and free gifts. See if you can find any publicity news stories in the mass media. Finally, you may even interview store managers to learn about the personal selling activities of each company.

Now evaluate the promotion mixes of the two companies. What similarities do you find? What are the differences? Why do you think these differences exist?

NOTES

1. "How four companies used strategic promotion planning." *Marketing News,* Oct. 30, 1981, p. 13, and "Coke's man on the spot." *Business Week,* July 29, 1985, pp. 56–61.

2. David B. Tinnin, "Porsche's civil war with its dealers." *Fortune,* Apr. 16, 1984, pp. 63, 64, 68.

3. "Community mental health centers must create promotions aimed at prospects and the public." *Marketing News,* Dec. 9, 1983, p. 7.

4. For further discussion of communications models see David A. Aaker and John G. Myers, *Advertising Management.* Englewood Cliffs, N.J.: Prentice-Hall, 1980, pp. 233–236.

5. "Who watches commercials." *Wall Street Journal,* May 20, 1982, p. 1.

6. This incident is reported in David A. Ricks, *Big Business Blunders: Mistakes in Multinational Marketing.* Homewood, Ill.: Dow-Jones Irwin, 1983, p. 56.

7. "Phone company finds direct mail is most efficient seller of service." *Marketing News,* July 22, 1983, p. 18.

8. Robert J. Lavidge and Gary A. Steiner, "A model for predicting measurements for advertising effectiveness." *Journal of Marketing,* Vol. 25 (Oct. 1961), pp. 59–62.

9. "Coke spurns cola wars, opts instead to run a foot race for diet drink sales." *Marketing News,* Oct. 26, 1984, p. 20.

10. Anna F. Ungar, "Creative's 'child' needs relevant research, not report card." *Marketing News,* Sept. 19, 1982, Section 2, p. 8.

11. For a discussion of expense categories for promotion other than personal selling see Charles H. Patti and Vincent Blasko, "Budgeting practices of big advertisers." *Journal of Advertising Research,* Vol. 21 (Dec. 1981), pp. 23–29.

12. "Study tracks housewives buying, information sources." *Marketing News,* Oct. 14, 1983, p. 16.

13. "Study finds 'information overkill'." *Marketing News,* Nov. 11, 1983, p. 7.

14. "How big business is carrying the Olympic torch." *Business Week,* Sept. 26, 1983, p. 96.

15. "How four companies used strategic promotion planning," op. cit.

16. Susan Bachsbaum and Mark K. Metzger, "Show and sell." *INC.,* May 1984, p. 73.

17. William G. Nickels, *Marketing Communications and Promotion.* Columbus, Ohio: Grid, 1976, p. 246.

18. Ibid.

19. Gerald S. Schwartz, "Public relations gets short shrift from new managers." *Marketing News,* Oct. 15, 1982, p. 8.

20. Thayer C. Taylor, "How's this for news? The sales cost barometer declines!" *Sales & Marketing Management,* Feb. 21, 1983, p. 9.

21. Thayer C. Taylor, "Sales call costs in a holding pattern." *Sales & Marketing Management,* Feb. 21, 1983, p. 36.

22. This figure is based on data from Executive Compensation Service as reported in "Rebirth of a salesman: Willy Loman goes electronic." *Business Week,* Feb. 27, 1984, p. 104.

23. Ibid., p. 103.

24. Sara Delano, "Turning sales inside out." *INC.,* Aug. 1983, p. 99.

25. Ibid.

26. Richard L. Bencin, "How to start a business-to-business telemarketing program." *Marketing News,* Mar. 16, 1984, p. 8.

27. "How four companies used strategic promotion planning," op. cit.

28. "Coffee companies pitch to a more discerning drinker." *Business Week,* May 28, 1984, p. 72.

Case 18.1

Goode Memorial Hospital

GOODE MEMORIAL HOSPITAL'S share of patients from its market area, a county in Tennessee, was slowly declining. Patients were choosing hospitals outside the county, and the hospital's administrators were concerned. To keep its prices in line with competition, Goode Memorial must meet marketing objectives concerning the percent of its beds in use (called the bed-occupancy rate).

Marketing research, conducted to find out why market share was declining, uncovered problems with county residents' impressions of the hospital and its services. They believed that the hospital was adequate for minor procedures (tonsillectomies, appendectomies, broken bones, and the like) but was not as equipped to treat serious disorders as other hospitals. Furthermore, the hospital's staff was rated to be not as friendly or concerned with patients' welfare as competing hospitals. Similar impressions were found among the county's business leaders.

Goode Memorial's administrators carefully assessed whether citizens' opinions were based on fact or were misconceptions. When problems were real, action was taken to correct them. For example, meetings were conducted with the staff to discuss and implement ways to improve interactions with patients and others coming to the hospital. A modernization program was also well under way and was expected to be completed soon.

After the necessary changes were made in Goode Memorial's service offering, a comprehensive promotion mix was planned. The research helped identify target audiences, one of which was the entire adult population of the county. Reaching as many citizens as possible with the hospital's message was considered important because friends', neighbors', and relatives' recommendations are primarily how patients choose their physicians and hospital. Another target audience was key managers in large firms with employee health programs.

Specific promotion objectives were set to guide the planning of the promotion mix. These objectives described what administrators wanted audiences to know

and understand about the hospital, and the competitive advantages on which the hospital wanted to establish its image. These objectives were as follows:

- Over the next two years, increase to 90 percent members of the target audiences who are aware of the improvement in specialist care provided by Goode Memorial Hospital

- Over the next two years, increase to 90 percent members of the target audiences who are aware of the improved facilities for all kinds of care, including specialists' care, provided by the hospital's new addition and equipment

- Over the next two years, increase to 75 percent members of the target audiences who rate the friendliness of nurses and technicians as excellent or good

- Over the next two years, increase to 70 percent the members of the target audiences who rate the willingness of Goode Memorial's doctors to explain problems and take an interest in the patient as excellent or good

- Over the next four years, develop awareness among at least 75 percent of target audiences that Goode Memorial is reaching out to the community with new services and programs that extend beyond the primary care of the hospital itself

- Over the next four years, persuade at least 50 percent of the target audiences that Goode Memorial Hospital has an area-wide reputation for quality specialty care in the treatment of at least one major health care problem

- Over the next four years, achieve recognition for at least one treatment area that Goode Memorial Hospital has specialty care superior to that of other hospitals in the area

- Over the next two years, establish a reputation for taking a strong interest in the health-related welfare of citizens in the county

- Over the next four years, continue developing a reputation for offering services out in the county that take advantage of the expertise of the hospital and its staff

- Over the next two years, improve the hospital's reputation for providing high-value treatment for the cost relative to its key competitive hospital

Hospital administrators carefully selected the promotion tools they thought were needed to achieve these objectives. Because of the professional nature of the service offered and the ethical concerns of the hospital's medical staff, advertising was not considered appropriate. Thus the promotion mix was limited to publicity, sales promotion, and personal selling.

The hospital assigned responsibility for publicity to one person who provided information to the local newspapers and television stations for news releases. In addition, the director of publicity arranged speaking engagements for the staff to local social, civic, and business organizations. The topics of the speeches generally concerned newsworthy events and issues in the field of health care (e.g., advancements in medical treatment, rising health care costs, the threat of socialized medicine). Speakers also were able to describe progress and improvements at Goode Memorial Hospital in the course of the talk.

Sales promotion was handled by an assistant administrator and was introduced in a small way. A brochure describing the hospital and its services was planned. The brochure was sent in billings and given to all patients and visitors to the hospital.

Finally, personal selling was planned by the top administrator and was implemented in two ways. Administrators increased calls on business leaders to discuss health care in the community and the hospital's programs for business employees. The staff was instructed to talk with patients and visitors about the programs of the hospital. The intent was to use the current staff to communicate the image and reputation of the hospital by informing people of the improvements in services.

QUESTIONS

1. What are the strengths of the hospital's approach to planning promotion? Do you see any weaknesses?

2. Do you believe that the promotion mix has been adequately coordinated? Why or why not?

3. Can the promotion mix be successful without advertising being included? Why or why not?

4. Has the promotion mix been coordinated with the hospital's marketing strategy?

Case 18.2

United States Army

THE SWITCH TO AN all-volunteer Army in 1973 had an impact, but the changes in the peacetime military extend beyond that. "We're no longer an all-volunteer Army," noted Maj. Ken Martell, chief of information and planning in the Program Analysis and Evaluation Directorate (PAE), U.S. Army Recruiting Command, Ft. Sheridan, Ill.

"Now, we're a regular institution."

If PAE is taken as a microcosm of today's Army, it's virtually impossible to distinguish the Army from the operations of any other large corporation. Just as a private company's marketing research department would be responsible for monitoring sales, analyzing the effects of proposed programs, and recommending marketing changes, PAE is responsible for monitoring recruitment, forecasting the effects of changes in recruitment policy, and recommending changes in those policies.

The Army's current recruitment budget totals $182 million, which underwrites marketing research activity, maintenance of recruiting offices, and a $62 million ad

SOURCE: "Today's Army relying on marketing research to attain recruiting goals," *Marketing News*, July 6, 1984, pp. 1, 16. Reprinted with permission of the American Marketing Association.

budget. That figure is meager when compared to Colgate-Palmolive's $300 million ad budget, Martell said, and it has only increased 62 percent since 1974, compared to a 430 percent increase in Anheuser-Busch's ad spending. But better marketing research is helping the Army get more out of the money it spends.

The Army has to make 780,000 "sales" a year, Martell said. The bulk of those come from soldiers who reenlist or have signed on for an extended hitch. The rest have to come from new recruits, and in fiscal year 1984 PAE is responsible for generating 138,892 contracts with new recruits.

Reaching that quota has proven routine for PAE in recent years. But instead of merely delivering warm bodies, PAE is recruiting soldiers from a variety of demographic groups, including the better educated recruits needed for a modern army.

PAE recommends changes in recruiting policy by spotting variables that can improve performance. For example, a 1981 study showed that the over-21 age group consistently scores higher in mental aptitude tests than younger recruits. Ads which appeal to this age group could improve the quality of recruits.

PAE increasingly is getting involved in Army ad efforts, such as the "Be all you can be" campaign developed by NW Ayer

Inc. There still was an anti-Vietnam backlash working against recruitment efforts when the campaign was developed in 1981, so the Army sought to emphasize adventure and the opportunity to grow while avoiding references to the military.

The campaign appeals to intelligent, highly motivated prospects by emphasizing the high technology career training available in the Army. It ranks as the most recognizable of all military ad campaigns, according to a 1982 survey, and the message appears on highly visible programs, such as a recent National Basketball Association play offs.

With its wealth of data, PAE is in a position to put a finer point on the targeting of Army ads, Martell said. "The current campaign is not as fine-tuned as it could be," he said. "The ad people are trying to segment the market with a meat cleaver.

"Advertising positioning is something we're getting more involved in. If you can find out what issues the individual with a propensity to join the military is interested in, you can emphasize those issues in recruitment ads.

"Although we're recruiting from one age group, we have a demographic field that is wider than the one most national corporations have."

QUESTIONS

1. In what ways should promotion be coordinated with recruitment strategy?

2. Should the entire promotional effort be allocated to advertising? Why or why not?

3. What kinds of promotion objectives are being set by the army?

4. What kinds of information can PAE supply to help improve the effectiveness of the advertising budget? Give examples to illustrate the information you recommend.

19 Advertising, Sales Promotion, and Publicity

When you finish this chapter, you will understand

☐ How advertising can be used to build demand for a company, product type, and brand

☐ The decisions that must be made to plan an advertising campaign

☐ The difference between sales-related objectives for advertising and communications objectives

☐ The advantages and disadvantages of different kinds of advertising media and how managers choose among them

☐ The strengths and weaknesses of alternative approaches to determining the size of an advertising budget

☐ Alternative approaches to testing advertising's effectiveness

☐ The decisions required to manage the sales promotion effort

☐ The decisions required to mange the publicity effort

If you want people to be aware of your product, inflate and fly it, whether "it" be a TV or a taco. Though some call these helium-filled advertising balloons mere novelties, the manufacturers (and many customers) see the balloons as a new, exciting, and legitimate promotional medium.

In 1982, seven persons in the Chicago area died from poisoned Tylenol capsules. Although Johnson & Johnson, the maker of Tylenol, was not at fault, many persons predicted that the brand was doomed because people would be afraid to use it again. One year later, Johnson & Johnson did what many said it could not do—brought Tylenol back from the brink of disaster.

At the heart of Johnson & Johnson's marketing strategy was strong consumer trust in the company. For years, management had meticulously built a widely accepted corporate reputation for quality health care products. Marketing research conducted shortly after the poisoning incident demonstrated that the public's trust in Tylenol was not destroyed by the tragedy.

New advertising was quickly prepared and tested. It emphasized three points: (1) tampering with the capsules was done outside the factory, (2) the incident was limited to the Chicago area, and (3) the company would replace all Tylenol capsules in consumers' possession. The advertisements tested well.

In the meantime, Johnson & Johnson developed new tamper-proof packaging.

Tylenol was temporarily withdrawn from the market and prepared for relaunching. Advertising was changed again. The new advertisements presented testimonials of people saying they did not blame the company for the poisonings, and they held the company in high regard. Coupons offering $2.50 off the purchase price were inserted into newspapers across the country. Management was pleased to see millions of these coupons redeemed as people purchased Tylenol again. The relaunching of Tylenol was a phenomenal success.[1]

WHEN SEVEN PERSONS DIED FROM contaminated Tylenol, instantaneously negative publicity was created for Johnson & Johnson nationwide. Management must have wondered whether consumers would ever trust Tylenol again. Yet, the company's reaction was swift and professional. First the company made sure that its facilities were not the source of the contamination. Then management turned to the task of restoring the public's confidence in its products.

Although effective promotion cannot take all the credit for the company's resurgence, it played a strong role. Management needed to communicate quickly with millions of persons across the United States. The company released information to the press as it tested plant facilities for possible sources of contamination and later as it developed tamper-proof packaging. Publicity was supported by the two advertising campaigns reinforcing the public's trust in Johnson & Johnson and Tylenol. As the publicity and advertising began to work, sales promotion was phased in to provide consumers with immediate incentive to buy Tylenol.

This chapter examines the marketing decisions that underlie effective use of advertising, sales promotion, and publicity. The perspective on promotion decision making developed in Chapter 18 is applied to managing these three promotion tools. In the first section, the entire process of planning an advertising campaign is reviewed, including the major decisions faced by managers. The next three sections examine in depth each of these decisions. Then sales promotion decisions are discussed, and their similarities and differences with advertising decisions are emphasized. Finally, decisions required for managing the publicity function are introduced.

PLANNING AN ADVERTISING CAMPAIGN

Types of advertising

You may recall from Chapter 18 that *advertising* is a paid form of nonpersonal communication that is usually carried by the mass media but can also be delivered through direct mail; receivers clearly understand that the message is coming directly from the source. There are three major types of advertising: (1) institutional advertising, which communicates about the organization as a whole; (2) product type advertising, which promotes a product type sold by an organization; and (3) brand advertising, which promotes a particular brand of the organization.

Institutional advertising (corporate advertising) promotes the image or reputation of an organization or an entire industry. Its purpose is not to sell products but to build a favorable relationship with various audiences including the general public, investors, and advocacy groups. Some institutional advertising is informative, describing a company's purpose, strengths, and philosophy of business. Other institutional advertising advocates a point of view held by the company's top management. Getty Corporation has used institutional advertising to explain the importance of free enterprise in an economic system, stressing the right of individuals to take risks if they choose to do so.

An advantage of institutional advertising is that it can develop a positive image in the minds of audience members, which can be a factor in obtaining desired behaviors such as buying the company's product and investing in the company. Thus institutional advertising is similar to an investment: The return is persons' making favorable decisions regarding the company as a result of its positive image. An executive at Compton Advertising, the agency that helped Johnson & Johnson recover from the Tylenol poisoning incident, commented on the value of institutional advertising.

> If a product or service has serious intent, the company should not be afraid to devote part of its effort to corporate image advertising that reinforces the trustworthiness of the company and its products. The reservoir of good will in the consumer population for Johnson & Johnson as a company was responsible in large part for the speed of the recovery. A campaign which focuses consumer trust in a human, involving way can be very beneficial to a company.[2]

Product type advertising helps build customer demand for a particular product type. It is important when target markets must be convinced

Corporate advertising has diverse audiences including individual investors, portfolio managers, customers, legislators, and employees. Generally, it tells what the company makes, how the company is doing, and something about the company's philosophy. Its objective is usually to enhance favorable awareness of the firm. To the degree that this is accomplished, the company or organization finds it easier to carry out its various activities, from marketing its products and services to raising money. (*Left*, courtesy of Lord, Geller, Federico, Einstein, Inc., copywriter Arthur W. Einstein, Jr., art director Richard Thomas, artist Roy McKie; *below*, courtesy of InterNorth)

The best way to im prove the post office is to build a new one.

Regarded as a desirable alternative to the sometimes slow U.S. Postal Service, the electronic mail business grossed $1.5 billion in 1983. MCI Mail has been spending heavily to develop, advertise, and promote its electronic mail service. In this ad, MCI compares (literally positions) its electronic mail service with the U.S. Postal Service. (Courtesy of MCI Mail)

that a product type is superior to other product types used for the same purpose. Cable television companies are using this kind of advertising to sell their data communications, teleconferencing, and teletext services to industrial firms. Top managers of many potential customer companies do not like the idea of their executives watching television in the office.[3] Cable television companies' advertising demonstrates the benefits of cable television services (a product type) and tries to convince executives of its practicality. Then a cable company can begin to sell its services.

Advertising aimed at building and maintaining demand for a particular brand is called **brand advertising.** It informs and reminds the target audience of the company's brand and helps persuade them to buy. Most brand advertising makes promises about the benefits of using a company's brand without mentioning the competition. Some companies directly compare their brands with those of competitors, which is called **comparative advertising.** Burger King successfully used this approach in the "Battle of the burgers" campaign to favorably compare its larger broiled hamburger with McDonald's fried product.[4]

Role of advertising

Underlying all advertising decisions is the role that management wants advertising to play in the promotion mix. Advertising's role is determined by how much weight is given to advertising relative to the other promotion tools. This role varies dramatically from company to company because of the tremendous differences in their environments. One company may have millions of customers, while another has only a few large customers. Buyers in one market may depend heavily on advertising as a source of product information; buyers in another market may not. One company's competition may use advertising extensively, while another company's competition may rely more on other promotion tools.

Exhibit 19.1 shows a list of the top ten advertisers in the United States. All these companies are manufacturers of consumer products with large and widely dispersed markets. Companies that must reach many different buyers at a low cost per audience member give considerable weight to advertising. It is also interesting to note that the top ten advertisers are all large companies with high sales volumes and market shares. Advertising's role also depends on what a company can afford.

Companies whose markets are primarily industrial, such as packaging, chemical, and steel companies, assign less weight to advertising than do many consumer-goods companies. Industrial-products companies have fewer customers, each one of which buys in large volume. Advertising's chief advantage of reaching large audiences economically is not as attractive in this situation. Most industrial-products firms rely heavily on promotion tools other than advertising. One survey of nearly 500 industrial-products firms showed that less than 7 percent spent more than $1 million on advertising, while almost half spent less than $100,000.[5] When advertising plays a small role, more weight is assigned to the other promotion tools because the communications task is important for both consumer- and industrial-products companies.

Exhibit 19.1   The top ten advertisers in the United States in 1983 (millions of dollars)

Procter & Gamble	$773,618.3
Sears	732,500.0
Beatrice	602,775.4
General Motors	595,129.5
R. J. Reynolds	593,350.3
Philip Morris	527,481.8
Ford	479,060.0
AT&T	463,095.5
K mart	400,000.0
General Foods	386,134.2

SOURCE: *Advertising Age*, Sept. 14, 1984, p. 1.

Advertising decisions

In Chapter 18, we discussed important decisions faced by managers who are planning an entire promotion mix. Not surprisingly, similar decisions are needed to plan for advertising. These decisions are shown in Exhibit 19.2. We now turn to examining each one.

SELECTING TARGET AUDIENCES AND SETTING ADVERTISING OBJECTIVES

Although any of the audiences selected for a promotion mix can be targets for advertising, most advertising is aimed at either a company's trade or its target markets. Thus the target audiences for advertising are usually dic-

Now last minute presentations can be made from your personal computer. In color. In house. In minutes.

Introducing Polaroid Palette.

Polaroid Corporation's ad for its Polaroid Palette was the 1984 winner of the Sawyer Award, which recognizes excellence in industrial advertising. This is regarded as an effective industrial ad because (1) the headline clearly and succinctly tells the Palette's benefit story in just seventeen words; (2) the picture, too, makes an unmistakable benefit statement; (3) the copy is flawless—it goes right to the point and is written much like the way one person would tell a friend about a good thing; (4) three bold subheadings answer questions likely to be the first a reader would ask; (5) the interested reader can't help noticing the large toll-free number and the coupon. (Reprinted courtesy of Polaroid Corporation and Doyle Dane Bernbach Advertising, Inc.)

tated by the overall marketing strategy of the company. A market opportunity analysis (MOA), which identifies target markets, plays an important part in advertising decisions at this step (see Chapter 4). Advertising managers must learn about these audiences, and then determine what advertising should accomplish.

Advertisers study audiences

Many of the ideas discussed in Chapters 4, 5, and 6 concerning analyzing market opportunity and the nature of buyer behavior are applied early in advertising planning. Two kinds of information are particularly important: descriptions of types of people in audiences and in-depth profiles of their behavioral makeup.

Describing people in target audiences relies heavily on discovering their demographic, socioeconomic, and life-style characteristics. Rather than getting to know each individual personally (usually impossible because audiences are so large), these characteristics help advertisers form a picture of what audience members have in common with each other. Understanding these similarities guides later decisions on messages and media. For instance, Dr Pepper recently expanded audiences for its advertising to include persons 25 to 34 years old. Previously, the audience had been limited to persons 12 to 24 years old, a very young target market. Persons 25 to 34 years old have a different life-style than persons in the younger group because they are developing families and careers at this stage in life. Noticeable changes in Dr Pepper's advertising have resulted, as illustrated by use of older actors in advertising scenes.[6]

Understanding who is in audiences is only a start. Advertising decision makers also want to know what interests and excites people in audiences. Information on a variety of factors—needs and wants, situations in which the product is used, benefits most desired, past purchases, and satisfaction with brands—form audience profiles that help managers understand what will and will not appeal to target audiences. Marketing research for Dr Pepper found out that price is an important consideration in soft drink purchase decisions. Managers also learned that less than 8 percent of soft drink users buy Dr Pepper on a regular basis, and that far fewer consumers had tried the brand than had tried the leading competitors. Thus advertising, through themes emphasizing price specials and out-of-the-ordinary taste, has been aimed at getting people to try Dr Pepper.[7]

Types of advertising objectives

Advertising objectives are statements of what advertising managers expect advertising to accomplish. Differences of opinion exist among advertisers as to exactly what kinds of objectives to set. One school of thought strongly supports using advertising to achieve sales-related objectives. Another is more interested in achieving communications objectives.

Sales-related objectives. Advertising objectives that direct advertising toward increasing sales or market share are *sales-related objectives*. Advocates of this point of view want advertising's performance tied directly to overall marketing strategy and corporate objectives. Sales-related advertising objectives have three drawbacks. First, managers should not expect advertising to

Exhibit 19.2 Steps in planning advertising

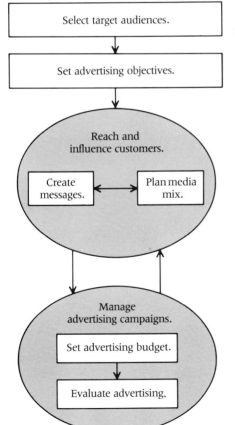

shoulder the load of increasing sales (or market share) by itself because so many other factors can also influence sales (see Exhibit 19.3). By itself, a sales-related objective is difficult to put into practice because managers are seldom sure how much advertising can really improve sales during a given period of time.

Second, sales-related objectives are usually short-run and cover a year or less. They are geared to the operating or planning period of a company. Yet, advertising can have a long-run impact on sales of a company's products. Advertising may spark customers' interest in a product, and they may buy two or more years after the advertising is run. This delay or lag is well known at American Motors. Advertising for its four-wheel-drive Jeep is aimed at encouraging former buyers to buy again and building favorable images among future buyers. To evaluate the success of these advertisements in terms of sales in the year in which they were run overlooks these long-term effects.[8]

Third, sales-related objectives provide little, if any, guidance on how to get sales. Suppose management expects advertising to increase sales by 10 percent in one year. This objective will not help advertising personnel decide which messages are best or select appropriate media to carry these messages. Sales-related objectives are not useful guidelines for any of the subsequent advertising decisions in the planning process.

Communications objectives. Everyone agrees that advertising should contribute to generating sales. However, many companies use *communications objectives* in addition to or in lieu of sales-related objectives. These objectives are based on a simple idea: The purpose of advertising is to communicate with audiences. Hierarchy-of-effects models discussed in Chapter 18 provide guidelines to help managers determine the types of communications tasks to try to achieve with audiences.

- Gain awareness for a product or company
- Build knowledge among the audience about the product or company

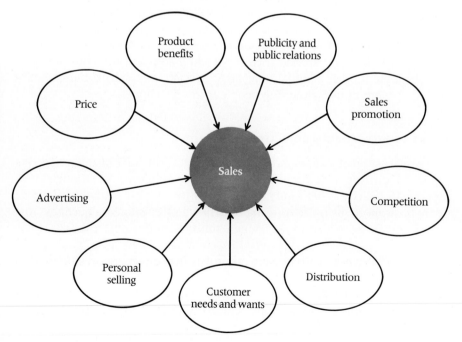

Exhibit 19.3 Advertising is one of many factors influencing sales

The Jeep CJ is part truck and part car; it is meant for hauling and off-road driving but is also found parked in the driveways of status-conscious Southampton, New York, and in the lots of glittering Los Angeles restaurants. (Courtesy of American Motors Corporation)

- Develop favorable attitudes (liking) toward the product or company
- Encourage preference for the product or company over its competitors
- Develop conviction that the company's product should be purchased

Communications objectives are derived from overall marketing objectives. Factors such as the newness of the product, the audience's knowledge of the company and its products, complexity of the product for the audience, and a host of others considered by managers when planning marketing strategy also help determine what advertising should accomplish. You can see these factors at play in the following situations and the resulting objectives:

> Waltec Industries, a Canadian manufacturer of faucets, developed a marketing plan to introduce a new washerless faucet into consumer do-it-yourself markets. Marketing research on the target market showed that less than 3% were aware of Waltec or its plumbing line. The company turned to consumer advertising on television networks, particularly during sports programs, to build the needed awareness. Later research showed that the advertisements successfully increased awareness by a factor of three during the year.[9]

> Marine Midland Bank, the 13th largest bank in the U.S., developed an advertising campaign to support the introduction of a new in-store banking service. Television advertisements were used to show how customers could use a card called the CashCard to access their checking and savings accounts from automated teller machines in supermarkets. An advertising objective was to make people aware of the service and to help them see how convenient and simple it is to use.[10]

Although both companies were introducing new products, their communications tasks differed. Waltec Industries was not well known in its target markets, so advertising was aimed at helping do-it-yourselfers get to know the company and its product line. The faucet product itself was simple enough for people to understand. In contrast, the public is very much aware of Marine Midland Bank, but the new service was difficult to understand. Thus communications objectives were aimed at building understanding of the service and how it works.

For communications objectives to be worthwhile, they must support sales-related objectives set by the marketing plan. According to the hierarchy-of-effects models, advertising that encourages target audiences to move along in the steps, from awareness to conviction, is doing just that. In practice, however, the link between communication and sales is not always clear. Managers may never know to what extent sales can be attributed to the communications task of advertising. And there is the nagging doubt that, as a senior vice-president for J. Walter Thompson (a large advertising agency) puts it: "Many people buy a product in spite of its advertising, not because of it." Uncertainty of the relationship between communication and sales explains why the controversy over whether to set sales-related or communications objectives continues.

REACHING AND INFLUENCING AUDIENCES

Achieving advertising objectives takes careful planning. The proper media mix must be selected and effective messages created. These decisions are related because media can enhance (or detract from) the ability of a creative communication to influence audiences. At the same time, media that are practical for a company to use may limit the kinds of creative appeals that can be made.

Advertising's media decisions

A relatively few classes of media are available to deliver advertising messages: television, radio, magazines, newspapers, outdoor billboards and signs, and direct mail. Exhibit 19.4 shows how much was spent on each class of media in the United States in 1983. Direct mail, television, and newspapers are the most-used media by a wide margin.

Exhibit 19.5 shows how the top ten U.S. advertisers for 1983 split their media dollars between eight classes of media. Notice that the percentages are different for these companies even though all sell consumer products or services to huge markets. This fact illustrates an important point: Companies choose a combination of media, called a **media mix**, to deliver their

Exhibit 19.4 Spending on classes of advertising media in the United States in 1983

Media Class	Expenditure (millions of dollars)	Expenditure (%)
Newspapers	$20,135	27
Magazines	4,210	6
Form publications	155	.2
Television	16,090	21
Radio	5,230	7
Direct mail	11,765	16
Business publications	1,876	2
Outdoor	805	1
Miscellaneous	14,794	20
Total	75,060	100

SOURCE: Estimates by *Advertising Age*, Jan. 2, 1984, p. 31.

Exhibit 19.5 How the top ten U.S. advertisers for 1983 allocated their media expenditures among five media

Company	Percent of Advertising Media Spending on*							
	Newspapers	Magazines	Farm Publications	Spot TV	Network TV	Spot Radio	Network Radio	Outdoor
Procter & Gamble	2	6	0	35	56	0.4	0.2	0.03
Sears	0	15	0	13	65	2	5	0.1
Beatrice	8	23	0.01	21	44	2	0.2	2
General Motors	20	20	0.4	6	45	6	2	0.9
R. J. Reynolds	24	33	0	8	15	0.8	0	19
Philip Morris	14	30	0	11	28	5	0	12
Ford	14	22	0.9	10	47	4	2	0.5
AT&T	20	17	0	12	41	8	3	0.1
K mart	0	22	0	20	47	10	0	0.4
General Foods	36	12	0	26	60	0.8	0.6	0.02

SOURCE: Derived from data in *Advertising Age*, Sept. 14, 1984, pp. 16–17.
* *Advertising Age* provides data on media expenditures for companies only on measured advertising expenditures, a figure that is less than total advertising expenditures. Thus percentage media allocations derived from these data are only approximate indicators of actual allocations, and at least in one case (K mart) they are quite inaccurate.

In the tough battle to be heard by consumers, some advertisers are returning to previously successful symbols. Proctor & Gamble has resuscitated Mr. Clean, the genie on its household cleaner of the same name, and Switzer Clark recently brought the character of Choo Choo Charlie back to life in ads for Good & Plenty Candy. Not all comebacks are successful, though. Miles Laboratories, Inc. has failed in its attempts to revive Speedy, the little character who appeared in more than 200 magazine ads for Alka-Seltzer between 1952 and 1964. (Courtesy of Miles Corporate Archives)

advertising messages. No one medium is best, but each has advantages and disadvantages when compared with the others. By using a mix of media, a company can gain additional advantages from the combination as well as counteract the disadvantages of any one medium.

Exhibit 19.6 summarizes some of the important advantages and disadvantages of each medium. Take a minute to review the differences between the media before reading further; this will help you better appreciate the task of choosing a media mix. Many of these differences affect the capability of the media to deliver messages effectively. For instance, the audiovisual capabilities of television are important for demonstrating how a product works in a use situation, which a newspaper advertisement cannot do as well. Other differences concern the cost and advertisement production tasks required to use these media.

Media mix decisions are far more complicated than simply allocating dollars between these six media classes. There are a wide variety of alternative **media vehicles** within each class. Hundreds of magazines, thousands of newspapers, dozens of major network television shows, hundreds of local television and radio programs, countless locations of billboards and signs, and hundreds of mailing lists for direct mail are available to a company. The media planner must examine these many vehicles to see which ones can best reach advertising's target audiences. Importantly, planners seek media vehicles that have the capabilities needed to enhance the communication ability of the message. Of course, costs of using each alternative must be considered.

Selecting the proper media mix

Most marketing professionals agree that selecting the best media mix is an art rather than a science. No one can be sure whether a particular mix is optimal. However, several criteria guide media planners, including: (1) audiences delivered by media vehicles, (2) media capabilities needed for a

Exhibit 19.6 Selected advantages and disadvantages of advertising media classes

Media	Advantages	Disadvantages
Television	Reaches large audiences Visual and audio capabilities Maximum flexibility for gaining attention Short lead time to place ad	Not easy to target selected audiences Relatively expensive Requires production specialists Short exposure time
Magazine	Reaches demographic and geographic segments High-quality reproduction Ad lasts as long as magazine is kept and read Magazine read by more than one person Ad benefits from magazine's credibility	Must place ad well in advance of publication Limited flexibility to gain attention No complete control of location of ad in magazine
Outdoor	Relatively inexpensive Many repeat exposures for one insertion	Only a very limited message is possible Cannot segment audience Very short exposure time
Radio	Audio capabilities Relatively low cost Short lead time to place ad Segments audiences demographically and geographically Reaches large audiences	No visual capabilities Short exposure time Little flexibility to gain attention
Newspaper	Reaches large audience Segments audiences by locale Short lead time to place ad Credibility of newspaper can benefit ad	May be expensive Little flexibility for creative messages Limited reproduction quality (e.g., use of color) Short life of newspaper carries over to ad
Direct mail	Flexibility in segmenting audiences No clutter from competing ads Easily personalized message and layout	Easily thrown away as "junk mail" Obtaining mailing lists can be expensive

Exhibit 19.7 Audiences of three magazines show differences in characteristics

Audience Characteristics	Percent of Readers		
	Sports Illustrated	New Yorker	Ladies' Home Journal
Gender			
Male	80.5	52.4	11.3
Female	19.5	47.6	88.7
Age			
18–24	28.4	16.3	13.6
25–34	30.4	29.1	23.8
35–44	17.2	17.1	17.3
45–54	12.3	13.7	16.1
Education			
College graduate	22.4	51.4	16.8
Attended college	24.8	25.0	19.8
High school graduate	40.1	18.6	44.7
Attended high school	9.6	3.2	11.9
Place of reading			
In the home	66.5	48.4	70.4
At work	12.0	17.0	6.0
While traveling	0.7	3.8	0.3
Elsewhere	23.5	32.6	25.2
Employment			
Full-time	67.9	61.6	44.1
Part-time	8.9	11.1	11.8
Not employed	23.2	27.2	44.1
Marital status			
Married	59.2	54.8	68.2
Single	32.6	31.1	14.2
Other	8.2	14.1	17.6
Number in household			
1	7.7	17.0	10.7
2	22.8	34.9	32.3
3 or 4	47.0	37.7	41.0

SOURCE: *The 1982 Study of Media and Markets*, Vol. M-1, Publications: Total Audiences, Simmons Market

message, (3) timing desired for advertisements, and (4) costs of alternative vehicles.

Media audiences. Each media vehicle reaches a different audience, so media planners select the vehicles with audiences that best match the company's target audiences. Fortunately, media vehicles do market research to find out what types of people are in their audiences. Furthermore, media research services, such as Simmon's *Study of Media and Markets,* can be purchased to provide similar data on many media alternatives. Media planners use this information to look for vehicles having the highest overlap with advertising's target audiences.

Look at the information in Exhibit 19.7. It compares the characteristics of people who read *Sports Illustrated, New Yorker,* and *Ladies' Home Journal.* Media planners typically use this kind of information, largely demographics, to find media having a high percentage of target audience members in their audiences. A company selling a product, such as deodorant, primarily to well-educated men, might choose *Sports Illustrated* as part of its media mix because of its high percentage of well-educated male readers. Notice also how much media audiences can differ from each other. You can easily see that *Ladies' Home Journal* reaches very different kinds of people than does *Sports Illustrated.*

Audience Characteristics	Percent of Readers		
	Sports Illustrated	New Yorker	Ladies' Home Journal
Number in household (cont.)			
5 or more	22.5	10.5	16.0
Number of children under 18			
1	24.4	17.9	17.0
2	19.7	14.6	16.7
3	6.1	3.1	7.7
4	3.1	0.8	1.1
Presence of children by age			
Under 18	54.3	36.8	43.5
Under 2	10.3	6.4	7.7
2–5	15.3	9.3	16.7
6–11	21.5	16.4	19.2
Type of dwelling			
Single-family	78.5	65.5	80.7
Two-family	6.5	9.1	4.9
Three-family or more	14.9	25.5	14.5
Occupation			
Professional/technical	15.6	25.7	12.4
Manager/administrator	12.5	20.1	6.4
Clerical/sales	15.6	15.4	20.1
Crafts/foreman	13.9	2.8	2.1
Race			
White	82.4	92.9	90.2
Black	14.8	4.6	7.9
Other	2.8	2.5	1.9
Census region			
Northeast	23.2	38.8	22.9
North central	26.3	20.3	29.9
South	30.9	21.2	26.8
West	19.6	19.7	20.4

Research Bureau, 1982.

Because media audiences are so frequently described using demographic characteristics—age, gender, income, education, and the like—companies are encouraged to describe their target audiences with these same characteristics. As illustrated in Chapters 4, 5, and 6, companies are making great strides in profiling their target markets with many more descriptive characteristics (life-style, attitudes, family buying roles, and others). Thus media selection decisions will improve as media audience information expands to provide more encompassing detail on vehicles' audiences (see Marketech for an illustration).

Enhancing messages. A properly selected media vehicle can increase the impact of an advertisement. Thus media managers look at characteristics of each medium that can add to the communication power of the message. One characteristic is the media vehicle's editorial content. The mood and

MarkeTECH

Audience research helps advertisers evaluate TV program quality

THE INCREASINGLY fragmented U.S. television audience is eroding the preeminence of measurements that only disclose the age, sex, and numbers of viewers of a program.

Programmers and advertisers are demanding research about program quality, and several companies are devising ways to provide it.

One alternative to the meter systems of Nielsen and Arbitron is the Voxbox, developed by R. D. Percy & Co., Seattle. The Voxbox combines a TV remote-control device with nine buttons which allow viewers to register favor or disgust with both commercials and programs they view.

Besides tracking who is watching a show, the system tracks "loyalty" and "stability" of the audience, including how many loyal viewers a show has, whether that number is growing, and how they feel about what they are watching.

Viewers respond to the program by pressing Voxbox buttons marked "excellent," "informative," "credible," "funny,"

SOURCE: Kevin Higgins, "Audience research services provide assessments of TV program quality," *Marketing News*, Jan. 22, 1982, Section 1, pp. 3, 6. Reprinted with permission of the American Marketing Association.

"dumb," "boring," "unbelievable," or "zap," which blots out the offensive segment.

The ninth button, marked "person," lets viewers react positively or negatively to the person on the screen.

Continuous monitoring of what is being watched and reactions to those shows is provided by Voxbox. Since channel switching is monitored, the loyalty of a program's audience becomes a factor in the evaluation of a commercial's effectiveness.

Another group trying to interject program quality information into TV rating is Television Audience Assessment Inc. (TAA), a nonprofit organization based in Cambridge, Mass. TAA's mission straddles the programming and commercial concerns of television. It was established partly to encourage greater program diversity and also to show program decision makers how information about quality can supplement traditional program ratings for cable and broadcast TV.

The introduction of new technologies and increasing advertiser sophistication are driving the development of such research, said Peter Lemieux, associate director of research for TAA. "The sophistication of advertisers has grown

dramatically," he said, "and big money is at stake."

How much attention the viewer gives a show directly relates to the impact of the commercials shown, TAA has found. For example, the organization has found that 69% of viewers who give a show "all" their attention remain in the room for all the commercials. By comparison, only 51% of viewers who gave "hardly any" of their attention remained in the room for the commercials.

Unanimity does not exist on the value of buying time on highly involving shows like . . . "Hill Street Blues," Lemieux concedes. Some advertisers only are concerned with buying numbers. Nonetheless, he believes there is intrinsic sales value in being associated with a quality program.

"Positive feelings about the program can translate into positive feelings about the advertiser," he said. "Being involved in quality programs rubs off on the advertiser."

As audiences become more fragmented through increased program offerings, Lemieux believes information about program quality will become more important to advertisers.

Considering the widespread popularity of exercising, a magazine ad showing an exhausted, perspiring jogger is an effective media vehicle for Gatorade. (Copyright Quaker Oats Co. 1984)

frame of mind created by the content should support, not detract from, the message in an advertisement. A television sports program may be an excellent medium for a Gatorade advertisement because the sports programming emphasizes the most important use of the product—to replenish vital nutrients after hard exercising. The same sports program is not the best choice for a commuter bus service because viewers, while watching a game, probably do not want to think about going to work.

Another characteristic is the capability of a media vehicle to present the message. The experienced media planner looks for technical factors such as use of sound, ability to reproduce colors, visual representations, and quality of advertisement reproductions to compare media vehicles. Television may be the proper choice for a product demonstration because it uses both sight and sound. In contrast, television may not be the best choice to list information about the stores in which the product can be purchased. That could best be done in a newspaper. Media planners rely heavily on experience to make these judgments.

Timing of advertisements. Media planners also consider timing of advertising messages. *Timing* concerns when and how often audiences are exposed to advertisements. As a general rule, an advertiser wants advertisements to reach buyers close to the time when they are making buying decisions.

Advertising managers have developed different types of schedules to coincide with various patterns of buying behavior. A *continuous schedule* runs advertising nonstop throughout a time period such as a year. Advertising might be scheduled evenly or be "pulsed" by having high frequency or bursts of heavy advertising during selected periods and low frequency the rest of the time. Pulsing can be timed to correspond with specific seasons or special events during the year. Automobile manufacturers have bursts of advertising during the fall when next year's models are introduced. Its For Levi, a chain of casual clothing stores, uses advertising pulses during the back-to-school season. And jewelry retailers advertise heavily during the Christmas season.

The alternative to a continuous schedule is an *intermittent schedule*—advertising is concentrated during predetermined periods. No advertising, sometimes called *flighting,* is run during the other times. Christmas trees and specially designed toys, for instance, are only advertised during the Christmas season.

Another aspect of timing concerns *frequency of exposures,* which is the number of times that the same advertisement reaches the target audience. Frequency is important because, up to a point, repetition of an advertisement increases the likelihood that a greater number of the target audience will see the advertisement. Repetition also helps people learn what the message has to say. Of course, too many repetitions simply duplicate previous exposures and may irritate people in audiences.

Media decisions also consider that vehicles have their own schedules: the television soap opera "Days of Our Lives" airs five days a week, *The New York Times* is published daily, the Miss America Contest is shown once a year, *Fortune* magazine is available every two weeks. A media mix coordinates the schedules of media vehicles with the desired advertising schedule. An income tax service such as H & R Block, with most of its business

Exhibit 19.8 Costs of running an advertisement in selected media

Media Vehicle	Rate
Network television (30-second prime time ad on CBS)	$295,000
Local spot television (30-second prime time ad in Knoxville)	1,200
Newspaper (full-page color ad in *New York Daily News*)	28,500
Newspaper (full-page, one-color ad in *Knoxville Journal*)	2,263
National magazine (one-page, one-color ad in *Time*)	81,590
Regional magazine (one-page, one-color ad in *Manhattan, inc.*)	4,875

SOURCE: *Standard Rate and Data Service,* Vol. 66, No. 11 (Newspaper Rates and Data, Consumer Magazine and Agri-Media Rates and Data, Spot Television Rates and Data), 1984.

coming during the spring tax season, does not advertise during baseball's World Series because it is televised in October.

Role of cost. Media fees vary widely, yet media planners have to decide which are the best buys (see Exhibit 19.8 for costs of several media vehicles). A common way to compare media vehicles is to use a **cost-per-thousand criterion** by computing the cost of reaching one thousand persons in a vehicle's audience. Suppose *Time* magazine charges $81,590 to run a full-page advertisement and has an audience of 4,600,000 persons. Its cost-per-thousand is $17.74 ($81,590/4,600,000 × 1000). This figure can be compared with cost-per-thousand figures for other vehicles with similar audiences to see which vehicles are the most economical.

The cost-per-thousand criterion is helpful but it is not a sufficient basis for choosing media. Unless other factors are considered as well, comparisons of vehicles can be misleading. One particularly important consideration is how many persons in the audience will actually read or listen to each advertisement. Some media are better at getting readership from its audience than others. Persons who read a hobby magazine such as *Golf Digest* are more likely to read the publication's advertisements than are readers of a news magazine such as *Time*. Audience makeup, technical media capabilities, and media schedules also must be weighed with cost. Thus cost per thousand is only one of several criteria that must be examined when a media mix is selected.

Computer models and media planning. The great number of vehicle alternatives in combination with so many factors to consider can make selecting a media mix seem overwhelming. Some advertising agencies and companies use computer models that assist in making many comparisons among the media vehicle alternatives.[11] Their main advantage is that the computer can compare alternative media vehicles using several criteria at the same time with great speed. The models can evaluate factors considered important such as cost, audience characteristics, and overlap among media audiences. The computer produces a list of media vehicles and a schedule of advertisement insertions in these vehicles. The models do not replace managerial judgment, however. Media planners can scan the computer-generated media mix and make changes based on experience.

Creating effective messages

Marketing managers spend much of their planning time defining market targets, developing strategies for positioning brands against the competition, and figuring out which product benefits to promise to customers. Translating product positions and benefits into effective advertising messages is often left to creative specialists.

Many managers believe that more attention needs to be paid to the creative development of advertising messages. If creative approaches are not successful, it does not matter how good the advertising strategy is. Yet evidence suggests that creative efforts in advertising are not all they should be. One source estimates that 85 percent of magazine readers and 75 percent of television viewers cannot recall an advertisement the day after they have seen it.[12] Advertising managers are responding positively to the situation.

> In corporate advertising offices all over the country, alarm bells are going off. The public has become so bored with television commercials that a growing percentage of consumers are successfully tuning them out. Advertisers, seeking to distinguish their messages from the general clutter, are searching for ways to make the viewer sit up and take notice. Along with such high-tech attention-getters as computer-generated graphics and slick special effects, advertisers are using humor and emotion to create more impact.[13]

Managing creativity. Creativity is not a well-understood process, and it is difficult to manage formally. However, there are several ways to get the most from the creative effort. First, inform creative specialists about the brand's major benefits when compared with the competition. Second, ensure that they understand the "flesh and blood" persons who are in the target audience. Marketing managers are responsible for providing MOA information on target audiences to creative designers. We can see this knowledge of markets being applied in FTD florist advertising. Buyers of floral arrangements use flowers to express their feelings for each other on special occasions such as Mother's Day, birthdays, hospital stays, or anniversaries. They want to be thought of as caring people.[14] Advertisements cater to this want by cleverly illustrating how flowers can help express these personal feelings.

Third, examine examples from past advertising that has been successful. Analyzing creative techniques that have worked well in the past yields useful clues to what will work well in the future. Exhibit 19.9 shows several

In the past, FTD and its competition have created ads and commercials that, though nice, look very similar. FTD's new ad campaign, which features sports celebrity and actor Merlin Olsen, represents a shift in strategy that resulted from insights the company gained from market analysis. Part of this new strategy is to convince consumers that they will be regarded as warm, caring people who demand the highest quality if they specify FTD. (Courtesy of Florists' Transworld Delivery Association)

"Turn the blues and blahs into ooohs and ahhhs." Know someone who's having one of those days? Send them the new Pick-Me-Up® Bouquet from your FTD Florist. Cheerful flowers in a coffee mug and a reusable tote bag. It's a sure cure for the blues.

Merlin Olsen

Lift someone's spirits with special care.™

FTD and the Mercury emblem are registered trademarks of Florists' Transworld Delivery Association.

Exhibit 19.9   Successful techniques for creative advertising appeals

Showing a problem solution

Using humor (if it is relevant to the message)

Developing relevant characters or personalities to associate with the product

Portraying a "slice of life" situation in which a person who originally doubted the product becomes a believer

Providing news about the product such as new uses

Showing candidly made testimonials

Demonstrating how a product works or is used

SOURCE: Adapted from findings of Mapes & Ross as reported in David Ogilvy and Joel Raphaelson, "Research on ad techniques that work—and don't work," *Marketing News*, Sept. 17, 1982.

*Marke*TALK ///

When politicians pitch a product

LAST YEAR GERALDINE Ferraro was trying to sell herself to the American people and making history.

This year she's selling Diet Pepsi and making money.

Is nothing sacred?

No.

Although the country's first woman candidate for vice president has everybody from feminists to Madison avenue hucksters debating her decision to hawk a soft drink, it should be noted that the lady does not hawk alone.

Former Senate Majority Leader Howard Baker is pitching USA Today, and former White House economic adviser Alan Greenspan is pushing Apple Computers.

Former Sen. Sam Ervin, who headed the Senate Watergate investigation, was featured in a 1976 American Express credit card ad ("Do you know me?"), as was William E. Miller, the Republican vice presidential candidate who ran with Barry Goldwater in 1964. Ervin also did an ad for National Home Life Assurance Co. of Valley Forge, Pa., talking up a policy that covered people to age 80.

SOURCE: Susan Trausch, "When politicians pitch a product," *Boston Globe,* Feb. 28, 1985, pp. 61–62. Reprinted courtesy of *The Boston Globe.*

The mix of politics and products dates back to the sainted Eleanor Roosevelt herself, who sold Good Luck margarine coast to coast in 1957 television ads for Lever Brothers.

Not even Winston Churchill was averse to the pitch, according to Ogilvy & Mather, the New York advertising agency that created the Roosevelt spot. An agency spokesman noted that Churchill was featured in a "Come to Great Britain" tourism ad.

So was Queen Elizabeth.

Nobody is sure exactly what the famous face does for the product or vice versa, although a spokesman for Lever Brothers did say Eleanor Roosevelt could not save the sagging sales of Good Luck, and Sam Ervin said the life insurance commercial did way too much for him. Ervin, 89, said he received 150 phone calls from people all over the country who wanted him to solve their life insurance problems.

"I haven't sold anything since," Ervin said in a telephone interview from his home in Morganton, N.C. He didn't get as much reaction from the American Express ads, which ran about the same time in the mid-1970s.

He said he did the ads because it was "very flattering" to be asked. But, like other people interviewed on the subject, he declined to discuss what he was paid and did not wish to comment on Ferraro's contract with the Pepsi-Cola Co., rumored to be around $500,000.

"That's her business and none of mine," Ervin said.

Tom Griscom, press secretary to Howard Baker, who joined the Washington law firm of Vinson & Elkins after leaving the Senate, said his boss agreed to do the USA Today radio and television commercials "because he gets the paper at home every day and likes it." Griscom said Baker did magazine ads for photography enlarging equipment and for a computer information service while he was in the Senate.

"He uses these products," said Griscom, adding that Baker received no compensation for doing the ads and didn't feel there was a conflict of interest.

"This is something that a public figure has to look at individually and decide for himself or herself whether or not it's a good idea," Griscom said.

Staff members in the House and Senate ethics committees said no rules prohibit legislators from doing commercials but said the practice is generally frowned upon.

Mark Elam, counsel to the House Com-

///

creative message appeals that have been successful in television advertisements. Variations on these techniques can be repeated with expectations that they will work well again.

Finally, creative specialists should understand what causes people to pay attention to and remember some advertisements and not others. The field of research on consumer behavior has discovered that people pay attention to words and scenes that are interesting and relate to some need or want.[15] They also pay attention to the unusual, something that is different or out of the ordinary. (See Chapter 5 for a discussion of these findings.) These principles lead advertisers to include humor, gimmickry, magic, well-known personalities (see Marketalk), and other attention-getting techniques in advertisements.

After Larry Hagman, the villainous J. R. Ewing of *Dallas,* slipped between a pair of Cannon Mills bedsheets for a new ad campaign . . . , the company got so many calls that its customer-service telephone broke down. One caller had to have the sheets he slept in.

Two of the most famous names in America sleep together.

CANNON MILLS

/ /

mittee on Standards and Official Conduct, said he knows of one newly elected representative who is being featured in a clothing store ad somewhere in the country, but he declined to identify state, store or seller.

"He's not violating any rule, but I'm sure this is embarrassing for him," Elam said. "I wouldn't want to have to explain this to the other clothing stores in my district."

Gary Orren, associate professor of public policy at Harvard's John F. Kennedy School of Government, believes that politicians promoting products only foster the cynicism Americans have about elected officials. He noted that the public accepts a politician trying to sell himself or herself, but that selling a product is "slightly tawdry and viewed as pure hucksterism."

He said damage would be particularly severe for Ferraro, who had set herself up as a symbol.

"All during the 1984 campaign, she claimed that she was more than just Gerry Ferraro," Orren said. "She said she was opening a door for immigrants and women. She represented a great moment in history. Having set herself up like that, the fall is greater. People who worked for her are feeling a little betrayed."

Orren, along with Stephen A. Greyser, Harvard Business School marketing professor, noted that the lack of a logical link between Ferraro and the Pepsi product would fuel these feelings.

"Howard Baker and USA Today are a tight personality fit," Greyser said. "You would expect someone in politics to read a lot." Greyser also noted that the American Express "Do you know me?" ads traded on the obscurity of people once in the public eye and soon forgotten, which is also suited to political life.

"But there's no particular reason why Geraldine Ferraro would drink Diet Pepsi," Greyser said. He pointed out that Pepsi and Coke ads trade on famous names to get the public to talk about the product—something the Pepsi ad has achieved in spades even before it's been aired.

Francis O'Brien, the Ferraro adviser who served as her press secretary during the campaign, said Ferraro decided to do the ad "because it was high-toned and tasteful, and Pepsi promised her she could say anything she wanted to."

He said speculation on whether this would hurt her political career and possible bid for a Senate seat is "ridiculous."

"The end result will be that this will

have absolutely no effect on her career," O'Brien said, "Not one iota."

Orren and other observers disagree, however, saying that the ad, along with a heavy lecture schedule and book promotion, indicates that she is not thinking seriously about pursuing a Senate seat. Orren said doing the commercial could add to the unfavorable impression created by the publicity surrounding the financial dealings of Ferraro's husband, John Zaccaro and her failure to report his income in congressional disclosure forms.

"That sounds like something that somebody at Harvard would say," said Michael Dowling, who heads Ogilvy & Mather's Washington office.

"Geraldine Ferraro will do for Pepsi what Michael Jackson did for Pepsi. I don't see this creating any fallout for her. The country accepts this kind of thing. It's just like a jock doing a beer commercial."

John Anderson, who ran for President in 1980 and is now teaching at Brandeis University, said he doesn't see anything wrong with politicians doing commercials, and he would be happy to do one himself.

/ /

◄ In addition to Larry Hagman, Cannon Mills Co.'s attention-getting ads feature *Dynasty* actress Joan Collins, chef James Beard, Brooke Shields, and Bob Hope posing with sheets and towels. With its aggressive and provocative ad campaign, Cannon hopes to make its brand name attractive enough to charge higher prices for its sheets and towels. "The real purpose of our advertising program," says Cannon president Harold Messmer, "is to prevent us from slipping into a commodity business." (Produced for Cannon Mills by Peter Rogers and Associates)

The ads have shaken up the staid world of home-textile advertising—and helped boost Cannon's sales of sheets and towels at a time when competitors . . . are reporting declines or slower growth.[16]

Selling points. Creative specialists are concerned with how to present a product's **selling points.** These are the major arguments for buying the product and are derived from the overall marketing plan. Information from an MOA describing customers' needs and wants as well as competitive strengths and weaknesses help marketing managers choose the best selling points to communicate with advertising. Wendy's advertising provides an interesting illustration. Management discovered that Wendy's hamburgers were larger than the hamburgers of competitors. They also knew that more meat in a hamburger is an advantage because consumers want more value for their money. The more-meat selling point was effectively communicated in the "Where's the beef?" advertising campaign. Humor was cleverly used to draw consumers' attention to Wendy's larger hamburgers. Exhibit 19.10 shows creative slogans that summarize several companies' presentations of product selling points.

Exhibit 19.10 Slogans that summarize creative presentations of selling points

Product	Selling Point	Creative Slogan
Wisk detergent	Powerful cleaner that attacks difficult-to-clean spots	"Ring around the collar"
Chevrolet pickup trucks	Trucks are built to last despite rough treatment	"Chevy Tough is taking charge"
Subaru cars	Quality and luxury extras at an affordable price	"Subaru: Inexpensive and built to stay that way"
The First National Bank of Chicago	To do business overseas takes help from a team of specialists	"First teamwork works"
Burroughs Corporation	Being a bigger firm does not mean having better business computers	"The question isn't who's bigger. It's who's better"
United Airlines	Flying is a comfortable and safe way to travel, especially with an experienced airline	"United flies the friendly skies"
Mars	M&M's are fun, but not messy to eat	"M&M's melt in your mouth, not in your hands"

Creative design and media. The way in which a selling point is communicated should take advantage of media characteristics. A versatile medium such as television gives maximum flexibility to creative specialists. When other media are used—billboards, radio, newspapers—there is less opportunity to apply many different creative techniques. Yet in an advertising campaign, in which advertisements are run in a mix of media, the same campaign messages have to be communicated in the different media. An increasing challenge for creative specialists is to work through these different media. As a vice-president of Wells, Rich, Greene, a New York advertising agency, said: "Creative people must become more adept at integrating campaign themes across media. For example, skills must be cultivated in the transference of TV images through radio and other ad media."[17]

MANAGING ADVERTISING CAMPAIGNS

Having planned an advertising campaign, advertising managers are then responsible for seeing that advertising accomplishes its objectives. The advertising plan must be put into practice and then evaluated to determine how well it is working. Let us examine some of the activities involved.

Budgeting for advertising

An advertising budget is a control device that puts a limit on spending. It also shows how advertising dollars are to be spent. While companies differ greatly as to what expense categories are included, most advertising budgets cover such costs as media time and space, advertising materials, direct mail postage, advertising research services, and advertising consultant fees.[18]

One of the more difficult budgeting decisions is establishing how much in total to spend on advertising. As we have seen already, advertising's impact on sales is hard to determine because it is only one of many factors influencing sales. This means that managers cannot always objectively calculate the return for a given size advertising expenditure. Some companies get around this problem by using "rules of thumb" to set the advertising budget.

Rules of thumb budgeting approaches. **Rules of thumb budgeting** use a step-by-step procedure for calculating a dollar amount to allocate to advertising. The rules generally do not require that a specific return from advertising be estimated when the budget is set. Unfortunately, once applied, a rule is often used repeatedly more through inertia ("that's the way we always do it") than because of any logical reason. Let us examine three such rules: (1) percent of sales, (2) what is affordable, and (3) matching competitors.

The *percent-of-sales* rule allocates a predetermined percentage of sales to advertising. The sales figure to which a percent is applied may be the current year's sales or a forecast of next year's sales. A jeans store chain uses this procedure by setting aside 7 percent of forecasted sales for its advertising budget. Suppose the sales forecast for the current operating year is $12 million. The chain's advertising budget for that year would be $840,000 (7% × $12,000,000).

Those who use this rule say it has several advantages. It is simple to apply and easy for managers to understand how the budget limit was set. Advertising expenditures depend on sales, which helps ensure that advertising costs do not get out of line with what the company can afford to spend. Furthermore, if percent of sales is used throughout an industry, competitive stability is ensured. Companies are less prone to engage in advertising "wars" by boosting advertising expenditures to an unusually high level.

Offsetting these advantages are a number of disadvantages. Too often the percentage is purely historical. At one time, someone in the company set a percentage that gradually became "cast in stone." The figure is used year after year (maybe because no one can think of a better percent). Such rigidity means that managers are not encouraged to consider the ways in which advertising can enhance the marketing mix. As we have seen, the task for advertising changes over time and the same percentage is not likely to be optimal year after year.

The percent-of-sales approach is also illogical because in spite of advertising's helping to create sales, the procedure requires that sales be calculated first, before an advertising budget is set. Thus sales are determining how much is spent on advertising, rather than letting managers devise an advertising budget needed to achieve a desired level of sales. Think about what happens in a period of expected low sales such as a recession. Advertising budgets are cut as company sales go down. Yet more, not less, advertising may be needed to keep sales from declining too fast or too much. Just the opposite happens in a period of high sales. Advertising budgets increase along with sales, whether more advertising is needed or not.

Another rule of thumb approach is to determine *how much a company can afford to spend* on advertising. A company manager such as a financial executive starts with a forecast of sales for the company. All costs except advertising are estimated and subtracted from forecasted sales. Then a target profit is established and subtracted from the forecast. The remainder is the amount that the company can afford to spend on advertising.

Interestingly, what a company can afford to spend on advertising may be either too much or too little. Management may never know which is the case without carefully analyzing how to use advertising to help with the sales effort. Notice that the advertising allocation varies up or down according to the fortunes of the company (advertising will be cut in recessionary times when sales are likely to be down, and boosted in growth periods). Again, advertising may be needed as much or even more in recessionary periods than in other periods, while boom sales periods may need less advertising.

The last rule *matches a company's advertising budget to the spending of competitors*. There are many ways to apply this rule. One company may try to set a budget that is a fixed proportion of the predicted budget of a competitor or in proportion to their relative market shares. Another company may set its advertising budget to match the average-size advertising expenditure in the industry. Some may argue that this approach yields an advertising budget that is based on the collective wisdom of the industry in determining advertising's worth. Furthermore, promotional wars are discouraged if the rule is widely used.

The major disadvantage of this approach is that it is based on the assumption that all firms in an industry can expect the same contribution from using advertising. In practice, this assumption rarely holds. Companies are typically trying to establish different selling points to build a competitive edge. They have different reputations and images, so advertising has different roles in the promotion budget. Furthermore, the firms in an industry are unlikely to be the same size or to have the same level of resources to commit to advertising.

All these rules of thumb have the same weakness. They are arbitrary procedures for setting an advertising budget because they do not explicitly consider how advertising can contribute to the sales effort. Companies seem to be increasingly aware of the deficiencies of budgeting rules of thumb. A recent study showed a substantial decline in the percentage of firms using them.[19]

A sound budgeting approach. A more defensible way to determine an advertising budget is to use **objective and task budgeting.** This approach determines a budget by summing the costs of advertising tasks required to achieve stated objectives. Exhibit 19.11 lists the necessary steps to determine a budget, and provides an illustration of its application by ItS For Levi, a regional chain of casual-wear clothing stores. Unlike the rules of thumb approaches, objective and task budgeting is not arbitrary. The opportunity to use advertising to achieve objectives important to a marketing strategy is explicitly considered. Additionally, management can compare the costs of advertising with the value of the objectives.

Clearly, objective and task budgeting is more difficult to implement than are the rules of thumb. The major problems are (1) assessing the value of achieving the objectives and (2) determining what is needed to accomplish the objectives. However, the required judgments can be made, and market research can assist managers in making them, as exemplified by advertising budgeting at Anheuser-Busch. This company's management has used experiments to find out how much different-sized advertising expenditures contribute to generating sales of Budweiser, its biggest-selling beer. Management had believed that advertising has a positive effect on sales increases up to a point. But beyond that point, spending more on advertising contributes little to sales and can even irritate people enough to

Exhibit 19.11 Objective and task approach to advertising budgeting

Steps in the Procedure	Illustration
1. Establish the objectives for advertising.	ITS For Levi wanted 90 percent of its target audience to be aware of and know about its expanded line of casual-wear clothing to complement jeans.
2. Determine the advertising tasks needed to accomplish advertising's objectives.	ITS For Levi developed an advertising campaign, including creative presentations and a media mix, to achieve the objective.
3. Estimate the cost of the advertising tasks.	ITS For Levi determined the costs of the message content and context design, testing of the design, and the media for delivering the message to its audiences.
4. Obtain approval of an advertising budget to cover the planned costs.	ITS For Levi's advertising manager submitted the cost of the campaign to the president and chief financial officer for approval.

SOURCE: Adapted from an unpublished application of a market opportunity analysis study to marketing planning by the Its For Levi retail chain.

cause decreases in sales. Results of the experiment showed that Anheuser-Busch had been spending too much on advertising and so reductions in Budweiser's total advertising budgets were made without losing sales.

Advertising agencies

In small companies, employees may effectively implement advertising plans if the advertising budget is small, messages are simple, and few media are used. Large companies find that it is not cost effective to have all the expertise they need on their staffs to put together and implement complicated advertising campaigns. They can buy this expertise more economically by hiring an **advertising agency.** A full-service advertising agency has (1) media experts who select media and arrange the placement of advertisements, (2) creative specialists who determine how to present messages and handle the production of advertisements, (3) marketing research experts who conduct studies on target audiences, and (4) account executives who help with developing advertising plans and serve as a liaison between the managers of the client and the agency's specialists.

For many years, advertising agencies have used a media commission system to receive payment for their services. Traditionally, 15 percent of media billings is paid to the agency, in effect, by the media rather than the client. Suppose an agency developed a media plan for a client company costing $20 million. The agency bills the company for the full $20 million, but then only pays the media $17 million for time and space. The difference of $3 million ($20,000,000 × 15%) is kept by the agency as payment for its services. If the company bypassed the agency and purchased straight from the media, it would still have to pay the $20 million.

Neither agencies nor advertisers are totally pleased with the 15 percent commission system. A recent study for the Association of National Advertisers showed that between 1976 and 1983, the number of advertisers using the commissions dropped from 83 percent to 71 percent. Paying fees for services is replacing the commission system.[21] Reasons seem to be that more advertisers feel they are being charged for services they did not use, and agencies have expanded their services well beyond creative design and media placement.

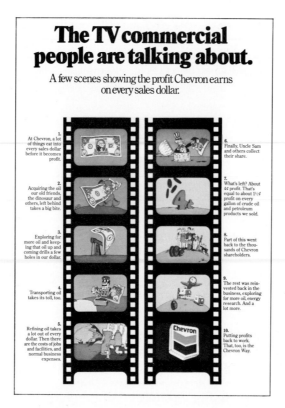

Chevron's pretests for its dinosaur animation campaign indicated that the message of the ad was convincingly presented. Furthermore, the post-tests for this campaign confirmed that it did make an impression on many of the people who saw it. (Courtesy of Chevron U.S.A. Inc.)

Evaluating advertising's performance

An executive from Ogilvy & Mather, a large and well-known advertising agency, estimates that the cost-per-thousand to reach an audience of men on network, prime-time television will jump from $7.86 to $25.34 during the decade of the 1980s; for reaching women the cost will go from $6.30 to $20.14.[22] Furthermore, the production costs alone for a typical thirty-second television commercial can be more than $100,000, which is more than double what that same commercial cost in 1980.[23] Faced by escalating costs, more and more advertising managers want to know what return they are getting for their money. Let us look at some of the ways in which advertising evaluation research can help.

What can be evaluated? Four aspects of advertising can be evaluated. First, managers may want to test the effectiveness of an **advertising concept,** which refers to the combination of selling points to be communicated by advertising. (Look again at Exhibit 19.10 for illustrations of selling points.) Second, an entire advertising campaign may be evaluated. Third, management may want to find out how much more effective one level of spending on advertising is than another level. Finally, individual advertisements may be tested to learn how effective the **advertising copy,** a combination of message content and context, is with target audiences.

Advertising research techniques are available for all these purposes. Interestingly, most advertising research is concerned with testing individual advertisment,[24] because effectiveness of individual advertisements is the easiest of all the tests to conduct and managers may assume that if individual advertisements are effective, the campaigns and the advertising concept will be also.

When should tests be made? Marketing research can be conducted at three stages: before, during, and after advertising is run. **Advertising pretests** are conducted before an advertisement is delivered to target audiences. A pretest's purpose is to help creative designers evaluate how effective a particular copy approach will be. Chevron conducted pretests to choose between two copy design alternatives intended to build consumer confidence in the oil company. One approach used a "dinosaur animation" to talk about the role of Chevron in the economy. Another approach, called the "talking heads" campaign, showed executives talking about various issues related to oil company operations. The pretests showed that the dinosaur animation was the more effective of the two design alternatives.[25]

 Advertising post-tests evaluate advertising's effectiveness during and after an advertisement has been run by the media. They help managers see what return the company is getting for its money. Equally important is the forewarning that management gets when a successful advertising campaign starts to lose its effectiveness. Chevron used post-tests for this purpose in evaluating the dinosaur advertisements. The advertisements were run for a five-year period, but were dropped in favor of a new campaign after post-tests revealed that awareness and attitude-change effectiveness was no longer up to standards set for the advertisements. Post-tests also can be used to see how well pretests predicted the effectiveness of the advertisements. Chevron has used post-tests in this way to choose between alternative kinds of pretests to evaluate future advertisements.[26]

Which kinds of objectives are tested? Drawing conclusions about the effectiveness of advertising requires a benchmark for comparison. The most important benchmark is the desired result stated in advertising objectives. It has long been a principle in advertising to set objectives in such a way that management can use evaluation techniques to see if the objectives have been met. The **DAGMAR** (*De*fining *A*dvertising *G*oals for *M*easured *A*dvertising *R*esults) approach was introduced years ago to focus attention on setting specific tasks as goals for advertising to enable management to evaluate the extent to which the tasks have been accomplished.

 Recall from our earlier discussion the two types of advertising objectives: communications objectives and sales objectives. Although there are many different kinds of tests from which to choose, they are all either tests of communications effectiveness or of sales effectiveness.

 An illustration of a **communications effectivenes test** is a **recall test.** Information is gathered to see the extent to which people remember the advertisement and its message. As an illustration, suppose the advertisement to be tested is a thirty-second television commercial. Shortly after the advertisement is run, a sample of viewers is asked if they were watching television at the time the commercial was run and if they were tuned to the correct channel. This information provides a measure of how many people were exposed to the commercial. Those who were exposed are asked if they can recall the advertisement and what it said. The percentage of exposed persons who can successfully answer the recall questions provides a measure of how effectively the advertisement achieved awareness objectives.

 Attitude change test, another communications effectiveness test, is more difficult to conduct. First, a benchmark is obtained by finding out what the audience's attitudes toward a company or its brand are before the advertising is delivered. After the advertising has been run for a period of time, another test measures the audiences' attitudes again. The amount by which the attitudes change from before to after the advertising is a measure of its effectiveness.

A **sales effectiveness test,** which measures advertising's ability to achieve sales objectives, is possible but can be expensive and difficult to conduct. Because many factors influence sales, it is difficult to attribute any improvement in sales just to advertising. One approach is to run experiments in which sales are measured after exposing audiences to advertisements. For this test to be effective, other influences on sales must be carefully controlled. The AUtel Company, a research firm, uses cable television hookups for sales tests. Different samples of people, called panels, are matched for similarity and asked to participate in the study. All these people agree to have AUtel control the advertisements they see. Each person keeps a record of purchases of selected products during the time spent on the panel. Suppose a company wants to see how much sales an advertisement can generate. One panel is exposed to the advertisement for a period of time, while another panel has it blocked out. The difference in the purchases of the company's brand by the two panels is the measure of sales effectiveness.[27]

SALES PROMOTION

Although sales promotion decisions are similar to those for advertising, there are some differences. Furthermore, sales promotion accounts for an important part of all promotion budgets in many companies. One source estimates that manufacturers typically spend 60 percent of their mass communications resources on sales promotion.[28] For these reasons, we now discuss the decisions concerning planning and evaluating the activities of *sales promotion*—the wide variety of short-term inducements to buy that receivers know are coming from the source.

Sales promotion audiences

Sales promotion, like advertising, can be targeted toward *end-user* audiences. For instance, Pepsi Cola supplemented national media advertising with sales promotion to introduce its Pepsi Free regular and diet caffeine-free colas. Samples of Pepsi Free were given away, coupons were inserted into media, and special displays were set up in stores. The purposes of both advertising and sales promotion were to build awareness among people in target markets, encourage them to try the new product, and eventually get them to purchase Pepsi Free on a regular basis.[29]

Sales promotion is also frequently aimed at the *trade,* distributors and retailers in a company's channel of distribution. These firms must be motivated to help with the total selling effort, and sales promotion can serve this purpose. In the grocery business, approximately 60 percent of all sales by manufacturers are made with a trade discount, one kind of sales promotion, that averages 12 percent off the manufacturers' list prices.[30] In exchange for the discount, manufacturers expect certain kinds of assistance such as the trade's passing on some of the discount to consumers, featuring the brand in newspaper advertisements, or setting up special displays of the product in the store.[31]

The third audience for sales promotion is a company's own *salesforce*. Again, motivation is the purpose. Tupperware is one company that must continually motivate salespersons. Management relies heavily on salespersons who only work part time and who must sell the company's plastic bowls and containers by hosting "Tupperware parties" for relatives, friends, and neighbors. As a sales incentive, Tupperware offers bonuses of merchandise premiums (e.g., refrigerators, televisions) to those with the best sales records.[32]

Companies may have sales promotions targeted at several audiences at the same time. A combination of different techniques may work better than concentrating on any one of them. Wrangler, a manufacturer of jeans, has applied this principle. Jeans sales are not increasing very much in the 1980s because people are buying primarily to replace their worn-out jeans. An interesting mix of sales promotions directed toward consumers and retailers has helped spur Wrangler sales in spite of this situation. As part of their promotions effort, Wrangler is

- Sponsoring rodeos
- Sponsoring a racing team and the "Wrangler Jeans Machine" race car
- Sponsoring twenty-six motocross motorcycle races
- Sponsoring tractor-pull contests
- Sponsoring "Wrangler Country Showdown," country music talent contests on 400 radio stations across the United States
- Providing specially designed store advertising and display materials to retail stores who offer a store sale to coincide with a Wrangler-sponsored event
- Providing free tickets to retailers to give away to their customers during a Wrangler-sponsored event in their area
- Providing back-to-school rebates for buyers of Wrangler jeans
- Holding a sweepstakes contest for consumers[33]

Setting sales promotion objectives

Although it is possible to set a number of different promotion objectives, they all involve encouraging immediate action from audiences. Examples of objectives aimed at the target market include getting customers to try a new product, send for further information on a product, buy a product immediately instead of waiting, or stock up on a product. Wrangler's objective of getting families to stock up on jeans during the months just before school opens in the fall is accomplished by back-to-school rebates.

Objectives for a company's trade and salesforce also specify similar desired actions. Some examples are to get the trade to feature a company's merchandise prominently and to encourage salespersons to meet or even exceed sales quotas.

The time horizon for achieving sales promotion objectives is usually quite short. A price-off sale or sweepstakes contest usually lasts no longer than a few months, spurring sales during that period. Other objectives may set somewhat shorter or longer time periods, but most are well less than a year. In this respect, sales promotion combines well with advertising. Advertising can be used to build long-term positive attitudes and image toward a company and its brands, while sales promotion provides the incentive for people to act now.

Determining sales promotion activities

Trying to classify the many and varied sales promotion activities is not easy. One way is to consider how sales promotions reach target audiences: (1) in-store promotions, (2) direct-to-audience promotions, and (3) trade shows.

In-store promotions. Many sales promotion activities are aimed at customers while they are shopping in a retail store. These include point-of-purchase displays and signs, in-store give-aways, live in-store demonstrations, trading stamps redeemable for merchandise, and audiovisual displays such as a television monitor showing a film describing how to use a product. These activities are expensive—the materials alone for point-of-purchase displays exceeded $6 billion in 1983.[34]

In-store promotions try to change customers' purchasing habits by offering incentives at the moment purchases are being made. Their purpose is to encourage activities such as stocking up on a product, switching brands, or drawing attention to a new product consumers may want to try.

Retail stores are bombarded with requests for in-store promotions. A large supermarket such as Kroger sells hundreds of brands, and most of the manufacturers of these brands want to run a promotion some time during the year. Manufacturers usually offer an inducement to retailers to get their cooperation. Consequently, consumer and trade promotions often are used in combination. A price discount or a merchandise allowance (e.g., offering free units of the product) induces a retailer to display the manufacturer's product prominently in the store. At the same time, a company's salespersons spend part of their time convincing retailers to cooperate with an in-store promotion. The store's manager wants to know how much the store will gain by using the promotion, usually in terms of increased sales.

Direct-to-audience promotions. Direct-to-audience promotion activities offer inducements directly to audiences with little or no involvement by retail stores. These include free samples sent by mail, coupons redeemable for a price discount, sweepstakes and contests, merchandise premiums (products given in addition to those purchased), and trade allowances (either cash discounts or additional product units given with a purchase). Some promotions, such as free samples, coupons, and sweepstakes, are targeted directly toward end-users, while others such as trade allowances are targeted toward the trade. A few promotions such as merchandise premiums and contests can be used equally well with all three sales promotion audiences: end-users, trade, and the salesforce.

Because retail stores are not involved in direct-to-audience promotions, managers look to other ways to reach audiences. Direct mail is frequently used to distribute free samples, coupons, and merchandise premiums. In fact, there are service organizations whose business is to handle promotional mailings. One such organization offers a service called Solo Pack Samples. Free samples of a manufacturer's product and a cents-off coupon are packaged together and mailed to designated areas ranging from an area as small as a single zip code to the entire nation.[35]

Direct-to-audience promotions are also tied in with advertising media. Coupons can be inserted into newspaper, magazine, or direct mail advertising. Sweepstakes and contests also use advertising media. Other media include using company personnel such as salespersons to communicate the promotion and attaching coupons and premium redemption announcements to the product package.

Trade shows. Companies use trade shows to exhibit their products to customers face to face. Sometimes the exhibits are set up at a business convention. Textbook publishers use this approach by attending meetings of academic associations such as the American Marketing Association. Space is rented for booths to display textbooks and other educational learning aids. Salespersons in the booths talk to potential adopters of these texts.

Trade shows are also planned as separate activities not tied to business conventions. Manufacturers of tennis equipment and clothing, for instance, participate in an annual trade show to introduce new lines for the year. People attending the trade show are not consumers, but are owners and managers of retail stores carrying these products.

Unlike other sales promotion activities, trade shows must draw customers to the exhibits. Considerable effort is often needed to encourage customers to attend. Direct mail announcements, advertisements, and contacts by salespersons may be used well in advance of a trade show for this purpose.

Budgeting for sales promotion

As with any promotion activity, costs of sales promotion should be planned and controlled using a sales promotion budget. The size of a sales promotion budget is determined in much the same way as is the advertising budget. Managers may use a rule of thumb such as a set percentage of past or forecasted sales. A more logical approach is to determine the specific activities needed to achieve sales promotion objectives, estimate the costs of these activities, and let the total of these costs be the expenditure limit. In this way, management lets the opportunity for sales promotion to contribute to company sales determine the expenditure limit.

Evaluating sales promotion

Managers want to know the extent to which sales promotion activities are achieving their objectives. The most straightforward measures are based on the frequency with which the action requested by a sales promotion activity is taken. These measures are often simple to obtain, as illustrated by an approach used by Chrysler Corporation. The company is using shopping mall shows to promote its Dodge automobile. Lifelike robots are placed in the cars to invite people to take test drives. A measure of the effectiveness of this sales promotion activity is the number of people who take test drives. Dodge expects the show to generate approximately 400 test drives per day. Careful record keeping will show whether this objective is achieved (see Marketalk).

Managers may also want to determine the sales effectiveness of sales promotion activities. A simple procedure is to measure the level of sales before, during, and after a sales promotion is run. Changes in sales during this period help managers evaluate the extent to which the promotion influenced sales. This measure should be used only with extreme caution. Many factors other than sales promotion affect sales and can cause changes. Colgate found this out when it introduced Peak toothpaste with little sales success. One reason for the poor performance was an allowance program

*Marke*TALK //

Dodge uses robots to attract buyers in shopping mall shows

STYLISHLY DRESSED, with neatly combed chestnut-brown hair, and rugged square jaw, Robert sits behind the wheel of a shiny new Dodge Daytona, talking about the car's styling, practicality, and performance. Revving the engine, he says contentedly: "This Daytona is outta this world."

And Robert could well be the quintessential Dodge customer—except that he is made of latex rubber and wire. He is a robot, and along with 23 companions is the newest spokesperson for Chrysler Corp.'s Dodge cars. This month, Robert and his pals will be tooting the company's horn in shopping malls across the country. The flashy ensemble is the most radical example yet of shopping-mall showcasing, now being given new emphasis by Detroit

SOURCE: "Detroit hits the road with new shopping mall shows," *Business Week,* Apr. 23, 1984, p. 47. Reprinted by special permission, © 1984 by McGraw-Hill, Inc.

auto makers. Without such extras to draw people, says Joseph N. Caddell, Dodge's general marketing manager, "You're just another pretty face in the crowd."

When the recession slowed auto-dealer showroom traffic to a crawl, auto makers began searching for ways to get potential customers to look at and test-drive their cars. They jazzed up the mundane exhibits that travel from one shopping center to another and found that consumers who are hesitant to step inside a showroom are willing to listen to a less formal sales pitch. Although showroom traffic has picked up, this year Detroit is relying even more heavily on the shopping mall shows as an important marketing tool.

The mini shows, by offering direct contact with the autos, are used to heighten the impact of television and print ads. On average, buyers visit only three or four showrooms before selecting a car. As Detroit's styles change in response to the inundation of foreign cars and evolving

consumer taste, exposure becomes increasingly important.

Dodge's robots are meant to underscore the division's high-tech ad theme of "Dodge: An American Revolution." After attracting attention, the robots invite passersby to step outside to the parking lot for a 90-second test drive through a mock town, complete with building facades. From behind the building, recorded voices extol the virtues of the cars. Dodge expects to generate up to 400 test drives a day with two separate traveling shows. "It's probably the biggest direct test-drive program the industry has ever had," boasts Caddell.

Dodge clearly believes the extra exposure will be worth the expense. The robots' $1 million price tag can be amortized over their five-year lifespan. And since the malls see the shows as a way to lure more shoppers, they do not charge Dodge the usual $3,000 to $5,000 for the exhibit space.

//

by Procter & Gamble to get retailers to stock up on Crest. Colgate could not overcome Crest's competitive advantage. Had Procter & Gamble not run their promotion when they did, Peak might have enjoyed a more successful introduction.

Market tests also help control other influences on sales so that management can get a clearer picture of a sales promotion's effectiveness. Sales from comparable geographic areas, which differ only in the amount or kind of sales promotion used, can be compared to see the impact of the test promotions. Furthermore, once sales effectiveness is known, managers can examine sales promotion profitability by comparing sales to costs.

PUBLICITY

A third tool in the promotion mix is *publicity,* nonpersonal communications primarily in the form of "news" items carried by the mass media, though the media are not paid by the source, and a message's origin is often perceived by receivers to be the media and not the source. Because publicity is included in the public relations function of a company, publicity helps increase sales for a particular product, and at the same time it can be part of the company's corporate image and reputation-building effort.

Of all the promotional tools, publicity is the least likely to receive a continuous and well-funded effort from organizations. Yet well-planned publicity activities can be beneficial to the company, sometimes gaining the product or company exposure that would cost many more thousands of dollars if advertising were used instead. Consider the experience of an executive for Ketchum Public Relations, a New York firm, that was gained from using publicity to promote apples.

> Big ad budgets which permit TV advertising on a wide scale can't produce the per-dollar return of a judiciously planned produce publicity program.
> An example is the Ketchum campaign on behalf of the International Apple Institute. Although it only cost $145,000, it was instrumental in building marketing support for apples, which have experienced dramatic sales growth in recent years.[36]

Publicity managers, like advertising and sales promotion managers, make decisions in the following areas: (1) target audiences, (2) objectives, (3) activities to achieve objectives, (4) budget, and (5) evaluating the impact of publicity.

Publicity's target audiences

Although media decide what publicity stories to carry, target audiences can be selected. When publicity is part of corporate image building, audiences can be wide ranging including the general public, stockholders, investors, employees, government officials, advocacy groups, and suppliers. On the other hand, publicity aimed at selling a product usually targets customer segments, special persons that influence customers, or the general public. In Ketchum Public Relations' apple publicity campaign, target audiences included consumers who buy produce in supermarkets and food editors for national magazines that publish recipes.[37]

As for the other promotion tools, targeting appropriate audiences depends on understanding who is involved in purchasing decision making. An MOA can help identify who is in markets and how they go about making purchase decisions. Managers need to know the nature and makeup of these audiences in the same detail as do advertising managers. Ketchum began planning its apple publicity campaign by conducting marketing research on apple buyers and conducting interviews with people leaving supermarkets with apples in their grocery bags.

Setting publicity objectives

Publicity is generally less versatile than is advertising in the types of objectives that can be achieved. Because the messages are carried by the media as part of news stories, there is little opportunity to present persuasive arguments for buying a product much less make a direct appeal to customers to buy the product. Thus publicity objectives usually entail informing and educating audiences. Achieving these objectives can and should enhance the likelihood of later sales.

Setting proper objectives depends on what management believes target audiences should know to influence sales. Again, an MOA can help uncover customers' current understanding of a product and what changes in their thinking and feelings would help the sales effort. Ketchum's marketing research discovered that people who buy apples view them as produce, much as they view other fruits and vegetables. Furthermore, consumers were not aware of the mány varieties of apples and their uses. These insights led to three major publicity objectives: (1) educating consumers about the sixteen varieties of apples, (2) making consumers aware of the use of apples as a snack food, and (3) helping consumers learn different ways to use apples in cooking.

Determining publicity activities

Successful publicity depends on finding topics that are newsworthy and at the same time inform and educate target audiences. A manager may look for these topics in the events happening in the company: a new product about to be introduced, a new use for an existing product, an unusually large sales order received, a breakthrough in research and development, opening of a new business location, and the like. Or the creative publicity manager may create an event to get media coverage. For instance, Manufacturers Hanover Corporation, the New York–based holding company, has been sponsoring long-distance challenge races for runners all over the United States. The races are tremendously successful in getting the company's name in the press in cities where it has not been well known. And they have led to identifying sales prospects among other corporate sponsors of racing events.[38]

Having found a topic, the next step is to prepare information for the media. Several techniques are used for this purpose including news releases, feature articles, press conferences, editorials, and records and films.[39] A *news release* is a short written description of the event, usually 300 words or less, that contains all essential facts. (The Marketalk in Chapter 9 about Service Corporation International is a news release.) It may also contain a photograph or drawing to enhance the copy. A *feature article* is a long article (up to 3000 words) that describes a story about the company or something the company is doing.

Press conferences are oral presentations by company spokespersons to the press. A company that wants to make an announcement arranges a public meeting and invites members of the press to attend. Well-planned press conferences also distribute written material summarizing the thrust of the announcement to those attending. *Editorials* are stories that usually advocate a point of view, written by a company for placement in the editorial sections of newspapers or magazines. While the company's editorial is almost never used verbatim, it can provide material for the press to use in the media's own editorial.[40] Finally, *records and films* can be made on interesting topics for use by the media in programs or to fill time between programs.

Editors of the media have complete control over which publicity items are used and which are not. Most of the publicity items that come across editors' desks are rejected either because they are judged not sufficiently newsworthy or are poorly written. Clearly, effective publicity requires well-written materials. Furthermore, publicity managers must develop contacts with the media's editors to influence use of this material. A strong working relationship between the company's publicity manager and the press can help the success rate of getting items into the media. This relationship is strengthened if the publicity manager understands what is interesting and informative to a medium's audiences and has a record of providing such items.

Budgeting for publicity

Because publicity is typically part of either advertising or public relations, it often does not have a separate budget of its own. The expense of creating the publicity items is likely to be included in budgets for these departments. In those companies in which publicity has a departmental identity, budgeting procedures are the same as those for advertising.

Evaluating publicity's effectiveness

As for any promotion tool, management should find out how effective the publicity effort has been. The most common measure of publicity's effectiveness is the amount of activity achieved. Activity refers to the number of items placed in the media. For example, a company may put together a "clippings book" of items actually printed in newspapers, magazines, and other forms of the print media. Though more difficult to do, records also may be kept of the amount of air time devoted to company publicity on radio and television. A summary measure of the worth of this activity is an estimate of the cost of the media coverage if paid for in the form of advertising.

An activity measure is not an entirely satisfactory way to evaluate the worth of publicity. Unfortunately, it does not indicate the impact of the material on target audiences. There is no way of knowing how many in target audiences saw the material, much less how much of it was comprehended or remembered. For this reason, activity measures should be supplemented by other indicators of effectiveness.

Similarity of publicity to advertising in its use of the mass media as well as its purpose of informing and educating audiences suggests what these additional measures might be. The advertising communication effectiveness tests can also be used for publicity. How much do target audience members recall from the publicity items? Did the publicity change audiences' attitudes? Answering these questions can give a manager much more insight into how much return a company received from its publicity dollars than measures of activity can.

SUMMARY

Advertising, sales promotion, and publicity—the tools in the promotion mix that are designed to reach large audiences and rely on nonpersonal forms of communication—are economical ways to communicate with many people at the same time. Furthermore, they support personal selling: Buyers who are familiar with the selling company and its products in a positive way, achieved through mass communications, are more likely to be receptive to the presentations of salespersons.

For each tool, essentially the same kinds of decisions are necessary to plan, implement, and control the effort. Audiences are selected, objectives set, budgets established, creative messages designed (including content and context), ways to deliver the messages are chosen, and measures of evaluation are selected by promotion managers. Underlying all these decisions is the need to understand the nature and makeup of the target audiences for the promotion activity. Because most of promotion is aimed at target markets or the trade, market opportunity analysis (MOA) is essential to help managers build and maintain this understanding.

Another similarity among the mass communications tools is the variety of audiences that can be reached. While most audiences are customers or the trade, others such as a company's suppliers, employees, stockholders, and investors are also possible targets.

Advertising, sales promotion, and publicity are also different. One of the most important differences is the way in which messages are delivered to audiences. Advertising relies on the mass media of television, radio, magazines, newspapers, billboards, and direct mail. Sales promotion may tie in with advertising and use these same media, such as when a coupon is inserted in magazine and newspaper advertising. However, the diversity of sales promotion activities requires different kinds of delivery techniques. In-store promotion tries to influence buyers at the place of purchase by engaging the assistance of retailers in delivery. Point-of-purchase displays and signs, trading stamps, and price-off promotions are illustrations. Obtaining the cooperation of the retailers is an important objective in these activities.

Direct-to-audience sales promotion activities are aimed at either end-users or the trade. Direct mail is especially important for this activity, as are salespersons, who play a major role in delivery to either audience.

Publicity largely works through the mass media. However, the delivery is through free news stories rather than paid advertisements. Thus obtaining media cooperation is an important aspect of publicity. Publicity managers must find material that is interesting and relevant to media audiences so editors and reporters will use it. Well-prepared news conferences, news releases, feature articles, editorials, and records and films are essential to encourage the media to use the material. Furthermore, publicity managers must build strong relationships with media editors and reporters to get publicity items accepted.

Another difference among the mass communications tools concerns the time horizon for planning. Advertising and publicity have long-run impact on audiences by building favorable attitudes and images for the company and its products. Thus effects of these promotion tools can carry over from one year to the next. On the other hand, sales promotion is typically short-term. Its purpose is to encourage immediate actions such as getting customers to stock up on the product, switch brands, and try a new product and encouraging the trade to offer a price reduction.

The differences among advertising, sales promotion, and publicity explain why companies use them in combination to achieve promotion objectives. For instance, publicity can get promotion messages into media and space that advertising cannot do. Advertising can help make audience members aware of a sales promotion—a coupon, free sample, or product premium—campaign going on. And sales promotion can provide an added boost to encourage the action from audiences promoted by advertising.

KEY TERMS

institutional advertising	media mix	rules of thumb budgeting
product type advertising	media vehicles	objective and task budgeting
brand advertising	cost-per-thousand criterion	advertising agency
comparative advertising	selling points	advertising concept

advertising copy   DAGMAR   attitude change test

advertising pretests   communications effectiveness test   sales effectiveness test

advertising post-tests   recall test

QUESTIONS FOR REVIEW AND DISCUSSION

1. What are the differences among institutional, product type, and brand advertising?

2. Is McDonnel-Douglas (manufacturer of airplanes) or Polaroid (manufacturer of cameras) more likely to assign a larger role to advertising in its promotion mix? Give reasons for your answer.

3. For which advertising decisions can a market opportunity analysis (MOA) help managers?

4. Are communications objectives for advertising better than sales-related objectives? Why or why not?

5. Because television is the most versatile communication media with both sight and sound capabilities, should all advertisers spend their media dollars entirely on television? Why or why not?

6. Given two media vehicles with similar audiences, should the one with the lowest cost per thousand be selected? Why or why not?

7. Why do advertisers use humor, magic, emotion, and gimmickry in advertisements?

8. How do selling points from a marketing plan show up in advertising?

9. Do creative specialists have to know what media will deliver an advertisement before the message content and context can be designed?

10. How can an advertising agency help a company make advertising decisions?

11. What is the objective and task approach to advertising budgeting? Is it better than the percent-of-sales approach?

12. Why should advertising be evaluated?

13. Are advertising objectives important for the evaluation of advertising? Why or why not?

14. How is a communications effectiveness test different from a sales effectiveness test?

15. Do audiences differ for advertising, sales promotion, and publicity?

16. In what ways are advertising, sales promotion, and publicity objectives different?

17. What are the ways in which salespersons might be used to assist in sales promotion?

18. What is a trade show?

19. What are typical objectives for publicity?

20. Does publicity offer any advantages over advertising?

21. How can a company know whether its publicity effort has been successful?

BUILDING YOUR PORTFOLIO

Pick two competing consumer-product or service companies in an industry. Gather information on their current advertising campaigns for directly competing brands. You may want to do library research on the companies by looking for periodical articles that discuss their marketing strategies. Also clip magazine and newspaper advertisements. Look for radio, television, and billboard advertisements and make notes on their content. Use the information to answer the following questions:

■ What are the selling points of each company? Are they the same or different?

■ What creative techniques are used to present the selling points?

■ Does each company make the same selling points when using different media?

■ Which company has the more effective advertising?

NOTES

1. "Tylenol restaging was made possible by firm's solid research and consumer trust." *Marketing News*, Oct. 28, 1983, pp. 1, 12.
2. Ibid.
3. Bob Woods, "Giving business the cable." *Sales & Marketing Management*, Mar. 14, 1983, p. 37.
4. "Comparative ads paying off for Burger King." *Marketing News*, Apr. 27, 1984, p. 18.
5. "Highlights of sales management and marketing survey on industrial advertising." *Sales & Marketing Management*, June 8, 1981, p. 53.
6. Al Urbanski, "Dr Pepper heals itself." *Sales & Marketing Management*, Mar. 14, 1983, p. 35.
7. Ibid., p. 36.
8. David A. Aaker and John G. Myers, *Advertising Management*. Englewood Cliffs, N.J.: Prentice-Hall, 1982, pp. 93–94.
9. Pete Mateja, "Maker of industrial product finds TV is viable alternative to trade promotion." *Marketing News*, June 10, 1983, p. 3.
10. Arup K. Sen, "Bank uses mall-intercept interviews to test ad concepts." *Marketing News*, Jan. 22, 1982, p. 20.
11. For a discussion of media models, see Aaker and Myers, op. cit., pp. 432–442.
12. David Ogilvy and Joel Raphaelson, "Research on ad techniques that work—and don't work." *Marketing News*, Sept. 17, 1982, Section 2, p. 2.
13. "The new TV trying to wake up viewers." *Business Week*, Mar. 9, 1984, p. 46.
14. "Research suggests using celebrity spokesman a focal point for floral group's consumer, trade ads." *Marketing News*, Nov. 11, 1983, p. 10.
15. This principle and others are discussed in James MacLachian, "Making a message memorable and persuasive." *Journal of Advertising Research*, Dec. 1983–Jan. 1984, pp. 51–59.
16. "Sleeping with the stars pays off for Cannon." *Business Week*, Sept. 24, 1984, p. 67.
17. "Two segmentation approaches combat fear and loathing of media fragmentation and cost hikes." *Marketing News*, May 11, 1984, p. 5.
18. For a discussion of expense categories in advertising budgets, see Charles H. Patti and Vincent Blasko, "Budgeting practices of big advertisers." *Journal of Advertising Research*, Vol. 21 (Dec. 1981), pp. 23–29.
19. Ibid., p. 25.
20. Russell L. Ackoff and James R. Emshoff, "Advertising research at Anheuser-Busch, Inc. (1963–68)." *Sloan Management Review*, Vol. 16 (Winter 1975), pp. 1–15.
21. These statistics are reported in Merle Kingman, "To fee or not to fee." *Advertising Age*, Aug. 29, 1983, p. M-24.
22. William E. Whitney, Jr., "15 ways to use your ad agency more productively." *Marketing News*, Mar. 18, 1983, Section 1, p. 10.
23. "Advertisers wrestle with issue of escalating production costs." *Marketing News*, May 11, 1984, p. 1.

24. Diane H. Schmalensee, "Today's top priority advertising research questions." *Journal of Advertising Research,* Vol. 23 (Apr.–May 1983), p. 55.

25. Lewis C. Winters, "Comparing pretesting and posttesting of corporate advertising." *Journal of Advertising Research,* Vol. 23 (Feb.–Mar. 1983), p. 29.

26. Ibid., pp. 25–26.

27. Fred S. Zufryden, "Predicting trial, repeat, and sales response from alternative media plans." *Journal of Advertising Research,* Vol. 22 (June–July 1982), p. 45.

28. Marji Simon, "Survey probes strengths, weaknesses of promotion." *Marketing News,* June 8, 1984, p. 3.

29. "Pepsi targets projected $3 billion segment of cola market with carefully plotted entry." *Marketing News,* Dec. 9, 1983, p. 16.

30. Monci Jo Williams, "The no win game of price promotion." *Fortune,* July 11, 1983, p. 93.

31. Ibid.

32. Gwen Kinkead, "Tupperware's party times are over." *Fortune,* Feb. 20, 1984, p. 114.

33. "Wrangler relying on multiple sales promotions to help it combat flat bluejean market." *Marketing News,* Mar. 4, 1983, p. 5.

34. Kevin Higgins, "In-store merchandising is attracting more marketing dollars with last word in sales." *Marketing News,* Aug. 19, 1983, p. 1.

35. "Flat-pack sampling helps marketers improve results from direct mailings." *Marketing News,* Mar. 30, 1984, p. 8.

36. Kevin Higgins, "Marketing becoming essential for commodity producer groups." *Marketing News,* Apr. 29, 1983, p. 1.

37. References to Ketchum's publicity campaign for the International Apple Institute are taken from ibid., p. 1, 4.

38. "What makes Manny Hanny run." *Business Week,* Aug. 22, 1983, p. 55.

39. Richard E. Stanley, *Promotion.* Englewood Cliffs, N.J.: Prentice-Hall, 1977, pp. 249–250.

40. Ibid.

Case 19.1 _____

Gillette Personal Care Division

TURNING OIL INTO GOLD is the aim of a $22.9 million product launch by the Gillette Co., Boston.

The spending will fuel consumer and trade promotions and advertising for a new brand called For Oily Hair Only (FOHO). The $12 million budget for national print and television advertising for the product represents one of the largest investments by Gillette's Personal Care Division in recent product introductions.

Gillette's marketing plan was prompted by research which showed oily-haired people constitute the largest segment of the $2 billion hair care market, surpassing the total of all antidandruff shampoos. Despite the segment's size, no one has marketed a product designed for these consumers' exclusive use until now, according to Gillette.

"Until now, people with oily hair could only use shampoos, cream rinses, or con-

SOURCE: "Gillette targets largest segment of hair-care market with $22.9 million new product launch," *Marketing News*, May 28, 1982, p. 16. Reprinted with permission of the American Marketing Association.

ditioners which evolved as extensions of brands designed for normal hair," said product manager Ellen Hoffman. "They also settled for some shampoos that over-strip hair or post-shampoo products that overcoat hair.

"For Oily Hair Only is the first brand exclusively designed to give oily-haired people real help."

FOHO, available as a shampoo and rinse in both seven- and 11-ounce sizes, is scheduled for national introduction in August. It will be sold oncounter in drug, food, and mass merchandising outlets.

Prime and daytime network TV spending will total $10.2 million in the first year. Introductory print ads will appear in six major consumer magazines and cost $1.8 million.

Consumer promotions designed to sample 78 million people will cost $3.1 million in the first year. The launch program has three key elements.

Two coupons good for a free trial-sized sample of the shampoo and rinse will be dropped to 18 million households as part of the "super coupon" program. The coupons also can be redeemed for $.50 off the regular price of $2.39 for a seven-ounce

bottle or $2.99 for an 11-ounce bottle of either the shampoo or rinse.

"Tip-in" cards will be inserted in five consumer magazines. They may be redeemed for a free trial-size bottle of either product. Cents-off coupons worth $.20 for either product will be included in trial-size product mailings.

Supporting the extensive advertising and sampling programs, trade allowances worth $7.8 million will be available. They include a 20% introductory off-invoice allowance and a 9% co-op advertising allowance. Placement allowances for counter and full-size floorstand displays also will be available.

Three display units have been prepared for FOHO. Full-size counter units will hold three bottles each of shampoo and rinse in both sizes, for a total of 12 units.

Floorstands which hold 36 pieces—18 seven-ounce bottles of each product—and trial-size floorstands also are being prepared. The latter stand holds 108 units, evenly divided between shampoo and rinse.

Full-color consumer brochures are included with the floorstands.

QUESTIONS

1. What tools in the promotion mix are being used in the introductory campaign? Give examples of each tool.

2. Has the target audience been sufficiently described for the promotion campaign? Why or why not?

3. Are sales-related or communications objectives more appropriate for the introductory advertising?

4. What creative messages should be used in the promotion?

5. How does Gillette's management know that $22.9 million is a proper budget for the promotion? Which of the budget procedures is best for this product?

6. Can publicity play a role in the new product introduction? Why or why not?

Case 19.2 _____

Legume

CHANDRI AND GARY BARAT assume that they can get Americans to eat bean curd and like it. They envision frozen products made of the white, cheesy, nearly

SOURCE: Sanford L. Jacobs, "Company finds a niche selling frozen foods made with tofu," *Wall Street Journal*, Jan. 25, 1983, p. 25. Reprinted by permission of the *Wall Street Journal*, © Dow Jones & Company, Inc. 1983. All rights reserved.

tasteless ingredient—properly known as tofu—selling briskly in supermarkets across the country.

Many businesses are started with such visions. Seldom do they succeed. Three out of four new frozen food products don't make it in the marketplace and disappear. Success usually must be bought with bundles of advertising dollars, but even such spending doesn't guarantee anything.

Many new products fail after millions have been spent on them. A few small concerns, however, find permanent places for their food products. Occasionally, one grows into a big company.

The Barats' company, three-year-old Legume, Inc., can't be counted a success yet. A private sale of stock last year raised $100,000 that saved it from bankruptcy. But the Bloomfield, N.J., concern has succeeded in placing its products in health-food stores across the country and in a few supermarket chains on both coasts. The Barats are talking to venture capital firms and a major food company about a $400,000 or $500,000 investment to be used primarily for promotion to build sales past the $1 million level by next year.

Hard work and good fortune have brought the Barats this far. Making tofu-based products has helped. Some food industry people say tofu could become as popular as yogurt, once an oddity sold mainly in health-food stores.

Made from the milk produced by cooking soybeans, tofu has been a dietary staple in the Orient for centuries. Occidentals usually encounter it in their soup in Chinese restaurants. It makes some people shiver.

Legume's success doesn't depend on people eating plain tofu. "Our idea," says 40-year-old Mr. Barat, "was to put it in finished products in ways that Mr. and Mrs. Average American can understand."

Tofu is low in fat and calories, hasn't any cholesterol and is a good source of protein. It can replace fat-rich cheese and eggs in many dishes, or be made into mock-meat dishes. In Legume's frozen lasagna, ravioli and pizza, tofu replaces cheese. The result is convenience food that is low in fat and calories, attributes that appeal to the growing number of health-conscious Americans.

A break moved the Barats quickly beyond the cottage-industry stage. A friend introduced them to a baker in New Jersey. He was impressed by their business plan and put $19,500 into the company and let them use his bakery after his daily baking was done. The professional facilities enabled the Barats to develop new products and produce more tofu baked goods, which they were able to sell to health-food stores.

Another fortuitous move was plucking Ira Shapiro's name from a list of food distributors and asking him to represent Legume. Mr. Shapiro is a veteran distributor who represents major low-calorie frozen food lines—something the Barats didn't know when they picked him out. He thought tofu-baked products could be big, but Legume was too small for his company then. However, his son, Robert, put $10,000 into Legume and became sales manager.

As luck would have it, a large Italian food company is near the bakery used by the Barats. Its owner was introduced to the couple by the baker, and they found that his philosophy of food coincided with theirs—his products contain no additives, sugar or artificial ingredients. The food company went on to make Legume's first tofu lasagna in May 1982, and now produces all its products. Eventually, the baked goods were dropped in favor of the Italian frozen products, which have gained supermarket acceptance quicker than quiches, muffins and desserts could have.

Legume's sales are only $40,000 a month, $20,000 less than the breakeven point. But the company will survive, Mr. Barat says, even if it doesn't get the money he is after. There's enough left from last year's financing to see it through to profitability. Sales could be built faster with funds for consumer advertising and store demonstrations. Giving out cooked samples has always increased Legume's sales in stores, but such promotions cost as much as $100 a day. The company also could use more sales people to make sure its products get into freezer cases.

QUESTIONS

1. Should Legume use a push or pull promotion strategy? Give reasons for your answer.

2. Does the financial condition of Legume affect the promotion mix that should be used? Give reasons for your answer.

3. How should a budget be determined for advertising? For sales promotion?

4. Should Legume use publicity in its promotion mix? Why or why not?

5. What promotion messages are appropriate for this product?

6. What types of advertising media and sales promotion activities should Legume use?

7. Does Legume need market opportunity analysis information to help with promotion decisions? Why or why not?

20 Selling and Sales Management

When you finish this chapter, you will understand

☐ The nature and scope of personal selling

☐ The steps of the personal selling process

☐ The differences between selling to business and government customers and selling to consumers

☐ The major activities that a sales manager performs in managing a salesforce

☐ Several key issues that confront sales managers

Formal training sessions to learn about new or modified products is one type of program in which an experienced salesforce participates. Salespersons must know their products to be effective with customers.

The NCH Corporation produces and markets more than 400 products, including specialized lubricants, cleaners, water treatments, pesticides, solvents, and other maintenance chemicals. Selling is a vital part of the company's marketing approach. NCH's selling strategy is centered on sales representatives gaining complete product knowledge and understanding of the customer's operations to enable salespersons to recommend systems that save the firm's 500,000 customers time and money. Customers are located primarily in the United States, Canada, Western Europe, Latin America, Australia, and the Far East. Ongoing training programs keep NCH's sales force current on the latest technological developments. Seminars are also conducted for customers. The nearly 4,000 salespeople are trained to help customers solve their maintenance problems. They study customers' unique maintenance requirements, responding with service, products, and equipment that meet their needs. Illustrative of NCH's commitment to improving customer service is the fact that sales representatives use a hand-held computer terminal to transmit orders to headquarters for immediate processing. This results in faster, more accurate service for NCH customers, building a strong relationship between the firm and its customers.[1]

SOME TOP SALESPEOPLE are paid more than $100,000 a year. For many companies, personal selling is the cutting edge of their marketing programs (although salaries of $100,000 are uncommon). There is a wide variety of selling positions ranging from the consultative positions used in NCH Corporation to door-to-door selling positions used in firms such as Avon.

Contacting customers directly using salespeople is an important marketing activity in fields such as real estate, insurance, industrial equipment, cosmetics, and stocks and bonds. Millions of persons are employed in selling. Avon alone had a salesforce of more than one million sales representatives worldwide in 1985.[2] Annual expenditures for personal selling by companies in the United States are approaching $200 billion.

In this chapter we examine the nature and scope of personal selling by considering its purpose and importance and the various types of sales positions that are used by business firms. Next, the steps in the selling process are discussed, followed by an overview of selling to business, industry, and government. Finally we look at the major activities of sales management, including establishing the role of the salesforce; recruiting, selecting, and training salespersons; and supervising, motivating, and evaluating salespersons.

NATURE AND SCOPE OF PERSONAL SELLING

Purpose of selling

Selling involves direct communications between buyers and sellers. Yet the selling process represents more than the flow of information between individuals. Personal selling is the process of interaction between a buyer and a seller of a good or service leading to an exchange that benefits each party.

Mutual advantage. An important point of this definition is that the exchange benefits each party. Situations in which one party does not deliver value to the other are fraud, not selling.[3] Unfortunately, there are some dishonest people in selling, and they can cause the public to question the ethics of salespeople. Although isolated events of fraud and dishonesty exist in the field of sales, most salespeople are highly committed professionals who recognize that both buyer and seller must benefit from the exchange.

Persuasive communication. At the heart of selling is persuasion; that is, convincing buyers that a product or service will meet their needs. An illustration from Quaker Chemical, a specialty chemical producer, demonstrates persuasive communication. A Quaker sales engineer was trying to persuade an appliance maker to use Quaker's primer to improve paint adhesion instead of the competitor's.[4] Such a salesperson functions as a problem solver, analyzing customers' operations, needs, and problems. The sales engineer determined through discussions with Quaker's laboratory staff that they could not provide a better primer. Instead, Quaker's sales strategy was to provide primer that could be applied at lower temperatures, thus reducing energy costs. Quaker got the business, which represented $250,000 in sales, and the customer gained a 20 percent energy savings.

Importance of selling

The importance of selling in business today is clearly illustrated by the number of persons employed in selling, annual expenditures for selling, and the role of selling in specific firms.

Persons employed in selling. The total labor force in the United States was 105 million in 1980 and is expected to increase to 122 million by 1990.[5] Selling accounts for approximately 7 percent of jobs in the United States. The number of sales employees of retail stores, manufacturing and wholesale firms, insurance companies, real estate agencies, and various other businesses will increase 28 percent from 6.9 million in 1980 to 8.8 million by 1990. Sales positions numbered 1.1 million in Canada in 1980, constituting approximately 10 percent of total employment.[6]

Personal selling expenditures. Though a precise estimate of total expenditures on selling is not available, using some conservative assumptions we can arrive at a rough estimate. If in 1986 there were 8 million salespersons each paid an average of $20,000 a year, total sales salaries were $160 billion. Assume that expenses, benefits, and other costs associated with personal selling amount to an additional one-fourth of the compensation of salepersons, or $40 billion. The total of these to figures equals $200 billion, the estimated expenditures for personal selling. Because industrial salespeople earn considerably more than $20,000 a year, our estimate is probably on the low side. For example, the sum of median annual expenses and compensation for salespeople in industrial-products firms was nearly $75,000 in 1983, split about equally between expenses and compensation.[7] Personal selling costs of $200 billion are quite large, dwarfing advertising expenditures by a substantial margin.

Selling in selected firms. A brief look at the role of personal selling in several firms will further demonstrate the importance of selling in the economy.

AT&T has a well trained professional salesforce of 6,500. They are called account executives. Commissions represent as much as 50% of an account executive's pay. They are targeted to 28 industry segments where salespeople concentrate on selling solutions.[8]

Personal selling is a major component of the marketing strategy of direct sales cosmetics firms like Avon, Mary Kay, and Lady Love. Small by Avon standards, Mary Kay Cosmetics, Inc., has an impressive record of accomplishment in both sales and profit growth. With only 4% of the total retail cosmetics market, the firm has nearly 200,000 part-time beauty consultants working under 4,000 full-time sales directors.[9]

At the age of 29, Kim Kelley, a computer salesman for Honeywell Inc. shook hands on an $8.1 million computer sale to the state of Illinois. His career was on the line in making the sale since he had been working three years laying the groundwork. During the last three months he was competing against other computer salespeople working six days a week, often 14 hours a day.[10]

Many other examples could be cited to highlight both the importance and variety of personal selling in business and industry. Let us examine how sales positions vary among companies.

Types of sales positions

A useful way to see the wide variation among sales jobs is to contrast order-takers in a Wendy's fast-food restaurant with consultative salespersons such as Kim Kelley, just described in the computer sales example. One widely used scheme classifies sales positions according to the technical knowledge and the creative skills necessary to sell the product or service.[11] The complexity and use of some products require the salesperson to have technical knowledge of the product. Creative skills are often needed to sell intangibles and products whose features must be communicated to the buyer. Based on these two factors, four general types of sales positions can be described: order taking, technical selling, creative selling, and consultative selling. You should recognize that use of such broad categories results in a variety of sales jobs within a category.

Order taking. Sales jobs that do not require the seller to have extensive technical knowledge or creative skills are generally known as **order taking** positions. Nevertheless, persons in these positions are important because they communicate with the buyer and execute the transaction. Many of the sales positions in retail stores fall into this category, as does trade selling, as illustrated by food products salespeople calling on retail supermarkets. The buying decision for many food products is often made by chain management or wholesalers rather than as a result of sales calls at the individual store level by order-taking salespeople.

Technical selling. Industrial sales positions that require the salesperson to understand how the product works and how it is applied are called **technical selling** positions. Some firms that sell complex equipment require salespeople to have engineering or science degrees. Others provide extensive product and applications training to their salespeople. For example, U.S. Surgical Corporation, the leading manufacturer of surgical stapling equipment, conducts a 240-hour training program for new salespeople covering basic anatomy, physiology, surgical terminology, scrubbing and gowning, and operating protocol in addition to the operation of the company's products.[12]

Creative selling. There are many products and services, such as life insurance and mutual funds, for which buyers have not established a definite need. In **creative selling** the salesperson must analyze how the product can meet the buyer's needs, encourage the prospect to recognize these needs, and then convince the buyer to purchase the product. Many intangibles are sold by the creative selling method such as security systems, financial services, and management-training programs.

Consultative selling. **Consultative selling** positions are the most demanding of all selling positions: Salespeople in these positions must have both technical knowledge and creative skills. Computer systems frequently are sold by consultative salespeople because they may help design products or systems to meet a client's needs. The NCH Corporation salesforce uses consultative selling. Because of the demands of consultative selling, salary and other compensation are often high.

THE PERSONAL SELLING PROCESS

What must a salesperson accomplish to make a sale? The major activities of the personal selling process are shown in Exhibit 20.1. A close examination of each stage provides insights into the salesperson's job. As you read about the selling process in the following discussion keep in mind that the entire process may occur quickly or it may span several days, weeks, or even months. Thus the nature and extent of the process depend substantially on the product or service and the particular selling situation.

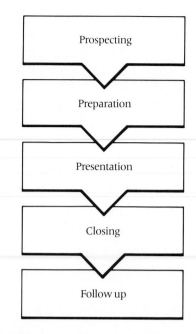

Exhibit 20.1 The personal selling process

Prospecting

Prospecting—finding potential buyers for your product or service—varies considerably from one business to another. Some businesses assign a salesperson to a geographic area called a *territory*. The salesperson must then identify possible buyers for his or her product. In other businesses specific customers (called *accounts*) are assigned to the salesperson. Increasingly, firms are providing salespeople with guidelines for targeting prospects. Time spent on accounts whose potential purchases do not justify the selling expenses is not profitable. For example, the management of Quaker Chemical has specified that a potential customer should have a need to purchase at least $50,000 of chemicals each year for a Quaker sales engineer to call on the prospect.

There are two important activities in prospecting: First, the salesperson must determine how and where to find prospective buyers, an activity that concerns *location*. Second, once identified, the salesperson must screen prospects to find out if they should receive further attention, an activity that concerns *qualification* of the buyer. Because a salesperson has a limited amount of time, allocating this effort to the most promising prospects is important.

Locating prospects. The objective of the search for prospects is to find consumer or organizational buyers that are willing and able to buy. Several techniques are used to find prospects including

Cold canvass. This method involves calling on all available people (or organizations) to uncover potential buyers. It is often used in door-to-door selling. Industrial salespeople may contact all available firms in a certain area or industry to determine which ones are promising prospects.

Referral. Prospects may be referred to salespeople as a result of inquiries from people interested in a product or service. Referral may come from advertising, friends of prospects, trade contacts, and shows and demonstrations.

Directories and lists. Various lists of people and organizations can be used to locate prospects. For example, during the late 1970s when purchase of precious metals was popular, some firms purchased mailing lists of investors from sources such as *Forbes* magazine and then followed up by contacting the people on the mailing lists by telephone.

Other specific techniques for locating prospects include company records, contests, parties (e.g., Tupperware parties), membership in civic and professional organizations, and newspapers.

Qualifying prospects. Once a prospect is located, the salesperson must determine whether further sales development effort is justified. Various factors are evaluated including the prospect's financial capabilities, extent and urgency of need, purchasing potential, and competition. Evaluating ability and willingness to buy are key factors in qualifying prospects.

Preparation

A salesperson should prepare for the sales presentation to the prospect. In some sales situations, only a single presentation is made. For technically complex or expensive products, such as a large computer system, several presentations may be necessary before closing the sale. Two essential aspects of **preparation** for a sales presentation are understanding the buyer's needs and wants and then developing a plan for selling the product.

Understanding the buyer. The more information the salesperson has about the buyer, the better equipped he or she will be to make a successful sale. The selling process in industry is often complicated because more than one person maybe involved in deciding what brand to purchase. (See Chapter 6.) Even in a household, more than one family member may be involved in purchase decisions. In preparing for a sales presentation the salesperson needs information on the buyer's intended use for the product, factors the buyer believes are important in selecting a brand, who influences the purchase decision, and competition. Carefully studying the potential buyer will guide the salesperson in deciding how to convince the buyer to purchase the product or service.

Developing the sales plan. Successful salespeople plan their sales presentations. A used-car salesperson may quickly formulate a plan while the prospect is on the lot. And the plan is probably a version of a successful selling approach that the salesperson has developed through years of experience. Alternatively, planning for the sale of a major computer installation requires extensive analysis and preparation. The objective of preparation is to decide how to match the buyers' needs and wants with the benefits offered by the product. The salesperson must also decide how to communicate with the prospect in a way that will enhance the chances of obtaining the sale. Planning for the presentation (or presentations) should incorporate information about the characteristics and preferences of the buyer, the use situation, and product characteristics. It is also essential that the salesperson be knowledgeable about the products of key competitors.

Since its purchase in 1980 by H&R Block Company, CompuServe Inc. has become a leader in providing videotext services to microcomputer users. In the past few years, its videotext subscription base has quadrupled to more than 200,000. CompuServe's advertisements contain toll-free 800 numbers, which is one way the company locates prospects for its service. (Reprinted with permission of CompuServe Incorporated)

Planning the presentation often involves using visual aids and other communications tools. (See Marketech for a description of how videoconferencing is being used in sales presentations.) Some companies provide salespeople with slide presentations, flip charts, display notebooks, samples, and other aids. When appropriate, the product is actually demonstrated. Some firms use so-called canned presentations, which are step-by-step presentation approaches that have proved successful through extended use. Salespeople are trained in how to use the standard approach, which is also called a *prepared sales presentation*. They are used in various industries including door-to-door selling, retail store sales, and some types of industrial sales. Prepared presentations assume that the prospect is typical or average and do not take into account specific needs and wants.

The *customized* approach recognizes that the needs of prospects vary and that the presentation should address the prospect's needs. This can also be called a need-satisfaction approach. A sales presentation can be designed for each customer and prospect or used for specific groups of customers.

Many selling approaches fall between the canned and customized approaches. The salesperson follows an organized approach based on knowledge of the general market situation and the common needs and wants of customers. This general guide is adapted by the individual salesperson to fit the particular selling situation. For example, the salesperson may be trained to recognize different types of buyers and follow a specific selling approach after identifying the buyer type.

An example of a sales plan for a salesperson's accounts is shown in Exhibit 20.2. The illustration highlights several important aspects of the selling process. Note that Sam has identified specific sales objectives including dates for accomplishment. He recognizes that more than one person will affect the purchase decision, and he has determined specific actions that are necessary to meet his objectives.

Marke**TECH** □ □ □ □ □ □ □ □ □ □ □ □ □ □ □ □ □

Using videoconferencing as a selling tool

AN IMPORTANT SELLING tool in many firms is *videoconferencing* (or *teleconferencing*). Today it is possible to transmit high-quality pictures at acceptable costs to a network of receiving locations. Although two-way conferencing is available, it is expensive. One-way video using private satellite transmission is gaining more rapid acceptance because of its relatively low cost. One-way direct broadcasting can cost as little as $30 an hour per site compared

SOURCE: "One-way video takes off like a rocket," *Business Week*, Nov. 12, 1984, p. 117; and Paul E. Gillette, "Picture this presentation,". *Sales & Marketing Management*, June 4, 1984, p. 57.

with more than $600 per hour for two-way, two-site networks.

Consider the following illustration:

When money market interest rates began to slide two years ago, Merrill Lynch & Co. produced a special hour-long presentation on "Strategies for High-Yield Investments" to try to keep big spenders in the fold. The live television show, broadcast to invited guests at 30 specially wired hotels around the country, did the trick: A solid 35% of the 30,000 viewing customers bought one of the products suggested. The company was so stunned by these results that this year it began a weekly broadcast to some of its sales offices. Now it is

installing a permanent video network that will encompass all 500 of its sales offices by next year.

A medical equipment manufacturer used videoconferencing to communicate with its wide customer base: 1000 orthopedic surgeons at twenty-six teleconference sites throughout the United States witnessed a demonstration of its new arthroscopic instruments in a delicate knee operation. Supplementing the surgical presentation was a three-hour live program explaining the latest advances in diagnosis and surgical techniques provided by local workshops at each of the receiving sites.

□ □

Exhibit 20.2 Illustration of a plan for an industrial account

SALES ENGINEER SAM DOAKS

Major Objectives	Date to Accomplish	Persons Affecting Decision(s)	Accomplish Objective	Date to Accomplish
1. Assure continued purchase of product "B" by convincing purchasing agent of the superiority of our paint.	10/1	John Jones, Purchasing Agent	1. Convince Jones to come to our plant for a visit—make appointment.	9/15
			2. Conduct tour of plant and demonstrate paint finish.	10/1
2. Obtain an initial order for product "C" of at least $5,000.	11/15	John Smith, Plant Engineer Jim Brown, Maintenance Superintendent John Jones, Purchasing Agent	1. Make appointment with John Smith to find current supplier and find out decision maker.	9/5
			2. Determine whether moisture or aging is most important problem to Smith.	9/5
			3. Get appointment for demonstration of product "C" to Smith, Brown, and Jones.	9/15
			4. Hold presentation and ask for order.	10/1

SOURCE: Robert A. Else, "Selling by measurable objectives," *Sales & Marketing Management Magazine,* May 14, 1973, p. 24. Copyright © 1973. Reprinted by permission.

Presentation and closing

After the salesperson has prepared, the presentation is made to the prospect, the prospect's objections (e.g., resistance) are countered, and the salesperson closes (or loses) the sale. These activities may occur at one point in time or instead may involve two or more contacts between the salesperson and the buyer, as illustrated in Exhibit 20.2.

Presentation. The **presentation** has four major parts: getting the buyer's *a*ttention, generating *i*nterest, stimulating *d*esire to buy, and finally causing *a*ction to purchase the product or service.[13] This is often called the AIDA model. Various techniques are used by salespeople to move the presentation toward ultimate action by the buyer. The most important rule of selling is that at the proper point in the presentation, the salesperson must *ask for the order.* Nothing happens unless the sale is closed.

Countering objections. One of the major strengths of personal selling, compared with advertising and sales promotion, is that the salesperson can interact with the buyer and respond to the buyer's questions. For example, if the prospect indicates that the price of the product is too high or that the product is too difficult to operate, the salesperson has an opportunity to overcome these objections. To properly respond to objections the salesperson must understand the buyer's needs and wants, the competition, the product, and the real reason the buyer is raising an objection.

Closing. **Closing** is the prospect's actual commitment to purchase the item the salesperson is selling. Your signature on an order form for a new automobile represents a closed sale. One frequent criticism of inexperienced salespersons is that they often fail to ask for the order, waiting instead for the prospect to indicate a willingness to buy. Successful salespersons are skillful in moving the selling process toward closing and have developed various techniques to assist in closing the sale. For example, an automobile salesperson may offer a final price concession to close the sale.

Postsale follow up

Successful salespersons know that the selling process does not end when the customer purchases the product. It is important that the buyer's experience in using the product be favorable. Depending on the product and the nature of the selling situation, **postsale follow up** can include activities such as offering application assistance, providing repair and service, handling complaints, obtaining names of other prospects, and acknowledging customers' suggestions for improving products. For instance, the word *guaranteed* plays a key role in the success of ChemLawn's services. The firm emphasizes the guarantee by painting it on each of its 3800 trucks. Trial of new services such as carpet cleaning and pest control is facilitated by eliminating the buyer's risk by offering the heavily promoted money-back guarantee.

Many businesses place a great deal of importance on postsale follow up, as illustrated by the practice of a large hospital in a metropolitan area. About ten days after each patient leaves the hospital, the administrator writes the person wishing them a speedy recovery, thanking them for using the hospital, and asking them to complete and return a short questionnaire evaluating the hospital stay. Hospital staff members follow up with personal contacts on any problems identified in the questionnaire. Excellent services, concern about patient care, and aggressive marketing have made the hospital one of the most successful in its market area.

This completes our look at the personal selling process. We next examine personal selling when the customer is an organization rather than a household. Because industrial-products selling differs in several ways from consumer products-selling, discussion of these differences will provide you with additional insights into the selling process.

SELLING TO BUSINESS, INDUSTRY, AND GOVERNMENT

Personal selling is a major part of the marketing budget for many firms that sell industrial products. This type of selling is sometimes called *business-to-business selling*. As we compare the process of selling industrial products with that of selling consumer products, look closely for some of the more important differences. Some aspects of industrial selling are discussed in Chapters 6 and 9: In Chapter 6 we consider key characteristics of industrial buyers, including how organizational buying differs from consumer buying, types of organizational buyers, how these buyers make purchasing decisions, and influences on organizational buying. In Chapter 9, the major categories of industrial goods and services are identified and described. Recall that the products used in producing and distributing goods include facilities, equipment, supplies, and services. Items incorporated into products consist of raw materials and parts and materials. Thus our objective in the following discussion is to look at how salespeople sell industrial products, emphasizing key differences between industrial and consumer sales. First, the types of industrial buyers are described. Next, characteristics of both market demand and the selling process are examined. Finally, characteristics of the promotional mix unique to industrial products are highlighted.

Types of buyers

Retailers and wholesalers. Buyers in these firms purchase for resale to consumer and industrial purchasers. Typically, purchases are made in large quantities, and a variety of criteria are important in evaluating suppliers. Purchase decisions for chains of retail stores are normally made for all stores in the chain. These decisions may be made by buying committees or by individuals, depending on the quantity and type of item. Because many of the products are purchased repeatedly, long-term relationships between buyers and sellers often make it difficult for new suppliers to make sales.

Consider this illustration. United Stationers, the largest independent office-products wholesaler in the United States, distributes 20,000 items made by 380 manufacturers to its 8500 dealers.[14] The primary mission of the firm's 125-person salesforce is to introduce and integrate various services into dealers' operations including store layout and design, merchandising and fixturing, and promotional assistance. More than 97 percent of the company's orders are received over telephone lines including dealer-based electronic order entry. Thus these salespeople work as management consultants to the firm's dealers, helping them build sales and efficiently process orders.

Manufacturers. Many manufacturers assign one or more persons the responsibility for purchasing the material needed to produce the firm's products. An important part of the salesperson's sales planning is determining and evaluating the nature and extent of influence on the purchase by each of the persons involved in the decision. A major distinction of purchasing by manufacturers compared with other organizations is that each item purchased is used to manufacture a product or becomes part of that product. Thus, a major criterion in the purchase decision is the competence and reliability of the supplier. An inexpensive item such as a switch in a piece of electronics equipment can cause the entire unit to break down if the switch is faulty. Accordingly, supplier evaluation is an essential part of many purchase decisions of manufacturers. Not surprisingly, when reliable sources of supply are established, manufacturers tend to repurchase from these suppliers.

Government. Federal, state, and local government agencies constitute a major market for potential suppliers. Purchases by various government units represent approximately one-fifth of the gross national product. Most salespeople responsible for government sales like the potential market the government represents but do not like the procedures, paperwork, and other red tape they must follow in the selling process. Each agency has its own purchasing practices and procedures. The buying situation varies considerably according to the item being purchased. Contrast, for example, the purchase of military aircraft with the purchase of paper clips. The process of buying an aircraft may take several years; it begins with requesting competitive bid contracts for the aircraft's development and ends with awarding a production contract. Even paper clips are purchased following routine bid procedures with price being a major factor in the purchase decision, providing the supplier is an acceptable source for paper clips.

Other organizational buyers. Examples in this category include sales to professional people such as doctors and dentists; not-for-profit organizations; professional services firms such as law firms, certified public accountants, and advertising agencies; and a wide variety of specialized firms providing such services as security, garbage collection, and transportation.

Demand characteristics

The demand for industrial products differs in some important ways from demand for consumer products. First, the driving force behind purchases of many industrial products is the demand for consumer products. Second, the volume of purchases by organizations is affected less by price changes than is the volume of consumer purchases. Third, purchases of many industrial products follow cycles of high and low sales.

Impact of consumer purchases. The market opportunity for products purchased by business ultimately depends on what and how much consumers are buying. In Chapter 6 the impact of derived demand on the automobile industry is discussed.

Impact of price on purchases. As long as consumer purchases stimulate organizational buying, price fluctuations of products purchased by organizations typically do not markedly alter the quantities purchased by an organization. If an industry needs a certain quantity of materials or parts to meet the demands of buyers of its products, this amount will be purchased even though the price of the material increases or decreases. Of course, if price increases a great deal and producers cannot pass the increases on to their consumers, then the producers may cut back on purchases. Similarly, major cuts in prices may cause organizational buyers to stockpile materials, parts, and supplies.

Cyclical purchases. In many industries purchases by organizations are subject to greater fluctuations than are purchases by consumers. When consumer purchases slow down or speed up, the quantity purchased by a manufacturer follows suit. Although not all industrial products are influenced by such shifts in buying, those affected may experience either very favorable or unfavorable sales conditions. Examples of industries affected include suppliers of homebuilding products, agricultural equipment, and machine tools.

Characteristics of the industrial selling process

Our discussion in Chapter 6 highlights the important characteristics of organizational buyers and the nature of the buying situation. We expand that discussion in this chapter to include some key aspects of the selling process.

The buying situation. Several factors may affect the buying situation including the amount of experience of the buyer, the newness of the purchase situation, the amount and type of information needed by the people involved in the purchase decision, and the purchase alternatives available to the buyer. Based on these factors, a buying situation can be designated as new task buying, modified rebuy, or straight rebuy as discussed in Chapter 6.

The salesperson has the greatest opportunity for new business in a new task buying situation and little or no opportunity in a straight rebuy unless his or her firm is one of the established sources of supply. If the salesperson loses a new task sale to a competitor or is trying to break into a straight rebuy situation, creating a modified rebuy may provide a possible sales opportunity.

Criteria for evaluating suppliers. What factors do organizational buyers use to evaluate new and existing suppliers? While the factors used to evaluate a firm's suppliers will vary according to the buying situation, several criteria are

Product or service quality
Application (use of product) and service assistance provided
Ability to meet the buyer's delivery requirements
Prices
Flexibility in responding to nonroutine situations
Communications and contact relationships between buyer and seller[15]

The National Can Company uses a set of criteria similar to these to rate each supplier. The firm's management provides a supplier with its evaluation and a comparison with its competitors. This information enables a supplier to find out its strengths and weaknesses as perceived by the buyer.

Sales development. Unlike selling to consumers, industrial sales normally involve several calls on the prospect before a purchase is made. Recall, for example, the sales plan shown in Exhibit 20.2. Several calls were planned

In a market as volatile as the computer industry, Wang realizes that good products alone do not ensure success. Services such as field service, support staff, and educational programs are added value that more and more today amount to the competitive edge. (Courtesy of Wang Laboratories, Inc. Copyright © 1984 Wang Laboratories, Inc.)

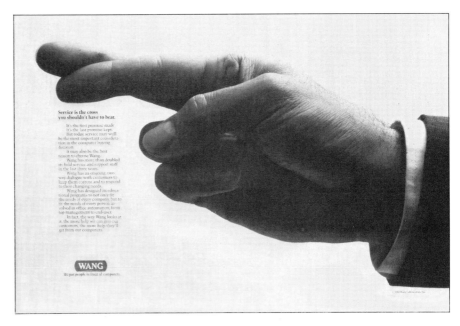

before the final presentation and the request for the order. Based on studies conducted by McGraw-Hill Research the average cost to close an industrial sale was $908 in 1981 and required an average of 5.1 calls. Only 4 percent of the firms included in the study reported closing sales with one call, and 7 percent indicated eleven or more calls were required.[16]

An interesting comparison of the cost per sales call for various industries in 1983 is shown in Exhibit 20.3. The overall average cost per call was $205 in 1983 compared with $67 in 1973.

Continuing buyer-seller relationship. Sales to consumers are often one-time experiences for both buyer and seller. Many industrial selling situations involve long-term relationships between buyer and seller. The new task and modified rebuy buying situations present a major sales challenge for a supplier trying to win over an account from a competitor. Consider, for example, Standard Register Company, the second-largest business-forms manufacturer in the United States. The firm's salespeople stress the savings

McGraw-Hill believes that many salespeople have been reduced to little more than wind-up toys by some marketing managers. A sales staff, this ad says, "should be supported by a multimedia customer-contact program that includes advertising, direct mail, and telemarketing." Let advertising locate new prospects and telemarketing and direct mail handle the smaller leads. An effective salesforce cannot rely on mechanical messages to existing and potential customers: It should concentrate its talents on major prospects and focus on negotiating and closing the sale. (Courtesy of McGraw-Hill Publications Company)

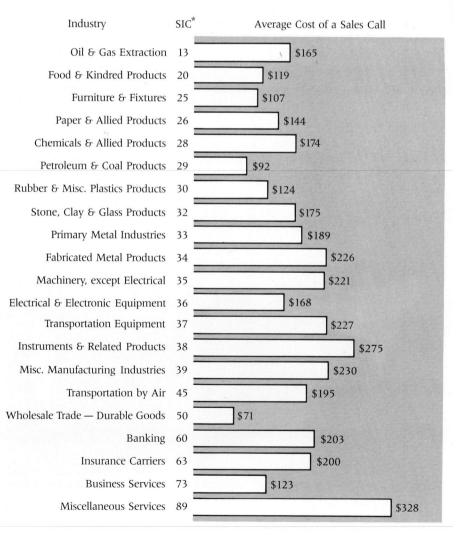

Industry	SIC*	Average Cost of a Sales Call
Oil & Gas Extraction	13	$165
Food & Kindred Products	20	$119
Furniture & Fixtures	25	$107
Paper & Allied Products	26	$144
Chemicals & Allied Products	28	$174
Petroleum & Coal Products	29	$92
Rubber & Misc. Plastics Products	30	$124
Stone, Clay & Glass Products	32	$175
Primary Metal Industries	33	$189
Fabricated Metal Products	34	$226
Machinery, except Electrical	35	$221
Electrical & Electronic Equipment	36	$168
Transportation Equipment	37	$227
Instruments & Related Products	38	$275
Misc. Manufacturing Industries	39	$230
Transportation by Air	45	$195
Wholesale Trade — Durable Goods	50	$71
Banking	60	$203
Insurance Carriers	63	$200
Business Services	73	$123
Miscellaneous Services	89	$328

*Only those SIC groups with five or more responses are included in this table.

Exhibit 20.3 Variations in cost of a sales call found from industry to industry
SOURCE: Reprinted from Laboratory of Advertising Performance Report No. 8052.2. McGraw-Hill Research. 1983 data.

that can be obtained by customers from simplifying and managing their usage of forms.

> While investigating how to save money for Earl Scheib, Inc., the national cut-rate car-painting firm, SR's salesmen learned that [Mr.] Scheib was a bit vain. So SR designed a form with Scheib's picture plastered over it and got the account.[17]

As you can see, personal as well as economic factors are involved in organizational buying.

Promotional mix characteristics

Consumer- and industrial-products firms often differ in the amount of their promotion budget allocated to advertising and personal selling. In many industrial firms, personal selling budgets are considerably higher than advertising budgets because the communications task between buyer and seller requires extensive personal contact to inform the buyer about the product, assist in applying the product, and provide after-the-sale service. The size of purchases by many industrial buyers provides sufficient margins for suppliers to pay for expensive sales calls (see Exhibit 20.3).

This completes our look at the personal selling process. Before turning to a discussion of managing salespeople, read Marketalk about Xerox Learning Systems' research results on knowing and using selling skills.

SALES MANAGEMENT

Role of the salesforce

Our earlier discussion of the major types of sales positions suggests that the job of *salesperson* may vary widely among companies. Marketing management must determine what role personal selling will play in the firm's marketing program, and from this decision guidelines that spell out the responsibilities assigned to the salesforce are set. For example, will the primary function of salespeople be to assist retailers in displaying the product line and other merchandising activities as do Revlon's salespeople, or instead to obtain orders, as do Avon's salespeople?

Salespeople may be assigned some combination of three major activities: obtaining sales, collecting market information, and providing customer service.[18] The selling process shown in Exhibit 20.1 describes the activities salespeople perform in obtaining sales. Market information responsibilities may include asking customers' opinions on product performance, evaluating key competitors, and providing feedback on customers' problems. Customer service may consist of merchandising assistance, service and repair, product application training, and various other aids to customers. The mix of selling, information, and service responsibilities vary depending on the role assigned to the salesforce by management.

Firms with several salespersons often use a job description to explain the role and activities of a salesperson. The **job description** indicates the specific responsibilities assigned to the salesperson regarding planning, organizing, selling, personal development, and organizational development. Examples of frequent topics included in job descriptions are shown in Exhibit 20.4.

Setting objectives

An important part of sales management's responsibilities is setting specific objectives for the salesforce. Depending on the role of the salesforce, objectives may be specified for total sales volume and market share, sales by product category, number of new customers, average sales by customer, number of calls per account, and other desired results.

*Marke*TALK //

Study reveals twenty-eight keys to customers' minds

KNOWING AND USING selling skills—28 skills in particular—make a significant difference in the average salesperson's call success, reports Xerox Learning Systems in research results announced in June.

Xerox Learning's in-depth analysis of more than 500 sales calls by 176 salespeople in 24 different companies also found that a salesperson's age, experience, education and gender is not a strong indicator of his or her ability to make successful calls.

Although the finding that skills rather than broad demographic characteristics create sales success is hardly new, Xerox Learning's statistical analysis of call information collected by trained observers provides new broadly-based information about an age-old marketing question.

Xerox Learning, which is in the sales training business, concludes that salespeople can improve their performance with:

- Natural, balanced dialogues with customers;
- "Probing strategies" to uncover information and reveal customer needs;
- Sensitivity to real customer needs and attitudes vs. "vague dissatisfaction";
- Benefit-oriented presentations; and
- A "close" that summarizes benefits and asks for customer commitment.

The study, based on observed calls in business services, chemicals, high technology, finance, manufacturing and many other industries, rated each call as "successful" (customer makes a commitment to take some action); "process-continues" (customer agrees to meet again); and "failed" (all other call results). Poor salespeople, the study says, aren't aware of sell-

SOURCE: *Business Marketing,* Aug. 1984, pp. 10, 12. Reprinted with permission from *Business Marketing,* Aug. 1984, copyright 1984 by Crain Communications Inc.

ing skills. Average salespeople know them but don't use skills efficiently. In contrast, successful salespeople constantly use the 28 critical skills and remain alert to closing opportunities throughout the call. The study also indicates a very strong relationship between the use of selling skills and salespeople's performance against quotas.

Among the findings Xerox Learning reported:

- There's no one best way to open a call, but successful salespeople prepare their opening in advance.
- The more successful the call on average, the more customer needs are identified during the call.
- The more successful the call, the more the salesperson acknowledges customer remarks.
- Failed calls discuss significantly fewer product/service features than "successful" or "process-continues" calls.
- The more successful the call, the more the salesperson discusses product/service benefits specific to a customer's expressed needs. But the number of generalized benefit statements made during the call apparently has little impact on its success.
- Failed calls contain significantly fewer "probes" in which the salesperson asks for information, compared to successful calls. But too many "closed probes" (which ask for a limited response) exert too much control, inhibit customer response, and tend to prevent a successful close. Too few "open probes" (which allow customers to respond freely) are also characteristic of failed calls. Xerox Learning recommends that salespeople avoid asking several closed probes in a row, and intersperse open probes into the call to encourage customer participation.

- The more a customer expresses acceptance for the sales proposition, the more successful the call.
- The more the customer expresses indifference, the less successful the call.
- Successful calls are more likely to contain customer objections, which are signs of involvement. They can have a positive or negative impact depending on how well the salesperson handles them.
- Customer skepticism also indicates involvement, and can have a positive or negative impact on the call depending on how it's handled.
- The more the customer asks questions, the more likely the call is successful. The relationship holds true even for questions raised near the end of a call.
- The more a salesperson exercises proper closing technique, the more successful his or her calls. The proper close, Xerox Learning says, summarizes customer benefits and suggests a customer action which requires commitment. (The research found customers taking the initiative to close in only 9% of all calls studies. On one call, the salesperson ignored the customer's statement that he'd take action, he kept talking about the product, and converted the positive response to a negative one.)

In addition to the skills cited, the research also found that success is more likely when salespeople:

- Have an appointment, rather than just "drop by";
- Call on established accounts;
- Call frequently at established accounts and on a particular individual at those accounts; and
- Call during the middle and late stages of the sales cycle at any type of account.

//

Exhibit 20.4 Frequent topics found in job descriptions

Title: Sales representative, territory manager, or account manager.

Objectives: Achieve assigned quotas within the assigned territory and within the approved level of expenses.

Responsibilities: Activities that a representative is obligated to perform in filling the role of a sales representative.

Planning:
Analyze market conditions and forecast future needs of customers and prospects.
Establish objectives for individual calls and for the territory that are consistent with district, regional, and corporate objectives.
Develop strategies for each account.
Develop tactics for each call.
Control expenses within approved budgets.
Maintain company supplies and equipment in an orderly and usable state.

Organizing:
Budget time and activities according to account potential.
Develop and maintain an attitude of cooperation with and support for other representatives, the field sales manager, and other company personnel.
Keep territory records current.

Selling:
Interact effectively with customers to develop a personal awareness of their operations and needs and to provide maximum consulting service.
Perform the steps in the selling process that are required by the selling plan.
Provide service that is appropriate for account potential.

Personal Development:
Develop skills in selling, planning, time and territory management, and communication.
Develop knowledge about the company, the industry, and competitive products.
Maintain a knowledge of current company policies, procedures, and programs.
Analyze success and failures to learn from previous experiences.

Organizational Relationships:
Reporting Relationships: Reports directly to the district sales manager. Communicates as necessary with persons in production, research and development, credit, and accounting.
Authority: The authority for performing activities, such as pricing or specifying delivery dates, without seeking permission is specified in the company policies and procedures for representatives.
Accountability: Representatives have an obligation to see that assigned activities are performed, and report the level of performance to the district sales manager and others through regular reports.
Communication: Communicate regularly and punctually with the field sales manager and other company personnel regarding performance, orders, complaints, inquiries, market conditions, the effectiveness of selling programs, and competitive activities.

Qualifications:
Job-Related Behaviors:
  a. Good oral and written communication skills
  b. A good planner
  c. A self-motivator
  d. Tenacious
  e. A realistic ego drive
Education: Some college education; a degree in business administration; a degree plus two years of selling; selling experience may be substituted for a completed degree.

SOURCE: G. David Hughes and Charles H. Singler, *Strategic Sales Management,* Reading, Mass.: Addison-Wesley, 1983, pp. 72–73. Reprinted with permission.

Objectives are sometimes used as a basis for measuring results for incentive compensation. For example, a sales volume objective, called a **sales quota,** can serve as a yardstick for determining incentive payments. Comparing the salesperson's actual sales with the sales quota indicates how well the salesperson is doing. The salesperson can be paid an incentive or bonus for meeting or exceeding quota. If management wants to ensure proper emphasis on each product, quotas can be assigned by specific product or product lines.

An illustration of how a pharmaceutical manufacturer ties quotas on specific products to incentive compensation is shown in Exhibit 20.5. This approach is particularly appropriate when management wants to ensure that new products or products in need of expanded selling effort receive adequate sales effort. Note the specific objectives for certain products in each product line plus overall sales objectives. The maximum opportunity for bonus compensation is $3.5\% \times 2$ (A and B) $\times$ 4 quarters, or 28 percent of annual salary.

Organizing the salesforce

In the following discussion we assume that a company is organizing a salesforce to cover a geographic area rather than a retail unit such as a department store. Three important aspects of organizing a salesforce are (1) deciding how many salespersons are needed, (2) determining how to allocate available selling effort, and (3) selecting the organizational structure to use in assigning salespeople to selling units.

Determining salesforce size. Salesforce size is an important management decision because both sales and expenses are affected by the number of salespersons employed by a firm. If more people are employed than needed to tap the available sales opportunity, then selling costs will reduce profits. Alternatively, if an insufficient number of salespersons are employed, the firm will not be able to take advantage of sales and profit opportunities.

Two popular methods for determining salesforce size include workload analysis and market potential. The objective of both methods is to base the amount of selling effort needed on some factor related to sales. **Workload analysis** can be determined by knowing how many calls are necessary to serve a firm's customers and prospects. Using the average number of calls that a salesperson can make during a time period, salesforce size can be estimated by dividing total required calls by average calls per salesperson. The average number of calls may be based on past experience, analysis of sales records, competition, and other factors. Suppose that Royal Food Brokers has determined that its 300 buying accounts should each receive ten sales calls per month. In addition, its fifty prospects should each receive six calls per month. Royal's total workload is 3300 calls per month ([300 $\times$ 10] + [50 $\times$ 6] = 3300). Assuming an average salesperson can make 100 calls per month, Acme needs thirty-three salespersons (3300/100 = 33).

Exhibit 20.5 Objectives linked to bonus compensation

Bonus Opportunity Available to Sales Representative Each Quarter	
Product Line A	**Product Line B**
1. 100% of *combined* quarterly sales objective for products A_1, A_2, A_3, and A_4 *1% of annual salary*	1. 100% *combined* quarterly sales objective for products B_1, B_2, B_3 and B_4 *1% of annual salary*
2. 100% of A_1 quarterly sales objective *0.5% of annual salary*	2. 100% of B_1 quarterly sales objective *0.5% of annual salary*
3. 100% of quarterly sales objective for all "A" products *2% of annual salary*	3. 100% of quarterly sales objective for all "B" products *2% of annual salary*
Total: 3.5% of annual salary	Total: 3.5% of annual salary

Different account categories can be established if the amount of selling effort should vary by type of customer. For example, if Acme's management feels that some accounts do not need ten calls per month, then additional account categories can be established.

An example illustrates how market potential can be used to help determine salesforce size. Suppose Acme Electronics, a distributor of electronics equipment, has twenty salespersons covering the Montreal, Canada, metropolitan area. Management has decided to expand operations to three other Canadian metropolitan areas. Experience indicates that industry sales of the equipment distributed by Acme are closely related to the number of people employed in an area. Employment levels in the three cities are: Toronto, 1.545 million; Ottawa-Hull, 0.344; and Vancouver, 0.632.[19] Employment in Montreal is 1.271 million. Using employment as a measure of market potential in Toronto, Acme will need

$$\frac{1.545}{1.271} \times 20 \text{ or approximately 24 salespersons.}$$

The salesforce estimates for Ottawa-Hull and Vancouver respectively are 5 and 10 (rounding to whole numbers).

Allocating selling effort. Companies use various bases for assigning the time of salespeople. Some of the more popular bases are geographic areas (territories), lists of customers and prospects, specific industries, and specialization by product line. The objective is to allocate available selling effort so that the greatest return is obtained from the effort.

Determining organizational units. A company's salesforce is normally organized into hierarchical selling units such as regions, districts, and offices with a region comprising several districts and a group of salespersons assigned to each district. For example, one medium-sized pharmaceutical firm has two regions, six districts in each region, and five to ten salespersons in each district. Firms with large salesforces may use additional organizational units such as branches and offices within districts. Note also that what one firm calls a branch may be equivalent to another firm's district in terms of sales volume and salesforce size.

RECRUITING, SELECTING, AND TRAINING SALESPEOPLE

Most companies are continuously locating people for sales positions, selecting those that qualify for available positions, and training both new and existing salespeople. Additions to a salesforce are necessary owing to increases in the size of the salesforce, retirements, resignations, promotions, and terminations of unsatisfactory performers. A discussion of these activities will help you understand their nature and scope.

Recruiting

Prospects for sales positions can be recruited from various sources including people seeking jobs, colleges, employment agencies, help-wanted advertisements, other departments within a company, and referrals by business associates, friends, and customers. Most companies have identified promising sources of prospects as a result of past experience. Likewise, recruiters have learned which sources to avoid.

Recruiting represents a major activity in firms that are steadily increasing the size of their salesforces. Similarly, high turnover stimulates recruiting efforts as illustrated in this description of Avon's recruiting challenge.

> Recruiting is tough—especially with a U.S. turnover rate of about 150%. Just to keep the sales force steady at last year's 435,000, Avon must add some 650,000 shiny new faces. Some are repeats—about 1 out of 8, the company estimates. But even so, that means that in 1981 one of every 60 women between the ages of 20 and 60 would have sold at least some Avon products.[20]

Avon's unusually high turnover is not typical, but all organizations experience some turnover of sales personnel.

Selecting salespeople

One of the major trends in salesperson selection is the rapid increase of women entering industrial selling. As women enter industrial selling in greater numbers than in the past, some interesting findings are being reported.

> Semispecialists of America, a Farmingdale, N.Y., electronic products distributor, says its average saleswoman earned $31,500 last year, compared with about $25,000 for men. . . . A 28-year-old saleswoman at TDX Systems, a Vienna, Va., long-distance phone service supplier, is making $60,000 a year after 18 months on the job.
>   . . . Allan Peyser, executive vice president at TDX, says women "get attention very quickly." Several companies find less turnover among women. IBM, which says it doesn't "see any differences in productivity" between the sexes, plans to hire more women. They make up 20% of its field sales force, compared with 12% five years ago.[21]

Three important aspects of salesperson selection are matching prospects to job requirements, considering legal aspects of hiring salespeople, and evaluating sales potential.

Matching prospects to job requirements. It is important to employ salespersons who are both qualified and motivated to perform the job assignment. Sales management is concerned with selecting people who have the potential to handle the sales position while avoiding applicants whose experience, salary expectations, and qualifications are greater than those for the position being filled. Hiring a person who is overqualified typically leads to job dissatisfaction and turnover.

Following a sequence of steps will increase the likelihood that qualified candidates will be recruited for sales positions.

- Develop a *job analysis* to identify the duties, requirements, responsibilities, and conditions involved in the sales job to be filled.
- Prepare a *written job description* so prospective sales applicants will know exactly what their duties and responsibilities will be and how they will be evaluated.
- Translate the duties and responsibilities set forth in the job description into a set of *sales job qualifications* that recruits should have to be hired.
- Attract a *pool of qualified sales recruits* from which to select.
- Evaluate each applicant through application forms, interviews, reference checks, and formal tests, and *select the most qualified.*[22]

It is essential that sales management specifies exactly what experience and qualifications are needed to perform the selling job in a particular firm.

Surprisingly, it is not unusual to find few guidelines regarding job qualifications in many firms, particularly small and medium-sized companies.

Legal considerations. There are several important legal considerations in recruiting and selecting salespersons. These include civil rights laws and regulations regarding minorities, age, national origin, handicap, and religion. Certain employment practices are prohibited, and those involved in recruiting and selecting salespeople must be familiar with relevant legal constraints regarding hiring. Firms with established personnel or human resources departments normally have experienced professionals who are familiar with relevant laws and regulations.

Evaluating selling potential. Because of the limited availability of experienced salespeople and their compensation requirements, many firms hire people who have no experience in selling. A major problem is determining what qualifications and experience are useful in predicting selling potential. While job qualifications as discussed earlier provide some guidelines, most do not specifically indicate what characteristics suggest a promise of sales success. Indeed, there is no commonly agreed on set of traits that are reliable predictors of sales success, although some general guidelines are available.

Two traits that are often cited as useful predictors of success in selling are empathy and ego-drive. **Empathy** is the ability to sense the reactions of another person. **Ego-drive** is the need of one person to persuade another and thus gain gratification.[23] Of course, other aptitudes, skills, and motivation are important as well. A field sales position is quite different from most other jobs. The salesperson operates away from supervision much of the time and must have a great amount of self-direction to perform the sales job.

Training salespeople

Training is essential to building and maintaining a productive selling organization.

Types of training. Inexperienced people that are new to a firm's salesforce often need training on various aspects of the job including

Selling methods and techniques
Allocating time and effort
Product information
Company policies and procedures

Training in these areas is accomplished through formal training programs, on-the-job training, or a combination of the two. New salespeople normally require training in all four areas. Existing salespeople receive much more limited training because of their training needs and the costs of training. Aspects of selling new and modified products is probably the most popular type of training for experienced salespeople.

Important training issues. A salesperson may require from a few weeks to several months of job experience before paying for his or her compensation and expenses. A good training program can reduce the time necessary to learn the sales job and can improve the quality of the selling effort. Yet training is expensive and should be concentrated in areas of greatest need and impact on salesperson performance. High training costs demand that management establish priorities regarding areas of training.

A related issue is deciding *how* training will be accomplished. For example, will formal training sessions be held? Or will the sales trainee be assigned to an experienced salesperson or manager for on-the-job training? Selecting the trainer (or trainers) is a key decision using either approach. The trainer should be competent. Selecting technical people as trainers because they know the product or using experienced salespersons to train because they know how to sell may not be successful unless the trainers are also trained.

SUPERVISING, MOTIVATING, AND EVALUATING SALESPEOPLE

American Business Products produces and markets business forms, specialty envelopes, mailers, and printing and binding in small to medium-sized businesses and towns using a salesforce of 700.[24] Serving a customer base of 80,000, the firm has positioned itself to handle an extremely large number of small and medium-sized orders. Personal selling represents an important part of American Business Product's marketing program. Supervising the salesforce, motivating and compensating each salesperson, and evaluating their performances are important parts of the sales management task. Increasing selling efficiency to the company's large customer base is also a critical management task in American Business Products as well as various other firms involved in salesforce management. Let us examine the nature and scope of these sales management activities.

Supervising salespeople

The sales supervisor's job is quite different in several respects from those of other supervisors. The people supervised are often located in several geographic areas, frequent contact with salespersons is not possible, the people supervised tend to be independent, and assessment of performance is difficult because of the variety of factors that affect salespersons' results. Compounding the supervisor's task is that many sales supervisors are expected to sell as well as to manage.

Supervision of salespeople includes the following important activities:

Coaching. Supervisors are normally expected to help salespeople learn and improve their selling capabilities.

Counseling. The nature of selling places the supervisor into a variety of advisory roles, both job-related and personal.

Controlling. Depending on the type of supervising position, this activity may require reviewing operating expenses, salesforce size, and direction of selling effort.

Evaluating. Appraising and discussing salesperson performance are essential supervisory responsibilities.

Administrating. These duties include determining sales territories, setting sales objectives (quotas), and reporting to higher-level sales management.[25]

Thus the sales supervisor must perform many roles including those of a teacher, advisor, controller, evaluator, and administrator.

Motivating salespeople

Whereas most sales management authorities agree that motivating salespeople involves far more than monetary compensation, analyzing the motivation-performance link is not simple. To understand the linkage we shall consider the performance determinants. Next, alternative rewards are discussed.

Determining performance. Several factors may contribute to the performance of salespeople in addition to motivation including the salesperson's personal characteristics, environmental conditions, and company policies and procedures.[26] The salesperson's aptitude and skills are clearly factors in his or her ultimate performance, as are the quality of supervision, intensity of competition, and company operating practices (e.g., type of incentive compensation plan). Thus it is important to recognize that money and other rewards interact with a variety of factors to determine the ultimate performance of salespeople.

Alternative rewards. What motivational tools are available to sales managers? Money is certainly an obvious means of motivating people, as are recognition and special rewards. Financial rewards are used extensively by sales organizations to motivate their salespersons. The same firms also typically incorporate recognition into the overall reward system. Some firms have placed salespersons and other employees in printed and electronic advertising. In addition to conveying messages to target audiences, such advertisements recognize particular employees.

Compensating salespeople

Salespeople may be compensated by a straight fixed salary, straight commission, or a combination of salary plus some form of bonus or incentive combination. Only 22 percent of the companies surveyed by the American Management Association in 1982 were using straight salary as a basis for compensating salespeople.[27] Salary plus some form of incentive was used by 72 percent, and 6 percent compensated with straight commission. Some form of incentive compensation is part of the compensation package in most firms. An interesting compensation trend has been reported by Dartnell Corporation.

> Some 21% still get paid solely through commissions, but that number has dropped sharply, from a peak of nearly 29% in 1973. The most popular form of compensation continues to be a blend of both approaches, typically 80% salary and 20% commissions. But as the popularity of full salaries grew, these combination plans declined, too.[28]

Designing a sound compensation plan for a salesforce should take into account desired qualifications of salespeople, their effect on sales results, the extent to which management can measure the results of salespeople, and the desired use of incentive compensation to direct the selling effort. Each type of compensation plan has certain features and limitations. For example, a straight salary provides management more control over how salespeople spend their time than the other methods. In contrast, a straight commission offers management little or no control over the selling effort.

Compensation for salespeople varies considerably by type of job, industry, method of compensation, and location. Some illustrations of salespersons' annual compensation are shown in Exhibit 20.6. Note that compensation of industrial salespersons is higher for all job categories.

Exhibit 20.6 Salespersons' total annual compensation: (1982 averages rounded to thousands of dollars)

	Consumer Products	Industrial Products
Sales trainee	$21,000	$23,000
Salesperson	28,000	30,000
Senior salesperson	33,000	37,000
Sales supervisor	37,000	44,000

SOURCE: American Management Association, *Executive Compensation Service,* as reported in *Sales & Marketing Management,* Feb. 21, 1983, p. 68.

Evaluating performance

Three important aspects of salesperson evaluation are purpose of evaluation, critical issues in evaluation, and methods of evaluation.

Purpose of evaluation. Salesperson evaluation is essential for several reasons. The basic objective is to keep desired and actual salesforce results as close together as possible. Another reason is to spot high performers so they can be rewarded and low performers so they can be assisted to improve performance. Incentive compensation adds an additional need for evaluation. Unless compensation is linked to performance, salespersons' morale may be adversely affected. Finally, the large investment that a firm makes in its salesforce demands that the resource be as productive as possible.

Issues in evaluation. When evaluating salespeople several issues must be considered. A basic problem in evaluating performance is that the salesperson often has only *partial* control over the results that are obtained in his or her territory or other assigned area of work responsibility. The market opportunity available, the company's position in the market, intensity of competition, and various other uncontrollable factors may cause two salespersons whose motivation and effort are equivalent to end up with different sales results. Deciding what to evaluate is another important consideration. Should evaluation focus only on sales or instead on other aspects of the job such as new accounts and product line coverage? Objectives and performance evaluation should be consistent. If a salesperson is assigned an objective, then his or her performance should be gauged against that objective.

Finally, it is essential that there be some way of measuring the results of performance. This is particularly important when incentive compensation is involved. Measurements should also adjust for factors beyond the control of the salesperson. Look at Exhibit 20.7. Using only the information shown in the exhibit, which salesperson would you rate the higher of the two, assuming sales volume is the primary basis of evaluation? Because both Mary and Harry sold the same amount, are they equal in performance? Compare Mary with Harry. Mary obtained the same sales volume in a territory with lower market potential, two years less experience, and the same number of customers. Overall, Mary seems to be producing sales equal to Harry in a territory with less sales opportunity and other factors about the same. Unless some reason other than the information shown in Exhibit 20.7 explains the difference, Mary should be rated higher than Harry.

Methods of evaluation. There are two primary approaches used to evaluate salespeople. One compares objective results with predetermined standards such as sales quotas. If the standards are adjusted to take into account factors uncontrolled by the salesperson, the comparison of actual results with the standard should provide a correct measure of performance. For example, suppose Mary had a sales quota of $400,000 compared with $500,000 for Harry. Mary achieved 125 percent of her goal compared with 100 percent for Harry.

When establishing objective standards is not feasible, subjective assessments of performance are used. These methods consist of rating forms completed by sales management. Subjective ratings can also be used in conjunction with objective evaluations of results.

Exhibit 20.7 Performance comparison of two salespersons

	Mary Jones	Harry Smith
Annual sales ($1000s)	500	500
Market potential ($1000s)	1800	2900
Number of competitors	10	10
Company market share (%)	28	18
Salesperson experience (years)	4	6
Number of customers	100	100

Increasing selling efficiency

Our earlier discussions of the average cost per sales call, calls necessary to close a sale, and compensation of salespeople clearly demonstrate the importance of trying to increase the efficiency of selling. Methods of saving time and making salespersons' efforts as effective as possible can return substantial savings in selling expenses. Consider this illustration:

> Mary Ellen Parulis, a saleswoman for Seaway Foods Inc., sweeps down the supermarket aisle carrying a calculator-like device in her left hand.
>
> Like a growing number of salespeople, Mrs. Parulis has adopted the portable data-entry terminal for recording sales. The terminals allow salesmen to enter information in their companies' computers directly, eliminating the need for key punchers. In addition, they increase the salesmen's productivity. According to Richard L. Nichta, Seaway's director of data processing, the average salesman at Seaway, a food and drug wholesaler, gains two to three hours a day for selling by using the terminals.[29]

Other methods of increasing selling efficiency include using the telephone, computer routing and effort allocation, automatic ordering, and screening accounts and prospects to target only those that justify call effort. (See Marketalk for still more information on how new technology will aid salesforce efficiency.)

*Marke*TALK ///

New technologies for complex organizations

LARGE ORGANIZATIONS exist today because complex tasks require the coordination of many people. This will be achieved in the future with the assistance of computer and communications links that can be extended directly to the individual, allowing him or her to plug in from anywhere, at anytime. Broad-band technologies, including cable, will provide ample opportunities for the transmission of data, text, graphics, voice, and even video. These links will tie workers not only to each other but also to major external data bases and services.

The emerging system will be more efficient than paper-based systems of memos and forms, and even more effective than the human linkages so prevalent now where layers of middle management too often distort communications to fit the world as they like.

Consider the case of an instrument salesperson in the field. In today's world, this person works out of a branch and reports to a sales manager who reports to a

SOURCE: Terrence E. Peal and Allan A. Kennedy, *Corporate Cultures,* Reading, Mass.: Addison-Wesley, 1982, pp. 189–190. Reprinted with permission.

branch manager who reports to a regional manager who reports to a national sales manager who reports to a marketing vice-president, and so on. All of these links in the middle-management chain are necessary to ensure two things: (1) that the salesperson does the job well—that is, calls on the right accounts, makes the right product pitch, wins the right orders, and so on, and (2) that strategic (for example, new products), tactical (for example, pricing), and operational (for example, inventory levels) decisions made on high are communicated as relevant. The chain is expensive, slow, and often inaccurate. For the organization to work well, elaborate bureaucratic procedures and relationships must be developed and followed. What a terrible way to get things done.

In the atomized organization, such salespeople will work in a little business—called a branch, perhaps—that is paid on the basis of the volume of product it moves per a pre-negotiated schedule of commissions. If they want details on a new product announcement, they will tune in to a videotape or cable-televised presentation of the new product that describes all its features. If they want to

know when they can deliver an instrument to a customer, they will hook into an inventory system and capture their machine. If they want to understand the company's new policy about replacement parts, they can tune on-line into the televised proceedings of the corporate policy committee and listen to the new CEO—as Cronkite—expound on why a new policy is needed. These tasks will all be done routinely, of course, because the salespeople will have worked with computers and video since elementary school.

And what if the salespeople are dealing with a new product? Today it can easily take eighteen months to collect centrally, interpret, and then disseminate the market feedback needed to adjust and make final commitments to full-scale production. We believe that they will participate, along with other salespeople of the future, in an electronic dialogue that will record their market experience and will respond almost immediately with ideas and answers from those facing similar situations. Adjustments in marketing strategy could be formulated as much as twelve months earlier, obviously with major financial implications. The technology exists today.

///

Productivity gains in selling effort are being achieved in the automobile industry. Automobile sales are moving into a new high technology era. Computers are being used to perform many of the activities previously handled by automobile dealers' salespeople. Illustrative functions include greeting customers, comparing features of competing models, computing operating costs, tabulating the costs of options, and estimating monthly payments. The objective of the new computer technology is to eliminate details for salespeople, making them more productive and effective in meeting customers' needs. The automobile industry is convinced that the baby boom generation will demand such high technology marketing. This age group will dominate the car market until the year 2000.[30]

SUMMARY

Personal selling is the process of interaction between a buyer and a seller that leads to an exchange that benefits each party. The importance of selling can be illustrated by the number of persons involved in selling—8.5 million by 1990—and the annual expenditures for selling—$200 billion in 1986. The major types of selling positions are order taking, technical selling, creative selling, and consultative selling.

Examining the personal selling process provides insights into the salesperson's job. The steps in the process consist of prospecting, preparation, presentation, closing, and postsale follow up. Prospecting involves the salesperson's determining how and where to find buyers and whether the prospect should receive organizational effort. Understanding the buyer and developing the sales call are essential aspects of preparation. The sales presentation has four parts: getting the buyer's attention, generating interest, stimulating the desire to buy, and causing action to purchase. This is called the AIDA concept. Closing is the prospect's commitment to buy, and postsale follow up is essential to ensure that the buyer's experience with the product is favorable.

The major differences between selling to consumers and selling to organizational buyers are in the areas of the role of demand, the selling process itself, and the promotional mix. Organizational buyers include retailers and wholesalers, manufacturers, and government.

Managing a salesforce includes establishing the role of the salesforce and setting objectives. These activities lead to important decisions regarding how to organize the salesforce, including determining how many salespersons are needed, where their efforts should be allocated, and what organizational units should be formed (e.g., districts, branches, offices).

Recruiting, selecting, and training salespeople are other essential management tasks, as are supervising, motivating, and evaluating salespeople. Supervising salespeople is a unique and demanding challenge compared with supervising people in an office, plant, or other installation because a field salesforce is typically spread over a wide geographic area and contact between salespeople and management is infrequent.

KEY TERMS

order taking   preparation   sales quota
technical selling   presentation   workload analysis
creative selling   closing   empathy
consultative selling   postsale follow up   ego-drive
prospecting   job description

QUESTIONS FOR REVIEW AND DISCUSSION

1. What is the purpose of selling?
2. What are the steps of the personal selling process?
3. Are all the components of the personal selling process always included in completing a sale? Why or why not?
4. Why is a postsale follow up necessary? What are the benefits for both the buyer and the seller?
5. Name the reasons why demand for industrial products differs from demand for consumer products.
6. What are the three buying situations in the industrial selling process? When does the salesperson have the opportunity to create new business and why?
7. Why are personal selling budgets for industrial firms sometimes higher than advertising budgets?
8. What are some of the ways that selling objectives are set?
9. What are the two most popular methods used to determine salesforce size?
10. Suppose you are recruiting new prospects for a salesforce. What are some possible sources of new salespeople?
11. What are some of the characteristics of a sales supervisor's job?
12. How should a sales compensation plan be designed?
13. Why is salesperson evaluation necessary?

BUILDING YOUR PORTFOLIO

■ You have just started working for Automotive Services, an automobile parts wholesaler. Your first assignment is to estimate how many salespersons should be assigned to each of the twenty largest cities in the United States. The sales manager has indicated that the number of people needed in each city should be proportional to population of each city. She considers the ten persons assigned to the Atlanta office to be the correct size for that market. Obtain population data for the twenty largest cities and estimate how many persons should be assigned to the other nineteen cities, assuming Atlanta has the proper-sized salesforce.

■ Identify a salesperson responsible for calling on customers and prospects. Ask the person to describe the way he or she plans how they will spend their time each day. Find out what problems the salesperson encounters in trying to follow the plan. Next, describe to the salesperson the selling process that is discussed in this chapter. Then ask the person to indicate the extent to which the selling process corresponds to his or her selling approach. Prepare a complete report of your findings. If available obtain a job description for the position to which the person is assigned.

NOTES

1. This illustration is adapted from NCH Corporation *1985 Report to Shareholders*, pp. 1–11.
2. *Value Line Investment Survey*, Edition 5, July 26, 1985, p. 813.
3. Ben M. Enis, *Personal Selling: Foundations, Process, and Management*. Santa Monica, Calif.: Goodyear, 1979, p. 6.
4. "Where sales engineers are superstars." *Business Week*, Sept. 10, 1979, p. 110D.
5. "Where new jobs will be in the 1980s." *U.S. News & World Report*, Feb. 7, 1983, p. 73.
6. Carolyn R. Farquhar, *Handbook of Canadian Consumer Markets, 1982*, 2nd ed. Ottawa: The Conference Board of Canada, 1982, p. 65.
7. "Rebirth of a salesman: Willy Loman goes electronic." *Business Week*, Feb. 27, 1984, p. 104.
8. "AT&T's bold bid to stay on top." *Business Week*, Oct. 11, 1982, p. 66.
9. "Mary Kay Cosmetics: Looking beyond direct sales to keep the party going." *Business Week*, Mar. 28, 1983, p. 30.
10. Thomas Ehrich, "Aiming high: To computer salesmen, the 'big-ticket' deal is the one to look for." *Wall Street Journal*, Jan. 22, 1974, p. 1.
11. Robert N. McMurray, "The mystique of super-salesmanship." *Harvard Business Review*, Mar.–Apr. 1961, p. 114.
12. "United States Surgical Corp.," in *The Value Line OTC Special Situations Service*. New York: Arnold Bernhard & Co., Apr. 28, 1980), p. A-97.
13. E. K. Strong, *The Psychology of Selling*. New York: McGraw-Hill, 1925, p. 9.
14. *1983 Annual Report, United Stationers*, p. 10.
15. David W. Cravens, "Supplier marketing strategies and their impact on purchasing decisions." *Atlanta Economic Review*, Jan.–Feb. 1977, p. 22.
16. McGraw-Hill Research Survey, 1981 data.
17. Steven Flax, "Win on price, lose on price." *Forbes*, Nov. 8, 1982, p. 108.
18. Kenneth R. Davis and Frederick E. Webster, Jr., *Sales Force Management*. New York: Ronald, 1968, p. 44.
19. Farquhar, op. cit., p. 72.
20. Rhonda S. Brammer, "Fresh look at Avon." *Barron's*, July 12, 1982, p. 8.
21. Bill Abrams, "Hair-care fears . . . license plates locate customers . . . sex and sales." *Wall Street Journal*, Feb. 5, 1981, p. 23.
22. Rolph E. Anderson and Joseph F. Hair, Jr., *Sales Management*. New York: Random House, 1982, p. 217.
23. G. David Hughes and Charles H. Singler, *Strategic Sales Management*. Reading, Mass.: Addison-Wesley, 1983, p. 231.
24. Frank W. Campanella, "Paper tiger." *Barron's*, Dec. 5, 1983, pp. 70–71.
25. Derek A. Newton, *Sales Force Management*. Plano, Tex.: Business Publications, 1982, pp. 54–56.
26. Gilbert A. Churchill, Jr., Neil M. Ford, and Orville C. Walker, Jr., *Sales Force Management*, 2nd ed. Homewood, Ill.: Irwin, 1985, pp. 623–625.
27. "Compensation." *Sales & Marketing Management*, Feb. 21, 1983, p. 70.
28. John A. Byrne, "Motivating Willy Loman." *Forbes*, Jan. 30, 1984, p. 91.
29. Michael L. King, "Computer age quickens pace of salesman." *Wall Street Journal*, Mar. 20, 1981, p. 27.
30. "Would you buy a car from a computer?" *Business Week*, Dec. 17, 1984, pp. 93, 97.

Case 20.1

Edwards Office Equipment Company

LINDA WALTER WAS completing her second month as a new sales representative for the Edwards Office Equipment Company. Edwards grossed about $3.1 million per year, selling office furniture, adding machines, office supplies, typewriters, and small hand-held calculators. Most of their customers were small businesses and professionals such as lawyers and doctors. Some of their biggest customers were insurance agencies, real estate brokers, and banks.

Linda had become fascinated by the new hand held calculator that had been designed for business use, was small enough to fit in a shirt pocket, and sold for less than $40. She had taken one of these machines home along with the instruction manual and played with it several evenings, much to her fascination. It seemed perfect for the businessperson because it would do all the functions that were needed for business analysis. It would perform the standard arithmetic functions of addition, subtraction, multiplication, and division, but it did much more than these basic functions. In one of its three calculating modes it could compute the cost, selling price, and margins that are calculated by retailers. The financial mode would calculate compound interest, annuities, amortization, bonds, and mortgage payments. With this calculator it would not be necessary for a loan officer or a real estate agent to carry a book that gives mortgage rates. A loan officer could quickly calculate different payments for varying interest rates and terms of a mortgage. Linda worked through the many examples in the instruction book that accompanied the calculator. She was amazed at how clearly the book explained financial calculations. It was practically a mini-financial course.

SOURCE: G. David Hughes and Charles H. Singler, *Strategic Sales Management,* Reading, Mass: Addison-Wesley, 1983, pp. 112–114. Reprinted with permission.

The third mode of the calculator was a statistical one. This mode permitted the calculation of the mean averages, standard deviation, linear regression, and trendline analysis. Following the simple examples in the manual, a businessperson could easily analyze and project sales.

Reflecting on the various prospects in her territory, Linda decided that bank loan departments would be the place to begin to try to sell those units. She decided to start with the Metropolitan Bank and Trust Company, a medium-sized bank in her territory. This bank had four retail loan officers who arranged loans for the public to purchase large items such as homes, automobiles, and boats. Metropolitan had seven commercial loan officers who arranged loans for business expansions, inventories, purchase of new equipment, etc., for the business community. Mr. Charles Monet was the Vice President in charge of the Commercial Loan Department. The bank had recently purchased office furniture for a branch from Edwards.

The economic outlook for the summer was not good. The prime lending rate for favored customers had been 18 percent and inflation was approaching 20 percent. The money market funds had siphoned funds out of savings accounts, thereby reducing the funds that were available for loans. There were indications that there would be a recession during the summer. The economic issues were clouded by the politics of a presidential election year. The Metropolitan Bank had recently introduced a new promotional campaign to commercial accounts titled "Creative Banking," in which it claimed it took its customers' needs to heart.

Linda began to map out her strategy for selling some of these calculators to Monet.

Charles Monet, Vice President of the Commercial Loan Department, had been in banking for twelve years, but he had not seen anything like this year. The prime lending rate for favored business customers was 18 percent, the inflation rate was approaching 20 percent, and the sales of some loan customers, such as automobile dealers, had dropped 25 percent. This was really a period for creative banking and identifying new market opportunities. A major dimension of the present job was keeping old customers happy when there was no money to lend. Mr. Monet reasoned that if there was a recession the situation could reverse quickly—the demand for commercial loans could drop quickly and the supply of money for lending could increase.

"Creative Banking" had become the theme of Metropolitan's Commercial Department during these difficult times. Commercial loan officers became more involved in the daily businesses of old customers and new prospects. They helped them with their financial decisions and showed them ways to make their investments work harder by such techniques as faster turnovers, taking discounts on invoices, etc. Thus these loan officers were engaging in the consultative selling of the bank's services.

During a recent board meeting, Mr. Monet had explained the strategies of creative banking and consultative selling. Other bank officials explained some of their strategies for solving their problems. For example, there was a promotional drive to increase the dollar deposit so there would be money to lend. Some of the strategies included certificates of deposit for the larger customers and premiums for the smaller customer.

One morning shortly after the bank opened, Mr. Monet received a call from Linda Walter, a sales representative of the Edwards Office Equipment Company, asking for an opportunity to present some ideas of how a new calculator might be helpful in Mr. Monet's daily operations. The Metropolitan Bank had bought some office equipment from Edwards when the bank opened a new branch office, so Mr. Monet decided to grant this representative an interview.

QUESTIONS

1. How should Linda go about making an appointment with Monet?

2. What must she do to prepare for this interview?

3. Assume you are Linda. How would you proceed when you walk into Monet's office?

4. If you were Charles Monet, what would be some of the problems that were on the top of your mind?

5. What benefits would you be looking for in a hand-held calculator?

6. How many of these calculators would you buy and how would you distribute them?

7. Could these calculators be a useful part of programs for creative banking and consultative selling?

A Special Look
Not-for-Profit Marketing

DR. CHARLES W. LAMB, JR.

A not-for-profit organization is any one of the hundreds of thousands of cultural, protective, religious, social, health care, educational, philanthropic, recreational, and political public and private institutions that exist for reasons other than making a profit. The *Encyclopedia of Associations'* list of national not-for-profit organizations is nearly 1500 pages long, and there are many more local than national not-for-profit organizations.

These organizations are critically important. Consider, for example, the impact that government has on the lives of everyone. The cost of government in the United States has become the top item in the family budget, more than housing, food, or health care. Federal, state, and local governments collect revenues that amount to one-third of the U.S. gross national product and employ one of five nonagricultural civilian workers. The U.S. Army spent $10.7 million on advertising alone during a thirteen-week period in 1971. In 1980 the military services had a recruiting budget of $825 million.[1]

Not-for-profit organizations affect our lives from the day we are born in one of the more than 6000 U.S. not-for-profit hospitals, through our education in some of the 44,000 not-for-profit elementary and secondary schools, and during our attendance at the 6000 not-for-profit museums and the performances of the 700 opera companies and 1400 symphony orchestras that are available for our education and enjoyment.[2] We attend not-for-profit churches, join associations such as the YMCA, contribute to the United Way, collect Social Security, and are buried in municipal cemeteries.

INCREASING INTEREST IN MARKETING

Adoption of marketing strategies and techniques among managers of not-for-profit organizations is one of the most exciting and challenging developments in marketing in recent years. Not-for-profit organizations are similar to profit-sector organizations in that they

1. Operate in dynamic, changing environments
2. Analyze present and potential customers (whether they call them clients, students, parishioners, members, recipients, passengers, supporters, citizens, taxpayers, or some other term)

About the Author: Charles W. Lamb, Jr., is the M. J. Neeley Professor of Marketing and Chairman of the Marketing Department at the M. J. Neeley School of Business, Texas Christian University. Professor Lamb is a frequent speaker on the subject of marketing for not-for-profit organizations and recently coauthored *Marketing Government and Social Services* with John Crompton (John Wiley & Sons, 1986). His book *Cases and Readings for Marketing for Nonprofit Organizations* with Philip Kotler and O. C. Ferrell (Prentice-Hall, 1983) is widely used in undergraduate and graduate courses in not-for-profit marketing. Professor Lamb also advises a wide variety of local and national not-for-profit organizations.

Count On Us For Outpatient Surgery.

Now, you can have your operation in the morning and be home in the afternoon! Thanks to advancements in surgical techniques, equipment and facilities, many operations which used to require overnight hospitalization can now be performed on an outpatient basis.

Union Hospital, an AtlantiCare Medical Center, has provided one-day surgery for over 10 years. This year, over 1,500 local residents will take advantage of this service, saving themselves time and money in the process. Some of the procedures you can have are dental surgery; vasectomies; plastic surgery; D & C's; hernia repair; and biopsies. In fact, over 100 procedures can qualify.

If you need an operation, ask your doctor if you might be a candidate for outpatient surgery at Union Hospital. For more information, call us at 596-2500.

Count On Us For Life.

Union Hospital

AtlantiCare Corporation • AtlantiCare Medical Centers • Lynn Hospital • Union Hospital
AtlantiCare Health Services • AtlantiCare Medical Treatment Centers • AtlantiCare Health Foundation

With bed-occupancy rates in decline, nonprofit hospitals are employing various strategies to reduce costs. Recently, Massachusetts' Union Hospital and Lynn Hospital (which were offering duplicate services in an area of decreasing population) joined forces to help meet ever-increasing competition and high operating costs. (Courtesy of Union Hospital)

3. Forecast demand for their services
4. Evaluate and select market targets
5. Develop, manage, and terminate programs
6. Develop pricing strategies and tactics (whether these are called fares, fees, tuition, taxes, charges, donations, tolls, assessments, dues, or some other term)
7. Schedule and locate programs and services
8. Communicate with potential users, supporters, and other constituents personally and through mass media

Surprisingly, it was not until the 1970s that managers of many not-for-profit organizations began recognizing the importance of marketing in achieving their organizations' missions.

Several factors account for the burgeoning interest in marketing among managers of not-for-profit organizations. Much of the stimulus to move from "business as usual" occurred as a result of dramatic shifts in the social and economic environments within which not-for-profit organizations operate. Executives became interested in marketing when they were faced with threats such as

■ Reduced availability of financial resources from traditional tax and philanthropic sources (the so-called taxpayers revolt led to the passage of Proposition 13 in California in 1978 as well as the presence on the ballot of tax and spending limit initiatives in fifteen other states during the same year)

■ Decreased customer satisfaction and participation (as many as 55 percent of all adult Catholics less than 30 years of age attended mass in 1966; by 1975 the rate had fallen to 39 percent)[3]

■ Increased competition from both profit and not-for-profit organizations (attendance at City of Dallas swimming pools decreased 16 percent in one year when commercial aquatic parks opened for the first time near the city)

■ Decreasing numbers in traditional market targets (American women gave birth to half as many babies in the late 1970s as they did in the 1950s)

■ Rapid technological change (the Educational Telephone Network at the University of Wisconsin has linked the university to more than 30,000 students statewide)

■ Vocal criticism from taxpayers, lawmakers, employees, clients, consumerists, and other affected and interested groups (one letter to the editor of the *San Francisco Chronicle* stated in part, "We are not anarchists, we are not radicals, and we do not think we are irresponsible. We are simply sick and tired of having our pockets picked at every level of government. We want only the most necessary government services.")[4]

Educational, health care, religious, and virtually all government-sponsored and government-supported organizations have been affected by rapid changes that have taken place in the 1980s. The changes, more than anything else, have led not-for-profit organization managers to begin asking the question, "How can marketing help us survive if not flourish?"

PROFIT VERSUS NOT-FOR-PROFIT ORGANIZATIONS

Profit-sector marketing knowledge is transferable to not-for-profit organizations, but it must be adapted and modified because there are substantial differences in the environments within which profit and not-for-profit organizations operate.

Target market

Many not-for-profit organizations must identify and attract people who are apathetic, disinterested, reluctant, or strongly opposed to accepting their offerings. Examples include services such as vaccinations, family planning guidance, drug or alcohol abuse assistance, or psychological counseling.

Distribution strategy

Profit-sector firms provide goods and services to customers on the basis of their *ability* and *willingness* to buy. Not-for-profit organizations such as public schools, libraries, and fire and police departments are usually expected to deliver service equally among all citizens regardless of their willingness or ability to ''buy'' or the amount that they pay in taxes. Like their profit-sector counterparts, not-for-profit organizations

- Establish distribution objectives (to have a neighborhood park within one mile of every residence in the city)
- Decide whether to distribute directly (social security payments) or indirectly (food to the needy using food stamps and grocery intermediaries)
- Choose to use exclusive (central libraries), selective (branch libraries), or intensive (bookmobiles) distribution.

They also must select locations where programs and services will be offered and schedule these events.

Intangible products

Not-for-profit organizations typically market services, ideas, and behavior patterns rather than physical goods. These services are intangible and cannot be seen, smelled, tasted, or felt. They cannot be produced and stored for sale and delivery at some later date. Interestingly, many services such as health care, the arts, recreation, garbage collection, and transportation are marketed by both profit and not-for-profit organizations.

Pricing strategies

Indirect payment for ''free'' services (e.g., libraries), separation between those who pay for and those who use services (e.g., welfare), and below-cost pricing (e.g., public universities) are just a few of the practices unique to not-for-profit organizations. Well-managed not-for-profit organizations do, however, follow a logical approach to pricing that is similar to profit-sector procedures. Yet not-for-profit organizations often seek to achieve objectives other than accruing revenues (e.g., income redistribution) and therefore may seek less than full-cost recovery.

Promotion strategies

Not-for-profit organizations engage in the full range of promotion activities that are available to profit-seeking organizations. College admissions staffs, for example, (1) travel around the country selling their schools; (2) advertise on billboards, on television, in newspapers, and elsewhere; (3) offer incentives such as scholarships; and (4) provide publicity releases to the media regarding their activities. Although some not-for-profit organizations are explicitly prohibited from advertising, the federal government is typically among the twenty-five largest advertisers in the United States. Some not-for-profit organizations are also quite effective in placing public service announcements in space donated by the broadcast media or in getting a voluntary organization such as the Advertising Council to contribute expertise and funds to promote their cause.

FUTURE TRENDS

At least five trends have been identified that will affect not-for-profit organizations in the near future. These are

- Rapid adoption of market-driven, clientele-based strategies
- More effective targeting to aid in resource allocation and market segmentation
- Rapid expansion of promotional activities
- Aggressive competition for scarce resources
- A substantial increase in the number of career opportunities for marketers interested in not-for-profit organizations

Notes

1. A. J. Martin, "Marketing and Manning the Military," in M. P. Mokwa and S. E. Permut (Eds.), *Government Marketing.* New York: Praeger, 1981, p. 88.
2. David L. Rados, *Marketing for Nonprofit Organizations.* Boston: Auburn House, 1981, p. 4.
3. Philip Kotler, *Marketing For Nonprofit Organizations,* 2nd ed. Englewood Cliffs: Prentice-Hall, 1982, p. 4.
4. This letter was cited in an article by Milton Friedman, "A progress report." *Newsweek,* Apr. 10, 1978, p. 80.

Part Seven

Marketing Planning and Control

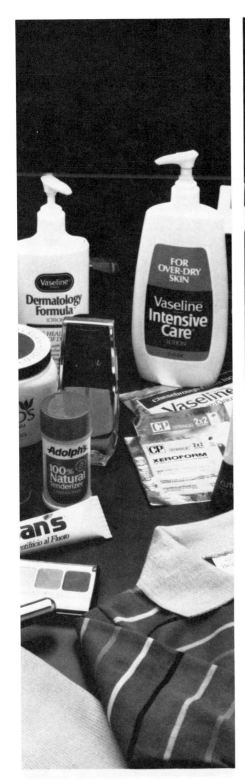

21 The Marketing Plan

When you finish this chapter, you will understand

☐ Several important marketing planning issues

☐ The major steps in preparing a marketing plan

☐ What information and decisions are included in a marketing plan

☐ How the marketing manager uses the plan to manage a marketing strategy

Monitoring market response to a new product or service is often accomplished through various kinds of test marketing. Here a home economist evaluates products in a test kitchen.

Glove makers, like many kinds of clothing manufacturers, have been bombarded by imports. These low-cost substitutes are threatening the future of many small glove makers in the United States, causing them to reduce output or close down. Glove imports in 1982 accounted for a 42 percent market share.[1] Galena Glove & Mitten Company of Dubuque, Iowa, is fighting the industry trend. The company is attacking the imports with an aggressive marketing plan. Galena's management approached the import challenge in the following way:

Situation Assessment   Management candidly assessed the situation faced by the firm, which revealed its strong financial position, skilled work force, and quality product.

Market Target   In deciding which customer needs to meet, management identified the high quality and price portion of the market as the primary market segment.

Objectives   Management developed a coordinated marketing program to achieve sales and profit objectives.

Action Plans   Galena's marketing mix included new glove lines, expanded retail distribution, advertising, and additions to the salesforce.

Budgets   Forecasts and planned budgets projected break-even sales in 1983 and profits in 1984 and beyond.

UNDERLYING MOST, IF NOT ALL, successful marketing efforts is a carefully designed and implemented marketing plan. Small firms such as Galena and giants such as AT&T need marketing plans to help guide their marketing efforts. The marketing plan pulls together management's decisions regarding the market target, objectives, and marketing program (product, distribution, pricing, and promotion) as shown in Exhibit 21.1. Note that the building blocks of the marketing plan are discussed in Parts Two through Six of the book. Our description of Galena's marketing plan highlights the major steps in building a marketing plan.

In this chapter we consider several important planning issues and guidelines. Next, the major steps in preparing a marketing plan are identified, described, and illustrated. As illustrated by Galena's marketing plan, the planning steps consist of assessing the situation; selecting market target; setting objectives; developing marketing mix action plans; and budgeting, implementing, and managing the marketing plan.

PLANNING ISSUES AND GUIDELINES

A marketing plan consists of management's decisions regarding the market target, objectives, and marketing program for a firm, a unit of the business, a product line, or a specific product. The plan indicates who is responsible for the various marketing activities, how these activities will be accomplished, time schedules, deadlines, and estimated costs (budgets).

Two major types of marketing plans are (1) the **strategic marketing plan,** which specifies marketing decisions two to five years into the future, and (2) the **annual marketing plan,** which indicates marketing actions to be taken over a twelve-month period. Additionally, some companies prepare **tactical marketing plans** ranging from one to three months.

Importance of the marketing plan

A good marketing plan contributes to the success of a marketing program, although poor planning may be worse than no planning. Let us examine the major advantages of good planning and some of the pitfalls to be avoided in developing marketing plans.

Exhibit 21.1 Building blocks of an integrated marketing plan

Advantage of planning. Marketing planning offers several specific advantages. These include

■ Establishing objectives, actions, responsibility and deadlines for various marketing efforts
■ Guiding the use of marketing resources (people and money) by allocating them to the most productive uses
■ Improving communication among marketing functions
■ Providing a basis for measuring results
■ Establishing a frame of reference for altering marketing strategy when contingencies are necessary

The alternative to planning is **crisis management,** which is reacting to problems or situations as they occur rather than deciding in advance what marketing actions to take. The danger, of course, is that by quickly reacting to a crisis, mistakes are likely to occur and the situation may be made worse. Planning forces management to analyze and coordinate the various decisions that make up the marketing effort. Decisions on products, prices, distribution, and promotion are integrated rather than treated independently. Although in a small firm, coordination may occur without a formal plan, in most organizations a marketing plan is essential to properly manage the marketing effort.

Consider, for example, Binney & Smith, the manufacturer of the Crayola Crayon brand that dominates the U.S. crayon market.[2] For decades the firm was successful without a marketing plan. Then, in the early 1970s as the baby boom leveled off and costs increased, profits declined. A new chief executive with a strong marketing background was hired in 1975. He implemented a new marketing plan.

> Binney & Smith is beginning to reap the benefits of a marketing program designed to gain sales outside its traditional crayon business. It has taken eight years to implement, but now Binney & Smith is plastering the green and yellow Crayola trademark on dozens of products that formerly carried other brand names. The strategy is beginning to pay off. Sales of watercolors, formerly sold under the Artista label, are up 20% in units. More important, Binney & Smith has developed a host of new products to put that trademark on.[3]

Marketing planning pitfalls. Formal planning does not guarantee success. Several areas in which problems may occur include the following:

- Decision making. Bad decisions, however skillfully blended into a plan, will not succeed.
- Planning. There is a danger in **over-planning**—developing a plan so detailed and complex that the marketing manager and staff must spend too much time trying to understand the plan rather than using it to manage the marketing function.
- Implementation. Implementation of the plan is crucial to its success. Faulty implementation will jeopardize the success of any plan.
- Participation. Successful marketing plans require the active participation of the managers responsible for selecting and implementing the actions contained in the plan.

How marketing plans are used

Planning levels. Marketing plans may be developed for an entire company, a unit of the business, a mix or line of products, or a single product or brand. Typically a specific plan is developed for a new product. Managers of major areas within the marketing function such as advertising and sales often prepare plans. For example, detailed plans for advertising programs and media selection are prepared each year, and the plans are updated each month or quarter during the year. Salesforce activities are typically planned and budgeted annually.

Planning guidelines are usually set by an organization's top management, although the actual development of marketing plans may follow one of two possible sequences. **Top-down planning** consists of management's developing plans at the highest levels of the organization and providing these plans to the next level down in the organization as the basis for preparing lower-level plans. **Bottom-up planning** consists of plans developed at the grass roots of the organization and funneled to the next level above until plans are collected at the top of the organization. The bottom-up planning approach is more participative in nature, encouraging lower-level involvement in planning.

Planning situation. The nature and scope of a firm's planning situation often vary depending on the extent of product and market maturity, competitive intensity, and environmental influences. Two strategy situations describe the opposite ends of a continuum of possibilities.

Balancing strategy is characterized by mature products in established markets in which competition is strong and marketing planning benefits from extensive experience. Controlling the marketing program to maintain a favorable balance between revenues and costs is a major concern of marketing management. Typically the planning process is well established, as is the content of the marketing plan.

New venture strategy is appropriate when the product and the market are new. The planning task is difficult owing to the firm's lack of experi-

At the 1983 Toy Fair in New York City, Binney & Smith presented ten new items to toy buyers from all over the country. At least three of these new products—Crayola Drawing Markers, a fine-tipped coloring marker; Crayola Designer Kit for Interiors, an activity set providing tools and instructions for home decoration and interior design; and DabberDoo, a kit that encourages self-expression through stenciling and decorating—were enthusiastically received. All of these new products carry the Crayola name and the familiar yellow and green package design. (Courtesy of Binney & Smith Inc.)

Our toys run on imagination.

Imagine you're a child, designing fabulous trend-setting homes for famous clients. Or imagine NASA has put you in charge of designing the ion powered inter-galactic spaceship that will put the first astronaut in another solar system.

One thing you won't have to imagine is how much fun your child will have with the Crayola Designer Kit for Interiors and the Crayola Designer Kit for Vehicles.

Because Crayola toys let a child's imagination run and hop and leap for joy. And how many toys give them a chance to do all that?

ence with both product and market. Some trial and error in planning may occur with management's adjusting the marketing strategy in response to information obtained from customers.[4]

Moving into a new market with a modified product involves less planning uncertainty than does a new venture but presents a more complex planning

Exhibit 21.2   Areas in which companies specify marketing objectives and strategies

Consumer-product manufacturers*		Industrial-product manufacturers†	
Activity or subfunction	Percentage of companies with plans including specific statement of:	Activity or subfunction	Percentage of companies with plans including specific statement of:
Profit margins	Objectives 71% / Strategies 61%	Profit margins	Objectives 74% / Strategies 54%
Sales promotion	Objectives 69% / Strategies 71%	Field sales effort	Objectives 72% / Strategies 59%
New-product development	Objectives 68% / Strategies 64%	New-product development	Objectives 70% / Strategies 61%
Pricing policy	Objectives 64% / Strategies 77%	Sales to major accounts	Objectives 61% / Strategies 51%
Advertising expenditures	Objectives 64% / Strategies 60%	Pricing policy	Objectives 54% / Strategies 63%
Field sales effort	Objectives 64% / Strategies 53%	Inventories/physical distribution	Objectives 45% / Strategies 36%
Advertising themes	Objectives 56% / Strategies 70%	Sales promotion	Objectives 44% / Strategies 45%
Marketing research	Objectives 50% / Strategies 42%	Marketing research	Objectives 44% / Strategies 38%
Sales to major accounts	Objectives 37% / Strategies 32%	Advertising themes	Objectives 41% / Strategies 42%
Inventories/physical distribution	Objectives 35% / Strategies 27%	Customer/product service	Objectives 41% / Strategies 38%
Packaging	Objectives 32% / Strategies 37%	Export sales	Objectives 40% / Strategies 37%
Customer/product service	Objectives 28% / Strategies 30%	Advertising expenditures	Objectives 39% / Strategies 26%
Distributor/dealer relations	Objectives 27% / Strategies 31%	Distributor/dealer relations	Objectives 34% / Strategies 34%
Sales training	Objectives 24% / Strategies 31%	Sales training	Objectives 31% / Strategies 23%
Export sales	Objectives 22% / Strategies 22%	Other marketing overseas	Objectives 26% / Strategies 26%
Other marketing overseas	Objectives 8% / Strategies 8%	Packaging	Objectives 7% / Strategies 4%

Objectives ☐   Strategies ▨

*Based on information provided by 98 companies.
†Based on information provided by 138 companies

SOURCE: David S. Hopkins, *The Marketing Plan*, New York: The Conference Board, 1981, pp. 23, 24.

challenge than a balancing situation. In general, marketing planning becomes increasingly difficult and uncertain as the planning task moves from a balancing situation toward the new venture.

Areas included in plans. In a major survey of consumer- and industrial-products firms, The Conference Board identified several areas included in marketing plans (see Exhibit 21.2). Depending on the size of the firm and the scope of products and markets, a company may develop more than one marketing plan. For example, Chesebrough-Pond's, a consumer-products firm, has marketing plans for Ragu sauce, Bass shoes, Q-Tips, and other specific brands.

Planning frequency. Long-range strategic marketing plans span two to five years. The short-term annual plan is used to implement the long-range strategies. Annual plans are often revised during the year to adjust for changing conditions and to incorporate necessary alterations. Changing a plan during the planning period does not indicate that the plan has failed. Such adjustments in plans are often a natural consequence of changing market and competitive conditions.

Planning steps. The steps in preparing the marketing plan are shown in Exhibit 21.3. First, assessing the situation outlines the conditions under which the plan is to be developed. The assessment should show the firm's strengths and weaknesses compared with competition, both present and future. Opportunities and threats in the marketplace should be indicated. Next, marketing management must determine the customer groups to be targeted and the objectives to be achieved. Action plans regarding products, distribution channels, prices, advertising, and personal selling follow in the planning sequence. Finally, the budgets necessary to carry out the action plans should be estimated, and the plan is implemented and controlled during the planning period.

Sound marketing planning consists of a carefully designed sequence of actions. Consider, for example, how Revco, the $1.3 billion retail drug store chain, plans its operations.

> Revco's planning is done with military precision at its unpretentious headquarters in Twinsburg, near Cleveland, Ohio. There, plans of each store are on file, and merchandising specialists dictate the offerings on each shelf inch by inch. Every time Revco figures out a new way of parting customers from their money, new computer-aided designs are dispatched almost immediately to every store. This way time taken up by merchandising decisions at the local level is kept to a minimum.[5]

In the remainder of the chapter we examine each of the planning steps shown in Exhibit 21.3.

ASSESSING THE SITUATION

The information shown in Exhibit 21.4 is needed by the marketing manager to help prepare the marketing plan. In a **situation assessment,** the environment must be analyzed by marketing management to gauge the opportunities and threats facing the firm. Furthermore, the firm's strengths and weaknesses must be considered.

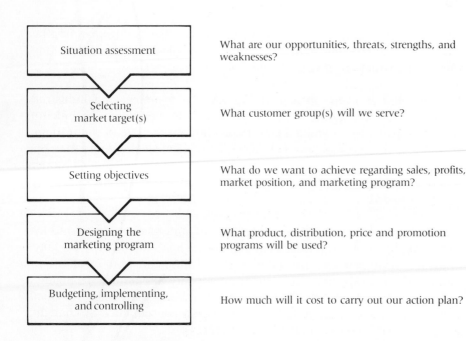

Situation assessment	What are our opportunities, threats, strengths, and weaknesses?
Selecting market target(s)	What customer group(s) will we serve?
Setting objectives	What do we want to achieve regarding sales, profits, market position, and marketing program?
Designing the marketing program	What product, distribution, price and promotion programs will be used?
Budgeting, implementing, and controlling	How much will it cost to carry out our action plan?

Exhibit 21.3 Steps in preparing the marketing plan

Study the past, present, and future

This part of the situation assessment involves analyzing the external factors that are likely to influence the firm's market and create both opportunities and threats. The objective is to study past, present, and future trends and new developments that may alter the firm's market opportunities and competitive situation.

The macroenvironmental analysis (see Chapter 3) should identify economic, governmental, technological, social, and physical environmental factors that may affect the firm's business situation. For example, the future trend in inflation rates will affect many companies. Similarly, deregulation of industries such as financial services is an environmental factor that dras-

Exhibit 21.4 Assessing the situation

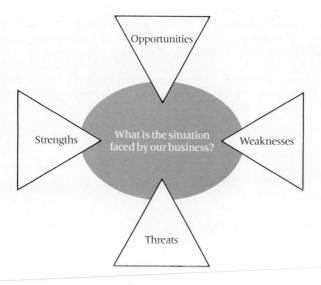

tically altered the business situation for financial firms. Tracking relevant environmental factors is an important part of the situation analysis. Management's task is to identify key environmental factors and then attempt to estimate future trends.

Market opportunity analysis (MOA) is concerned with identifying markets, analyzing customers, evaluating competition, and forecasting sales. Chapters 4, 5, 6, and 7 provide important guidelines for obtaining information about these aspects of the situation. For example, an important part of the marketing plan is estimating the size and composition of the market and market growth trends. A rapidly expanding market will create a planning situation different from a slowly growing or declining market.

The second part of the situation analysis is to determine the firm's advantages and limitations compared with competition. A firm's advantages may be based on financial resources, location, operating (cost) efficiencies, experience, or marketing capabilities. It is also important to recognize a firm's limitations. For example, a small bank or savings and loan typically does not have the financial resources to launch an extensive advertising program. Other promotional activities such as direct sales contacts with key customers are probably more appropriate.

Decide what action to take

The situation assessment serves as the foundation for the marketing plan. Typically, short-range (one to two years) and long-range (two to five years) plans are developed. The situation assessment should yield information on macroenvironmental factors, markets, competition, industry, and the company itself. Marketing management must analyze information about the situation and then decide what action to take. The situation should be appraised on a regular basis—usually annually when the marketing plans are prepared for the coming year.

As we discuss the steps of preparing the marketing plan, a company's actual plan will be described to illustrate the content of a marketing plan.* The company is a large savings and loan institution located in Texas, which we call R$T Savings to avoid direct comparisons with existing institutions.

The general situation faced by R$T was favorable, although the competitive environment for financial institutions owing to deregulation was changing rapidly and creating both opportunities and threats. Some examples drawn from the situation assessment for R$T conducted in early 1984 are shown in Exhibit 21.5. Also indicated are the marketing plan implications for each of the situation factors. Using information such as marketing research studies and published data for financial institutions, R$T's management evaluates the market and competition on a regular basis. For example, in early 1984 a large bank holding company in Texas began offering radios, televisions, and other premiums to attract savers. No other financial institution in the market areas was using premiums. R$T's marketing research director quickly set up a monitoring program to determine the amount of savings deposits withdrawn from R$T to establish new accounts with the holding company banks and obtain premiums.

---

* This illustration is based on information provided by the marketing vice-president of a large savings institution located in Texas and research conducted by the authors.

Exhibit 21.5 Examples of R$Ts, situation assessment in 1984

Situation Assessment	Marketing Plan Implication
Opportunity The population of Texas is expected to grow from 14 to 19 million between 1980 and 1990, creating a major opportunity for financial institutions to attract new customers.	Obtain market coverage by expanding retail outlets in high-potential geographic areas.
Threat Branch banking laws were expected to change to allow banks to open branches in any location desired by management.	Determine locations where R$T's market coverage should be strengthened.
Strength Offers a full line of financial services at very efficient operating costs compared with most other financial institutions.	Develop innovative and aggressive marketing program to attract new accounts.
Weakness High turnover of tellers in several branch offices.	Analyze causes of turnover and develop program for reducing turnover.

SELECTING MARKET TARGETS

Market targeting, or deciding which people or organizations to serve in the marketplace, is an important decision in the marketing plan. Whether to take a mass market or segment approach, as discussed in Chapter 8, must be determined. If market, competitive, and product conditions favor segmenting, three segment options can be considered.

1. Targeting one segment in the market
2. Targeting a small portion of the segments in the total market (selective coverage)
3. Targeting all or most of the segments in the total market (extensive coverage)

Segmenting is a logical market target strategy for serving many markets (see Marketalk).

Jazz, the software program that was introduced by Lotus Development Corporation in 1985, is expected to help increase sales of the Macintosh computer to businesses. It remains to be seen whether Apple and Lotus, by targeting the work world for their products, will achieve the sales they have estimated. Jazz was designed to be used at work, but so far the Macintosh is largely perceived as a home personal computer. (Courtesy of Lotus Development Corporation)

MarkeTALK ///

European retailers target U.S. market

U.S. CONSUMERS are about to discover a way of shopping that Europeans have know for years.

One example: An Italian clothing manufacturer named Benetton is overrunning Fifth Avenue in New York City. Shops sporting the green-and-white Benetton logo have sprung up so quickly that seven now grace the fashionable thoroughfare. Half a dozen more dot nearby neighborhoods of Manhattan's monied Upper East Side.

"I'd be hard-pressed to come up with the name of another chain that does something like this," says Kurt Barnard, publisher of Retail Marketing Report. "They capture an entire area."

Some U.S. retail chains will tailor their stores to the whims and character of a city. But Benetton adapts them to individual neighborhoods and sometimes even a single block. Benetton developed the strategy in Europe, where it has 2,500 shops. Now, the company has transplanted its approach to the U.S. Starting with five U.S. shops in 1979, Benetton reached 200 by the end of last year. It expects to hit 400 before 1985 is out.

Benetton is in the vanguard of a new wave of European retailers rolling across the U.S. Using distinctive retailing approaches that propelled their expansions in Europe, the companies are tackling the large and potentially lucrative American market. Their novel approach, each hopes, will allow them to stand out amid the clutter of stores that already glut America's main streets and malls.

These newcomers differ markedly from an earlier generation of European retailers, which bought their way into the U.S. by acquiring existing retailers. And though the newcomers haven't yet spawned American imitators, some think that's inevitable.

"Retailers look at them as trend-setters," says Victor Politis, executive vice president of New York Land Co. and a consultant for several European retailers.

Britain's Laura Ashley Ltd., has shunned Benetton's avant garde approach and instead has found a niche with subdued traditional designs. Ashley's toiletries, dresses and home furnishings all are redolent of Victorian London. "What we like to think we're selling is an English lifestyle," says Peter D. Revers, president

of Laura Ashley Inc., the U.S. subsidiary.

Ashley currently has 55 stores here and plans to double that by next year. U.S. sales grew 48% last year to $52 million, and Mr. Revers expects a 40% gain this year.

Some European companies are just getting a toehold. A French retailer named Euromarche last fall introduced the U.S. to a concept familiar in France, the *hypermarche,* or "hypermarket." The first store, in Cincinnati, is called Bigg's, and it's exactly that: a cavernous building containing an oversized supermarket and a huge department store under a single roof.

A Swedish furniture retailer called IKEA also has grand plans for the U.S. Already a household name in Europe, IKEA this summer intends to open a store in the Philadelphia suburb of Plymouth, Pa., that will cover three acres. It will sell contemporary furniture and home furnishings at prices "at least 20% less than the competition," says Bjorn Bayley, president of IKEA's North American operations. Prices are held down, he says, by manufacturing in large production runs and by cutting service costs. For example, customers will pick out their merchandise with few sales people present, pull it out of the warehouse by themselves and assemble it at home.

The European retailers are crossing the ocean now partly because the purchasing power of the dollar has been so great. But many of them also are bumping up against the limits of growth in Europe and look upon the U.S. as virgin territory.

Their main advantage in the U.S., Mr. Politis says, comes from "carefully targeting their audience" and from controlling the design and manufacture of their merchandise. Through the latter, he says, "they avoid the pitfall of so many other retailers, whose merchandise is 70% the same as everyone else's."

Because stores tend to be smaller in Europe than in the United States, the European companies also "know how to market their retail space aggressively," Mr. Politis says. "American retailers are satisfied, or seem to be satisfied, with (annual sales of) $300 a square foot, where European retailers, such as Benetton or Laura Ashley, have achieved $1,000 a square foot or more."

One way they do that is by stacking merchandise higher "without losing the design element, the beauty of the display," Mr. Politis says.

Nevertheless, the Europeans have had to make some adjustments. Laura Ashley spent its first two years here "making a lot of mistakes, learning about doing busi-

ness in America," says Mr. Revers, its U.S. president.

For instance, in Europe, Laura Ashley locates its stores in older, renovated buildings off the beaten track. That both lowers overhead costs and provides old-world charm. But when it tried that with its first U.S. store, in an out-of-the-way section of San Francisco, few customers took the trouble to find it. The store later closed. Ashley now opens most of its American stores in malls.

Laura Ashley also has had to adjust to U.S. retailing seasons, which start earlier here, by shipping new collections sooner. And it has begun producing a line of clothing exclusively for its 15 stores in the Sun Belt. Though that region stays warm most of the year, customers there still like to feel that the seasons are changing, Mr. Revers says. So, Ashley now makes a line of clothing using summer-weight fabrics but winter colors and patterns.

Benetton also has had to adjust. In Europe, where shoppers prefer intimate boutiques, Benetton's stores are small—usually only 600 to 700 square feet in area. But "American people like more open spaces," so Benetton's stores here tend to be around 800 to 1,000 square feet, says Mr. Della Barba, the U.S. executive. Benetton has even begun opening a limited number of U.S. "super stores" with as much as 4,000 square feet.

Some skeptics suggest Benetton's saturation strategy could backfire in the already-crowded U.S. market. Benetton is opening so many stores that they are fighting each other for the same business. The manager of one Benetton store on Fifth Avenue, for example, says her biggest competitor is another Benetton franchise store across the street.

The battle is never over price. Benetton executives decline to say how they are set, but "somehow we all seem to arrive at the same prices," one shop owner notes.

The rivalry is moderated somewhat by tailoring each store's decor and merchandise to its clientele. Though all Benetton franchises can buy the same merchandise, each is urged to select styles and colors that best suit its neighborhood. So, for example, the window of the Benetton shop at Fifth Avenue and 48th Street, a prime tourist spot, shouts with red-striped sweatshirts, blue polka-dotted blouses and lemon-yellow jumpsuits. But the shout becomes a whisper of pink, beige and powder-blue sweaters in the Benetton store at Madison Avenue and 70th Street, a far tonier neighborhood.

///

Describing target customers

Market analysis activities aided R$T's management in selecting the customer group to be targeted by the firm. A key decision was to concentrate on attracting people that require a new banking relationship. People select a new financial institution because of geographic relocation, marriage, or divorce. R$T's marketing management estimated that attracting new customers in these categories would be more feasible and less costly than trying to persuade people to change banks without any reason. Management had conducted studies to determine the costs of both attracting people seeking a new banking relationship and attracting new customers from competing financial institutions.

R$T's market target customer group is described as middle income, twenty-five to forty-nine years of age, and relocating to or living in the urban areas in the band from the Red River in North Texas to Corpus Christi, including the Dallas–Fort Worth metroplex, Austin, San Antonio, and Houston. Also targeted are persons eighteen to twenty-four years of age in newly formed households. Management was convinced that trying to attract business from established banks in small and medium-sized cities east and west of this band would not be successful. Population growth in these areas would be small through 1990. Moreover, people in the these communities are loyal to the home town bank, so it would be difficult to convince them to change their banking relationship.

Marketing mix guidelines

The market target decision provides important guidelines for preparing the marketing plan. It indicates the size of the market opportunity and the characteristics of the people to be served by the firm. The market target profile should indicate where customers and prospects are located, their demographic and socioeconomic characteristics, buying habits, and other information useful in developing the marketing mix. For example, expansion of R$T's banking facilities can be concentrated in major metropolitan growth areas in the state. Advertising messages and media selection are guided by a knowledge of customer needs and their characteristics. As we discuss later in the chapter, the market target description is essential to planning decisions for each component of the marketing program. Determining what products to offer, where and how to distribute, how to price, and how to promote depends substantially on the characteristics and needs of the customers and prospects targeted by the firm.

SETTING OBJECTIVES

Selecting the market target (or targets) should be followed by establishing objectives. Marketing objectives are statements about performance that are realistically obtainable providing the proper amount of marketing program effort is expended on the market target. Objectives are guides for action in the areas of financial performance, market position, and marketing program results. Sales, market share, profit contribution, and new customers are typical areas in which firms set objectives. Exhibit 21.2 illustrates the wide range of objectives used by the firms surveyed by The Conference Board.

Levels of objectives

Marketing objectives are often set for the marketing department, market targets, product lines, specific products, and marketing mix areas such as advertising. For example, general objectives may be set for the entire marketing function and then specific objectives for each major marketing activity (e.g., pricing, marketing research). Suppose R$T's marketing department has a certain dollar deposit objective for next year. This overall deposit objective would then be allocated to one or more market targets such as commercial and consumer accounts, specific products such as certificates of deposit, geographic sales areas, and finally each branch will be responsible for a portion of the sales objective. Because R$T has salespeople assigned to certain types of accounts, each of these persons is given a deposit sales quota.

Financial institutions such as R$T typically set annual objectives for volume of deposits, market share, number of new customers, and various marketing mix components. For example, increasing awareness of the financial institution's name is frequently an advertising objective. This objective might be stated as increasing awareness of R$T in the target market from 54 percent to 65 percent by December 31, 1986. Objectives and results of a new financial service introduced by R$T are shown in Exhibit 21.6. The example indicates how objectives can be used for both planning and evaluating results. Note the use of quarterly (three-month) objectives. This helps marketing management gauge how the new service is performing during the annual planning period. As you can see in Exhibit 21.6, R$T completed the first year with results above objectives although deposits and new accounts were below objectives in quarters 1 and 2.

Characteristics of good objectives

Exhibit 21.6 highlights three important characteristics of good objectives. First, objectives should be explicit and measurable so marketing management can determine if they have been achieved. Unless an amount is specified, actual results cannot be compared with desired results. The objectives set by R$T's management for new accounts and deposits indicate the results necessary to make the new service profitable.

Second, objectives should be achievable. Stating a result that is hoped for but really impossible to achieve is of no value. What is more, such an objective can be demoralizing for those responsible for achieving the result. Suppose you are a salesperson for a computer manufacturer and you have

Exhibit 21.6 Customer and dollar deposit objectives and results for R$T's new financial service

Quarter*	Objectives		Results	
	Number of Accounts	Deposits (millions of dollars)	Number of Accounts	Deposits (millions of dollars)
1	500	2	529	1.8
2	1400	4	1297	3.7
3	2500	8	2731	8.3
4	3500	12	3733	12.7

* Three-month period.

been assigned a sales quota (objective) for next year of $850,000. You know, based on past experience and current market and competitive conditions, that you will be doing extremely well if you sell $675,000 of equipment. What would you do? You might be inclined to leave the company if you were convinced that sales management would consider sales below the $850,000 objective unsatisfactory.

Third, objectives should be relevant to what marketing is trying to accomplish through the marketing plan. For example, an objective of a bank that specifies increasing the number of depositors without regard to the size of the deposits could lead to the bank's attracting customers with small deposits (less than $100) that would be unprofitable.

Setting objectives is discussed further in the next section as we examine the preparation of action plans. Marketing mix activities such as advertising require objectives to guide action and measure the extent of accomplishment. The marketing budget also represents the financial objectives that management wishes to accomplish.

*Marke*TALK ///

ChemLawn Corporation: programmed for success

Company Profile

KEY ACCOMPLISHMENTS in the 15 years since the company was founded:

- Market leader in the $.5 billion residential lawn-care market, holding a 40% market share.

- Serving 1.4 million households in 106 North American markets.

- 1983 sales were $228 million, up 24% from 1982 and 262% from 1979. 1983 profits were $13 million, up 24% from 1982 and 262% from 1979.

Company Units

ChemLawn Lawn Care: ChemLawn is the only company providing lawn-care service to major markets from coast to coast. Services include fertilization and weed and insect control applications using materials formulated for the agronomic needs of each local area. The customer base increased 20% in 1983.

ChemLawn Tree and Shrub Care: Services

SOURCE: *ChemLawn Annual Report 1983*, Jan. 9, 1984.

were offered in 53 markets in 1983. Sales increased 53% over 1982, growing to 132,000 customers.

ChemLawn CarpetClean: Test marketing continued in 18 markets in 1983. Results to date encourage the belief that by providing guaranteed satisfaction in carpet cleaning and using strong introductory marketing support, ChemLawn can achieve a leadership share in this large, fragmented market.

ChemLawn Pest Free: Introduced in one midwestern and five southern test markets. Preliminary market targets are southern states where indoor pests are a year-round problem and the food and lodging industries across the country. Test marketing will continue in 1984 to confirm operations and marketing strategies in preparation for expansion in 1985.

ChemLawn Commercial Services: A separate sales force sells all of the ChemLawn services available in each market to large commercial accounts, such as office buildings, apartments, and restaurant and motel chains. Market segments with the highest market potential for ChemLawn services have been identified through extensive marketing research.

Marketing Plan

- Selective targeting of customer segments with targeting decisions guided by marketing research.

- Expansion into related services using the ChemLawn name and customer base. Marketing research supported use of a common name for all new services.

- Use of carefully trained personnel committed to customer satisfaction and services backed by a strong money-back guarantee.

- Aggressive advertising to household markets. Over 35 million brochures were mailed in 1983. This mail program benefits from ongoing marketing research and analysis of advertising concepts, materials, and distribution list selection criteria to produce maximum advertising effectiveness and efficiency.

- Marketing support expenditures were $16.5 million in 1983, up 57% over 1982.

- Ongoing research and development programs are conducted to assure continued technical leadership in agronomics and horticulture and to establish leadership in carpet cleaning and pest control.

///

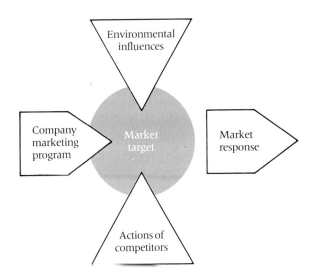

Exhibit 21.7 Factors affecting market response

DESIGNING THE MARKETING PROGRAM

The targeting decision and objectives set the stage for developing action plans to accomplish the objectives in the market served by a company. (As Marketalk reveals, ChemLawn Corporation's success and rapid growth represent what can be accomplished by designing a sound marketing program.) Marketing management must estimate how the market target will respond to alternative marketing programs under consideration to select the program that is expected to generate the greatest sales volume less marketing costs. In designing the marketing program, decisions must be made concerning how much to spend and how to allocate portions of the total program expenditure to each marketing mix component. First, we explore these marketing program decisions. Next, the variations in the composition of the marketing mix over the life cycle are considered. Finally, marketing mix variations among firms are illustrated and discussed.

Estimating market response

Market response is the amount of specific goods or services sold to buyers who make up a firm's market resulting from the firm's marketing efforts.

As shown in Exhibit 21.7, factors other than the firm's marketing program may affect the market response obtained by the firm's marketing program. As is explained in Chapter 3, various environmental factors such as economic conditions, social influences, technology, and government all may influence how people respond to marketing efforts. The marketing programs of the competition also affect market response. Although competition is considered an environmental influence, because of its central importance in marketing program planning we have shown it as a separate influence in Exhibit 21.7.

Why estimate market response? It is important to know something about how the market target is likely to respond to a planned marketing program. Suppose the marketing manager is considering three different marketing programs, A, B, and C. Assume that he or she can estimate the amount of market response that will result from each marketing program. The marketing manager's sales and cost estimates are shown in Exhibit 21.8. Which marketing program would you select to obtain the highest sales net of marketing program costs?

Program B yields the highest sales but when marketing program costs are subtracted from sales, B yields less net sales after marketing costs than C. Thus, of the three alternatives, program C appears best. While admittedly oversimplified, the example illustrates the key issue in estimating market response to a marketing program. Different programs will yield different sales results. The objective is to select the program that will provide the greatest increment of sales in excess of marketing costs. Note that we are assuming that the increment of sales net of marketing costs will yield a profit to the firm after nonmarketing costs are subtracted.

How do you estimate market response? Market response can be estimated in three ways: past experience, customer intention surveys, and test marketing.

Using *past experience,* management draws from the knowledge of market behavior gained from analyzing the market response of marketing programs used in the past. Consider this example. Revlon introduced Charlie perfume in 1973, and it became one of the most successful new product introductions in the highly competitive women's fragrance industry. The success of Charlie is attributed to the keen sense of market response of Charles Revson, the chairman of Revlon, who seemed to know what women wanted in a fragrance. Revson believed that women wanted a life-style product that would convey a liberated image, and he sensed that women would respond favorably to a perfume named for a man. Charlie was introduced using a very large promotional program.[6] Sales of Charlie reached $10 million in the first year. Competitors such as Fabergé, Coty, and Max Factor tried to duplicate the success but were unable to do so.[7] Revson had an impressive understanding of consumer behavior. An intuitive sense of what buyers want is important in marketing planning although most marketing managers require more than judgment and experience to help guide their marketing program decisions.

The original Charlie woman was aggressive, self-confident, and pleased with being single. She was seen walking into nightclubs and sitting down with a mass of male admirers. During the 1980s, however, due to changing preferences and life-styles, Revlon realized that its image of women needed to be rethought. The new Charlie woman was more romantic and wore seductive clothing. No longer alone, she was seen walking around town with her boyfriend and by the end of the 30-second commercial had accepted his proposal of marriage. (Courtesy of Revlon)

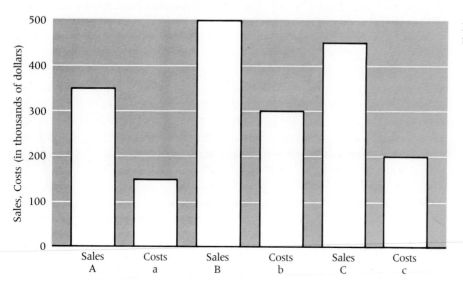

Exhibit 21.8 Market response for marketing programs A, B, and C

Marketing research techniques such as *customer intention surveys* can also be used to help estimate market response, particularly for new products. Prospects in a market are surveyed to determine their purchasing preferences and other information, which is used to help management gauge market response.

Probably the most accurate method of estimating response is to try a proposed marketing program in one or more test markets. Although a market test is costly and more limited than a full-scale market introduction, the test provides some indication of what market response is likely to be on a national basis. Test marketing can be used for existing products as well as new products.

An interesting test marketing service is offered by Information Resources. Called BehaviorScan, the service uses consumer panels in several test cities, where most of the residents have cable television in their homes, and tests the marketing mixes for new or existing products. BehaviorScan is described by Gian Fulgoni, president of the firm.

> Cable is necessary, says Mr. Fulgoni, because BehaviorScan can then insert test ads for its clients which will show only in that small market.
>
> It can help a client choose the ad consumers reacted most favorably to, judging by the purchases of the panelists as well as the total purchases made at the store. "The system allows the manufacturer to measure the purchases of products under different marketing plans," says Mr. Fulgoni.
>
> He points out that a company "may find that an ad campaign that would cost $5 million works just as well or better than the marketing plan that would cost $20 million.
>
> "It is important because a company can increase the chance of having a successful product once the right marketing plan is known," he adds.[8]

Thus marketing management must choose among various methods to help estimate how buyers in the market will respond to different amounts of marketing program expenditure and different marketing mix combinations. (See Marketech for a description of some alternative testing methods.)

Marke**TECH** □ □ □ □ □ □ □ □ □ □ □ □ □ □ □ □ □

New methods for gauging consumer preferences

CONVENTIONAL TEST marketing offers important advantages over full-scale introduction of new products. Nevertheless, running tests in one or more cities is expensive, reliable feedback often requires many months of testing, and tests are subject to sabotage by competitors. Because of these limitations, companies are using alternative methods to estimate customers' response to new products. These techniques offer cost-effective options to conventional tests in certain situations such as

SOURCE: Eleanor Johnson Tracy, "Testing time for test marketing," FORTUNE, Oct. 29, 1984, pp. 75, 76. Reprinted by permission from FORTUNE Magazine.

weeding out products not likely to succeed before investing in conventional market tests. Firms using the new methods include Procter & Gamble, Consolidated Foods, and Quaker Oats.

One less expensive and faster alternative to traditional test marketing is *simulated test marketing*. Consumers at a shopping center are recruited. The participant reads an advertisement for a new product and receives a free sample of the product. The research firm handling the test calls the person after sufficient time has elapsed for the product to be tried. Sales potential is estimated based on the responses of test participants. Such tests, costing approxi-

mately $40,000, are primarily useful for eliminating products likely to fail rather than accurately predicting sales potential.

Another method of gauging market performance of new products is the use of *scanner-linked feedback* at supermarket checkout counters. A sample of consumers in selected test cities is exposed to advertising messages using cable television. Response to the new product is monitored by special cards inserted at the checkout stand by sample participants at supermarkets. Because these people are ongoing members of a panel, they are not aware that their response to the new product is being measured.

□ □

Designing the marketing program

It should be clear by now that understanding market response is a key factor in planning the marketing program. The marketing manager must decide how much to spend on the marketing program and how to allocate the expenditures to each marketing mix component. Let us look into what must be accomplished for each of these decisions.

Deciding how much to spend

The description of BehaviorScan gives reasons why determining how much should be spent on the marketing plan is important. For new products, test marketing may assist management in making this decision. The dilemma facing marketing management is that if too much is spent profits will be adversely affected, and if not enough is spent the market may not respond adequately. At the crux of these issues is estimating market response to marketing program expenditures. In many firms, marketing program expenditures for new products are guided by test market findings or by sales forecasts and expenses needed to obtain the sales forecasted. Management may be willing to incur losses in the early stages of market introduction to gain market position. Sales and expense projections are initially set and adjusted based on actual sales. For existing products, marketing program expenditures normally do not change substantially from year to year unless unusual conditions are experienced or marketing strategies are modified.

Church's Fried Chicken, the fast-food retailer, provides an illustration of how major changes in marketing program expenditures may occur. Declining sales and profits and a top management shift in 1983 led to the following changes made by the new chairman and cofounder, J. David Bamberger:

> "We have not been marketing-oriented enough," says Bamberger. He immediately boosted the company's 1983 advertising of $6 million—itself a radical increase from earlier years but still only 1.3% of sales—with a supplemental $700,000 in December. That, he says, is why Church's sales rose in the quarter, and he plans to double the ad budget this year to $12 million.[9]

Allocating expenditures. Test marketing findings or past experience often provides an indication as to how much of the total marketing program expenditure should be allocated to each part of the marketing mix. Nevertheless, marketing management should regularly consider possible adjustments in the marketing mix in attempting to improve marketing results. Changes in the marketing mix may be appropriate because of

1. Experience gained in marketing a product. Management may learn that one mix component (e.g., personal selling) is more effective than another (e.g., advertising). Consequently, expenditures may be increased on one component and decreased on another.
2. Changes in the effectiveness of mix components as the product moves through its life cycle. For example, price may decline (using inflation-adjusted dollars) as the product moves toward maturity.
3. Competitive actions. For example, R$T Savings, recalling our earlier discussion of a competitor's gift premium program, may find it necessary to introduce a premium program (or make other mix adjustments) to avoid losing deposits to the competitor.

A look at the contents of a firm's action plans for the marketing mix components will indicate the kinds of information that are included in the marketing plan. Excerpts from the product line marketing plan for a home-furnishing products company are shown in Exhibit 21.9. Note the various actions that are indicated for the product line, advertising, sales promotion and display, packaging, trade selling, marketing research, pricing, and cost reduction.

To gain further insights into how firms decide to allocate their financial resources to the marketing mix components, we examine two influences on marketing mix composition: the product life cycle and variations among firms.

Marketing mix and the product life cycle

Several important characteristics of marketing mix components affect how they are used in marketing plans. As a product and market move through different stages in the product life cycle, the composition of the marketing mix often changes as a consequence of these characteristics.

Mix component characteristics. The marketing planner must take into account several features and limitations of marketing mix components.[10] Results from marketing expenditures do not always occur immediately. Normally there is a *time lag* between marketing actions and results. For example, a salesperson may require several months on the job before becoming productive. Advertising messages may need to be repeated several times to trigger actions of buyers.

One marketing mix component (e.g., advertising) may serve as a *substitute* for another (e.g., personal selling). Thus the marketing manager may decide to substitute more of one marketing mix component for another.

Combinations of marketing mix components also often *complement* each other: Two or more mix components such as price and advertising may work more effectively together than alone.

Marketing mix components sometimes *lose their effectiveness.* Advertising programs must be revised, salespeople trained, and other changes made in the marketing mix components to avoid their effectiveness decay. Finally, *scale economies* sometimes affect the decision to use (or not use) components of the marketing mix. For example, small manufacturers cannot support the size salesforce needed to sell their product and must sell through independent manufacturer's agents who represent several different manufacturers.

Understanding these features and limitations is useful in developing the marketing mix and adjusting it over the life cycle of a product.

Product life cycle considerations. Several characteristics of the marketing mix during the life cycle are highlighted in Exhibit 21.10. Note, for example, the transition from an emphasis on heavy planning in the introduction and growth stages of the product life cycle to concern over cost control and efficiency in the maturity and decline stages. Similarly, the role and importance of each mix component often change as the product moves through the product life cycle.

The following changes in mix components occur as the product moves through the life cycle:

- As the product moves toward maturity, modifications and improvements are typically made to help retain its attractiveness to buyers.

Exhibit 21.9   Action plans for marketing mix components for a product line marketing plan

1. *Product Line Plans*
   a. New product objectives
   b. New product positioning vs. identified product needs of consumers
   c. New product specifications
      - Style, weight, size, finish, etc.
      - Manufacturing cost
      - Selling price
   d. New product budgets
      - Exploration and screening
      - Development
      - Market introduction
   e. New product event schedule
      - Design releases
      - Designs complete
      - Market tests complete
      - Production releases
      - Advertising planned and scheduled
      - Selling aids complete
      - Distribution achieved
      - Commencement of consumer advertising, promotion, and selling
   f. Planned deletions and accompanying phase-out program

2. *Advertising Plans*
   a. National advertising (by individual campaign)
      - Definition of consumers and their buying motivations
      - Message theme and objectives
      - Reach and frequency objectives
      - Budgets
      - Preparation and execution schedules
      - Creative plans
      - Media plans
   b. Cooperative advertising programs
      - Trade participation objectives
      - Budget
      - Relationships to other marketing programs
      - Preparation and execution schedule   *(cont.)*

SOURCE: David S. Hopkins, *The Marketing Plan*, New York: The Conference Board, 1981, pp. 116–118.

Exhibit 21.10   Illustrative characteristics of the marketing mix at product life-cycle (PLC) stages

Introduction stage
Developing marketing mix plans are critical concerns of management.
Marketing management is unsure of the effectiveness of the marketing mix components.
   Substantial adjustments in the mix are often necessary.
Informing customers of product availability and features is essential.
Prices typically are highest in this PLC stage.

Growth stage
Expansion into new markets often occurs in this stage.
Multiple market targets may require different marketing programs.
Marketing mix adjustments may occur based on experience gained during the introduction stage of the PLC.

Maturity stage
Marketing management is more concerned with cost control than with planning.
The marketing mix is relatively stable during this stage.
Aggressive price competition often occurs at this PLC stage.

Decline stage
Product elimination may be under serious consideration by some firms in the industry.
Downward pressures on prices are likely to continue in this stage.
Cost reductions are of primary concern to management to gain as much profit contribution as possible from the product.

   c. Trade advertising (by individual campaign)
- Message and audience objectives
- Budgets
- Preparation and execution schedules
- Creative plans
- Media plans

   d. Trademark changes

3. *Sales Promotion and Display Plans*
   a. Consumer and trade promotion objectives
   b. General description of promotion program, budgets, and calendar
   c. Fixturing programs and budgets

4. *Major Packaging Plans*

5. *Trade Selling Plans*
   a. Description of significant changes in distribution policy
   - Approved outlets
   - Distribution methods

   b. Distribution coverage objectives
   c. Account coverage objectives
   d. Selling expense budgets
   e. Specific new account targets
   f. Special trade merchandising programs and calendar
   g. Field selling programs and calendar
   h. New services for trade customers
   - Delivery service
   - Inventory backup
   - Selling support, or the like

   i. Sales quotas for each representative by product line

6. *Special Market Research Projects*
   Include a general description of each project, its objectives, budget, and timetable

7. *Pricing Recommendations*

8. *Special Cost Reduction Programs*
   Include a general description of each program, its expected dollar savings, and an assignment of responsibilities.

- Distribution may not change for many products. In some instances marketing management may work toward more intensive distribution.
- Typically, prices decline (in real dollars) over the product life cycle owing to cost reductions and competitive pressures.
- The role of promotion often changes from initially informing buyers of a new product's availability to stressing features of one brand versus another during the maturity and decline stages.

Perhaps the most important implication of our discussion of the marketing mix and the product life cycle is that a mix is rarely fixed over time. Adjustments in the amount spent on the mix and the allocation to mix components are inevitable as a product moves through life-cycle stages.

Marketing mix variations among firms

One question that has probably occurred to you is why do firms in the same industry use different marketing mixes?

Marketing mix variations within industries. Variations in market targets served and management's choices regarding the substitution of one mix component for another help explain why firms in the same industry have different marketing mixes. For example, consider Avon and Revlon. Avon uses direct selling as a major part of its marketing mix. In contrast, Revlon spends much more than Avon on advertising. The difference is explained by the targeting of different customers by the two firms. Also contributing to the difference is marketing management's preference for heavy use of one marketing mix component instead of another: Avon's management is convinced of the merits of direct selling; Revlon's management has developed the firm's marketing effort around a mass merchandising distribution strategy.

Risk of following competition. One dangerous pitfall that should be avoided is blindly adopting a competitor's percentage allocation to the marketing mix components. Just because R$T Savings spends a certain percentage of its marketing budget on advertising does not necessarily indicate that XYZ Savings should spend the same percentage on advertising. R$T could be spending too much or not enough on advertising. The two financial institutions also may have different market targets and different advertising objectives.

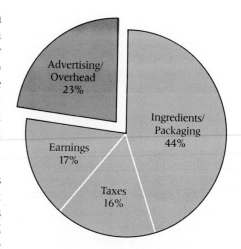

Exhibit 21.11 Marketing mix for WD-40 (percent of each $1.00 of sales)
SOURCE: Ellen Paris, "The one-mystique company," *Forbes,* Apr. 26, 1982, p. 103.

Industrial- versus consumer-product mixes

You are probably familiar with the lubricant WD-40 that is packaged in a blue and yellow spray can (WD-40 stands for Water Displacement Formula No. 40).[11] An analysis of how the sales dollar is expended by the WD-40 Company is shown in Exhibit 21.11. As is typical of other consumer-products firms, advertising is the major portion of the firm's marketing program. Most orders are received by mail from distributors and wholesalers.

There are wide variations in the marketing mixes used by consumer-products firms, and the same variations occur for industrial-products firms. Nevertheless, some general differences can often be found between the marketing mixes of the two groups. Recall, for example the section Selling to Business, Industry, and Government in Chapter 20. Perhaps the most striking difference is that industrial-products firms tend to spend more of their marketing budgets on personal selling and less on advertising than do customer-products firms. Yet, a substantial number of exceptions exist such as Avon.

Budgeting, Implementing, and Controlling

The final step in developing the marketing plan is estimating the revenues and costs associated with the planned actions. Whereas analyzing forecasted revenues and marketing costs occurs in the earlier steps of marketing planning, we are concerned at this point with actually preparing the marketing budget. First, several aspects of budgeting are considered. Then, the process of implementing the marketing plan is described. Finally, the important task of keeping the plan on target is discussed.

The marketing budget

The budget is an essential tool for managing marketing expenditures. Expenditures for marketing are substantial in many companies so it is important to plan how the money will be used. For example, in early 1984,

Anthony J. F. O'Reilly, president and chief executive officer of H. J. Heinz Company, announced that spending to market the firm's food products could climb by 17 percent in fiscal 1985 to $340 million.[12] (Heinz's budget was $290 million in 1984, and actual expenditures totaled $253 million, or 6.8 percent of sales, in 1983.) Heinz's management had projected expenses more than one year into the future.

What is budgeting? Budgeting is selecting and assessing the resources required to achieve marketing objectives. Normally budgeting begins with forecasts of sales. Budgeting is projecting revenues and expenses into the future. When expenses are combined with sales forecasts, profits also can be projected. The budget comprises dollar estimates for each major activity in the marketing plan. For example, from Heinz's total marketing budget for 1984 of $290 million, specific expenses were budgeted for advertising, salesforce, marketing research, and other marketing activities. Detailed budgets are also typically prepared for each major function such as advertising. An example of a small retailer's revenue and expense budget is shown in Exhibit 21.12. Note that the budgeted income statement shows specific expense categories above and below the budgeted amounts. This annual budget can be broken down into months or quarters and actual sales and expenses compared with budgeted amounts during the year. Adjustments in planned expenditures may be necessary during the year based on sales.

Purposes of budgeting. The marketing budget serves two main purposes. First, budgets translate planned marketing actions into their financial consequences. For example, what are the revenues, costs, and estimated profits (or losses) expected during the first year of introducing a new snack food? In some instances, after budgets are prepared, management may decide to adjust planned marketing actions because the costs are too high when combined with the total budget. Second, budgets enable the marketing manager and staff to monitor actual results during the planning period.

Exhibit 21.12 Susie's Dress Shop: Budgeted income statement for the year 1987

	Budgeted	Actual	Variance
Gross sales	$200,000	$250,000	$50,000
Less: sales returns and allowances	10,000	30,000	20,000
Net sales	$190,000	$220,000	$30,000
Less: cost of goods sold	85,000	102,500	17,500
Gross margin	$105,000	$117,500	$12,500
Less: Operating expenses			
Salaries	41,500	42,500	1,000
Sales commissions (5% of gross sales)	10,000	12,500	2,500
Advertising	2,500	2,000	(500)
Promotional gifts	500	500	0
Rent	6,000	6,700	700
Utilities	3,500	3,000	(500)
Miscellaneous	2,000	1,000	(1,000)
Total operating expenses	$66,000	$68,200	2,200
Income before taxes	$39,000	$49,300	$10,300

When variances between budgeted and actual expenses are excessive, adjustments may be made in the remaining planned expenses. Thus budgeting performs vital planning and control functions.

Implementation

The marketing plan is useless unless it is put into operation. Effective implementation is critical to the success of marketing plans. Consider these planning decisions.

> Should we emphasize price or quality? Do we want to stay with smaller, upscale retailers or seek market expansion through large discount chains? Will our proposed new product take sales away from our existing line? These are the kinds of questions—ones of strategy—that marketers agonize over. But what happens once a particular strategy is agreed to? Will marketers effectively turn drawing-board strategy into marketplace reality? Too often a seemingly effective strategy fails to do what it is supposed to do, and marketing executives immediately assume that the strategy is at fault.[13]

The issue, of course, is implementation. Unless the plan becomes actionable, nothing happens. Implementation difficulties with marketing plans can result from a variety of organizational and structural problems and inadequate personal skills.[14] A closer look at some implementation guidelines will highlight some major aspects of effective implementation.

Implementation guidelines. Four questions must be answered before marketing plan **implementation**.

1. What is to be implemented? (Specific actions should be indicated.)
2. Who will be responsible for implementation? (Putting the plan into operation is accomplished by people.)
3. When and where will implementation occur? (Dates, schedules, and locations for each event in the plan are essential.)
4. How is implementation to be accomplished?

Answering the *what, who, when, where,* and *how* questions is an important first step in implementation.

Implementation skills. After answering these questions, many specific decisions and tasks occur while plans are implemented. The managers responsible for implementation should possess certain skills to move the process toward success. These include

Interacting. The marketing job by its nature is one of influencing others inside and outside the corporation.

Allocating. The implementor must divide time, assignments, and other resources among the marketing jobs to be done.

Monitoring. It is by using monitoring skills that a manager can do the most to reconstruct degraded corporate information and control systems.

Organizing. Good implementors have an almost uncanny ability to create afresh an informal organization or network to match each problem with which they are confronted.[15]

Interestingly, executives who are good planners are not necessarily good implementors. Those responsible for executing marketing plans should possess skills in interacting and influencing people, effectively allocating assignments, monitoring results, and establishing organizational networks to facilitate implementation.

Keeping the plan on target

Beyond the communications and human aspects of implementation, the type of organization adopted and the management practices used by the marketing manager and staff are important determinants of the success of the marketing plan. These topics of organizational design and marketing control are discussed in detail in the next chapter. At this point we need to examine one key issue associated with planning and control.

Marketing plans often need to be adjusted during implementation. This is particularly the case when new products are introduced. Poor sales results with existing products also may cause drastic alterations in marketing plans.

Consider, for example how Victor Kiam turned around ailing Remington Products after purchasing the firm from Sperry Corporation in 1979.

> It's a familiar turnaround because Kiam himself appears in the company's TV commercials, proclaiming that he bought the company because he believed in its electric shavers. Kiam's faith in the product—and his skill at selling it—have been handsomely rewarded. Since 1979, Remington has earned $30 million and last month retired the last of its bank debts. Marketing share has improved dramatically, though the subject is touchy because of competitor's counterclaims. But in the crucial Christmas period, Remington's share of men's razors climbed to 38% last year, from 20% in 1978. Similarly, women's razors rose to 48% of the market, from 27% in the same period.
>
> "The whole turnaround was due to the marketing concept," Kiam says. Accordingly, a complete turnover of sales and marketing managers followed Kiam's arrival, while most financial managers stayed. The impact of a new marketing outlook was felt from the start in all areas:
>
> - Remington forewent a price increase planned by prior management, achieving a price advantage over competitors.
> - The product line was curtailed and costly product introductions abandoned.
> - Packaging was revamped and an enigmatic three-letter trademark discarded.
> - Advertising was refocussed, both to attract customers and to reassure the trade. An old slogan, "Shaves as close as a blade or your money back," was reinstated.
>
> Largely as a result of these measures, Remington's financial picture improved rapidly. When Kiam took over, sales were $49 million. Last year, they were $100 million, up 35% from 1981.[16]

Marketing planning is a continuing process with adjustments being made to cope with changing conditions.

SUMMARY

The marketing plan pulls together managers' decisions regarding the market target, objectives, and marketing program. Planning is decision making. It is an ongoing process of making decisions, implementing them, and evaluating results.

The major building blocks of the marketing plan are decisions about market target, objectives, and the marketing program for a firm, a unit of the business, a product line, or a specific product. A good marketing plan offers several key advantages to the marketing manager including improving communication, providing a basis for measuring results, and establishing a frame of reference for changes. Typically, the planning horizon for a short-term marketing plan is one year. Long-range strategic plans are prepared two to five years or more into the future.

The marketing plan is prepared in five steps. Step 1 consists of assessing the situation, and the results indicate the conditions under which the plan is to be developed. The assessment should highlight opportunities and threats faced by the firm and indicate key advantages and weaknesses of the firm compared with competition. Steps 2 and 3 indicate the customer groups to be targeted and the objectives to be achieved. A description of the market target is critical to guiding the development of the marketing plan. Obtaining descriptive characteristics of buyers and their needs and wants is essential in planning the marketing program. Explicit, achievable, and relevant objectives indicate what the marketing plan is intended to accomplish in the market served by the firm.

In step 4 the marketing program is designed to accomplish the objectives formulated by marketing management. The decision maker must estimate how the market target will respond to alternative marketing programs under consideration. The marketing program mix that will be most effective in achieving the marketing plan objectives must be selected. Past experience, customer intention surveys, and test marketing to estimate market response are ways to gauge market target response. Designing the marketing mix also involves deciding how much to spend and how to allocate it. Many managers look at variations in the marketing mix over the product life cycle and variations among the marketing mixes of various industries to gain insight as to how to allocate funds.

The final steps in developing the marketing plan are budgeting, implementing, and controlling. The marketing budget translates planned marketing actions into their financial consequences. Budgets also enable the marketing manager and staff to monitor actual results during the planning period. Budgeting is essential in both planning and control. Effective implementation is critical to the success of the marketing plan. Only by monitoring the plan does a marketing manager know when changing it becomes necessary. Nothing happens until the plan becomes actionable.

KEY TERMS

strategic marketing plan	over-planning	market response
annual marketing plan	top-down planning	implementation
tactical marketing plan	bottom-up planning	
crisis management	situation assessment	

QUESTIONS FOR REVIEW AND DISCUSSION

1. What are the five major steps in building a marketing plan?

2. Describe a marketing plan and indicate examples of the types of activities that are included in a marketing plan.

3. Explain the term *crisis management*. How does a marketing plan help avoid this situation?

4. Establishing objectives, actions to be taken, responsibility, and deadlines for managing various marketing efforts are specific advantages offered by marketing planning. List other advantages of marketing planning.

5. What are some marketing planning pitfalls?

6. Why is a situation assessment necessary? What information does it yield for marketing decision making? How often should a situation assessment be made?

7. R$T Savings has a competitor that is giving away premiums to attract customers. What should be the marketing plan implication of this aspect of R$T's situation assessment?

8. We saw how R$T Savings identified their target customers. What guidelines does the market target decision provide for building the marketing plan?

9. Indicate typical areas in which firms set objectives. For what levels of operations are marketing objectives set?

10. Explain the three characteristics of good objectives.

11. What is market response? What are the factors that influence market response?

12. What are three ways to estimate market response? What does each approach entail?

13. How do firms' marketing program expenditures differ from new and existing products?

14. Five characteristics of marketing mix components affect how they are used in marketing plans. Discuss these characteristics.

15. The marketing mix is rarely fixed over time. Adjustments to mix components are inevitable as a product moves through the product life-cycle stages. Give examples of changes that are made in each stage.

16. Why do firms in the same industry use different marketing mixes? What is often a marketing mix difference between consumer- and industrial-products firms?

17. The marketing budget is an essential tool for managing marketing expenditures. What does budgeting consist of?

18. What are the two main purposes the marketing budget serves?

19. Effective implementation is critical to the success of marketing plans—unless a plan is actionable, nothing happens. What are the four key aspects or guidelines of implementation?

20. The managers responsible for implementation should possess certain skills owing to the specific decisions and tasks that occur during implementation of plans. Give examples of these skills.

BUILDING YOUR PORTFOLIO

- Select a product category such as ready-to-eat cereals, coffee, or automobiles. Conduct library research to determine the market share of the companies that produce the product you have chosen. Compare market share position of the major firms for a five- to ten-year period up to the present time. If market share has changed, indicate possible reasons for the change or changes. For example, were the changes caused by the firms' faulty planning?

- Prepare a description of the marketing strategy for a company of your choice. Use Exhibit 21.3 as a guide for collecting and analyzing information about the company. Indicate the approximate amount of the marketing budget allocated to each marketing mix component. Possible sources of information include annual reports, *Business Week, The Wall Street Journal,* and other business publications. After you have prepared the strategy description, critically evaluate it indicating what you consider to be strengths and weaknesses. As an alternative to library research, you may select a company in your city and interview the chief marketing executive.

NOTES

1. This illustration is based on Dedra Hauser, "Glove makers seek niche for survival." *Wall Street Journal,* Nov. 10, 1983, pp. 33, 51.
2. Steven Flax, "The greening of Crayola." *Forbes,* Apr. 12, 1982, pp. 190, 192.
3. Ibid.
4. David W. Cravens, "Marketing strategy positioning." *Business Horizons,* Dec. 1975, pp. 53–61.
5. Eamonn Fingleton, "Knocking off Head & Shoulders." *Forbes,* June 7, 1982, p. 162.
6. "A whiff of immorality." *Forbes,* Sept. 15, 1975, p. 36.
7. Stanley H. Slom, "Taking fragrance to market isn't easy: Making them successes is even harder." *Wall Street Journal,* Aug. 16, 1978, p. 46.
8. Eileen Norris, "Product hopes tied to cities with the 'right stuff.'" *Advertising Age,* Feb. 20, 1984.
9. *Business Week,* "Church's Fried Chicken: Cutting loose from its penny-pinching past." Feb. 27, 1984, p. 72.
10. The following discussion is based on R. P. Willett, "A model for marketing programming." *Journal of Marketing,* Jan. 1963, pp. 42–44.
11. Ellen Paris, "The one-mystique company." *Forbes,* Apr. 26, 1982, p. 103.
12. "Heinz expects a jump in marketing outlays." *Wall Street Journal,* Mar. 16, 1984, p. 37.
13. Thomas V. Bonoma, "Making your marketing strategy work." *Harvard Business Review,* Mar.–Apr. 1984, p. 37.
14. Ibid., p. 69.
15. Ibid., p. 75.
16. Steven Mintz, "Sales and marketing to the rescue." *Sales & Marketing Management,* Apr. 4, 1983, p. 37.

Case 21.1

Marketing Planning at a Rubber Company

MARKETING PLANS ARE prepared annually, and in recent years have become more closely tied to the company's strategic plan objectives. . . .

Marketing planning is preceded by establishment of strategic objectives for each marketing division. Senior executives representing marketing, manufacturing and administrative services meet in formal planning sessions to consider progress against past objectives, the changing competitive and business environment within which the company operates, and forecasts relating to markets served. Updated and revised strategic objectives are arrived at, giving consideration to the following:

1. Profitability history of marketing units measured by net profit to sales, manufacturing costs trends, and return on investment.
2. Market position history—an assessment of each marketing operation's current share position relative to competitors and progress against share objectives.
3. Long-range market growth prospects.
4. Product cost review—consideration of

SOURCE: David S. Hopkins, *The Marketing Plan*, New York: The Conference Board, 1981, p. 21.

significant design or process improvement plans.
5. Manufacturing capacity—current and projected.

From these deliberations, strategic objectives are set stating sales growth, market share, and profit goals for each marketing unit. Sales divisions then prepare marketing plans designed to meet the targets stated in the strategic objectives. These plans do not follow a set format but all include most of the elements listed below. Plans are prepared by the manager directly accountable for the sales operations covered by the plan. Plans generally include the following:

1. A restatement of strategic objectives.
2. Analysis of these objectives' potential effect on future profits.
3. A presentation of elements of the marketing plan. These vary depending upon the characteristics of the markets for which each sales operation is responsible, but may include the following:
   a. Training—special training plans for field sales personnel and/or customers.
   b. Pricing plans.
   c. Identification of target markets or

customers. These may be industries or individual accounts where improved sales penetration is required to meet objectives.
   d. Field sales programs—identification of programs planned for sales personnel.
   e. Promotion programs—identification of planned advertising and promotional programs.
   f. Product plans, including new products. Includes product design changes, product deletions, and planned new introductions.
4. A presentation in greater detail of selected key elements in the marketing plan.
5. Presentation and discussion of next year's sales budget, with some product detail and consideration of its fit to strategic objective.

Marketing plans are presented in person to senior executives annually. Agendas for these market planning sessions include all marketing units, and are restricted to consideration of each marketing operation's plan and its fit to strategic objectives. A summary of decisions made and actions required is prepared at the conclusion of the meetings.

QUESTIONS

1. Evaluate the company's approach to marketing planning.
2. What improvements can you suggest to the marketing manager?
3. What specific information would you expect to find in the part

of the marketing plan covering field sales programs?

4. Suggest how a market target might be identified in the plan.

Case 21.2

Gillette Safety Razor Division

THE MARKETING STRATEGY used for Gillette's TRAC II razor is described by Derek W. Coward, vice president of marketing.

SOURCE: Reprinted from the January/February 1983 issue of *Marketing Times*, update for the sales management and marketing professional published by Sales and Marketing Executives–International, pp. 38–40.

"When the Gillette Company's Safety Razor Division started researching and developing the world's first twin-blade razor—TRAC II (our acronym for twin-blade razor and cartridge) we knew we had a winner. But it took a successful product introduction in 1971 and then another 10 years of aggressive marketing for the TRAC II to change the face of shaving in America and around the world.

"Always highly competitive, the razor and blade market include such heavyweights as Warner-Lambert (Schick), Colgate (Wilkinson) and Philip Morris (American Safety Razor) when Gillette introduced TRAC II.

"But we have remained firmly committed to a long-time marketing philosophy: There's always a better way to shave. Grounded in that notion, our marketing program encompassed:

"1. *Thorough research.* By 1957, Gillette researchers had already begun to develop and test razor designs based on the simple concept that two blades properly placed in tandem would give even a closer shave. Original designs went through a myriad of phases, including a razor which had blades facing one another.

"By the early 1970s, research had given the twin-blade concept credibility. High-speed, high-magnification photography revealed as a blade passes through the whisker, it also lifts the hair out of the facial cavity and exposes—for a fraction of a second—part of the whisker previously below the skin. A second blade placed in tandem behind the first one could cut the extended whisker after the first blade had initially trimmed it, Gillette theorized.

"Engineers developed a final razor design applying twin-blade theory giving birth to TRAC II and twin-blade shaving.

"As part of ongoing research in our South Boston Shave Test Center, hundreds of Gillette's male employees came to work every day unshaven to test the new razor. These tests, along with highly confidential consumer usage and reaction tests, provided resounding evidence that the as-yet unnamed razor had the potential to revolutionize shaving.

"2. *Introduction.* Our marketing team made plans to introduce the new shaving product through press conferences, advertising and promotion, all highlighted by the advertising slogan: It's one blade better than whatever you're using now.

"The goal: to win immediate acceptance for TRAC II among males 18–34.

"As a major part of its marketing plan, Gillette turned to a venerable success strategy it has often employed over the years: sports marketing.

"Major league baseball's world series seemed like a natural platform for introducing and promoting TRAC II to consumers.

"With a $4 million advertising and sales promotion budget for a four-month introductory period in late 1971, we put the following activities into motion as world series time rolled around:

- A heavy advertising campaign on network television and radio during the world series

- Print advertisements in national magazines

- Launch of a sampling program that would eventually result in the distribution of over 12 million samples

- A $1 consumer refund offered at special world series counter displays in stores

- Retail promotional aids such as streamers and flags for high point-of-purchase impact during the world series

"Result: almost overnight TRAC II became the bestselling razor in the nation.

"3. *All-Star promotion.* In 1972, its first full year on the market, TRAC II had a $10 million advertising and promotional budget. We built on TRAC II's introduction by making it a focal point of Gillette's most elaborate consumer promotion: sponsorship of baseball's All-Star Election in which fans help select the players who represent the American and National League teams in the annual all-star game.

"We offered ballot forms at special retail displays featuring TRAC II—drawing attention to the new razor and encouraging consumers to make a purchase.

"By the end of 1972, TRAC II refill cartridges had captured a full 10 percent of the blade market—an unusually dramatic share in the shaving industry so soon after the launch. TRAC II blades had doubled to 20 percent of the blade market by the end of 1973, becoming a key part of Gillette's 60 percent overall market share for blades.

"4. *Demonstration.* While capitalizing on its association with baseball, TRAC II advertising has featured demonstrations—through animation—of twin blades in action.

"The success story continues today. Since introduction in late 1971, Gillette has sold more than 3.6 billion TRAC II blade cartridges and 64.5 million razor handles, accounting for $845 million in retail sales of blade cartridges and $180 million in razor handle sales.

"5. *One step further.* In 1977, Gillette took the TRAC II marketing legacy one step further by introducing the Atra razor—combining twin-blade

technology and pivoting head to hug the contours of the face.

"The five-year-old Atra has become Gillette's premier razor, already on a market share parity with TRAC II.

"Since TRAC II has remained popular and has accumulated a vast franchise of users, we continue to promote it aggressively through year-round trade and consumer promotions—including Super Bowl, all-star and world series tie-ins.

"A Gillette brand frequently does 25 to 33 percent of its volume during one of the company's sports promotions, which generally run only 45 to 60 days. With this ongoing promotional effort, TRAC II and Atra have the highest level of consumer awareness among all major razors and the major share of Gillette's shaving business.

"For the future, we plan to continue support for TRAC II while building share for Atra—our leading blade and razor system. Gillette will also continue to offer consumers the convenience of Gillette disposable shaver products—Good News!, Daisy and Swivel.

"This combination of twin-blade products has prominence on blade and razor racks of drug stores, supermarkets and convenience stores across the United States—at in-aisle locations, front-end checkout stands and special end-aisle displays featuring world series, all star games or Super Bowl promotions.

"Our brand management team continues to evaluate strategies to supplement our sports promotions. We recently added auto racing to our family of sports marketing programs—specifically to promote the growing use of the Atra razor.

"Auto racing matches baseball in attendance and auto racing fans exhibit high brand loyalty to supporting companies. Moreover, professional auto racing has a male audience—60 to 80 percent of the 50 million fans who turn out for auto races each year fall into Atra's target market: the 18 to 34 age group.

"During 1983, the Atra professional auto racing program will include product sampling of 1.2 million Atra razors at 22 races. The program also includes awards for racecar drivers, on-track identification through signage and announcements, off-track media coverage, and ongoing involvement with the National Association for Stock Car Auto Racing, International Motor Sports Association and the Sports Car Club of America."

QUESTIONS

1. Critique Gillette's marketing plan for TRAC II.

2. What problems might the TRAC II razor create for Gillette's existing line of razors?

3. How could Gillette's marketing strategy for TRAC II be changed in an attempt to appeal to women as well as men?

22 Marketing Organization and Control

When you finish this chapter, you will understand

☐ The alternative ways in which companies organize the marketing function

☐ Why managers must look for performance problems after implementing marketing plans

☐ The steps in a control activity

☐ How performance standards are developed

☐ How marketing managers discover marketing performance problems

☐ How marketing managers find causes of performance problems

☐ The alternative ways that marketing managers correct performance problems

In a creative business like Binney & Smith's (manufacturers of Crayola crayons), the organizational culture is likely to be less structured than in other companies.

General Electric handles in-warranty repair calls for its consumer appliances, service contracts, sales of parts to do-it-yourselfers, and repair of out-of-warranty appliances through local branches blanketing 80 percent of the United States. Unfortunately, several performance problems with the out-of-warranty segment were discovered: (1) few people were aware of the service, (2) market share was low—8 to 10 percent of repair requests for GE, (3) the number of repair requests was not increasing, and (4) potential sales were limited because a repair is only requested when an appliance fails.

GE's management pondered the causes of these performance problems. Stiff competition was coming from local businesses that repaired all brands. Sales growth could be achieved only by expanding into new geographic areas, not by building share in existing areas. Furthermore, profit responsibility was under the control of operations managers, not marketing. Operations managers put great emphasis on cost savings, which often limited the capacity of GE service branches to handle repair requests from consumers by limiting telephone capacity, call-takers, order processing, and other capabilities.

A new advertising campaign was tried. Its objectives were to attract more first-time sales in existing areas and to encourage more people to switch to GE's repair service. Evaluation of the impact of advertising on performance showed, however, that its cost exceeded increases in sales. Advertising alone could not increase sales. Something else needed to be done.

After extensively testing marketing strategies and further analyzing markets, GE settled on a marketing approach centered on expanding service quality. Emphasis was placed on improving the ability of GE branches to efficiently handle larger volumes of requests for service from consumers. At the same time, quality of the repairs was carefully controlled to meet customers' expectations. Advertising was continued, but at a lower level, freeing funds for the service quality program. This marketing strategy worked—sales and profitability climbed.[1]

MARKETING PLANS DO NOT ALWAYS work as well as managers expect. Even a well-managed company such as General Electric experiences problems. GE managers, however, had enough foresight to evaluate marketing strategy for the out-of-warranty appliance repair segment of their service business. Performance problems were discovered. Only after careful evaluation and trial and error experience with advertising did managers hit on marketing strategy improvements that corrected problems and improved both sales and profitability.

Discovering and solving performance problems are control activities. **Marketing control** is concerned with analyzing the performance of marketing decisions, uncovering performance problems and their causes, and taking actions to correct these problems. Essential to control is management's ability to quickly find performance problems. A **marketing performance problem** occurs whenever a marketing decision leads to performance that does not measure up to management's expectations.

Performance problems do not automatically surface. A problem in one area of a business can be hidden by high performance in other areas. Suppose GE's managers had lumped together sales and profits from its out-of-warranty segment with performance of its other, more successful services. They might not have noticed the segment's low performance.

This chapter will help you understand how managers can control marketing performance. First we examine different ways in which a company organizes the marketing function to assist in all phases of marketing management: planning, implementing, and controlling marketing strategy. Next, we identify key steps that make up the marketing control activity. Finally, in the remainder of the chapter, we discuss how each of these steps is carried out in practice.

MARKETING ORGANIZATION

Marketing management is responsible for several components of marketing mix strategy including products and services, pricing, distribution, advertising, sales promotion, publicity, and a salesforce. Companies devise **mar-**

keting organizational structures to formally assign the responsibility for each component to various managers. This structure is shown in a company's organizational chart and in the job titles and lines of authority that are established for all functions including marketing, research and development, financial control, manufacturing, and physical distribution.

Purpose of marketing organization

A marketing organizational structure offers two important advantages to a company. First, structure divides a large responsibility into small, manageable responsibilities. For all but the smallest companies, planning, implementing, and controlling a total marketing strategy is a large responsibility that can overwhelm one or a few managers. Organizational structure makes managing the marketing function of a huge, multiproduct company such as RCA easier by dividing it among many managers, each of whom has responsibility for part of the total strategy.

The second advantage of an organizational structure is that each manager of the various components of the marketing strategy can specialize, and marketing specialists are created. An advertising manager, for instance, can become skilled at making advertising decisions by not being sidetracked by decisions on other parts of the marketing mix.

Marketing organizational structure also creates problems, such as how to coordinate the decisions made by various managers. Effective marketing strategy demands that each component of a marketing mix be coordinated with the others. Consider the problem of building selling points into marketing strategy. Both advertising and personal selling should emphasize a product's selling points. Yet, product design, advertising, and personal selling decisions are made by managers in different departments. Coordination needs are great because each of the many components of a marketing strategy is dependent on the others to work effectively. Organizational structure must provide for this coordination.

Types of marketing organizations

Functional marketing organization. Many companies, particularly small ones, create functional managers to head up each marketing component. This approach is called a **functional marketing organization** and is illustrated in Exhibit 22.1. Notice that pricing and distribution—two components that we have considered part of marketing management—are missing. Although marketing managers influence pricing and distribution decisions, these two activities typically are included in other functions of a company. Pricing decisions may be made by top management, a chief marketing executive, managers in a functional department all its own, or managers in the financial control function of a company. Distribution can be part of manufacturing or, like pricing, have its own functional manager.

As companies grow, they eventually become too unwieldy for a simple functional structure. It would be extremely difficult for a single sales manager to plan and control performance for a geographically widespread salesforce or an extensive product line. A marketing organizational structure is expanded to accommodate decision making by forming activity centers. A **marketing activity center** is a subdivision of a marketing function that is assigned to an individual manager. The manager is responsible for the performance of the center, typically sales or profit performance,

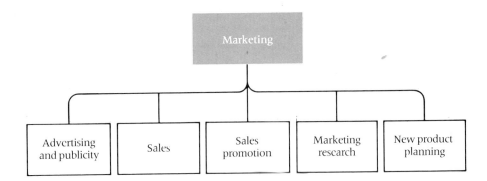

Exhibit 22.1 Functional marketing organizational structure

and given a portion of the function's resources to accomplish objectives. Common activity centers are organized by (1) product and brand, (2) geographic area, (3) market segments, (4) customer, and (5) distribution channel. Suppose the geographically widespread salesforce is broken down into geographic subdivisions such as districts so that each district can be controlled by a district sales manager. Districts become the activity centers.

All marketing functions are not necessarily organized in the same way. In fact, top management may decide to install a new arrangement in one function before considering what to do with the others. This enables the company to see how the activity center arrangement works. Personal selling is often the first function to get attention. Large companies with national salesforces, such as Procter & Gamble, IBM, and American Hospital Supply Corporation, organize geographically by dividing the country into regions, forming districts within regions, and sales territories within districts. Exhibit 22.2 illustrates how the sales organizational structure provides managerial positions corresponding to these geographic area activity centers.

Another approach is to create specialized salesforces to contact market segments. In this case, the market segments become activity centers. National Cash Register, a manufacturer of data entry and processing equipment for business customers, has adopted this approach by assigning a well-defined customer industry segment, such as supermarket operations or financial companies, to each sales staff.[2] Exhibit 22.3 shows the general structure for a market-based sales organization.

Product manager organization. Companies with a growing number of products and markets find that even the expanded functional structures are not adequate. Planning, implementing, and controlling marketing strategies demand increased specialization in all the marketing functions. One alternative is to create a product function and then divide it into product-based activity centers in which managers are responsible for performance for individual products and their markets. You can see the need for these centers at Miles Laboratories, which has several separate product lines such as adult vitamins, chewable vitamins for children, and antacids. Each product line has several brands—chewable vitamins include Flintstones and Bugs Bunny brands. Product managers are assigned to each product line and are expected to achieve sales, market share, and profitability objectives. Exhibit 22.4 shows the form of a typical **product manager organization.**

The product manager organizational structure has the distinct advantage of concentrating managers' attention on the unique opportunities and

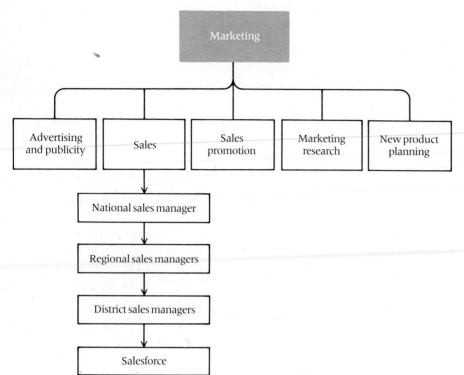

Exhibit 22.2   Functional organizational structure with geographic sales activity centers

problems of each product and its markets. An information base is built for each product, and the company is assured that someone is managing the business that every product is bringing in. Product managers develop marketing strategies for their products, coordinate the plan's implementation, and control how well the strategies are performing. They typically have direct authority over the mass communications components of promotion in the marketing mix—advertising, sales promotion, and publicity. In fact, when product manager activity centers are formed, promotion functions are shifted from functional managers to product managers, whereas prod-

Exhibit 22.3   Market activity centers for the sales function of a marketing organization

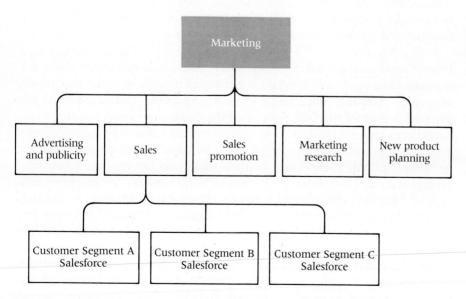

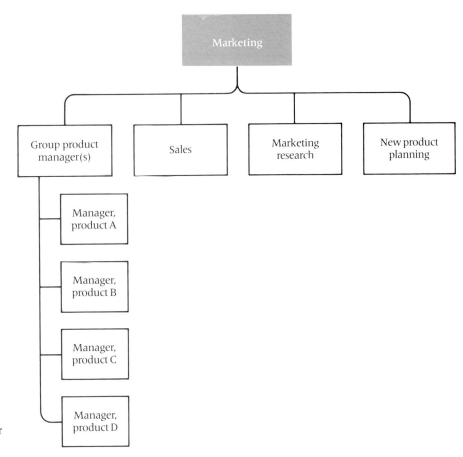

Exhibit 22.4 Product manager organizational structure

uct managers are given little or no authority over the salesforce, pricing, or distribution. Each product manager is expected to work closely with these functions to get product plans implemented. Thus product managers must be particularly adept at gaining cooperation from others in the company, primarily through personal persuasion.[3]

Divisional organizational structure. Larger, multiproduct companies often deal with decision-making complexity by dividing the company into separate divisions—a **divisional organizational structure.** Each division has responsibility for all marketing functions for a group of related products. If the structure is carried out to the fullest extent, manufacturing and all other nonmarketing functions may also be integrated into each division as well. Corporate headquarters provides services such as marketing research, media buying, and financial assistance that a division may choose to use. Exhibit 22.5 illustrates the divisional organizational structure.

General Foods uses a divisional organizational structure. Originally organized around product lines based on similarity in the way products are manufactured—Birds Eye, Jell-O, Post, and Kool-Aid Divisions—the company faced problems managing the many products. Often General Foods would find that it had products from different divisions targeting the same markets. Powdered dessert mixes were handled by Kool-Aid and frozen desserts were the province of Birds Eye. Switching to a market-based organizational structure helped resolve these problems. General Foods reorganized into three large divisions, each of which could concentrate on serving

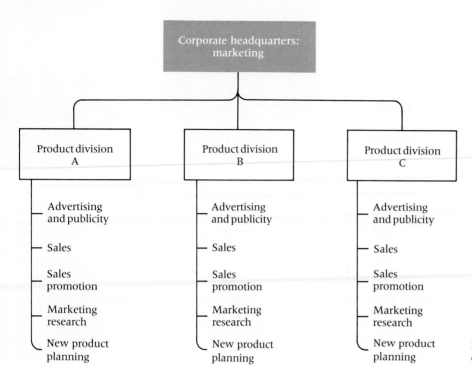

Exhibit 22.5 Divisional marketing organizational structure

the needs of a specific market—Food Products Division, Beverage and Breakfast Foods Division, and Pet Foods Division.[4]

Matrix organizations. A company may try a complicated, hybrid organizational structure to deal with complex market situations. This structure is called a **matrix organization** because it combines functional organization and activity center subdivisions. A matrix organization using both functional and product manager structures is shown in Exhibit 22.6. Its advantage stems from specialization in the several activity centers simultaneously. You can see from Exhibit 22.6 that the product manager organization ensures that sufficient attention is focused on individual products and their markets, and at the same time, product managers can draw expertise from specialized managers in each of the marketing mix functional components.

Matrix organizations are difficult to make work because they violate a cardinal rule of management: Each employee should report to only one boss. As you can see, the matrix organization sets up two or more bosses for employees in the functional components. A manager who specializes in advertising reports to the head of the advertising function and is assigned to a product manager at the same time. The same holds for managers in the other functional departments. Each department has different goals, and so conflicting demands can easily be made on the manager's time and energy. Special procedures have to be developed so the structure will operate efficiently. An employee's performance, for instance, should be jointly evaluated by the heads of each area.[5]

Matrix organizations are also costly to set up and to manage. Top management must be committed to making the organization work. Managers must be trained to cope with the overlapping lines of authority between the activity centers. Furthermore, the number of managers is greater than for other organizational forms. Nevertheless, there is likely to be greater emphasis on achieving performance objectives throughout the organization.

In general, organizing by well-defined activity centers enables marketing managers to concentrate on manageable units of the company's sales. Coordinating small units is achieved by grouping them under a higher-level marketing manager. For this reason, many organizations have levels of managers, each with control responsibility. These levels effectively decentralize management authority by spreading control of marketing decisions.

Matching organizational structures to environments

No one organizational structure is best for an organization. Instead, management searches for the structure that best responds to the decision-making environment facing the company. Over time, most organizations must change their marketing organizational structure as their environments change. Let us briefly examine two of the more important of these environmental factors.

The *size of a company* affects its organizational structure, particularly when products and markets for which marketing strategies are needed are added. Simple organizational structures work well when there are few products and markets, but become less efficient when marketing managers must divide their attention among an increasing number of products and markets. Generally, structure is increased in complexity to match the greater complexity of the product and marketing environment.[6] For instance, large multiproduct companies such as Procter & Gamble and Miles

Exhibit 22.6 A matrix marketing organizational structure

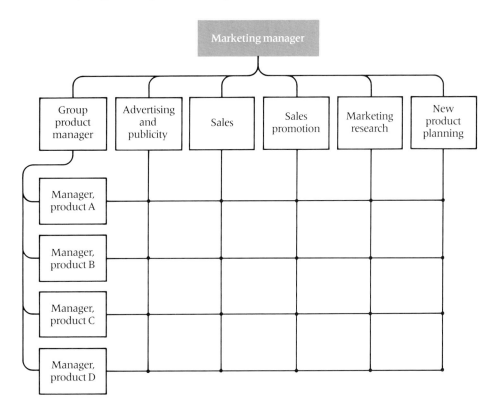

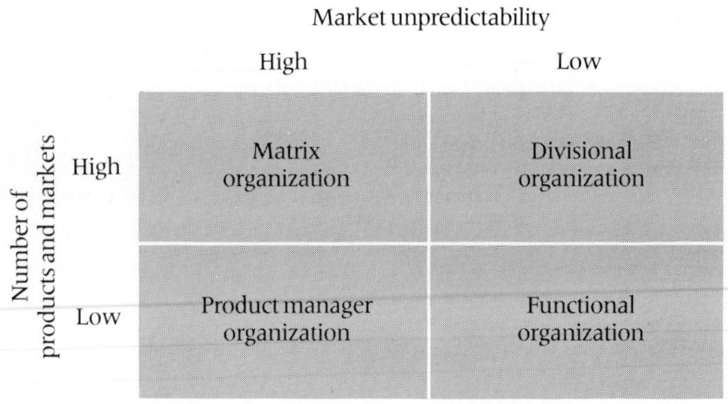

Market unpredictability

	High	Low
High	Matrix organization	Divisional organization
Low	Product manager organization	Functional organization

(left axis label: Number of products and markets)

Exhibit 22.7   Matching marketing organizations with environments

Laboratories use the product manager organizational structure to ensure that the unique aspects of each product and market are looked after by marketing managers.

Another environmental factor concerns the *complexity of a company's individual markets*. Markets are complex when they are changing and managers have difficulty predicting what is going to happen. Just consider the rapid changes in information technology and information needs that make the markets served by computer companies such as AT&T, IBM, and Hewlett-Packard unpredictable. The functional marketing organization is not well suited to companies making decisions in this environment, because the marketing manager cannot process all the information necessary to determine the appropriate marketing strategy. Again, increasingly complex organizational structures are needed.[7]

Exhibit 22.7 suggests the types of environmental situations in which each organizational structure is likely to work best.[8] Both the number of different products and markets entered and the unpredictability of these markets combine to determine appropriateness of different marketing organizational structures. The complicated matrix organization is best suited to companies with many products and many unpredictable markets. Product manager organization is also suitable for coping with unpredictable markets, but only for companies with relatively few entirely different products and markets. Divisional organizational structures are effective for companies targeting so many predictable markets that separate marketing functions are needed. The simple functional organization is best when there are few products and few predictable markets, as when a company is small and targets local markets. Furthermore, as a company's environment changes in complexity, top management should be prepared to shift the marketing organization in response. Thus for successful companies, the struggle to decide when to make a change as well as to what kind of organizational structure is faced repeatedly.

Informal marketing organization

So far we have discussed only the part of a marketing organization that shows up on organizational chart, that is, formally assigned responsibility. Another, less visible part of an organization is every bit as important. The **informal marketing organization** is made up of the many working relationships that develop among managers regardless of the formal lines of authority. These relationships develop over time from the process of implementing marketing strategies. We have already noted one illustration:

Product managers must have strong support from managers outside the product and marketing structure (see Exhibit 22.8).

> Products often are viewed as the responsibility of the product manager while sales are looked upon as the responsibility of the sales force.
>
> Although these perceptions are true in an organizational sense, it's highly important to develop and maintain strong cooperation and communication between the product manager and the sales force, since one cannot function profitably without the other.
>
> An excellent product, regardless of how effective the product manager's strategies, will not go very far without an effective sales effort. Likewise, the best sales effort cannot compensate, in the long run, for an uncompetitive, ill-conceived, or misunderstood product.[9]

The need for coordination in an organization has led companies to experiment. Informal committee and team arrangements are common. Many companies such as International Telephone and Telegraph, Apple Computer, and Hewlett-Packard use *venture teams* (see Chapter 10) to explore new product opportunities. The typical team draws people from many areas of the organization for temporary assignment and is given resources and time to look into a new product idea. Committees have also been used to coordinate promotion in functional and divisional marketing organizations by bringing together the heads of each of the promotional departments.

Management also should be concerned with establishing the proper **organizational culture,** which refers to the working-related values and

Exhibit 22.8 The product manager's informal marketing organization

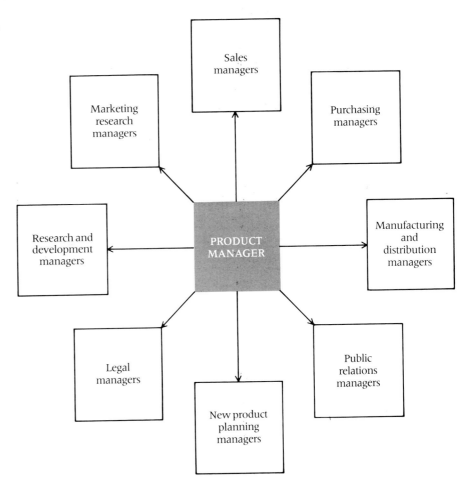

Decisions are easy
if you no it all.

A company called TRW is very much concerned with revealing to potential investors and current and future employees its organization's culture. Print advertisements like this one discuss the corporate environment of a company that nurtures ideas and whose business is creativity. (Courtesy of TRW Inc.)

beliefs held by all members of an organization (see Marketalk). A desired value might be that achieving corporate objectives should take precedence over achieving a department's objectives. Training sessions with employees may be needed to influence managers and employees to adopt the desired values. The reward system may also be used, as Emhart Corporation did by tying compensation to long-run growth to encourage managers to make decisions based on long-run considerations. The result of learning a culture can effectively complement the formal and informal marketing organizations by ensuring a common base of values and beliefs among managers during interactions.

CONTROLLING MARKETING PERFORMANCE

Throughout the text so far our discussion has emphasized planning and implementing marketing strategies. No less important is control. A marketing manager must be skilled at discovering and correcting performance problems before they become a serious threat to a company. Although control may seem less glamorous than planning a marketing strategy, continually looking for performance problems and their causes is essential to keeping them manageable.

Effective control requires a well-developed approach to keep on top of performance at all times. This approach consists of a logical series of steps (see Exhibit 22.9), and an unrelenting willingness to follow them from start to finish. Harold S. Geneen, former chief executive of ITT, describes the essence of this process.

> What do you do if your company or your division or your department has not made its quota for the quarter? First of all you locate the problem. Then you find the cause. Then you fix it. That is why we had the controllers of every ITT company sending us in headquarters the figures of their companies every week. Less than satisfactory results showed up in those reports very clearly.

Exhibit 22.9   Steps in a managerial control process

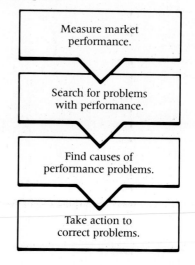

Measure market performance.

Search for problems with performance.

Find causes of performance problems.

Take action to correct problems.

That's why our line managers "red-flagged" their major problems for immediate attention. That's why we held monthly managers' meetings. We wanted to pinpoint the causes of the problems and find the best possible solutions as quickly as possible.[10]

Organization and control go hand in hand. The organizational structure assigns responsibility for control to managers of the various activity centers, so it is clear who is accountable for each and every aspect of a company's total performance. Although the control steps are essentially the same regardless of the activity center, the information used differs. A sales manager is likely to work with sales information when examining performance, while a product manager routinely focuses on sales, market share, and profit information. In the remainder of this chapter, we discuss what is involved in each step of a control process.

MEASURING MARKETING PERFORMANCE

Experienced managers expect marketing performance problems to arise from time to time. Thus proper control starts by setting in motion procedures to look regularly for problems. An early warning system is needed because managers want enough time to take corrective action before the problem gets out of hand. Early warning comes from monitoring actual performance regularly. An **index of performance,** usually one or more numbers measuring the magnitude of performance, direction of performance, or both, must be selected as the focus for the monitoring activity. Control actually begins when a manager asks two questions: (1) What should the index or indexes of performance be? and (2) How will information needed to provide an index on a regular basis be gathered?

*Marke*TALK //
Marketing cultures vary by company

"MARKETING CULTURES" vary greatly in different companies, according to Howard Bratches, partner, Thorndike Deland Associates, New York.

Two distinct cultures, however, predominate among packaged goods companies—analytically driven and advertising-driven. *"Analytically driven organizations,"* he said, "are characterized by a strong, financially based planning process in which the marketing staff plays an integral role" (italics added).

Marketing executives at these companies tend to be MBAs with strong planning and financial credentials.

"There are no better archetypes of this data-intensive marketing culture than Procter & Gamble and General Foods," Bratches said.

Advertising-driven organizations, by contrast, are more open in their approach to marketing and less preoccupied by figures (italics added).

"These companies tend to be copy oriented and almost fascinated by imagery," he said, citing National Distillers, R. J. Reynolds, and Revlon as prime examples of "companies that match great sophistication with an equal degree of imagination. Their marketing people tend to start out in advertising agencies."

Marketing preculture—a more primitive approach to marketing common among companies in which the discipline has not fully integrated into corporate planning—also was characterized by Bratches. In these companies, marketing is primarily sales- and promotion-driven (italics added).

Many banks, financial services institutions, and apparel companies fall into the marketing preculture category.

"These organizations," he said, "will use specific marketing tools, such as direct mail and point-of-sale promotion, but they've yet to make marketing their central focus.

"Still in transition, they too often fail to comprehend all that's involved in developing a true marketing culture or orientation."

SOURCE: "Executives need to fit corporate 'marketing culture,' " *Marketing News,* Oct. 26, 1984, p. 4. Reprinted with permission of the American Marketing Association.

//

Marketing objectives specify performance

Every marketing manager is expected to achieve the performance stated in marketing objectives. In fact, how well managers are judged by their superiors depends in part on how well these objectives are met or exceeded. For this reason, marketing objectives dictate the important kinds of performance, and therefore the indexes, used for control.

By now you know that many different kinds of objectives can be set by a company. In our discussion of control, we consider three ways to measure performance derived from common marketing objectives: (1) revenue-related performance, (2) profit contribution performance, and (3) market support performance.

Revenue-related performance. Most marketing managers are evaluated according to how well their activity centers achieved sales and sometimes market share.[11] These objectives specify that managers control **revenue-related performance.**

A **sales performance index** is the unit or dollar volume of one or more products sold less returns (unsold or defective products returned to the company) and other adjustments. Marketing managers have primary responsibility for controlling the sales aspect of a business, and so this index is commonly used. Sometimes, however, examining sales alone is misleading. Sales may be increasing and making performance look good. But if the market is growing faster than are company sales, true performance is not satisfactory. This situation happened to Waterford, the maker of fine crystal. Although Waterford's sales grew by 20 percent between 1979 and 1983, the entire market for crystal grew considerably more than that as sales of imported products tripled.[12]

To supplement sales indexes, marketing managers frequently use a **market share index** to compare a company's performance with competition. It measures the percentage of total sales of a defined product in a defined market that has been captured by a company.[13] Waterford saw its market share drop for several products, including stemware, the share of which dropped from 30 to 25 percent.[14] Notice that market share can decrease as sales increase.

Profit contribution performance. An increasing number of companies are also concerned with the profit contribution (and sometimes return on investment) from marketing. This trend stems from top management's concern for the relationship between marketing and financial strategies. Marketing's **profit contribution index** is measured by revenue for an activity center less cost of the products sold and marketing expenses incurred to generate that revenue. The amount by which a center's revenue exceeds its costs makes a contribution to the company's general overhead costs and profits.[15]

Revenue-related and profit contribution performances are the bottom line for marketing managers. These objectives must be achieved if a company is to perform well.

Market support performance. Marketing is expected to create favorable impressions of the company and its brands in the minds of potential customers. These impressions lead to sales because customers are likely to buy brands they hold in high regard. A **market support index** specifies the nature of the impressions management wants customers to have. These impressions are usually

- *Awareness.* What should customers be aware of about the company and product?
- *Understanding.* What should customers understand about the company's and product's ability to meet needs?
- *Attitude.* What should customers like most about the product or company?
- *Preference.* What percentage of a market preferring our product to competitors' do we aim for?
- *Customer satisfaction.* What percentage of a market expressing high satisfaction with the company or product do we aim for?

The impact of achieving market support objectives on company sales performance is aptly illustrated by AT&T, which has benefited greatly from customers' satisfaction with its telephone service. Despite increased competition from other telephone manufacturers, many people are reluctant to switch to other services because of this satisfaction.[16]

Market support indexes are typically used in addition to, rather than instead of, revenue-related and profit contribution indexes. They can be similarly controlled by measuring the percentage of a market holding a stated impression. But market support indexes are derived from objectives that offer important guidance to marketing managers who are planning a marketing mix. For instance, AT&T wanted to reinforce consumers' positive attitudes toward the quality of its telephones. This objective was instrumental in keeping the company from lowering price and quality of its product in the face of intense price competition, and led to creative advertising presentations showing "smarmy salesmen pushing 'cheap' phones."[17] It is just as important to control performance of marketing in achieving these support objectives as for any other kind of objective.

Marketing budgets set cost limits

Controlling costs of marketing decisions is as important as controlling revenue-related performance. Large insurance companies recognize this fact by emphasizing cost control in their selling activities to counter new competition coming from the increasing number of banks selling insurance. Because the insurance industry relies so heavily on more than 250,000 insurance agents, companies are looking for ways to cut costs and improve productivity of these agents. At the same time, more insurance companies are experimenting with lower-cost selling channels including brokerage houses such as E. F. Hutton & Company.[18]

Cost control begins with budgets developed during the planning of marketing strategy. By setting a limit on the costs for a marketing function, a budget establishes indexes for performance. Managers are expected to implement decisions while staying at or under these cost limits. Cost control also helps determine marketing's profit contributions. Achieving profit contribution means that managers must simultaneously meet revenue objectives (sales and market share) and cost objectives. Performance indexes that combine both revenue and costs are needed, such as **sales-to-cost ratios**: sales of marketing function ÷ cost from the function. Sales managers frequently use this kind of index when they examine the cost of supporting each salesperson compared with his or her sales for a period of time. Similarly, an advertising manager may use an advertising sales-to-cost ratio.

After performance indexes to measure performance are set, information on actual performance as specified by each index is gathered and periodically delivered to managers of the appropriate activity centers. Two main sources of this information are the record-keeping system of a company and marketing research.

Record-keeping system measures performance

When designing a record-keeping system, accountants usually try to balance information needs for two different purposes. First, a system must supply information on the financial condition of an organization. Financial statements such as income statements and balance sheets are generated for external use by stockholders and government agencies like the Internal Revenue Service. Second, a record-keeping system must supply information for internal management decision making. Operations managers such as those in production and distribution have historically been the primary users. More recently, marketing managers are increasing their demands on record-keeping systems for decision-making information.

Marketing's need for recorded information is illustrated by the following situation:

> Product X was generating an annual profit of $800,000, and Product Y was losing money at the rate of $600,000 per year—and management was totally unaware of the situation, just pleasantly happy to be making $200,000! They were simply astounded when a little accounting by product line revealed Product Y to be such a drain."[19]

Exhibit 22.10 A modular accounting system shows managers how two product activity centers are contributing to company profits

	(A) Company (000)	(B) Model 1 (000)	(C) Model 2 (000)
Net sales	$800	$300	$500
Less cost of goods sold	500	210	290
Gross margin	300	90	210
Direct expenses			
Commissions	10	3	7
Advertising	40	22	18
Promotion	12	8	4
Shipping	25	10	15
Warehousing	22	10	12
Product improvement	3	3	0
Model profit contribution	188	34	154
General expenses			
Market research	2		
Factory overhead	88		
Administration	42		
Net profit (before taxes)	56		

To make a record-keeping system useful for marketing, both sales and cost data must be assigned to activity centers so performance can be measured for each center. A system designed for this purpose is a **modular record-keeping system** because each activity center has a module of stored performance data. By requesting performance data modules, managers can analyze performance corresponding to the activities they have responsibility for.[20]

The income statement data in Exhibit 22.10 illustrates the advantage of having a modular record-keeping system. Precision Instruments has two models of an instrument for measuring pressure. Column A of Exhibit 22.10 shows the income information provided for managers by a nonmodular record-keeping system. Notice that the company is making a profit on the product line.

Now look at columns B and C. Because production, distribution, and selling costs as well as revenue have been assigned to each product model, the data show how much profit contribution each one is making to total company performance. Model 2 contributes almost five times as much to general expenses and profits of the company as does model 1. Apparently, model 1 requires a disproportionate amount of company resources given both models' relative sales volumes, a fact that managers could not know without the product activity center breakdown.

Marketing research measures performance

Sometimes a company's record-keeping system cannot keep track of sales or costs fast enough or in sufficient detail for managers' needs. In addition, the exact data needed may not be available in the system. Suppose a sales promotion manager is trying to find out how a trade discount is performing in individual retail stores. Even the best record-keeping system could not provide data on sales of the company's product to consumers by store, and yet they are the data needed to decide how long to keep the promotion going (see Marketool). Furthermore, a record-keeping system usually does not measure market support performance (customer awareness, understanding, attitude, preference, and satisfaction). In all these situations, marketing research supplements company records by providing additional measures of performance.

Managers for Domino's Pizza must control specific marketing performances for which the record-keeping system is not an adequate source of control information. The company developed a marketing strategy with a successful competitive advantage: More than 90 percent of sales are derived from its home delivery service. Management believes that high consumer awareness and satisfaction with the service are essential to support sales performance. Domino's uses several different marketing research studies to measure the strategy's actual performance.

- Studies are conducted each year that measure the percentage of consumers in markets who are aware of Domino's service.
- A "Mystery Customer" program is used in which a sample of consumers in an outlet's trading area are recruited and paid (with free pizza) to order pizzas from Domino's for a three-month period; these consumers comment on the quality of service (e.g., speed of delivery, courtesy of employees, whether pizza arrived hot).
- Questionnaires are sent with each pizza to measure customers' attitudes and satisfaction with Domino's home delivery service.[21]

MarkeTOOL

Marrying shipments data with consumer purchases data helps spot sales promotion problems

BRAND MANAGERS OF packaged-goods products typically sold through supermarkets and drug stores periodically run sales promotion activities to stimulate consumer sales. A brand manager, for example, may offer a trade discount to retailers with the expectation that they will, in turn, use an advertising boost, price-off specials, or some other means to attract consumers to the brand. The trade, however, may just buy higher volumes during the sales promotion to get the lower per-unit price, but then sell the brand to consumers without any special promotion. This practice is called *inventory loading* because the trade is merely loading up on inventory, but not helping push the brand as expected.

To control the performance of sales promotions aimed at the trade, a brand manager monitors sales data before, during, and after the sales promotion. Readily available data consist of how much of the brand was shipped from the company's warehouses to the trade; these data are obtained from internal records. In addition, brand managers may choose to buy consumer purchases data from marketing research firm sources such as SAMI, Niel-

SOURCE: Arthur I. Stern, "Computer marketing analysis system slices promotion budget 25%, without slicing sales," *Marketing News*, Sept. 14, 1984, p. 13.

	Time Periods									
	1	2	3	4	5	6	7	8	9	10
Product shipments	125	115	118	120	144	143	149	146	112	118
Consumer purchases	119	122	121	117	120	116	118	121	125	119
					Sales promotion begins		Sales promotion scheduled to end			

sen, Majers, and NABSCAN (NABSCAN USA Inc.). These data are gathered from checkout scanners or from physical counts of products sold from stores' inventories.

Suppose a brand manager decides to run a four-month trade discount to boost consumer sales. The promotion begins in period 5 and is scheduled to end in period 9 (see illustration). Shipments and purchases data for periods 1 through 4 provide a baseline showing sales levels without the promotion. Analyzing the data during and after the trade discount by comparing sales with the baseline enables the brand manager to see how well the sales promotion is working.

In the accompanying table, notice that the shipments data increase 20 percent as the promotion begins in period 5. The consumer purchases data show no corre-

sponding increase, however. This comparison suggests that the trade is just inventory loading and not doing any more than it normally does to push the company's brand. The data for periods 5 through 10 show what would happen if the brand manager did nothing, as might be the case if only the shipments data were available and the manager did not see the inventory loading taking place. Yet, notice that with both kinds of data the brand manager can spot this problem shortly after the trade discount promotion begins—by period 6 or 7. Corrective action, such as halting the trade discount or sending salespeople into stores to encourage store mangers to cooperate, can be started immediately after spotting the problem to prevent further losses.

SPOTTING MARKETING PERFORMANCE PROBLEMS

With both performance indexes established and regular performance information flowing in, managers are in the best possible position to see performance problems as they arise. Let us examine how managers use these data to spot problems.

When marketing performance does not meet standards

Earlier we defined a performance problem as performance that did not meet managers' expectations. Thus managers' expectations form **control standards** against which measures of actual performance are compared. Problems are revealed when actual performance falls above (in the case of costs) or below a standard. Consider the performance problem that caught the computer company Atari by surprise. The company saw its sales drop from $2 billion in 1982 to $1 billion in 1983. For 1984, management expected sales to level off at $1 billion. Performance in the first half of the year, however, showed that sales would be considerably lower. Atari had overpriced computers, and apparently computer buyers knew it. The company was sold, and new management revamped marketing strategy around a better value-for-price home computer product line.[22]

Control standards can be set by marketing plans, findings from marketing research, competitive performance, and past performance.

Marketing plans. Planning provides the most important impetus for establishing standards. Marketing objectives and budgets in plans formalize management's expectations and are the source of control standards. Well-formulated marketing objectives should have certain characteristics.

1. They state the type of performance expected.
2. They quantify expectations by using numbers to express expected performance.
3. They set a time limit for meeting the standard.
4. They specify the target market in which performance is to be achieved.

Domino's management established a well-formulated objective for its home pizza delivery service that had all four of these characteristics: 80 percent of its target consumers should be aware of the company's home delivery service by 1985.[23] This objective set a clear and definite target for the company's promotion managers to work toward. Furthermore, marketing research could unambiguously determine whether the objective was achieved.

Findings from marketing research. Marketing managers want standards that are realistically achievable with the resources available and, of course, hard work. Information is needed to determine what kinds and levels of performances are, in fact, realistic, and because most control standards are concerned with customers, marketing research can make this information available. Finding out that too few people are aware of your company and its products, for instance, suggests that awareness objectives should be set from which performance indexes can be drawn.

Competitive performance. Marketing managers often select important competitors and set standards based on their performances. A market share objective illustrates a comparative marketing performance standard because it states how well the company is expected to do against the competition. Many managers believe that there is a strong relationship between having high market share and being profitable in the long run.[24] Sometimes a company will sacrifice immediate profits to achieve high market share for this reason. As Thomas S. Monaghan, owner of Domino's Pizza, says, "My competitors want a return on investment. I don't care about that. I just want to be No. 1 in every market we're in."[25]

Past performance. Very often exceeding past performance is uppermost in the minds of marketing managers. This objective is evident when *Marketing News*, a trade newspaper read by marketing professionals, recently announced "record-breaking" growth in advertising sales (a major source of the newspaper's income comes from sale of its advertising space). The

1983–1984 sales record of $530,000 was evaluated by comparing it with the previous year's sales, showing a 20 percent growth.[26]

Marketing performance that does not exceed past years' performance typically is seen by management as a problem. In general, growth is an important objective for business. Only when the cause is uncontrollable (e.g., increasing competition, declining customers' buying power owing to the economy, slowing population growth in key groups) will no growth be accepted.

Comparing marketing performance

Looking for problems primarily involves comparing numbers—each performance standard is compared with the corresponding actual performance index measure. For middle- and upper-level managers who have many activities to control, analysis can be quite time consuming and tedious. Nevertheless, these comparisons are absolutely essential. According to Harold S. Geneen, former chief executive of ITT,

> There is a price to pay for all this analysis, of course: paying attention to the numbers is a dull, tiresome routine—it's drudgery.
>
> If you are running a well-managed company, most of the numbers will be those you expect. That makes them even more mundane and dull. But you cannot skip over them; you dare not allow your concentration to flag. Those numbers are your controls, and you read them until your mind reels or until you come upon one number or set of numbers that stand out from all the rest, demanding your attention, and getting it.[27]

Essentially two types of comparisons can be made: static control comparisons and control comparisons over time.

Static control comparisons. **Static control comparisons** are made for a single time period such as a month, a quarter, or a year. A sales manager for an automobile dealership, for instance, sets monthly sales objectives (i.e., quotas) for each salesperson. These quotas are the performance standards. At the end of each month, the salespersons' actual sales are compared with these quotas (see Exhibit 22.11). Take a minute before reading further to see if the data in Exhibit 22.11 reveal performance problems.

Exhibit 22.11   Using monthly reports on sales and preset sales quotas to control salesperson performance in an automobile dealership

Salesperson	August's Sales (no. of cars)	August's Quotas (no. of cars)	Percent of Quota Met
Alan Jones	5	4	125
Sheri Smith	4	4	100
Tom Lortz	1	3	33
Felix Bourne	7	5	140
Jim Mitchell	6	8	75
Sharon Campbell	5	3	167
Anton Jackson	3	3	100
David Frederick	4	4	100
Total	35	34	103

Exhibit 22.12 Controlling selling expenses for an automobile dealership

Selling Expense Item	August's Actual Expenses	August's Budgeted Expenses	Percent Actual to Budgeted
Salaries: regular	$5200	$5200	100
Salaries: overtime	800	200	400
Commissions on sales	3500	3400	103
Displays and signs	300	100	300
Sales training	50	50	100
Trade subscriptions	53	53	100
Total	$9903	$9003	

Two of the salespersons, Tom Lortz and Jim Mitchell, did not meet their quotas for the month. Notice that Mitchell had the second highest sales among all salespersons for the month and Lortz had the lowest. Yet both are below quota and are flagged by the sales manager, using the percent-of-quota data, as having a performance problem. Without the standard provided by the quotas, the sales manager probably would not have spotted a problem with Mitchell's performance because his sales were high.

In a similar way, a single time-period comparison can be made for marketing costs. Here a manager looks for costs that are exceeding the budgeted limits for the given time period. Suppose the sales manager of the automobile dealership has a selling budget to control. Exhibit 22.12 shows the cost performance for the same one-month period.

Marketing managers must interpret performance data carefully. Not all deviations of actual performance from standards necessarily indicate a problem. Notice that three expense items in Exhibit 22.12 are above budgeted expenses: overtime salary, commissions, and displays and signs. Only two of the items flag performance problems, however. Overspending on commissions occurred because sales were slightly higher than planned (see Exhibit 22.11). The sales manager is not going to consider overspending caused by higher-than-budgeted sales a performance problem. On the other hand, the overspending on overtime salary and displays and signs are problems to look into.

Control comparisons over time. Another way to search for marketing performance problems is to track actual performance over several time periods. This approach, called **control comparisons over time,** is used so past performance patterns can provide a standard for comparison. These patterns are noted when a regular up or down change occurs in the performance data. Returning to the automobile dealership illustration, the sales manager may track monthly sales for each salesperson during the year (see Exhibit 22.13). He is looking for consistent or regular changes in the period-to-period sales.

Tracking salespersons' sales confirms the performance problems identified earlier for Tom Lortz and Jim Mitchell (compare Exhibits 22.11 and 22.13). More insight, however, is obtained from the data about the nature of the problem. The eight months of sales performance data for Tom Lortz show a steady decline in sales performance. The sales manager must look into this problem. For Jim Mitchell the picture is somewhat different. He

Exhibit 22.13 Tracking sales performance of an automobile dealer's salespersons

Salesperson	Monthly Sales in Units							
	Jan.	Feb.	Mar.	Apr.	May	Jun.	Jul.	Aug.
Allan Jones	3	2	3	4	4	3	4	5
Sheri Smith	3	3	4	4	4	3	4	4
Tom Lortz	5	4	4	3	3	3	2	1
Felix Bourne	5	4	3	4	5	5	5	7
Jim Mitchell	6	5	7	8	9	9	6	6
Sharon Campbell	2	3	3	4	3	3	4	5
Anton Jackson	1	1	2	2	2	3	3	3
David Frederick	2	2	3	4	3	4	4	4

appears to have had a spurt in performance between March and June, but since June has fallen back to pre-March sales levels.

Managing by exception

When making both static and tracking comparisons managers must look for the *unusual* marketing performance. Standards determine what is unusual and what is not. This approach is called **managing by exception** because managers look for performance that is out of line. They then spend their time trying to bring the "exceptional performance" back in line.

Reports of performance should be organized to help managers find the exceptions by highlighting deviations from standards. Consider the way in which information has been organized in Exhibit 22.14, a comparison of

MarkeTALK ///

Controlling performance in retail stores of the future

TODAY'S RETAIL-STORE manager is a hands-on, shirt-sleeves fellow who worked his way up through the ranks. His managerial style is tactical and reactive. If he were in the military, he'd be a sergeant.

The store managers of the future will be analytical, pinstripe-suit types with college degrees. Their managerial style will be strategic and predictive. If they were in the military, they'd be captains.

So predicts Arthur D. Little Inc. (ADL), the Cambridge, Mass. based consulting firm, in a recent study conducted for the Coca-Cola Research Council. The bottom line: the emergence of *megastores* is forcing

SOURCE: "Megastores need strategic, not hands-on, managers," *Marketing News*, Sept. 14, 1984, p. 45. Reprinted with permission of the American Marketing Association.

substantial changes in retail management.

The manager of the future, the report states, will oversee a store with more customers, higher sales volume, greater product diversity, and more capital investment. "Managing this store will involve less of a hands-on approach, with more attention being given to delegation and management-by-exception," the ADL consultants said.

Today, control is frequently informal, marked by managers "walking around store aisles." In the store of the future, control will be based on scanner data and computer analysis. "Management by walking around" will remain important, but will focus on staff development rather than attention to operating details.

Tomorrow's managers will *have* to be more professional, simply because they'll

be controlling megastores with 45,000 to 100,000 sq. ft. of floor space, $20 million to $75 million of sales volume, and 50 to 100 full-time and 100 to 200 part-time employees.

Store managers today, the report states, gauge their performance primarily by relating to past performance and doing well in relation to other stores in the chain. Most employees have fixed salaries, with bonuses for store managers. Recognition, if it comes at all, is an informal pat on the back.

In the future, however, performance measures will be based on competition and the store's specific strategies. More employees will be eligible for incentive pay. Managers will be expected to take a more systematic approach to recognizing achievement.

///

Exhibit 22.14 Profit contribution comparisons for a retail store chain

Store Location	Profit Contribution Objective	Actual Profit Contribution	Deviation From Objective
Wilmington	$12,000	$12,818	+818
Charlotte	9,400	9,456	+56
Greenville	7,200	2,328	−4,872
Knoxville	13,800	15,653	+1,853
Fayetteville	10,900	7,865	−3,035
Tuscaloosa	6,700	8,469	+1,769
Lexington	11,400	11,479	+79
Kingsport	4,700	4,722	+22
Total	$76,100	$72,790	−3,310

profit contribution margins for store activity centers in a chain (see also Marketalk). Notice how quickly and easily managers at the chain's headquarters can spot the Greenville and Fayetteville stores' performance problems by scanning the "deviations" column. The deviations show both how much actual performance is off and whether performance is above or below the standard. Stores having high deviations, particularly those with profit contributions well below the standard, are the exceptions, and should get managers' attention. Well-organized reports are essential when there are many activity centers to evaluate.

By their very nature, problems are unexpected. But a problem, when first discovered, has yet to have its cause explained. Before taking any action to correct it, the manager must find out what has caused a performance problem to arise.

FINDING CAUSES OF PROBLEMS

Experience with the workings of an activity center is very important to the task of finding causes of problems. Managers who understand the important influences on performance can more easily search for the ones that account for the unexpected performance. Essentially two types of influences must be examined by marketing managers: (1) components of the marketing mix used to achieve performance and (2) outside factors that influence performance (e.g., competition, market characteristics, economic changes).

Detailed evaluation of performance

Performance data that are aggregated over an entire activity center or even a broad component of a center can hide the real nature of a problem. Thus detailed analyses of performance are often needed to pinpoint the source of a problem.[28] Performance data are further broken down within the marketing activity center so a manager can see what aspects of performance appear to be weakest. An illustration should help you see how this search works.

Let us start with the performance data presented in Exhibit 22.14. Activity center analysis is shown by the profit contribution breakdown by store. To find the source of the overall problem (shown in Exhibit 22.14 as a negative deviation of $3310 from companywide planned profit), management looked at each store's performance. The Greenville and Fayetteville stores were quickly discovered to be the sources of the profit contribution problem.

Using the control-by-exception principle, headquarters concentrated its attention on these stores. One possible cause of the profit contribution problems could be the stores' marketing mixes: merchandise assortment, salespersons, prices, advertising, store sales promotion, or location. Several of these possibilities could be tested by using performance data from the chain's record-keeping system.

First, management wanted to see how well the stores' salespersons were doing. Data showing sales by salesperson were examined. Because no sales quotas were set, management simply looked at each salesperson's sales performance for the past six months (see Exhibit 22.15).

Jeff Roberts' sales performance is not satisfactory. Not only are his sales substantially lower than the others, but his sales increases are too small for the seasonally high sales months of August, September, and December. To follow up on this analysis, central office managers talked to the store manager and to Roberts himself to explore why he is not doing well. How management is to handle Roberts depends on why he is doing so poorly.

Before discussing the problem with Roberts, management wanted to see how he allocated his time to different merchandise items in the store. This step involves further dividing an activity center into more detailed performance categories. Exhibit 22.16 shows a breakdown of Roberts' sales by merchandise line. This breakdown suggests that salespersons have been specializing in certain lines. Batten is concentrating his sales effort on men's clothing, particularly jeans and suits. Jacobs and Smith have been selling mostly women's and children's clothing. Roberts' sales show an emphasis on children's clothing and, to a lesser extent, on women's clothing.

Although the store promotes "clothing for the whole family," management knows that most sales are clothes for adults. Roberts therefore seems to be allocating too much of his selling time to the merchandise line with lowest potential. Also notice that only Batten is selling much men's wear. Management may want to encourage Roberts to spend more of his time selling men's wear.

Looking externally for causes of problems

At some point, further analysis of performance data sheds no more light on causes of problems. Causes of problems could be external—the task environment of markets, competition, or both could be changing. If a

Exhibit 22.15 Sales track records for salespersons in the Fayetteville store

Salesperson	Six Month Sales ($000)					
	Jul.	Aug.	Sep.	Oct.	Nov.	Dec.
Jan Jacobs	3.2	8.9	7.3	6.2	6.2	9.3
Jeff Roberts	2.1	3.5	2.9	2.5	2.2	4.5
Sharon Smith	3.6	9.4	8.9	7.4	7.3	9.9
Bill Batten	4.2	7.9	7.5	7.2	6.7	8.5

Exhibit 22.16 Salespersons' sales broken down by merchandise line

Merchandise Line	Percentage of Salesperson Sales			
	Jacobs	Roberts	Smith	Batten
Men's jeans	5	3	4	34
Men's shirts	4	8	3	15
Men's suits	0	3	1	26
Men's accessories	9	6	5	10
Men's swimwear	1	5	2	8
Women's jeans	23	16	29	5
Women's blouses and shirts	18	10	15	0
Women's accessories	12	6	14	1
Women's swimwear	14	8	12	0
Children's wear	14	35	15	1
Totals	100%	100%	100%	100%

company's marketing strategy has not kept up with these changes then performance problems are sure to result. Borden's marketing managers experienced this kind of problem when they did not detect consumers' changing taste preferences for premium, ultrarich ice cream. Consequently, its dairy products division lost ground to new premium ice cream brands such as Häagen-Dazs.[29]

Market opportunity analyses are a key source of information on outside task environmental causes of performance problems. Marketing research studies are particularly useful because they can measure customers' reactions to a company's marketing strategy or to the strategies of competitors. As an illustration, look back to Exhibit 22.14. A number of possible outside factors may have caused the Greenville store to perform poorly. Changes in the store's trading area such as deterioration of customers' attitudes toward the store and changes in consumers' preferences for merchandise are factors to explore. A study of consumers' attitudes toward the store's merchandise, service offering, or location may find out if a deterioration in consumers' attitudes is causing the performance problem.

Management may also study available information on the population or the economy to see if changes are taking place. Studying census data for Greenville may reveal population changes shrinking the store's market. The area may be losing population or the population mix may be changing. Finally, management may simply observe what is happening in markets or talk to people who are close to markets such as distributors. A manager may visit the Greenville area, for example, and discover more competition from other stores than previously recognized.

When problems recur

When marketing managers find that problems are recurring, they may become overwhelmed as they try to solve these problems and keep marketing performance on target. Too many problems may signal that the entire approach to planning and implementing marketing strategies by the marketing organization is weak. Without noticing it, marketing decisions may have become unduly influenced by inertia ("that's the way we have always done it"), by indifference, by lack of information on changing market opportunity, by company politics, or by procedures that no longer work.[30] To discover the effectiveness of the marketing function, a marketing audit is needed.

A **marketing audit** is a thorough evaluation of the external environment in which marketing is operating; the objectives, strategies, decision-making procedures, and organization of the marketing function; and the performance contribution of marketing to the company.[31] It should be conducted by people who are not involved in the marketing function, such as an outside consultant or managers from nonmarketing departments, to ensure an unbiased evaluation. Top management will make decisions on how best to change the marketing function based on the results of the audit, so they must have confidence in the auditors.

One purpose of a marketing audit is to determine whether current marketing strategies are appropriate for markets. A company's strategies may not have kept up with changes in the task environment. Auditors can use a market opportunity analysis to examine what is happening in markets and with competition. Then forecasts are made to see the impact of changes on sales. Components of the marketing mix (products, promotion, channels, pricing, services) are evaluated according to the results of the MOA.

Another purpose of an audit is to evaluate how well marketing managers are equipped to make important decisions. Auditors examine the organizational structure to see if proper coordination among the different marketing functions is taking place. They may examine the coordination between the salesforce and advertising, between sales and distribution, or any other pair of functions. Auditors may also assess procedures for developing marketing plans as well as those for implementing the plans. Ways to improve the organization and procedures can lead to better marketing strategies in the future.

TAKING CORRECTIVE ACTION

The payoff from analysis comes when decisions are made to correct marketing problems. Two kinds of decisions must be considered: (1) whether to change the standards so marketing performance will have a better chance of meeting them and (2) whether to change marketing organization or strategy to improve performance. Either approach is intended to correct the problem by bringing marketing performance in line with standards.

Sometimes causes of marketing problems cannot be dealt with by managers, such as changing markets or competition. Standards set previously, under different task environment conditions, may now be unrealistic. Atari faced this situation in 1984 when it found that its sales objective of about $1 billion was unachievable. The market for video games had fallen off, and Atari could not do anything about it. A new and more realistic sales objective of $500 million was set as a result. At the same time, marketing budgets were lowered to provide cost limits more in line with the lower sales objectives.[32]

When problem causes are correctable, marketing managers modify marketing plans. Corrective action may involve any or all parts of a plan from changing market targets to adjusting the components of the marketing mix. Consider the following illustrations:

Spinnaker Software, the Cambridge, Mass., firm that developed and marketed the first PCjr programs, expected to lose several thousand dollars in 1985 because IBM halted production of the PCjr. Though best known for its children's educational games, Spinnaker may try to compensate for this loss by developing business software for a more powerful version of the Apple II computer. (Courtesy of Spinnaker Software Corp.)

IBM made several changes to improve poor sales performance of its PC Jr personal computer. An improved keyboard was added, its memory capacity was expanded, and prices were reduced. Later, the company withdrew the product from markets to halt the poor performance.[33]

Waterford Crystal Inc. saw sales level off and market share decline even though crystalware sales in the United States were expanding impressively. An important part of management's solution was to redefine market targets to include the affluent baby boomers—the so-called yuppies—who had become important buyers of crystal. Formerly, target markets were limited to brides and well-off middle-age women.[34]

When a sale is chalked up on Circuit City's computerized cash registers, the information travels by phone to central computers—one on each coast. If a store is getting low on, say, Sony color TVs, the computer signals a warehouse that a batch must go out on the next truck. If the computer discovers the Sonys aren't moving, headquarters can send an electronic message to one or all stores to put the sets on sale.[35]

Circuit City's system of control is particularly interesting because it shows that computers can take over routine control activities. The company's central computers are programmed with sales standards, and data on sales performance are electronically gathered and compared with the standards to identify problems. The computer also is programmed to recommend corrective action such as putting slow-selling television sets on sale. Notice that the computer cannot find causes of problems. It only recommends predetermined marketing mix changes to react to recurring problems.

The results of a marketing audit may also lead to permanent changes in the marketing organization or decision-making procedures. New assignments of performance responsibilities or new ways to improve performance may be needed. When faced with increasing competition from other communications companies, AT&T responded in this fashion by reorganizing its marketing function to put managers in charge of marketing to different customer groups. The organizational change led to separate planning for individual markets.

Having implemented corrective actions, the control activity starts over again. New decisions must be controlled using the same sequence of steps. In this way, control is a never-ending activity.

SUMMARY

Managers plan, implement, and control marketing strategies for marketing activity centers. Responsibility for marketing activity centers are assigned to managers by the company's marketing organizational structure. Depending on the environmental situation faced by the company, several different forms of organizational structure are found in practice: functional, product manager, divisional, and matrix. The number of a company's products and markets as well as the complexity of markets and competition dictates which structure is best suited to a company.

Effective marketing control for an activity center enables a manager to regularly search for marketing problems. Performance indexes are established to monitor implementation of a marketing plan. These indexes are taken from the performance expected as stated in marketing objectives or from cost limits set in a marketing budget. This step ensures that control is linked directly to marketing planning.

Marketing managers use the company's modular record-keeping system and marketing research to provide data that measure the marketing plan's actual performance in areas such as sales, market share, profit contribution, marketing costs, and customer awareness, understanding, attitude change, preference, and satisfaction. Performance is compared with standards set by objectives, budgets, competitors' performance, and the company's past performance to see if performance is as high as expected. Deviation of actual performance from the standard suggests a problem.

Before correcting a problem, managers must learn what has caused it. A detailed analysis of performance may help find the source of the problem. Managers also use other sources of information such as marketing research, personal observation, interviews with distributors and employees, and reports from other organizations (e.g., government, research firms) to uncover causes.

When causes are known managers can take corrective action. Standards may be changed if causes of the problem are beyond control of the company. If causes can be acted on, then managers may change marketing strategy. In the most serious cases, managers may decide, based on a marketing audit, to change the marketing organization, decision-making procedures, or both to improve the chances of the success of future marketing strategy plans and implementation.

KEY TERMS

marketing control	functional marketing organization	divisional organizational structure
marketing performance problem	marketing activity center	matrix organization
marketing organizational structures	product manager organization	informal marketing organization

organizational culture
index of performance
revenue-related performance
sales performance index
market share index

profit contribution index
market support index
cost control
sales-to-cost ratios
modular record-keeping system

control standards
static control comparisons
control comparisons over time
managing by exception
marketing audit

QUESTIONS FOR REVIEW AND DISCUSSION

1. What kinds of companies are most likely to use functional marketing organizational structures?

2. Under what environmental circumstances would a company want to use a product manager organizational structure?

3. Compare the merits of having a divisional marketing organizational structure instead of a product manager organizational structure for a company with many products.

4. What are the advantages and disadvantages of a matrix organization?

5. What is the purpose of having marketing activity centers in a marketing organization?

6. Why should marketing managers set up an ongoing step-by-step control procedure for each activity center?

7. Which performance indexes are better: revenue-related or market support?

8. How is a profit contribution index different from a measurement of revenue-related performance?

9. How can marketing budgets help set marketing performance indexes for control?

10. What are the sources of information for measuring marketing performance?

11. Why would a marketing manager want to use a modular record-keeping system?

12. What are the different ways in which managers set standards for marketing performance?

13. Suppose a marketing manager had the following sales information:

    | Product A | $303,500 |
    | Product B | $500,520 |
    | Product C | $268,400 |
    | Product D | $345,200 |

    How could the manager determine whether there is a performance problem with any of these products?

14. What does *managing by exception* mean?

15. How can marketing research help a marketing manager control a marketing activity center?

16. What is a marketing audit? Under what circumstances would a marketing audit be used?

17. What are the different ways in which a marketing performance problem can be corrected?

BUILDING YOUR PORTFOLIO

Choose a manufacturing company in your area, and set up an interview with its marketing or sales manager. Develop a list of questions for the manager aimed at finding out how the company has organized the marketing function. Who makes decisions on the product (or products), pricing, advertising, sales promotion, personal selling, and distribution? How are these decisions coordinated?

After the interview, use the information to evaluate the marketing organization. Try to explain why it is structured as it is. Consider factors that you believe are important such as the size of the company, the number of products in its product mix, size of markets, and changes going on in markets. Do you think that another form of organization would work better?

NOTES

1. This illustration is based on a discussion in "GE generates service business by shifting dollars from advertising to order-capturing." *Marketing News*, June 24, 1983, pp. 12, 13.
2. Mack Hanan, "Reorganize your company around its markets." *Harvard Business Review*, Nov.–Dec. 1974, p. 66.
3. For more discussion of the role of product managers, see Victor P. Buell, "The changing role of the product manager in consumer goods companies." *Journal of Marketing*, Vol. 39 (July 1975), pp. 3–11.
4. Hanan, op. cit., pp. 68–70.
5. William C. Goggin, "How the multidimensional organization works at Dow Corning." *Harvard Business Review*, Jan.–Feb. 1974, pp. 59–60.
6. Barton Weitz and Erin Anderson, "Organizing the Marketing Function," in Ben M. Enis and Kenneth J. Roering (Eds.), *Review of Marketing 1981*. Chicago: American Marketing Association, 1981, pp. 134–142.
7. Ibid., p. 138.
8. Ibid., p. 137.
9. Linda Richardson, "'Profile system improves product manager sales force communication." *Marketing News*, Mar. 18, 1983, Section 1, p. 21.
10. Harold S. Geneen, "The case for managing by the numbers." *Fortune*, Oct. 1, 1984, p. 78.
11. Frederick E. Webster, Jr., James A. Largay, III, and Clyde P. Stickney, "The impact of inflation accounting on marketing decisions." *Journal of Marketing*, Vol. 44 (Fall 1980), pp. 13–14.
12. "Waterford learns its lesson: Snob appeal isn't enough." *Business Week*, Dec. 24, 1984, p. 63.
13. For a discussion of measures of market share see Bernard Catry and Michel Chevalier, "Market share strategy and the product life cycle." *Journal of Marketing*, Vol. 38 (Oct. 1974), pp. 29–30.
14. "Waterford learns its lesson," op. cit.
15. Webster, Largay, and Stickney, op. cit., p. 14.
16. Linda J. McAleer, "Service marketers should weigh levels of customer satisfaction." *Marketing News*, Apr. 27, 1984, p. 4.
17. Brian O'Rielly, "Lessons from the home phone wars." *Fortune*, Dec. 24, 1984, p. 84.
18. "Upheaval in life insurance." *Business Week*, June 25, 1984, pp. 60–61.
19. Patrick M. Dunne and Harry I. Wolk, "Marketing cost analysis: A modularized contribution approach." *Journal of Marketing*, Vol. 41 (July 1977), p. 83.

20. For more discussion of modular record-keeping systems for marketing, see Jimmy D. Barnes and Douglas V. Leister, "Profitability Accounting: Implications For Marketing Management," in Neil Beckwith, Michael Houston, Robert Mittelstaedt, Kent B. Monroe, and Scott Ward (Eds.), *1979 Educators' Conference Proceedings.* Chicago: American Marketing Association, 1979, pp. 562–566; and Dunne and Wolk, op. cit., pp. 83–94.

21. Bernie Whalen, " 'People-oriented' marketing delivers a lot of dough for Domino's." *Marketing News,* Mar. 16, 1984, Section 2, pp. 5–6.

22. Gary Hector, "The big shrink is on at Atari." *Fortune,* July 9, 1984, p. 23; and "How Jack Tramiel hopes to turn Atari around." *Business Week,* July 16, 1984, p. 30.

23. Bernie Whalen, op. cit., p. 5.

24. For a discussion of this idea, see Robert D. Buzzell, Bradley T. Gale, and Ralph G. M. Sultan, "Market share—a key to profitability." *Harvard Business Review,* Jan.–Feb. 1975, pp. 97–106.

25. Bernie Whalen, op. cit.

26. "Marketing News enjoys 12th consecutive year of record-breaking advertising sales." *Marketing News,* June 8, 1984, p. 1.

27. Geneen, op. cit., p. 81.

28. This idea and the ensuing illustration are based on a discussion in Barnes and Liester, op. cit., pp. 564–565.

29. "Borden: Putting the shareholder first starts to pay off." *Business Week,* Apr. 2, 1984, p. 101.

30. Hal W. Goetsch, "Conduct a comprehensive marketing audit to improve marketing planning." *Marketing News,* Mar. 18, 1983, Section 2, p. 14.

31. For additional discussion of the marketing audit see Goetsch, ibid.; and Alice M. Tybout and John R. Hauser, "A marketing audit using a conceptual model of consumer behavior." *Journal of Marketing,* Vol. 45 (Summer 1981), pp. 82–101.

32. Hector, op. cit., p. 23.

33. "How IBM made 'Junior' an underachiever." *Business Week,* June 25, 1984, p. 106–107.

34. "Waterford learns its lessons: Snob appeal isn't enough," op. cit., p. 63.

35. Brian Dunaine, "Circuit City's secret for electrifying sales." *Fortune,* Jan. 7, 1985, p. 72.

Case 22.1

Precision Instruments

PRECISION INSTRUMENTS manufactures, distributes, and sells a quality control device that measures temperature precisely. Its initial market comprised manufacturers located within a 250-mile radius of Precision Instrument's plant. These firms manufacture drugs for which sterilization of containers is part of the production process. The president set the price at $2600, which was one of the higher-priced instruments available. However, it had several benefits that customers liked including being easy to use, rugged, and easily adapted to different production line configurations.

The company was founded by three men who set up the organizational structure. The chart on the right shows this structure.

Over the past five years, the company has prospered and grown. The product line now includes seven instruments ranging in price from $900 to $8500. Markets have expanded to include more than half a dozen industry groups including utilities, processed foods, chemicals, and electronics. University and government testing laboratories are also being served. Precision Instruments has also branched out into different types of instruments for different purposes, including measuring pressure and materials strength. Finally, a new service has been introduced in the last year that provides consulting to companies faced with a quality control or other problem centering on measuring physical forces such as temperature and pressure.

Competition has also been intensifying in many of the markets. Additionally, the technology of the measurement techniques is changing.

The president of Precision Instruments has been wrestling with the inadequacy of the current organizational structure. He is particularly concerned with the organization of the marketing activities, because marketing has become more important to the overall strategy of the company.

PRECISION INSTRUMENT ORGANIZATIONAL CHART

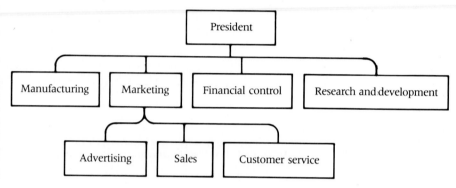

QUESTIONS

1. Should the president consider expanding the marketing function to include other components?

2. What other organizational structures for the marketing function are better suited for the company than its present one?

3. Which organizational structure would you recommend and why?

Case 22.2

Saga Corporation

WHEN CHARLES LYNCH took over as president of Saga Corporation, he inherited four restaurant chains located on the West Coast of the United States. One chain, The Straw Hat pizza chain, had unspectacular growth and was sold. Another

SOURCE: Kenneth Labich, "The dean of college cuisine smartens up," *Fortune*, Aug. 6, 1984, p. 30.

chain, The Velvet Turtle, attracts older, white-collar customers. Mr. Lynch decided to keep this chain in the product mix for the time being because it gives the company a good reputation for managing fine restaurants. The other two chains, the Black Angus restaurants and The Refectory, are under review.

When Mr. Lynch took over, Black Angus comprised forty-eight steakhouses.

Each has a bar with recorded music and a dance floor for the more energetic crowd, and a large dining area for customers wanting a meal. Prices for meals are moderate compared with competitive restaurants. The Black Angus concept in dining has worked well, meeting and even exceeding management's performance expectations. Each unit in the chain, on the average, provides up to $2 million in sales, which is very high for this type of restaurant. The restaurants' active bars account for much of this performance.

Another chain, The Refectory, comprised ten units, each generating about $950,000 in sales. Refectory restaurants offer sit-down table service, tablecloths, and decor intended to create a more formal dining atmosphere than that for Black Angus. The market group attracted by Refectory restaurants primarily were young, blue-collar customers. Mr. Lynch became convinced, after looking at marketing research studies, that the Refectory units were attracting the same kinds of customers as the Black Angus chain. Surprisingly, even though the two restaurant chains had different appearances, they were in direct competition with each other.

In relation to costs of building and operating a Refectory unit, sales generated were not high enough to be in line with company profit growth objective of 15 percent annually. Clearly, Black Angus and other restaurant chains were able to do better than the performance shown by the Refectory units to date. Saga had a limited amount of resources to put into its restaurant operations. Thus Mr. Lynch had to decide what to do with the two restaurant chains.

QUESTIONS

1. What step in a marketing control process has the president, Mr. Lynch, reached with regard to the Black Angus and Refectory restaurant chains?

2. Is Mr. Lynch faced with a problem, opportunity, or both? What are the indicators that you used to arrive at your answer?

3. Does Mr. Lynch need more information before making decisions concerning the two restaurant chains? Why or why not?

4. What are the alternative marketing strategy decisions that Mr. Lynch can make with regard to the Black Angus and Refectory chains?

23 Marketing's Strategic Role

When you finish this chapter, you will understand

☐ What takes place in developing strategic plans for businesses

☐ The paths that businesses may follow in their development

☐ The nature and scope of business mission and objectives

☐ How business unit portfolios are analyzed and business strategies are selected

☐ Marketing's strategic role in the modern corporation

To grow faster, General Mills diversified from food processing into restaurants. The Red Lobster specialty seafood chain is in a rapidly growing segment of the market.

Strategic planning by top management charts the future course of a business. The outcome of these strategic plans determines whether the business will be successful. Dayton Hudson Corporation, the diversified retailer, doubled its sales from 1980 to 1985, reaching nearly $9 billion in 1985. Profits also expanded rapidly during this same period. Strategic planning was an important factor in Dayton Hudson's impressive sales and earnings growth. Moving from a retail base of traditional department stores, diversification into Target, Mervyn's, and B. Dalton Booksellers has enabled the firm to attract new customers. In contrast, giant Exxon's diversification into electrical equipment, office automation, and shale oil and synfuels was not successful because of poor acquisitions, management problems in office automation, and declining oil prices.[1]

AS THE EXPERIENCE OF THESE FIRMS demonstrates, strategic planning, or the lack thereof, is often a key factor affecting business performance. Marketing strategy plays a vital role in a company's achieving corporate strategic goals. Contrast, for example, the Great Atlantic & Pacific Tea Company's struggle during the 1970s to keep from going under with the impressive performance of Dayton Hudson. A&P's poor financial performance and loss of market position clearly indicate the dangers of faulty corporate and marketing strategies. Strategic planning for a business requires that management have perceptive insights into customers' needs and wants and ways of achieving customer satisfaction through the firm's marketing offer (product, distribution, price, and promotion strategies). Thus a close working relationship between executives responsible for strategic planning and marketing managers is essential.

So far in this book we have been concerned with how marketing management carries out its functions in an organization. The purpose of this chapter is to describe the planning process for the entire business, highlighting marketing management's role in business strategy. Our first task is to consider the various paths corporations follow when moving into new markets and products. Then we examine the activities that make up business planning, illustrating why it is a critical business activity. A discussion of the steps involved in strategic planning—conducting environmental analysis, determining corporate mission and objectives, determining business composition, analyzing the business portfolio, and developing business strategy for each unit of the business—follows. The chapter concludes with an examination of marketing's role in strategic planning.

HOW BUSINESSES DEVELOP

When a business is first formed operations are concentrated in a particular product and market area designated the **core business.** The Limited, a women's fashion apparel retail chain, began its core business in 1963 with a single store in Columbus, Ohio. The company experienced rapid growth in the 1970s. By 1985 the chain had more than 2000 retail stores and had acquired Lane Bryant, a retailer of special-sized clothing for women, with nearly 300 stores. Lane Bryant represented movement beyond the core businesses into a different, yet related, business area. Victoria's Secret, specializing in the sale of European and American designer lingerie through specialty retail stores and mail order, was also acquired in 1982. The Limited's sales exceeded $2 billion in 1985. Often movement beyond the core business occurs as a company grows.

Companies have several avenues for business development beyond the core business. While some organizations never move away from the core

```
                    ┌─────────────────┐
                    │                 │
                    │  Core business  │
                    │                 │
                    └─────────────────┘
              ↙              ↓              ↘
      ╭──────────────╮ ╭──────────────╮ ╭──────────────╮
     ( New markets for)( New products  )( New products for)
     ( current products)( and markets  )( current markets )
      ╰──────────────╯ ( (diversification))╰──────────────╯
                        ╰──────────────╯
```

Exhibit 23.1 Paths for business development

business, many firms expand into other products and markets for a variety of reasons, usually to achieve one or more of the following objectives:

- Increase the rate of growth in sales and profits
- Reduce the firm's dependence in the future on the core business
- Use available cash that is not needed in the core business

The major paths for corporate development are shown in Exhibit 23.1. We are assuming that product or market expansions, such as extending the line of existing products, do not move the firm out of its core business. Sometimes it is not easy to establish whether a product or market is clearly new or whether it is an expansion. As we examine the business development options shown in Exhibit 23.1, we cite several examples to clarify the distinction between what is an expansion and what is totally new. The Limited's acquisition of Lane Bryant is best designated as an expansion because The Limited did not move beyond its core business, women's apparel, although the acquisition did position the firm in a new market niche, special-sized clothing for women.

New markets, existing products

When a firm serves a new market with an existing or modified product, it expands its opportunity for corporate growth while using its knowledge and experience with the product. Polaroid's management adopted this strategy in the late 1970s when it pursued industrial applications for products initially developed for consumer markets. Other firms that expanded into new markets are A. T. Cross, which markets writing instruments to both consumers and business, and Maytag, which offers both commercial and household laundry products. This option reduces dependence on the core business as do the other options shown in Exhibit 23.1. Entering a new market requires a new or altered marketing program because the target customers are different. New market entry also consumes financial resources. Interestingly, during the early 1980s several companies cut back the areas in which they did business by concentrating on the core business. Diversification has not been as profitable as the core business for several companies. For example, in the late 1960s, the Cummins Engine Company expanded from its core business of diesel engines, acquiring companies

Polaroid Corporation is targeting its products to business as well as consumers. For instance, market research showed that the company could sell more of its 35mm film to industrial and commercial users if it fit any 35mm camera. So it now does: In the medical use of its Instant Slide film, Polaroid identified a new market by modifying an old product. (Courtesy of the Polaroid Corporation).

A $1 million TV commercial in the action/romance spirit of movies like *Raiders of the Lost Ark* and *Romancing the Stone* recently inaugurated a major change in Wrangler's marketing strategy. Well known as a manufacturer of denim apparel, Wrangler is now trying to position itself as a leader in casualwear. In addition to TV commercials, posters like this one are being used to communicate the company's "fashion forward" approach to its customers. (Courtesy of Blue Bell, Inc.)

making products as diverse as skis and computer software. By 1984 management had decided to concentrate on a single product—diesel engines.[2]

New products, existing markets

Offering new products to a market presently served by a corporation shares many of the features and limitations of a new market entry. The major difference is that a new product must be developed instead of a new market. Procter & Gamble has aggressively pursued a strategy of developing new products, using its strong marketing and distribution capabilities to rapidly gain market position. Products are both internally developed and acquired. Examples include Pampers diapers (developed), Folger's coffee (acquired), and Pringles' snack foods (developed). Procter & Gamble's skills in analyzing consumers' needs and wants have been a major advantage in guiding the firm's new product planning. (See Marketalk for a description of how Komatsu is expanding its product line.)

Diversification

Moving into a new market with a new product represents diversification from the core business. Although a company that chooses any of the options of business development risks poor financial performance, diversification is the most risky because only limited use of existing capabilities and experience can be made. Diversifications may be related or totally unrelated to the core business. General Mills has diversified from its core business (consumer foods) into the areas of restaurants, toys, fashion, and specialty retailing. General Mills' president describes the logic of the firm's consumer goods concentration.

*Marke*TALK ///

Komatsu's corporate strategy

KOMATSU, FOUNDED IN 1921, is Japan's leading manufacturer of construction equipment and a major supplier to 150 other countries. Komatsu produces a full line of construction equipment, including bulldozers, excavators, wheel loaders, dump trucks, and motor graders. The firm also manufactures industrial machinery, such as presses, machine tools, and industrial robots, and is rapidly expanding into machinery components including engines and hydraulic equipment. These lines offer promising growth oppor-

SOURCE: Komatsu Ltd., *1983 Annual Report.*

tunities, counteracting intensified competition and slow growth in construction equipment markets throughout the world.

Komatsu's strategy to sustain growth on a worldwide scale is based on studying customer needs and strategic planning to meet new areas of demand. Management's plans include both diversification and refinement of construction equipment. An illustration is the industrial machinery series. Komatsu has pioneered various products developed with state-of-the-art technology. A robot press production system developed with Toshiba Corporation in 1983 is an example. This computerized

system enables fully automated press operation, from the changing of dies to the switchover of material supply. The rapidly expanding market for industrial robots is a promising growth area for Komatsu.

An important objective of Komatsu's corporate strategy is *customer satisfaction.* Management believes that complete customer satisfaction is the foundation of company growth. To achieve this objective Komatsu is expanding equipment lines, strengthening the worldwide sales and service network, improving existing products using advanced technology, and developing new products.

///

The focus has allowed us to build strong market positions and a very experienced management team. The fact that these five areas are big, comprising nearly two-thirds of the consumer goods segment of the gross national product, gives us plenty of room to grow. But the real attraction for us is the continual shifts in consumption patterns, caused by changing demographics, lifestyles, and economics. These provide dramatic opportunities for marketers who can anticipate and take advantage of changing consumption patterns.[3]

While General Mills' strategy of diversification was successful in moving the firm toward growth in both sales and profits, management decided in 1985 to reduce the firm's mix of businesses because of declines in profits. Units that were candidates for divestiture included the toy group, fashion businesses, and some restaurant and retail stores. General Mills' actions followed a trend of other companies in the food processing industry such as Quaker Oats and Beatrice Companies—dropping extraneous business units and concentrating on core business operations.[4] Diversification offers excit-

Procter & Gamble virtually created the disposable diaper business when it introduced Pampers in 1961. But nearly twenty years later, Kimberly-Clark came out with Kleenex® Huggies®, a better diaper. Recently, Procter & Gamble responded with Luvs®, still another new diaper product. (*Left,* Courtesy of The Procter & Gamble Company; *right,* courtesy of Kimberly-Clark Corporation)

ing growth and profit opportunities but the strategy is often difficult to implement successfully. Many companies have attempted diversification but relatively few (such as Dayton Hudson) have achieved success through movement into new areas of business.

Some modern conglomerates (diversified corporations) are made up of unrelated businesses. The major distinction of this development strategy is that there is little or no relationship between the business units in the corporation. Sometimes referred to as **multiform corporations,** this diversification strategy became quite popular in the 1960s. Many multiform corporations performed poorly in the 1970s. For example, Singer's fragmented diversification from the core business, sewing machines, led to major losses in the late 1970s. During the last decade a major shakeout occurred with conglomerates selling unprofitable units in an effort to strengthen the total corporation. Examples of multiform corporations include the Avco Corporation (financial services, engines, military products, and real estate), Bangor Punta (Piper aircraft, guns, boats, and industrial products), and Greyhound Corporation (food, transportation, consumer products, financial services, business services, and bus manufacturing). Greyhound moved back toward the core business in 1983 with the sale of its food-processing division.

What Is Strategic Planning?

The Norton Company manufactures abrasives, products for oil and gas well drilling, and other industrial products. Sales in 1985 were $1.3 billion. Norton's top management is responsible for the company's strong performance record during the last decade. Robert Cushman, chairman and chief executive officer, describes strategic planning as answering the following questions for the corporation: Where and what are we now? Where do we go? What do we want to become? How can we best get there?[5]

Although these questions seem simple and logical, answering them correctly is a major challenge to the chief executive officer of every corporation as well as of nonbusiness organizations such as universities and charities. **Strategic planning** consists of

1. Analyzing the environment
2. Defining the nature of the organization
3. Formulating basic goals
4. Identifying, evaluating, and selecting the fundamental courses of action for the organization.[6]

A strategy is a group of interrelated decisions intended to accomplish an organization's goals or objectives. For example, Dayton Hudson's management has pursued a corporate strategy of aggressive new business development to contribute to the growth and profitability of the corporation. The decision to acquire and develop the Mervyn's chain represents one part of the execution of this strategy.

Why planning is important

Business planning is important because (1) intense competition in many mature markets demands carefully designed and implemented business strategies and (2) business environments are changing rapidly and causing top management to continually update their strategies. Overwhelming evidence indicates that strategic planning is one of the high-priority management activities of U.S. business today.[7] The reason is clear: Top managers are entrusted with the success and survival of their firms. Compare, for example, Delta Airlines to Braniff International. Both were strong performers in the late 1970s. By 1982 Braniff was bankrupt, while Delta continued to retain a strong market position amid turbulent economic conditions, intense competition, and deregulation. Clearly, Delta's management recognized the forces of change and developed strategies to position the airline favorably in a competitive environment. Unfortunately, the glamour and mystery often associated with strategic planning mask what is a demanding yet logical process of determining the mission and objectives of an organization and then devising strategies for reaching objectives. In corporations that have two or more business units, top management must also determine the corporate strategy for each unit of the corporation such as Dayton Hudson's Mervyn's chain. Each unit operates as a separate business activity, performing the functions of accounting, finance, marketing, and operations.

As we move toward the twenty-first century it is becoming increasingly clear that the business environment will be turbulent, rapidly changing, complex, and often threatening. Slow growth in many industries will intensify competition, making corporations' business strategy decisions critical for survival and prosperity. Consider AM International, formerly known as the Addressograph-Multigraph Corporation. Bankrupt in April 1982, management filed for protection under Chapter 11 of the Federal Bankruptcy Act in an attempt to reorganize the company. The following account illustrates the importance of correctly charting a company's course:

> The decades of success are now just feeble memories for the office products company that changed its name to AM International, stumbled in a desperate effort to migrate from the mechanical to the electronic age, lost a whopping $245 million last year and yesterday ingloriously announced that it was seeking protection under the bankruptcy laws while it reorganized.
>
> The collapse of AM International, a company only marginally profitable for most of the last decade and that came to be labeled the "Addressogrief-Multigrief" company, is a classic case of a thriving company's failure to cope with a new environment.
>
> The failure makes the AM company the best-known office product concern to succumb to the high-technology wars.[8]

Management's failure to assess the impact of electronic technology on addressing machines and copiers and to devise strategies for coping with this threat eventually led to the failure of the firm.

Steps in strategic planning

The steps of preparing a strategic plan are shown in Exhibit 23.2. The starting point is opportunity and threat analysis of the various external factors that were discussed in Chapter 3 and an evaluation of company strengths and weaknesses. Strategic planners often refer to this activity as the WOTS (*weaknesses, opportunities, threats,* and *strengths*) analysis. Next, management must determine the future direction of the business and what objectives to work toward. Although company purpose (mission) usually is not altered once it is established, top management may decide to make changes because of anticipated opportunities and threats. It is impor-

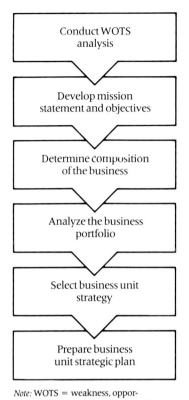

Conduct WOTS analysis

Develop mission statement and objectives

Determine composition of the business

Analyze the business portfolio

Select business unit strategy

Prepare business unit strategic plan

Note: WOTS = weakness, opportunities, threats, and strengths.

Exhibit 23.2 Steps in strategic planning

tant to determine the composition of the business because business units, sometimes called strategic business units (SBUs, defined later in the chapter), form the basis for developing corporate strategies. An important part of strategic planning is analyzing the corporation's portfolio of business units. The result of this analysis is the selection of a strategy for each business unit (e.g., Mervyn's). These decisions are then translated into a strategic plan for each unit. Most of the remainder of the chapter is devoted to examining the planning steps shown in Exhibit 23.2.

BUSINESS MISSION AND OBJECTIVES

WOTS analysis

At the heart of strategic planning is the **WOTS analysis,** periodic assessments of corporate and business unit weaknesses, opportunities, threats, and strengths. Because rapid change in the business environment has become the rule rather than the exception, regularly assessing the situation faced by the firm is essential. The result of WOTS analysis may be to change some aspect of the firm's business strategy or to strengthen an existing strategy.

The following examples will help you understand the nature and importance of WOTS analysis to corporate survival and prosperity. As you can see from the examples, an important part of WOTS analysis is monitoring market trends and competition.

■ *Weakness.* The Great Atlantic & Pacific Tea Company's poorly located, small, and deteriorated supermarkets in the early 1970s contributed to the firm's dramatic loss of market position.

■ *Opportunity.* U.S. Surgical Corporation's founder recognized in 1964 the potential for using stainless steel staples instead of needle and thread to close skin openings after surgery. Surgeons saw the advantages of the new closure technique. By 1984 the firm's sales had grown to more than $200 million.

■ *Threat.* Today, quartz crystal technology dominates the watch industry. Seiko's management saw its potential and was able to gain top position in the industry. Many other firms, including the Swiss, did not recognize the threat of quartz crystal movements. Some firms failed (Gruen) and many other conventional watchmakers lost business position.

■ *Strength.* John Roach, chairman of Tandy Corporation, correctly estimated the potential of the small computer and recognized Radio Shack's opportunity to reach the market through its strong retail store network. The company quickly gained an early leading position in the market.

When the WOTS analysis is completed management should develop a statement of the corporate mission and objectives. The analysis may indicate a need to alter the mission or, instead, to continue as in the past.

Corporate mission statement

The **corporate mission** of a firm establishes its reason for existence. Hershey Foods Corporation for three-quarters of a century was a manufacturer and distributor of chocolate and confectionery products, meeting people's wants for candy.[9] Several years ago management began to alter the mission of the firm. Today, Hershey has evolved into an aggressive and dynamic enterprise by diversifying into pasta products, retail food services with the 600-store Friendly Ice Cream chain, international operations, and a number of new confectionery products.

The mission of any corporation is to a large extent determined by management. Available resources place limits on the speed and direction of corporate development, and sometimes external factors force management to modify corporate mission. In one company, mission simply may be the chief executive's general idea of where he or she wants to go with the firm, such as, "I want this business to become a large retail grocery chain." In another company, mission may be a written statement indicating management's purpose for the corporation. Typically, when a written mission statement is made available outside the firm, it is stated in general terms. Nevertheless, such expressions give an indication of how management plans to develop the corporation.

The mission statement should indicate what management wants the corporation to be. It provides a **business definition** indicating purpose and scope of operations. The following are examples of what is contained in a mission statement:

- Why the company is in business and its responsibilities to the stakeholders (owners, customers, suppliers, employees, society, etc.)
- The firm's areas of product and market concentration
- The nature and direction of diversification
- Management's performance expectations for the corporation
- The role of research and development and other general guidelines for business strategy[10]

Hospital Corporation of America defines its corporate mission as follows:

- To attain international leadership in the health care field.
- To provide excellence in health care.
- To improve the standards of health care in communities in which we operate.
- To provide superior facilities and needed services to enable physicians to best serve the needs of their patients.
- To generate measurable benefits for: The Company, The Medical Staff, The Employee, The Investor and, most importantly, The Patient.

(Courtesy of Hospital Corporation of America)

Payless Cashways defines its business as a building materials specialty retailer. The company has always concentrated in this type of business and it remains fundamental to the corporate culture. Nevertheless, management recognizes that change is the only constant in the marketplace. In moving toward the company objective of becoming a multibillion-dollar specialty retailer, management is committed to being alert to consumers' needs and responsive to their changing preferences.

> Payless Cashways' emphasis on long-term planning as a key management tool has enabled the Company to devise a number of strategies to meet the requirements of a growing store network and changing competitive forces. Most notable among these are: the selection and prioritization processes associated with new markets and store sites, size, configuration, and potential return-on-investment analysis; the design and development of the new management information system; the introduction of coherent marketing and merchandising programs sensitive to the consumers' needs and expectations; and the continuing commitment to the issues of human resources and development.[11]

Although this general description of Payless Cashways' future plans must be translated into specific objectives and strategies, it indicates a sense of direction for the company.

Management's view of the purpose of the business may be narrow or broad. Marketing myopia is the term used to describe the dangers of defining a business too narrowly. Marketing myopia is illustrated in the following example:

> The railroads did not stop growing because the need for passenger and freight transportation declined. That grew. The railroads are in trouble today not because the need was filled by others (cars, trucks, airplanes, even telephones), but because it was not filled by the railroads themselves. They let others take customers away from them because they assumed themselves to be in the railroad business rather than in the transportation business. The reason they defined their industry wrong was because they were railroad-oriented instead of transportation-oriented; they were product-oriented instead of customer-oriented.[12]

Of course, defining the business too broadly can be equally dangerous for firms with limited resources and management. Genesco Corporation's management in the late 1960s set out to rapidly become an apparel conglomerate. Rapid expansion of the firm from its core shoe business (Jarman and Johnston & Murphy brands) through acquisition took the firm into several areas including retailing and clothing manufacturing. After a decade of financial problems including the threat of bankruptcy, in 1985 top management was trying to turn the company around. Some divisions had been sold. The huge debt incurred to achieve rapid expansion, poor choice of acquisitions, and lack of management depth all contributed to Genesco's problems.

Objectives

An **objective** is something a person or organization intends to accomplish (an objective you may have is to complete an undergraduate business degree by a certain date). Objectives may be broad or specific and may be set for the corporation as well as for its individuals, functions, and units. Sometimes, the term *goal* is used to denote broad targets of accomplishment. In this book, the words *objective* and *goal* are used interchangeably.

One of Payless Cashways' key objectives is profitable growth, emphasizing expansion in existing market areas. The annual sales volume of an average Payless Cashways retail facility in 1984 was $8.3 million with $347 of sales per square foot of retail area. During the period 1980 to 1984 total sales increased from $0.4 billion to $1.2 billion, and profits increased from $13 million to $37 million.[13]

To give you an idea of the scope of objectives, several examples are shown in Exhibit 23.3. Accomplishing an objective at a low level should contribute to accomplishing higher-level objectives. For example, in Exhibit 23.3, achieving the advertising objective should help achieve the $12 million profit contribution for the business unit. Objectives should also be measurable so progress toward them can be gauged, and they should be achievable.

Business composition

Businesses that have expanded beyond the core business are operating in more than one business area. It is important that you understand the composition of a diversified corporation. Each unit of the business requires specific business and marketing strategies. Unless the units are clearly identified and their strengths, weaknesses, opportunities, and threats analyzed, developing effective strategic plans for the components will be difficult if not impossible. Let us examine the categories that are often used to describe the business components of a company.

Business segment, group, or division. In general, a **business segment** is a substantial part of the entire corporation often containing a related mix of products. Power, building systems, defense, industrial, and controls are business segments of United Technologies. Specifically, United Technologies' building systems segment includes Carrier Air Conditioning, Otis elevators, Essex wire and cable, and the Building Systems Company. There may be large differences in the sales accounted for by business segments. Some firms use the term *group* or *division* instead of segment. Segment is becoming the more widely used term because the Financial Accounting Standards Board's guidelines for preparing financial reports indicate that the reports should be broken out into business segments. Our use of the term *business segment* should not be confused with *market segment*, which is a part of a total market.

Strategic business unit. A business segment often comprises two or more business areas or units, and each is called a **strategic business unit**

Exhibit 23.3 Some examples of objectives

Business unit:	Make a profit contribution to the corporation of $12 million in 1986, and increase this by 10 percent each year for the following 4 years.
Marketing department:	Hold marketing expenses in 1986 at or below 14 percent of sales.
Advertising:	Increase consumer awareness by the end of 1986 of brand X from 18 percent to 30 percent in U.S. households with family incomes between $20,000 and $30,000.
Salesperson:	Increase unit sales of small electrical motors by 10 percent in 1986, compared with 1985.

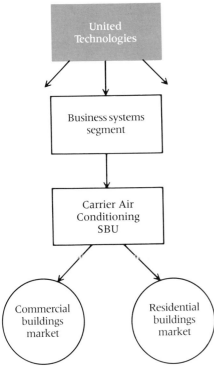

Note: SBU = strategic business unit.

Exhibit 23.4 Examples of business composition

(**SBU**). An SBU is "a single product or brand, a line of products, or a mix of related products that meets a common market need or a group of related needs, and the unit's management is responsible for all (or most) of the basic business functions."[14] Let us look at how SBUs were formed for the General Foods Corporation.

> We started out with four divisions: Kool-Aid, Birds Eye, Jell-O, and Post. Among the products in those four divisions, we saw five basic menu segments in addition to coffee: dessert, main meal, breakfast, beverage, and pet food. We combined these five strategic business units—SBUs—into three new divisions: main meal and dessert SBUs became the food products division; beverage and breakfast SBUs were combined into one division, and pet foods—which we considered a major growth opportunity—was put into a third division.[15]

At General Foods, the SBU represents a group of brands linked by their natural relationships on the consumer's menu rather than because the brands are all manufactured in the same plant or process. For example, frozen foods and instant rice are part of General Foods' main meal SBU, although extremely different manufacturing processes are involved.

Brands, product-market segments, and other subunits. When an SBU contains a mix of products, a mix of markets, or both, it may be useful to identify subunits within the SBU. A brand (e.g., Jell-O) is one example of a subunit. Another basis of forming subunits within an SBU may be according to market segments. The airlines service three market segments: commercial, group tour, and household.

An example of United Technologies' levels of business composition are shown in Exhibit 23.4. A large corporation with many products and markets may use different designations than a firm with a more simple business composition for exactly the same business activity. For example, a single brand in a corporation might be designated as an SBU or even a business segment if it is the only brand offered by the firm in that particular product and market area. In another company, a group of brands could fall into one SBU.

BUSINESS UNIT STRATEGY

Analyzing the business portfolio

A **business portfolio** is the group of SBUs that make up a corporation or major business segment within the corporation. An example is Canadian National's business portfolio. Canadian National is wholly owned by the government of Canada but is managed much like a private enterprise, and its business portfolio includes a railroad system, trucking, communications, hotels, ferry services, consulting services, real estate, industrial development, and fifteen other SBUs. The business portfolio is similar in concept to an investment portfolio of stocks and bonds with each unit reflecting different degrees of risk and opportunity. When a company is made up of more than one product targeted at one market, management must develop a group of strategies, one for each SBU. The basis for developing these strategies is analysis of the business portfolio. Portfolio analysis has as its purpose

- Determining the weaknesses, opportunities, threats, and strengths of each business unit

- Evaluating business unit performance during the past three to five years
- Estimating the future market opportunity for the business unit
- Evaluating the future competitive situation faced by the business unit
- Deciding the future strategy of the business unit over the next three to five years[16]

The strategy may be encouraging aggressive growth for the SBU, managing it to retain market position and generate cash for use in other SBUs, reducing resources allocated to the SBU, or selling or liquidating the SBU. **Business portfolio management** consists of following a management plan for each SBU that, when combined with the plans for all other SBUs in the portfolio, will lead to the most favorable overall corporate financial performance. Each SBU's strengths, weaknesses, threats, and opportunities are compared to determine the appropriate strategy for each.

An illustration will show the consequences of business portfolio management. In mid-1982, after struggling for several years to improve company performance, the diversified typewriter corporation SCM appeared on the brink of a turnaround. SCM's major segments include chemicals, coatings and resins, paper products, typewriters and appliances, and Durkee Foods. The following is a description of management's efforts to select the proper strategy for each business unit:

- An aggressive restructuring program began in 1972 that included getting rid of thirty-six business operations and streamlining all that remained.
- Research and development was aimed at moving the SCM typewriter business into the electronic age. New products included electronic typewriters and printers for word processors.
- During 1982 alone management closed an overseas typewriter plant, two paint plants, and an edible oil plant.
- Although the 1981–1983 recession had a negative effect on most of SCM's businesses, profits for fiscal year 1983 were expected to signal a turnaround for the company.[17]

SCM clearly illustrates the challenge of managing the business portfolio, using corporate strengths and deemphasizing weaknesses to capitalize on opportunities and avoid threats. The example also shows the long time span often needed to move a group of businesses toward acceptable performance.

The shakeout of weak business units is likely to continue through the 1980s. It is clear that the business environment of the past decade has made managers much more cautious than in the past about adding new business units. While growth continues to be important in most companies, the prevailing complex business environment and the demise of W. T. Grant, Osborne Computer, AM International, and others demonstrate the importance of gaining a strong competitive advantage and not spreading financial and management resources too thin.

In the 1980s, SCM's typewriter business unit was strengthened after a multimillion-dollar research and development program yielded a new line of home and office electronic products. These typewriters are "sound driven"; that is, they use ultrasonics—high frequency sound waves that replace a multitude of mechanical parts found in other typewriters. (Reprinted by permission of SCM Corp.)

Analysis methods

Management is concerned with evaluating the performance of each unit in the portfolio and then deciding what future action to take. During the last decade several strategic planning aids have become popular for analyzing business portfolios. To gain an insight into how these aids are used we examine two of them: grid analysis and profit impact of marketing strategy (PIMS).

Grid analysis. **Grid analysis** is positioning (plotting) a business unit on a two-way axis. One axis denotes the extent of opportunity in the unit's market and the other denotes business strength compared with competition. Typically, the area of the grid covered by the business unit indicates its size based on sales volume. Suppose the four business units of PDQ (hypothetical company) have been analyzed and positioned on the grid shown in Exhibit 23.5. Assume that each business unit comprises a single product serving one specific market. The circular areas denote sales in dollars for units A, B, C, and D. Suppose that product-market attractiveness is based on the average annual growth rate of the product and market, and that business strength is gauged by relative market share (company market share divided by market share of the largest competitor). (See Marketool in Chapter 1, page 20, on how to calculate market share.) A unit with more market share than all competitors would fall into the high category, as do units A and D. Unit A is both strong and in an attractive market. Unit D has a strong business position in a slow-growing mature market. Unit C has a low relative market share in an unattractive market. Unit B is a small factor in an attractive market.

Given this diagnosis, what strategy should management follow for units A, B, C, and D? Unit A is clearly in a favorable position. The future growth of the market is high, thus indicating that the product is relatively new. Unit A also has a leading position relative to competition. Of PDQ's four units, A is positioned most favorably, suggesting that management should continue allocating resources to build or improve its position. Unit B is in a position that suggests either building business strength or possibly selling the unit. If business strength is not improved as the product matures, unit B is likely to deteriorate into a position similar to that of unit C. The appropriate strategy for unit C will depend on management's assessment of

Exhibit 23.5 Strategic analysis of PDQ's business units (size of circles is proportional to sales)

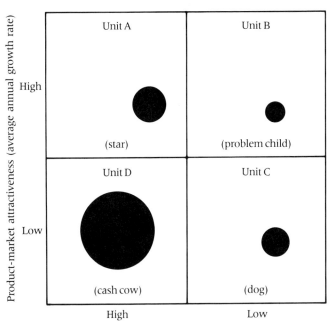

the competitive situation. Management may continue to support unit C because there may be a market niche or segment where it has unique advantages over other competitors. An alternative would be to sell the unit. Unit D is what strategic planners call a *cash cow*. It generates more cash than is needed to maintain its strong position over competition. Further growth is probably limited and incurring additional costs to obtain additional sales will not be profitable. Unit C is called a *dog* because both opportunity and business strength are low. Unit A is called a *star* because it occupies the highest grid position. Unit B is a *problem child* because management must decide whether to attempt to build business strength or exit from the business area.

The example in Exhibit 23.5 is an illustration of one strategic analysis tool, the Boston Consulting Group's growth-share matrix. Several other grid or matrix approaches are available that position the business units or product-market segments in the firm's portfolio. An example of how the planning grid was used in the mid-1970s by the Norton Company is shown in Exhibit 23.6. More recently, Norton has further developed the matrix analysis to include additional strategic factors beyond market growth and market position. The theory underlying the strategies (e.g., build, maintain, harvest) is that a firm with a leading position in a market has more experience in producing the product than the competition, and thus its costs are likely to be lower. Although the cost advantage is not present in all industries, it apparently applies to certain situations such as a high-volume business. Having a strong cost advantage in a rapidly growing market should place a company in a very favorable position. The grid analysis suggests what should be done but not how to accomplish it. Thus the tool has not eliminated management's responsibility for selecting business unit strategies. We discuss this issue in more detail in the section The Business Plan.

PIMS analysis.   Another popular planning tool is the **PIMS** (profit impact of marketing strategy) **analysis** devised by the Strategic Planning Institute of Cambridge, Massachusetts. PIMS is a computer model developed using data from more than 2000 businesses. The model indicates relationships between financial performance and several marketing strategy determinants of performance such as advertising, salesforce, and research and development expenditures. Values of the determinants for a firm's business unit are fed into the computer model to evaluate the business unit's strategy. Several diagnostic comparisons are provided to the participating company, and strategic actions are recommended (e.g., increase product development expenditures) based on the results of the computer analysis.

Companies pay a fee for the analysis and must complete a lengthy series of five questionnaires. The PIMS analyses have identified the following factors as strong predictors of business unit financial performance listed in approximate order of importance. *Plus* indicates that increasing a factor contributes to high performance and *minus* indicates just the opposite.

1. Investment intensity (minus)
2. Productivity (plus)
3. Market share (plus)
4. Market growth rate (plus)
5. Product or service quality (plus)
6. Innovation and differentiation (plus)

7. Vertical integration (plus)
8. Costs pushed to customers (plus)[18]

The direction of change also affects profitability. For example, if a business has a large but declining market share, then the decline will adversely affect profits.

As you may have determined all analysis methods are concerned with two factors: (1) the attractiveness of the market opportunity and (2) the advantage a firm has over competition. You can see why marketing managers play an important role in developing business strategy since market and competition analysis is a marketing activity (see Chapter 4). In general, the more favorably a firm is positioned relative to these factors, the better its financial performance is likely to be. Each analysis method is useful to determine how favorable a business appears at a particular point in time. None of the methods is helpful in telling management how to improve or maintain business position. Nevertheless, one of the major consequences of the rapid adoption of formal strategic analysis methods is that they have caused management to critically examine the business units that make up the corporation. This, in turn, has focused attention on how to gain advantage over competition.

Exhibit 23.6 Norton Company as a portfolio of businesses (size of circles is proportional to sales)

SOURCE: Presentation by Robert Cushman, Chairman, Norton Company, at the North American Society for Corporate Planning, Oct. 19, 1978. Reprinted with permission of the Norton Company.

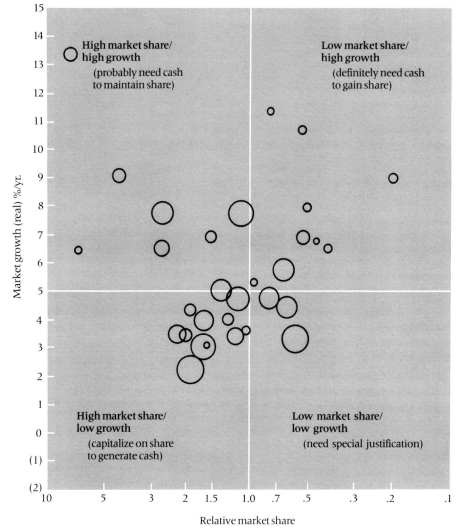

Finding an advantage over competition

Few business situations are protected from competitors; although the intensity of competition varies among types of businesses, it is typically most intensive in mature markets. Gaining an advantage over competition is influenced by the nature and scope of the industry and the markets it serves. Four strategies that have been found useful for gaining an advantage over competition are innovation, low costs, market segmenting, and marketing strength. Often a combination of these strategies is used.

Innovation. Having a new product—particularly one not easily duplicated—gives a firm an important advantage over competition. A successful new product introduction can pump new life into a mature market or create a totally new market opportunity. Research and development play important roles in industries such as electronics, drugs, chemicals, and aerospace. In Chapter 3 we examine some of the technological changes that are predicted for the next decade.

An illustration will demonstrate how developing successful new products create new opportunities for businesses. The Film Tec Corporation was founded in 1977 and has become a leading manufacturer of membranes (ultrathin porous film materials) used for purifying and treating seawater, brackish water, tapwater and wastewater. Film Tec's products are key components of desalting systems that produce drinking water from seawater and brackish water; yield high-purity water from tapwater for industrial, laboratory and institutional applications; treat waste water for reuse; and purify home drinking water. Research and development has launched an exciting new business of developing and marketing membranes for use in filtering water and other liquids. Film Tec's sales of $5.5 million in 1983 were nearly double 1982 sales, and 1983 net income of $0.9 million was three times the 1982 level. More than 40 percent of sales were to the export market.[19]

Low cost. A company with the leading market share position will often have the lowest costs in its industry because through experience the firm has learned how to produce the product more efficiently. By producing more than its competitors, the experience enables the firm to further improve efficiency. Although the high-volume producer does not always have the lowest costs, it is clear that the low-cost producer has a keen edge over competition. (See Marketool for a description of how to calculate comparative advantage.) One company that has demonstrated that small firms in an industry can beat the giants on costs is Nucor Corporation, a minimill steelmaker. Through shrewd management, modern technology, employee incentives, and product specialization, the company has gained a strong cost advantage over larger firms. A company with lower costs can attract customers through lower prices or can obtain larger profit margins than competitors with competitive prices.

Market segmenting. Concentrating on a special group of customers in a market has proved profitable for many firms. Nucor specializes in producing steel joists for industrial construction, and it holds the leading position in this market segment. Ethan Allen in furniture has been very successful, in part, because management decided to target people wanting mid- and upper-priced and high-quality traditional American furniture and fixtures.

MarkeTOOL

How to calculate comparative advantage

THE ESSENCE OF comparative advantage begins with the idea of a competitive advantage, which means that one party can accomplish a task at a lower cost than another party. It follows that comparative advantage is a comparison of these competitive advantages. Consider this illustration:

Product	Man-hours to produce 1 unit	
	Mexico	UK
Stereo speakers	1	4
Stereo receivers	4	8

Mexico has the comparative advantage in the production of both speakers and receivers. With 48 man-hours, Mexico can yield twenty-four speakers and six receivers while the same number of man-hours in the United Kingdom gives just six speakers and three receivers. It follows then that when we add, 96 man-hours will

yield thirty speakers and nine receivers. With the onset of free trade, though, with the same production requirements the combined efforts can produce thirty-two speakers and ten receivers. How can this be?

Based on comparative advantage Mexico and the UK must reallocate their resources to their optimal use. The UK will cease production of speakers and with 48 man-hours will produce six receivers. Mexico will then devote 32 man-hours to speakers for which it has the greatest competitive advantage, and the other 16 man-hours to receivers. This will produce thirty-two speakers and four receivers. This yields more goods, yet will Mexico and the UK be better off in the long run? Price relationships can give us the answer (the dollar sign is the symbol for peso).

	Mexico	UK
Stereo speakers	$24,000	£ 500
Stereo receivers	96,000	1200

A retailer in Mexico can obtain a receiver for $96,000 or £1200 giving an exchange rate of 80:1. A retailer in the UK can purchase a speaker for $24,000 or £500. The rate here is 40:1. Based on this exchange rate calculation, the opportunity to buy and sell currencies is created. To put it more simply, the two retailers in each of the countries will be content if the peso/pound rate is between 40:1 and 80:1.

Suppose the exchange rate is 60:1. Before free trade, a Mexican retailer could buy twenty speakers and five receivers for $960,000. After free trade, here is the savings calculation for the Mexican retailer:

20 speakers × $24,000	$480,000
5 receivers × £1200 × $60	360,000
	$840,000

Savings: $960,000 − $840,000 = $120,000

Leica cameras occupy the high-priced portion of the camera market (see Marketalk). Dollar General Corporation has been successful as a self-service discount department store chain in marketing low-priced clothing and health and beauty aids.

Marketing strength. Marketing capabilities can offer a business a strong advantage over competition. For many years Deere and Company has been envied by its competitors in the farm equipment industry because of the firm's powerful network of independent dealers. Being extremely competent in distribution, advertising, selling, marketing research, and other aspects of marketing management can provide a strong advantage over competition. Ask a competitor what Procter & Gamble's advantage is and the response is likely to be that Procter & Gamble has strong marketing capabilities.

Most of the ways of finding an advantage over competition are related to markets and marketing, which demonstrates the close relationship between marketing management and business planning.

The business plan

The final step in strategic planning is assembling the various corporate, business unit, and functional decisions into a formal business plan (see Exhibit 23.1). The **business plan** sets forth the results of the situation

*Marke*TALK ///

Leica: The "Rolls-Royce" of 35mm cameras

WHY PAY $1,600 for a 35-millimeter camera when a professional-quality 35-mm can be bought elsewhere for as little as $200? And why continue to manufacture such an expensive camera when it isn't wildly profitable?

The Leica simply is different. "Our niche in the photo market is populated by people who want and need a little bit more; price isn't as important as in other areas," says Karl Heinz Hormel, head of the U.S. subsidiary of Ernst Leitz Wetzlar G.m.b.H., the West German firm that makes Leicas.

World-wide, the company expects about 30,000 people to fork out that $1,600—or more—this year for a Leica single-lens-reflex camera. Another 7,500 or so are expected to buy the slightly less expensive Leica rangefinder, which is focused through a viewfinder rather than through the lens.

The Japanese camera makers deal in much larger production volumes and have gone after the mass market with lower-priced instruments. But Leitz, says Mr.

Hormel, is "tied to the Leica; it's part of our tradition." There are other motives. Leitz's chief interest is scientific instruments such as microscopes and binoculars, and the research and development done for Leica, says Mr. Hormel, "helps to keep our expertise up."

One professional photographer says the Leica has a "Rolls-Royce" image. Most Leica buyers are advanced amateurs. A survey taken several years ago showed that Leica owners used an average of 13 rolls of film a month, about twice as many as other camera hobbyists. And they usually owned other cameras.

Until well into the 1950s, Leicas were the standard by which other 35-mm cameras were measured. "It's a mystique," says Ken Hansen, a New York camera dealer who specializes in Leicas. Professional photographers, he says, claim that a Leica "feels different; it's more solidly built, more solid in operation."

Michael D. Sullivan, a photographer based in Austin, Texas, says he still uses his first Leica, bought in 1962. In the meantime, he has worn out Japanese cameras. "You pay for quality, though," he comments. Compared with lenses on some Japanese cameras, he says, Leica lenses are "slow," meaning that they require a longer exposure time. "They're

heavy and they're expensive, but they're awful dependable," says Mr. Sullivan.

Mr. Hansen says photographers tell him of getting deeper, warmer colors with Leica lenses. Fred Maroon, a Washington, D.C., photographer, calls it "clearer color," and says he especially noticed it at the Watergate hearings. The lighting was the same every day, and Mr. Maroon says film shot with cameras other than Leicas came out with a slight yellow tone. Mr. Sullivan, the Texas photographer, says, "Occasionally you can say, 'That's a Leica picture' . . . there's a sparkle. . . . It's either that or an incredible P.R. job."

Rangefinder cameras (Leitz is one of the few companies that still makes them) make less noise than single-lens-reflex instruments, because they don't have mirrors flopping up and down to reflect the image coming through the lens. Photographers say Leica's SLR is quieter than other models, too. Working quietly can be important in a church or courtroom, or when photographing wild life.

Mr. Hormel, the Leitz executive, says that with the possible exception of Hasselblad, a Swedish camera of comparable quality and price that uses larger film, "We really do have a niche nobody else bothers about, or could."

///

analysis, mission, objectives, and strategies for a company, business segment, or SBU. The following items are often included in an SBU's strategic plan:

- WOTS analysis summary spells out the business unit's weaknesses, opportunities, and strengths that should be considered in the plan.
- Mission statement defines business activity.
- Objectives specify what top management expects from the unit during the time period covered by the plan.
- Strategy for achieving objectives specifies the overall game plan for the business unit (e.g., growth, retrenchment).
- Plans for functional areas indicate what will be accomplished by each business function (marketing, operations-production, accounting and finance, human resources, research and development).
- Contingency plan indicates what will be done if the future turns out differently than planned.

All business plans should include contingency plans. For example, the business plan might be developed assuming that business conditions will be favorable over the next three years. The contingency plan indicates what will be done if unfavorable business conditions occur during the planning period. Thus the contingency plan is simply an alternative plan developed for a different set of assumptions about what will happen in the future.

MARKETING MANAGEMENT'S ROLE IN BUSINESS PLANNING

Marketing management and business planning

It should be apparent by now that marketing management participates in business planning in various ways. Marketing research may be needed in conducting the WOTS analysis. Use of the grid and PIMS planning tools require market analysis to estimate market attractiveness. Strategies used for business units to gain an advantage over competition may be market centered—for example, segmenting markets and building strong marketing capabilities. When the business unit's strategy is developed, marketing management must prepare and implement a strategy for carrying out the marketing function. Marketing management is increasingly being asked to participate in business planning as well as to be responsible for managing the marketing function.

There is probably no better example of the critical role of marketing management in the modern organization than Texas Instruments. Historically, Texas Instruments developed products from a technology point of view instead of from the point of view of customers' needs and wants.[20] In 1982 it launched a major reorganization stressing decentralization and a new respect for marketing. Looking back on the company's failure with digital watches, erosion of market share position in semiconductors, and other problems, management was attempting to return the company to the performance levels of the early 1970s. It is clear that marketing management will be called on to play a major role in Texas Instruments' future. The firm's huge losses in 1983 in the personal computer market further highlighted its marketing weaknesses. The departure in June 1983 of a top management executive credited with shifting Texas Instruments toward a market-oriented strategy raised new questions about the performance of the Dallas-based company.[21] In the spring of 1984 Texas Instruments stopped producing home computers, apparently signalling an end to the firm's efforts to move into consumer-products markets.

Illustrative corporate profiles

An analysis of four kinds of companies is shown in Exhibit 23.7. Companies that decide to become more consumer oriented, such as Texas Instruments, are likely to work toward the characteristics described in the right-hand column of Exhibit 23.7. Companies that are production, sales, or technology oriented will find competing with consumer-oriented companies difficult, if not impossible, if the business environment of the early 1980s continues. Note that the consumer-oriented company does not neglect manufacturing, sales, or research and development. Rather, market-centered strategies are used to guide manufacturing, sales, and research and development. Marketing management can contribute to all the activities we have discussed in this chapter. Some companies are assigning strategic planning responsibilities to the chief marketing executive to facilitate adopting a marketing orientation. Many other firms are calling for marketing's participation in business planning.

Marketing's relationships with other business functions

Marketing management also has various relationships with the other business functions. Several examples of areas involving mutual responsibility, cooperation, and sometimes conflict are shown in Exhibit 23.8. Many business activities require that two or more functional areas work together. Because of differences in objectives, conflicts occur and compromises may be necessary. Discussing a situation that involves operations and marketing can illustrate the kinds of differences that occur.

To gain cost advantages many manufacturing firms produce batches or groups of products. A furniture manufacturer may only produce a certain style of furniture two or three times a year. Suppose a retailer orders a particular style of bedroom furniture and it is out of stock. Production is not scheduled for ninety days. The retailer's customer is unwilling to wait and decides to shop other retailers. The issue is how much inventory to produce to meet future needs. The inventory costs of meeting high levels of customer satisfaction (e.g., eliminating out of stocks) are high as we saw in Chapter 15. Marketing, of course, is concerned with customer satisfaction; opera-

Exhibit 23.7 Four kinds of companies compared

	Production Oriented	Sales Oriented	Technology Oriented	Consumer Oriented
Typical strategy	Lower cost	Increase volume	Push research	Build profitability
Normal structure	Functional	Functional or profit centers	Profit centers	Market or product or brand; decentralized profit responsibility
Key systems	Plant profits and losses; budgets	Sales forecasts; results versus plan	Performance tests; Research and development plans	Marketing plans
Traditional skills	Engineering	Sales	Science and engineering	Analysis
Normal focus	Internal efficiencies	Distribution channels; short-term sales results	Product performance	Consumers; market share
Typical response to competitive pressure	Cut costs	Cut price; sell harder	Improve product	Consumer research; planning, testing, refining
Overall mental set	"What we need to do in this company is get our costs down and our quality up."	"Where can I sell what we make?"	"The best product wins the day."	"What will the consumer buy that we can profitably make?"

SOURCE: Adapted from Edward G. Michaels, "Marketing muscle," *Business Horizons*, May–June 1982, p. 72. Copyright, 1982, by the Foundation for the School of Business at Indiana University. Reprinted by permission.

Exhibit 23.8 Illustrative relationships between marketing and other business functions

Functional Area	Illustrative Relationship
Accounting and finance	Expense control Sales forecasting Credit approval of new customers Collecting of bad debts
Human resources	Recruiting of salespeople Wage and salary administration Employee benefits Equal Employment Opportunity
Operations/production	Product quality Inventory requirements Product availability Packaging
Research and development	New product needs Feasibility studies Product use tests
Physical distribution	Warehouse location Shipment of products

tions is concerned with the costs of producing and storing products. Some give and take is often necessary to resolve issues between functional areas.

SUMMARY

Business planning is vital to the survival and prosperity of the modern corporation because of intense competition and the rapidly changing business environment. The business planning process is being adopted in many nonbusiness organizations such as hospitals, universities, and government agencies. Business planning is essential in small firms as well as in large ones. Understanding the various paths of business development beyond the core business is important to devising a strategic plan. These paths include moving into new markets, introducing new products, and diversifying.

The first step in business strategic planning calls for a candid and objective analysis of company weaknesses, opportunities, threats, and strengths. The WOTS analysis provides a springboard for developing (or altering) the corporate mission statement and objectives. The mission establishes the reason for the firm's existence and spells out what management wants (and does not want) the corporation to be. Objectives are something a person or organization wants to accomplish. They may be set for the corporation as well as its individuals, functions, and units. Next, the composition of the business is determined, and the business is broken out into strategic business units (SBUs).

Business unit strategy is developed by analyzing the business portfolio to determine the best strategy for each unit, given the objective of maximizing the performance of the total portfolio. Two of the more popular methods of portfolio analysis are grid methods and PIMS analysis. The major strength of these tools is that they diagnose problems rather than show management how to develop a strategy for the future. A strategy may include finding an advantage over competition. The final step of strategic planning is preparing the business plan. The plan often includes the WOTS analysis summary, the mission statement, objectives, strategy for achieving objectives, plans for functional areas, and contingency plans.

Marketing can contribute to many of the steps of the business planning process. Tracking opportunities and threats, performing business unit analysis, and finding a strategic advantage frequently require the participation of marketing management.

KEY TERMS

core business	business definition	business portfolio
multiform corporations	marketing myopia	business portfolio management
strategic planning	objective	grid analysis
WOTS analysis	business segment	PIMS analysis
corporate mission	strategic business unit (SBU)	business plan

QUESTIONS FOR REVIEW AND DISCUSSION

1. A strategic plan consists of the decisions that are made to achieve the goals or objectives of the organization. Describe the strategic planning process.

2. Why is strategic planning a high-priority management activity?

3. What management errors caused AM International to file for protection under Chapter 11 of the Federal Bankruptcy Act?

4. What is the purpose of a WOTS analysis?

5. What is meant by the term *core business*? Why would a firm expand beyond its core business?

6. In corporate development, clarify the distinction between what is an expansion and what is totally new.

7. The mission of any corporation is largely determined by management. What other factors influence the corporate mission statement?

8. The mission statement should indicate what management wants the corporation to be. Identify areas illustrative of what may be contained in a mission statement.

9. Suggest some business definition guidelines that might be appropriate for a small computer accessory manufacturing firm.

10. What does the term *marketing myopia* mean?

11. An objective is something a person or organization intends to accomplish. For whom are objectives set? What relationship is there between lower-level objectives and higher-level objectives? Why should objectives be measurable?

12. What is an SBU? Why would General Foods include such different products as frozen foods and instant rice in the same SBU?

13. What is the purpose of portfolio analysis? What is the objective of business portfolio management?

14. The Boston Consulting Group's growth-share matrix is an example of grid analysis. How can this strategic planning aid be used by management?

15. What does PIMS stand for? How does this planning tool analyze a business?

16. A contingency plan is often included in a business unit's strategic plan. What is the purpose of the contingency plan?

17. In what ways does marketing management participate in business planning?

18. Exhibit 23.7 compares four kinds of companies. What are the typical strategies of companies in each category?

BUILDING YOUR PORTFOLIO

Select a corporation large enough so that published information will be available on the firm. Identify various sources of information such as magazine and newspaper articles, company annual reports, investment analyses, and other relevant information. If the firm has offices in your city, you may also want to contact the local office or write the corporate headquarters. Using the information you have identified, prepare a complete analysis of the firm's mission, objectives, and business composition, indicating the products offered and markets served. You may find that a review of the company's annual report (or reports) will provide sufficient information for the assignment. Be sure to identify the company's business units.

NOTES

1. "The new breed of strategic planner." *Business Week,* Sept. 17, 1984, pp. 64–65.
2. Harlan S. Byrne, "Cummins decides to go with its strengths as it pins hopes on diesel truck engines." *Wall Street Journal,* July 3, 1984, p. 21.
3. Bruce Atwater, *1981 General Mills Annual Meeting Report.* Nov. 6, 1981, p. 10.
4. "General Mills outlines a plan of divestiture." *Wall Street Journal,* Mar. 27, 1985, p. 2.
5. Robert Cushman, "Norton's top-down, bottom-up planning process." *Survey of Business,* Spring 1981, p. 11.
6. Don Hellriegel and John W. Slocum, Jr., *Management,* 3rd ed. Reading, Mass.: Addison-Wesley, 1982, p. 159.
7. David W. Cravens, "Strategic marketing's new challenge." *Business Horizons,* Mar. 1983, p. 19.
8. N. R. Kleinfield, "AM's brightest years now dim memories." *New York Times,* Apr. 15, 1982, p. 29.
9. *Report of Annual Meeting of Stockholders.* Hershey Foods Corporation, Apr. 28, 1980, p. 4.
10. David W. Cravens, *Strategic Marketing.* Homewood, Ill.: Irwin, 1982, p. 50.
11. Payless Cashways, *1984 Annual Report.* p. 5.
12. Theodore Levitt, "Marketing myopia." *Harvard Business Review,* Sept.–Oct. 1975, p. 26.
13. Payless Cashways, op. cit., p. 24.
14. Cravens, *Strategic Marketing.* p. 54.
15. "James L. Ferguson: General Foods' super-marketer." *MBA Executive,* Mar.–Apr. 1980, p. 6.
16. Cravens, *Strategic Marketing.* p. 107.
17. Judy Greenwald, "Turnaround at SCM?" *Barron's,* June 21, 1982, pp. 37, 56.
18. *THE PIMSLETTER on Business Strategy,* No. 1. Cambridge, Mass.: The Strategic Planning Institute, 1977, pp. 3–5.
19. *Film Tec Corporation Annual Report 1983.* p. 1.
20. "An about-face in TI's culture." *Business Week,* July 5, 1982, p. 77.
21. Jeffrey M. Guinn, "Texas Instruments loses a staunch supporter." *Fort Worth Star-Telegram,* Aug. 6, 1983, p. 10B.

Case 23.1

Domino's Pizza

EVER ORDER A PIZZA from your local Mom-and-Pop pizza store, and ask that it be delivered to your doorstep?

Millions of American consumers do just that every week. Sometimes they're satisfied with the results . . . many times they're not.

Two hours after the initial phone call, the delivery person rings your doorbell. The pizza is cold, stuck to the lid of the box, or piled up on one side of it. You ordered sausage and mushroom; you got pepperoni and anchovy. It's hard to be sure.

Perhaps that's why home delivery accounts for only 16% of the $7-billion pizza market. Restaurant orders and carry-outs account for 30% each; frozen and packaged pizzas represent 24%, according to *Restaurant Business* magazine.

Aha! A smart marketer would see that there's a profitable market here and a consumer need that isn't being satisfied. Why, a marketer who could ensure consistent, prompt delivery of tasty, piping-hot pizza could make as much money as Mama Celeste.

In 1960, Thomas S. Monaghan and his brother James scared up $500 and bought a tiny Italian (mostly pizza) restaurant near the campus of Eastern Michigan University in Ypsilanti. Tom was hoping the profits from the store (named Dominick's) would fund his academic aspiration: a degree in architecture.

Eight months later Jim grew weary of the restaurant business. He opted out of the partnership, his only compensation a battered Volkswagen that had been used for deliveries. In 1961, Tom took on another partner and opened stores in Ann Arbor (University of Michigan) and Mount Pleasant (Central Michigan University).

Dormitory food, it seems, contributes to the popularity of pizza on college campuses.

"I knew very little about business, especially the pizza business, and it showed," Monaghan said. "However, I was anxious to succeed, and even sold pizza below cost in the beginning. I made a lot of mistakes, but I kept going, probably because I was too stubborn to know when to quit."

In 1965, Monaghan once again found himself partnerless, and thousands of dollars in debt. Drastic measures were called

SOURCE: Bernie Whalen, " 'People-oriented' marketing delivers a lot of dough for Domino's," *Marketing News*, Mar. 16, 1984, pp. 4–5. Reprinted with permission of the American Marketing Association.

for. He crossed out every entree on his menu, except pizza; tossed out the tables and chairs; changed the company name to Domino's; and started to specialize in pizza take-out and delivery. The company logo became a red domino with three white dots—one for each store.

Sales doubled that year and Monaghan opened four other Domino's outlets near college campuses and military bases (mess hall food isn't much better than dormitory food). In 1967, Domino's sold its first franchise, and opened a commissary to supply pizza ingredients. The first out-of-state Domino's was opened in 1968.

Then the road to success got rocky. A fire destroyed the company's headquarters and Monaghan was unable to fulfill the promises he had made to franchisees. "We just went too far, too fast, without being ready," he recalls. Debts (totaling $1 million) piled up, the franchisees and creditors filed 150 lawsuits, and Domino's was taken over by a bank.

Monaghan went back to working in the restaurants, slowly paid off his debts, and regained control of the company in 1971. Over the next four years, he embarked on another expansion program, boosting the number of franchises to 100.

"I began rebuilding by staking out a business niche—free delivery—and doing it better and faster than anyone else," Monaghan said.

In 1975, the Amstar Corp., maker of Domino Sugar, filed suit against Domino's, alleging trademark infringement. A judge forced Monaghan to use a different name for his new stores. He chose Pizza Dispatch. The dispute wasn't settled until 1980, when Monaghan agreed to use the name Domino's Pizza Inc. (rather than just Domino's).

The litigation over, Monaghan took stock of his progress: 398 outlets throughout the country and system-wide sales of $98 million. It was clear that if Domino's Pizza was to go any further, it would have to penetrate the lucrative residential market, lessening its dependence on the college and military locations. Monaghan decided to stress good management and marketing—a focus on the consumer.

"It was 'plow ahead' in the early days," recalls Joyce Julius, Domino's national marketing director. "But about four years ago we decided we needed a more scientific approach, a calculated marketing plan."

One of Monaghan's first moves was to decentralize the company to get rid of the excess layers of management that had accumulated over the years. He established

six regional offices to work directly with the franchise network.

Regional vice presidents are given policies to follow, but operate autonomously. To instill pride among regional executives, the regions are named for them. For example, the "Orcutt" region is the Atlanta-based southeastern region managed by Mike Orcutt.

Twenty-four commissaries (which comprise a wholly owned subsidiary) supply all the pizza ingredients, including fresh dough, to the franchises. Laboratory research and taste tests are conducted to control quality and improve the product. Another subsidiary supplies store equipment, signs, uniforms, and promotional materials.

As Domino's started moving into the residential market, management decided to emphasize the firm's unique selling proposition: the pizza will be delivered hot in 30 minutes, or it's free of charge to the consumer (a Domino's pizza costs $8–$12, including delivery). "All our studies show that taste and prompt delivery are the key buying criteria," Julius notes.

Domino's has designed its stores and product offerings, and trained its employees to ensure that few pizzas are given away. First of all, store owners specialize in delivery, although they offer carry-out service (but it's not promoted). As a result, home delivery accounts for more than 90% of sales.

Only two sizes of pizza are offered: thin-crust 12-inch and 16-inch. Toppings can be altered to fit local tastes (jalepeno peppers are popular in the southwest, pineapple is big in California and Hawaii), but the number is limited, usually to eight or nine. The beverage list has one item: cola. Stores open at 4:30 p.m. and close between midnight and 2 a.m., when consumption is highest.

When the phone rings, the consumer's order is recorded by a dispatcher, who uses a blow-up map of the surrounding community for routing. The 30-minute guarantee is only offered to homes within a two- or three-mile radius of the store, and can be lifted during inclement weather.

The order is turned over to employees who work at the "make-line." Pizza ingredients are assembled along the line in the order in which they appear on the pizza: dough, sauce, cheese, toppings. "It takes one minute to make the pizza and six minutes to bake," Julius said.

The finished pizzas are placed in rigid corrugated boxes (a Monaghan innovation) and put in racks designated for certain delivery routes. That leaves 10–20 minutes to get the pizzas to the consumers. Delivery cars contain portable ovens (called "hot boxes") to keep the pizzas warm en route.

If a delivery person misses the deadline, he's not punished financially. "Only 1½% of our pizzas are given away for failure to meet the 30-minute guarantee," Julius said. "That isn't much of a loss. If you get a free pizza, chances are you'll call again and give Domino's another shot at it."

Are consumers sticklers about the 30-minute rule or do they pay for the pizzas, even if delivered a few minutes late? "People are always testing us to see if we can get there in 30 minutes," she said. "If we're late, even by a minute, people want the pizza for free. Most consumers aren't that good-natured about it."

To ensure prompt delivery, Domino's also issues five instructions on its menu:

1. Know what you want before ordering (size of pizza, toppings, beverages).
2. Know the phone number and address of the residence from which you are calling.
3. When placing an order, let us know if you have large-denomination bills.
4. Remain by the phone after ordering. We may call back to confirm the order.
5. Turn on your porch light.

"The instruction about staying by the phone is aimed at discouraging crank calls," Julius explains. "We also try to limit large-denomination bills for the protection of the driver." The menu states: "Our drivers carry less than $20."

Mom-and-Pop pizza stores, as a rule, prefer to operate on a carry-out-only basis, Julius said. They offer home delivery basically for competitive reasons. As a result, they tend to have low-paid delivery personnel. Turnover is high.

Domino's, realizing the importance of employee dedication, has created a system which attracts aspiring entrepreneurs to the position of deliveryperson.

"The only way you can become a franchise owner is to work for Domino's," Julius explains. "You can't buy a franchise on the open market. You start out as a delivery person, you learn how to make pizzas, you become a management trainee, then an assistant manager, then you get a chance to run your own store.

"As a result, our deliverypeople work hard—they have a great opportunity in the company. We have a couple dozen millionaires in the system, and they all started out delivering pizzas." "Field consultants" from the regional offices visit franchisees monthly to provide supervision and training.

Domino's headquarters in Ann Arbor, Mich., conducts a "Mystery Customer" program. Consumers in each franchise area are recruited through newspaper ads. They get a free pizza if they promise to order at least twice a month, for three months, from the local Domino's.

"The program's designed to keep the deliverypeople on their toes," Julius said. "If the deliveryperson gets a Mystery Customer on his route he can win a prize by delivering the pizza on time, saying thank you, and so forth."

A questionnaire is delivered with each pizza. It asks the consumer about the demeanor of telephone personnel, pizza quality, delivery time, etc. "As a personal thank-you for completing this flyer, you will receive a 50¢ discount on your next pizza ordered from our store. Just present this card with your next order," the questionnaire notes.

Data gathered from the questionnaires are turned over to the regional offices for analysis. Results are used to identify and correct problems at the store level.

Direct mail and door-hangers are used to distribute discount coupons ($1 off, free drinks, etc.). Delivery personnel also give customers Domino's keyrings, auto litter bags, and plastic beverage containers. Regional offices place newspaper ads with the slogan "Domino's Pizza Delivers!"

Marketing efforts are designed to reach and appeal to the core consumer group (ages 18–34) and the secondary group (age 35 and up). Other demographic factors—income, occupation, family size, etc.—don't seem to affect buying behavior, Julius said.

"Some of the suburban areas we're penetrating are generating high volume," she said. "But our best stores are still in college areas where you have a concentrated group of younger consumers. That's why we're in every major college market in the nation."

Stores are allowed to adjust their offerings to meet local tastes and conditions. In the Southwest, especially Oklahoma, pizzas are made with barbeque sauce rather than conventional tomato sauce. In traffic-congested Manhattan, one Domino's store specializes in on-foot delivery, and still offers the 30-minute guarantee.

It costs about $160,000 to open a Domino's outlet; franchise fee is $3,500 plus 5.5% of annual sales. Franchisees who train managers, only to see them leave to open up their own stores, are compensated for the loss: they receive a 1% share of the new store's royalties for four years. This policy encourages store owners to move managers up through the system.

The average Domino's outlet takes in $9,000 a week. About 3% of each store's sales are earmarked for a corporate advertising fund, half of which is used for local radio and print ads. This year a nation-wide TV ad campaign, the first for Domino's, will be introduced. "I can't discuss it in detail," Julius said. "But it looks a lot like Wendy's current campaign." Agency is Group 243 Design.

Two years ago, consumer awareness in Domino's markets was only 7%. Now it's about 40% and the goal is 80% by 1985.

This increased emphasis on marketing has worked, according to the table. Since the late 1970s, Domino's has grown steadily both in number of units and gross sales (about a third of the outlets are company-owned). The firm has stores in every state, except Alaska.

DOMINO'S PIZZA INC.

Year	No. of units	Retail sales
1984	2,000	$600
1983	1,180	366
1982	831	256
1981	582	154
1980	398	98
1979	292	61
1978	215	38

NOTE: Retail sales in millions, excluding national commissary sales; 1984 figures are estimates.

Domino's is opening up an outlet per day and hopes to have 2,000 by the end of the year. The company is also going international. It opened a store in Winnipeg, Canada, late in 1983 and plans outlets in Great Britain, France, Hong Kong, the Philippines, West Germany, Denmark, Belgium, and Australia.

"We'll keep the product the same overseas," Julius said, "but we'll have to make other adjustments for the local cultures. The ads and prices obviously will differ.

"Last year was fantastic for us in terms of growth and sales. But we have a long way to go. We're still in the entrepreneur stage of the company life cycle. I think we can hit sales of $1 billion a year."

She said Domino's ranks second behind Wichita, Kan.-based Pizza Hut Inc. in the retail pizza market. Pizza Hut, a subsidiary of Pepsico., has more than 4,000 outlets and annual sales of $2.6 billion. No. 3 Godfather's Pizza Inc., Omaha, Neb., has 800 stores.

As a rule, Pizza Huts don't offer home delivery, so Domino's isn't worried. "There are imitators out there, but they don't compete with our 30-minute guarantee," Julius said. "That's why we say we're the No. 1 pizza-delivery company in the world."

The firm plans to stick to that specialty. In the 1970s, it experimented with offering a frozen version of its product for sale in grocery stores. The idea was scrapped.

Domino's is privately owned, and Monaghan wants to keep it that way, despite rumors to the contrary on Wall Street. He says he's paid off virtually all the firm's debts. Corporate profits are plowed back into expansion, leaving annual earnings in the $3-million range.

Monaghan has openly stated his company goals: 5,000 outlets by 1987, one in every community with 10,000 or more population. If that comes true, Domino's will be neck-and-neck with Pizza Hut.

"My competitors want a return on investment," he has announced. "I don't care about that. I just want to be No. 1 in every market we're in." Currently, Domino's has 4% of the national pizza market, he figures.

As a child growing up in Michigan, Monaghan dreamed of playing shortstop for the Tigers, Detroit's American League baseball team. Last October, he made national headlines when he plunked down $43 million to buy the team. He says he likes sports because there are clear-cut winners and losers, which isn't always the case in the world of big business.

Domino's has retained former Tiger star Al Kaline as a corporate spokesman. He'll appear in commercials and at store openings. Tie-in promotions are planned between Domino's and the Tigers, Julius said.

The company also uses sports events to build awareness among consumers. It sponsors an Indy-500 racing team as well as the Michigan 500, Domino's Pizza 500, and collegiate track-and-field. The Domino's Indy car is called "The Hot One" (representing the firm's pledge to deliver piping-hot pizza). Its number is 30—representing the 30-minute delivery guarantee.

Domino's success rests heavily on its marketing—promotion, public relations, advertising, consumer research—"which we've done for the long term," Monaghan says. He also credits his management style, which he describes as "informal." Monaghan's office doesn't have a desk, just a big, round table "so everyone feels equal."

Although he never was able to pursue his goal of an architecture degree, he's received several honorary degrees and is planning to build a huge tower, based on a Frank Lloyd Wright design, in Ann Arbor.

He's a heavy reader of self-help books and biographies and autobiographies of Horatio Alger–types. His heroes are Wright, Henry Ford, Howard Hughes, Hugh Hefner, Stanley Marcus, and Ray Kroc, the late founder of McDonald's.

"I want to be the largest pizza chain in the world, passing Pizza Hut. I want to be one of the top dozen privately-held companies in the world, or at least in the U.S. I want to move up the Maslow pyramid of self-actualization," he once told the *Detroit Free Press*.

In a service business, he feels, success is highly based on a firm's ability to manage and motivate people.

"I had a vice president who gave all his people the day off to read the book *The One-Minute Manager*," Monaghan said. "When he told me that, I actually cried. It was such a great idea. That's what I call management.

"People are a company's most important natural resource. . . . Success in business *is* possible, through fairness and honesty to employees and customers."

QUESTIONS

1. What is Domino's corporate strategy?

2. What are the major components of Domino's marketing strategy?

3. What changes should Domino's management consider making

in the firm's corporate and marketing strategy to achieve future goals? Should diversification be considered?

4. Why is it important for Domino's to monitor the environment?

Case 23.2

Guest Supply

IN 1979, GUEST SUPPLY, Inc. entered an undefined segment of the lodging-hospitality industry as a pioneering company with a sound marketing strategy and a strong belief in the future of hotel amenities. Today, its amenity products and programs are in more than 2,300 hotels and lodging establishments, including hotel properties owned or operated by 15 of the 25 largest hotel chains in the United States.

SOURCE: Guest Supply, Inc. Reprinted with permission.

Guestroom amenities are designed to increase comfort and make hotel guests feel more at home during an away-from-home stay. To hoteliers, amenities also function as an important marketing tool, designed to increase occupancy rates and add to bottom-line profitability. They can influence a guest's perception of a hotel property, and set a hotel distinctly apart from its competition.

Guest Supply amenity programs consist primarily of design and color-coordinated sets of toiletries including shampoos, hair conditioners, soaps, bath gels, hand and body lotions, and colognes. The firm's marketing strategy emphasizes nationally known brand-name products, including toiletries manufactured under such names as Vidal Sassoon and Roger & Gallet. More than 50 different amenity and accessory items are offered—most of which have been designed and developed expressly for use in hotel guestrooms. Guest Supply's customized and coordinated amenity programs have helped to set the standard for what has become one of the fastest growing segments of the lodging-hospitality industry.

From small, independent hotels to major hotel chains, from completely customized programs to economical stock amenities and accessories, Guest Supply is a full-service company with complete capabilities to create, coordinate, produce and deliver unique and affordable amenity programs to the lodging industry.

Guest Supply takes every opportunity to broaden its client base and has adopted an aggressive marketing program to reach new customers. Professional design capabilities, the wide selection and consistently high quality of products, the expertise and efficiency of account services, along with competitive pricing, are among the advantages the firm offers its customers.

The strength of the business lies in a solid customer base that includes major hotel chains as well as small chains, independent hotels and international cruise ship lines. Accounts are serviced with a high degree of professionalism by Guest Supply management and are supported by key members of the sales and design staffs.

Amenities have grown to a level within the hotel industry where they are no longer considered a luxury, but more a necessity. Guest Supply takes into account changing demographics and lifestyle trends to develop amenity products and programs that will help the hotel industry reach its marketing goals and profit potential.

Excellence is a high priority at Guest Supply. Quality products and servicing are assured by the stringent control maintained over all aspects of the business.

Guest Supply's operations are finely tuned to deliver the finest quality products in the most timely manner with the most efficient pricing. Design, development, manufacturing, production, warehousing, distribution—all are controlled by the highest quality standards and totally integrated to support the sales effort.

Rising product demand has already spurred Guest Supply's plans for expanded physical growth. Management will be moving into new corporate headquarters with expansive facilities for program presentations, as well as market research and new product development. Also scheduled for 1984 is the completion of a state-of-the-art distribution center for Guest Supply products that will be the prototype for a network of warehousing and distribution centers in key market areas across the country.

QUESTIONS

1. What is Guest Supply's mission?

2. What role does marketing strategy play in the firm's corporate strategy?

3. Is Guest Supply production, sales, technology, or consumer oriented (see Exhibit 23.7)?

4. At what level is Guest Supply in its channel of distribution? Discuss.

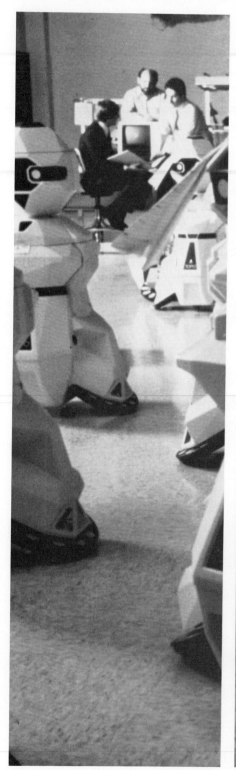

Part Eight

Marketing in a
Changing World

24 International Marketing

When you finish this chapter, you will understand

☐ Why a company would want to move from national into international markets

☐ How marketing principles can be applied to marketing internationally

☐ The role played by market opportunity analysis in international marketing decisions

☐ How companies decide which international markets to serve, and how they can enter those markets

☐ The advantages and disadvantages of global and international marketing programs

☐ Problems faced by marketing managers as they analyze international market opportunities

☐ Some of the complexities of trading internationally that differentiate international marketing from national marketing

A bus company in Hong Kong that transports an average of 2½ million passengers a day keeps 1800 buses rolling with the help of a U.S.-made computer.

Black & Decker, the worldwide maker of power tools, faced lackluster performances in the early 1980s. Its most important market of do-it-yourself home-repair consumers was saturated. A drill as well as other power tools could be found in almost every household, and competition was intensifying. Japanese-based Makita Electric Works was taking business away from Black & Decker in U.S. markets and in other countries around the world. Makita produced lower-cost tools and had successfully pressed this advantage in Europe before entering U.S. markets.

Black & Decker did not have good communications with its international subsidiaries. Each organization had control over marketing in its own country. There was little coordination among countries.

A new chairman dramatically changed marketing strategy. Black & Decker purchased General Electric's small appliance operation to gain distribution of a new product line in the United States. This strategy of purchasing a domestic small appliance line to gain established distribution is being used in other countries.

Black & Decker is also moving toward standardizing its product lines. Makita Electric is already using this approach successfully to gain cost advantages in power tools. Basically the same product is sold everywhere, rather than offering substantially different products to different countries. Using the cost savings from standardization, price is kept low. Black & Decker is banking on markets being similar enough around the world to make this strategy work.[1]

DEMAND FOR PRODUCTS AND SERVICES extends beyond national boundaries. Finding and tapping this demand can be an important growth strategy for many companies. When markets in one country become saturated or dominated by strong competition, other countries may be ripe for a sound marketing program. Black & Decker's management saw this opportunity and strove to improve its position in all markets, domestic and international. Being able to engage in **international marketing** by planning, implementing, and controlling marketing strategies for foreign markets as well as home country markets will increasingly characterize the well-managed organization in the 1980s and beyond.

Our purpose in this chapter is to help you gain an appreciation for the role that marketing can play in a corporation's international strategy for growth. Although international business decisions go well beyond considerations of marketing strategy, marketing plays an important role.

In the first section, the growth of international marketing is examined. Then we discuss the function and environment of international marketing and how international environments differ from country to country. In the third section we consider how the decision to enter international markets is made with particular emphasis on marketing's contribution. In the last section we discuss several special challenges for marketing in the international environment.

GROWTH OF INTERNATIONAL MARKETING

Dominating the field of international marketing are large **multinational companies**, which routinely do business in many countries and obtain a high proportion of their sales from markets outside their home countries. U.S. corporations such as General Motors, Ford, IBM, and Coca-Cola have long been multinational companies. Companies from all over the world such as Royal Dutch/Shell Group (Netherlands/Britain), Nestlé (Switzerland), Toyota (Japan), Renault (France), Volkswagenwerk (West Germany), and Volvo (Sweden) are participating in international market opportunities see (Exhibit 24.1).

No longer can we think of only the large corporations in the economically strong countries of North America, Western Europe, and Japan as the ones benefiting from worldwide business. The developing countries in the Middle East, the Far East, and in Latin America also have corporations doing business throughout the world. With so much income from oil, Saudi Arabia and other Middle Eastern countries for years have been making investments in the rich Western markets. More recently, corporations head-

Exhibit 24.1 The twenty-five largest industrial companies outside the United States

1983 Rank	Company	Country	Industry	Sales ($000)
1	Royal Dutch/ Shell Group	Netherlands/ Britain	Petroleum	80,550,885
2	British Petroleum	Britain	Petroleum	49,194,886
3	ENI	Italy	Petroleum	25,022,358
4	IRI	Italy	Metal manufacturing	24,518,447
5	Unilever	Britain/ Netherlands	Food products, soaps, cosmetics	20,291,583
6	Toyota Motor	Japan	Motor vehicles	19,741,094
7	Francaise des Petroles	France	Petroleum	18,350,186
8	Elf-Aquitaines	France	Petroleum	18,188,156
9	Matsushita Electric Industrial	Japan	Electronics, appliances	16,719,440
10	Petrobras	Brazil	Petroleum	16,258,011
11	Philips' Gloeilampen-fabrieken	Netherlands	Electronics, appliances	16,176,941
12	Pemex	Mexico	Petroleum	16,140,013
13	Hitachi	Japan	Electronics, appliances, office equipment	15,804,301
14	Siemens	Germany	Electronics, computers	15,724,273
15	Nissan Motor	Japan	Motor vehicles	15,697,733
16	Volkswagenwerk	Germany	Motor vehicles	15,693,352
17	Daimeer-Benz	Germany	Motor vehicles and parts	15,660,437
18	Bayer	Germany	Chemicals	14,615,594
19	Hoechst	Germany	Chemicals	14,558,235
20	Renault	France	Motor vehicles and parts	14,467,765
21	Fiat	Italy	Motor vehicles and parts	14,466,548
22	Nestlé	Switzerland	Food products, beverages	13,303,618
23	BSAF	Germany	Chemicals	13,250,424
24	Volvo	Sweden	Motor vehicles and parts, energy	12,963,008
25	Imperial Chemical Industries	Britain	Chemicals	12,750,075

SOURCE: "The international 500," *Fortune*, Aug. 20, 1984, p. 200. © 1984 Time Inc. Reprinted from the World Business Directory, *Fortune* Magazine.

Exhibit 24.2 The world's largest trading companies

Company	Revenue (millions of dollars)	Corporate Headquarters	Industry
Mitsui & Co.	63,149	Japan	Wholesaler
Mitsubishi Corp.	62,831	Japan	Wholesaler
C Itoh & Co.	48,436	Japan	Wholesaler
Marubeni Corp.	46,816	Japan	Wholesaler
Sumitomo Corp.	45,806	Japan	Wholesaler
Nissho Iwai Corp.	34,039	Japan	Wholesaler

SOURCE: "The ever-rising sun," *Forbes*, July 2, 1984, p. 134. Reprinted with permission.

quartered in South Korea, Taiwan, Hong Kong, Singapore, the Philippines, India, Mexico, and other developing countries are also going beyond their national boundaries. Multinational companies are a part of the growing economic strength of these countries.[2]

Not all companies engaging in international marketing are true multinational companies. **International companies** do business in foreign countries but concentrate primarily on sales in their home countries. A company does not become a multinational overnight. Typically a firm begins to market internationally with products already being sold in its home country. Thus an international focus can be a step toward becoming a multinational. On the other hand, the difficulties of competing in foreign markets, such as coping with language and cultural differences, can keep some companies from pursuing extensive international sales and they may never become multinationals.

Companies other than manufacturers also are involved in international marketing. Services such as advertising, consulting, and financial assistance are becoming an increasingly important aspect of international trade. Furthermore, companies that are primarily part of international channels of distribution assist in trade. Huge trading companies, most notably those headquartered in Japan (see Exhibit 24.2), are part of channels for many products and services sold worldwide. They perform a host of services such as buying and selling products, offering trade financing, managing construction projects, conducting marketing research, and consulting with other companies. The operating concept of the trading company is to center in one corporation the complex of services that together facilitate international trade. As an executive at Sears World Trade, a trading company headquartered in the United States, explains,

> If you engage in enough activities, including shipping, insurance, placing of goods, brokerage, commissions on the equipment, design of equipment, installation of equipment, export of the product—if you get your arms around enough of the project, you can make a lot more than if you try to do it with several different institutions.[3]

Partly because of the increasing strength of multinational and international businesses headquartered in other countries, the United States has been losing its dominance in world trade. Between 1950 and 1980, the U.S. share of the world's gross national product (GNP) went from 40 percent to 21.5 percent, and its share of world trade went from 20 percent to 11 percent.[4] A new and increasingly difficult competitive environment exists for U.S. multinational and international companies serving world markets.

MARKETING MANAGEMENT IN INTERNATIONAL BUSINESS

Decisions to do business on an international scale are made at the highest levels of a corporation. Financial, legal, political, marketing, and a host of other considerations are taken into account. Marketing's contribution is to help management see market opportunity in foreign markets and develop strategy to tap it. Exhibit 24.3 shows important decisions that must be made when a company considers moving across national boundaries. Many of the marketing management skills that we have examined throughout the text are used when these decisions are made.

Functions of international marketing

Throughout this text, we have examined the functions of marketing management. These functions include (1) finding and analyzing markets for opportunity, (2) developing a marketing plan describing the strategy for tapping opportunity, (3) implementing the marketing plan, and (4) controlling performance of marketing strategy. We have also examined the skills that marketing managers need to carry out these functions. A professional marketing manager must know how to find and use information for making decisions, understand how to use tools such as forecasting techniques, and have systematic, logical approaches to solving problems and taking advantage of market opportunities.

Marketing's functions do not change when a company expands its business internationally. The same basic steps and skills must be applied everywhere. In fact, marketing may be even more important to a company's international sales effort than it is to its national effort. The challenge of finding and taking advantage of market opportunities is often magnified as a company moves from national to international markets.

Environment of international marketing

International marketing is different from national marketing because the environment changes from country to country. Several of the more important areas of change include (1) government's role in business; (2) population, cultural, and buying patterns; and (3) business customs and practices.

Exhibit 24.3   Marketing plays an important role in international business decisions

Business Decisions to Go International	Marketing's Contribution to Decisions
1. Decide which countries offer the best opportunity to meet corporate goals	Analysis of market opportunities
2. Decide which markets to go after within a country	Analysis of market opportunities
3. Decide how to take advantage of opportunity in markets	Marketing strategy planning
4. Decide what type of organization is needed	Marketing organizational structures that coordinate marketing mix components such as distribution and promotion
5. Decide how to manage an international business operation	Marketing strategy implementation and control procedures and techniques

Government's role in business. As more companies and nations expand their world trade, government increasingly is influencing international business decisions. One way government influences international trade is by regulating imports and exports. **Import quotas** are restrictions on the number of units of a product that may legally be brought into a country and are common worldwide. In 1984, for instance, the U. S. annual import quotas for Japanese automobiles were 350,000 for Honda, 450,000 for Nissan, and 500,000 for Toyota.[5] These quotas were intended to protect the domestic automobile industry in American markets from foreign competition. Unfortunately for American consumers, quotas cause prices of Japanese cars in high demand to soar.[6] Of course, Japan also sets import quotas, which limit sales of American products.

The ultimate quota is an **embargo,** in which a nation completely restricts imports or exports of a product. Although embargoes are uncommon between countries in the free world, they do happen. The embargo during the mid 1970s on oil shipments between the oil-producing nations of the Middle East and the United States is one that had far-reaching consequences for the economies of all countries involved.

A **tariff** is a tax on imported products imposed by a nation's government. Although its purpose may be to provide the nation with a source of revenue, a tariff is usually imposed to protect a national industry. Its net effect is to raise the price of an imported product relative to the domestically produced competition. Motorcycles and steel are two of many products for which the United States sets tariffs on imports.

Quotas, embargoes, and tariffs are often accompanied by other rules that limit international trade in a country. Government may restrict the amount of currency exchange between its country and others, require that facilities be built in the country before foreign companies can sell their products there, require that joint ventures be set up (a business arrangement discussed later in the chapter), or any of a host of other rules that limit or even act as barriers to sales by foreign companies. The purpose of these rules is usually to keep money or expertise from flowing out of a country.

Many governments also try to encourage international trade. The **General Agreement on Tariffs and Trade (GATT)**, signed by more than eighty countries, has had a positive impact on trade. Through periodic "rounds" of trade negotiations, the latest being the Tokyo round in 1979, GATT has been instrumental in limiting the size of tariffs and nontariff trade barriers. The agreement has a "most-favored nation" clause that does not allow a nation to impose higher tariffs on some of the signing countries than it does on others. Furthermore, a wide variety of regulations and rules are used to further trade, and each one is typically aimed at a particular product or service. The Canadian government recently increased the legal limits on the amount of assets that can be held by foreign banks in the country for two main reasons: to encourage more competition in Canada's banking system, and to keep other countries from restricting the amount of assets held by Canadian banks abroad.[7]

Individual regulations and formal agreements are the more visible parts of government's influence. Nations also set policy that determines how active government is in planning strategy for economic development. At one extreme are **centrally planned economies**—countries such as Russia and Cuba where government does the bulk of economic planning. Foreign companies must negotiate directly with government agencies to do business in these countries. Business organizations within these countries are primarily responsible for implementing economic plans. At the other extreme are **market economies**—free world nations that do not centralize planning for economic development and rely on the market forces of supply and demand to determine economic growth. In the United States, the epitome of this approach, the government acts as a protectionist for certain industries able to show a need for relief from foreign competition.

A growing phenomenon among nations is a developmental approach in which government and business serve as partners in planning a **national strategy** for economic growth.[8] The strategy is worked out in discussions between government and business leaders. Products and markets with opportunity for growth are selected, and resources are marshaled to develop the needed capability to exploit these opportunities. Great care is taken to find products or services that the country's business base can develop to advantage over other countries. Japan has been especially successful in using a national strategy. Government and business have combined forces to build world trade leadership in areas such as automobiles, consumer electronics, atomic reactors, optical and medical instruments, semiconductors, and supercomputers. Economic success in Japan, France, and developing economies such as Taiwan and Korea may lead to more widespread adoption of national strategies. Already, some are calling for the United States to use a national strategy to regain dominance in world markets.[9]

Countries may form an **economic alliance**—an agreement to reduce trade and tariff barriers to participating nations—to foster international trade. Probably the best known alliance is the European Community or European Common Market, but there are others: the Central American Common Market, the British Commonwealth of Nations, the Afro-Asian Organization for Economic Cooperation, and the Latin American Integration Association, for example.

Population, cultural, and buying patterns. Most companies build a successful marketing strategy in a home country before moving into international markets. With success in home markets comes familiarity with the buying patterns and characteristics of local customers. Market opportunity analyses (MOAs), trial-and-error experience in seeing what works with customers, or both help managers become market experts concerning home country (i.e., local) markets.

Transferring local market knowledge to markets in other countries can be a serious problem. Market characteristics are not the same in all countries. Population, cultural, and buying patterns may be sufficiently different to affect how well a particular marketing strategy works. Consider the experience of General Foods as it tried to sell Jell-O in Great Britain in the same form as is sold in the United States. Americans were used to powdered gelatin but British consumers were accustomed to buying gelatin already jelled. Powdered gelatin was not appealing to them and so the product did not sell well (see also Marketalk).[10]

Marketing managers can encounter rather startling differences in populations when moving from one country to another. Demographic characteristics such as age, income distribution, education, and family size must be scrutinized to assess their impact on buying. Consider China with more than 1 billion people. More than 80 percent of the population is employed in agriculture where incomes are traditionally low. In contrast are the

Because China's door is open to suppliers of industrial products and technology, McGraw-Hill is publishing Chinese language issues of five of its magazines, including *Modern Plastics International* and *American Machinist*. With $16.7 billion in reserves, the Chinese are on the brink of a spending binge. (Courtesy of McGraw-Hill Publications Company)

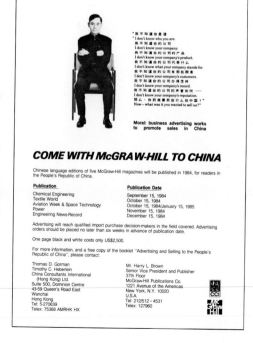

*Marke*TALK //

Grappling with the intricacies of international marketing

A COMPANY MAY ENTER international markets by taking a product or service selling well in its home country into markets in foreign countries. This approach can succeed if the company's managers have thoroughly analyzed the macroenvironment and task environment in these foreign countries. The field of international marketing, however, is strewn with blunders because managers overlooked an important factor affecting the success of the marketing strategy. Consider the following instances:

A prominent manufacturer of water recreation products was puzzled when its Malaysian distributors said they wanted to stop handling the company's line. Later the manufacturer discovered that in Malaysia, where a large number of people are illiterate, color and shapes take on an increased meaning. Unfortunately, the manufacturer's emblem was green, which symbolized jungle dangers and disease—something to fear, not to buy.

Campbell's Soup, which dominates the U.S. soup market, lost $30 million in ten years of doing business overseas. One of its problems concerned a failure to educate people about the concept underlying its soups. In England, for instance, people are accustomed to buying ready-to-eat Heinz soups. Campbell's tried to introduce its condensed soup, which was packaged in a smaller can but priced about the same as Heinz. Marketing strategy did not include any effort to educate the British about the condensed form of their soups, which was the reason for the smaller can. People simply could not justify the higher cost of Campbell's when it appeared that they were buying less soup. After two years of frustration, Campbell's finally began a program to educate the English about condensed soups.

Simmons Company, a manufacturer of quality beds, failed to realize the importance of tradition in Japan. The company organized a subsidiary in Tokyo to produce, distribute, and sell beds. While production went smoothly, sales were not up to expectations. Management had hired an eight-person, Japanese salesforce and rigorously trained them before sending them into the field. More than a month passed before Simmons learned that none of its salespersons had ever slept in a bed. In Japan, there is a centuries-old tradition of sleeping on a floor pallet.

Colgate-Palmolive took its Cue toothpaste to France. An advertising campaign was translated into French without error and announced the arrival of the toothpaste brand. Only later did management discover that Cue is also the name of a widely circulated French pornographic magazine.

Even a world marketer such as General Motors can make a mistake in international markets. The company introduced its successful small car, Nova, into markets in Latin America, but sales were unexpectedly low. Management later found out that the brand name when spoken as two words, no va, means "it doesn't go." General Motors quickly changed the name to Caribe, and sales picked up.

Too often a company's managers assume that what works in their home country will also work the same way abroad—the so-called self-reference criterion. This assumption often does not hold. Proper analysis is essential for marketing in foreign countries. Understanding the environments of markets can make the difference between success and embarrassment.

SOURCE: The first three extracts were taken from Gerald H. Graham, *The World of Business,* Reading, Mass., Addison-Wesley, 1985, p. 652, and the last two extracts were based on Kathleen Wisniewski, "Corporations prepare future generation of cross-cultural employees," *Marketing News,* Sept. 14, 1984, p. 43.

//

higher-income middle class of managers and professionals, a small group, representing less than 1–1.5 percent of the total population. The impact of these population differences on markets is staggering. Of the population as a whole, only 5 percent owns a television; of the small middle class, 75 percent owns a television.

All people have beliefs and values that are part of their country's culture. These aspects of culture are important because they influence what people will and will not accept. Consider Strohs' recent use of a dog in its beer advertisements. The American belief that a dog is man's best friend is not shared by Islamics who believe that a dog is dirty and should not be a pet.[12] In America, the company has successfully used Alex, a dog with humanlike intelligence and fondness for beer, to add humor to its advertising. Using Alex in advertising scenes, regardless of the product promoted, would not be well received in Muslim countries.

Surprisingly, cultures do share some values and beliefs. Being young and attractive and having status are important in many cultures. Quality is also widely desired. At the same time, each culture has its own unique values and beliefs. Thus a major challenge facing marketing managers is to decide whether cultural similarities or differences should be reflected in international marketing strategy. This issue is discussed later in the chapter in the section Global and International Marketing Strategies.

Business customs and practices. The culture and traditions of a country affect not only the lives of citizens but also the way business is done. Marketing managers must understand these aspects of culture to communicate effectively with business managers in other countries. Arranging distribution, negotiating partnerships with foreign counterparts, and discussing contractual agreements with industrial customers are a few of the more important situations in which understanding local business customs and practices can make the difference between success and failure. Arabs, for instance, do not like setting deadlines as American do. Backing an Arab manager into a corner by setting deadlines can lead to problems during negotiations, but the same approach with an American manager may be effective.[13]

Customs and traditions also can explain why countries' business systems differ. One of the most important parts of a business system is the distribution channels for reaching local markets. Though all countries have wholesaling and retailing organizations, distribution channels in a foreign country can be unlike those in a company's home country. Knowing how to use the local distribution system can make the difference between success and failure. An illustration comes from the Japanese distribution system.[14] Japanese markets are increasingly attractive for Western countries because their products are becoming popular in Japan. Yet Japanese distribution is difficult for Westerners to understand. The channels are considerably longer than those in Western countries. Channels for consumer products such as food, cosmetics, clothing, textiles, and pharmaceuticals may have as many as five intermediaries between manufacturer and consumer.

Though Japan is famous for its huge trading companies, most Japanese distribution companies are small. To handle the many transactions required for a population in excess of 100 million, the distribution system relies on a vast number of these small companies. Japan's complex distribution network evolved as a result of cultural, economic, and political factors. Many Japanese have a strong desire to own a business, although most have little income or financial resources. Distribution is a relatively inexpensive business to start, and Japanese entrepreneurs entered distribution in large numbers. Many of these small businesses are run by owner-managers who are conservative and reluctant to change, even though the economic benefits of larger size are great. The large number of distribution companies effectively copes with Japan's long-term unemployment by offering jobs to the unskilled. Interestingly, however, the government has provided most of its assistance to the manufacturing sector to build a powerful industrial base. The distribution system has not had to change because government has not intervened.

Importance of analysis

Our discussion of environmental differences among countries raises an important point for persons interested in international marketing. Analyzing foreign markets is essential so managers know what to expect. James A. Thwaits, president of international operations and corporate staff services for Minnesota Mining and Manufacturing Company (3M), explains,

> The essential requirement for any company doing business abroad is the same as in the United States: sound intelligence about the marketplace. However,

Terrorists and even governments can cause political risks, typhoons and fires can cause natural disasters, and unfamiliar customs and cultural gaps can cause social embarrassments. By providing insurance policies to protect business from these forces, CIGNA Corporation acknowledges that international business can be very much affected by environmental disturbances. (Courtesy of CIGNA Corporation)

when you step outside of your native land, you also need to acquire more than just a superficial understanding of the people, their value standards and driving forces.[15]

Each country may have a different environment, and market opportunities often have to be analyzed from scratch to describe the countrywide forces that influence opportunity. Some of these forces, such as political risks,[16] may be unlike those with which managers have previous experience. IRA terrorist attacks in Northern Ireland, racial strife in South Africa, and emotional outbreaks of French nationalism in Canada are but a few illustrations of particularly dangerous political events that may put international and multinational companies at risk. Such events can cause work stoppages, boycotts, governmental expropriations of assets, kidnapping of employees, and other disasters. Consequently, analysis of political risk is often part of the astute company's evaluation of a country's environment.

International macroenvironmental market opportunity analyses apply the approaches we discuss in Chapters 4 and 5. Markets must be found, customers' requirements identified, competition evaluated, and market size forecast. Special emphasis should be placed on cultural, political and legal, business practice, and economic factors to familiarize managers with the unique characteristics of that country.

ENTERING INTERNATIONAL MARKETS

Becoming an international or multinational company is the result of many management decisions. Three of the more important marketing-related decisions concern (1) which international markets to enter, (2) how to obtain distribution abroad, and (3) how to plan for growth (see Exhibit 24.4). To help you fully grasp the nature of the decisions, we start by examining the different types of countries encountered by companies selling abroad.

Exhibit 24.4 Marketing-related decisions to enter international markets

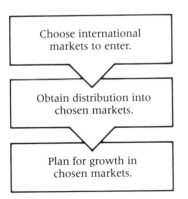

Choose international markets to enter.

Obtain distribution into chosen markets.

Plan for growth in chosen markets.

Types of economies

There are more than 125 countries around the world, and each is a potential source of market opportunity. One way for managers to deal with so many alternatives is to classify them into groups. Ideally, each group should include countries with similar characteristics suggesting the nature and degree of market opportunity. Two factors determine the classification we use in this book: (1) whether the country has a market or a centrally planned economy and (2) the stage of a country's economic development. (Market and centrally planned economies are defined earlier in the section Environment of International Marketing.) Although economic development progresses through many stages, it is common to distinguish between developing and developed countries.[17] The distinction is based on a country's GNP (a measure of people's income) and on how this GNP is spread among the population.[18] Together these factors lead to four groups of countries: developing market economies, developed market economies, and developing and developed centrally planned economies (see Exhibit 24.5).

Developing market economies. **Developing market economies** have quite low annual income per person compared with developed economies, and income is unevenly distributed. Still, the category is very broad. Some countries are extremely poor, with annual per capita incomes of $500 or less. Others, such as Brazil, Mexico, South Korea, Taiwan, Singapore, and Hong Kong, are rapidly becoming industrialized and have annual per capita incomes of $1500 or more.[19] Most developing countries share a national objective of growth to increase their standards of living.

Within many developing countries are two very different economies, a situation that is called a **dual economy.** A high percentage of people live in small rural villages and are very poor and dependent on the land for their livelihood. In stark contrast, a relatively small percentage of the people live

	Market economies	Centrally planned economies
Developing economies	India Zaire Pakistan Zimbabwe Thailand Mexico Brazil South Africa Hong Kong Israel	China Vietnam Cuba North Korea Romania Yugoslavia
Developed economies	United States Japan Canada France Italy Spain United Kingdom Australia Federal Republic of Germany	Poland USSR German Democratic Republic Bulgaria Czechoslovakia Hungary

Exhibit 24.5   A classification of economies of the world with selected illustrations
SOURCE: Derived from data in *World Development Report 1982,* New York: Oxford University Press, 1982, pp. 110–111.

in cities, which may be quite modern, and have much of the country's income. Thailand, Ethiopia, and Mexico have dual economies as do many countries in Asia, Africa, Latin America, and other parts of the world.

Markets in the cities of developing countries are typically easier to reach than are those in the rural areas. Yet large percentages of the population live in the rural areas. A challenge for marketing in these countries is how to serve both the urban and rural markets. Marketing researchers must devise new ways to analyze rural markets (see Marketool for an illustration).

The developing countries account for more than 70 percent of the world's population, and this percentage is increasing.[20] Through sheer numbers and rising income, developing countries will increase in importance as sources of market opportunity. Furthermore, international and multinational companies based in developing countries will increasingly compete with companies in other parts of the world.

Developed market economies. **Developed market economies** are in the most advanced industrialized countries of the world. Income is more evenly distributed than in developing countries, and per capita annual income is so high that large percentages of the population have considerable discretionary income. Although the developed market economies have less of the world's population, because the per capita income is high they are attractive markets for many products and services. Not surprisingly, the United States is one of the largest, richest markets in the world although it only has about 5 percent of the world's population.

Interestingly, international and multinational companies in the more advanced developing countries do a great deal of business in the United States. South Korea, Taiwan, Hong Kong, and Singapore, called the Four Tigers because of their explosive growth in export trade, ship more manufactured products to the United States than do Great Britain, Germany, and France. Because buying power is so important to determining market opportunity, all the developed countries will continue to be targets for companies from everywhere around the world.

Centrally planned economies. International trade with the centrally planned economies is more controlled by government than is typical for other types of countries. Foreign companies must go through government agencies such as Amtorg Trading Corporation in Russia, which handles imports and exports with the United States. Special problems arise when dealing with these agencies: For instance, the seller may have difficulty determining what objectives drive central planners. The profit objective is common in the free market but not in centrally planned economies. Selling points built around cost savings may not have the appeal that they do elsewhere in the world.[21]

Centrally planned economies engage in countertrade, the practice of trading products between buyer and seller without relying on money as a medium of exchange. Trading helped Occidental Petroleum consummate a deal with Russia. Occidental agreed to take ownership and then try to sell Soviet ammonia in Western countries in exchange for Russia using its phosphate fertilizer. Although the practice of countertrade adds considerably to the complexity of negotiations between buyer and seller, it is attractive to centrally planned economies because of problems they face. They have had trouble obtaining credit for purchases, and countertrade alleviates this problem. Countertrade also opens up international markets for prod-

MarkeTOOL

Identifying market opportunities in rural areas

ALTHOUGH VAST NUMBERS of people live in rural areas in developing countries around the world, analyzing whether a particular area has sufficient market opportunity for particular products or services is a formidable challenge. Problems such as lack of published information on rural populations, high illiteracy rates, language dialects, and few telephones severely hinder application of conventional marketing research techniques. Marketing researchers must be resourceful by devising new ways to identify market opportunities in these areas.

One promising approach is based on research procedures used by anthropologists who study the growth of communities. Because community growth also is a major factor in the attractiveness of a rural area's market opportunity, the procedure is applicable for marketing. It is based on a simple idea—growth of a community is indicated by the presence (or absense) of certain specialized kinds of institutions such as a school with more than four grades, telephone service, governmentally designated officials, electric power facilities, a doctor, and retail stores. As a community grows, increasingly specialized institutions arise to serve the population. Thus, a community can be categorized at a given level of growth by noting which of these institutions it has.

Before collecting information on a particular community, a scale must be developed to designate stages of growth based on the presence of the institutions. The information is gathered for an entire coun-

SOURCE: Richard P. Carr, Jr., "Identifying trade areas for consumer goods in foreign markets." *Journal of Marketing*, Vol. 42 (Oct. 1978), pp. 76–80. Reprinted with permission of the American Marketing Association.

Differentiation scale of rural Thailand and associated markets

Step	Item Content	Estimated Population	Market Opportunities
1	Market square	1000–3000	Piece-good cloth and light agricultural implements (e.g., shovels)
2	Fair ground; agricultural support shops (e.g., hand forges, wheel wrights); food shops	3000–8000	Manufactured clothes (e.g., work clothes, sandals); canned or dried foods (e.g., evaporated milk, dried shrimp and squid); radios, bicycles, and mopeds
3	Raimie fiber mill and pond, Buddhist temple, elementary school; urban support shops (e.g., auto repair shop)	5000–10,000	Service for mopeds; hardware (e.g., hammers, saws, roofing material); school supplies; one-man motorized agricultural equipment (e.g., front end tiller)
4	Government administration building; ambulatory health care, secondary school, police services	7000–10,000	Window and door screen material, glass; social dresses; primitive plumbing equipment (e.g., lavatories, shower heads with support piping)
5	Raimie sack mill and water reservoir; high school and/or technical college; sewer and water purification systems	22,000–30,000	Light industrial machinery (welding, pipe threading equipment); air conditioning; cement; construction services; office supplies and equipment

try. The scale for rural Thailand, constructed from information provided by Thailand experts in the U.S. Department of Commerce, shows steps in community growth from 1 (low) to 5 (high) and probable marketing opportunities at each step.

With scale in hand, data pinpointing the specialized institutions are collected on particular rural areas in the country by taking aerial photographs, either by satellite or airplane, of communities in the areas. The photographs are analyzed for evidence of institutions, such as building shapes and locations, visible from the air. Or actual visits may be made to each community to take a physical inventory of its specialized institutions. Each community is then positioned at its proper place on the growth scale so that probable market opportunities can be identified.

ucts that the country's producers would otherwise have trouble selling abroad.

The centrally planned economies hold vast markets for many products and services. Their populations, in total, are huge, and as their per capita incomes increase, so will the needs and wants of their citizens. Yet governmental philosophy in these economies often runs counter to some of the practices of marketing accepted in much of the rest of the world. Advertising, letting supply and demand set prices, and making a profit are viewed with disdain. More recently, however, many centrally planned economies are relaxing some of these policies, and it is becoming easier for foreign businesses to gain access to their markets.[22]

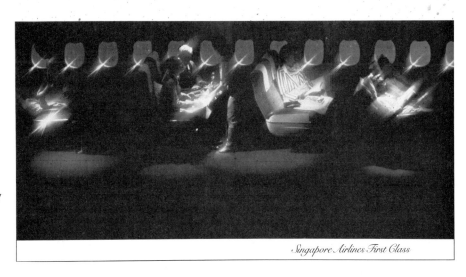

Singapore Airlines First Class

A barrage of brand-name goods and services from South Korea, Taiwan, Hong Kong, and Singapore (known as the Four Tigers because of their dynamic economic growth) is trying to achieve the same status as have Sony, Toyota, and others from Japan. Four Tigers brand names are being promoted vigorously in the United States: TV commercials for Singapore Airlines Ltd. feature the "Singapore Girl" in a brightly patterned national dress, and in Times Square a huge billboard pictures a woman advertising Gold Star TVs from South Korea. (Courtesy of Singapore Airlines)

Selecting international market opportunities

Selecting international market opportunities can be more difficult than selecting markets in a home country. Need for information is greater because the environments are likely to be less well understood. At the same time, obtaining the right information can be a problem. Management's having a systematic procedure for evaluating opportunity in international markets is especially important for these reasons.

One way to evaluate international market opportunities is to use a series of screening steps, which enable managers to systematically sort through the many possible options. Exhibit 24.6 shows a screening procedure actually applied by many companies in practice that incorporates some of the market opportunity analysis ideas presented in Chapter 4.[23]

Screening countries. Before seeking markets for products, managers should quickly screen whole countries for market opportunities. The classification of countries into developing, developed, and centrally planned categories is a practical starting point. Management may want to begin by analyzing countries in one or two of the categories in which the opportunity is likely to be greatest. Factors such as the nature of the product (e.g., whether it is a basic necessity or a luxury product), the willingness of the company to deal with governments, likelihood of obtaining financial backing, and the economic wealth needed to provide markets can help managers select which of the four categories are most likely to contain countries with attractive market opportunity.

For each country in the category, information is gathered to help judge its suitability as a source of market opportunity. Economic factors are a first consideration. 3M applies a screening procedure that uses three measures of a country's market potential: (1) GNP; (2) "market intensity," which is GNP divided by total population; and (3) projected GNP growth. By considering all three indicators, 3M's management can identify the largest markets with most growth opportunity.[24]

Management may also look at other factors. Regulations such as tariffs and quotas, governmental support of local industry, stability of government, political risks, and potential barriers to trade are evaluated. Cultural characteristics are also important.

Exhibit 24.6 Screening steps for finding international market opportunity

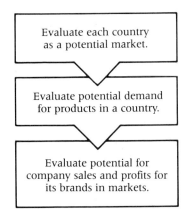

Evaluate each country as a potential market.

Evaluate potential demand for products in a country.

Evaluate potential for company sales and profits for its brands in markets.

At this point, countries having inadequate market opportunity or where political risk or other barriers are apparent are eliminated.

Evaluating demand. The next step is to evaluate potential for products in markets within the remaining countries. Not surprisingly, companies rarely consider products other than ones already in their product lines. This fact is aptly illustrated by the strategies of Japanese multinational companies. They concentrate on products that have already proved successful in their home markets.[25] A product may have to be modified for a foreign market, but which products to sell abroad is set by a company's mission and product mix.

Data on factors affecting market opportunity such as statistics on local production, imports and exports, number of competitors and distribution channels are needed to estimate demand for the products selected. Marketing research may have to be conducted to learn about customers' values, use situations and buying habits, attitudes toward foreign brands, and other buyer behavior characteristics. Visiting the country to talk with customers and distributors is also helpful.

The result of this evaluation is that countries with insufficient market opportunity are eliminated. Those countries remaining offer the best chance for successful entry.

Evaluating sales and profitability. The success of a company in an opportune foreign market depends on several factors. First, a competitive advantage must be found. Using a market opportunity analysis, markets for the product are identified, important customer market requirements are sought, and competitive strengths and weaknesses are assessed. This analysis will help management determine whether the company can use its strengths to establish an edge over the competition. Many Japanese manufacturers have been particularly adept at finding a competitive advantage in foreign markets. They create an advantage based on superior product quality at impressively low prices compared with local competition.[26]

Second, costs of entering and doing business in a foreign market are evaluated. These costs include advertising expenses, margins required by distribution organizations, tariffs, and taxes. Management must compare these costs with sales to estimate profits from the foreign market.

Finally, management must examine the ways in which distribution can be set up in the country. Should the company set up its own distribution system or rely on local distribution channels? A survey showed that multinational companies see cost advantages to using local distributors rather than using company-owned sales and service operations.[27] Yet there can be problems in evaluating and training local distributors. If a distributor in a country is effective because it is given special privileges by the government, then a change in government can cause a decline in performance.

In general, the three screening steps gradually reduce the number of alternatives to the most promising products and markets. Many countries will be eliminated quickly without extensive and expensive market analyses. Opportunities that get past the first step are subjected to even more demanding criteria. In the final decision, only the most promising products and markets are compared using the factors of competitive advantage, profits, and performance of distribution channels.

Information sources in foreign countries. Some countries such as the United States, Canada, and those in Western Europe have an abundance of published information that can be used to evaluate their market opportunities. Evaluating many other countries is usually not as easy, however, because they do not have or make available a similar wealth of information. Furthermore, because many developing countries are changing rapidly, evaluating their market opportunities is even more difficult because what little published information there is becomes so quickly outdated.[28]

Although marketing research can obtain information not found in published sources, conducting research in the developing countries is difficult for several reasons. High rates of illiteracy often preclude written questionnaires, and the small number of telephones seriously limits the use of telephone surveys. Thus personally interviewing consumers and distributors may be the only alternative. Even here, interviewers must be familiar with the nuances of local culture. In some countries, for instance, the husband controls income and makes all spending decisions for the family. Interviewing wives in these countries about demand for a product, as is so commonly done in the United States, yields unreliable data. In this case, interviewing husbands is necessary. Marketing researchers must adjust research procedures to take into consideration these unique economic and cultural characteristics of the country.

Ways to enter international markets

Having chosen a foreign market, company managers must decide how to enter it. As Exhibit 24.7 shows, access to another country's markets can be gained in many different ways. They differ primarily by where decisions on production, marketing, and distribution will be made—at the home-country headquarters or by managers in organizations located in the foreign countries.

Exporting. The easiest way to enter a foreign market is by **exporting.** Products produced in the home country are shipped to markets in foreign

Exhibit 24.7 Ways to enter international markets

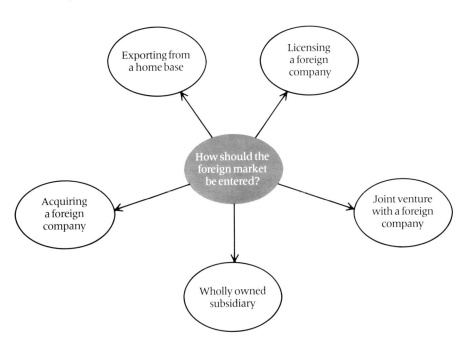

Americans roast,
Russians toast,
Englishmen pour, Frenchmen adore,
Argentinians drink, Dutchmen clink,
Chinese serve, Germans deserve,
Italians expect, Japanese select,
Swedes sip
and Brazilians ship

the best coffee in the world!

Brazil ships yearly more than 18 million 60-kilo bags of coffee, its leading commodity export. According to the Brazilian Coffee Institute, no other country sells a greater variety of coffee bean. (Courtesy of Brazilian Coffee Institute, Rio de Janeiro, Brazil)

countries. Toyota Motor Corporation, for instance, exports cars produced in Japan to the United States, Canada, and many other countries around the world. A company that exports from its home country retains control over production, distribution, and marketing strategy. Management usually has difficulty in dealing with local market conditions, however, because important decisions are made far away in the home country.

Exporting requires special expertise to get products from one country to another. A company may hire an exporter middleman to handle tariffs, duties, and other regulations that are imposed by governments trying to control trade. Management may alternatively create an export department to deal with international sales.

Exporting may also be facilitated by a company located in the foreign country that engages in **importing** products. The importing company buys products from foreign manufacturers, arranges for their distribution into the country, and may even handle the sales effort to local markets. The importer, instead of the foreign manufacturer, has control over the marketing functions. An advantage to working with an importer is that the manufacturer does not face all the problems of distributing to and selling in an unfamiliar foreign country.

Licensing. An alternative to exporting is licensing, which is a foreign company's agreeing to take responsibility for producing and distributing the product. The foreign company is given rights to a product or a production process through a licensing contract that sets the conditions for the arrangement such as meeting standards for product quality, quality control, and distribution. Many companies, from European clothing manufacturers such as Ellesse to beer companies such as Loewenbrau, have successfully used this approach.

Licensing greatly reduces the distribution costs of getting products to foreign markets. It also reduces or eliminates the problems (tariffs, duties, etc.) encountered with export. To get these benefits, some control over product and distribution is given up. Licensors periodically evaluate the performance of licensees to see whether the contract is being fulfilled.

Joint ventures. A company's management may want to get the benefits of local know-how in a foreign market by entering into a **joint venture.** Companies from each country agree to share the management of a product or product line in the designated market. Each company provides part of the needed expertise. A widely publicized joint venture was arranged by Toyota Motor Corporation and General Motors Corporation to produce, distribute, and sell a subcompact car in the United States. Toyota designed the car, and GM supplied the plant. Running the venture is shared equally through a new organization called New United Motor Manufacturing Corporation.[29]

Both companies in a joint venture benefit from the relationship. The foreign company gains access to a local market without having to deal with governmental regulations. Furthermore, management and production expertise is shared between the companies. GM will learn about small car production techniques from Toyota, and Toyota will get GM's expertise in local U.S. car markets. Of course, the companies are risking the possibility that the management teams from each country may not work well together.

> Success or failure depends not on a venture's underlying strategic rationale, Ohme [Kenichi Ohmae, a Tokyo director of McKinsey & Co.] says, but on how well "companies with different blood types, different ways of doing things, can work together." The action of such corporate chemistry is difficult to predict and control, but it is critical because joint venture agreements usually give both partners an ongoing role in management.[30]

Because joint ventures share decision-making responsibility, a disagreement could hurt operations.

Wholly owned subsidiary. A **wholly owned subsidiary** is a separate company formed in the foreign country by an investment of the parent company. Some subsidiaries are limited to handling a few business functions, for example, a sales office or a manufacturing plant set up to serve a foreign market. Other management functions are retained at a company headquarters. In contrast, a subsidiary may be a complete business unit handling most or all business functions needed to serve a foreign market. Black & Decker uses this approach by selling power tools to world markets through full-functioning subsidiaries such as Black & Decker of West Germany. Coca-Cola, Procter & Gamble, Volkswagen, and many other companies also have full-function subsidiaries. Subsidiaries require a larger investment than the other alternatives, but control is easiest to maintain over the business.

Acquisition. Finally, a foothold in a foreign market may be established through **acquisition,** buying into a local company either partially or completely. Immediate access to markets is gained. Saatchi & Saatchi, a London-based multinational advertising agency, gained market share in U.S. markets by buying into two New York advertising agencies—Compton Communications and McCaffrey & McCall.[31] Acquiring a business in a foreign country buys an already established competitive position in markets, but management of the parent company faces the problem of changing the operations of the local company to fit its own style.

Going international in stages

Most companies do not enter international markets on a large scale immediately; instead, they gradually increase their business abroad in stages.[32] The first stage occurs when a company recognizes the opportunity to go international. Requests for products may come from customers in foreign countries or from middlemen with international sales. A company's management may also realize that markets in its home country are becoming saturated and begin looking for growth opportunities in foreign markets. For example, the Japanese telephone equipment manufacturer NEC Corporation began looking overseas when it realized that almost everyone in Japan was part of the telephone system and growth was limited.[33]

At this initial stage, easy and inexpensive ways such as exporting, licensing, and joint ventures are likely to be used to reach foreign markets. If growth is likely, a company may set up an exporting department to handle the increased distribution abroad. Management may also see the need for sales and service offices close to markets.

In the second stage, as the international portion of a company's business grows, organizational changes usually have to be made. Sales and service offices may be expanded to become full-function subsidiaries. If international business includes several foreign countries and extensive product offerings, management becomes concerned with planning strategy on a grand scale. A division of the company may be set up to deal only with worldwide sales.[34]

In the third stage, a company has evolved into a multinational company with many products being sold in many markets. Controlling performance becomes a substantial challenge. Foreign subsidiaries are common, and local companies may be acquired. Several divisions may be needed to manage so many far-flung businesses. 3M is faced with this challenge because it has nine major product divisions that operate in forty-eight countries. These divisions operate company-owned subsidiaries.[35]

MANAGING MARKETING PROGRAMS INTERNATIONALLY

Managing international marketing programs has much in common with managing domestic programs. Marketing plans must be developed and implemented, and performance must be evaluated and controlled. Two unique issues arise concerning a company's international operations: First, how much planning and control should be centralized in a company's headquarters? Second, should marketing strategy be different for every foreign market entered?

Centralizing international marketing

When international operations are small, companies usually plan and control marketing strategy from a home country office. Of course, the plans must be implemented in the foreign market. Working primarily out of a central office becomes increasingly difficult as international business grows.

As mentioned previously, organizational changes are made at different stages of growth to cope with the larger volume of business. At each stage, the question of how much should the home country management be involved in planning and control recurs.

Companies differ greatly in how they approach this issue. Some continue to maintain a central planning and performance control responsibility at a home headquarters. For instance, Moet-Hennessy, the French-based international seller of Dom Perignon champagne, Christian Dior perfumes, and other products, runs its international operations from headquarters in France.[36] At the other extreme, a company may give responsibility to each of its foreign subsidiaries as Ford Motor Company has done. Which approach is taken depends on management styles and how unique top management believes each country's markets are.

The relationship between a headquarters and foreign managers can change depending on how well home country operations are performing relative to the performance of international businesses. When Ford Motor Company was having difficulty in U.S. automobile markets in the 1970s and early 1980s and Ford of Europe was doing well, managers in the European subsidiary were left alone by headquarters. In the mid-1980s the situation was reversed. U.S. automobile sales grew and Ford of Europe began having difficulty. U.S. headquarters started paying more attention to Ford's European operations.[37]

A challenge for management is to work out a proper relationship between headquarters and the local operations in foreign countries. When strategies in more than one foreign market can be coordinated, the company can take advantage of economies of scale. On the other hand, local managers must be able to react to local market conditions as they shift over time.

The degree to which headquarters controls foreign operations differs dramatically among companies. A study of planning in Brazilian subsidiaries of multinational companies from the United States, Europe, Canada, and Japan showed varying degrees of home office involvement. Exhibit 24.8 shows the typical planning sequence for their subsidiaries. The circles and dotted lines are the areas in which headquarters' involvement varied the most. Home office input into information collection, for instance, varied from providing goals and objectives for the subsidiary to achieve, to only sending economic outlooks for the world, region, or country, to having no input at all.[38]

Global and international marketing strategies

How much to centralize management's marketing strategy decisions is closely related to another issue now being debated: whether a company should develop one or multiple marketing strategies for its various worldwide markets.[39] A **global marketing strategy** calls for the same product, or at least very similar designs, to be offered to world markets with essentially the same promotional strategy. A company that uses this strategy is a form of multinational company called a **global company.** Companies such as Coca-Cola, Campbell's Soup, and Union Carbide have been successful with global strategies for a long time. Others such as Black & Decker and the advertising agency Saatchi & Saatchi are only recently discovering its benefits. The alternative to a global marketing strategy is an **international marketing strategy,** in which different product designs and pro-

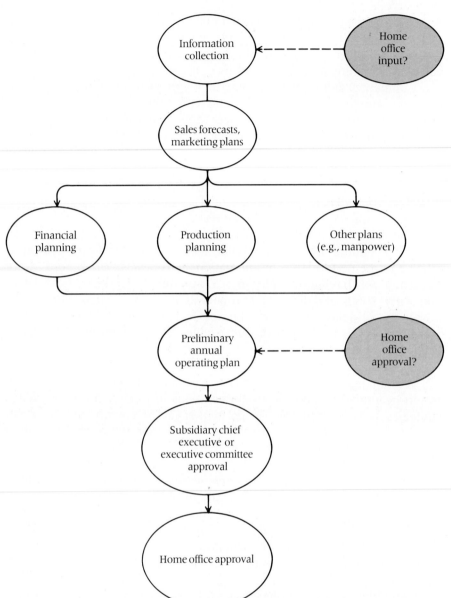

Exhibit 24.8 **Typical planning procedure for Brazilian subsidiaries of U.S., European, Canadian, and Japanese multinational companies**
SOURCE: Adapted from James M. Hulbert, William K. Brandt, and Raimar Richers, "Marketing planning in the multinational subsidiary: Practices and problems," *Journal of Marketing*, Vol. 44 (Summer 1980), p. 9. Reprinted with permission of the American Marketing Association.

motion are developed for each foreign market. Ford Motor Company employs this approach by designing and selling different types of cars for different countries.

International marketing strategies. Managers who adopt this approach believe that cultural, political, competitive, and other differences among markets in various countries outweigh any similarities. Products, advertising, prices, and the other aspects of a marketing offer must be tailored to meet the unique conditions of each market. For example, knowing that Germans like heavy, durable, high-powered drills and other power tools and Americans prefer light power tools would cause a manufacturer to design different tools for each market.[40]

International strategies are more expensive than global strategies. Because more decision-making responsibility must be given to managers in each local market, achieving coordination among local managers can be difficult. For example, Black & Decker decreased the number of motor sizes for its power tools from 260 to 10 after switching from an international strategy to a global strategy.[41]

International strategy advocates argue, however, that the extra expense is needed to respond to the unique requirements of markets in each country. Sales from tailoring marketing offers to each individual market should be higher, offsetting higher costs. Furthermore, managers located in the foreign market are most familiar with local market conditions, explaining why autonomy from headquarters' management is needed. A majority of companies with international business hold this view.

Global marketing strategies. A trend toward adopting standardized marketing strategies for international markets is growing. Rather than looking for differences among customers in foreign markets, managers search for their similarities on such factors as product needs, wants, and uses. Global strategies gain economies of scale for a company by allowing it to make the same offer to customers in many foreign markets. Essential to many global marketing strategies is having a high-quality, highly reliable product at a competitive price. Obviously, for the strategy to work, customers must place great importance on quality, reliability, and price benefits.

A global marketing strategy also enables decision making to be more centralized than is possible for an international marketing strategy. In fact, centralized company planning is necessary to make sure that foreign operations follow the standardized strategy. Coordinating operations in foreign countries is greatly eased because each one is striving to achieve the same broad goals and objectives. For example, 3M Company develops global strategies for each of its product lines in its U.S. headquarters, and all subsidiaries are expected to implement these strategies.[42]

Successful global strategies are not rigid. They do allow differences in those components of the marketing offer when characteristics of markets warrant them. The differences are usually not great, however, as illustrated by Toyota, which makes the same cars for world markets but varies the location of driver controls depending on which side of the road cars are driven (e.g., right side of the road in the United States and the left side in England).

Advertising as well can be standardized yet tailored to accommodate individual markets. Global strategies use the same buying proposal that presents the main selling point or reason for buying. At the same time, media as well as the context dictating how the selling points are to be communicated can be varied to fit cultural differences of markets. Lufthansa German Airlines' selling points stress punctuality of flight arrivals. This benefit appeals to businesspersons in all countries. At the same time the scenes, models, and language of the advertisements are tailored to suit the cultural characteristics of local markets.[43]

Which marketing strategy is best? Both strategies work given the right market conditions. Current trends, however, suggest that the global strategy will continue to increase in importance. A major factor is technology. Worldwide communications through satellite television and interconnected media services enable people to see with ease what is happening in all parts of the world. The availability of international travel is having a similar impact. The result is rising demand for the benefits of modern economies with the most advanced technology for producing products and services. As demand

"The best advertisement for a Lufthansa flight is a Lufthansa flight."

This is an authentic passenger statement.

Lufthansa
German Airlines

A 1985 survey of 120 marketing executives revealed that the products and services rated most appropriate for global marketing strategies include computers, airlines, cameras, heavy equipment, and machine tools. Rated least suitable were beer, household cleaners, toiletries, food, and clothing. (Courtesy of Lufthansa German Airlines)

Lufthansa

becomes more similar, the opportunity to use standardized marketing strategies will increase.[44] At the same time, important political, economic, cultural and other differences will remain, making international strategies work well, too, and cautioning the global companies to be flexible in the way strategies are implemented in different markets (see Marketalk).

SUMMARY

Business is rapidly moving into an era in which managers must adopt an international view of their responsibilities. The well-managed company seeking growth sooner or later will investigate international market oppor-

*Marke*TALK //

The ad biz gloms onto global

THE COMMOTION resounding from the direction of Madison Avenue these days is the sound of the latest advertising industry bandwagon: global marketing. If the trade press and executives at some big agencies are right, "global" is about to transform the way U.S. corporations sell their products and services overseas. The bandwagon could also, its riders say, squash small agencies that lack vast networks of offices abroad. Underneath all the banners, bells, and whistles, however, is a pretty creaky cart.

The guiding principle of global marketing—selling the same product in essentially the same way everywhere in the world—is hardly a new idea. Exxon, for instance, has been selling motor oil globally since 1911, while Coca-Cola has been ubiquitous for over 40 years. Notes William Phillips, chairman of Ogilvy & Mather International, "Talking about global marketing as though it had come into existence yesterday is a bit like announcing that water puts out fires."

Nobody in the ad business gave much thought to global marketing's potential, though, until the summer of 1983. Then Theodore Levitt, a Harvard Business School marketing professor, wrote an article for the *Harvard Business Review* that he's since worked up into a book called *The Marketing Imagination*. Levitt's apocalyptic premise: companies that do not become true global marketers will perish on the rough seas of what he calls "the new global realities."

Just as Levitt was making his case, young, brassy British ad agency Saatchi & Saatchi was staking out global advertising as its own preserve. The Saatchi brothers, Charles and Maurice, latched on to Levitt's theory and ran with it—noisily. Full-page, double-spread ads appeared in newspapers in London and New York, implying that Saatchi was the only truly global ad agency. Giant U.S. competitors saw red—many of them have been quietly running global ad campaigns for years. Smaller agencies, with less international clout, did a fair job of feigning unconcern.

Levitt's vision of total worldwide standardization is global marketing at the extreme. He argues that, thanks to cheap air travel and new telecommunications technology, consumers the world over are thinking—and shopping—increasingly alike. "The new Republic of Technology," according to Levitt, "homogenizes world tastes, wants, and possibilities into global market proportions, which allows for world-standardized products."

A company that sells the same thing in Copenhagen or Cleveland, says Levitt, can achieve economies of scale that let it lower prices and, presto, whomp the competition. Interestingly, he has no quantitative proof that global marketing works. "Innovation," he says, "is by definition a reach beyond the self-evident or the immediately provable. All new things are in some way an act of faith."

Philip Kotler, a professor of marketing at Northwestern University's Kellogg School, is among Levitt's fellow academics who remain skeptical. He champions the tried and true method of international selling: each national market is different,

hence products—and, yes, advertising—need to be tailored to the local culture.

Even the agencies that claim to have invented global marketing don't seem totally committed to its strict interpretation. McCann-Erickson Worldwide, the agency that adapted Coca-Cola's "Mean Joe" Greene commercials for use in 14 countries, is among the most ardent believers in the notion that U.S. ad agencies that don't own their foreign offices are headed for the boneyard because they aren't equipped to sweep the planet with identical sales pitches. Yet McCann's president, Robert James, concedes that most companies don't need a truly global approach to advertising.

Executives at Madison Avenue's biggest agencies agree that some products are better suited to selling worldwide than others. Asked for ideal examples of standardization, Ogilvy & Mather's Phillips replies, "The Israeli UZI submachine gun, the French Exocet missile, and the Russian Kalashnikov rifle." He then removes tongue from cheek and names De Beers diamonds, Chivas Regal scotch, and BMW autos. Agency heads also maintain that a company can't be an effective global marketer unless it replaces its patchwork of 50 or 100 local agencies with a single worldwide one.

Persuasive as the advertising crowd can be, there's little evidence so far of a great rush toward globalization. According to one survey, about 20% of large U.S. corporations now consider themselves bona fide global marketers. Many of those—Eastman Kodak, Gillette, and Timex—have been selling standard products in similar fashion worldwide for decades. Yet some

//

tunities. The growing number of international, multinational, and global companies from the developing as well as the developed countries attests to this fact.

Marketing plays an important role in expanding business across national boundaries. Moving into international markets means introducing new environments with which managers must cope. Differences in the role of government in business; population, cultural, and buying patterns; and business customs and practices must be understood before decisions are made. The marketing manager's expertise in locating markets, analyzing them for opportunity, planning strategies to service markets, and controlling market performance are equally if not even more essential skills for success in foreign markets than in home country markets.

///

global companies seem to have a far less exalted notion of the effectiveness of global advertising than their agencies do. Saatchi & Saatchi tells prospective clients that its famous TV commercial showing the island of Manhattan cruising in for a landing at London's Heathrow Airport may have brought British Airways an extra $50 million in revenues.

The goal for a true global marketer is what Coca-Cola calls "one sight, one sound, one sell," so that a traveler in any part of the world can instantly recognize a brand. The more pervasive the image, the better the product's "share of mind"—an ad industry catch phrase—that leads inexorably to a bigger share of market.

The trouble is, a welter of obstacles to standardization—in manufacturing, selling, and advertising—get in the way. Black & Decker, for example, has "globalized" its operations abroad in an effort to hold out against Japanese competition in power tools. Black & Decker tools now *look* the same everywhere—but because electrical outlets and voltages vary, the circuits and cords of those drills and sanders must be different from one country to another.

Government restrictions on advertising can also undermine the notion of "one sell." The Marlboro cowboy, arguably the most peripatetic of global ad symbols, was banned in Britain on the ground that children worship cowboys and might thus be moved to take up smoking. Philip Morris, Marlboro's maker, replaced the cowboy with only his saddle and riding gear, but authorities complained that still smacked of range riding and roundups. What finally showed up on Britons' screens were

commercials showing non-cowboys driving around Marlboro Country in a jeep.

The biggest hindrance to global marketing is still cultural differences among people. Europeans may watch *Dallas* as avidly as Americans do, and a campaign that features actress Victoria Principal (Pamela Ewing on the show) sells Jhirmack shampoo pretty well all over the world. But no Yankee glamour could sell razors to European women, many of whom don't shave.

Executives at advertising agencies can reel off long lists of well-known brands that have flopped for cultural reasons, some of them downright baffling. When J. Walter Thompson tested Unilever's Lifebuoy soap in Britain some years ago, the agency discovered that shoppers were lukewarm toward Lifebuoy because it reminded them of something Army corporals would use. That's right, Army corporals. No one quite knows why.

Global marketing seems especially hard for food companies. Kool-Aid, for example, is a big hit in Venezuela, where the Kool-Aid Man—the same fellow shaped like a frosty pitcher who appears in U.S. commercials—answers to children's cries of "Epa Kool-Aid!" (Roughly "Hey Kool-Aid!") But General Foods has given up trying to sell it to Europeans.

Nestlé, which sells coffee in every country in the free world, doesn't try to standardize. Says François Perroud, an executive at the company's Vevey, Switzerland, headquarters: "The Nescafé you buy in Switzerland tastes very different from the Nescafé you buy a few kilometers away across the French border." The advertising is different too. "If I may say so," adds Perroud, "I think we are proving Levitt

wrong." Kotler of Northwestern would agree. "There are only a very few products, if any, that you can safely standardize," he says. "I really think the whole global marketing craze is just a ploy by advertising agencies to get new business."

This is not to say that there have been no global-marketing success stories. Coca-Cola got a big boost from World War II, when GIs spread the Coke habit from the cliffs of Dover to downtown Tokyo, and it's still the quintessential global product. By repeating the same advertising theme everywhere, executives at the company's Atlanta headquarters estimate they save more than $8 million a year in the cost of thinking up new imagery.

The best reason to take global marketing with a big lump of salt may well be that Levitt's "new global realities" aren't realities yet, and perhaps never will be. Jerry Wind, who heads the Joseph H. Lauder Institute of Management and International Studies at the Wharton School, points out that no hard evidence exists to show that consumers everywhere are becoming more alike. Rather, the overwhelming bulk of academic and market research suggests that, as people around the globe get better educated and more affluent, their tastes actually diverge. Besides, says Walter O'Brien, vice chairman of J. Walter Thompson, "Consumers don't live globally, and they don't care that you're running the same ad campaign in 40 other countries. Ads have to talk to you on a one-to-one basis." Companies and ad agencies that can manage that always-tricky task should prosper even after the global marketing bandwagon trundles out of earshot.

///

Entering international markets begins with a search for foreign market opportunities. Markets are evaluated by a series of screening steps. First, countries are examined for market size and growth. Second, each country passing this initial screening is analyzed further to find markets with demand for the company's products. Finally, the opportunity for sales of company brands having attractive potential is evaluated. Importantly, the screening process is based on market opportunity analysis ideas introduced in Chapter 4.

Having found international markets, a company must decide on the best way to enter them. Several ways are widely used in practice including exporting, licensing, joint ventures, wholly owned subsidiaries, and acquisition of local companies. The simpler alternatives of export, licensing, and joint ventures are more likely to be used in the earlier stages of growth into international markets. Company investment in foreign operations becomes more prevalent as the international portion of the business becomes much larger.

The marketing management responsibilities of planning, implementing, and controlling performance are just as necessary in international markets as in domestic markets. Two issues arise because of the wider-spread operations characteristic of international marketing. One issue concerns where responsibility for decisions is placed—with managers in home country headquarters or with managers located in each foreign market. In practice, each company must balance decision responsibility between headquarters and the local markets.

The second issue is related to how much to centralize decision making: Should a company standardize marketing strategy on a global scale or customize marketing strategy for each individual foreign market? Because of the impact of technology, which creates similarity among peoples of the world, there is a trend toward global marketing strategies. The challenge for marketing managers will be to determine what aspects of strategy can be standardized and what components must be tailored to the unique characteristics of each foreign market.

KEY TERMS

international marketing	centrally planned economies	importing
multinational companies	market economies	joint venture
international companies	national strategy	wholly owned subsidiary
import quotas	economic alliance	acquisition
embargo	developing market economies	global marketing strategy
tariff	dual economy	global company
General Agreement on Tariffs and Trade (GATT)	developed market economies	international marketing strategy
	exporting	

QUESTIONS FOR REVIEW AND DISCUSSION

1. How do multinational companies differ from international companies? Are multinational companies only found in developed Western countries?

2. Suppose a national company is considering doing business abroad. What decisions would have to be made for the company to engage in international marketing? How can marketing contribute to these decisions?

3. Is the marketing management function as applied to marketing within a company's home country different from marketing management in international markets? Explain the reasons for your answer.

4. What makes international marketing different from marketing in a company's home country?

5. What are the ways that government can influence international trade?

6. What is a national strategy? Do countries of the free world have national strategies?

7 What role should cultural values and population characteristics play in developing international marketing strategies?

8. Are distribution systems the same in all countries?

9. How is a market economy different from a centrally planned economy?

10. Are markets the same in developed and developing economies? Why or why not?

11. What are the ways in which a foreign country's markets can be entered?

12. What are the advantages and disadvantages of licensing compared with joint ventures as ways to enter foreign markets?

13. What are the advantages and disadvantages of exporting from the home country?

14. Compare using a wholly owned subsidiary with acquiring a foreign company as ways to enter foreign markets.

15. How does a global marketing strategy differ from an international marketing strategy?

16. Suppose your company wants to use a global marketing strategy. What are the factors that management should consider before deciding whether to use the global strategy?

BUILDING YOUR PORTFOLIO

Choose a country of interest to you, other than your home country. Using available information in library sources, analyze the country for market opportunities. Search for information on geographic location, geographic features, population size, population composition or makeup, population distribution over the land area, type of economy, GNP, GNP per capita, type of government, business characteristics, cultural and social characteristics, and any other factors you believe are important. What kinds of products and services do you think would sell well in the country? What kinds of products and services would not do well?

NOTES

1. Bill Saporito, "Black & Decker's gamble on 'globalization.'" *Fortune,* May 14, 1984, pp. 40–48.
2. David A. Heenan and Warren J. Keegan, "The rise of third world multinationals." *Harvard Business Review,* Jan.–Feb. 1979, pp. 101–102.
3. John W. Dizard, "Sears' humbled trading empire." *Fortune,* June 25, 1984, p. 74.
4. Bruce R. Scott, "National strategy for stronger U.S. competitiveness." *Harvard Business Review,* Mar.–Apr. 1984, p. 77
5. Henry Scott Stokes, "Honda: The market guzzler." *Fortune,* Feb. 20, 1984, p. 106.
6. Ibid.
7. "Ottawa throws a bone to foreign bankers." *Business Week,* Apr. 30, 1984, p. 54.
8. For an excellent discussion of national strategies, see Scott, op. cit., pp. 77–91.
9. Ibid.
10. David A. Ricks, *Big Business Blunders: Mistakes in Multinational Marketing.* Homewood, Ill.: Dow Jones-Irwin, 1983, p. 24.
11. Hans B. Thorelli, "First survey of China's 'middle-class consumers' finds 8% own refrigerators, but 75% own TVs." *Marketing News,* Feb. 18, 1983, p. 16.
12. Ricks, op. cit., p. 66.
13. Ibid., pp. 7–8.
14. The discussion of the Japanese distribution system is based on information in Mitsuaki Shimaguchi and William Lazer, "Japanese distribution channels: Invisible barriers to market entry." *MSU Business Topics,* Winter 1979, pp. 49–62.
15. "Global marketing success is contingent on a solid bank of foreign market intelligence." *Marketing News,* Dec. 23, 1983, p. 1.
16. The following discussion is based on information in F. J. Rummel and David A. Heenan, "How multinationals analyze political risk." *Harvard Business Review,* Jan.–Feb. 1978, pp. 67–76.
17. Heenan and Keegan, op. cit., p. 1.
18. For a more detailed discussion of classifying economies, see Philip R. Cateora, *International Marketing.* Homewood, Ill.: Irwin, 1983, pp. 315–320.
19. Ibid., p. 317.
20. Heenan and Keegan, op. cit., p. 102.
21. Cateora, op. cit., p. 324.
22. This idea is discussed in G. Peter Lauter and Paul M. Dickie, "Multinational corporations in Eastern European socialist economies." *Journal of Marketing,* Vol. 39 (Oct. 1975), pp. 40–46.
23. S. Tamer Cavusgil, "Exporters wrestle with market and distributor selection problems in penetrating new markets." *Marketing News,* Dec. 23, 1983, p. 10.
24. "Global marketing success is contingent on a solid bank of foreign market intelligence," op. cit.
25. David L. Snyder, "React quickly when Japanese enter your industrial market." *Marketing News,* June 25, 1982, p. 1.
26. Ibid.
27. Cavusgil, op. cit.
28. James M. Hulbert, William K. Brandt, and Raimar Richers, "Marketing planning in the multinational subsidiary: Practices and problems." *Journal of Marketing,* Vol. 44 (Summer 1980), p. 11.
29. "Are foreign partners good for U.S. companies?" *Business Week,* May 28, 1984, p. 58.
30. Ibid.
31. Myron Magnet, "What makes Saatchi & Saatchi grow." *Fortune,* Mar. 19, 1984, p. 46.
32. William H. Davidson and Richard Harrigan, "Key decisions in international marketing: Introducing new products abroad." *Columbia Journal of World Business,* Vol. 12 (Winter 1977), pp. 23–32.
33. Lee Smith, "Japan's two-fisted telephone maker." *Fortune,* June 24, 1984, p. 31.
34. Davidson and Harrigan, op. cit., pp. 28–29.
35. Ibid.
36. "Moet-Hennessy: The king of champagne uncorks a campaign to extend its U.S. realm." *Business Week,* June 25, 1984, pp. 146–147.
37. "Detroit takes the wheel at troubled Ford." *Business Week,* June 25, 1984, p. 45.
38. Hulbert, Brandt, and Richers, op cit., pp. 7–16.
39. An argument for global marketing strategies is made by Theodore Levitt, "The globalization of markets." *Harvard Business Review,* May–June 1983, pp. 92–102.
40. Saporito, op. cit., p. 40.

41. Ibid., p. 42.
42. "Global marketing success is contingent on a solid bank of foreign marketing intelligence," op. cit.
43. James Killough, "Improved payoffs from transnational advertising." *Harvard Business Review*, July–Aug. 1978, pp. 105–106.
44. This argument is made by Levitt, op. cit.

Case 24.1

Matsushita Electric

JAPANESE AIR CONDITIONER manufacturers have long been cool toward the U.S. market. They had no experience making the big central air conditioners and heavy window units that roomy American houses require, and successive recessions shrank U.S. demand. Now the market is growing again—up a torrid 25%, to $4.5 billion, in 1983—and the Japanese are blowing in. They're bringing American-style window units and a new product, a hybrid of room and central air conditioning that is popular in Japan.

Matsushita Electric, the Japanese giant (1983 sales: $16.6 billion), is leading the charge in window air conditioners under its Panasonic brand name. Last summer it marketed four models priced 20% higher than comparable ones made by Whirlpool and General Electric. Dealers praised Panasonic's quality and extraordinary quietness—Matsushita has an original design for air passages that reduces whooshing—but sold only a few thousand. "That was a test," says Panasonic marketing director

Maurice J. Guiheen. "Now we're beginning our entry."

Panasonic has 12 models this year, with prices in line with American brands. The company's marketing strategy calls for 1,000 appliance dealers who already sell Panasonic's fast-moving microwave ovens to pitch its air conditioners as representing better quality for the same price as American makes. If the Matsushita machines sell well, other Japanese producers are likely to follow. Sanyo already is test-marketing three inexpensive models on the East Coast.

Perhaps the boldest Japanese entrant is Daikin Industries, a $700-million-a-year Osaka company little known in the U.S. Daikin is eyeing the market for central air conditioning, but its beachhead product is a kind of heat pump called a multizone split system. In Daikin's system, as in a typical heat pump, a condensing unit sits outside the house on a concrete slab. But a conventional heat pump uses one central fan indoors, while Daikin has up to five compact, wall-mounted satellite boxes, one for each room. These boxes are tethered to the outside unit by copper tubing that carries coolant. Daikin's system costs as much as a heat pump to install. But Daikin says its systems are cheaper to op-

erate because satellites can be switched off in rooms not in use. Eleven major distributors mostly in Sunbelt states have already snapped up the product for sales to contractors.

The new imports are expected to account for no more than 2% of this year's U.S. sales, but Japanese cooling companies have already given American producers headaches. Three years ago Japan overtook the U.S. as world leader in room air conditioners, trouncing the Americans in the Middle and Far East. U.S. manufacturers insist that they'll be ready when competition heats up at home. "We compare ourselves to GM, Kodak, Xerox, and RCA before the Japanese came," says James F. Lyons, executive vice president at Carrier, a United Technologies subsidiary. "We're more automated, more productive, and better attuned to global strategy than they were." But a Harvard Business School study published in 1983 suggests there's reason to sweat. Comparing room air conditioners from seven Japanese and nine American companies, it found that the American cooling units required first-year service calls at a rate nearly 17 times that of the Japanese machines.

QUESTIONS

1. Would the marketing management function as needed for selling air conditioners in Japan be different than the marketing management function for sales in the United States? Why or why not?

2. What are the alternative ways that Matsushita can enter the U.S. market?

3. What would be the advantages and disadvantages of setting up a joint venture with a U.S. air conditioner manufacturer as a way of entering the U.S. market?

Case 24.2

Loewenbrau AG

IN ITS NATIVE LAND [Germany], Loewenbrau beer is a regional brew, confined mostly to Bavaria. Take the Loewenbrau name abroad, however, and beer

drinkers around the world would probably recognize it. Such are the vagaries of international marketing.

But Loewenbrau AG here knows something about the field of international brand marketing. Markets abroad have served the company well in the past and put it in a good position to continue succeeding in the future. That's to be expected, perhaps, for a company that is no

novice in expanding its business beyond its borders. Of the 4.7 million barrels of the brand sold worldwide, only 1.53 million barrels actually are brewed in Munich. The rest—3.17 million barrels—is produced by licencees the world over.

The company had sales of $82 million in the fiscal year ended September, 1983, according to a German analyst's report.

The biggest licensee is Miller Brewing

Co., Milwaukee, the Philip Morris Inc. unit that is a leading brewer in its own right. It's estimated that 10% of Loewenbrau sales come from licensees, of which 78% comes from Miller. A recent venture into Canada eventually may catch up to the size of the Miller stake in Loewenbrau. In early May, Loewenbrau signed a licensing agreement with Molson Breweries, Montreal, to brew a Loewenbrau-branded beer there, and observers expect it to run neck and neck with Millers's Loewenbrau some day. Other licensees are in Greece, Hong Kong, Japan, Panama, Sweden, Turkey and the U.K. Just recently, Loewenbrau added a tenth member to its family, Tenerife.

How large that family grows is a subject Johann Daniel Gerstein, marketing director of Loewenbrau AG, refuses to discuss. But it's safe to assume that negotiations are going on with more brewers. As one source said, "Some German competitors are eyeing Loewenbrau's profitable licensing business most enviously." Said another, "Not only the big German breweries, but the big European ones were asleep at the switch when licensing came along."

International marketing to Loewenbrau actually means two things. Along with the frothy licensing business, the company has been successful with exports, sending its product to 140 countries, the most important being Austria, Italy, Switzerland and the U.K. The long-standing export business, in fact, is one reason why Loewenbrau enjoys international prominence. The first bottles were sent beyond Bavarian borders about 1850, and the first barrels went to America before the century was out.

In Munich, company executives point with pride to the slogan, created in New York two decades ago, "If you run out of Loewenbrau, order champagne." Or as one source said, "Loewenbrau is simply identical with beer from Bavaria, and even in the remotest corner of the world people know that Bavaria is the beer country par excellence." Naturally, Loewenbrau does not taste the same everywhere. German beer drinkers who have tried the Miller version greatly prefer the Munich original.

"We aren't just sitting here waiting for the quarterly licensing fees to roll in," Mr. Gerstein said. "We have about 10 people in Munich working full-time on licensing;

most of them are usually somewhere on the road. The right to use the name Loewenbrau is tied up with a lot of stipulations, which we keep constant check on." The brewing process itself is one. Samples have to be sent to Munich every month for checking, and there is a constant exchange of technical staff between Munich and the licensees. The international marketing scheme requires bottles, logos, labels and other elements to be uniform all over the world, with a few trifling deviations. The lettering on Loewenbrau trucks also has to be the same everywhere.

Licensing agreements specify minimum ad expenditures, and Loewenbrau has a voice in the creative product. "It wouldn't do," Mr. Gerstein said, "for Loewenbrau to advertise anywhere in the world with naked women." The brand is not, however, uniformly positioned everywhere. In Germany, the slogan is "A beer like Bavaria." That message gets across in the U.K., but in Japan it doesn't. In other countries, therefore, the pitch is "Loewenbrau, a pure, international beer."

QUESTIONS

1. What does Loewenbrau gain from licensing as a way to enter foreign markets?

2. Should Loewenbrau rely so heavily on licensing? Why or why not?

3. Should Loewenbrau use a global strategy? Why or why not?

25 Marketing and Society

When you finish this chapter, you will understand

☐ How and why marketing management practices are being applied in several nontraditional areas such as professional services, medical care, religion, and politics

☐ Some major criticisms that have been charged against marketing and the key issues underlying each criticism

☐ That evaluation of marketing's performance in an organization, a society, and the world depends substantially on the criteria used and for whom the evaluation is intended

☐ Several actions that are under way to improve marketing's effectiveness and efficiency

☐ The nature and scope of challenges and opportunities for marketing that may occur in the next decade

The shift in the 1980s from an energy crisis to a worldwide oversupply of petroleum affected many markets, some favorably and others unfavorably.

Those who find the phrase "global marketing" replete with excitement and opportunity are advised to study Nestlé's experience in misapplying global marketing for its infant formula. In aggressively employing Western advertising, marketing, and sales promotion techniques, Nestlé became a third world market leader. Its tactics, however, aroused the criticism of numerous organizations and governments. A worldwide boycott of Nestlé was begun in 1977.

Nestlé used Western marketing techniques to sell its infant formula to third world mothers. Much of the water in third world countries is contaminated with bacteria, and because the formula had to be mixed with water, many infants became sick and died.

Nestlé has adopted the World Health Organization's infant formula marketing code, which recommends that direct advertising of infant formulas be prohibited and that consumers be informed that breast milk is normally the best food for infants. The boycott leaders suspended the boycott and planned to monitor Nestlé for six months before deciding whether to lift the boycott entirely. Thus a complex marketing impasse involving two issues of supreme importance—infant mortality and malnutrition—was resolved.

Regardless of the actions taken, the proper use of infant formula is important in the struggle against infant mortality in third world nations. Properly designed information programs are in the public interest. Nestlé's challenge is to devise educational and constructive marketing programs consistent with social conscience.[1]

NESTLÉ'S EXPERIENCE ILLUSTRATES how marketing practices can generate societal conflicts, particularly when human life is involved and potential problems in product misuse exist. Some critics have argued that Nestlé's experience with infant formula is a "classic case history of mismarketing a good product, then ignoring the ensuing problem, and finally, mismanaging the inevitable crisis."[2] Other observers are concerned that Nestlé's compliance with the World Health Organization's standards will result in third world mothers who are not able to produce enough milk not getting the information and education they need concerning use of the formula.[3]

Marketing infant formula is one of many issues and concerns about marketing and society. Often the issues have sound arguments supporting both sides. Our objective in this chapter is to explore some of the more important aspects of marketing from a societal perspective. First, the application of marketing beyond the traditional turf of business is examined. Next, criticism of marketing is considered, and evaluating marketing's performance in an organization, society, and the world is discussed. An analysis follows of several actions intended to overcome the criticisms. Finally, some important challenges and opportunities for marketing that are likely to occur in the future are identified and evaluated.

DOES MARKETING APPLY TO EVERYTHING?

If we consider marketing as a process of meeting peoples' needs and wants, then marketing extends far beyond its traditional role and scope in a business firm. Throughout the book several nonbusiness applications of marketing practice are examined. As one considers broadening the scope of marketing, several issues emerge. We first explore some examples of nontraditional marketing applications. Then the question of whether social and ethical limits should be placed on marketing is discussed.

Beyond marketing's traditional turf

Some of the areas in which the business sector's use of marketing has been questioned include professional services such as medicine, dentistry, law, architecture, and accounting; products that involve potential health hazards such as cigarettes and alcohol; and items such as Kung-Fu weaponry, stun guns, birth control products, and abortion services. Expanded applications in the nonbusiness sector include venereal disease treatment and special causes such as campaigns against drunk drivers and population control. Many of the historical barriers against marketing these products and services have been removed, although there is clearly resistance in some business sectors and by some people. A look at these areas will demonstrate some of the concerns that have been expressed about expanding marketing into such new areas.

Medicine. The issue of hospitals and doctors competing for patients has become a major controversy in the medical services industry. Some industry members believe that active competition should be encouraged, whereas others are fighting to preserve the professional nature of medical services in which patients seek doctors' services who in turn specify a hospital when needed. The general trend in medical services is toward more active competition for services.

> Albuquerque, N.M., gynecologist Steven Konadina advertises on his hot-air balloon, which is emblazoned with a stork. His car license plate reads "STORK." He and his medical group also employ a full-time teacher to give classes on such subjects as pregnancy, prenatal care and nutrition. Dr. Konadina is up against a hefty advertising campaign by Lovelace Medical Center, which markets itself in newspaper ads as "an alternative to bring life into the world in a joyous manner at a reasonable price."[4]

Much of the competition is due to overcapacity in the health care industry. There are too many hospital beds and facilities in several areas, and the number of physicians is expanding rapidly. The Department of Health and Human Services estimates that by the year 2000, more than 700,000 active physicians will be practicing in the United States compared with a national need of about 672,000.[5]

Law. Too many lawyers resulting in a battle for legal services has encouraged lawyers to adopt marketing methods. Some prominent persons, including a member of the U.S. Supreme Court, have gone on record against the advertising of legal services. A 1977 Supreme Court decision made it legal for lawyers to advertise, although prior to this decision more than a few perceptive attorneys skillfully used the news media to promote their services. Defending nationally recognized clients, for example, has often generated favorable publicity for attorneys. Today, marketing efforts of attorneys extend beyond public relations to include advertising, price competition, personal selling, and other promotional tools. Consider the following description of industry marketing efforts in a very competitive environment:

> Once anxious to avoid publicity, and required by law to seek assignments only through social contacts and professional reputation, lawyers are now embracing promotion to sell their services. And all their messages say the same thing: Hire us. "In its own way," says Robert B. Krueger, a Los Angeles attorney, "every firm of any size in the country is out there marketing like hell." After making an unsolicited presentation, Krueger himself recently won the business of a corporation that controls vast natural-resource reserves.[6]

In 1985 a Supreme Court decision expanded the right to advertise that was granted lawyers in 1977. Lawyers may now use pictures in advertisements to attract clients and may advertise by soliciting clients to sue specific companies.

CENSORSHIP IN A FREE SOCIETY. IT'S A BAD MATCH.

Censorship is the greatest tragedy in American literature. It constricts the mind, teaches fear and leaves only ignorance and ashes.
Today, all over the country, books are being banned, burned and censored. Teachers, students, librarians, and book and magazine publishers are being harassed.

The attacks of these self-appointed censors are endorsed by our silence.
The freedom to read is one of our most precious rights. Do something to protect it.
Contact:
People For The American Way, P.O. Box 19000 Washington, D.C. 20036 or call 202/822-9450

People For The American Way

A First Amendment citizens' organization, People for the American Way (which was founded by Norman Lear and has more than 150,000 members) concerns itself with promoting and protecting First Amendment freedoms. Along with censorship issues, the organization publicizes its concern over the improper mix of religion and politics as well as the independence of the federal judiciary. (Courtesy of People for the American Way, 1424 16th St., N.W., Suite #601, Washington, DC 20036)

Exhibit 25.1   Examples of unmentionables

Products	Personal hygiene articles
	Birth control products
	Some "defense" products, e.g., napalm, germ and chemical warfare
	Drugs for terminal illness
Services	Abortion
	Vasectomy and sterilization
	Venereal disease treatment
	Treatment for mental illness
	Material preparation for death (funeral arrangements, wills)
	Artificial insemination
Concepts	Extreme political ideas
	Emotional preparation for death
	Unconventional sexual activities
	Racial or religious prejudice
	Terrorism

SOURCE: Reprinted by permission of the *Harvard Business Review*. An exhibit from "The Marketing of Unmentionables" by Aubrey Wilson and Christopher West (January/February 1981). Copyright © 1981 by the President and Fellows of Harvard College; all rights reserved.

Unmentionables. The category of unmentionables includes "products, services, or concepts that for reasons of delicacy, decency, morality, or even fear tend to elicit reactions of distaste, disgust, offense, or outrage when mentioned or when openly presented."[7] Several examples are shown in Exhibit 25.1. Unmentionables include products and services such as pornography and prostitution that are generally rejected by society but sought by a minority of individuals, or items such as birth control and personal

This ad was written by a parent who has a child with cystic fibrosis. By marketing awareness of the dreaded disease, the ad's creator (who insists on remaining anonymous) hopes to inform people about the genetic disease from which more children have died than from the most common forms of childhood cancer. "If this helps bring attention to an illness that takes the lives of three children a day," he says, "then it will be worth it. If it helps raise funds for research, that would be even better." (Courtesy of Parents for Cystic Fibrosis Research)

hygiene products that are acceptable to society but typically not discussed by the buyer.

Many issues must be considered when deciding what unmentionables should be actively marketed. An interesting analysis of products and services that fall into different categories of acceptance by society and by the buyer is shown in Exhibit 25.2. Suggested marketing situations include products that are not marketable, **hypermarketing** (making special efforts to market a product or service), and **demarketing** (discouraging the purchase of products or services through marketing efforts). An example of demarketing was natural gas companies' discouraging energy use during the energy shortage of the late 1970s.

Are there social and ethical limits?

Exhibit 25.2 highlights three important issues regarding what should be marketed. First, the product, service, or concept should be considered from the point of view of the buyer, the seller, and society. Second, should consumption be encouraged or discouraged? Third, is marketing the product or service socially acceptable? There is no definitive answer to what should not be marketed. In general, the tendency appears to be toward marketing products and services that have historically not been actively marketed.

Some people are beginning to question the wisdom of marketing products and services that may exacerbate certain social problems. Project SMART is a coalition of allies—consumer activists, the National Congress of Parents and Teachers, the Seventh-Day Adventist and Methodist churches, and various other groups—that is bent on banning the advertising of beer and wine on radio and television. SMART, which stands for Stop Marketing Alcohol on Radio and Television, is well on its way to collecting a million signatures on petitions to remove beer and wine advertisements from the airwaves. Last year, SMART was instrumental in persuading Congress to withhold federal highway funds from states that do not raise their legal drinking age to twenty-one by late 1986.

Though distillers of hard liquor have not been allowed to broadcast their products on the air for some years, beer and wine companies spent more than $700 million to advertise over radio and television in 1984. Especially popular with the makers of Budweiser and other producers of beer and wine is the use of athletic scenes and celebrities in alcohol commercials.

> [Though] still-active sports figures can't be used in such ads under present rules, Project Smart has been pushing for a broader ban, arguing that beer and wine advertising built around sports glorifies drinking, particularly in the minds of impressionable young viewers.[8]

In some applications, however, marketing has contributed to solving important social problems. Consider, for example, third world population control. In Bangladesh, Population Services International (PSI) has used "social marketing" with a goal of population control. Robert L. Ciszewski describes PSI's marketing approach.

> "We set the price high enough that it will represent something significant in the mind of the consumer, yet low enough so that he can afford it, while allowing retailers an attractive margin.
>
> "A local marketing/advertising firm is used to introduce the product, and package design and a brand name are selected in the same way Procter & Gamble would do it.

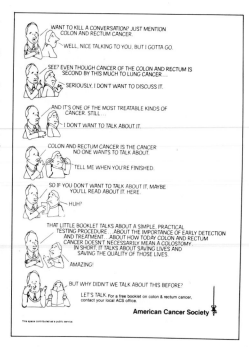

In 1985, when President Reagan had a cancerous polyp removed from his intestinal tract and when Rock Hudson was diagnosed as having AIDS, the news media didn't shrink from broadcasting the stories. Nor does the American Cancer Society, which, though it may offend some sensibilities, tries to bring to our attention a disease that few of us want to hear about. As this ad suggests, some forms of cancer are truly unmentionable. (Courtesy of American Cancer Society)

"In Bangladesh, for instance, card playing is popular among the poor, so we market our condoms under the name Raja, meaning king. The king of spades appears on each package."

Salespeople and supervisory staff are recruited from major multinational corporations, and the profit motive ensures the best results from them.

"Our key people around the world have been associated with Lever Brothers and other major corporations," he said. "They're paid well if they produce."

Marketing research paved the way for PSI's Bangladesh project.

"When we started we did a lot of marketing research, particularly to select a name that wasn't repugnant," he said.

"Interestingly enough, our marketing manager did not feel Raja was the right name for the product. Rather than take the research at face value, we did limited testing and let the consumer vote with his nickels."

The Raja name outsold the No. 1 pick for a brand name by two or three to one, a difference Ciszewski attributed to the universal recognition of a picture of a king on the package.

Research also favored a bright red color for the product.

Shopkeepers often string the condoms around their stores as a kind of homemade point-of-purchase display, Ciszewski said. PSI supplies other p-o-p materials, as well.

"A shopkeeper truly can't afford not to stock them," he said. "He only makes a fraction of a cent on each sale of a package of three, but he complains if he dosen't get service from salesmen."

Ad spending for Raja is concentrated in radio spots and ads shown between movies at movie theaters. An illiteracy rate of 85% precludes much print advertising, although outdoor ads in the form of product pictures on sailing vessels are used.

"We keep our ads very tasteful and free of sensationalism," Ciszewski said. "We use American style advertising—concrete and immediate—and we put

Exhibit 25.2 The unmentionable matrix: Situations and examples

SOURCE: Reprinted by permission of the *Harvard Business Review*. An exhibit from "The Marketing of Unmentionables" by Aubrey Wilson and Christopher West (January/February 1981). Copyright © 1981 by the President and Fellows of Harvard College; all rights reserved.

	BUYER		
SOCIETY	Accepts	Indifferent	Rejects
Accepts	Normal Marketing Toothpaste	Hypermarketing Venereal disease treatment	Hypermarketing Racial tolerance
Indifferent	Moderate Marketing (by suppliers) Demarketing (by public authorities) Tobacco	Strong Supplier Marketing Contraceptives	Hypersupplier Marketing Sanitary napkin disposal services
Rejects	Demarketing Hard drugs to hard-core socially condemned	Demarketing (moderate) Soft drugs to moderately socially condemned	Not Marketable Murder for hire

condom ads on the radio and no one ever thinks anything about it. There's nothing startling about it, except from the American perspective.

In contrast, governmental family planning relies on patriotic exhortations and does not appeal to the individual.

"We've got six mobile film units which travel around the country and show educational films on farming and other topics," he said. "Included in those presentations are some very strong messages about our products," which include birth control pills and spermicidal tablets.

"If that film unit is in town, everybody goes to see it, and it's really the only way you can talk to women" in a Muslim country.[9]

The PSI marketing program produced impressive results by inexpensively pricing a product previously distributed free by the government. Both PSI's and the government's condoms are supplied by the U.S. government. The key difference is that PSI has established a brand identity for its product.

CRITICISMS AIMED AT MARKETING

The conduct of marketing activities has been criticized. Charges have been made that marketing is wasteful, stimulates excessive demand, is deceptive and unethical, and is too powerful.

Wasteful?

Because of the large advertising budgets for some consumer products, marketing is often criticized as being wasteful. We are convinced that competitive pressures normally force prices down, and that firms with advertising budgets that are excessive will eventually bring them in line. Many people argue that if $15 million were not spent on advertising for a new shampoo, the price of the product could have been lowered. But will buyers become aware of a product and purchase it if they do not receive promotional information? Normally, competitive pressures demand efficient use of marketing resources. Competitive advertising may also help lower prices, as was the case when Datril entered the nonaspirin pain reliever market against Tylenol and MCI entered the long-distance telephone service market against AT&T.

In fairness to the critics, some marketing activities are wasteful. Firms may overspend on advertising and some new products do not generate enough revenues to cover their costs. The stakes are high when new products are launched. For example, RCA introduced its videodisk player in 1980, and lost nearly $300 million by 1983.[10] In early 1984, RCA announced that it would discontinue production of the product. Some waste owing to failures and poor allocation of resources is inevitable in a free enterprise system.

Stimulates excessive demand?

Critics have charged that the marketing efforts of firms cause people to buy more than they need. Consider this description of an advertisement.

The camera revolves slowly around a sculpture of a middle-aged woman's face, wrinkled and creased. Over soft music, a sympathetic voice asks: "How do you feel inside? Youthful, vibrant, up-to-date? But the aging face often leaves a different impression on others or affects the good feelings we have about ourselves."

This is one of Dr. Donald Levy's attention-getting ads. Effective though the ad is, probably few people hate their noses. But another ad reads: "Do you have wrinkles?"—a malady from which all of us eventually suffer. The question really is, though we may have wrinkles, do we want or feel a need for plastic surgery? (Courtesy of The Clinic of Cosmetic Plastic Surgery and McDonald Davis & Associates)

Then the scene shifts to a man in doctor's whites. "I'm Dr. Donald Levy," he says. "Your face is your billboard to friends, co-workers and loved ones." Next comes the tag line: the Clinic of Cosmetic Surgery, Milwaukee, Wis.[11]

The reason for this promotional effort is competition. By 1990 there will be 45 percent more plastic surgeons than are needed. Some, like Dr. Levy, are aggressively promoting face lifts, breast enlargements, body contouring, and hair transplants. Such efforts may stimulate demand. For example, Dr. Levy's $100,000 a year advertising campaign helped double referrals, increase operations by 58 percent, and increase the number of people on the waiting list for consultation to 110.[12]

The crux of the charge that marketing efforts stimulate unnecessary demand is whether people can make their own decisions about what to purchase. Our position on this issue is that marketing efforts simply are not powerful enough to make people buy what they do not want or need. Marketing may be able to push or nudge someone into buying a product or service, but only if the basic want is present. People are not going to subject themselves to plastic surgery unless a want is triggered by promotional efforts like those described. Clearly, some exceptions exist.

Deceptive and unethical?

Deception pertains to marketing activities that mislead or deceive the buyer. Unethical actions are those that vary from accepted standards of business conduct. Deceptive or unethical actions on the part of a business cause criticism by customers, industry observers, and competitors.

Deceptive actions. Deception in marketing often pertains to advertising and other promotion claims. Practices of marketers that are considered deceptive may also include pricing actions such as inflated "list" prices and packaging that is misleading (e.g., a large box half filled with cereal). Perhaps the most perplexing issue in this area is what constitutes deception. The **Federal Trade Commission (FTC)** is the government agency responsible for enforcing laws preventing deceptive marketing practices. The FTC policy statement on deception is based on three concepts. Deception exists if

> (1) There is a claim, act, or failure to give information that (2) is likely to create a wrong impression in the minds of reasonable consumers and (3) if the misimpression would concern a material feature of the product or service advertised.[13]

The policy statement was adopted in late 1983 by a 3 to 2 vote of the members of the FTC. The difficulty of determining what practices are deceptive is illustrated by the five commissioners' being unable to agree on a policy statement. The two dissenting commissioners were unable to accept totally the third concept. The new standard requires proof of consumer detriment (injury) before deception can be established.

Deception in advertising is clearly a major problem in industry, evidenced by FTC efforts to develop a policy statement and by the various cases brought to trial by the FTC each year.

Unethical practices. Unethical practices fall into a gray area regarding acceptability. There are few laws concerning unethical practices, and it is often difficult to determine whether a practice is acceptable or unacceptable. Nevertheless, proported unethical actions by individuals and firms have generated criticisms. Examples of situations that may be considered unethical include accepting gifts from suppliers by purchasing agents, not informing a consumer that a product being purchased has been discontinued, and informing a buyer that the ordering time for an item out of stock will be shorter than is actually the case. The line between ethical and unethical practices is often difficult to establish, and what one person considers an acceptable practice may be viewed as unethical by another. For example, some college coaches accept money from athletic shoe manufacturers for promotional assistance whereas other coaches do not believe that they should accept the money.[14]

Several examples of the range of marketing actions from acceptable to unacceptable are shown in Exhibit 25.3. The question mark after "Unethical actions" means that most of these practices are considered both acceptable and unacceptable by different people.

Too powerful?

The criticism is often made that large firms that control substantial portions of the market are too powerful. In the United States, government antitrust agencies police the market share position of industry leaders such as General Motors and U.S. Steel to prevent the development of monopolies. When monopolies are allowed, they are heavily regulated to protect consumers' interests and to control price increases.

Throughout the world there are examples of very powerful marketing organizations. Some markets are controlled by cartels such as the Organization of Petroleum Exporting Countries (OPEC) and De Beers in diamonds.

A recent public service campaign from the American Association of Advertising Agencies takes a lighthearted approach to the ad industry's image. These four ads created by Fallon McElligott Rice deal with some common misperceptions about advertising and note how advertising benefits consumers. (Courtesy of American Association of Advertising Agencies)

Exhibit 25.3   The range of marketing actions—from acceptable to unacceptable

Acceptable Actions	Unethical Actions?	Deceptive Actions	Unacceptable Actions
□ Patenting a new product	□ Paying fees to college coaches to promote athletic shoes	□ Promoting product performance features that cannot be delivered (e.g., instant weight loss, breast augmentation, and cure for baldness)	□ Payoffs of public officials
□ Increasing prices to cover costs of higher wages	□ Delaying the processing of an order placed by a competitive firm		□ Price fixing by competing firms
□ Terminating a contract with an independent agent	□ Subsidies by foreign governments, allowing their firms to sell at prices less than competition.	□ Door-to-door salespersons claiming to be conducting a market research study	□ Theft of product designs
□ Advertising a brand's advantages over competing brands			□ Divulging of trade secrets of ex-employer to a competitor by an employee
		□ Advertising items at discounts that are not in stock	

(Marketalk examines De Beers global operations and demonstrates the marketing power of this organization.) Although few firms possess the global power of De Beers, there is no question that selected industries do have power based on size, market control, or both. Surprisingly, De Beers is not subject to government regulation as a monopolist.

ISN'T IT FUNNY HOW STEREO ADS ARE BORING UNTIL YOU WANT A STEREO?

We admit it. There are times when advertising isn't especially interesting.

For instance, stereo ads when you're not looking for a new stereo. Or insurance ads when you're not looking for a new insurance company. Or detergent ads when you're not looking for a new detergent.

But suppose your stereo breaks down. Or your insurance rates go up. Or your laundry comes out gray. All of a sudden, stereo ads, insurance ads and detergent ads start looking a lot more interesting.

It's one of the basic truths of advertising. We try to be entertaining, but that's not really

our job. Our job is to help you make the right choices when you're in the market for any kind of product or service.

Of course, when you're not in the market, we recognize that advertising may seem beside the point. In that case, you're free to pretend it isn't there. In fact, you're free to ignore advertising for as long as you choose.

Right up until your stereo breaks down.

ADVERTISING.
ANOTHER WORD FOR FREEDOM OF CHOICE.
American Association of Advertising Agencies

WITHOUT ADVERTISING, EVEN THE BEST IDEAS TAKE AGES TO CATCH ON.

Every now and then, a new product becomes popular by word of mouth alone. But that process usually takes many months. Sometimes years. By then, the company that makes the new product may be in serious trouble — if they're around at all.

Advertising is the surest way to get an idea to the public. By advertising a new product or service, more

people are able to try it more quickly than if it were allowed to "catch on" by itself.

Good ideas become popular right away and bad ideas...well, who needs a square wheel anyway?

ADVERTISING.
ANOTHER WORD FOR FREEDOM OF CHOICE.
American Association of Advertising Agencies

*Marke*TALK ///

A gem of a global operation

DE BEERS CONSOLIDATED Mines controls the supply and wholesale distribution of at least 85 percent of the world's uncut diamonds and has maintained this market position for more than fifty years. Several events that occurred in the early 1980s, including Zaire's dropping De Beers as its marketing agent, threatened De Beers' monopoly position.

De Beers fought back in a globe-spanning campaign that involved smugglers

SOURCE: John R. Emshwiller and Neil Behrmann, "Restored luster: How De Beers revived world cartel after Zaire's pullout," *Wall Street Journal,* July 7, 1983, pp. 1, 14. Reprinted by permission of the *Wall Street Journal,* © Dow Jones & Company, Inc. 1983. All rights reserved.

and heads of state, diplomacy and threats, and a diamond hoard worth over $1 billion. It appears to have paid off. Late last year, Australia signed with the De Beers cartel. In March, Zaire returned to the fold. And in the past few months, the diamond business has regained some of its former luster.

De Beers marketing strategy over the years has been to regulate the supply of diamonds and to gradually increase prices so diamonds will continue to appreciate. From 1973 to 1983 the prices of uncut diamonds increased 160 percent, compared with 1000 percent for OPEC. Most observers rate the actions of De Beers as acceptable, although its actions in the marketplace illustrate the incredible power wielded by the firm.

De Beers obtains uncut diamonds either from its own mines or other mines that sell through the cartel. It offers the diamonds to the dealers it invites to periodic gatherings known as "sights." Each dealer is offered a box containing various uncut diamonds. De Beers determines which diamonds go into which box, and assigns a single price to each box.

A dealer generally must accept or reject the box he is shown; De Beers rarely negotiates. Those who don't buy risk not being invited back. This arrangement allows De Beers to parcel out diamonds in such a way as to maintain price stability.

Thus this powerful firm clearly dictates how business will be conducted in the diamond industry.

///

Entire industries are judged by some observers to have too much power over political processes. The most frequently cited industries are large oligopolistic industries dominated by a few firms such as the oil and steel industries.

EVALUATING MARKETING'S PERFORMANCE

Marketing's performance can be considered from organizational and societal perspectives. We examine both points of view, indicating how marketing performance can be evaluated at each level.

Evaluating marketing's organizational performance

Our previous discussion of several criticisms of marketing practices indicates some of the concerns people have about the marketing practices of organizations. When problems become apparent, faulty performance of a marketing function usually can be identified. A basic issue is to establish the criteria for evaluating marketing's performance in an organization.

The logical way to measure marketing performance is in terms of customer satisfaction. As is discussed in Chapter 1, the philosophy of the marketing concept is to achieve customer satisfaction and at the same time meet the objectives of the organization. *How* to measure customer satisfaction is difficult to determine. Extreme cases of customer dissatisfaction are usually apparent by the product's failure in the marketplace and, in some instances, the organization's failure. A more difficult task is measuring how well a typical organization is satisfying its customers.

Financial performance. One way to evaluate a business organization's success in satisfying its customers is to look at the firm's financial performance. The argument is that if the firm is profitable then it must be delivering customer satisfaction. While profit performance may be a useful general measure of marketing performance, it has three important limitations.

1. When profits decline or losses occur, it may be too late to take corrective action.
2. A poor profit performance may not be the consequence of the firm's failure to provide customer satisfaction. For example, management may have spent too much money on other business activities.
3. In the case of a not-for-profit organization such as the American Cancer Society, financial performance is not a very useful measure of the extent of satisfaction provided by the organization to its clientele.

Marketing research. Many companies conduct marketing research surveys on a regular basis to measure customer satisfaction. For example, Procter & Gamble obtains feedback from customers regularly by printing toll-free numbers on the package or label of its products. Procter & Gamble also conducts extensive marketing research to measure customer satisfaction with its products and to obtain customers' suggestions for product improvement and other marketing actions.[15] These monitoring techniques can be used by nonbusiness organizations such as churches, social organizations, and special interest groups.

Evaluating marketing's social performance

Many of the issues that involve the social performance of marketing are concerned with **social responsibility,** the extent to which marketing actions are consistent with the needs and priorities of the society. Lazer and Culley comment that marketing extends beyond a managerial focus to include social dimensions as well.

> The societal aspects of marketing will complement the managerial aspects as social dimensions are factored into marketing decisions. Products, costs, and profits will be seen in terms of their social costs and benefits. Marketing executives will be challenged to achieve an appropriate balance between organizational goals and society's goals and between private marketing concerns and public marketing involvement.
>
> New standards will be developed to appraise the social effects of marketing decisions in such areas as new-product development, pricing, and advertising. Profit goals will continue to lose force as a guiding principle, and social marketing audits will be conducted regularly as marketing leaders accept their new social roles.[16]

Clearly, measuring consumer satisfaction is more difficult at the societal level than at the organizational level. Moreover, what is considered social responsibility in one country or for a particular group of people may be unacceptable in another nation or group. For example, Sweden and Albania are the only two countries in Europe that do not allow any form of broadcast advertising.[17] The Swedes frown on drinking, and advertisements for hard liquor are forbidden by the same government that distills and sells Vodka nationwide. In contrast, nudity and sexual permissiveness in advertisements are common.

Social responsibility and marketing actions. One of the more impressive recent actions of social responsibility by a company was Johnson & Johnson's response to the 1982 deaths from Tylenol capsules contaminated with cyanide.[18] The firm responded with an immediate and massive effort to remove all Tylenol capsules from retail stores and throughout the product's distribution channels. This was followed by a crash program by package design-

Exhibit 25.4 The marketing mix and social responsibility

Component of Marketing Mix	Related Social Issues
Product and service	Unclear warranties and guarantees Misleading packaging Poor quality Poor service Environmental pollution Waste of resources Injuries to health Product obsolescence Costly repairs High maintenance costs
Pricing	Monopoly profits Price maintenance Misleading pricing tactics Phony list prices Phony sales Price discrimination Price rigidity and inflation No price competition
Distribution	Maldistribution (gasoline and other supplies) High middlemen margins Profiteering Inefficient distribution Price fixing After-sale service Handling of consumers' complaints Credit practices
Communication	False and misleading claims Manipulative advertising Advertising aimed at children Misrepresentation High-pressure sales tactics Credit sales Omission of information Brand monopolies Phony sales deals Banning of advertising by professional associations

SOURCE: William Lazer and James D. Culley, *Marketing Management: Foundations and Practices*, Boston: Houghton Mifflin, 1983, p. 71. Copyright © 1983 by Houghton Mifflin Company. Used by permission.

ers to develop a tamper-resistant container. Finally, a huge (and expensive) marketing communications program was planned to help restore the trust of doctors and buyers in Tylenol. Although Johnson & Johnson was not responsible for the contamination of its products, the firm assumed full responsibility and immediately worked toward eliminating the problem.

Several examples of social issues that may be related to marketing management actions in business are shown in Exhibit 25.4. As is apparent from the illustrations, there are many ways that the marketing actions of organizations may conflict with social issues. Often the conflicts do not involve unethical, deceptive, or illegal actions by marketers. Instead, the conflicts may be due to communications gaps and lack of information about the social consequences of marketing actions. For example, the risks of certain fertilizers, DDT insecticides, and Rely tampons were not apparent even after the extensive testing that was conducted before the products were introduced. (See Marketech for an interesting discussion of a new type of advertising that some people may consider too powerful.)

Measuring social performance. Spotting obvious problems generated by the marketing actions of firms is not difficult, once the consequences are apparent. A more basic issue is determining how well an organization is contributing to the needs of society. The *social audit* has been proposed to evaluate corporate social performance. Although the social audit is not widely used,

Marke**TECH** □ □ □ □ □ □ □ □ □ □ □ □ □ □ □ □ □ □ □

Ads against wall in video background

IMAGINE A CLUB pulsating with 1,000 demographically luscious bodies—all 18 to 34, good earners, high consumers, all frustratingly hard-to-get at home, at least through tv.

They can be yours! That is, if all goes according to plan at Entertel Inc., a video production and distribution company run by 32-year-old Stuart Young in New York.

Mr. Young, a fast-talking, clean-cut fellow who looks like the ventriloquist he was in junior high, creates "ambient video," otherwise known as "video wallpaper"—the visual equivalent of Muzak. His silent, hourlong montages of old movies, video art and laser shows serve as backdrop to a club's music.

Depending on the age and club clientele—gay, straight, teenybopper, suburbanite—Mr. Young can offer an appropriate tape mix, from "Hodge Podge Montage" to "Cartoon Classics," "Symphony of Slapstick," "Fabulous Females" and "Beefsteak Brigade." The long-playing tapes have one thing in common: Versatility.

Unlike music videos, short clips created by a particular rock group for a particular song, Mr. Young's videos are generic. They look right with any music, from rock to reggae to rap. "Your brain coordinates your eye and your ear," says Mr. Young. "That's the secret." In other words, when Fred Astaire is dancing on the screen and Kiss is shrieking from the speakers, they'll look coordinated.

What does all this mean for advertisers? Plenty, insists Mr. Young. Until now, the entrepreneur has been selling his tapes for $200 an hour to about 400 discos across the country, most of them outside of New York. However, at least 1,500 clubs are what Mr. Young considers to be video-capable, and he is soliciting them. "If I told

1,500 people that I could give them one of my tapes for free, I'd mail out 1,200 to 1,500 next week." And the way to make them free is to get them to carry . . . advertising.

"The advertising industry, whether it likes it or not, will have to come to grips with a whole new way of advertising," Mr. Young believes. For an ad to work on a silent "fun" video it must blend in with the rest of the fare and convey its message without words—even without a story. And, confesses Mr. Young, "It's bordering on subliminal advertising."

For example, a jeans company recently approached him to find out if they could slip a commercial into his hourlong color montage of "Fabulous Females." "Fabulous Females," a video he commissioned for Entertel, shows lithe lady torsos wriggling in bathing suits, shorts and skirts (when you shoot torsos without showing heads "you don't need release forms"). Mr. Young decided he definitely could splice in a minute's worth of jeans advertising—although he has not done so yet—providing the spots are provocative and not blatantly commercial. Furthermore, when he does, he will weave them in as four 15-second cuts to keep the show moving. "People in clubs don't want to see ads," he explains. "But girls dancing on a beach for 15 seconds . . ." who just happen to be sporting, say, Calvins? Who could object to that?

Meanwhile, adds Mr. Young, bartenders using his videos in their lounges have suggested inserting some liquor ads into his film. Mr. Young finds this idea eminently appealing, murmuring, "Budweiser could just show their Clydesdales . . ." With no Federal Communications Commission guidelines to block him, he figures the hard-liquor industry, too, might one day enjoy his videos.

But bar and club venues represent only the first battleground of the coming revolution. In Mr. Young's mind, video soon may become as all-pervasive as outdoor advertising—only indoors. Bank lines,

cruise ships, department stores, international flights, restaurants, beauty salons—wherever there's a captive audience, there's a video opportunity, he believes.

Thus the man who claims, "The most important thing is to be productive" has begun creating "seamless wallpaper" and "video postcards" for these incubating markets. Seamless wallpaper is a series of video clips that flows from one to the next with no beginning and no end. These can be abstract images created by lasers or computers, or more movie snippets expertly spliced. Video postcards are longer clips: Four minutes of a sunset, perhaps, followed by four minutes of waves crashing on California shores. These postcards someday may take the place of aquariums in doctor's waiting rooms and already have replaced the convention of paintings on the walls of some trendy restaurants, says Mr. Young.

In the forefront of these experiments is the California-based Black Angus restaurant chain, which has installed large-screen videos in all 100 of its outlets, according to Tom Koranda, entertainment manager. The chain now produces its own videos, buying only raw footage from Entertel.

Mr. Young recites the demographics: 14 million people a year, average age, 26. "If I asked an advertiser, 'How would you like to reach them, ridiculously cheap?' what do you think they'd respond?"

Mr. Young's videos also are cropping up in the lobbies of some Holiday Inns, Ramada Inns and Marriotts. Like the disco-goer and Black Angus diner, the traveling businessman is another tough guy to reach. Videos in public places will hit these moving targets.

Ten years ago patrons would not have tolerated electronic advertising in taxis as they do today, or inflight ads or commercials on baseball and football scoreboards, Mr. Young said. But today's consumer has come to understand that if you can catch him, he's fair game. And catching him, he believes, is the videogame of the future.

SOURCE: Lenore Skenazy, "Ads against wall in video background," *Advertising Age,* Feb. 28, 1985, p. 6. Reprinted with permission from the Feb. 28, 1985, issue of *Advertising Age.* Copyright 1985 by Crain Communications, Inc.

□ □

some firms are reporting social responsibility actions in their annual reports. McDonald's, the fast-food restaurant, is recognized as a leader in
practicing social responsibility. The scope of marketing's social actions is
described.

> Social marketing is more than just the marketing of social programs and ideas.
> It also is the use of marketing assets in a way that makes social sense, making
> marketing decisions on the basis of social as well as economic criteria. Social
> marketing stresses the interface between marketing management and such
> goals as improving community relations, developing human and natural re-
> sources to the fullest, protecting consumers, advancing health, and preserving
> the environment. In broad terms, the goal of social marketing is to improve
> the quality of life.[19]

Using this perspective marketing's challenge is to move beyond a response to specific problems and instead play a lead role in helping improve
the quality of life in society. Our final task in the chapter is to examine how
marketing's performance can be improved.

Marketing's Social Challenge

Responsibility for improving marketing's contributions to society extends
beyond business firms. Improving the societal effectiveness and efficiency of
marketing practices is also the responsibility of industry, special interest
groups, consumers, and government.

Business and nonbusiness organizations

Organizations can contribute to marketing's social challenge in three
important ways. First, improving business performance by eliminating inef-
ficient practices should continue to receive a high priority by business executives. Second, ethical marketing practices should be demanded from all
employees. Third, management should include social responsibility as an
organizational objective.

Improving organizational performance. There is ample evidence of faulty
marketing decisions that have been costly. Improving marketing decisions
will benefit both business firms and customers. Products such as RCA's
videodisk player, Texas Instrument's home computer, and Polaroid's instant movie system are examples of major product failures. Unfortunately,
major disasters divert attention from many small decisions that prove
faulty. For example, aggressive lending practices of financial institutions
may lead to extending loans to poor credit risks. In severe cases such
practices may cause bankruptcy.

Failing to evaluate market opportunity is frequently a reason for marketing failures. Firms too often assume that they know what buyers want
instead of analyzing market needs in advance of developing new products.
Faulty execution of business plans is also a major cause of poor performance in the marketplace. Improving management skills and practices is a
major challenge facing marketers in the decade ahead.

Following marketing ethics. Several examples of ethical issues have already
been cited. Employees of businesses that are in contact with buyers encounter situations that may involve choices based on ethical considerations.

Exhibit 25.5 The American Marketing Association code of ethics

As a member of the American Marketing Association, I recognize the significance of my professional conduct and my responsibilities to society and to the other members of my profession:

1. By acknowledging my accountability to society as a whole as well as to the organization for which I work.

2. By pledging my efforts to assure that all presentations of goods, services and concepts be made honestly and clearly.

3. By striving to improve marketing knowledge and practice in order to better serve society.

4. By supporting free consumer choice in circumstances that are legal and are consistent with generally accepted community standards.

5. By pledging to use the highest professional standards in my work and in my competitive activity.

6. By acknowledging the right of the American Marketing Association, through established procedure, to withdraw my membership If I am found to be in violation of ethical standards of professional conduct.

SOURCE: Courtesy of the American Marketing Association, Chicago, Ill.

Offering gifts to industrial buyers is prohibited by many companies. The ethical aspects of such decisions are not always apparent to the employees. Some firms prepare guidelines for business conduct to emphasize the importance of ethics in business practices. Some industry and professional organizations have developed codes of ethics. For example, the American Marketing Association's ethical conduct guidelines for its members and their professional responsibilities are shown in Exhibit 25.5.

Practicing social responsibility. A growing number of firms such as Alcoa, McDonald's, and PepsiCo are assuming active roles regarding social responsibility. (See Marketalk about PepsiCo's corporate citizenship policies.) Practicing social responsibility is a voluntary action in many instances. The managements of corporations could choose not to participate in helping solve social problems.

Because you will probably work for a company someday, you should recognize some of the hazards that may be encountered when changing jobs. Consider the experience of a former McDonald's expert in market research.

> He quit to join a competitor a few years ago, taking with him a large batch of papers. McDonald's soon served up a lawsuit, alleging he walked away with company secrets.
> Before launching the lawsuit, within a few days of his leaving, McDonald's sent a letter to McEx warning him not to divulge any "confidential information" regarding a number of activities. Among them were marketing, advertising, training methods, profit margins, raw materials prices, selling prices and operations procedures.[20]

The information that a person has about company operations may place him or her in a difficult position when changing jobs. Some firms use contracts to require employees to promise not to divulge secrets when leaving the firm.[21] The contract may even prohibit your accepting employment with a competitor. Typically, high technology industries such as computers, pharmaceuticals, toys, defense equipment, and electronics are likely to use employee secrecy agreements.

*Marke*TALK //
Corporate responsibility

IN ORDER TO FULFILL the primary responsibility of maximizing the return over time for its shareholders, PepsiCo believes in preserving and enhancing the environment in which its divisions operate.

In recent years PepsiCo has carefully defined principal areas of corporate involvement. This, plus the substantial increase in the PepsiCo Foundation's gifts and grants, has allowed the corporation to make a growing impact in the areas of health and human services, education and the arts.

In the area of preventive medicine, PepsiCo has established with the Boys Club of America the SuperFit All-Stars program, a health-related fitness education effort for youth.

PepsiCo Fellows at Duke University Medical Center, Harvard Medical School, Mayo Clinic and Stanford University School of Medicine are now conducting

SOURCE: *1983 PepsiCo Annual Report.* Courtesy, PepsiCo, Inc.

research into the relationship between exercise and fitness.

PepsiCo's support of education includes scholarships, and a 10-year commitment totaling $1 million to the United Negro College Fund. PepsiCo provides financial and program sponsorship for the Leadership, Education and Development (LEAD) program at Columbia Unversity, an effort to widen the pool of future minority business leaders.

Programs at a variety of undergraduate and graduate schools and on the high school level are designed to improve the quality and availability of educational opportunities. PepsiCo provides research and professorship support in the areas of marketing, food service, economics and international management. A commitment to Columbia University's Center for Research in Career Development has led to important studies on such subjects as human resource functions and male and female career patterns.

PepsiCo's continued interest in the arts is best represented by support of PepsiCo

Summerfare, one of the leading performing arts festivals in the United States, produced by the State University of New York at Purchase.

The PepsiCo Foundation works with PepsiCo's operating companies to actively develop national and regional programs. Beyond this the Foundation matches employee gifts to educational and arts institutions. This year an Awards to Volunteers program was launched to recognize and support employee volunteer activities and to provide funds to additional nonprofit organizations.

PepsiCo's divisions also work independently to provide support for social agencies, projects and programs. For example, since 1975 Pepsi-Cola USA has sponsored "Tony Brown's Journal," the country's leading television program on black affairs. Frito-Lay's involvement with the Adopt-A-School program in Dallas has been nationally recognized.

These and many other programs are helping to demonstrate PepsiCo's corporate citizenship.

///

Industry

Certain industries have initiated actions to encourage socially responsible behavior by industry members. In some industries, review boards have been established to monitor the business practices of firms within the industry. Let us look closer at industry efforts regarding social responsibility and self-regulation.

Social responsibility. The alcoholic beverage industry faces a dilemma: The per capita consumption of most alcoholic beverages has either declined or leveled off during the past few years. Amid a weak market for its products, the industry is being assaulted by special interest groups seeking to control and reduce consumption of alcoholic beverages. The rapid development of these powerful groups is impressive.

> Mothers Against Drunk Drivers [MADD], founded less than four years ago, now has 266 chapters in 44 states. Students Against Driving Drunk, organized in late 1981, counts between 5,000 and 6,000 high-school chapters. Their efforts are being aided by the largest public-awareness campaign ever conducted by the insurance industry, which provides form letters, speeches and television spots to citizens pushing for reform in their hometowns.
> The campaign helped bring about tougher drunk-driving laws in 40 states last year, and judges are meting out harsher sentences. Since January 1983, 11 states have raised their minimum legal drinking age.[22]

Note the involvement of the insurance industry with the social problem. Its actions are aimed at discouraging excessive consumption of alcohol.

Not only is there MADD, there is BADD. Bartenders Against Drunk Drivers has been broadcasting its concern about drinking and driving since 1984. (Courtesy of Mothers Against Drunk Drivers)

ONE FOR THE ROAD "KILLED" IS ONE TOO MANY.

Jodi Ann Southard
Age 8
Killed by a drunk driver with 3 previous DWI offenses

MADD
Mothers Against Drunk Drivers

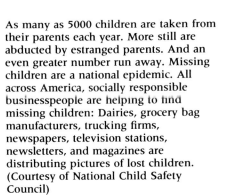

As many as 5000 children are taken from their parents each year. More still are abducted by estranged parents. And an even greater number run away. Missing children are a national epidemic. All across America, socially responsible businesspeople are helping to find missing children: Dairies, grocery bag manufacturers, trucking firms, newspapers, television stations, newsletters, and magazines are distributing pictures of lost children. (Courtesy of National Child Safety Council)

Though Joseph E. Seagram & Sons has long shown a certain social responsibility by placing ads like this, the company today is being traumatized by an American shift in drinking habits. What's more, with increasing public sentiment against drunk driving and "happy hours," further declines in brown liquors—Seagram's traditional strength—seem destined. (Courtesy of The House of Seagram)

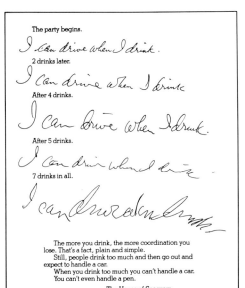

The consumption of alcoholic beverages is part of a serious social problem that, if curtailed, will reduce industry market opportunity. How do you think the industry should respond? Clearly, prohibition is not the answer. People will find a way to obtain alcoholic beverages if their sale is prohibited. The industry has responded with modest financial support for combating drunk driving.

The Wine Institute, a trade group, has held wine tastings to benefit Mothers Against Drunk Drivers. Miller Brewing Co. has given about $1 million in the last few years to such groups. In 1983, Anheuser-Busch increased its donations to Students Against Driving Drunk to $178,000 from $10,000 the year before.[23]

Some industry members are promoting moderation in drinking in their advertising.

Self-regulation. A few industries have established groups for monitoring industry practices. For example, the advertising industry monitors the advertising practices of its members. The **National Advertising Review Board (NARB),** established in 1971, performs a self-regulatory function for the industry regarding deceptive or misleading national advertising. The NARB refers offenders to the appropriate government agency if corrective action is not taken immediately by the advertiser. Several hundred cases are processed by the NARB each year, many initiated by unhappy competitors.[24]

Consumers

The consumerism movement that developed in the late 1960s was perhaps an inevitable response to the increasingly complex and impersonal society of our times.[25] Consumers also have a responsibility for informing themselves about important social issues and for conducting their affairs in a socially responsible manner.

Consumerism is a social force designed to aid and protect the consumer by exerting legal, moral, and economic pressures on business.[26] Individuals, politicians, and special interest groups engage in various consumerism-related actions. Examples include Ralph Nader, citizen groups such as environmentalists, and elected officials that champion specific consumer issues. The organization of consumers to bring pressures on business firms and government has proved to be an effective means of attacking social problems. Some results have been positive while other actions have probably created more problems than have been solved. Consider this analysis:

> The need is clear for improved communication and information feedback among all parties involved in the consumerism movement. Debate has been based far too often on superficial response and emotion rather than on an objective assessment resulting from carefully formulated and executed research. Fragmented actions on the part of consumer interest groups without the benefit of information concerning their effects could result in overcontrol and a hampering of the important forces and influences that comprise our socioeconomic system. At the same time, however, all groups should be aware of the potential value of achieving certain consumerism goals. The trade-offs must be weighed carefully for each specific issue and action taken which will tend to benefit both business and consumers over the long run.[27]

Informed consumers. Our complex and rapidly changing society requires that everyone become better informed about the use and misuse of products. For example, few of us really understand the issues associated with atomic power. Not surprisingly, much of the negative reaction to the use of atomic energy is emotional rather than objective. Nevertheless, the resistance is real and presents a major obstacle to utilities that plan on expanding nuclear power facilities. A 1983 public opinion poll commissioned by *Business Week* and conducted by Louis Harris & Associates, using a sample of 1200 Americans, obtained these findings:

- Fifty-one percent oppose building nuclear power plants.
- Fifty-four percent believe that nuclear-generating plants are dangerous.
- Seventy-four percent think that disposal of radioactive wastes is a major problem.
- Seventy-five percent are concerned about the escape of radioactivity into the atmosphere.[28]

The potential of the personal computer and the use of available data banks offer a major opportunity for consumer education. Far too often, lack of information about a social issue may lead to overreaction by uninformed individuals.

Socially responsible consumers. People must act in a socially responsible manner if social problems are to be eliminated. Actions by business, government, and other organizations are not sufficient to overcome social problems. The previously cited *Business Week* survey found that 36 percent of the respondents will use less energy if the price of energy goes down by 10 to 20 percent in the next few years.[29] Approximately one-third indicated greater use of energy if prices declined. Thus, a sizable portion of the sample responded in a socially responsible manner (assuming energy conservation is socially desirable). Interestingly, almost as large a group planned *greater* usage of energy if prices declined.

Government

Government has at least five responsibilities regarding the social challenge of marketing: (1) eliminating waste, (2) implementing needed legislation, (3) deregulating when appropriate, (4) participating in market development, and (5) deciding whether to respond to the pressures of special interest groups.

Eliminating its own waste. The U.S. Mint produced approximately 780 million Susan B. Anthony dollars with perhaps one-third initially circulated.[30] By 1980 the failure of the new coin was apparent. Today the coin is rarely seen; most are stored in Federal Reserve vaults or at the mint. You need only to glance at the coin to understand why it was a failure: It looks and feels much like a quarter. People did not want the coin because of possible confusion. Businesses likewise avoided using the coin. The experience stresses the responsibility of government to eliminate waste. The total cost of this product failure was absorbed by taxpayers.

Regulating. Government regulates business by enacting antitrust laws and consumer legislation. Both contribute to consumer welfare in various ways. Legislation that regulates marketing management decisions is discussed in other chapters. Areas regulated include price fixing, price discrimination, patents and trademarks, product labeling, product safety, relationships among distribution channel participants, and deceptive promotional practices. Government legislation and regulatory activities are important mechanisms for eliminating some of the criticisms aimed at marketers. Legislation, however, should be the exception rather than the rule. Problems should be allowed to work themselves out in the competitive marketplace. Government should participate when too much market power is held by one or a few firms and when marketing practices occur that are not in the best interests of society.

Deregulating. Government has a responsibility to deregulate industry when it would be beneficial to society. By 1985 major deregulation benefits were being gained from the series of activities shown in Exhibit 25.6. Deregulation of financial, telecommunications, and transportation industries appears to have been beneficial by lowering prices, revitalizing industry, and stimulating innovation.

> Long-distance airline fares, adjusted for inflation, have declined by almost 50% in the past seven years. Many trucking rates have skidded down 30% in real terms since 1980. The costs of standard telephones in 1983 have fallen by one-third, compared with last year. And today, the cost of buying stock for small investors using discount brokers is 60% below the commissions charged by old-line houses.[31]

The consequences of deregulation have not been favorable for all the parties involved. Some people have lost their jobs. Some companies have gone bankrupt, and consumers cannot obtain all the services that were previously available. Acknowledging these problems, the benefits of deregulation appear to be greater than the social losses incurred.

Adoption of some free enterprise practices in China offers an interesting illustration of the benefits of deregulation. In 1979 in the Sichuan Province, China, the Steel Goat People's Commune installed a responsibility system involving quotas, contracts, incentives and rewards, profit shar-

Exhibit 25.6   Major steps toward deregulation

1968 The Supreme Court's Carterfone decision permits non-AT&T equipment to be connected to the AT&T system.	**1978** Congress deregulates the airlines.
1969 The FCC gives MCI the right to hook its long-distance network into local phone systems.	**1979** The Federal Communications Commission allows AT&T to sell nonregulated services, such as data processing.
1970 The Federal Reserve Board frees interest rates on bank deposits over $100,000 with maturities of less than six months.	**1980** The Federal Reserve Board allows banks to pay interest on checking accounts.
	1980 Congress deregulates trucking and railroads.
1974 The Justice Department files antitrust suit against AT&T.	**1981** Sears, Roebuck becomes the first one-stop financial supermarket, offering insurance, banking, brokerage services.
1975 The Securities and Exchange Commission orders brokers to cease fixing commissions on stock sales.	**1982** Congress deregulates intercity bus services.
1977 Merrill Lynch offers the Cash Management Account, competing more closely with commercial banks.	**1984** AT&T divested itself of its local phone companies.

ing, and even some private enterprise and free trade.[32] Consider this profile of one commune family.

> On the Good Virtue commune, Mr. Huang, his wife and their two children each are allotted 1/100 of an acre, and after converting a corner of their house into a sty they're also raising six pigs. The pork, the garlic shoots, the lettuce, the chives will find their way to the free market—a capitalist crime a few years ago. "The policy now is to let the peasants become rich," says Mr. Huang, and on the modest scale of a poor country, that is what is happening in parts of China.[33]

Participating in market development. Governments in some countries around the world play an active role in market development by encouraging joint ventures of competing firms to develop new technologies, offering incentives to new ventures, and other actions to stimulate economic growth. Japan has been particularly active in this area. Antitrust legislation in the United States severely limits the opportunity for cooperative efforts between competing firms. U.S. efforts to stimulate market development have typically been centered on providing tax incentives.

Restraints on cooperative research were reduced in the United States in 1983. Cooperative research and development gained some momentum with the consortium of twelve companies founding Microelectronics and Computer Technology Corporation (MCC), headed by former CIA associate director Admiral Bobby Inman. MCC conducts research on computers. While it will be several years before the success of this venture can be evaluated, its potential is encouraging.

Applying pressure on goverments. Special interest groups sometimes attempt to influence governments about important social issues. Possibly more than a billion people throughout the world in 1985 watched sixty of the most prominent rock acts via live satellite as a part of Live Aid, a program intended to keep the African famine issue in the public eye.[34] The Live Aid telethons raised over $50 million to help feed starving Africans. Another group, USA (United Support of Artists) for Africa, initiated the "We Are the World" project, including a record made by popular recording stars. The two groups were exploring how to cooperate in keeping the famine issue alive. Leaders of the two groups believed that their political pressure influenced President Reagan to increase the U.S. goverment's aid in 1985 to $800 million for famine relief.[35]

SUMMARY

The scope of marketing is clearly expanding to encompass several new areas including professional services, social causes, government, politicians, and unmentionables. Products and services fall into categories of acceptance by society and the buyer. Recommended marketing approaches range from normal marketing to not marketable. These decisions depend on the point of view of the buyer, the seller, and society; whether consumption of the product or service should be encouraged or discouraged; and whether marketing the item is socially acceptable.

Marketing has received several criticisms. Some of the more frequently encountered charges are that marketing is wasteful, that it stimulates excessive demand, and that it is deceptive, unethical, and too powerful. These charges are justified in some situations; for example, firms may overspend on advertising, deceptive and unethical practices do exist, and certain oligopolistic industries are judged by some observers to have much power over the political process. Each situation must be evaluated in terms of the relevant factors, and some criticisms are a consequence of the type of economic system that exists in the United States.

Marketing's performance can be considered from the perspective of an organization and the society. The task of measuring marketing's performance at the organizational level is more straightforward than at the societal level. Firms must look beyond financial performance to judge their success in satisfying customers. At the organizational level, spotting obvious problems is often not too difficult. A more demanding activity is determining how well an organization is contributing to the needs of society. The social audit offers a potentially useful means of accomplishing this evaluation.

Improving marketing's contributions to society is the responsibility of business, industry, special interest groups, consumers, and government. Business should work toward improving organizational performance, following marketing ethics, and practicing social responsibility. Industries should also be socially responsible and practice self-regulation. Consumers have responsibility for initiating actions against social abuses, keeping themselves informed, and behaving in a socially responsible manner. Government should be concerned about eliminating waste, regulating and deregulating industry, and participating in market development.

KEY TERMS

hypermarketing   social responsibility   consumerism
demarketing   National Advertising Review
Federal Trade Commission (FTC)   Board (NARB)

QUESTIONS FOR REVIEW AND DISCUSSION

1. What are some reasons for the increase in marketing among those offering professional services (doctors, lawyers, certified public accountants, etc.)?

2. What are the limitations of the use of profit performance as a means of measuring marketing success or failure?

3. What are the techniques that firms can use to measure customer satisfaction?

4. Why has social marketing become such an important concept?

5. What are some reasons for the rise of consumerism?

6. Why must the government become involved in the social challenge of marketing?

7. What are some common criticisms of current marketing practices?

8. How might a U.S. firm go about selling its product or products in a third world country?

9. Why are unmentionables frequently not actively marketed?

BUILDING YOUR PORTFOLIO

Conduct a survey of ten of your friends who are not business majors. Ask each person for examples of business practices they consider to be unethical. Be sure to ask each person *why* the practice is unethical and what they believe should be done to correct the problem. Tabulate the responses to determine the extent to which your friends have identified similar problems. Try to place similar situations into categories. Analyze each practice considered to be unethical. Indicate why you agree or disagree that the practice is unethical. Try to explain any differences that exist between you and your friends.

NOTES

1. "Meeting a global marketing challenge." *Advertising Age,* Feb. 6, 1984, p. 18. Reprinted with permission from the Feb. 6, 1984, issue of *Advertising Age.* Copyright 1984 by Crain Communications, Inc.
2. Richard K. Manoff, "Learning a lesson from Nestlé." *Advertising Age,* Feb. 13, 1984, p. 16.
3. Rance Crain, "From nonmarketing to nonselling." *Advertising Age,* Feb. 13, 1984, p. M-30.
4. Laurel Sorenson, "Medical test: Hospitals and doctors compete for patients, with rising bitterness." *Wall Street Journal,* July 19, 1983, p. 15.
5. Ibid., p. 1.

6. "The blue-chip lawyers discover marketing." *Business Week,* Apr. 25, 1983, p. 89.
7. The following discussion is from Aubrey Wilson and Christopher West, "The marketing of 'unmentionables.'" *Harvard Business Review,* Jan.–Feb. 1981, p. 93.
8. Craig C. Carter, "Sudless sports?" *Fortune,* Jan. 21, 1985, p. 84.
9. Kevin Higgins, "Marketing enables population control group to boost results." *Marketing News,* Oct. 14, 1983, p. 12. Reprinted with permission of the American Marketing Association.
10. Laura Landro, "RCA reaches crossroads on future of its troubled videodisk player." *Wall Street Journal,* Sept. 13, 1983, p. 35.
11. John Bussey, "Ads for plastic surgery stir medical feud." *Wall Street Journal,* Mar. 13, 1984, p. 31.
12. Ibid.
13. George W. Douglas, "Who is being deceptive." *Advertising Age,* Feb. 13, 1984, p. M-27.
14. Steve Swartz, "Athletic-shoe concerns' payments to college coaches draw criticism." *Wall Street Journal,* July 26, 1983, pp. 31, 41.
15. John A. Prestbo, "Good listener: At Procter & Gamble, success is largely due to heeding consumer." *Wall Street Journal,* Apr. 29, 1980, pp. 1, 35.
16. William Lazer and James D. Culley, *Marketing Management: Foundations and Practices.* Boston: Houghton Mifflin, 1983, p. 57.
17. Mark Goldsmith, "Sweden puzzling to U.S. marketers." *Advertising Age,* Apr. 16, 1984, p. 46.
18. Michael Waldholz, "Tylenol maker mounting campaign to restore trust of doctors, buyers." *Wall Street Journal,* Oct. 29, 1982, p. 25.
19. Lazar and Culley, op. cit., p. 88.
20. Kevin McManus, "Who owns your brains." *Forbes,* June 6, 1983, p. 174.
21. Ibid., p. 178.
22. Trish Hall, "Industry headache: Americans drink less, and makers of alcohol feel a little woozy." *Wall Street Journal,* Mar. 14, 1984, p. 19.
23. Ibid.
24. Priscilla LaBarbera, "Advertising self-regulation: An evaluation." *MSU Business Topics,* Summer 1980, pp. 53–63.
25. David W. Cravens and Gerald E. Hills, "Consumerism: A perspective for business." *Business Horizons,* Aug. 1970, p. 21.
26. Ibid., p. 24.
27. Ibid., p. 28.
28. "Energy-guzzling: Most consumers are cured." *Business Week,* Apr. 4, 1983, p. 16.
29. Ibid.
30. "U.S. Mint to suspend production in March of Anthony dollars." *Wall Street Journal,* Feb. 20, 1980, p. 48.
31. "Deregulating America." *Business Week,* Nov. 28, 1983, p. 80.
32. June Kronholz, "Profits for peasants: China's communes get a lot less communal as incentives bloom." *Wall Street Journal,* July 18, 1983, p. 1.
33. Ibid., p. 15.
34. "Rocking the global village." *Time,* July 22, 1985, pp. 66–67.
35. Steve Morse, "Keeping the Live Aid issue alive." *Boston Globe,* July 16, 1985, p. 15.

Case 25.1

Tulsa Motor Inn

MR. JIM BAGGETT had heard about Oklahoma's penal reform plans. One phase of the plan involved the establishment of prisoner prerelease centers in both Tulsa and Oklahoma City. This idea seemed to make sense in some ways: the cost of rehabilitating a man might be lowered, and the percentage of parolees who made the transition from tax-using regimented prisoner to useful tax-paying citizen might be increased.

But as Jim scanned the newspaper that morning, his attitude toward one particular prisoner prerelease center (PRC) began to change. The headline catching his eye read: TULSA MOTEL TO BECOME PRISONER PRERELEASE CENTER. The article went on to explain the state had entered into a long-term lease with the owners of a mismanaged and floundering motel to use that facility as the Tulsa PRC. Another PRC was to be located in Oklahoma City. The most important information in the article to Jim, however, was the location of the PRC motel. It was *next door*, not 50 yards away from his own motel, the Tulsa Motor Inn.

The Baggetts had acquired the Tulsa Motor Inn 18 months prior to the PRC announcement. After successfully managing a motel in the Oklahoma City area, they had purchased one in Tulsa, which at the time was also mismanaged and losing money. Jim carefully planned and financed its remodeling and renaming under a nationally franchised motel chain. After investing $1,250,000 and a year and a half of hard work, the operation was beginning to show promise of success. "And

SOURCE: This case was prepared by James C. Johnson, St. Cloud State University, and Howard A. Thompson, Eastern Kentucky University.

now the state wants to locate 20 to 30 parolees within 50 yards of my guests, dozens of new cars, vacation-enlarged billfolds, and dressed-for-the-pool swimmers!" The thought brought with it a vision of empty rooms, forced room-rate reductions, and higher overhead stemming from new security precautions.

During the last 12 months the Tulsa Motor Inn had grossed $197,000, permitting a net profit before taxes of $41,000. Although he considered this to be less than half of its potential profitability, assuming occupancy percentages continued to improve, Baggett believed the Motor Inn to be "on target" according to his forecast nearly two years earlier. The PRC, however, was definitely not part of the "game plan." He had little doubt but the excellent repeat business with commercial travelers (sales representatives), now believed to constitute about one-half of total revenue, would shift to a "safer" location once the prisoners were known to be 50 yards away. An earlier advantage of being located near an expressway within 15 minutes of downtown Tulsa while still out of the congested part of the city now seemed almost a disadvantage.

Baggett's business associates counseled him to seek an injunction to prevent the state from locating an "undesirable" facility next door. He, with his son, a management major at the University of Tulsa, had been wrestling with questions of social responsibility, environmental pollution, and the like only a few weeks ago. He was very much in favor of business committing itself to the pursuit of these goals and ideas. But if he failed to act quickly against the state's announced plan for the new PRC, Baggett was certain this could mean a severe financial reversal for the Motor Inn.

Two broad types of travelers are customers of the Tulsa Motor Inn, transient or through travelers and business travelers making frequent trips to Tulsa. In terms of room-occupancy percentages, the business traveler is slightly more important. This is true except during the summer months when through travelers are most numerous. Through travelers, however, are most important in terms of annual gross rental income. During the only full calendar year of operational experience under the present management, 56.8 percent of gross rental income was from through travelers and 43.2 percent from business travelers. Multiple occupancy among through-traveler customers creates a total gross rental income greater than that received from the more numerous business traveler rentals.

Average monthly room occupancy increased from about 30 percent at the time of purchase to 60.2 percent last year.

At the present the Tulsa Motor Inn enjoys a fine reputation with its repeat customers, the business travelers. Comments such as "clean," "well-managed," "best beds in town," and "best motel for your money in the area" are frequently filled in on rating cards left in their rooms by business travelers.

Among business travelers "previous experience" was a strong factor influencing the choice of the Tulsa Motor Inn. Approximately 72 percent indicated that this was the reason which drew them back to Tulsa Motor Inn whenever they were in the Tulsa area. Other business travelers volunteered the information that they had only recently started staying at the Tulsa Motor Inn as a result of advice from other salesmen. Such indicators as these suggest that the present business volume at the Tulsa Motor Inn is healthy and growing, especially among this customer group.

QUESTION

What counsel would you give Baggett?

Case 25.2

Apex Bank

ANDY BROWN, PRESIDENT of Apex Bank, is working on a difficult presentation to be made to his board of directors next week at the quarterly directors' meeting. In a recent analysis of savings account deposits he learned that more than 40 percent of depositors had deposits of less than $100, many of which were less than $25. These low-income depositors were using the savings account as a way to get the bank to cash payroll, social security, and other checks. Several of the bank's business customers and consumers with large deposits have complained to management about the crowded conditions inside the bank, at the drive-in window, and in the parking lot during heavy check-cashing periods. Management's estimates clearly indicated that savings accounts below $100 cost the bank far more than the return obtained by loaning the money.

Andy is concerned about two issues. First, if the bank increases the minimum deposit to $200 or $300, some of the under-$100 depositors will not have enough cash to maintain the account. A substantial amount of criticism of the bank could occur in the community. While this adverse public opinion will not have a direct effect on the bank, competitors might take advantage of the opportunity to try to attract some of Apex's better customers. Second, the dissatisfaction of the bank's important business and retail customers will probably result in the loss of several of these accounts, unless the overcrowding problem is reduced soon.

Andy has identified three possible alternatives. The bank can continue operations as in the past, informing the customers who have complained that the adverse social impact of increasing the minimum deposit will reflect unfavorably on the entire community. Another option is to increase the minimum deposit and suffer the consequences of possible criticism in the community. Finally, Andy can recommend building another drive-in facility or branch to help overcome the overloaded conditions. It is doubtful that the expansion will attract enough new business to cover capital and operating costs. Net profits for Apex had been less than the national average for banks of comparable size for the last four years.

QUESTIONS

1. Indicate the important issues that should be considered by Apex's management in deciding which alternative to select.

2. What alternative should Andy Brown recommend to Apex's board of directors?

3. Should a bank be expected to provide a subsidized check-cashing service to low-income consumers?

4. What responsibility should the bank's more affluent customers have regarding the problem described in the case?

Appendix A
Financial Analyses for Marketing Decisions

MARKETING MANAGERS ARE increasingly required to know the financial implications of their decisions. Although marketing managers need not be financial specialists, they must be able to use information from financial statements when weighing decision alternatives. A very important statement for this purpose is the operating or income statement. In this appendix, we discuss the application of information from the operating statement to marketing decisions. In addition, we examine other selected kinds of financial information including break-even analysis and pricing calculations.

OPERATING STATEMENT

The operating statement portrays the results of a company's efforts to obtain profits from its operations. Its primary purpose is simply to show how much profit (a measure of results) was achieved from operations. Profit is calculated by subtracting costs from revenue: Revenue − costs = profit. Thus an operating statement is divided into three parts corresponding to these components. Managers usually want to know how revenue was obtained and what costs were incurred to get that revenue. To provide this detail, an operating statement can show supporting information about revenue and costs. Exhibit A.1 illustrates how profits were achieved by a computer store. Revenue comes from net sales of computers and related products sold by the store. As is common on operating statements, costs are divided into two categories: cost of goods sold and the expenses related to storing, displaying, and selling these products and the general operations of the business.

Operating statements more detailed than Exhibit A.1 can provide additional information about net sales, cost of goods sold, and expenses. Exhibit A.2 is an expanded operating statement for the computer store. Notice that it shows how net sales and cost of goods sold were calculated and separates expenses into the various categories or types of costs that were incurred. This greater breakdown of information is useful to the owners who want to evaluate how well the store did and to control its performance. Let us briefly review the meaning of each category listed in the operating statement.

Net sales

Revenue for the store comes from gross sales of computers and related products such as programs, disks, printers, and add-on circuit boards. The amount of gross sales, $345,000, is determined by adding together the quantity of all products sold during the year times the prices received for them. This total, however, is not the exact amount of revenue that the store

Exhibit A.1 An operating statement

Computers for Everyone: Operating Statement for the Year Ending December 31, 1985

Net sales	$336,500
Cost of goods sold	−$149,700
Gross margin	186,800
Expenses	−134,400
Net profit (before taxes)	52,400

actually generates. To keep customers happy, the store takes back merchandise customers were unhappy with or gives an allowance or discount off the merchandise's price. By subtracting the amount of these returns and allowances, net sales are determined. The amount of net sales more accurately than gross sales shows the revenue available to the store.

Cost of goods sold

An important cost of being in business is the cost to the store of the products that are sold during the period covered by the operating statement. To calculate cost of goods sold, we first have to calculate the cost of products that were available for sale during the period. This cost is determined by the quantity of products in inventory at the beginning of the period plus the quantity of products that were purchased and delivered during the period.

Exhibit A.2 Expanded operating statement

Computers for Everyone:
Operating Statement
for the Year Ending December 31, 1985

Gross sales			$345,000
Less returns and allowances			8,500
Net sales			$336,500
Cost of goods sold			
Beginning (1/1/85) inventory at cost		$ 56,000	
Purchases at billed cost	$124,700		
Less purchase discounts	3,000		
Net purchases	121,700		
Add freight cost	3,100		
Net cost of delivered purchases		124,800	
Net cost of goods available for sale		180,800	
Less ending (12/31/85) inventory at cost		31,100	
Cost of goods sold			149,700
Gross margin			$186,800
Expenses			
Selling expenses			
Sales salaries and commissions	$ 36,000		
Advertising	24,000		
Promotions	4,000		
Delivery and installation	1,200		
Total selling expenses		65,200	
Administrative expenses			
Office salaries	$ 28,500		
Office supplies	1,500		
Miscellaneous expenses	800		
Total administrative expenses		30,800	
General expenses			
Store rent	$ 18,500		
Utilities	9,500		
Insurance	2,200		
Depreciation of assets	5,400		
Miscellaneous	2,800		
Total		38,400	
Total expenses			134,400
Net profit (before taxes)			$ 52,400

Cost of beginning inventory as of January 1, 1985		$ 56,000
Purchases during the period	$124,700	
Less purchase discounts	3,000	
Net purchases	121,700	
Add cost of freight	3,100	
Net cost of delivered purchases		124,800
Net cost of goods available for sale		$180,800

The cost of purchases includes the cost of freight to get the products delivered. It also considers prices actually paid to suppliers after deducting purchase discounts received from the sellers. Of course, not all of the available products will actually be sold during the year; some will still be in inventory at the end of the year. The cost of the products in ending inventory is subtracted from net cost of goods available for sale to get cost of goods sold:

Cost of goods available for sale	$180,800
Less ending inventory as of December 31, 1985 at cost	31,100
Cost of goods sold	$149,700

Exhibit A.2 shows the typical way that cost of goods sold is displayed for a retailer or wholesaler. Retailers and wholesalers buy finished products from manufacturers and resell them to customers without changing the form of the products. Thus the cost of goods sold is determined by the prices paid for these products. Cost of goods sold by a manufacturer is calculated similarly, but takes into consideration that the costs are those incurred in actually making the product. Rather than having a cost of purchases, the manufacturer figures the cost of goods manufactured. Exhibit A.3 shows this calculation.

Gross margin

As shown in Exhibit A.2, net sales minus cost of goods sold equals gross margin, also sometimes called gross profit. It is the amount of revenue, after cost of goods sold is deducted, that remains to cover expenses and, it is to be hoped, to provide a profit.

Expenses

All costs of the business, other than cost of goods sold, are accumulated into the expenses section of the operating statement. In Exhibit A.2, these expenses have been placed into three broad categories: selling, administration, and general. Selling expenses are those that are incurred to generate sales and include the salaries and commissions earned by salespersons, the costs of advertising and sales promotion, and the cost of delivering products to customers. Administrative and general expenses are costs that support the sales effort and keep the business running from day to day.

Net profit

Net profit (before taxes) is the amount of revenue left over after costs of goods sold and all expenses of the business are deducted from net sales. The computer store made a before-tax profit of $52,400 as a return for the effort

Exhibit A.3   Cost of goods sold for a manufacturing firm

Cost of goods sold

Beginning finished goods inventory	$ 70,000
Add cost of goods manufactured (see schedule below)	243,800
Total cost of finished goods available for sale	313,800
Less ending finished goods inventory	62,500
Cost of goods sold	251,300

Schedule of cost of goods manufactured

Beginning work in process			$ 24,500
Raw materials			
Beginning raw materials inventory		$ 8,400	
Net cost of raw materials purchased		110,000	
Total cost of materials available		118,400	
Ending raw materials inventory		9,300	
Cost of materials placed into production		109,100	
Direct labor		125,000	
Manufacturing expenses			
Indirect labor	$23,000		
Maintenance and repairs	7,500		
Factory supplies	3,500		
Utilities	12,000		
Miscellaneous	700		
Total manufacturing expenses		46,700	
Total manufacturing costs			280,800
Total work in process during period			305,300
Less ending work in process inventory			61,500
Cost of goods manufactured			$243,800

expended during the year to get the $336,500 net sales. This effort of running the business is represented on the operating statement by all costs (cost of goods sold plus expenses) of $284,100. By deducting all costs from net sales, management can evaluate how well the business profited from operations.

Detail needed for operating statements

How much detail to include on an operating statement depends on whom the information is for. An operating statement sent to stockholders in an annual report may have only the major categories of net sales, cost of goods sold, gross margin, expenses, and net profit. Stockholders typically want only a general picture of how well the business is doing. On the other hand, a marketing manager will want more detailed financial information to evaluate the business and particularly to control the sales- and cost-incurring activities. We can better see this application of the operating statement by examining its analysis.

ANALYZING OPERATING STATEMENT RATIOS

An operating statement can be difficult to use if there are many sales and cost categories and the numbers are large. Managers simplify the task of interpreting the data in the statement by calculating ratios. A ratio divides one number from the operating statement by another and is usually expressed as a percent. Two kinds of ratios commonly used are operating ratios and stockturn ratios.

Operating ratios

Operating ratios compare various operating statement categories, such as returns and allowances, cost of goods sold, gross margin, expenses, and net profits, with net sales. Net sales are a good basis for comparison because all other numbers in the operating statement are directly related to sales volume. Some categories such as cost of goods sold are determined by sales volume. Other categories such as selling expenses are costs used to generate sales volume. The ratios are expressed as percentages of net rather than gross sales (multiplying by 100 gets rid of the decimal):

$$\text{Returns and allowances ratio} = \frac{\text{Returns and allowances}}{\text{Net sales}} \times 100.$$

$$\text{Gross margin ratio} = \frac{\text{Gross margin}}{\text{Net sales}} \times 100.$$

$$\text{Operating expense ratio} = \frac{\text{Operating expneses}}{\text{Net sales}} \times 100.$$

$$\text{Net profit ratio} = \frac{\text{Net profit}}{\text{Net sales}} \times 100.$$

These ratios help a manager review performance of the company. To interpret what a ratio means, the manager compares the ratio for the current period with a similar ratio from past time periods or with an industry average. Suppose the manager of the computer store wanted to evaluate gross margin performance. The gross margin ratio based on the operating statement in Exhibit A.2 is

$$\text{Gross margin ratio} = \frac{\$186,800}{\$336,500} \times 100 = 56 \text{ percent.}$$

If the store's gross margin ratio for the last five years were 38 percent, 38 percent, 40 percent, 39 percent, and 41 percent, respectively, then the current percentage of 56 indicates improved performance in controlling cost of goods sold. On the other hand, suppose that the computer store's returns and allowances ratio also is compared with past years.

	1981	1982	1983	1984	1985
Returns and allowances percentage	1%	1.5%	1%	2%	3%

The general pattern of increasing percentages suggests that returns and allowances are exceeding historic levels, which may signal a problem such as low merchandise quality or salespersons' not matching products with customers' needs. The out-of-line ratio alerts the manager to a problem.

Operating ratio analysis proceeds in this fashion, calculating ratios for the key categories on the operating statement and then comparing them with standards. The analysis alerts managers to problems that need further scrutiny. Thus ratio analysis is an important part of the marketing control process.

Stockturn ratio

Another type of ratio that is commonly used for control is the stockturn ratio, sometimes called the inventory turnover ratio. This ratio is the number of times that average inventory is sold (i.e., turned over) during the time period. Average inventory can be calculated by adding together beginning and ending inventories and then dividing by 2:

$$\text{Average inventory} = \frac{\text{Beginning inventory} + \text{ending inventory}}{2}.$$

Stockturn ratio can be calculated in three distinct, but similar ways.

$$\text{Stockturn at cost} = \frac{\text{Cost of goods sold}}{\text{Average inventory at cost}}.$$

$$\text{Stockturn at selling price} = \frac{\text{Net sales}}{\text{Average inventory at selling price}}.$$

$$\text{Stockturn in units} = \frac{\text{Sales in units}}{\text{Average inventory in units}}.$$

Stockturn is a measure of efficiency. Because holding goods in inventory is expensive, management usually wants to have a high stockturn. High stockturn means that average inventory is small relative to sales volume. Using data from Exhibit A.2, the stockturn for the computer store at cost can be calculated as follows:

$$\text{Stockturn at cost} = \frac{\$186,800}{\dfrac{\$56,000 + \$31,100}{2}} = \frac{\$186,800}{\$43,550} = 4.3.$$

Historic or industry average stockturns can be used as the basis to analyze operating ratios. The computer store manager, for instance, can compare the stockturn of 4.3 with previous years' stockturns to see if inventory management is getting more or less efficient.

RETURN ON INVESTMENT RATIO ANALYSIS

The net profit figure from the operating statement can be evaluated by comparing it with the amount of investment required to generate that profit. The comparison can easily be made by calculating a return on investment (ROI):

$$\text{ROI} = \frac{\text{Net profit}}{\text{Investment}} \times 100.$$

Net profit is usually measured as after-tax net profit. Investment is the dollar amount of resources that a company has allocated or "invested" in a product, a project, or the entire business. Investment is calculated differently among companies, and special calculations may be required to determine the figure that management wants to use. Investment might be figured as total money invested in the business as measured by assets. Or investment might be measured by the equity that owners have in the business. Assets and equity are numbers taken from the company's balance sheet, a statement of assets, liabilities, and owners' or stockholders' equity. Measuring return on assets (ROA) and return on equity (ROE) each leads to a different kind of ROI:

$$\text{ROA} = \frac{\text{Net after-tax profit}}{\text{Net assets}} \times 100, \text{ and}$$

$$\text{ROE} = \frac{\text{Net after-tax profit}}{\text{Owners' equity}} \times 100.$$

ROA is calculated by using figures from the operating statement (net profit) and the balance sheet (investment in assets). Suppose the computer store has $250,000 in assets. The ROA (in this illustration ROA is a before-tax percent) is

$$\text{ROA} = \frac{\text{Net profits}}{\text{Net assets}} \times 100 = \frac{\$52,400}{\$250,000} \times 100 = 21 \text{ percent.}$$

ROI is a revealing measure of the efficiency with which management used the company's resources. Like any ratio used for control, it can be compared with historic ROIs for the company or with an industry average. Furthermore, ROI can be compared with other uses of funds open to a company to see if the current use is best. A low ROI relative to the ROI that could be obtained from other uses is an indication of current operations' inefficiency or lack of opportunity. In this case, management may have to look for ways to increase efficiency or to reallocate resources to a more opportune area, such as getting into new markets or bringing out new products.

Even more revealing is a breakdown of the components of ROI: net profit margin and investment turnover. Net profit margin is a net profit-to-sales ratio, and turnover is a sales-to-investment ratio (similar to stock-turn). Putting these two component ratios together reveals how ROI is obtained:

$$\text{ROI} = \text{Net profit margin} \times \text{investment turnover} \times 100$$

$$= \frac{\text{Net profit}}{\text{Net sales}} \times \frac{\text{Net sales}}{\text{Investment}} \times 100$$

$$= \frac{\text{Net profit}}{\text{Investment}} \times 100.$$

Again, let us look deeper into the ROA for the computer store:

$$\text{ROA} = \text{Net profit margin} \times \text{asset turnover} \times 100$$

$$= \frac{\$52,400}{\$336,500} \times \frac{\$336,500}{\$250,000} \times 100$$

$$= .156 \times 1.346 \times 100$$

$$= 21 \text{ percent.}$$

Net profit margin is an indication of how efficiently costs were employed to generate sales. Investment turnover concerns the efficiency with which assets were managed. Notice that ROI can be improved in either of two ways: reduce costs relative to sales to increase net profit margin or reduce investment in assets relative to sales to increase turnover. Increasing sales alone will not necessarily improve efficiency unless the costs of achieving the higher sales do not increase as much proportionately.

BREAK-EVEN ANALYSIS

Break-even analysis uses information on costs and price to determine the revenue that is needed to break even, or just cover costs. Break-even analysis has been applied in several places in the text to help evaluate new products (see Chapter 10) and to help set price (see Chapter 17). It has other uses as well.

Before reading further, you may want to review the explanation of direct fixed costs and variable costs in Chapter 16. Break-even analysis compares revenue with these costs to determine the break-even sales volume. The equation for break-even volume (BE volume) is

$$\text{BE volume} = \frac{\text{Direct fixed costs}}{(\text{Unit price} - \text{unit variable cost})}$$

$$= \frac{\text{Direct fixed costs}}{\text{Unit contribution margin}}.$$

Suppose the manager of an industrial instruments manufacturer wants to know how many units of a new instrument would have to be sold to break even at a price of $1,200 per unit. The annual fixed costs for the product are estimated to be $500,000. The per unit variable cost is $650. Thus, break-even volume in units would be

$$\text{BE volume} = \frac{\$500,000}{(\$1,200 - \$650)} = \frac{\$500,000}{\$550} = 909 \text{ units.}$$

The instruments manufacturer must produce and sell 909 instruments at $1,200 each to bring in enough revenue to just cover the $500,000 of direct fixed costs and the $650 variable costs per unit produced. If more than 909 units are sold at $1,200, then the company will make a profit, assuming that fixed and variable costs do not change. If less than 909 units are sold at that price, then the company will lose money on the product.

The relationships among direct fixed costs, variable costs per unit, and revenue are shown in Exhibit A.4. Part A of the exhibit shows fixed costs over a range of units produced. For simplicity the graph shows no change in fixed costs over the entire range. In practice, of course, fixed costs may change over different ranges of units produced. Part B illustrates total variable costs over the same range of units produced. Notice that per unit variable costs are assumed not to change over the entire range, so total variable costs are shown to increase at a constant amount.

Part C overlays revenue on the direct fixed and variable costs lines to show what happens to profit over the range of units if they are sold at a price of $1,200. You can see that the variable cost line has been added to the fixed cost line to get total cost at all unit volumes in the range. Revenue is shown as a line because price is assumed to be the same over the whole range of units. The break-even volume is found by looking for the unit volume immediately below the point at which the revenue line crosses the

A. Direct fixed costs

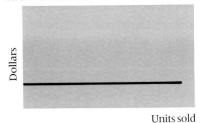

Dollars

Units sold

B. Variable costs per unit

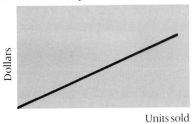

Dollars

Units sold

C. Revenue and costs to break even

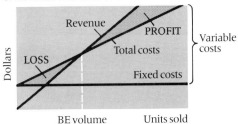

Dollars

Revenue

PROFIT

LOSS

Total costs

Variable costs

Fixed costs

BE volume

Units sold

Exhibit A.4 Break-even (BE) relationships

total cost line. At volumes above the break-even point, the revenue line is above the total costs line, indicating that profit is made. Conversely, at volumes below the break-even point, the total cost line is above the revenue line showing that losses are incurred.

Break-even analysis only shows what would happen to profits if the volumes included in the graphs are actually sold at the price assumed. The revenue line will change if a different price is charged. If fixed or variable costs change, the break-even volume also will change.

Break-even analysis is a flexible tool for helping managers make important decisions. Because it is difficult to estimate sales and costs precisely, break-even analysis can be used to examine alternative figures. Suppose the manufacturer of the industrial instrument wants to know how many units would have to be sold at $1,200 to get a return of 15 percent of sales. Break-even analysis can be used to answer this question:

$$\text{BE volume} = \frac{\text{Fixed costs} + 0.15\ (\$1{,}200 \times \text{BE volume})}{\text{Unit contribution}}$$

$$= \frac{\$500{,}000 + (180 \times \text{BE volume})}{(\$1{,}200 - \$650)}$$

$$= \frac{\$500{,}000 + (180 \times \text{BE volume})}{\$550}.$$

Therefore,

$$(\$550 \times \text{BE volume}) - (\$180 \times \text{BE volume}) = \$500{,}000$$

$$\$370 \times \text{BE volume} = \$500{,}000$$

$$\text{BE volume} = \frac{\$500{,}000}{\$370}$$

$$\text{BE volume} = 1352 \text{ units.}$$

Knowing that 1352 units of the instrument must be sold at $1,200 to get a 15-percent return on sales, managers must estimate whether this volume of sales is possible. Only if this number of units is sold at $1,200 will the return be achieved.

Break-even analysis is a versatile management tool that is used to help answer a variety of questions related to costs and sales, such as the following: (1) If fixed costs increase by a given percentage, how much must sales volume increase to break even? (2) If variable costs decrease by a given percentage, how much can sales volume decrease to break even? and (3) How much must be sold to achieve a higher sales-return objective?

PRICING CALCULATIONS

Markups

Marketing managers are acutely aware of the necessity of pricing products so that costs are covered and a contribution is made to the return for being in business. No company can operate for long if prices are not covering costs. Thus marketing managers look at price as made up of two components: cost and markup. The markup is the amount by which price of a product exceeds its cost. A markup allows the product to contribute to the company's unallocated overhead cost and to profits. If the computer store buys a software program from a supplier for $20 and then sells it to a customer for $45, the markup on that product is $25: $45 minus $20.

For convenience, markup is usually described as a percentage. (Percentage is a small number and therefore easy to remember, and percentages can be compared across products more easily than dollar amounts.) The most common markup percentage is a ratio of dollar markup to selling price, called markup on price:

$$\text{Markup on price} = \frac{\text{Dollar markup}}{\text{Product price}} \times 100.$$

The markup on price for the software program sold by the computer store is

$$\text{Markup on price} = \frac{\text{Dollar markup}}{\text{Software price}} \times 100$$

$$= \frac{\$25}{\$45} \times 100 = 55.6 \text{ percent.}$$

Markup can also be calculated as a percentage of cost of the product:

$$\text{Markup on cost} = \frac{\text{Dollar markup}}{\text{Product cost}} \times 100.$$

To illustrate, the software program's markup percentage on cost is

$$\text{Markup on cost} = \frac{\text{Dollar markup}}{\text{Software cost}} \times 100$$

$$= \frac{\$25}{\$20} \times 100 = 125 \text{ percent.}$$

If a manager knows the markup percentage that a product should make, then markups can be used to determine selling price. The following equation will yield the price derived from a known markup:

$$\text{Selling price} = \text{Cost} + \frac{(\text{Markup} \times \text{selling price})}{100}$$

$$\text{Selling price} - \frac{(\text{Markup} \times \text{selling price})}{100} = \text{Cost}$$

$$\text{Selling price} \left(1 - \frac{\text{markup}}{100} \right) = \text{Cost}$$

$$\text{Selling price} = \frac{\text{Cost}}{1 - (\text{markup}/100)}.$$

Suppose that the manager of the computer store wants to make a 70-percent markup on selling price on a computer model that has a delivered cost of $875. Applying the equation to the computer model pricing decision yields a price of $2,916.67.

$$\text{Selling price} = \frac{\text{Cost}}{1 - (\text{markup}/100)} = \frac{\$875}{(1 - 0.70)}$$

$$= \frac{\$875}{0.30} = \$2,916.67.$$

It is easy to convert from markup on selling price to markup on cost and vice versa. The relationship between the two kinds of markups is

$$\text{Markup on cost} = \frac{\text{Markup on selling price}}{(100\% - \text{markup on selling price})}, \text{ or}$$

$$\text{Markup on selling price} = \frac{\text{Markup on cost}}{(100\% + \text{markup on cost})}.$$

Suppose the manager of the computer store learned that a competitor has a 100-percent markup on cost for the same software product that the manager's store is selling for a 50-percent markup on selling price. How close are the markups between the competitors? Beginning with the competitor's markup on cost, the manager can convert it to a markup on selling price to see that the two markups are the same.

$$\text{Markup on selling price} = \frac{\text{Markup on cost}}{(100\% + \text{markup on cost})}$$

$$= \frac{100\%}{(100\% + 100\%)} = 50\%.$$

Markdowns

Pricing to get a particular markup does not guarantee that the markup will be achieved. Only if the product is sold at that price does the company get the markup. When a product does not sell at the original price, management may lower price to move the product out of inventory. The amount by which price is lowered is a markdown. For instance, at the end of the year, five units of a software program priced at $45 remained in inventory. To clear the program out of inventory, the manager of the computer store lowered price to $30 and then sold the five units. The markdown on each of the five units is $15: $45 minus $30.

Markdowns are usually monitored because they represent how efficiently a company purchases the quantity of a product wanted by customers or sets a price that customers are willing to pay. Although managers expect to have some markdowns, too much hurts the ability of the company to achieve profit objectives. Markdowns can easily be evaluated by computing a markdown ratio of net sales for individual products or for the company as a whole:

$$\text{Markdown ratio} = \frac{\text{Dollar markdowns}}{\text{Net sales}} \times 100.$$

Suppose the computer store manager wanted to know the markdown ratio for the software program. Total sales for the product, including one hundred units sold at the original price of $45, and five units sold at the markdown price, is $4,650. The dollar markdown is $75: 5 units $\times$ ($45 $-$ $30). Thus, the markdown percentage is

$$\text{Markdown ratio} = \frac{\text{Dollar markdowns}}{\text{Net sales}} \times 100$$

$$= \frac{\$75}{\$4,650} \times 100 = 1.6 \text{ percent.}$$

To evaluate the 1.6 percent markdown, the manager compares it with a standard such as historic markdowns for this product or similar products.

Appendix B
Sources of Information for Analyzing Marketing's Environment

A MARKETING MANAGER IS responsible for understanding the external environment in which his or her company operates. The macroenvironment contains many influences that affect customers' purchase decisions as well as the actions of competitors. The task environment comprises markets and competitors and is the immediate world in which marketing strategy operates. In many ways, dealing with the external environment makes marketing exciting and challenging. Marketing plays a major role in guiding the company through the maze of environmental forces, some of which can be influenced by what the company does while others are largely uncontrollable.

Being able to analyze the external environment is an important skill for marketing managers. Analysis means gathering information about environmental forces and drawing conclusions from that information about how the forces will affect the company's efforts to achieve its goals. Obviously, analysis can be little better than the quality of information on which it is based. Thus the ability to get and use relevant, accurate, and timely information can have an important effect on successfully planning marketing strategy. A professional marketing manager knows where to get this information.

Marketing managers have several sources of information on the external environment. First, information can be found in *published sources,* or secondary information sources (see Chapter 7). Every marketing manager should know how to locate these sources. Second, information is readily obtained from *personal observation* of environmental forces at work. This observation forms much of the experience of managers brought to bear on planning marketing strategy. Finally, marketing managers sometimes use *primary marketing research* to gather information not obtainable from the other two sources (see Chapter 7).

PUBLISHED SOURCES

Published information sources, which are in print and generally available to users, include periodicals and newspapers, books, government reports, reports of private companies including marketing research firms, and trade association reports. A combination of these sources provides a wealth of information about a company's external environment. Because there are so many sources, however, managers need diligence to locate them all. Several aids to getting access to the variety of sources include (1) libraries, (2) computerized search services, and (3) other information services.

Libraries

Fortunately, so many city and university libraries are located in the United States that almost all marketing managers are near one. Furthermore, many large companies have developed their own libraries of business and technical information sources for their employees' use. Libraries not only store information but also offer several aids, such as librarians, indexes and bibliographies, computerized search services, encyclopedias and directories, and card catalogues, to help users find the information they are looking for.

Librarians. Libraries are staffed by experts trained in the systems by which information sources are stored to facilitate retrieval. Large libraries can have hundreds of thousands or even millions of separate information sources, and getting to them easily can be a monumental task. Some libraries are designated by the U.S. government as repository libraries for government documents, and these libraries receive thousands of documents monthly. Because of the constant flow of documents into repository libraries, getting access to this information is especially difficult. Assistance from a trained librarian is practically essential.

Indexes and bibliographies. Indexes and bibliographies are another access aid and are particularly important for locating information in periodicals, newspapers, and books. They are easy to use because information sources are organized by author or subject. The subject indexes and bibliographies are especially helpful for external environmental analyses because they steer the user toward sources that contain information on particular topics such as population, economy, product, competitors, and industry. The widely used *Reader's Guide To Periodical Literature* is only one of many indexes that are available. Many indexes and bibliographies are needed because each one lists somewhat different information sources. Some of the more important ones for marketing analyses include

Business Periodicals Index. A cumulative subject index to English language periodicals in the fields of accounting, advertising and public relations, automation, banking, communications, economics, finance and investments, insurance, labor, management, marketing, taxation, and specific businesses, industries, and trades. Periodicals such as *Journal of Marketing, Journal of Retailing, Fortune, Forbes,* and *Business Week* are listed.

Business Index. A cumulative subject and author index to business periodicals. Some books are included as well as newspapers such as *The Wall Street Journal* and the business section of *The New York Times.*

Public Affairs Information Service *Bulletin* (PAIS). A selective subject index to the latest books, pamphlets, government publications, reports of public and private agencies and periodical articles relating to economic and social conditions, public administration, and international relations.

Predicasts *F & S Index United States.* Index to products, company and industry information from more than 750 financial publications, business-oriented newspapers, trade magazines, special reports, as well as sources reporting on corporate acquisitions and mergers.

The Wall Street Journal Index. Subject index of news items appearing in

The Wall Street Journal. There are two parts: general news and business news. The names of public figures and those appearing frequently in the news are carried by name under a "Personalities" heading.

Conference Board's *Cumulative Index.* The Conference Board is an independent organization that conducts an extensive research and conference service to provide industry with information on economic issues and trends as well as on management practices. One area of research concerns marketing administration, marketing planning, sales management, distributor relations, marketing and advertising research, and marketing cost analyses. The *Index* is a guide to the publications of the Conference Board.

Marketing Information Guide. An annotated bibliography of various publications arranged by broad subject areas.

Consumers' Index to Product Evaluations and Information Sources. A subject index to product evaluations and descriptions contained in product-testing periodicals such as *Consumer Reports.*

The New York Times Index. A monthly index to all of the articles that have appeared in *The New York Times.*

Monthly Catalog of United States Government Publications. An alphabetical index to all government publications published by the U.S. Superintendent of Documents. It is also indexed by author, title, subject, and series or report.

Computerized search services. Increasingly libraries are turning to the computer to help users search for information sources. The sources are contained in data bases, which are similar to indexes but placed in computer retrieval form. The user submits one or more code words and the computer then searches through a data base to find all information sources that have those code words in a title or abstract. The user gets a computer printout of the information sources that are located by these code words. The computer search saves the user's time that would have otherwise been spent going through the various indexes. Its cost can range from $3 to more than $100 depending on the data bases searched and the number of sources located.

Encyclopedias and directories. A marketing manager may want to know the names of organizations that may have and be willing to share information on request. Sources that list these organizations are called encyclopedias and directories. In addition to the name and location of the organizations, some encyclopedias and directories also have selected information on the organizations. Some of the more widely available encyclopedias and directories include

Encyclopedia of Associations. A listing of national trade associations and professional and other organizations in the United States. It contains the name of the associations and organizations, their addresses, and listings of their publications.

Thomas Register of American Manufacturers. A directory of manufacturers with company names, local office addresses, telephone numbers, capital ratings, and company officials.

Standard Directory of Advertisers. A listing of more than 17,000 companies that advertise as well as their advertising agencies. The companies are arranged by product and include name, address, telephone number, and product or service. Companies are also arranged by state and city.

Dun & Bradstreet's *Million Dollar Directory*. A listing of businesses (manufacturers, utilities, transportation companies, banks and trust companies, stockbrokers, mutual and stock insurance companies, wholesalers, and retailers) with a net worth in excess of $500,000. Includes some executives' names, number of employees, and sales. The companies are arranged alphabetically, geographically, and by product.

Poor's Register of Corporations, Directors and Executives of the United States and Canada. A listing of businesses that includes name, address, telephone number, and name, title, and functions of officers and directors. Arranged by Standard Industrial Classification (SIC) code, geographic location, and alphabetically.

Card Catalogues. When the user knows the name of the information source, it can be easily found in the library through the card catalogue system. A card catalogue lists sources and special numbers that indicate where in the library each source is kept. It is arranged by subject, author, and title. The card catalogue is a master listing of all library information sources.

Computerized search services

Libraries are not the only organizations providing computerized search services. As more and more companies become adept at using information for managerial decision making, private organizations are moving into the business of establishing data bases for this purpose. The data bases range from information source index services such as those used by libraries, to government data on populations and business, to statistical information on companies and industries. Largely because of the popularity of the personal computer, these private computerized services can be accessed by managers at their desks. Fees and time-oriented costs are charged for the services, but they are very convenient and fast to use. An illustration is PTS Prompt provided by Predicasts. Its data base comprises abstracts of important information compiled from various sources on a dozen or more industries including computers, chemicals, electronics, and food.

Other information services

Many organizations provide services allowing managers to receive information sources directly on a timely basis. Some of these are available in libraries and some are not. You are already familiar with the subscription services of periodicals and newspapers. Similarly, governments, trade associations, professional organizations, and private research firms also offer information reports that can be purchased on a one-time or subscription basis. These organizations are in the business of collecting, organizing, and selling information either for profit (e.g., private research firms) or nonprofit (e.g., governments, trade association and professional organizations). Government information services include

U.S. Industrial Outlook. A review of developments in more than 200 industries including both manufacturing and nonmanufacturing.

Census of Population. A compilation of demographic, socioeconomic, and other characteristics of the U.S. population published every ten years. The last census was in 1980.

Census of Housing. A compilation of housing characteristics of the U.S. population published every ten years. The last one was in 1980.

Censuses of Business. There are six censuses of business that survey retail trade, wholesale trade, manufacturing, transportation, selected services, and construction industries. They provide a variety of statistics such as number of establishments in each category, number of employees, and sales. The business censuses are done every five years; the last one was in 1982.

Statistical Abstract of the United States. Annual summary of statistics on the social, political, and economic characteristics of the United States. It is a convenient source for many statistics and also is a guide to other sources of statistical data.

Survey of Current Business. Published by the U.S. Bureau of Economic Analysis, this source provides current statistics on the U.S. economy including general business indicators, labor force, employment and income, foreign trade, and on individual products.

10-K Reports. Publicly held companies in the United States are required to file extensive financial and operating data with the Securities and Exchange Commission. The data are more extensive than that typically contained in company annual reports. Because 10-K reports are public information, they can easily be obtained by company managers.

Private research firms that provide information include

Editor & Publisher's *Market Guide.* Provides information on more than 1500 individual geographic areas and includes location, transportation facilities, population, households, banking, passenger automobile registration, utilities, principal industries, climate, and retail trade.

Sales & Marketing Management Magazine's *Survey of Buying Power Data Service* and *Survey of Buying Power Forecasting Service.* Provides data on population, households, effective buying income, retail sales, and a buying power index for both the United States and Canada. Geographic subdivisions covered include states, counties, and metropolitan areas. The data service has current statistics, and the forecasting service makes future projections.

Standard & Poor's Industry Surveys. Provides data on sixty-nine U.S. industries. Prospects for the future as well as historical trends and problems are reviewed. Also includes a comparative analysis of selected companies in the industry.

Predicasts Basebook and Forecasts. Provides in two volumes historical data series and forecasts of economic indicators and industry product sales.

Standard Rate and Data Services. Provides data on cost of advertising space in various publications such as newspapers, magazines, radio, and television; their circulations; and demographic and socioeconomic data on areas.

Rand McNally and Company's *Commercial Atlas and Marketing Guide.* Contains demographic and socioeconomic data on states and cities.

Simmons Market Research Bureau's *The Study of Media and Markets.* Results of Simmons' annual survey of product and media usage by people in the United States. The results of each survey are published in forty volumes organized by product. Each report provides data on demographic and socioeconomic characteristics of product and media users.

Moody's Manuals. Six manuals provide historical, business operations, and financial data on major corporations in an industry. The manuals are the Municipal and Government Manual, Bank and Finance Manual, Public Utility Manual, Transportation Manual, Industrial Manual, and OTC Industrial Manual.

Dun & Bradstreet's *Key Business Ratios.* Data are reported on selected business ratios for wholesaling, retailing, manufacturing, and service industries.

PERSONAL OBSERVATION

Published or secondary information should be supplemented by regular and systematic observation by managers. A wide variety of activities fall into this category. Buying a competitor's product or service to see the quality, materials, and performance characteristics provided to customers is one way to observe. Another is to regularly monitor the advertising of companies in the industry. Advertising is like a window into another company's marketing strategy planning function because advertising communicates important information about the company or its products to audiences. Interviewing personnel in companies making up a channel of distribution for a product, both suppliers and middlemen, also enables a manager to observe what is taking place in the task environment.

Using personal observation requires skill to get the maximum benefit from this source. A manager must become accustomed to looking for clues to environmental forces from everyday observations. For instance, a manager may learn to quickly scan competitors' advertising to see what prices are being changed, what product benefits are being stressed, what types of audiences are being reached, and whether facilitating services are being offered.

A single manager does not have the time or opportunity to observe all that is going on around the company. Thus managers must rely on the company's information agents, such as salespersons, to see and pass on information to managers. These agents must be identified, trained to recognize important observations, and given incentives to direct the information back to the company.

PRIMARY MARKETING RESEARCH

Published secondary and personal observation sources provide the majority of information for marketing analyses. Primary marketing research supplements these sources by getting data that are not otherwise available. The application of primary marketing research data to marketing decision making is discussed in Chapter 7, and we do not describe its characteristics here. These data are generally expensive and take considerable time to collect, and so primary marketing research is usually the last resort as an information source for information essential for an important decision.

Appendix C
Careers in
Marketing

THE FIELD OF MARKETING offers today's graduate a wide range of opportunities. No longer are positions limited to sales and advertising. Various career paths lead to many challenging jobs. A marketing education is also excellent preparation for the aspiring corporate executive. A recent study by a worldwide executive search firm revealed that many chief executive officers of major U.S. corporations have backgrounds in marketing or sales.[1] Thus, a marketing career provides one fast track to the executive suite.

JOB OPPORTUNITIES IN MARKETING

The sluggish job market in the early 1980s affected marketing as well as the rest of the business world. The experts, however, believe that marketing hiring will suffer only in the short term and will experience phenomenal growth in the future owing to increased consumer sophistication, heightened corporate competition, and the complexity of products and services.[2] Marketing experience offers a strong base for moving into top management in many firms. Wholesalers and retailers are essentially marketing organizations (see Chapters 13 and 14). Marketing executives have moved into key positions in the deregulated industries. A look at several types of marketing jobs illustrates the nature and scope of the career options that are available.

Selling

In Chapter 20 we describe the scope of responsibilities of a salesperson and the types of sales positions that are available. A career in selling can take one of two directions: personal selling and sales management. In most firms employees are required to have sales experience before they become managers. Several companies, including Procter & Gamble, prefer that all marketing staff and management personnel obtain a few years' sales experience before moving into other marketing positions. Thus experience in sales may also provide a springboard for upper-level marketing and general management positions.

Sales also offers more jobs than any other area of marketing. If you are a marketing major the odds are high that your first job will be in sales. Most of the companies that interview marketing majors on your campus are looking for salespeople. Jobs in advertising, marketing research, and other marketing areas are a relatively small proportion of total marketing jobs compared with those available in selling. Typically, a person enters selling as a sales trainee and advances to a sales position, senior salesperson, and sales supervisor. Sales trainee jobs for college graduates in field salesforces had compensation levels in excess of $22,000 per year in 1985.

Advertising and public relations

Activities related to advertising and public relations are discussed in Chapters 18 and 19. Jobs in advertising are available with companies that use advertising as a part of their marketing programs and with advertising agencies that help companies create advertising programs. Corporate jobs consist of advertising planning and management, agency coordination, and liaison with other marketing activities. Agency assignments include account management (marketing and advertising planning and coordination between the agency and client company), creative work, media selection, and research. There are approximately 8000 advertising agencies in the United States, staffed by an estimated 100,000 professionals. Additional jobs exist in corporate advertising departments, public relations agencies, and the advertising departments of the print and broadcast media.[3]

Advertising is an exciting but demanding career for people who have creative skills and an understanding of mass communications. Typically, competition is strong for the 1200 agency openings each year.[4] College graduates with summer or part-time job experience often have an advantage over others seeking professional careers in the field.

Many of the college graduates going into advertising are journalism and communications majors. Business administration students seeking an advertising career should consider taking courses offered in advertising departments and colleges of communications. Advertising also offers positions in commercial art.

Public relations work is more specialized than advertising although the two areas are similar. Some agencies offer both advertising and public relations services. Career opportunities in public relations are more limited than advertising.

Marketing research

Marketing research, which is discussed in Chapter 7, involves planning, conducting, and interpreting research studies. Analysis of published information is also part of marketing research. Positions exist in corporate marketing research departments and consulting firms such as A. C. Nielsen. Statistical and computer skills are required for many research positions. A graduate degree may be needed for some jobs. The University of Georgia offers a master's degree in marketing research.

A career in marketing research in a corporation tends to be rather specialized. For persons who like planning and conducting studies, research offers an interesting and rewarding career. Moreover, the number of research jobs is increasing each year. People have found it difficult to move from research into other marketing areas unless the change was made after only a few years of experience. If you want to work toward a top management position in a manufacturing or distribution firm, research is probably not a good career choice.

Product and brand management

Our discussion of product management in Part Three considers many of the responsibilities of product and brand managers. Job responsibilities include coordinating new product planning, conducting test market studies, designing packing, and making branding decisions. It is often difficult to obtain a product management position without prior experience in a related area of marketing such as sales or advertising. Product and brand management experience is valuable in preparing for higher-level marketing management positions. A master of business administration (MBA) degree may enable you to obtain a product management position, particularly if you have sales experience from summer or part-time work. It is often necessary to have a technical background in engineering or science to qualify for product management positions involving complex products such as computer systems, electronic equipment, and manufacturing equipment.

Purchasing

Acquiring supplies, components, and finished goods creates a need for buyers, purchasing agents, and directors of purchasing in manufacturing and distribution firms (see Chapter 6). These professionals and executives are responsible for purchasing items and services necessary for operating a business. Employees responsible for purchasing in retail stores are called buyers. In retailing, buying experience is often necessary to move into high-level general management positions such as store manager and corporate vice-president.

Distribution

Several types of jobs are essential to move goods and services through distribution channels, a process we discuss in detail in Chapters 12, 13, 14, and 15. Examples include warehouse supervisors, transportation managers, service managers, and inventory control managers. There are a wide range of jobs for persons wishing careers dealing with transportation in shippers' firms and transportation service firms (railroads, airlines, truckers, etc.).

Marketing manager

Marketing managers coordinate two or more marketing mix components such as sales, advertising, research, and pricing (see Chapter 2). These responsibilities may apply to a line of products, a business unit, or an entire corporation. Illustrative positions are marketing manager, director, and vice-president. The designation *marketing manager* is used for a wide range of marketing jobs—including both line and staff positions—that cover many various responsibilities. Some marketing management positions do not include line responsibility for organizational units such as the salesforce. It is essential to review the job description of the marketing management position to understand the nature and scope of the job.

How Much Can You Earn?

Compensation for top marketing jobs compares favorably with compensation for managers in production, engineering, personnel, finance, and accounting. Although entry-level salaries in sales and other marketing jobs are somewhat lower than the pay in accounting and engineering, marketing professionals at middle and top management levels of responsibility receive compensation that is generally comparable to other professional management positions as shown in Exhibit C.1.

The increasing importance of marketing in business firms today provides executives with marketing experience a promising opportunity to move into chief executive positions. One study of the career tracks of top executives in Fortune 500 companies found that marketing and sales represented the most common route to the top. The results of the study covering industrial firms indicated the percentages of top executives from the following areas:[5]

Marketing and sales, 31 percent
Accounting and finance, 25 percent
Manufacturing and operations, 21 percent
Engineering and research, 12 percent
Legal and other, 11 percent

The percentage represented by marketing and sales in nonindustrial firms was 34 percent. Interestingly, the chief executives responding to the study

Exhibit C.1   Salary ranges for selected middle management positions in medium and large companies, 1982

Position	Range for Top Third of Managers
Technical	
*R&D executive	60,000–79,000
*Corporate construction director	60,000–77,000
Chief industrial engineer	50,000–63,000
Finance	
*Security investments manager	50,000–76,000
*General accounting (report to controller)	45,000–68,000
*Tax compliance manager	50,000–66,000
Financial planning officer (report to controller)	50,000–62,000
Bank manager (at least $10 million deposits)	46,000–61,000
*Chief internal auditor	40,000–53,000
Sales	
*National account manager	50,000–69,000
Brand manager (sales over $5 million)	30,000–63,000
International sales	45,000–59,000
Sales promotion	40,000–56,000
Personnel	
*Management training specialist/dept. head	50,000–76,000
*Personnel/human resources manager	50,000–68,000
*Labor relations executive	45,000–68,000
Employee training specialist/dept. head	35,000–47,000
Planning	
*Corporate strategic planner	50,000–70,000
Corporate economist	50,000–61,000
Manufacturing	
*Plant manager	40,000–69,000
Quality assurance & reliability	35,000–60,000
Other	
*Management Information Systems specialist/data proc.	45,000–77,000
Federal relations executive	50,000–64,000
Corp. insurance/risk manager	45,000–63,000
Contract administrator	40,000–54,000
Purchasing manager	35,000–53,000
Media manager	30,000–53,000

* The top dozen career slots for current middle managers of above-average abilities in medium and large-size companies.

SOURCE: Steven S. Ross, "The 12 top money-making careers of the '80s," *Business Week's Guide to Careers*, Spring 1983, p. 9. Reprinted from Spring 1983 issue of *Business Week's Guide to Careers* by special permission, © 1983 by McGraw-Hill, Inc. All rights reserved.

Exhibit C.2. Average 1985 starting salaries for selected academic fields

Engineering and science	$23,000–28,000
Finance and accounting	19,000–20,000
Sales and marketing	19,000
Business administration	18,000
Personnel administration	17,000
Education	17,000
Communications	16,000
Liberal arts	15,000

SOURCE: "Bright job prospects for the class of 1985," *U.S. News & World Report*, Dec. 17, 1984, p. 65.

were not job hoppers. Less than one-fifth had worked for more than three full-time employers. Staying with the same company may therefore be better than moving around if you want to move to the top.

Starting salaries

Average starting salaries for college graduates have generally increased each year for several decades. Average expected 1985 annual starting salaries for selected academic fields are shown in Exhibit C.2. Starting salaries are higher for those with graduate degrees such as the MBA. Starting salaries for persons with MBAs from accredited programs range from 20 to 40 percent higher than for persons with only undergraduate degrees.

Illustrative pay levels

Illustrative marketing career routes and compensation levels are shown in Exhibit C.3. Because compensation varies substantially by type of industry, size of firm, and job responsibilities, the figures shown in Exhibit C.3 should be considered illustrative. Probably the best source of reliable compensation data is the *Executive Compensation Service* published by the American Management Associations.

Shifting career paths is also possible. For example, a salesperson might move into advertising or product management after gaining a few years' experience in sales. Some companies consider sales experience essential to move into marketing management positions. This is particularly true in firms in which the sales function represents the major portion of the marketing mix.

Typically, compensation for sales positions includes incentive payment such as a commission or bonus. Compensation in some sales positions is entirely based on commissions earned from sales. Earnings from commission sales can be high in fields such as real estate and insurance, although few achieve earnings levels in excess of $100,000 per year. Lois Zambo is one of a few top performers in sales. She joined a commercial real estate broker in 1975 as a $6000-a-year receptionist, eventually moving into sales. In 1984 at age 38 her earnings reached seven figures, placing her in the exclusive millionaire broker status.[6]

Exhibit C.3. Illustrative marketing career routes and compensation levels

Sales	Senior	Field	Sales
Salesperson	salesperson	manager	vice-president
$20,000–	$ 30,000–	$30,000–	$ 40,000–
30,000	100,000	50,000	150,000+
Advertising*			
Account	Account	Management	Senior
executive	supervisor	supervisor	vice-president
$14,000–	$25,000–	$45,000–	$ 40,000–
40,000	48,000	75,000	130,000+
Marketing research			
Research	Account	Project	Research
analyst	manager	director	director
$15,000–	$20,000–	$25,000–	$30,000–
25,000	30,000	40,000	50,000+
Product-marketing management			
Product-brand	Product group	Marketing	Marketing
manager	manager	director	vice-president
$30,000–	$50,000–	$ 70,000–	$ 90,000–
60,000+	80,000	100,000+	180,000+

* 1983 salaries from *Advertising Age,* Jan. 2, 1984, p. M-17.

WHERE THE JOBS ARE

You should recognize that job prospects vary a great deal owing to inbalances in the supply of job candidates and in the demand for people by businesses and other employers. Let us look closer at the occupational outlook for the next several years and some industries that offer promising job opportunities.

Outlook for selected occupations

The Labor Department offers a comprehensive analysis of the employment outlook for a wide variety of occupations in its *Occupational Outlook Handbook.* Major growth is anticipated in service-related occupations. Some jobs that are expected to grow at an above-average rate through 1995 are shown in Exhibit C.4. As you consider alternative career fields, review the

Exhibit C.4 Jobs expected to grow at an above-average rate through 1995

	Jobs in 1995 (in 1000s)
Accountants	1200
Bank managers	617
Buyers	332
Designers	253
Electrical engineers	529
Health-service administrators	478
Real-estate agents	449
Securities salespeople	106

SOURCE: "Hunting for a job? Here's where to look," *U.S. News & World Report,* Aug. 13, 1984, pp. 62–63.

Labor Department's occupational outlook information to help you spot promising occupations. Several professional organizations also prepare job forecasts for specific types of jobs. Another excellent source of career information is the magazine *Business Week's Guide to Careers* published four times a year.

Promising industries and areas

Job opportunities are often affected by economic conditions in specific industries. For example, automobile imports and the 1981–1983 recession lowered sales of U.S. manufactured automobiles, reducing the hiring plans of these companies during this period. By 1985 the automotive industry was planning to substantially increase its hiring of college graduates. One useful guide to industry hiring plans is to review the list of companies planning interviews on your campus. These firms normally specify in their interview schedule the types of jobs they have available. Hiring plans of all companies vary from year to year as a consequence of economic conditions and other factors. Thus you should monitor how the economy is performing during the period you are seeking employment. For example, hiring of college graduates in 1983 was down substantially compared with 1982 whereas 1985 was up substantially compared with 1983 and 1984.

Job prospects are generally good in areas where the population is expanding. Many of the Sun Belt states are growing rapidly. Industry continues to expand into these states. Prospects are less attractive in many of the northern states, although jobs exist throughout the United States. International employment prospects are promising in selected fields. Often training and experience are necessary before moving into international jobs. Several of the information sources discussed in Appendix B contain useful information on industries and companies.

MARKETING YOURSELF

The job-hunting experiences of people who have obtained promising career positions suggest that you will benefit by applying some of the basic marketing principles to marketing yourself. A wide variety of students' experiences have provided several guidelines that should prove helpful to you as you move into the job market.

Study your strengths, weaknesses, and preferences

Few of us are likely to be effective and successful in a wide variety of occupations. For example, the discussion of personal selling in Chapter 20 may have attracted you to the field. Some people like selling, whereas others dislike the personal contacts, travel, attempts to close sales, and regular contact with new people. An essential first step in finding the right job is candidly evaluating your own strengths, weaknesses, and preferences. Here are some examples of questions you will need to answer about yourself before moving into the job market:

- How effective am I in communicating with individuals and groups?
- Am I able to work with computers?
- Where do I want to live?

- How do I feel about frequent travel?
- Am I willing to relocate several times during my career?
- Am I good at handling details?
- Do I have leadership potential?

Prepare a list of what you consider to be your strengths, your weaknesses, and your job preferences. Then discuss these with your teachers, friends, parents, and others who can help you take an objective look at yourself. When you start to interview, prospective employers try to find job opportunities that correspond to your strengths and preferences and are not heavily dependent on skills that you do not have. Also recognize that your capabilities will improve over time. For example, few people are natural salespeople; most of these skills are developed through experience. Management capabilities similarly are developed through learning and experience. Few of us are natural managers. Finally, self-confidence is important. Do not be too critical of what you think are your weaknesses.

Prepare for interviews

The initial interview has two objectives. The company representative must decide whether to continue discussions with you; you must determine if you have an interest in the company. Typically, the representative's interest is the most critical because you probably would not ask for the interview unless you were considering the company. College recruiting is a popular method by which companies screen job candidates and students screen companies, so we concentrate our discussion on this activity. Nevertheless, you should not restrict your job-hunting to campus interviews. Make some direct contacts with firms that are of interest to you. Remember that college recruiting is conducted primarily by large corporations. Many excellent small and medium-sized firms do not recruit on campuses.

Your primary strategy should be to convince the campus interviewer, normally in twenty to thirty minutes, that the company should talk further with you. Before you go to the interview learn some basic information about the company, its products, and activities. Review a recent annual report. Literature on the company may be available in your placement office. Try to think of questions you will likely be asked and prepare answers for them. Often these questions will be applicable to several prospective employers. Here are some examples.

How did you happen to select this field (e.g., sales) as a career choice?
What are the qualities necessary for success in this field?
What capabilities can you contribute to this profession?
What are some of your weaknesses that might hinder your success?
Why should we consider you over other applicants?
What are your career plans?
Why do you want to work for our company?[7]

You should also identify a few questions to ask during the interview, because you will probably be given an opportunity to ask questions. Ask only one or two questions. Review the questions before the interview so that you will not have to refer to a list during the interview. The questions should reflect your interest in the company and should convince the interviewer that you have thought seriously about important career and employment issues. Examples of areas in which you might ask questions are how you would spend your first few years with the company, the availability of training programs, career progression stages, the future outlook for the company and industry, and the characteristics the firm is seeking in job candidates.

Prepare your resume

At some point in seeking employment you will need a resume. You should talk with your college placement officer and faculty advisor about preparing a resume. A friend or relative who is a personnel or human resources executive is also a good source of advice. A poorly prepared summary of your experience, education, and interests is a liability rather than an asset. Here are some general suggestions.

- Target your resume to the job opportunity, particularly regarding the discussion of the type of position you are seeking. Companies normally are trying to fill specific positions. You may need more than one resume.

- Describe all of your previous experience, including summer jobs. While your part-time job in a fast-food restaurant may not seem important, it is better than indicating no job activity.

- Organize and properly sequence the information listed. Some experts suggest including your grade average; others advise against it. If the average is low, wait until the information is requested.

- Have the resume printed on good-quality paper. Many duplication centers offer inexpensive high-quality copying.

- Rather than include references it is better to prepare a separate list with three or four names, addresses, and telephone numbers. The list can be supplied on request. Be sure to obtain permission from the persons you are using as references.

There are various other considerations in resume preparation. Get some help and spend enough time to develop a complete, well-organized, and attractive resume.

Get experience

It is important for you to obtain as much experience as possible before graduation. Summer and part-time jobs and class projects involving business firms and other organizations can be useful. Experience will give you an advantage over other candidates. Responsible positions in school activities also will strengthen your job credentials and develop your self-confidence. If feasible, try to gain experience in more than one type of job.

Several universities offer co-op programs enabling students to incorporate work experience into the formal educational process. These programs offer an excellent opportunity to gain work experience. Building a portfolio of your accomplishments during your college studies may be useful in showing employers examples of the work you have done. The portfolio may include special project reports, research studies, and student activities projects.

CAREER PLANNING

It is not too early with your first job to start planning your career. Although a complete examination of this important activity is beyond the scope of our discussion, some key issues can be highlighted.

Set realistic objectives

A small number of people achieve high levels of success in only a few years. For most people progress to the top jobs typically requires several years. Be realistic in your job aspirations. Try to maximize your experience. In ten years you do not want to look back and realize that you have gained one year of experience repeated ten times. Evaluate your experience at the end of each year. If you are not doing something better, different, or more efficiently, a change may be indicated. Your value should increase with the scope and depth of your experience. You should explore this point with a prospective employer. Find out what is likely to be your experience path during your first years on the job.

Deciding if and when to change jobs is an important career consideration. People sometimes change jobs to improve salary and opportunity. Deciding whether a change is appropriate depends on a number of factors such as the present job situation, opportunities with the new firm, costs and financial benefits of a change, the people you will work with, and anticipated future of the industries you are leaving and joining. A carefully evaluated change can sometimes be advantageous. Too many changes will earn you a reputation as a job jumper.

Graduate school

Students often raise questions about graduate school: (1) What is the need and value of a graduate degree? and (2) Should I work a few years before returning to school? The need for graduate work depends on various factors, many of which are specific to the firm in which you are seeking employment. Some companies seek people with graduate degrees such as the MBA for management-training positions. Other firms concentrate on hiring candidates with undergraduate degrees. An MBA typically commands a higher starting salary but there are not as many jobs available for MBAs as for people with undergraduate degrees. Also, the loss of income during the time in graduate school and experience that would have been gained on the job must be considered in comparing undergraduate and graduate degree salary differences. An advanced degree may give you an advantage over other people in some situations. For example, it is not uncommon, in reviewing the educational background of middle and top management executives, to find that many have MBAs.

Assuming you decide that you want a graduate degree, should you work a few years before returning to school? Some job experience will probably enable you to gain more benefit from graduate study. Some of the top schools consider experience very favorably in making admission decisions. On the negative side, you may find it difficult to break away from a challenging job. One option is part-time study, although the work load of graduate study and full-time employment is very demanding. Finally, do not rule out graduate study immediately after receiving your undergraduate degree, particularly if you have summer and part-time work experience.

NOTES

1. ''What is the fastest track to the executive suite? Sales/marketing.'' *Marketing News,* July 6, 1984, p. 7.
2. Daniel Burstein, ''When the smoke clears, the jobs will appear.'' *Advertising Age,* Jan. 2, 1984, p. M-9.
3. Janine Linden, ''The exciting world of advertising.'' *Business Week's Guide to Careers,* Spring-Summer 1984, p. 33.
4. Ibid., p. 34.
5. ''What is the fastest track to the executive suite,'' op. cit.
6. ''Careers.'' *Forbes,* Dec. 17, 1984, p. 206.
7. Marcia Fox, ''Interview do's and don'ts.'' *Business Week's Guide to Careers,* Spring-Summer 1984, p. 54.

Glossary

Glossary

acquisition (24) Entry by a company into a foreign market by buying into a local company either partially or completely.

advertising (18) A paid form of nonpersonal communication, carried by the mass media (e.g., television, radio, newspapers, billboards, and magazines) or by direct mail. Receivers clearly understand that the message is coming directly from the source.

advertising agency (19) An organization hired by a company to assist in the selection and placement of advertisements, to create advertising messages, to produce advertisements, to do marketing research, and to help with development of marketing and advertising plans.

advertising concept (19) The combination of selling points to be communicated by advertising.

advertising copy (19) The combination of message content and context contained in an advertisement.

advertising post-tests (19) Tests to evaluate advertising effectiveness during or after an advertisement has been run by the media.

advertising pretests (19) Tests of advertising effectiveness conducted before an advertisement is delivered to target audiences.

agricultural cooperative (14) An organization formed by a number of small farmers enabling them to achieve some of the advantages of large-scale marketing.

AIDA model (18) A hierarchy-of-effects model, the steps of which are awareness, interest, desire, and action.

analysis models (7) A description of a relationship between selected environmental factors.

anchor stores (13) Department stores that are located within shopping malls to attract customers to mall locations.

annual marketing plan (21) The marketing actions that will be taken within a twelve-month period.

assorting (12) Assembling various stock items to satisfy the needs of customers.

attitude change test (19) A communications effectiveness test that measures change in attitudes of the target audience from before to after the advertising.

attitudes (5) Feelings of like and dislike toward something such as a product, a company, an idea, or a person.

banked trademark (11) A trademark for which a firm has obtained registration even though management has no immediate plans to launch a major marketing effort for the brand that is registered.

bartering (16) An exchange in which one product or service is traded for another.

basing-point pricing (17) A variation of delivered pricing policy in which the seller establishes one or more locations from which to calculate transportation costs.

beliefs (5) Opinions or facts a person holds to be true.

bidding (6) A procedure for getting offers from suppliers to sell at a specified price.

birdyback (15) A combination of air and land distribution services.

bottom-up approach to promotion budgeting (18) A promotion plan developed by deciding what combination of message content, context, and media is required to achieve specified promotion objectives. The total cost of the plan becomes a recommended promotion budget and is reviewed by top management.

bottom-up planning (21) Origination of plans at the lowest level of the organization and funneling of plans to the level above until plans are collected at the top of the organization.

brand (4) A combination of attributes and benefits, including image, that is offered for sale by a particular organization. Also a name, term, symbol, or design, or a combination of them that is intended to identify the goods or services of one seller or groups of sellers and to differentiate the goods or services from those of competitors.

brand advertising (19) Advertising that is specifically aimed at building and maintaining demand for a particular brand.

brand competition (3) Competition between different brands of essentially the same type of product.

brand loyalty (11) A customer's predisposition to purchase the same brand repeatedly.

brand manager (3) A manager in the marketing department who holds responsibility for a particular brand.

brand mark (11) A particularly distinctive name or physical symbol that is associated with a product.

brand name (11) A particularly distinctive name or physical symbol that is associated with a product.

brand sales forecast (4) An estimate of how many units (or dollars) of a brand will be sold.

break-even volume (17) The total number of units of a product that must be sold if revenue is to equal costs exactly, with no profit or loss.

brokers (14) Agents who act as go-betweens for buyers and sellers and receive commissions for the goods they sell.

budgeting (2) A transition step between planning and implementation that occurs when managers convert a plan into a budget, indicating the resources required to achieve objectives.

bulk-breaking (12) The intermediary function of breaking down large quantities of goods purchased from producers into smaller quantities for redistribution to users.

business analysis (10) An estimate of the financial attractiveness of the new product to the firm after it is introduced into the market.

business definition (23) The mission statement that indicates the purpose and scope of the firm's objectives.

business plan (23) The situation analysis, mission, objectives, and strategies for a company, business segment, or business unit.

business portfolio (23) The composition of a corporation in terms of business segments and strategic business units.

business portfolio management (23) A management plan for each business unit that, when combined with the plans for all other business units in the portfolio, will lead to the most favorable overall corporate financial performance.

business segment (23) A substantial part of the entire corporation often containing a related mix of products.

buyer behavior (5) The actions of persons directly involved in purchasing and using a product or service including the decision processes that lead to a purchase choice and the satisfaction or dissatisfaction experienced as a result of the purchase.

buying center (6) All members of an organization who participate in a purchase decision.

buying committees (6) Collections of individuals assigned responsibility for purchase decisions.

buying units (6) Households or organizations that provide the setting in which purchase decisions are made.

cannibalization (9) The loss of sales of a firm's existing brands due to the introduction of a new brand.

carrying costs (15) Costs associated with maintaining inventory stocks such as financing, storage, insurance, and obsolescence.

cash and carry wholesaler (14) Wholesalers who do not utilize salespeople but instead allow customers to pick up the merchandise from the wholesale location in return for immediate cash payment.

cash discount (17) A reduction in price offered to encourage the trade or end-user to pay for purchases within a specified period of time.

catalogue showrooms (13) Small retailers that offer low prices and national brands and that have warehouse space adjacent to retail display area.

central business district (CBD) retailers (13) Stores located in downtown areas that sell to consumer end-users.

centrally planned economies (24) Countries in which the government decides how the nation's resources are to be allocated and local business organizations implement these plans.

channel captain (12) A channel member who coordinates, supports, and controls the activities of other channel members.

channel of distribution (12) A network of cooperating organizations that together perform the activities required to link producers of goods and services to users and end-users of those goods and services.

channel flow (12) The movement of some good or service between two or more channel participants within the distribution network.

channel cooperation (12) The practice of one channel member assisting another by providing sales incentives, training, cooperative advertising, and other forms of cooperation.

Clayton Act of 1914 (16) Federal law that prohibits price discrimination and other acts that have the effect of substantially lessening competition or creating a monopoly.

closing (20) The actual commitment of a prospect to purchase an item a salesperson is selling.

combination branding (11) An approach to product marketing that stresses both the company name and the individual or family brand name.

combination export manager (CEM) (14) A person or organization that is experienced in selling to foreign markets, has an established network of overseas distributors, is familiar with export procedures and requirements, and represents several noncompeting organizations with related products.

combination stores (13) Stores that offer both grocery and drug items. These stores are larger than supermarket or superdrug stores but are similar in pricing strategies and operating policies.

commercialization (10) The final stage in new product planning that results in roll-out or full-scale introduction of the product into the market.

commission merchants (14) Agents who handle competing product lines, often take possession of goods, and charge the producer commission and expenses once the goods are sold.

communication of a plan (2) The conveying of information about a plan to those who are responsible for its implementation.

communications effectiveness test (19) A test used to evaluate the ability of advertising to communicate with target audiences.

communications promotion objectives (18) Statements of desired awareness, belief, and attitudinal reactions of people to promotion.

communications channel (18) A means of delivering a message to the audience.

company sales forecast (4) The sum of all brand sales forecasts.

comparative advertising (19) Advertising that compares a company's brand with competitors' brands.

competition (3) The marketing actions of all organizations that are aimed at taking sales from a company's target markets.

competitive dominance strategy (17) A marketing strategy that aims at building and maintaining the largest target markets.

component parts and materials (9) The items that are assembled into products during the production process.

concept testing (10) Measurement of customer reaction to a proposed new product.

concentrated marketing (8) Design of a firm's marketing program to meet the needs of the people or organizations in a single market segment.

consultative selling (20) The most demanding sales positions, requiring both technical knowledge and creative skills.

consumer (1) An individual, household, or organization that uses goods and services to satisfy needs and wants.

consumer buyers (5) Persons in family and nonfamily households who purchase goods and services for personal use to satisfy needs and wants.

Consumer Credit Protection Act of 1968 (16) Federal law that requires lenders to fully disclose annual interest rates and other financial charges.

Consumer Goods Pricing Act of 1975 (16) Federal law that supersedes state laws that had legalized price-fixing between different levels in a channel of distribution (e.g., between manufacturer and wholesaler or retailer).

consumer market (5) A group of people in households having both the ability and willingness to buy a product or service to satisfy a need or want.

consumer orientation (1) Marketing that is directed at discerning and satisfying consumers' needs and wants.

consumer perspective (1) Marketing from the point of view of the consumer involving activities that are directed toward satisfying needs and wants through the exchange processes.

consumer products (9) Goods and services purchased for consumption by a person, family, or household.

consumerism (25) A social force within the economy designed to aid and protect the consumer by exerting legal, moral, and economic pressures on business.

containerization (15) Combination of several loads organized in units.

containerized freight (15) Goods placed in a storage unit that is smaller than a railroad car.

contractual purchase agreement (6) A negotiated agreement to purchase over a period of time.

contribution pricing (16) A pricing structure whereby price is set to yield enough revenue to cover direct costs and make a contribution to indirect costs and profits; does not consider indirect costs.

control comparisons over time (22) The tracking of performance of marketing decisions over several time periods.

control standards (22) Managers' expectations concerning performance of a marketing decision.

convenience products (9) Relatively inexpensive purchases for which the consumer makes a limited effort to identify and evaluate purchase alternatives.

convenience stores (13) Retail outlets that are smaller than supermarkets and that offer a limited range of food items.

conventional channel (12) Firms that buy from and sell to one another and cooperate in the performance of various channel functions. This type of channel is characterized by independence of the firms and easy entry to and exit from the channel.

coordination of a plan (2) Organization of the people involved in a plan's implementation so that each person does the assigned activity on a schedule and in the proper sequence.

core business (23) A business that concentrates in a particular product and market area.

corporate branding (11) Establishment of product identity with the corporate name.

corporate mission (23) The established reason for a firm's existence.

cost control (22) The procedure by which managers use budgets to set limits on the costs of decisions and then maintain spending at or below these limits.

cost-per-thousand criterion (19) The cost of reaching one thousand persons in a media vehicle's audience.

cost-plus pricing (17) See *target markup pricing*.

countertrade (16) Bartering between nations.

corporate-owned and franchised chains (13) Retail stores that are owned by a channel member (e.g., manufacturer) or operate through a contractual franchise agreement with a channel member.

creative selling (20) A sales technique in which the salesperson analyzes how a product will meet the buyers' needs, encourages prospects to recognize these needs, and then convinces the buyers to purchase the product.

crisis management (21) Reaction to problems or situations as they occur rather than deciding in advance what marketing actions to take.

cross-sectional study (7) A study in which respondents are observed or questioned once and then data from that single session are analyzed for information.

culture (3) The values, ideas, beliefs, and attitudes about a wide variety of issues, appropriate behavior, and objects that are shared by people in a country.

cumulative discount (17) A reduction in price given when large purchases are not practical and based on the volume of purchases throughout a time period, such as a year.

customary pricing (16) The practice whereby price setters maintain the same price over a long period of time.

customer profile (4) A compilation of all information collected by a market opportunity analysis that describes customers in markets.

customer satisfaction (1) A measure of the ability of a seller to meet customers' needs.

customer service level (15) A company's standards for performance in making its product available to buyers when and where they want them.

customer testing (10) An evaluation of a new product idea from potential customers.

DAGMAR approach (Defining Advertising Goals for Measured Advertising Results) (19) A procedure for defining advertising goals so that advertising can be tested for effectiveness in reaching these goals.

data (7) Facts and opinions about marketing's environment.

data analysis (7) The process of compiling and studying data to provide summaries, descriptions of relationships, and conclusions.

data interpretation (7) The process of drawing conclusions from data analysis.

dealer (13) A type of retailer that often handles goods or services purchased by business end-users.

deceptive pricing (16) The practice of quoting a price in such a way that the customer is misled about what he or she is actually paying for the product.

decline stage (9) The point at which product sales begin to decline, often resulting in product elimination or reduction of marketing expenditures.

decoding (18) The task of interpreting the meaning of a message.

delivered pricing policy (17) A policy decision that determines the amount of transportation cost to be paid by the seller.

demand curve (16) A graphical representation of the schedule of quantities of a product or service that customers in a market are expected to buy at different prices.

demand-oriented or value pricing (17) The practice of setting the price for a product according to the value customers place on the product.

demarketing (25) The practice of discouraging the purchase of a firm's products or services through marketing efforts.

demographic characteristics (3) Data about people that describe (1) their innate physical characteristics (age, gender, race), (2) their key possessions (education, income, occupation, type of housing), and (3) their social arrangements (marital status, family size).

demographic segmentation (8) The process whereby variables such as age, income, and gender are used to divide markets into segments.

depth of the product line (9) The variety of sizes, colors, flavors, and other characteristics of a particular product line marketed by a manufacturer.

derived demand (6) The concept that industrial buyers adjust their purchases according to the outlook for their sales, buying more when sales are growing than when sales are declining.

descriptive research (7) The process whereby managers collect information about a particular environmental factor that they believe is important.

desk jobber (14) A merchant wholesaler who rarely takes physical possession of goods. Instead, customers receive goods directly from the producer, who bills the merchant wholesaler; the merchant wholesaler in turn bills the customer.

developed market economy (24) The economic structure of the most advanced industrialized countries of the world, where income is high and more evenly distributed than in developing market economies.

developing market economy (24) The economic structure of nations that have quite low annual income per person compared with developed economies and where income is unevenly distributed among the population.

direct costs (16) Costs that can be traced directly to the product being priced.

direct marketing (13) Selling goods and services to buyers without the use of stores; making contact by mail, telephone, face to face, vending machine, or electronic methods.

discount department stores (13) Stores that offer large discounts, few services, austere facilities, and self-service checkout counters.

discrepancies or gaps (1) Differences in preference between producers and consumers based on what is produced, where it is produced, or when it is produced.

distribution (2) The network of company departments and other businesses that make products available to buyers.

distribution warehouses (15) Warehouse facilities that are owned and operated by the firms whose products are stored in them.

divisional organizational structure (22) An organizational structure in which each division is responsible for all marketing functions for a group of related products.

drop shipper (14) A merchant wholesaler who rarely takes physical possession of goods. Instead, customers receive goods directly from the producer, who bills the merchant wholesaler; the merchant wholesaler in turn bills the customer.

dual economy (24) The existence of both a rural and an urban economy in one developing country.

durable products (9) Items that are used many times and have a relatively long life.

economic alliance (24) An agreement to reduce trade and tariff barriers among participating nations to foster international trade.

economic environment (3) The actions of business that directly affect the purchasing power of organizational and consumer buyers.

economic-order quantity (EOQ) model (15) A representation of an economic balance between ordering costs and inventory carrying costs. Commonly, the model identifies the level at which stock should be reordered.

economies of scale (16) The phenomenon whereby per unit fixed cost decreases as the volume of a product increases and variable costs go down due to volume discounts on materials and supplies.

ego-drive (20) The need of one person to persuade another and thus gain gratification.

electronic order entry (15) Use of an electronic device to record and transmit a customer's order to the distribution location where the order will be filled.

embargo (24) Restriction by a country on imports or exports of a product.

empathy (20) The ability to sense the reactions of another person.

encoding (18) The task of putting ideas into words, pictures, and sounds that have meaning.

environmental analyses (2) A look outside a company to find and assess external forces that affect marketing strategy.

equipment (9) Industrial products used to perform functions such as manufacturing, movement and storage, maintenance, and office services for industrial firms and other organizations.

exchange (1) A transaction in which a supplier provides some good or service to a consumer in return for a payment.

exclusive distribution (12) The use of only one outlet for sales within a defined trading area.

experience curve (16) A graphical representation of the effect of experience on per unit cost in constant dollars.

experimental research (7) Research in which cause and effect objectives are set and data are collected to show how one factor will cause a change in another factor.

exploratory research (7) Research that helps managers discover environmental forces affecting marketing decisions.

exporting (24) The shipping of products produced in one country to markets in foreign countries.

extensive segmenting (8) The targeting of many different segments to expand sales and profit opportunities.

F.O.B. (free on board) with freight allowed (17) A method of transportation in which the seller includes transportation costs in the price of goods and at the same time lets the buyer pay the shipper.

F.O.B. (free on board) origin (17) A method of pricing in which the seller's price is quoted from the point of shipment and does not include transportation costs.

facilitating organizations (12) Organizations such as banks, marketing research firms, insurance companies, and advertising agencies that provide specialized assistance for regular channel participants in moving products from producers to users.

facilitating services (2) Activities that sellers perform to help customers after the sale to get full benefit from using a product.

facilities (9) Buildings and other parts of the physical plant used to produce and store products.

fads (9) Products that quickly become popular and then just as quickly fade from popularity.

family branding (11) Placement of one or more entire lines of products under one brand name.

fashions (9) Styles or trends in clothing and accessories that gain acceptance and grow to a peak in sales and then disappear as they lose their appeal.

Federal Trade Commission (FTC) (25) The government agency responsible for enforcing deception violations and antimonopoly laws.

Federal Trade Commission Act of 1936 (16) Federal law that established the Federal Trade Commission to enforce the Clayton Act.

fishyback (15) A combination of truck and water distribution services.

fixed costs (16) Direct costs that do not vary with the volume of a product produced.

fixed-order quantity model (15) A representation of an economic balance between ordering costs and inventory carrying costs. Commonly, the model identifies the level at which stock should be reordered.

focus group interview (7) A technique in which a small group of respondents (typically ten to twenty people) are asked questions and are encouraged to talk with each other about their answers.

food and drug retailers (13) Supermarkets, superdrug stores, convenience stores, and combination stores.

forecasting (4) The process by which predictions are made of the amount of sales that markets will yield.

franchise extension (11) The use of an existing brand name to identify a new product, often not closely related in function or use to the original brand.

franchising (12) A contractual arrangement in which a parent company (franchisor) grants a small company or individual (franchisee) the right to do business in a specified manner for a specified period of time in a specified location.

full-markup retailers (13) Retailers who price their products to maintain substantial margins between the cost of the merchandise and the selling price.

functional marketing organization (22) An organizational structure in which functional managers head each marketing component.

General Agreement on Tariffs and Trade (GATT) (24) An agreement signed by more than eighty countries that has limited the size of tariff and nontariff trade barriers; it includes a ''most-favored-nation'' clause that does not allow the imposition of higher tariffs for some signing countries than for others.

generic product (11) A specific product item that has no brand name and typically has a lower price than an equivalent brand-name product.

geographic pricing policy (17) A policy for setting prices that reflects the cost of transporting products from the seller to the buyer.

geographic segmentation (8) The process of dividing national markets into regional, state, and local segments.

global company (24) A form of multinational company that uses global marketing strategy.

global marketing strategy (24) A strategy in which the same product or very similar products are offered to world markets with essentially the same promotional strategy.

going rate pricing (17) A pricing strategy that sets price to closely match the prices of competitors.

grid analysis (23) A graphical technique in which one axis denotes the extent of opportunity in a business unit's market and the other denotes business strength compared to competition.

growth stage (9) The stage in the product life cycle at which revenues should increase faster than expenses and the product should be generating profits.

hierarchy-of-effects model (18) A flow diagram that describes a sequence of mental steps people go through leading to a purchase.

high-involvement decision making (5) A decision-making process used for purchases that are related to important motives or values or are significantly relevant to a life-style.

horizontal conflict (12) A dispute between channel members at the same level in the channel, such as two wholesalers.

horizontal dimension (12) A particular channel level consisting of participants that are usually similar in type and function.

hypermarket (13) A giant mass merchandizing retail outlet offering a wide merchandise mix, from groceries to soft goods, and operating on a reduced-price, self-service basis.

hypermarketing (25) Unusually extensive efforts to market a product.

idea generation (10) The process of producing new product ideas.

implementation (21) The process of putting a marketing plan into action.

import quotas (24) Restrictions on the number of units of a product that may legally be brought into a country.

importers (14) Organizations that specialize in purchasing goods from all over the world and whose negotiating skills may also be useful in exporting.

importing (24) The purchase of products from foreign manufacturers for sale in a company's home country.

independent retailers (13) The most common group of retailers, accounting for approximately 25 percent of total retail sales.

index of performance (22) A measure of the magnitude of performance, direction of performance, or both.

indirect costs (16) Costs that cannot be traced directly to individual products produced (usually called overhead).

individual branding (11) Use of a brand name for a single product item.

industrial buying (6) The purchasing of goods and services by organizations.

industrial buying behavior (6) The actions of organizations and their employees directly involved in purchasing and using a product or service, including the communication and decision processes that lead to the purchase choice and the satisfaction or dissatisfaction resulting from the purchase.

industrial products (9) Products purchased by an individual or organization for use in producing or distributing goods and services.

informal marketing organization (22) The part of the organizational structure consisting of the many working relationships that develop among managers regardless of formal lines of authority.

informed judgment techniques (4) Use of the opinions of knowledgeable people to forecast sales.

institutional advertising (19) Advertising that promotes the image or general reputation of an organization or an industry.

intensive distribution (12) Placement of products or brands in as many retail outlets as possible.

internal data (7) Information accumulated and recorded by a company to describe its transactions and activities.

international companies (24) Companies that do business in foreign countries but concentrate primarily on sales in their home country.

international competition (3) Competition that overlaps all other competition and comes from brands and product types sold by companies from many countries.

international marketing (24) The planning, implementing, and controlling of marketing strategies for foreign markets.

international marketing strategy (24) An approach whereby different product designs and promotion are developed for every foreign market.

interview study (7) A study in which people are asked questions and their answers are recorded as data.

intraorganizational environment (3) All forces that arise from the formal organizational structure and from interactions with employees.

introduction stage (9) The beginning of the life cycle of a product or service.

job description (20) The specific responsibilities assigned to a salesperson regarding planning, organizing, selling, personal development, and organizational development.

joint venture (24) An agreement between companies from different countries to share the management of a product or product line in a designated market.

just-in-time (JIT) inventory system (15) The practice of ordering supplies and parts frequently and in relatively small quantities from suppliers located as close as possible to production centers.

learning (5) Changes in what consumers believe, in their attitudes, and in how they behave that occur through experience.

legal and political environment (3) The actions (laws, regulations, decrees, and political influence) of decision makers in governmental positions that affect the strategies of an organization.

level (12) The position or location of the marketing intermediary within the channel of distribution (wholesale, retail, or broker level).

licensing (11) The sale to another party, including a foreign country, of the right to use a brand name for purposes not in competition with the original brand use.

life-styles (3) The particular ways that people lead their lives including time, money, and energy spent on work and leisure activities.

line expansion (9) The practice of increasing the depth of a product line by adding different or varied products.

line extension (11) The expansion of a company into new product areas through the leverage of its most valuable asset: the consumer awareness, goodwill, and impressions conveyed by its brand name.

list price (17) A preestablished price normally communicated to customers.

logistics (15) The flow of raw materials, supplies, and parts to producers as a part of the physical distribution network.

loss-leader pricing (17) The practice of setting a low price for one product to increase sales of other, related products in a line.

low-involvement decision making (5) A decision process used for purchases that are not very relevant to the consumer.

macroenvironment (3) The more general forces, lying beyond the task environment, that may eventually affect suppliers, customers, and competitors and their actions.

macroenvironmental scanning (3) The process of gathering and using information on macroenvironmental forces to identify new trends, project these trends into the future, and analyze their implications for corporate and marketing decisions.

macromarketing (1) The whole marketing system, with the total mechanism of institutions involved in the marketing process and how marketing should be carried out to meet the goals of society and to optimize social benefits.

mail-order house (14) A retailer or wholesaler specializing in the sale of goods through orders received by mail.

mail questionnaire (7) A list of questions designed so respondents can answer the questions without assistance.

managerial perspective (1) Business executives' management of their organization so that customers will be satisfied and the organization's performance targets will be reached.

managing by exception (22) A process by which managers look for the unusual marketing performance or performance that deviates from standards.

manufacturers' agent (14) A salesperson outside the manufacturing organization who performs the selling function for the producer as an alternative to a factory salesforce.

manufacturer's brand (11) A product brand that belongs to the manufacturer.

manufacturers' representatives (14) Salespersons outside the manufacturing organization who perform the selling function for the producer as an alternative to a factory salesforce.

margin (16) The per unit price that a seller receives from customers less the per unit cost of that product to the seller.

marginal analysis (17) A process that evaluates changes in revenue and costs for price increases and decreases to find the price that maximizes profits.

marginal cost (17) The amount by which total cost changes with a change in price and quantity sold.

marginal revenue (17) The amount of change in total revenue caused by a change in price and quantity sold.

market (4) A group of people or organizations with the ability and willingness to buy a product or service for consumption.

market conditions (4) Factors that influence the amount of sales a market will yield.

market economy (24) The economy of nations that do not centralize planning for economic development but rely on the market forces of supply and demand to determine economic growth.

market forecast (4) An estimate of the sales for a product type; the total sales for all companies selling similar brands forming the product type.

market niche (8) A target group of customers with specific characteristics and needs. Same as market segment.

market opportunity (4) The opportunity to convert potential sales into actual sales in a defined market for a product or service.

market opportunity analysis (MOA) (4) The gathering and analysis of information about products, buyers, and competition to determine which marketing strategy is needed to convert potential sales into actual sales and the amount of sales to expect.

market position (2) The way in which a company uses its marketing mix to create in customers' minds an important advantage or combination of advantages for buying from the company rather than from its competitors.

market potential (4) The upper limit or maximum level of sales that a market can yield.

market requirements (4) Expectations that customers have about a product or service when they purchase and use it.

market response (21) The amount of a specific good or service that customers purchase, constituting a firm's market resulting from the firm's marketing efforts.

market segment (8) A target group of customers with specific characteristics and needs. Same as market niche.

market segmentation (1) The targeting of one or more specific groups within a market.

market segmenting (8) The process of dividing the total market into two or more parts so that the people in each part have relatively similar needs and wants for a particular product or service.

market share index (22) The percentage of total sales of a defined product in a defined market that has been captured by a company.

market support index (22) A number that specifies the nature of impressions of the company and its brands in the minds of potential customers.

market target (1) The group of people or organizations to which a company decides to market its product or service. Same as target market.

market targeting (21) The process of deciding which people or organizations to serve in the marketplace.

marketing (1) The process of planning and executing conception, pricing, promotion, and distribution of ideas, goods, and services to create exchanges that satisfy individual and organizational objectives.

marketing activity center (19) A component of a marketing program to which a portion of company sales can be assigned.

marketing agents (14) People who perform all or most of the marketing functions for a producer including pricing, advertising, selling, and distribution.

marketing audit (22) A thorough evaluation of the external environment in which marketing is operating; the objectives, strategies, decision-making procedures, and organization of the marketing function; and the performance contribution of marketing to the company.

marketing budget (21) The resources required to achieve marketing objectives and the projection of revenues and expenses associated with those objectives.

marketing concept (1) A belief about the proper way to manage a business or an economic system.

marketing control (22) The process of analyzing the performance of marketing decisions, uncovering performance problems and their causes, and taking actions to correct the problems.

marketing functions (1) The activities of product development, distribution, pricing, promotion, and after-sale services that bring buyers and sellers together.

marketing information planning (7) The control of the flow of information from its various sources to the managers who use it.

marketing information system (MIS) (7) A combination of people and equipment organized to systematically gather data about marketing's environment, to analyze the data for information, and to deliver the information to managers who use it for marketing decisions.

marketing institutions (1) The group of organizations that aids in the exchange process, including wholesalers, retailers, financial institutions, and transportation firms.

marketing intelligence (7) The scanning of events in the macroenvironment and task environment by employees and other people.

marketing intermediaries (1) The organizations that link producers with end-users of goods and services. Also referred to as middlemen, or specialists who perform functions such as distribution, pricing, and promotion.

marketing management (1) The managers who consider the various issues, problems, and decisions associated with marketing.

marketing mix (1) A combination of the product, its distribution, price, advertising and sales promotion efforts, and after-sale services to enhance the product's use. Same as marketing program.

marketing myopia (23) Concentration of too much effort and attention on a firm's products rather than on the generic needs satisfied by alternative products.

marketing objective (2) A statement about the kind and level of performance that are realistically attainable by the company's marketing mix aimed at target markets.

marketing organizational structure (22) A formal assignment of responsibility for each component of marketing to various managers.

marketing performance problem (22) A situation in which a marketing decision leads to performance that does not measure up to management's expectations.

marketing plan (2) A blueprint for action establishing the company's market targets, setting objectives in the markets, and specifying how the marketing mix will be used to achieve the objectives.

marketing program (1) A combination of the product, its distribution, price, advertising and sales promotion efforts, and after-sale services to enhance the product's use. Same as marketing mix.

marketing research (4) The systematic gathering, analyzing, and reporting of data to answer managers' questions concerning a specific marketing problem, opportunity, or decision.

marketing strategy (2) A set of decisions managers make to select the customers whose needs and wants a company can profitably meet, to set objectives for desired performance, and to explain how the company is to use the marketing mix to achieve these objectives.

marketing system (1) The network of organizations such as manufacturers, distributors, wholesalers, and retailers who together perform the essential functions needed to move goods from production point to consumption point.

marketing's environment (3) The set of forces, external to the marketing manager's job position, that are either partially or completely uncontrollable but that have a substantial impact on the success of decisions made by the manager.

markup (17) The amount added to cost to determine price.

mass marketing (8) The process of serving all or most of the people that have needs or wants for a specific product.

mass merchandisers (13) Stores that price goods lower than traditional department stores, provide fewer services, and process sales through the use of checkout counters.

mathematical forecasting techniques (4) Procedures that use mathematically stated relationships or models to derive a forecast from data describing historical market conditions.

matrix organization (22) A complicated organizational structure that combines two or more organizational marketing activity centers.

maturity stage (9) The point in a product's life cycle where product sales reach their highest level and intensive competition often develops, bringing pressure on prices and profit margins.

media mix (19) A combination of media used to deliver advertising messages.

media vehicles (19) Alternative means of delivering advertising messages within a media category.

megamarketing (1) The process whereby organizations anticipate, influence, and help direct environmental change rather than merely respond to changes after they occur.

merchandise mart (14) A facility where producers display their goods and organizational buyers such as retailers can examine the lines of several manufacturers.

merchant wholesalers (14) Companies that buy, sort, assemble, grade, and store goods in large quantities and sell these goods to retailers and to institutional, farm, government, professional, and business users.

message content (18) The meaning of ideas that are to be communicated to target audiences.

message context (18) The way in which the message content is to be communicated to the target audience.

middleman's brand (11) Some organization in the distribution channel (other than the manufacturer) that owns the brand.

middlemen (12) The organizations that link producers with end-users of goods and services. Also referred to as marketing intermediaries.

modified rebuy decision (6) A decision to repurchase a product or service to replace one that has been used in the past, after considering alternative products.

modular record-keeping system (22) A system that assigns both sales and cost data to activity centers so that performance can be measured for each center.

monopolistic competition (16) A situation in which an industry is made up of many small firms, no one of which is large enough to stand out as a price leader.

monopoly (16) A situation in which only one company in an industry provides a product or service and customers have no choice of companies to buy from.

motivation (2) The process of giving incentives to those people who are responsible for carrying out plans.

motives (5) Predispositions that direct behavior toward certain goals.

multiform corporations (23) Business conglomerates composed of unrelated businesses.

multimodal services (15) The use of a combination of distribution methods.

multinational companies (24) Large companies that routinely do business in many countries and obtain a high proportion of their sales from markets outside their home countries.

multiple branding (11) The process of marketing several brands of a single item in an effort to gain different market segments.

multiple channels of distribution (12) A system in which more than one type of intermediary exists at a particular level.

multiple-zone pricing (17) A pricing structure that establishes more than one geographic zone for quoting delivered prices.

National Advertising Review Board (25) A self-regulatory agency for the marketing industry that monitors deceptive or misleading national advertising.

national brand (11) A brand that is sold throughout a country.

national strategy (24) A strategy that is developed by government and business serving as partners in planning for economic growth.

natural environment (3) The forces of nature as well as availability of natural resources that influence the success of company strategies.

need competition (3) Competition between products or services designed to meet differing needs of customers.

needs and wants (1) Uncomfortable feelings of deprivation or desire that can cause people to act, usually by purchasing and consuming goods and services.

new product (9) An item that has not been previously offered for sale by a company and that substantially differs from existing products in function, design, features, or method of production.

new product committee (10) A team of executives representing functions such as finance, marketing, operations, and human resources with responsibility for new product planning.

new product department (10) An organizational unit responsible for planning, coordinating, and managing new product activities.

new task decision (6) A purchase decision managers must make for a product or service for which they have little or no previous purchasing experience.

noise (18) Anything that causes a message to go unnoticed or to be misinterpreted.

noncumulative discount (17) A discount off-price given for volume buying on a particular purchase order.

nondurable products (9) Products that are fully consumed immediately or after a limited number of uses.

nonprobability sampling (7) The selection of people as respondents based on the researcher's judgment about the types of people that are important to study.

objective and task budgeting (19) A procedure for determining an advertising budget by summing the costs of advertising tasks required to achieve stated objectives.

objective (23) A goal that an individual or organization intends to accomplish.

observation study (7) A type of study in which people's behavior is observed and recorded.

odd pricing (16) The practice of setting prices ending in odd numbers.

off-price outlets (13) Retail outlets that operate at the low end of the pricing spectrum, marketing irregular merchandise, manufacturers' close outs, or otherwise low-cost merchandise.

oligopoly (16) A market situation in which a few large sellers control a high percentage of the supply of a product or service.

opinion leaders (5) Persons whose opinions a consumer seeks.

opportunity (7) A set of environmental circumstances that enables the company to improve its performance.

order processing (15) The transmission by electronics or paper of customers' purchase orders.

order taking (20) A sales situation in which the buyer rather than the salesperson initiates the purchase.

ordering costs (15) The expenses of placing and processing orders.

organizational culture (22) The working-related values and beliefs held by all or most members of an organization.

out-of-stock costs (15) Costs incurred when a customer becomes dissatisfied or purchases from another source if he or she is forced to wait for goods to be ordered.

over-planning (21) The process of writing such a detailed and complex marketing plan that the marketing manager and staff find it difficult to understand and implement.

patent (11) An exclusive property right to an invention that is issued by the Commissioner of Patents and Trademarks, U.S. Department of Commerce.

penetration pricing (17) The practice of setting a low price relative to prices of competitive products.

per unit cost (16) The total direct cost divided by the volume of the product produced.

per unit fixed cost (16) The total fixed cost divided by the volume of the product produced.

per unit variable cost (16) The total variable cost divided by the volume of the product produced.

perception (5) The process by which people receive, interpret, and remember information from the world around them.

personal interview (7) An interview in which an interviewer asks questions of respondents face to face and records their answers.

personal selling (18) The process of interaction between a buyer and a seller of a good or service leading to an exchange that benefits each party.

personality (5) Reaction tendencies that an individual exhibits in different situations.

physical distribution (15) The movement of goods from origin to destination.

physical distribution management (PDM) (15) The planning, implementation, and control of the physical flow and storage of materials and finished goods from suppliers, manufacturers, and middlemen to end-users.

piggyback (15) The use of a railway flatcar to haul loaded trailers to a destination where they are unloaded and then hauled by truck to distribution stores.

PIMS analysis (23) A computer model that indicates the relationship between financial performance and several business and marketing strategy determinants of performance such as market share and research and development expenditures.

population analysis (4) A procedure for using information about citizen and business populations to look for indications of market opportunity.

positioning (8) The buyer's overall perception of a firm's brand, product line, or the entire company that results from the impact of the firm's marketing mix on the buyer.

postsale follow up (20) A salesperson's contact with a buyer after a sale regarding product satisfaction, maintenance, customer suggestions, and so on.

predatory pricing (16) Unfair pricing by one company to injure a competitor.

preparation (20) Analysis of the buyer's needs and wants and subsequent development of a plan for selling the prospect.

presentation (20) Formal communication from seller to prospective buyers regarding product characteristics, buyer preferences, product use situation, and so forth. These communications normally incorporate use of a wide range of visual aids along with verbal communications.

price (2) The value that a buyer exchanges for the benefits of a seller's product or service.

price band (17) The price range that customers establish based on how they perceive competitive intensity and value of the product and within which they will buy the product.

price change policy (17) A policy that determines the frequency and time period over which price can be changed.

price discount policy (17) A policy that controls the amount, timing, and terms of discounts offered.

price discrimination (16) The practice of charging different prices to different customers.

price elasticity (16) The sensitivity of customers to price as measured by the percentage of change in quantity purchased relative to the percentage change in price.

price fixing (16) A type of pricing whereby managers from different companies jointly agree on the prices each company will charge.

price gouging (16) The practice of charging an unusually high price relative to a product's cost.

price leadership (16) The situation in which one or a few usually larger companies are consistently first in an industry to change price.

price lining (16) The setting of specific prices for a line of products with no prices in between.

price negotiation policy (17) A policy of setting boundaries around the authority of a salesperson to reduce price.

price-quality relationship (16) A psychological meaning attached to price whereby customers use price to judge quality of a product.

pricing objectives (17) Statements describing a price's effect on a product's performance.

pricing policies (17) Specific rules to guide managers faced with recurring pricing issues.

pricing strategy (17) Guidelines that specify how price is to achieve its objectives.

primary data (7) New data collected expressly to assist managers in making specific marketing decisions.

private brand (11) A brand owned by a retailer or other distributor of products.

private warehouses (15) Warehouse facilities that are owned and operated by the firms whose products are stored in them.

probability sampling (7) Systematic procedures to select members of a sample which ensure that every person from the population being sampled has a known probability of being selected for the sample.

problem (7) A situation in which the performance resulting from implementing a previous decision is not meeting the standards set for it.

producer (1) An organization or individual that creates goods and services.

producers' cooperative (14) An organization formed by a number of small farmers enabling them to achieve some of the advantages of large-scale marketing.

product (2) A combination of tangible or intangible performance capabilities or benefits that are designed to meet particular customer needs or wants.

product development (10) The process of transforming an idea into a product.

product item (9) A specific unit or model within a product line.

product life cycle (9) The various stages a product moves through from its initial introduction into the market throughout its life.

product line (9) A set of specific product items that logically fall together because of one or more common bonds such as performing the same function, meeting the same user need, or having a comparable price range.

product manager (3) A manager who has marketing planning and coordinating responsibility for one or a group of related brands of a company.

product manager organization (22) An organizational structure in which managers are assigned to products and are expected to achieve sales, market share, and profitability objectives for those products.

product mix (9) The total product offering of a particular firm comprising lines of products and individual items.

product modification (9) The redesign of a product to make it better and more attractive to buyers.

product performance specifications (6) Benefits important to the user of a product as well as nonproduct criteria important to a buying organization.

product portfolio (9) The entire product offering an organization such as a business firm or a division unit within an organization.

product positioning (8) The image or perception of a product in the mind of the buyer that distinguishes it from the competition.

product rejuvenation (9) A product modification intended to help extend the product's life cycle.

product type (4) A combination of attributes and benefits that similar competing brands have in common.

product type advertising (19) Advertising whose purpose is building customer demand for a particular product type.

product type competition (3) Competition between products that do not look similar but are bought and used for essentially the same purpose.

product warranty (11) A written statement provided by a manufacturer to a buyer that spells out the firm's responsibilities if the product or service proves to be defective.

production costs (15) The ratio of cost per unit to the number of units produced at a given time.

production orientation (1) The selling of a product that the producer decided to make with little regard for the buyer's desires.

profit contribution (16) The amount obtained by multiplying quantity times margin.

profit contribution index (22) The revenue for an activity center less the cost of the products sold and the marketing expenses incurred to generate that revenue.

profit-maximizing price (17) The price at which marginal revenue equals marginal cost.

promotion (2) A company's most important tools for delivering information to customers and other audiences.

promotion discount (17) A discount to encourage wholesalers and retailers to advertise, set up in-store displays, or otherwise promote a product in their area.

promotion mix (18) The tools—advertising, sales promotion, publicity, and personal selling—that deliver information to a company's audiences.

promotion objectives (18) Statements specifying exactly what actions are desired by management as a result of promotion.

prospecting (20) The act of finding potential buyers for a product or service.

psychographic segmentation (8) The process whereby variables such as life-style, social class, and personality are used to divide consumer markets into segments.

public relations (18) A function that gains public understanding and acceptance of an organization's goals and image and of management's point of view on issues of concern to the welfare of the organization.

public warehouses (15) Independently owned storage facilities that are rented to other firms.

publicity (18) Nonpersonal communications primarily in the form of news items carried by the mass media. The media are not paid by the source, and the message's origin is often perceived by receivers to be the media and not the source.

pull promotion strategy (18) A strategy whereby promotion is aimed at end-users as target audiences and the promotion mix is dominated by advertising, sales promotion, and publicity.

purchasing agents or managers (6) Managers who typically are responsible for identifying suppliers and their products, negotiating price for a purchase order, and working with suppliers' salespersons.

purchasing offices (14) Buying units located in market centers to take advantage of direct and regular contact with suppliers.

pure competition (16) A situation in which there are many small sellers with no differences between their marketing offers.

push promotion strategy (18) A technique whereby promotion is dominated by personal selling, trade advertising, and sales promotion and the promotion mix is aimed primarily at the trade in a company's channel of distribution.

quantity (16) The estimated number of units of a seller's brand that can be sold.

quantity discount (17) A price reduction to encourage customers to buy in volume from the seller.

rack jobber (14) A wholesaler who supplies merchandise, sets up displays, and receives payment only for items sold.

raw materials (9) Various substances such as metals, woods, agricultural produce, chemicals, and other goods that are transformed through production processes into products.

recall test (19) A communications effectiveness test that measures how many members of the target audience can remember an advertisement and its message.

receiver (18) A person in the target audience for a message.

reciprocal demand (6) A situation in which two companies are simultaneously both buyer and seller, but for different products.

reference groups (5) Groups of two or more people who share values and beliefs concerning acceptable behavior.

regional brand (11) A brand that is sold only in a particular geographic area of a country.

regional distribution centers (RDC) (15) Large private distribution warehouses located within a geographic area served by a manufacturer, wholesaler, or retailer.

request for proposal (6) An invitation to suppliers to suggest how all order specifications will be met and at what price.

resale price maintenance (16) The practice by a firm of fixing the price of a product that a firm at another level in a channel of distribution can charge.

research design (7) A plan for conducting a marketing research study.

research objectives (7) Statements specifying what is to be learned about selected marketing environmental forces likely to affect marketing decisions.

retailer (13) A middleman who sells products that are purchased by individuals for their own use and not for resale.

retailer cooperatives (13) Organizations that provide the advantages of retail chains to their members but allow them to operate independently.

retailing (13) The activities involved in selling goods and services to end-users, including households, individuals, and others who are purchasing for final consumption.

revenue-related performance (22) Returns to a company measured by sales and market share.

Risk Retention Act of 1981 (14) Federal law to help wholesalers overcome the rapidly escalating costs of product liability through group insurance arrangements.

Robinson-Patman Act of 1936 (16) A federal law that specifies the activities considered to be price discrimination.

role of price (17) The weight that managers place on price relative to other components of marketing strategy.

roll-out (8) Product introduction into a market one area at a time rather than simultaneous introduction into all markets.

rules of thumb budgeting (19) A step-by-step procedure for calculating a dollar amount to allocate to advertising.

sales branches (14) Organizational units that sell and service a manufacturer's products and often provide financial services to customers.

sales effectiveness test (19) A marketing research test that measures the ability of advertising to achieve sales objectives.

sales offices (14) Organizational units that typically perform only a selling function.

sales orientation (1) Heavy emphasis by the seller on only the functions of selling and distribution.

sales-oriented promotion objectives (18) Statements of overt kinds of behavior expected as a result of promotion, such as customers' redeeming a coupon, making an inquiry about a purchase, going to a dealer, or buying the product.

sales performance index (22) The unit or dollar volume of one or more products sold less returns (unsold or defective products returned to the company) and other adjustments.

salespersons (18) Individuals paid by a company to deliver the company's messages through oral communications with receivers who clearly understand that the messages are coming from the company.

sales promotion (18) A wide variety of short-term inducements to buy, including coupons, point-of-purchase product displays, free gifts, signs, contests, and trade shows. Receivers know that the inducement comes from the source.

sales quota (20) A sales volume objective often used to determine incentive payments and to measure desired performance.

sales-to-cost ratios (22) Numbers that compare the cost of each marketing function to sales from that function.

sample (7) A subset of people selected from a population for study.

screening (10) The placing of new product ideas into one of two categories: (1) ideas that will receive more comprehensive evaluation before making a go/no go decision regarding development or (2) ideas that are to be rejected.

secondary data (7) Data that have been previously collected but not specifically to assist in making a particular marketing decision.

selective distribution (12) Limitation of product distribution to a specific number of outlets within a defined geographic region.

selective segmenting (8) Targeting of a few segments within a total market.

selling agents (14) Agents who perform all or most of the marketing functions for the producer including pricing, advertising, selling, and distribution.

selling points (19) The major arguments for buying a product that are communicated in a message.

service contracts (11) A form of service insurance that provides service for a specified length of time to the purchaser of a product.

service mark (11) A particularly distinctive name or physical symbol that is associated with a company's service.

service retailers (13) Business organizations that sell an intangible rather than a tangible product. Banks, airlines, and movie theaters are examples.

service (9) An intangible that provides benefits that satisfy consumer and organizational user needs.

Sherman Act of 1890 (16) A federal law that outlaws any action specifically intended to restrain national or international trade or to create a monopoly.

shopping products (9) Goods involving comparisons of brands and/or stores on the basis of price, quality, style, and other features.

single segmenting (8) Marketing directed to only one specific group or segment within a total market.

single-zone pricing (17) The practice whereby a seller quotes one list price and the same transportation cost for all customers regardless of their location.

situation assessment (21) The process of determining market target, objectives, action plans, and budgeting and of implementing and managing the marketing plan all within the scope of the environment.

skimming pricing (17) The practice of setting a high initial price for a new product relative to the price of a competitive product used as a reference by customers.

social class (5) A large group of people who are held in approximately equal esteem; share similar cultural values, ideas, beliefs, and attitudes; and tend to socialize among themselves rather than with people from other social classes.

social environment (3) The cultural, demographic, and life-style characteristics of people in a geographic area that influence consumer demands.

social responsibility (25) The extent to which marketing actions are consistent with the needs and priorities of society.

societal perspective (1) A view of marketing from a total or aggregate perspective rather than a specific activity of a company.

sorting (12) Establishment of grade categories, primarily for mineral or agricultural products.

source (18) The originator or sponsor of a message.

specialization (1) Concentration on a particular work activity to satisfy one need rather than trying to provide for all needs.

specialty products (9) Goods that involve special effort to obtain because they are carried in only a few stores in a trading area.

specialty stores (13) Stores that typically concentrate on only one line or a few lines of merchandise.

staffing (2) The process of assigning persons with appropriate expertise to individual tasks.

Standard Industrial Classification (SIC) codes (6) A classification scheme used by the U.S. government to group U.S. organizations into categories for purposes of organizing and presenting statistical information about them.

static control comparisons (22) Comparisons of performance to standards during a single time period such as a month, a quarter, or a year.

statistics (7) Manipulations that summarize data and help discover important differences among them.

storage warehouses (15) Independently owned storage facilities that are rented to various firms.

straight rebuy decision (6) A purchase decision made when the product or service being purchased has been bought frequently in the past.

strategic business unit (SBU) (23) A single product or brand, a line of products, or a mix of related products that meets a common market need or a group of related needs; the unit's management is responsible for all of the basic business functions for that product or mix.

strategic marketing plan (21) A plan that specifies marketing decisions two to five years into the future.

strategic planning (23) The procedure that consists of analyzing the environment, defining the nature of the organization, formulating basic goals, and identifying, evaluating, and selecting the fundamental courses of action for the organization.

strict liability (11) The situation in which a manufacturer is responsible, regardless of the precautions taken, if a defect in a product is established legally.

strip developments (13) Groups of retailers who locate along street and highway segments.

subculture (5) Groups of people in a country who share values, ideas, beliefs, and attitudes different from the dominant culture of the country.

supermarket and super drug stores (13) Large, self-service stores that sell high-volume foods or drugs at low margins.

superstores (13) Large combination food and nonfood retailers.

suppliers (6) Companies that sell products being considered for purchase by other organizations.

supplies (9) The many and varied items used in production and distribution operations.

tactical marketing plan (21) A short-term marketing plan ranging from one to three months in duration.

tactics (2) Decisions managers make to put strategy into operation by choosing components of the marketing mix that determine how strategy will be carried out.

target audience (18) The particular persons that promotion is designed to communicate with.

target markets (2) Groups of people or organizations to which a company decides to market its product or service. Same as market targets.

target markup pricing (17) A prespecified (target) amount to be added to the per unit cost of a product to determine price.

target rate-of-return pricing (17) The practice of setting price for each product so that the quantity sold will yield a revenue and cost relationship achieving the targeted rate of return.

tariff (24) A tax on imported products imposed by a government.

task environment (3) The forces attributed to suppliers, competitors, and customers, the groups that most directly affect a company's success in serving its markets.

task force (10) A group of executives responsible for planning and coordinating a particular business project such as a new product.

technical selling (20) An industrial sales situation in which salespersons must understand how a product works and how it is applied to specific situations.

technological environment (3) The capabilities of a country and its industries to produce and distribute products and services.

teleconferencing (18) A technique whereby salespersons make direct contact with customers through television and telephone hookups. Salespersons in one location can see and talk with several customers in different locations, eliminating the need for travel.

telemarketing (18) A technique whereby salespersons make contacts with customers by telephone rather than in person.

telephone interview (7) An interview technique in which people in a sample are called and asked questions over the phone.

test marketing (10) The introduction of a new product or service in a limited market area to help a company measure the ultimate success of the product when introduced nationally and also to test planned market strategy.

time series study (7) A series of cross sectional studies done at regular intervals.

top-down approach to promotion budgeting (18) A procedure applied when top management sets an upper limit on spending for promotion with little or no directives given to middle or lower management on how the money is to be spent.

top-down planning (21) A procedure whereby plans are developed at the highest levels of an organization and then presented to the next lower level as the basis for preparing lower-level plans.

total cost (17) Fixed costs plus variable costs.

total cost pricing (16) A pricing procedure that allocates all indirect costs to all products before setting prices.

total direct costs (16) The sum of fixed and variable costs for a product.

total revenue (17) Price times quantity sold.

trade or functional discount (17) A price reduction given in exchange for the trade performing specified functions such as storing the product, providing warranty repairs, training dealers, and marking price.

trade show (18) A sales promotion activity where sellers set up exhibits to show their wares to dealers or end-users.

trademark (11) A legally protected name or symbol for a product.

trading companies (14) Middlemen companies that are part of the channels for products and services sold worldwide and that perform services such as buying and selling products, offering trade financing, managing construction projects, conducting research, and consulting with other companies.

traditional department stores (13) Stores offering a wide range of merchandise sold in various departments at prices yielding high margins, utilizing sales clerks, and providing numerous customer services.

transaction (1) An exchange between a buyer and a seller of a good or service in return for something considered of equal value.

truck jobber or wholesaler (14) A merchant wholesaler who combines the activities of salesperson and delivery person, who usually sells for cash, and whose stock is usually limited to nationally advertised specialties and fast-moving semiperishable or perishable items.

unitizing (15) The practice of combining as many packages as possible into one load or pallet.

upscale discounters (13) Retailers who locate near full-price retailers and use lower prices to attract business from full-price department and specialty stores.

use situation (5) Those characteristics of the immediate time and place in which a person will use a product or service.

use test (10) A gauge of how an intended user feels about a new product after actually using it.

validity (7) A characteristic present in data that measures what the data were intended to measure.

value (5) A very important feeling about how good or bad performing an activity or achieving a goal is.

value analysis (6) A study of the function that a product must perform.

variable costs (16) Direct costs that vary with the volume of a product produced.

venture team (10) A group of key people representing various business functions such as manufacturing, research and development, marketing, and finance that work with the product venture from idea stage to commercialization.

vertical conflict (12) Disputes between channel members at different levels such as retailers and distributors.

vertical dimension (12) The alignment within a channel of different organizations from producer to end-user.

vertical marketing system (12) A professionally managed system of marketing intermediaries that is engineered and operated to achieve operating economies and optimum impact in the channel.

videotex (13) A form of electronic shopping whereby households and businesses retrieve various kinds of information from remote data bases using a terminal, television set, or telephone lines.

warehouse retailers (13) Retailers that offer lower prices than upscale discounters and operate in more austere surroundings.

wheel of retailing (13) A concept that suggests that low-margin and low-price competitors force their way into the marketplace because of the high margins and high prices of existing retailers.

wholesaler (14) A distributor who performs various functions necessary to supply retailers and other organizational buyers with producers' goods and services.

wholesaling (14) The activities of establishments that sell to retailers, merchants, industrial, institutional, or commercial users but do not sell a significant amount to ultimate consumers.

wholly owned subsidiary (24) A separate company formed by an investment of a parent company.

width of product mix (9) The number of different product lines offered by a company.

workload analysis (20) The number of salesperson calls necessary to serve a firm's customers and prospects divided by the number of salespeople.

WOTS analysis (23) The evaluation of weaknesses, opportunities, threats, and strengths within a company.

Indexes

Name Index

Subject Index